Some Recent Publications
of the Bureau of Business and Economic Research

MONETARY POLICIES AND FULL EMPLOYMENT
by William Fellner (1946, 1947)

CRISIS IN BRITAIN: PLANS AND ACHIEVEMENTS OF THE LABOUR GOVERNMENT
by Robert A. Brady (1950)

SCIENTIFIC METHOD FOR AUDITING
by Lawrence L. Vance (1950)

APPLICATION OF LINEAR PROGRAMMING TO THE THEORY OF THE FIRM
by Robert Dorfman (1951)

UNCLE SAM IN THE PACIFIC NORTHWEST. FEDERAL MANAGEMENT OF NATURAL RESOURCES IN THE COLUMBIA RIVER VALLEY
by Charles McKinley (1952)

HOUSEBUILDING IN TRANSITION

Publications of the
Bureau of Business and Economic Research
University of California

HOUSEBUILDING IN TRANSITION

Based on Studies in the
San Francisco Bay Area

BY

SHERMAN J. MAISEL

UNIVERSITY OF CALIFORNIA PRESS
BERKELEY AND LOS ANGELES
1953

UNIVERSITY OF CALIFORNIA PRESS
BERKELEY AND LOS ANGELES

CAMBRIDGE UNIVERSITY PRESS
LONDON, ENGLAND

The opinions expressed in this study are those of the author. The functions of the Bureau of Business and Economic Research are confined to facilitating the prosecution of independent scholarly research by members of the faculty.

To the memory of my father

LOUIS MAISEL

Preface

The purpose of this book is explained in chapter 1. As the reader progresses, it will be clear that in order to describe the housebuilding industry to economists and other interested observers, such as materials suppliers, lenders, government personnel, and legislators, I have included descriptions of technical processes which may be basically familiar to builders. I felt it necessary to furnish sufficient technical facts so that students and other readers can understand why certain procedures are employed. At the same time, I felt that these descriptions are also important to builders. An orderly presentation of the actual steps in constructing a house will enable them to reexamine their own operations with a view to improving their methods, by offering an insight into the logic of many procedures that are frequently taken for granted.

Even an abbreviated list of acknowledgments must be long. The basic research for this book was performed under contract (No. O-E-50) with the Administrator, Housing and Home Finance Agency, results of which were submitted in a report dated August 31, 1951. I am particularly indebted to that agency and to the University of California Bureau of Business and Economic Research, which was a joint sponsor of that project. Their staffs, under the direction of Dr. Richard Ratcliff and Dr. Frank Kidner, respectively, aided greatly in the furtherance of this study. Mr. Jack Rogers, my associate in the above project, gave valuable assistance throughout, particularly in connection with the Statistical Appendixes, many of which stand in the approximate form in which he developed them. Mrs. Betty Ballantine Hogan assisted in the writing of the results. Mr. George Pucci, Robert Williams, Wells Keddie, Fred Maisel, Willard Wall, and many others shared in gathering the basic data. Mrs. Jerry Honeywell Hobbs and Mrs. LaVerne Rollin performed the initial editorial and secretarial work.

The complete coöperation of the builders of the Bay area—essential to this first accurate, composite picture of who housebuilders are and how they operate—was freely accorded. Above all, I am indebted to my wife, Lucy Cowdin Maisel, for aid in a myriad of ways. I have imposed upon her time and good nature for aid and comfort, as well as for a large amount of skilled technical work.

Sherman J. Maisel

University of California
Berkeley, March 1953

Contents

PART I

1. *Introduction* 3
2. *The Housebuilding Industry* 10
3. *The Small Builder* 31
4. *The Medium Firm* 67
5. *The Large Firm* 95
6. *Supply of Factors* 134

PART II

7. *Evaluating the Efficiency and Performance of Housebuilding* 167
8. *How Efficiency Grows with Size* 189
9. *Effect of External Restrictions* 223
10. *Performance of Housebuilders* 256
11. *The Future* 287

APPENDIXES

A. *General Method of Procedure and Reliability of Estimates* 303
B. *Housebuilding Production* 312
C. *Size and Type of Housebuilding Firms* 315
D. *Housebuilders' Operations* 318
E. *Information on Firms' Age, Characteristics, Ownership, and Financial Operations* 321
F. *The Product* 323
G. *Structure of the Trade-Contracting Industries* 325
H. *Pricing of the Composite House* 327
I. *Materials Supply* 332
J. *Data on the Labor Force, Entry, and Profits* 334

TABLES

1. Confidence intervals of estimates 339
2. Fiducial limits for percentages estimated from Bureau of Business and Economic Research survey data 340
3. Increase in population and dwelling units 1930–1950, United States and San Francisco metropolitan area 341
4. Nonfarm residential construction begun, 1946–1951 342
5. Medium and large-sized housebuilders in the United States . . 342
6. Houses built by nonprofessionals in 1949, by area 342
7. Housebuilders in 1949, classified by size and by area 343
8. Houses built in 1949, classified by size of builder and by area . . 343
9. Houses built operatively in 1949, classified by size of builder and by area 344
10. Houses built in Bay area in 1949, classified by size of builder, by type of building, and by location 345
11. Bay area housebuilders in 1949, classified by dollar volume of all production and by size 346
12. Bay area housebuilders in 1949, classified by number of employees and by size 347
13. Bay area housebuilders in 1949, classified by per cent of houses each built operatively and by size 347
14. Bay area housebuilders in 1949, classified by per cent of houses each built in tracts and by size 348
15. Bay area housebuilders in 1949, classified by per cent that new housebuilding formed of total production and by size 348
16. Bay area housebuilders in 1949 completing dwelling units in addition to houses, by size 349
17. Bay area housebuilders in 1949, classified by number of permit centers in which they built and by size 350
18. Bay area housebuilders in 1949, classified by number of months active during year and by size 350
19. Bay area housebuilders in 1949, classified by average price of house built and by size 351
20. Bay area housebuilders primarily engaged in housebuilding (more than 90 per cent) in 1949, classified by off-site personnel and by size 351
21. Bay area housebuilders in 1949, classified by main determinants of existing size and by size 352
22. Bay area housebuilders in 1949, classified by number of integrated trade contractor operations and by size 352

23. Bay area housebuilders in 1949, classified by channels of materials distribution and by size 353
24. Bay area housebuilders in 1949, classified by age of the principal and by size 353
25. Bay area housebuilders in 1949, classified by age of firm and by size 354
26. Bay area housebuilders in 1949, classified by years principal worked in building industry before establishment of firm, and by size 355
27. Bay area housebuilders in 1949, classified by type of ownership structure and by size 355
28. Bay area housebuilders in 1949, classified by total assets and by size 356
29. Bay area housebuilders in 1949, classified by current assets and by size 357
30. Bay area housebuilders in 1949, classified by net worth and by size 358
31. Bay area housebuilders in 1949, classified by net worth as a per cent of sales volume and by size 359
32. Bay area housebuilders in 1949, classified by value of equipment owned per unit completed and by size 359
33. Bay area housebuilders in 1949, classified by net profit and by size 360
34. Bay area housebuilders in 1949, classified by net profits as a per cent of sales volume and by size 360
35. Bay area housebuilders in 1949, classified by net profits as a per cent of net worth and by size 361
36. Comparison of characteristics of one-family houses started in 15 metropolitan areas and in the San Francisco area in the last half of 1949 362
37. Per cent distribution by price class of new one-family houses completed in last half of 1949 in Bay area 363
38. Characteristics of one-family houses started in the San Francisco area in the last half of 1949 classified according to size of builder 363
39. Houses constructed by Bay area builders in 1949, classified by price class and by size of firm 364
40. Selected mortgage characteristics of mortgaged houses completed in last half of 1949, in 15 metropolitan areas and San Francisco area 365
41. Financial data classified by income group of purchaser in last half of 1949 for 15 metropolitan areas and San Francisco area . . . 366
42. Estimates of number of Bay area trade contractors in 1949 with housebuilding specialties 367
43. Bay area trade contractors in 1949, classified by dollar volume and by trade 367

44. Bay area trade contractors in 1949, classified by average number of site employees and by trade 368
45. Bay area trade contractors in 1949, classified by average number of overhead personnel and by trade 368
46. Bay area trade contractors in 1949, classified by per cent work on new housing formed of total volume and by trade 369
47. Bay area trade contractors in 1949, classified by per cent new housing formed of total production, by trade, and by size 370
48. Bay area trade contractors in 1949, classified by number of areas worked in and by trade 371
49. Costs of the composite house classified by main expenditures and by size of builder 372
50. Labor costs of the composite house by contractor and trade, and by size of builder 373
51. Materials costs of the composite house by contractor and by size of builder 374
52. Overhead and profit on site work of the composite house, by contractor and by size of builder 375
53. Concentration ratios in 1947 of industries manufacturing building materials 376
54. Distribution of housebuilding materials by concentration ratio classes, 1947, based on use of materials in composite Bay area house 378
55. Distribution of housebuilding materials by concentration ratio classes, 1947, based on value of products of materials supply industries 378
56. Revised wholesale price index and building materials price indexes 379
57. Construction employment in 1940 and 1950 for United States, California, and San Francisco metropolitan area 379
58. Average earnings and average hours worked, for building and all manufacturing employees, in United States and California, selected years 380
59. Number of work stoppages and man-days idle, 1946–1950, United States and California 381
60. Comparative profit rates based on total sales, construction, and other industries 382
61. Net profit as a per cent of net worth, in selected industries and years 383
62. Rates of net growth, entry, and discontinuance, for selected industries, areas, and years 384

FIGURES

1. Housebuilding in the San Francisco Bay area in 1949 24
2. Financial balance sheets for a typical housebuilder of each size . 39
3. Operations in the construction of a typical Bay area house . . . 51
4. Construction estimate sheet 62
5. Age, background, and type of ownership of Bay area housebuilders in 1949, by size 70
6. Typical organization of large firm 100
7. Wholesale price movements—all commodities, lumber, and other building materials 140
8. Paths to greater efficiency through improved functioning of housebuilding firms 172
9. Plan and elevation of the composite house 186
10. Major payments for the composite house, by size of builder . . 190
11. Costs of building the composite house by builders of different sizes 197

PART I

1

Introduction

This book is aimed at increasing the reader's knowledge and heightening his understanding of the housebuilding industry. New knowledge and better understanding are fundamental to any effort to improve the methods by which houses are produced. Because of the importance of housing to all, and because of general dissatisfaction with the achievements of this industry, interest in the problems of housebuilding is widespread. For these reasons, this book is addressed not alone to specialists with a particular interest in housing, but to a broad range of readers who seek a clearer comprehension of one of the country's most basic industries.

There are various possible paths to improved housebuilding, and the selection of those which may be expected to lead to best results requires accurate information. The lack of valid information in this field is great. Housebuilding, as one of the oldest, largest, most diverse, and most troubled and troublesome of all industries, has been the subject of much writing, especially in recent years; yet facts about how it actually functions, analysis of why it operates as it does, and evaluation of results and of prospects are exceedingly sparse. These gaps in knowledge and understanding, this book attempts to fill.

In assembling the needed information, this study undertakes a threefold approach. A specific description of how houses are built in the San Francisco Bay area is presented to meet the need for facts about what exists; analysis explains why operations take their present form; and evaluation of housebuilders' performance judges the effectiveness of today's results and points toward possibilities for future betterment. This approach makes use of a great many data which illumine the structure of the industry, the interrelationships of the men who manage it, their methods of production, their products, the results they have achieved, and their expectations.

The desirability of research into the organization and operations of housebuilding is highlighted by the fact that this industry is one of the most important in the nation in terms of dollar volume, employment, and contribution to the nation's wealth, and that from one-fourth to one-sixth of each family's income is spent for shelter. It is evident from either the consumer's or the industrial point of view that any improvements in housebuilding and any reductions in the cost of shelter will raise the general standard of living. In addition, many believe that fluctuations in housing production have been a major factor in introducing and spreading instability throughout the economy. If this is true, knowledge leading to stabilization of housing production would, again, be a prime economic and human benefit.

Knowledge about the housebuilding industry, however, has been too sparse for any effective application. Probably less is known about housebuilding than about any other major industry. Myths, dogmas, and pat solutions of the housing problem have been offered in place of facts.

Existing knowledge in the field is summarized in two excellent, fairly recent works. The first, *American Housing*,[1] a comprehensive survey of known conditions, presents a typical picture of what most people—even experts—believe the industry to be like. The second, *Production of New Housing*,[2] brings together the results of earlier research in housing and analyzes current problems. Both of these works will be referred to throughout this study as reflecting the facts and views about housebuilding that existed when this book was written.

Inadequacies of the state of knowledge are described by Leo Grebler in *Production of New Housing*:

> The student in this field is confronted, in the existing literature, with a great many conflicting assertions, generalizations often drawn from inadequate evidence, *ex parte* statements, and analyses obviously designed to support one kind of public policy or another. He finds few undisputed data and little analysis of a scientific nature.

[1] Miles L. Colean, *American Housing: Problems and Prospects*, (New York: The Twentieth Century Fund, 1947).

[2] Leo Grebler, *Production of New Housing*, (New York: Social Science Research Council, 1950).

> A few examples of the assertions found in the literature will illustrate the point: Housing production is inefficient and uses largely the handicraft methods of a hundred years ago; methods of housing production have changed a great deal and are as efficient as they can be considering the nature of the product and the market. New houses are within the reach of only a small proportion of families in the upper income brackets; new houses are within the reach of a large proportion of families in all but the lowest income groups. The cost of distribution of building materials is excessive; the cost of their distribution is low considering the functions performed in the distribution process. Labor union restrictions are responsible for high costs and impede technical progress; labor unions exercise no restrictions except those dictated by considerations of health and safety and do not stand in the way of progress. The list could be extended indefinitely. There are few observations in this field which may be considered more than untested hypotheses.[8]

No one familiar with the literature can quarrel with this statement. For example, a look at the many congressional investigations into housing makes it evident. Although much time and money have been spent on almost annual hearings, few facts of value have been added since the hearings of the Temporary National Economic Committee in 1939, with the exception of the 1940 Census data. Beliefs and dogmas have been restated in more detailed and sometimes more elegant language, but they still remain untested generalizations. Repetition has won their acceptance as facts.

It is the purpose of this book to cut through outmoded data and to clear at least one corner in this morass of misinformation for inspection of actual facts. Concentration on collecting statistics as complete as possible about the housebuilding industry in one area—the San Francisco Bay area—has made it possible to go to primary sources, the builders themselves, for the basic material. Examination of the structure of the housebuilding industry and the methods of construction employed by it in this area and comparison of the actual facts found with known data in other areas have made possible some evaluation of the importance of many issues under continual discussion.

---

[8] Grebler, *op. cit.*, p. 2.

Inspection of actual facts is the crux, because understanding of them can improve the performance of the industry. The facts are crucial to management, which requires them for important daily decisions and which all too often makes its decisions without the guidance of the experience of others. Knowledge of how fellow builders solve similar problems can improve day-to-day operations.

The facts are crucial, too, in the formulation of public policy. Questions concerning changes in the policies of government lending agencies, enforcement of antitrust laws, expenditures of public funds, and changes in building codes and zoning ordinances arise every day and need answers. Information required for making wise decisions has, on the whole, been lacking. It is hoped that pragmatic answers may be made possible through some of the information that this book offers, and that, consequently, improvement in public policy decisions will aid the performance of the housebuilding industry.

Beyond advances in knowledge and understanding of the housebuilding industry in general, this study is directed toward the broader target of adding to knowledge of the free enterprise system, of which the housebuilding industry is so competitive a part. Most attention in industry studies has been paid to the workings of oligopolistic industries, with far less heed given to the results obtained in the more competitive sector of the economy. In this time of social and political struggle, when the entire system of competition and free enterprise is under fire, the survival of the system depends upon its capacity for improvement—and its capacity for improvement depends upon better knowledge of the methods by which the competitive system performs, and of its strengths and its weaknesses.

To accumulate all the facts about an industry is a long and complex project. It confronts the investigator with questions such as these: Why is this particular industry characterized by its particular type of behavior? What are the factors in its history, in its markets, in its relationships that cause present results to emerge? What are the best possibilities for its improvement? Can certain basic changes be made that would benefit everyone interested in this industry?

The answers to these questions depend upon many variables. The performance of an industry is composed of many kinds of action taken at all levels. Its factors include the industry's over-all organization, its market structure, its type of products, its method of production, the entrepreneurs and their organization, the supply of the components of production, and the channels through which they move.

In the gauging of performance, attempts to evaluate the results also raise many questions. What has been the price history of the industry? How do its prices relate to its costs? How do the products rate in terms of quantity, quality, and fulfillment of consumers' needs? What is the optimum size for a plant or firm in this industry? How does its technological progress relate to available potentialities? Are avoidable wastes limiting performance and dissipating results?

In answering these and other questions for the housebuilding industry, this book offers a complete description of structure, organization, and operations, before presenting any analysis and evaluation. The description covers the size, type, and geographical relationships of the firms active in the housebuilding market; the dynamic forces at work, such as changes in demand, changes in population, and changes in financing which have occurred during the past decade; the product itself and what it contains; the background and ability of the men who run the firms; the differences between contractors and merchant builders; the ways of organizing firms in terms of legal structure and of overhead structure; the manner of meeting financing problems and marketing problems; the methods of production and the changes which have developed; and the handling of purchasing, records, and controls.

Because the level of the industry's performance and the price of its product depend to a great extent upon the supply of materials and services, a brief description of some aspects of the industries supplying housebuilders with factors of production is offered.

It is the purpose of these descriptions to show by data what housebuilding is, how it works, what its problems are, what its relationships are, what improvements are being made, and what possible improvements remain to be achieved. The descriptions are based upon data gathered through field research. So far as possible, they are unalloyed with interpretation or opinion.

The second part of the book is based upon these descriptions and upon additional statistics gathered specifically for the purpose of analyzing and evaluating the industry. Here, however, because of a lack of absolute standards of judgment, some admixture of interpretation and opinion is necessary. The analysis and evaluation focus upon the measurement of efficiency and performance, in the belief that if housebuilding is to be improved and if housebuilding costs are to be brought as low as possible, the industry must use the productive resources available to it as efficiently as possible.

Popular discussions of the problems of housebuilding efficiency have followed three main channels: the rationality or irrationality of the structure of the industry and the methods used by individual firms; the effect of size or scale on the efficiency of production; the wastes and excess costs resulting from restrictive forces outside the building firms.

The first stream of thought holds that housebuilding is industrially retarded, organizationally inefficient, and lags behind other industries in application of machine techniques. The second is similar, adding the belief that efficiency will increase only as the size of firms increases. For example, C. Abrams asserts:

> The housing need will be met neither quantitatively nor qualitatively as long as this little speculative industry continues to block up the flow and hold down the quality of homes for the American people. Greater efficiency would follow if the builder were to set up as a large-scale producer on a parity with the automobile manufacturer.[4]

The third stream of ideas holds that the industry is subject to an unusual number of institutional restraints both from inside and outside. Miles L. Colean lists seven elements exercising influence, each of which seems to operate in its own interest alone and to help inflate production costs.[5]

Because these opinions are so widely held, it was believed worth while to test each a priori hypothesis separately against the available facts and against new information which was developed. At the same time, new hypotheses were formed and tested in conjunction with those that had already gained wide acceptance. All possible sources of information relating to the housebuilding industry in the San Francisco Bay area were examined, new methods and procedures for

[4] C. Abrams, "Housing—The Ever-Recurring Crisis," in (S. Harris, ed.) *Saving American Capitalism,* (New York: Knopf, 1948), p. 185.

[5] Colean, *op. cit.,* pp. 314, 329. For additional analyses, cf. R. U. Ratcliff, *Urban Land Economics,* (New York: McGraw-Hill, 1949), pp. 200–201, 454, 477; "Housing: Puny Giant," *Wall Street Journal,* Oct. 9–20, 1947; U. S. Temporary National Economic Committee, *Toward More Housing,* Monograph No. 8 (Washington: Government Printing Office, 1940), pp. 126–141; G. Greer, "Housing: Let's Not Kid Ourselves," *Survey Graphic,* Vol. XXXVI, No. 9 (September, 1947), 470, 495; "The Industry Capitalism Forgot," *Fortune,* Vol. XXXVI, No. 2 (August, 1947), 66.

gathering data were developed, the collected data were tabulated, and from this reservoir of facts flowed the procedures of description, analysis, and evaluation.

This investigation stressed the gathering of new data through the use of large-scale statistical surveys. It employed the accumulation of a large group of case histories obtained through interviews and site observations. It collected a large amount of cost data so that statistical cost functions could be derived. The investigation was limited to a single metropolitan area so that problems of geographical differences would not arise.

This new information, it is believed, results in a far more accurate description of the industry and its structure and operations than has hitherto been available. It makes possible analysis (based perhaps for the first time on reliable statistics) of the effects of changes in scale, of external restrictions, and of the effect of improvement in techniques and management on efficiency and costs. It enables a more accurate evaluation to be given of how the system is working and of its pressure upon the interests of the public.

From this diagnosis of the industry's condition, it is possible to make some prognoses pertaining to the industry's progress. The first part of the book shows the actual manner in which the housebuilding industry is using its resources, and the second indicates areas in which resources might be used more efficiently. With the reader in possession of all the facts in the existing situation, his coöperation is enlisted for exploration of the realm of what may come in the future. Pertinent policies may be suggested to him which, in the hands of the housebuilder himself or in the hands of the public, might eventuate in the improvement of housebuilding, and, therefore, of the living standards of all Americans.

2

The Housebuilding Industry

Forces Shaping the Industry

A grasp of the general institutional patterns and major forces shaping the industry is essential for a perceptive examination of housebuilding. This study describes and analyzes the structure and organization of the San Francisco Bay area housebuilding industry in 1949 and 1950. Since this was a period of transition, the details of the firms' operations reflect many stages of growth and development. The most important force shaping firms' activities was the tremendous expansion which the industry had just experienced. A huge increase in housing demand had taken place. Pressure for shelter had generated opportunities for dynamic development both of scale of operations and of technology. The rate at which this pressure was assimilated varied from firm to firm but is exhibited in all phases of the industry's structure and operations.

In addition to the acceleration in demand typified by the period, the particular area selected for this study exerted a strong influence on the manner in which builders operated. Every metropolitan area differs somewhat in its background, population, habits, climate, wealth, and institutional composition from every other area. These conditions contribute to the way in which the industry in each area develops.

The forces of growth and the regional characteristics are molders of the type of builders at work as well as of their size and of their product. These influences affect the mode of entrepreneurship, and the degree of initiative, in fact, the builders' ability to plan and control their own future. In addition, they change the fashion of houses produced, in style, materials, price range, and site.

To depict the actual functioning of these forces, the national housing scene will be described in general terms, and the specific features of the Bay area housebuilding industry will be outlined and related to the national scene. From these data, the reader may note the areas in which generalization from the local to the national situation appears possible, as well as areas of probable contrast and conflict. They are offered as a basis for the more intensive descriptions and analyses which follow—a panoramic background for the detailed picture.

Growth in Production

Immense growth nationally in production of housing marked the decade 1940–1949.[1] This vast increase in volume created significant changes in the structure of the housebuilding industry. Of necessity, the forces of growth which were at work throughout the country were exerting their influence on the Bay area.

During this decade, between 8,000,000 and 9,000,000 dwelling units were added to the nation's housing inventory (table 3). Between 6,000,000 and 7,000,000 were newly constructed units, and the rest were conversions and marginal additions to the supply. This record stands in dramatic contrast to the inventory change for the period 1930–1939, when the increase was about 5,000,000 of which 2,730,000 were newly constructed units.[2]

The important story told by these figures is that the rate of building of new dwelling units was approximately 2½ times as rapid in 1940–1949 as in 1930–1939. The same story of increase is told by the figures for the terminal years of the two decades. In 1939, 515,000 dwelling units were started, whereas in 1949 the number was more than 1,025,000.[3] The increase was large both relatively and absolutely.

The gain in production in the 1940's was not spread evenly throughout the period. Under the impetus of the defense economy, large gains in housebuilding had been made in 1940 and 1941, but when the war started, housing was cut back to such a degree that 1944 was one of the lowest years ever recorded. The low level continued until the war ended. Then, of course, there was a tremendous upsurge. In the year 1946, housing production was almost quadrupled. Further gains of

[1] Data used in this section can be found in Appendix B and tables 3 and 4.

[2] Colean, *American Housing*, p. 365; F. W. Dewhurst, *America's Needs and Resources* (New York: Twentieth Century Fund, 1947), p. 142.

[3] *Housing Statistics* (January, 1951), table 23.

10 to 20 per cent were experienced annually through 1949, and another sharp increase amounting to 35 per cent took place in 1950. More than 60 per cent of the decade's new construction was concentrated in the last four years. One striking statistic sums up this production boom: more houses were built in America in the five years from 1946 to 1950 than had been constructed in the entire preceding 15 years (tables 3 and 4).

The production situation in the Bay area was roughly similar to the national picture. The number of dwelling units in the Bay area increased by 247,000 between 1940 and 1950, in contrast with the increase of about 90,000 between 1930 and 1940 (table 3).

In the local situation, however, there was a relatively smaller concentration of building at the end of the decade. Since the Bay area had been a major war production center which had experienced a sudden, massive influx of population, comparatively more emergency housing had been authorized and produced in this locality during the war than elsewhere. For example, 48,000 units, or one-fifth of the total increase in the decade, consisted of public war housing. This was probably the largest concentration of war housing in the country, and its presence diminished the intensity of demand for new housing when the war ended. It must be emphasized that this moderation of demand was strictly relative, since the Bay area's hunger for housing was far from satisfied by war housing projects. Residents of the Bay area were crowded in apartments, living with in-laws, accepting makeshift arrangements, just as were the residents of every other area; and when the pent-up pressure for "a home of one's own" was undammed, the flood of demand for new housing was only slightly less urgent locally than nationally.

The enormous increase in production—when war's end made production possible—to meet the acute demand altered the cost structure as well as the type of markets and the organization of firms. The effect on costs and prices was naturally inflationary. Building cost indexes, which are based on weighted averages of quoted materials, rose by approximately the equivalent of the increases of wholesale prices in general.

The estimated cost of one-family dwelling units actually constructed increased somewhat less than the change shown in the cost indexes. It rose from $4,000 for the average one-family unit in 1939 to $7,625 in

1949, or 90 per cent compared with 108 per cent for the price index.[4] This difference may reflect either a change in size of the units built in the two periods or, perhaps, a change in efficiency.

Even more important than its effect on cost structure was the effect of the increased rate of production on builders' size and methods. What has emerged from the war and postwar periods is the large-scale operative builder. War experience gave the initial impetus to the growth of the big merchant housebuilding firms. Although the war imposed a decrease in the amount of housebuilding, that which did take place was more concentrated among the larger firms than it had been in the past. Builders who could work with government agencies in obtaining permits, priorities, and contracts were able to augment greatly their dimensions of operation. Problems of financing and marketing which had plagued them and kept them small in the prewar period were removed through the receipt of government aid and a ready-made market. Although the war ushered a large number of firms out of the industry through its restrictions and regulations, it abetted the growth of many which were able to hold on. Among the advantages gained by those firms which remained and grew was the opportunity to experiment with new techniques based upon their increased scale. Those who built at all had a ripe market of war housing demand, and, aided by the government, they built on a grand scale.

These advantages were carried over into the postwar period. The initial situation which gave momentum to the growth of the large firms was altered only in degree. A huge backlog of demand, aided and increased by government-guaranteed and insured credit, eliminated most of the prewar marketing and financing problems. The financial position of many firms had improved as a result of the war. They had more capital. The assured market, together with definite government commitments to insure loans on completed houses, greatly eased credit problems. Builders who had been active during the war had gained experience with larger operations and knew the advantages to be gained from increased size as well as the techniques necessary for successful large-scale operations. Other builders observed their success, recognized the new opportunities, and hastened to exploit them.

The structure of the housebuilding industry, as this study found it, manifests all these influences: war-induced growth; a marketing situa-

---

[4] *Housing Statistics* (January, 1951), tables 3 and 6.

tion rooted in widespread, unsatisfied demand; the stimulus of easy credit. This picture was practically unaltered until 1951. At that point, there was a tightening of credit and some slackening of demand. Since this book is a report on the industry as it existed during 1949 and 1950, the bulk of the text is focused on that period. Only after the status of the industry as it stood at that time has been completely presented do we permit ourselves guesses concerning meanings of changes and their possible indications for the industry's future.

The Area of This Study

The geographical location of the housebuilders described in this study[5] strongly influences their operations. They are all based in the San Francisco–Oakland metropolitan area. The most important aspect of this geographical influence is the fact that these are metropolitan builders. It is clear from an examination of all data that there is a vast difference in the problems of the building industry inside and outside metropolitan areas. Differences in concentration of population, number of units built per year, unionization, codes, traditions, and style of houses, all aggregate to make important organizational and structural variations.

San Francisco is considered typical of the standard metropolitan areas which the government has established throughout the country for statistical purposes. Each of these, by definition, must include at least one city with a population of 50,000 or more. An attempt is made to include in a single area those contiguous counties that are economically and socially integrated. These boundaries are continuously reëxamined in order to make these groupings as currently logical as possible.

The San Francisco–Oakland metropolitan area comprises the counties of San Francisco, San Mateo, Alameda, Contra Costa, Solano, and Marin. The area has 52 building-permit centers, which include most of the incorporated cities and towns, as well as a major center in each county handling all its unincorporated parts. The total land area is 3,300 square miles. Since San Francisco Bay lies in the midst of the area, the total expanse is far larger. Communication difficulties created by the Bay as well as by several mountain ranges have tended to separate some builders into those specializing in the East, West, or

[5] See Appendixes B and F, and tables 3 and 4.

North Bay area. The general homogeneity of the area is sufficient to make these difficulties easily surmountable by the larger operators. The communities' dependence on San Francisco for most services acts as a centralizing factor so that firms desiring to do so can work throughout the area. Such universality is accomplished by many large builders, trade contractors, and suppliers.

The climate is mild, with a mean temperature of 59 degrees. Rainfall varies from 12 to 46 inches a year in different parts of the area, but is almost entirely concentrated in the winter months. More important, as far as building is concerned, is the almost complete absence of freezing and snow. This climatic situation permits a simpler type of construction than is required in regions of rugged weather extremes. Another effect of the temperate climate on building is that outdoor work rarely has to be suspended because of rain, except in the three winter months, and no special heating precautions are required during construction.

The terrain is a hilly one, with few level areas. Three mountain ranges run through the region. These have a Protean influence upon housing, resulting in unique styles of construction in the major cities. Special planning of each house to its own lot is almost a topographical prerequisite in many places. The hilliness tends to limit somewhat the maximum size of tracts, even in the more nearly level areas, and frequently imposes special problems of site planning. As a result, site planning itself is probably more advanced than in most other regions.

The total population of the area on April 1, 1950, was 2,240,000. This represented an increase of 808,000, or 56.4 per cent, in the past decade, compared with an increase of 14.4 for the country as a whole. Although part of this increase resulted from more births than deaths, the principal part of it was due to a heavy immigration (table 3).

The average age in the Bay area is slightly higher than for the country as a whole, whereas the average household size is smaller. Probably more important, as it affects housebuilding, is the generally high level of income. The median family income in 1949 was $3,817, or 17 per cent higher than the national nonfarm average. On the other hand, there is virtually no difference in income when comparison is made with other major metropolitan areas (table 41 and sources cited therein).

This kaleidoscopic glimpse of the Bay area has shown certain local variations from the national average in design for living. Despite these individual differentiations of the locality, a more careful look at the Bay area housebuilding pattern will show its many similarities to the national average in sizes and types of builders and kinds of units produced.

Types of Builders

Is there such a thing as a housebuilding industry?[6]

Before the industry's structure and organization can be described, the question of whether the housebuilding industry exists as an entity apart from the construction industry as a whole must be answered.

This study takes the position that the housebuilding industry does exist as an entity, separable from general contracting at one extreme, and from owner-builders at the other.

The opposite answer to the question has been given by many previous writers. Miles L. Colean has written:[7]

> In discussing housebuilding, it is necessary to deal largely with the processes required rather than with producing organizations. Centralized producing organizations, combining all or even most of the essential processes, are extremely rare in housebuilding. Ordinarily, housebuilding must be defined as a series of activities that ultimately result in the production of houses. . . .
>
> Basic to centralized control (in other industries) is producer initiative—that is, the determination by the producer of both the quantity and nature of his product in advance of sale. This contrasts with buyer initiative commoner in custom industries like . . . housebuilding.

The survey on which this study is based indicated that housebuilding operations are identifiable as an industry; that in discussing housebuilding it is possible to deal with the producing organizations rather than merely with processes; and that, as will be seen, "producer initiative" is a dominating characteristic of postwar housebuilding comparable with the predetermination of product in other industries. Contrary to previous assumptions[8] that dwellings are not commonly constructed by a special class of producer, and consequent tendencies

[6] See Appendixes B and C, and tables 6, 9, 10, 13.

[7] Colean, *op. cit.*, pp. 59–60; cf. also Grebler, *Production of New Housing*, p. 6.

[8] Colean, *op. cit.*, p. 63.

to lump together statistics on all types of construction, this research developed the fact that, at least in the Bay area, the overlap between housebuilders and others in the building industry is not great.

In 1949, 90 per cent of the houses built by firms in the Bay area were constructed by businesses which did only housebuilding or received less than 10 per cent of their income from other types of building. Of the remaining 10 per cent of houses, half were built by 200 firms which also did general building, but whose housing volume made up from 60 to 90 per cent of their total. Only the final 5 per cent of the houses were built by general contracting firms which did more work on other types of building than housing. There were 238 of these; but one-third of their production was contributed by two large general contracting firms which also did tract building. These figures are evidence that it is correct to speak of a housebuilding industry as such, though classifying building firms as members or nonmembers of the housebuilding industry on the basis of a set percentage of total volume devoted to housebuilding must be somewhat arbitrary (tables 10 and 15).

The number of general contractors who engaged in housebuilding but whose housing volume made up less than half of their business is too small to affect the picture of the industry as portrayed through statistical surveys. Where their structure is such as to influence the attributes of firms, attention is called to this fact as well as to the manner in which they affect the statistical tables. In effect, they are segregated where necessary, and for purposes of analysis they are not allowed to alter the true picture of housebuilders.

At the opposite end of the scale from general contractors are owner-builders. Housebuilding is an exception among major American industries in that a significant proportion of all houses built in the United States are constructed by individual households or nonprofessionals. The day when families can build their own shelter has not yet passed in this country, frontierlike as that may sound in a machine-age culture. For purposes of industry analysis, it is vital that these individuals be separated from the firms before any statistical measures are derived; otherwise, since their number is so large, it will bias all results and negate most interpretations. Failure to make this separation is the cause of many of the weaknesses in the prewar data of the Bureau of Labor Statistics.[9]

[9] Cf. Grebler, *op. cit.*, p. 6.

In 1949, more than a fourth of all privately financed nonfarm dwellings started in the United States were built by amateurs. These owner-builders numbered 265,600 and built approximately an equivalent number of units, or 33 per cent of all houses constructed. Nationally, owner-builders outnumbered actual building firms by more than two to one (tables 6 and 7).

The prevalence of owner-builders is much greater in nonmetropolitan than in metropolitan areas. Sixty-four per cent of the owner-built units were constructed in the nonmetropolitan areas, whereas these same areas accounted for less than 35 per cent of total housing production. The preponderance of the owner-builder pattern in the country, rather than the city, is illustrated by the fact that in nonmetropolitan areas 60 per cent of the houses are built by owner-builders; in metropolitan areas only 18 per cent are put up by owner-builders.

In the metropolitan areas, there were 96,000 nonprofessional builders. This means that there were nearly one and one-half times as many amateur builders as there were active firms in these areas, although the amateurs accounted for less than one-fifth of the total units produced.

The figures for the San Francisco Bay area resemble the average of other metropolitan areas. There were 2,002 nonprofessionals, compared with 1,658 firms which completed houses in 1949. These individuals exceeded the number of firms by 22 per cent and actually accounted for about 11 per cent of all residences constructed.

In the Bay area, two-thirds of these "homemade" houses were built by people with no relation to the industry whatsoever. They were primarily amateurs who read a book or had a friend with some experience and set out to build their own homes. The remainder of these houses were built by craftsmen whose jobs and skills were related to the industry—maintenance carpenters, building inspectors, or mechanics working for others, who frequently used their own time to build for themselves.

Usually individuals built in their leisure hours—week ends, vacations, or after work. Six per cent, however, put in full time on the job. Most of the nonprofessionals did a large part of the basic work, assisted by their families and friends, but they subcontracted plumbing, electrical work, and sometimes other specialties. In 12 per cent of the cases, they merely acted as general contractor and supervisor, hiring carpenters, subcontractors and laborers.

Although a significant segment of the nation's housing demand is supplied by individuals, these amateurs ordinarily appear in the market only once in their lifetimes. They are not part of the actual industrial process. Their problems differ greatly in kind and degree from the problems of members of the industry. For the remainder of our discussion, our references are only to those firms building houses as a business.

In turning from general contractors, on the one hand, and owner-builders, on the other, to the housebuilding industry as an entity, we find that professional housebuilding firms are divided into two principal types—the contractor and the merchant or operative builder. The distinction between these two types of operation is as essential to a study of the housebuilding industry as is the separation from it of owner-builders and the segregation of general contractors. In the public mind, the small housing contractor is the symbol of the housebuilder. He is the man who builds on a lot which the owner has bought, builds to a design which the owner has selected, accepts payments for his work as it is installed in the house, and risks very little in terms of decisions or capital. The public has given comparatively little thought to the merchant builder who acquires the site, determines the design, puts out his own money as the work progresses, and assumes the risk of losing his entire investment if the house does not sell.

Many who have studied the contractual relationships which exist between the contractor and the owner of a house have believed that the housebuilding industry has been afflicted with undermanagement because too many functions and controls remain in the hands of the owner. But these criticisms clearly need not apply to the merchant or operative builder, who does make all necessary decisions and offers a completed product to the final purchaser. The dependency in functions represented by the contractor, as contrasted with the independency in functions of the operative builder, has prompted a number of housing critics to generalize that the industry would necessarily remain inefficient as long as it remained influenced by custom building, and progress could take place only with a shift to merchant building.

If these generalizations are at all accurate, the stage has certainly been set for progress. New statistics indicate that the shift has occurred.

In the Bay area and throughout the country, the majority of houses built by firms are constructed by merchant builders. In 1949 merchant builders constructed 71 per cent of houses built by firms nationally, 75 per cent of houses built by firms in the nation's metropolitan areas, and 78 per cent in the Bay area (table 9). These are the firms, determining the nature and quantity of their product in advance of sale, which are increasing in number and increasing in size. Although yesterday belonged to the contractor, this study shows that the contractor is not growing; that the merchant builder, taking advantage of today's techniques in mass production and mass merchandising, is moving in on tomorrow.

SIZE OF BUILDERS

When housebuilders are examined as to number and classified as to size,[10] two striking facts stand out: first, the large number of active housebuilding firms and their wide diversity of size and type; second, the importance in production of medium- and large-sized firms, particularly in contrast with previous experience.

The number of firms signifies the ease of entry into the industry and is an important determinant of its flexibility and its profit structure. The increased prominence of the larger-scale producers signifies a change in the structure of the industry which has greatly influenced all methods, techniques, and operations in housebuilding.

The Bureau of Labor Statistics estimates that there were 119,600 active housebuilding firms in the United States in 1949. These firms constructed 540,000 dwelling units, or an average of approximately five each.

In the Bay area, 1,658 firms built 17,485 houses in 1949, or an average of more than 10 each (tables 7 and 8). For purposes of analysis, some basis of classification of these firms is necessary, since the organization and functioning of each cannot be discussed individually.

Before our surveys, there was no existent information and no ready-made system of classification. Therefore, in the course of our field research, we tried various classifications in order to find a method of presentation which would bring out significant differences most vividly. The most satisfactory system seemed to be that based upon size.

---

[10] See Appendixes B and C, and tables 5–10, 13, 14.

Having determined to use size as a method of classification, we still had various possibilities of definition. Familiar studies in other areas classify size of firms by value of production, by value of assets, by number of employees, or, after Sombart, by type of management. Besides these categories, in many previous studies of housebuilding the method of size classification used was that of the number of units produced in a given year.

Fortunately, the degree of correlation among these various methods is so high that choosing any one will give results varying only slightly from any of the others.

A firm can be defined as small if it builds between one and 24 houses per year, does less than $200,000 in total volume of business, employs fewer than 10 men, has less than $100,000 in total assets, or is owned and managed by a craftsman who spends most of his time actually working on the job.

A firm can be defined as medium-sized if it builds between 25 and 99 units a year, does between $200,000 and $1,000,000 in business, hires between 10 and 99 employees, has from $100,000 to $600,000 in total assets, and is owned and managed by an executive who has little or no staff and performs almost all overhead work himself, while also spending a good deal of his time on actual job supervision.

A firm can be defined as large if it completes 100 or more houses a year, has a volume of business of more than $1,000,000, hires 100 or more employees, has more than $600,000 in total assets, and maintains a large overhead staff.

Variations in one or two of these attributes do occur, but they are unusual, and often reflect a condition external to the organic situation under study—the firm may conduct other businesses in addition to housebuilding; or on the day when it reported, its functioning may have been atypical because it was working at less or more than its normal rate.

In order to maintain a constant category throughout this study, we have classified all firms by the number of houses completed in 1949. This measure was readily available in all cases and appeared to have fewer ambiguities than other means. At the same time, as has been mentioned, it is highly correlated to the other criteria of size most frequently employed.

For most purposes, we designate firms as small, medium, or large, according to whether they completed between one and 24 houses, between 25 and 99, or more than 100, in 1949.

It is necessarily somewhat arbitrary to draw a sharp line between these groups. The transition in type of organization is gradual. In some cases, firms close to each other in size but placed in separate statistical classes by our arbitrary division, may actually be more alike in type of organization than are firms lying at the far extremes within a given class. Certain kinds of overlap cannot be avoided. The important point is that when firms are divided according to the number of completions, there occur significant differences between classes which are more meaningful than the differences existing within a class.

When size differences within a class alter organizations, or when other attributes become important, these facts will be given. For example, we subdivide small firms into two classes—those building less than 10 houses a year, and those building from 10 to 24—when the variations of a particular characteristic are so great over the whole range of these firms that lumping the firms together gives a meaningless average. Similarly, in discussing certain characteristics of small firms, we divide the firms into categories of merchant builders and contract builders, because these two builder types differ significantly in certain functions. The purpose of our system of classification and of our interpretations of statistical results has been to bring to the reader as meaningful a picture as possible.

Using this system of classification, we find that of the 119,600 housebuilders in the United States in 1949, more than 115,000 were small, and less than 4 per cent of all housebuilding firms were in the medium-sized or large classifications. There were only 720 large builders, and 3,030 medium-sized firms. Despite this discrepancy in number, the medium-sized and large groups of firms accounted for 45 per cent of the units built by firms. Large builders constructed 24 per cent of the 540,000 units; medium-sized firms built 21 per cent (tables 7 and 8).

These figures represent a dynamic increase in the number of units built by larger firms as well as in the number of large firms in the market since the war. It is clear that an important increase in the concentration of production among the larger firms has occurred, though its exact magnitude cannot be measured because of the lack of comprehensive statistical information for the prewar period.

Prewar data on number and size of housebuilding firms are extremely sketchy. In fact, only our recent increase in knowledge makes it possible to select among the prewar figures with any confidence that we are obtaining a true picture. A statistical description of the prewar industry requires selecting data from several sources. As a result we can be certain only that it is relatively accurate. We cannot depend upon specific individual figures.

We estimate that in 1939 there were only about 90 to 110 large builders (that is, who started more than 100 houses a year) and only about 400 to 600 medium-sized builders (that is, who constructed between 25 and 99 units a year) (table 5). The large builders started from 15,000 to 18,000 units in 1939, and the medium-sized from 18,000 to 27,000. These represent less than one-tenth of all units (including owner-built) constructed in 1939, compared with the large and medium builders' 1949 percentage of nearly one-third. The large- and medium-sized builders constructed less than one-fifth of the houses started by firms in 1939, compared with nearly half of those started by firms in 1949. The total number of units built by large- and medium-sized firms was at least six times as great in 1949 as in 1939. These figures dramatize both the increase in total production and the increase in the number of larger firms. Both the relative and the absolute changes are striking in the nation as a whole.

The increased importance of large firms is even more impressive when we examine metropolitan areas and the San Francisco Bay district, since it is the less-populated regions which contain the bulk of owner-builders and the metropolitan areas where the larger firms are located. There are no large builders in the sparsely habitated, nonmetropolitan areas, and only about 6 per cent of the new units in these places are constructed by medium-sized builders. In the limited markets of small towns it is difficult for large builders to arise, because the necessary output for their scale of operations would exceed the total demand of the local markets.

Approximately two-thirds of all houses started in 1949 were built in metropolitan areas. Included were nearly 80 per cent or 429,000 units of the national total constructed by firms. At the same time, the number of firms active in these areas was only 66,000, or about 55 per cent of the national total. Metropolitan firms built an average of about seven houses each. The large firms built 31 per cent and the medium-sized firms built 25 per cent, whereas the 95 per cent of the firms which

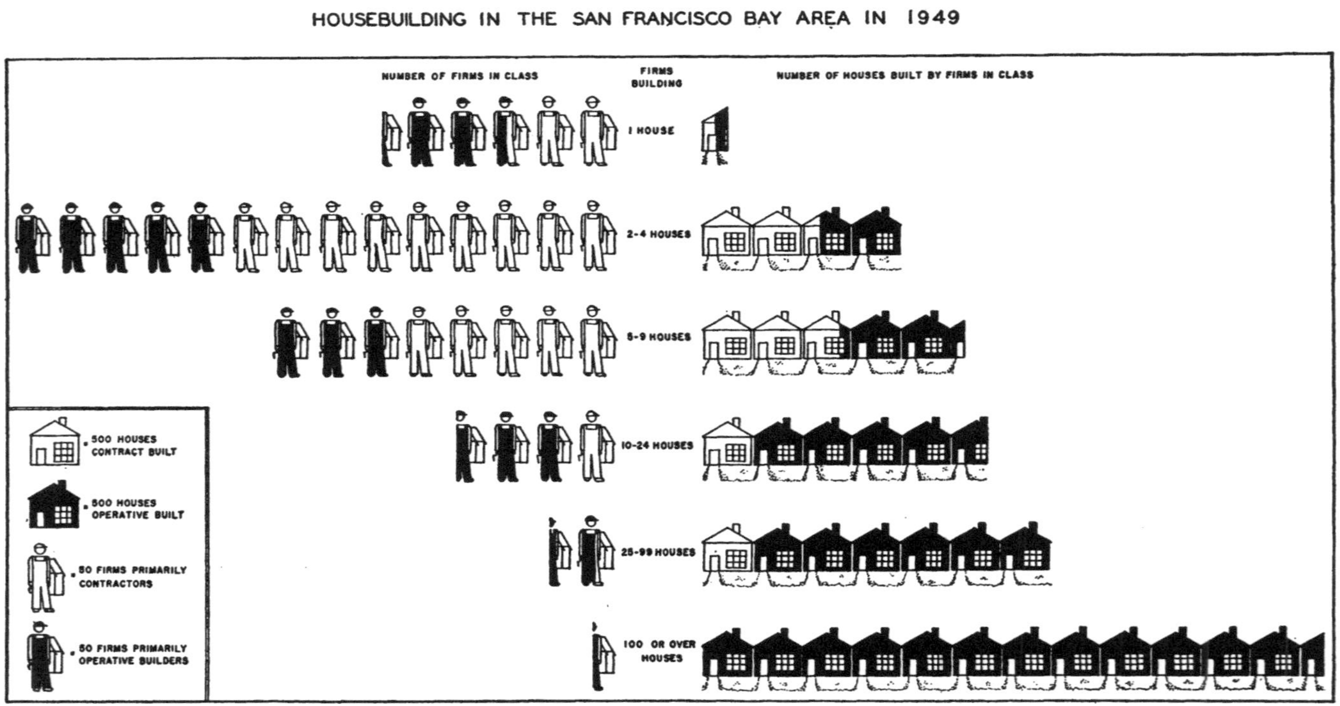

Fig. 1. Housebuilding in the San Francisco Bay area in 1949.

built less than 25 units each in the year accounted for only 44 per cent of the houses that were professionally constructed in metropolitan areas (tables 7 and 8).

The story for the San Francisco Bay area is similar to that of the other metropolitan regions. A graphic picture of the Bay area situation is presented in figure 1. In 1949, there were 1,658 firms in the area building houses. These firms completed 17,485 structures in that year. Divided by size, there were 30 large firms, 77 in the medium classification, and 1,551 small builders. In other words, 2 per cent were large firms, 5 per cent were medium-sized, and 93 per cent were small, compared with the national averages in metropolitan areas of 1 per cent large firms, 4 per cent medium-sized firms, and about 95 per cent small firms.

Large and medium firms together accounted for 55 per cent of the houses produced by firms. The breakdown was 35 per cent for the large firms and 20 for the medium (tables 8, 9, and 10).

In metropolitan districts throughout the nation, as well as in the Bay area, it was the medium-sized firm which built the average or median house—that is, the house which is found midway through a table cumulating units completed, according to builders' size. In the Bay area, the median house was built by a firm which constructed 40 other units in the same year, whereas in most other metropolitan areas the median house was built by a slightly larger producer. This means that in 1949 the odds were even that anyone buying a house from a metropolitan housebuilder purchased from a firm which had constructed close to 50 other houses (table 8).

A similar picture is received if one compares present data with the prewar permit surveys of the Bureau of Labor Statistics, which have usually been quoted as among the best estimates of the sizes of housebuilding firms. Again, one finds the relationship between the two periods to be comparable both on the national and the Bay area levels. The average number of completions per builder in 1938 was estimated at 2.2 nationally, and at 4 houses per Bay area builder.[11]

Omitting the builders of single houses to correct roughly for individuals—not enterprises—included in the 1938 study, the averages would be 4.8 per builder nationally, and 7.6 for the Bay area builder

[11] "Builders of 1-Family Houses in 72 Cities," U. S. Dept. of Labor, *Monthly Labor Review* (September, 1940), "Operations of Urban Home Builders," *Monthly Labor Review* (May, 1941).

in 1938, as compared with averages of 10 nationally and 12.4 for the Bay area in 1949.

When changes in inequality of production between 1938 and 1949 are compared, it is found that inequality has increased. In 1949, builders of more than 100 houses accounted for more than 35 per cent of completions in the Bay area and for 24 per cent of completions throughout the country, in contrast with 16 per cent for Bay area firms of this size shown by the permit data in 1938 and with less than 5 per cent for the large firms in the 1938 national total.[12] These firms which have increased in number and in size are operative or merchant builders in type.

A high correlation between size of firm and type of building was found by our survey. At one extreme, the firms which completed more than 100 houses per year did about 1 per cent of their work on contracts, or about 99 per cent of their work operatively, and only 5 per cent of their houses were not in tracts. At the other extreme, the firms which completed fewer than 10 houses per year did more than 55 per cent of their construction on contracts, and almost all their houses were built on individual lots (tables 10, 13, and 14).

The correlation of size and type of builder is illustrated by the fact that 78 per cent of the units constructed by firms in the Bay area in 1949 were operatively built, with 56 per cent of professionally built units constructed in tracts. This is indicative of the greater importance of larger firms in the building industry. Conversely, the diminished importance of the smallest firms is shown by the fact that only 22 per cent of the Bay area units completed by firms in 1949 were done on contract, principally on individual lots, compared with more than 50 per cent in 1938.[13]

House Characteristics

A final important force in forming the housebuilding industry's organization is the house itself. In fact, the prevalent size and type of builder and the type of house produced are interrelated factors influencing each other as well as the structure of the industry. The predominance of large merchant builders throughout metropolitan areas means that a large number of units produced tends to acquire a uni-

[12] "Builders of 1-Family Houses in 72 Cities," *loc. cit.*, pp. 6–8.
[13] "Operations of Urban Home Builders," *loc. cit.*

form style, often called the "builder's house," and, in its more mundane aspects, nicknamed the "GI house." Certain information on characteristics of houses started during the last half of 1949 was gathered in 15 metropolitan areas by the BLS and was expanded for the San Francisco area as part of the research for this study.[14]

This information makes it apparent, again, that the San Francisco area is typical in the kinds of units being produced by merchant builders, though its climate is more temperate than the average, and its local tradition prompts a few unusual and often more expensive features than are found elsewhere.

The typical Bay area house built in 1949 was a one-story detached unit with garage, having five rooms with an area of 1,010 square feet. It had a median price of $10,750. Although the house was built in the rural nonfarm or suburban areas, in 97 per cent of the cases it had both a community water supply and a community sewer system. It was almost always a frame house. Forty-three times out of a hundred this house had a stucco exterior and was often sheathed only with wire and building paper. When it was not stucco, the exterior was usually redwood siding or shingles. In 83 per cent of the houses, dry walls were used. Sixty-eight per cent had only a floor or wall furnace, rather than central heating. A similar percentage had a fireplace (tables 36, 38, and 39).

Most of these features are typical of all metropolitan houses. Certain characteristics, chiefly related to climate, make Bay area houses simpler than most others. Because of the mild climate, the percentage of houses without central heating and without a basement or utility room is far higher than the national average. For the same reason, the percentage of Bay area houses containing masonry walls or plaster is much lower than the national average. Nevertheless, the Bay area is closer to the national average in all of these features than are Southern or some other Western cities.

Other characteristics related to the pattern of life and local tradition make the Bay area house more expensive than others. Almost every house has a garage or carport; this is true only of about half the typical houses in other areas. More than two-thirds of the Bay area houses have fireplaces, whereas less than half as many, on the national average, have them. Bay area houses are larger than those in nearly all

[14] See Appendix F.

other areas. Of the 15 metropolitan areas studied for the last half of 1949, the Bay area was found to have the second largest average house. The Bay area house was about 13 per cent or 120 square feet larger than the median house of the other cities. All this added up—perhaps together with differences in wage rates or efficiency—to a $1,100 difference in the mean price of the Bay area house over the average of the other areas. The Bay area ranked fourth from the top of the 15 metropolitan areas in price of units built, surpassed only by Cleveland, Chicago, and Washington. This same general type of cost relationship for the Bay area has existed throughout the postwar period (table 36).

Consideration of the kinds of houses also discloses that many features of the houses produced in the Bay area vary with the size of firm producing them. These facts are significant in that they show that in 1949 builders of different sizes were not primarily competing with each other, but were fulfilling the needs of rather distinct and separate markets.

Small builders, who do the bulk of custom work, erected houses with more space, more expensive details, and almost certainly finer quality. Proportionately more houses constructed by small builders have basements or utility rooms, central heat, extra bathrooms, and costlier surfacing for both the exterior and interior walls than do the houses built by the medium-sized and large firms. All these features indicate greater value in the house of the small-sized group of firms.

These small firms produce houses on contract for a small, select market which can afford, and usually demands, many special services. It is a custom market which parallels the high-priced custom market in many other commodities, in contrast with the cheaper, mass production market (table 38).

Bay area builders of more than 100 houses sold about 47 per cent of their total production for less than $9,000. More than two-thirds of their houses were priced under the general average. The median-priced house sold by the smallest builders—of less than 10 houses—cost $13,000, with nearly 40 per cent of this group's production reaching more than $15,000. Remembering that the median house among all groups sold for $10,750, it is possible to conclude that the concentration of the large producers is in the mass market, whereas the smaller the builder, the more expensive a house he is likely to produce, and the more select his market (table 39).

A similar relationship exists with respect to type of land and area in which the various sizes and types of builders work and corroborates the conclusion about the separateness of the markets served by the various size-classes of builders.

The large-scale builder, interested principally in large expanses of relatively cheap land for tract development, must go outside the cities to obtain it. The percentage of small firms building primarily in the central cities is three times as high as the percentage of large firms. When the small builder utilizes land in built-up areas, he is not competing with the large firm at all, but actually is dealing in an entirely different product in a separate market.

The relationship between size of builder and type of land area is reiterated by the relationship between type of land area and price of house. For example, 40 per cent of the houses built by firms in the nonurban sections of the Bay area sold for less than $9,000. Only 24 per cent of the houses built in incorporated areas with less than 50,000 population sold for less than $9,000. Only 5 per cent of the houses built in the central cities sold for less than $9,000.

The interrelationships just observed among size of builder, area and market, and price may be an important explanation of the increased movement of population outside the city. Much attention has been paid to signs of this population movement throughout the nation. In the central cities of the Bay area, one new house was completed in 1949 for every 464 persons; one new house was built for every 62 persons in the suburbs; and there was a new house for every 49 persons in the nonincorporated areas. This shows that the rate of building outside the central cities is more than seven times as great as inside. These results of our survey confirm the preliminary census reports of the movement of population from the central cities to the suburbs, nationally, and underscore the conformity of what is happening in the Bay area to what is happening in the rest of the nation.

Because of this conformity, observable in many aspects of the housebuilding situation, some readers may find certain Bay area data offered by this study useful for reckonings about the industry as a whole.

This study confines itself, for the next three chapters, to an examination of the Bay area housebuilding industry in terms of size of builders. The high intercorrelation between number of units produced and all other measures of size makes unit production a workable criterion;

and the high intercorrelation between size of builders and all other factors involved in housebuilding makes size a usable statistical lens for X-raying the structure and organization of the industry. The following chapters present, in order, the small builder, the medium-sized builder, and the big builder in three statistical profiles describing the problems and solutions of each in respect to typical background, organization, financing, market, production, labor relations, purchasing, and controls.

It should be emphasized that though these facts are presented in narrative form, they are based on a statistically reliable survey of the entire housebuilding industry in the Bay area. The description of methods and organization of each size of firm is based upon case studies and interviews. The statistical appendix describes in more detail the methods used in these case studies. It also presents tables that enable the reader to estimate the reliability of each statement (tables 1 and 2).

3

The Small Builder

Although their role has decreased, small firms continue to play an important part in the housebuilding industry.[1] Their chief characteristics are simplicity, flexibility, and direct control over their workers and subcontractors, with resulting advantages inherent in personal relations. Although extremely elementary, their organization in relation to their labor supply, trade contractors, and materials distributors is sensible and properly performs the functions required of it. As with many informal organizations, theirs has far greater efficiency and stability than is commonly recognized.

Because of their small scale, these firms cannot adopt many of the cost-saving procedures of the other classes. However, much of their relative inefficiency in purchasing and in the use of major factors required for production is compensated by low charges for profits and overhead. Because of their simple form, they operate without exact records and cost information, but thus far their techniques of control have been fairly adequate for the demands placed upon them.

Opportunities for research and development of new procedures are practically nonexistent for small firms, but they contribute to the industry's progress by building experimental units and those of new design created by architects. In the postwar period they have adopted many new techniques rapidly. They also fill an important role as custom builders who furnish for upper-income groups better quality houses on scattered sites. Unlike larger firms, they can produce individual units in any location without further loss of efficiency.

These firms exist for personal and historical reasons, not because they are particularly efficient. Although it is possible that some are

[1] See Appendix C, and tables 10, 11, 13, 18, 39.

founded with hopes of winning in the grand lottery and of becoming the rich successful firms of the future, most reflect, rather, their owner's desire for independence and self-employment. These firms used to be dominant in the building industry. They still are, in terms of number, but not in actual production.

Small firms are those which build between one and 24 houses in a single year. Their total sales are less than $200,000. They are the firms usually owned by former carpenters who still work on the job as foremen and are their own best workmen. Only toward the top of this bracket do the owners spend their full time in direct supervision. A majority of these firms are contractors, but among them are some small operative builders, constructing individual houses primarily on a speculative basis.

There were 1,551 small housebuilding firms (93 per cent of the total) active in the Bay area in 1949. They produced 7,778 dwelling units (45 per cent of the total), or an average of five units per firm. Their distribution by size was J-shaped, with the largest number of firms those which completed only one house in the year. For many of the firms included in the small-sized classification, housebuilding was either a secondary interest, or the firm spent only part of the year in building (tables 10, 15, 16, and 18).

Among them were general contractors who received most or a sizable percentage of their incomes from constructing buildings other than houses. In addition, some firms had incomes from real estate or land development activities. More than half the firms in the small classification were in business only part of the year (nine months or less). If a firm builds during only part of the year, size when measured by yearly volume is obviously smaller than its monthly rate of construction. The net effect of all these factors is that measuring by completions understates somewhat the actual size of the firms. The firms in business for only part of the year reflect the rapid rate of turnover of housebuilding firms. Housing has had a larger percentage of turnover than any industry in most postwar years. Turnover in building is due not only to the attrition normal in all industries through death, sickness, failure, and so on, but also to the fact that low capital requirements induce many mechanics to set up their own enterprise when a favorable contract or speculation is available and then allow it to fall into disuse until the next advantageous opportunity arises.

The interaction of these various factors is apparent. Only 16 of 270 firms completing a single house reported that they were in business for the entire year and did not have income from other types of building. The other firms which did no other building were in existence six months or less. Within the whole group of firms falling in the 1–9 unit bracket, only 340, or one-fourth of the total, reported that they did only housebuilding and were in business for the complete twelve months (table 18 and Appendix C).

Since important managerial changes take place at around the ten-unit-per-year level, it is logical for many purposes to subdivide small builders into two homogeneous classes. First, there were 1,362 firms which completed less than ten houses in the year. Together they built 4,842 units. In this smallest-size bracket, 424 of the firms were primarily operative builders, 716 were primarily contract housebuilders, and 222 were general contractors who built some houses but did more of their work on other types of buildings. These last two categories, containing nearly 70 per cent of the total, conformed to the usual picture of the traditional housebuilder as a small firm working primarily on contracts from the plans of others. As firms expanded into the 10–24 classification, their methods of operation began to change. In this second group of 188 firms, 132 were operative housebuilders whereas the remaining 56 did most of their work on contracts. Together they completed 2,936 units (tables 11, 13, and 15).

As mentioned previously, the custom houses produced by small builders contained more space and had more expensive features than those built by larger builders. The median house produced by this group cost $12,400 as compared with a median of approximately $9,800 for the larger firms. Perhaps more important, more than 40 per cent of the units built by firms completing less than ten per year and 20 per cent of the units built by those in the 10–24 classification cost more than $15,000. This compares with a total of less than 9 per cent of expensive houses constructed by medium and large firms (table 39).

Background and Organization

Small builders operate in the craft tradition. The average owner had 14 years of building experience, principally as a carpenter working for others, before he started his present firm. Most firms have been founded since the war—only one-fourth date from the prewar period.

The recent tremendous expansion of demand, the availability of somewhat simpler financing, and increases in their own capital resulting from the general prosperity allowed these men to leave their employers and branch out on their own.[3]

With a median age of four years, firms in this class are somewhat younger than are those of the larger groups. So, also, are their owners, despite a long background in building. Owners of the firms in the 1–9 classification have a median age of 43, and those in the 10–24 group average 48 (tables 24 and 25).

Among the youngest of the new owners is a sprinkling of nonmechanics who have established housebuilding firms since the war. Not being tradition-bound, they have hoped to improve the industry through the introduction of new techniques and ideas. This younger group includes some recent college graduates and a small percentage of men from other industries. (Seven per cent of small builders are college graduates and 9 per cent did not start as mechanics.) Still, the great majority of owners have spent all their time in building, most of it in working for others.

Small size is a matter of choice for many of these firms. Their owners have no wish to pyramid themselves into great or powerful enterprises. Their thinking and planning is on a small scale. They take pride in their craft and like housebuilding. They enjoy working with tools and materials and are satisfied with their existing size and independence from worry and stress.

The organization of these firms, in their executive and management functions and their legal form, remains as simple as possible. Unincorporated proprietorships predominate in the smallest-size group, with 904 firms, or 66 per cent of the total, in this category. Next most important are partnerships, totaling nearly one-quarter of the firms. The prevalence of partnerships is a striking feature of the building industry, noticeable at all size levels. Apparently, partnerships are a particularly logical form of structure. Duties and responsibilities of ownership are diverse and can be split rather simply. At the same time, partnerships increase the possibility of raising capital, and some such increase over individual holdings is necessary for growth. Finally, fewer than 100 firms building less than 10 units per year are corporations, and these frequently are general contractors for whom housebuilding is of minor importance. As would be expected in small firms,

[3] See Appendixes C and E, and tables 21, 24–35.

few intercorporate relationships exist. The only exceptions are those firms established as housebuilding affiliates of a real estate business (table 27).

The executive functions of small firms remain uncomplicated also. In 76 per cent, or more than 1,000 firms, the owner is a working foreman spending six to seven hours each day on the job as a carpenter and foreman. The owner uses the remainder of the construction period, hours after work, and some time in the evening in record-keeping, searching out and negotiating with subcontractors, and handling other overhead details. Although in some small firms a part-time bookkeeper or secretary may be regularly employed, frequently either the owner or his wife does all the bookkeeping and secretarial work (table 20 and Appendix D).

In most of these firms, the owner's home is his office. In many cases, the only cash payments for overhead personnel go to an accountant or bookkeeper, who checks the books and prepares the tax records on a fee basis.

In 24 per cent of the firms completing less than ten houses per year, the owner acts as a full-time executive rather than as working foreman. In these firms, the builder usually either has other interests, such as real estate, which occupy part of his time and furnish him additional income, or he is a contract builder working on expensive units. In the latter instances, more time must be spent in obtaining bids and in negotiating with owners or architects, and the higher price of the units includes the necessary payments for this additional overhead.

This lack of a complicated overhead structure is simultaneously the source of greatest strength and greatest weakness of these firms. The strength exists because only extremely low overhead charges need enter into the price of their houses. The weaknesses lie in the fact that the management effort and skills bestowed on these firms are also minimal.

Firms must add overhead to their direct costs. It includes all costs of supervision above the level of working foreman, all office expenses, depreciation of equipment, selling costs, rent, and the cost of capital not borrowed specifically for the construction of a particular house. Because of the great difficulty of separating on an economic basis profits and overhead in these firms, both returns are considered together.

How large is each main component of overhead in a small firm? A very simple estimate can be made for those 900 firms in which the proprietor is a working foreman who performs management functions in his spare time. Such firms have no off-site employees; the owner or his wife handles the paper work. They pay no rent for their office, which is usually the dining-room table. In these firms, which are unincorporated, the cost of supervision, the return on capital (which is primarily working capital), and the owner's wages as foreman are lumped together. This total sum was estimated from financial records of the builders (Appendix E). In this estimate it was assumed that the first $5,000 of the proprietor's income covers his wages as a working foreman. In reality, this is somewhat less than he would have received in wages if he had been a foreman working for another firm.

According to the builders' financial records, the median small builder (1–9 units) received $2,800 above his estimated salary. (In partnerships, estimates are after their joint salaries have been withdrawn, and in the few corporations, after all expenses.) This net profit before taxes averaged approximately 5.7 per cent per dollar of sales. It was a return of approximately 13 per cent per annum on the net worth which the builder risked in his operations (tables 33–35).

This so-called net profit had to cover both the necessary return for the risk of the builder's investment and any cash compensation for the many extra hours he and his wife put in on management functions. In reality, since it was only about half the rate of return received by those who had invested in larger building corporations, it may not have been even a normal return on capital.

The small builder was getting little or no compensation for the time spent in managerial and overhead functions. He was paid for his actual labor as a carpenter foreman and for the use of his equity, but that was all. All his executive work was a labor of love. The cost for management in small firms was approximately zero.

Many feel that there is something basically wrong in this situation. The builder spends ten to twenty hours of his free time in overhead functions, and certain observers believe, therefore, that this must be a cost. They feel that in some way he is being exploited because he gets no monetary return for his work. They fail to recognize that he is paid in nonmonetary satisfaction. If he demanded money in addition to his present returns, he could not compete and could not remain independent. The incentives of ownership and self-employment cause people to work longer hours and for less pay from themselves than they would for others. The small builder pays for the privilege of ownership and self-employment, just as the owners of the small corner grocery, the little hardware shop, the variety store, and many other independent purveyors of goods and services pay for the privilege of independent operation. The returns to management may actually be negative.

The remaining items of overhead—depreciation, selling costs, and fees for outside clerical help—are also minor factors for the small builder. Depreciation is low. Excluding the owner's personal auto, it is probable that the total cost of equipment charged per house is less than $100. The small builder is usually a contractor and therefore has few if any selling costs. When he does build for his own account, he is as likely as not to sell the house himself without payment of fees. He uses little or no other outside help. All these overhead items together average about 2.5 per cent of selling price. When overhead is added to profits, it appears that the small builder's total margin between price and direct costs, even in the very prosperous postwar period, is slightly more than 8 per cent. This covers all charges for supervision, profit, depreciation, rent, and other overhead (Appendix E).

How can this 8 per cent figure be reconciled with the 15 per cent frequently quoted as a fair or proper charge for these items? The housebuilding industry is simply too competitive in the lower levels for any such return to exist. Among small firms, increased demand and boom conditions have been reflected primarily in a decrease in the number taking losses and an increase in the number making moderate profits. Only a few firms have made percentage profits even approaching what many consider necessary.

A somewhat different picture of overhead costs and profits exists in those small firms in which the owner has become a full-time executive. As volume increases, overhead structure also develops. In the 10–24 completion group nearly a third of the owners operate as working foremen; somewhat more act as job superintendents and full-time executives, no longer using tools but neither employing additional aid; and fewer than a third of them not only spend full time on executive duties but also hire an assistant. In these firms, if the owner performs direct construction supervision, assistants usually help in estimating or expediting; if the owner specializes in the non-technical aspects of the job, the assistant may be the primary site supervisor (table 20 and Appendix D).

As size increases, legal structures change also. Only 38 per cent of these 10–24 unit firms are still sole proprietorships; one-fourth are partnerships; and nearly one-eighth are corporations. The incidence of affiliated firms is also greater, nearly one-fourth being related to some other type of business. The firms in the 10–24 group build, on the average, $200,000 worth of units per year. The total return to the proprietor has averaged $18,400. Because he no longer works as a carpenter, this is all charged to overhead. After again subtracting the $5,000 assumed necessary to cover his actual wages as a supervisor, his net profit is at the rate of 6.7 per cent per sales dollar (tables 27, 33–35).

Other overhead expenses are again insignificant. Depreciation on equipment averages about 0.5 per cent per sales dollar. The firms in this group are still most likely to have their headquarters in the owner's home and to use only part-time clerical help. The owner himself probably does a good deal of selling. Assuming that $4,000 will cover all of these incidental expenses, and adding this to the $18,400, it appears that total overhead and profit in these firms have risen to about 11 per cent per sales dollar.

All these facts indicate that small housebuilders have brought overhead charges and profits close to a minimum. Difficulties still exist. Adequate management and supervisory skills are a luxury that small firms cannot purchase with the small sums available—a fact that becomes apparent in a discussion of their records and controls.

Financing

For an industry in which the average firm is commonly supposed to live a hand-to-mouth existence, builders' total assets are surprisingly high. This is indicated in the first column of figure 2—the balance sheet of an average small builder. The balance sheet is composed of the median holdings for each type of asset or liability found in an examination of builders' financial reports.[8]

The median small builder (1–9 units completed) had total assets of $36,500. A frequency distribution of this item in all firms bears out the fact that in the postwar period builders have been relatively

[8] See Appendix E, and tables 28–35.

affluent. Only 5 per cent of the small firms had less than $10,000 in total assets, whereas more than 17 per cent had more than $100,000 in assets.

These figures are influenced by the fact that small firms are predominantly unincorporated proprietorships rather than corporations, and therefore their balance sheets contain both business and personal

FIGURE 2

FINANCIAL BALANCE SHEET FOR A TYPICAL HOUSEHOLDER OF EACH SIZE

Item	Median holding of builders in size class			
	1–9	10–24	25–99	100 and over
	in dollars			
Current assets	15,200	42,700	160,000	562,000
Tools and equipment	2,700	4,000	8,500	17,500
Real estate and buildings	16,200	27,600	30,500	310,000
Miscellaneous assets	2,400	13,700	58,000	190,500
Total	36,500	88,000	257,000	1,080,000
Liabilities	6,300	36,200	145,000	661,000
Net worth	30,200	51,800	112,000	419,000
Total liabilities and proprietorship or capital	36,500	88,000	257,000	1,080,000

SOURCE: Tables 28–32.

assets. No simple method exists of separating in financial statements builders' personal property, which includes such assets as their homesteads and savings, from those used in their business. For many purposes, of course, no real division is desired. Personal property is not available for use in construction, but it does serve as additional security against which working capital can be borrowed. In addition, since these enterprises are unincorporated when the builder enters into any venture, all his assets, no matter of what type, are at stake.

It is noteworthy that builders own most assets outright. The ratio of their net worth to total assets is high. The median small builder borrows only between $6,000 and $7,000 compared with an average net worth of more than $30,000. For an industry in which credit supposedly plays such an important role, this is a small amount. The distribution of net worth among small firms follows the same relative characteristics as that of assets. Virtually no firm is worth less than $5,000; somewhat more than one-third have holdings between $5,000 and $20,000; nearly 40 per cent have a net worth between $20,000 and $50,000; and more than a quarter of even these small firms are worth more than $50,000 (table 30 and fig. 2).

Net worth is important, but it is not the prime factor that determines the amount of work the builder can perform. Because much of his net worth is frozen, it is his working capital—mainly cash—which is of primary importance in determining his financial ability to handle work.

At any given time, the small builder's working capital is likely to include about $5,000 in cash plus another $1,000 or $2,000 in war bonds or similar assets. In addition, he is owed an equivalent amount for work in process. His current assets, representing both cash and the work for which he has not yet been paid, are slightly more than $15,000. Because of the mixture of personal and business assets, his percentage of total assets currently available is somewhat less than for other categories of building. A builder's current and working assets pass through a continuous cycle. In the process of building, cash is drawn and becomes work in process. Then when payment is received for work completed, the amount of work in progress is decreased and the cash item again increases.

Because of the relatively low percentage of his total current assets, the small builder (completing 1–9 units) has a low turnover of his capital, his sales-equity ratio being approximately two and a half to one, compared with a median ratio of five times per year for the large firms. This slow turnover, plus a relatively small profit on sales, results in the low return on net worth made by the small firm (tables 31, 34).

The second item in the builder's balance sheet consists of tools and equipment. This item averages $2,700 and emphasizes the low level of mechanization existing in the industry. Even so, the average small firm has an amount of equipment nearly five to ten times as high per completion as do the larger firms in the industry, a discrepancy which reflects the lumpiness of equipment expenditures. The small builder's high equipment ratio compared to the large builders' is not caused by the magnitude of his own holdings but simply by the extremely low level of theirs. The small builder's equipment usually includes a pickup truck, a car, a power saw, and hand tools. These are almost the minimum necessary to operate. As size increases, additional equipment is added but at a very slow rate. Since even for the small builder equipment costs are slight (depreciation averages only $100 per house) any spreading of this overhead item is comparatively unimportant (table 32 and fig. 2).

In addition to current assets and tools and equipment, the average small builder owns about $16,000 in real estate and buildings and $2,400 in miscellaneous assets. The real estate is usually his own home, though occasionally he holds a few building lots for speculation. Miscellaneous assets include minor investments in other ventures.

Although the builder's net worth is larger than might have been expected, it still does not suffice to cover his financing needs. The average house contract is large and takes a long period to complete. Therefore, a procedure is necessary whereby builders can collect on work in progress and replenish their cash; otherwise practically none could accept jobs as large as a house.

The problems of the small contractor in construction financing are discussed at this point, and in the next chapter the construction financing of operative builders is discussed. On contracts, final financing is the responsibility of the owners, who, in most cases, use either a conventional loan or have sufficient funds to pay for the entire cost of the house themselves. Since it is a luxury market, owners who contract for houses are likely to have adequate financial means.

By exercising diligence and assuring himself that he is dealing with a responsible party, the contractor can be certain that adequate funds for final payment on the contract are available before he starts. He need not concern himself with the problems of the buyer's financing. All he has to do is provide sufficient capital to meet his own current bills between receipt of payments against the contract. The amount of capital he requires will depend upon the rate at which he expends funds for a house, and the rate at which he receives payment for it from the owner, plus some additional amount to meet unknown contingencies such as an increase in costs above his original estimate.

To keep the amount of capital invested in any job as low as possible, the contractor wants to be paid for each item as soon as it is placed in the house. In this, his interests are opposite to those of the owner, who is interested in security. The contractor wants the least possible investment in any single building so that he can handle the maximum number of jobs with his limited capital. The owner wants to be sure that the contractor has sufficient funds to finish the job. He worries lest he finds himself with a partly finished job, no contractor, and no funds. Such a situation may arise if he pays the contractor for all or more than the work put in place, or if the contractor estimated incorrectly.

A compromise between these divergent interests is found in the normal system of "draws," or partial payments against the agreed upon contract price. Under this system, the owner deposits with a bank or other escrow agent sufficient funds to cover the contract. Where a loan is involved, a bank usually performs this function. At the start of construction, the bank holds the owner's equity and, in addition, his signed note to cover a loan to pay for the remainder of the contract. As the house is constructed, the bank lends against the work actually completed. The contract agreement specifies the rate at which payment for the work will be made. Many possible payment methods exist: for example, the monthly percentage of completion achieved may be estimated and an equivalent percentage of the contract paid out; payments may be based on bills paid by the builder; or agreed-upon payments may be made each time a particular stage of the house is reached. The last method is most common in this area. Agreements normally state that the bank will pay to the contractor 20 per cent of the contract price at each of five stages of construction. Normally the completion of a stage is certified by the architect or the owner. The stages used in this area are usually: (1) upon completion of foundation and rough flooring, (2) at completion of roofing, (3) at completion of plastering, (4) at completion and acceptance of job, and (5) after the lien period, which in this case is thirty-five days after completion of the job.

The decision as to whether or not the contractor has sufficient working capital to undertake a job is made by the owner or bank after a credit investigation. Infrequently a performance bond is required. These apparently have not been used in the average case in the postwar period on the assumption that contractors who could obtain a bond usually would not need it, and that the system of partial payments adequately protects the owner.

The use of the five-payment system means that a contractor may have a personal investment up to 20 per cent of the value of a contract in each job at any time. When his investment has reached that amount, he should have reached the next stage and should be able to draw against the contract. Since this is true, his total contracts under construction at a given time should be limited to five times his working capital. Otherwise there are likely to be periods when he cannot meet his bills because his investments in work in progress exceed his available capital. He may be solvent but illiquid. Also, of course, some additional capital should be available if unforeseen adverse happenings develop, and he actually loses money on a contract. If this occurs, both his solvency and liquidity may be in danger.

Actually, the required amount of working capital may be somewhat less than 20 per cent of each contract. There may be a lag between installation of work in a house and his payment of bills. Thus at a certain stage, he may be paid for materials installed and subcontracts for which he still owes the trade contractor or material dealer. At any time, he is the beneficiary of an average of two to three weeks' credit from his workers, trade contractors, and materials dealers, which, in effect, increases his working capital. By adjusting his work properly and using this additional credit, he may be able to handle contracts equal to ten times his working capital instead of the five considered normal.

Such an expansion would be, of course, dangerous for the owner even if favorable to the contractor. The owner may find he has paid for a house which, because of mechanics' liens, he only partly owns. If the owner has paid the contractor upon completion of a certain stage, but the trade contractors and material supply houses have bills outstanding, the owner may find that he buys his house twice, through having to pay the bills of these firms in addition to what he has paid to the builder. For this reason, in certain instances payments to cover materials and trade contract bills are not made directly to the contractor, but instead a system is set up whereby he submits these bills to the escrow agents and they send the checks directly to the subcontractor or dealer. Such systems are not common in the Bay area. The average contractor, even if short of working capital, usually has other securities adequate to insure proper completion. In fact, in many cases banks will lend contractors working capital on personal notes with this other security in mind. Other loans may be secured by chattel mortgages against tools and equipment.

Contractors on the whole have had adequate capital for their operations. If, however, they attempt to become operative builders or to expand operations, the problem of capital, and especially that of construction financing, becomes critical. The average builder finds that his capital is not sufficient, and he cannot borrow enough additional to handle the jobs he might obtain. The firm would like to expand but is not able to because it has no method of raising additional capital.

The Market

The problems of marketing, land, and product development are completely interrelated for small builders. Firms must decide upon the type of building they wish to perform and also upon the market for which they aim.[4] If a firm decides to become an operative builder it must obtain land and plan its houses. If it does not wish to perform these merchant-building functions it can enter the contract field and concern itself with the problems of bidding.

As with most functions of small firms, these problems are handled in a rather elementary fashion. The decision as to the type of building is far more likely to be based upon the firm's past history than upon any economic considerations or ideas of what might be most profitable. However, depending upon whether its decision favors contracting or merchant building, the firm's course of action will be markedly different.

Firms that undertake operative building are hampered in all their decisions by a lack of market knowledge. Little basis exists upon which to choose designs, and builders have difficulty deciding whether or not to adopt innovations in style or material. Key factors shaping decisions are the availability of land, the selling history of the selected location, and the current selling rate for new houses in the area.

The first of these factors—land—is most important. The small builder in the Bay area searches constantly for advantageously priced lots in new expanding areas or in old familiar ones. If he can afford to, he will attempt to maintain a small inventory of lots. He buys those that look promising and that can be had at a reasonable price. The location and price will have an important influence on the units he builds.

[4] This section and the remainder of this chapter are based on the survey described in Appendix D.

Given available lots, the builder will determine the style and price class of his units in accordance with his and others' past experience. The price range will be established by the general rule of thumb which relates proper land costs to selling price and acts as a guard against over- or underdevelopment of a particular lot. Percentage rules attempt to insure a proper blending of the house into the neighborhood. If necessary the arbitrary ratios will be relaxed to insure such conformity.

If a builder uses a design which has sold easily in the past, risk of serious error is reduced. In addition, the technical building process will be somewhat simplified because the design will be familiar to both his crew and himself. If, however, a new design or style has become popular in the area (frequently as a result of changes introduced by architects and owners working through contractors), or if a particular new feature strikes his eye, he may adopt it. Stock plans are adjusted to introduce these new ideas and to conform to particular sites. The builder roughs out his ideas and turns them over to a draftsman for incorporation into final plans. He may continue to adjust the plan during the process of building. Decisions about materials innovations follow the same path as design; they will be introduced if they seem to be economical and have gained popular acceptance.

As a result of this type of analysis, houses similar in style and price will be built until a few remain unsold on the market for above-normal periods. When houses back up in this manner, the builders will attempt to find a new style or a price range that does sell. Changes or innovations are likely only when the market situation shifts and the builder must find a new solution to the altered conditions or fail.

When a house is completed, the operative builder still faces the problem of sales. The small firm has the choice of attempting to sell the house itself or of paying a real estate broker for this service. Half the builders use one method and half the other. A builder puts out a "For Sale" sign when he starts to build. If no sale takes place before the house approaches completion, he may advertise. The period in which he will attempt a sale without brokerage depends on his estimate of the market, time, and his cash needs. If the last prove pressing, he may hand the sale over to a real estate broker on a brokerage basis. In the remaining cases, the house is put in the hands of a real estate broker at the outset. Frequently this is on a *quid pro quo* basis.

The agent is given the listing in return for service he has performed in finding suitable lots, assisting with financing, or furnishing usable market information. As firms expand and tend toward the upper limit among small builders, the payment of a regular broker's fee becomes less frequent. In the group from 10 to 24 completions per year, the builder is likely to sell the units himself, hire a salesman, or enter into an agreement with a broker to handle them on special terms. In each method, the cost of selling will be somewhat less than normal brokerage fees.

The problem of the contract builder is obviously different. He is not concerned with market analysis but with successful bidding. The opportunity to bid usually comes through informal channels. Invitations to bid come from architects with whom the builder has previously worked or from prospective owners referred by friends or attracted by the contractor's sign on houses he is building.

In these instances, the design and approximate cost will have been decided before the builder enters the picture. He may, however, be asked for suggestions or, if the cost of the initial design is too high, as has been frequent in the postwar period, he may suggest possible alternatives.

The time and effort spent on a bid will vary depending on the complexity of the design and the number of new and unfamiliar materials proposed. The estimate forms and methods used by contractors are discussed in a following section.

Preparation of a bid for an average house takes from two to three days. The time required for small commercial buildings may be double this. Half the time is spent on the take-offs and estimates of direct costs; the other half in dealing with the subcontractors and materials suppliers. This two-to-three-day period includes only the builder's effort and not the work of these other groups.

Total bidding time depends on how long it takes to prepare a single bid and on the ratio of successful to unsuccessful bids. For contractors as a group this derives directly from the number bidding on a particular job as well as on the number of jobs on which bids have been taken but which never reach the construction stage. The individual builder considers his chances on any bid as average and therefore believes his ratio of successful to unsuccessful bids will be approximately the same as the number bidding. If there is an average of three bidders per job, he will expect to be successful in one out of three bids; if five bidders, one out of five, and so on.

This provides a basis for estimating bidding costs. The interest in this problem is so great that it is worth while to digress somewhat to obtain such an estimate. For example, the small contractor who is a working foreman, will start about four houses per year. If, on the average, he is one of three competitors for each job, his total time spent in estimating will be 4 times 3 (the number of jobs he has to bid on to gain a single success) times two and one-half days (the average amount of time he spends on each bid). He therefore spends about thirty days a year on bidding. Very little of this effort will appear as overhead, since most of the work will be done at night or week ends. If the number bidding on each job is six, the amount of time spent on bidding to obtain the same jobs would double. If the bidder has to spend sixty days per year in bidding, not all of it could be accomplished in spare time and part would be charged against construction.

This analysis applies also to the small contractor who spends his full time as a supervisor rather than working foreman. Assume that he starts 10 houses per year, is one of five bidders each time, and spends two and one-half days per bid. His total bidding time is then one-hundred and twenty-five days. Slightly more than one-third of his effort goes into bidding. To estimate the cost of the contractor's bids per house, assume he charges $5,000 per year in wages. Then one-third of this, or $1,700, must be spread over his ten successful bids. This amounts to $170 per house to cover his bidding labor. If this time were not spent in bidding, he could work on more houses, and the overhead charge against each would be reduced.

To arrive at the total economic cost of bidding, the bidding costs of subcontractors and materials dealers must be added to the builder's direct costs. Their charges are slight since, especially in stable periods and on fairly routine houses, only a few formal estimates will be required. The costs which the subcontractors and dealers must cover will run from $50 to $100. Adding these to the contractor's direct costs, we find that the total bidding cost per house will be from $220 to $270. This, applied to the median-priced contractor house, means that 2 per cent of the price of this type of house goes to defray the costs of the bidding system. Actually, this overestimates the true costs, because the first group of contractors does not charge for its time and others reduce their charges below this percentage through the following procedures.

Contractors recognize that the cost of bidding is a function of their successful bid ratios. Three methods are commonly used in an attempt to keep this ratio high and the bidding cost low. (1) The contractor will refuse to bid for an owner or architect who, he believes, has requested too many bids. Thus if most jobs have only three or four bidders, he will be loath to compete with more than six and will do so only if forced by unusual circumstances. (2) Many contractors have tie-ins with real estate brokers for what is called a "package deal." The owner approaches the broker, who shows him various lots and stock plans. Eventually they arrive at an approximate over-all price for a particular type house. The builder is then called in and stock plans are adjusted to meet the purchaser's desires and price limit. If the price is satisfactory, the owner makes the purchase from the broker, who arranges financing, and the contract is awarded to the builder directly without consideration of other bids. (3) In the final method, the owner approaches the builder directly with some idea as to the type and price of house he wants. Either the owner or the builder furnishes the lot. The house is then designed by the owner and builder together, usually from stock plans or from magazine clippings and ideas brought by the owner. Occasionally, an architect is called in. If an agreement is reached, a contract is awarded directly without any call for bids.

An important difference should be noticed between contractors working on bids and those working on deals of the type discussed above. Custom houses cost more, not primarily because of the bidding effort expended on them but because additional risks, delays, and training required in their construction affect both the bids and actual work. When builders have to perform different or unknown functions, they are on slippery ground. They lack knowledge, and as a result, unfamiliar work such as is found in many custom jobs is likely to cost more.

The unexpectedly high costs of what appear to be simple jobs and the very great variety in bids from supposedly competent contractors have frequently been commented upon. These are basically due to two factors. (1) Contractors may differ in their estimates of the cost of unknown contingencies, depending partly upon their own particular needs and desires for new work. (2) The cost of work on contracts of a design new to a particular builder varies. The builder must spend more time on planning, supervision, and actual experimentation on the site when he undertakes types of jobs new to him.

Even if the profit level is the same on work performed on bids as on work done operatively, the former is likely to cost more. Innovations and specification of custom details not familiar to the builder raise his costs, and these must be paid for. As a result, contract work is primarily limited to the high-priced market which is willing and can afford to pay for extra details.

Production

Observers watching an average small builder during the construction process are struck by how traditional and familiar his production techniques appear to be. The assertion is frequently made that only a few changes in methods have occurred since Egyptian days. Building is performed by about the same number of men, each going his own way. There are few obvious changes in the tools used or in the types of materials employed. The number of subcontractors arriving and leaving at various times has increased, not diminished.

Such observations, however, do not penetrate below the surface. Important changes have taken place in the housebuilding process, even among smaller firms. The organization of the production process has improved. Preplanning, in use of both manpower and materials, is commonplace. There is a decided increase in mechanization. Perhaps more important, far more of the total house is purchased in fabricated form.[5]

[5] It should be noticed that this book deals only with the problems of housebuilders who construct and assemble houses at the site in the conventional manner. Conventional—so-called on-site—builders should be differentiated from prefabricators. In this book, following the custom in the Bay area, precutting is considered a basic conventional method, as is the purchase of fabricated subunits such as windows and cabinets, or the preassembly of major sections at or near the site. Prefabrication is used to refer to the construction of most or all of the major assemblies, such as walls, in a factory or some other location away from the house site. The number of houses built by any type of prefabrication in the Bay area was extremely small, and the number which were factory fabricated was virtually nil. Obviously the methods and problems of builders as discussed in this book will not apply completely to the prefabrication industry. A comparison with that industry shows many similarities but some important differences. Cf. Burnham Kelly, *The Prefabrication of Houses* (New York: John Wiley and Sons, 1951).

With today's techniques, the small builder is primarily an assembler of wood products and a coördinator for the installation of other parts of the house, particularly equipment and finishes. The amount of actual fabricating he does has steadily decreased. Building consists of purchasing finished or semifinished products, performing some cutting, a minimum of planing, and a great deal of nailing to arrive at the completed house.

This change is most obvious in the case of lumber. At one time, not so long ago, the builder would have bought logs and finished them himself. Somewhat later he still would have made his own doors and windows and cabinets. Now, however, he purchases his lumber finished and frequently already cut to the required sizes. Wallboard comes in long sheets, a fair percentage of which requires no cutting. Windows, doors, cabinets, and trims are purchased ready for installation.

As a result of this trend, the builder's on-site costs are decreasing. Only 24 per cent of the cost of a typical Bay area house is value added by the small builder himself. Another 24 per cent covers his purchases of materials, and 35 per cent, or the largest sum of all, goes to subcontracts. Finally, 13 per cent is required for the land and 4 per cent for incidentals (table 49).

This breakdown somewhat underestimates the importance of site work because, in addition to that of the builder, a major part of the work of the subcontractors also takes place there. Together they produce 43 per cent of the final value, with 28 per cent covering their joint site labor, and 15 per cent their profits and overhead. The remaining 57 per cent pays for purchases of materials, land, and other services (tables 46, 50, 51, and 52).

Fewer changes have occurred in the actual organization of the production process than in the types of materials purchased. Figure 3 shows the thirty principal operations typically performed on houses built by small builders in the Bay area. The small builder performs sixteen with his own crew and subcontracts the rest. For planning and organizational purposes, these operations are divided into four main categories.

The first group includes the preparation of the site and the construction of the foundation. After the site is laid out, grading is done, usually by a subcontractor. Thereupon, the builder starts the actual foundation process. The trenches for footings and foundations are

FIGURE 3

OPERATIONS IN THE CONSTRUCTION OF A TYPICAL BAY AREA HOUSE

Direct labor	Subcontracted
Site preparation and foundation	
Building layout Foundation excavation Form work Placing mudsills	Grading Concrete and cement finishing
Framing	
Placing joists Subfloor Framing Roof framing Roof sheathing	Plumbing Electrical Sheet metal and heating
Walls and roof	
Placing building paper Siding Installing windows and doors Dry wall installation Exterior trim	Roofing Drywall taping Masonry
Finish	
Interior trim Cleanup	Plastering Painting Hardwood flooring Linoleum and asphalt tile Ceramic tile Shades and blinds

SOURCE: Appendix D.

marked out and dug, usually by hand, following which the builder and one or two carpenters make the forms for concrete and tie in the necessary steel reinforcing rods. This is rough carpentry, quickly and traditionally done, with few if any innovations in the process. Boards are cut to size by hand, and the necessary supports are driven with sledges.

When the foundation forms have been prepared, the concrete is poured. Depending on how busy he is, the builder may perform this job with his own crew or may sub it out. The task is relatively simple and no longer involves mixing the concrete on the site, as was common before the war. In most cases the concrete is purchased already prepared and delivered in a transit-mix truck. The builder needs only to be certain that the trucks can get onto the site and that necessary troughs are available to take the concrete to each of the forms. If this is impossible, the concrete is distributed by wheelbarrows. The concrete is pushed through the troughs and tamped by hand. Before it hardens, the wood mudsills are placed in it.

Mudsills have to be anchored in by bolt. Frequently, the holes for the bolts are drilled electrically, though in the majority of cases the old-fashioned bit and auger are still used. In either method, the small builders make certain that by this time there is electricity at the site. The electric wires entering the job mark a step forward in mechanization and reflect the increased importance of power tools on even the smallest job.

The second group of jobs in house construction centers around erecting its frame. This involves putting in the joists and subfloor, placing studs which have to be braced and have firestops installed, and finally erecting the roof rafters and roof boards. These processes have been improved through important changes in construction technique.

Since each house built by a small builder differs from all others, he and his carpenters have to refer constantly to the blueprints and have to do a large amount of hand measuring and cutting. This hand work, however, is decreased whenever possible by preplanning. Joists are used as they come from the lumber yards. The subfloor is nailed on with boards of odd lengths and then all projecting ends are cut off at one time with a power hand saw. The same method is used for the roof boards. Studs are ordered either precut from the lumber yard or they, plus most of the fire-blocking, are cut by power at the site.

Wall frames are assembled in horizontal positions on the subfloor, where studs are nailed to the bottom and top plates. Necessary headers, cripples, sway bracing, and other parts of the frame are installed. When one wall of the frame has been completely nailed together, it is lifted into place. The other exterior and interior walls are similarly nailed, raised, and joined together. During the framing, as well as in construction of the roof, hand and power sawing are intermingled.

The amount of power used will depend upon the efficiency of the individual builder as well as on his and his crew's familiarity with the job in hand.

While the builder is framing the building, trade contractors, particularly plumbers, electricians, sheet metal and heating men, are also at work. They, too, mix old-fashioned and modern techniques. Electric drills and electric handsaws are used side by side with hand tools. Since each house differs so much in design, these trade contractors cut and fit all their pipes, wires, conduits, and the like on a completely individual basis.

In the third part of the production process, the house is actually enclosed. In this group of jobs, the division of work between builders and trade contractors depends upon the particular materials used. Some parts are almost always subcontracted, as for example, roofing, plastering, and stuccoing. However, if, as is common in this area, siding and wallboard are used in place of plaster and stucco, the builder will normally perform these functions with his own crew, and there will be fewer subcontractors at work on the house.

In enclosing the house, except in expensive units or in certain areas where codes require it, sheathing is not used. Wood siding is usually installed directly over building paper, and stucco is installed over linewire and building paper.

The builder's decision as to whether to use his own men to install wallboard is difficult. His own carpenters can do the job adequately. However, carpenters specializing in wallboard have become so expert that their wages plus the trade contractor's overhead and profit still average less than the builder has to pay his own men. His decision may hinge on his time schedule. If he is running out of work, he will perform this function with his own crew in order to keep them steadily employed and together. Alternatives such as this are important in adding flexibility to the builder's work schedules.

Included in the enclosing process are the installation of window frames, windows, door jambs, and outside doors. In small firms, these jobs are almost always done by the builder's own men. For the majority of houses the windows arrive with the prime coat of paint already on and frequently are preglazed, thus eliminating another subcontract.

The final phase of the house is the finishing and installation of equipment. Except the finish carpentry work, which includes hanging doors, installing cabinets, trim, bookcases, and hardware, this phase is almost entirely subcontracted. Whether performed by the builder's or trade contractor's labor, finish work is mainly a hand process, partly because of a belief that handwork is quality work and machine work is not, but also because for many purposes the use of a complicated tool in houses built individually on scattered lots is not economically sound. In certain instances, it may reflect restrictions of unions against machine work.

Establishing the production process is primarily a problem of the builder's use of labor, and here the greatest organizational differences occur between the small and large builders. The average small builder in the Bay area employs only a small, unspecialized crew of two carpenters, one laborer, and the owner himself as foreman-carpenter, whereas the larger builders use a far more complicated system.

The average level of skill on small jobs is high. Carpenters on custom jobs have to be able to work on their own without making errors. These houses are individually designed and must be erected from blueprints. Since plans are really shorthand notes rather than spelled-out instructions, the carpenters have to be able to understand what is desired and use their heads as well as their hands. In addition, the level of quality has to be high. Finally, since there are no efficiency standards to measure the amount of work to be accomplished, each worker must be willing to apply himself to the job in hand.

Finding and holding skilled men is one of the major problems of the small builder. It is accomplished primarily on a personal basis. The builder has usually been a carpenter and knows others. He asks among his friends and urges them to let him know if they or other good men are available. Frequently several carpenters working on a house may actually be licensed builders, who periodically take work for their own account.

The similar background of the owner and his men results in a rather informal relationship. The builder has been an employee. He works side by side with his men and frequently does more work than any of the others. As a result, personal loyalties develop, and the carpenters tend to identify themselves with the firm and with the task in hand.

A builder who has found skilled, efficient, and reliable men will go to great lengths in his attempts to keep them employed. This usually means arranging schedules so as to give continuous employment. Since changing men costs money and lowers efficiency, it may be worthwhile to take certain jobs at a slight loss. Men get used to working with each other and in addition become familiar with the firm's methods. A change of crew is expensive not only because of the time and effort required to break new men into one's way of doing things, but also because a long search may be necessary to find equally skilled and efficient men. In addition to steady employment, small builders frequently hold their men by paying bonuses above scale so that wages will equal efficiency. On the job themselves, they are able to recognize the value of the individual to the firm and pay accordingly.

The informal relations and identification of the individual employee with the firm lead in general to a minimum concern with union rules and regulations. Frequently, for example, the carpenters will perform odd jobs technically falling under other jurisdictions. Cutting corners in this manner saves the firm the extra trouble and expense of hiring special mechanics for small tasks and generally expedites the entire process. Small firms are so spread out and their relationships with their own employees are of such a close nature that problems with the union are rare. Most unions fail to check work at scattered sites. Difficulties arise only if a dissatisfied employee complains. These firms pay union rates. Their employees are all union members, and they maintain union conditions, but this is the extent of their labor relationships with outside organizations.

The less strict adherence to union regulations and the greater individual efficiency of the small firm's carpenters all aid in keeping labor costs down. Even so, because they cannot take advantage of the efficiency resulting from division of labor, the average small firm's costs are higher than are those in the larger categories. The greater skill of the average small firm's employees is a necessary condition to its continued survival. It does not succeed in giving them as low unit labor costs as can be achieved with specialization.

The problem of making available to these scattered sites the greater mechanization and specialization now being employed in large tracts is the main one facing the small firm. Unless his production improves, the small builder can never compete in efficiency, and he must reconcile himself to that small market which is willing to pay a premium price for custom work. Experience in other fields has shown that this custom market is extremely vulnerable, especially in periods of economic fluctuations, and for this reason the small builder is in a dangerously exposed position.

Purchasing

In purchasing both materials and subcontracts, the small builder again finds himself limited by size. He has no choice but to continue to buy in the traditional manner from the wholesale-retail lumber yard. When a builder buys from a retailer, however, he does not—as has so often been alleged—pay the retail or over-the-counter price. Instead, he gets a builder's discount, varying from 5 to 20 per cent, depending on the particular item. Eighty per cent of small firms purchase through the retail channel. Only as firms approach the top of this size class are certain items—particularly lumber—purchased at wholesale. One-third of the builders in the 10-to-24-per-year class do buy lumber at wholesale, and about 5 per cent buy hardware directly from a wholesaler or broker (table 23).

Four basic materials—lumber, hardware, millwork, and wallboard—are purchased directly by the small builder. All are normally carried by and bought from a lumber yard, though sometimes millwork or cabinets are ordered directly from specialty shops. About half of the small firms trade regularly with a single building-materials dealer. The builder takes his material lists to the dealer, asks him to figure the price, and then arranges for delivery to the site. Delivery is usually made in two or three loads, planned to arrive at the site as required.

The other half of the small builders tend to shop around, to compare price quotations, and to ask for competitive bids on their materials list from two or three dealers. This is a particularly prevalent practice among contractors who are themselves bidding on jobs, and who find that small variations in materials cost may suffice to win or lose a bid. In addition, since the builder agrees to a definite price for his work, he wants to cover himself by having a definite materials price quotation in hand. A definite price is not as important to the operative builder, who may be able to pass on in his sales price any cost increases he is forced to incur during construction.

Builders who do not shop around claim that they obtain better quality and service. They have dealt with a particular firm and have been satisfied. They believe that they are better off paying slightly higher prices, if necessary, to receive assured service and to maintain a source of supply which will be open to them even in periods of shortages. The other half disagree, finding that by demanding bids from several firms, they increase competition and obtain their goods at slightly lower prices. Their payments depend upon the market and the need of several dealers for business rather than upon one lumber yard's estimate of the current situation.

Why does the small builder buy materials from retail dealers and not directly from the mill? The reasons are primarily convenience, required quantities, perhaps credit, and quality. The small builder purchases materials only about once a month. He needs many different types. It is convenient for him to make all his purchases in one spot at one time without wasting hours shopping. He succeeds in doing this by taking his materials list to his habitual supplier or suppliers. By using a dealer he eliminates the necessity of maintaining inventories. He does not have to be concerned with coördinating shipments from distant sources. The problems of unloading, handling, and delivery are arranged for at one time. The material dealer's crews specialize in this work and can do it for less than the builder would have to pay if he set up a special handling crew each time.

Even more basic than convenience is the problem of quantities. Most manufacturers deal in carload lots, the minimum amount usually purchased by a dealer. This allows savings in freight, in handling, and in selling costs compared with smaller units. Small builders cannot use full carloads of most items, and manufacturers are not interested in selling smaller quantities.

The importance of the credit furnished by the materials dealer has perhaps been overemphasized. Although the contractor does not have sufficient working capital to tie up large sums for long periods in inventories, as would be necessary if he bought in large quantities direct from manufacturers, he still is currently as well off as purchasers in other fields and can meet his bills promptly. The dealer furnishes the capital while goods are in transit and storage and for an additional two to three weeks after the material has been delivered to the builder's site.

The problem of quality is mainly important in lumber, the largest item purchased. Since it is available in single truckloads from brokers or truckers, lumber could be bought wholesale by even the smallest of Bay area builders. In using a wholesale channel, however, the builder finds that he cannot complain about deliveries of poor quality, which are not infrequent. The problem is serious to a small builder because his purchases are small and take place only at intervals of one or two months. Any losses on individual loads cannot be made up in the course of the year. Big builders, on the other hand, can demand better quality because a large number of deliveries are made under a single agreement. Furthermore, even if they do receive a poor load, it is not wasted because they can use it on jobs which do not require high grade lumber.

The small builder recognizes that he is paying for special services; and since the cost of these services, plus the dealer's profits, is reflected in the price, he wishes that they were not necessary to him. On the other hand, he realizes that with another type of distribution he might be neglected in favor of the larger builders. If he were unable to get these services when he needs them, his costs would be higher.

The problem of small size also affects the builder's relations with his trade contractors. His difficulties do not arise, as many have believed, because he is forced into a poor bargain by larger and stronger trade contractors; even small builders are as large as the average trade contractor. He is handicapped because he cannot spend enough time in coördination and in making certain that his trade contracts are carried out in the most efficient manner.

Subcontracting is prevalent even in the largest industries. The main reason that so much more attention has been called to it in housebuilding would appear to be that it is more apparent when men from many trades and under different managements all work on the same building at one time. This intermingling of different subcontractors is a situation created by site assembly. Otherwise, subcontracting in housebuilding hardly differs from that in the other parts of the economy.

Subcontracting is a necessary step toward efficiency and is not a system imposed on the small builder by outside forces. As long as houses require many different skills in their assembly, a builder is better off using specialists rather than Jacks-of-all-trades. The question is simply whether it is more efficient to hire the specialists himself or to let trade contractors do the jobs.

The average house requires ten to fifteen specialists, some of whom may spend as little as half a day working on the unit. The builder cannot take time and does not have the skill to hire and supervise each of these specialists directly. If he attempts it, he finds himself spending full time in labor negotiations and in finding the necessary men. If he finds the men, he then discovers that the amount of work each has to do in the house does not come out in even units a day. If he hires the men directly, he has to pay for nonproductive time while the worker stands idle waiting for another job, or moves to another site.

By subcontracting, the builder can eliminate these wastes. The trade contractor coördinates all jobs of a particular type. He is able to assure the most skilled workers in the craft steady employment by scheduling them from one builder's job to the next. For this necessary function, the trade contractor charges relatively small sums. Trade contractors, like small builders, tend to be working foremen who perform their overhead functions in their spare time and do not charge very much for their supervisory work.

The problems of the builder's relation with his trade contractors are complex, but they are not as difficult as many have believed and stressed. For example, it has been claimed that the system is inherently expensive because the builder must obtain bids from three or four subs for each of his ten or fifteen subcontracts. Obviously, such a system would be extremely inefficient. Both builder and trade contractor would be spending most of their time in bidding and very little of their time actually on the job, with a consequent loss of time and money that could hardly be estimated.

Actually, this type of problem does not arise. The relationships between the builder and the trade contractors with whom he works are stable. Practically no shifting of trade contractors occurs as the builder moves from one job to the next. He tends to work very closely with a picked group of subs and does not seek independent bids for each job. A change in subcontractors is uncommon. Some firms boast of having operated with the same group for twenty years. Subcontractor prices (in 85 per cent of firms) result from direct negotiation rather than from a formal bid system. During stable periods, the trade contractor will not even be asked to figure jobs beforehand. He will be informed of the location of the job, and it is assumed that previous prices will prevail.

A change in subcontractor is in order if the latter cannot or does not meet existing competition. Especially in a fluctuating market, but occasionally in normal periods as well, a builder may test the market or he may be approached by independent trade contractors offering favorable terms. If his own man cannot stand up to these other offers, a change is made. Dissatisfaction with service, delay, disagreement, or deterioration in quality of work may also prompt a substitution in trade contractor. Such occurrences are infrequent. Small builders average less than one change per house among the 12 trade contractors employed on the average job.

For new work, for unusual work, for work during periods of shifting prices, and for the tasks which vary with the design of the house, especially if these are contract houses, the trade contractor will be asked to quote a price in advance. Formal bids from competing contractors will be used primarily on houses on which the builder himself is bidding. This type of bidding is, of course, far more common on nonresidential work and frequently is required on public works.

Among small builders the coördination and control of subcontracting also constitute a simple process. When a house is begun, the sub is informed of the approximate time his services will be required. He is again alerted a week or so in advance and a day or two before needed. The work schedule is usually sufficiently flexible to permit a delay of two or three days between the time the sub is supposed to appear and actually does. The trade contractor makes an effort to meet any pressing needs promptly. At the same time, builders recognize that certain delays are inevitable and, providing they are not too long and that urgent requests are handled promptly, work does not suffer as a result of this flexibility.

The work of the subcontractor is supervised by the builder in the same informal manner. The small builder is either working on the job near the trade contractor or else he checks sometime during the process or after the job is finished. If he believes it does not meet proper standards, he will hold back payment until the work is corrected or a satisfactory agreement is reached.

This system is not, of course, highly efficient, any more than are the small builders' purchases through a long distribution channel. This inefficiency is not a result of poor management or of external influences forcing the builder to use channels which he does not desire, but rather, a function of his scale. The small builder solves his particular problems in the only way open to those of his size. As long as he has a function to perform in the housing field, this problem of scale and therefore of relative inefficiency in purchasing will probably persist.

Controls

The problems of estimating, budgeting, and accounting remain difficult for the small builder. Marked improvement is required if his planning, analysis, and financial judgments are to be more effective. The small builder faces the same conflict that confronts small firms in many industries. How much time can he afford for overhead functions? How can the small owner develop the necessary management skills to perform a whole group of ancillary processes required if he is to do his job successfully? In large firms, various people can be hired, each trained to perform a specialized task which the small man must perform himself.

Outside pressures have brought about progress toward improving control functions.[6] Lending institutions have required builders to prepare preliminary cost estimates. The Bureau of Internal Revenue and the State Licensing Authority require that he maintain a record of all costs for tax purposes. To meet these requirements, most builders now prepare detailed estimate sheets for each house, as well as a record of historical costs, through a set of double-entry accounting books with a column or sheet for each house.

The main factors itemized in both sets of controls are shown in the example of a typical estimate sheet (fig. 4). The builder must estimate and account for his direct labor costs, his direct materials costs, his subcontracts, his direct incidental expenses, and his overhead and profit. Each of these items appears on the sheets in some detail. They summarize the builder's labor and materials take-off and the bid prices received for subcontracts and materials. The complexity of the estimate will vary from firm to firm. Many—especially contract builders—use a complete, detailed estimate of the type found in a standard estimating manual such as Walker's.[7] Others—builders who are continuously producing houses of approximately the same type—may simply base their estimates on previous performance.

[6] This section is based on the case studies and survey described in Appendix D.

[7] Frank R. Walker, *The Building Estimator's Reference Book* (Chicago: Frank R. Walker Co., 1948).

FIGURE 4
CONSTRUCTION ESTIMATE

Job Number........................ Owner...........................

Location.......................... Date.............................

Item	Quantity	Labor	Material	Total	Actual
Excavating					
Concrete					
Foundation					
Slab					
Flatwork					
Lumber					
Rough					
Finish					
Millwork					
Windows					
Jambs					
Doors					
Garage					
Cabinets					
Hardware					
Nails					
Rough					
Finish					
Gypsum board					
Electrical					
Wiring					
Fixtures					
Fireplace—chimney					
—mantel					
Floors					
Hardwood					
Tile					
Linoleum					
Heating					
Painting					
Plastering					
Plumbing					
Roofing					
Shades and blinds					
Sheet metal					
Wallboard taping					
Miscellaneous					
Permits					
Sewers					
Power and water					
Insurance					
Title fees					
Recording fees					
Interest					
Commitment					
Plans					
Survey					

When money is being advanced by a lending institution, this estimate will be used as a proposed budget. The agency will use it and whatever other work the builder has in prospect in relation to his working capital as the basis for its decision to lend or not.

Accounting records follow the same form as estimates. A column or card is allocated to each item on the estimate sheet. When payments are made for materials and subcontracts, the voucher or check shows the appropriate job against which they are to be charged, and these are carried to the proper card and column. The foreman who keeps the timecards also records the amount of labor time spent on each job. When the payroll is made out, the total payments are subdivided and charged against the proper house. In this way, when a house is finished the builder's accounting records show all direct costs incurred. He can, if he desires, also allocate indirect charges to the house. Total costs are then compared to the original estimate which serves as a check on the causes of variations and as a means of improving future estimates. Virtually no other accounting or production records are maintained.

Although these records constitute improvements over those used by small builders in the past, they are still not sufficiently accurate to answer many of the questions whose answers the builder needs to know if he is to operate efficiently. *Ex post* he can find out where he has made estimating errors, but this may be too late. In addition, these records are not accurate enough to enable him to measure the many variables with which he deals. As a result, his estimates for his next job will have to be approximations with a rather wide possible margin of error.

Although in this area there is great need of and room for progress, a solution is not obvious. Some improvements will take place as the small builder becomes better educated and as new devices for overhead control are developed which will better meet his needs, but the problem is almost certain to continue as long as he remains small in size.

Determination of Size of Firm

A final, interesting question is why these firms, many of which have been very successful, have not expanded more in the recent dynamic period when opportunities were so great. An explanation obviously includes psychological and sociological factors which do not belong in our analysis. Builders of this size frequently state that they limit the amount of work undertaken because of the worries and headaches which they feel come with larger size. Their present income is sufficient for their needs, and expansion is not worth the effort and strain necessary to achieve it. There are also, however, certain economic factors which play an important and sometimes dominant role in determining whether a firm will expand (table 21).

Of a somewhat mixed nature is the question of the possible supervisory span of existing management. Nearly a third of the small firms report that there is a discontinuity in the supervisory cost curve which, added to the other factors, determines their size. These builders feel that, given their present organization, they have reached their maximum managerial span. If they expanded their firms, a working foreman would have to lay down his tools and become purely an executive, or a present executive would have to add an assistant. The builder may feel that such a change would exceed his capabilities or would present other problems. He also may recognize that such an increase in overhead would not pay off unless his volume nearly doubled, but would only raise the charges of supervision on each job.

At the same time, the expanded overhead would increase risk. Any downward changes in volume with larger fixed charges would rapidly lower his operating profits. Because of personal experience or the experience of friends or fellow-builders in the prewar period, the small contractor is very conscious of risk in any event. His capital is not large and a few errors in calculation, either on contracts or on speculatively built houses, can rapidly push him under. About 20 per cent of the small builders indicate that the additional risk is the dominant factor preventing their expansion. Small builders frequently are pushing against a capital ceiling. Since banks and bonding companies allow a builder to proceed on a house or contract only if they feel he has the necessary capital, their decisions become the determining factor limiting expansion. One-third of the small builders say this lack of credit has forestalled possible expansion.

A final factor is discussed by builders in terms of available skilled mechanics. This item reflects the prevailing shortage of good carpenters in the postwar period. Most small firms compete in the market on the basis of craftsmanship, finish, and efficiency among workmen. A firm achieves a standard of quality by carefully building up its crew of carpenters. If the firm now wishes to expand, it has the problem of recruiting men of similar skills and, once recruited, of guaranteeing them a stable level of production. Because the level of skill of men recruited on a temporary basis will be too low, the firm cannot attempt to expand by hiring men for an additional job and then letting them go. This ranks among the most important factors currently inhibiting expansion of small firms.

SUMMARY

The small builder, though still important, is playing a diminishing role in housebuilding production. Whereas thirty years ago he was the industry, in 1949 in the Bay area he produced 45 per cent of the units built by firms and in 1950 only about one-third of the total. This tendency toward greater size and concentration exists even among the smaller firms. The 8 per cent of small firms which completed 10 or more houses in the year constructed nearly 40 per cent of the group's total production. In contrast with this diminishing share of the market, more than 93 per cent of all firms were still small.

The small firm has not suffered from inadequate financing. It has the advantage of extremely low overhead costs, much of this work being performed by the unpaid labor of the owner and his wife. It has not fallen far behind in the amount of equipment it uses or in its techniques. Although its owners—primarily craftsmen tied to their jobs—are not innovators, and some lag does occur in their adoption of new techniques, on the whole the use of new materials and machinery has spread at a rapid rate. The average small firm adopts any innovations within its scope within a year or two after they become general among the larger firms.

The small firm's problems stem primarily from the fact that its organization cannot be stretched to make many necessary improvements. Given its maximum size of overhead, labor force, and purchases, the small firm has only a limited number of possible solutions to the problems of organization and methods of production which face it. It cannot specialize its labor to any extent. It cannot obtain quantity discounts on its purchases. It might improve its records somewhat; but without losing its chief advantages as a minimum overhead unit it cannot make them entirely adequate to handle the job it faces.

If it cannot solve its problems within these limits, then the only other way it can improve its position is to alter the functions it performs in the market. Its present specialization in custom work is logical. In addition, other changes in its province appear probable. These will be discussed more fully in the final chapter dealing with current trends. New functions might include working in a partnership with large firms or changing the type of product and material purchased.

Its situation in the future appears uncertain. The small builder has a function in the industry, but the size of this function is not clear. Recent history has witnessed improvements in his efficiency, but at a slower rate than that of other firms. As a result, he finds that he cannot compete in the large-scale mass market introduced by cheaper financing aids, but is relegated to the custom market or to building on small scattered lots in more densely populated areas. During the postwar period the larger builder was not interested in these special markets, which are most likely to be affected by economic fluctuations and also carry the greatest risks. The small builder has kept the most dangerous market. Even here he is not secure, for if any large builders decide to enter this market their greater efficiency might furnish such competition as to make his position barely tenable.

4

The Medium Firm

A composite picture of the housebuilding industry is reflected in the activities of the medium-sized housebuilding firm. What is happening in the housebuilding industry generally is happening most typically at this level.[1] Like the industry, this group of firms is in a transitional state, on its way from contract building to operative tract building. This group crystallizes the housebuilding pattern because it is the connective link in the evolution of the industry from the small custom contractors who still stand in the public mind as typifying housebuilders—since they did compose the housebuilding industry of the past—to the big-scale, mass-production tract operators who are changing the shape of the housebuilding industry and giving form to the future.

The two extremes, small contract builders and tract operators with mass-production techniques, are represented at each end of the group of medium-sized building firms. What makes this dichotomy significant of the direction being taken by the industry as a whole is the fact that the firms among the medium-sized builders which have remained contractors have reached their terminal size and volume, whereas the firms which have turned to merchant or operative building have increased in size and number and appear to contain the genes of greater dynamic development.

The medium-sized firm has been defined as one building between 25 and 99 houses per year. The production median of this group of firms is the production median of the industry, a fact which underscores the role of this group as dramatizing the trend of housebuilding. The median medium-sized firms produced 40 houses a year; similarly,

[1] See Appendix C, and tables 10, 11, 13–15.

half the houses built in the Bay area in 1949 were produced by firms completing more than 40 units in the year, and half by those producing less.

Using another measure of volume, if the medium-sized firm were classified by the value of the work produced during the year rather than by the number of units, it would be found that the range runs from $250,000 to more than $1,000,000, with the heaviest concentration around the median of $500,000 (table 11).

There were 77 firms in this group in the Bay area in 1949. They produced 3,512 houses or 20 per cent of the total. Most of these firms were operative builders, taking the first steps toward the potential economies of large-scale operation, though often these steps were hesitant and did not go the full distance toward fulfilling the potentials. Some, however, were already well on their way to real mass production (tables 10 and 13).

One of the characteristics of the group, typifying its transitional state, is a lack of innovation in design or technique. The medium-sized operative builder has grown too big for the directly supervised, individual blueprint work of the contractor, with its originality of design; but he is not yet big enough, does not have the necessary staff, nor is he sure enough of himself, to undertake the advanced innovations in mass-production techniques of the large-scale builder on tracts. The medium-sized firms copy in design and technique. They do not often risk originality or experimentation.

Although many of them have begun to work in tracts, this development is not complete. A few build scattered houses on speculation. Medium-sized firms often build in small groups, with other builders. They can utilize odd, favorably priced lots in the neighborhood of other similar work. Some do small scattered groups of units in cities. Others work on single tracts in suburbs. Of the operative builders in this group in the Bay area in 1949, a tenth of the firms did most of their building on separate lots; about a third built primarily in tracts, but also worked on separate lots; the remainder worked only in tracts. About one-quarter of the units completed by medium-sized firms were outside of tracts (tables 10 and 14).

Only 13 out of the group of 77 medium-sized builders built primarily on contract. Because their supervision of individual work could be direct, these contractors retained the tradition of custom building, concentrating on craftsmanship and quality. Although in comparison with other house contractors they were the largest, their number of completions were at the bottom of the classification of medium-sized firms. Only 16 per cent of the units completed by medium firms were produced on contract. Attempts to expand house contracting further in terms of volume of production run against obstacles rising out of the nature of the operation. These obstacles include such problems as direct supervision of atypical and "different" houses, of building on unusual lots, of maintaining custom-quality tradition, working to individual blueprints, and giving personal attention to owners' wishes in luxury detail. These problems require individual solution and cannot be determined in terms of a volume operation. Contractors, however, could and did increase their total volume by doing other types of building. Since these buildings and their houses had high unit values, these builders are found near the top of the entire group in dollar volume (tables 10, 11, 13, and 15).

The inevitably greater expense involved in building to individual contract is unquestionably an important factor in the trend away from contract building. It is the merchant builder, in the group of medium-sized firms, who can effect certain economies by adopting some—though not all—of the techniques of the mass producers yet retaining some of the advantages of the small producers. Like the small contractor, his overhead remains low. Because of his larger size and merchant operation he can get materials at a lower cost by buying wholesale. He can organize his labor force more efficiently. He can strike better bargains with his subcontractors. His controls and his possibilities for introduction of new patterns in style and method are limited, but he can offer a satisfactory product, at lower cost, to the consumers who feel that they cannot afford the luxury of custom quality. It is this group which produces the most typical houses, and it is this group which, apparently, is a key factor in the market's price determination.

Background and Organization

Who are the owners of the medium firms?

They are usually men about fifty years old. Their past experience in the industry is shorter than that of either the small or the large builder. They have been active in other fields of business, sometimes as close to building as real estate or building materials, sometimes as remote as dairying or banking. Their experience has been practical and diverse. On the average, they have spent some six years in building before establishing their firms, though more than a quarter of them started their firms without any previous building experience (tables 24–26 and fig. 5).

Many of them look at building as a place for investment, or as a business, rather than as a craft. From previous experience and from

FIGURE 5
AGE, BACKGROUND, AND TYPE OF OWNERSHIP OF BAY AREA HOUSEBUILDERS IN 1949, BY SIZE

Item	Size of builder		
	Small	Medium	Large
Principal's age, average in years	44	50	52
Firm's age, average in years	4	6	15
Principal's previous building experience, average in years	14	6	5
Proprietorships, single, number	976	11	..
Partnerships, single, number	331	23	1
Corporations, single, number	74	5	2
Combinations of firms, number	170	38	27

SOURCE: Tables 24–27.

personal choice, they desire to be executives rather than craftsmen or working foremen. They cannot be full-time executives in a small-sized firm which does not produce enough units to support executive overhead. They must start with a volume of production sufficient to carry at least one executive salary and perhaps more. The medium bracket is the first with volume sufficiently large to afford executive personnel and room for expansion. Their background in business and their performance in building make it possible to speculate that the men coming into this group of builders from outside the industry bring new blood, new vitality, new attitudes, which make them potentially the big builders of the future.[3]

The medium builders are almost equally divided among three types of firms.

First are the old established building firms which, by steady production, have grown to medium size. These often began as small con-

[3] See Appendix D and E, and tables 20, 24–26, 32.

tracting firms. A majority of the medium-sized contractors have this background. In reaching their present size, they have gone as far as they can. Others have turned to operative building and changed in structure as well as type of work.

Second are the firms of former mechanics who started their organizations after the war, with enough capital and enough drive to put themselves in the medium bracket. These are men who know the processes of building, literally from the ground up, and are ambitious for growth.

Third are the firms formed by men from outside the industry, men who have been successful in other businesses (frequently real estate) and, for one reason or another, wish to invest their capital in house-building. They are the men with versatile knowledge of other fields and business relationships. They are the promoters for whom the medium bracket is the minimum feasible size.

The medium-sized firms, as a group, are relatively young, with a medial age of six years (table 25).

When a firm gets into the medium bracket, its legal structure becomes more formal and its overhead structure more complicated than in the small building group. Only 14 per cent of the firms in the medium group are individual proprietorships without affiliates, and similarly, 30 per cent are lone partnerships and 6 per cent are single corporations.

A marked characteristic of the legal structure in this group is association of the building firm with another firm in a related field, such as a firm conducting a real estate or land development business. Half of the medium-sized firms in the Bay area have affiliates. Although most affiliates are real estate firms, a few are building materials or trade-contracting businesses. In many instances, this trait of duality stems from the building firm's beginning as an offshoot of a previous business; perhaps more often, however, it reflects an initial attempt to diversify risk and gain certain tax advantages.

The overhead structure of the medium-sized firms is more elaborate than that of the small firms because, in this bracket, the executive duties are so numerous that it is no longer possible for the builder or principal to act as working foreman, even if he wants to. The head man has to lay down his tools, if he is a former working foreman, and become a boss. All firms in this group have a full-time executive. In most cases this necessitates having an office and an office staff, though in about a quarter of the firms the office work is still carried on single-handedly from the home. Where an office and office staff are used, both are small and frequently share quarters with a real estate business or other sales outlet. In about half the firms, the executive or principal acts as his own construction superintendent, but in the other half a construction superintendent is hired. Even in the largest of the firms in this group, the total personnel overhead rarely exceeds five people (table 20). The medium-sized classification divides in this manner:

In 25 per cent of the firms, the owner acts as executive, manager, and supervisor, with no additional off-site personnel. He hires an on-site working foreman, or, when necessary, foremen.

In 25 per cent of the firms, the owner, in addition to performing these supervisory functions, hires a single full-time office employee, bringing his overhead staff to two.

In the next 25 per cent of the firms, the owner-executive is aided in his supervisory work by a full-time assistant, who may be either an expediter-estimator or a construction superintendent. These firms usually have a full-time office employee, too, so that their total overhead staff comes to three.

The final 25 per cent of the firms have an additional staff member or two handling sales, purchases, and similar functions.

The salaries of overhead personnel for medium-sized firms run, as a general rule, between 2 and 4 per cent of the selling price of the houses they produce.

Equipment is a minor aspect of overhead expenses. The investment in equipment is relatively small, with a median value in the group of $8,500 per firm (fig. 2). This usually includes the personal automobile of the owner or owners, a pickup truck, a power handsaw, probably a full-sized power radial saw, and a few hand tools such as wheelbarrows and shovels. When specialized equipment, such as a bulldozer or heavy truck, is required, it is either rented or obtained by subcontract.

The amount of equipment does not increase proportionately with the size of builder. Additions to equipment over that of the small builder consist primarily of more and larger power tools. Altogether, cost, replacement, and depreciation of equipment are likely to represent no more than $50 in the selling price of a house constructed by a medium-sized builder (table 32).

The amount of plant and equipment investment per unit for these firms remains so small that it is a negligible influence in determining the rate or scale of operations. Capital requirements for equipment are no bar to expansion, and conversely, capital sunk in equipment exerts no pressure for maintaining output.

What is the total cost of overhead in a medium-sized firm? How can an exact figure be determined? Serious difficulties beset the statistician in attempting to arrive at an exact figure reflecting the items in total overhead. These difficulties proceed, primarily, from the form in which the material concerning overhead costs is available.

If statements about efficiency are to have validity, the overhead cost estimates should reflect economic costs and true profits. Data based on accounting records are notoriously poor for this purpose. For many reasons, the lines between economic costs and profits are blurred in the accounting statements studied. The use of the terms "net" and "gross" profit varies from report to report. "Net" may refer to net before or after taxes or before or after withdrawals in proprietorships and partnerships. Similarly, the factors included in "gross" will vary.

Examination of profit-and-loss statements of individual firms shows that the allocation of operating margin between costs and profits is extremely arbitrary. In closely held corporations such as building firms, it is common practice to minimize corporate profits in order to avoid the double taxation of dividends. For this reason, executive salaries in corporations of this type are frequently high and reflect a return on equity and compensation for entrepreneurship in addition to payments for services as executive. This factor does not apply to the majority of firms, which remain unincorporated proprietorships or partnerships. Since salaries and profits are combined and taxed at the same rate in these firms, either may be carried at nominal figures.

Another difficulty arises when firms have affiliates. Prices charged in transactions between affiliates reflect purely bookkeeping decisions. Instead of showing costs as they would be reflected in the market, they may aim at dividing profits so as to minimize either taxes or problems with lending agencies.

Indirect expenses, too, present a problem. In all types of firms there are decided advantages in claiming as expenses as many borderline items as possible, though it is perhaps easier for large corporations to justify claims for personal entertainment, travel, transportation, and so on, as legitimate "expenses" for purposes of tax deductions. This is another hazard for the statistician who is attempting to combine all actual items of overhead costs into an exact total.

To circumvent these various statistical pitfalls pragmatically, the operating margin—the gross amount between direct costs and selling price—has been taken by this study as the most workable figure for purposes of calculating profit and computing total overhead. We also give some data on net profit, but this figure is even more subject to error and therefore we use it more discriminately.

For the medium-sized firms estimates of operating margins were taken directly from operating statements. A sample of firms in this class showed operating margins ranging from 6 to 31 per cent, with a median of 13.7 per cent of the sales dollar. The distribution was somewhat skewed, so that the mean was 2.5 per cent above the median. These firms reported a median net profit of 8.5 per cent per sales dollar (table 34). When this is subtracted from the operating margin, total overhead, including selling costs, is found to be 5.2 per cent per sales dollar. The arbitrariness of this division is acknowledged.

Financing

Significant changes take place in financing as the scale of housebuilding operations increases.[8] Here the medium-sized housebuilding firms have more problems in common with the large firms than they have with the small ones. This is because they are primarily operative builders, making larger capital investments and taking larger risks, whereas the small firms are primarily contractors whose investments and risks are comparatively minor.

The operative builder must obtain sufficient equity to assume the initial risks of unexpected costs in the construction of the house or unexpected losses in the sale of the house. In addition he must obtain sufficient funds to finance the construction of the house and to enable him to hold the house until it it sold. Finally, he must arrange the purchaser's financing or permanent loan—the so-called take-out money.

These three aspects of financing are, in their general outlines, similar for all operative builders. In this chapter, the manner in which the medium-sized builder meets his problems of equity financing and

[8] See Appendixes E and F.

construction loans are discussed. The third phase of financing, the permanent loan, is examined in the next chapter, which is devoted to the big builder for whom this plays an even more important part.

How do the medium-sized firms raise their capital?

Equity capital, in all cases, is raised entirely on a personal basis without recourse to public financing. No funds are raised through public offering of stocks and bonds. Ownership of most firms, whether they are single proprietorships, partnerships, corporations, or corporate groups, does not exceed four principals. The owners make an initial investment, but in the medium and larger firms the bulk of equity capital has come from reinvestment of profits.

A typical balance sheet (fig. 2) for a medium-sized firm shows $257,000 in total assets, of which the builder's equity or net worth is $112,000. Current assets of $160,000 representing the principal assets used in the production process, consist almost entirely of cash, completed work in place, units for sale, and inventories about to go into units. Total assets include current assets together with equipment ($8,500), real estate and buildings ($30,500), miscellaneous assets ($58,000) such as deposits for water service and other utilities, notes on units sold or from affiliated firms, and outside investments such as savings bonds. Liabilities to others of $145,000 are primarily loans secured by mortgages on units under construction but include amounts owed to all other claimants, such as trade credit and loans secured by notes on the general assets of the firm.

Although equity funds have been adequate for the present operations of builders, the difficulty of expanding equity has been responsible for preventing a majority of medium- and large-sized builders from greatly expanding their operations. Available assets are correlated to volume and do not allow much expansion. Most firms press closely upon their capital ceilings. Because of this, the growth of many of these firms has depended upon their ability to achieve a high rate of capital turnover. When firms approach their capital limits, those making the best use of their available resources most easily increase their relative size.

The ratio of sales dollar to net worth shows the number of times during a year a firm turns over its net worth. In respect to turnover, the medium-sized firms were found to be divided into nearly equal groups, with a third having a turnover rate higher than five to one, a third having a rate slower than three to one, and the remainder between. Although more than 20 per cent of the large firms had a sales volume more than ten times as great as their net worth in 1949, only 10 per cent of the medium-sized firms were in this bracket. This would indicate that existing equity capital was sufficient for some increase in output if firms increased their rate of capital turnover, but not for much more than doubling it. If we assume that a volume to equity ratio of 10 is close to the maximum, then without new capital, about 40 per cent of the medium-sized firms were limited to doubling their 1949 volume or less, whereas most of the remaining could not have increased their volume by more than three times.

This problem of limited capital makes examination of the ratio of total liabilities to net worth (its leverage) an important means of interpreting the financial structure of a firm. The greater the leverage, the higher the firm's risks and prospective profits. Leverage increases with size of firm. As firms grow larger, they increase their use of borrowed capital both relatively and absolutely.

A large number of medium firms made a high rate of return. In the majority of these, high profits on net worth reflect a high rate of capital turnover with a comparatively high profit on sales. The combination of these two factors gives a high return on capital and appears to mark the most daring as well as the most efficient firms.

The medium-sized firms averaged 23 per cent return on their net worth, and their profit on sales was 8.5 per cent (tables 34 and 35).

Equivalent in importance to equity financing in these firms' operations is construction financing. Financially, the period covered by this study was an exceptional one. Although the problem of construction financing has been the subject of much concern throughout the history of the building industry, it was not, during the period of this study, a critical matter.

The issue of construction financing is traditionally vital to the builder because his unit investments and sales are so large. At any time, about one-quarter of his yearly volume of sales is tied up in partly completed units. Few builders, and no large or medium ones, have sufficient working capital to cover the differences between the rates of their income and outlays. As a result, they must borrow money on various types of security to augment their working capital and aid in bridging the gaps. Borrowings were primarily from financial institutions on mortgages against houses in process, during the period under study.

The summary balance sheets show that less than 45 per cent of the average medium-sized firm's assets at any time are covered by its own equity; in other words, more than 55 per cent of the amount used by these firms is owed to others.

In spite of this proportion of debts, the old picture of housebuilders as an overextended group, who had great difficulties in meeting their current bills and to whom the credit they could obtain from material suppliers and subcontractors was crucial, became outmoded in the postwar period. During this time, most builders had adequate capital or bank credit to meet their trade bills promptly, and in the larger firms they not only frequently furnished financing for subcontractors but also built up sizable inventories of materials. When the current trade payment policies of firms were investigated, it was found that almost all were meeting their bills on a discount-to-prompt basis.

The main influence on construction loans during the postwar period was the government's participation in the financing market. This influence was experienced in three ways. (1) Construction loans were made less risky when the costs of credit to final purchasers, as well as their equity requirements, were greatly reduced, and the government insured lenders against losses if houses could not be sold by the builders. (2) The percentage of value that builders could borrow for construction was increased by government participation. (3) Available funds were increased when establishment of insured loans enabled lending institutions from outside the area to participate more freely in the market.

These effects of government policy and participation channeled from the programs of both the Veterans Administration and the Federal Housing Administration. It was the FHA program which had the greater effect in the construction financing sphere. The Federal Housing Administration gave lending institutions commitments to insure final loans before construction even started. In a majority of cases, these commitments were "firm"; that is, they would be honored either in the name of the builder or any other qualified buyer. This greatly increased available construction funds, since it meant that lenders of construction money were not assuming risks of a deflation in the house market. If the builder completed the house, the government guaranteed the lender against loss. The lender risked only a failure of the borrower to complete the house.

From the builder's point of view, FHA-insured construction loans had additional advantages. Conventional noninsured construction loans carry a lower loan-to-price ratio. On conventional loans, builders could borrow only 50 to 65 per cent of value in contrast to a theoretical 85 per cent of value in certain cases under the Federal Housing Administration. Besides the lower loan-to-price ratio, conventional construction loans often carry a higher interest rate to offset the lender's somewhat greater risk. As an additional advantage, according to relevant FHA regulations, the amount of the insured loan could be increased if approval was obtained before construction started and if inspections took placed during construction. These features were so advantageous that more than 64 per cent of the houses built by operative builders in the Bay area were constructed on that basis. The remaining 36 per cent of the operative builders' production consisted mainly of houses built singly rather than in tracts, or houses which, because of their style or price, could obtain only a conventional loan.

The Market

Market problems of the medium-sized housebuilding firm take their configuration from the dimensions of the enterprise.[4] The transition from simplicity in smallness to a more complicated structure in largeness engenders problems of land planning, unit designing, market analysis, and sales techniques. The fact that the transition is incomplete—that the medium-sized firm has not gone all the way to mass production and mass merchandising—sets limits on its possible solutions to these problems.

Solutions are limited by lack of scale. With respect to land, these firms are not large enough to develop whole new areas of their own. In design, they do not have sufficient total volume to afford specialized assistance, and so they must continually imitate designs that are familiar to them. In market analysis, they seldom do any scientific research, and so they rely on guesswork. With respect to sales techniques, these firms do not have the capital to invest in all-out sales efforts, and so they fasten their hopes to underpricing the prevailing

[4] The description in the remainder of this chapter is based on the case studies and surveys described in Appendix D.

market in a familiar area, with a type of house which conforms to the area and to the area's previous experience. All these restrictions confine the medium-sized builder to constructing the most conventional housing produced by the industry. This group, by attempting to create the most salable units at a minimum of expense, operates with a minimum of originality.

The most basic decisions of firms that do merchant building in tracts are those relating to land. The medium-sized firms are the first, in the ascending scale of size, for whom land is of cardinal importance. Except for contractors and the smallest firms within this group, there is not enough land already developed to meet the needs of the medium-sized merchant housebuilders.

Land creates a severe financing problem for a firm of any size, but especially for a firm with capital limitations. Land uses a large part of a firm's equity because unimproved land is usually not considered a suitable security for bank loans, and frequently large amounts of equity are required for financing improvements. This means that the amounts tied up in land are frozen and are hard to thaw for other uses. The carrying costs on land are an important segment of all indirect charges. The costs to the builder—especially the opportunity costs—are high. If builders hold large amounts of land for future development, this greatly diminishes their liquidity. At the same time, if they do not plan their development for large blocks of land they are likely to lose some of the most important advantages of large-scale building. The fluctuations in value of the land may be great. If the cycle is favorable, land may return high capital gains, but if building declines rapidly, the firm's position may be endangered. The only item of equal potential danger is an inventory of unsold houses.

Land development for the medium-sized builders conforms to a typical pattern. Vacant land is usually found in an area where building is already taking place. The medium-sized builders do not develop new communities. Instead, they depend on a ready-made situation, initiated by others, for such community facilities as shopping centers, schools, parks, churches, transportation conveniences, and so on. By having to rely on others for these facilities, they lose part of the profits which accrue to those who develop them. The medium-sized merchant builder usually works on units of from 10 to 50 lots. He often tackles a tract together with other builders of his own size.

The cost of developed land runs from $30,000 to $150,000 a year for builders in this group. About half this amount represents the cost of the raw land. Land must be bought and development planned or begun at least six months, and preferably a year, in advance of construction. It is necessary for a builder to have this much land ahead at all times, because before he can move his construction crew onto a lot, he must have taken many time-consuming steps—steps involving site plans, financing, planning commission approval, line-up of materials, and preliminary work. This means that if a builder's crew is working on a six-month project, he must be actively engaged in the development work on the next project that will follow. For smoothest operations at this level, at least three or four projects a year are desirable.

The matter of keeping ahead of himself in land, if it involves investment of his own funds in raw land and land development, is the heaviest claim on capital confronting a builder. In seeking to solve the problem of land planning with limited capital, builders use several means.

One method to control land for future use without at the same time tying up capital is through the purchase of options. By this means the total tract is divided into segments, each with an agreed price, and the builder takes options upon them which he can pick up as he requires the land. In other cases the owner of the property assumes part of the risk, either by entering into an agreement whereby the builder pays for the developing and the owner receives his payment as each house is sold, or the owner takes back a large mortgage which again is released as the houses are sold. This method is affected by both Federal Housing Administration and state regulations. If a firm commitment is to be obtained, the owner of the land or its mortgage holder must subordinate his interest to the construction and permanent loan. In addition, the builder must be able to give clear title to every house. No house can be sold still subject to a general mortgage on the entire tract. Any of these methods of obtaining the use of land short of outright purchase decreases the builder's equity requirements and increases his potential volume.

Another solution of the problem is offered when a development company takes responsibility for land development, financing, and sales, with the builder responsible only for construction. In this situation, the builder and land development company divide profits on a predetermined basis which is frequently 40–60 or 50–50, since both carry the burden of the risk of their own equity.

In a third of the firms there is a related land development affiliate. These affiliated firms frequently represent the real estate interests and additional capital of the owners. The duality of corporate existence allows a different sharing of risks, experience, and profits, and in some cases eases the problem.

Still other approaches are based on efforts to have outsiders hold or share the land risks, receiving payment if the ventures are successful.

Some firms which have sufficient money handle their own land purchasing and development. But the prevalence of risk sharing is evidenced by the fact that the median builder in this group actually holds only $750 worth of land per completion. This reflects the complete absence of land holdings on the part of nearly half the medium-sized building firms. Twenty per cent of the medium builders hold a year's supply, and another 20 per cent hold about two years' supply.

The actual physical planning of the land is almost always done by an engineering firm acting as a consultant on a fee basis. This firm is responsible for all plans, required surveys, maps, and so on, and frequently handles all negotiations from the beginning right on through the required approval of the planning commission, sometimes even supervising the installation of utilities. Construction work involved in the land development, such as building roads and sewers, is subcontracted to firms specializing in these operations. This construction work goes on simultaneously with housebuilding except when the terrain requires roads to be built first to get trucks onto the site.

The design of the house usually follows those which have already been completed successfully by the firm. Builders do not know what the consumer wants. They guess. Their guess usually is that he wants what he used to want. The medium-sized builder imitates and copies and offers more of what has been bought. If his guess is right, he is lucky. If his guess is wrong, he goes out of business.

Ideas are often sketched out in rough form by the owner and turned over to a draftsman for final drawings. Some attempt is made to design for simplicity of construction, and to simplify a new design more than its predecessor. New ideas may be derived from reading trade magazines, from listening to salesmen interested in promoting certain materials, or from observing the work of others. In general, new ideas are incorporated very slowly by the medium-sized builder. He is used to following a certain plan and utilizing a certain material; it has worked and it has sold in the past; he must be thoroughly convinced of the soundness and salability of an innovation. He would rather not engage in experimentation, himself. If the innovation is to be tried out, he would prefer to see it put to test by other builders in the area, and to observe their experience with it before he ventures to depart from his accustomed way.

The sales of the medium-sized builder are usually placed with a particular real estate broker on a special basis or put in the hands of a land development firm. Building firms in this group are almost equally divided in their choice between these two relationships. Since land development for builders of this size is commonly handled by a separate firm, the sales function can easily be performed by this same development unit. Whether the development unit is owned by the principals of the building firm or is an unrelated real estate firm which assumes part of the risk, the building firm, in effect, pays a fixed fee for the job of developing the land, arranging the financing, negotiating with the Federal Housing Administration and Veterans Administration if necessary, and selling.

Some firms may hire a broker and pay a fixed selling fee per house. If there are two or more principals of the firm, one may hold a real estate license and sell the unit himself. Or, finally, a firm may furnish office space to a real estate broker who handles the firm's sales on a special fee basis while conducting his private business on the firm's premises. Only the smallest firms of this group pay a regular brokerage fee for sales.

As a sort of substitute for market research, medium-sized firms often test the market by selling from a model home. The objective is to make sure that there is demand, and that the builder is not ahead of the market. The difficulty is that the builder has to plan the whole project in advance, and has to be working on it while the model home is in construction and while the sales effort is under way. The model home does test the market, but the builder is frequently so committed that he could not back out, even if the test turned out "negative," and sales very slow. The chief purpose served by the model home technique is that the sales effort can be begun sooner, with the result that later homes may be sold before their construction is completed.

Production

The medium-sized firm is at the halfway mark of expansion in the manner in which it organizes its production as well as in most other aspects of its operations. It continues to perform primarily carpentry work, subcontracting out the rest of the production processes. Thus the surface organization of production is similar to that of the small firm. The same tasks are still performed by the builder's direct labor; the same jobs are still subcontracted; and materials are bought with about the same degree of finish. The internal organization of production, however, begins to show some similarity to that of the large firms. This is seen particularly in utilization of labor.

The medium-sized firm's labor force is still small, averaging 15 mechanics (table 12). These are divided into four crews, each of which does only one of four major jobs—foundation, framing, walls, and finish. Their specialization begins and ends here. Within each crew, there is virtually no specialization. All members, for example, of the framing crew pitch in to do whatever is needed to build, raise, and place the frame.

When firms reach this size of operation, their labor relations become somewhat more formal. They have more turnover of men, with the result that they have to hire those available in the labor market, probably taking whatever carpenters the union sends them. This makes the relations less personal, as well as less permanent, than those of the small builder and his crew.

Since it pays to keep labor turnover as low as possible, medium firms try to plan their rate and system of work to fit and hold onto permanent crews. These firms try to maintain a steady production schedule. Crews must be scheduled in proper rotation. A crew works on a group of three or four houses, and then the next crew moves in to work on that group, while the first crew goes on to another group. If the schedule does not permit retaining a full permanent crew, these firms always seek to hold at least four or five crew leaders. To do this, they may have to slow down work and delay completion of units. For example, if a firm has enough work to keep 16 men busy for a week, it has enough work to keep four men busy for a month; therefore, if a gap occurs in the production schedule, the firm, instead of using 16 men for a week, may let four men do the job in a month, in order to keep the four crew leaders permanently on the payroll. The increased carrying costs and less liquid capital imposed by the slower rate of work may be compensated for by better efficiency resulting from utilization of men whose skill and reliability have been demonstrated.

In addition to increased specialization of crews, medium firms also use better and more efficient techniques. Among new techniques, precutting and preassembling are becoming increasingly common, though prefabrication is virtually nonexistent. As pointed out in the preceding chapter, the term prefabrication is used here to designate the assembling of a complete wall or final unit in some type of centralized manufacturing process, with the unit brought to the site ready for final erection. Many firms of all sizes attempted prefabrication in the postwar period. Currently, all but two have either gone out of business or returned to the usual amount of precutting.

In precutting, lumber is usually sawed to predetermined lengths by some type of power machinery. The lumber is placed on a saw table where it is forced by hand against a stop at the desired length from the fixture carrying the saw. The mechanism can be extremely simple. The stop is usually just a piece of lumber or a nail set in cuts which have been made at fixed distances along the table. The setting can be changed rapidly for each desired cutting. The fixture includes either a large-sized radial saw or the simple power handsaw (Skil). Other types of precutting use angle cuts made either with a pattern or by setting of the saw to cut at a given angle.

This cutting may take place immediately adjacent to the house site, or in a builder's yard, on or near the tract but at some distance from the site where the lumber enters the house, or in the yard of the materials dealer.

Cut pieces are either tossed directly to the work point on the house or, if cut in a yard, are binned and distributed later. They may or may not be numbered and marked individually, depending on the complexity of the operation.

In preassembling, lumber or other materials are placed on jig-tables where the jig outlines the desired pattern, and the pieces are nailed together. The units are placed in piles from which they are distributed to the individual house site either by trailer or skid. They are then incorporated into the house in a manner similar to other units.

The amount and type of precutting or preassembly vary greatly from firm to firm. Most small firms use precut main items, such as studs and headers. As the size of a project increases, more and more items tend to be precut, until at the maximum almost all lumber is so handled. Ultimately, only the plates, subflooring, and sheathing are left to be sawed during erection. The question at this stage is simply one of whether it is easier to cut an item before fitting or after fitting.

The amount of preassembling is less correlated with size than is precutting. Some firms do almost no preassembly work, though certain units such as cabinets and garage doors are bought ready-made from the dealer. Other firms preassemble such wall sections as openings for windows and doors; sometimes doors are fitted to the jamb, and entire window units, including decorations and window boxes, may be preassembled also. The shop preparation of sheet metal for all units is a somewhat similar operation. Finally, some firms preassemble the complete framing for a wall and move it to the site.

Specific procedures are determined by variations in particular cost factors. Precutting is adopted because of the advantages of power over handsawing and mechanical over handmeasuring, because of the great saving of time and materials through repetition and proper planning of cuts, and because of the increase in labor output which results from setting work standards.

Disadvantages also exist. Precutting requires some increase in the cost of handling and transportation, since items must be classified, binned or stacked, counted, and distributed. There is also an overhead cost in the purchase and maintenance of equipment.

Similarly, for preassembly, when measurements are made and lumber is marked mechanically, repetition sets in and work standards can be established; but the problem of transportation is accentuated because the assembled units are awkward and must be handled with some care.

The total procedures of the firm will determine the relative efficiency of each method. The increased speed that comes with repetition and use of a pattern can rapidly be offset by larger handling costs. Depending upon the general methods of the firm, its scheduling ability, and its available labor and supervision, builders of similar size will find different systems more efficient at different times, and a single firm may change its methods as its supervisors and labor change.

Improvements similar to those of precutting and preassembling are brought about by the use of patterns and templates. These add the related economies of demonstrating the most efficient cuts and utilization of surplus cutoff ends to the time which they save in measurement.

The simplest type of template is that employed in marking off the position of studs, doors, windows, and the like. These are simply bars approximately six feet in length, with crosspieces the width of the stud, and possibly other standard distances marked off. With this template and a crayon, a man can rapidly indicate the exact location of each stud on the plates. When he is familiar with the plan from previous experience, he can also indicate the proper location of all necessary openings and cuts.

Once constructed, the template reduces the problem of exact measurement for each house. Templates are often used for laying out foundation forms, and they can indicate the location of the interior position of the fireplace, porches, and so on.

Templates may further be used in hanging doors to show the correct location of the hinges and hardware. In this latter case, the template is a rod fitting exactly into the jamb, with spaces of the right size cut out at the right spot for hinges. It is nailed temporarily against the jamb and furnishes a guide for routing. After a number of jambs have been routed, the doors can be treated in the same manner.

Since templates change from plan to plan, they cannot be used in scattered building. It is not worth the time and overhead to make, store, and then search them out for intermittent use on individual houses every few months.

A pattern is invaluable when a large number of pieces are to be cut or notched. For example, roof rafters have to be sawed to meet the ridgepole at the proper angle, and notched to fit properly over the top plate. The cuts can be made with a minimum of measurement on the saw table or marked off from a pattern and cut with a power handsaw at the site.

As his scale increases, the medium builder gains increased opportunity to use these timesaving procedures. They mark important improvements in technique, but unfortunately they cannot be fully utilized until a builder's size is large enough to employ better production planning and controls than the medium-sized builder can. Before that point, some of these new methods aid in reducing his costs, but large potential areas for improvement still remain.

PURCHASING

Salient organizational changes in the transition from small to medium-sized building operations occur in materials supply. Here there is tangible evidence of increasing economy and efficiency commensurate with increasing scale of production.

It is in the medium-sized group that wholesale buying, discount prices, and direct purchases of materials from mills become common. The medium-sized builder is ordinarily able to by-pass the retailer. He does not require the usual dealer's services which were valuable to the small builder. This builder buys the same four items that the small builder buys, but usually he is able to take advantage of his larger-scale operation to obtain lower unit prices for quantity purchases.

The medium-sized builder almost always buys his lumber and hardware at wholesale or at a wholesale price. He usually obtains his millwork and cabinets from a specialist and receives a quantity discount. Gypsum is his greatest materials problem, because it is the most closely controlled of the materials. On gypsum, some medium-sized builders obtain a discount, and some do not (table 23).

Very few medium-sized builders are directly affiliated with a supply source, but the simplification and economy of wholesale and quantity discount purchasing represent an important innovation at this level in the scale of housebuilding operations and indicate marked increase in efficiency.

The medium-sized builder shops around, since quantities are large and small savings per unit add up, so that he may choose the yard, broker, or wholesaler whose price is best. Because of the amount of each order, he has more bargaining power than the small builder. Whole channels of distribution may be cut out because their services are no longer necessary.

Illustrative of savings resulting from increased scale is the comparative cost of lumber purchased at retail and at wholesale. In January, 1951, the single-house builder was charged $97 per thousand board feet at retail, though the wholesale price of this lumber on a Bay region siding was about $82 per thousand. Most medium-sized builders who produced as many as three houses per month purchased through a broker or wholesaler at the lower price. The larger ones among them who bought direct from the mills saved an additional 5 per cent. Similarly, millwork which cost the small builder $725 for a typical house cost the medium-sized builder $580; hardware which cost the small builder $185 could be bought in quantity by the medium-sized builder for $155. In sum, the medium-sized builder saved about 14 per cent on all of his direct materials purchases (table 51).

Another economy, and consequent increase of efficiency, made possible by the medium-sized builder's greater volume of production is found in his relation to subcontractors. The number of subcontractors used by the medium-sized builder does not differ because of his larger scale from the number used by the small contractor. He still enters into from 10 to 15 subcontracts per house (table 22). The important change in the medium-sized firm's relationships with subcontractors is that this firm has acquired bargaining power and has begun to use it to make savings and thus to increase efficiency. The builder's subcontract charges are reduced by sums equivalent to the savings he makes possible for his trade contractors. These occur in four major ways (tables 49–52).

First, the subcontractor in medium-sized tracts saves by more efficient use of labor. The largest reduction in labor cost comes from decreasing lost time rather than from changed techniques and methods. Except for painters, the amount of labor each subcontractor furnishes to a given unit is not large. At the same time, in several trades this small amount may be spread over several visits. This means that for jobs in scattered houses, the ratio of nonproductive time—time spent in getting to the house and getting equipment out and set up—to productive time is high. Further, when jobs are not an even multiple of the working day and the amount of time left is too short to move to another location, the men will tend to stretch into a full day's work the job they have in hand. An example of this may be taken from masonry. In ceramic tiles and masonry, the labor cost for a small builder's single house is often estimated as two full days' wages for a mason and his helper. The work could be done more quickly, but doing so would not leave enough time to move to a new location, start preparations, mix mortar or mastic, and accomplish any work. On the other hand, for a medium builder's small or medium tract, if two houses are worked in a row, the time saved in setting up and preparation usually allows the two units to be completed in three days instead of four—a labor saving of 25 per cent.

Second, subcontractors' savings in materials purchases occur when a tract project is large enough to permit buying in bulk quantities. As quantities grow large, the trade contractor can buy in carload lots or in standard packages, which means lower prices. For example, for the typical house in a medium-sized builder's operation, oak flooring costs $198 that would cost the small builder $224; plumbing materials cost $450 that would cost the small builder $495; paint costs $135 that would cost the small builder $144. Savings in purchases of trade contractors' materials for the medium-sized tract come to 6 per cent.

Third, the medium tract saves for the subcontractor by making more accurate his estimating, scheduling, and production controls. On a tract, the subcontractor knows just what to expect and can plan and pace his work more efficiently because the work is similar from one house to the next. Furthermore, he can afford to spend more time on his planning, thus doing better, more economical planning. On an individual house, each subcontractor's task is too small to allow for detailed thought and supervision.

The fourth cost-saving feature of increased scale is a sharp reduction in the trade contractor's charges for overhead and profit. The medium-sized builder is charged about $100 less by his subcontractors for overhead and profit on the typical house than the small builder is charged. As one example, the plumber's overhead and profit charge to the small builder on a typical house is $200; to the medium-sized builder it is $148.

There are three main reasons for these reductions. Because overhead and profit are some type of function of the payments for materials and labor, since magnitudes of these amounts determine necessary capital and supervision, payments for overhead fall at least proportionately with the fall in direct costs. The amount of estimating, supervising, purchasing, and bookkeeping time required to handle a large job is less proportionately per house than that required for a small one, the amount of effort spent on each task being spread over more units.

And because the medium-sized builder is able to make savings for the subcontractors in the four ways described, and offers larger volume, the subcontractors are willing to take lower profits. Subcontractor competition for jobs of larger volume is sufficient to cause them to pass along to the builder the savings which the builder has made possible, and they often go beyond this by shaving their own profit margin.

In a highly competitive situation or when building is slow, subcontractors may cut their profits to nothing, simply to go on working and to retain their permanent crews.

The medium-sized builder has not actually introduced any new methods in his trade contractor relationships. No real changes or improvements in the system of subcontractual relations or the subcontractors' methods have taken place. The difference from the small builder is one of degree rather than one of kind. The medium-sized builder's advantageous position derives from greater volume of production.

The control by medium-sized firms over their subcontractors' work remains slight. These firms are not large enough to plan subcontractors' methods. They do not have time. All their available time must be spent on controls of their own direct operations. Such supervision as there is by the builder is handled informally. In their relationships with and dependence on the ability of their subcontractors, the medium-sized firms are not very different from the small firms.

Controls

The transitional position of the medium-sized builder is seen again in his methods of estimating, accounting, and controls.[5] These methods differ somewhat from those of the small builder. The differences arise mainly from the operative nature of his work and his increased volume of production. The medium-sized builder must work out a preliminary budget covering total tract costs, since his projects are speculative. He usually sets his selling price before he knows his actual costs. In addition, his estimate, based upon one house, must show the total quantities of materials required for the tract as well as funds necessary for all purposes.

Estimating in this manner enables him to decide what bulk purchases of materials should be attempted, and to budget his total financial requirements more completely. His capital must be carefully rationed to the most profitable uses. The medium-sized builder is also required to organize his time more comprehensively in advance than the small builder. His work is done in groups—he may have several groups of houses under construction at once—and he must be able to schedule his foundation, framing, wall, and finishing crews, as well as

[5] The description in this section is based on the case studies and surveys described in Appendix D.

purchases and deliveries, in the proper sequence. If he produces 50 houses a year, he may have four groups of 4 or 5 houses each in various stages of completion at the same time, and the efficient rotation of his crews necessitates detailed preliminary planning as well as close supervision.

Medium-sized firms frequently have a small yard and warehouse, which require a simplified inventory system. A purchase-order plan is likely to be used. Accounting for supplies is on a more formalized basis than is that of the small builder. Here the group is the accounting unit. Deliveries are checked in at either the yard or warehouse on duplicate order forms and are reported to the bookkeeper. Materials are charged to a group of houses. Labor and overhead are also calculated on a group basis. When the total costs for the group of houses are tabulated, they are then allocated back and prorated to the individual houses.

Although some kind of production schedule is necessary, it has been difficult for builders to work out a completely satisfactory system of suitable and inexpensive production controls. Most firms make time estimates when they start a project and then depend on personal supervision to keep up their labor effectiveness. Completed work is posted to a chart. In addition, progress payments and required inspections for each house are recorded on the chart. These serve as bench marks and proof that the work has been completed. The charts show progress at about eight stages for each house. Any delay in schedule can be checked.

Labor is accounted for by the foreman of each crew, who records by timecard the hours expended on each group of houses. The time is then charged accordingly, the group again being used as the accounting unit. This is a compromise between the expensive ideal of accounting for labor on each house and the dangerous short cut of calculating labor costs only when the whole project is completed. This system permits the cost per crew per phase of work to be calculated as soon as a group of houses is completed. The result gives the executive a set of figures that he can use for control purposes. He checks the actual work figures against his original estimates and if the standards that he set up have not been met, he finds out why.

Subcontractor payments and incidentals are charged by medium-sized firms (as is also true with small firms) directly against particular units. When all direct costs have been tabulated for the group of houses that make up a given accounting unit, the results are compared with selling prices, and the difference is the gross margin on sales. From this gross margin, indirect construction costs such as supervision and depreciation and all other overhead expenses including office salaries, sales costs, licenses, and the like are then subtracted to give the profit per individual house.

The controls are actually the minimum necessary to keep this size of builder from losing control of his operations. Doing a half-million-dollar business, he obviously must have improved his accounting methods over those of the small builder. At the same time, the controls rarely are sufficiently detailed to aid him in production planning. His assignment of crews, checking their work, and determination of production methods remains almost entirely on a personal and hit-or-miss basis.

Determination of Size of Firm

The medium-sized firms have already made the transition from small size to a more complicated structure. If they are to expand further they must meet and solve an entirely new and different set of problems. They have passed the hurdle of the owner's laying down his tools to become an executive; the principal of these firms is already an executive. Changing the nature of the operation from contracting on individual houses to operative and tract building is behind them; the majority of these firms are already engaged in operative and tract building. Only about 20 per cent claim that their expansion is limited by managerial span; that is, a reluctance to bring in an additional principal or executive (table 21).

Credit, risk, and land present the prevailing impediments to further expansion and of these, credit is the most common. This usually means that the firm is already pressing the limit of extension allowed by the financial institutions. It might desire to expand but does not have the working capital to make this possible.

Among that half of the firms who do have some funds available for enlargement, the lack of suitable land or the fear of overexpansion—in some cases both—are the prime deterrents. As has already been indicated, these companies have a difficult land problem because they need large amounts and yet cannot develop entirely new areas. Those firms which are building for others, such as separate land development organizations or property owners who assume the risks, are dependent for their rate of expansion on the risks the others are willing to take.

To go into their own land development would require a very substantial addition of capital. It would also require a readiness to tie up the additional capital in a slow-moving asset, one on which banks are not willing to make loans, and one which is hard to thaw for other uses. Further, it would subject the additional capital to serious risks because the value of land is susceptible to extreme fluctuations. Hence, even the firms which are not tightly pressing their capital limits are hesitant to freeze their available funds in an investment which is hard to liquidate and is subject to market hazards.

The risk element in expansion plays a determining role in the decisions of many firms in this bracket. They have kept their overhead and invested capital comparatively low and enjoy the resultant feeling of security. They are not eager to jeopardize it through expansion.

Increased production frequently requires a jump of many units; it is not possible simply to add one or two houses a year to output. This discontinuity in the production curve means that firms which appear to have more than ample resources at their present level still do not have enough to bridge the gap to the next feasible size.

Summary

The evolution of the housebuilding industry can be observed in the structural and organizational changes in the medium-sized building group, as compared with small builders. Starting with the small builder, the change which has taken place in the medium-sized bracket is introductory to the development of the big builder. The medium-sized builders mark the mid-point in the development of the housebuilding industry.

The production median of this group is the production median of the industry. At the lower end are the contractors, a minority which appears to be at a dead-end of production development; at the higher levels of this group are the operative tract builders, and this majority evidences the genes of greater growth.

The men who compose the firms of this latter group are businessmen first, then builders. They bring to building the vitality of new business attitudes and methods. They form partnerships and corporations. They affiliate with firms in related fields. They establish themselves as executives and develop overhead structure. They meet the challenge of more complicated financing problems and greater risk. They supply sufficient equity capital to finance the house from the ground up and hold it until it sells. They secure construction loans and arrange the permanent loan for the final consumer. Their leverage is greater than that of small firms; their turnover is more rapid. They reap the reward by averaging 23 per cent return on their net worth, compared with 13 per cent among the small builders.

They are confronted by a new set of market problems—land planning, unit designing, market analysis, and sales techniques. To meet these, they adopt some, but not all, of the methods of mass production and mass merchandising, but they do not innovate. The result is the most conventional product of any class of builder.

The first steps toward mass production are seen in some specialization in organization of the labor force and off-site fabricating. The first steps toward the economies of mass purchasing are seen in wholesale buying, shopping for discount prices, and making direct purchases of materials from mills. The first steps toward increased bargaining power are utilized to gain lower prices from subcontractors.

Estimating, accounting, and controls have become more complicated for the medium-sized builder. More budgeting, planning, scheduling are required for production of groups of units than for single units.

At the same time, the inability to support any sizable overhead staff keeps these controls at a minimum. These controls serve a negative rather than a positive function. They guard against depletion of money at crucial times and against too lengthy waiting periods and delays for the crews. They do not, however, enable the builder to plan and control more efficiently. Primarily he is still using the same methods and techniques as the small builder, though he has gained some purchasing and other advantages which arise with scale.

The medium-sized firms could become more efficient and more profitable if they could carry their incipient organizational and structural adaptations from the present rudimentary stage to a maximum evolvement. This is impossible with their present scale, however, because this higher organization would require larger indirect expenses than could be carried efficiently by their existing volume. To achieve a higher volume would require an altered organization and more credit, more capital, more land. If these become available, some builders will attempt to move up, whereas others, who are satisfied with their existing size, will not take the additional risk.

5

The Large Firm

At the top of the housebuilding pyramid is that group of firms whose number narrows to smallest though its production rises to highest. There are only thirty firms in the classification of Bay area businesses which produce more than 100 houses a year.[1]

The big 30—representing but 2 per cent of Bay area builders—constructed 6,195 houses in 1949, or 35 per cent of all units produced by the industry. These are the new giants in an industry once populated by pygmies. Here, at the very peak of the pyramid, are the leaders of construction who are not content merely to build houses. They construct communities (table 10).

These firms personify housebuilding's answer to the dynamic pressures at work in the past decade. They have developed new techniques, new processes, and new forms of organization in response to a new market situation. The metamorphosis of the market came about through a tremendous demand kindled by easier financing and the big backlog from the war, when new housing production fell far behind new family formation.

It is true that these firms would not be considered colossal if they existed in the automobile or steel industry or other areas of manufacturing titans. They are mammoth, however, in relation to the industry's past history, the type of market in which it operates, and in their method of organization.

Their silhouette shows that they have developed in a rather lopsided manner. They too are still in transition. What they required for success in the postwar market was, primarily, skill in purchasing and financing. In this direction, they overspecialized. They under-

[1] See Appendixes C and F, and tables 10–17, 38, 39.

specialized in such directions as production management and design, elements which the market did not require them to develop to any great extent. Their imbalance faces them with serious problems both of present efficiency and future progress, giving rise to the question of whether these firms took advantage of their position to make the most of their potentialities while the market was most favorable to their growth. What of the present and the future? Is it probable that the best aspects of present operations will spread from the large firms to most other firms? Will the large firms continue to develop as they move into a future of more competitive conditions? This chapter does not attempt an easy "yes" or "no" answer to these questions. It is hoped that the description of the large builders' operations, structure, and organization will suggest tentative answers to the reader.

The large firms are all merchant builders in type, producing the bulk of their units in tracts by operative methods. Only two firms in this group built more than one or two houses on individual contracts, and in both instances the amount of contract work was minor. Only six firms in the group did any building in addition to houses. Three of these were general contractors who did all kinds of building; for two of these three, housebuilding was only a sideline furnishing a small part of their total volume (tables 10, 13–16).

The three other firms which erected units other than houses built multifamily and commercial structures. Most of this building consisted of their own shopping centers and apartment houses in or near their own main tracts. This work was part of the construction of a complete community.

There was appeal to all large builders in the rich potentialities of creating a whole community—particularly of capturing, through commercial development, the enhanced values which they brought to an area by their own construction of houses. At the time of our survey, many large firms planned, or had already completed, such commercial developments. Consequently, though they remain housebuilders, the number of firms doing this other type of building varies from year to year.

The total dollar volume of business produced by the large firm in 1949 ranged from $1,000,000 to $5,000,000, though three of the concerns fell just below the bracket and four topped it. None attained the maximum size of $25,000,000 to $30,000,000 in annual volume achieved by housebuilders in a few other areas (table 11). (It was possible, however, to draw upon some of the experience of those still larger firms in parts of the discussion which follows.)

Most large firms concentrated their building in the nonurban or small suburban parts of the metropolitan area. Even the few firms which found sufficient land to develop within the major cities usually had other and lower-priced projects in the outlying districts. Operation of two or three tracts in adjacent sections was rather common. Half the large firms built in two or more permit centers. Because several of their tracts were in near-by counties beyond the census boundaries of the area, 20 per cent of the units built by the large Bay area firms were on land outside the official limits of the Bay area. This tendency to spread out, however, did not represent real dispersion. Almost all tracts were within an actual economic market. Only rarely did firms work on sites more than 15 to 20 miles apart (tables 10, 17).

It was the large firms which built the least expensive houses. The median-priced house sold by these firms in 1949 cost the buyer $9,250. This compares with the median price of $12,400 for the small builder and $10,500 for the medium-sized firm. The large builder's houses tended to be stripped of all extras, and their merchandising was pointed toward the mass market. Besides their skimpiness in quality and detail, they were frequently built on newly developed land of the least expensive kind (tables 38, 39).

The large builders' concentration in low-priced houses was not exclusive. A few firms did build houses in the higher price brackets, though in most cases they also worked in the cheaper, more active market.

"Mass" is the key to most of the operations of this group of firms—mass production and mass merchandising for the mass market.

BACKGROUND AND ORGANIZATION

These tallest trees in the housebuilding forest have, as a group, the deepest roots in the building business. The average age of the large firms is 15 years—nearly three times that of the other groups. This average is somewhat misleading, however, because the age distribution is U-shaped. Half of the large firms were flourishing before the war. Most of these had been started in the 1920's and had had the stamina to survive the depression. Several stem back to the century's first decade. The other half, however, are new shoots, born of the war and the postwar boom (table 25).

The older firms had developed gradually, building up their experience and capital over the years. They had grown to medium size, and in a few cases, to large size, before the war began, and were in readiness to expand to meet the new demand.[2]

The newer members of the large group had originated, in many cases, as medium-sized firms. The owners of these firms frequently came to building from a background of real estate or financing which helped them to recognize the opportunity and need for development of large-scale firms. These men either had capital of their own or attracted partners who could furnish sufficient funds so that it was not necessary for them to start as small firms and grow gradually. At the outset they were able to hire construction superintendents to handle technical details, and they, as principals, undertook executive and supervisory duties. Several of the postwar firms were formed by younger men who had been trained in engineering or other professional fields which enabled them to bring fresh and original ideas to the business of house production.

It is these newest members of the large group who have shown the most dynamic growth. They are the ones most willing to take greater risks and to operate on lower equities. They are the ones who often bring invigorating new concepts—or new applications of existing practices in other fields—into housebuilding. They are often the innovators for the industry. Often, growth of their firms has been accelerated because they have reinvested in their businesses most of their substantial profits.

The owners of the large firms are slightly older than are the principals of the smaller firms. Their average age is 52. These extra years signify extra experience. The owner may have grown gray with his firm, steering it through the vicissitudes of the depression and recurring business cycles, in the case of an old and well-established business; or, in the case of a newer building firm, the owner may be a veteran of another profession—banking, savings and loan, real estate, retailing—and bring to building a knowledge of other business techniques (tables 24, 26).

Only 40 per cent of the owners of large firms have worked as build-

[2] See Appendixes D and E, and tables 24–27, 32.

ing mechanics. This experience frequently consisted only of work for their father or another relative who was the firm's founder. In contrast with this traditional path of entry were those with a general business background, and a final 20 per cent who were graduate engineers.

The operating structure of firms building more than 100 houses a year becomes much more complex than that of firms with a smaller volume of production. Multiplication of business entities is characteristic of operating structure in this bracket. The average is nearly three legal entities per large-sized builder. Apparently builders at this level find that it pays to multiply corporate units in order to spread the risk and also, probably, to solve certain problems connected with taxes, with building supply, and occasionally with union restrictions.

Forty per cent of the large firms have more than two entities, and the very large ones usually have five or more related corporations. The 30 firms in this group actually perform their functions through at least 80 separate corporations, partnerships, or proprietorships. A maximum of 10 to 15 companies in a single group occurs in several cases in the Bay area, but this is still a small figure compared with the forty-three corporations with which the 1951 national president of the Homebuilders' Association is credited (table 27).

The uninitiated might inquire as to what separate functions so many different firms could perform for what is, essentially, one business. A large combine might consist of the construction company itself, a real estate and insurance firm, several firms handling individually the land development for each separate tract or subdivision, several realty firms each owning and operating a separate apartment house or shopping center, one or two trade-contracting firms, a materials-supply firm, and several materials-producing units such as millwork firms and lumber mills.

These cases are unusual, as is evident from the median. The most typical operation is corporatively divided three ways: (1) construction; (2) land development, property ownership and management; (3) building materials and supply. It should not be supposed that each corporation requires separate personnel. Usually the separateness of the corporations is a convenient legal fiction. Each member of the main firm dons the hat of a given corporation, as required, from time to time. Except for accounting and other financial considerations, little effort is made to divide the actual workings of the individual units.

The main firm in a typical large-scale operation frequently has from two to four principal members who assume the primary executive positions. Although some single-ownership firms do exist, most companies have several nearly equal owners active in the business. This coöwnership allows an active part in management to the men who furnish funds, thus facilitating raising capital.

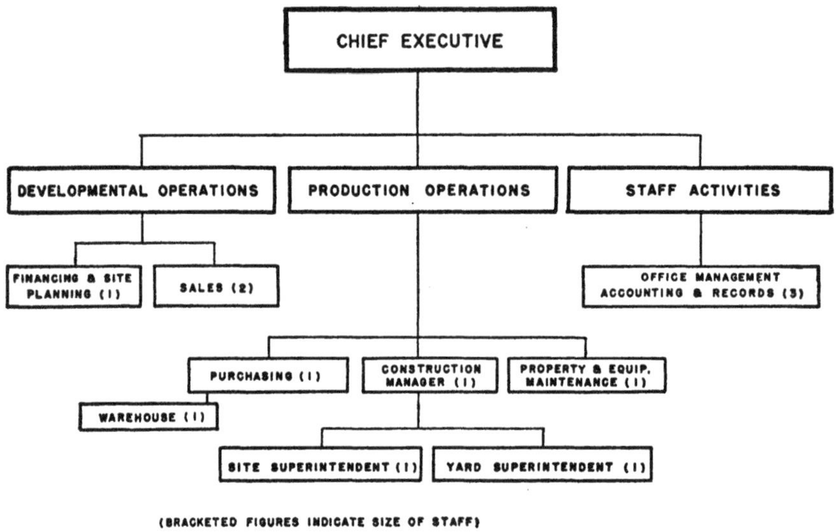

Fig. 6. Typical organization of large firm.

A total of thirteen off-site or supervisory personnel is average in the group of firms producing between 250 and 300 houses annually. There is little formality in either the organization or business procedures of these firms. The relatively small size of the management group encourages personal contact. Few, if any, special organizational techniques are used.

A typical pattern of organization for such firms operating in the Bay area is charted in figure 6. The figure shows the allocation of duties among the dozen supervisory personnel. The duties allocated are those which must be accomplished in operations of any size. In small firms all are performed by a single person. In these larger firms they are fragmented, with the division of work depending upon the skills possessed by the particular executives of the firm.

Ordinarily the chief executive administers the over-all operation. His two main assistants—or the other principals in a multiheaded firm—handle the production operations including construction management, and the remaining line functions such as planning of tracts, financing, sales, and purchasing. Staff duties, such as office management and records and accounting, can be handled at a subsidiary level. The decisions requiring executive skill as well as some vision are the forward planning, negotiations for important purchases of land, materials, and trade contractors' services, and frequently dealings with financial institutions and particularly government agencies. Certain functions of the typical firm of this size, such as design, estimating, and production control, do not appear in the chart as specialized supervisory functions because they do not have individuals assigned to them.

The firms that have widened their scope to do general contracting or community development have a somewhat larger overhead structure, necessitated by their larger dollar volume of building and by the increased functions they perform. When firms add functions and reach a building volume of about $5,000,000, their overhead staff expands to approximately 50 people.

The general organizational structure of these largest firms remains practically the same as that shown by the chart for the 250- to 300-house firms, but all sections are expanded. The supervisor in charge of staff activities has a much bigger job. His is now an executive function. The office unit handles rental matters for the shopping center and apartment units. The record-keeping functions expand and become a full-fledged business operation. The task of keeping track of funds and equipment is greater. The amount of correspondence and the number of tax and financing problems increase. A larger maintenance crew is required. The general office staff averages about 15 people in these larger firms instead of the three shown in the figure. The sections under developmental operations assume greater importance, particularly planning. Advance land planning, design, and estimating work become so voluminous that the firm performs many of the related functions itself rather than farming some of them out to consultants on a fee basis, as is common among the smaller large firms. The planning section includes estimating, drafting, and architectural design, and requires about five men, one of whom has professional responsibilities. The purchasing and warehousing sections may have as many as seven men between them instead of two. This is accounted for partly by the increase in volume and partly by reason of more bulk purchases further back along the distribution line; more time is spent at the mills and in finding alternative channels of supply. The sales force expands proportionately for similar reasons.

Overhead on production operations is obviously increased as well. Here the problem is simply one of performing a larger volume of work in more areas, but personnel increases more than proportionately. Although one might expect expansion in production overhead personnel to be approximately equivalent to the expansion in scale of operations, a disproportionate increase takes place because production has spread beyond the area of simple visual control by the owner or owners.

The personnel for supervision of construction for these largest firms increases to a total of 11 men from the three—the construction manager and two superintendents—noted on the figure for the average large firm. These 11 men include a construction manager, three superintendents, four assistant superintendents or nonworking foremen in charge of specific types of operations, and three timekeepers and production-control clerks. Although the number of supervisory personnel more than triples at the same time that the volume only doubles, the supervisory payroll may expand dollarwise simply in proportion to volume—in other words, may only double. The reason for this is that the three original supervisors required by the average large firm must be of high caliber—one probably an owner or executive and the others either drawing high salaries or working on a bonus basis—whereas the new men added by the very large firm draw only foremen's or clerk's wages. Consequently the salaries of the additional eight may aggregate no more than those of the first three.

The overhead cost per dollar of sales may not increase in these larger organizational structures, even though expansion brings about a somewhat incommensurate growth in the number of overhead personnel as compared with output. This is a consequence of the largest firms' capacity to spread a few high-cost executive skills over more units by adding a larger number of low-cost specialized personnel to assist them.

The economy of spreading overhead costs over a larger number of units is particularly noticeable in respect to equipment. The big builder uses the least amount of equipment per unit of all firms. The average big builder owns $17,500 worth of equipment. His investment in equipment represents an average of $60 per house he completes. The amount of capital used, equipment-wise, per unit has fallen below that used by the medium-sized and small builders (table 32 and fig. 2).

The large firms have not taken advantage of the opportunity available to them of appreciably adding to their machinery as their scale has increased. They simply add more small and inexpensive power tools rather than shifting to more complicated and costly machinery. The most substantial increase in equipment is found in a few examples of materials-handling machinery acquired by the largest builders, but even these are rare. Other tools and machines used by the large builders are about the same as those employed by the medium-sized firms.

In this, housebuilding differs from many other industries. It is a common industrial pattern to find that as size of firms increases and individual operations become more specialized, new types of equipment are devised which perform these operations more efficiently. Many observers have believed that the failure to develop more costly specialized machinery in housebuilding was due to the inability of small firms to spread its costs over sufficient units. Whatever may have been the truth of this observation in former periods, it is obvious that it does not apply to the large builder of today. Other explanations must be sought. Perhaps housebuilding is simple enough not to require intricate specialized equipment. Building firms doing general contracting have far larger investments in plants and equipment. Apparently the more complex structural problems of large buildings have led to a greater stress on modern methods and machinery in the commercial building field. Perhaps the small investment by housebuilders follows from a desire of the firms to sink as little capital as possible in overhead because of the risks of fluctuations in housebuilding demand. Certainly the existing investment in equipment is so small that the need to obtain a return on it exerts no pressure on firms to maintain production. In contrast to other industries, large housebuilding firms can disregard the problem of fixed costs if they wish to remain idle.

The task of ascertaining the exact cost of the expanded overhead of the large housebuilding firms is again, as it was with the medium-sized firms, a matter of correctly translating accounting costs into true economic costs. The total reported operating margins of these large firms average 18 per cent—the difference between their direct costs and their selling prices. In a necessarily rather arbitrary division, 10 per cent of this is assigned to profits and 8 per cent to overhead. It must be recalled that some additional amounts properly attributable to the operating margins of these firms may actually be shown in affiliates, since assets transferred between affiliates will be carried at nominal prices not necessarily expressing their actual economic value (tables 34 and 49).

FINANCING

If total assets had been used as a measure in categorizing Bay area housebuilding firms by size, large firms would have been defined as those with assets of more than $600,000. This method of classification would have increased by 13 the number of large-sized firms, because the largest of the medium-sized housebuilders and a few general contractors who built fewer than 100 houses a year have assets surpassing $600,000. This classification would also have transferred out of the large group seven firms which actually completed more than 100 units but had assets of less than $600,000 (table 28).

To use this figure as a criterion of bigness would appear preposterous in many industries. Part of this nonconformity to industrial pattern is based on the local scale of housebuilding, and part reflects the relatively small amount of assets required to carry on a large housebuilding business.[8]

Three firms were found to have more than $5,000,000 in assets. These are the Goliaths in an industry whose history is one of Davids. Measured by assets, most of the large firms are in the brackets between $1,000,000 and $5,000,000. The median large firm had $1,080,000 in total assets. Net worth was $419,000 with the remaining $661,000 owed to others. More than half the total assets were current—representing units in construction and inventories of materials. Real estate or land held for development constituted the next largest item in total assets, and, as discussed above, represented one of the greatest problems. The median land holding of large firms was valued at $310,000. These firms also had substantial miscellaneous assets, with a median of $190,000, covering investments in affiliates, utility deposits for improvements which are repaid over several years, notes on previous sales, and similar items. Finally, the item of equipment remains extremely small, as we have seen, at $17,500 (fig. 2).

[8] See Appendix E.

The large firms turn over their capital an average of five times a year—the highest turnover of all the groups. Combined with the highest rate of profit on sales, this gives them the greatest return on net worth—an average of 30 per cent per annum (tables 31 and 35).

These averages tend to conceal almost as much as they reveal, because of the breadth of the gamut run by this group of firms in assets. Because the total assets range from $350,000 to more than $10,000,000, an examination of the firms ranked by asset size yields interesting results which may be more telling than averages (based on survey given in Appendix E).

The most striking fact is the high correlation between large asset size and age. The firms which have been in the business the longest have had the most time to accumulate assets and have done so. The ten richest firms average twenty-six years of age, whereas the ten least wealthy in this category of large firms average only eight years. The average assets of the top ten are almost seven times as large as those of the bottom ten. There is some correspondence between assets and number of completions. The wealthiest firms completed about 30 per cent more houses, on the average, than did those at the other extreme in this group. Their houses tended to be somewhat more expensive—built on costlier land, often within cities, thus requiring more formal structure—and they also developed more communities. This meant that their total dollar volume of sales was more than double that of the group with less assets. A few of the firms with the smallest assets, however, were among the highest in number of completions, thus injecting an inconsistency. In all respects the middle ten fell between the top ten and bottom ten—in assets, age, and number of completions. In comparison of firms within the group by assets and by volume of production, it is observed that assets increase more rapidly than volume. Put another way, the wealthy firms' assets per unit completed are larger. This calls attention to the immense variation in turnover of capital characterizing the firms at the extremes of the large group—a variation which extends to relative risks and profits. The formula for the variation appears to be: the smaller the capital, the greater the turnover, risk, and possible rate of profits.

To enter the category of large firms at all, many firms must accept the affliction of continuous anxiety about capital. These are, of course, the firms which come in at the bottom of the classification in terms of total assets. They must utilize their capital as efficiently as possible, turn it over as fast as they can, and consider its status in all their decisions. This means that they are living on the edge of danger at all times, since if they miscalculate to any great extent or if sales are held up by a slow market, a materials shortage, or a labor delay, their income may not meet their necessary outlays.

The 10 firms in the group with the least assets turned their capital over 8 times during the year; 6 of these firms had a turnover ratio higher than 10 times a year. One of the factors making possible the rapid turnover was a far lower investment in land and real estate by these firms compared with the firms possessing the greatest assets. The bottom 10, in assets, had real estate holdings representing only 6 per cent of their annual volume, compared with 40 per cent for the top 10. This meant that the owners of the firms with the smaller assets had to act as promoters and had to bring in other persons who would share their risks by holding part of the land necessary to their operations.

These firms also had a higher rate of profits on sales. They averaged about 14 per cent profit per sales dollar compared with 5 per cent for the more highly capitalized firms.

This higher rate of profits on sales combined with their much more rapid rate of turnover of capital brought the average rate of profit on net worth for the low-capital firms to nearly 12 times that of high-capital firms in the group—170 per cent compared with 14.

The firms at the lower end of the group of large builders, by assets, have been expanding as rapidly as their capital can bear. The wealthier firms in the group, on the other hand, have slowed down their rate of expansion. They have the riches and resources which would potentially allow them to grow even larger, but they have not used them.

The relatively high profits of the whole group of large builders are explained primarily through the presence of the expanding firms. Instances of a five- or tenfold increase in the net worth of these firms during the first four postwar years are not uncommon, although these dramatic increases have usually been built on a comparatively small base ($25,000–$50,000). Whereas the total profits of the wealthier firms have been as large, the relative rate of profits has not been as spectacular because they have been based upon a much greater net worth. It should be pointed out, however, that these large postwar equities need not, and in fact usually do not, represent large initial investments. They frequently result from large capital gains made in land or shopping center holdings. Their size is a result of reinvestment of profits rather than large initial investments.

When firms have a healthy equity and, as in the case of the most heavily capitalized firms, have reached a point of slower turnover, they find that their construction financing is somewhat simplified. The firms with large equities are sufficiently sound so that banks will grant them credit based on notes against their general assets. These advances can ease the strain of credit for land development and relieve similar operating difficulties which harass the smaller builders. They also cost the large firms much less than regular mortgage credit because of savings in title fees, taxes, and similar expenses. The large firms still, however, use the Federal Housing Administration commitment and construction advances almost exclusively when houses are actually in process of being built.

The largest builders occupied a highly favorable bargaining position in relation to lenders after the war because they could generate a large volume of loans which could be placed on the books inexpensively. Instead of requiring a separate negotiation with the bank, the Federal Housing Administration, and the Veterans Administration over commitments for each house, loans for the large builder could be handled in groups of 25 to 100 units with corresponding savings in time and effort. Any builder who could promise a quantity of mortgages was sought after, since lenders were actively pursuing outlets for funds. Furthermore, it was worth the large builder's time and effort to use his bargaining power to get the best financing deal, in view of his great volume. A difference of $100 a house in financing costs on 250 units amounted to $25,000.

For these reasons, the largest builders spent more time on financing problems than did the others. If they could not get satisfactory terms in the local market, it was worth while for them to travel to other areas, especially New York. Their volume was large enough to enable them to operate as mortgage brokers, if necessary. As happens in most situations of strong bargaining power, such steps were usually not necessary. Satisfactory accommodations were usually available in local banks, and in only a few cases during the period under study did large builders go outside the Bay area for funds for their permanent loans.

The large builder's problem was to obtain the necessary permanent loan at the best possible terms. The fact that the best terms were available only on government-insured or guaranteed loans limited his area of maneuver and reduced his loan campaign to two fronts: (1) to obtain the commitment of an institution to lend on insured or guaranteed loans; (2) to obtain the highest possible appraisal from the government.

In the first place, the commitment was crucial because the relation between the permanent and the construction loan was inseparable. The builder required a commitment for the permanent loan before he could obtain his construction money. The reason for this is the fact that the equity upon which the operative builder works is too small for him to keep much money tied up in houses upon which he has received a deposit while the prospective owner searches for financing. If he had to wait on such terms, there would be little or no large-scale building. Twice during the postwar period the large builder's operations were seriously affected by conditions in the permanent loan markets. The first occasion was in 1948, when the supply of 4 per cent money for Veterans Administration guaranteed loans dried up. The second was in the spring of 1951, when both 4 and 4.25 per cent money became extremely tight. The first money shortage mainly affected the rates for which builders could borrow their construction money and the terms for which they could sell their houses. The second affected their ability to build at all.

In the second place, the highest possible appraisal was important because if a builder planned to avail himself of terms made possible by the Veterans Administration guarantee, his selling price could not exceed their estimate of fair value. The Federal Housing Administration, though not fixing a maximum price, did set a maximum loan, thus affecting the amount of equity required by both the builder and the eventual purchaser. Hence the builder had to make certain that the design of the house was one which would obtain a maximum appraisal. He also had to spend time in negotiations if appraisals fell below his expectations. Failure to obtain a sufficient appraisal seriously limited the builder's ability to sell.

During the times of shortage, builders did more shopping for terms and funds. Since Veterans Administration and Federal Housing Administration terms are the same for each borrower, identical conditions for final financing were offered during most of the period. Occasionally, however, certain institutions were willing to make 4 per cent loans though others insisted on 4½ per cent. Occasionally, some institutions allowed lower down payments than others. There were likely to be differences in the premiums charged or granted the builder. And there were some variations in service, such as the speed with which loans were handled and payments made.

Except during shortages, these differences were not sufficient to cause most builders to shop the market assiduously. The average builder was inclined to continue his customary relationship with his regular bank, unless some very strong incentive for change arose. Only those builders most conversant with financing took advantage of differences in the market. As the size of the builder grew and he became more familiar with how to flex his bargaining power, he began to deal more freely in a wider market.

Even so, the large builder was not always pleased with his changed financial situation, nor sure that it was advantageous. The large-scale operative builder deals in a financial market which is much more sensitive to governmental action than that of his contemporaries of lesser size and other types. His is the money market which has changed most rapidly and received the greatest attention. This is the sphere of financing which has made possible the growth of large builders. But its dependence on government support puts the large builder in an ambivalent situation. His livelihood depends upon government aid, but he fears its potential competition, and also the possibility that it may enforce regulations which will cause him difficulties.

The Market

Where? What? How many?

These questions, and usually in this order, characterize the large firm's approach to marketing.[4]

Since the large firms are all engaged in merchant building, their executives must determine at the outset the location, the type of houses to be built, and the number of units before a project can start. On the success or failure of their answers will depend the end result of all their efforts—the sales.

[4] The description in the remainder of this chapter is based on the case studies and surveys described in Appendix D.

In the majority of cases, builders have concurred in the nature of their answers to these questions. Builders in the category of large-sized firms may be divided into two kinds of businessmen: the leaders, who search for innovations, hazard new techniques, test new materials, try organizational experiments, and, above all, who risk departures in design to improve their product; and the followers, who take the course of least resistance and imitate past performance. The majority of large builders have been followers and are thus largely to blame for the fact that housebuilders as a whole during the postwar period brought on themselves the accusations of fostering atrociously bad design and of building the slums of the future.

Firms acting as followers have had smooth sailing in the postwar market. They ran before a good breeze of spontaneous demand and were able, with the aid of government guarantees, to sell financial terms—the appeal that monthly payments amount to less than rent—rather than having to depend upon any ingenuity of their own to sell their product. With the need for shelter and the attractiveness of the financial situation (in which ownership appeared to cost less than tenancy) fanning the market, the product sold itself. The follower firms had only to observe the type and price range of houses selling rapidly, including their own previous years' production. They had only to find suitable land as close as possible to the earlier units. They had only to put a similar house in a similar area and count on a similar buyer to come and get it. It was that simple. This method of close copying is the classical case of a monopolistic competitor who wants to cut into another's market.

The follower firms paid little or no attention to the development of their product. They did not have to. They merely copied existing designs or stock plans. They spent minimal amounts on site-planning, on architectural variations, or even on such details as color differences. Public appetite for housing was so ravenous that it was not necessary to change the icing—much less the cake—to tempt consumers. Even the few flashy changes for advertising purposes, which are familiar in a competitive situation in most fields, did not take place in their housebuilding.

Since the firms which were only followers did not invent or devise or innovate, the pivots in their operations were primarily purchasing and production. Unless they made some large error in judgment in purchasing land and locating their product, or some great miscalculation in production, they had units which automatically sold in a seller's market. Only a rapid shift in demand could have caused difficulties. The nearest thing to a market shift developed in 1949, when, before the easing of credit, demand slackened. Robbed of their ready-made breeze, some of these firms began to founder in marketing difficulties, but a new burst of demand put them back on their course. A few firms of this follower type did make location errors which retarded their sales. None, however, was serious to the point of submerging a builder, and the lowerings of value resulting from these mistakes were more than offset by rising prices and general boom conditions. In a more competitive situation, of course, either the shifts in demand or the mistakes in locations could have wrecked a housebuilding business.

In contrast to the majority that have just been described as followers, about a third of the large-sized builders did assume leadership in blazing new trails of product development and marketing. A listing of some of their innovations, to give an idea of their approach, includes: (1) developing a new area or town, (2) designing a new low-cost unit, (3) specializing in modern design, (4) using hitherto unused titles of government financing, (5) specializing in housing for minorities, (6) bidding on Wherry Act housing, (7) attempting a very high-cost exclusive development, (8) entering into areas where no large-scale builders were operating.

Each of these innovations involved a certain amount of risk. One of them—the high-cost exclusive development—turned out rather disastrously. Apparently buyers with sufficient income to afford high-cost housing did not, generally, choose to buy it in a tract. Another innovation for housebuilders—entering the FHA 608 field, apartment house building—looked, for a period, as though it might damage the reputation, if not the pocketbooks, of certain firms; but this situation may have been corrected by the defense inflation.

The method used by most innovators contemplating a departure from established pattern in site, size, type, or price was to attempt some sort of market analysis, even on an elementary level, and to begin experimental projects with only limited investment so as to keep risk as low as possible. The attempted market analysis was commonly of the back-of-an-envelope kind, or, more exceptionally, involved the summoning of specialists for consultation. In either case, the object of the market analysis was to estimate the number of families within certain income brackets who might desire to live in a given area or who might be in the market for a particular type of home. If the back of the envelope, or the consultant, convinced the builder he had found a new market, he tested it. When adequate financing existed or could be found by persuading the lenders, including Federal Housing Administration or Veterans Administration, that the idea was sound, the firm could proceed. The next steps would ordinarily consist of buying a minimum of land outright and the rest on options, building a model house or houses, and starting construction on 25 or 50 units more. If these sold well, operations would be expanded as rapidly as possible.

The physical planning of new projects was handled partly by the firm and partly by its consultants, working on a fee basis. The firm often roughed out its own ideas as to the site development and house design. Then it would call in an architect or engineering firm to check its plans and offer criticism and advice. Houses are usually designed to a price. The frame of price might require paring certain features off the original design, or in rare cases adding features. If costs changed, an effort was usually directed toward offsetting increases by altering the design rather than by raising the price.

Architectural assistance was usually paid for on a straight fee basis. There were a few exceptions at either extreme. Some firms had complete architectural and planning staffs, and some took the opposite course and hired outside architects to assume responsibility for the whole job. Whatever the arrangement, the use of architectural service was generally held to a minimum by builders, who held the view that architects are not interested in the mass market, are not sympathetic with what the builder is trying to do, and do not know enough about housebuilding anyway to hold costs down. Here is one area where a popular theory—that of lack of coöperation between builder and architect because of dissimilar aims and language—is borne out in professional practice.

The one-third of the large builders who were progressive in their attitude toward experimentation and product development kept abreast of material and design innovations by reading the trade journals and technical press and by attending association meetings. Successful ideas can and have spread rapidly after having been proved economical and salable. The challenge to the industry is to find the first few who will risk a new idea.

The fact that some innovators have existed, have been willing to try out new ideas, and have spent larger sums on design, has meant a gradual improvement in the product. Most critics believe that Bay area builders have generally been more dynamic and inventive and have done a far better job in improving their product than house-builders as a whole. Unhampered by the architectural strait jacket of "the Cape Cod house," local builders were able to start with a freer prototype for the Bay area house. Their site design, too, has been more creative, forced into new patterns by more difficult land problems. The same critics who admire these features state, however, that the ease of selling the houses has removed incentive for further improvements which would have been both desirable and possible.

This lack of incentive produced by a seller's market was also responsible for the general inattention to marketing problems. Little was done in the field of marketing because little had to be done. Large firms usually handled their own sales directly or through a land-development affiliate. Sales effort consisted almost entirely of the insertion of a small display advertisement in the Sunday newspapers when the model home was completed, and the presence of salesmen or clerks equipped to accept down payments when customers appeared.

This system made for very low selling costs with consequently high efficiency, relatively speaking. It did not increase a firm's ability to sell in other than a seller's market. Neither did it lead to any increased understanding by builders of what buyers want. With the exception of the guesswork engaged in by some of the innovators, virtually no efforts were made in the direction of market analysis.

Production

It is in the production process that some of the most conspicuous differences between the small- and the large-sized builder may be seen. The source of these differences is size: with increased scale, builders can specialize the functions of their labor. The larger size of operations does not merely permit the employment of more efficient methods of production—it forces them. In the sphere of labor utilization, the big builder is forced to adopt mass-production industrial methods to compensate for the lack of highly developed individual skills among his workmen. The large firm does not have access to the skilled craftsmen who are available to the small builder. The small builders and often the medium-sized firms can hold on to their most able and satisfactory mechanics; the large firms, which employ between 100 and 200 workmen, cannot. Although the large firms would like to keep all their men from project to project, such continuity of employment is seldom possible. The best they can do is to retain their key men by slowing up the work at particular times, using their foremen and crew leaders as regular carpenters and maintenance men, assigning them to small jobs, or even giving them paid vacations if necessary.

In keeping their key men, they maintain the best of the know-how and systemization of their labor force, but when they must build up crews for a full-scale project, they have to draw in new men. Men who are immediately available in the labor market are ordinarily those who have not been considered sufficiently valuable to be held in steady jobs. In addition, when a firm is expanding rapidly, it may have to bring into the labor force workers who have had no previous housebuilding experience. The actual skills thus available are not of the highest level, and the individuals are not likely to be versatile. If these men were required to perform all types of carpentry, as do carpenters on the smaller jobs, their efficiency would be extremely low. To keep their labor costs down and still obtain sufficient labor as needed, the large firms must resort to a breakdown of tasks. In effect, they "de-skill" jobs. For example, they have carpenters use only one tool or do a single type of operation instead of the great variety of tasks expected of a trained carpenter. A man can be trained in a short period to do one thing well. This, of course, is familiar industrial practice. It may be recalled that the rate at which pattern- and tool-and-die-makers were turned out during the war astonished everyone. These men did not have the high level of skill previously required in the trade; usually they learned to do just one thing. This is now true of many carpenters doing a satisfactory job on tract work.

This increase in specialization does more than merely make up for lack of previous skill, experience, or versatility. It is actually more efficient. After the first two or three months of training crews and setting work standards on a tract, the labor cost falls to such an extent that the large firms save about 26 per cent compared with the wages expended by a small firm building a similar house (table 50).

How is this increased specialization accomplished and how does it work for greater efficiency?

The first step in accomplishing it is the organization of the work force into small crews, each of which handles only a single task. The factors which influence the decisions as to the number and content of these crews, with maximum efficiency in view, are diverse. They are psychological as well as organizational.

Psychologically, though a man acquires skill and speed by repetition of a task, his output falls if the job becomes too boring and routine.

Organizationally, time losses from waste motion, misused skills, and poor job coördination must be guarded against. In terms of motion, either the mechanic must move from one house to another, or a method must be devised for delivering his completed work, performed at one site, to the various houses. If each job per house is too small, his waste motion will mean serious time loss. In terms of use of skills there must be a proper relationship between supervisors, skilled, and unskilled men, since each receives a different wage rate. It is desirable to use as much unskilled labor and the least supervision possible. This standard suggests using fairly small crews under working foremen who perform supervision as an added duty. An unskilled laborer's time may be shared among the crews, thus keeping the crew's time confined to specialized work. In terms of job coördination, each crew must hold its pace and yet be kept busy at all times; it should not finish a job too soon or too late. Even very small waiting periods cumulate to large wastes. Tasks must be planned in relation to each other, and add up to a complete day's work. Jobs must be organized to allow leeway for normal errors, inspections, and inspection delays without wasting time or capital in needless slack.

These considerations lead to an increase in the number of crews and in the amount of specialization as the size of a project grows. Medium-sized tracts may use from three to five crews having no specialization within each crew, but when a tract is large there must be as many as ten crews with some job specialization within each one. As an example of intracrew specialization, in the finish crew one man may hang doors, one windows, one do the trim, and so on. The number of crews performing each task can be varied. It is possible that some rather rapid jobs, like sawing, can be performed by one crew on all houses, whereas the next task—framing—may be performed by four crews each working on a separate house.

A builder with about the maximum number of crews has one each for sawing or cutting; for foundation forms and mudsills; for subfloors; for layout and raising; for rafters and roofs; for roof sheathing; for exterior trim, door jambs, and casings; one for clean-up and one for finish. The size of the crews varies from two to five men. Each has a working foreman who reports directly to the site superintendent. If several crews are used for the same task at the same time, as in framing, there may be a foreman over each group of crews.

Jobs are planned on a large project so that no two crews work on the same building at the same time. A waiting period ranging from half a day to a day between tasks allows sufficient slack to iron out minor irregularities. This kind of organization requires especially careful scheduling to insure the proper work coördination among the various crews.

In theory, it might seem simple to set up and schedule crews; in practice, this is one of the most difficult jobs in the entire planning process. It is a job which points up the great differences between firms and has an important influence on the entire efficiency of the building industry.

Part of its difficulty arises from industry adjustment to a new situation, with lack of precedent for it. As a firm expands, the shift to crew work and more detailed scheduling requires skills and information different from those employed in the past. When the firm's operations were small, slight attention was paid to losses resulting from a break in the job rhythm or from waste handling and lost motion. Since no exact standards existed, the general basis for supervision was determined by visual inspection of how hard a man was working, rather than how efficiently. The new situation produced by large volume operations demands new standards of supervision.

In acquiring more size, a large firm's specialization of labor functions is only half of the change in its production picture; mechanization is the other half. Like the organization of the work force into specialized crews and the coördination of the crews, mechanization requires careful planning and involves many decisions. The decision as to the type and quantity of machinery to be used on any job depends on such factors as the number of times an operation is performed, the decrease in labor time achieved by the machine, the initial cost of the equipment and its upkeep, and the experience and planning ability of the supervisory staff.

The first mechanization question concerns the foundation. For the individual house constructed by the small builder, the foundation trenches and the trench for the main soil line of the house are almost always dug manually. Machines are not very effective because the tolerances are small; the effects of boulders, roots, mud, and the like are pronounced; the cost of the machine, even if rented, would be large compared with the total trenching cost ($30–$50) on a single house; and moreover, the work is usually done by a common laborer who might otherwise be idle. In a medium-sized operation, the possibilities for mechanization are greater. More units are worked on in a given period, and thus the machine overhead is spread further. It is not so important to find a job for a common laborer because the ratio of unskilled labor to skilled workers is decreased, leaving those on the payroll with less free time. Consequently, a simple machine, usually a pneumatic jackhammer, is used effectively to break and prepare the soil for lifting. Actual lifting of the soil is still done by hand. Finally, in some of the most efficient large tract operations, when the amount of work is sufficient to offset the costs of time lost in transportation of equipment, the trenching may be done by small mechanical trenchers using revolving wheels and buckets which both dig and throw out the soil—a much speedier process than hand trenching.

The next mechanization question on the builder's production schedule concerns the machinery for transportation and materials handling. When houses are built individually or lumber is transported directly from the lumber yard, machinery is limited. For the medium-sized builder with yard and warehousing facilities, transportation may be handled by the high-leg lumber carriers—"Hysters"—which simplify the loading problem by picking up and carrying a load suspended. Skids and trailers may also be used, since they can be loaded or unloaded easily and may be left at the house site until discharged. As the size of a firm's operations increases, materials-handling equipment—fork lift trucks, similar units equipped with a shovel or loader, fixed roller conveyors and tractors—may also be added for use both at the site and in the yard. All yard operations use some of this equipment, and many of the largest and the most efficient of housebuilders' operations use all of it.

The next opportunity for mechanization occurs in the rough carpentry phase of production. Here is found the maximum use of machinery and its maximum variety. All operations, regardless of size, use a certain amount of power equipment. Although many builders, especially the small ones, still depend largely on hand equipment, in certain projects every part of the process except hammering is mechanized. Even hammering is partly mechanized by some large firms which use pneumatic hammers for nailing the subfloor.

In every house, the number of cutting operations bulks so large that it is obviously worth while to mechanize them, especially given the comparatively low overhead and maintenance costs of a single power handsaw. Almost all projects, including the single houses produced by the small builder, provide for the power sawing of studs, subflooring, and sheathing.

Variations begin to occur when scale of operation makes it necessary to decide to what extent power should be employed on cutting lumber for small items such as fire-blocking and bridging, or for such pieces as headers and cripples, as well as for the cutting of special notches and forms. The number of each of these cuts in a house may be so small or an operation may be so limited that special planning for mechanization hardly seems worth while. Most of these jobs on the individual house are performed by hand. Even in the medium-sized tract, such operations as cutting off stakes for forms, cutting occasional boards, and the like are done by hand. In larger units, however, this kind of process is simplified either through design to insure a minimum number of odd-shaped pieces or by cutting similar units for many houses at one time, though each appears only once or twice per house.

The final phase of the builder's direct operations concerns the finish carpentry. In a tract operation, in contrast with scattered houses, doors and windows are ordinarily hung with the aid of power equipment including small power saws, a power router and drill, a power plane, and templates. The complete process of cutting, planing, routing, and drilling is performed by machine.

The use of machinery on trim and baseboards is uncommon. The pieces have to fit exactly and cover any small variations which occur in placing the studs and so on. These pieces, being small and thin, can be cut nearly as fast by hand as with machinery.

Although the builder's use of mechanization on most of his direct operations increases with his increase in scale, with consequently heightened repetition and specialization of tasks, the methods of the subcontractors do not change much in relation to the size of the tract because the subcontractor is already a specialist doing repetitive tasks. There are a few exceptions. For example, the use of machines to tape wallboard is just becoming popular on tract work. Aside from the fact that the mechanism is somewhat cumbersome, there is no apparent reason why it should not be used in individual houses. In a similar manner, an electric sander is sometimes used for sanding down the taped joint.

Another exception is the extent to which machinery is used in plumbing. This also varies with the size of the project. On some individual jobs, pipe is still cut by hand. On others, a portable pipe cutter is attached to and powered by a truck. On tracts, however, it is customary to install heavier pipe-cutting machinery either in a temporary shop in the yard or in the main shop. Certain standard lengths and joints can thus be fabricated repetitively.

Whatever the size of the project, digging for main sewer, water, and gas lines is always done by machine, usually on subcontract to a firm specializing in this work, of which there is a large amount.

Except in unusual cases, excavating and grading are power operations on all projects. For this work, tractors have either a scraper or loader blade, and the excess material is removed with dump trucks. On larger-scale operations there is the advantage of working on several sites at once, with spread of the overhead and setup time over more units, and the possibility of saving on hauling and backhauling when excess material from one unit can be utilized by an adjacent one.

The pouring of concrete and the finishing of flatwork use a great deal of mechanized equipment. Almost all concrete for jobs of all sizes is delivered ready-mixed in the now familiar transit mix truck. The finishing of flatwork requires some hand labor, but this operation, too, is in the process of mechanization. If the amount of tamping is large, it is frequently done with a pneumatic tamper. On the larger tracts finishing is speeded up with a combination of power and hand trowels.

Another type of equipment comparable to machinery is special scaffolding and similar gear designed to save labor effort in larger tracts. Since crews follow each other rapidly, the equipment can remain in place to serve several purposes.

Contrary to popular assumptions, it is apparent that the use of machinery in housebuilding is following a path of dynamic progress and that hand power is far less important than is supposed. Part of the increased popularity of mechanization is due to new inventions and the simplification of equipment to permit its use on individual houses; part arises from the ability to distribute its cost over more units when projects are larger.

PURCHASING

The most important progress toward increased economy resulting from increase in scale of operation has taken place in the field of purchasing. Here the large builders have devised new methods of materials distribution and developed new relationships with subcontractors. These changes have led to impressive cost reductions. The big builder needs and gets far less service. In addition, he can absorb items of lower quality than can be furnished to the builder of individual houses. Simplification in the distribution and trade contracting system, as well as economies, have contributed to heightened efficiency (table 23).

The new distribution system is primarily based upon direct purchase and direct delivery from the mill. Orders are placed at the mill itself, or are placed through a broker or a wholesaler, with shipments straight from the mill to the builder. One-quarter of the large firms have established building-supply affiliates in whose names goods are purchased. About a quarter of the firms—with some overlap between the two groups—go beyond this and actually own or control the mills from which they draw their supplies. These innovations eliminate one or more of the traditional distribution channels.

At the same time, a standardization has taken place. Special brokers who handle only items for tract houses have come into being. Their tract-house items are frequently standard goods which have been redesigned to give minimum quality at a minimum cost. The broker or wholesaler specializing in materials for tract work builds up a large volume in a few selected commodities and thereby lowers his margins. The conventional or traditional wholesalers state that they cannot compete with these specialty jobbers because the type of service rendered and the kind of goods offered by the specialists are too dissimilar from the service and goods used by the traditional trade.

For example, large builders have found that they can strike a better bargain by purchasing steel kitchens in carload lots rather than buying the traditional plywood cabinets, which must then be painted and covered with tile or similar materials. The carload price on such items as standardized steel kitchens may run 20 per cent or more below normal wholesale prices. The savings effected by purchase in carload lots combined with elimination of additional treatment such as tiling and painting represent an important economy, much more than offsetting the cost difference between metal and wood.

To obtain the substantial savings on materials by buying in carload lots (or for a few specialty items, in standard packages) often involves buying for as many as 40 or 50 houses at once. This presents the builder with the problem of storage and warehousing, but storage is done on the tract and the complications created are few. The increased expense incurred by storage is insignificant compared with the possible savings inherent in quantity purchases. Compared with the small builder, the average large builder saves $410 on materials purchased for a typical house, and the largest builder may save an additional $130, or a total of almost a quarter of the small builder's materials cost (table 51 and Appendix H).

The progress in relationship between the large builder and his subcontractors follows the lines already begun by the medium-sized builder. New developments stress a growth in subcontractors' specialization and controls parallel to the growth in the builders' own production processes. In addition, the large builder-subcontractor relationship is likely to be closer, sometimes exclusive.

To a great extent, the reduction in charges of the subcontractor to the big builder—equivalent to increase in efficiency—stems from the same four factors in larger-scale operation which are responsible for the subcontractor's reduction in charges to the medium-sized builder. These are (1) more efficient use of labor; (2) savings on materials purchases; (3) better controls; (4) lowering of overhead and profit. Since these factors are progressively more important as sources of savings when scale of operation grows, they result in even lower prices to the large builder than to the medium-sized firm.

A fifth factor enters the situation for the large builder. This is better management arising from increased size. The large builder who, himself, has reached the level where better management is possible, is likely to have trade contractors who also operate more efficiently, either because the builder is dealing with a large trade contractor who needs and can afford better management, or because the builder aids in his subcontractor's operations in order to protect himself.

Contrary to a popularly held belief that the big builder takes over a greater and greater share of the production process as his scale of operations expands, there has been only a slight tendency for large builders to assume directly, through crews of their own hiring, production jobs which are traditionally handled by subcontractors. Half the large housebuilding firms in the Bay area did not handle directly any processes which are typically subcontracted during the period studied. Most of the remaining half had their own crews perform only one or two of the 12 to 15 possibilities ordinarily subbed out. None of these firms made it a matter of policy to attempt to integrate as many processes as possible (table 22).

What are the factors which determine whether or not integration is worth a builder's efforts? In theory, integration appears attractive. Most large firms indicate that they have tried integrating various processes at one time or another, and on occasion have even been forced to do so by the dearth of good subcontractors. But they have usually returned to the minimum list of functions directly performed and subcontracted out the rest. This is significant in showing that the existing situation is not due to inertia but is a policy pursued after testing of other possibilities.

Even counting the cases of integration of a few functions, it was found that the total number of subcontracts entered into by the typical large firm is often actually above average. As scale increases, some tendency exists toward further specialization and breaking off of additional functions. For example, the forming of foundations, hanging of cabinets, installation of window sashes and garage doors, landscaping, window cleaning, and clean-up are likely to be done on subcontract for large firms, whereas they are almost always handled by the builder's own crew in small units. Such proliferation of subcontracts increases the total for large firms, even when some of the subcontracts on the initial list are eliminated through integration of the processes by the builder's own crews.

An exception to this tendency toward breaking off of additional functions and proliferation of subcontracts occurs among some of the larger firms which practice a form of quasi-integration. Certain big builders prefer to deal with subcontractors who expend most of their effort on the builder's tract alone, and retain only sufficient reserve business to hold together their crews during slack periods on the big job. These builders feel that such arrangements enable them to insure better coördination and at the same time to make a better bargain. To promote this type of relationship, the builder may aid a mechanic to establish himself as a trade contractor, or he may help small trade contractors to expand their size, furnishing, if necessary, financial or managerial assistance. Frequently there are no direct formal agreements, financial or otherwise, but prices charged by the trade contractor will be low. Sometime trade contractors established in this manner branch out until eventually they may have no commitments with the builder who gave them their original chance at expansion.

In many of the trades, a single contract to handle a large builder's annual business will put the subcontractor into the large or medium class. This fact has stimulated many subcontractors to spend more time on perfecting production techniques for fulfilling large contracts. Several trade contractors specialize in tract work and are able to insure a large volume of business for themselves by obtaining the contracts for several tracts.

When the large builder prefers to work with a smaller contractor willing to concentrate exclusively on his own tract, it pays the builder to furnish planning assistance. The advantage here is that while he is planning his own production, he can, at the same time, plan that of his dependent trade contractors. Since any failure of the subcontractor to keep up to schedule is a threat to the builder's own progress, the builder can investigate difficulties directly and help solve problems.

As a result of the savings which have been discussed, the trade contractors working in tracts tend to be the most efficient. It is also true that variations in efficiency exist among the trade contractors on tracts just as they do among large builders themselves. The best methods, though available, are not used by all of them. Some trade contractors are more efficient than the builders for whom they work, and vice versa.

Controls

It is in the control of the building process that the largest firms differ most from the small- and medium-sized firms and also from the less large firms within the category of large-sized builders.[5] About 25 per

[5] This section is based on the case studies and surveys desdribed in Appendix D.

cent of the big builders use a fairly complex and detailed system of production controls which, they believe, aids them in increasing efficiency and lowering costs. Another 25 per cent of the large-sized firms employ a quasi-control method, but it actually has little influence over their construction processes. The remaining half of the large builders resemble most of the medium-sized and small firms by using only the most rudimentary system or dispensing with any system at all.

What functions can a control system perform? The six major ones are: (1) keeping track of the value of the firm and of its profits or losses through accounting; (2) keeping track of all physical property by an inventory subsidiary to the general bookkeeping; (3) budgeting to enable the firm to estimate money requirements; (4) programming work so that purchases are made at the proper time, and labor and trade contractors arrive at the site when required; (5) determining the true costs of all the components, sections, and separate features of the house through cost accounting; (6) scheduling work to insure performance of tasks in the proper manner, order, and with the best techniques and equipment, and thus increase the efficiency of labor.

The first four functions of control are found, in simple form, in all large firms. But most firms make little or no effort to integrate these fragmentary functions into a whole control system, coördinating every aspect of the building process. Most builders believe they have a control system when they set up a general estimate and time schedule. Actually, they do not have a complete and workable control system at all. Lacking any real control of production, they lack knowledge of how to improve their efficiency.

The activities which make up any system of production control are routing, scheduling, dispatching, and reporting. Routing is a planning step which consists of mapping the course of the product through the production process—deciding what operations will be performed, how they will be performed, and in what order. Scheduling is also a planning step and provides the timetable of operations—it is the selecting of the times for performance. Dispatching is the issuing of orders, authorizations, and instructions to production centers at the times specified in the scheduling. Reporting is the reciprocal function of transmitting production information from the production centers to those who route, schedule, and dispatch.

These activities may be carried out in a simple, informal manner without the aid of specialists or detailed record-keeping systems. The complications introduced into most industrial production-control systems arise from the necessity of closely controlling varied and complex production processes which require a large volume of information to be handled rapidly and accurately. This necessity is not present in housebuilding. When the production process is simple, as in housebuilding, the volume and frequency of the clerical tasks of control can be correspondingly simple.

The advantages of production control to management are obvious. A serviceable system can facilitate intelligent establishment of operating requirements and proper utilization of productive facilities, can simplify order giving, and can quickly make known any deviation from established output standards. Still more importantly, it can promote efficiency by compelling more intensive consideration of the technical organization of production. Procedures which have been matters of custom or which have been left unspecified, and hence have been improvised in the process of direct supervision, are likely to be scrutinized more carefully in terms of their necessity, the time required for their performance, their method, and their relation to other parts of the process. This is particularly true when the system includes accurate cost data.

Production scheduling and setting of output standards usually require a detailed study of jobs and groups of jobs to eliminate superfluous tasks, reduce idle time, secure the advantages of repetitive processes, and gain the best balance among operations. Production control for the housebuilder necessitates an examination of methods and consequent decisions as to the best technological processes. Such analysis of procedures and processes benefits management by weeding out waste.

Large firms, as well as the medium-sized and small firms, which do not give much attention to the planning and control process must operate in a dappled light or in the dark. Without a production control system, they cannot be certain that the plans which they devise will work. A large part of their planning is guessing. At the end of a project, they can check their results back with their guesses, but it is too late then to correct any mistakes made on that project. They have to chalk up what they have learned to experience and hope that they may apply it better to the next project. To paraphrase the old barnstorming pilots, these firms build by the seat of their pants.

The top quarter of the large-sized firms, which have adopted highly organized production control systems, find that their systems keep them in the light as to what they are doing throughout the entire course of their operations. Their systemization enables them to plan wisely at the outset as to methods, costs, coördination of crews, scheduling of subcontracts, placing of orders for materials, and receipt of supplies. It permits them to know at every stage of the production process how much work has been accomplished, how much money has been spent, how much money has been received, what materials have been delivered, and what supplies are due. It makes possible a daily check of performance against plan. It gives the firm an opportunity to correct deviations from schedule as they occur. It assures the firm of results corresponding to expectations.

A comparison of the three-quarters of large firms which use only fragmentary control methods with those firms which employ a full-scale production control system shows that these advantages are principally generated by more accurate and more complete estimating and scheduling, based on better cost accounting records.

In the average large firm ordinary accounting records are hardly usable in operations and production. Although the accounting records of a firm grow in volume as the firm's production grows in volume, these records may be even less applicable for management decisions than are the accounting records in smaller firms. The volume of business and the complexity of the corporate structure require more bookkeeping for large firms, but the accounts contain merely historical costs for large groups of houses because they are maintained on a tract basis rather than on a house or group-of-houses basis. They are not detailed enough to be very valuable for management's future planning.

It requires an outright decision to change and great effort for the firm to develop its accounts to a point where they are helpful for cost analysis purposes. The firm must delve deeper than the payroll and similar financial records and develop special data. It is not sufficient to know what costs have been in general. Exact costs must be obtained for each specific operation, for each segment of the finished house.

A usable system of cost analysis in production control starts with accurate estimates for each part of production. This requires breaking down the construction process into a series of fundamental steps which correspond generally to the distinct operations found in standard estimating manuals—trenching, installation of joists, hanging of windows, and the like.

The total carpenter hours and total laborer hours required for each step are estimated initially on past experience, for which complete cost records have been kept. When a new design is produced, extra care is taken with supervision and timekeeping during the early weeks to record the amount of labor actually utilized for each task. The number of men in each crew and the amount of work they are expected to complete are revised, as work proceeds, in accordance with the recorded results. Estimates and revisions are not creatures of formal time-and-motion studies but are the products of actual performance under strict supervision and "pushing" by the foremen. The estimate is tied directly into a scheduling and reporting system. From the completed estimate a weekly time schedule or operations-planning sheet is prepared together with a cost budget. The schedule separates the process of construction into logically sequential or self-contained steps, in the same fashion as was done for estimating purposes. The schedule is translated into a Gantt-type bar chart of man-days and materials quantities or some similar chart on which progress can be recorded.

In typical cases, progress is posted to the chart either daily or weekly. The posting to the production control chart is usually done from timecards, prepared by the foreman on the site, and from materials invoices, or it may be handled by special assistants who do only production control work. Timecards and invoices carry code numbers equivalent to the operations listed on the time schedule. This coding system is used both in accounting for labor and materials and for cost-control purposes. The schedule readily provides the needed job-progress information.

The posted chart enables the work supervisors to check anticipated against actual performance. If the men are kept off the job for some reason such as weather, this shows up in both anticipated and actual production and cost columns. If costs are running higher than budgeted, the line in the chart showing actual costs outruns anticipated costs. If work is slower than scheduled, a line shows actual production running short of planned production. These lines notify the firm that it must take action to restore efficiency in terms of lowering costs or improving the rate of production or both. If performance is shown by the chart to be surpassing work standards which have been set, supervisory action may be taken to determine whether this is merely the result of some exceptionally felicitous circumstances, or whether work standards should be reëxamined as to their correctness.

In addition to job-progress information, the schedule indicates materials-purchase and delivery dates, and dates at which the various subcontractors should begin and finish their jobs. The estimate sheet, previously discussed, becomes the basis for the materials-purchase program, and orders are placed to cover an entire project with delivery as needed.

Any discrepancy between planned progress and achieved progress in any aspect of the operation becomes apparent on such charts and calls for expediting action by the site superintendent, office force, or top executive. Tighter control is possible with more frequent posting and with perhaps a finer breakdown of operations, but even the most progressive firms consider systems such as that just described to be adequate and the expense of a more detailed job-progress reporting system to be unnecessary.

In contrast with such a system, the estimates in the majority of firms are rough, although developed with the design. Their previous data are not accurate enough for fine cost analysis. Although materials and subcontract prices may be made definite before starting, direct labor costs and overhead charges are estimated on assumptions from past experience. Estimates are in terms of probable costs per house and for the project as a whole. Schedules are not precise but are of the one-house-a-day type. The combination of these inexact estimates and schedules gives a projected budget which magnifies all the inaccuracies in its sources.

These firms are handicapped by their lack of knowledge throughout their operations, from design and planning to price. Their dearth of information ultimately lowers their return on investment and weakens their capital position.

Almost every firm must pay special attention to its working capital position. A firm is in constant danger of becoming illiquid if there is any pile-up of inventory, whether this consists of unused materials, unsold houses, or work in progress. Money has a very high marginal value in the housebuilding industry, since the average firm ordinarily has large areas of possible investment which it is not exploiting, such as speculative land, materials, apartments, and so on. Yet these firms are not able to budget properly or to make the most efficient use of their capital when emergencies arise. They may have to maintain an oversupply of materials, for example, to guard against materials shortages; they may have to engage in an overdrastic retarding action, when delays occur; they can never be certain their budgets will work.

Implementing the budget is a firm's time schedule. This, too, suffers—and, in turn, makes trouble—when a builder's knowledge of his own operation is inadequate. The schedule must include planning, financing, and preparation of land as well as the actual construction of the house. The ideal time schedule is organized to speed up the turnover of money and at the same time to allow slack for unforeseeable delays. High costs can result from delays for which no slack has been provided in the schedule—delays associated with slow materials deliveries, subcontracting problems, labor difficulties, and the like. The most highly organized time schedule strikes a flexible medium between tautness for turnover and slack for emergencies. This may require overtime in certain critical areas or a retarding action in others.

When the firm's schedules are not precise they cannot accomplish their purposes effectively. For example, purchase orders may be incorrectly geared to production if not closely regulated by schedules. When firms buy from retailers, purchases may be made only a day or two before use. When materials come direct from mills, the length of time between order and delivery increases. Variations in this length of time occur especially when the mill is on some sort of allocation basis. The perfected schedule helps not only with appropriate timing for placement of orders but also with follow-up dates on slow orders. The rough schedule may not allow for unusual lag in deliveries; thus the firm may have to stockpile unnecessarily in advance to provide for possible excessive lags, or it may be forced to buy materials more expensively on an emergency basis when something is needed in a hurry to keep production going.

Firms with a relatively casual schedule attempt to have their subcontractors at the right place at the right time and to be ready for them when they arrive, but they are not in the best position to inform their subcontractors well in advance of the definite dates when the subs are expected, or of the rate of progress expected of them. A firm can do this only if it knows, itself, the exact progress on the project at each point. Since delays are costly to subcontractors as well as to builders, and since subcontractors, too, must plan labor and purchases, a subcontractor is likely to make a better price and do a better job for a builder on whose schedule he can depend.

All these factors lead to more efficient production in those firms with the best cost analysis and control systems. The amount of attention given to the planning and control of the building process seems to increase with the progressiveness of the management and the size of the enterprise. Association of lower costs with more detailed planning and tighter control gives evidence of not being accidental. Although statistics to support this view are not completely available, our impressions and management opinion agree that if the large-sized firms were segregated according to those with low and those with high production costs, more of the firms relying on planned controls would be found in the low-cost division.

Determination of Size of Firm

The year 1950 is a revealing period in which to study the determinants of size of housebuilding firms. In 1950, although concentration of production among the large firms increased, expansion was primarily among firms which became large for the first time. On the average, the firms which were already large in 1949 did not increase their share of production; many of these remained constant in size, though the total output of the area was expanding. Even those among the already large firms whose production increased still stayed within the same general size range. The maximum size remained below three starts a day, or 700 completions for the year. In the Bay area, no firms reached the 3,000 to 4,000 units-per-year mark which a few firms in other areas have done.

It may seem strange that these large firms in the Bay area did not further increase their size in a boom market. To understand why housebuilding does not follow the familiar trend of industry toward greater and greater concentration into fewer and fewer hands, it is necessary to think in terms of the trend of costs of firms in this industry.

Apparently, no great change in costs is probable with further increase in size within the ranges of possibility immediately available to local firms. These firms have reached a point where with additional volume they simply duplicate production methods and where added advantages in spreading of overhead, purchasing, financing, and so on are slight. Firms would make about the same amount of profit per unit on each additional house sold.

At the same time, further expansion is troublesome. It increases their local competition. It requires more executive time. It is more risky for their capital situation. Because of taxes, it does not offer greatly increased personal income (table 21).

A factor in deterring large firms from becoming yet larger seems to be that the executive and managerial functions in this industry are still very personal. The average firm has from one to four principals, with an average of two. These principals own the existing organization completely. They make all the primary decisions and many of the detailed ones. If the firm is to expand much beyond present size, it must increase its top-level executive staff. In view of the personal nature of management in this industry, this can be done, ordinarily, only by taking in additional principals. Adding principals means dilution of control and of returns. The increase in returns, by the addition of one person, would probably not be sufficient to offset splitting them more ways.

It seems to be the concensus of the men who have built their hundred houses or more a year that unless some personal force is driving toward increased size, expansion is unnecessary. If expansion is stopped, then the capital position improves and the risk of a total loss diminishes. There may be, in addition, advantages in investing available capital in other related activities, such as property ownership, which may show a larger net return after taxes. For these reasons, the large firm tends to expand into related fields rather than further increasing the size of its own building operations. All these factors at work account for the failure of the existing large firms to grow much greater in volume even while the industry was expanding rapidly, and account, therefore, for the high number of large firms in the industry (table 21).

Summary

The postwar market, based on the need for housing and the money to get it, produced the big builder. He was the answer to the mass market's demand for mass production. There were 30 housebuilding firms in the Bay area which were able to build a hundred houses or more a year to satisfy the hunger for housing. They represented only 2 per cent of the Bay area builders, but they built 6,195 houses in 1949 or 35 per cent of the industry's output. With average assets of more than $1,000,000, each produced a total dollar volume of business that year ranging from $1,000,000 to $5,000,000 and sold Bay area homeseekers their cheapest house—at an average price of $9,250.

It may not have been much of a house, measured by some standards, since it was located on newly developed tract land and was meager in quality and detail; some critics thought it had atrocious design. But the builders did not have to worry about design and quality; it was a seller's market and the buyer took what he got. The product sold itself and the firms concentrated on aspects of business other than design, market analysis, or merchandising.

They concentrated, for example, on operating structure, increasing their business entities to three, to help solve problems of risk, taxes, supplies, and labor. They developed additional functions such as warehousing and production control which increased their total overhead costs but made more han equivalent savings in direct costs. They spent more time on money matters, since, on the average, they owed $660,000 to others, and had to guard their capital position. By turning over their capital an average of five times a year and obtaining the highest rate of profit on sales, they received an average 30 per cent return on net worth. The firms with the lowest net worth turned over their capital fastest, made the greatest profits, and did the most expanding.

In financing, all large firms were preoccupied with the necessity of obtaining permanent loans before they could obtain construction advances, and with negotiations for highest possible Veterans Administration and Federal Housing Administration appraisals. Because they generated a great number of mortgages, the largest firms were in a favorable bargaining position in 1949, in a narrow money market sensitive to government action.

In production, they specialized the functions of their labor force, increased their use of mechanization, took advantage of more precutting and preassembling, more laborsaving devices such as patterns and templates. These innovations increased their efficiency, saving 26 per cent in labor costs compared with those of the small builder.

In purchasing, they saved 18 per cent on supplies compared with the small builder, by inaugurating a new distribution system based on direct buying of materials; and saved 21 per cent in subcontracting costs by developing new and more efficient subcontractual relationships. A few firms adopted production control systems which appeared to aid in increasing efficiency and lowering costs.

Through taking advantage of the economies inherent in their greater scale of operations, the large firms averaged 10 per cent profit on sales. The largest firms seemed satisfied with that. Observing that yet further expansion in housebuilding only increased effort, strain, and risk without appreciably increasing net return after taxes, the largest firms showed a tendency to stabilize their capital in housebuilding and to expand in related fields.

6

Supply of Factors

Only part of the building process is determined by the housebuilder's own organization. A significant part of it is shaped by his factors of supply—factors such as materials, labor, subcontractors, financing, and land. The housebuilder's freedom of choice is limited by the availability of production factors he can purchase and the prices he must pay for them. Although he can select any particular mixture of available factors he desires, the final product he offers the public is as much influenced by the supply schedules offered to him as by his own decisions and organization.

Most discussions of housebuilding stress the importance of this role played by the factor suppliers in the structure and efficiency of the housebuilding industry itself. Many previous studies have argued that efficiency in housebuilding cannot be improved until a solution is found of the problem of control by suppliers over building processes.[1]

This study has already described housebuilders' uses of the particular factors of supply and housebuilders' relations with suppliers. To evaluate the specific influence of factor supply on housebuilding efficiency, we also need to have at least a partial picture of the supplying industries themselves. The description of their organization which follows is confined to data required for the subsequent efficiency evaluations.

Materials and Their Distribution

The fact that 40 per cent of the selling price of the small builder's typical Bay area house is expended for materials purchased by the builder and his subcontractors dramatizes the predominance of the

[1] For a basic statement of this thesis, cf. the conclusions of Colean, *American Housing*, pp. 314–315; cf. also Grebler, *Production of New Housing*, p. 53.

materials factor in the supply picture. The efficiency and organization of the materials-supply industries have an important bearing on the efficiency and organization of the housebuilding industry (table 51).[2]

Studies of the building materials industries have tended to be very critical, but they have often been superficial, lacking detailed and accurate data. One source of this hostility was the price situation, in which many building materials prices seemed to be administered and rather inflexible. Furthermore, charges of monopoly and restraint of trade have been brought against building materials firms, with decisions in many cases won by the government. These suits have been directed against control of patents, basing point systems, joint selling agencies, and illegal use of trade associations.[3]

No attempt can be made here to discuss all these charges in detail, since each would require information as extensive in scope as this entire study. It should be observed, however, that present opinion recognizes the complexity of the problems involved and is not willing to condemn the industries on the extraneous bases previously used.

This discussion is restricted to three areas in which sufficient data are known. The first is the type of industries producing building materials and particularly the type of market control existing within them. The second is the number and variety of the local channels of distribution for building materials. The third is the recent price history of building materials. Rather than covering all the hundreds of possible products which might be used in a building, this description concerns the 23 major industries, as defined in the Standard Industrial Classification of Manufacturing Industries, which furnish the principal items entering into Bay area houses.

In examining a conglomeration of factors such as building materials, it is vital that some attempt be made to relate them quantitatively. The importance of each on the total must be considered; monopoly in marble, for example, would affect housing prices only slightly if at all, whereas one in lumber would have immediate and large-scale repercussions.

One approach to the problem of these industries is through a consideration of their markets. Recent discussion indicates that market

[2] See Appendix I.

[3] Cf. Thurman W. Arnold, U. S. Attorney General, "Restraints of Trade in the Building Industry," address at New York Building Congress, N.Y.C., June 21, 1939 (mimeographed by Department of Justice).

control and characteristics are strategic in explaining differences in competitive and price behavior.[4] This appears to hold true in the building materials industries. Those which have similar market characteristics follow like paths in competition and price patterns. All building materials are, of course, producers' goods, and the amount of product differentiation is slight. Several carry brand names, but they disappear into the final unit and are not known to the ultimate purchaser.

By means of data recently made available on the ratio of concentration of output in industries, it is possible to classify building materials producers in accordance with their degree of market control.[5] It appears from this classification that housebuilding materials are produced in far less concentrated industries than most industrial goods, and consequently firms producing them have less than an average degree of market control (tables 53–55).

Lumber, millwork, building paper, cast-iron pipe, paint, lighting fixtures, bricks, and furnaces and hot water heaters—items making up 60 per cent of the cost of the building materials going into a Bay area house—all come from industries in which the eight largest firms controlled only minor proportions (less than 36 per cent in 1947) of total production. These industries produced more than half the value of output of the 23 industries making housebuilding materials.

In each of these industries with a low concentration of output, competition has been relatively intense. Prices have varied and have tended to fluctuate rapidly. Attempts to diminish competition have been made primarily through trade associations. Except in shortage periods, they have not been very successful. In most of these industries, large builders can and frequently do enter into the fabricating end themselves. As a result, they can combat restrictions directly. Whether for this or other reasons, builders report that effective competition exists in most of these industries.

It may be argued that including all these industries in the nonconcentrated group is ambiguous because some of them are industries for which the national concentration is low but which have high re-

[4] Joe S. Bain, "Price and Production Policies," in (Ellis, H., ed.) *A Survey of Contemporary Economics* (Philadelphia: Blakeston, 1948).

[5] Subcommittee on Study of Monopoly Power, House Committee on the Judiciary, *Study of Monopoly Power* (81:1), Serial No. 14, Part 2-B, p. 1436.

gional concentration, whereas others may have great concentration in the particular sphere of our interest (Appendix I).[6]

Industries for which the national concentration ratio is low, but which produce primarily on a local or regional basis include cement, lighting fixtures, and bricks. The latter is particularly typical of this group. Whereas the country's 8 largest brick firms control only 17 per cent of national output, the 6 brick manufacturers in the Bay area—and there are only 6—control 100 per cent of local production. Because of high transportation costs, competition from distant producers is negligible. Industries in which a variety of products is manufactured at different levels and in which the concentration ratio may consequently not be significant include steel water pipe, sheet metal, electrical wiring, and warm-air furnaces and hot-water heaters (tables 53 and 54).

Removal of these seven regionally concentrated and mixed-product industries from the previous totals causes no important change in the general picture. Altogether they make up only 14 per cent of the materials going into the typical house and 29 per cent of the value of all building materials manufactured. Even excluding these industries producing 14 per cent of a house's materials because they are local or special cases, 74 per cent of the materials going into the house still have a concentration ratio of less than 70 (51 per cent less than 30) and only 12 per cent have a ratio of more than 70 (table 54).

The industries in which concentration is high and entry appears to be difficult include gypsum with a concentration ratio (8 firms) of 94 per cent; plumbing fixtures, 82 per cent; window shades, 83 per cent; linoleum, 94 per cent; window glass, 98 per cent; and ceramic tile, 70 per cent. As mentioned above, these make up less than 12 per cent of the materials cost of the house. Close behind these is roofing material, whose concentration ratio is 65 per cent. Its market behavior is similar to the more concentrated group. Most of these high concentration industries would be considered oligopolistic, and observed market results appear to follow the pattern found in other goods with concentrated control—relatively stable prices, use of basing points, strong distributor tie-ups, and the like (table 53).

[6] For a discussion of these problems, cf. Joe S. Bain, "Relation of Profit Rate to Industry Concentration: American Manufacturing 1936–1940," *Quarterly Journal of Economics*, Vol. LXV, no. 3 (August, 1951), 293–324.

Finally, there are the items whose concentrations fall in between the high and low concentration groups. These are primarily steel products and also electrical supplies and building hardware. They follow a mixed market pattern. Mill prices on these items are usually regulated, making it difficult for builders to obtain discounts at that level. On the other hand, their distribution—through jobbers, wholesalers, or direct from the mill—is far more flexible, so there is variation in delivered prices, and the bargaining power of the individual builder helps to determine his delivered price.

Differences in the market control of building materials are frequently reflected in the second area under discussion—distribution channels. Most important in this area are the materials dealers who furnish goods to the small builders and trade contractors. These are called either retailers or wholesalers, depending on their particular line. But irrespective of the name, they generally perform the same functions. They receive car lots from the manufacturer, store them, and deliver the desired quantity to the contractor at the site of construction. They may or may not also sell over the counter to individuals.

Another group which sometimes appears in the chain of distribution comprises the brokers or wholesalers who sell to materials dealers and occasionally to the large builders. In certain cases they own warehouses and carry stocks. For example, in specialty millwork and hardware, where the materials dealer does not use enough of certain items to make carload purchases, a wholesaler handles the assembling and stocking of the items. In other instances, the wholesaler is a mere broker or salesman, taking the place of direct factory agents. He does not accept title, furnish warehousing, or perform any similar functions. His pay must be competitive with the cost to the factory of performing this function through its own staff. Margins paid to the broker for the performance of these services normally run from 3 to 5 per cent, rising to 8 or 10 per cent on items which the wholesaler carries in stock.

In the San Francisco area in 1948 there were at least 625 wholesale dealers in building materials. About two-thirds of them were merchant wholesalers with warehouses or yards, and the rest of them were divided quite evenly between manufacturers' sales branches which also carried stocks, and brokers or agents who did not.[7]

[7] 1948 Census of Business, *Wholesale Trade,* Bulletin No. 1-W-4, table 102.

The business of these wholesale dealers was not, of course, confined to selling to housebuilders. In several lines, such as electrical supplies and hardware, sales for installation in new houses made up only a minor part of the dealer's total business. In other cases, however, many wholesalers in particular lines did most of their business with builders or trade contractors.

In addition to buying through wholesalers, many builders bought from retail lumber, hardware, and building materials dealers, of whom there were more than 800 in the area. At the other extreme, some of the largest builders bought directly from mills.

The number of possible sources of supply for most items had an important bearing on the actual channels used by builders and on the prices they paid. The more sources a builder has available to him, the less likely it is that uneconomic methods of supply will continue to exist. Where numerous alternative sources of supply exist, it usually requires illegal collusion to maintain inefficient systems, and where the number of firms involved is large, it is difficult for illegal practices to be carried on successfully. The large total number of sources, however, is not in itself a guarantee of alternative sources for each material. The number of wholesalers of a product is related directly to the number of producers of that item. Products stemming from highly concentrated industries were likely to be distributed through a minimum number of trading units, whereas items originating among a large number of producers were likely to be channeled through a similar proliferation of distributors.

The final important area of the materials industries under discussion is their type of price movements. Figure 7 shows the movement of all wholesale prices, of wholesale prices excluding farm and food products, of all housebuilding materials prices, and of lumber prices.

Costs of building materials have depended upon the type of industry from which they were drawn. Relative price changes for these supplies have been determined by the kind of material going into the product, the importance of raw materials compared with plant and labor costs, and the competitiveness of the particular industry. These elements have also affected the particular building material industry's ability to expand. The less competitive industries generally have been those using materials which require more work to be done in plants and furnish more highly fabricated products. Because of fixed plant costs, they have expanded more slowly, and their prices have been more stable, but there have been occasional shortages and resultant black or gray markets for these goods. The more competitive industries have been those furnishing goods in a form closer to the raw material. These have expanded more rapidly, and their price fluctuations, moving in

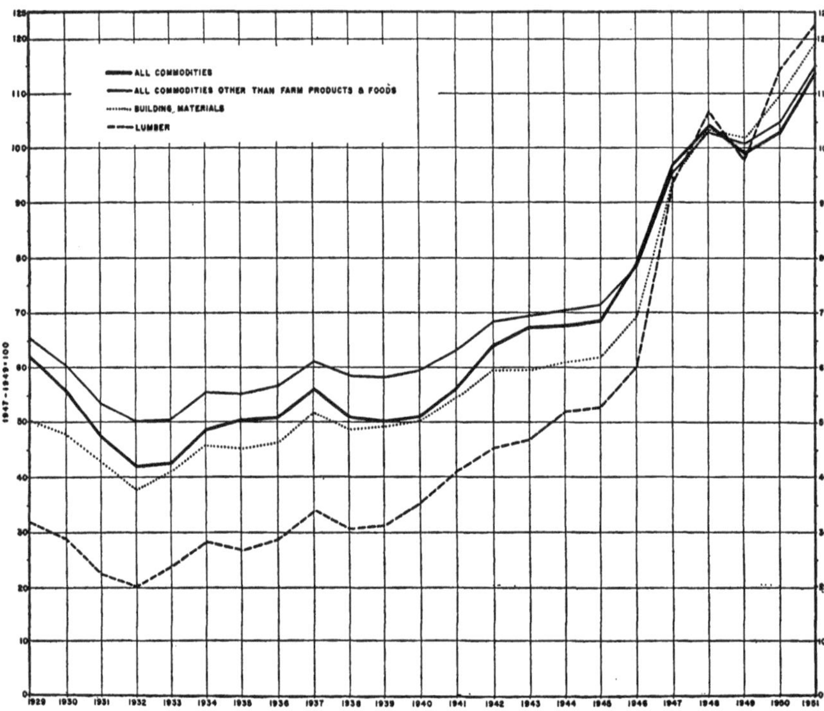

Fig. 7. Wholesale price movements—all commodities, lumber, and other building materials. Source: Bureau of Labor Statistics.

accordance with those of other raw materials, have been wider. Also, there has been a somewhat more elastic supply.

Most vivid is the manner in which lumber prices have differed from other wholesale prices (fig. 7). Lumber prices have moved in a far more volatile manner than other prices, and since 1940 they have become relatively much higher. Lumber has had large demand fluctuations, and it is produced in a very competitive industry, falling between farming and mining in its mode of production. Some lumber comes from large commercial operations in which the basic cost is labor and stumpage. Some comes from individual farm wood lots.

The impact of large demand changes on lumber is similar to that on many farm products with resultant wide price fluctuations. At the same time, a greater rise in price has occurred because of a rapid increase in rates paid labor, together with a decrease in accessible stands of trees. As a result, lumber prices have fluctuated sharply but around a steadily increasing level.[8] Lumber prices rose by 250 per cent in the decade of the 1940's—the largest increase for any major commodity.

Other building materials are produced in industries whose price movements differ but little from the average of the economy. The price fluctuations for these other materials have not varied much from those of other commodities except in the two periods when building demand rose more rapidly than general demand. From 1932 to 1937, other building materials rose more slowly in price than the total wholesale price index but somewhat faster than nonagricultural products. From 1937 to 1947, these materials again rose more gradually than the total index, but at the same rate as nonagricultural products. Then from 1947 through 1951, as a result of the concentrated increase in construction demand, the prices of building materials, excluding lumber, rose at a more rapid rate than did those of other commodities.

Price movements of these other housebuilding materials fall between those of lumber and those of all other materials. Since lumber represents nearly 40 per cent of the total cost of housing materials, it is plain that building materials as a whole have risen far more rapidly than wholesale prices in general.[9]

The Trade Contractors

Next in importance to building materials as a supply factor in housebuilding is subcontracting, which accounts for almost half the builder's direct costs. Thirty-six per cent of the final sale price of the typical house is paid to the subcontractors.[10] It is, therefore, important

[8] For a complete description of the industry and a discussion of these points, cf. "The Lumber Industry of the Pacific Coast," *Monthly Review of the Federal Reserve Bank of San Francisco,* Supplement, December, 1950.

[9] The reactions of prices of building materials to change in demand are similar to what would be expected on a theoretical basis. Prices react to many variables, but particularly to changes in factor price and demand. For an exposition of this whole topic and the unreliability of attempts to equate price movements and concentration or competition, cf. Alfred C. Neal, *Industrial Concentration and Price Inflexibility* (Washington: American Council on Public Affairs, 1942).

[10] See Appendix G.

to understand the working and organization of this major element in the housebuilding process.

Many writers have denounced the subcontracting system as a hindrance to the development of efficient construction methods. They charge that the builder, by involving himself in difficult problems of coördination, loses direct control of essential parts of the building process and plunges himself into an unstable situation. In the discussion of the operations of the various sizes of builders, however, it was brought out that the relations between builders and subcontractors are normally quite stable. Together, the builder and his subcontractors form an organizational unit, albeit an informal one. No serious difficulties arise in this organization except in periods of shortages. Although coördination of subcontractors' work does at times become troublesome, the system is thought to be more efficient by even the largest builders than the alternative policy of integration, under which the builder would attempt to handle the specialized jobs himself. Integration remains very rare at all size levels.

Assuming, therefore, that subcontracting is more efficient than integration, there are two aspects of the actual workings of the system to be considered here: (1) the structure of the trade-contracting industries and the relative bargaining strength of the builder vis-à-vis his trade contractors; and (2) the manner in which the trade contractors perform their tasks.

If previous information on housebuilders was slight, that on trade contractors, both in this area and elsewhere, was almost nonexistent. No one has known how many trade contractors there are, which types are the most numerous, what the size of their businesses is, how they divide their work between housebuilding and other activities, or how they operate. In order that information might be obtained on these fundamental points, a special survey of trade contractors in the San Francisco Bay area was conducted. The methods used and the tables showing the exact results may be found in Appendix G. (As indicated because of cost limitations, the survey covered only 5 of the trades which work on houses. These trades, however, contained a majority of all licensees and accounted for about 72 per cent of the cost of subcontracts for the typical house. The appendix describes the manner in which the data for these trades have been applied to the totals.)

About 75 per cent of all firms holding a trade-contracting license indicated that they were actively working in the trade as a separate proprietorship, partnership, or corporation. The remainder of license holders did not use their licenses; they were retired, working for others, or working in other trades. Statements here about the number and attributes of trade-contracting firms are based on the percentage reporting active use of licenses. The picture which develops is one of firms very similar to housebuilders themselves, with related problems of size and methods (table 42).

By far the largest category of trade contractors is painters. It accounts for 36 per cent of the outstanding licenses and nearly as high a percentage of active firms. Next most numerous are plumbers, with about 11 per cent of the licensees, and electricians with the same percentage. Following this in terms of licensees come the plasterers and roofers, with about 6 per cent, and the ceramic tilesetters with about 4 per cent of the total. The masonry, wood flooring, sheet metal, and cement and concrete firms each have between 3 and 4 per cent, and the excavating, landscaping, and warm-air heating specialists claim between 2 and 3 per cent. Finally come the cabinetmakers, glazers, lathers, sewer installers, and soft tile and linoleum workers, each with less than 2 per cent of the total.

What do these trade-contracting firms consist of? How large are they, both absolutely and relative to each other and to housebuilders? The various types of trade contractors have been divided into four groups according to the total annual volume of business reported: (1) smallest firms doing less than $10,000 in volume (these are primarily one-man firms doing repair and maintenance); (2) small firms whose volume was between $10,000 and $50,000; (3) medium-sized firms with business running between $50,000 and $200,000; and (4) large firms which top that amount (table 43).

Important variations exist among trades. Most conspicuous is the average size of the painters, half of whom are in the smallest category as compared with about 20 per cent for the other trades. Floorlaying has nearly as high a percentage of small firms as painting, though a far lower one in the very small group. The cement and concrete contractors and the plumbers have the largest percentage of very large firms. These distributions are directly reflected in each group's median volume, which ranges from $10,000 for painting and $24,000 for floorlaying, to cement and concrete at $37,000, masonry at $38,000, and plumbing at $41,000.

Dollar volume as a measure of size has the disadvantage of being affected greatly by the magnitude of purchases made by the firm. This is a business component which varies according to the type of work done. For example, the painters' materials cost relatively only half as much as those of the other trade contractors; consequently their size appears small on the basis of dollar volume, but less small when based on a measure more nearly reflecting actual work, such as labor. For this same reason, trade contractors appear small in comparison with builders when measured by dollar volume. Since the builder's sale price includes payments for subcontracts and land, his dollar volume per employee is relatively high. Only 38 per cent of builders have a volume less than $50,000 as compared with 71 per cent for trade contractors; 45 per cent of builders have a medium dollar volume compared with 19 per cent for the subcontractors; and 17 per cent of the builders are in the large category as compared with 10 per cent of the subcontractors. The number in the largest group with a volume of more than half a million does not differ greatly. The median volume for all builders is about $72,000, or more than twice as high as the median volume for trade contractors (tables 11 and 43).

If the number of employees is used as a measure of size, the relationships among trade contractors appear slightly altered. Such a distribution brings out, too, the prevalence of firms with no employees, in which the owner does all the work himself. Firms with fewer than 5 employees may be considered as small. By this measure, the disparity between the painters and the other trades diminishes. On the other hand, the masonry contractors have an even greater concentration in the larger-sized groups. Based on employment, the size distribution of builders and trade contractors is roughly similar. Omitting painters, the majority of whom are engaged in repair and maintenance work, and considering only firms active in housebuilding, it is found that trade contractors usually have more employees and are somewhat larger on the average than the builders (tables 12 and 44).

The number of small trade contractors is not surprising, but it is economically significant, when coupled with the large number in each trade-contracting group. It indicates the possibility (and also probability) of competition with fairly equal bargaining power. The large number of small trade contractors also indicates the possibility of large builders being able to bargain with fairly small subs. This is a major factor in making nonintegration cheaper than integration.

The generally high correlation in size of firms by both dollar and employment measures, as well as the somewhat lower volume of business per employee in painting, is illustrated again when painting contractors and cement and concrete firms are cross-classified by dollar volume and number of workers at the site. In cement and concrete, firms with a volume of business less than $10,000 all consist of self-employed workers acting as trade contractors with no other employees. In the painting business, though most of the smallest firms are also simply self-employed mechanics, in about a third of the cases small employers do have an assistant working with them. This same tendency of painting firms with a given volume of business to have more employees than contractors in other trades is noticed throughout the field.

In the subcontracting picture, the relationship of trade contractors to the housebuilding industry is of primary concern to this study. All firms surveyed were requested to report the division of their volume between work on new houses, on new buildings of other types, and on remodeling, repair, and maintenance. What is the relative size of the trade contractors specializing in work on new housing? It was found that this varies from trade to trade (tables 46 and 47).

About a third of the active trade contractors in the area do little or no work on new houses, about 26 per cent concentrate 70 per cent of their work primarily in the new housing field, whereas the remainder have their work spread evenly over both fields with the importance of housebuilding in their total volume varying from 10 to 70 per cent. Conversely, about 36 per cent of the firms concentrate primarily on repair and maintenance, about one-fourth do no repair and maintenance work, and the remainder spread their work over both.

Translating these percentages into the number of active trade contractors in the area shows that about 1,100 trade contractors concentrate most of their effort in housebuilding, about 1,300 do mainly repair and maintenance, and the remaining 1,200 split their effort between the two types of work. This means, then, that there are about as many trade contractors active in housebuilding as there are housebuilders. Each trade contractor works on many more houses than each builder, but puts in correspondingly less work per house.

The importance to housebuilding of various-sized firms in any category of trade contracting depends upon the relative volume of work on new housing compared with remodeling, repair, and maintenance jobs and with nonresidential building performed by the trade as a whole. In addition, the type of organization and skill required to do large commercial, institutional, or industrial jobs will affect the size of firms.

In almost all trades the smallest (primarily one-man) firms are concentrated in remodeling, repairs, and maintenance. The only exception is masonry and, to a certain extent, floorlaying, where the amount of repair work is not great and where, therefore, even the smallest firms do a large amount on new buildings.

In masonry, a sharp dichotomy occurs between the small and medium firms and the large ones. The small and medium firms concentrate almost entirely in new housing, whereas the large ones specialize in big nonresidential projects. The building of fireplaces is the primary masonry job in new houses, and in this the small and medium firms appear to be most efficient. Bigger jobs require the capital and organization of the large firms.

Floorlaying firms form another pattern. Here, firms of every size work primarily in new housing. Even the largest are concentrated in housebuilding, presumably because of the relative unimportance of hardwood floors in nonresidential buildings.

Painting and plumbing firms resemble each other in organization. In each, total volume is characterized by a large amount of maintenance and repairs. For each, the organization required for handling large industrial and commercial buildings is rather great. As a result, firms active in new housebuilding fall primarily into the small- and medium-size classifications. Even among these, however, the actual number of firms specializing in housing is still only 15 to 25 per cent.

Almost no large painting firms specialize in housing; they depend upon maintenance work or specialize in large new commercial building. Painting in the new nonresidential work seems to be concentrated in the larger firms. Large plumbing firms are divided into three nearly equal groups—one specializing in new housing, one in other new buildings, and one doing all types of work including a good deal of repair on existing buildings. Again, the problem of bidding and successfully completing work on large structures apparently requires a special type of knowledge and organization so that only large plumbing firms enter this field.

Cement and concrete contractors are about average in size distribution compared with the other trades. The smallest firms do little work on new buildings. About 31 per cent of the small and medium firms concentrate on houses, and almost all in these size groups do a fair percentage of work in new housing. The large firms are spread evenly through the three types of work.

In summary, it is apparent that most trade contractors working on new houses come from the small- and medium-sized firms in each specialty. About 40 per cent of the firms in these groups do specialize in housing work. On the other hand, the smallest firms in every category work primarily on maintenance, repair, and remodeling jobs. Among the largest firms, most flooring outfits specialize in work on housebuilding. Large cement and concrete, painting, and plumbing firms do some work on houses, whereas very few masonry firms do any.

Although the absolute number of large and medium trade contractors at work on new housing may be relatively small, as with housebuilders, their percentage of the total volume may still be high. In flooring and plumbing, the large firms account for more than half the total work on new housing, partly because the volume of work per house in these trades is high, and partly because the methods and type of organization used on tract work differ markedly from those used in scattered houses. Specialists in tract work have arisen particularly in plumbing. If a firm obtains the contracts on several tracts, its volume becomes large. Since the average house built in the Bay area is in a tract, it is easy to see how such firms can account for more than half the total house-plumbing volume.

In cement and concrete and in painting work, the largest firms account for only 20 to 30 per cent of total work in new houses. In both these trades as well as in masonry, the medium-sized firms do the bulk of the housebuilding jobs. The small firms are primarily important in masonry (40 per cent of dollar volume). In the remaining trades, though the small firms comprise more than 50 per cent of the firms working in houses, their percentage of dollar volume is less than 10.

Trade-contracting firms, like housebuildings firms, have a very small number of overhead workers. Firms were asked to state the number of employees or members of the firm working in a supervisory, sales, or other off-site position and doing no direct labor at the site; or, alternatively, to indicate whether the firm had no off-site employees and the owner did all off-site work in his spare time. The latter proved to be the more prevalent situation; in almost three-fourths of the firms, off-site work was performed by the owner in his spare time (table 45).

The one important exception to this general proportion occurs in the plumbing trade. The plumbers' union has a rule that a union employer may not work with the tools for more than four hours on a job, and then only on maintenance and repair work. This regulation accounts for the much smaller percentage of plumbing contractors reporting overhead work done in spare time. In fact, the question may well be asked: How does one account for the large number of plumbing contractors who report that they spend full time on the site? One-tenth of the number is simply accounted for—they are self-employed plumbers with no employees. The remaining firms average a single employee, and are probably nonunion shops working chiefly on repair and maintenance jobs. Because of a shortage of journeymen during the period surveyed, the union was not strictly enforcing the regulation against an employer's working.

One-third of all firms reporting no overhead personnel were self-employed owners with no additional employees. The percentage without employees was lowest among the masons where, except for very simple jobs, a hod carrier increases efficiency. In addition to the 70 per cent of firms having no overhead workers, 12 per cent reported that the owner spent full time on overhead functions but had no additional aid. The remaining 18 per cent had employees doing overhead work, but their number remained small. Only 6 per cent of all trade contractors had five or more people in their overhead structure.

Trade-contracting firms do their work over a much wider area than builders. With the exception of plumbers, a majority of all trade contractors worked in at least two or three counties. (It will be recalled that only 10 per cent of housebuilding firms worked in more than one county.) Furthermore, the large trade contractors frequently may take work anywhere in the state and occasionally outside it (table 48).

The spread in area occurs partly because of the need to work on many more jobs than do builders, since each job is smaller. At the same time, it is made easier by the relative lack of heavy equipment that has to be moved. This ability to move around increases the competition in these trades. It may also bring in some problems of labor jurisdiction and may require numerous nuisance outlays in the form of licenses and permits in every area in which work is done.

In their methods of estimating, bidding, controlling, and scheduling their work, trade contractors divide sharply into two groups, depending upon the manner in which their work is performed in the house. The first group includes the trades whose tasks are simple, specialized, and done in a uniform manner even though performed on all sorts of houses. The problems of laying floors and linoleum, of shingling or roofing, of plastering, and of finishing cement do not vary. In this group, estimating, bidding, controlling, and scheduling are based almost entirely on a unit-in-place method. All controls are built up from knowledge of a standard basic unit. Thus the floorlayer, roofer, or plasterer knows from past experience the labor cost for installing a square foot of floor, a square yard of plaster, or a square of shingles, and the prevailing materials costs. His estimating job is fairly easy. The second group of trade contractors includes the trades whose tasks are somewhat different in every house, though variations may not be great. These are trades such as plumbing, electrical work, excavating and grading. Their estimating job is more difficult.

Over and above these differences, both these groups take greater care in estimating when they are planning work on a tract for a medium-sized or large builder than when they are planning work for a small builder. It is, naturally, more worth their while to take the extra pains in planning for the larger number of units. This additional effort often pays off in time, labor, and materials savings. The estimates in both groups serve as the chief guide in production control and scheduling.

For the first group of trade contractors, whose work is figured in standard units, the repetition of jobs throughout a tract facilitates controls. The trade contractor can estimate the exact amount of materials that will go not only into each house but into the entire group, and the exact amount of labor time to put them there; he can use his best workers in the first several houses to develop a labor pattern for the tract; he can instruct his less skilled, or new men, to follow this pattern; he can schedule all his men so that they have a specific amount of work to do per day; and he can control their work by seeing that the amount of time they claim does not exceed his estimate.

For the second group of trades, whose tasks vary somewhat for each differently designed house, the factor of repetition in tract work is even more important to scheduling and control. For instance, in plumbing there is a definite change in technique as scale increases. Since every job differs on scattered houses, work is done on a custom basis. Measurements are taken, pipes are cut to length, and joints made in the house. In a tract operation, the plumber sets up a site fabricating shop. All steps for the entire unit are carefully planned. Within the shop, heavy pipe-cutting machinery is used to cut almost all pipes to their proper length. At the same time, a certain number of the main joints are prepared. The material is then distributed to each house ready for final installation. This change in technique can save 20 per cent or more in labor. As with carpentry, precutting and preassembling enable the plumber to use less skilled mechanics on the more repetitive tasks. At the same time, it increases the efficiency of scheduling and control.

Emerging from an examination of trade contractors is the close resemblance that they bear to builders in most aspects of their operation. In both cases, the smaller firms exhibit the problems of lack of management skill engendered by low overhead. In both cases, the larger firms display the advantages of dynamic growth and of improvement in methods. In the case of trade contractors, however, the level of increase in efficiency with increased size of firm probably remains below the average for large builders. Trade contractors, on the whole, have not adopted new methods with increased scale as rapidly as builders, perhaps because of their still low overhead. They use approximately the same amount of machinery on all jobs and often hesitate to adopt new machines and methods of materials handling.

It should be stated, in fairness, that variation in methods is great, and that the knowledge required to test the efficiency of any specific potential change is frequently lacking. In some instances it may be that, being specialists, they are already using highly specialized methods and equipment. In addition, there are important recent examples of increased use of machinery with scale, such as heavy pipe-cutting equipment on large plumbing jobs, taping machines, and machine trowels.

Whatever the efficiency of the trade contractor may be, it is only rarely that the builder can exercise any influence toward improving it. Most builders do not have the time or supervisory personnel to analyze the trade contractors' problems. Only a few large builders would be in a position to do this, and for them it probably would not be necessary, since the trade contractors on large-scale projects doubtless have grown sufficiently to perform this task themselves. Most builders must accept what the subcontractors offer and content themselves with the knowledge that it is probably better than they could do themselves.

LABOR

Twenty-eight per cent of the cost of the typical house is paid to on-site labor.[11] This amount varies somewhat, depending on the degree of custom work, the degree of finish of materials when they are purchased, and the efficiency of the firm's management. A description of the factor of labor in housebuilding's supply picture must include discussion of four questions: the amount of labor available; the type of workers; the wage rates charged; and finally, the manner in which the workers are organized. These elements comprise the relationships with which the builder must deal in planning his organization and production processes. If the supply, quality, or price of a particular kind of labor is unsatisfatcory, the builder may attempt to substitute other factors by changing the production process, altering the location at which labor is applied, or varying the type of skills required. His ability to make such changes depends upon the institutional structure of labor's organization.

The first condition to be considered is the size of the labor force and the changes that have occurred in it. This condition affects the number of houses that can be built as well as the efficiency wages that will have to be paid. A problem common to most other factors of supply arises again in studying the housebuilding labor force—the difficulty of defining the group concerned and of separating labor employed in the housebuilding industry from construction labor in general. It has been observed that trade contractors move freely among housebuilding jobs, other construction, and maintenance or repair work; it follows that the labor they employ performs its tasks on the same diversified projects. Workers who do not remain with one firm but migrate from job to job find themselves engaged on all kinds of construction which can use their particular skill. Organization of labor in the construction industry takes account of this overlap between types of work. Unions recruit workers employed on all kinds

[11] See Appendix J, and tables 57–59.

of construction work, and labor contracts are entered into between unions and employers representing all types of construction firms.

For estimating the number of workers employed in housebuilding, the basic source is the preliminary report of the last Census, which enumerated 68,000 people engaged in the construction industry in the San Francisco Bay area in April, 1950. Approximately 10,000 of this number are estimated to have been employers and own-account or force-account workers. The remaining 58,000 were engaged by private firms in the construction and housebuilding industry. Of this number approximately 40,000 worked on new houses, though they may also have done other kinds of construction work. These workers were approximately divided evenly between those employed by housebuilders and those employed by special trade contractors (table 57).

The number of construction workers reported by the Census for California was 316,000 whereas the national total was 3,480,000. These figures include all types of workers besides those engaged specifically on housebuilding.

Data on which to classify construction employees nationally are difficult to obtain. The Bureau of Labor Statistics reports, based on Social Security bench marks, indicate that more than 80 per cent of workers in the construction industry are employed by building contractors or special trade contractors. Of this number, about 42 per cent (35 per cent of the total) are employed by builders and the remaining 58 per cent work for trade contractors. They construct all types of buildings and do maintenance and repair work as well. Work on new housing actually takes slightly more than half their effort.[12]

The employment figures for the San Francisco Bay area reflect both the increased importance of construction in the postwar period and the general expansion of California's and the nation's labor force. In 1950, construction employment both in the Bay area and in California was up more than 105 per cent compared with 1940, whereas the total United States construction force rose 70 per cent in the same period. At the same time, total employment in California rose 58 per cent, compared with 25 per cent for the country as a whole. In both the Bay area and the State of California, construction employment in 1950 made up about 8 per cent of the total employment—a much

[12] Construction employment is reported in the *Monthly Labor Review*, June, 1951, table A-2. Relation of labor to value of work is reported in *Construction* of January, 1951.

greater percentage than construction workers manifested nationally (6.2 per cent) or in the Bay area and state in 1940 (6 per cent) (table 57).

The rapid growth in the labor force has played an important part in the total housebuilding field. Although construction is usually considered to be a skilled trade requiring long practice, the need for labor can be met fairly well when demand rises. During most of the postwar period, the labor supply was tight but, except for a few special crafts, the tightness was no worse for building trades than for skilled labor in general. In addition to drawing from other fields, housebuilding gains additional flexibility by being able to hire workers rapidly from other types of building. These shifts within the building field can be particularly important in local areas.

As might be expected, the rapid increase in the number of workers affected the second labor condition under discussion. Both the composition and quality of the whole shifted greatly. The influx of new workers caused a general lowering of labor quality and efficiency, marked by a decrease in the level of skill. Men had to be, and were, trained rapidly, but there was not time to develop them into the versatile craftsmen found among the old-timers in the trades.

The labor force of the construction industry differs in two important respects from that of other industries. First, because of the heavy nature of the work, construction labor is composed almost exclusively of men, whereas in many industries, such as manufacturing, nearly a quarter of the employees are women. Second, the average skill—and consequently the average age—of construction workers is higher. In California in 1947, even with the tremendous influx of laborers which had already occurred, the average age of male construction workers was 38.2 years. Those employed by builders were somewhat older than those employed by special trade contractors—38.8 as compared with 37.4 years. The average age for all male workers in the state was 37.1, whereas in manufacturing employment it was 36.7 years.[13] Thus it may be seen that the average employee of a building contractor is two years older than his counterpart in other industries, although the work he does is likely to be more exposed and more difficult than elsewhere. Another statistic pointing up this age differential is that 25 per cent

[13] Department of Employment, State of California, Research & Statistics Section, *Bulletin 31*, table 29, "Workers with Earnings Sufficient to Qualify for Benefits in Insured Employment in 1947."

of building employees are more than 50 years of age, compared with 20 per cent of those employed in manufacturing.

The third condition of the labor supply—cost—affects housebuilding directly. Changes in payments for labor vary with efficiency as well as with wage rates. The efficiency with which employees work is difficult to measure, and the only knowledge available on labor cost is of the actual changes in wage rates on the basis of hourly or weekly earnings.

The earnings of construction workers are somewhat higher than are those of employees in other industries. For instance, employees of builders in the United States earned an average of $68.56 per week worked in 1950 and those of specialized trade contractors earned $77.77 per week, compared with an average of $59.33 for all employees in manufacturing industries. This means that builders' employees earned 16 per cent more per work week than manufacturing labor, and special trade mechanics earned 31 per cent more. To achieve these earnings, building workers put in, on the average, fewer hours per week than other employees. In 1950 employees of building contractors worked 35.8 hours and those of special trade contractors 36.7 hours a week, compared with 40.5 for manufacturing workers. These lower average hours reflect not only a shorter work week, but also weather and scheduling problems and more time between jobs (table 58).

Since the work week is shorter and the average weekly earnings greater in construction, it is plain that the hourly pay rates are higher than in other industries. Builders' employees make an hourly rate 31 per cent higher than manufacturers'. The increase in hourly earnings of building employees since 1940 has been slightly less than that of manufacturing employees—109 per cent as against 122—but the increase in the postwar period from 1946 to 1950 has been nearly equal at 36 per cent.

All the foregoing figures and comparisons should, of course, be considered with care and discrimination and in their context. Although they are indications of the cost of labor to housebuilders, they are not an indication of greater annual earnings over a long period of time or of undue prices for building labor. The statistics report the earnings of those actually employed in selected weeks. If building workers had had more weeks of unemployment than those in other industries during the period studied, as they probably did during the prewar period, their total incomes would be relatively less. But since the war, unemployment has not been a characteristic of the construction industry, particularly for the special trade employees, who have both higher earnings when working and a higher likelihood of uninterrupted employment. With regard to actual rates for building labor, the differential must cover the costs of the sex and skill differences between construction and manufacturing workers. In other industries whose labor force is primarily made up of skilled male workers, a similar differential is noted; for example in copper and bituminous coal mining, brewing, printing, industrial chemicals, petroleum products, and various metal and machining industries that have the same type of sex and skill requirements as the building industry, workers' earnings are equivalent to those of building workers.

The statistics just presented are based on national payrolls and earnings. California building workers received somewhat higher wages, as did California workers in general. Specifically, builders' employees in California earned $73.05 per week in 1950, or $4.49 (6.5 per cent) more than the national average. Employees of special trade contractors in California earned $85.51, or $7.74 (10 per cent) per week more than the national figures.

It has already been pointed out that this higher average earning figure may be reduced to some extent through time lost between jobs. It is known that the turnover rate for building employees is somewhat higher than that for other workers, but the rate is not as high as is frequently supposed. In 1947—the only year for which figures are available—the average worker employed by builders worked for 1.63 employers in each quarter. As would be expected, trade contractors' mechanics had a lower turnover rate, averaging 1.48 employers per quarter. Although this rate may look very high to the inexperienced eye, it is not much higher than that for other groups. The rate for all employees in industries covered by unemployment insurance was 1.32 per quarter, whereas in other service industries it was 1.45—close to the rate for building. It should also be noticed that it is the rate per quarter that is important; the rate cannot be multiplied by four to get an annual rate because, for instance, a man working for the same employer throughout the year would appear as one in each quarter, and it is only on the quarterly rate that figures are available.

In addition to the number, characteristics, and earnings of building labor, it is important to know something of the unions into which these employees are organized, since unions constitute a most important determinant of labor supply conditions.

The housebuilding industry in the Bay area is almost completely unionized. There are no known open-shop projects. On only a few jobs, and even then in only some crafts, are nonunion men employed. These exceptions to the general unionization are found in the small nonunion shops doing primarily maintenance and repair work. Unions in many crafts exclude small one-man firms which do not ordinarily work on new housing, as a matter of policy, but these small, nonunion shops do occasionally accept subcontracts on individual new houses. Consequently, such houses are built under partial nonunion conditions, but their number is so small and their importance so slight that no one pays much attention to them. Typically, the nonunion sub comes on the site when no others are there, does his work, and departs before others arrive.

In the Bay area, the union men in the industry are divided into twelve international groups with about 85 locals. The internationals are as follows:

- Bricklayers, Masons and Plasters' International Union of America
- United Brotherhood of Carpenters and Joiners of America
- International Brotherhood of Electrical Workers
- International Union of Operating Engineers
- International Hod Carriers, Building and Common Laborers' Union of America
- Wood, Wire and Metal Lathers International Union
- Brotherhood of Painters, Decorators and Paper Hangers of America
- Operative Plasterers and Cement Masons' International Association
- United Association of Journeymen and Apprentices of the Plumbing and Pipefitting Industry of the United States and Canada
- United Slate, Tile and Composition Roofers, Damp and Waterproof Workers Association
- Sheet Metal Workers International Association
- International Brotherhood of Teamsters, Chauffeurs, Warehousemen and Helpers

Each of these unions has its own complex set of rules and procedures differing in varying degrees from the regulations of each of the others. They are all, of course, extremely important to housebuilders since they determine to a large extent the supply and cost of his labor.

The building unions have a reputation for ruthlessness, for striking over minor issues, and for becoming involved in an excessive number of jurisdictional disputes. The record of the postwar period, however, does not bear this out.

In the first five postwar years there were 1,126 strikes in all California industries. Of these, a total of 145, or nearly 13 per cent, were in construction. The number of man-days lost through strikes was 14,982,000 for all industries, of which 920,000, or 6.1 per cent, were in construction (table 59). These percentages should be considered in relation to the fact that about 8 per cent of all workers were engaged in construction and that the total employment figure includes those engaged in trade and agriculture, where strikes are very unusual. It is possible that, since this was a period of prosperity and labor shortage, building employers may have been more willing to agree to labor's demands whether they believed them reasonable or not. If so, this might account for the fact that construction strikes became an increasing part of the total, as prosperity and labor shortage diminished over a period of time.

The strike picture for the Bay area is similar, or possibly slightly more favorable. There were 12 strikes in the construction industry in this area in 1949 and 1950, costing a total time loss of 20,203 man-days, or about an hour of strike time per construction employee per year.[14] Of the 12 strikes in the Bay area, 11 were for wages or so-called fringe benefits, primarily travel pay and welfare funds. Only one major strike was jurisdictional. This occurred on a project where a fight developed between the carpenters and the roofers as to which group should lay composition shingles. Building on a large tract was halted off and on for short periods over a period of six months. A decision was finally handed down in favor of the roofers by the National Joint Board for Settlement of Jurisdictional Disputes.

FINANCING

The structure of the financing system for housebuilding is somewhat simpler than the organization of the industry's other factors of supply,

[14] Based on information in the files of the California State Division of Labor Statistics.

and a good deal more information about it is available.[15] The basic problem in financing houses is dual: to find sources of money for loans during the course of construction and to carry the owners of the new dwellings. Both construction and final loans are essential because usually neither builders nor ultimate buyers have sufficient funds to pay cash for such expensive items as houses.

In considering, first, the problems of construction loans, one finds that a narrow market for these funds is a striking characteristic of the Bay area. There were only about a dozen sources of money supply for tract-construction loans in the Bay area during the postwar period. These included six banks, one savings and loan company, two insurance companies, and three mortgage companies. The six banks actually accounted for about 90 per cent of the loans, and the two largest banks furnished more than half the total.

This allocation of sources in the Bay area construction loan market differs so sharply from the pattern in the rest of the country that it is worth examining. In most areas of the country, the construction-loan market is about evenly divided among banks, savings and loan companies, and insurance companies or mortgage companies. In the Bay area, where the market share differs so drastically, the savings and loan companies are much smaller and are chiefly interested in conventional loans at higher interest rates, particularly on older houses. Only one of these companies has actively entered the tract market. The Bay area mortgage companies and insurance companies have not, apparently, attempted to compete actively with the banks for construction loans, but instead have operated with or through them.

What accounts for the large share of the banks in this construction loan business? A chronology of the local market may help give the answer.

At the beginning of the postwar period, the banks were eager to obtain permanent government-guaranteed or insured loans. To attract the builders who generated many mortgages, and thus to obtain the permanent loans, the banks were willing to make construction loans without premiums and at low interest rates. The Bank of America, largest bank in the world as well as in the Bay area, was particularly active during this period. Other banks followed suit. After about two years of vigorously increasing mortgage accounts, the Bank of America

[15] See Appendix F, and tables 40 and 41.

apparently decided that its mortgage loans were sufficient for its portfolio. The other banks still desired loans, but no longer at the rapid rate at which they were being offered.

At this time, Eastern insurance companies still had large amounts of uncommitted funds and were willing to pay a premium on permanent government-guaranteed and insured loans. Local banks, which were doing business with the local builders, apparently decided to go on using their own funds for construction loans but to obtain the permanent financing from Eastern institutions. They continued to make construction and permanent loans, but they sold or assigned the permanent loans from their portfolios in the Eastern market at a rate which kept their loan portfolios constant.

When premiums for selling permanent loans began to disappear from the market, the local bankers were still willing to make construction loans, provided a firm commitment was obtained from some other source to take the permanent loan. In some instances, the builders obtained these promises of funds directly from the final source; in others, the banks continued to act and obtained the commitments for them.

During this period, the banks began to demand fees on construction loans. These fees plus possible servicing fees on the final loan apparently made such transactions profitable, even when premiums on the final loans had disappeared.

During most of 1949, nevertheless, Bay area builders were hampered by the unwillingness of local lenders to make 4 per cent Veterans Administration loans. For this reason, none of the tract houses built carried the more favorable terms that would have been available if the entire loan had been guaranteed by the Veterans Administration. The best terms were obtained by a combination of the Federal Housing Administration loan with a Veterans Administration secondary loan. This allowed almost as low a down-payment as an original Veterans Administration loan, but required nearly a 20 per cent increase in interest payments (table 40).

In contrast with the Bay area situation, in Los Angeles and in most other large metropolitan areas 20 per cent or more of houses in the second half of 1949 were sold on Veterans Administration guaranteed loans. This seems to indicate that in other areas there was somewhat more competition. Mortgage companies and savings and loan associations were willing to make Veterans Administration loans because they had advance commitments from the government to buy them through the Federal National Mortgage Association. In the Bay area, on the other hand, virtually no loans were sold to the Federal National Mortgage Association. Bay area lenders found that it was not necessary to use this source because as long as they could restrict the market to the higher interest rate loans, all loans offered could be absorbed in the private secondary market.

During the first half of the period, the builder had to pay only for title insurance, appraisal and recording fees, and interest on the money actually advanced. The total cost to the builder was an annual rate of about 7.5 per cent. In 1949, fees or premiums to the lenders became common. Since the money was borrowed for only three months, the effective interest rate was actually 13 per cent per year. In extreme cases, this rate went to 25 per cent per year, amounting to 4.5 per cent of the selling price of the house. Under normal circumstances, all construction-financing costs average between 2 and 3 per cent of the sales price. These figures indicate that though the cost of construction borrowing is high compared with borrowing in many other industries, only in extreme cases does it become a significant factor in the selling price.

Turning from construction loans to permanent loans, one finds that the market for permanent loans is somewhat wider than the market for construction loans. In the six counties of the San Francisco–Oakland metropolitan area, the institutions making permanent house loans can be classified as follows: 32 commercial banks, including 16 national and 16 state, with a total of about 250 offices; 5 state savings banks with 15 offices; 29 savings and loan associations; and 30 life insurance companies, each of which did more than $100,000 in loan business in the area during each year of the postwar period. In addition to these lending institutions, mortgage houses, real estate brokers, and individuals lending their own money may play a role in the permanent financing picture.

Potentially each buyer had nearly 100 different loan sources from which he could select terms for permanent financing; actually, his range of choice was not as broad as might be supposed since the competition among these sources was not great. Only a few differences existed in the interest rate, the amount of down payment, and the amortization time, and during many parts of the period certain lenders were out of the market, thus further limiting choice.

The permanent loan market differs in degree for four groups of builders. Those feeling most intensely the influence of permanent financing are the operative builders doing a large mass-volume business, who must obtain the commitments for the final loan before they even start to build. Next are operative builders who construct more expensive houses; for them the final financing has not been so critical a factor because the actual terms may be arranged after a prospective buyer appears. Third are contractors for whom the permanent financing is usually arranged before construction starts, with the lender paying as work is put in place. Finally, there are those owners or contractors for whom no loan is required.

Although permanent as well as construction loans on tract houses were restricted to the 12 largest sources previously mentioned as covering most of the merchant-built units in the area, a different picture is found when we consider permanent loans based on houses built by owners, contractors, or the smaller operative builders. Only about one-third of these houses were covered by government-insured or guaranteed loans. Another third were covered by conventional loans. The final third were financed by the owners entirely with their own funds. In 1949, these nontract units accounted for about half the production in the total market, so that the actual share of each kind of financing amounted to approximately one-sixth of the whole market. The scattered-lot market was far less affected by fluctuations in funds available under government guarantees, or by the government's appraisal methods, than was the tract market.

Combining all types of builders and all types of financing, one finds that in the last half of 1949 banks made permanent loans on more than half the houses built. These were almost entirely insured or guaranteed and a large percentage of them was resold in the secondary markets. Savings and loan associations made about 4 per cent of the loans, more than 80 per cent of which were guaranteed or insured. Insurance and mortgage companies accounted for loans on about 30 per cent of the houses, and of these 80 per cent were also insured. Individuals made loans on 2 per cent of the houses, and these were almost entirely uninsured. The final 9 per cent of the houses were bought for cash (table 40).

Role of Local Governments

A description of the factors of supply in housebuilding would not be complete without mention of the part played by local units of government in the issuing of licenses and permits and in the administration of building codes. By issuing building permits, these governmental units supply the right to use the land, and, together with private companies, they furnish the necessary utilities.

The total number of building-permit issuing centers in the Bay area is 52, but the average firm deals with only a few of these centers. Only about 30 firms built in more than three permit centers. In addition to building permits, however, firms frequently require a business license and permit to obtain utilities. If the firm is developing new land, the number of governmental agencies involved increases, since the layout of the site and the type of streets and utilities have to be approved by planning commissions and by the water and sewer districts, and the state has to approve the financial aspects of the subdividing.

With the exception of negotiations over approval for new sites, relations between builders and local government authorities tend to be harmonious and stable. Conflicts over new building sites sometimes arise because there is a divergence of viewpoint among the builders, who are concerned primarily with opening up new building sites at the lowest possible cost, and the planning authorities, whose preoccupation runs more in the direction of aesthetics and future development of the community.

Builders in many parts of the country charge that codes imposed by local authorities are too diverse and too unrelated to the practical requirements of housebuilding. This is not true in the Bay area, though there are 52 code authorities each of which has a separate building, electrical, and plumbing code. The differences between the codes are rather minor, since almost all areas use the same uniform codes, and the number of variations adopted within the uniform codes is very small.

For building code purposes, the Bay area divides into five groups: (1) the bulk of the area, which has adopted by reference the Uniform Building Code of the Pacific Coast Building Officials Conference; (2) San Francisco; (3) four small centers which have not adopted the

Uniform Code and where less than 130 houses were constructed in 1949; (4) a few small cities and towns planned as high-priced suburbs, which have adopted the Uniform Code but with a few significant amendments; and (5) certain parts of the rural nonfarm areas hitherto operating without codes, now in process of adopting the Uniform Code. This means that by far the largest percentage of houses built in the Bay area are built in accordance with the Uniform Code without additional restrictions.

The Uniform Code is revised every three years. But how carefully do areas adopt the latest revisions? Slightly more than a year after the 1949 revision of the code, it was found that 13 centers containing 50 per cent of the housebuilding of the area had adopted the new revision. Twenty-four centers in which about 40 per cent of the houses were constructed were still operating under the 1946 revision, and 9 centers, with about 10 per cent of the building, operated under earlier editions. It might be mentioned that the number of changes affecting housebuilding from revision to revision is not great. In addition, local building officials can and usually will allow use of changes which appear in the new editions even if the municipal ordinance has not been amended.

As with the building codes, all areas have adopted the basic principles of the National Electrical Code by reference, with individual municipal ordinances including some additional restrictions over and above the minimum requirements of the National Code. About one-third of the houses built in 1949 were constructed in areas which had adopted the National Code without amendment; about one-third were constructed in localities which had adopted a slightly more restrictive code in a form known as the Uniform Electrical Code of the Pacific Coast Electrical Bureau. (It is predicted that in the future this code will no longer include any variations from the National Code so far as housing is concerned.) The final third of the houses were constructed in areas which had adopted amendments requiring a marked variation in methods from the National Code, but even in these areas the effect on the cost of the house was not significant.

Somewhat greater variations occur in plumbing codes, though the pattern is similar to the other codes in uniformity of adoption. Again, the city of San Francisco has its own. The entire county of San Mateo and most of its cities, accounting for about 30 per cent of the housing construction in the area, also have their own. For the past year, committees have been trying to obtain a unified code for the East Bay, which is the largest remaining part of the area. These codes, in relation to housebuilding, are basically similar to the Uniform Plumbing Code of the Western Plumbing Officials Association.

Chapter 9 analyzes the costs imposed by the differences between these areas, and it is found to be slight. The variety and number of local governments may have important indirect effects upon the building industry, but their direct effect is not great.

PART II

7

Evaluating the Efficiency and Performance of Housebuilding

Part I of this study presented a picture of the Bay area housebuilding industry. The structure of the industry and the manner in which it functions were described, together with the problems faced by builders and their methods of meeting them. The remainder of the book evaluates the skill with which housebuilders perform their functions.

Such an evaluation of performance must be based largely on judgment, since neither the available facts nor the criteria of what constitutes good performance are of a nature to supply clear-cut answers. Still some kind of evaluation is necessary for a meaningful explanation of what has already happened to housebuilding, for an understanding of what is currently taking place, and for formulation of future policies if these are to be sound. This study was engineered so that specific data to test hypotheses concerning problems of performance and related policy suggestions could be gathered at the same time that basic descriptive material was being made available.

The chapters which follow contain both the results of these tests and certain conclusions drawn from them. They point to present trends in the industry's development and potential areas for improvement in efficiency. Because the evaluations rest on both judgments and facts, individual readers may, of course, question particular lines of analysis. To aid each one to form his own opinion, the basic information is presented factually in the succeeding chapters, as well as the conclusions from it.

STANDARDS OF PERFORMANCE

The housebuilding industry has been subjected to severe criticism. It has been called a relic of ancient days, untouched by the industrial revolution and still operating in a medieval fashion. As a result, it is claimed, the level of performance attained by builders is far lower than that of any other industry, and houses are so expensive that the simple furnishing of shelter for the population continues to be a crucial economic problem. It is frequently stated that the only means of attaining satisfactory performance in housebuilding is through a rationalization of the entire industry.

Performance in an industry has many dimensions—many more than can be examined in a limited space. Among the most important are those concerned with efficiency, the industry's product, the distribution of its output, the distribution of its income, and its dynamic qualities.[1]

The chapters which follow present the available data concerning performance. In certain cases, these consist primarily of time series based on national averages. In other cases, they are either time series or cross-section data especially collected and compiled for this study. A final group of data is mainly descriptive, with no statistics.

The type of data encountered varies according to the topic under discussion. For example, information on the quality of product—a major area of performance—is purely descriptive. Judgment in this sphere must, on the whole, be subjective, because though some elements of quality are capable of exact measurement, it is not possible to measure precisely the quality of the total unit. There are no absolute standards for design; they vary from person to person, from area to area, and from time to time. At best, one can only report the facts and the opinions of so-called experts, but neither should be accepted as authoritative.

Again, in the realm of progress and technology, it is necessary to inject the element of personal judgment. Performance here depends upon progress shown over a period of time; more specifically, on the rate at which innovations are adopted compared with the number

[1] For a discussion of the problem of measuring industrial performance, see Grebler, *Production of New Housing,* chap. 2; Alfred R. Oxenfeldt, *Industrial Pricing and Market Practices* (New York: Prentice-Hall, 1951), pp. 90–93; Hiram F. Davis, *Industrial Study of Economic Progress* (Philadelphia: Univ. of Pennsylvania Press, 1947), p. 5.

available for adoption and compared with the rate of acceptance of new ideas by other industries. It is possible to measure and describe the way in which technology is changing, but opinions as to whether these changes are adequate must remain primarily personal.

In the field of profits, distribution of product, and opportunities for entry, more information is available. The data describe existing conditions in these fields and also provide a basis for appraising changes over time. But again, present knowledge is insufficient to permit formulation of true standards. Consequently judgments are bound to be subjective and open to argument because of the lack of real standards.

The final area of evaluation—that of changes in efficiency or productivity—is the one which has generally received the most emphasis. It is considered by many to be the most important because, if efficiency is improving rapidly enough, many other problems of performance may gradually dwindle away. An examination of the ways in which performance can be altered may provide a background for fuller discussion of efficiency evaluation.

Determinants of Performance

The actual performance of any industry depends on the movements of many separate and sometimes conflicting forces, each of which often makes several alternative courses of action available. The course adopted in each area separately as well as the interactions of the various decisions determine the final results for the industry as a whole.

Although the number of areas open for action can be classified and subdivided in innumerable ways, economic analysts have fixed upon certain broad categories as most important. These include: (1) the management of firms in the industry, (2) the scale of the enterprise, (3) the structure and influences of the factors used in production, and (4) the over-all organization of the industry.

In attempting to judge performance as a whole, one is concerned with the use made of the potentialities available in each category. Although theoretical concepts have been developed to explain why certain actions occur, their application will vary in all industries and at all times. The unique features of each industry cause it to meet its problems in different ways. An exploration of the determinants of the level of performance in each of the four main categories, and their effects on the housebuilding industry, may prove revealing.[2]

Management.—The skill, ability, and goals of the owners and managers in any industry are frequently considered to be the most important forces determining its efficiency and good performance. The managements (which in housebuilding are identical with the owners and entrepreneurs) make the day-to-day decisions which shape performance. These decisions—resulting in action or failure to act—cumulatively determine the whole industry's policies and its over-all direction toward progress, stagnation, or retrogression.

In their decisions, the managers are not, of course, free from all restraints. Their choices are limited at least initially by certain elements outside their control, and much of the total performance of the industry depends upon these other factors. Management is presented with particular situations and can only attempt to maximize performance with respect to the variables that it can influence. It is important to observe, however, that factors outside the owners' control in the short run are often amenable to modification over a longer period of time.

Most important of the elements outside management's control is the supply of the labor and materials needed in production. Firms find themselves with a limited range of possibilities as to the type and cost of the factors which can be used in a house. These are given parameters, each of which has a large weight in determining total performance. The firm can choose and substitute among these factors, but at least in the short run its influence on their availability, prices, and basic efficiency is slight.

The next most important outside element in circumscribing management's operations is the available technical knowledge. At any given time the number of production possibilities is limited. Houses can be constructed economically only from a certain group of materials and by particular methods. Again, the firm can choose among these possibilities, but can expand its field of choice only gradually.

These two elements—supply and technology—limit the range of sizes of operation open to the firm. The existing relationships between

[2] For basic statements, see Committee on Price Determination, *Cost Behavior and Price Policy* (New York: National Bureau of Economic Research, 1943); E. A. G. Robinson, *The Structure of Competitive Industry* (New York: Pitman, 1948); and J. Steindl, *Small and Big Business* (Oxford, Basil Blackwell, 1947).

factor prices and technical possibilities (the production function) determine the relative efficiency of particular firm sizes or scales of operations. If the firm wants to produce at the optimum point, it may find itself forced to a particular size of organization.

Finally, there is a whole group of constraints resulting from the industry's (as differentiated from the firm's) over-all organization. This organization is influenced by the builders, the factors of supply, the methods of production, the characteristics of the product, and the market.

Although these limitations on the action of housebuilding firms are important, it is a mistake to believe, as many have done, that they are the main determinants of performance. Housebuilders still have wide latitude for decision, and the available avenues open for action are, on the whole, probably more important than those which are closed.

The choices offered to management may be examined in terms of the various levels of organization at which the managers operate. These many possibilities are shown in figure 8, which presents some of the most obvious ways in which performance can be improved.

The simplest approach is at the house or project level (equivalent to the plant in other industries). This is where production actually takes place. Here the firm can choose among many technical processes available at any given time. It can examine the technical potentialities of various materials, machines, and types of labor in the light of their costs. It can determine the proper proportions or mix of the factors of production so as to give lowest costs. Although this problem is frequently excluded by assumption in theoretical analysis, it is practically one of the most important in the determination of efficiency.

Having decided upon the general method of production to use, the firm can then establish particular systems and production controls to achieve lowest costs. Its methods of operation can determine to what extent the waste of labor, of material, and of other factors will be curtailed. The prices paid for labor and materials may be outside the scope of the firm's management, but the value received and the method of utilization are not. The diagram shows many of the potentialities for cost reduction at the plant or project level which have been important in recent periods.

Above the project or projects, there is another group of functions

FIGURE 8

PATHS TO GREATER EFFICIENCY THROUGH IMPROVED FUNCTIONING OF HOUSEBUILDING FIRMS

I. At project or plant level
   A. Cut waste of materials
   B. Lower supervision and overhead costs
   C. Reduce costs of land and incidentals
   D. Improve use of labor
      1. Reduce movement of men and equipment
      2. Reduce idle time
      3. Diminish reading of blueprints
      4. Increase skill by repetition
      5. Increase tooling
      6. Improve supervision
      7. Set work standards and improve controls
      8. Cut handling of materials and equipment
      9. Reduce turnover

II. At firm level
   A. Better choice of technology
   B. More accurate choice of inputs
   C. Research for improved technology
   D. Design
      1. Better site planning
      2. Reduce size of structure
      3. Reduce variety of plans
      4. Substitute more efficient materials
      5. Rational arrangements of elements
      6. Simplify construction
      7. Increase livability
   E. Lower costs of materials
      1. Cut out distribution channels
      2. Increase bargaining power
      3. Save on freight and handling
      4. Reduce waste
   F. Lower overhead and profit
      1. Spread overhead over more units
      2. Reduce selling costs
      3. Obtain cheaper financing
      4. Reduce profit margin

III. In scale and depth
   A. Obtain optimum scale
      1. Production or technical costs
      2. Selling and purchasing costs
      3. Financing
      4. Management
      5. Risk
   B. Integrate or disintegrate
      1. Materials suppliers
      2. Trade contractors
      3. Other inputs

IV. Change in organization of industry
   A. Change type of market
      1. Amount of competition
      2. Fluctuations in demand
   B. Create coöperative organizations
      1. Research
      2. Marketing
      3. Purchasing
   C. Alter governmental policy
      1. Credit
      2. Codes
      3. Guaranteed market
   D. Change relationships to suppliers
      1. Improved bargaining
      2. Technology

which are commonly spoken of as those at the firm level. Here, again, a wide choice is available to managers. This is the field in which purchases of the direct factors of production are made. The firm is presented with many different ways in which it can arrange for these purchases. Some cost less than others. It is at this level, too, that the builder determines the design of his project. Design influences the production costs, but, perhaps more important, it determines the value of the product he makes. The builder's control over his output may be more important than that over his inputs.

The firm also has more influence than is commonly recognized on the actual technical processes or technology available for use. Most obviously, it has the ability to affect, through research, the state of technical knowledge. Just as important as new research, on the level of performance, is the adoption of the most advanced of already existing knowledge—for example, adoption of machinery already in use in other industries. This path toward greater efficiency is one which builders have been slow to follow. Potential changes in technology have frequently existed for long periods, but because of lack of systems for examining them and of willingness of the builder to experiment, they have been overlooked.

Other vital decisions made at the firm level for housebuilding managements concern overhead structure and use of capital, including such issues as the relationship between fixed and variable costs, the amount of management and executive time purchased, and the ratio of equity to borrowed capital. The judgments on each of these matters will affect costs and the efficiency of the firm. Crucial in this field are price and marketing policies. The management determines the level of performance in these areas by deciding to what class of market its appeal shall be pitched, the type of appeal (either price, advertising, or product differentiation), and the amount to spend on the appeal. It also determines what type of markup and profit level it will seek.

Finally, management has the choice of determining the scope of the firm. Firms are not limited to their present scale, their present depth, or the existing organization of the industry. They can change their scale and obtain any advantage which might accrue to them thereby. They can increase their depth by vertical integration to include more of the building process in their own hands. If housebuilding managements did this, they would then assume the responsibility for the efficiency of certain factors, such as trade contractors' supervision or fabricating of materials, now supplied by others. The builder, by changing his depth, can work with a new set of factor costs and technical possibilities.

Over a period of time, the builder can exert a great deal of influence on the industry's organization as a whole. He can enlarge the functions of his trade associations and assume greater responsibility for the rate of technical change and market knowledge. He may alter the labor structure of the industry through collective bargaining. He may influence the land and capital supply curves by political action. All these are real possibilities for promoting efficiency, and all have actually been attempted in the recent past.

The last two chapters contain an evaluation of the extent to which firms have used the possibilities open to them. In some instances, actual measurements of changes and improvements are possible. In others, all that is found is a potential area of action which has been completely neglected or only now is beginning to be exploited by the most advanced firms. It is from an examination of these facts that trends can be perceived and lines of action for the future can be projected.

Scale.—Among the factors which no housebuilding management can change is the important one of relative efficiency of firms of different size. Builders can pick the particular scale they desire, but related to each size is a certain potential level of efficiency. Although the builder can choose the amount of the factors of production he wishes to use and can also select among various technical possibilities of production, the resultant ratio of output to inputs (or efficiency) shifts in relation to the firm's size. As a corollary, it is evident that some of the changes in efficiency which take place in a dynamic situation are due simply to increases or decreases in scale rather than to any change in the builder's own performance.

The reasons for the changes in efficiency which accompany changes in scale have been detailed many times. In addition to the opportunity for specialization of labor and management which size makes possible, there is the fact that certain indivisibilities exist in the way in which the factors of production can be used and mixed. Consider, for example, what happens in management and overhead. The small builder is tied to his hammer and saw. As a working foreman, he has only his nights and Sundays to devote to off-site and executive functions. The medium-sized builder, who has laid down his tools, is still swamped with details of supervising construction, doing his own purchasing and subcontracting, keeping his records and accounts. He does not have assistants to attend to routine off-site chores while he streamlines his organization. It requires the added capital and large sales volume of a big builder to afford sufficient off-site assistance to free the manager himself to such an extent that he can explore new paths to efficiency. The result is that many types of management organization are open only to large firms. If these organizations are more efficient, the value received per unit of expenditure for overhead in the large firm will be greater than in the others.

Similar problems arise with all other factors of production. In each case some levels of output are more efficient than others because of indivisibilities. The most efficient scale for the firm (its optimum size) will be at the point where the proportions of all the factors are best—that is, where their total costs are lowest. This, of course, may not coincide with the lowest cost point for any specific factor. The essence of efficiency is that total unit costs be at a minimum, rather than that any single factor be used most economically.

Total unit cost depends upon payments for many kinds of service. Since the cost of each category of service reacts differently to changes in scale, total unit costs may fall either because the costs of all categories are falling or because some categories are falling faster than others are rising.

Economic literature is replete with discussions of the particular cost functions for each factor as well as with assumptions as to the way in which they react to changes in scale. Production or technical costs are the most important and have received the most attention. Since Adam Smith's description of the manner in which production costs fall with specialization and gradual mechanization in the pin industry, it has been common to ascribe a falling cost per unit to the production cost category.

The second major cost category—marketing—is also believed to fall rapidly in relation to growth of size. Methods of buying and selling improve as firms grow larger, bringing about lower costs per unit. Clearly, however, marketing costs cannot continue to fall in relation to unlimited amounts of output. If too many houses are produced in any market, their value will decrease, as will the builder's ability to sell them. Similarly, if labor and materials purchases take too much of the available supply, each additional unit of the factors of production purchased by the builder must carry a higher price than the previous one. Consequently, after some point, the builder's marketing cost must begin to rise.

Financing, which is the third cost category, could continue to drop in relation to any amount of growth in housing production, since the amount of financing required for housing is only a minor part of the total available. The larger the builder, the wider the financial markets open to him.

The fourth cost category—management—decreases at first with scale, as has been seen, but most theorists believe it would begin to go up again at a fairly early stage of further scale increase because of the increased difficulty of coördination and the complexity of making decisions as the size of facilities grows. This is true also of the fifth cost category, capital cost, which includes the price that must be paid for assumption of risks and losses due to potential economic fluctuations.[8]

The actual cost curve for any firm depends upon the interaction of these five categories. All are changing at different rates and in separate ways. Economists have traditionally held that the cost curves resulting from these separate movements are U-shaped: as size increases, unit costs fall; if size continues to increase, unit costs will start to rise at some point.

In addition to these effects of scale, observable among firms of various sizes in a static situation, certain other advantages might arise with growth of size in a dynamic situation. In the real world, management's influence on technology and the general organization of the industry increases with size. It is, therefore, possible—though not inevitable—that larger scale could bring about further reductions in costs through changes in the production function and in factor prices.

Factors of Supply.—The vital part in housebuilding performance played by the factors of supply has already been discussed. From 80 to 90 per cent of the total cost of a house is spent for the direct costs of construction. The total cost of these factors will be influenced by the management's efficiency in purchasing and combining them, but it can also change independently.

---

[8] Cf. Robinson, *op. cit.*, and Committee on Price Determination, *op. cit.;* for a fuller explanation of these points.

The housebuilder's own position is such that he cannot change basic prices of supplies and labor. At the most, he can change the total expenditure by substituting one factor for another or by altering the proportions within a given element. For example, he may reduce his labor bill by making use of unskilled in place of skilled labor, but he usually cannot change the basic price he has to pay the skilled or unskilled men. These prices are determined by the impact of all builders together and of the entire economy.

Although the builder's influence on the cost of the factors of production is minor, the effect exerted by these factors on the total performance of the housebuilding industry is great. In addition to setting up the basic frame within which prices of houses are established, the supply industries are important determinants of technology and the organization of the industry itself.

The extensive changes that have occurred in the prices of the factors of production in recent years have already been discussed. In any period, changes in these prices are likely to outweigh all other cost factors.

In technology, though housebuilders themselves have done practically no research, the supplying industries have. A large share of new technical processes, new methods, materials, and machines have entered the house because of progress in the supplying industries. Examples include the recent development of simple power tools, of transit-mix concrete, of effective dry walls. Even more progress along these lines appears possible.

In the general organization of the industry, the factors of supply form an important part and affect the builder's ability to change the shape of the industry as a whole as well as that of his own firm. It was observed that when a builder expands his firm in depth he assumes some of the functions of the existing suppliers. The suppliers may acquiesce in such changes, or they may obstruct changes until the builder will not even attempt them. Some changes in organization require approval of financing institutions, labor unions, or of the government. Any of these may raise objections, or, as has happened in the postwar period, some of the most important impetus toward change may arise in these fields. Chapter 9 will discuss some of the main constraints imposed upon builders from these sources as well as their effects on general performance.

Organization.—The over-all organization of the housebuilding industry, which is the final determinant of its performance to be considered here, is the result of the interplay of many forces. The groups which control factors of production and those which implement public policy, as well as market conditions, the type of product, production methods, and the historical development of the industry, all add their weight to the individual decisions of housebuilders to determine what the organization of the housebuilding industry shall be.

The market for housing is competitive, varied, local, and fluctuating. The industry is fragmented into thousands of firms, none controlling an important share of the national market. Even in local areas there are few dominant firms. Entry is simple. The industry is subject in almost all areas to potentially fierce competition, though during the postwar period, because of the tremendous increase in demand, competition was for the most part moderate.

Housebuilders' associations have had little effect on competition or other aspects of market conditions. Large- and medium-sized firms, joined by some small ones, have only recently united in local and national organizations. The purpose of such groups is primarily to exchange information, publicize the industry, and exert political pressure. They have made rapid progress, but are still in an embryonic stage compared with many other industrial associations.

The local nature of the demand for houses is, of course, a dominating characteristic of the market. Houses are sold on a local basis. Every market has unique tastes and idiosyncracies. Consequently, intimate knowledge of local conditions is required for success. In addition, because demand for housebuilding has experienced fluctuations that rank among the sharpest known to our economy, great flexibility is also a requisite for success in the field.

In addition to the market, the nature of the product is, of course, a major determinant of housebuilding performance. The house is bulky and complex, with a great multiplicity of parts and materials. It is durable and is produced in great variety, with every house differing from every other in some way.

A further factor influencing the industry's structure is its production technique. Traditionally, housebuilding has been a combination of fabrication and assembly. In recent years, builders are becoming to a greater extent assemblers. Since assembling is done with a minimum of equipment, this trend works to decrease the maximum size of firm necessary to produce houses.

The historical background of the industry also plays a part in its present-day structure and performance. Housebuilding is one of the three or four oldest occupations. Houses very similar to modern ones have been constructed and lived in since ancient times. The long and slow development of man's ideas about proper shelter obviously affects his ideas of shelter today. This is also true of construction methods. Present materials and methods have been tested through a long period of time. Although this fact does not preclude the introduction of radical innovations—the transportation industry proves the opposite—it does mean that technical progress, unless of a revolutionary type, is likely to be slower because knowledge of various possibilities has existed for many years and much time has already been spent on improvements.[4]

Another important historical factor is the background of most of the entrepreneurs in the housebuilding industry. The fact that the majority of builders were formerly mechanics or craftsmen who have grown out of that class has an important effect on their planning and methods of operation. Professor F. H. Knight's suggestion that the relation between efficiency and size of firm is largely a matter of personality or historical accident rather than of intelligible general principles is illuminated by many of the traits noticed in housebuilding firm managements.[5]

Apart from historical considerations, in today's economy the factor of capital requirements has a telling effect on the form of the housebuilding industry. Clearly, a different type of industrial structure will develop when a successful firm may be established with from $1,000 to $2,000 capital, as in housebuilding, rather than $100,000,000 or more as required in an industry like automobiles. The amount of capital required to enter an industry is determined by the amount of plant and equipment needed for production as well as by the need for working capital and the methods of financing common to the industry. The amount necessary to meet each of these requirements tends to be minimized in housebuilding.

The forces that have been cited affect performance directly in many cases. The market influences the level of profits and prices. By requir-

[4] Davis, *op. cit.*, p. 40.

[5] Cf. Committee on Price Determination, *op. cit.*, p. 228.

ing flexibility, it exerts large pressures on the way in which firms organize. It also controls the rate of entry. These things, in turn, affect technology, methods of marketing, and distribution of the product. But the market should not be considered as the only influence.

Many forces affecting performance have frequently been ignored, and performance left to market determination alone, since the builder has not been equipped to deal with the other elements or has not considered them important. Such neglect is not, however, necessary. When problems are too big for an individual builder, they could be approached through the combined efforts of many builders or through public policy. Recently, certain attempts have been made to influence performance along these lines. Examples may be found in the use of government research to improve technology and in the use of the Federal Housing Administration and the Veterans Administration to widen the market. Other possibilities, such as joint-selling campaigns and attempts to reduce demand fluctuations, will be considered later.

The organization of the industry is a fixed structure only in short-run terms. In the long run, it is subject to the influence of individual builders, their associations, associations of the supply factors, and the public. Throughout a discussion of performance, it should be kept in mind that potential action might come through any or all of these channels.

Measurement of Efficiency

Based on the background of the preceding examination of the determinants of performance, a more detailed exposition of the measurement of efficiency may be offered.

Because of the great interest in the measurement of efficiency, much effort was expended in this study on devising methods of measuring it. Since the difficulties which were encountered, as well as the ways in which they were surmounted and the reasons for arriving at the final method, have strong bearing on the analysis in succeeding chapters, these problems receive a fuller discussion than has been given to the other measures.

In theory, efficiency is relatively simple. It is measured by the ratio of real output to real input, but the problem is complicated by the fact that there are so many determinants of the level of efficiency. For some purposes it may be enough to know simply that efficiency has changed, but for most, some measurement of the effect of the different forces is desired. For instance, the changes in efficiency over the past ten years might be due to opposing movements in the performance of management and of the factors of supply. In this case, one could arrive at two quite different understandings of the situation depending on whether one proceeded from knowledge of the amount of each separate movement or from knowledge of their aggregate results alone.

Unfortunately, the ideal measurements are simply not possible at the present time. There are no available statistics showing how total housebuilding efficiency has changed, let alone data on the individual components. Furthermore, even measurement of the level of efficiency now existing is difficult. Such a measurement requires a scale or standard. Yet, since every industry has its own particular background, product, organization, and market, such standards vary from one industry to another. Comparisons are frequently made with another industry or with a list of suggested improvements, but such comparisons may be invalid because no one knows whether or not a technique is applicable until it has been tried. The history of the past twenty years is littered with suggestions for improvements in housebuilding, most of which were not usable. People thought they knew exactly what ailed building, but their ideas were often based on too little knowledge or on false analogies. Interindustry comparisons contain many such fallacies. For these reasons, even with data collected especially for the purpose, quantitative measurements are limited in their scope.

The ensuing discussion will present facts which may be more pertinent. In the first place, the estimate of the effect of scale on efficiency is based upon a cross-section analysis of existing firms of different sizes. Since it is known that larger-sized firms have developed only in the recent past, this estimate also measures the effect of the growth of such firms. On a more speculative basis, it gives some of the facts necessary for an analysis of possible future trends in scale.

In the second place, measurements of some of the influences on efficiency exerted by the factors of production outside the firm are based on results of the known inefficiencies and constraints in these factors. These measurements provide estimates of potential changes, as well.

In the third place, estimates of the performance of management in housebuilding are based either upon a comparison of the average with the best now active, or upon a set of subjective standards which have struck the main observers of the industry as applicable.

The combination of the various types of measurement and evaluation gives more workable knowledge than was previously available of the significance of changes that have already taken place as well as of the major problems facing the industry in the future.

In combining types of measurement, this study gave heed to the great amount of discussion in the past as to how changes in efficiency could be evaluated. To obtain a valid measurement, it is necessary to have a series showing the changes in outputs and inputs either over periods of time, or among firms of various scales, or among firms facing particular external problems, depending on which of these influences is to be separated out and measured. Special problems were faced in devising a pragmatic scheme of measuring housebuilding efficiency.

As to inputs, the productive resources used by a housebuilding firm are varied. First come those required to perform the overhead or indirect functions of the firm. These include the management and executive staffs with a small group of salaried assistants, the capital investments, a very small amount of equipment and real property, and the sales staff. In the next group of resources is the direct labor hired by the firms. Finally come all the purchases made by builders, including their materials, subcontractors, financing, and other incidentals. Some basis for judgment of efficiency might be obtained by calculating the ratio of each of these specific inputs to outputs measured in physical terms. For example, some industries measure output per man-hour or output per unit of equipment and speak of the changes in these ratios as measurements of efficiency. This simplified procedure is far from satisfactory, however. In building it would have little value, because no factor is paramount in the production of the house. A change in the ratio of a particular input might always be offset by changes in other factors. In addition, it is difficult to obtain measurements for many of these inputs in physical units.

For these reasons, it appears necessary in measuring building's efficiency to aggregate all input in dollar terms and to compute changes in the total dollar value of input. To be of value, each input must obviously be expressed in dollars of a constant value before aggregation; otherwise the comparison might simply reflect changes in prices and profits instead of efficiency.[6]

[6] This is the method approved by the primary experts in this field. Cf. Davis, *op. cit.*, p. 25; Committee on Price Determination, *op. cit.*, p. 154.

Still more difficult problems arise in the measurement of output. Houses are usually measured in units, or occasionally in units of a certain average price, but everyone knows that houses can vary greatly in their size, design, and workmanship. As a result, either of these measurements is extremely inaccurate. The output which is used in finding efficiency ratios must represent a fixed bundle of utilities, or the measurement makes little sense. This difficulty of stabilizing the measurement of output is, of course, not unique in housebuilding.[7]

Other obstacles occur in attempts to measure efficiency. The number of variables in the production process is endless. Ideally, we should observe production in controlled experiments in order to gauge the manner by which the ratio of output to input changes with each variable. This is the method of the laboratory. It is remotely possible, at great expense, to duplicate such conditions in the building field, and such experiments have potential value.

Such experiments were not, however, possible for this study because of their great cost, and also because the setting up of the experiment actually might have had more influence upon the variables being examined than any changes observed in the process of the work. For these reasons, and others, we found it necessary to base our measurements upon accounting records in the actual field, rather than on any test-tube situation.

Turning to the actual accounting records of firms, there were again several potential approaches and even greater difficulties. The entire housebuilding industry in the postwar period has been in a state of turmoil. Firms have been growing rapidly, and their methods of production have been undergoing constant change. The prices paid for factors were fluctuating almost every day.

It was possible to obtain some aggregate figures for changes in the costs of a firm over a period of time, and also some figures which would have allowed comparisons of the costs of many firms at the same time. What, however, would have been the value of either of these measurements?

Changes were so rapid that it would have been impossible to isolate any of the variables under consideration. An example was the problem

[7] Davis, for example, states: "In the study of productive efficiency it may be that for practical purposes one needs to be more concerned about the inaccurate measurements of output than about the complete measurement of input." *Op. cit.*, p. 35.

of material purchases. Five firms, each building houses in the same period, all paid different amounts for their materials. To what factor should these cost differentials have been ascribed? Part of the difference was obviously due to changes in scale, or to the differences in the amounts purchased by a firm in a given period. A part arose from the fact that though the period covered was the same, materials prices changed daily and even hourly. Thus unless the firms were all buying at the same moment from equally well-informed sellers, part of the variations were simply due to differences in time. Other variations resulted from the fact that the products actually received by the firms were not identical. They varied in grade and in the services furnished. Finally, some firms paid less because they had better or more efficient managements, able to shop more effectively in the existing market. These problems are typical of those which arise in an attempt to compare prices actually paid. They could not be resolved because of the imperfect knowledge existing in most of the housebuilding materials market.

Similar difficulties exist, of course, in measurement of output. Although a firm may have built nearly the same house from period to period, there was no way of isolating the effects of whatever changes were introduced. This was also true of comparisons among firms. No two housebuilding firms ever build the identical product.

In seeking to solve the foregoing difficulties, we arrived at the device of measuring the effects of changes upon the costs of a composite house which any firm might have built. We developed a synthetic cost curve drawn from many accounting sources rather than a cost curve based upon an attempt to rectify the figures of a single firm. This composite house index or synthetic cost curve serves two purposes: (1) It provides a method of weighting all the various elements that go into the house so that each appears in its proper perspective, and (2) it results in a comparison of over-all costs and efficiency.

The procedure used in developing this index was to obtain for large, medium, and small builders average prices paid for each basic element of a typical house. Actually about 100 different elements of direct and indirect costs were priced separately. Prices for each element were obtained from enough sources so that the resulting average price for each class of builder was thought to be accurate. (See Appendix H for a complete description of the method used.)

The plans for the structure used in obtaining these prices are shown in figure 9. It was designed with the typical characteristics of a Bay area house. It is completely undistinguished in design and character. On the other hand, it is typical. It meets the FHA minimum construction requirements. It is of median size. It is of minimum quality. No one would be surprised to come upon this house anywhere in the area.

The plans for the house, the list of materials required, and the quantities and specifications for each subcontract were taken into the field where prices were obtained for each element. The labor costs and incidentals were taken from the builders' records, corrected as necessary to account for differences in specifications. The materials and subcontract prices were derived from those reported by dealers and trade contractors. Since these men actually sell materials or bid for jobs with various types of builders each day, it was assumed that their knowledge of the discounts and other savings available to various-sized builders was more accurate than that of builders who enter the market only periodically and then are not certain whether they are obtaining the best possible deal.

The profit and overhead figures were also taken from actual operating statements as described in previous chapters. We have used typical figures rather than following the common practice of assigning an arbitrary value for these components. In fact, the only cost not based upon a survey is that for land. (The reason for using a single figure for this item for all builders is explained later.)

The prices or costs of every element to each class of builder were averaged separately. These element prices were then added together to give the total amount an average builder of each size would have had to pay in building this same structure (fig. 10). Since average operating margins were added to the builder's direct cost, the index shows the total price each size of builder charged for his product as well as the costs for each major expense in the house.

The cost curves are synthetic because they are derived from many separate sources. In addition, they apply to an imaginary house, rather than a real one. The composite house is simply a method of assigning weights to each factor in the building process so that over-all comparisons can be made. It is believed to be a representative index. Inherent in it are all the problems familiarly encountered in the use of index numbers. But it does, we believe, serve its purpose. It demonstrates

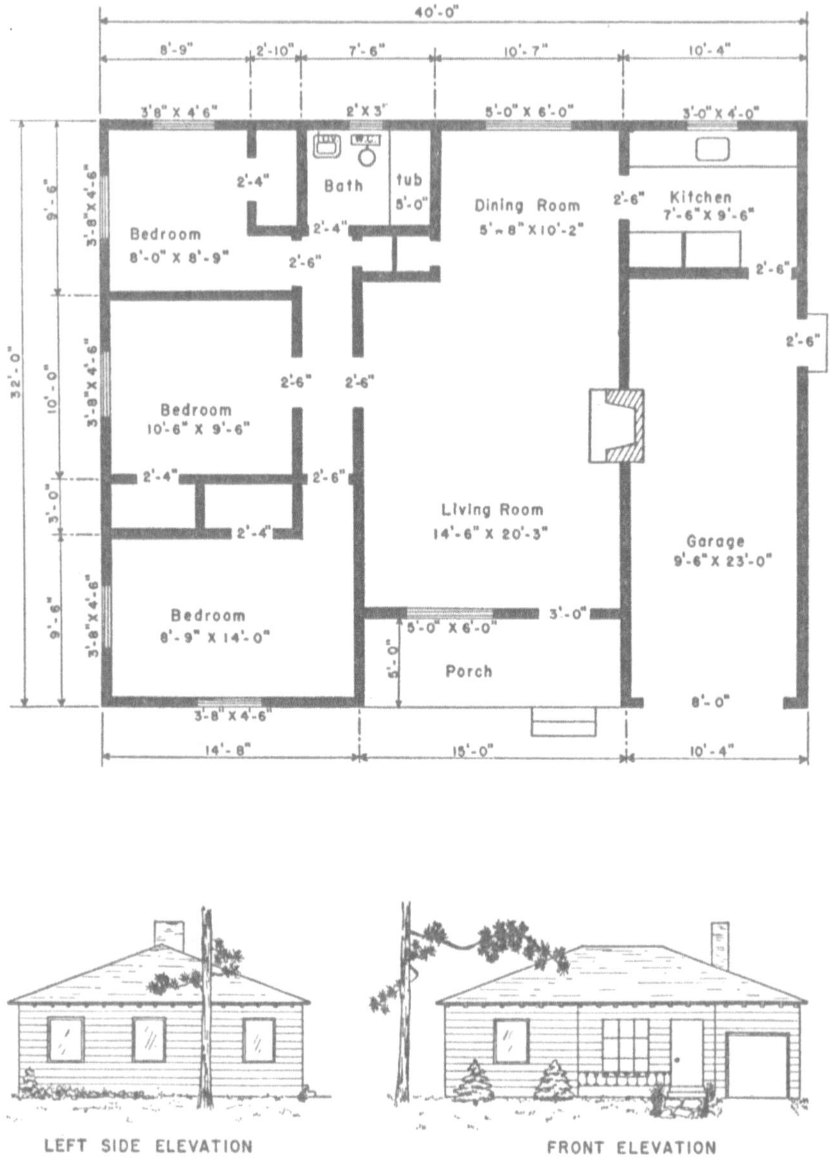

Fig. 9. Plan and elevation of the composite house.

the relative costs for materials, subcontracts, and labor to average builders of each class. It also shows the relative importance of each element of cost in typical Bay area construction.

Through its use, variations in efficiency accompanying changes in size can be measured directly through comparison of the cost of each specific input and through comparison of the price that would have been charged for the composite house by the average firm of each size. Its data also make possible measurement of the importance of any supply restrictions. This can be done by relating a restriction's effect upon the factor's own cost to the total cost for the typical house. In this way the supply restriction's relative weight can be found. Finally, though the index does not measure internal efficiency, these data make it possible to judge the relative importance of particular problems facing a firm's own management. Thus the index may prove of use to a study of the industry as a whole or to an examination of practical issues confronting an individual firm.

The dangers of this approach are obviously great. Many of the men in the industry who aided us with cost data voiced skepticism as to whether there were such things as typical or average prices or conditions. They felt that the individual circumstances surrounding each price were such as to invalidate comparisons. On the other hand, as we continued to amass our research data, we found that costs tended to cluster, to form definite distributions, and therefore averages appear to show a true picture of the underlying relationships.

Certain important qualifications of this analysis must naturally be made. The index is for an average builder of each size and therefore might apply only partly to any real firm. Depending on the know-how and ability of the particular owner, production methods used varied greatly. The range in production efficiency due entirely to the skill of management at any level of output appeared to be as high as 50 per cent. This meant that comparisons of the most to the least efficient builder at any level, or between levels, might show so great a difference. In measuring the effect of size on efficiency, the management skill factor was held constant by using the builder of average efficiency at each level.

The actual practices employed by any firm also depend upon the conditions of supply and demand in the markets for materials and labor. Cost-saving devices which are possible when ample supplies are available may be discarded during other periods in favor of costlier methods which seem to insure a more certain flow of materials. Channels of materials distribution described in this study were those available immediately before the Korean war, from July, 1949 to June, 1950, when, on the whole, the greater part of materials and labor were in adequate supply and the most efficient channels for materials purchases could be employed.

It is possible that the use of the composite house as an index may raise the question that since no firm has necessarily constructed a unit identical with it, its concreteness is illusory. This is not important. Every builder has purchased most of the items included in it. Each has entered into subcontracts calling for approximately the same amount and quality of work by each type of trade contractor as required for this house. All have hired labor to build units of about the same size. The pricing of fixed quantities and specifications allows comparisons.

8

How Efficiency Grows with Size

Effect of Scale on Costs

Differences in costs due to size of operation reflect the effect of scale on the level of efficiency. The extent to which costs vary with scale can be measured by the composite house price data. These show the actual expenditures by builders of each size group at the start of 1951 for all of the main building components, as well as the prices at which they would sell the house. A comparison among the columns of figure 10, giving the specific amounts, shows how costs change with size. (See Appendix H for a description of the method of compiling the index.)

Increased size has led to decided savings for builders in purchasing, financing, and the production process. It is true that most of these savings have been offset by higher payments to the owners and managers of large firms, so that, to date, only about 8 per cent of the reductions in direct costs have been passed on to the ultimate consumer.

This composite house index may, however, understate the real growth of efficiency which has occurred with size. The indirect costs shown for large firms may well be excessive and peculiar to the period under study because of a lack of competition. In addition, certain factors such as design and land, which increase the advantages of large firms, are omitted from the index.

There are clear indications that the total margin charged by large firms over direct costs was abnormally high during the period studied. Demand was so strong, and competition, therefore, so weak, that the large builder's margin could rise to engross most of the difference between his costs and those of the small builder. In a noncompetitive situation, increased efficiency led to greater profits instead of to lower prices—a result that would be predicted in normal economic analyses. This special situation may have distorted the true picture of efficiency in relation to scale.

The omission of exact estimates for design and land must also be considered in evaluating costs and efficiency. The cost figures show the amount of money required to produce an identical house by firms in each size group—a situation which, of course, did not occur in reality. In 1949 the median house sold by small builders was priced at $12,400; by medium-sized builders at $10,500; and by large builders,

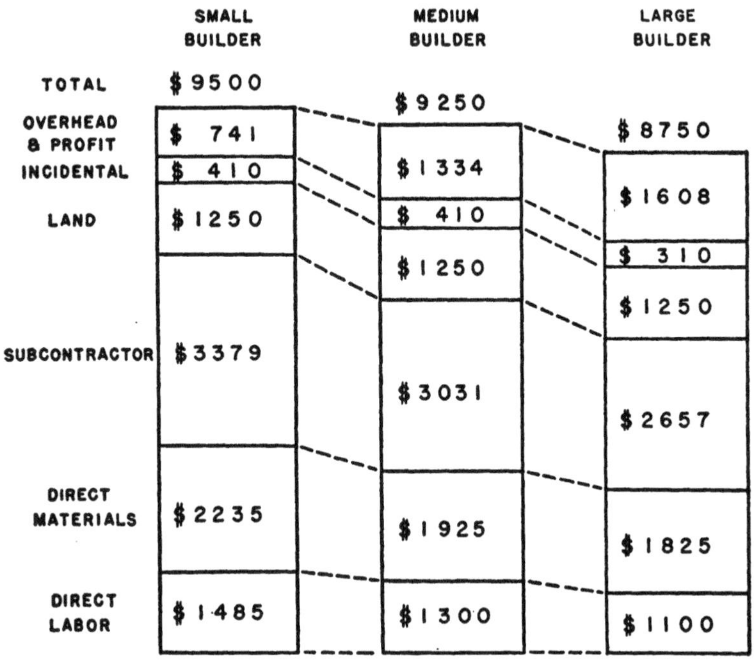

Fig. 10. Major payments for the composite house, by size of builder. Source: Tables 49–52.

at $9,250. These figures, which refer to houses actually constructed, reflect great differences in the design of the units and in their land costs, factors excluded from the composite house index. Differences in design can cause much greater variety in average costs to builders of each size than do changes in the efficiency of producing like units (table 39).

Good design is one of the main factors affecting true efficiency. Within the various limits imposed by codes, planning commissions, banks, Federal Housing Administration, and by the paramount requirement of salability, a builder erecting houses for sale and not on contract can plan the structure as he desires. He is able to plan so that building costs are reduced to a minimum. Although this statement applies to both large and small builders, it is more important in larger operations, since the greater the number of units constructed, the greater is the total potential saving obtained through better planning and the more funds are available for spending on it.

The following methods of reducing costs through proper design have frequently been publicized:

(1) The large-scale merchant builder can save costs on land, improvements, and house construction by correctly gearing the size and location of lots and the type and amount of improvements to the nature of the prospective house. He may also improve its salability thereby.

(2) The builder can reduce the cost of materials by decreasing the total size of the house; by keeping the types and quality of materials to a minimum (e.g., all millwork may be of the simplest type); and by cutting down waste in making certain that no studs, joists, and the like, are unnecessarily duplicated, and that the unused scrap is minimized. When new, cheaper, or more efficient materials are discovered, they are included in the plan.

(3) Additional features can be incorporated which reduce both materials and labor, as, for example, the use of slab floors with asphalt tile in place of the more conventional foundation and hardwood floor, and the use of an exposed beam ceiling-roof combination ("single roof").

(4) The house can be designed to simplify construction and save as much labor as possible through the simple repetition of a basic design and the use of standard items.

(5) Finally, the amount of value in a given quantity of materials and labor can be augmented. This is familiarly known as increasing the livability. Through better design, the buyer may receive more for his money. Conversely, if the design calls for poorer quality, he may find himself with greatly increased maintenance costs and with less actual value.

Although good design can obviously reduce costs in several directions, no attempt has been made in the composite house index to express the potential savings in dollar terms. It is probably not valid to compare the designs evolved by small builders with those of large builders because each may be constrained by market considerations.

Builders of large numbers of units tend to produce "minimum" houses for a low-priced field, whereas builders of small numbers of units typically produce a more expensive and less standardized dwelling.

The small builder typically builds a custom house in the more expensive areas. The buyer of this house pays for location, greater space, a large amount of finish work, and other custom details. The medium-sized builder comes much closer to building the composite house, though it may be on more expensive land than would be considered typical.

The large builder, on the other hand, is likely (or was, during the period of this study) to build a unit that has many more cost-saving features than the composite house we have used. The composite house has hardwood floors, a fireplace, and a redwood-siding exterior; the house built by the large builder may have a slab floor, no fireplace, and may use stucco. All these features will lower the cost of the unit. Other materials—for example, millwork and cabinets—are also produced at low prices especially for the tract home. These, too, will reduce comparative costs, though they will not necessarily improve efficiency.

The kind of land used by different types of builders is, like design, a major cause of variations in actual prices, reflecting differences in value rather than in efficiency. Although a few of the big builders specialize in expensive homes on high-cost land, most of them are likely to build on less expensive land than that used by other classes. The average house of the large builder is usually on a smaller lot, in a tract, and probably has less value.

Our study shows that there is likely to be but little relation between the type of land used by operative builders and by single-house builders. Each concentrates in his own area. In addition, in tract developments the financial arrangements for the preparation of the land are likely to be done in a special way each time, and the manner of raising funds and allocating possible cost savings will vary from job to job.

Small builders' costs reflect large differences in land prices depending upon the area in which they are active. The medium and large builders' land costs are usually arbitrary, expressing only an internal accounting decision by the development company as to what price the building firm should be charged. Land can be a profitable source of income, and in certain instances the profit on this item may be more than that on building. For these reasons, we have not attempted to price land for our composite house.

Other profits similar to those on land may accrue to the large builder, but likewise are not reflected in the costs of the composite house. Most important has been his ability to capitalize on the movement of population into an area by building a shopping center. Such a venture is almost always handled separately so that the bulk of eventual profits can be shown as a capital gain with consequent tax advantages. The large builder can capitalize on this possibility, but it is not available to the small one.

Along the same line is the chance for profits on originating a large volume of loans. The index shows somewhat lower financial charges for the large builder. However, during periods when government-insured loans have sold at a premium, the big builder has made additional profits as an agent arranging the final mortgage loans. Similar possibilities for profits also exist in selling insurance and in brokers' fees paid for resale of houses.

These other sources of income have at times been so large that builders enjoying them would have been willing to operate their actual construction enterprises without any profit. None of them, in practice, felt called upon to go to this length, but the possibility of such a development points up the fact that large scale engenders certain savings and profits not measured by the composite house index. It also indicates that in a more competitive situation the charges for profit and overhead attributed to construction in the large-scale operation might be greatly reduced.

Effect of Size on Direct Cost Categories

The theoretical basis for changes in costs as size of operations increases has received ample attention from economists. Labor costs fall when workers repeat the same task rather than perform a variety of operations; when less time is lost in moving from task to task; when the amount of mechanization is increased; and finally, when scheduling and supervision are thoroughly organized. The cost of materials and subcontracts is reduced by institution of more economical purchasing methods. As operations grow in size, quantity purchases become feasible and the buyer can drive a harder bargain. Through better planning and scheduling, the cost of financing may be reduced.

Figure 10 showed that direct costs—labor, materials, subcontracts, and incidentals—in the composite house index amounted to $7,509 for the small builder, $6,666 for the medium builder, and $5,892 for the large. In other words, these costs fell by $843, or approximately 11 per cent, with the first increase in scale and by an additional $774, or about 10 per cent, with the next increase. Those who built at a rate of more than 100 units per year averaged approximately 21 per cent less in direct costs than did the builders whose rate was less than 25 units per year.

Examination of each of these cost components in turn will show how its cost changes with scale, the reasons for such changes, and some of the problems encountered in measuring these variations.

Direct Labor Costs.—The average small builder paid out $1,485 to his own crews to construct the typical house. The operational problems of the small builder have been described so frequently that they form for most people a stereotype of the building industry. There is little specialization. Each man must be a craftsman able to perform all tasks. Most pieces of lumber must be cut to fit, the process consisting of finding a piece of lumber, carrying it to its destination, measuring it, sawing it, and then hammering it into place. Much time is lost in movement, in measurement, in picking up and laying down tools, and in the change of tempo as a worker goes from one task to another, never getting into the swing of a process. Very little mechanized equipment is used, partly because it is not worth carrying the overhead of expensive tools which will only be used occasionally, but mostly because a power tool requires more time to move and set up than a hand tool, and does not pay unless it can be used steadily for several operations. Finally, since every job is different, it is impossible to set good work standards. The work accomplished is checked by a visual inspection to ascertain whether the carpenter is "putting out" or not.

This stereotyped picture is somewhat overdrawn. The composite builder of single houses in the Bay area, from whom the $1,485 figure is taken, had as minimum mechanized equipment a hand-power radial saw which he used to trim the subfloor, sheathing, and siding and possibly to cut studs. In many cases, he also employed a large power saw to cut studs, blocking, bridging, and the like. He recognized the need to minimize materials-handling and waste, and he attempted to save carpenters' time by having the laborer carry as much material as possible close to its point of use.

As the size of operations increased, more efficient methods were adopted. Medium-sized firms divided their men into several crews, each of which worked on only one part of the house. By the time the rate reached one house a day, there were as many as ten crews with work quite specialized, each crew gaining greater proficiency at its particular task. Since all the houses were similar, a worker continually repeated the same task, building up his skill and speed and developing a rhythm and tempo which increased output and thereby lowered the costs. In place of blueprint reading and laborious measurements, templates and patterns were used. Mechanization was increased.

Such a reorganization of their technological methods and the functions of their labor force resulted in a saving for the average medium-sized builders of slightly more than 12 per cent, or $185, of the $1,485 the small builder spent on direct labor. For the average large builder, the saving in labor cost amounted to $385, or 26 per cent, which is about one-quarter of his total savings resulting from scale. This saving was made without any appreciable difference in unit costs of equipment or supervision.

Such advantages cease after size has increased to 500 units a year. Experience indicates that when the volume of construction of the most efficient large firms grows beyond the level of one to two houses per day, few, if any, further savings can be realized through labor specialization. Most efficient firms of this volume are already operating in an area where labor costs may rise rather than fall as operations increase. Exact costs depend upon particular conditions in the labor market. When labor is tight, any expansion in the size of large firms means hiring additional personnel who are less efficient and cause greater turnover.

Beyond this, with increased size, costs of supervision rise slightly, whereas few offsetting advantages result from better available techniques or increased mechanization. In fact, firms moving within the range of one to 20 houses per day have experienced practically no change in the type and amount of equipment used or in the production process. Most firms find that four to five men for any particular operation are about the maximum, and that by the time production is one unit per day, they have divided the construction process into about as many operations as practicable. This means that, considering only the builder's direct labor, the most effective amount of specialization is reached when there are between 50 and 100 men on the project. After this point, the same organization is simply repeated as many times as necessary to reach any desired level of output. Approaching their minimum when volume is near one house per day, labor costs stay at this low level for larger outputs as long as an adequate labor supply is available.

Changes in methods and costs of materials distribution.—It has been pointed out that as the builder increases the size of his organization, he also changes the methods and channels through which he buys materials. The small builder buys his supplies almost exclusively from retail lumber yards. The medium-sized builder uses both retail and wholesale channels, whereas the large builder purchases almost entirely from mills or wholesalers. Basically, similar changes occur when trade contractors purchase for jobs of various magnitudes.

What effect do changes in purchasing methods have on prices? Survey data showed that costs fell rapidly as the size of purchases grew, primarily because the services required by the builder progressively diminished. The actual decreases in costs are shown in figure 11.

In brief, the figure shows that for the typical Bay area house, the average small builder spent $2,235 on items purchased directly—mainly lumber, millwork and cabinets, wallboard, and both rough and finish hardware. On these items the large builder was able to save $410, or 18 per cent. This same percentage, amounting to a total of $669, was saved on all the 15 major materials in the typical house, including those bought by trade contractors. The total amounted to $3,759 in the house constructed by the small builder (table 51).

The source of these materials-cost reductions is found in the four basic factors leading to greater efficiency and lower costs with increased size—namely, reduced wastage, bulk handling, simplified distribution channels, and increased bargaining power. The following discussion presents the reason why materials prices to builders and trade contractors fall with size, with examples of the most important changes which occur in individual materials.

(1) The simplest cost reductions are based on less wastage. When several houses are built at one time, bits and pieces left over from one

frequently can be used on the next. This is the basic reason for the indicated savings on concrete and paint between the small- and medium-sized job. Concrete is furnished in fixed units. When a single house is built, if all is not used, the balance is wasted. When two houses

FIGURE 11

COSTS OF BUILDING THE COMPOSITE HOUSE BY BUILDERS OF DIFFERENT SIZES

Component	Size of builder (In dollars)			Size of builder (In per cent)		
	Small	Medium	Large	Small	Medium	Large
Labor						
Direct	1,485	1,300	1,100	16	14	13
Trade contractors	1,161	1,010	944	12	11	11
Subtotal	2,646	2,310	2,044	28	25	24
Materials						
Direct	2,235	1,925	1,825	24	21	21
Trade contractors	1,524	1,427	1,265	16	16	14
Subtotal	3,759	3,352	3,090	40	37	35
Trade contractors' overhead and profit	694	594	448	7	6	5
Builders' overhead and profit	741	1,334	1,608	8	14	18
Land	1,250	1,250	1,250	13	14	14
Financing and incidentals	410	410	310	4	4	4
Total	9,500	9,250	8,750	100	100	100
Subtotals						
Subcontracts	3,379	3,031	2,657	35	33	30
Direct costs[a]	7,509	6,666	5,892	79	72	68

[a] Includes labor, materials, subcontracts, and incidentals.
SOURCE: Tables 49–52.

are poured one after the other, as occurs in a tract, this wastage is eliminated and costs are reduced. Similarly, small amounts of paint are not wasted when the same color is used again and again.

(2) More important are the savings made in bulk or quantity purchases. Most familiar and significant of these is the price differentiation between carload (C.L.) lots and less than carload (L.C.L.). Somewhat

similar are discounts that depend on the method of packaging. Prices differ between standard packages and broken lots and between units sold in drums and in cans. Finally, discounts may apply to the amount purchased on a given bill or according to volume during a given period.

An example of the savings to be realized through quantity handling was found in roofing. Roofers could buy in four different quantities and pay four different prices for the same product. Bay area dealers in roofing products quoted the following types of price differentials to all dealers and trade contractors. The basic price was that for deliveries of more than 1,000 pounds to the building site or to retail dealers. If the order was for less than 1,000 pounds, this price was increased by a cartage charge of $2.50. On the other hand, if the order was for a full carload spotted at the tract, yard, or wherever the builder chose, the basic price would be reduced by 16.5 per cent. The builder was then responsible for unloading the car and moving the material to the site, so that his actual savings on quantity purchases would run from 12 to 14 per cent. The fourth price was intermediate. If the builder wanted to pick up his order at the warehouse, he would pay 5 per cent less than the price delivered at the site. Savings in this case would depend on the quantity involved and on his own handling costs. (Based on the survey for Appendix H.)

The carload savings for plumbing and heating equipment, for asphalt tile and linoleum, and also for ceramic tile follow a similar pattern and are of the same magnitude. Other items such as paint, electrical supplies, paper, mastics, and so on usually were not purchased in carloads, but reductions were available for buying standard packages, pallets, or drums. In these cases, the standard package reduction was about equivalent to the difference in L.C.L. and carload prices just described for the more bulky items. Some carried an additional discount based on the total size of a given order.

An illustration of the standard package saving is found in the electrical field, where discounts on either wire or standard items such as outlets and fuse boxes were based on standard packages and on volume of the total order. For instance, the price of No. 12 "Romex" type nonmetallic cable when sold in cut coils of less than 500 feet was $73; if 11 or more coils were purchased, the price would be $55. Similarly, a common piece of electrical equipment packed 10 units per carton and 50 cartons per standard package cost 40 cents per unit when bought in less than carton lots, 35 cents if bought in cartons, and 30½ cents if bought in standard packages. The saving through purchasing standard packages rather than cartons was 13 per cent. Approximately 40 houses could be equipped from a single standard package.

In certain cases, discounts based on the volume of each order and sometimes on the volume for a period were superimposed on these standard ones. These discounts were based on fixed units such as $100, $1,000, or $2,500 per order. Depending on the size of the order, they might run from 3 to 10 per cent additional. In a competitive situation, if the volume of an order was large, this type of discount might go even higher, with bidders figuring on some type of cost-plus basis.

(3) The third type of cost reduction stems from a reduction in the services required in the channels of distribution. When builders become large enough, they no longer require an intermediary to furnish credit, pool orders, maintain inventories, and give site delivery. Small builders do require these services, and the cost of the services is added to their price. Taking the small-dealer price as the base price, manufacturers grant part of this total price to others in the channel of distribution to repay them for the tasks they perform. These are spoken of as trade-channel discounts and may pay for retailing or wholesaling services. They will vary for such functions as difficult brokerage duties, acceptance of title and granting credit, and maintenance of a warehouse and inventories. When a builder or trade contractor assumes any of these functions or removes them, he may expect to have the base price reduced by amounts equivalent to the discounts granted those who normally perform these services.

Lumber, the most important material in the house, furnishes a good example of this type of saving. Since retail lumber dealers purchase in quantity, they pay the prevailing mill price and usually no further volume discounts are available to anyone. But if the large builder performs the dealer's functions, he can purchase at the same price as the retail dealer and can reduce his price by their normal markup. He can absorb the margin usually charged for performing the distribution function. Of course he also has certain additional costs for handling and overhead. After these were accounted for, the builder buying lumber in bulk saved in the vicinity of $10 per thousand board feet, or about 11 per cent. The actual saving would vary somewhat depending on the particular channel or services used, but once the stage of direct purchases was reached, would not vary much with the builder's size.

The other items bought directly by the builder—millwork, cabinets, and hardware—showed reduced costs resulting from a combination of both trade-channel and quantity discounts. Small- and medium-sized builders usually bought these goods from retail lumberyards which, in turn, purchased either from wholesalers or from the mill. As the builder increased in size, he found these same channels open to him. As a result, his costs were first reduced by increased quantity purchases and then, if these became large enough, by elimination of a trade channel.

A standard interior fir door is a good illustration of how this worked in practice. This door, when bought singly from a lumber yard, cost $10.25. The yard's price to builders for doors bought for one house at a time was $9.50. On the other hand, the medium-sized builder purchasing for five to ten houses at a time might have paid as low as $8.25 per door from the retail yard, because the yard could get quantity discounts from the mill. The carload price on the doors would have been about $7.25 each, and to obtain it, a builder would have had to buy a minimum mixed carload of doors and windows containing enough items for 40 or 50 houses. This price would therefore be possible only for the fairly large builder. The largest builders buying carloads at frequent intervals might have received a price as low as $6.60 per door.

Nails provide an example of similar discounts available in the hardware field. The individual purchaser of 8d. nails paid 15 cents per pound. If he bought a 100-pound keg over the counter, he would still have paid $12.50 per keg. The small builder, on the other hand, buying from the same retail lumberyard but including it in his total materials purchases, would have paid about $11.35 per keg. The medium-sized builder who dealt directly with a wholesale hardware house would have paid, on the average, about $9.70 a keg. As scale increased and purchases became larger, the builder buying greater quantities might have been able to obtain a price as low as $8 per keg. If he got into the carload-lot bracket, he could then buy from a manufacturer, special jobber, or wholesaler, and would pay between $7.25 and $7.75 per keg. Since there are 400 kegs in a car, a direct purchase would entail an investment of about $3,000 plus warehousing while the nails were being used.

Cabinets, on the other hand, were almost always bought directly from the cabinet shop or mill even by the small builders. For this item, the medium-sized builder buying for a small tract at one time would usually receive an additional discount of from 10 to 15 per cent. But for the large builder, cabinets are an example of products which follow an entirely different channel of distribution. As mentioned in the chapter on the large builder, many tract builders have switched from the plywood cabinet to steel kitchen fittings purchased in carload lots through special brokers who handle only items for tract houses.

It is also possible for builders to purchase their own lumber, millwork, and cabinet mills. They can use their assured markets to attempt integration of the fabricating process, with a view to further cost savings. Decisions as to whether builders should integrate the mill operations are difficult. The cost of mills is not great, but on the other hand, they tend to be a boom-or-bust operation. At various periods in the past, builders have been attracted by high milling profits or have wished to assure themselves of a guaranteed source of supply. Consequently they have actually purchased mills, or have become the sole selling agents for a mill, withdrawing the products necessary for their own use and selling the rest on the open market. The results of these operations even in the postwar boom period appear to have varied, and several firms have sold their mills.

The problem of reducing trade channels was a sore subject with respect to gypsum products, certain types of lumber, and many of the items purchased by trade contractors. Manufacturers in some of these fields refused to sell direct to builders under normal circumstances, asserting that it was unfair competition for their dealers. Chapter 9 will show that such restrictions apparently depend upon the amount of monopoly control in the individual products and were not important in most of the postwar period.

(4) The final cost reductions, though significant, are the hardest to ascertain and generalize. These reductions depend upon individual discounts which firms enjoy as a result of their purchasing power and bargaining ability. That such discounts exist and are important has been demonstrated by many studies, and examples were found to be exceedingly common in housebuilding. They are primarily a reflec-

tion of particular competitive situations. A survey by interview or questionnaire is, however, not a very effective method of ascertaining the amounts in question because price cutting of this sort may be considered illegal, unethical, or unfair. Neither the seller nor the buyer in such cases wants to publicize his special discounts; the former for fear of alienating other customers, the latter for fear of jeopardizing this good deal. From information obtained, however, it appears that such "deals" were not very prevalent in the more oligopolistic building-materials fields during the period studied. Supply and demand were sufficiently balanced to offset the necessity of offering special discounts. As soon as supply exceeded demand, special discounts did appear. Occasionally carloads of plumbing pipe sold at 5 to 10 per cent below normal carload levels, and though during most of the period prices were firm, this was true for most other items.

In the case of the more competitive items, such discounts (usually the result of special arrangements with small mills or suppliers) occurred frequently. If the contractor would pay cash and furnish transportation, it was possible at times for him to buy lumber and shingles far below the prevailing prices. Such an arrangement was common in flooring and paint and, when competition became intense, in hardware. Volume discounts were proof of a firm's bargaining ability and also at times implied the threat that purchases would be made direct from the mill or manufacturer. For example in flooring, medium-sized firms buying in large volume were likely to be quoted a price midway between the small buyer's and the carload price. During the period under consideration, the carload price ranged from 20 to 25 per cent less than the small contractor's price. Because of problems raised in attempting to justify these discounts under the Robinson-Patman Act, this type of arrangement did not usually appear in published price lists.

Certain qualifications should be mentioned in connection with the way purchasing changes with size of firm and the cost reductions obtained. The methods and results described here, though typical, vary from builder to builder. Some builders avail themselves of all the economies engendered by scale and some do not. As the size of the builder increases, so does his buying flexibility. A large builder may purchase through a regular yard if it will grant him quantity discounts, or buy from the same broker or wholesaler who sells to the retail yards. He may often set up building affiliates in whose names the goods are purchased, but who do little or no retail business. The affiliate is mainly used as a protection in case supplies become tight, or perhaps for tax purposes.

The builder may also buy directly from the mills. The particular channel he decides to use will depend on the amount of service he desires and his ability to make a deal. All channels are probed, and, though it may appear improbable on the surface, some of the lowest prices are obtained through retail yards which may take only a wholesaler's markup on large quantities and furnish them for less than it would cost the builder to perform these functions himself. Some builders will receive prices lower than those typically prevailing because of superior bargaining ability. Also, when a builder uses a purchasing subsidiary, the splitting of cost reductions between the two firms becomes an accounting and tax problem. The value of the reduction can be used as the builder sees fit and may not be fully reflected in the accounts of the building firm.

Furthermore, discounts sometimes are not net reductions in costs. If a builder purchases a carload of lumber or gypsum board, for instance, he must pay for unloading and transportation to the site. The direct expenditures of the builder which may derive from his assuming such functions as transportation, warehousing, and handling are included here as part of his materials costs. Estimates of indirect overhead costs such as additional bookkeeping or funds tied up are not included, since these amounts are slight and are accounted for as part of the total difference in overhead which exists between firms of varying size.

One difference should be noted between trade contractors and builders with respect to purchasing discounts. Discounts obtained by trade contractors depend not on the size of the contractor himself, but on the size of the job for which he is purchasing. Since a large trade contractor can work on jobs of any size, it might be expected that his materials costs would be the same no matter what size unit he was working on, but for various reasons, this is not true. For certain items, the diversity of small jobs is so great that no large quantities can be purchased, as for example, with paint or plumbing fixtures. With other items, the problem of distribution to individual lots is likely to eat up much of the potential quantity savings. When bricks, for instance, are shipped directly to a tract, it becomes worth while to purchase in quantities, since the distribution problem consists simply of unloading pallets at several adjacent houses. But it is not worth while for the contractor to buy a carload of bricks, stock them in his own yard, and reload for each individual job.

In some cases, a large subcontractor who saves through bulk purchasing does not pass this saving on to the small builder of individual houses, whereas he does give the large builder the benefit of his lower cost. This discriminatory policy is possible because his smaller competitors must pay higher prices for the same material. For example, medium-sized floorlaying firms paid $198 and small ones $224 for the materials they used in houses built by both small- and medium-sized builders. Since on the small jobs the medium floorlayers were competing with small ones who had to pay the higher price, they did not pass on their materials saving, whereas on larger jobs they did.

To sum up the effects of size on materials purchasing, it was found that in this realm firms achieved their most spectacular savings from scale. When a firm expanded from the small to medium category, a saving of $400 was made on materials, almost half of the total cost reduction realized by scale. A builder in the large class saved nearly $700 over the small in materials outlays, or about 40 per cent of his total savings. Moreover, it is possible that even greater savings in materials purchasing might come with further increase in scale. The largest firms in existence at the time of this study made greater savings than the average in their group and possibly could buy at still lower prices if their size expanded further. Since these possibilities are projections beyond the range of existing knowledge, their magnitude is not certain. It appears probable, however, that simply through increased size alone materials prices for the items purchased in this study might fall an additional 10 to 20 per cent (fig. 11 and table 51).

The above figures represent a true cost saving because the distribution system has been simplified. It is, in effect, an increase in efficiency resulting from innovations in supply channels. The large builder needs and gets less service, and, in addition, he can absorb items of lower quality than can be furnished to the builder of individual houses. This means that a new system dealing in somewhat different items is in the process of being established alongside the traditional materials distribution system.

Effect of Scale on Subcontracting Costs.—In general, the effect of increased volume on subcontractors' costs is the same as that on the costs of the original builder. The builder pays the subcontractor for an installed job, which must cover the subcontractor's purchases of materials, direct labor costs, and overhead and profit. As the size of the project increases, the subcontractor enjoys the same cost-saving possibilities as the builder, and in a competitive situation these savings will be reflected in a lower price.

It should be mentioned again that savings depend on the scale of the housebuilding project and not on the scale of the trade contractor. Until tracts become very large, there is no necessary relationship between the size of the trade contractors operating within the tract and its own size. Similarly, there may be no relationship between the size of the trade contractor and the size of the housing jobs he undertakes. In many trades, large firms do no housing work, whereas in certain others only a few large firms specialize in tract work. In many tracts, the trade contractors are small firms doing almost all their business in the one project.

The small builder of the individual house paid out $3,379 to his subcontractors for the typical house used in this study. This figure covered the subcontractors' payments for direct labor of $1,161 (34 per cent); for materials, $1,524 (45 per cent); and $694 (21 per cent) for overhead and profit. (tables 49–52).

Figure 11 shows the effect of changes in scale on the subcontractors' charges. It shows that the builder of a medium-sized tract paid about 10 per cent less for the identical work than did the small builder of houses on scattered lots. The large tract builder found his costs reduced by $722, or nearly 22 per cent less than those of the small builder, and if he was an extremely able bargainer, he may actually have saved somewhat more.

Of the amount saved by the medium builder, about $97 was due to savings in the subcontractors' materials purchases, $151 to more efficient use of labor, and $100 to savings on supervision, overhead, and profit. The large builder saved $259 on the materials purchased by his subcontractors, $217 on their use of labor, and $246 on overhead and profit.

Chapter 4 explained in detail the origin of these savings. The transition from work on scattered houses to jobs in tracts allowed the trade contractors to use their labor more efficiently, to improve their estimating and controls, to save on materials, and to cut their charges for overhead and profits.

A good example of the more efficient use of labor and of an improved system of controls which become possible with increased size is found in the schedule of the floorlaying contractor. The average labor time on a typical flooring job is about 4 man-days, or 32 hours. Yet men must go to each job at four different times. Allowing a half-hour for moving from one job to the next on scattered jobs, the total wasted travel time is two hours, or 6 per cent. Added to this, there will be extra unproductive time in loading and unloading, getting into the house, and getting acquainted with the job and its layout. In a tract, however, where the houses are adjacent to each other and the layout of the jobs is similar in the houses, most of this time will be saved. Furthermore, the builder can make certain that all potential savings are achieved by using better controls. Since the jobs are identical, it is worth while spending more time and money in establishing the proper rate of work,—this overhead cost will be amortized from the savings on all future jobs—and the rate can be more easily controlled. In addition, the knowledge that future jobs are assured makes the mechanics more amenable to working at a faster rate.

Passing over the savings realized by trade contractors in their materials purchases, which were discussed in the preceding section, we find that their saving on the final cost category—overhead and profit—is, percentagewise, the greatest of all. Although the absolute money saving accompanying growth in size is of about the same magnitude for this factor as for labor and materials, the percentage of reduction is much greater, running about 35 per cent as compared to a 17 per cent fall in materials costs and 20 per cent in labor.

In reality, the amount of cutting of overhead and profit may exceed the typical amounts shown. Discussions with individual builders indicated that when there is a great deal of competition among the trade contractors, the charge for profits falls nearly to zero, and overhead is also greatly reduced. Interestingly enough, however, the exceptionally low prices may not be available to the largest of the large firms, since these very low prices arise primarily from small trade contractors competing vigorously to obtain a large job. The largest firms cannot afford to take a chance on these small trade contractors who operate without overhead or much system. Their jobs are too big. They must have the assurance that the trade contractor will complete his work on time. Therefore, they frequently attempt to decrease their risk by paying somewhat higher prices to larger and better-established trade contractors.

Incidental Costs.—There is a final class of miscellaneous direct costs, mostly minor, which have been grouped together. Included are charges for permits, utilities, surveys, plans, and—most important—the charges for financing construction. The total amount of these charges is about $410 for the small builder of the composite house, or slightly more than 4 per cent of all costs.

Many of the items of this group are charged on a per unit basis; consequently, no saving is realized through increased scale. In others, such as surveys and plans, there may be variation with size, but the items are small, and important differences occur only when an architect is employed. In an architect-designed custom house, of course, plans and design are a major cost but usually are not assumed by the builder. On the other hand, small and medium operative builders cannot afford custom design. This is not true of the builder on a large tract job; if an architect is employed, his overhead can be spread so that custom design will cost no more than stock plans on the smaller jobs, and, as suggested earlier, his design may bring improved efficiency.

The principal differences in incidental costs were found in direct financing charges—that is, in the amount which must be paid for the construction loan on the house. Financing payments included the amounts required for title insurance, appraisal and recording fees, lending fees, and interest on the money actually advanced. They averaged slightly more than 2 per cent of the total cost of the house.

The advantageous position in financing enjoyed by the large builder has already been described. In addition to the benefits accruing to him indirectly, through land profits, ability to expand, and so on, he also profited directly through his ability to initiate a large volume of loans. The cost of a construction loan to the large builder averaged only about half of that to the small, the difference lying in the fees paid by the builder or the premiums paid to him. At various times, builders have collected as much as $300 per house for originating the loans. At such times, the builders' incidental direct expenses would have totaled zero—obviously a decided saving due to scale.

Effect of Scale on Indirect Costs

The difference between the direct costs of a firm and the price at which it sells its product is its operating margin. Figure 10 showed that these indirect costs rose from $741 for the small firm to $1,334 for the medium firm, and to $1,608 for the large. While direct costs fell with increase in scale, indirect costs rose by 117 per cent. The percentage of the total index going to indirect costs rose even more rapidly because the higher dollar expenditures in these categories were combined, for the larger builders, with lower expenditures in the other classifications.

For several reasons, explaining why indirect costs change as they do is far more difficult than analyzing the reasons behind the fall of direct costs. In the first place, though it is certain that increases in indirect costs accompany growth, the estimates of the dollar magnitudes of the changes are subject to a larger error than in direct costs. In the second place, because these values as they appear on balance sheets are not those required for economic analysis, dividing indirect costs into the basic components of overhead and profit is hard. Finally, a comparison of the values and services received by different firms for the sums expended is made difficult by the heterogeneity of the factors. It is hard to decide whether differences in the sums spent for overhead and profits reflect variations in efficiency or changes in the nature of the inputs purchased.

Overhead Costs.—There are really two questions to be answered in analyzing overhead charges. To the first—Does the amount spent change with scale?—the answer is, yes. To the second—Does the amount spent increase faster than the benefits realized?—the answer is not clear. Great variation is found in the overhead services to firms. Some firms cut direct costs by increasing overhead, as, for example, in replacing labor by expanding plant. In other cases, overhead increases the efficiency of the direct factors and thus reduces the amount paid for them; for example, improved organization may make possible a cut in the amount of labor used. Such considerations make it difficult to measure whether the efficiency of overhead changes with scale.

The importance of overhead costs in our modern economy is a familiar idea. Most discussions of decreasing costs and simplified explanations of the advantages of large-scale production assume that firms have falling unit costs because the charges for important indivisible factors, such as management and plant, are spread over more units as production increases. If no indivisibilities existed, all units could be produced at a constant cost. In addition, it is overhead (especially if it is truly fixed) that causes problems in slack periods. The costs of the overhead must be met, and if this cannot be done, the firm loses money. The size and inflexibility of the overhead, therefore, are important factors in determining risk.

Overhead costs are frequently defined as those which are common and cannot be allocated to individual units. They also tend to be fixed over quite wide areas of production. When a firm is organized, a decision is made as to the manner in which the overhead or management functions will be performed. The structure decided upon can then be used to handle a rather large number of units, but at certain levels, if production is to be further increased, revisions must be made to expand overhead.

We consider as overhead all costs of supervision above the level of working foreman, all office expenses, depreciation of equipment, selling costs, rent, and the cost of capital not borrowed specifically for the construction of a particular house.

In the chapters devoted to the small, medium, and large builder, a description of the organization and overhead costs of each type of firm was included. The overhead structure of building firms starts at an extremely simple level and never becomes very complex. Its cost in the smallest firms ran about 2.5 per cent of the total, and in firms completing between 10 and 24 houses per year it had risen to about 4.3 per cent. In medium-sized firms, overhead cost was approximately 5.2 per cent, whereas in the largest category it amounted to 8.0 per cent. The dollar expenditures at each size level were about $240, $410, $480, and $700 respectively. The problem of overhead in housebuilding is not so much one of the magnitude of these expenditures as it is of the value received. Charges for overhead and profits average only about a third to a half of those for many manufacturing industries (tables 34 and 52).

The small firm pays very little for overhead, but at the same time gets very little in return. Its equipment is simple. Its records are sketchy. Whatever time the owner can spare for management must be used only for the most vital functions. No time is available for planning and study.

The situation has not changed radically in the medium firm. Here, expansion allows a small amount of warehousing and, consequently, some bulk purchasing. An office is rented, taking the place of a desk in the builder's home. Slightly more equipment is employed. The owner spends full time on management and may have one or two assistants. These changes enable the firm to make some savings through improvements in the production process and better bargains in purchases.

Among the firms classified as large, great variety is found in the size and activities of the overhead organization. Their staffs range from 3 to more than 50 in number. Some firms possess only small yards and storage facilities, but others handle all their own materials. Some deal directly with mills for all purchases; a few even own and operate their own mills. Some have their own subcontracting affiliates, perform their own architectural and site-planning work, and maintain complex systems of production control. Others still operate in the simple direct fashion of the medium and small builders.

Are the extra costs of overhead a sign of more difficult management problems in the larger firms and therefore an indication of a lower efficiency in the use of this factor, or does the increased overhead save enough of other variables to more than compensate for its additional cost? It is clear that without a minimum increase in overhead large firms could not make the savings they do in purchasing and labor organization. In such cases, the change in the function of overhead brings greater returns; the increased charges pay for more value received, and there is consequently no indication of any fall in efficiency with scale.

More importantly, within the group of large firms with the highest overhead expenditures, the quality of services received from the overhead is often superior. As a result, these firms get more for their money relatively than the firms which have remained as simple as possible. This is true when the larger overhead goes to purchase management capable of developing skills and techniques hitherto neglected by most housebuilding firms.

Profits.—Problems also arise in attempting to analyze profits. Profits, being residual, cover payment for the activities of the firm's entrepreneurs but may also include unearned income arising through accidental circumstances. In considering the way in which costs vary with scale, we are interested primarily in those profits which are a necessary part of the cost curve. The synthetic cost curve for each size of builder should include only those profits received for essential functions and not those which were the result of windfall gains. At the same time, essential profits must include sums to pay for dynamic changes in the industry. They must not only compensate firms for their present effort, but also keep the industry alive and progressive. They must attract adequate capital and skills for future development. At present, the history of progressive housebuilding firms is too short to permit accurate judgment as to whether or not the portions of the existing profit level which appear to be windfalls in a static analysis are required payments for progress.

The median firm in the 1–9 class made net profits before taxes equivalent to 5.7 per cent of its sales volume. The median in the 10–24 bracket made 6.7 per cent. Both of these returns included profits in the normal sense but also compensation for the overtime work of the proprietors. Medium-sized firms averaged 8.5 per cent on sales, and large firms 10.0 per cent. In these two categories of firms, it is probable that, to avoid double taxation, the owners may have drawn amounts in salaries and expenses which overcompensated them for their actual managerial functions, and hence their profiits on sales may be understated. This, together with the fact that large firms were likely to have minimized their real profits by listing them with affiliated enterprises, indicates a sizable increase in profits as scale increased—even greater than that shown (table 34).

If these large profits were all essential for the efficient functioning of the larger firms, then is much of the apparent efficiency of large scale, as measured by direct costs, illusory? Is it true that most of the savings in purchases of the factors would suffice only to pay for the unearned profits needed to operate larger enterprises? What is the answer to the level of profits required by these larger businesses?

The answer should be geared to a number of requirements. Profits are required to pay a return on invested capital, to reward innovators, to attract skilled management, and to compensate investors for possible future losses. Such payments are real costs, and if they vary with scale, would change the efficiency of various-sized firms.

The increased profits of large firms were not due to variations in the amount of capital invested per unit of output; in fact, the opposite is true. Small firms have a larger investment per house produced than do large, and their return on net worth is less, rising from 13 per cent for the smallest to 20 per cent in the 10–24 bracket, 23 per cent in the medium classification, and to 30 per cent in the large (table 35).

Some of the added profits were certainly payments for innovations. The large builders made important shifts in the production function. Until these changes became widespread, the innovators made increased profits. Whether or not these payments for innovation were a necessary cost, they still tend to disappear if all firms use more efficient production functions.

The two final factors compensated for by profits may, however, require differential rates. Higher payments may be needed to attract to housebuilding skilled managements with adequate investment funds, and to compensate them for the additional risks that come with scale.

The small builder is attracted to the housebuilding industry partly for noneconomic reasons. Having been employed in it and being already familiar and at home in it, he naturally chooses to remain in it in his new status as a self-employed owner. He is willing to accept low profits, but does not contribute much in return. His participation is welcome, but he does not bring much management experience or funds—lack of which has been a major problem—to the industry.

Skilled managers with funds sufficient to operate large firms may not enter the industry if it offers only limited opportunities. At the same time, they supply needed services, an expansion in the scale of operation, and an accompanying decrease in direct costs. If they would not be attracted by the low profits earned by small firms, as appears probable, then some increase in the profit rate is a necessary condition for their entry and offsets the savings they bring in other costs.

The higher return of large firms may, in addition, be required to compensate for additional risks. If risk increases with size (as is discussed in the following section), then large firms must receive higher returns in prosperous periods, and these returns must be included in the cost curve.

It appears, however, that some of the differential profits were not of the required type, but were a combination of windfall and temporary monopoly returns. The tremendous surge of postwar demand clearly increased the profits of the entire housebuilding industry. Because of the way in which it made itself felt on the market, this demand resulted in greater windfalls for large firms than for the smaller. The big builders were the ones which could answer the demand of the mass market, the area in which the largest growth occurred. Until sufficient expansion could take place to meet all the new demand, those already in the market reaped windfall-monopoly returns.

Although this discussion of profits must remain inconclusive, it does appear probable that the existing profit rate overcompensated large firms during the period of this study. Many of them, in fact, stated their personal belief that this was the case. If so, the total amount of necessary indirect costs is overstated in the synthetic cost curves of the composite house. One may still conclude, however, that the increase in efficiency from scale is less than the reduction shown in direct costs.

Effect of Further Increases in Size

Large builders as classified in this study build 100 to 1,000 houses per year. To date, few firms have surpassed this rate. No radical changes in the maximum size or type of housebuilding firms have occurred in the postwar period. Although larger firms are more important than in the past, prototypes of existing firms could be found in the prewar period. No Bay area builder, and none elsewhere, has jumped into a new super-large or colossal class. Few extend into more than two or three local markets, and none has spread over wide areas.

The principal difference between the largest Bay area firms and the largest firms elsewhere is to be found in the size of the particular markets in which they operate. A few large firms in other areas have produced 3,000 to 4,000 units in a year. Such a production rate is simply due to the fact that they are located in larger metropolitan areas and have a more populous market to draw upon. Their share in their own markets is roughly the same as that of the San Francisco firms that produced 700 to 800 units per year, and their methods and techniques are also of approximately the same scale.

It is worth while to speculate on what factors have hindered the growth of much larger firms. Why does no firm in the housebuilding industry hold a position comparable to that of General Motors in the automotive industry? The answer depends primarily on the manner in which costs change as scale increases still further, and therefore it must be considered as part of the present discussion. If costs continued to decrease with scale, one would expect larger firms to develop.

The reasons already outlined for cost changes would apply as well to changes with future growth. If firms became much larger, some of their costs for the factors of production might fall and others might rise, actual variations depending on the specific magnitudes involved. The problem of estimating the effect of still greater scale is simply that of determining the shape of the individual cost functions at higher levels of production and again aggregating them. Such estimations require extending existing cost curves beyond the limits of present data—an extremely risky procedure, since a further change in the size of builders might so alter the organization of the building process as to render current data irrelevant. Still, because of the intense interest in this question, the risk appears to be worth taking.

Turning first to the probable effect of future growth on the items making up direct costs, it has been observed that even within the size reached by existing firms, few additional economies of scale alone appear possible in the field of labor or subcontracting costs. Firms of existing size have already attained most of the economies of scale related to production on a given site. When a firm builds in projects of 200 to 500 units, it employs as much specialization in methods as is now known to be efficient. When it increases its size beyond this amount, it simply duplicates the same procedures. More crews perform identical functions instead of new processes being added. This holds true both for direct labor and for that of the subcontractors.

Since increasing the size of existing projects is not more economic, greater efficiency with scale would appear to depend either upon greater advantages which would accrue to firms running many plants all of the same maximum size as now exist, or upon radical innovations which would change the whole organization of the production process and make larger plants more efficient.

As the size of firms increases and they operate more plants over a wider area, some additional economies of scale in the purchasing of materials appear possible. For some items, even the largest existing firms are not yet purchasing in sufficient quantities to obtain the greatest possible discounts; and in some, they are still forced to go through distribution channels that are not the most efficient. Further increases in size would improve their purchasing power and result in somewhat lower materials prices, estimated to be from 10 to 20 per cent less.

As to other direct costs, since the cost of incidentals (e.g., surveys, utilities, financing) is already close to zero, further increases in size would have little effect on them. In land, far from bringing about any saving, increased scale would cause costs to rise; for it becomes progressively harder to find good, unused land in tracts of the size required for large-scale operation. Even now, the largest firms usually build in several separate areas in an attempt to overcome this problem.

When all these direct costs are considered together, it appears probable that any additional economies of scale would be from 3 to 5 per cent. These savings would result primarily from more efficient materials purchases, since the other direct costs would, if anything, have a tendency to increase with further growth.

Does the sphere of the indirect-cost functions hold more promise for further efficiencies with scale? It has, in other industries where the most important efficiencies of scale have been brought about primarily through better management and more efficient use of capital funds. Contributions to efficiency have also been made elsewhere through the ability of extremely large firms to wield an effective influence on the over-all organization of their industry.

In housebuilding, the most promising increase in efficiency appears to lie in better management. Even the largest housebuilding firms have spent relatively little time on planning and working out their production process. They have done virtually no research work in methods, designs, or materials. Increases in size beyond present limits might facilitate these activities by permitting greater specialization in management and the hiring of more skillful men. Large firms in other industries have discovered significant economies through improvement in these lines, and it would seem that larger housebuilding firms might profit by following their example.

Larger scale might also give managements greater scope for their activity. In a dynamic situation, large firms can alter the existing technology, as well as conditions in the supplying industries, and the market. It has been the hope of many that increased scale might bring about a snowballing of more effective action along these lines. This problem is dealt with more completely in the final chapter. There is nothing within the present situation, however, that makes such changes appear probable.

If there are possible sources of greater efficiency to be found in increased size, there are also important inefficiencies which may accompany growth of firms. The four most important of these are loss of flexibility, increased marketing difficulties, production problems, and greater capital problems.

Housebuilding firms need both quantitative and qualitative flexibility.[1] Their total amount of output varies seasonally and cyclically; consequently, increasing their size and overhead will mean more unemployed resources and higher average costs when production is low. Qualitative flexibility is required (1) because the people purchasing houses have demanded variety at any given time, and if their tastes are catered to, many of the advantages of large-scale organization are lost, and (2) because there is a problem of reacting to changing tastes and styles. A firm organized to turn out a vast number of the same unit will find it very expensive to change if that unit suddenly ceases to meet with public acceptance.[2]

One of the most important advantages of existing firms may lie in their ability to react quickly to changing conditions. When fashion, techniques, and markets are in a state of flux, entrepreneurial decisions must be made frequently and rapidly. Small rather than large firms have a decided advantage here because the entrepreneur is less inhibited in his functioning. Examination of industries in which large firms fail to predominate shows that most turn out nonstandardized products in which this type of decision is important. Hoover sums up this factor as follows:

> In some businesses there are so many unpredictable variables in the production process (including procurement and distribution as well as processing) that the limits of ordinary human administrative capacity seem to be reached in a small enterprise operating only a single plant. Only a few enterprisers who possess exceptional abilities or have developed some relatively protected or stable line can operate on a larger scale.[3]

This quotation goes beyond the problem of flexibility and introduces the second limit to larger size, that of marketing. Houses are sold in a local market. They are attached to the ground; they meet

---

[1] E. M. Hoover, *The Location of Economic Activity* (New York: McGraw-Hill, 1948), p. 81; Committee on Price Determination, *Cost Behavior and Price Policy*, pp. 223–225.

[2] P. S. Florence, *The Logic of Industrial Organization* (London: Kegan Paul, Trench, Trubner and Co., 1933), pp. 42–44, 262.

[3] Hoover, *op. cit.*, p. 82.

with many prejudices and peculiarities of local taste and custom. These facts cause difficulties and high costs for firms entering a new market. The skills of determining suitable areas for new tracts, of negotiating for land, of getting necessary approval, of fitting the houses to local taste—these have not been systematized. They are arts, not sciences. Successful firms know their own areas and can meet such problems through their past knowledge and intuition. But when they enter new areas, their existing knowledge is no longer serviceable. They can obtain the necessary data with which to enter new areas, but it is costly and risky. Therefore, they have done so only when they intend to produce an important number of units in the new location. This is a major deterrent to increased size. Unless firms can enter many new markets on either a regional or national scale, their maximum size cannot increase far beyond that of existing firms.

The third deterrent to size is the fact that expanded production and entry into new localities may also be accompanied by production problems. New labor must be recruited and trained in the firm's methods. Particular traditions and customs in working methods, inspections, safety regulations, and the like, may force changes in the firm's basic production procedures. It may have to train new subcontractors and materials suppliers, or else persuade the previous ones to move into the new area. All these problems again mean that expansion is expensive and may lead to marked diseconomies of scale.

Several facts seem to indicate, however, that the limit set by marketing is more important than that of production. In general contracting, where the marketing problem does not arise, experience shows that firms can spread over the whole nation without significant losses of efficiency. It is the merchandising problem for houses that causes the main cost increases. Housebuilders do spread out when particularly advantageous marketing conditions are available to them or when they get an opportunity to bid on houses which are purchased in a block by the government. Housebuilders have bid on Army or Atomic Energy Commission contracts all over the country. They also have established new tracts far from their headquarters when the demand was evident and very great, as, for example, when a new defense plant moved into a certain area.

The fourth and final factor which may lower the efficiency and hinder the arrival of still larger firms is the problem of capital and profits. There is the question of whether firms can raise sufficient capital to increase their size. There is also the question of additional risks involved in expanded size, or, in effect, how risks affect the cost curve for capital. Thus far, all housebuilding firms have been personally owned and financed. The jump to any larger scale of production would require much larger amounts of capital, which would be difficult to obtain. The generally unsuccessful record of those builders in the 1920's who were able to issue stock and appeal for wider ownership would make it hard for new firms to attempt a public issue. This, in effect, means that firms face a capital limit or capital rationing.

After a certain point, capital costs rise either because of the need to pay higher interest rates for more risky borrowings or to offer especially advantageous terms to prospective investors. There is also a point at which the cost curve for capital becomes vertical, indicating a complete lack of further available investment funds at any price. This point would be reached quite rapidly by most housebuilding firms.

This capital limitation and the failure of so many large builders in the past are primarily due to the great risks inherent in the building industry—risks which would deter firms from expanding even if they could obtain additional financing. Even the largest firms at present still remain comparatively flexible financially. Their overhead is larger, but they have a very small amount of sunk capital. If they have to contract rapidly, they can do so. The larger they get, however, and the more spread out their work, the more difficult would a contraction become. It is almost certain that the amount of risk rises faster than size and thus becomes another diseconomy of scale.

The increase in risk is connected with the fact that large firms have a higher leverage ratio (ratio of assets to net worth) than do smaller housebuilding firms or firms in most other industries. If these firms tried to expand rapidly in size and maintained the same type of high leverage, they would be increasing their risks at an even faster rate. A high leverage ratio means that firms make higher profits in a boom, but also sustain greater losses in a depression.[4] Any great expansion, therefore, means sacrificing safety margins for the possibility of additional profits, and this fact may act as an important brake upon the desire of a firm to increase past a given size.[5]

[4] Steindl, *Small and Big Business*, p. 43.

[5] Cf. W. Fellner, "Average-Cost Pricing and the Theory of Uncertainty," *Journal of Political Economy*, Vol. LVI, No. 3 (June, 1948), 250. See also the excellent discussion of the liquidity-solvency motive in R. A. Gordon, "Short Period Price Determination," *American Economic Review*, Vol. XXXVIII (June, 1948), 271.

Even if greater efficiency could arise with much larger size, it is still uncertain as to whether such a change would actually occur. Most observers are struck by the close relation in building between the size of a firm and the personality of its owner. This may tend to make the optimum size indeterminate within rather wide limits. Housebuilders are not drawn primarily from a group skilled in management; many are happy to have achieved as much as they have and feel little desire to expand.

Large firms experience continuous pressure caused by the rapid rate of entry of new units into the industry. The personal drives and desires of individuals to be entrepreneurs may bring about actual negative management costs in some small firms, whose owners work harder than paid managers and take out very little in expenses. Competition from firms such as these may make it difficult for large firms to expand their management staffs, yet such an expansion might, if it took place, lead to far greater efficiency and much larger size. The growth of large-scale production is a dynamic factor.[6] It does not proceed in any simple manner. Cost curves are not continuous but may have several ups and downs. This means that if a more efficient scale did exist with much larger size, firms would not, on this account alone, break into the lower area farther along the cost curve; it might require some fortunate coincidence of circumstances to achieve it.

All these factors point to the conclusion that unless a new, radically different, and much cheaper method of production develops, it appears likely that, though housebuilding firms may continue to expand somewhat beyond their present size, they will not rise into the super or colossal group and will remain much smaller than major firms in other large industries.

Summary

Growth in the size of housebuilding firms, at least within their present size range, is accompanied by improvements in efficiency resulting from division and specialization of labor, increased bargaining power of the firm, and elimination of certain processes.

Division of labor saves costs because each man does a specialized task, repeating it at more frequent intervals. This permits more mechanization to be used, together with simplifications in the form of

[6] Cf. K. E. Boulding, "Proceedings," *American Economic Review*, Vol. XXXVIII (May, 1948), 165.

patterns, templates, and other measuring aids. Materials prices decrease because the large builder requires fewer services in the distribution of his materials, and also because his bargaining power is greater. Especially when there is competition either at the manufacturing or distributing level, he can obtain price concessions because of the desirability of volume orders. For the same reasons, a decrease in the prices of subcontracts also occurs with increased size. The trade contractor can save on his labor, material, and overhead costs when he works on a large tract. He is forced to pass on these savings because of the competition for such large jobs.

The cost of incidentals and land also decreases with scale. Financing is easier for the large builder. Since rates vary from bank to bank and from area to area, the large builder has an advantage in that he can spend more time exploring the financial markets.

Because design and land were considered as constants in the composite house index, no specific estimates of cost changes in these spheres were made. The discussion showed, however, that here, too, important advantages accompany increased scale. Better design can increase efficiency through lowering the costs of the inputs required. Ownership of large tracts by the large firms enables them to capture some of the changes in land values that are lost to the smaller firm.

While direct costs were decreasing, indirect costs rose with scale. Small firms are characterized by an almost total lack of any real management. They also attract owners who will accept a low rate of return on invested capital. These two conditions are not true of larger firms, which must have expanded management staffs in order to operate at all and which must offer larger profits to attract competent executives and adequate funds.

The net result (fig. 10) of these conflicting forces was that costs of the large builder (including his operating margin and excluding changes in land and design) were 8 per cent less than those for the small firm and 5 per cent less than those for the medium builder. If possible windfall profits made during this period are excluded and allowances are made for varying design and land, the actual changes in efficiency due to increased scale would range from 12 to 15 per cent. This is the amount that can be saved in the building of a typical house by a large firm. Such a house must be built in or near a tract and cannot include custom changes. Those desiring custom features and houses built on more expensive lots must hire a small builder and must pay additional amounts over and above these differences arising from scale. If they can afford such increased amounts, they may, of course, receive additional real value and personal satisfaction for their higher expenditures.

There is no indication that further important decreases in costs would occur if large firms continue to increase in size, unless further growth brought a complete change in the housebuilding process. Most of the direct costs approach their minimum point within the size of existing firms, the main exception being the cost of materials, which could continue to fall slightly. There is a drop in production costs at the site until production reaches a rate of two or three houses a day. After that point, additional economies are small, and the cost curve levels off with only a slight further decline as size increases.

Meanwhile, in opposition to the down curve in production costs, a point is reached where indirect costs turn up. As firms grow, they lose flexibility, which thus far has been vital in building. Marketing costs also rise. Housebuilding remains—and must remain—a local industry, and local markets are not limitless. A firm which arrogates to itself a greatly increased share of the local market will face added pressure of competition and higher sales expenses, which will shoot up as a power curve rather than rising simply in proportion to the firm's greater size.

The hazards of expansion are compounded not only with increased competition and marketing costs, but with increased capital risk. The larger the number of units under construction, the more dangerous become the possibilities of a decrease in demand, a shift in building cycle, labor troubles, supply difficulties, and so on. In theory, a very large firm might guard against labor and supply adversities by integration both vertically and horizontally. In practice, this effort is questionable because, though it might by-pass obstacles existing on the outside, it might also lead to too great inefficiency in operations inside the firm.

None of these cost changes takes place abruptly. The range over which the minimum cost for each factor applies is large. It is, therefore, conceivable that by husbanding their financial resources and improving their management and marketing organizations, the largest of existing firms could expand to four or five times their present size. Such an expansion would not, however, bring about any important changes in efficiency. A firm expanded to this point would still supply only about 2 per cent of the national market and would still be about the size of a small automobile manufacturer. The difference in potential size between these two industries and the contrast between housebuilding and others appear to follow directly from the nature of the products involved.

9

Effect of External Restrictions

There is a widespread belief that a major source of the high cost of houses today is a drain by outside forces exerting various forms of extortion. Critics subscribing to this belief hold that the first step in reducing building costs should be the removal of external restrictions. The business and professional press frequently gives voice to this idea, and it is the main thesis of *American Housing*.

Although few specific estimates of the amount of inefficiency caused by restrictive forces can be found, the impression is common that probably half or more of the cost of a house is wasted in this manner. As an example, a conference held by the *Magazine of Building* reported its belief that savings of from 20 to 40 per cent would result merely by removing a few of the chief restrictions.[1]

Each of the principal suppliers to housebuilding has been accused of specific restrictions which result in inefficiency. It has been stated that materials manufacturers and suppliers have engaged in price fixing to keep prices high and have thus reaped excess profits, at the same time avoiding the necessity of introducing new materials and techniques. They have enforced distribution policies to bolster established groups against efforts to reroute materials around them and have hindered the opening of new channels of distribution and the elimination of unnecessary steps. In short, their policies are said to have made impossible the most efficient and economical supply of materials to the house.

Subcontractors, it has been stated, have upheld and profited from the cumbersome system of materials distribution, and their resistance to the integration of building operations has resulted in severe sched-

[1] "Round Table Report," *The Magazine of Building*, February, 1951, p. 116.

uling problems, jurisdictional conflicts, wastes, and damage. Critics declare that the use of many subcontractors and the bidding system lead to a lowering of quality and to instability in production relationships in place of the efficiency that comes with familiarity and continuity of association.[2]

The widespread accusations to which organized building labor has been subjected by the general public are certainly familiar to all. The main complaint against the unions has been that they needlessly increase the cost of housebuilding by their working rules and at times by limiting output per hour directly. Their practices are said to lower the actual output of units of work per dollar, in a market where hourly wage rates are thought by many to be already staggeringly high. It has also been claimed that the number of different crafts and their high degree of organization lead to frequent strikes and jurisdictional conflicts. Rationalization of the building process is hampered, it is said, by the problem of craft lines and the desire of the workers to maintain the existing number of jobs per house. Finally, critics aver that the practice of making entry difficult into the building trades has lowered the general efficiency of labor and kept the average age of artisans higher than it would otherwise be.

Building codes and the policies of financial institutions cause wastes when they require an excess amount of materials and of labor. In addition, they impede progress toward the most efficient design. Codes also help in enforcing the restrictions initially imposed by various groups. Since wastes and restrictions in any given area of supply are supposed to reinforce those of the others, the cumulative effect of all the restrictions is said to be greater than simply a summation of each. It is believed that the effect of this cumulation is to freeze the pattern of the housebuilding industry in its local mold and to deprive it of the flexibility and growing space that an aggressively expanding industry must have. New types of producing organization, new techniques and materials, and alternative methods of distribution consequently have a hard time making headway, according to many critics.

The leading reasons advanced for the prevalence of these restrictive practices are: (1) Since each part of the industry supplies only a small fraction of the final product, it neglects the effect of its price policy on total demand. (2) The amount of insecurity in the industry has

[2] Colean, *American Housing,* chap. 4.

been so great that all its components are willing—in fact, eager—to sacrifice potential expansion for increased security.

The first type of action is explained by the principle of derived demand. Because a house is composed of several hundred items of material and types of labor, each supplier's demand curve is derived from—but is different from—the general demand for housing construction. Since each individual is concerned with his own demand rather than with that of the industry, each will take action which, though appearing best for himself, may in the aggregate prove to be worst for all.

For example, a supplier of a certain material may furnish 1 per cent of a house. By doubling his price, if his unit sales remain constant, he would double his revenue, but would increase the price of the house by only 1 per cent. This small price rise would not appreciably change the total demand for the product. The supplier's demand curve depends upon the possibilities of substitution of other products and the competition of other dealers rather than on the primary demand for housing.

If this supplier operates in accordance with the general principle of free competition and attempts to maximize his profits, he will pay attention only to his demand curve, since his actions are too slight to influence the total demand.[3]

Some suppliers may even go beyond the limits of free competition and enter into restrictive price agreements. Since the price at which they sell is so important to their own income but so insignificant a part of the final unit, why should they not combine with their nominal competitors so that all may obtain a higher price? This solution is made more attractive by the second force—the desire for security. In this connection, *American Housing* states:

> Restraints in housebuilding can be partially explained as efforts of the subsidiary groups in the industry to acquire stability and security that cannot be obtained from chronically weak and unstable management in a restricted local market. Each group strives to protect itself as best it can. But interests are diverse and alliances shift. Manufacturers of building materials strengthen themselves by mergers or mutual agreements. These, in turn, endanger the position of local dis-

[3] This problem of maximization is, of course, basically similar to the problem of large group equilibrium in monopolistic competition. See E. H. Chamberlain, *The Theory of Monopolistic Competition*, 5th ed. (Cambridge: Harvard University Press, 1946), pp. 74–94.

tributors, who consequently combine in self-protection. Subcontractors generally cannot individually resist the price pressures of distributors of materials on the one hand and of general contractors on the other. Hence they make intra-trade agreements. Finally, labor unions, faced with seasonal and sporadic employment, have often consented to act as the enforcing agents for restrictive agreements of subcontractors or suppliers in the hope of protecting their jobs and earnings.[4]

Finding the actual extent and effect of restrictions is of major importance in any study of housebuilding. If these forces cause significant inefficiencies, then the improvement of housebuilding requires the removal of the restrictions or the discovery of methods to circumvent them.

In this study of Bay area housebuilding, therefore, great emphasis was placed on scrutinizing these restrictions and estimating their total effect on housing costs. Previously there were no accurate data for this purpose. Careful examination of the plethora of statements on the subject revealed that few, if any, of them were based upon sound fact. It became clear that most estimates of losses due to restrictions were based on a few specific cases located in isolated cities, which might or might not have general application. For example, the problems of plumbing in Chicago, the use of wood in Denver, and of electrical installations in New York are cited over and over again. Is each of these situations found in all areas of the country? To establish the great loss of efficiency alleged, each of these conditions, and many more, would have to apply to every house built. Is this the case?

To answer this question, the external restrictions which the builder faced were examined in detail and an attempt was made to estimate their effect on cost. The study was based on the observed operations of builders and on their reactions to the groups with which they dealt, as well as upon specific surveys of each of these other classes.

The San Francisco–Oakland area is a good locale for such a study. It is one of the most highly unionized areas for housebuilding in the country. In many materials and service industries there is a long history of lack of competition, fostered in many cases by state laws aimed at reducing competition. Financial institutions wield a dominant influence on building. The area is split into at least 52 administrative

---

[4] Colean, *op. cit.*, p. 101.

units, each with separate jurisdiction over building. Only its codes, as we have seen, are atypical. They are probably somewhat more progressive than those in the rest of the country and may reflect benefits which other areas hope to reach in the next few years. But even this advantage is not an absolute one, since if one examined only the largest city in every metropolitan area, this region would appear no better than the rest.

It is possible that the results are less applicable to other areas than are most data in this study. Other cities may have different underlying situations. The particular time studied may also cause variances. For example, labor conditions differ greatly from what they were in the prewar period and may change still more in the future. During most of the postwar period there has been such a serious shortage of competent men in all trades that the unions have been less strict in enforcing rules and have maintained open rolls to qualified applicants, thus removing two important sources of friction from the scene. Contractors have been eager for men. With adequate labor and materials and as long as they paid no more than their competitors, they could make money no matter what the wage scale. The result of this situation is the common practice of paying above scale for efficient men, with the union scale acting as a floor. The labor shortage has also left building labor in an anomalous position with respect to the Taft-Hartley Act. Builders have not wanted to rock their profitable boat by demanding ambiguous rights. Rights to use certain materials, methods, and so on, theoretically guaranteed under the Act, have not been claimed. What might happen in a later, more competitive situation cannot be predicted from present circumstances.

Even taking into consideration possible divergencies caused by time and geography, it is believed that on the whole the following picture of inefficiency resulting from external restrictions is accurate for the Bay area, and that it reflects the situation in other areas more correctly than do most discussions.

Materials Distribution

Restraints in building materials can occur only if there is an absence of competition in a particular industry and then only if the housebuilder lacks sufficient economic strength to strike a fair bargain with the monopolists. Competition can be absent when a few manufacturers control most of an industry or when illegal price and distribution agreements exist among manufacturers or local distributors.

It has been believed that housebuilders have faced restrictions from each of these sources. Some materials had concentrated production, some were controlled by illegal agreements, and sometimes the builder's bargaining power was weak. Examination of the Bay area situation indicated that restraints currently existed only in materials having a limited number of manufacturers. In other materials, either illegal agreements were not common, or else builders had sufficient strength to thwart them. Furthermore, even in the cases where a few firms did control the entire output, the larger builders were still able to obtain reasonable prices.

At least two-thirds of the materials going into the house come from competitive industries. Large- and medium-sized builders are frequently bigger than producers in these industries. (For example, even the smallest of large builders uses more lumber than is turned out by 90 per cent of the mills in the country.) As a result, these builders could use their bargaining power to the hilt, could obtain rock-bottom prices, and could insist upon the most economic channels of distribution.

Although certain large firms in these competitive materials lines sometimes set up distribution policies which theoretically prevented the builders from obtaining lowest prices, their attempts were not successful. If there is enough competition, the builder with sufficient purchasing power will either refrain from dealing with such firms and will get his supplies from the smaller, less established producers, or special deals will be made allowing him to get approximately the same prices from the firms which theoretically will not grant them.

It is in the one-third of the materials supplied by industries with concentrated control that real problems arise. Since competition in these industries is either indirect or oligopolistic, the controlling firms can establish price and distribution policies that are best for themselves, but are inefficient from the consumer's point of view. Little is known about the true efficiency of these pricing policies. Prices in these industries are more stable than competitive industries in periods of either rising or falling prices. Whether on balance this is good or bad for the economy is uncertain.

More can be said about their marketing policies. It is argued, for example, that because of their market control, suppliers in these industries can insist upon unnecessary steps in the distribution channel, thereby raising the costs of materials. It is claimed that the prices quoted to builders do not vary with builders' size and that firms are forced to purchase through middlemen whether or not they require the services of these marketing groups. Those who believe that this constitutes a restraint state that prices should depend upon the quantity purchased and not upon the functions for which the purchasing firm is established. They say that a carload lot should be sold at the carload price whether to a dealer or to a builder. This point has been a subject of bitter debate, rising even into the realm of congressional investigation. No decision has as yet been reached.

Several industries have maintained that dealers' discounts are justified because a retail distribution system is necessary to handle the requirements of the small builder and the individual homeowner, and any attempt to short-circuit the system endangers it and constitutes unfair competition. Therefore, these industries established their discount arrangement on a purely functional basis.

In certain trades, sales are made by the manufacturer only to bona fide retail dealers. To qualify, dealers must sell lumber and building materials at retail. They must maintain and keep open to the public a yard, office, and sales force. They must carry sufficient inventories for a general public trade. In other industries, manufacturers have set up a firm distribution channel by agreeing to sell on an exclusive basis to a given wholesaler or to a selected group of wholesalers. When large builders approach manufacturers in industries where these practices prevail, they are referred to the dealer in their area, or the order may be accepted at the normal retail price with the difference turned over by the manufacturer to the dealer.

Builders and contractors hold that such a system is inefficient and needlessly raises the price of materials and therefore the final cost of the house. They maintain that when builders become large enough to purchase in the same quantities as the dealer, the latter's functions have atrophied and should be excised. They speak of any sums paid to the dealer on quantity-direct-shipment purchases as a rake-off or holdup paid without justification.

In certain instances this conflict is a semantic one. Some manufacturing firms do not set up any sales staff of their own, but prefer to delegate sales functions to a broker or wholesaler for an entire area. These manufacturers are usually not equipped to deal directly with purchasers. In such cases the earnings of the wholesaler are usually equal to or less than the amount the manufacturer would have to pay for his own staff. This kind of arrangement is common. Some firms shift back and forth between some such exclusive distributorship and their own branches. In these arrangements wholesalers have a true economic function which is not a waste.

Even if these distributors maintain rigid prices and are less amenable to bargaining pressure from the builders, inefficiency cannot be proved. Manufacturing firms in concentrated industries make their firm price policies effective by limiting their distributorships. The fact of limited distribution is not in itself a waste. It may even raise efficiency.

There are other cases, however, where the mill or wholesaler is equipped to deal with builders but still insists that the additional channel of a retailer be used. Most observers think this a less desirable state of affairs. In the previous example, the wholesaler's markup includes only minor profits, selling, credit, and bookkeeping expenses—usually 3 to 5 per cent—which could not be eliminated, no matter who performed these functions. In the second case, the retailers' markup includes payments for handling, storage, delivery, and other services not required by the builder. It is a much larger and more important sum.

Although this controversy has not been settled, it was a somewhat academic question during the period of this study. This was not true in the immediate postwar period, when materials were in such short supply that, instead of obtaining discounts on volume purchases, builders frequently had to pay black market prices. During 1949 and most of 1950, however, supplies of many items had become adequate. Builders reported that they were able to make quantity purchases of formerly short items at discounts approaching those of the normal dealer. These discounts were obtained in three principal ways: (1) Firms theoretically wedded to the idea of giving only functional discounts, in actuality accepted builders' orders under various pretexts. (2) Builders established or purchased building materials supply affiliates which met the definition of dealers and therefore were eligible to purchase at dealers' discount. (3) Approved dealers were willing to accept builders' orders for carload lots shipped directly to the builder's siding and on these to charge only a nominal (5 per cent) markup.

The results of these possibilities are reflected in the gypsum industry, where there is nominally complete protection of the distribution channel. The few large manufacturers state they will sell only to established dealers. Therefore, it might be supposed that all builders of whatever scale would have to pay the retail price. With adequate supplies, this was not true. In the period 1949–1950, medium-sized builders obtained occasional direct shipments and purchased others at a discount below that normally available to small builders. Average large builders received carload shipments upon payment of a nominal fee to retail dealers. The largest builders bought directly and paid the lowest price. Similar results also were obtained in the other concentrated industries.

The over-all situation, then, was one of active competition in industries producing the bulk of the materials for a house and limited competition in the others. In these latter industries, manufacturers do set price and distribution policies which might be inefficient for housebuilding. If the distribution methods are very inefficient, however, larger builders can secure relief. There is no clear indication as to whether or not the results of the remaining price and selling policies are wastes. It is probable that because of the large sector of supplies which is competitive, the total costs of materials are not unduly raised by restrictions.

SUBCONTRACTORS

Many popular assumptions about subcontracting—that it lowers efficiency, raises costs, and leads to instability—are contradicted by our study in the Bay area of the reasons for subcontracting and its efficiency relative to its alternatives. Building appears to be one of the many industries where vertical disintegration increases efficiency and lowers costs without lessening stability. The fact that most large firms have tried integrating various of the processes normally subcontracted but have usually returned to subcontracting them, is of great importance because it shows that the present prevalence of subcontracting is the result of a policy deliberately adopted by builders after testing alternative possibilities. It would seem, therefore, to be based on solid economic foundations of greater efficiency.

The logic of trade contracting has developed as follows: (1) Efficiency reaches its maximum under specialized labor. (2) Specialized labor reaches its maximum effectiveness when applied regularly on many units. (A carpenter who specializes in dry-wall installation is most effective if he hangs only gypsum boards and hangs them continuously.) (3) The problem of sustaining specialized jobs as well as the coordination of the movement of men among them requires special supervision, usually performed by the trade contractors. (4) The trade contractor further assumes the function of furnishing materials and certain equipment, since he can frequently concentrate purchases of a given item for many houses.

Given a need for specialized mechanics, the builder gains greater flexibility and a decrease in the problems of supervision through subcontracting. Large firms have a sufficient volume of work in many of the subcrafts to warrant hiring mechanics on a full-time basis if they so desired. Ordinarily they would be allowed to do this, though in a few cases union regulations require the purchasing or establishing of a specialized subsidiary. However, experience shows that hiring directly is usually not worth while. The average skill of the men available would be far less than that of the men working for subcontractors. A firm attempting to handle specialized tasks directly would find its cost for skilled labor running higher on an efficiency basis than that paid by subcontractors. This is because subcontractors, by working for many prime contractors, can maintain a steadier work load. They retain their most efficient men on a full-time basis and turn to the less skilled labor pool only in unusual circumstances. Even when new men are hired, the fall in average efficiency will be slight since it will depend on the ratio of new men to the total number of employees; and indeed such a fall need not occur at all since the temporary employees can be given relatively unskilled jobs. In contrast, since builders cannot guarantee steady work over any long period, they must reconstruct their specialized crews frequently, and so their entire labor force will be drawn from the pool of unskilled men.

The planning for and supervision of a large number of different skills and crafts can also be handled more efficiently by subcontracting. If the builder hires labor directly, it must be supervised. Most trade contractors charge approximately the same amounts as the builder would have to pay for his own supervisors. Furthermore, the subcontractors' supervision and planning are likely to be more effective. A Jack-of-all-trades will usually prove less efficient than a man skilled at one. In addition, the trade contractor has a ready-made profit incentive for cutting costs, which the builder would have to attempt to duplicate by some sort of bonus or profit-sharing arrangement.

These are the reasons for the existence of subcontracting. What, however, of the claims that the trade contractors raise their prices unduly by carving out private preserves from which they bar house-builders? Given the need for trade contractors, it is not surprising that they may attempt, like other businessmen, to combine to lower competition. Since entry into these activities is so easy that competition in most periods is extremely active, combines are frequently believed desirable by both the trade contractors and the unions.

The purpose of the combine is usually said to be simply assurance that all active contractors in the trade will use a sound basis for figuring their costs. It is claimed that with unrestricted bidding, those accepting contracts at less than cost, probably because of error, will skimp on the job, will attempt to correct their error through sweating their labor, or will go broke, causing losses to labor and suppliers. Although many of these claims are undoubtedly true, a serious problem exists, as was evidenced in the history of the NRA, in determining when restraints really correct existing evils and when they lead to monopolistic profits.

For any type of combination to be effective, entry must be restrained. This is why trade contractors have in the past attempted to control the issuance of licenses, materials distribution, or the supply of labor. However, although these potential methods of restraining entry may exist, their importance in the period of our study has apparently not been great. In almost all trades, competition was keen. In most, both materials and labor were fully available to builders.

Builders in this area state that the only instances where subcontractors have been at all successful in restricting entry into residential trade contracting for any periods have been in plumbing, electrical work, and lathing. The methods used have been primarily through control of materials supply or labor. Even in these instances, however, rather large numbers of trade contractors remain outside the trade associations. Where bid depositories exist, as for example in the electrical field, they are mainly effective on public or large commercial and industrial buildings. They do not apply in the housing market.

In addition, the large builder has the opportunity, if he desires, to set up his own firm in these fields or to take over an existing firm, thus placing himself beyond the reach of possible gouging.

The picture does change, however, when entry into a subtrade is limited or scarce materials are channeled through existing firms. The balance of power swings, and the big builder may no longer be able to obtain low prices through his wide bargaining power. The profits of the trade contractor rise sufficiently for the builder to attempt integration. In shortage periods, the quality of performance may fall so that the builder feels it necessary to control particular subtrades in order to guard against delay on his whole schedule. Some large firms in the immediate postwar period assumed additional functions for these reasons, but by the period of this study they had almost completely dropped them. Such functions might well be assumed again in a new shortage period.

The absence of integration during most of the period, even though it could have been present, leads to the conclusion that the subcontracting system flourishes not because the builders are its helpless victims, but because they have found in the vast majority of cases that they are better off using subcontractors than attempting to perform the same functions directly. The fairly low average markup to large builders of only 15 per cent, which must cover the trade contractors' cost of equipment, overhead, and profits, is an indication that competition rather than restraint characterizes the field. In addition, the relationship between a builder and his subcontractors is stable, with bidding the exception, not the rule. It thus appears that the subcontracting system does not lead to excessive costs either in efficiency or in stability.

Labor

The attempt to measure labor efficiency exemplifies the difficulty of ascertaining appropriate standards. Far different judgments would result if measurements were made against an absolute standard instead of a relative one. Because no absolute standard exists, however, the best that can be done is to settle for relative criteria and compare the efficiency of housebuilding labor with that of other industries.

It is outside the scope of this study to discuss or judge the aims of the labor movement in general. Such labor aims as union recognition, good working conditions, security, adequate wages, no speed-up, and premium pay for overtime are the equivalent of standards in other areas and industries, and are not treated here as sources of inefficiency, though they may raise costs. Rules that might be listed as restrictive are those which aim at unnecessarily increasing the amount of work, requirements that an excessive number of men be hired, jurisdictional conflicts, and attempts to keep wages above the competitive level by restriction of entry. It is often very difficult to draw the line between the two types of regulations. For instance, is the prohibition of incentive wages a method of halting the speed-up or of restricting output? Are the existing overtime provisions reasonable, or do they stem primarily from a make-work and share-work tradition?

The method followed in this study was first to list the restrictions most commonly attributed to unions, and then to check these by a survey of the unions' rules and practices. Information was elicited through discussions with both the unions and the builders. In addition to specific questions on restrictions, contractors were asked about their general problems and attitudes toward labor. Finally, all this material was put together by relating it to the costs of building the composite house.

Some method of summarizing various practices had to be found. Each of the twelve international unions and the approximately eighty-five locals involved in the construction industry in the Bay area has its own set of rules and regulations. Not only does each of these differ from the others on paper, but there are many variations in interpretation and procedures, and in the enforcement of regulations among locals and with respect to individual builders and specific jobs. It is usual, for example, to find that regulations are enforced with much greater thoroughness on commercial building than on housing. A potential restriction may apply in one union but not in another, in one local of a union but not in the adjacent one, to a particular builder or only to a particular job. It is important to keep in mind this lack of uniformity when making statements about labor efficiency, since the situation tends to be oversimplified in the minds of many. It is possible to find examples to support almost any view for or against labor efficiency, but it is erroneous to use isolated instances, as has frequently been done, to draw up a sweeping indictment. The effect of each type of regulation on individual houses and its total importance to the entire cost structure must be ascertained if a true picture of the situation is to be drawn.

Those rules and regulations which are claimed to be restrictive and to raise costs fall into six rather distinct categories, namely: (1) prohibitions against owners working with tools; (2) "upgrading" of specific tasks; (3) prohibitions against use of particular tools, equipment, and methods; (4) excessive jurisdictional requirements leading to conflicts and strikes; (5) limitation of output, and (6) constriction of entry. Every one of the unions can differ with respect to each of these conditions.

In the first case—the working on the job by owners and employers—regulations run from one extreme to the other, from complete freedom for the employer to complete prohibition. A good example of the first type is the bricklayers. A large number of masonry firms working on new houses consist only of the owner (who must be a union member) plus a hodcarrier. These firms specialize in work on fireplaces and are a major influence in the field. The carpenters, laborers, carpet layers, and teamsters also allow the owner to work, though they specify that only one owner-member of the firm can work, and usually he must belong to the union.

In the next group are the painters, plasterers, cement finishers, roofers, and sheet metal men. In these trades the employer may work on the job if he employs a journeyman to work with him. Finally, lathers, electricians, and plumbers have a strict rule against the employer's working with tools.

The reasoning behind these restrictions on working employers usually goes back to the union's fear of piecework or lumping of labor. It is claimed that if a man is allowed to contract simply for the sale of his own labor, there is no way of insuring against his accepting a job that will actually net him far less than the standard wage rate. Such competition would gradually erode the union scale.

The rule obviously has little or no effect on housing costs and efficiency except for the three unions which prohibit the employer from working at all. No matter what the regulations might be, single-man firms are not important in work on new buildings. On the other hand, we have seen that owners performing site labor and handling their overhead functions in their spare time make up the most common type of shop. In the three trades where the union forbids such action, isn't overhead raised unnecessarily? The answer is yes, but for small firms only. The net effect is primarily to strengthen the importance of medium and large firms in these trades. These larger firms start with a basic cost advantage in purchase of materials and use of labor. Small firms, to offset this advantage, must have a lower overhead. If the owner cannot perform overhead functions in his spare time, lower overhead is impossible to achieve.

It is probable that in any case the prevailing price for subcontracts would be that set by the medium or large firms who do the bulk of work, whether or not aided by such a regulation as this. If the competitive price would be set by the firm in which the owner is spending full time on supervision, the restrictions against small firms would have no direct effect.

These regulations do mean, however, that the competitive fringe of one- or two-man firms is removed. Smallest firms are restricted to the repair and maintenance field and can work on new houses only on a nonunion basis. This may account for the fact that it is in the three trades with this type of regulation that most complaints have occurred about lack of competition in periods of shortages. When the smallest contractor is not available for bargaining purposes, a competitive price exists only so long as there is competition among the larger firms. A competitive situation did exist during 1949 and 1950, but builders stated that it was not apparent during the war nor the immediate postwar period. They expressed fears for what the present and future crises might bring. This working rule and potential lack of competition were cited as among the factors leading to integration or quasi-integration of electrical and plumbing work, and as responsible for the complete absence of lathing in many units after the war.

The second problem is that of upgrading of work. This can take either of two forms. In one it is claimed that too many foremen (who receive a higher wage) are required and their work is too limited. In the other it is claimed that work which could be done by semiskilled or unskilled men must be done by journeymen. The question as to when regulations of this type actually become restrictive is most difficult. Unions enforcing such rules usually claim that they are necessary to keep up the level of skill.

It is fairly clear that in the aggregate the first form of upgrading is not important. Half the unions leave the hiring of foremen to the employers, though they do specify a higher pay scale when one is appointed. The remainder insist that a foreman be designated when there are three or more men in the crew. The amount of regular work the foreman can do is limited only in isolated cases. As a result these regulations do not increase costs in the majority of cases, though when they do, it can be extremely annoying.

Upgrading of work often involves an interdiction against the handling of materials by common labor beyond a certain stage of production. These instances are not numerous and, because of the nature of housebuilding, are not important in this industry. Most housing crews are too small to make it worth while to hire common laborers to do tasks in which upgrading is a problem. Moreover, in shops with permanent crews, these restrictions are overlooked and jobs are handled in the most convenient manner. Regulations of this type become more important (and will be discussed) when the question of innovations is raised.

Again, in the third type of restriction—prohibiting use of particular tools, equipment, and methods—actual cases exist only in certain trades. Unfortunately, the trades in which they may be most prevalent are those which bulk largest among the trade contractors on the average house—plumbing, painting, and masonry.

As examples, the plumbers, in addition to requiring skilled men to handle certain jobs, have also traditionally required that fabrication be performed on the site. This apparently has limited the amount of prefabrication and standardization on rough plumbing installations. A new agreement allows work to be done in shops or factories anywhere in the 46 counties of northern California, providing that the employees doing the work are members of the union and receive the union scale. This, for the first time, permits prefabrication for an entire area. Whether it will be used is still not certain, as previous agreements limiting prefabrication to the shop on the site are still followed. Under these agreements, the employer is allowed to introduce any tools or methods he desires. Most plumbing work for tracts is done through a form of shop prefabrication, but possibly, under the new rules, a standardized system could also be developed for scattered houses.

The painters' agreements also appear to include certain restrictions. The most common and important are those forbidding the use of spray guns and of brushes of more than a certain designated size (varying from local to local). The reason for these rules and the effect on painting efficiency have been debated vehemently for the past thirty years. Contractors in the area feel that the rule on size of brushes is unimportant. They believe, however, that some cost savings would be possible if sprays could be used.

Most other union agreements specify that there will be no limitation on the use of new tools and equipment. Whether this provision is followed is hard to determine. It is clearly followed in some trades, such as carpentering, where the job has become almost completely mechanized. In others, however, new mechanized tools have made an appearance but are not widely used. This is true of mechanical trowels in cement finishing and of taping machines for dry walls. It is usually explained that the lag is caused by the difficulty of training both the employee and the trade contractor in new methods. Both are slow to adopt innovations. The lag may also reflect an unwillingness of labor to work with new tools. It is not possible to judge from existing data whether the adoption of such tools or similar ones is being retarded by union opposition. A possible test of whether union opposition is responsible for lag in use of tools which have frequently received a big play in the press (mechanical bricklaying methods, for instance) might be an inquiry as to how extensively such methods have been adopted in nonunion areas. If mechanical methods are not in use outside the union's jurisdiction, they probably have simply been overpuffed and are not truly efficient, rather than being held up by union objection. One must distinguish between paper ideas and true innovations.

The fourth complaint against unions in the building field has been the claim that they are too prone to strike, and that a large percentage of their strikes is over jurisdictional matters in which the builder is only an innocent bystander caught in the middle of labor's own wars. As we have seen, however, in the postwar period, this has apparently not been true. The number, importance, and duration of strikes in building have been roughly the same as for other industries.

Of course it is possible for jurisdictional problems to be cost consuming and lead to inefficiency even if there are no strikes. A prime complaint of builders is the difficulty of taking workers into the jurisdiction of other locals of the same union. If a mechanic has to be paid a day's wages to do only a few minutes of work, this, too, will increase costs. However, on most housing jobs where these situations occur, the jurisdictional rules that are onerous are usually overlooked. As a rule, there is only one craft in a house at a time. The crews are small and have worked together. They do not stand on formality or trade rules, but get the job done.

The fifth point is concerned with specific limitation of output. This has been a controversial point for years, but one on which little information is available. Almost all union contracts have a specific ruling against limitation of output, and unions claim they adhere to this ruling. On the other hand, employers frequently feel that their employees could do more work if they wished.

All contracts give the employer the right to hire and fire as he sees fit. This is, of course, the main stimulant to efficiency. The mechanic must meet average production rates or lose his job. The problem is really whether or not these averages are held down by tacit agreements among the workers. Most feel that specific limitation does not exist, but that as a result of a general labor shortage, efficiency has fallen. Since men are not worried about getting another job, there is no great pressure to exceed the average rates unless bonuses are paid.

Related to this is the question of travel and show-up time. Employers hold that it is inequitable for them to be required to pay excessive travel time or for whole days of which the men work only part. The men, on the other hand, see no reason why they should go unpaid simply because the job is at some distance or the employer is too inefficient to arrange a full day's work.

The final major complaint concerns restricted entry. It has been stated again and again that unions have ignored the public welfare in regulating the number of workers in the labor market, preferring to keep low the number eligible for work so as to maintain high wages. Entry has been held down, it is claimed, by long apprenticeships, by high initiation fees, and by closing the union rolls.

The actual number engaged in construction in California increased by 108 per cent between 1940 and 1950, whereas the number employed in all industries was increasing by slightly less than 60 per cent and the total civilian labor force increased by less than 50 per cent (table 57). Obviously, the construction labor force expanded far more than did the general labor force. But in addition, during this period, the members of the trade unions in the building field increased by more than 350 per cent.[5]

At the moment, most unions are working under preferential union agreements. Under these agreements, employment preferences are given to members of the union, but if the union cannot furnish an adequate labor force, the employer may hire anyone he pleases. When this occurs, the man is usually required to join the union within thirty days.

All unions state that their rolls are open to new members. If a man is qualified, he has the right to join. Qualification in a skilled craft usually means four or five years' previous work in the field and either a testimonial of skill or a satisfactory examination.

The initiation fee and dues of the unions have not changed much since the prewar period and thus are relatively lower, since present wage rates are so much higher. The majority are set at $100, though some are as low as $50, and others require ten days' base pay, which could amount to $200. Normally, these fees can be spread over long periods by depositing an application fee of $10 or $20 and then paying 10 per cent or a similar ratio of earnings until they are cleared. The rates are not likely to exclude mechanics seriously wishing to join.

The area has a very active apprentice program. Under state aid, it is run by joint committees of the contractors and the unions in each trade. The apprenticeship agreements are formal, outlining the topics to be covered, the hours of specific types of work to be accomplished, and the amount of formal schooling required during the apprenticeship period. There are more than 3,000 apprentices in the Bay area in the building trades, compared with no more than 200 in 1940.

The training periods are still long. They average four years in most trades, with a proviso that a year can be eliminated if sufficient skill is demonstrated by that time. Many claim that this amount of time is far too great in proportion to what is actually learned. It is also felt that even the present number of apprentices is not sufficient to furnish the number of journeymen required for replacement and expansion in these trades.

This brief survey has shown that some of the complaints against labor inefficiency appear justified. Many of the specific charges can be

[5] Department of Industrial Relations, State of California, *Union Labor in California, 1940–1949* (Sacramento: State Printing Office).

proved in individual cases. Some unions do prohibit owners from working with tools; some require an excessive number of foremen; some prohibit use of the best tools; the apprentice program is long; piecework is not allowed. On the other hand, the number of strikes and of jurisdictional conflicts has, at least in the postwar period, been greatly overemphasized. When restrictions of various kinds do apply, they usually apply only to two or three of the twelve crafts. The number of men who have entered the industry and the unions has been large compared with the general increase in the labor force.

The attitude of builders toward their labor reflects the accuracy of the above observations. In addition to the specific problems which have been discussed, builders were asked for more general comments, with questions such as: How are the firm's relations with unions? How often do unions check work? Do working rules hinder operations? How does the firm rate the efficiency of its men? What are the chief problems? Would the firm like to make any changes in its method of operations? In what manner is the firm affected by restrictions? The general organization of the labor force was brought out through questions on turnover, methods in hiring, and so on (Appendix D).

Builders had few complaints against working rules or restrictions in the two unions (carpenters and laborers) whose members they hire themselves. More than 95 per cent of the firms replied that their relationships with these unions were good. The small percentage that had difficulties was concerned primarily with jurisdictional problems. Both the carpenters and laborers pride themselves on stressing increased efficiency, on having no rules against power tools, new methods, or the like. The builders were aware of this, but they did complain that the average mechanic was not worth the rate he received. The war and postwar carpenters' boom brought in many relatively unskilled men. (In this area, they are spoken of as "men from the shipyards.") A comparison of efficiency wages in the postwar and prewar periods showed why owners have been driven to distraction. It was not evident, though, that their complaints were any louder than those of employers in other industries. The condition reflected a seller's market for labor—a fact implicit in the familiar statement that all that is needed to improve efficiency is a 10 per cent unemployment rate.

In general, the trade contractors' reactions followed those of the builders, though they were not as satisfied with their labor relations as the builders were. They dealt with a multiplicity of crafts and unions and, as stated, the number of rules is great. Complaints about cost-increasing restrictions were more common among trade contractors, though they varied from craft to craft.

The relation between builder (or trade contractor) and mechanic differs somewhat from the popular idea. Basic labor skills were likely to vary with the size of the firm. Most small builders (60 per cent) maintained their same crew constantly. They felt that these employees were skilled; they were used to working with them, and they attempted to give them steady work. It was not a case of calling the union and asking them to send out available men for a day or a week. Even when they did not keep the same crew constantly, most contractors were able to hold their best man or men. Only about 15 per cent of the small firms changed their crews after each job or group of jobs.

This stability of the working relationship was important. With small crews, many were willing to perform jobs normally falling under other jurisdictions. When the men would not do these jobs, the owner frequently did them himself. This eliminated a problem which could become troublesome and expensive if it entailed hiring a special mechanic for some small job. The ability to disregard craft lines was simplified by the fact that with adequate work, unions checked the jobs of small builders only infrequently. About half the small builders reported that the job was rarely, if ever, visited by union business agents. One-fourth stated that such visits did occur occasionally, and the other one-fourth had rather frequent contacts with one or the other of the unions.

Larger projects were much more closely supervised by the unions. The informal breaking of rules common on small jobs was no longer possible. As many builders stated, when one gets 10 or more men on a job, someone carries the working rules in his pocket. Then crafts have a steward on each job, and his relationship with the management becomes more formal, since he goes more by the book.

All contractors also believed that they might solve part of their problem if it were not for the unions' restrictions on incentive wage plans. In many nonunion areas, mechanics are hired on a piecework basis. This, it is held, eliminates the question of inefficiency. The unions, however, forbid piecework on the traditional grounds that it leads to a speeding up which is disastrous for the workers' health and welfare. Unions claim that builders have the right to fire anybody not putting out a full day's work; they are at liberty, further, to hire anyone more efficient, who will then be taken into the union. In addition, builders can, and many do, pay for efficiency, though bonuses must not be based on piece rates.

Another practice to which the builders objected was the charging of very heavy premiums for overtime. They claimed that the current system, which calls for time and a half for the first four hours of overtime with double time for the remainder, Saturdays, Sundays, and holidays, was wasteful. They stated that the stress on the short five-day week was a carry-over from the period when jobs were short and that it had nothing to do with health or welfare needs. With the shortage having become one primarily of labor, builders would like to have Saturday pay revert to time and a half with double time prevailing only after a certain number of extra hours.

In addition, small contractors complained about jurisdictional conflicts between adjacent locals of the same union. (As an example, the laborers' union in one county has been unwilling to grant working permits to men from locals in the adjoining ones.) The regulation in this matter varies from union to union. Some have no restrictions against men from other locals, whereas in many, complete freedom of transfer is permitted only if the local cannot meet the demand. Others permit only 50 per cent of the men on the job to come from outside the area, and some allow only the foreman to be brought in. With small, closely knit crews especially, this need to add men from outside the home county could become a decided hindrance.

The problem of weighing the validity and quantitative importance of these various claims is extremely difficult. It is clear that the main question is that of the average efficiency of men receiving the union scale. Are they less efficient than those in other industries? Could their efficiency be improved by piecework without causing a speed-up? Is existing inefficiency the result of poor management, poor workers, or poor union regulations?

Measurement requires a shift from the theoretical discussion of labor costs to an examination of the costs attributable to various kinds of labor and the restrictions which affect each. This shift can be accomplished through use of the composite Bay area house which was developed for the purposes of this study and which has already been discussed. It is important to know the relative importance of the crafts in the total labor picture in determining the effect on efficiency of their union regulations. Obviously, even if a trade near the bottom of the list is completely inefficient, it adds only very little to the cost, whereas any cost-increasing rules instituted by the carpenters or painters would have a significant effect.

The carpenters received $1,372 out of a total labor bill of $2,646 paid by the small builders, or slightly more than half the total wage bill (table 50). The painters received 14 per cent of all wages, the laborers 10, the plumbers and masons 7 per cent each, the electricians 3 per cent, and all the remaining crafts received slightly more than 7 per cent.

It has already been stated that few, if any, restrictions were imposed by the carpenters and laborers. The earnings of masons, who were primarily self-employed, were directly related to their own effort and efficiency. These crafts accounted for 69 per cent of the total labor cost of the house.

It is probable that a slight increase in efficiency of the direct labor would result if all restrictions were removed. Some increases may, of course, occur as time passes and the vast number of new men become adjusted to the new trade. On the other hand, even under the existing system, the most efficient of the large firms have been able to reduce their direct labor cost to about 8 per cent of the final price. These are organizations which, because of their size, must adhere strictly to all union regulations. Considering the large amount of work done on the site, it is difficult to imagine any significant reduction below this level. Failure of other firms to obtain equal efficiency might well be attributed to their failure to adopt the best possible procedures rather than to union restrictions.

Thus, the problem of labor restrictions comes down to a question of the severity of their effect in the remaining trades employed by the subcontractors. The total wage payments to these eight groups vary from $819 in the small builder's house to $687 in the large. Several of the unions do seem to have rules and regulations which many outside observers believe restrictive. What proportion of their total wages can be ascribed to restrictive regulations and how much would they receive if their tasks were done under the most efficient conditions?

Although this whole subject is one of conflicting testimony, it does seem important to set some outside limit to the possible extent of inefficiency imposed by these external factors. Failure to do so leads to probable overemphasis.

Ascribing one-third of the total amount received by these trades to union restrictions would be a high estimate and more than adequate to cover the true situation. Eliminating this proportion for these trades would mean a possible saving of from $230 to $275 per house. In addition, it is possible that even the other three trades against whom no complaints have been made do have some restrictions which lead to inefficiency. Assuming that these are from 10 to 20 per cent, and eliminating this percentage for these three trades, would mean a further saving of $100 to $250, depending on the size and efficiency of the individual builder. Adding the two estimates, to account for possible wastes in all crafts and all labor costs, it would appear that a maximum estimate of labor inefficiency would run from $330 to $525 per house, or from about 3.5 to 5.0 per cent of the total cost.

Local Governments

Although there are several possible areas of conflict in interests between builders and local government units, the principal governmental constraint upon builders occurs in the sphere of building codes. It is widely believed that unsatisfactory building codes cause houses to be built inefficiently; that the builder is forced to use poor designs or to waste materials and labor. If the codes were changed, it is held, important sums could be saved.

This problem of building codes breaks down into three parts: (1) Can good basic uniform codes be prepared with the existing technical knowledge, and can they be as efficient and practical as possible? (2) Given good basic national codes, are they adopted locally? If not, how do local codes compare in costs with national ones? (3) How well are codes administered?

The first of these questions is probably the most important, but it is outside the scope of our study. There is widespread dissatisfaction with codes throughout the country, particularly because of the belief that they require too much structural strength. Sufficient data to judge the validity of these opinions, however, are not available. There is very little knowledge as to what a good building code should or should not include.

About the only thing on which general agreement can be found is that building codes are necessary. For lack of a better standard, therefore, in judging performance, in this study the uniform national codes are accepted as adequate but not excessive in protecting health, safety, and efficiency. Of course, to the degree that the uniform national codes are poor and inefficient, so, too, is their local effect. This is a sphere where more efficiency may be brought about through greater technical knowledge.

If, however, the level of knowledge embodied in the various uniform codes is accepted as a standard then the question arises as to how the Bay area codes compare with this standard. Chapter 6 pointed out that almost all Bay area localities adopted the uniform codes by reference. Adoption was without amendment in areas where one-third of the houses were built. Amendments were minor in areas where half of new housebuilding took place; in the remainder, somewhat greater restrictions applied. The problem, then, is one of ascertaining the potential wastes caused by these variations. For this purpose, a comparison can be made with the uniform codes, even though it is recognized that some of the local variations may actually be justified. So far as this is true, the following discussion actually overstates the amount of waste and inefficiency.

In discussing wastes, it is important to differentiate between wastes of specific items and inefficiencies in terms of total inputs. Certain codes may be relatively wasteful with respect to a given material, all materials, or labor, but they may still be efficient in cost terms. The latter is our concern here. Do codes increase the inefficiency of building by raising its costs? The problem of wastage of materials is far more complex than is the problem of economic efficiency. Certain codes may require use of the same material but in different sizes, as, for example, 4-inch pipe instead of 3-inch. In this case, a direct comparison of the excess amounts required by the more restrictive code is possible. In other cases, however, if codes require different materials, the attempt to relate them directly makes no sense unless some outside criteria are established. For example, on a cost basis, a code that requires galvanized steel pipe for water pipes is restrictive because the total cost of such an installation is somewhat greater than one made with copper. If, however, it is desired to save copper as a critical material for defense purposes, obviously the code would be justifiable.

Another factor to observe is that since metals are relatively cheap, large savings in materials may have little or no effect on cost. It is impressive to say that if the electrical codes in this area requiring rigid conduits for service entrances were amended, the total amount of steel required would be cut by 50 per cent. It is somewhat less impressive to say that as a result of this change, the total savings for all units built in the San Francisco Bay area in a given year would be about 50 tons of steel. Perhaps even less impressive is the statement that such simplification would mean a saving in the cost of the electrical installation in a house of between 1 and 2 per cent, and that the saving in the total cost of the house would be between two and four hundredths of 1 per cent (i.e., 0.0002).

An illustration of the effect of code amendments may be found in the code for San Mateo, a small city on the peninsula south of San Francisco, and the area with the most amendments to the building code. Relating the changes its code requires to the typical house used in our study, it was found that the effect would be to require the foundation of the typical house to be increased by 6 inches and to require ratproofing. The stucco variant of the typical house would also be required to use either wood or composition sheathing instead of stretched wires. These restrictions would raise the cost of the typical house by something less than $100 for the first items and something less than $250 with the special sheathing. These figures are representative of the largest increase in costs resulting from the most restrictive building codes in the area.

Similar minor differences were found with respect to the electrical and plumbing codes. The two main electrical codes in use resulted in variations in total installation costs for the typical house of between two and four dollars. In fact, because of the rough estimating system used by most electricians in scattered houses, it is probable that there would have been no difference at all in quoted prices. The most restrictive code in the area might have required about a $10 cost increase, but this would be extreme.

The facts with respect to plumbing are the same. Although the code variations were more numerous, plumbers in the area stated that the differences they made in the cost of building were nominal. In one or two areas, costs may have been increased by $25, or about 3 per cent of plumbing costs. But since some of the rural areas with a large amount of tract housing have had less stringent requirements, total costs for the area were probably slightly less than those which would have prevailed if all had adopted the uniform code.

In summary, in houses built in the localities where the uniform codes applied without changes—some 33 per cent of the total number built in the area—no inefficiency could be charged to the restriction of codes. Fifty per cent had their costs raised by less than 1 per cent for the typical house through code alterations. Even in the case of the final 15 to 20 per cent, where greater code restrictions were in force, the increased costs did not run more than 3 per cent above the uniform code areas.

The final question concerns the administration of codes. Are delays incurred as a result of the necessity of obtaining permits or inspections? Are inspectors arbitrary in their interpretations so that procedures which would be allowed in most areas are banned under the identical code elsewhere? Finally, what about the possibility that costs will be higher because of the necessity of working in areas with different regulations?

Although some instances of delays and arbitrary rulings were reported, most builders in the area stated that neither was of any consequence in the total cost of the building. Between 5 and 10 per cent of the builders reported that they had occasional difficulties in obtaining inspections on time or in having their plans approved, but the remainder said any delays or problems were unusual. They pointed out that they had worked with the various inspectors over long periods and that they knew what was expected. Occasionally, a new inspector might raise some question over what had been traditional methods, but these were usually ironed out amicably without serious delays or expense.

Part of this satisfaction may, of course, simply indicate that the average builder was not an innovator. He was building a house in a traditional manner, familiar both to himself and the inspector. When a new design was desired, the first one or two units might require discussion with the inspector and perhaps a few small adjustments, but these played a minor part in the over-all picture. What would happen if radical innovations were attempted cannot, of course, be predicted from previous experience. The average builder has not desired to make any startling changes, and, therefore, the administration of codes has not been a problem.

Difficulties which might have been expected to arise when builders and trade contractors worked in various localities under separate codes and inspectors were not important either. This follows from the fact that builders and trade contractors, being small on the average, usually operated in only a few localities. Factors other than codes localized work.

Because of this pressure toward localism, a trade contractor normally will not leave his usual neighborhood for a single job. He will enter a new area only if he intends to do a fair amount of work there or to undertake a tract or a group of houses. In this new location, some problems of code interpretation may exist for the first job or two. After a few jobs, however, he will have adjusted himself to the new code and administration.

The difficulties encountered in working under two or three separate codes were irritating, but most firms agreed that the problem is usually so minor that it does not enter into cost estimates.

Under this heading of administration and differences between localities, it may be said that codes are an important factor to builders only if they expand their operations into new areas covered by different codes than the ones under which they have previously worked. But even in this case, as firms increase in size and acquire large tracts in the new area, the problems raised by the new codes quickly lose their importance. It is necessary and worth while for such builders to become familiar with the codes in the new area, but the differences are so slight that it is not necessary for them to undertake expensive studies or make costly errors.

In the Bay area, at least, the restrictive effect of codes has been greatly overemphasized. Less than 1 per cent of the money spent for housebuilding was attributable to known code inefficiencies. It must again be stressed, however, that this estimate does not take into consideration possible improvements in the national uniform codes, the efficiency of which it is not possible to judge in this study.

The Efficiency of Financing

The actual sums paid out by builders for financing the construction of their houses constitute the least important of the factors which make up the cost of a house. Before the imposition in 1949 of service charges on borrowers, the financial charges against the house were only about

1.5 per cent of the selling price. Some then doubled or, in extreme cases near the end of the period, tripled, reaching a high of 4.5 per cent of the selling price; but the average went up only to slightly more than 2 per cent.

These costs, which include title insurance, appraisal and recording fees, as well as interest on the money actually advanced, were rather high compared with interest rates paid in other industries; however, there are several elements which differentiate housebuilding loans from other industrial loans. The builder was able to borrow larger amounts with less equity than most other industrialists, a fact of great advantage to him since his business was more risky than most. His high costs were incurred so that firm liens might be placed against his property under construction, giving a great deal more security to the lender than notes secured only by the firm's general assets. If the builder had had to increase his equity, he might have had to offer returns far larger than the interest payments, or again, he might have found it impossible to expand at all.

For these reasons, the fact that the builder's rates are high compared with those of other industries does not necessarily imply inefficiency. The cost of borrowing was not a main factor affecting his efficiency, but the conditions imposed on him by the lenders and his relations with them, particularly with the Veterans Administration and the Federal Housing Administration, were important. His encounters with the regulations of these agencies were frequent and complicated.

More than half the builders in the Bay area reported difficulties in dealing with the Veterans Administration and the Federal Housing Administration which they felt raised costs or lowered efficiency. These problems are of two types: (1) those of purely procedural nature, and (2) those involving rulings and interpretations.

During the spring and summer of 1950 when the interviews for this study were conducted, the outstanding complaint of the builders concerned a procedural problem—the processing of applications. During this period, the government agencies had some of the largest processing backlogs in their history, and processing periods exceeded two months and, in some cases, extended to four or more. This was a serious handicap to builders.

The period of processing affects building methods and costs at two main points. The first is in the timing of the starting dates for individual projects and units. The builder must have a firm or conditional commitment before he starts work. If this is delayed, he may have to break up his organization, have his overhead continue uselessly, and then build up his labor force *de novo*. Such a situation was apparently not uncommon during this period. Resources were wasted and costs increased. The second impact of processing delays hits the builder who is awaiting the return of his equity funds. After a house has been completed, a builder has equity tied up until the sale is concluded and he receives payment. His equity funds are then freed for a new project, and, at the same time, the borrower begins to meet the interest payments. When the processing of purchasers' applications is delayed, completed houses stand vacant until the applications are approved. The builder has the choice of slowing up the construction process or allowing the vacancies to exist. Either is obviously inefficient and wasteful. If the delays average two months beyond the normal period, the waste might easily add $100 to the cost of a house.

Another difficult procedural issue primarily concerned the small builder. This involved methods of filing plans, making corrections, and so on. It appeared that large builders, who had men specializing in handling their applications for financing, were not bothered by such mechanics. Smaller builders had difficulty meeting the processing requirements. When their applications were rejected for procedural reasons, they were bewildered as to what steps to take.

The second main type of problem, concerned with the method and content of the rulings and interpretations made by these agencies, is even more important. A sizable percentage of builders believed that current appraisal methods lowered the efficiency of building and led to higher costs and lower value for the ultimate consumers.

The problem is actually one of design. Do the existing appraisal methods lead to the most efficient methods of design in the sense that the purchaser gets the maximum value for his housing dollar, or do they penalize good design by lowering the return to the builder who puts better value in his products?

The builders who objected to present appraisal methods stated that they believed the net effect was to lower the quality and value of housing and also to block any innovations that builders might wish to make. It was generally believed that appraisals were based upon a standard minimum house, similar to the typical house of this study. As long as a builder constructed a minimum house of this type, he had smooth sailing; any deviations would cause difficulties.

Appraisals made no allowances for higher costs resulting from differences in quality. Therefore, builders furnishing above-minimum quality would either have to absorb cost differences or attempt to sell houses with larger down payments. Since quality was not credited in appraisals, the small builder either had to lower his standards or restrict his operations to higher-priced houses. Traditionally, most small builders have specialized in higher quality units both in materials and workmanship, but many were forced to lower their standards.

A cursory examination of appraising and inspecting methods of government agencies indicates that these criticisms are probably valid. It was extremely difficult to judge quality either by plans or during construction in the rapid inspections made by these agencies. Appraisals were made on a purely quantitative basis. Builders recognized that in the type of market that has existed, in which sales have been based primarily on monthly and down payments, any who priced above the appraisal level were penalized. As a result, there is evidence that the minimum standards tended to become the maximum.

The still more complex problem of innovations in design has received some national attention but no adequate solutions. The Federal Housing Administration has traditionally followed the line that any innovations must be appraised from the viewpoint of a conservative financial institution. Since any innovation obviously is more risky from this vantage point (even though it might be less so from the viewpoint of general government policy), it must be given a lower appraisal. This means that any changes in design away from the conventional standard minimum house have been penalized.

Designs that might either lower the cost of building or increase the value of a house have led to lower appraisals. When a firm has slight tendency to change, the conservatism of financial institutions makes little difference. When it is intent on innovations, it may resort to great effort and adroit maneuvering and pressure on the government's financial institutions. The most serious effect will be felt among those firms in the middle, who might occasionally have been willing to attempt something new but who have been deterred because of this financial pressure toward greater standardization. As a result, design has probably lagged behind its normal rate of progress.

The Net Effect of Inefficiencies in Factor Supply

This discussion of inefficiencies imposed on the housebuilder by outside elements has been limited to a consideration of the problems and relationships existing within the present framework of the industry. It is possible, of course, that efficiency would be increased by alteration of the entire organization of the building process, and that inefficiency is increased by the inability of housebuilders to change the make-up of the factors going into their product. Perhaps the inflexibility of each factor reinforces that of the others so that the whole is much greater than the sum of its parts. Although such a possibility exists, the next chapter indicates that it is not a strong probability. The total effect of restrictions in the factors of supply does not appear to exceed the aggregate of the impacts of the respective factors. Therefore, a simple addition of the restrictions as they have been shown to exist gives a fair indication of their total effect.

The most important point, observed repeatedly in each area of potential restriction, is that results will vary with the times and even more with the state of supply and demand for materials and labor. Thus, with adequate available supplies in both materials and subcontract prices, the large contractor paid no excess costs. He was able to get a competitive price. Only when shortages occur is the builder forced to go through high-cost channels.

The small builder bought his materials from retail dealers and did not enjoy the bargaining power with trade contractors possessed by the large builder. This might raise materials prices and the cost of a few subcontracts. There is no indication, though, that either of these groups in this area was less competitive than business as a whole. In fact, the contrary is probably true. A larger percentage of items going into a house is probably produced under conditions of more vigorous competition than is true in most other parts of the economy.

In labor relations, the same story of variations emerged. The postwar period has been one in which there were more than sufficient jobs to go around. As a result, many so-called restrictions have been relaxed, particularly for carpenters and building laborers who do the bulk of work in the house. The principal problems in these trades concerned the inability to use incentive-wage plans, the apparent lowering of efficiency as a result of rapid expansion in the postwar labor supply, the conditions of entry, and the rigorous rules for overtime.

Certain additional restrictions appeared to exist in other trades, as observed, for example, in the prohibitions by painters with regard to sprays and certain size brushes, the demands of other unions that jobs be handled by journeymen and not by laborers, that foremen be hired, and so on. These, it appears, do increase the cost of the house.

When it became necessary to estimate the cost of these restrictions, any figure was at best only an approximation and subject to wide error. Certain magnitudes had to be kept in mind. The total labor content of the median house in the area was about 24 per cent of its cost. How much, then, of the amount going to site labor was due to outside restrictions? Guesses ran all the way from zero to 20 per cent of labor costs, or from zero to 5 per cent of the total cost of the house. The latter should probably be taken as an outside estimate. If all possible restrictions on the use of labor were removed and labor became as efficient as it is in other industries, the total cost of the house might be reduced by 5 per cent. The possibility of checking such a guess is not great, however. Various methods could be tried. It might be possible to compare costs on similar union and nonunion jobs; but even here, other factors are likely to be more important in determining actual results.

The next most important items of waste result from unnecessarily restrictive building codes. Totaling all types of variations, we found that combined inefficiency or additional costs attributable to failures to adopt the national building codes exactly was less than 1 per cent for the area as a whole.

The inefficiency of the government agencies in the financing field was of a different sort. During much of the period under discussion, inability to process applications rapidly enough may have increased costs of the particular units being processed by as much as $100, with the average per house running to about $50. In addition, there are some indications that improvements in design may have been retarded.

Summing up these restrictions, we find that by making the estimate purposely high so as to show the outside limit of the problem, perhaps as much as 7 per cent of the cost of the house, or $650, was due to restrictive forces outside the firm. This estimate, if anything, overstates the problem for the housebuilding industry. Most industries have similar problems.

10

Performance of Housebuilders

Workable or Effective Competition

The final step in evaluating the performance of housebuilding is concerned with management and the over-all organization of the industry. Although housebuilders play the leading part, the way in which they play it and the results which they obtain are affected by their own interrelationships as well as by the action of other groups and forces. The men and firms composing the industry are only partial masters of their own efforts. The present picture of the housebuilding industry, in addition to being a creation of housebuilding management, also reflects the interplay of the basic competitive situation, changes in the scale of operations, and workings of the factors of production—forces over which the managements have little control. Reflected also are the results of increased demand and of shifts in the government's programs.

Attempts to evaluate performance in an industry are commonly spoken of as the determination of the requirements for "workable competition," as well as the measurement of the actual situation based on these requirements.[1] This terminology is used because, in most industry studies, the problem under consideration is whether or not there is sufficient competition to insure adequate performance. In housebuilding, though the same language can be used, much of the discussion has been concerned with the opposite problem of whether there is not too much competition to give best results. Many observers have believed that the industry is so competitive that the quality of the product, of progress, of management, and of use of resources suffers. In evaluating performance of the industry, therefore, one must consider both the possibility that there is not enough as well as the possibility that there is too much competition to insure the best level of product, selling costs, profits, flexibility, and efficiency and progress.

[1] Cf. Joe S. Bain, "Price and Production Policies" in (H. Ellis ed.) *Survey of Contemporary Economics;* Edward S. Mason, "The Current Status of the Monopoly Problem in the United States," *Harvard Law Review,* Vol. 62, No. 8 (June, 1949), 1266–1285.

The Position of the Product

The first criterion against which performance in the housebuilding industry must be measured is the adequacy of its product. The primary question is: Does the industry offer the best possible product in terms of what consumers would want if they were well informed of all the possibilities which exist for changes? The quality of the product depends upon its design, materials, and method of fabrication. It also depends upon meeting certain standards about which an average consumer cannot be expected to be informed.

Adequate performance requires that the industry meet three separate product desiderata. First, the product should furnish maximum livability through good design, both in its internal and external arrangements. This means the best possible use of space within the house, the proper location of the house on the site, and the suitable layout of the neighborhood. Second, the product should be designed to facilitate the most efficient methods of construction with the least possible waste of resources. Third, the quality of the house must be such as to permit low maintenance costs and minimum obsolescence. The costs with which the average house buyer is concerned are not only the immediate payments but also those expenses which will extend throughout the future. The gratifications in which he is interested are not merely the immediate pleasures of home ownership but the future stream of satisfactions. He wants the greatest shelter satisfaction for his money, maximum utility in terms of livability, and minimum total expenditures for the life of the house, obtained through a proper relationship between initial costs and future expenses for maintenance, depreciation, and obsolescence. Low initial charges and gingerbread ornaments for immediate sales appeal are not adequate. Experience in many fields has shown that a minimum cost product is not necessarily the least expensive, for if its low-cost production depended on use of shoddy materials and workmanship and a skimping on size and design, its future costs would be far higher than they should be and its satisfaction less.

The problem of quality is double-barreled. Builders attempting to furnish a good product and buyers attempting to acquire one, both encounter difficulties. The inherent nature of the problem itself acts as an obstacle to good design.

For the builder's part, his ability to affect or improve the design of his product is, to a large extent, dependent on his size. If he is a small contractor, he has little or no design function, since he works from the architect's or owner's plans. If he is a small- or medium-size merchant builder, his design function is circumscribed again, because he builds in settled neighborhoods where houses must fit into already established surroundings and have the widest possible appeal. He believes he cannot risk an appeal to the small segment of the market possibly interested in innovations in design. Such buyers usually can afford and do demand the right to participate in their planning, rather than buying another man's ideas already built. Hence, the small- and medium-sized builders seldom innovate. The large builder, on the other hand, has a high enough volume so that even a high initial cost for planning can be spread until the cost per unit is low. He develops new areas and usually assumes the responsibility for the land planning and selection of sites as well as the design of the individual structure.

It is the large builder, then, who can innovate, but even he does not receive as much guidance as he might hope from the market. He does not know what consumers actually desire in housing. Consumers' choice is constrained by a limited market, by factors of financing and price, and by the fact that they are offered only packaged products with a largely predetermined neighborhood environment. Their actual purchases give little indication as to whether or not they are satisfied.[2]

On the buyer's part, even his limited powers of choice may not be fully exercised. People remember with nostalgia the houses they grew up in, much as they recollect mother's cooking, a fact which makes most attitudes conservative and traditional. Changes in design, even if they hold promise of great improvements, may meet with prejudices and resistance. Furthermore, homeseekers are usually not well informed as to the true value of houses. They do not know whether the design and construction of the house meet the desiderata for the best product.

This lack of consumer knowledge makes the builder's attempts to change his product more difficult. If the builder's existing product is selling, investment in product change will increase his costs and may decrease existing demand, lower profits, and increase risk. The builder who navigates by records and controls knows that as soon as he changes

[2] Catherine Bauer, "Social Questions in Housing and Community Planning," *Journal of Social Issues*, Vol. VII, 1 and 2 (1951), 3–6.

from his existing pattern, he is on an uncharted sea and may founder. New costs can be estimated only roughly from the old. He has to train his crews and trade contractors in new ways, thereby incurring another expense. Supply sources are used to the old methods, distrustful of the new, and may cause him additional troubles. As stated previously, financial institutions also may create breakers.

Since the builder may receive no increased returns but will certainly encounter additional costs, risks, and headaches through improvement in design, such expenditures frequently strike him as wasteful. All these difficulties have diverted builders' attention from the quality of their product. Being human, they have been interested in building the units that involve the fewest problems. The result has been a continuation of existing design and a neglect of innovation until some change was forced, either by a more progressive builder who did change, by the need for a new selling point, or by the appearance of a proven, sure-fire, cheaper method.

Performance in the whole area of product has suffered as a consequence of this static design policy. The answer to the primary question on product is: No, consumers have *not* received the best product available.

Most observers believe that neither the structure, design, nor the site plan of the average builder utilizes the best techniques. It has been pointed out that the typical large-scale builder's house lags far behind developments in architectural knowledge. Some improvements have been made, but they have come slowly. Critics, comparing the average house with the exceptional one, show that though some builders have invested in good design and have been able to achieve more livable space at less cost, the average builder still has far to go.

Other types of product improvement suffer the same disabilities as does design. For example, the few builders who have experimented have demonstrated that a slab floor or an integral ceiling-roof (flat-top) is cheaper and can win consumer acceptance, and that improvements can be made in windows and in other phases of the product. But the majority's organizations and methods are not geared to innovations, and they have adopted such improvements only slowly.

Again, the static situation which obtains in the area of innovation for product improvement prevails in the field of product quality. Most of the larger builders have tended to build minimum quality units. The majority of builders sell to a given buyer only once and do not think of developing a continuous market. It is difficult for the average buyer to judge quality, anyway. The type of paint job, finish of millwork, extras in foundation or framing are not obvious to him, and they do not affect the price the builder can obtain. For these reasons, most builders have offered, as a rule, only that quality necessary to obtain lenders' approvals and sales, without considering the effect on future costs of any particular material or method. By comparison with the average and poorest performers, the exceptions dramatize how much progress the industry as a whole could still make in product quality.

The improvements in quality which have taken place have most often occurred when new materials or techniques were shown to be both better and cheaper. In addition, some firms have deliberately maintained a higher quality of product than the regulations or the market required, sometimes in the belief that offering better houses might maximize future earnings, and sometimes simply as a carry-over of the craft tradition. In still other cases—the small minority—there have been true innovators who have had daring and the desire to try new ideas. These few entrepreneurs have found that the traditionalism of the over-all organization of the industry was not as great and insuperable as it seemed. If they were determined to institute changes, nothing actually halted them. They faced greater problems in innovating than they would have if they had been satisfied with traditional methods; but this was part of the game, and these men enjoyed matching wits against odds. For the majority, however, to whom the course of least resistance was the pleasantest, the prospect of greater problems increased their own inertia and reinforced their reasons for not making changes. Neither housebuilding managements nor other parts of the over-all organization were interested in innovation. In fact, the contrary was more nearly true of all groups. Consequently, the housebuilding picture has included no element concerned with the product. There has been little to guarantee the consumer a best buy, and good quality has been a hit-or-miss proposition.

The Question of the Market

Closely related to the question of creating the most desirable product is that of the most desirable method of marketing it. Although the problems of quality may not be wholly in the hands of housebuilders to solve, it is in their province to determine the methods by which houses are merchandised. In determining their merchandising methods, they face three issues: the costs of selling, the breadth of the market, and the satisfaction of consumer wants. How they meet these issues spells market performance.

The issue of distribution cost is the most important determinant of merchandising performance in many industries. In housebuilding, however, since houses are a necessity, particular interest has been expressed in the breadth of market, and more attention has been paid to the housebuilder's choice of the market to which he will appeal than to any other criteria. The least emphasis has been given to the issue of satisfying consumer wants because a minimum of information about who the consumer is and what he wants is available.

Reliable information about what the market is and what it demands is essential to wise selection of merchandising methods. The skill of a producer in obtaining market knowledge is his key to successful market performance. Better market knowledge might enable housebuilders to answer such questions as these: Would larger investments in distribution costs improve performance? Should houses be produced for all segments of the population—the broadest possible market—or for limited groups? Are consumers satisfied with what they are getting, or should designs and locations be changed to suit different wants and needs?

If selling costs alone are considered, housebuilders' marketing performance would appear extremely efficient. There is no significant wastage in distribution costs. The actual expense of selling the finished product is one of the lowest of all industries. Two forces previously mentioned—the huge postwar demand for houses and the government's credit policy facilitating financing—have combined to simplify sales problems and lower selling expenses. Sales effort has almost simmered down to making known the availability of houses and accepting the orders. Often, the total sales expenditure has been as low as $75 per house, or less than 1 per cent. Seldom has it risen to 5 per cent. The probable average in the postwar period has been about $200 per house, or 2 per cent of the final selling price. This low percentage may be compared with the 15 to 25 per cent in automobile distribution, and the 35 to 40 per cent for distribution of most durable household appliances.

Although the house is a much larger item than an automobile or refrigerator and should, therefore, carry relatively a lower sales markup, its dollar costs for distribution are low even in absolute terms. It actually costs fewer dollars to sell a house than an automobile, and a householder pays almost as much for the marketing cost of an electric clothes washer and drier to go into his house as he does for the house itself.

At the same time that housebuilders have enjoyed these low distribution costs, they have succeeded in increasing the breadth of their market. Builders in the past have been sharply criticized for appealing only to a custom market and neglecting the mass market. Whether or not this criticism was justified in previous periods, it was not valid during the postwar housing boom. During this period, thanks to lower financing terms based on government insurance, the mass market was the most active market. In the San Francisco area in 1949, large firms aimed at this market with houses in the $8,000–$9,000 bracket and produced more than 45 per cent of their units for less than $9,000. The result of the improvement in financing terms and the concentration on production of lower-cost houses was that builders succeeded in reaching all of the top 70 per cent—by income—of the families in the area.[8] Within this range, houses are purchased in nearly proportional amounts by all income classes. This increase in the range, or breadth, of the market is not peculiar to the San Francisco Bay area. Most other metropolitan districts have produced houses at even lower prices and thus have reached an even higher percentage of the families in the $2,000–$3,000 per year income group (tables 39 and 41).

Although the housebuilding industry's performance appears efficient—on the surface, at least—in distribution costs and breadth of market, the third issue of merchandising—satisfaction of consumer wants—has been virtually ignored. There has been an almost complete lack of market information. In the San Francisco Bay area, neither individually nor as a group have builders made the effort to find out what buyers desired. Even the largest firms have been indifferent to market research.

---

[8] Based on a comparison of purchase prices of new houses in the last half of 1949 and the census distribution of families by income. The top 75 per cent of families had an income per family of over $2,800 in 1949. Bureau of Labor Statistics, *Sales Prices and Financing of New Homes in Four Western Metropolitan Areas 1949–1950*, table 5b; and Bureau of the Census, 1950 Census, *1950 Census of Population—Preliminary Reports Series PC-5, No. 45* (June 6, 1951), table 13.

No one knows whether buyers would have been happier with other designs or sites than those which they purchased. Selection of locations was made with such disregard of buyers' preferences that even in a boom market, some sites turned out to be unwanted. Sales cannot be interpreted as testing consumer taste because there is no way of knowing whether the houses offered really suited the tastes of prospective buyers, or whether the latter merely took whatever was offered because they were hungry for housing and could afford it, though preferring and ready to pay more for something different. When sales slowed down, no one knew whether the relapse was temporary, or what caused it; whether the builder had produced in a poor site, or from an undesirable design, or for a nonexistent sector of the market. Whatever the cause, the builder had lowered the value of his completed unit and endangered his own economic health. Without market analysis, he could not know why.

It seems obvious that performance would be improved if the industry would find out what types of houses are most needed and desired, and then plan its houses accordingly. Such market research would, of necessity, be expensive. It might be too costly for individual firms, since each covers only a small part of the total market. But market research could be conducted through builders' local organizations on a coöperative basis similar to joint-selling campaigns. With better knowledge of the market, better performance by all would follow. This sequence could take a variety of forms. For example, the knowledge of the types of houses which people really want could be applied to influencing people to fulfill these needs at the expense of other, less necessary, desires. The knowledge could be channeled into a campaign to increase house buying. Increased house buying might improve the welfare of the nation as a whole, in addition to that of the individual builder and the industry.

Speculate, for a moment, on the possibilities that might develop if housebuilders spent sums on advertising—influencing public taste and buying—comparable with the sums now spent for these purposes by the cigarette, beer, whiskey, or automobile industries. If, as many claim, too little is now being spent by the public on housing to achieve necessary housing standards and general well-being, then every dollar transferred to housing from some other less essential use would improve the national well-being. At the same time, increased expenditures for housing might stimulate the industry's ability to produce better and higher quality houses more efficiently. If the increased demand for more and better houses was timed so that necessary supply adjustments could be made, it is possible that the cost of market research and advertising could be offset by lowered production prices.

Many observers would claim that such a theoretical possibility could not become a practical reality—that either it would be a wasted effort failing to stimulate demand, or, if effective, the greater demand would merely be met by higher prices and higher profits. Such skeptics would contend that the current convention of accepting the demand for housing as a given factor over which the industry has no control is more efficient. They would argue that performance would be lowered rather than raised by increasing marketing effort and expense.

A tolerant glimpse of the positive possibilities, however, reveals the fact that low marketing cost is not necessarily an assurance of high efficiency. Although the builder pays only slight sums for his selling effort, he receives only slight returns in market knowledge, and, therefore, uncertain returns in profits. It is questionable whether the minimal marketing costs really mean adequate marketing performance.

It is also questionable what breadth of the market represents adequate performance. Lack of data makes it impossible to ascertain whether the entire population should be included in the range reached by housebuilders, rather than the top 70 per cent—by income—as at present. No one knows whether the families in the lower quarter of the income distribution should be in the market for new houses. These are mainly atypical families, with partial or irregular incomes, many of them relief or borderline relief cases. It is possible that their living requirements and capacities would be better served by other types of dwelling units than new houses. It is further possible that the subject of their housing represents a problem for public concern and policy, rather than a market for the housebuilding industry. With respect to breadth, as in regard to costs, consumer needs, and other problems, the complete question of the market cannot be answered until more market knowledge is acquired.

The Problem of Profits

Study of the adequacy of the product and of the methods of marketing leads directly into a third aspect of an industry's performance—the problem of profits. Here the criterion is often expressed by the word "fair." Is the industry making "fair" or excessive profits? A fair profit is a condition which exists in the minds of men and varies with each individual's personality, his position in the scheme of things, and the state of his purse. It is a condition which is rarely, if ever, defined. Moreover, relative profit data which would permit comparisons to be made are inadequate.

Profits are necessary to attract a capital supply for production, to insure continuation of production, and to make expansion possible. They serve as the reward for efficiency and for successful innovations. They are, however, suspect when they occur as the result of a monopoly or windfall.

There is need for some standard. Housebuilding may be inefficient if profits are too low, or unstable, thus failing to attract good management and necessary capital to the industry. Housebuilders have often complained that their industry was thus afflicted.[4] Housebuilding may also be inefficient if profits are too high. Experience shows that firms making windfalls, or high profits for other reasons, may waste large amounts of resources and may charge prices far higher than necessary.[5] The problem is that of the correct or appropriate level between high and low.

Although the pressure toward efficiency in our economy is composed of fear of loss and hope of gain, criteria for appropriate gain are not easy to apply. They occur in general terms and are not quantitative. Consequently, the commonest method of judging profits is comparison with profits earned at other times or by other firms. This may be the best approach for housebuilding. The profits of the postwar period may be compared with the profits in building's own past history and with the profits earned in other, similar industries, and a comparison may be made among various building firms at the present time.

These comparisons will allow some judgments to be made, though not completely accurate ones. In general, if the profits of building firms are low compared with firms in other industries, then one may judge that housebuilding's performance is probably high. Such a judgment, however, must be viewed in the light of the industry's own organization and history, and also in the light of comparison among similar firms at present—a light that may disclose inefficiencies.

[4] Ian Bowen, "The Case for Rationalization of the Building Industry," *The Manchester School of Economic and Social Studies,* Vol. XIX, No. 2 (May, 1951), pp. 170–189.

[5] Oxenfeldt, *Industrial Pricing and Market Practices,* p. 120.

Taking a look at the record (table 60), the history of construction corporation profits recounts much famine but little feast. In 1929, corporate profits were approximately 4.3 per cent of sales. By 1932, losses ran nearly as high as 7 per cent and continued through 1935. The peak year for profits in the 1930's was 1937, and then they reached only 1.9 per cent. In the 1940's, the story was different, of course. In 1943, for reasons of war, profits rose to nearly 6 per cent, and they reached 7 per cent during the years of our study, 1949 and 1950.

Comparing building with other industries, the percentage of gross income going to profits in construction companies has been far less than the percentage for manufacturing firms, and has been much less than the returns for all corporations combined. Perhaps more signficantly, in comparison with other durable goods industries that have experienced the same kind of sharp fluctuations as construction, the ratio of profits to sales volume in building has been lower. Corporate profits of construction firms have been only one-third to one-half those of the machinery and automotive industries in the postwar period. Because this comparison excludes nonincorporated firms in housebuilding whereas production in these latter industries is almost entirely in the hands of corporations, it may be that the disparity is actually larger.

The above comparisons of profits have been based on the profit percentage of sales. If a profit comparison were based on the profit percentage of owner's equity, the change in perspective would yield a different picture. Bay area builders received a return of from 20 to 25 per cent of their net worth in 1949, a slightly higher percentage of equity than was earned by manufacturing industries in general (table 61).

By way of statistical apology, it should be noted that all these comparisons are necessarily rough, because based on inadequate data, but they are probably of the proper order of magnitude, even if not exact in detail. Any errors are in the direction of understating the degree by which profits on sales in other industries surpass those of housebuilding and overstating the actual profits of the housebuilding industry.

These possible biases occur because profit data, both historical and current, have had to be based chiefly on corporate profit tax payments made to the Bureau of Internal Revenue, an unsatisfactory source for two reasons. First, Bureau statistics omit any distinction between housebuilders and other types of builders and contractors. Second, and more important, their profit information is derived from the returns of corporations and omits unincorporated enterprises which form a large part of the housebuilding field. Only about half the total amount of housebuilding is accounted for by corporate returns, whereas almost the complete output in manufacturing and other industries is produced by corporations.[6]

Since it is probable that the two statistical inadequacies of this source work in opposite directions, the actual figures as reported by the Bureau of Internal Revenue may be a fair estimate of housebuilders' profits. On the one hand, housebuilding firms in the postwar period have probably been more profitable than other types of contract construction firms and, on the other hand, unincorporated firms have a lower profit rate than corporations. This well-recognized fact that unincorporated firms get lower profits was corroborated in our San Francisco Bay area sample, where a high correlation occurred among profit, size, and incorporation.

Analysis of the available figures indicates that builders' profits have been reasonable in comparison with other industries. Traditionally a competitive, low-profit, high-risk field, building has a past history of profits too poor for best performance. In the postwar period, when demand boosted housebuilders' profits together with those of most other industries, there is no evidence that the rise was excessive or out of line, particularly considering the greater risks and the longer years of the locust in housebuilding compared with the others. Total profits for housebuilding firms of all sizes in the Bay area in 1949, before taxes, were about $15,000,000 on gross housing sales of close to $200,000,000. Since this profit covered 17,500 houses, the actual profit per house sold in 1949 was about $845 (tables 11, 33, and 34).

Even higher housebuilding profits might have benefited the economy. Because outside capital is reluctant to enter the housing field, it is profits that permit firms to expand. Since increased efficiencies come with increased size of firm, sufficient profits to support expansion can lead to more competent operation and more and better housing for all.

Whereas returns on net worth in housebuilding are higher than profits expressed as a percentage of sales, these also appear not to have been excessive. Because of the large risk in housebuilding, an even

[6] United States Department of Commerce, *National Income Supplement* (Washington: U. S. Government Printing Office, 1951); tables 29, 31, and 16.

greater return on equity than the 20 to 25 per cent earned might have been expected. Builders operate with a high ratio of debt to equity, a hazard that would justify high returns on capital. Builders increase their risks to turn over their equity at a rapid rate, and this—despite the moderate profit per sales dollar—results in a relatively higher profit on their actual investment.

It is only when one turns from comparing housebuilding with other industries and with its own past history to a comparative study of profit distribution among Bay area firms that the profit performance appears unsatisfactory. Here, certain dangers in the present picture become evident. It is seen that in addition to the reasonable rise in average rate of profits as size of firm increases, exceptionally big profits both on sales and on invested capital were received by a number of large- and medium-sized firms. These facts probably indicate that the average efficiency in management for which average profits are paid falls very short of the efficiency of the best firms and that which might be prompted industry-wide by a more competitive market situation.

The present picture is explained by the existence of a profit "umbrella" which protects the efficient and the inefficient alike. The profit umbrella was raised by those two forces mentioned earlier—the push of powerful demand and the spread of easy credit. In 1949 and 1950, since houses sold readily if they had government guaranteed and insured loans, the factor which set prices was the appraisal policy of the Federal Housing Administration and the Veterans Administration.

The actual methods of appraisal followed a type of bulk pricing system. The price was set so that the bulk of houses needed for the market could be produced under average conditions with a "fair" profit. The set price allowed the average firm (a medium-sized one) a fair profit allowance over and above its necessary costs. In such a bulk-pricing system, firms which were more efficient than average because of larger size or better management had costs well under the price and made high profits, although less efficient firms crowded their price line and received a lower return.

On the surface, this looks like an equitable system because it expands the idea of a fair profit to include the possibility of higher reward for greater efficiency. Closer scrutiny, however, shows that this type of pricing may lower the total efficiency of the industry if the market does not put pressure on individual firms. Under the protection of this profit umbrella, firms need not be really efficient but only as efficient as other firms to receive a profit. To be as efficient as the average firm may mean little because there is no guarantee that the average firm will be performing well.

This seems to have been true. The fair level of profits set to compensate the average firms did not require them to be efficient. The level and distribution of profits tended to retain in the industry a large number of small firms, plus many larger firms which had no prod to improve their performance. Large and efficient firms reaped much higher profits without being pushed to increase their efficiency, expand output, or substantially lower their prices.

If demand for housing decreased, making the market more competitive, this situation would change. Sales and prices would depend less on credit and appraisal and more on ability to sell at the proper price in the market. The general level of profits would fall. The least efficient firms would be weeded out. The potentially more efficient firms would have to realize their possibilities and cut costs to remain in business. Even the most efficient firms would have to bestir themselves, keeping down their costs and cutting their profits too. These cuts would, of course, accrue to the advantage of house buyers. If, on the other hand, demand were to rise still further beyond recent heights, and the prices people were willing to pay were reflected in higher appraisal levels, the "umbrella" would grow to shelter decreases in performance and efficiency, together with increases in profits.

The Dynamics of Demand

Housebuilding is one of the industries most immediately and intensely affected by changes in the general demand. Because the product is extremely durable and the existing stock is large compared with annual new production, a period of deflation will wipe out the demand for new houses, and the onset of inflation will stimulate demand more drastically in this field, in relation to normal new production, than in most others. That small shifts in the general demand cause tremendous shifts in the demand for the construction of new houses is dramatized by the facts that the amount of building required can fluctuate from almost zero to more than a million units, and that year to year changes of 300,000 to 400,000 are not uncommon.[7]

[7] S. J. Maisel, "Variables Commonly Ignored in Housing Demand Analysis," *Land Economics* Vol. XXV, No. 3 (August, 1949), 260–274.

Flexibility is, therefore, a prerequisite to successful performance. To perform well, an industry must be geared to come to grips with the fluctuations which appear inevitable in our economy. In housebuilding, so especially sensitive to economic change, this is particularly true, since this industry's total performance is vitally affected by its flexibility in meeting demand shifts.

In this connection, ease of entry into the industry is also important. In the first place, flexibility itself is enhanced the more simple entry is made. In the second place, ease of entry improves the health and performance of the industry by providing the economic advantages which are normally associated with free competition. Monopoly cannot exist in an industry where entry is easy. In the third place, besides such economic grounds, there are important social and political reasons for applauding the ease with which new firms can come into being. Socially, it is desirable for the so-called small man to have a chance to become his own boss and rise in the world; politically, it is desirable that wealth be distributed rather than overconcentrated.

Housebuilding compares favorably with other industries with respect to these criteria. Entry is simple since initial capital requirements are low, resources are not restricted, and the amount of requisite investment in plant and equipment is negligible. The power of existing organizations is not of a nature to make others fear to compete. Even the legal requirements of licensing are minor. For similar reasons, expansion of output by existing firms is not difficult.

The record of housebuilding spells flexibility. The industry has been able to cope with its kaleidoscopic shifts in demand with as fluid shifts in production as have been accomplished by any other industry. It increased the number of dwelling units produced by more than 250 per cent in the periods 1921–1923 and 1933–1936; and from 1944 to 1948 the increase was more than 550 per cent. The industry experienced the largest production in its history in 1949, and still was able to expand its capacity by more than 40 per cent in 1950. There are few heavy goods industries which can lay claim to surpassing their peak production by nearly one-half in a single year, even under the forced draft of a war or a defense program (table 4).

Figures to define ease of entry are equally plain. Between 1940 and 1950, the number of firms engaged in construction on the national scene increased by 85 per cent. This was almost three times as great an increase in participation as was experienced by any other industry. This rapid growth nationally was reflected in California, where the number of licensed contractors nearly doubled between 1945 and 1950, and the number of active firms probably increased somewhat more (table 62 and sources cited therein).

This spectacular expansion was made possible by the inherent factors listed above. Because little expensive equipment is required, and working capital is replenished by customers or lenders after work has begun, the financial resources of most individuals with experience in building and a will to become independent are sufficient to start a contracting firm. The small builder can almost literally start on a shoestring—or, at any rate, on a single set of tools—if he uses his own home as a base of operations, does his own record-keeping, and holds all fixed expenses to the minimum. Although a house is a complex product, so many of the tasks involved in its construction can be performed by subcontractors that most problems of recruiting, training, and maintaining a work force are eliminated. Product development, sales effort, and other such costly functions can be omitted. The entrant need not be an innovator, under present market conditions. He needs neither wealth nor imagination but just a little knowledge of his craft. In California builders must be licensed, but the requirements of four years experience and ability to pass a fairly easy written examination are not onerous. The small-scale entrant is reasonably safe; he can revert to his former status without much loss if things go badly or build up his firm if things go well.

In addition to entering the industry with ease, builders of all sizes can increase production easily and rapidly. Expansion can occur with little increase in the overhead per unit. Housebuilders are not hampered by the bottlenecks in fixed plants and equipment which hold back other industries. Simple overhead structures and low capitalization permit as flexible an increase in production as demand invites. It is true that most newly formed building proprietorships feel some discomfort from lack of capital, but these disabilities can be overcome by partnerships or by pooling of the capital of several investors; and when earnings are good, the capital shortage need not last long.

In the postwar period, when housebuilders bought supplies at rapidly rising prices, they themselves were rapidly increasing in scale—and with increased scale, they could lower their internal cost curve so as to offset some of the higher supply prices. Housebuilders have sufficient opportunity to substitute among their factors of supply so that they can increase flexibility from those sources also.

This pattern of flexibility and the ability to cope with problems of factor supply were especially visible in relation to labor. The number of workers employed in construction dropped from 1940 to 1945 and then more than doubled from 1945 to 1950. In the San Francisco Bay area, the number of workers employed in construction increased by more than 100 per cent from 1940 to 1950 and by 25 per cent in 1950 alone. During the peak of expansion, labor was scarce in particular trades, but because of builders' substitutions of skills and materials, the labor shortage did not form a bottleneck (tables 57 and 58 and sources cited therein).

At the same time, efficiency wages were rising. While wage rates were increasing at about the average rate for the economy as a whole, wage payments tended to rise faster for the builders, because the new men coming in at the new wage rates were less skilled, and the more skilled men obtained bonuses above the union scale. In addition, there was a general fall in output per wage unit because of the individual slackness that normally accompanies noncompetition for jobs in an overemployed market.

Despite the impediment of a labor supply which was hard to get, cost more, and produced less, the flexibility of the industry enabled it to reduce actual labor costs. This was done by changing the process of production through use of specialization and mechanization so that more actual output could be obtained from a man, though his skill and desire to work were small.

A comparable change is less visible in relation to materials supply. The wholesale prices of building materials rose by nearly 100 per cent from 1945 to 1951, compared with increases of about 66 per cent for prices in general (table 56). Housebuilders were able partly to offset this relative rise by changes in the channels of distribution, and somewhat by certain substitutions among goods. It is not clear whether their flexibility enabled them to offset the total rise, however. The fact remains that though their factors of supply rose more rapidly than prices in general, housebuilders held increases in construction costs during the postwar period to about the same rate as wholesale prices in general, and thus to a slower rate than that of the supply factors.

Besides labor supply and materials supply, a third major factor affecting expansibility of housebuilding firms has been money supply. It has been seen that financing was not a critical problem in terms of firm equity, but it was necessary to have adequate financing for the final sale. During most of the postwar period, there were sufficient mortgage funds available to take care of the industry's need for expansion. At certain times, however, mortgage funds became temporarily scarce, and on these occasions, the industry had difficulty in adjusting. Absence of mortgage money can be a serious impediment to sales.

The other cost factors have, on the whole, been flexible. With the ease of adding to overhead for both builders and trade contractors and the economies inherent in larger scale, expanded production brings greater overhead efficiency, in striking contrast with those industries which have fixed plant and overhead costs. When these other industries reach their limit of expansion, their costs shoot up almost vertically because of lack of flexibility.

Sufficient flexibility is good, but it also may pose difficult problems. With a high rate of entry, there is also a high exit rate. Men may be attracted to the business simply through the hope of making a rapid dollar, and may run out just as fast when the promise glimmers. During their period in the industry, they are not interested in performance and do not add much to the industry's reputation. At the same time, since many elements in ease of entry increase risk, they may deter sound businessmen from taking advantage of it.

Another deterrent is the difficulty of investing in research and similar activities which require some type of protected market for amortization of the investment. In housebuilding, even if a firm makes an important discovery in processes or techniques, its share of the market is so small that its gains from its discovery may be small and only sufficient to pay for a fraction of any expenses incurred in making it. This disadvantage of ease of entry suggests that if the familiar Schumpeterian thesis of the importance of monopoly gains can be applied anywhere, it is here.

Housebuilding meets fluctuations in demand with good performance, but would not performance be still better if housebuilding were so organized as to halt the fluctuations? This question could receive a realistic answer only if a way were found for the industry to level out the changes in demand. The difficulty is that the waves of demand are impelled by external forces.

Some might suggest that increased size and overhead would help housebuilding firms to overcome the ebb and flow of demand. Although the risks of fluctuations tend to hold down the overhead size, there is no indication that additional size of overhead would diminish the fluctuation processes. The fact that steel or auto companies have had large overhead plants has not lessened their output fluctuations, but has only augmented their financial difficulties.

Suggestions have been made that housebuilding fluctuations might be diminished by a more flexible price policy. But there is no evidence that additional demand would result from lowered prices. Price elasticity does not appear to be great. Houses now are a necessity within the purse reach of most families. Even if firms attempt to lower prices, their ability to do so would be slight because only a small percentage of the final price returns to housebuilding firms. Flexible price policies are possible primarily when firms can change their products so as to reduce production and factor costs or their share of the final price to an extent not possible for housebuilders. And furthermore, flexible price policies might have an effect the reverse of that desired. Since a house is a durable object which can easily be stored, buyers and speculators might attempt to anticipate price changes, thus accentuating existing fluctuations.

Since fluctuations are largely due to forces outside the industry's control, the most feasible methods for lessening them would also appear to lie largely outside. Stability might be improved through a shrinking in the fluctuations of national income, and perhaps through the setting up of some type of guaranteed housing market with government support. This latter possibility, which appears best, would depend upon the trend of industry-government relationship. Until recently, it appeared probable that some type of increased demand during depressions would be forthcoming from government sources. Now it is not as evident. In any case, these problems are those of the performance of the economy as a whole. Housebuilding appears to have done its share in meeting the fluctuations in demand which have faced it in the past.

Efficiency

The problem of efficiency has already been dealt with at length. It is recognized that good performance in this field consists in an increasing productivity ratio (output over input) over time, together with a proper utilization by industry of the potential changes in productivity available to it. These changes, of course, may lie within the province of management or they may depend upon developments in some other parts of the housebuilding organization.

The growth of efficiency in housing has followed four separate paths. First, there has been a general increase in mechanization and improvement in the techniques used at all levels. Second, cost reduction has been achieved by the moving of a larger share of production off the site and into plants, where lower costs are possible through better controls and deskilling of labor. Third, cheaper financing and easier selling have made savings possible. Fourth, the greater specialization engendered by increased scale has cut costs.

All builders have introduced greater mechanization into their construction process. Small power hand tools have been perfected and used for an increasingly large number of operations, thus cutting down the units of labor required. At the same time, more attention has been paid to the efficient planning of the entire construction process, with even the smallest firms attempting to use procedures and techniques with the lowest costs.

The pushing back of the production process from the site into the mill or factory has meant that many assemblies formerly produced by craftsmen with hand tools are now manufactured under factory conditions and arrive at the house in a nearly finished state. Steel and aluminum windows, complete with glazing and screens, are a good example of this type of item. In addition, the use of more completely finished materials that are simpler to install has increased. The advantages of dry walls and tile floors fall into this category. The result of these changes has been to make the builder increasingly an assembler rather than a fabricator. At the same time, the amount of handwork, and with it, the amount of skill required, has been reduced, with a consequent increase in efficiency.

There has been a change for the better in the field of financing since the prewar era, when all studies stressed the poor financial condition of builders. For example, *Housing America* estimates that during the 1920's financing made up more than 20 per cent of the final costs of a house,[8] and builders were believed to be dependent on their suppliers

[8] Fortune, editors of, *Housing America* (New York: Harcourt, Brace & Co., 1932), pp. 67–68.

for credit, thus paying higher prices. In earlier periods, the financing cost was so high because buyers and builders had to pay exorbitant fees to obtain necessary financing, frequently through the use of junior liens.

In contrast with this, financing made up only about 2 per cent of the cost of houses in 1949 and 1950. The saving was realized in lower costs for the final consumer financing, more available construction credit, and lower payments to suppliers. Improved financial position enabled builders to realize additional cost reductions because they were no longer dependent on their suppliers for credit and because the hazards of liens, failures to carry out contracts, and steps aimed at avoiding such failures were all reduced. With improved capital conditions, the industry simplified its credit structure and problems.

Finally, there are savings due to the increase in the size of builders and their assumption of responsibility for the complete housebuilding process. The rapid increase in demand which characterized the war and postwar periods became the most powerful force behind the industry's progress. And this progress manifested itself most significantly in the strong trend toward merchant building and the concentration of production into the hands of large firms, run often by shrewd successful businessmen exploiting a new mass market. The largest firms employed 40 or 50 people spending full time on management and executive functions—a far cry from the small firm whose owner performed all overhead duties himself in his spare time. Managements of this size can enjoy the benefits of specialization within themselves and have been able to evolve better financing and land development methods as well as production techniques. The improvements and cost reductions realized through bulk purchasing and better relationships with subcontractors have already been stressed. Most important of all has been the greater degree of rationalization of the production process.

"Rational" organization of the work force tends to be self-reinforcing. Specialization leads to greater efficiency and increased volume which, in turn, make possible the use of more repetitive and routine operations. Increased mechanization begins to pay dividends as tools can be kept in more constant use and their cost per unit of output falls. Inclusion of standardized product elements, such as precut or preassembled components, becomes more feasible with expanded output. Standardization, too, allows extensive employment of patterns and templates and various work-holding or work-positioning devices to reduce work effort. At the same time that direct productive efficiency is increased, the opportunity arises for more effective use of the supervisory force through tighter job scheduling, decreased necessity for direct supervision by major executives, and higher worker-supervisor ratios. Last, but not least, it becomes worth while to utilize more rigorous accounting procedures in conjunction with other management controls (such as production and inventory controls) so that costs are known in the fine as well as the gross, so that cost standards can be set up, and so that concrete information for making decisions is available.

Although not all these changes are measurable, they have meant important improvements in efficiency. It is probable that as a result of changes in the production process, the efficiency in the use of direct labor by large firms was at least a third higher than that found in the average housebuilding firms of the prewar period. Such an increase in labor efficiency means that improvements in the housing process during this period probably compare favorably with those in other industries. If the estimate of *Housing America* was approximately right, there was an additional decrease of at least 15 per cent of the total cost simply through improved financing. Finally, since at the start of the decade of the 1940's few, if any, large firms existed, an improvement in efficiency must have occurred at least equal to the 6 to 12 per cent reduction in costs which resulted from larger scale.

These four lines of efficiency growth demonstrate increased efficiency over the past, but they do not show whether or not housebuilders are actually using their existing potential to the fullest extent. They may be efficient compared to their own past performance, but inefficient compared to other industries or to their own possibilities. Such inefficiency appears particularly acute in management, which remains one of the weakest parts of housebuilding performance.

The growth in size of housebuilders brought about far less improvement in management than might have been expected. The average firm is still not run efficiently, and the contrast between good management and average management in every size class is great. Perhaps this lag is not surprising in view of the rapid and incomplete transition just gone through by many housebuilding firms, which mushroomed from businesses spending next to nothing on management to operations requiring and able to afford a high degree of managerial skill. The development was so rapid that it was next to impossible to meet the requirements for good management. Not only was there a shortage of men with the necessary knowledge and talent, but the executives of the rapidly expanding firms were primarily concerned with entrepreneurial problems. They frequently did not have either the time or the necessary background and organizational skills required for efficient operation of their firms. Furthermore, no external impetus toward better organization was provided by competition during the period, and consequently, development has been slow.

The greatest management weaknesses seem to lie in the realms of cost data and research and in a failure to reëxamine the over-all problems of the organization and functions of the firm.

(1) Perhaps most important has been the failure to develop adequate record-keeping and methods of production control. Management has remained on a very personal basis. Scheduling has been too often hit-or-miss, and knowledge of what actually occurred during the production process has been haphazard and loose. Many of the advantages of specialization, which firms in other industries are quick to exploit, have been neglected through inertia and ignorance.

Weaknesses of this kind in management are difficult to measure. Since no two industries function alike, interindustry comparisons are suspect. Our belief that housebuilding has proceeded only part way toward comparative management efficiency is based not on an ideal borrowed from other fields, but rather on comparison among building firms in the San Francisco area. Even among the big firms, wide differences exist in methods of planning, controlling, and supervising production. The majority had no adequate cost accounting or production controls. As a result, their efficiency was lower; they received less output for their labor expenditures and wasted more of other production items than the few firms with better management.

Housebuilding firms have accurate records of their total costs, but have failed to break them down to show the costs of specific parts of their operation. Many examples can be found where builders in the area have not known whether or not they should adopt a specific technique because they had no way of comparing relative costs. Consequently, many innovations are adopted only by those with the best information and may later be copied by others if they appear to bring about savings.

(2) Related to this lack of knowledge about costs has been the failure of firms to reëxamine their complete job organization and to introduce new methods and materials. It is true that large builders have emphasized standardization, simplification, and the logic of their production processes to some extent, but on the whole, the field has received far less attention than is its due. If builders knew more about their actual costs in terms of components and individual sections of the house, as compared with their present knowledge of what they spend for materials, labor, and trade contracts, they might find it advantageous to modify and revamp their whole construction process to a great degree.

New procedures have been developed in the most efficient firms, and it is probable that, in time and with more intensive competition, more effort will be made to develop management skills by all firms in the industry; otherwise, many may fall by the wayside. If the gap can be closed between the best-run firms and the average firm, the entire efficiency of the industry will be greatly improved. More important even than the acquiring by inefficient firms of the techniques already in use is the development of new management methods and skills by all.

The obvious reluctance of large firms to increase their overhead has been a major drag on progress toward better management. Expanding overhead has meant taking additional risks, which firms have naturally been hesitant to do unless forced by competition or led on by hopes of much larger profits. Unlike many manufacturing industries, where expanding firms can find already developed successful techniques to incorporate into their own overhead, housebuilders have no assurance that money spent in expansion will not go down a rathole. Until more firms make concerted efforts to develop better methods, progress will remain slow.

Progress

The final—and, to many, the most important—criterion of performance is progress. The whole economic history of the United States is characterized by giant increases in productivity, with even average industries developing new methods and better technology at a rapid rate. Simply to hold its place in the industrial scheme, an industry must show constant improvement.

Builders have not closed the door on progress in the past decade. They have shown great willingness to adopt methods proved by others. When techniques have appeared promising, they have spread quite rapidly. A fair percentage of builders, though perhaps not the average, has made an effort to keep abreast of current developments through the technical press and their trade associations. A certain number of builders have experimented with new techniques, and if they were successful, the use of the innovations has become widespread. The rate of progress in recent years has been greatly accelerated over that of the past. Even so, this progress has primarily taken the form of more skillful performance of the same traditional housebuilding processes.

Innovations, or cost-reducing or output-increasing changes, can come about in a variety of ways. There can be (a) an introduction of a new method of production involving changes in the manufacturing processes or their organization; (b) discovery or creation of a new market for the industry's output; (c) development of a new source of supply or factors; (d) creation of a new product or a significant change in quality of existing ones; and (e) a change in the industry's organization or distribution methods.

Examining the record of the housebuilding industry with respect to this list, and especially comparing it with the record of other industries, one is struck by the relatively unchanging nature of its product, processes, and organization. Perceptible changes have taken place both in the construction process and the product it has evolved in the Bay area in recent years, but they have not been revolutionary.

This conservative record is disappointing to many observers, whose minds have long pictured the rosy possibility of a suddenly different and radically better housing industry. They feel that it has missed a great opportunity, seized by many other industries, to live up to its own potentialities, to introduce dynamic changes, to take the large view. Ford revolutionized auto-making. Where is the Ford of building? Many candidates have come forward seeking this honor; why have they failed?

There are two possible explanations for the stability and relative lack of progress in the housing industry. The first is that possibly the most efficient firms, using present production methods, have already brought the cost per unit of output as low as it can be with existing knowledge; that further reorganizations, changes in factor use, and other innovations would not actually bring about a sufficient cost reduction in the final unit to justify the upheavals attendant upon instituting them. The second is that, assuming there is ample room for real growth in efficiency, no one has had the vision to perceive in what areas changes should be brought about; or, if they have such insight, have not had sufficient influence or strength to bring them about within the existing organization of the industry. In terms of the earlier analysis, there is some scale of firm that is far more efficient than the present optimum size, but it cannot be reached because of the intervening, less efficient size ranges, which a firm cannot push through without being given a strong shove by some external force.

Those who hold the first view claim that the present structure of the industry, with its small overhead, great flexibility, and low profits, is efficient, and that the production process is better than most critics realize. Wood is basically an efficient material, cheap, easy to handle and to work with. A wood frame has great advantages over other materials. A competent large firm can complete the shell of a $10,000 house, including foundation, subfloor, framing, siding, and roofing, for less than $2,000—a figure extremely difficult for other procedures to compete with.

Those adhering to the second point of view, however, maintain that this appearance of efficiency is an illusion, and that the cheapness of the frame of the house is deceiving. Builders comparing other methods of production find that they cannot beat their present framing costs, and, therefore, continue as before. They ignore the fact that the big expense of a house is the equipment and finishing, which are purchased from subcontractors and do not enter the picture when the builder calculates new methods. Efficiency can be increased, but only if someone takes an entirely new view of the complete building process, looking toward elimination of some of the present steps rather than continuing merely to develop gradual improvements in the present methods of performance. A radical shift in the method of production (the production function) is called for.

The proponents of this second explanation have, on the whole, held that a basic prerequisite to important shifts in the production function is probably that firms much larger than those of the present must come into existence in order that the potentialities for new production methods can be perceived and brought about. Connected with this belief is the idea that the housing industry is too competitive to operate efficiently. Those who advance this theory state that, contrary to most industries, housebuilding has suffered because of a lack of firms with a monopoly position. Firms are required which could furnish leadership, understand the need for change, undertake necessary research, and introduce radically new methods that would achieve greater efficiency. The present state of housebuilding, characterized by intense competition, diversity of organization, extreme flexibility, and an unstandardized and complex product, is not conducive to the development of such firms.

The excess of competition, it is claimed, leads to a general absence of money for research and a consequent following of a one-at-a-time approach which fails to encompass the building process as a whole. It is claimed that many of the factors which make entry easy tend at the same time to slow down innovation. Where entry is too free, industry members may undertake few departures, realizing that new entrants will adopt them and their favored position will be "competed away." In addition to possible rapid erosion of profits of innovation in an easily entered industry, there is a strong possibility that firms may find it hard to accumulate funds to finance the research from which new products or new methods of production can stem. Lacking firms with a protected position, the industry requires either an outside force, such as aid through governmental policy, or the emergence of an entrepreneur with unusual ability, drive, and luck to achieve any important changes in the production function.

The present relative inertia of housebuilders is not illogical. When comfortable profits can be made by being only as efficient as the bulk of the industry; when the nature of the product is still largely dictated by common acceptance of an indifferently designed and executed product; when any one producer controls only a small part of the industry output and not all the processes of production; and when concurrent innovation is lacking in supplying industries, the urge to innovate is weakened. When, further, introduction of new materials or methods of production must be pushed past stiff institutional resistance, the prospective net gain of innovation appears small.

The argument for larger size and greater monopoly in housebuilding is also advanced on the grounds that the present relationship between housebuilders and the suppliers of factors is unsatisfactory.

This line of reasoning follows partly from the belief that monopoly is widespread among the supplying industries. It was brought out earlier that this is far from the case, but it is true that whatever restrictions the industry does feel might be reduced if housebuilding firms enjoyed still greater bargaining power. Perhaps, too, though no single source of supply of a necessary factor has been able to hold back progress, the cumulative effect of all factors may have been to discourage builders from upsetting the status quo. A builder might be willing to battle a labor union or a code authority to adopt an innovation, but would shrink from arousing the combined opposition of all his suppliers, including labor, materials, codes, and financing institutions. If he is making adequate profits, he would probably lack the necessary drive to attempt any such total innovations.

In opposition to this idea of housebuilding's difficulties arising because of too much monopoly on the supply side, the problem may be one of too much fragmentation leading to the same lack of progress noticed for builders. Since no one supplier furnishes a preponderant amount of the total product, none is moved to look far beyond his own immediate interest, and thus no impetus toward improving the over-all performance comes from this source. Technical research among the supplying industries, as well as among the housebuilders themselves, may be lagging. In lumber, for example, almost the only research has been conducted by the government. In codes, where the government has the main responsibility, the lack of knowledge is almost complete. Only recently has the rate of development of construction machinery accelerated. Other material industries show similar lacks.

If, however, depth were increased and the entire process from raw material to finished house were controlled by a single firm large enough to integrate all parts of the production process, any disadvantages due to either too much monopoly or too little cohesion in the factors of supply might be offset. In theory, such a firm could be run by a management capable of planning the entire process in the most efficient way, and it could succeed in combining and streamlining the many diversified actions now taking place. Although belief in this type of advantage has been advanced by many, in the actual development of the industry to date, no concrete advantages of this type have appeared. The theoretical benefits of better management and stepped-up research and development programs have yet to be seen in practice. Nor has integration proved to be more efficient. In contrast with these illusory advantages, the greater risks and higher marketing costs attendant on increased scale are clear and ever-present.

Experience alone can prove or disprove the arguments of those who propound the necessity and possibility of revolutionizing the industry to achieve greater efficiency. It is impossible to combat an assertion of what might be that is not based on existing facts. Time may bring about radical changes; the fact that it has not as yet done so cannot prove or disprove the possibilities for the future. All that can be done is to look again at experience and try to see what hints it may hold.

In view of the facts that, with current housebuilding procedures, further increases in scale carry with them as many drawbacks as advantages, the main opportunity for increased efficiency would seem to lie in more rapid technical progress with the existing organization. Here, the lack of faster progress may well reflect the state of the product and the market structure of the industry. The materials used by the industry have developed over a long period of time and are efficient. The fact that they are produced and consumed primarily in competitive industries may, however, be hampering faster development.

The history of attempts at innovation in housebuilding in recent periods is extremely interesting. Attempts have been made to develop modern production methods, some of them backed by the resources of the country's largest firms. They have failed, primarily because other materials, more suitable for mass production, have difficulty competing on a price basis with wood. Increased production efficiency has not been able to offset increased material and overhead costs. This has been the experience both in England and in the United States.[9]

On the other hand, where funds have been available in the supplying industries, important improvements have been made. In some of the specific parts of the house—for example, in interior walls, window casements, and certain types of flooring—new products have been developed. Individual firms supplying these products had a sufficiently protected position to recoup their costs of innovation. In parts of the house constructed from materials produced by the less oligopolistic

[9] Cf. Kelly, *The Prefabrication of Houses;* Herbert G.Heavenrich, Jr., *Housing in Great Britain,* mimeographed (Cambridge: A. F. Bemis Foundation, 1952).

industries, improvements have, on the whole, resulted primarily from governmental research. Examples may be found in work on plywood, nailing, lumber strengths, plumbing, and work methods. These are areas in which no individual firm has had the interest to attempt research on the necessary scale, and even firms much larger than present-day ones would not be of sufficient size to undertake it.

The type of results that have been obtained to date may well indicate what progress to expect in the immediate future, given the structure of the housebuilding industry and of the lumber industry, its chief source of material. Individual firms, limited in their scope, can continue to perfect their own individual skills, particularly in the production process and in design. Their suppliers can continue to improve their products and to develop new machinery. But work on major innovations in the over-all structure of the industry is beyond the scope of individual firms and may well depend on the organization of some kind of coöperative efforts among housebuilders and on government leadership.

In fact, the encouragement of some type of joint research is probably a much more logical basis for bringing about growth in efficiency than is promoting expansion in the size of firms. The latter means is fraught with uncertainties, involving as it would the replacement of the present known advantages of easy entry and free competition by monopoly. It is an indirect route, which might lead to greater inefficiencies in other spheres than would be justified by the results of the research it might make possible.

On the whole, the organization of the housebuilding industry and the institutional setting in which it operates do not appear to be conducive to rapid change. Some of the very factors that make for ease of entry militate against further dynamic behavior, and some of the developments that make for safety of enterprise (e.g., spreading risk by trade specialization) also make for limitation of enterprise. The industry has not reacted readily to suggestions for change, perhaps in part because many of the changes advocated have been put so broadly that industry members cannot evaluate their worth. The ideas for a completely reorganized and different industry probably fall in this category of not being feasible, even though they cannot be ruled out completely. There are too many lessons from other fields to allow anyone to scoff at those who believe they have found new solutions of the building process. Granted the possibility of rapid change, those who believe in it must still explain why it has not occurred, and it does not appear that they have succeeded in making such an explanation. There is no indication that the persistence of existing methods is not simply a victory of the most efficient means in a competitive market.

11

The Future

Bases for Change

It requires not merely self-control but a break with tradition to conclude a study on housebuilding without prescribing a procession of panaceas which, if taken, would quickly cure all the housing ills of the economy. Since this study has shown that the housebuilding industry still has before it broad opportunities for betterment, a parade of alluring short cuts toward a happy and easy solution might seem called for. Unfortunately, such an optimistic pursuit of the future would run counter to all the body of facts which the statistical method has marshaled. These painstakingly gathered data teach that progress in housebuilding, as elsewhere, must make haste slowly, with knowledge and wisdom.

Housebuilding is in transition. The many forces whose ferment has formed the industry's past and present are at work determining its shape in the years immediately ahead. These years hold out hope for far greater progress than has yet been achieved. Although the housebuilding industry has made a better showing under postwar pressures than its critics will concede, its accomplishments are still not up to the peak which its advocates boast. There are yet higher levels of performance within its grasp. These levels will ultimately be attained. The immediately challenging questions concern the way in which they will be attained, and how soon. There is a broad range of possibilities as to the form and pace that change will take, based on the existing situation.

With its flexibility and freedom of entry, housebuilding remains one of the prime strongholds of free competition in the economy. Although the impact of a tremendous demand for housing on an initially limited supply did allow some firms to reap large gains and did decrease

applying it to housebuilding. Management can raise its whole achievement level by concentrating more attention on those performance aspects which were neglected in the postwar boom when firms centered on increasing production and profits. Although the housing shortage may have made maximum production a suitable goal for performance during that period, such aspects of performance as quality of product, the market, and efficiency will have more weight in the future.

Builders can face the future with more security when they have worked out the problems of the over-all organization of their industry, as well as the structure of their individual firms. With the industry remaining a conglomerate of competitive firms of all types, there will be opportunities for progress which can be grasped only by the industry as a whole. More coöperative action among firms appears both necessary and probable. In addition to strengthening their own operations and their bargaining power vis-à-vis their suppliers, builders through coöperation may expect to increase their influence on government policy. The trend is already apparent and may be expected to become an important area of action in the future.

Looking at the possibilities of industry bargaining power vis-à-vis its suppliers, it is conceivable that builders can help themselves by taking some initiative in stimulating improvements in the factors of supply to housebuilding. Any progress in the supplying industries would, of course, aid building. Given the existing structure and problems of the supplying industries, the extent of the important changes they will make on their own volition may be limited. These suppliers operate in accordance with their traditional part in the economy of a free enterprise system, and appear no better and no worse than the average industry. Progress at an average rate may be expected of them, but any more rapid change would need to be at the instance of the builders probably operating through their industry organizations.

Looking at the relationship between the industry and the government, it is clear that the federal government, especially in recent years, could make or break progress in housebuilding. In many cases its actions have been ambiguous. It has had too little concern with the effect of its actions on competition or performance. If progress is to go into high gear, the government must develop more logical and consistent policies than in the past, and must consider more carefully the results of its actions.[1] There are also wide areas for possible action not yet explored. Many areas where builders cannot possibly succeed as individuals, such as in production for atypical markets or for periods of depression, may be possible with government coöperation.

Closely related to the question of government policy is the problem of the market. The market was, of course, abnormal in the postwar period. Builders had no occasion to compete for sales; if houses could be built, they could be sold. No one was taking another's market. Such competition as existed was among buyers. This extreme demand was modified by 1950 when the supply began to meet the need. Once again builders had to worry about sales. Firms which had increased their volume and capacity had to seek sales in a more limited market. If normal conditions return to the housebuilding market, this acceleration of competition is likely to be the most potent single pressure in the near future.

Although all these forces will probably be important in an evolutionary way, there is no sign of a development apt to produce a revolution in housebuilding. The generally diverse conditions appear likely to continue for the immediate future unless an entirely new technical situation develops. The history of radical innovations indicates that they cast their shadow before them, and no prefiguration in the existing situation hints of sudden or extreme change. For a drastic force to be effective in the near future, it would have had to spark already, since the interval from drafting board to actuality is long. Likewise, it appears improbable that there will be any snowballing effects of change through tremendously increased scale. Housebuilding is not geared to develop huge firms. The same factors which have put a ceiling on the size of the largest firms continue to exist. In general, improvement will depend upon continued development along existing lines.

The Scope of Change

If progress proceeds along the lines indicated—toward better management, better performance, and better organization of the industry—what may be expected in terms of net results? These may be summarized as a change in the size distribution of firms, an improve-

[1] Cf. Leo Grebler, "Stabilizing Residential Construction—A Review of the Postwar Test," *American Economic Review* (September, 1949), pp. 898–910; and S. J. Maisel, "Policy Problems in Expanding the Private Housing Market," *American Economic Review Proceedings* (May, 1951), pp. 598–611.

ment in product and in marketing methods, increased research, a shift in profit rates, and probable advances in production processes.

With respect to size distribution, a more rapid polarization of the industry into large merchant firms, at one extreme, and small contractors, at the other, may be expected. The industry is still highly heterogeneous in sizes and types of builders, all in sundry stages of development. More vigorous competition should speed concentration at the two poles. If the housebuilder's evolution follows a survival-of-the-fittest pattern, many medium-sized firms, unable to stand the test of a stabilized or decreased demand, may become extinct.

The survival of competent small contractors seems unquestioned, not only because of their enduring role in the custom market, but also because of their potential role in the erection of prefabricated structures on scattered sites. For example, many small contractors might operate on houses designed, precut, and delivered to scattered sites by the large firms, with subcontracts handled by a constant group of trade contractors who would perform the same work for various small contractors. Such an operation would combine the advantages of both the large and the small firm, for the small firm's problems of purchasing and design would be solved through a central source, whereas its greater flexibility, lower overhead, more efficient labor, and better quality control would continue to offset many of the advantages of larger scale.

Survival of the large merchant firms is an obvious evolutionary certainty, since increased scale represents housebuilding's adaptation to the economy. Certain big building firms are likely to grow somewhat bigger than they are, but an octopus-like development—concentration of the national market into a few hands—appears improbable, at least in the near future. The prospects are rather that in most metropolitan areas a few large firms will take over more of their local markets, under the pressure of greater competition and more stress on efficiency. No single firm, at present, has a maximum share of more than 4 or 5 per cent of its local market. In the San Francisco Bay area, large firms offering a superior product made with more efficient methods will be able to double or triple this percentage, and, in addition, to hold a similar percentage of several adjacent markets. This will mean fewer and larger firms. A likely possibility is that the San Francisco Bay area, instead of having more than 100 large and medium firms with an average output of 90 houses each, as in 1949, will have only 20 or 25 such firms, with an average output of 400 or 500 each. By taking a share in adjacent markets, the largest of these firms might strike an output of from 2,000 to 5,000 units per year, in contrast with the present Bay area maximum of 1,200.

Turning to product improvement as the next net result of evolutionary forces at work, it may be expected that the house of tomorrow will rise above today's standards in design, quality, and spaciousness. With their increased emphasis on management and performance, the larger firms will pay more attention to building livability into their homes.

They will have to do this, for the protection of their reputations, if they are to remain large over a long period of time. It is only possible to milk the market in the short run, such as the recent period of excessive demand. For long-run success, large firms will have to introduce innovations and improve their merchandise. Builders' mistakes are impressed durably on the landscape. Although such mistakes did not deter the eager postwar homeseekers from buying, the return of more normal market conditions will compel builders to offer a satisfactory product if they are to attract new purchasers or to resell to previous customers.

Product improvement will require research and market analysis, activities on which housebuilding has spent only minor sums compared with other industries. Housebuilders have conducted virtually no research into materials, methods of production, or the market. The only study in these fields has been carried out by materials producers and by the government. As a result of heightened public interest in housing, Congress has appropriated funds for housing research, and helpful results have already been obtained.

Better industry organization and coöperation among firms can be expected to bring about important advances on these lines. Although research seems hardly worth undertaking to the individual builder because of its high cost compared with the returns to himself, research takes on greatly enhanced values when conducted collectively for builders as a group. Builders have already banded together for advertising and promotional purposes in Pacific coast areas, and progress in market analysis is a logical next step. Most builders are more interested now than formerly in market conditions and consumer needs.

When the industry as a whole is prepared to take a more active part in studying its methods and its market, both under its own power and in coöperation with others, better materials and means of production will develop at a faster rate. Present technological lags will be shortened. Even in the local market, builders acting coöperatively through joint organizations will be able to make long strides in market analysis. When they find out exactly what buyers want, and offer it, there will be a real improvement in housing. This improvement will benefit the builder as well as the buyer. There will be an increase in the amount of money spent for housing, because more buyers will enter the market and invest larger sums when they can obtain the values they really desire; and there will be a decrease in the cost of producing housing, because builders will avoid losses of energy and wastes of materials due to poor guessing.

The market forces of the future will probably bring profits, as well as the product, more into line with the consumer's standards. In the seller's market, builders have obtained large profits without having been pressed to increase efficiency, improve quality, or substantially lower prices. In a buyer's market, not only will efficiency have to be increased and quality improved, but firms may well have to shave their prices and profits in order to insure a stable sales volume.

Although builders' profits on sales were not unduly high in the postwar period, home buyers were paying more in profits during these years than they had paid in the past and more, in all probability, than they will in the future. Builders were both surprised and pleased by their profit rates after the war, and they did not expect them to last. They recognized that they were in an extremely fortunate position because of high demand, and that it was a make-hay-while-the-sun-shines situation. To risk a forecast—past experience suggests that a drop from a median of 8.5 per cent on sales to 3 or 4 per cent might be expected and that a spread around this level would be narrow. Such a fall in profits would be dangerous only if it retarded additional investment in the industry, or drove out of the industry the progressive entrepreneurs and innovators who were attracted to it by the chance for high profits on low investments—and who have done the most to increase housebuilding's efficiency.

Turning, finally, to the effect of the evolutionary forces on the production process, increased size of firms and improved management may be expected to bring about better standardization, controls, and job organization; new materials, tools, and techniques; advances in design, and greater ease of building.

At the present level of management skill, many executives are so ignorant of their own production process that they cannot improve it. They are not able to calculate the best mixture of inputs or the best technology to adopt. They cannot decide whether or not it is advantageous to substitute certain amounts and types of labor and materials for others. With more management knowledge and skill, developed through experience, research, and increasing initiative, firms will be able to determine both the best design and the most efficient approach to their organization for production.

Simplification of the production process is an important possibility for progress. Although building trends have moved in the direction of simplification, there continues to be a tremendous amount of departmentalization, a large use of skilled labor, and a heavy movement of men to and from the site. This is a complexity reflecting the continuation of the small craft tradition amidst the general transition to larger and more effective operations. Departmentalization costs too much. In an economy which pays higher and higher prices for skilled labor, those products with the highest skilled labor content are the most costly. To make houses cost less, ways must be found to use less skilled labor and fewer men per job.

Decreasing departmentalization can be accomplished by a consolidation of many of the production steps which now exist. Introduction of new tools, techniques, and materials, better coördination of trade contractors, use of fewer trade contractors, and movement of more production off the site will make this simplification possible.

The rate of introduction of these means for lowering production costs appears to be increasing. New tools include power saws, power planers, power routers, and other equipment which speeds up performance of the traditional jobs of the housebuilding process. More important than these, which merely enable existing processes to be done faster, is introduction of new materials which can eliminate some of the crafts and skills now employed. New inexpensive plastic materials which can be handled by carpenters replace tiles in many low-cost houses, thus doing away with the labor and materials cost of the tilesetter. Similarly, plasterers and masons no longer appear in many houses. When walls are ultimately simplified and made of a single material, two men of a single craft will erect a wall at one time, in place of the ten or more men of four crafts who now make eight to ten visits to a house to perform the several applications of different layers and final expensive finishing. It awaits only further research, knowledge, and skill to achieve this and other economies with materials in the house of tomorrow.

Economies similar to consolidation of production steps occur when more of the production process is moved off the site. Work done in factories can be performed under more efficient conditions, with more mechanization, more specialization, and less skilled labor. In the case of prefabricated cabinet work, which arrives at the house ready for installation, unskilled machine operators in the factories replace several crafts of skilled workmen on the site.

Off-site production of plumbing units appears to be another cost-saving procedure which is developing. With prefabrication, pipe and fittings can be cast in such a way that the number of necessary joints can be reduced; the amount of machine work can be increased; the skill needed to put together the parts can be decreased; the general level of workmanship in the finished product can be improved. Several of the largest builders have already designed complete plumbing units and have made attempts to manufacture them. They have met difficulties with unions, materials suppliers, codes, and financial institutions.[2] If they prove as efficient as seems probable, it is only a matter of time until the restrictions will be removed. In certain instances of off-site fabrication of plumbing installations in the San Francisco Bay area, restrictions have already been dropped.

The main obstacle to further progress in moving more fabrication off the site is transportation costs. As the size of prefabricated and pre-assembled units increases, the cost of hauling them rises rapidly. This is the chief reason that so many assemblies are still site-assembled.

There is a possible collision of interests in the future development of the prefabricator and the large-scale builder. Already the type of work done at the site and the type done at the factory have occasionally overlapped. This is because prefabricators seek to move as much of the production process as possible back into the factory, including the assembling of major components such as the whole wall. Meanwhile, conventional builders have continued to do the major part of their

[2] Kelly, *The Prefabrication of Houses*, pp. 153, 262–264.

assembly work at the site, although they have wanted increased off-site fabrication and have hoped that more of their subassemblies could come to them in a finished condition.

The issue of site versus factory poses important questions as to the relationship of the one to the other and to the market in general. Would it be more economical to have a greater concentration and specialization of firms fabricating subassemblies? For example, would the country benefit by having firms specialized in plumbing assemblies, chimney assemblies, electrical installations, and the like, selling their finished products to operative builders for incorporation in their houses? Or would the country gain more advantage from having building firms specialized in the entire factory fabrication of a house, including the major subassemblies?

The answers to these questions will be determined by conditions existing in local marketing, transportation, and overhead. In these fields, the conventional builders' advantages over complete prefabricators have been great. If builders maintain their marketing advantages and their low overhead, the answer will be that movement of work off the site should continue primarily in the form of subassemblies rather than complete units.

The increasing fabrication of subassemblies off the site will, of course, reduce the number of trade contractors working in the house, by reducing the number of skilled crafts required. Thus the purpose of simplification of the production process will be served.

Even if the number of skilled trades is not reduced greatly, better planning of the work of the trade contractors offers an important opportunity for lowering production costs. Only in the most skillfully managed firms is much emphasis given to the proper production integration of the trades. With management's increased competence, reëxamination of the trade contractors' work methods and their relationship to the whole problem of building a house will bring about closer coördination, better techniques, and more mechanization, thereby contributing to the streamlining of the production process and heightening the over-all efficiency of housebuilding.

Conclusions

The critics of housebuilding have been sharply divided—the prophets of gloom who have cried havoc, chaos, and confusion in terms of profiteering, inefficiency, and waste, and the smiling optimists who have promised palaces for all the people at half the price of huts.

Somewhere in between the forecasts of the two groups lies the truth. Relying on the data in this volume, we may visualize the essence of what lies ahead. A new estimate of the future may be formulated—still, of course, not without risk of error. Such an estimate would run somewhat as follows:

(1) Increased scale of operation and intensified competition will lead to greater efficiency. Removing the umbrella of protection will force the average efficiency level of all firms close to the level of efficient operation which is now achieved by a small minority. Future elevation of average firms to the level of the present efficient minority should improve the production process sufficiently to lower construction costs by 5 per cent.

(2) As keener competition compels the most efficient firms to give up part of their wide profit margins, and at the same time keys them as price setters for the industry, the selling price of houses should be lowered by an additional 5 per cent.

(3) Through the greater bargaining ability and buying power which will come with increased size of firm, it is probable that economies in materials purchases amounting to from 3 to 6 per cent may be realized.

(4) By reduction of external restrictions, whose maximum costs were calculated at 7 per cent, additional savings can be made.

When all these factors are added up—improved performance, lower profits, better purchasing, fewer restrictions—it appears that a concerted effort to bring peak efficiency to the housebuilding industry, with existing methods and knowledge, could lower average costs by about 20 per cent.

Beyond these identifiable economies, a gradual introduction of new methods would occur—similar to the innovations for individual parts of the house which have taken place in the past decade—and each of these changes would further increase the efficiency of the whole operation. Finally, of course, there are the possibilities of far-reaching reorganization and radical improvement which, though not visible on the horizon today, are always a possibility.

Although it is hoped that improved efficiency will result in equivalently lower prices, this would not necessarily be the case. In a dynamic situation, the costs of the factors required to build a house may change again as they have in the past through forces outside the industry. Housebuilders cannot control the prices of their inputs, but only the efficiency with which the inputs are used. Although improved efficiency will not guarantee lower actual prices, it does mean that prices will be lower than would otherwise be the case.

The improvements in total performance which have been estimated here as probabilities for the future may come as a disappointment to those who have been captivated by the glittering hopes of the optimists. The failure of the housebuilding industry to revolutionize itself for the welfare of mankind appears, however, to be not so much an indictment of the industry's accomplishments as it is a reflection on the wisdom of the prophets.

Where the prophets have failed by promising too much progress, it is hoped that estimates based on facts will succeed. The facts show no shake-up to be likely in the housebuilding industry, no revolution in production, methods, organization, costs, or prices. Evolution is the order of the day—in housebuilding, as elsewhere. Progress in the future will depend upon improving efficiency along paths already staked out. That even more spectacular gains in efficiency cannot be predicted on the basis of analysis and evaluation of the facts is, in a sense, a tribute to the present level of development of the housebuilding industry; that a gain of at least 20 per cent in efficiency is foreseeable represents a realistic hope for better housing in America. The speed with which the housebuilding industry brings about these gains for itself and the householders of its country will depend upon the rate at which it gathers available knowledge about itself and puts that knowledge to intelligent use.

APPENDIXES

Appendix A. General Method of Procedure and Reliability of the Estimates

The main purpose of this study was to measure fictions, beliefs, and hypotheses against facts. For this purpose, it was necessary to have accurate data and to have them in a form that was useful for analysis. Although information in the housebuilding field has improved, it is still woefully short.[1] Most data are concerned with existing houses and not with the industry which produces them. Whatever estimates exist for housebuilding are usually for the entire nation. Because of the lack of uniformity in the industry, difficulty is experienced in applying them locally.

Whatever data were available have been used in this study and are presented in the following sections. Basic, of course, are general statements as to population, housing, and income made available through the decennial censuses of the United States. These sources appear in Appendixes B and F. Census data on the materials manufacturing industries are also valuable and are used in Appendix I.

Perhaps more helpful was the fact that this area was one in which the United States Bureau of Labor Statistics had gathered housing data. This meant that sample information existed on the characteristics of houses constructed and on the methods of financing the purchases of these houses. It meant also that there was an independent estimate of the number of houses constructed in the area based upon monthly reports of all building permit centers. Finally, the Bureau of Labor Statistics gathered information on the prices of building materials. (Data from this source are described in Appendixes B, C, F, and I.)

More information was available on labor than on any other phase of the study. The United States Bureau of the Census, the California State Department of Employment, and the California State Department of Industrial Relations all compile and publish labor data. It is possible to obtain labor facts in the construction industry both for the state and the area on the numbers of men employed; on wage rates, earnings, strikes, and work stoppages; and to a certain extent on agreements, turnover, and annual income (cf. Appendix J).

[1] For a complete review of available data, cf. E. E. Ashley "Recent Developments in Government Construction Statistics," address, American Statistical Association, Dec. 29, 1951, Boston, Mass., mimeographed, United States Housing and Home Finance Agency.

Financial institutions, including the Federal Housing Administration and the Veterans Administration, title companies, and credit-reporting firms gather financial data, information on the background of firms, and some operating information, particularly with respect to costs and volume. Information of this type was made available through the Bay Area Residential Real Estate Committee and directly by the agencies concerned. While this study was under way, a similar project aimed directly at the problem of financing was in process which made available additional information in that field (cf. Appendix E).

In addition, a small amount of knowledge on over-all profits and movement in and out of the industry becomes available through the publications of tax-collecting agencies. This type of data is discussed in Appendix J.

The available data, though improved, still fell far short of the amount required for an adequate industrial study. For most questions on which information was required, no secondary sources existed. The bulk of the information on housebuilding rests with the individual firms. To obtain it, one must approach the firms through a series of surveys, case studies, and interviews. That was the primary method used in this study. Necessary data were collected from individual firms by field surveys.

In the past it was impossible to make any precise statements about the structure or operations of housebuilding firms because no one knew how many there were, which were typical, or what part each played in the entire building scene. Our primary aim in this study was to avoid this difficulty by establishing a complete universe and enumeration of all builders in the area. The objective was a complete representation of all types of firms active in all sizes and sorts of localities.

The following sections report the manner in which this aim was achieved. With a complete initial listing, information was then obtained by extensive mail surveys, followed by interviews with initial nonrespondents. Information on operations, methods, structure, background, and so on, was obtained by drawing further samples and subsamples from the original universe. The size of each sample depended upon the amount of variation in replies and the cost and difficulty of obtaining the information. In each case, the method was first to obtain as much information as possible from intensive case studies of a small group of firms. Following this, those variables that seemed significant were included on shorter questionnaires to an expanded sample of firms.

Five separate surveys were conducted during this study and they constitute the basic research underlying this report. In chronological order, they were:

1. A mail survey of housebuilders in the San Francisco metropolitan area during the years 1949 and 1950, designed to obtain information about the size, location, general method of operation, price class, and so on of firms constructing dwelling units in 1949 (Appendix C).

2. An interviewing survey during 1950 of a sample of housebuilding firms for the purpose of obtaining detailed information on the organization, method of operation, relations with suppliers and subcontractors of building firms (Appendix D).

3. An analysis of the financial and operating records for 1949 and 1950 of a sample of housebuilding firms to procure data on the ownership and financial structure, revenue, profitability, age of enterprise, characteristics of the management, and the like of building firms (Appendix E).

4. A mail survey of trade contractors in the Bay area during 1950 and 1951 for information relating to their volume of business, method of operation, and so on in 1949 (Appendix G).

5. A study of the potential cost of construction of a "composite house" for the purpose of determining the influence of a builder's size on building cost and the quantitative effect of various restrictions in the housebuilding field (Appendix H).

The subject matter of these surveys covered 15 major facets of the housebuilding operation, more than 60 different topics, and several hundred individual items. All this material is important, and most of it is necessary, in obtaining a proper perspective of the industry and its operations and functions. The following list shows the questions asked and the information obtained. The letter or letters following each item indicate which survey was used to gather the necessary data. The letter "C" after each item in the first group, for instance, indicates that this information came from the mail survey of all housebuilders.

I. Classification
1. Name (C)
2. Number of units completed in 1949: (*a*) by price; (*b*) operative; (*c*) contract; (*d*) tract (C)
3. Total volume of building: (*a*) new houses; (*b*) multifamily; (*c*) other new buildings; (*d*) additions, remodeling, repair, and maintenance (C)
4. Total employees on October 15, 1949: (*a*) on site; (*b*) off site (C)
5. Area or areas in which building was performed (C)

II. Organization and Management
1. Type of firm: (*a*) individual proprietorship; (*b*) partnership; (*c*) corporation; (*d*) group of affiliates (D, E)
2. Functions performed: (*a*) building; (*b*) real estate; (*c*) land development; (*d*) insurance; (*e*) rental; (*f*) materials supply; (*g*) mills; (*h*) trade contracting; (*i*) other (D, E)
3. Organization chart including number of employees in each category (D)
4. Age of firm (E)
5. Management experience: (*a*) age; (*b*) education; (*c*) years as as employer; (*d*) years in industry; (*e*) experience outside industry; (*f*) interruptions in career as builder; (*g*) failure and cause; (*h*) relatives who aided (E)
6. Determinants of size: (*a*) land; (*b*) credit; (*c*) risk; (*d*) managerial span; (*e*) availability of personnel; (*f*) satisfaction; (*g*) other (D)
7. If no longer active, reasons for halting (D, E)

III. Production, Development, and Design
1. Market analysis (D)
2. Determination of design: (*a*) stock plan; (*b*) architect; (*c*) own design (D)
3. Computations with respect to new materials and methods (D)
4. Information on new developments and products (D)
5. Information on bids: (*a*) method of seeking bids; (*b*) procedure; (*c*) time and cost (D)
6. Characteristics of units: (*a*) price; (*b*) location; (*c*) basement or utility room; (*d*) number of rooms; (*e*) livable floor space; (*f*)

wall construction; (*g*) heating; (*h*) plumbing; (*i*) fireplace; (*j*) garage; (*k*) type and style of roof; (*l*) type of floor (C, F)

IV. Organization of Production
   1. Integration (D, E)
   2. Method of operations: (*a*) conventional; (*b*) type of precutting; (*c*) type of preassembly; (*d*) prefabrication (D)
   3. Organization of crews (D)
   4. Techniques: (*a*) machinery; (*b*) patterns, templates, and jigs; (*c*) special design (D)

V. Records
   1. Estimating procedures (D)
   2. Materials-purchase program (D)
   3. Inventory controls (D)
   4. Operations-planning schedules (D)
   5. Performance controls (D)
   6. Cost records (D)

VI. Sales
   1. Method of handling: (*a*) self; (*b*) own staff; (*c*) special deal with broker; (*d*) affiliated firm; (*e*) part of land development; (*f*) normal brokerage; (*g*) other (D)

VII. Purchasing
   1. Source of supply: (*a*) retail; (*b*) wholesale; (*c*) producer; (*d*) produces own; (*e*) trade contractor (D)
   2. Reasons for method used: (*a*) credit; (*b*) convenience; (*c*) risk; (*d*) comparative cost; (*e*) restricted channels (D)
   3. Costs for each material through each possible channel (H)
   4. Land: (*a*) developed; (*b*) undeveloped; (*i*) amount; (*ii*) method of development; (*c*) effect of land on operations (D)

VIII. Subcontracts
   1. Items integrated and those subcontracted (D)
   2. Reasons for subcontracting: (*a*) restricted entry; (*i*) unions (*ii*) supplies; (*b*) credit; (*c*) supervision; (*d*) comparative costs (D)
   3. Relations to subcontractors: (*a*) frequency of change; (*b*) method of price negotiations; (*c*) direct relationships; (*d*) costs; (*e*) supervision (D, G)

IX. Trade Contractors' Operations
   1. Classification: (*a*) volume; (*b*) distribution of volume (*i*) new

houses (*ii*) other new buildings (*iii*) additions, remodeling, repair, maintenance; (*c*) number of employees (*i*) on-site (*ii*) off-site; (*d*) location of work (G)

2. Operations: (*a*) crews; (*b*) equipment; (*c*) plans (G, H)
3. Cost and effect of scale of job: (*a*) labor costs, reasons for cost variations; (*b*) material; (*c*) overhead and profit (G, H)
4. Materials purchases (G, H)
5. Labor relations (G)
6. Relations with builders: (*a*) method of obtaining jobs; (*b*) estimating (D, G)

X. Labor Relations

1. Kind and quantity of labor hired directly (C, D)
2. Method of hiring (D, H)
3. Turnover of crews (D)
4. Efficiency of men (D)
5. Relationship with union, main problems (D)
6. Effect of working rules and jurisdictions (D)
7. Figures on productivity and costs (D)
8. Union regulations: (*a*) employer working; (*b*) working permits; (*c*) overtime pay; (*d*) foreman; (*e*) entry; (*f*) restrictions on tools and methods; (*g*) hiring hall; (*h*) travel time; (*i*) regulations on output; (*j*) apprenticeship program (D, H)

XI. Building Codes

1. Problem of obtaining permits and inspections (D)
2. Problems in content of codes (D, H)
3. Problems in administration (D)
4. Restrictions imposed by codes (D)

XII. Financing

1. Method of obtaining construction credit: (*a*) cash; (*b*) suppliers; (*c*) FHA firm commitments; (*d*) conventional mortgage; (*e*) loan on general assets; (*f*) other (D, E)
2. Source: (*a*) bank; (*b*) savings and loan; (*c*) insurance company; (*d*) other (D, E)
3. Cost (D)
4. Consumer financing: (*a*) FHA; (*b*) VA; (*c*) conventional; (*d*) source (D, F)
5. Any problems with FHA or VA or bank (D)

XIII. Firm's Financial Structure

1. Balance sheet: (*a*) total assets; (*b*) current assets; (*c*) tools and equipment; (*d*) real estate and buildings; (*e*) net worth (E)

XIV. General

1. Chief problems (D)
2. Ideas on industry (D)
3. History of firm (D, E)

For each survey, group of case studies, or interview, common statistical techniques were followed under careful controls, so that final results could be given in absolute terms, and statements could be made as to the confidence which is attached to each figure. Both the descriptive material in the body of this book and the tables are based on these studies.

The following appendixes give information as to the specific methods used in obtaining universes and drawing samples. In each case, however, the same fourteen basic steps were followed, namely: (1) listing the population of sampling units (frame), usually business units; (2) deciding what kinds of information were to be secured, that is, the potential variables for analysis; (3) developing the method of data collection, such as mail survey questionnaire, interview blank, record analysis form, and the like; (4) pretesting, where possible, the method of data collection by a small-sample pilot survey; (5) dividing the population into strata or categories (subframes), selecting sampling ratios for the strata and drawing, by a random process, the required number of sampling units; (6) collecting the complete data from responding sampling units where the survey process was used or recording data from primary and secondary records; (7) calling back on nonresponding sampling units for further data; (8) preliminary analyzing of the information and extending the sampling, if necessary; (9) transcribing the data to I.B.M. punch cards or to analysis sheets, directly or after coding; (10) setting up cross-classifications for the variables and carrying out machine or manual sorting and tabulation processes; (11) inflating the sample results to secure full population distributions; (12) calculating estimates of population parameters such as the arithmetic mean, median, etc.; (13) computing confidence limits for population parameters; (14) preparing tables in final form for inclusion in this book.

Although the preponderance of the quantitative (and much of the qualitative) information contained in this report was obtained under strict statistical controls, a few figures are presented which were based on small, nonrandom samplings, and their reliability cannot be accurately assessed by standard statistical methods. These cases, mostly occurring in the estimation of the cost of the composite house, are explicitly noted in the text and require no comment here beyond the observation that inferior accuracy is not necessarily implied.

Even where complete population listing, stratification, random drawing of sample units, and comparison with independent estimates can be rigorously enforced, results are still subject to sampling variability, and only ranges within which "true" values lie can be given with assurance. Where it is necessary to base statements on more limited observations, the judgment of the observer as to their consistency and representativeness replaces the objective reliability measures derivable from the variability of random sample values. An observer familiar with the field and armed with supplementary information may draw inferences from sparse data which prove as valid as those based on more extensive surveys, particularly if nonnormal distributions prevail.

Two of the surveys listed above—the mail surveys of housebuilders and trade contractors—may be regarded as "complete" surveys in terms of the effort spent in establishing the extent of populations to be surveyed. Although data were then gathered by contacting of randomly selected sampling units, the fraction of universe members reached was generally high. Additional authority was lent to the data by stratifying of builders according to size and increasing the sampling fraction in the strata of large builders with greatest influence in the industry totals, whereas in the trade-contracting survey, the more important categories were covered intensively in preference to the covering of all categories thinly. In both surveys the possibility of bias from nonresponse was reduced by the following up with personal calls on a substantial percentage of nonrespondents, both to secure answers to the questionnaires and to ascertain the causes for failure to answer.

The interviewing survey of builders and the analysis of financial and operating records might be called "small sample surveys," since industry members were selected for these further studies by subsampling of the housebuilder population. Aproximately one-tenth of the active builders in the area were reached in the former; one-sixth in the latter. Here again, however, coverage of the more important strata was emphasized, and the samples were statistically adequate, being "small" only in relation to those used in the preceding surveys.

The last of the projects mentioned can be classed as a "very small sample" survey. The "composite house" study was essentially a cost-index problem, and the measure evolved has the deficiencies common to all such indexes, including, perhaps, undersampling. As stated above, no reliabilities have been calculated for this particular study. Enough price and cost data of sufficient homogeneity were collected on each of the house components to assure that ruling prices and cost levels were reasonably well approximated, and it was not considered worth while to make further expenditures of time and effort for an almost certainly small return in increased accuracy.

Since all the estimates in this book are based on samples, they are subject to sampling variability. In addition, of course, any survey or census is subject to normal biases in response which would appear even if the population were completely enumerated. Every effort was made to keep these normal biases as small as possible, including re-checks where independent data indicated that some errors might have occurred. As a result of this care, the amount of response bias is believed to be minimal. This belief is reinforced by the fact that all data have been checked against other sources and rechecked with the men in the industry wherever possible, and, to date, no important biases have been discovered.

The amount of sampling variability depends on the size of the sample and the method by which it is drawn. When samples are drawn on a probability basis as they were in these surveys, it is possible to make statements concerning the degree of uncertainty associated with the estimates.

Table 1 shows the confidence intervals for the estimates of the number of builders and trade contractors, as well as certain other parameters. It will be observed that most of the major estimates fall within a range of plus or minus 5 to 10 per cent at the 95 per cent probability level. This means that 19 of 20 samples drawn from the same universe would be expected to fall within the given confidence intervals.[2]

In addition, it is possible to state the confidence intervals which apply to the sampling of attributes of the builders and trade contrac-

[2] The estimates in tables 1 and 2 were derived by use of the formulae for estimating sampling errors as described in F. Yates, *Sampling Methods for Census and Surveys* (London: Charles Griffen and Co., 1949), sections 7.5 and 7.7.

tors. Much of the description in this book was based on tabulations showing the percentage distribution of various attributes found among builders of a given size. The more important of these data are presented in the tables which follow.

Since these distributions are based on samples, they, too, may vary from the true values existing in the universe. The reliability of an estimated percentage depends both upon the size of the percentage and the number of replies upon which the distribution is based. Since the number of replies in the surveys conducted for this study varied both with respect to the particular characteristic being examined and the size classification of the builder, there is a difference between the reliability of separate tables as well as of the columns in a given table. The classification in table 2 enables the interested reader to determine exactly the reliability of any percentage based upon the surveys conducted at the University of California. Reliability of data taken from other sources may be found in the cited references.

Table 2 contains a list of the tables based upon original data which follow in the statistical appendix. The stub is divided into sections based upon the size classifications used for builders with an additional section for trade contractors. In each section, there is a listing of all tables in which the specific size classification is used. The columns are divided to list possible percentages which appear in the following tables.

To find the confidence interval for any estimate for which this book is the original source, find the proper row in table 2 based upon the appendix table in which the estimate appears, as well as the size of builder classification to which it applies. Then if the figure shown under the proper column is added and subtracted from the estimated percentage in question, it will give the range within which the percentage would have fallen in 19 out of 20 samples drawn similarly from the same population.

Appendix B. Housebuilding Production

The term "house," as used in this study, means a one- or two-family dwelling unit, as opposed to a multifamily unit or apartment. Apartment houses differ in form, in type of materials, in methods of construction, and in costs from houses. They are as remote from the house to construct as, for instance, a store building would be, and are, therefore, considered in the category of "other building" in the cases of housebuilders who did both. Previous studies in the field, particularly the *Census of Business: 1939, Construction* (see also *American Housing*, p. 379), also define housebuilders as builders of one- and two-family structures. Although the production of two-family units in the area was low, several firms concentrated work in this field, and neglecting their production of two-family houses would have given an incorrect picture of their operations.

Most existing statistical data are not concerned with houses as such. They are concerned with shelter and, therefore, deal with dwelling units, the basic unit of shelter. Dwelling units can be rooms, caves, houses, or the like. The number of dwelling units in a given house can, and does, change frequently. Table 3 shows the changes in the population and in the number of dwelling units from 1930 to 1950, both for the United States and for the San Francisco–Oakland metropolitan area. These data are taken from the decennial censuses, the primary source of such information.

The monthly and annual production of new nonfarm dwelling units are estimated currently by the U. S. Bureau of Labor Statistics with national estimates available back as far as 1900 (cf. *American Housing*, table 10). Data for the nation, metropolitan areas, and selected standard metropolitan areas are reported periodically in *Construction*. Table 4 shows this information for recent years. It includes data both for all dwelling units and for houses.

Because no regular information is collected about housebuilders, far less information is available on the size group that builds these units. Existing data depend upon special compilations made nationally by the Bureau of Labor Statistics for 1938 and 1949 and by the Bureau of the Census for 1939, and made as part of this study for the San Francisco standard metropolitan area in 1949.

Estimates of housebuilders for 1938 are based on a survey of building permits issued for one-family houses in 72 cities (cf. "Builders of 1-Family Houses in 72 Cities," *Monthly Labor Review*, September, 1940 [R. 1151] and "Operations of Urban Home Builders," *Monthly Labor Review*, May, 1941 [R. 1313]). The total number of builders in the medium and large classifications has been estimated (cf. table 5) by dividing all urban areas of the country into population size groups and considering the reports obtained from the enumerated areas as a subsample for their own particular size groups. The estimate for the number of builders in each classification was obtained by multiplying the number of builders reported in the subsample by a blowup ratio obtained by dividing the number of completed houses in the whole population size group by the completed houses in the subsample.

This estimate is thought to have a downward bias because: (1) The use of permits in the original survey may underestimate actual sizes because some firms may have used different names and built in other areas. (2) Houses built in rural nonfarm areas are not included. (3) The enumerated subsamples may underrepresent urban suburbs of large cities. On the other hand, all cities of more than 500,000, the only ones where large firms were reported, are completely enumerated. (For a discussion of this entire problem, as well as an independent survey confirming the approximate level of these estimates, cf. *American Housing,* Appendix C.5.)

The data for 1939 are estimated from the *Census of Business: 1939; Vol. IV. Construction.* The Census enumerated all operative builders. Although the coverage of the census is thought to be somewhat incomplete in the lower brackets, there is no indication of any unusual bias for the medium- and large-sized firms discussed in this section. The Census reports by size-groups the number of operative builders in the United States, as well as the total value of work each group performed on one- and two-family houses.

In order that the data might be used, it was necessary to convert the value of work figures into house units. This was done by assuming that a house was completed for every $2,000 of work performed (including materials and values added) by an operative builder. The average construction cost of houses in 1939 was $4,000 (cf. *Housing Statistics*). The average builder performed half the work on houses he built and subcontracted half (*Census of Business: 1939; Vol. IV,* table 9A).

Based on this estimate, medium-sized builders were those whose volume of work exceeded $50,000 in 1939, and large-sized ones were those with a volume of work of more than $200,000. The estimates for table 5 were derived from table 5A of the 1939 Census. This estimate is for operative builders only, and, therefore, again is biased downward. For purposes of comparison, it may be observed that when builders were completely surveyed in 1949, 83 per cent of the large firms and 65 per cent of the medium firms reported that they did only operative building. This means that some nonoperative builders should be added to the estimate if the complete number of housebuilding firms is to be arrived at. If the same ratio held in 1939 as in 1949, the estimate for all large housebuilding firms would be 111 in 1939, and for all types of medium-sized housebuilding firms would be 600. The additional firms would have been included under the heading "General contractor" rather than "Builder" in the census, and thus would not be included in table 5.

The figures for 1949 are based on a special compilation for this study from the results of the 1951 Builders' Panel Survey of the Bureau of Labor Statistics. This special compilation was necessary to meet the definition of a house as a one- or two-family structure.

Appendix C. Size and Type of Housebuilding Firms

In the past, the size, structure, and attributes of housebuilding firms were unknown. In order that this gap in knowledge might be filled, it was necessary to survey the actual firms in the industry. This was done for this study by a mail and interviewing survey of all housebuilders (C) in the Bay area.

A complete listing of all housebuilders was obtained by the copying of names, addresses, and other pertinent data from all housebuilding permits issued in any or all of the 52 permit centers of the San Francisco standard metropolitan area during the period October 1, 1948 to September 30, 1949. All permits issued to a builder in any center were combined. When all permit recipients had been listed and all obvious duplication or errors eliminated, the resulting initial population was divided into eight strata; nonprofessionals (i.e., unlicensed individuals) and seven size classes of firms—those taking out 1, 2–4, 5–9, 10–24, 25–49, 50–99, and 100 and more permits.

The original population contained 4,430 permit recipients. A questionnaire was mailed to all firms which had received 5 or more permits and to a 50 per cent random sample of those that had received less than 5. A total of 2,791 questionnaires were mailed. Of the total who received questionnaires, 643 replied by mail. A random sample was then drawn of the nonrespondents in each stratum and these sampling units were checked in person. The efficiency of this sample was increased by having the number drawn from each stratum depend upon its importance and variability. A total of 319 replies to the questionnaire was obtained through personal calls. The total number of replies received ranged from 20 per cent among the smallest builders to 90 per cent among the largest.

The replies were then edited and processed through machine tabulations. In each case, sample results were blown up by factors which weighted responses in each stratum according to whether they came from original mailed replies or call-backs. The estimates of confidence limits were also derived from data by individual stratum.

Data on builders' operations for the entire United States and for all metropolitan areas are based upon the 1951 BLS Builders' Panel Survey which followed a basically similar method. The main difference in method was the fact that the Bureau of Labor Statistics combined both area and size stratification in its sampling. Their initial estimates were obtained for a group of selected areas which were then blown up to a national total. In addition, the Bureau of Labor Statistics counted the number of houses started during 1949 and classified builders on this basis, whereas our study counted and classified by units completed.

Table 6 compares the number of units built by nonprofessionals in the United States, in metropolitan areas, and in the San Francisco area. The continued importance of nonprofessionals in housebuilding is clear. However, the BLS estimate that more than 60 per cent of the houses built outside of metropolitan areas were built by nonprofessionals appears unusually high.

Table 7 shows the number of firms distributed into size classifications. The BLS distribution is based on all housebuilding firms classified according to the number of dwelling units started in 1949. The San Francisco distribution includes all housebuilding firms classified according to the number of houses completed in 1949. Per cents here, as elsewhere in the tables, may not add to 100 because of rounding.

Tables 8 and 9 show the number of houses erected by the builders within each size group, as well as the number built operatively within each size group. The Bay area survey defines as operatively built all units constructed for the firm's own account and not on an individual contract. The Bureau of Labor Statistics considers a house as built on contract if the land was owned by others. This excludes from the operative class those units built by a large-scale builder where the land was owned by a development firm. The differences in definition are not important either in practice or in the estimate. All data clearly show the importance of medium- and large-sized operative builders in the present market.

The reason for the variations in the number of houses shown in tables 6, 8, and 9 results from the fact that different groups are under consideration in each table. Table 6 includes all houses built within the area, whether built by nonprofessionals or by housebuilding firms. Table 8 includes only units built by the firms based in the particular area. Table 9 includes only those units built operatively by these firms. The footnote for table 10 shows the relationship among these totals for the Bay area.

Table 10 presents the same information for the Bay area in more detail and, in addition, shows the number of units built in tracts and outside the area by size groups. This table demonstrates the more complete distribution which was used for most of the analysis. The tables printed in this book are all contractions of the original distributions.

Tables 11 and 12 show Bay area firms cross-classified by separate measures of size and, therefore, also show the firms distributed by their dollar volume and their number of employees. The correlation between the measures of size is high, but not perfect. The variations are primarily accounted for by the fact that firms did other types of building in addition to houses, or that firms were not equally active during the whole year. Firms which were small when classified by houses built, but were large in volume and employees, were primarily general contractors for whom housebuilding was only a minor function. These firms are atypical, and the statements made concerning the operations of the average small firms do not apply to them. Their presence was one reason for using the median instead of the arithmetic mean in analysis, since they wield an undue influence on all means.

The small number of employees compared with completions for some firms is accounted for by the fact that firms were asked to report only employees on their October 15, 1949, payroll. For firms in business only part of the year or with an uneven seasonal distribution, a sizable difference would exist between this figure and their average number of employees with the latter more nearly correlated to completions.

Tables 13, 14, 15, and 16 furnish additional information on the type of building performed by housebuilding firms. Tables 13 and 14 show the increased concentration on operative building and tract building which takes place as the size of firms increases. Only the smallest firms are primarily contract builders, whereas among the largest, many do no contract work whatsoever.

Table 15 shows the amount of work on other types of building (non-housebuilding work) done by housebuilding firms. It is clear that most of these firms concentrate primarily on housebuilding, though some are general contractors who build houses while doing all other types of building jobs. Table 16 shows that frequently this other building consists of apartment houses. The total number of dwelling units constructed by housebuilding firms was about 10 per cent higher than the number of houses they built.

The final group of tables discussed here, 17, 18, and 19, detail other facts about the makeup of housebuilding firms. Table 17 shows the distribution of firms by the number of permit centers in which they operated. Although most firms operate in only one location, a few built houses in more than five different cities or towns. Table 10 showed that nearly 10 per cent of the houses built by these firms were actually outside the metropolitan area. Most of these houses out of the area were in locations in adjacent counties.

Table 18 classifies firms by the number of months they were active, as well as by their size. The data in this table primarily reflect the rapid turnover in housebuilding firms. Some of the firms not active for the entire year, however, may simply have been dormant while in the process of reorganization or finding new projects. Some turnover exists at all levels. Less than full-time production is common among small firms, where owners work as mechanics for others between their own projects.

Table 19 shows the average price of houses built by each firm classified by size. Although exceptions exist, the most obvious relationship is the concentration of the small firms in the high price market. This fact is made clear also by table 39, which shows the actual distribution by price and firm size of each house completed.

Appendix D. Housebuilders' Operations

Although the mail survey of housebuilders was broad in terms of its coverage, reaching a significant proportion of all active housebuilders, the range of information sought had to be fairly narrow, since response to mail questionnaires is determined partly by the length and apparent degree of complexity of the questionnaire form. Therefore, in order to gather additional data on the details of housebuilders' operations, the mail survey was followed up with a series of interviews conducted in a sample of housebuilding firms.

The interviewing survey was begun with a preliminary interviewing program in which periods of time ranging from an hour to several days were spent with members of building firms. It was felt that subsequent, shorter interviews could be carried on more efficiently if the principal variables to be examined could be discovered in these beginning interviews, and possible deviations from common practice focused upon in a standardized interview form. The preliminary interviews were more or less free in form and indefinite in length, nondirective, and aimed at obtaining as much information as possible; the shorter, more directive interviews were intended to secure a definite set of facts and figures and, only secondarily, where the interviewees were willing, to obtain broader statements of opinion, illustrative anecdotes, and the like.

The first step in the survey after preliminary interviewing was to draw a subsample sufficient to obtain replies from 150 builders by random selection from the population established in the mail survey. The original population, rather than the population of initial mail respondents, was used so as to avoid the possibility of bias arising from probable differences between the operations of those who answer readily and those who do not. In accordance with the scheme of stratification earlier applied, the sampling fraction was increased in the strata of larger builders. Taking for denominators the numbers of builders in the respective strata as determined in the mail survey, the sampling ratios in the 1–9, 10–24, 25–99, and 100-and-over size class strata were $^{78}/_{1362}$, $^{30}/_{189}$, $^{24}/_{77}$, and $^{18}/_{30}$.

Step two consisted of sorting the sampling units by location, laying out routes for calls, and arranging appointments with firms. The third step was the interviewing process in which the field man, guided by the interview form, asked questions of the building firm member, listened, observed; and recorded data. Since the majority of the interviews occurred at building sites, the interviewers had opportunities to watch work in progress, note the methods used, and ask supplemental questions about operations. In many cases, the interviewer was "passed around" among members of management to obtain information about particular functions from the men responsible for them. Each interview was summarized upon the field man's return to the office so that the information could be evaluated and useful leads noted.

These surveys resulted in a large number of case studies as well as specific statistical information. The statistical data were tabulated covering 30 points of the firms' operations. From the case studies and the tabulations, descriptions of typical operations and of major variations in them were written for each size of firm. These descriptions were then submitted to a group of selected builders of each size for comment. Such checking was employed to insure against important errors in interpretation or emphasis in the transfer of the data from the surveys to final form.

Sections 4–8 of chapters 3, 4, and 5, which are descriptions of the operations of the firms, and certain sections of chapters 8 and 9 are based on these surveys. Tables 20–23 are examples of some of the more important statistical tabulations derived from these data. Because much of the other data showed only a small amount of variation within classes, the results have been incorporated directly in the descriptive chapters and no separate tabulations are printed.

Table 20 lists the variations in overhead personnel which occur with size. The table contains data only for those firms which did 90 per cent or more of their volume in housebuilding. If the firms that did large volumes of other types of building were not considered separately, their overhead staff primarily engaged in other functions would have been reflected in this table, and the true relationship between size and overhead for housebuilding would not have been clear. The supreme importance of owners working as foremen and handling executive functions in their spare time, as well as the growth of overhead with size, are both clear. Figure 6 in chapter 5 shows the division of this personnel in typical large firms.

Table 21 shows the replies of housebuilders to a question aimed at discovering the main factors that led firms to maintain their present size instead of expanding. The figures in each column add to more than 100 per cent, since each firm could list several reasons for not expanding.

Tables 22 and 23 are based on some of the information gathered on the relationship between housebuilders and their subcontractors and materials suppliers. Table 22 shows the number of housebuilders who integrated certain trade contracting functions by directly hiring their own labor to perform any of the functions usually performed by trade contractors (figure 3 shows a list of these trade contractor functions). Concrete work and hanging of dry walls have been excluded from this compilation because these two items vary so much from firm to firm and also within a firm from house to house, depending on scheduling problems, that no generalization as to the most common channel for these functions can be made. It is clear that some integration of functions occurs with size, but the amount remains slight. As noted in the text, there is an offsetting trend, with large firms subcontracting some additional items which small firms perform with their own crews. Table 23 shows the number of firms using traditional channels of materials distribution. As is clear from the text discussion, when firms buy some products at wholesale, there can still be some variation in the number and type of products purchased at this level. In addition, cost differences can occur within a given channel depending on bargaining and the particular outlet employed. Thus the fact that firms buy only at retail may not necessarily mean that they get no quantity reductions.

Appendix E. Information on Firms' Age, Characteristics, Ownership, and Financial Operations

For the analysis of housebuilders' characteristics and financial and operating figures, a special survey was required. This survey was based on financial reports filed with financial institutions. The sample taken was not completely random because only sampling units were selected for which a mail survey return (initial mail response or call-back) or completed interview form was available. A search through all the available financial records was made to determine for which of the firms represented by earlier returns further data were available, and 266 eligible cases were found. The distribution of firms was practically identical with that of the original universe, with an exception of a slight underrepresentation in the smallest-size category. That the smallest-size stratum was not fully represented can be explained by the lesser probability of established small firms rendering full financial reports or of newly formed small firms yet having had a chance to appear. In the 1–9 size class, sampling ratios varied from $^{78}/_{1362}$ to $^{132}/_{1362}$, in the 10–24 class from $^{42}/_{189}$ to $^{60}/_{189}$, in the 25–99 class from $^{26}/_{77}$ to $^{48}/_{77}$, and in the 100-and-over class from $^{16}/_{30}$ to $^{26}/_{30}$, depending on the item of information considered.

The aim in assembling the data was to tie together the aggregates derived in the mail survey of housebuilders and the details accumulated in the interviewing program with information showing in quantitative terms the influence on financial affairs of size, method of operation, and other variables. Also, it was considered desirable to fill in the background on different sizes and types of firms in terms of length of existence and growth, source of management skills, and so on.

Information which reveals the financial structure and operating position is the data most closely guarded by housebuilding firms. They are often understandably reluctant to give complete and specific cost data[3] or indicate operating margins, and there is small likelihood of many making statements regarding profitability without strong reason. Even where firms are willing on principle to divulge such information, it may be necessary for them to go to more trouble to get it together than they think reasonable. For these reasons, and because tentative investigations confirmed the probability of restricted response, the collection of general financial data was confined to the secondary, though reliable, detailed financial information that builders filed with credit-reporting agencies, lending institutions, and government agencies. It was necessary, of course, to guarantee the anonymity of individual firms in the final presentation of data, but this was not an important impediment.

Although the number of statements (266) checked in our survey was sufficient to give a high degree of reliability in sampling variability, possible statistical pitfalls in relying on such sources of information are apparent. Certain firms may have reported incorrectly, or their data may have been incorrectly analyzed. There is no way to estimate reporting bias. A large percentage of returns is prepared by public accountants or may be true copies of the firm's income tax reports. Most firms recognize the seriousness of credit and financial reporting. Accuracy is as high as the industry's general standards of integrity.

[3] We circumvented this difficulty in the composite house and price survey, however, by asking each contact about only a few cost items and building up the total cost structure by aggregating data from firms equivalent in all important respects.

After selection of the most frequently occurring items of information in the firms' financial records, coding instructions were drawn up, and the information for each firm in the sample of 266 was analyzed and recorded on a coding sheet. The data were then punched into the I.B.M. cards for subsequent machine cross-classification for ultimate translation into population distributions.

The tabulations which follow were derived from the cross-classifications mentioned above and are distributions applicable to the population of housebuilders in the Bay area as established by the mail survey of housebuilders. This was accomplished by calculating the percentage distributions by strata of the sample data and applying the percentages to strata totals (numbers of firms) found in the mail survey.

Tables 24–27 present certain data on the age and background of housebuilders. Among the facts that stand out are the young average age of firms, the middle-age and craft background of the owners, and the concentration of ownership into proprietorships and partnerships. At the same time, important variations in all these attributes exist, related to size of firm.

Tables 28–35 all give information on the financial operations of builders. The first three tables deal with balance sheet items. They, plus similar less important tables not shown, enable one to draw up the typical balance sheet for firms of each size, as has been done in figure 2.

Tables 31 and 32 show the relationship of certain of these assets to sales volume. They thus indicate the manner in which these assets have actually been used. Finally, tables 33, 34, and 35 all present data on the profit experience of firms. These show both actual profits and their relationship to sales volume and net worth. Net profit is defined for corporations as the profit before taxes. For proprietorships and partnerships, it is the net return before taxes minus an imputed wage of $5,000 per year for the proprietor or per partner. These returns are related to total net worth and sales volume, including that part arising or used in other building operations.

Appendix F. The Product

Information on the characteristics, prices, and final mortgage financing of houses in this study is based on data gathered by the Area Housing Program of the Bureau of Labor Statistics. Since this program was gathering complete information on these characteristics for all one-family houses started in the San Francisco area in the last half of 1949, it was decided not to duplicate collection of similar information.

The survey of housing characteristics by the Bureau of Labor Statistics and purchasers' financing was similar to the Bureau of Business and Economic Research Survey described earlier, except that it was based on a study of individual houses drawn from a universe of all building permits instead of on a study of builders. Complete details of these surveys, as well as estimates of their reliability, can be found in *Construction,* February, 1951, pp. 6–14.

The BLS surveys did not attempt to estimate characteristics for all houses built in the United States, but only for those built in the 15 large metropolitan areas actually surveyed. Approximately one-third of all nonfarm single-family houses started in the last half of 1949 were constructed in the areas surveyed. They accounted for half of all house-building which took place in metropolitan areas. (Cf. *Housing Statistics,* January, 1951, tables 1–3, and *Construction,* August, 1951, table 6.) The San Francisco area accounted for about 6 per cent of the production in the 15 areas. Its production, therefore, was 3 per cent of all metropolitan building and 2 per cent of all nonfarm housing.

The houses built in these large metropolitan areas are not typical of the entire national production. Known differences exist with respect to both construction costs and prices. The average construction cost in the 15 areas was $8,500 in the last half of 1949, whereas it was $7,250 for all other nonfarm houses. These differences probably reflect variations in both unit costs and characteristics.

Table 36 compares some of the main characteristics of San Francisco houses with those of the other areas. It is evident that San Francisco houses rank at or near the top in space and other special items, but they are at or near the bottom in those features necessitated by rigorous weather. The Bay area has the lowest number of small houses and is second highest in both median and mean space. It is similarly high in garages, fireplaces, and community water and sewers. On the other hand, it is low in basements, extra bathrooms, and central heating.

As a result, the construction cost and price of the Bay area house are slightly above average. The exact amount is not clear from the table because only arithmetic means are available; and these, because the cost and price distributions are skewed, are not suitable for accurate comparisons. This fact is demonstrated in table 37 which gives a frequency distribution of prices and shows the gap between the median and mean.

Additional information on the characteristics of the houses is presented in table 38 which is based on the same survey as table 36, but in this case, the replies have been classified also by size of builder. It is clear that the houses built by the smallest builders have a much higher percentage of expensive and custom features.

This same variation in cost and size is observed in table 39 which is based upon the Bureau of Business and Economic Research survey of Bay area housebuilders described in Appendix C. Another factor worth noting is the great similarity in the price distributions of tables 37 and 39. These are independent estimates of the price of houses produced in the Bay area. They are very similar in results, even though the data from the Bay Area Survey cover more houses and a longer period of time than do those of the BLS.

Table 40 contains data on selected mortgage characteristics as well as on the type of lending institutions and type of loans made for the purchases of single-family houses. Table 41 presents similar data classified by the income level of the house purchaser. It also shows the estimated income distribution in 1949 for all families based on census data. This table enables a comparison to be made between the income distribution of all families in the area and those who purchased new houses.

Appendix G. Structure of the Trade-Contracting Industries

Because general ignorance of the number, type, and operations of trade contractors was, if anything, greater than that concerning housebuilders, this study included a detailed mail and interview survey of trade contractors. The method followed was identical with that used for housebuilders. A universe was established, and questionnaires were mailed to each firm in the universe. After mail replies had been received, a sample of nonrespondents was drawn, and these firms were called on in person. The editing, tabulation, and analysis also followed similar lines.

The universe in this case was established through the fact that all trade contractors in California must secure operating licenses from the Contractor's State License Board. This Board publishes a directory showing the names and addresses of all licensees. All firms in the categories covered who had addresses in the six Bay area counties were included in the universe, with the exception of painting for which only Alameda and Contra Costa counties were used.

Because of limitations of cost and time, the survey covered only 5 of the 17 building trades which perform trade contract work on houses. The 5 trades surveyed—painting, plumbing, flooring (wood), cement and concrete, and masonry—made up 58 per cent of the licensees in the area and accounted for about 72 per cent of the cost of subcontracts for the typical house.

Table 42 shows the number of licensees in the various trades. It also shows the number of active licensees in the trades surveyed. The trades selected require application of a fairly wide range of skills, and it is believed that their characteristics are representative of trade contracting firms in general. The average results obtained for four surveyed groups (excluding painting) have been applied to the number of licensees in the remaining trade contracting categories. This is considered as an estimate of the probable values for this "all other" category. In this manner, it is possible to obtain some idea of the total trade contracting picture. It will be inexact, however, so far as the surveyed groups do not accurately represent "all others." The 26 per cent of licensees not active include those retired, those working as mechanics for others, those temporarily out of the industry but retaining their license, and those engaged in partnerships where several individuals are licensed but operate together as a single firm.

Some estimate of the accuracy of these estimates may be obtained by comparison with the figures of the State Department of Employment in its report on the average number of trade contracting firms who had one or more employees in 1949. (Cf. *California Employment and Payrolls, 1949* [State of California, Department of Employment].) The average number of firms reporting in each quarter was 3,059. This includes special trade contractors who were not of a type to work on houses and, therefore, were excluded from our survey. This compares to an estimate of 2,779 ± 410 for housebuilding trade contractors without employees from this survey (col. 3, table 42 minus col. 2, table 44).

Tables 43, 44, and 45 show respectively the size distribution of trade contracting firms by volume of sales, by all employees, and by overhead employees. Comparison may be made between these tables and tables

11, 12, and 20 which give the same type of information for housebuilders. In making this comparison, it must be remembered that housebuilders' dollar volume is higher per employee because of their payments to the trade contractors and for land.

Tables 46 and 47 indicate the percentage of their volume performed on new houses by trade contractors. This amount varies with the trade (in some, maintenance and repair work makes up the bulk of their work) and also with the size of the firm. This latter relationship fluctuates from trade to trade, and for that reason table 47 portrays the specific cross-classification in selected trades.

The final table in this group, 48, demonstrates the greater spatial flexibility of trade contractors compared to housebuilders. Since their average job is far smaller than that of a housebuilder, they must work on many more jobs. Frequently, this requires spreading into several adjacent areas. In addition, because the trade contractor's work is similar throughout the region and because his marketing problem is simple, since he has to deal only with other builders, it is easier for the trade contractor to work over a larger area if he so desires.

Appendix H. Pricing of the Composite House

Certain chapters of the text (particularly 7 and 8) have already given a good deal of information about the method of pricing the composite house. It will be recalled that the house is essentially an index which allows weights to be assigned to prices for each separate element.

Plans for a typical 1,000 square-foot house were drawn up; a complete materials take-off was made as well as a listing of the required amounts and specifications for each subcontract. Costs were divided into five groups: direct materials purchased, subcontracts, direct labor, incidentals, and profits and overhead. Data for each group were obtained separately.

For materials, the composite house required 30 major items to be purchased by the builder. A list was made up showing the exact amount of each required. This list was then taken to ten retail lumberyards, five wholesalers, and several mills and mill representatives. In each case, the dealer was requested to report the prices of each item as well as any quantity discounts he allowed. If the dealer was a wholesaler or mill owner, information was requested as to the circumstances under which he would or would not sell to a builder.

These figures were then checked from other sources. A selected group of builders was requested to report the prices paid for materials; all builders in the subsample (Appendix D) had previously been asked the channels through which they purchased their materials. Other groups, including the Bureau of Labor Statistics, the Veterans Administration, and major banks in the area, all of whom gathered similar price data, made available their reports on typical prices.

The final estimates shown in this report were based upon the most typical prices charged in whichever channel was used by the majority of builders of a given size. As indicated previously, variations were found between dealers at each level, but these variations were not great. Also, experience in this and other fields indicates that markups in any field tend to be standardized and that those found in one group of firms are likely to be duplicated in all.

The second group of costs contained subcontract prices. The exact amounts and specifications for 15 subcontracts were listed. This list, with a copy of the house plan, was taken to between 5 and 10 trade contractors for each type of work. These contractors were selected to represent all sizes of firms active in the new housing field. Each trade contractor was asked to estimate his charges for the required item if it was installed in a single house (scattered sites), a tract of 30 houses, and a tract of 100 houses. Wherever possible, these estimates were checked against recent bids for similar work. At the same time, we discussed with him the breakdown of the estimate into labor, materials, and profit and overhead, and we asked an explanation as to why the charges varied by size.

The final estimates for each trade again came from the most typical figures. These figures were also checked with builders, with materials suppliers, and with the other agencies gathering similar information. They were also scrutinized for internal consistency.

The third set of costs—for direct labor—was harder to obtain. The difficulty of making estimates of this type, with the large opportunity for error involved, should be apparent to anyone familiar with building practice. To ascertain the differences in costs or labor inputs achieved on the average as a result of changed scale, we had to obtain recorded outputs and inputs for various-sized firms. These outputs and inputs had to be comparable to be useful. However, it is clear that comparability can differ widely for at least three basic reasons: (1) Inputs within a given firm will vary with weather, with available labor supply, and with other factors in the labor market. (2) No two firms produce identical units. For example, there are obviously tremendous differences between the typical so-called GI house with minimum fittings and the expensive mansion filled with all types of hand-finished items. (3) Finally, not only will specific functions differ among firms, but in each, direct labor costs will depend upon which functions are handled by the concern itself and which subcontracted.

How, then, did we arrive at our estimates of labor saving? The first problem was met by use of a uniform period of one year, 1950, for all firms. In a given year, it may be assumed that all firms in the area experienced approximately the same conditions of weather and labor supply. At the same time, firms were asked to report average direct labor costs for the period. This, it was hoped, would remove the problem of fluctuations from house to house within a firm because of unusual internal conditions. Since labor costs within the same firm may fluctuate 10 per cent on either side of their average, failure to use the average can lead to decided biases.

The problem of variation in types of houses was met by limitation of the study to houses of approximately the same class, built on flat land in roughly the same areas. At the same time, we attempted to handle the problems of other variations in the houses by expressing labor inputs as a percentage of dollar and unit outputs for each particular firm. Comparison of the input-output ratio instead of direct labor costs is believed to have ironed out many of the differences arising from house to house variations.

To gain similarity, we used a fairly narrow range for selling price and gross floor area, including, in the latter, both living space and the garage. The price range of the houses selected was $8,400 to $12,800, with most houses falling between $8,900 and $10,000. Gross areas ranged from 1,000 to 1,400 square feet. The average price and area range compared favorably in each size class. Average price of the houses handled by small firms was $9,600; for the medium firms, $9,700; and for the large firms, $9,800.

It is possible, of course, that neither price nor area is a good index of comparability. Firms of a certain class could include more value in a house of a given price. However, examination of actual units produced and other data indicate that this did not occur. Whereas size and price of house are inversely correlated to size of firm, when a selection is made of units of the same size, price, and location, characteristics, and workmanship are approximately equal. Individual differences that might exist between firms are resolved by use of the class averages.

As for the third problem, in operations performed directly, wide variations are not usual. Principal differences occur when firms do or do not perform their own concrete work, hanging of wallboard, and painting. When firms included other items under direct labor, we did not attempt to use their reports. For the typical house, it was assumed that a firm hangs its own wallboard but subcontracts concrete and painting. In this case, which held for the majority of firms, reported labor costs could be used without adjustment. When a firm reported variations from items normally handled, correction factors were used to make its report comparable to the standard. These were obtained from data showing the ratio of each of these variables to all costs for particular firms.

In practice, obtaining labor data was a fairly simple and clear-cut procedure. Personal interviews were arranged with 52 firms to obtain figures on average labor costs per house. These firms were asked to describe their most typical house built in 1950: its gross area and selling price, labor cost, operations included in labor cost, and any other pertinent information. Replies were then screened to eliminate inadequate figures, extreme deviation from the average in type or price of house, and the inclusion of unusual operations in direct labor.

As a result, only half the replies were used. They included ten large firms, six medium, and ten small. The reported figures were then adjusted by percentage correction factors to give the direct labor costs for performing identical operations. At this point, we had a labor cost based upon a like set of operations but performed in houses with different gross floor areas and a different selling price for each firm. To correct for the variations, we divided the labor cost by the gross floor area to obtain a cost per square foot for each firm. These were then arranged and averaged by class of firm. At the same time, the labor cost was expressed as a percentage of selling price for each firm, and these results were also arranged and averaged. This, then, gave us the average direct labor cost per foot or per dollar of sales value for performing identical operations. This is the figure necessary for comparing the average input in each size class for an identical unit of output.

For the small firms, the average direct labor cost per gross square foot was \$1.15 with a range between \$0.97 and \$1.39. For the medium firms, the average was \$1.01 with a range from \$0.80 to \$1.39. For the large firms, it was \$0.85 with a range from \$0.60 to \$1.04. In all cases, the mean and median were approximately the same (within 3 per cent). Of the total selling price, direct labor costs averaged 14.6 per cent in the small firms with a range from 12.4 to 17.8 per cent. It was 13.1 in the medium firms with a range from 9.2 to 17.2, and 10.9 in large firms with a range from 6.0 to 13.9 per cent. It should be noticed that the results obtained by both methods are practically identical.

As we stated initially, the specific figures obtained through these selected reports are obviously subject to error. The number of usable cases is not large. The method of insuring comparability also can give variation. On the other hand, the results confirm the observations in the case studies which are based on a much larger sample. In addition, they agree with informed opinion.

Information on incidental costs—the fourth item—was obtained directly from builders as part of the survey described in Appendix D. The final estimate for the operating margin was obtained from the survey of financial statements discussed in Appendix E. After all direct costs had been obtained for the average builder of a given size, this amount was increased by the average percentage operating margin for builders of the same size. This total was then considered as the typical cost for the particular size group.

Table 49 shows the amounts paid by the builders of different sizes for each major cost of the house, including each of the major subcontracts. These figures, it must be recalled, are averages within each group based upon the plans for the composite house just discussed.

Tables 50, 51, and 52 show these figures in greater detail. The first shows the way in which total labor costs vary with size. In this, it should be noticed that the small amount of building labor hired by many trade contractors is not separated out from the main trade employed by the particular contractor. Table 51 demonstrates the way in which each materials cost varies. Table 52 shows overhead and profits. Land, which is the final cost, was assumed constant in all cases. The reasons for all these cost variations were discussed at length in chapter 8.

Appendix I. Materials Supply

In discussing the supply factors to the housebuilding industry, a distinction must be made between exclusively housebuilding materials and materials used both in construction and other purposes, since the picture obtained of structure and price movements will differ, depending on the manner in which this division is made. This problem arises because the standard classification of industries is based primarily on characteristics and not on use. Some industries produce mainly construction materials, but in others, such as steel, the amount going to housebuilding forms only a small part of the total. If, however, steel is included in an aggregate index of construction materials in accordance with its over-all importance to the economy, it will overwhelm the movement of other materials which actually have far greater influence on housebuilding.

This point is made clear in the last two columns of table 53 which compares the percentage importance in production of different materials used in buildings with their actual importance in the typical Bay area house. The amount of difference is slightly understated in the case of value assigned for steelworks and rolling mills, where the computations are based on value added rather than on total production, as it true of all other items.

The difficulty of defining an industry creates another problem in discussions concerned with the structure of industries. Certain products which go into houses are not produced in homogeneous national markets. Some (such as bricks), because of transportation costs, are restricted to relatively local or regional sales. In other cases, for various reasons, the industrial classification is not homogeneous, but contains many different types of products. In these industries, a national concentration ratio is likely to be ambiguous, because in the case of regional products or those with mixed outputs, particular companies could control a much larger share of specific markets than would be indicated by the national data.[4]

The industries which seem to fall into these classifications are cement, lighting fixtures, bricks, sheet metal, electrical wire, water pipe, and furnace and hot-water heaters. These items are footnoted in table 53.

[4] Joe S. Bain "Relation of Profit Rate to Industry Concentration: American Manufacturing, 1936–1940," *The Quarterly Journal of Economics*, Vol. LXV, No. 3 (August, 1951), 299–304.

In general, classification rests on the distinctions made in *The Structure of the American Economy* among industries that are national or regional and "straight" or "mixed."[5] An industry was considered non-homogeneous if it was not both national and straight. An industry considered homogeneous satisfies, in general, the requirements of a theoretical industry; that is, "a group of outputs which to all or most buyers of each are generally close substitutes for each other and distant substitutes for all other outputs."[6]

Cases were included as homogeneous where the industry was mixed, but the concentration ratio of the specific building material product under consideration had a concentration ratio approximating that of the industry.

Also, four industries—millwork, plywood, vitreous plumbing fixtures, and ceramic tile—which were classified as mixed in *The Structure of the American Economy,* have been reclassified as homogeneous for this work because their definition and coverage were changed by the time of the 1947 census.

The use of industries for concentration ratios raises other problems, but none believed important enough to invalidate the very general statements made concerning them. For example, the amount of competition in lumber is somewhat overstated because lumber is produced in different parts of the country, and certain types are not complete substitutes for others. On the whole, though, the degree of substitution possible and the very large number of firms clearly support the accuracy of the contention that there is only slight concentration of control in lumber.

The breakdown of materials in table 53 is somewhat more complete than in table 51, because hardware, plumbing, millwork, and electrical materials draw from several industrial classifications. In these cases, the totals shown in 51 have been distributed to their component industries. In addition to weights, table 53 also indicates the number of companies in each industry and the concentration of market control among the 4, 8, and 50 largest firms in each industry. The figures are based on the total share of the industry's production manufactured by these firms. One point worth noting is that when concentration is low for the first 4 or 8 firms, then even the 50 largest will usually not control a large share of the market. On the other hand, in those cases

[5] U. S. National Resources Committee, *The Structure of the American Economy* (Washington: Government Printing Office, 1939).

[6] Bain, *op. cit.*, p. 298.

where 4 or 8 firms have a medium control, then the top 50 will usually control almost all output. This is even more true, of course, when the first 4 or 8 firms start with an important share of the total market.

Tables 54 and 55 show the distribution of building materials by the percentage of production concentrated in the 8 largest firms. We have constructed the first of these tables using as weights the importance of the materials furnished by an industry for the typical Bay area house. In the second we have used as weights the industry's share of the total production of all 23 industries. The first two columns in each table are based on those materials which do not fall into the ambiguous market group, and the second two columns show the distribution of all materials, with this group included but shown separately.

Table 56 records the wholesale price movements of building materials as reported by the Bureau of Labor Statistics. These figures, of course, are subject to all of the problems normally contained in data from this source. The BLS new index was not carried back before 1947 for subclassifications. For this reason, it was necessary to construct specially the building materials index. The method used was to change the old subgroup relatives to the new base and then to multiply these relatives by the new weights. The results obtained by this procedure will differ slightly from a complete reconstruction of the index. The reason is that weights within the subgroups have also been changed. As a result, simply shifting the base year of the old relatives will not give the same results as reconstructing them. The two methods were, however, compared for three overlapping years, and differences were found to be small.

Appendix J. Data on the Labor Force, Entry, and Profits

The remaining tables contain data drawn from various secondary sources. These data suffer from the fact that they, as a rule, do not differentiate between information for housebuilders and that for other types of builders and trade contractors. Furthermore, most of the data are available only on a national basis, with not more than occasional glimpses of the actual situation in the Bay area.

The failure to differentiate between housebuilding and other building data is least important in the labor field. In the first place, most of this information does separate facts on those employed by builders and those working for trade contractors. In addition, previous information showed that trade contractors' work, and consequently their labor, was spread among new housing, other building, and maintenance, and, therefore, no real differentiation was possible. Although employees working for housebuilders were most likely to work only on houses, their next job might be for a general contractor on other types of building. Even when there was little interchange between these groups, the existence of the other workers and the fact that union agreements normally were negotiated for and covered employees of all builders mean that, for many purposes, the figures covering both groups are satisfactory.

The failure to separate out housebuilders and the lack of even state data, let alone local, are far more serious faults with respect to entry and profit information. These figures are primarily based upon Social Security and Internal Revenue data as adjusted for the National Income Accounts. For both entry and profits, rates applying to housebuilders and general contractors are likely to be quite different. In addition, the profit data are based only on corporations, though at least half the volume in housebuilding is performed by noncorporate firms. Since there is a correlation between size, incorporation, and profits, this would be likely to bias the figures upward. If an upward bias exists, it acts primarily to add further emphasis to the analysis of chapter 10.

Table 57 shows the changes and relative changes which have taken place in the construction labor force. It is clear that construction has seen a more rapid expansion in employees than most other industries.

Table 58 reports wage data for construction employees in general as well as for California. Construction workers make a higher weekly return than do other groups, though working fewer hours. For each item, construction workers in California are better off than are those in the rest of the country.

Table 59 presents data on work stoppages in the postwar period. Such data are necessary in the determination of the relative effect of strikes in building as compared with other industries.

Tables 60 and 61 show profit rates on income and equity for construction corporations as compared with other selected groups. The data for profits on income come from the Bureau of Internal Revenue as adjusted and estimated by the Bureau of Foreign and Domestic Commerce. The data for profits on net worth are collected by the Securities Exchange and the Federal Trade Commissions.

Table 62 shows the net growth and the rate of entry and discontinuance for all contract construction firms as well as all manufacturing firms and all nonfarm firms in the United States. In addition, net growth rates are available for Bay area construction firms showing the difference between the growth of building firms and special trade contractors. Since housebuilders comprise about 80 per cent of all building firms, these data also allow a more direct estimate of the change in housebuilding firms.

TABLES

TABLE 1

CONFIDENCE INTERVALS OF ESTIMATES

(95 per cent probability)[a]

Estimate for number of	Value of estimate	Confidence interval
Small builders (1–24)	1,551	1,446–1,656
Medium builders (25–99)	77	61–93
Large builders (100 and over)	30	25–35
Cement and concrete contractors	116	105–127
Flooring contractors	123	105–141
Masonry contractors	119	108–130
Painting and decorating contractors	1,232	1,119–1,345
Plumbing contractors	423	384–462
Above five trade contractors	2,013	1,893–2,133
Houses built in Bay area in 1949	17,799	16,823–18,767
Houses built by Bay area builders and nonprofessionals in 1949	19,487	18,137–20,847

[a] Estimates from 19 out of 20 samples would be expected to fall within the confidence interval shown.

TABLE 2

FIDUCIAL LIMITS FOR PERCENTAGES ESTIMATED FROM BUREAU OF BUSINESS AND ECONOMIC RESEARCH SURVEY DATA
(95 per cent probability)

Size-class and appendix table	Estimated percentage[a]					
	5 or 95	10 or 90	20 or 80	30 or 70	40 or 60	50
1–9 Completions						
Tables 10–19	2	3	3	6	6	6
24–27, 30–31	4	5	7	8	9	9
20–23, 28–29, 32	4	6	8	9	10	10
33–35	5	7	9	10	11	11
10–24 Completions						
Tables 10–19	4	5	7	8	8	9
20–23	4	6	8	9	10	10
24–32	5	7	9	10	11	11
33–35	6	8	11	12	13	13
25–99 Completions						
Tables 10–19	4	5	6	7	7	8
24–27	4	5	7	8	9	9
30–31	4	6	8	9	10	10
28–29, 32	5	7	10	11	12	12
20–23, 33–35	7	9	13	15	15	16
100 and over						
Tables 10–19	3	4	5	5	6	6
24–27	3	4	6	7	7	7
30–31	4	6	8	9	10	10
28–29, 32	6	8	11	12	13	13
20–23	7	9	13	15	15	16
33–35	8	11	14	17	18	18
Trade contractors						
Tables 43–48						
Cement and concrete	5	7	9	10	11	11
Flooring	6	9	12	13	14	14
Masonry	5	7	9	11	11	12
Painting	4	5	7	8	9	9
Plumbing	4	5	7	8	8	8

[a] The figures in the table show the range (plus and minus) within which 19 out of 20 samples would be expected to fall.

TABLE 3

INCREASE IN POPULATION AND DWELLING UNITS 1930–1950, UNITED STATES AND SAN FRANCISCO METROPOLITAN AREA

Year	Population				Dwelling units			
	Number		Per cent increase in decade		Number		Per cent increase in decade	
	United States	San Francisco area	United States	San Francisco area	United States	San Francisco area	United States	San Francisco area
1930	122,775,046	1,323,288	....	....	32,027,894[a]	398,327[a]	....	....
1940	131,669,275	1,432,211	7.2	8.2	37,325,470	485,991	16.5	22.0
1950	150,697,000	2,240,800	14.4	56.4	45,875,000	742,800	22.9	50.0

[a] Estimated. Since data on occupied units were available only for 1930, estimate was based on assumption of same vacancy rate in 1930 as in 1940.

SOURCE: Bureau of the Census; 1950 Census; Series PC-5, No. 45; HC-7, No. 5; 1940 Census of Housing.

TABLE 4

NONFARM RESIDENTIAL CONSTRUCTION BEGUN, 1946–1951

Year	Dwelling units			Houses	
	United States	Metropolitan areas	San Francisco area	United States	San Francisco area[a]
1946	670,500	b	17,290	602,100	15,127
1947	849,000	b	19,470	757,200	16,791
1948	931,600	629,761	19,910	790,000	16,775
1949	1,025,100	718,595	20,240	805,600	15,706
1950	1,396,000	1,000,932	30,170	1,179,000	25,992
1951	1,090,000	b	24,000	920,000	19,000

[a] Estimated.
[b] Not available.
SOURCE: *Housing Statistics*, HHFA, December, 1951, p. 2, and *Construction Supplement*, U. S. Department of Labor, BLS May 1951, pp. 6, 7.
Construction, Annual Review, 1950. Figures for 1951 are preliminary.

TABLE 5

MEDIUM- AND LARGE-SIZED HOUSEBUILDERS IN THE UNITED STATES

Year	Number of firms by houses built		Number of houses built by size class of builder (in thousands)	
	25–99	100 and over	25–99	100 and over
1938	358	33	13.9	5.3
1939	388	92	17.8	14.7
1949	3,030	720	114.2	132.2

SOURCE: Compiled from data of the Bureau of Labor Statistics and the Bureau of the Census. For detailed explanation see Appendix B.

TABLE 6

HOUSES BUILT BY NONPROFESSIONALS IN 1949, BY AREA

Area	Total by builders and nonprofessionals	Owner-built	Per cent owner-built
United States	805,600	265,600	33
Metropolitan areas	525,000	96,000	18
San Francisco area	17,799	2,002	11

TABLE 7

Housebuilders in 1949, Classified by Size and by Area

Area	Number of firms by houses built				All firms	Per cent of firms				
	1–9	10–24	25–99	100 and over		1–9	10–24	25–99	100 and over	All firms
United States	109,170	6,680	3,030	720	119,600	91	6	3	1	100
Metropolitan areas	57,650	4,810	2,920	720	66,100	87	7	4	1	100
San Francisco area	1,362	189	77	30	1,658	82	11	5	2	100

TABLE 8

Houses Built in 1949, Classified by Size of Builder and by Area

Area	Number of houses by size class of builder (in thousands)				All houses (in thousands)	Per cent of houses				
	1–9	10–24	25–99	100 and over		1–9	10–24	25–99	100 and over	All houses
United States	216.8	76.9	114.2	132.2	540.0	40	14	21	24	100
Metropolitan areas	122.1	65.7	109.0	132.2	429.0	28	15	25	31	100
San Francisco area	4.9	2.9	3.5	6.2	17.5	28	17	20	35	100

TABLE 9

Houses Built Operatively in 1949, Classified by Size of Builder and by Area

Area	Number of operatively built houses by size class of builder (in thousands)				All houses (in thousands)	Per cent of operatively built houses				Operatively built as a per cent of all houses in class				
	1–9	10–24	25–99	100+		1–9	10–24	25–99	100+	1–9	10–24	25–99	100+	All houses
United States	106.2	56.0	96.3	124.5	383.0	28	15	25	33	47	73	84	94	71
Metropolitan areas	61.9	44.6	92.1	124.5	323.0	19	14	29	39	51	68	84	94	75
San Francisco area	2.1	2.3	3.0	6.2	13.6	16	17	22	45	45	80	84	99	78

TABLE 10

HOUSES BUILT IN BAY AREA IN 1949, CLASSIFIED BY SIZE OF BUILDER, BY TYPE OF BUILDING, AND BY LOCATION

Size class by houses built	Number of firms in class	Number of houses built by size class of builder			
		In all areas	On contracts[a]	In tracts[a]	Outside Bay area[a]
1	270	270	143	.....	.....
2–4	694	1,985	1,139	.....	18
5–9	398	2,587	1,405	254	83
10–24	189	2,936	585	1,067	22
25–49	56	2,030	492	1,263	84
50–99	21	1,482	58	1,349	130
100 and over	30	6,195	45	5,860	1,351
Total	1,658	17,485	3,867	9,793	1,688
	Percentage distribution				
1	16	2	4	..	..
2–4	42	11	29	..	1
5–9	24	15	36	3	5
10–24	11	17	15	11	1
25–49	4	12	13	13	5
50–99	1	8	2	14	8
100 and over	2	35	1	59	80
Total	100	100	100	100	100

[a] To obtain number built by complementary method, subtract figure in this column from that shown on same line under All areas; Examples:

On contract... 3,867	In tracts... 9,793	Outside Bay area... 1,688
Operative.....13,618	Scattered... 7,692	In Bay area........15,797
17,485	17,485	17,485

To obtain total units completed in Bay area add:
In Bay area by firms.............15,797
In Bay area by individuals........ 2,002

17,799

TABLE 11

Bay Area Housebuilders in 1949, Classified by Dollar Volume of All Production and by Size

Total volume of production (in dollars)	Number of firms by houses built				All firms	Per cent of firms in class				
	1–9	10–24	25–99	100 and over		1–9	10–24	25–99	100 and over	All firms
Less than $50,000	627	..	..	..	627	46	..	..	..	38
50,000–199,999	657	93	..	..	750	48	49	..	..	45
200,000–499,999	68	84	40	..	192	5	45	52	..	12
500,000–999,999	8	12	28	3	51	1	6	36	10	3
1,000,000 and up	2	..	9	27	38[a]	[b]	..	12	90	2
Total	1,362	189	77	30	1,658	100	100	100	100	100

[a] Of this number 4 firms produced more than $5,000,000.
[b] Less than one-half of 1 per cent.

TABLE 12

Bay Area Housebuilders in 1949, Classified by Number of Employees and by Size

Number of employees	Number of firms by houses built				All firms	Per cent of firms in class				
	1–9	10–24	25–99	100 and over		1–9	10–24	25–99	100 and over	All firms
0–2	648	8	2	..	658	47	4	3	..	40
3–9	553	106	11	..	670	41	56	14	..	41
10–24	87	64	38	..	189	7	34	49	..	11
25–99	70	11	26	11	118	5	6	34	37	7
100 and over	4	..	..	19	23	[a]	..	..	63	1
Total	1,362	189	77	30	1,658	100	100	100	100	100

[a] Less than one-half of 1 per cent.

TABLE 13

Bay Area Housebuilders in 1949, Classified by Per Cent of Houses Each Built Operatively and by Size

Per cent of houses built operatively	Number of firms by houses built				All firms	Per cent of firms in class				
	1–9	10–24	25–99	100 and over		1–9	10–24	25–99	100 and over	All firms
0–14.9	547	16	5	..	568	40	8	6	..	34
15–54.9	308	30	8	..	346	23	16	10	..	21
55–74.9	42	5	..	..	47	3	3	..	..	3
75–94.9	82	40	19	2	143	6	21	25	7	9
95–100	383	98	45	28	554	28	52	59	93	33
Total	1,362	189	77	30	1,658	100	100	100	100	100

TABLE 14

Bay Area Housebuilders in 1949, Classified by Per Cent of Houses Each Built in Tracts and by Size[a]

Per cent of houses built in tracts	Number of firms by houses built				All firms	Per cent of firms in class				
	1–9	10–24	25–99	100 and over		1–9	10–24	25–99	100 and over	All firms
0–14.9	1,313	102	13	..	1,428	96	54	17	..	86
15–54.9	22	20	8	1	51	2	10	10	3	3
55–74.9	3	32	9	1	45	b	17	12	3	3
75–94.9	1	8	20	3	32	b	5	26	10	2
95–100	23	27	27	25	102	2	14	35	84	6
Total	1,362	189	77	30	1,658	100	100	100	100	100

[a] A tract is defined as an area in which a single firm built 5 or more houses.
[b] Less than one-half of 1 per cent.

TABLE 15

Bay Area Housebuilders in 1949, Classified by Per Cent That New Housebuilding Formed of Total Production and by Size.

Housebuilding's per cent of total production	Number of firms by houses built				All firms	Per cent of firms in class				
	1–9	10–24	25–99	100 and over		1–9	10–24	25–99	100 and over	All firms
0–14.9	71	..	..	..	71	5	..	..	..	4
15–54.9	151	13	1	2	167	11	7	1	7	10
55–74.9	94	14	12	..	120	7	7	15	..	7
75–94.9	205	25	12	4	246	15	13	16	13	15
95–100	841	137	52	24	1,054	62	73	68	80	64
Total	1,362	189	77	30	1,658	100	100	100	100	100

TABLE 16

BAY AREA HOUSEBUILDERS IN 1949 COMPLETING DWELLING UNITS IN ADDITION TO HOUSES, BY SIZE

Size-class	Number of firms	Units completed	Per cent	
			Firms	Units
1–9	87	1,145	66	64
10–24	22	155	17	9
25–99	17	223	13	13
100 and over	6	259	4	14
Total	132	1,782	100	100

TABLE 17

Bay Area Housebuilders in 1949, Classified by Number of Permit Centers in Which They Built and by Size

Number of permit centers	Number of firms by houses built				All firms	Per cent of firms in class				
	1–9	10–24	25–99	100 and over		1–9	10–24	25–99	100 and over	All firms
1	1,068	106	27	15	1,216	78	56	35	50	74
2	190	50	30	8	278	14	27	39	27	17
3	98	15	19	4	136	7	8	25	14	8
4	5	12	..	1	18	1	6	..	3	1
5 and over	1	6	1	2	10	[a]	3	1	6	[a]
Total	1,362	189	77	30	1,658	100	100	100	100	100

[a] Less than one-half of 1 per cent.

TABLE 18

Bay Area Housebuilders in 1949, Classified by Number of Months Active During Year and by Size

Number of months active	Number of firms by houses built				All firms	Per cent of firms in class				
	1–9	10–24	25–99	100 and over		1–9	10–24	25–99	100 and over	All firms
1–4	139	1	..	..	140	10	1	..	..	8
5–6	152	..	5	..	157	11	..	6	..	9
7–8	139	26	5	4	174	10	13	6	13	10
9–10	194	2	2	..	198	14	1	3	..	12
11–12[a]	738	160	65	26	989	55	85	85	87	61
Total	1,362	189	77	30	1,658	100	100	100	100	100

[a] No firms reported 11 months' activity.

TABLE 19

Bay Area Housebuilders in 1949, Classified by Average Price of House Built and by Size

Average house price (in dollars)	Number of firms by houses built				All firms	Per cent of firms in class				
	1–9	10–24	25–99	100 and over		1–9	10–24	25–99	100 and over	All firms
Less than $9,000	153	15	9	9	186	11	8	12	30	12
9,000–10,999	324	46	32	12	414	24	24	41	41	25
11,000–12,999	237	31	14	7	289	17	16	18	22	17
13,000–14,999	122	40	9	1	172	9	21	12	4	10
15,000 and over	526	57	13	1	597	39	31	17	3	36
Total	1,362	189	77	30	1,658	100	100	100	100	100

TABLE 20

Bay Area Housebuilders Primarily Engaged in Housebuilding (more than 90 per cent) in 1949, Classified by Off-site Personnel and by Size

Number of off-site personnel	Number of firms by houses built				All firms	Per cent of firms in class				
	1–9	10–24	25–99	100 and over		1–9	10–24	25–99	100 and over	All firms
Owner only in spare time	729	52	..	..	781	76	32	..	..	65
Owner only full time	67	61	19	..	147	7	38	33	..	12
2–4	164	42	25	2	233	17	26	43	10	20
5–9	...	6	14	5	25	..	4	24	20	2
10 and over	...	...	...	17	17	..	..	..	70	1
Total	960	161	58	24	1,203	100	100	100	100	100

TABLE 21

BAY AREA HOUSEBUILDERS IN 1949, CLASSIFIED BY MAIN DETERMINANTS OF EXISTING SIZE AND BY SIZE

Determinant of size	Number of firms by houses built[a]			Total	Per cent of firms in class			
	1–24	25–99	100 and over		1–24	25–99	100 and over	Total
Land	155	31	15	201	10	40	50	12
Risk and credit	776	62	18	856	50	80	60	52
Managerial span	714	15	4	733	46	20	13	44
Personnel	388	23	5	416	25	30	17	25
Other	418	23	9	450	27	30	30	27

[a] Columns add to more than 100 per cent because each firm could list several reasons.

TABLE 22

BAY AREA HOUSEBUILDERS IN 1949, CLASSIFIED BY NUMBER OF INTEGRATED TRADE CONTRACTOR OPERATIONS AND BY SIZE

Integrated operations	Number of firms by houses built			Total	Per cent of firms in class			
	1–24	25–99	100 and over		1–24	25–99	100 and over	Total
0	1,303	49	15	1,367	84	64	50	82
1	140	19	6	165	9	24	20	10
2	108	9	5	122	7	12	17	8
3 and over	...	..	4	4	..	..	13	[a]
Total	1,551	77	30	1,658	100	100	100	100

[a] Less than one-half of 1 per cent.

TABLE 23

BAY AREA HOUSEBUILDERS IN 1949, CLASSIFIED BY CHANNELS OF MATERIALS DISTRIBUTION AND BY SIZE

Materials channels	Number of firms by houses built				All firms	Per cent of firms in class				
	1–9	10–24	25–99	100 and over		1–9	10–24	25–99	100 and over	All firms
All retail	1,090	117	27	3	1,237	80	62	35	10	75
Some wholesale	272	72	50	27	421	20	38	65	90	25
Total	1,362	189	77	30	1,658	100	100	100	100	100

TABLE 24

BAY AREA HOUSEBUILDERS IN 1949, CLASSIFIED BY AGE OF THE PRINCIPAL AND BY SIZE

Age of the principal in years	Number of firms by houses built				All firms	Per cent of firms in class				
	1–9	10–24	25–99	100 and over		1–9	10–24	25–99	100 and over	All firms
Less than 30 years	74	6	2	..	82	6	3	3	..	5
30–39	437	49	17	3	506	32	26	22	10	31
40–49	372	52	19	10	453	27	27	24	33	27
50–59	298	62	29	14	403	22	33	38	47	24
60 and over	181	20	10	3	214	13	11	13	10	13
Total	1,362	189	77	30	1,658	100	100	100	100	100
Median (in years)	43	48	50	52						

TABLE 25

BAY AREA HOUSEBUILDERS IN 1949, CLASSIFIED BY AGE OF FIRM AND BY SIZE

Age of firm in years	Number of firms by houses built				All firms	Per cent of firms in class				
	1–9	10–24	25–99	100 and over		1–9	10–24	25–99	100 and over	All firms
Less than 5 years	794	85	30	9	918	58	45	39	31	55
5–9	206	63	22	5	296	15	33	28	16	18
10–14	145	13	7	1	166	11	7	9	3	10
15–19	52	6	2	5	66	4	3	4	17	4
20 and over	165	22	15	10	212	12	12	20	33	13
Total	1,362	189	77	30	1,658	100	100	100	100	100
Median (in years)	4	5	6	15						

TABLE 26

BAY AREA HOUSEBUILDERS IN 1949, CLASSIFIED BY YEARS PRINCIPAL WORKED IN BUILDING INDUSTRY BEFORE ESTABLISHMENT OF FIRM, AND BY SIZE

Principal's previous building experience in years	Number of firms by houses built				All firms	Per cent of firms in class				
	1–9	10–24	25–99	100 and over		1–9	10–24	25–99	100 and over	All firms
Less than 1 year	128	46	21	3	198	9	25	27	10	12
1–5	152	35	16	12	215	12	18	20	40	13
6–9	244	15	10	5	274	18	8	13	17	16
10–19	442	31	13	6	492	32	16	18	20	29
20 and over	396	62	17	4	479	29	33	22	13	30
Total	1,362	189	77	30	1,658	100	100	100	100	100
Median (in years)	14	9	6	5						

TABLE 27

BAY AREA HOUSEBUILDERS IN 1949, CLASSIFIED BY TYPE OF OWNERSHIP STRUCTURE AND BY SIZE

Type of ownership	Number of firms by houses built				All firms	Per cent of firms in class				
	1–9	10–24	25–99	100 and over		1–9	10–24	25–99	100 and over	All firms
Proprietorship	904	72	11	..	987	66	38	14	..	60
Partnership	281	50	23	1	355	21	26	30	3	21
Corporation	52	22	5	2	81	4	12	6	7	5
Multifirm combinations	125	45	38	27	235	9	24	50	90	14
Total	1,362	189	77	30	1,658	100	100	100	100	100

TABLE 28

BAY AREA HOUSEBUILDERS IN 1949, CLASSIFIED BY TOTAL ASSETS AND BY SIZE

Total assets (in dollars)	Number of firms by houses built				All firms	Per cent of firms in class				
	1–9	10–24	25–99	100 and over		1–9	10–24	25–99	100 and over	All firms
Less than $40,000	755	45	..	..	800	55	24	..	..	48
40,000–199,000	540	116	32	..	688	39	61	42	..	41
200,000–599,000	61	18	41	7	127	5	9	52	23	8
600,000–999,000	6	3	2	5	16	[a]	2	3	17	1
1,000,000–10,000,000	...	7	2	18[b]	27	..	4	3	60	2
Total	1,362	189	77	30	1,658	100	100	100	100	100
Median ($000)	36.5	88	257	1,080						

[a] Less than one-half of 1 per cent.
[b] 3 firms had more than $5,000,000 in total assets.

TABLE 29

Bay Area Housebuilders in 1949, Classified by Current Assets and by Size

Current assets (in dollars)	Number of firms by houses built				All firms	Per cent of firms in class				
	1–9	10–24	25–99	100 and over		1–9	10–24	25–99	100 and over	All firms
Less than $20,000	905	46	..	..	951	66	24	..	..	57
20,000–99,000	406	112	27	..	545	30	60	36	..	33
100,000–199,000	39	17	22	3	81	3	9	28	10	5
200,000–499,000	6	10	19	11	46	[a]	5	25	38	3
500,000–5,000,000	6	4	9	16[b]	35	[a]	2	11	52	2
Total	1,362	189	77	30	1,658	100	100	100	100	100
Median ($000)	15.2	42.7	160.0	562.0						

[a] Less than one-half of 1 per cent.
[b] 6 firms had more than $1,000,000 in current assets.

TABLE 30

BAY AREA HOUSEBUILDERS IN 1949, CLASSIFIED BY NET WORTH AND BY SIZE

Net worth (in dollars)	Number of firms by houses built				All firms	Per cent of firms in class				
	1–9	10–24	25–99	100 and over		1–9	10–24	25–99	100 and over	All firms
Less than $20,000	503	32	2	. .	537[b]	37	18	2	. .	33
20,000–49,000	519	61	7	. .	587	38	32	10	. .	35
50,000–199,000	325	78	42	9	454	24	41	54	30	27
200,000–499,000	10	14	22	10	56	1	7	29	33	3
500,000–7,500,000	5	4	4	11	24[b]	[a]	2	5	37	2
Total	1,362	189	77	30	1,658	100	100	100	100	100
Median ($000)	30.2	51.8	112.0	419.0						

[a] Less than one-half of 1 per cent.
[b] 14 firms had a net worth less than $5,000, and 7 firms had a net worth more than $1,000,000.

TABLE 31

BAY AREA HOUSEBUILDERS IN 1949, CLASSIFIED BY NET WORTH AS A PER CENT OF SALES VOLUME AND BY SIZE

Net worth as a per cent of sales	Number of firms by houses built				All firms	Per cent of firms in class				
	1–9	10–24	25–99	100 and over		1–9	10–24	25–99	100 and over	All firms
Under 14.9	207	35	19	11	272	15	19	24	37	17
15–34.9	376	95	30	14	515	28	50	39	48	31
35–54.9	316	25	17	3	361	23	13	22	9	22
55–84.9	236	15	9	..	260	17	8	12	..	15
85 and over	227	19	2	2	250	17	10	3	6	15
Total	1,362	189	77	30	1,658	100	100	100	100	100
Median (per cent)	42	25	27	21						

TABLE 32

BAY AREA HOUSEBUILDERS IN 1949, CLASSIFIED BY VALUE OF EQUIPMENT OWNED PER UNIT COMPLETED AND BY SIZE

Value of equipment per unit (in dollars)	Number of firms by houses built				All firms	Per cent of firms in class				
	1–9	10–24	25–99	100 and over		1–9	10–24	25–99	100 and over	All firms
Less than $200	75	54	48	17	194	5	29	62	57	12
200–399	138	67	18	7	230	10	35	23	23	14
400–999	515	51	11	2	579	38	27	15	7	35
1,000–1,999	326	14	..	..	340	24	7	..	..	20
2,000 and more	308	3	..	4	315	23	2	..	13	19
Total	1,362	189	77	30	1,658	100	100	100	100	100
Median ($)	940	320	130	60						

TABLE 33

BAY AREA HOUSEBUILDERS IN 1949, CLASSIFIED BY NET PROFIT AND BY SIZE

Net profit (in dollars)	Number of firms by houses built				All firms	Per cent of firms in class				
	1–9	10–24	25–99	100 and over		1–9	10–24	25–99	100 and over	All firms
Loss	152	13	..	..	165	11	7	..	..	10
0–4,900	698	22	3	..	723	51	12	4	..	43
5,000–19,900	439	101	6	..	546	33	53	8	..	33
20,000–49,900	73	53	35	4	165	5	28	45	13	10
50,000–and over	...	..	33	26	59	..	..	43	87	4
Total	1,362	189	77	30	1,658	100	100	100	100	100
Median ($000)	2.8	12	49	150						

TABLE 34

BAY AREA HOUSEBUILDERS IN 1949, CLASSIFIED BY NET PROFITS AS A PER CENT OF SALES VOLUME AND BY SIZE

Net profit as a per cent of sales	Number of firms by houses built				All firms	Per cent of firms in class				
	1–9	10–24	25–99	100 and over		1–9	10–24	25–99	100 and over	All firms
Loss	152	13	..	..	165	11	7	..	..	10
0–4.9	431	50	6	7	494	31	26	8	23	30
5–9.9	555	67	38	8	668	41	35	49	27	40
10–19.9	178	54	30	12	274	13	29	39	40	17
20–29.9	46	5	3	3	57	4	3	4	10	3
Total	1,362	189	77	30	1,658	100	100	100	100	100
Median (per cent)	5.7	6.7	8.5	10.0						

TABLE 35

Bay Area Housebuilders in 1949, Classified by Net Profits as a Per Cent of Net Worth and by Size

Net profit as a per cent of net worth	Number of firms by houses built				All firms	Per cent of firms in class				
	1–9	10–24	25–99	100 and over		1–9	10–24	25–99	100 and over	All firms
Loss	152	13	..	..	165	11	7	..	..	10
0–9.9	442	37	5	2	496	32	19	6	7	30
10–39.9	504	64	36	11	615	37	34	47	37	37
40–99.9	210	56	25	8	289	16	30	33	26	17
100 and over	54	19	11	9	93	4	10	14	30	6
Total	1,362	189	77	30	1,658	100	100	100	100	100
Median (per cent)	13.1	20.5	23.0	30.4						

TABLE 36

Comparison of Characteristics of One-Family Houses Started in 15 Metropolitan Areas and in the San Francisco Area in the Last Half of 1949

House characteristic	Per cent of all houses: In all 15 areas	Per cent of all houses: San Francisco area	Rank of San Francisco in the 15 areas
Detached	95	96	13
One story	83	91	7
No basement or utility room	32	71	3
Garage	51	96	1
More than one bathroom	11	8	13
Community water supply	94	99	2
Community sewers	75	97	1
Fireplace	28	68	2
Central heating	66	32	11
Floor or wall furnace	24	68	2

House characteristic	Average of all houses: In all 15 areas	Average of all houses: San Francisco area	Rank of San Francisco in the 15 areas
Construction cost, mean	$ 8,500	$ 8,900	6
Purchase price, mean	$10,905	$12,005	4
Number of rooms, median	5	5	2
Floor area (sq. ft.), median	890	1,010	2
Floor area (sq. ft.), mean	[a]	1,072	2
Floor area (sq. ft.)	Per cent in class		Rank
Less than 800	30	7	15
800–999	35	37	4
1,000–1,199	18	37	1
1,200–1,599	12	13	7
1,600 and over	5	6	6

[a] Not available.
Source: *Construction*, February, 1951, tables 4–17; August, 1951, table 6.

TABLE 37

PER CENT DISTRIBUTION BY PRICE CLASS OF NEW ONE-FAMILY HOUSES COMPLETED IN LAST HALF OF 1949 IN BAY AREA

	Purchase price class, dollars							Median	Arithmetic Mean
	Less than 8,500	8,500–9,499	9,500–10,499	10,500–12,499	12,500–14,499	14,500–18,499	18,500 and over		
Per cent of houses	19	17	12	21	7	12	12	$10,600	$12,005

SOURCE: "Sales Prices and Financing of New Homes in Four Western Metropolitan Areas"—U. S. Bureau of Labor Statistics, Western Region.

TABLE 38

CHARACTERISTICS OF ONE-FAMILY HOUSES STARTED IN THE SAN FRANCISCO AREA IN THE LAST HALF OF 1949 CLASSIFIED ACCORDING TO SIZE OF BUILDER

Characteristic	Per cent of houses having characteristic by size class of builder					
	1–9	10–24	25–99	100 and over	Non-professionals	All houses
No basement or utility room	53	63	82	71	71	71
Stucco exterior	37	56	58	49	29	43
Dry wall construction	66	81	70	91	76	83
Central heat	37	37	32	27	25	32
More than one full bath	24	9	6	1	5	8
More than 1,500 square feet	24	3	5	1	14	10
Median size (in square feet)	1,070	1,033	974	1,002	950	1,010

TABLE 39

HOUSES CONSTRUCTED BY BAY AREA BUILDERS IN 1949, CLASSIFIED BY PRICE CLASS AND BY SIZE OF FIRM

Price classes (in dollars)	Number of houses by size class of builder				All houses	Per cent of houses in class				
	1–9	10–24	25–99	100 and over		1–9	10–24	25–99	100 and over	All houses
Less than $9,000	517	264	963	2,904	4,648	11	9	27	47	27
9,000–10,999	1,328	1,048	1,041	1,499	4,907	27	36	30	24	27
11,000–12,999	554	528	549	1,148	2,779	11	18	16	19	16
13,000–14,999	533	508	330	388	1,759	11	17	9	6	10
15,000 and over	1,910	588	629	265	3,392	40	20	18	4	20
Total	4,842	2,936	3,512	6,195	17,485	100	100	100	100	100

TABLE 40

SELECTED MORTGAGE CHARACTERISTICS OF MORTGAGED HOUSES COMPLETED IN LAST HALF OF 1949, IN 15 METROPOLITAN AREAS AND SAN FRANCISCO AREA[a]

Mortgage characteristic[b]	In all 15 areas	San Francisco area	Source of first mortgage	Per cent of total		Type of financing	Per cent of total	
				In all 15 areas	San Francisco area		In all 15 areas	San Francisco area
Amount	$8,410	$8,970	Mortgage company	31	9	VA guaranteed	19	2
Duration in years	22.0	22.0	Bank	37	57	FHA–VA combination	33	47
Initial equity	$2,220	$2,730	Savings and loan associations	15	4	FHA insured	23	27
Monthly mortgage payment	$52.50	$58.35	Insurance company	10	21	Uninsured	18	15
No down payment	25%	8%	Individuals	3	2	Unmortgaged	7	9

[a] Does not include nonprofessionally built.
[b] Based on arithmetic means.
SOURCE: "Purchasers' Incomes and New-home Financing," *Monthly Labor Review*, July, 1951, (R.2051), and *Construction*, February, 1951, table 7.

TABLE 41

FINANACIAL DATA CLASSIFIED BY INCOME GROUP OF PURCHASER IN LAST HALF OF 1949 FOR 15 METROPOLITAN AREAS AND SAN FRANCISCO AREA

Income group of purchaser	Per cent of buyers in group		Average price paid by group		Per cent in group using mortgage		Average per cent of price covered by mortgage		Ratio of mortgage to income		Ratio of mortgage payment to income		Per cent of all families in income group	
	In all 15 areas	San Francisco area	In all 15 areas	San Francisco area	In all 15 areas	San Francisco area	In all 15 areas	San Francisco area	In all 15 areas	San Francisco area	In all 15 areas	San Francisco area	In all 15 areas	San Francisco area
Less than $2,000	2	2	$9,525	$10,455	66	..	63	..	..	..	..	..	18	14
2,000–2,999	12	5	8,560	9,390	95	76	86	82	2.9	2.8	0.22	0.23	14	14
3,000–3,999	36	33	9,240	10,155	97	93	87	88	2.3	2.4	0.17	0.18	22	25
4,000–4,999	23	26	10,570	11,455	96	91	81	81	1.9	2.0	0.14	0.15	16	17
5,000–5,999	13	14	12,115	12,670	93	95	75	73	1.6	1.7	0.13	0.13	11	11
6,000–7,499	6	8	13,935	17,445	95	91	69	60	1.4	1.5	0.11	0.12	8	9
7,500–9,999	3	6	16,385	15,715	78	77	68	67	1.3	1.2	0.10	0.09	6	4
10,000 and over	4	3	22,985	20,365	70	88	57	61	...	...	....	....	5	4
All	100	100	10,905	12,005	94	91	79	77	...	...	....	....	100	100

SOURCE: "Purchasers' Incomes and New-home Financing," *Monthly Labor Review*, July 1951, (R. 2051); Bureau of Census: *1950 Census of Population*, Series PC-5.

TABLE 42

ESTIMATES OF NUMBER OF BAY AREA TRADE CONTRACTORS IN 1949 WITH HOUSEBUILDING SPECIALTIES

Type of Contractor	Licenses		Active firms	
	Number	Per cent active	Number	Per cent of all active
Painting	1,720	71.6	1,232	35
Plumbing	544	77.7	423	12
Flooring (wood)	168	73.0	123	4
Cement and concrete	164	70.5	116	3
Masonry	152	78.5	119	3
All others	2,036	74.9	1,525	43
Total	4,784	74.0	3,538	100

TABLE 43

BAY AREA TRADE CONTRACTORS IN 1949, CLASSIFIED BY DOLLAR VOLUME AND BY TRADE

Type of contractor	Number of firms in trade	Per cent of firms performing total work of a value				
		$0–9,999	$10,000–49,999	$50,000–199,999	$200,000–499,999	$500,000 and over
Painting	1,232	50	36	10	4	[b]
Plumbing	423	28	27	33	5	7
Flooring (wood)	123	19	63	4	14	[a]
Cement and concrete	116	24	33	27	8	8
Masonry	119	6	54	25	15	[a]
All others	1,525	19	44	22	10	5
Total	3,538	31	40	19	7	3

[a] Included in previous class because number is so few that confidential information might otherwise be divulged.
[b] Less than one-half of 1 per cent.

TABLE 44

BAY AREA TRADE CONTRACTORS IN 1949, CLASSIFIED BY AVERAGE NUMBER OF SITE EMPLOYEES AND BY TRADE

Type of contractor	Number of firms in trade	Per cent of firms with number of employees				
		Owner only	1–4	5–9	10–24	25 and over
Painting	1,232	31	44	13	4	8
Plumbing	423	17	43	20	10	10
Flooring (wood)	123	19	51	14	9	7
Cement and concrete	116	20	47	8	13	12
Masonry	119	9	31	30	24	6
All others	1,525	16	43	18	14	9
Total	3,538	22	44	16	10	8

TABLE 45

BAY AREA TRADE CONTRACTORS IN 1949, CLASSIFIED BY AVERAGE NUMBER OF OVERHEAD PERSONNEL AND BY TRADE

Type of contractor	Number of firms in trade	Per cent of firms with number of off-site personnel			
		Owner in spare time	Owner only	2–4	5 and over
Painting	1,232	81	5	10	3
Plumbing	423	47	25	19	8
Flooring (wood)	123	77	9	1	13
Cement and concrete	116	68	10	13	9
Masonry	119	69	15	15	1
All others	1,525	65	15	12	8
Total	3,538	70	12	12	6

TABLE 46

BAY AREA TRADE CONTRACTORS IN 1949, CLASSIFIED BY PER CENT WORK ON NEW HOUSING FORMED OF TOTAL VOLUME AND BY TRADE

Type of contractor	Number of firms in trade	Per cent of firms performing new housing equal to per cent of total volume				
		0–9	10–39	40–69	70–89	90–100
Painting	1,232	60	16	12	2	10
Plumbing	423	37	15	28	11	9
Flooring (wood)	123	13	34	13	12	28
Cement and concrete	116	29	21	28	9	13
Masonry	119	16	7	15	20	42
All others	1,525	24	19	21	13	23
Total	3,538	38	18	18	9	17

TABLE 47

BAY AREA TRADE CONTRACTORS IN 1949, CLASSIFIED BY PER CENT NEW HOUSING FORMED OF TOTAL PRODUCTION, BY TRADE, AND BY SIZE

Size class (in dollars)	Percentage distribution of firms in each size class											
	Cement and concrete, Per cent of work on new housing				Masonry, Per cent of work on new housing				Plumbing, Per cent of work on new housing			
	0–9	10–69	70–89	90–100	0–9	10–69	70–89	90–100	0–9	10–69	70–89	90–100
$ 0–9,999	78	22	..	..	50	..	50	..	63	37	..	..
10,000–49,999	17	43	20	20	..	12	26	62	24	46	11	19
50,000–199,999	3	72	3	22	7	56	20	17	24	52	17	7
200,000–499,999	..	67	33	..	89	11	..	..	61	28	6	5
500,000[a] and over	75	25	..	..	..	..	..	..	41	22	34	3
Total	30	47	10	13	17	22	21	40	37	43	12	8

[a] Masonry firms of this size are included in previous class so that confidential information may not be divulged.

TABLE 48

BAY AREA TRADE CONTRACTORS IN 1949, CLASSIFIED BY NUMBER OF AREAS WORKED IN AND BY TRADE

Type of contractor	Number of firms in trade	Per cent of firms working in number of areas				
		1 county	2-3 counties	4-6 counties	Rest of bay area	Outside area
Painting	1,232	48	39	1	5	7
Plumbing	423	66	20	3	4	7
Flooring (wood)	123	22	49	..	19	10
Cement and concrete	116	41	32	8	14	5
Masonry	119	20	44	5	10	21
All others	1,525	37	36	4	12	11
Total	3,538	43	36	3	9	9

TABLE 49

COSTS OF THE COMPOSITE HOUSE CLASSIFIED BY MAIN EXPENDITURES AND BY SIZE OF BUILDER

Expenditures	Size of builder			Size of builder		
	Small	Medium	Large	Small	Medium	Large
	(in dollars)			(per cent of total)		
Direct labor	1,485	1,300	1,100	16	14	13
Direct materials	2,235	1,925	1,825	24	21	21
Subcontracts						
Plumbing	889	765	640	9	8	7
Painting	626	587	537	7	6	6
Flooring	396	370	343	4	4	4
Cement and concrete	314	285	259	3	3	3
Masonry	235	205	180	2	2	2
Sheet metal and heating	225	212	175	2	2	2
Electric wiring and fixtures	220	207	180	2	2	2
Ceramic tile	180	141	130	2	2	1
Roofing	174	168	148	2	2	2
Grading	52	33	19	1	[a]	[a]
Linoleum	35	31	24	[a]	[a]	[a]
Shades and blinds	33	27	22	[a]	[a]	[a]
Subtotal subcontracts	3,379	3,031	2,657	35	33	30
Incidentals	410	410	310	4	4	4
Land	1,250	1,250	1,250	13	14	14
Overhead and profit	741	1,334	1,608	8	14	18
Total cost	9,500	9,250	8,750	100	100	100

[a] Less than one-half of 1 per cent.

TABLE 50

LABOR COSTS OF THE COMPOSITE HOUSE BY CONTRACTOR AND TRADE, AND BY SIZE OF BUILDER

Contractor and trade	Size of builder			Size of builder			Size of builder		
	Small	Medium	Large	Small	Medium	Large	Small	Medium	Large
	(In dollars)			Per cent of total labor cost			Per cent of total cost of house		
Direct Labor									
Carpenter	1,266	1,101	909	48	48	44	14	12	11
Laborer	219	199	191	8	8	11	2	2	2
Subtotal direct	1,485	1,300	1,100	56	56	55	16	14	13
Trade contractors									
Painting (painters)	360	338	322	14	15	16	4	3	4
Plumbing (plumbers)	194	167	159	7	7	8	2	2	2
Flooring (carpenters)	106	93	88	4	4	4	1	1	1
Masonry (masons)	100	72	72	4	3	4	1	1	1
Tile (masons)	88	59	51	3	3	2	1	1	1
Wiring (electricians)	80	74	66	3	3	3	1	1	1
Sheet metal and heating (sheet metal)	60	55	50	2	2	2	1	1	1
Cement and concrete (cement finishers)	50	43	39	2	2	2	1	a	a
(laborers)	41	41	41	1	2	2	a	a	a
Roofing (roofers)	42	40	37	2	2	2	a	a	a
Grading (excavators)	18	9	5	1	a	a	a	a	a
Linoleum (painters)	15	12	9	1	1	a	a	a	a
Other labor	7	7	5	a	a	a	a	a	a
Subtotal subcontracts	1,161	1,010	944	44	44	45	12	11	11
Total	2,646	2,310	2,044	100	100	100	28	25	24

[a] Less than one-half of 1 per cent.

TABLE 51

MATERIALS COSTS OF THE COMPOSITE HOUSE BY CONTRACTOR AND BY SIZE OF BUILDER

Material	Size of builder			Size of builder			Size of builder		
	Small	Medium	Large	Small	Medium	Large	Small	Medium	Large
	(In dollars)			Per cent of total material cost			Per cent of total cost of house		
Direct									
Lumber	1,085	970	970	29	29	31	11	11	11
Millwork	725	580	510	19	17	16	8	6	6
Gypsum board	240	220	205	6	7	7	3	2	2
Hardware	185	155	140	5	5	5	2	2	2
Subtotal direct	2,235	1,925	1,825	59	58	59	24	21	21
Trade contractors									
Plumbing	495	450	405	13	13	13	5	5	5
Flooring (oak)	224	198	185	6	6	6	2	2	2
Concrete	179	168	153	5	5	5	2	2	2
Paint	144	135	108	4	4	4	2	1	1
Sheet metal	113	113	97	3	3	3	1	1	1
Roofing	99	99	87	3	3	3	1	1	1
Electrical	96	96	83	3	3	3	1	1	1
Masonry	80	80	63	2	2	2	1	1	1
Ceramic tiles	61	60	59	2	2	2	1	1	1
Shades	19	14	14	[a]	[a]	[a]	[a]	[a]	[a]
Linoleum	14	14	11	[a]	[a]	[a]	[a]	[a]	[a]
Subtotal trade contractors	1,524	1,427	1,265	41	42	41	16	16	14
Total	3,759	3,352	3,090	100	100	100	40	37	35

[a] Less than one-half of 1 per cent.

TABLE 52

OVERHEAD AND PROFIT ON SITE WORK OF THE COMPOSITE HOUSE, BY CONTRACTOR AND BY SIZE OF BUILDER

Contractor	Size of builder			Size of builder			Size of builder		
	Small	Medium	Large	Small	Medium	Large	Small	Medium	Large
	(In dollars)			Per cent of all overhead and profit			Per cent of total cost of house		
Builder	741	1,334	1,608	52	69	78	8	14	18
Trade contractors									
Plumbing	200	148	76	14	8	4	2	2	1
Painting	122	114	107	9	6	5	1	1	1
Flooring	66	79	70	5	4	3	1	1	1
Cement and concrete	44	33	26	3	2	1	[a]	[a]	[a]
Masonry	55	53	45	4	3	2	1	1	1
Sheet metal	52	44	28	4	2	1	1	[a]	[a]
Electrical	44	37	31	3	2	2	[a]	[a]	[a]
Ceramic tile	31	22	20	2	1	1	[a]	[a]	[a]
Roofing	33	29	24	2	2	1	[a]	[a]	[a]
Grading	34	24	14	2	1	1	[a]	[a]	[a]
Linoleum	6	5	4	[a]	[a]	[a]	[a]	[a]	[a]
Shades and blinds	7	6	3	[a]	[a]	[a]	[a]	[a]	[a]
Subtotal trade contractors	694	594	448	48	31	22	7	6	5
Total	1,435	1,928	2,056	100	100	100	15	20	23

[a] Less than one-half of 1 per cent.

TABLE 53

CONCENTRATION RATIOS IN 1947 OF INDUSTRIES MANUFACTURING BUILDING MATERIALS

Material	Industry	Classification number	Number of firms	Concentration ratio—per cent of output supplied by: 4 firms	8 firms	20 firms	50 firms	Relative importance: By material in Bay area[a] house (in per cent)	By value of shipments in 1947 (in per cent)
Lumber and flooring	Saw and planing mills	2,421	19,223	5.4	7.2	11.0	17.9	34.1	14.1
Millwork	Millwork plants	2,431	2,276	7.4	13.0	23.8	38.8	13.3	2.9
Cabinets	Plywood plants	2,432	142	21.9	33.6	55.7	83.4	5.4	1.4
Gypsum products	Gypsum products	3,272	33	84.6	94.1	99.7	100.0	6.4	0.7
Hardware									
Nails and spikes	Fabricated wire products	3,481	63	39.6	59.6	85.6	99.3	1.9	0.2
Rods	Steel works and rolling mills	3,312	111	44.7	62.8	81.1	94.2	1.3	12.7
Finish	Hardware, n.e.c.	3,429	717	28.5	39.9	52.7	69.8	1.9	3.2
Building paper	Paper and board mills	2,616	453	15.6	23.7	36.5	56.4	0.7	15.7
Plumbing									
Metal plumbing fixtures and fittings	Metal plumbing fixtures	3,431	263	34.7	48.3	67.9	85.7	5.3	1.6
Vitreous plumbing fixtures	Vitreous plumbing fixtures	3,261	26	57.9	81.7	99.6	100.0	1.9	0.4
Pipe, cast iron	Gray iron foundries	3,321	1,554	16.3	23.6	35.3	48.1	2.1	6.5
Water pipe, galvanized steel	Steelworks and rolling mills[c]	3,312	111	44.7	62.8	81.1	94.2	2.6	12.7
Concrete									
Cement, hydraulic	Cement,[c] hydraulic	3,241	73	29.5	45.1	70.0	93.3	2.4	2.3
Aggregates[b]	.....	....	.....	....	....	....	....	2.4	....
Paint	Paints and varnishes	2,851	1,154	27.3	35.7	48.2	60.9	3.8	6.9
Sheet metal	Sheet metal work[c]	3,444	1,665	20.5	28.5	37.8	48.3	1.2	2.4
Roofing, asphalt	Roofing felts and coatings	2,952	104	41.7	64.8	87.3	98.7	2.4	1.9

Electrical									
Wiring	Insulated wire and cable [c]	3,631	150	40.7	57.4	80.5	95.6	1.1	1.7
Lighting fixtures	Lighting fixtures [c]	3,471	1,198	18.1	25.8	38.6	55.0	1.[illegible]	2.6
Masonry, red brick	Brick and hollow tile [c]	3,251	574	9.7	16.6	29.8	46.5	2.1	0.8
Ceramic tile	Floor and wall tile	3,253	34	50.9	70.3	96.4	100.0	1.6	0.2
Window shades	Window shades	2,562	103	71.7	83.4	93.0	98.3	0.5	0.4
Linoleum	Hard surface floor coverings	2,274	14	80.3	94.5	100.0	100.0	0.4	1.0
Window glass	Flat glass	3,211	15	88.1	98.5	100.0	100.0	0.6	1.4
Heating									
Furnace and water heater	Heating and cooking apparatus except electric [c]	3,439	792	11.7	20.2	37.1	57.4	3.1	6.3
Total	.....	.....	.....	.....	.....	.....	.....	100.0	100.0

[a] Total value of materials in San Francisco Bay Area House is $3,759.00.
[b] Concentration ratio not available.
[c] Nonhomogeneous.
SOURCE: "Study of Monopoly Power," *Hearings*, Subcommittee on Study of Monopoly Power, U. S. House Committee on The Judiciary (81:2), p. 1437 ff.

TABLE 54

DISTRIBUTION OF HOUSEBUILDING MATERIALS BY CONCENTRATION RATIO CLASSES, 1947, BASED ON USE OF MATERIALS IN COMPOSITE BAY AREA HOUSE

Concentration ratio first 8 companies	Homogeneous industries[a]		All industries[b]	
	Per cent	Cumulative per cent	Per cent	Cumulative per cent
0.1–10	40.8	40.8	35.0	35.0
10.1–20	15.9	56.7	13.6	48.6
20.1–30	3.4	60.1	2.9	51.5
30.1–40	13.2	73.3	11.3	62.8
40.1–50	6.3	79.6	5.4	68.2
50.1–60	2.4	82.0	2.0	70.2
60.1–70	4.5	86.5	3.8	74.0
70.1–80	1.9	88.4	1.7	75.7
80.1–90	2.8	91.2	2.4	78.1
90.1–100	8.8	100.0	7.6	85.7
Nonhomogeneous	....	....	14.3	100.0
Total	100.0	100.0	100.0	100.0

[a] Calculated from material values totaling $3,145.00; the value of all materials in the composite house equal $3,759.00.
[b] Calculated from material values totaling $3,669.00 for which concentration ratios were available; the value of all materials in the composite house equals $3,759.00.

TABLE 55

DISTRIBUTION OF HOUSEBUILDING MATERIALS BY CONCENTRATION RATIO CLASSES, 1947, BASED ON VALUE OF PRODUCTS OF MATERIALS SUPPLY INDUSTRIES

Concentration ratio first 8 companies	Homogeneous industries[a]		All industries[b]	
	Per cent	Cumulative per cent	Per cent	Cumulative per cent
0.1–10	19.9	19.9	14.1	14.1
10.1–20	4.1	24.0	2.9	17.0
20.1–30	31.4	55.4	22.2	39.2
30.1–40	16.4	71.8	11.6	50.8
40.1–50	2.3	74.1	1.6	52.4
50.1–60	.2	74.3	0.1	52.5
60.1–70	20.5	94.8	14.6	67.1
70.1–80	.3	95.1	0.2	67.3
80.1–90	.6	95.7	0.4	67.7
90.1–100	4.3	100.0	3.4	71.1
Nonhomogeneous	....	....	28.9	100.0
Total	100.0	100.0	100.0	100.0

[a] Calculated from value of products shipped of $12,783,440,000.
[b] Calculated from value of products shipped of $17,946,824,000 which includes all industries supplying materials for the composite house, except Aggregates, for which no data are available.

TABLE 56

REVISED WHOLESALE PRICE INDEX AND BUILDING MATERIALS PRICE INDEXES

Year	All commodities	All commodities other than farm products and food	Building materials[a]	Lumber[a]
1929	61.9	65.5	51.4	32.1
1930	56.1	60.9	48.2	29.3
1931	47.4	53.6	43.1	23.8
1932	42.1	50.2	38.7	20.0
1933	42.8	50.9	41.6	24.2
1934	48.7	56.0	46.2	28.9
1935	52.0	55.7	45.6	27.7
1936	52.5	56.9	46.9	28.9
1937	56.1	61.0	52.2	34.1
1938	51.1	58.4	49.8	30.9
1939	50.1	58.1	49.8	31.9
1940	51.1	59.4	51.5	35.2
1941	56.8	63.7	55.4	41.9
1942	64.2	68.3	58.7	45.4
1943	67.0	69.3	59.0	47.3
1944	67.6	70.4	61.4	52.2
1945	68.8	71.3	62.4	53.0
1946	78.7	78.3	69.8	61.0
1947	96.4	95.3	94.0	94.5
1948	104.4	103.4	104.0	107.3
1949	99.2	101.3	102.0	98.2
1950	103.1	105.0	109.5	114.5
1951	114.8	115.9	119.6	123.6

[a] Years 1929–1945 calculated by linking old BLS wholesale price relatives of major classes to 1947–1949 = 100, and using new class weights prevailing in 1947.
SOURCE: Bureau of Labor Statistics, U. S. Department of Labor.

TABLE 57

CONSTRUCTION EMPLOYMENT IN 1940 AND 1950 FOR UNITED STATES, CALIFORNIA, AND SAN FRANCISCO METROPOLITAN AREA[a]

Area	Employment (in thousands)		Per cent increase		Per cent of employed labor force	
	1940	1950	1940	1950	1940	1950
United States	2,056.3	3,480.0	.....	69.3	4.6	6.2
California	151.9	316.0	.....	108.1	6.1	8.1
San Francisco	33.1	68.1	.....	105.9	6.0	8.0

[a] Includes employers, own-account workers, and so on.
SOURCE: Bureau of the Census; 1950 Census: Series PC-5, No. 45; PC-6, No. 1; PC-7, No. 2.

TABLE 58

AVERAGE EARNINGS AND AVERAGE HOURS WORKED, FOR BUILDING AND ALL MANUFACTURING EMPLOYEES, IN UNITED STATES AND CALIFORNIA, SELECTED YEARS

Year and area	Building general contractors[a]			Building trade contractors[a]			All manufacturing industries		
	Earnings (in dollars)		Hours worked per week	Earnings (in dollars)		Hours worked per week	Earnings (in dollars)		Hours worked per week
	Weekly	Hourly		Weekly	Hourly		Weekly	Hourly	
United States									
1940	30.56	0.92	33.3	33.11	1.01	32.7	25.20	0.66	38.1
1946	53.33	1.42	37.6	59.52	1.54	38.6	43.82	1.09	40.4
1950	68.56	1.92	35.8	77.77	2.12	36.7	59.33	1.47	40.5
California									
1950	73.05	2.21	36.4	85.51	2.41	35.5	65.39	1.65	39.7

Indexes 1940=100

Year and area	Building general contractors[a]			Building trade contractors[a]			All manufacturing industries		
	Earnings		Hours of work	Earnings		Hours of work	Earnings		Hours of work
	Weekly	Hourly		Weekly	Hourly		Weekly	Hourly	
United States									
1940	100	100	100	100	100	100	100	100	100
1946	175	155	113	180	153	118	174	164	106
1950	224	209	108	235	209	112	235	222	106

[a] In private building.

SOURCE: U. S. Bureau of Labor Statistics, *Handbook of Labor Statistics, 1947, 1950;* California Department of Industrial Relations, *Handbook of California Labor Statistics, 1949–1950.*

TABLE 59

NUMBER OF WORK STOPPAGES AND MAN-DAYS IDLE, 1946–1950, UNITED STATES AND CALIFORNIA

Year and area	Work stoppages			Man-days idle		
				(In thousands)		
	Total all industries	Construction	Construction per cent of total	Total all industries	Construction	Construction per cent of total
United States:						
1946	4,985	351	7.0	116,000	1,450	1.3
1947	3,693	382	10.3	34,600	2,770	8.0
1948	3,419	380	11.1	34,100	1,430	4.2
1949	3,606	615	17.1	50,500	2,760	5.5
1950	4,843	611	12.6	38,800	2,460	6.3
California:						
1946	246	19	7.7	6,082	29	0.5
1947	247	18	7.3	2,440	42	1.7
1948	178	27	15.1	2,790	72	2.6
1949	217	43	19.7	2,040	109	5.3
1950	238	38	16.0	1,630	668	41.0

SOURCE: Bureau of Labor Statistics, *Handbook of Labor Statistics;* California Department of Industrial Relations, *Handbook of California Labor Statistics, 1949, 1950.*

TABLE 60

COMPARATIVE PROFIT RATES BASED ON TOTAL SALES,[a] CONSTRUCTION, AND OTHER INDUSTRIES

Industry classification	Net income as a per cent of sales volume in year:									
	1929	1932	1938	1940	1943	1945	1947	1948	1949	1950
Construction	4.3	− 6.8	1.5	2.8	5.7	3.3	5.6	6.3	6.9	6.8
All industries	7.1	− 4.4	3.1	6.9	10.7	8.2	8.8	8.7	7.7	9.8
All manufacturing industries	7.2	− 4.2	3.2	8.5	10.3	7.5	9.8	9.7	8.2	11.1
Machinery (except electrical and transportation)	11.3	−15.5	6.7	15.1	14.1	9.1	11.7	12.2	10.8	13.4
Automobiles and equipment	7.7	−13.6	2.2	11.5	8.9	5.7	11.0	12.3	13.9	17.7
Furniture and finished lumber products	3.1	−16.9	1.2	5.1	7.3	7.0	8.4	7.0	4.5	6.8
San Francisco Bay area housebuilding	....	......	....	....	....	....	....	....	8.5[b]	....

[a] Total sales of corporations are used since gross income of corporations for all above years is not available.
[b] Profit rate for medium size builders, see table 34.
SOURCE: National Income Supplement to *Survey of Current Business*. The profit rate is the ratio of corporate income before taxes to corporate sales.

TABLE 61

NET PROFIT AS A PER CENT OF NET WORTH, IN SELECTED INDUSTRIES AND YEARS

Industry classification	Profit as a per cent of owners' equity			
	1947	1948	1949	1950
Bay Area housebuilding	a	a	23.0	a
All manufacturing industries	25.5	25.6	18.5	27.8
Machinery (except electrical and transportation)	26.4	27.3	19.3	25.8
Motor vehicles and parts	29.2	34.7	37.6	52.9
Furniture and fixtures	30.5	26.8	14.6	26.9

[a] Not available.

SOURCE: Securities Exchange Commission–Federal Trade Commission: *Quarterly Industrial Financial Report Series for All U. S. Manufacturing Corporations.* Bay Area data based on table 35 of this report. The profit rates are before federal income taxes.

TABLE 62

RATES OF NET GROWTH, ENTRY, AND DISCONTINUANCE, FOR SELECTED INDUSTRIES, AREAS, AND YEARS

Area and industry	Percentage rates of change of industry populations					
	1945	1946	1947	1948	1949	1950
	Net growth rate					
Bay Area						
Contract construction	a	a	a	14.9	0.5	5.7[b]
Building contractors	a	a	a	22.2	1.1	6.5[b]
Special trade contractors	a	a	a	11.4	0.3	3.9[b]
United States						
Contract construction	22.5	29.9	13.5	6.3	3.5	8.3
All manufacturing industries	8.3	16.3	2.7	− 3.0	− 6.6	− 2.0
All industries	7.1	11.2	4.7	0.5	− 0.7	1.0
	Entry rate					
United States						
Contract construction	33.2	41.5	26.5	20.7	17.6	20.4
All manufacturing industries	18.6	26.3	15.1	12.1	10.1	12.2
All industries	13.4	17.6	12.3	9.9	9.0	10.0
	Discontinuance rate					
United States						
Contract construction	10.7	11.6	13.0	14.4	14.1	12.1
All manufacturing industries	10.3	10.0	12.4	15.1	16.7	14.2
All industries	6.3	6.4	7.6	9.4	9.7	9.0

[a] Not available.
[b] Preliminary.
SOURCE: National data: *Survey of Current Business*, May, 1950, pp. 12–20, and "Business Statistics," 1951. Bay Area data: *California Employment and Payrolls*, State of California, Department of Employment. Bay Area data are based on changes in average number from previous year; national data are based on changes from March 31 to March 31.

INDEX

INDEX

Abrams, C., 8
Accounting, 61–63, 91–92, 124, 126, 277
Age: of firms, 34, 70–71, 96–97, 354; of wners, 34, 69–70, 98, 353
Appraisals, 108, 252–253; and profits, 268–269
Architects, 48, 112, 207. *See also* Design
Assets: current, 39–40, 75, 104, 357; total, 38–39, 75, 104, 356

Background of housebuilders, 33–34, 69–70, 97–99, 355
Bain, J. S., 136 n., 137 n., 256 n., 332 n.
Balance sheet, 38, 39, 75, 104
Bauer, C., 258 n.
Bay area, 14–16
Bidding, 46–49; subcontracts, 59–60; depositories, 233
Boulding, K. E., 219 n.
Bowen, I., 265 n.
Budgets, 63, 90, 124, 126
Builders, types of, 16. *See also* Housebuilders
Building. *See* Housebuilding
Building codes. *See* Codes
Bureau of Labor Statistics, 20, 25, 313–314, 316

Capital, 39, 41, 73, 75, 218; availability of, 44, 64, 75, 92, 105–106, 131, 218, 271; leverage of, 76, 218; turnover in, 40, 75, 76, 105, 359; working, 39–40, 42, 43
Chamberlain, E. H., 225 n.
Channels of distribution, 138–139, 196. *See also* Materials
Codes, 162–164; administration of, 249; restrictive practices in, 224, 246–249
Colean, M., 4, 134 n., 224 n., 226 n.
Committee on Price Determination, 170 n., 179 n., 182 n., 216 n.
Community builder, 96. *See also* Housebuilders, large-sized
Competition, 189; and entry, 270–271; and innovations, 282–283; and labor, 236–237; effective, 256; in financing, 158–160; in materials, 136–138, 140, 227–228, 270; in subcontracts, 144, 233; workable, 256. *See also* Concentration; Monopoly
Composite house, 184–188, 311, 327–331; costs of, 190, 197, 372; labor costs in, 373; material costs in, 196–197, 204, 374
Concentration, 136–138, 333–334; in housebuilding, 22–26; in materials, 136, 228, 376–378
Confidence intervals, 311–312, 339, 340
Construction. *See* Housebuilding
Construction financing. *See* Financing
Contractors, 19, 32, 69, 292; general, 17, 32, 96
Controls, 61–63, 90–92, 123–130; of subcontracts, 149–150, 297
Cost analysis, 126, 276–277, 278–279
Cost curve, synthetic, 184
Costs, 12; and flexibility, 272–273; direct, 194–207, 214–215; fixed, 103; indirect, 73–74, 103–104, 189, 208, 215, 322, 375; median, 25, 190; overhead, 38, 72, 102–104, 208–210, 375; of bidding, 46–48; of composite house, 190, 196–197, 204, 372, 374; of custom work, 28, 33, 48, 69; of financing, 107, 160, 207, 251–253, 275–276; of incidentals, 207; of labor, 153–154, 194–196, 244–246, 373; of materials, 121, 196–204, 374; of restrictive practices, 244–249, 254–255; of selling, 37, 261–262; of subcontracts, 204–207, 372. *See also* Prices
Credit, 77; lack of, 64, 92; of materials suppliers, 57. *See also* Capital
Crews, size of, 54, 83, 115–116, 195–196
Custom work, 28, 33, 48, 69

Davis, H. F., 168 n., 178 n., 182 n., 183 n.
Demand, 10–14, 111, 264, 269, 273–274
Depreciation, 37–38, 41, 72
Design, 45, 48, 81–82, 110–113, 168–169, 190–191, 207, 252–253, 257–259; of site, 113
Determinants: of performance, *see* Performance; of size, *see* Size
Development companies, 80–81, 99
Discounts, 87; builders', 56; dealers', 229–231; quantity, 120–121, 197; special, 201–202; trade channel, 199–201; volume, 199–201
Distribution. *See* Channels of distribution; Materials
Draws. *See* Payments, partial
Dwelling units: definition of, 313; number of, 341

Efficiency, 85, 114, 274–279, 280–282, 299; and profits, 265; and scale, 174–176, 189–222; and subcontracts, 58–59, 122–123,

Efficiency (*cont.*)
142, 231–233; measurement of, 180–188; of financing, 250–253, 275–276; paths to, 172; problems of, 8; range in, 187. *See also* Restrictive practices
Entry: in housebuilding, 270–271, 384; in labor, 240–241; in subcontracting, 233–234
Equipment, 37, 39–41, 72, 75, 102–104, 359; restrictions in use of, 238–239
Equities, 39–40, 74–75, 77, 104, 218, 252, 271, 358, 359, 361. *See also* Capital
Estimates, 61–63, 90, 128–129; of subcontracts, 149–150
Executives, 35–37, 71–72, 100–101. *See also* Management; Overhead

Factors, supply of, 134–164
Federal Housing Administration, 77–78, 107, 159, 251–253, 268. *See also* Financing
Federal National Mortgage Association, 160
Fellner, W., 218 n.
Financing, 38–44, 74–78, 104–108, 157–161; construction, 41, 76–78, 107, 158–160, 207; cost of, 107, 160, 207, 250–252, 275–276; efficiency of, 250–253, 275–276; land, 79–81, 92–93; permanent loans, 108, 158–161, 365–366
Flexibility, 216, 232, 270–273
Florence, P. S., 216 n.

Gordon, R. A., 218 n.
Government, 162–164, 290–291; and financing, 77–78, 159; and restrictive practices, 246–250. *See also* Federal Housing Administration; Veterans Administration
Grebler, L., 4, 5, 17, 134 n., 168 n., 291 n.

Heavenrich, H., 284 n.
Hoover, E. M., 216 n.
House: characteristics of, 27–30, 323–325, 362, 363; definition of, 312; median, 25; prices of, 27–28. *See also* Composite house; Product of housebuilders
Housebuilders: areas worked in, 350; definition of, 21; completing other dwelling units, 349; in metropolitan areas, 23–24; in 1949 by size, 343; median, 25, 67–68; months active, 350; number of, 20, 22, 23, 343; number of employees, 347; other buidling, 348; overhead employees, 351; prior experience of, 33–34, 69–71, 97–99, 355
Housebuilders, contractors, 19, 32, 69, 292
Housebuilders, large-sized, 95–133; characteristics of, 98; definition of, 21–22; number of, in 1938, 1939, and 1949, 342; summary of, 131–133
Housebuilders, medium-sized, 67–94; characteristics of, 67–69; definition of, 21; number of, in 1938, 1939, and 1949, 342; summary of, 93–94
Housebuilders, operative. *See* Operative housebuilders
Housebuilders, small-sized, 31–68; characteristics of, 31–33; definition of, 21; house characteristics, 33; problems of, 55–56, 63, 65–66; summary of, 65–66
Housebuilding: as an industry, 16–20; custom, 28, 69, 192; forces shaping, 10; in Bay area, 25; in metropolitan areas, 23; problems of, 8; trade contractors in, 370; volume of, by nonprofessionals, by size, by size and area, by size and contract, by size and tracts, 342–345

Income, of house buyers, 15, 262, 366
Innovations, 45, 65, 68, 79–82, 87, 110–113, 120, 204, 212, 239, 249, 253, 258–259, 278–279, 280–282, 284–286, 291
Index, cost, 184
Integration, 122–123, 142, 144, 201, 231–233, 283–284, 352

Jurisdiction, problems of, 55, 148, 157, 239–240

Kelly, B., 49 n., 284 n., 296 n.

Labor, 151–157; and owner-workers, 236–237; by size of housebuilder, 347; costs, 151, 153–154, 194–196, 244–246, 373; earnings, 154–155, 380; entry, 240–241; jurisdictions, 55, 148, 157, 239–240; of trade contractors, 144, 368; relations, 54–55, 83, 113–114, 242–244; restrictive practices of, 224, 234–246; skills of, 54, 64, 114, 153, 243; specialization of, 84, 102, 113–115, 122, 195, 276–277; strikes, 157, 239–240, 381; supply of, 114, 151–153, 272, 379; unions 156–157; upgrading, 237–238
Land, 29, 44–45, 78–81, 92–93, 106, 192–193, 215; and price, 29; financing, 79–81, 92–93
Legal structure, 34, 38, 70–72, 99, 355
Leverage of capital, 76, 218
Livability, 191, 257
Lumber, 56–58, 87–88, 136, 140–141, 199–200

Maisel, S. J., 269 n., 291 n.
Management, 35–37, 71–72, 100–102, 170–174, 176, 210, 215, 288, 295; and progress, 289–290; efficiency of, 170–174, 268, 277–279; span of, 64, 92
Margin, operating, 73–74, 103–104, 189, 208, 322, 375
Markets, 28, 44–48, 78–82, 109–113, 178, 260–264, 291; analysis of, 82, 111–113, 262–264, 293–294; control of, 136–138
Marketing, 113, 175–176, 216–217, 260–262. *See also* Markets; Sales
Mason, E. S., 256 n.
Materials: channels of distribution, 138, 139; competition in, 136–138, 228, 270; concentration in, 136, 228, 333–334, 376–378; costs of, 121, 196, 204, 374; in composite house, 196–197, 204, 374; monopoly in, 135–138, 270; prices of, 139–141, 379; restrictive practices in, 135, 227–231; purchases of, 56–58, 87–88, 120–121, 227–231
Mechanics' liens, 43
Mechanization, 39, 55, 116–120, 275; among trade-contractors, 118–119, 150
Merchant builder. *See* Operative housebuilders
Method, statement of, 30
Monopoly, 135, 270; profits of, 212–213. *See also* Competition; Restrictive practices
Mortgages, 158–161, 365–366. *See also* Financing

Neal, A. C., 141 n.
Net worth. *See* Equities
Nonprofessionals, 17–19; number of, 342

Operations. *See* Production
Operative housebuilders, 19–20, 26, 96, 109–113, 292; financing of, 74–75; number of, 344, 347; volume of housebuilding, 344
Organization: of firms, 34, 38, 71–72, 99–101, 355; of industry, 178–180, 293–294
Overhead, 34–35, 38, 64, 71, 99–104, 274, 351; costs, 38, 72, 102–104, 208–210, 375; of trade-contractors, 147–148, 368
Owner-builders. *See* Nonprofessionals
Oxenfeldt, A. R., 168 n., 265 n.

Patterns, 86
Payments, partial, 42
Performance: determinants of, 169–180; evaluating, 256; standards of, 168–169
Population, 15, 341
Preassembling, 84–85, 296
Precutting, 84–85, 150
Prefabrication, 49 n., 84, 292, 296–297
Preplanning, 49, 52, 115, 123
Prices: elasticity of, 274; of houses, 27–28, 351, 363, 364, 379; of labor, 380; of materials, 135, 138–141. *See also* Costs
Product of housebuilders, 256–260, 323–325, 362. *See also* House
Production: growth in, 10–12; process, 49–56, 65, 83–86, 113–120, 275–279; schedules, 83–84, 90–92, 116–117, 124–130, 149–150, 278; simplification of, 84, 114, 295–297
Profits, 36–38, 73, 76, 104–106, 193, 210–213, 264–269, 294, 322, 360–361, 382–383; in composite house, 375; in subcontracts, 206; umbrella, 268; windfall, 265
Progress, 279–286; and profits, 211; factors in, 299; in mechanization, 119–120; paths to, 289–291
Purchases, 56–61, 87–90, 120–123, 227–231; bulk, 197–204; wholesale, 87. *See also* Discounts; Materials; Subcontracts

Ratcliff, R. U., 8 n.
Restrictive practices: and progress, 282–283; costs of, 244–246, 247–249, 254–255; external, 223–255; in codes, 224; in government, 224, 246–250; in labor, 224, 234–246; in materials, 135, 224–225, 227–231; in subcontracts, 231–234; in use of equipment, 238–239
Risks, 93, 105–106, 131, 212, 218. *See also* Capital
Robinson, E. A. G., 170 n., 176 n.

Sales, 37, 45–46, 82, 110, 261–262. *See also* Markets; Marketing
Sampling variability, 311–312
San Francisco–Oakland metropolitan area, 14–16
Scale, 174–176; and direct costs, 193–207; and efficiency, 189–222; and indirect costs, 208–213; and labor, 113; and materials, 87–88, 121, 196; and purchasing, 120–123; and subcontracts, 119–123, 204–207; further increases in, 213–219. *See also* Mechanization; Size; Specialization
Schedules, 83–84, 90–92, 116–117, 126–130, 278; of trade-contractors, 149–150
Self-employment, 37, 236–237
Size, 20–26, 343; and design, 258; determinants of, 34, 63–65, 73, 75–76, 92–93, 130–131, 213–219, 352; growth of, 22–26; optimum, 175, 219; war's effect on, 13. *See also* Scale

Specialization, 55, 84, 102, 113–115, 122, 195, 276–277
Standards of work, 85, 124, 127
Steindl, J., 170 n.
Strikes, 157, 239–240, 381
Structure of ownership, 34, 38, 70–72, 99, 355
Subcontracting, 58–61, 89–90, 142, 206; and scale, 119–123, 204–207; bids, 59–60, 233; control of, 60, 90, 123, 149–150, 297; estimates, 59–60, 149–150; list of, 51; mechanization in, 118–119, 150; overhead in, 147–148, 368; relationships, 59–60, 90, 121; restrictive practices in, 231–234. *See also* Trade contractors
Supply: of labor, *see* Labor; of materials, *see* Materials
Surveys, methods of, 304–312

Templates, 86
Tracts, 68, 97, 147, 348. *See also* Land
Trade contractors, 141–151; by area of work, 371; by volume, 144, 367; employees of, 144, 368; housing volume, 369–370; number of, 367; overhead of, 147–148, 368; size of, 143, 146–147, 367; survey of, 325–327. *See also* Subcontracting
Turnover: of capital, 40, 75–76, 105, 359; of labor, 155

Unions, 156–157. *See also* Labor

Veterans Administration, 77, 107, 159, 251–253, 268. *See also* Financing

Walker, F. R., 61 n.
Wholesale, purchases at, 57, 87, 120, 138–139, 199–204, 228–231

Yates, F., 311 n.

www.ingramcontent.com/pod-product-compliance
Ingram Content Group UK Ltd.
Pitfield, Milton Keynes, MK11 3LW, UK
UKHW040234290926
15471UKWH00002B/182

9 780520 349384

Schellmann, Baumann, Gläser, Kegel

Handbuch Medien

Medien
verstehen – gestalten – produzieren

6., erweiterte und verbesserte Auflage

VERLAG EUROPA-LEHRMITTEL • Nourney, Vollmer GmbH & Co. KG
Düsselberger Straße 23 • 42781 Haan-Gruiten

Europa-Nr.: 35210

Die Autoren

Schellmann, Bernhard, Kißlegg i. A.
Baumann, Andreas, Wangen i. A.
Gläser, Martin, Prof. Dr., Dettingen/Erms
Kegel, Thomas, Konstanz

Lektorat und Leitung des Arbeitskreises:
Bernhard Schellmann

Informationen und Anfragen: www.medien-verstehen.de

Titelblatt: Thomas Kegel
Buchlayout: Andreas Baumann, mit freundlicher Unterstützung von Rainer Leippold, Stuttgart; Daniela Schreuer

Bildentwürfe und Fotos: Autoren
Weitere Fotos und Grafiken: Leihgaben der Firmen (s. Verzeichnis am Ende des Buches)

6. Auflage 2013
Druck 5 4 3 2 1
Alle Drucke derselben Auflage sind parallel einsetzbar, da bis auf die Behebung von Druckfehlern untereinander unverändert.

ISBN 978-3-8085-3526-4

http://www.europa-lehrmittel.de
Umschlaggestaltung: Thomas Kegel, 78464 Konstanz; Media-Creativ, 40723 Hilden
Satz: Daniela Schreuer, 65549 Limburg
Druck: M. P. Media-Print Informationstechnologie GmbH, 33100 Paderborn

Eine große Zahl interessierter Menschen setzt sich mit den Medien in Schule, Studium, innerhalb einer Umschulungsmaßnahme oder autodidaktisch im Beruf und in der Freizeit auseinander. Um die medialen Bausteine auswählen und einsetzen, um mit ihnen produzieren zu können, wird ein breit gefächertes Wissen vorausgesetzt. Das Buch bietet umfangreiche und fundierte Einblicke in die spannende Medienwelt. Einsteiger wie Fortgeschrittene finden die vielen Sachverhalte schlüssig und praxisnah beschrieben. In der 6. Auflage wurden die Inhalte im Teil A neu gegliedert, durch eine eingehende Betrachtung des Journalismus ergänzt und damit den „Rundumblick“ auf 360° geschlossen. Nun kann unser Medienbuch mit Recht den Titel „Handbuch Medien“ tragen.

Wie gewohnt werden die kompakten Texte durch zahlreiche aktuelle Abbildungen anwendungsbezogen ergänzt, so dass sich die Inhalte auch nachhaltig einprägen. Die 6. Auflage wurde mit neuen Zahlen und Fakten auf den neuesten Stand gebracht, der uns aktuell vorliegt. Besonderer Dank gilt den Agenturen und Firmen, die uns mit Bildmaterial und Produktionsbeispielen unterstützt haben. Die inhaltliche Aufbereitung entspricht dem zum Zeitpunkt der Manuskripterstellung aktuellen Stand der technischen Entwicklung und der wissenschaftlichen Erkenntnisse. Ständig wechselnde Daten und Fakten finden Sie auf unserer Website www.medien-verstehen.de. Zu den entsprechenden Kapiteln gelangen Sie dort über eine benutzerfreundliche Navigation oder über den entsprechenden QR-Code am Anfang des Kapitels.

Viele Anwendungsbeispiele bedürfen der visuellen Unterstützung durch Hard- und Softwareprodukte, die wir aus einer breiten Palette von Angeboten beispielhaft herausgesucht haben. Die erwähnten Soft- und Hardwareprodukte sind in den meisten Fällen eingetragene Warenzeichen und unterliegen als solche den gesetzlichen Bestimmungen.

Die in sich abgeschlossenen Kapitel enden jeweils mit einer Aufgabensammlung, die als Anregung dienen soll, die behandelten Inhalte im Versuch und in der Produktion anzuwenden. Dadurch wird die Auseinandersetzung mit dem Thema intensiviert und neue Erkenntnisse und interessante Erfahrungen gewonnen. Für das praktische Arbeiten in den einzelnen Themengebieten bietet sich häufig eine einschlägige Vertiefung an. Aus dem großen Angebot an Literatur haben wir die, nach unserer Ansicht, wichtigen Werke in einem Literaturverzeichnis zusammengefasst, das jedem Kapitel anhängt.

Das Lehrbuch eignet sich für alle medienorientierten Schularten und Ausbildungsberufe. Ein zweiter Schwerpunkt des Grundlagenwerks liegt im Bereich medienbezogener Fachschulen, Akademien und Hochschulen mit dem Schwerpunkten auf den Medien und für das Selbststudium.

Die Verwendung der maskulinen Form bei der Beschreibung von Berufsbildern und Personen geschieht aus rein praktischen Erwägungen.

Unser Dank gilt unseren Familien und allen die mit hilfreichen Gedanken und Beiträgen dieses Buch in die nun 6. Auflage mit begleitet haben. Über Anregungen, Hinweise und neue Ideen zu den Inhalten freuen wir uns. Sie erreichen uns über die Internetseite www.medien-verstehen.de.

Kißlegg, 2013 Die Autoren

A

1 Theoretische Grundlagen 12
2 Medien im Kommunikationsprozess 60
3 Medien in der Praxis 120

Grundlagen

Zu Beginn des vorliegenden Lehrbuchs soll Klarheit darüber hergestellt werden, was Medien eigentlich sind, welches ihre Leistungen sind, die sie erbringen, und welche Rolle sie im Leben der Menschen spielen. Es geht um ein vertieftes Verständnis der Rolle und Bedeutung von Medien für die Gesellschaft, die Wirtschaft und die Politik.

In diesem Zusammenhang ist viel von Kommunikation die Rede. Der Grund ist, dass die zentrale Aufgabe der Medien darin besteht, als ein wichtiges Bindeglied in der Kommunikation der Menschen zu fungieren. Der Großteil der Kommunikation innerhalb unserer Gesellschaft findet nicht direkt zwischen den Menschen statt, sondern als sog. mediale Kommunikation.

In Kapitel 1 wird dargestellt, was man sich unter dem Begriff der Medien alles vorstellen kann und wie man die Medien in der Theorie erklären kann. Medien kann man nur verstehen, wenn man sich klar macht, welche Funktion sie im Hinblick auf die Kommunikation der Menschen ausüben. Hierzu braucht man Theorien.

Kapitel 2 beleuchtet in vertiefter Form die Rolle der Medien im Kommunikationsprozess. Dies geschieht methodisch anhand der berühmten Lasswell-Formel: „Wer sagt was über welchen Kanal zu wem mit welcher Wirkung?".

Das abschließende Kapitel 3 beschreibt alle wichtigen Medienmärkte, wie man sie in der Praxis vorfindet. Der Bogen spannt sich von Zeitungen über das Fernsehen bis zum Internet. Jeder einzelne Bereich wird mit seinen Besonderheiten aufgezeigt. Vorangestellt ist in kompakter Form die hoch interessante Geschichte der Medien.

1 Theoretische Grundlagen

Webcode: A0100

Für weitere Infos zu diesem Kapitel mit dem Smartphone einfach QR-Code scannen oder auf www.medien-verstehen.de den Webcode eingeben.

80 Prozent der Deutschen lesen mehrmals in der Woche Zeitung, 50 Prozent lesen Zeitschriften, ein Fünftel der Bevölkerung liest mehrmals in der Woche Bücher. Der Durchschnittsbürger hört dreieinhalb Stunden täglich Radio, ebenso lang sieht er fern, fast eine Stunde täglich nutzt er das Internet. Die Medien haben daher für den Einzelnen und für die Gesellschaft größte Bedeutung und es ist es wichtig zu verstehen, was Medien sind, welche Wirkung sie ausüben und welche Rolle sie spielen, das heißt, man muss sie zunächst einmal theoretisch beleuchten.

1.1 Medien als Phänomen

1.1.1 Definition von Medien

Der Begriff **Medien** ist uns alltäglich und selbstverständlich. Wir verwenden ihn, ohne viel nachzudenken. Da sie überall präsent sind, ist uns das Phänomen der Medien längst in Fleisch und Blut übergegangen. Völlig zu Recht bezeichnet man unsere Epoche daher auch als das „Medien- und Informationszeitalter". Doch Vorsicht! Bei genauerem Hinsehen zeigt es sich schnell, dass der Medienbegriff gar nicht so einfach zu fassen ist. Es gibt ziemliche Unschärfen im Gebrauch. Alles Mögliche bekommt das populäre Etikett Medien angeheftet, ohne dass dies immer zweckmäßig ist. Deshalb muss man sich ausführlich mit dem Begriff des Mediums bzw. der Medien befassen.

Ursprung des Wortes Medien

Das Wort „Medien" stammt vom lateinischen Adjektiv „medium" ab, was so viel bedeutet wie „in der Mitte befindlich", „mittlerer" ❶. Die Verwendung des Begriffs steht in Verbindung mit „der Idee der Vermittlung, der Idee des Zentrierens, der Idee eines Trägersystems geistigen Ausdrucks, das sich von örtlicher und zeitlicher Gebundenheit löst" ❷.

❶ **medius, media, medium (lat.)** = in der Mitte befindlich, mittlerer

❷ Quelle: Wiegerling , Klaus: Medienethik, Stuttgart 1998, S. 7. In unserer Sprache haben sich verschiedene verwandte Begriffe zum Medienbegriff eingebürgert, die auch den Sachverhalt der Vermittlung kennzeichnen: **Mediation** = Vermittlung in einem Streit, z. B. zwischen Staaten, Unternehmen oder Einzelpersonen (Scheidung); **Medium** = Mittel, Mittelsperson (bei spiritistischen Sitzungen) zwischen dem Fragenden und der Geisterwelt, auch Experimentierperson bei Varietévorführungen, Hypnosen und dergleichen.

Definitionen im Alltagsgebrauch

Der Medienbegriff wird im Alltagsgebrauch vorrangig als Sammelbegriff für die technischen Mittel oder Instrumente verwendet, die der Verbreitung von Aussagen dienen. Dies zeigen **Lexikon-Definitionen**:

- Meyers Enzyklopädisches Lexikon 1975: „Medium (Plural: Media) [lat.: das in der Mitte Befindliche], allgemein: Mittel, vermittelndes Element; insbes. [in der Mehrzahl]: Mittel zur Weitergabe oder Verbreitung von Information durch Sprache, Gestik, Mimik, Schrift und Bild (...)".
- Bertelsmann Universal Lexikon 1993: „**Massenmedien, Massenkommunikationsmittel**, alle Einrichtungen, die bei der Massenkommunikation zur Vermittlung oder Übertragung von Aussagen dienen; sie sind technische Instrumente oder Apparaturen, mit denen Aussagen öffentlich, direkt, und einseitig (d. h. ohne Dialog zwischen Publikum und Medium) an ein disperses ❸ **Publikum** verbreitet werden. Zu den Massenmedien werden Presse, Rundfunk, Film und Fernsehen gerechnet, neuerdings auch Schallplatte, Buch und Video."

❸ **dispers** = verstreut

Vertiefende Definitionen der Wissenschaft

Auch die Wissenschaft stellt die **Vermittlungsfunktion** der Medien bei ihren Analysen in den Vordergrund, wie man aus verschiedenen Definitionen ersehen kann:

- Die Medien sind die „technische und organisatorische Infrastruktur für die **Kommunikation**." ❶
- Ein Medium umfasst „alle jene technischen Instrumente und Apparaturen, mit deren Hilfe publizistische Aussagen an die Öffentlichkeit weitergeleitet werden." ❷
- „Medien sind Vermittlungsinstanzen. Zur Vermittlung benötigen sie nicht nur eine Öffentlichkeit, eine Präsentationsstätte für das Mitzuteilende und eine Transportkapazität, sondern auch einen Inhalt. Was Medien transportieren, sind Bedeutungen, die auf einen Gegenstand oder einen Sachverhalt verweisen." ❸
- „Unter Medien werden in unserem Zusammenhang materiell-mechanische oder energetische (elektrische, elektromagnetische, elektronische, opto-elektronische) Träger und Übermittler von Daten bzw. Informationseinheiten und mechanische sowie elektronische Mittel der Datenverarbeitung verstanden, dies im Sinne der drei medienlogischen Grundphänomene der Speicherung, Übertragung und Bearbeitung." ❹

❶ Quelle: Hunziker, Peter: Medien, Kommunikation und Gesellschaft, Darmstadt 1988, S. 15

❷ Quelle: Pürer, Heinz: Einführung in die Publizistikwissenschaft, 4., überarbeitete Auflage, München 1990, S. 42

❸ Quelle: Wiegerling , Klaus: Medienethik, Stuttgart 1998, S. 17

❹ Quelle: Hiebel, Hans H. / Hiebler, Heinz / Kogler, Karl / Walitsch, Herwig: Die Medien, München 1998, S. 12

Allerdings weisen viele Ansätze über die enge Vorstellung, Medien seien lediglich so etwas wie „Transport-Unternehmen für Botschaften zwischen den Menschen", hinaus. Die Wissenschaft sieht die Medien auch noch in einem größeren Zusammenhang, und hier vor allem als wichtige **Einrichtungen der Gesellschaft**:

- Medien sind nicht nur **Kommunikationskanäle**, die geeignet sind, Zeichensysteme zu transportieren. Sie sind auch Organisationen, also „zweckerfüllende Sozialsysteme", und zwar komplexe Systeme. Diese Systeme haben eine große Wirkung „in alle erdenkliche Schichten des gesellschaftlichen Seins" hinein. Und es sind institutionalisierte Einrichtungen, die innerhalb des „gesellschaftlichen Regelungssystems" eine Rolle spielen. ❺
- „Damit ein Kommunikationsvorgang zustande kommt, bedarf es eines Mediums, d. h. einer Veranschaulichung der zu übertragenden sprachlichen Zeichen. Die Gestalt der Medien hängt von der Art der verwendeten Zeichensysteme sowie von der Art des sozialen Kontakts zwischen den Kommunikationspartnern ab." ❻
- Medien sind u. a. „technologische Artefakte" (z. B. Kabel, Satelliten), von der Gesellschaft abhängige publizistische Arbeitsorganisationen (Redaktionen, Nachrichtenagenturen, Rundfunkorganisationen, Pressedienste, Vertriebssysteme) und auch gleichzusetzen mit „Berichterstattung", das sind die verbreiteten Ergebnisse der Auswahlentscheidungen der Redaktionen. ❼

❺ Quelle: singgemäß nach Saxer, Ulrich: Konstituenten einer Medienwissenschaft, in: Schanze, H. und Ludes, P. (Hg.): Qualitative Perspektiven des Medienwandels, Opladen 1997, S. 21

❻ Quelle: Hunziker, Peter: Medien, Kommunikation und Gesellschaft, Darmstadt 1988, S. 15

❼ Quelle: singgemäß nach Rühl, Manfred: Kommunikation und Öffentlichkeitsarbeit, in: Bentele, G. und Rühl, M.: Theorien öffentlicher Kommunikation, München 1993, S. 79

1.1.2 Klassifikationen

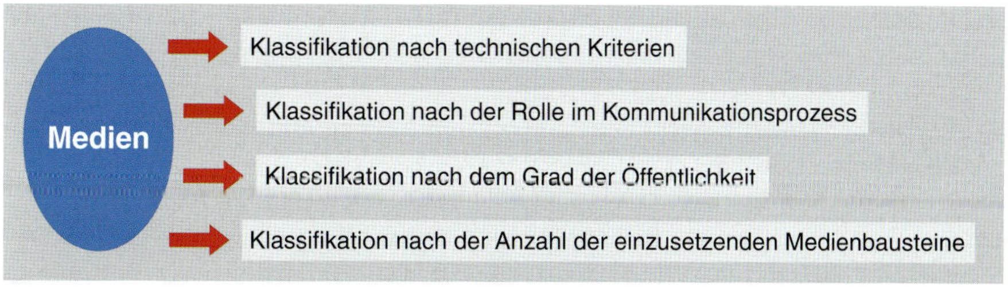

Klassifikation nach technischen Kriterien

❶ Quelle: Maletzke, Gerhard: Kommunikationswissenschaft im Überblick, Opladen, Wiesbaden 1998, S. 53

❷ „Es gibt keine unvermittelte Kommunikation; alle Kommunikation bedarf des Mittels oder Mediums, durch das hindurch eine Nachricht übertragen bzw. aufgenommen wird." Quelle: Graumann, Carl Friedrich: Handbuch der Psychologie, Bd. 7, Göttingen 1972, S. 1182

Medien kann man aus ganz unterschiedlichen Blickwinkeln betrachten. Man kann sie z. B. danach unterscheiden, inwieweit die Sender und Empfänger von Botschaften bei ihrer Kommunikation **technische Hilfsmittel** einsetzen. Grundsätzlich gibt es hierbei **drei Möglichkeiten** ❶:

- Fall 1: Weder Sender noch Empfänger setzen technische Hilfsmittel ein. Beide beschränken sich auf die dem Menschen von Natur aus gegebenen Möglichkeiten der Kommunikation, nämlich auf die menschliche Stimme, die Gestik und die Mimik. Die Transportmittel der Kommunikation sind also die natürlichsten Medien, die es gibt, nämlich die Medien des „menschlichen Elementarkontakts", die „Mensch-Medien" ❷. Man nennt sie **primäre Medien**.
- Fall 2: Nur der Sender setzt technische Hilfsmittel ein, der Empfänger kann darauf verzichten. Zu denken ist an Printprodukte wie Zeitungen, Zeitschriften oder Bücher, die einen hohen technischen Aufwand zur Herstellung erfordern, vom Leser aber ohne Technikeinsatz genutzt werden können. Diese Medien nennt man **sekundäre Medien**.

Primäre Medien

- Körperbewegungen, v.a. Gesichtsausdruck, Handbewegungen, Haltung
- Lachen und Weinen
- Geräusche (so weit sie noch nicht codiert sind) wie Zischen, Blasgeräusche, Pfeifen, Stöhnen, Seufzen, Glucksen, Kichern, Zungenschnalzen
- Demonstrative Kopf- oder Handbewegungen
- Gerüche wie z.B. Deodorants
- Gesprochene Sprache
- zu beachten: Lautstärke, Tonfall

Sekundäre Medien

- Frühe sekundäre Medien: Megafon (Hebung der Lautstärke der menschlichen Stimme), Glocken-, Trommel-, Feuer- und Rauchzeichen, optische Telegrafie, Signalmasten, Flaggen
- Sekundäre Medien auf der Grundlage von Bildern, Schrift und Buchstaben: Handschriften, Briefe, Druckerzeugnisse: Buch, Presseorgane wie Zeitungen und Zeitschriften, Werbebroschüren, Plakate, Fotografien

Tertiäre Medien

- Frühe tertiäre Medien: Kabelübertragungen, Telegrafie, Fernübertragung über Telegrafenmasten, Morsezeichen, codierte optische Telegrafie, Telefon
- Jüngere tertiäre Medien: Radio, Fernsehen, Schallplatte, Tonband, Cassetten für Video, Film und Ton, Compact Disk
- Zu beachten: Fernsehen ist das Leitmedium!

- Fall 3: Sowohl Sender als auch Empfänger bedienen sich bei der Kommunikation technischer Hilfsmittel, und auch die Übertragung der Botschaften erfordert technische Unterstützung. Typische Beispiele für diese Medienform sind die elektronischen Massenmedien Radio und Fernsehen sowie das Internet. Medien dieser Kategorie nennt man **tertiäre Medien**.

Diese Dreiteilung geht von der Unterstellung aus, dass jede Kommunikation ein medialer Vorgang ist. Jeder Austausch von Botschaften zwischen einem Sender und einem Empfänger benötigt danach ein Medium, egal ob es sich um die direkte Kommunikation von Mensch zu Mensch handelt oder um indirekte Kommunikation im Wege des Einsatzes von Technik.

Klassifikation nach der Rolle im Kommunikationsprozess

Wenn Menschen miteinander in Kommunikation treten, werden Botschaften ausgetauscht, die in irgendeiner Form transportiert werden müssen. Dies geschieht zum einen mit Hilfe elektromagnetischer Wellen, zum anderen durch den Einsatz von langlebigen Trägermaterialien. Demnach können Medien auch unterschieden werden in ❶:

- Übertragungs- oder Transportmedien
- Speicher- oder Fixiermedien

Unter den **Übertragungs- oder Transportmedien** ist das natürlichste die menschliche Sprache. Erfolgt ein Technikeinsatz, so sind vor allem das Telefon, Radio und Fernsehen und das Internet zu nennen. Zahlreiche weitere Übertragungsmedien sind denkbar, insbesondere solche, bei der die zu transportierende Botschaft in die Form eines Symbols gekleidet ist, z. B. die Beflaggung von staatlichen Gebäuden an wichtigen weltlichen Feiertagen oder zu besonderen Anlässen (Staatsbesuch, Katastrophe). Zu denken ist auch an Hornsignale wie das Blaulicht von Polizei und Feuerwehr oder das Läuten von Kirchenglocken an Sonn- und Feiertagen. Zahlreiche solcher „Symbol- oder Signalmedien" sind heute nicht mehr in Gebrauch, hatten aber in der Vergangenheit zum Teil höchste Bedeutung erlangt. Ein prominentes Beispiel ist die Errichtung eines Systems der optischen Telegrafie im Frankreich des 18. Jahrhunderts ❷.

Eine immer größere Rolle im Leben der Menschen spielt der zweite hier genannte Medien-Typ, nämlich die **Speicher- bzw. Fixiermedien**. Bei ihnen handelt es sich im einzelnen um:

- Handschriften
- Druckwerke
- Bilder
- Fotos
- Ton-, Film-, Videobänder oder -cassetten
- Audio-, Video- oder Multimedia-CDs, DVDs
- Online-Systeme
- Datenbanken

❶ Quelle: Winterhoff-Spurk, Peter: Medienpsychologie, Stuttgart, Berlin, Köln 1999, S. 13ff.

❷ Die **optische Telegraphie von Chappe**: „Betrachtet man nur einmal das von Claude Chappe entwickelte System der optischen Telegraphie, bei dem mit Hilfe fester Relais-Stationen auf Kirchtürmen oder Bergkuppen ein begrenztes aber wohldefiniertes System von 77 Zeichen (...) über längere Distanzen übertragen wurde. Das 1793 vom Nationalkonvent der Französischen Republik für die Strecke Paris–Lille erstmals genehmigte System wurde anfangs ausschließlich für militärische und politische Zwecke benutzt; es beruhte auf einem Code-Buch, in welchem häufig wiederkehrende Botschaften in bestimmte Stellungen der beiden Signalarme des Systems übersetzt wurden. Den Bedienungsmannschaften des optischen Telegraphen wurden vom Leiter der Telegraphenstationen lediglich die Abfolgen der Einstellungen mitgeteilt, die diese ohne Kenntnis des zu übermittelnden Inhalts in einer bestimmten zeitlichen Reihenfolge einstellten. Hatte die nächste Relaisstation die Einstellung übernommen und dadurch quittiert, wurde die nächste Kombination hergestellt. Eine mit diesem System übermittelte Nachricht war von Straßburg nach Paris nur 37 Minuten unterwegs." Quelle: Winterhoff-Spurk, Peter: Medienpsychologie, Stuttgart, Berlin, Köln 1999, S. 13

Klassifikation nach dem Grad der Öffentlichkeit

Eine weitere Einteilung der Medien bezieht sich auf die Anzahl der Personen, die von einer Botschaft angesprochen werden sollen. Es geht also um die Frage, ob eine Person, mehrere, viele oder sehr viele Personen vom Kommunikationsvorgang betroffen sind. **Vier Grundformen der Kommunikation**, auf die sich Medien beziehen können, lassen sich unterscheiden ❶:

- Interpersonale Kommunikation
- Kleingruppenkommunikation
- Organisationskommunikation
- Massenkommunikation

Medien in der **interpersonalen Kommunikation** beziehen sich auf die Kommunikation von Mensch zu Mensch ❷, vor allem in der direkten privaten oder geschäftlichen Begegnung. Hier steht das für den Menschen typische und zugleich am weitesten entwickelte Kommunikationsmittel, nämlich die Sprache, im Mittelpunkt. Aber auch die technisch vermittelte Individualkommunikation über Telefon oder Online ist hier zu nennen.

In der **Kleingruppenkommunikation** sind Medien dazu da, den Austausch (die „Interaktion") zwischen Personen in kleinen Gruppen zu befördern, normalerweise mit dem Ziel, die Entscheidungsfindung zu unterstützen. Angesprochen sind Themen wie das Arbeiten im Team im Bereich des Projektmanagements oder der Einsatz von Software für Gruppenarbeit ❸.

Im größeren Zusammenhang steht der Einsatz von **Medien in der Organisationskommunikation**. Hier geht es um die Unterstützung großer kooperativer Netzwerke innerhalb von Unternehmen, Behörden oder anderen Organisationen. Alle Aspekte der interpersonalen und Gruppenkommunikation sind betroffen. Die Medien greifen stark in die Organisationsstruktur ein.

Schließlich spielen die Medien in der **Massenkommunikation** eine Rolle. Im Gegensatz zur Individual-, Gruppen- und Organisationskommunikation ist die Massenkommunikation auf ein großes Publikum ausgerichtet, das sich nicht an einem Ort versammelt, sondern weit verstreut ist („disperses Publikum"). Bei der Massenkommunikation geht es um öffentliche Kommunikation. Die Massenmedien zielen darauf ab, Öffentlichkeit herzustellen. Es handelt sich ferner um eine einseitige Kommunikation, bei der so gut wie keine Interaktion stattfindet ❹.

Den **Massenmedien** kommt bei der Behandlung der Medienthematik eine herausragende Bedeutung zu. Das Leben jedes einzelnen und die ganze Gesellschaft ist stark von den Massenmedien geprägt. Massenmedien machen einen hohen technischen Einsatz zumindest auf der Produktionsseite erforderlich, so dass es verständlich ist, dass die Grundlage für das Entstehen von Massenmedien – beispielsweise Tageszeitung oder Hörfunk – die technischen Entwicklungen am Ende des 19. und zu Beginn des 20. Jahrhunderts waren ❺.

❶ Quelle: Littlejohn, S.W.: Theories of Human Communication, zit. nach Maletzke, Gerhard: Kommunikationswissenschaft im Überblick, Opladen, Wiesbaden 1998, S. 41

❷ Direkte Kommunikation von Mensch zu Mensch = **Face-to-Face-Kommunikation**

❸ Software dieser Art wird **Groupware** genannt.

❹ „Unter Massenkommunikation verstehen wir jene Form der Kommunikation, bei der Aussagen
- öffentlich (also ohne begrenzte und personell definierte Empfängerschaft
- durch technische Hilfsmittel (Medien)
- indirekt (also bei räumlicher oder zeitlicher oder raumzeitlicher Distanz zwischen den Kommunikationspartnern)
- und einseitig (also ohne Rollenwechsel zwischen Aussagendem und Aufnehmendem)

an ein disperses Publikum vermittelt werden."
Quelle: Maletzke, Gerhard: Kommunikationswissenschaft im Überblick, Opladen, Wiesbaden 1998, S. 46

❺ Quelle: Funkkolleg Medien und Kommunikation, Weinheim und Basel 1990, Studienbrief 3, S. 14

Klassifikation nach dem Kriterium der Anzahl der eingesetzten Medienbausteine

Im Hinblick auf den Umfang der eingesetzten Medienbausteine können **drei Typen von Medien** unterschieden werden: Monomedien, duale Medien und Multimedia.

Monomedien betreffen jeweils nur ein einziges Medium wie z. B. Bild, Ton oder Text. Zu denken ist an eine Audio-CD oder ein nur aus Text bestehendes Buch. Angesprochen wird also der Nutzer des Mediums auf einen einzigen Sinn hin, z. B. auf das Gehör oder das Auge. **Duale Medien** stellen eine Verbindung zwischen zwei Feldern von Medien her und führen damit zu einer neuen Qualität der Mediennutzung. Vorwiegend treten duale Medien als audiovisuelle Medien in Erscheinung. **Multimedia** ist schließlich die Verknüpfung mehrerer Medienelemente auf einer gemeinsamen **digitalen Plattform**. Ziel ist es, den Nutzer über mehrere Sinne gleichzeitig anzusprechen. Dies erfolgt in Kombination statischer und dynamischer Medienbausteine ❶. Bei Multimedia werden in der Regel drei Merkmale miteinander verbunden ❷:

❶ **Statische Medien** sind: Texte, Daten. **Dynamische Medien** sind: Töne, Animationen, Bewegtbilder

❷ Quelle: Bruhn, Manfred: Kommunikationspolitik, München 1997, S. 824f.

- Multimodalität: Mehrere Sinne werden gleichzeitig angesprochen.
- Integration: Die Bausteine werden auf einer digitalen Basis zusammen geführt, was die Möglichkeit bietet, inhaltlich und zeitlich beliebige Kombinationen zu erzeugen.
- **Interaktivität**: Die Benutzerführung erfolgt dialogorientiert über Eingabemechanismen wie z. B. Tastatur oder Touchscreen. Informationen können nach individuellen Bedürfnissen abgerufen und bearbeitet werden.

Ausgangspunkt für das Entstehen von Multimedia ist das Zusammenwachsen der **„TIME"-Branchen**, d. h. der Telekommunikation (T), der Informationstechnologie (I), der Medien (M) und der Unterhaltungselektronik (E für Elektronik).

1.1.3 Medien: Ein vertieftes Verständnis

Medien als Teil des Kommunikationsprozesses

Medien sind Bestandteil der Kommunikation. Sie sind ein wichtiger Teil der Kommunikation innerhalb der Gesellschaft und zwischen den Menschen. Medien werden eingesetzt, um das Gelingen der Kommunikation sicher zu stellen, sei es im Bereich der Individual- oder der Massenkommunikation. Medien sind also immer untrennbar mit der Frage der **Kommunikation** verbunden.

Die zentrale Bedeutung der Medien liegt also darin, dass sie eine Leistung erbringen, die zum Gelingen von Kommunikation beiträgt. Diese Leistung besteht in der Vermittlung. Es ist wichtig, das Phänomen der Kommunikation nachfolgend näher zu beleuchten.

Kommunikation – Begriff und Bedeutung

Ein Wissenschaftler hat über 160 Definitionen für Kommunikation ausfindig gemacht. Gleichwohl besteht eine gewisse Einigkeit darüber, was unter dem Begriff „Kommunikation" zu verstehen ist ❶: „Kommunikation steht für die Tatsache, dass Lebewesen untereinander in Beziehung stehen, dass sie sich verständigen können, dass sie im stande sind, innere Vorgänge oder Zustände auszudrücken, ihren Mitgeschöpfen Sachverhalte mitzuteilen oder auch andere zu einem bestimmten Verhalten aufzufordern."

❶ Maletzke, Gerhard: Kommunikationswissenschaft im Überblick, Opladen, Wiesbaden 1998, S. 37

Mit Burkart ❷ lassen sich **sechs Merkmale** anführen, die das Wesen von Kommunikation ausmachen:

❷ Quelle: Burkart, Roland: Kommunikationswissenschaft, 4. Aufl., Wien, Köln, Weimar 2002, S. 20ff.

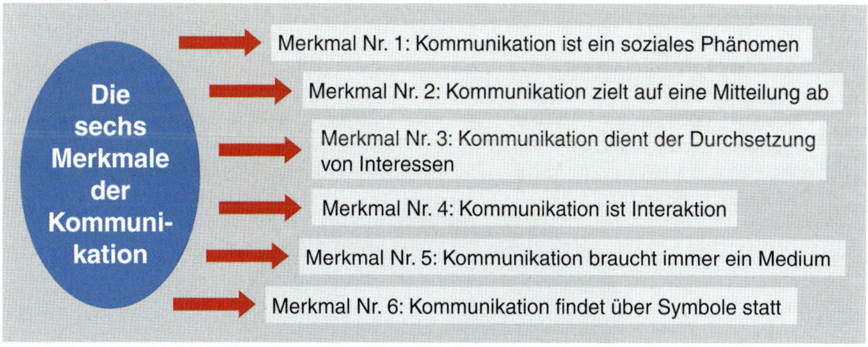

Merkmal Nr. 1: Kommunikation ist ein soziales Phänomen
Kommunikation ist ein Ausdruck sozialen Verhaltens und hat daher immer mit Lebewesen zu tun ❸. Sozial sind Verhaltensweisen von Lebewesen dann, wenn sie aufeinander bezogen sind, aufeinander ausgerichtet, mit der Zielrichtung der gegenseitigen Beeinflussung. Unter diesem Blickwinkel ist es daher nicht zweckmäßig, z. B. von „Mensch-Maschine-Kommunikation" zu sprechen. Maschinen sind keine sozialen Wesen und kommunizieren infolgedessen nicht.

❸ **Kommunikation** kommt vom lat. Adjektiv „communis"= gemeinsam. Kommunikation sorgt für Gemeinsamkeit. Kommunikation ist Bedeutungsvermittlung zwischen Lebewesen.

Merkmal Nr. 2: Kommunikation zielt auf eine Mitteilung ab

Menschliche Kommunikation ist auf eine Handlung ausgerichtet, sie ist „intentional". ❶ Kommunikation ist also kein Selbstzweck, sondern stets Mittel zum Zweck: Wenn ein Mensch kommuniziert, verfolgt er immer ganz bestimmte Ziele. Auch wenn er es wollte, kann er sich diesem intentionalen Charakter der Kommunikation nicht entziehen.

Hauptstoßrichtung der Kommunikation ist die Mitteilung. ❷ Derjenige, der kommuniziert, will einem anderen etwas mitteilen, genauer: er will bestimmte Bedeutungen „mit ihm teilen". Hinter dem Anliegen, dem anderen eine Mitteilung zu machen, steht das Ziel der Verständigung. Er will Verständigung zwischen sich und seinem Kommunikationspartner herstellen. Sich mit dem anderen zu verständigen, gelingt dann, wenn die Kommunikationspartner die vermittelten Bedeutungen auch tatsächlich miteinander teilen. ❸

❶ Manfred: „Monika, schließe bitte das Fenster"

❷ Manfred verfolgt mit seiner Äußerung das Ziel, dass Monika versteht, was er meint. Er sucht die Verständigung mit ihr.

❸ Quelle Grafik: Burkart, Roland: Kommunikationswissenschaft, 4. Aufl., Wien, Köln, Weimar 2002, S. 20ff.

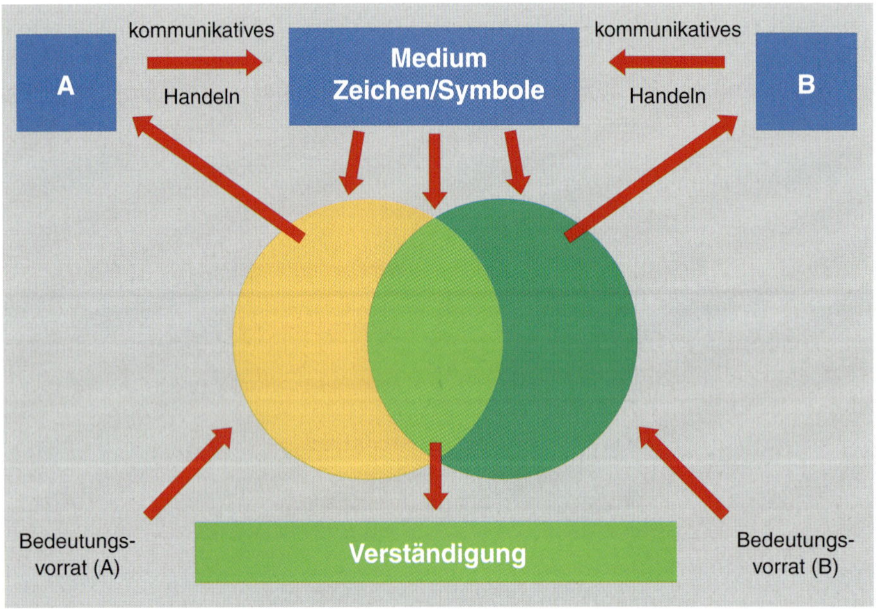

Merkmal Nr. 3: Kommunikation dient der Durchsetzung von Interessen

Weiterer Zweck der Kommunikation ist die Durchsetzung von Interessen. Neben der Mitteilung mit dem Ziel der Verständigung verfolgen die Kommunikationspartner also immer auch spezielle Interessen. ❹

Insofern hat Kommunikation im Sinne einer sozialen Handlung immer zwei Aspekte:

- Mitteilung mit dem Ziel der Verständigung
- Interesse mit dem Ziel der Interessensdurchsetzung

❹ Manfred will erreichen, dass Monika das Fenster schließt und die störende Zugluft ausbleibt. Das Ergebnis der Kommunikation soll sein, dass Manfred sein Interesse durchgesetzt hat.

❶ Manfred will, dass Monika ihn versteht und auf seine Äußerung reagiert.

Merkmal Nr. 4: Kommunikation ist Interaktion

Damit man von Kommunikation sprechen kann, bedarf es der sog. **Interaktion**, d. h. Kommunikation liegt nur dann vor, wenn die Kommunikationspartner in eine wechselseitige Beziehung zueinander treten und sich austauschen. Nur so gelingt es ihnen, zu einer Verständigung (Merkmal Nr. 2) zu gelangen. Kommunikation ist also ein doppelseitiges Geschehen. ❶

Merkmal Nr. 5: Kommunikation braucht immer ein Medium

Jede Kommunikation benötigt ein Medium, also eine Instanz, über die der Austausch der Botschaften zwischen den Kommunikationspartnern abläuft und die für die Vermittlung zwischen den Kommunikationspartnern sorgt. Dies gilt auch für die direkte persönliche Kommunikation.

❷ Manfred setzt das Medium Sprache ein, um die Kommunikation mit Monika zu gewährleisten. Die gemeinten Bedeutungsinhalte sind mit der Lautabfolge z. B. „F-e-n-s-t-e-r" greifbar und wahrnehmbar.

Es geht also bei der Kommunikation darum, dass wir mit Hilfe von Medien Botschaften übermitteln, also mit Hilfe von Mimik, Gestik, Sprache, Schrift, Bild oder Ton, von Angesicht zu Angesicht oder über papierene oder elektronische Übertragungs- und Speichertechniken. Medien sind die Transportmittel für die Botschaften bzw. für die zu vermittelnden Bedeutungsinhalte. Medien sind Vermittlungsinstanzen, ohne die Kommunikation nicht möglich ist. Es gibt keine unvermittelte Kommunikation. ❷

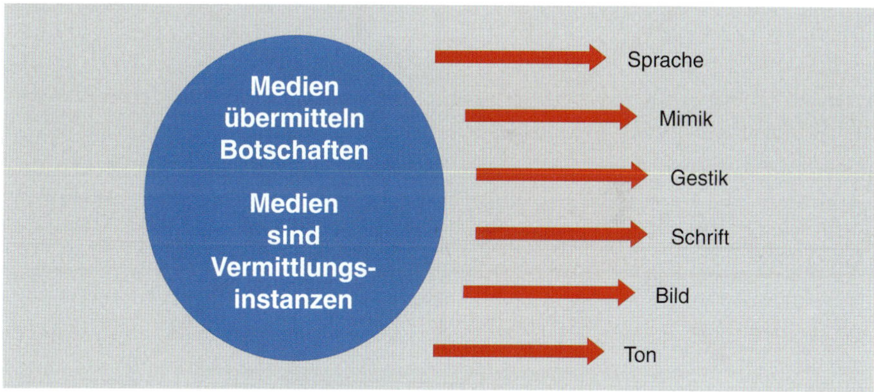

❸ Manfred und Monika verstehen einander, weil die Aussage „Fenster schließen" eine gemeinsam vorrätige Bedeutung, ein Symbol, das für einen Gegenstand steht, „treffsicher" ins Bewusstsein ruft.

Merkmal Nr. 6: Kommunikation findet über Symbole statt

Menschliche Kommunikation ist schließlich als ein Interaktionsvorgang zu verstehen, der über Symbole vermittelt wird. Gemeint ist dabei eine wechselseitige Beziehung zwischen den Kommunikationspartnern, bei der ein gemeinsam verfügbarer Zeichenvorrat aufgebaut wird, den beide verstehen. ❸

Ein Zeichen, das einen Gegenstand, einen Zustand oder ein Ereignis repräsentiert, nennt man Symbol. Ein Symbol übt eine Stellvertreterfunktion aus, indem es stellvertretend für den Gegenstand, auf den es verweist, steht. Das bedeutet, dass die Symbole anstelle des jeweiligen Gegenstandes im Bewusstsein der Kommunikationspartner Anschauungen, Vorstellungen und Gedanken hervorrufen können, die sonst eigentlich nur der Gegenstand selber hervorrufen könnte.

1.2 Direkte persönliche Kommunikation

Die Medien sind nach dem Grad der Öffentlichkeit in die vier Grundformen unterschieden worden (s. o.): interpersonelle Kommunikation, Kleingruppenkommunikation, Organisationskommunikation und Massenkommunikation.

Es ist naheliegend, dass man mit zunehmendem Öffentlichkeitsgrad – also je mehr man sich in Richtung der Massenkommunikation bewegt – technische Mittel der Verbreitung einsetzen muss, um die gewünschte Kommunikation sicher zu stellen. Auf Technik kann man nur in der unmittelbaren, persönlichen Kommunikation von Mensch zu Mensch verzichten – wobei es selbst dort oft zweckmäßig ist, die Kommunikation technisch zu unterstützen ❶.

Im Hinblick auf den notwendigen technischen Medieneinsatz sind also die beiden folgenden **Kommunikationsformen** zu unterscheiden:

- Direkte persönliche Kommunikation ❷
- Mediale Kommunikation

Die nachfolgend näher zu beschreibende **direkte Kommunikation** geschieht persönlich zwischen Menschen, ohne dass es dabei eines technischen Transportmittels zwingend bedürfte. Technik dient höchstens zur Unterstützung der Wirkung der Sprachkommunikation, der Kontext des persönlichen Zusammentreffens der Kommunikationspartner wird aber nicht aufgehoben.

Demgegenüber ist es bei der **medialen Kommunikation** zwingend notwendig, dass Technik eingesetzt wird, um Kommunikation überhaupt erst möglich zu machen, wie es z. B. im Fernsehen, Radio oder im Internet der Fall ist.

❶ Man denke z. B. an den Einsatz von Mikrofonen bei einer Rede oder an ein Megafon bei einem Polizeieinsatz bei einer Demonstration.

❷ Dieser hier gewählte Begriff wird nicht einheitlich verwendet. Die folgenden Begriffe sind auch gebräuchlich:
interpersonale Kommunikation,
Individualkommunikation,
natürliche Kommunikation,
unvermittelte Kommunikation,
informelle Kommunikation,
Face-to-Face-Kommunikation,
dyadische Kommunikation.

1.2.1 Bedeutung des Kontexts

Direkte Kommunikation verläuft unterschiedlich, je nachdem, in welchem Kontext man sich befindet. Nach der Anzahl der beteiligten Personen kann man unterscheiden:

- Die Zweierbeziehung (auch „**Dyade**" genannt): Sie ist logischerweise die kleinste Einheit. Nur zwei Personen sind unmittelbar beteiligt.
- Kleingruppe: Sehr kleine Gruppen umfassen 3 bis 6 Personen. Von Kleingruppen kann man bei ca. 10 bis 15 Personen gerade noch sprechen.
- Großgruppe: Eine Gruppengröße von 20 Personen und größer bezeichnet man bereits als Großgruppe.

Innerhalb dieser Kontexte findet jeweils ein direkter kommunikativer Austausch statt, wobei die Beteiligten stets die Möglichkeit, sich gegenseitig wahrzunehmen und aufeinander einzugehen. „Direkte Kommunikation ist also jede Form des Austauschs zwischen zwei oder mehr Personen, die sich gegenseitig wehrnehmen und die aufeinander eingehen können (aber nicht zwingend müssen!)" (Quelle: Hillebrecht 2009, S. 18 f.).

1.2.3 Verbale und non-verbale Kommunikation

❶ „Es gibt drei Gattungen öffentlicher Reden, die Volksrede, Festrede und Gerichtsrede. Abarten dieser Reden gibt es sieben, die empfehlende und warnende, preisende und scheltende, anklagende, verteidigende und prüfende Rede, sei es an sich oder vergleichsweise. Das also ist die Zahl der Abarten aller Reden. Man wird sich ihrer bedienen in öffentlichen Auseinandersetzungen, in Gerichtsverhandlungen über Verträge und im persönlichen Verkehr" (Aristoteles: Rhetorik an Alexander, zit. nach Merten, Klaus: Einführung in die Kommunikationswissenschaft, Bd. 1, Münster 1999, S. 123).

Wird Sprache als gesprochene Sprache verwendet, versteht man sie als ein Instrument der **verbalen Kommunikation**. Dies kann die verschiedensten kommunikativen Kontexte bzw. Typen kommunikativer Gattungen betreffen: Vortrag, Präsentation, Rede, Gespräch, Klatsch, Gerücht, Small Talk.

Ein **Gespräch** ist eine auf ein Thema hin vorsätzlich und gezielt geführte Kommunikation mit hohem Informationsgehalt und bindender Wirkung auf die Kommunikationspartner. Demgegenüber ist der Small Talk eine informelle Kommunikation ohne eine definitive Absicht und erschöpft sich in der Unverbindlichkeit.

Ein prominenter Fall der verbalen Kommunikation ist die **Rede**. Sie ist bewusst darauf ausgerichtet, eine bestimmte und gewollte Wirkung beim Publikum zu erzielen, sei es bei einer politischen Wahlversammlung, vor Gericht als Plädoyer oder als Tischrede bei einer Hochzeitsfeier. Die Bedeutung der Rede wurde schon im Altertum sehr hoch gehandelt. So hat bereits Aristoteles (384-322 v. Chr.) eine Theorie der Rede entwickelt, die er als Rhetorik bezeichnete ❶. Berühmt für ihre **Redekunst** waren u. a. Demosthenes, Cicero, Augustinus, Jefferson, Napoleon, Rosa Luxemburg, Churchill, de Gaulle, Mao-Tse-Tung, Dale Carnegie.

Sprachliche Kommunikation muss nicht unbedingt auf der Grundlage der gesprochenen Sprache erfolgen, sie kann sich auch **non-verbal** vollziehen. **Non-verbale Kommunikation** kann einerseits dazu dienen, einen Sachverhalt gänzlich ohne Worte auszudrücken („beredtes Schweigen") oder andererseits das gesprochene Wort in seiner Wirkung zu unterstützen. Letzteres ist die Regel. Und man kann hinzufügen: es findet keine persönliche Kommunikation ohne non-verbale Elemente statt. Der berühmte Kommunikationspsychologe Paul Watzlawick hat dies so ausgedrückt: „Man kann nicht nicht kommunizieren!"

So darf die verbale Kommunikation nicht isoliert betrachtet werden, da bei der Verständigung der Kommunikationspartner stets auch nicht-verbale Formen der Kommunikation eine bedeutende Rolle spielen. Es ist geradezu eine Zwangsläufigkeit, dass bei der sprachlichen Kommunikation – soll sie gelingen – nicht-sprachliche Elemente bedacht werden müssen. Dabei sind die folgenden **Aspekte** zu nennen ❷:

- **Körperkontakt**: Als positiver Grundtypus des sozialen Verhaltens gilt in Deutschland z. B. das Händereichen als Grußform. Ansonsten ist der Körperkontakt in der Gesellschaft in der Öffentlichkeit geradezu tabuisiert.
- **Nähe/Distanz**: Es ist wichtig, gegenüber dem Mitmenschen eine ausreichende körperliche Distanz zu wahren, was als ein Zeichen von Wertschätzung und Respekt gilt. So entsteht z. B. ein Gefühl des Unwohlseins, wenn jemand in einem persönlichen Gespräch so nahe „auf die Pelle rückt", dass er die intime Distanz – die bei einem Abstand von ca. 46 cm verläuft – verletzt. Man weiß, dass persönliche Interaktion zwischen Menschen am reibungslosesten in einer Distanz zwischen 46 cm und ca. 1,20 Metern geschieht. Die sog. öffentliche Distanz beginnt ab ca. 3,60 Metern. Sie wird immer dann wichtig, wenn eine größere Anzahl von Menschen zusammen kommen.

❷ Quelle: Neuhäuser-Metternich, Sylvia und Witt, Frank-Jürgen: Kommunikation und Berichtswesen, München 1997, S. 15ff.

- **Körperhaltung**: Von ihr wird angenommen, dass sie die innere Einstellung eines Menschen zum Ausdruck bringt. Nicht von ungefähr spricht man z. B. von „aufrechter Haltung“. Geöffnete Arme gelten allgemein als Zeichen von Sympathie und Offenheit, verschränkte Arme sollen auf Verschlossenheit, Unsicherheit und Hemmungen hinweisen.
- Äußere Erscheinung: Diese wird meist gezielt eingesetzt, um den Erwartungen der sozialen Gruppe zu entsprechen, z. B. durch Tragen eines dunklen Anzuges und Krawatte bei Geschäftsleuten. Hier ist die Gefahr groß, dass man einer vorschnellen Einschätzung eines Menschen unterliegt.
- **Mimik**, **Gestik**, **Pantomimik**: Wichtig sind auch der Gesichtsausdruck, das Gebärdenspiel bzw. die „Sprache“ der Hände und die Bewegung des Körpers.
- Blick: Der Blickkontakt spielt eine wichtige Rolle beim Aufrechterhalten eines Gespräches. Allerdings verursacht es Stress, wenn man als Gegenüber einem unausgesetzt andauernden Blick ausgesetzt wird.
- Non-verbale Aspekte der Sprache: Einflüsse gehen schließlich von der Sprechweise, der Stimme, der Sprechgeschwindigkeit und der Tonhöhe aus.

Vor diesem Hintergrund ist es daher zweckmäßig, zwischen sprachlicher bzw. verbaler Kommunikation einerseits und nicht-sprachlicher (nicht-verbaler bzw. non-verbaler) Kommunikation andererseits zu unterscheiden. Nicht-verbale Kommunikation ist deswegen so bedeutsam, weil sie das, was über die verbale Schiene zum Ausdruck kommt, unterstützt, interpretiert, bestätigt und unterstreicht. Sie wirkt gewissermaßen als „Flankenschutz“, um das Gesagte besser zu vermitteln. Manchmal ist es allerdings so, dass zwischen dem, was gesprochen wird, und dem, was die Körper-„Sprache“ verrät, ein Gegensatz ist.

Gestik

Mimik

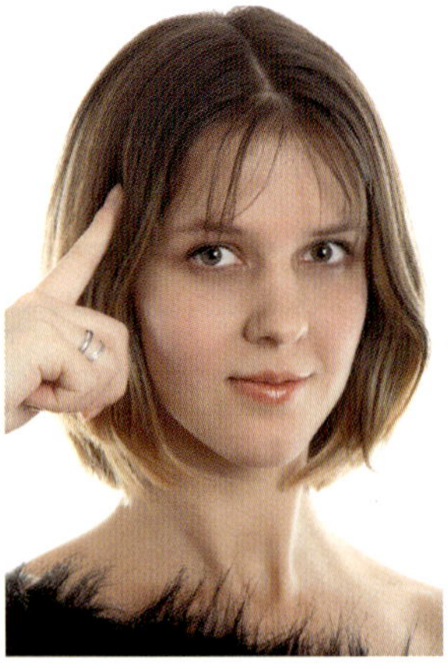

Blickkontakt

Einsatz medientechnischer Hilfsmittel

Oft ist es in der direkten persönlichen Kommunikation hilfreich oder sogar notwendig, die Sprache durch medientechnische Hilfsmittel zu unterstützen. Dies kann akustisch oder visuell durch den folgenden Medieneinsatz geschehen:

- Handout: Das „gute alte“ Papierdokument kann eine Präsentation unter Umständen in hervorragender Weise unterstützen.
- Verstärkung durch Mikrofon und Lautsprecher. Das Spektrum reicht hier von der Ein-Personen-Präsentation bis hin zu großen Events wie Pop-Konzerten, wo der audiovisuelle technische Aufwand gigantische Ausmaße annehmen kann.
- Tafel: Klassisches Medium im Schulungsbereich.
- Flipchart: Großformatiges Papier, Einsatz für Besprechungen in Kleingruppen.
- Pinn-Wand: Große Weichfaserplatte, die mit Packpapier bespannt wird, als Ergänzungsmedium zum Flipchart.
- Whiteboard: mit abwaschbarem Marker beschreibbare weiße Kunststofffläche.
- Beamer: Projektion digital aufbereiteter Inhalte, z. B. Power-Point-Präsentationen, Filme oder Internet-Content über Beamer.

Der Medieneinsatz erfolgt zur Unterstützung der Wirkung des gesprochenen Wortes oder der Darbietung. Bei Präsentationen verfolgen sie zumeist den Zweck, die Aufmerksamkeit der Zuhörer oder Zuschauer von der Person des Vortragenden weg und hin zur Sache und zum Thema zu lenken. Man macht sich dabei die Erkenntnis zunutze, dass Lerninhalte und Botschaften durch Visualisierungstechniken deutlich besser behalten werden können.

Kriterien für den Einsatz von Medien

Nachfolgende Liste stellt einen Katalog von Empfehlungen dar, wie man mit Medien zur Unterstützung der Wirkung des gesprochenen Wortes umgehen sollte: ❶

❶ Quelle: Schuhmann 2008, S. 33.

- Medien sollen motivieren und emotionalen Widerstand abbauen.
- Medien sollen an die Erfahrungen der Hörer anknüpfen.
- Sprache und Gestaltung sind adressatengerecht zu gestalten.
- Medien sollen z. B. durch Fragen, Impulse oder Aufgaben zur Aktivität anregen.
- Die Größe und Zusammensetzung der Gruppe sind zu berücksichtigen.
- Orientierungspunkt ist das Ziel der Veranstaltung.
- Ein Medium pro Thema soll genügen.
- Klare Gliederung und einfache Darstellung helfen.
- Abwechslungsreiche Gestaltung wirkt belebend, z. B. durch Bildhaftigkeit, Grafiken, unterschiedliche Schriftgrößen.
- Wenig und leicht lesbarer Text in großen Buchstaben erleichtert das Behalten.
- Der Redner/Gesprächsleiter muss das Medium vorher ansehen bzw. anhören und sich mit der Handhabung des Mediums auskennen.
- Medien sollen methodisch sinnvoll eingegliedert werden.
- Der Aufwand darf nicht zu hoch sein.

Die Rede

Besonders bei einer Rede ist es von großer Bedeutung, die Erfolgsbedingungen für eine gute und gelingende Kommunikation zu beachten. Reden kommen in **drei Formen** vor: Information, Ausdruck, Appell (vgl. hier und nachfolgend Schuhmann 2008, S. 8 ff.).

Die **informierende Rede** spielt im Berufsalltag: zu denken ist an Erläuterungen von Sachverhalten, Darstellung von Problemen und Lösungsvorschlägen, Überzeugungsarbeit von Sachfragen im Beruf. In der Ausbildung: Lehrer Unterricht, Schüler mündliche Prüfungen. Wichtig ist der Nutzen für den Zuhörer. Die Glaubwürdigkeit der Aussagen ist mit Daten und Fakten zu belegen.

Anders bei der **Ausdrucksrede**, wo Gefühle im Vordergrund stehen sollen. Bei Geburtstagen, Jubiläen, Verabschiedungen, Beerdigungen. Gefühlsregungen bei den Zuhörern hervorrufen und eigene Gefühle äußern.

Schließlich die **appellierende Rede**, die zu Handlungen auffordern will. Beispiele sind die politische Rede, etwa im Wahlkampf, das Verkaufsgespräch

Nachfolgende Übersicht zeigt die einzelnen Bausteine, die man bei der Gestaltung einer Rede beachten soll, darüber nachdenken soll. Entscheidungen treffen.

Das Gespräch

Gespräche erfolgreich zu führen, gelingt häufig nicht. Man denke z.B. an Nachbarschaftsstreitigkeiten, Erbauseinandersetzungen, Gerichtsverhandlungen. Oft bekommt man die Beteiligten nicht einmal an einen Tisch. Sich verständigen können ist neben diesen großen Themen aber auch im ganz normalen Alltag eine Herausforderung. Der Hauptgrund liegt darin, dass im direkten persönlichen Gespräch neben der Sache, um die es geht, immer auch die Beziehung zwischen den beteiligten Personen und damit deren Emotionen eine Rolle spielt. Man sollte immer darauf gefasst sein, dass es zu Störungen kommen kann.

Die folgenden **Arten von Gesprächen** lassen sich unterscheiden (vgl. Schuhmann 2008, S. 57 ff.):

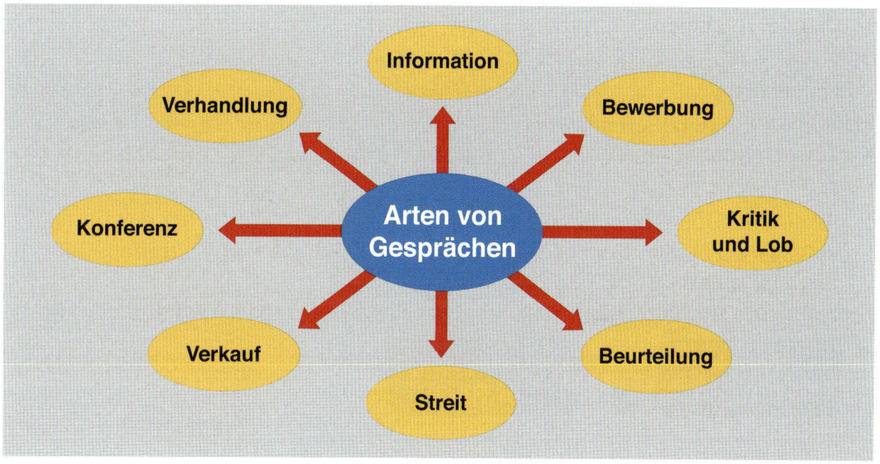

Im Hinblick auf die Gefühle, die bei den Gesprächspartnern aufgerufen werden , sind besonders die Kritik-, Beurteilungs- und Streitgespräche, aber auch manche Verhandlungen, als „brisant" einzustufen. Hier einige allgemeine **Empfehlungen**, wie man ein **Gespräch konstruktiv gestalten** kann:

Bezogen auf die **Sache**, um die es geht:

- Das Ziel des Gesprächs klar benennen
- Sachlich bleiben: Fakten, Daten; keine persönliche Kritik, Aussagen begründen
- Ausreichend Zeit für das Gespräch vorsehen

Bezogen auf die **Beziehung** zwischen den Gesprächspartnern:

- Wertschätzung: Jederzeit dem anderen durch Worte und Körpersprache Wertschätzung zeigen, positive Gefühle zum Ausdruck bringen, aktives Zuhören, Anerkennung durch positive Zeichen geben
- Äußerer Rahmen: positive Atmosphäre schaffen (Raum, einladende Umgebung)
- Konstruktive Werte: Ehrlichkeit, Offenheit, Integrität
- Gemeinsamkeiten betonen

1.3 Mediale Kommunikation

Bei der medialen Kommunikation (andere Bezeichnungen: vermittelte Kommunikation, indirekte Kommunikation) vollzieht sich die Kommunikation zwischen den Menschen mit Hilfe von **Medien** (Geräte, Apparate, Vorkehrungen), die **als Transportmittel der Botschaften** dienen. Anders als bei der direkten persönlichen Face-to-Face-Kommunikation, bei der bestenfalls eine medientechnische Unterstützung erfolgt, geschieht die Übermittlung der Botschaften vollständig medial. Dies bringt einige wichtige **Vorteile** mit sich: Möglich wird die zeitliche und räumliche Trennung der Kommunikationspartner. Möglich wird auch die Speicherung, Konservierung, Bearbeitung und Übertragung von Kommunikationsinhalten. **Nachteilig** ist aber, dass ein unmittelbares Feedback erschwert oder gar unmöglich wird.

➲ **Mediale Kommunikation ist medienvermittelte Kommunikation, bei der die Beteiligten zeitlich und/oder räumlich getrennt sind.**

„Unter medialer Kommunikation verstehen wir die (sich mehr und mehr verbreitende) Form der Kommunikation, bei der
- Zeichen (also Texte, Grafiken, Töne, Bilder)
- privat oder öffentlich (in allen denkbaren Graden und Versionen)
- durch technische Verbreitungsmittel (Medien im weitesten Sinne)
- analog oder digital und vernetzt (also ohne oder mit Unterstützung elektronischer Datenverarbeitung [Computer] und Netzsystemen
- anonym, verschlüsselt oder explizit simultan oder zeitversetzt bei räumlicher Distanz ein- oder wechselseitig (also ohne oder mit Rollenwechsel der Kommunizierenden, wobei letzterer auch als Interaktivität bezeichnet wird)

an einzelne, mehrere oder viele (Adressaten/Zielgruppen) vermittelt werden" (Kübler 2000, S. 15).

1.3.1 Grundformen medialer Kommunikation

Mediale Kommunikation lässt sich aus verschiedenen Blickwinkeln betrachten: Zum einen kann man die Art der Wahrnehmung der Botschaften betrachten und fragen, mit welchen Sinnesorganen die Kommunikation realisiert wird. Zum anderen kann man auf die Medien blicken und damit auf den Informationsträger, mit dem die Botschaften im Kommunikationsprozess ausgetauscht werden.

Nach den **Art der Wahrnehmung** (auch **Modalität** genannt ❶) lässt sich die mediale Kommunikation nach den folgenden **Grundformen** unterscheiden:

- **Textkommunikation**. Anwendungen: Gedruckte Bücher, Fachliteratur, E-Books
- **Bildkommunikation**. Anwendungen: Bildbände, Fotografien
- **Text-Bild-Kommunikation**. Anwendungen: Zeitungen, Zeitschriften, Prospekte
- **Auditive Kommunikation**. Anwendungen: Radio, Musik, Audio-CD, Hörbücher
- **Audiovisuelle Kommunikation**. Anwendungen: Fernsehen, Film, Kino
- **Multimodale Kommunikation**. Anwendungen: Spiele, Gaming

❶ Die „Modalität" (oder der „Modus") stellt auf die menschliche Wahrnehmung mit den Sinnesorganen ab: so wird Musik fast immer akustisch wahrgenommen, Filme audiovisuell, Texte visuell. Der visuelle Modus bei der Wahrnehmung von Texten muss aber nicht der einzige sein: Texte können auch vorgelesen werden (akustischer Modus) oder sogar taktil (durch Berührung) bei der Blindenschrift (Braille-Schrift).

1.3.4 Unternehmenskommunikation

Ausrichtung der Kommunikation auf die Stakeholder

❶ „Stakeholder" heißt übersetzt „Anspruchsgruppe" oder „Interessengruppe"

Die mediale Kommunikation in Form von Journalismus hat – wie oben gezeigt – den Anspruch, die Gesellschaft mit glaubwürdigen und seriösen Informationen zu versorgen – sozusagen der Gesellschaft einen „guten Dienst zu erweisen". Ein diametral entgegengesetztes Ziel verfolgt die mediale Kommunikation, wenn sie ganz spezifische, vor allem wirtschaftliche Interessen verfolgt. Diese **interessengeleitete Kommunikation** wird von Wirtschaftsunternehmen betrieben mit dem Ziel, erfolgreich am Markt bestehen zu können. Sie wird als **Unternehmenskommunikation** bzw. **Kommunikationspolitik** eines Unternehmens bezeichnet. Die Kommunikationspartner des Unternehmens sind alle Gruppen, die in irgendeiner Beziehung zum Unternehmen stehen. Diese Gruppen werden als **Stakeholder** bezeichnet ❶. Vier zentrale Stake-holder-Gruppen lassen sich unterscheiden, mit denen das Unternehmen jeweils zielgruppenorientiert kommunizieren muss:

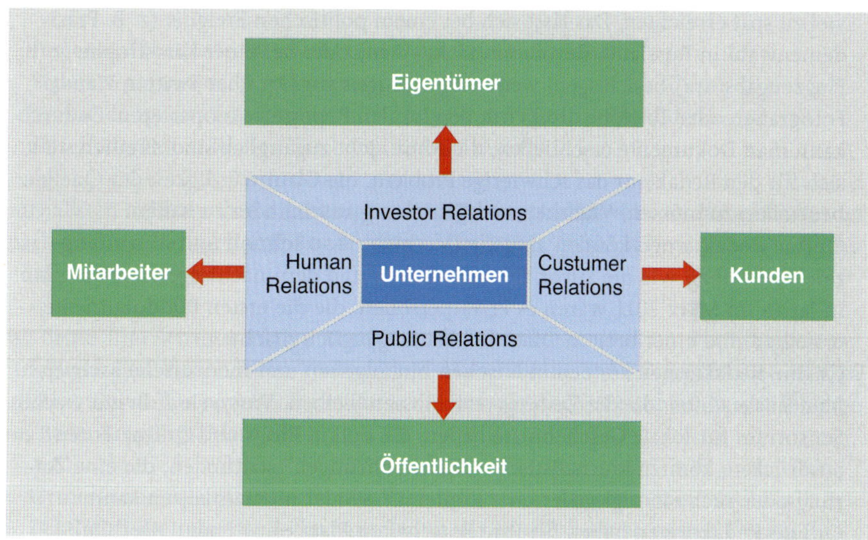

- **Eigentümer:** Sie stellen das Eigenkapital des Unternehmens zur Verfügung und haben ein großes Interesse daran, dass ihre Investition gut und sicher angelegt ist. Das Unternehmen wird sich also bemühen, den Eigentümern gute Informationen über die Rentabilität und Wirtschaftlichkeit des Unternehmens zu liefern. Die Kommunikation mit den Eigentümern hat den Fachbegriff **„Investor Relations"**.
- **Kunden:** Sie sind für den Absatz der Produkte die zentralen Ansprechpartner. Deren Interesse ist es, ihre Bedürfnisse mit möglichst guten und preiswerten Produkten zu befriedigen. Das Unternehmen muss also alles daran setzen, mögliche Interessenten für seine Produkte gezielt anzusprechen. Die gute Information über die Produkte (z. B. durch Werbung) ist die Grundvoraussetzung, damit die Interessenten am Ort des Kaufs (**„Point of Sale"**) geneigt sind, das Produkt auch tatsächlich zu kaufen und zu Kunden zu werden. Die Kommunikation mit den Kunden wird auch als **„Customer Relations"** bezeichnet.

- **Mitarbeiter:** Ein weiterer sehr wichtiger Ansprechpartner für das Unternehmen sind die eigenen Mitarbeiter. Nur wenn diese verstehen, was das Ziel des Unternehmens ist, wie die Ertragslage aussieht, welche Chancen und Gefahren am Markt bestehen, und auch wie gut sie für ihre Leistungen bezahlt werden, sind sie bereit, sich für das Unternehmen mit allen ihren Kräften einzusetzen. Diese von persönlicher Motivation getragene positive Einstellung ist Grundvoraussetzung für den Erfolg und das Überleben des Unternehmens. Es ist daher nicht überraschend, dass die sog. interne Kommunikation (**„Human Relations“**) als eine „Königsdisziplin“ der Kommunikationspolitik eines Unternehmens angesehen wird!
- **Öffentlichkeit:** Nicht zuletzt ist es für ein Unternehmen wichtig, in der Öffentlichkeit gut dazustehen. Nur wenn das Unternehmen Vertrauen und Glaubwürdigkeit in der Öffentlichkeit genießt, wird es auch als Marktpartner geschätzt. Ein Unternehmen, das z. B. wegen seiner schlechten Bezahlung der Mitarbeiter oder wegen dubioser Geschäftspraktiken ins Zwielicht gerät, ist in seiner Existenz gefährdet. Das Instrument, das für Vertrauen in der Öffentlichkeit wirbt, nennt man **„Public Relations“**.

Instrumente der Unternehmenskommunikation

Dem Unternehmens steht ein breites Spektrum **kommunikationspolitischer Instrumente** zur Verfügung. Gemeinsames Ziel ist es, dem Unternehmen und seinen Produkten ein klares und von der Konkurrenz unterscheidbares **Profil** zu verleihen. Das Unternehmen und seine Produkte sollen in den Köpfen der Interessenten und Kunden als wichtige „Persönlichkeiten“ verankert werden. Der „Instrumentenkasten“ stellt sich in der Übersicht wie folgt dar:

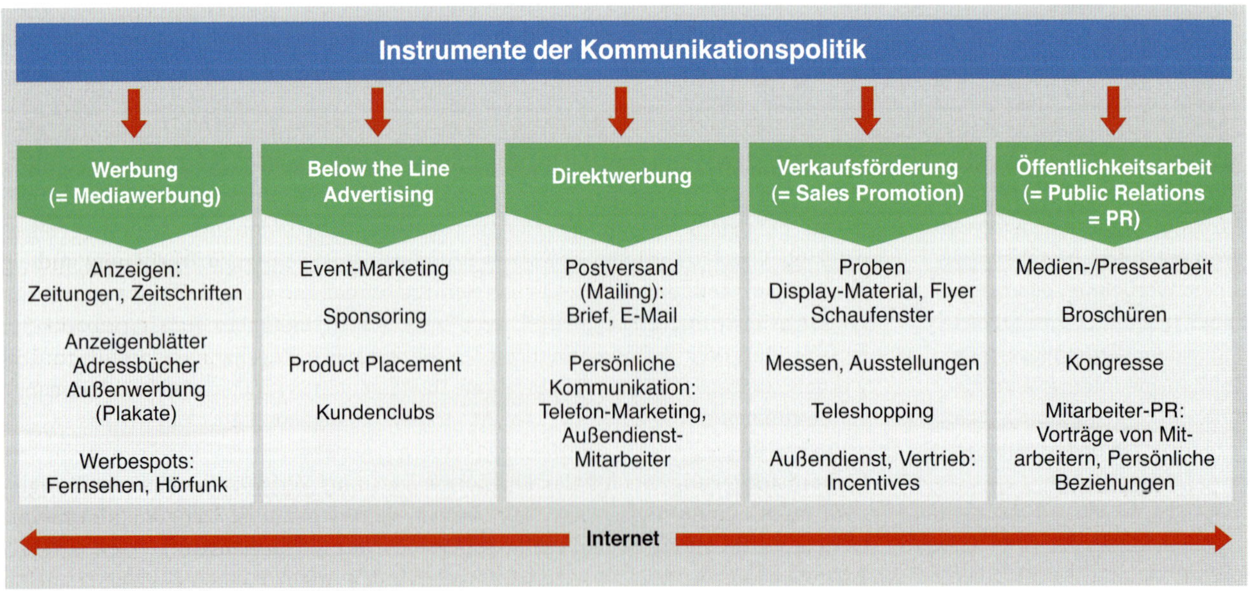

❶ „Media" deswegen, weil sich dieser Typ der Kommunikationspolitik der Medien als sog. „Werbeträger" bedient. Die Medien wie Zeitungen, Zeitschriften, Fernsehen oder Hörfunk sind die Träger bzw. „Überträger" der Werbebotschaften.

Die **Werbung** (auch als **Mediawerbung** bezeichnet ❶) wird herkömmlicherweise als das bedeutendste kommunikationspolitische Instrument eines Unternehmens angesehen. Man versteht darunter die bezahlte Form der unpersönlichen Präsentation von Produkten. Als klassische Werbung gilt Anzeigenwerbung in Zeitungen und Zeitschriften, Anzeigenblätter und Adressbücher, Werbung im Fernsehen, Radio und im Kino sowie Plakatwerbung (Außenwerbung). Erheblich an Boden gut gemacht hat in jüngster Zeit die Online-Werbung in Form von Werbebotschaften auf den Websites von Verlagen, Sendern, Suchmaschinen, Portalen oder Plattformen. Sie kann inzwischen schon zur klassischen Werbung gezählt werden. Als Hauptziele der Mediawerbung stehen im Vordergrund:

- Bekanntmachung: Bei den potentiellen Kunden wird bekannt gemacht, dass es das Produkt gibt und dass es erhältlich ist.
- Information: Dem Kunden werden Produktinformationen mitgeteilt wie Preis, Bezugsquellen oder technische Daten.
- Image: Bei den Umworbenen soll das Produkt einen guten Eindruck hinterlassen. Es soll als eine starke und überzeugende Produktpersönlichkeit wahrgenommen werden.
- Kaufhandlung: Der potenzielle Kunde soll zum Kauf bewegt werden.

➲ **Werbung ist das klassische kommunikationspolitische Instrument.**

Below the Line Advertising: Alternativ zu den klassischen Werbeformen sind die sog. Werbekonzepte zu sehen, die sich „below the line", also unterhalb der Linie zu den herkömmlichen Werbeinstrumenten, abspielen. Dies sind vor allem Sponsoring, Product Placement und Kundenclubs, aber auch die Veranstaltung von Events. Unter Sponsoring versteht man die Förderung von Personen oder Organisationen mit dem Ziel, das eigene Unternehmen zu kommunizieren. Im Vordergrund steht das Sponsoring in den Bereichen Sport, Kultur, Soziales und Umwelt. Mit Product Placement wird die Platzierung eines Markenartikels als Requisit in der Handlung eines Spielfilms bezeichnet.

❷ Eine typische diesbezügliche Werbeform ist das Mail Order Package. Dies ist eine adressierte Werbesendung, bestehend aus einem Werbebrief, einem Prospekt, einer Rückantwortkarte und einem Versandkuvert. Im Zeichen von Internet wird die Antwort (der „Response") des Interessenten online erfolgen.

Unter **Direktwerbung** (auch als **Direct Marketing** bezeichnet) versteht man die individuell auf ganz bestimmte Zielgruppen ausgerichtete Werbung. Das Konzept besteht darin, Zielpersonen ganz gezielt anzusprechen, verbunden mit dem Ziel, einen direkten Kontakt zu ihnen herzustellen und mit ihnen in einen Dialog einzutreten. Das Hauptanwendungsfeld der Direktwerbung ist der Postversand ❷ oder online. Ein wichtiges Instrument ist auch die Direct-Response-Werbung, bei der beispielsweise in Fernsehspots oder Zeitungsannoncen Telefonnummern eingeblendet oder abgedruckt werden; Ziel ist es, bisher nicht bekannte Interessenten in einer anonymen Zielgruppe zu identifizieren und einer direkten Ansprache zugänglich zu machen.

Verkaufsförderung (auch **Sales Promotion** genannt) verfolgt das Ziel, das Produkt zum Interessenten hin zu „drücken". Man spricht daher auch vom „Push-Konzept". Der klassische Ansatz besteht darin, am Ort des Verkaufs bzw. Kaufs („Point of Sale") zusätzliche Kaufanreize zu setzen und dadurch den Absatz zu fördern. Eine Fülle von Möglichkeiten bieten sich hierzu an, wie z. B. Produktvorführungen, Sonderpreisaktionen, Gewinnspiele, Rabattgutscheine, Probiertische oder Zugaben.

Schließlich ist **Public Relations** (auch **Öffentlichkeitsarbeit** oder kurz „PR“ genannt) zu nennen, ein Instrument, das für das Unternehmen in seiner Ganzheit von höchster Bedeutung ist. Ziel von Public Relations ist es, ein positives Bild vom Unternehmen in die Öffentlichkeit hineinzutragen. Das Unternehmen soll sympathisch und liebenswert erscheinen, es soll von möglichst vielen Gruppen der Gesellschaft als glaubwürdig eingestuft werden, es soll in allen seinen Aktionen als seriöser Geschäftspartner erkannt werden. Kurz: es geht darum, in der Gesellschaft um Vertrauen in das Unternehmen zu werben. Als besonders wirksame Instrumente der PR bzw. Öffentlichkeitsarbeit bietet sich Medien- und Pressearbeit an (Pressekonferenzen („PK“), aber auch die Durchführung von Veranstaltungen (z. B. Tag der offenen Tür, Jubiläen, Vorträge), gezieltes Sponsoring und Publikationen (vor allem Geschäftsbericht, Firmenbroschüren, Mitarbeiterzeitung). Von besonderer Bedeutung sind immer auch die persönlichen Beziehungen führender Mitarbeiter des Unternehmens.

Alle PR-Anstrengungen haben letztlich zum Ziel, die Identität des Unternehmens nach außen darzustellen – und dabei im bestmöglichen Licht erscheinen zu lassen. Die Identität des Unternehmens ist mit dem Fachbegriff der **Corporate Identity** belegt. Sie gliedert sich in die folgenden vier Teilbereiche:

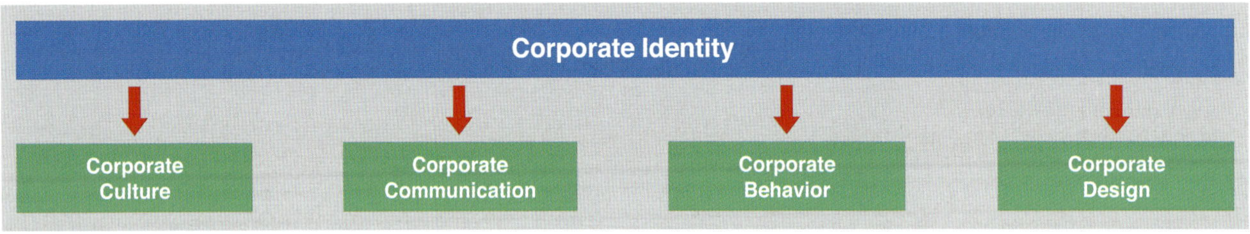

- Unter **Corporate Culture** versteht man die Summe der Werte und Normen, die das Zusammenleben innerhalb des Unternehmens bestimmen. Sie verkörpern die Denk- und Verhaltensmuster der Mitarbeiter.
- **Corporate Communication** verdeutlicht die Art und Weise, wie das Unternehmen mit seinen Stakeholdern kommuniziert. Wünschenswert ist eine offene, widerspruchsfreie und im Einklang mit der Strategie stehende Kommunikation. Eine hohe Bedeutung kommt dabei den Werbeaussagen zu: Der Slogan „Spiegel-Leser wissen mehr“ legt die Messlatte hoch und zwingt den Spiegel-Verlag in eine Bringschuld, diesem Anspruch auch gerecht zu werden.

DER SPIEGEL

- Mit **Corporate Behavior** wird das Verhalten des Unternehmens gegenüber den externen und internen Stakeholder bezeichnet. Positiv ist das Corporate Behavior, wenn das Unternehmen ein schlüssiges, stimmiges und durchgängiges Verhalten an den Tag legt.
- Schließlich bezeichnet das **Corporate Design** das visuelle Erscheinungsbild des Unternehmens, wie es im Firmenlogo, im Firmennamen, in Farbe, Schrift, in Prospekten, aber auch z. B. in der Dienstkleidung zum Ausdruck kommt. Ziel ist es, die Unternehmensidentität auch durch eine unverwechselbare äußere Form zu unterstreichen und wiedererkennbar zu machen.

Die Frage des optimalen Einsatzes der Kommunikationsinstrumente

Der Einsatz von Kommunikationsinstrumenten ist für das Unternehmen nur so gut, wie sie auch eine Wirkung erzielen. Eine der wichtigsten Voraussetzungen dafür, dass die Instrumente die gewünschte Wirkung erzielen, ist ihr integrierter, auf einander abgestimmter Einsatz. Es geht also darum, ein durchdachtes Konzept der **integrierten Kommunikation** zu entwickeln.

Wie ein solches Konzept aussehen kann, zeigt die nachfolgende Abbildung (Quelle: Bruhn 2005, S. 32):

Kommunikationsinstrumente / Funktionen	Werbung	Verkaufsförderung	Messen/Ausstellungen	Direct Marketing	Sponsoring	Multimediakommunikation	Event Marketing	Persönliche Kommunikation	Public Relations
Kundenakquisition									
Bekanntmachung von Produkten	●	◑	●	○	○	○	○	○	◑
Image/Markeneinführung	●	◑	◑	○	◑	○	◑	○	●
Unternehmensdarstellung	●	○	◑	○	○	◑	●	◑	●
Hineinverkauf Handel	◑	●	●	○	○	○	○	◑	○
Abverkauf Endabnehmer	●	●	●	◑	○	○	○	○	○
Kundenbindung									
Wiederverkauf	●	○	●	●	●	◑	◑	◑	○
Weiterempfehlung	○	◑	●	●	○	○	●	●	◑
Cross Buying	◑	◑	◑	◑	○	◑	○	◑	○
Kundenrückgewinnung									
Fehlerkorrektur	◑	○	○	●	○	○	◑	●	●
Wiedergutmachung	○	○	○	●	●	○	●	◑	◑
Überzeugung	●	◑	●	●	○	○	●	●	●
Stimulierung	●	●	◑	◑	○	○	●	◑	◑

Wirkungsintensitäten: ● überdurchschnittliche ◑ mittlere ○ geringe/keine

Aus dieser Darstellung wird deutlich, dass jedes einzelne Kommunikationsinstrument im Hinblick auf die Funktionen eine **unterschiedliche Wirkungskraft** entfaltet. So leistet zum Beispiel die klassische Werbung besonders wertvolle Dienste bei der Bekanntmachung und dem Image-Aufbau von Produkten, kann aber nichts bei der Kundenrückgewinnung ausrichten. Die Unternehmenskommunikation steht also vor schwierigen Fragen: Wie sollen die einzelnen Instrumente aufeinander abgestimmt werden? Wie lässt sich die Wirkung maximieren? Stehen die einzelne Instrumente im Widerspruch zueinander? In welche Instrumente soll man investieren, in welche nicht?

1.4 Modelle der Medien

1.4.1 Bedeutung der Perspektive

Metaphern

Jede theoretische Erklärung, sei es in Form eines einfachen oder komplexeren Modells, sei es in Form eines ganzen Theoriegebäudes, hängt davon ab, von welchem Standpunkt aus die Erklärung vorgenommen wird. Der **subjektive Standpunkt** des Betrachters bestimmt die Erkenntnis. In der Medien- und Kommunikationstheorie wird dieser Sachverhalt mit dem Begriff der **Metapher** bezeichnet.

➲ **Eine Metapher ist die ganz spezielle Perspektive, aus der heraus wir einen interessierenden Gegenstand (hier die Medien) betrachten.**

Es ist wichtig, sich stets bewusst zu machen, dass wir die Dinge immer aus einer bestimmten **Perspektive** heraus betrachten und dass es notwendig ist, die jeweilige Perspektive, aus der wir ein Thema beleuchten, zu verdeutlichen.

Die Erklärung von Rolle und Bedeutung der Medien kann aus den unterschiedlichsten Perspektiven heraus erfolgen. Als grundlegende Sichtweisen kommen zahlreiche **Metaphern** in Frage ❶:

❶ Quelle: Funkkolleg Medien und Kommunikation, Weinheim und Basel 1990, Studienbrief 3, S. 18ff.

- Im Altertum steht die Metapher von der Bewahrung erinnerungswürdiger Ereignisse, Personen oder Errungenschaften im Vordergrund: Kommunikation ist die Schaffung von zeitlosen Monumenten (Inschriften in Grabkammern, auf Obelisken, in Stein gemeißelt, zur Verewigung z. B. des Pharao). Die monumentalen Inschriften hatten im Übrigen auch die Funktion, das Volk gefügig zu machen.
- Die Metapher der Schaffung von (kognitiven) Gemeinsamkeiten („cognitive sharing") besagt: Kommunikation ist etwas, das bei den Kommunikationspartnern zu Gemeinsamkeit führt. Sie drückt sich in Form einer Mitteilung aus. „Mit-Teilung" bedeutet „Teilung" von etwas Gemeinsamem. Diese Metapher unterstellt, dass es im Kommunikationsvorgang nur eine einzige Bedeutung gibt, die von jedem der beteiligten Kommunikationspartner erkannt und begriffen wird.
- Die Metapher vom physischen Transport („Container-Metapher") besagt: Kommunikation ist die – physikalisch messbare – Übertragung von Botschaften. Ein Medium ist gleichsam ein Container, der Botschaften von einem Ort zum anderen transportiert. Umgangssprachliche Redewendungen, die auf diese Optik hindeuten, sind z. B.: „Was steht in dem Brief?"; „Der Artikel enthält nichts Neues"; „ein bedeutungsvoller Satz!"
- Die Metapher vom Kanal besagt: Kommunikation wird als ein physikalischer Fließvorgang von Signalen verstanden, der in einem rohrartigen Kanal stattfindet. Die Botschaften werden als Flüssigkeit von einem Ort zum anderen geleitet. Menschliche Kommunikation ist in diesem Bild eine Erscheinung, die sogar mehrere Rohre benötigt, entsprechend der Vielfalt der Kommunikationsformen (verbal/nonverbal; Kanäle des Sehens, Hörens, Berührens, Riechens, Schmeckens). Sprachlich kommt diese Metapher z. B. im Bild vom „Informationsfluss" zum Ausdruck.

Sind wir Opfer unserer Metaphern? Oder erkennen wir sie und können damit umgehen?

❶ Dabei spielen Begriffe wie Informationsmengen (Bits), Kanalkapazität, Übertragungsmenge oder Redundanz eine Rolle.

❷ In vielen alltäglichen Redewendungen ist diese Metapher lebendig, z. B.: „Dann schieß mal los!"; „Ihre Behauptung ist unhaltbar"; „Seine Worte haben ins Schwarze getroffen"

❸ **Metaphern** leiten unser Bild von Kommunikation. Herauszufinden, wie wir zu Wissen und Vorstellungen gelangen, ist Aufgabe der sog. **Erkenntnistheorie**.

- Das vorgestellte Shannon-Weaver-Modell folgt – wie gezeigt – einer Metaphorik, bei der die Kommunikation als ein mathematisch nachvollziehbarer Vorgang verstanden wird ❶.
- Metapher vom Argument als Krieg: Kommunikation wird als ein Instrument der verbalen Kriegführung begriffen ❷.
- Kontroll-Metapher: Kommunikation ist nach dieser Vorstellung ein Instrument zur Lösung menschlicher Probleme bzw. zur Erreichung von Zielen. Kommunikation ist Ursache. Im Extrem kann Kommunikation sogar eine Technik zur Manipulation sein. Umgangssprachlich finden sich viele Beispiele: „Das Fernsehen wirkt sich auf die Schulleistungen aus"; „Der Brief machte mich glücklich".

Anhand dieser Aufzählung möglicher Metaphern wird deutlich, dass es immer höchst unterschiedliche Vorstellungen über das Phänomen der Kommunikation und der Medien geben wird ❸. Es wird nicht möglich sein, sich auf eine einzige Sichtweise zu verständigen. Je nach Gesellschaft, Situation oder Fragestellung wird die eine oder die andere Sicht bevorzugt.

➲ **Wer kommuniziert, muss sich bewusst sein, dass er sich – ob er will oder nicht – einer ganz speziellen Metapher bedient, die von der Vorstellung eines anderen abweichen kann.**

Viele Metaphern werden von vielen Menschen – bewusst oder intuitiv – häufig verwendet. Sie sind dann wie ausgetretene Pfade, denen viele folgen. Das gilt sicher für die Container-Metapher oder die Metapher vom Fluss von Informationsmengen. Es ist offenkundig, dass eine solche physikalisch-mathematische Sicht der Dinge problematisch sein kann. Ebenso ist es offenkundig, dass es ein einziges, allgemein gültiges Kommunikationsmodell nicht geben kann.

In der Medien- und Kommunikationstheorie haben sich aber dennoch **zwei theoretische Grundkonzeptionen** herausgebildet, die sich gewissermaßen als Leitlinien für den Aufbau von Theoriegebäuden eignen. Es handelt sich um die beiden folgenden Konzepte:

- Reiz-Reaktions-Schema
- Konstruktivismus

Das **Reiz-Reaktions-Schema** geht davon aus, dass eine Wirkung immer auch eine Ursache haben muss. Die Wirkung (= „Response", „Reaktion") ist also immer die Folge eines Reizes (= „Stimulus"): Man verwende bei einer Anzeigenwerbung eine knallige Farbe, und schon steigt der Grad der Aufmerksamkeit beim Leser! Der Ansatz wird daher auch Stimulus-Response-Ansatz genannt. Auf die Medien übertragen, stellt er die Frage: Was machen die Medien mit den Menschen?

Im Gegensatz zu diesem theoretischen Ansatz steht der Ansatz des **Konstruktivismus**. Dieser geht nicht davon aus, dass der Mensch ein passives Wesen ist, das nur darauf wartet, von den Medien beeinflusst zu werden, sondern unterstreicht die Vorstellung, dass sich jeder Mensch seine eigene Wirklichkeit – aktiv – selbst konstruiert. Die zentrale Frage ist nicht: Was machen die Medien mit den Menschen? Sondern: Was machen die Menschen mit den Medien?

Reiz-Reaktions-Schema

Das Reiz-Reaktions-Schema bezeichnet eine Denkhaltung, die sich in den Kategorien von **Ursache** (Reiz) und **Wirkung** (Reaktion) bewegt. Nach diesem Denkmodell hat jede Erscheinung, die wir beobachten können, immer eine Ursache, oder auch „**Stimulus**“ genannt, und eine Wirkung, als „Response“ bezeichnet. Ein Beispiel:

Reiz bzw. Stimulus: Ein Kind sieht fünf Stunden am Stück fern.
Reaktion bzw. Response: Am nächsten Tag zeigt das Kind ein aggressives Verhalten, das in der Schule allen Lehrern und Mitschülern auffällt.

Man spricht in diesem Zusammenhang auch vom Denken in den Kategorien von Kausalität (Ursache) und Finalität (Wirkung) ❶.

❶ **kausal** = ursächlich von lat. „causa“ = der Grund
final = zielgerichtet von lat. „finis“ = das Ende

In der Medien- und Kommunikationstheorie werden Modelle, die dem Reiz-Reaktions-Schema folgen, als **„S-R-Modelle“** oder **„S-O-R-Modelle“** bezeichnet
(S = Stimulus, O = Organismus, R = Response).

Ein Organismus ist z. B. der Mensch, von dem man wissen will, wie er sich verhält. Es kann auch eine ganze Gruppe von Menschen angesprochen sein, z. B. in der Werbung, wenn man sich eine Vorstellung darüber machen will, wie eine Werbekampagne im Fernsehen auf die Zielgruppe wirkt.

❷ Quelle: Merten, Klaus: Die Wirklichkeit der Medien, Opladen 1994, S. 294ff.

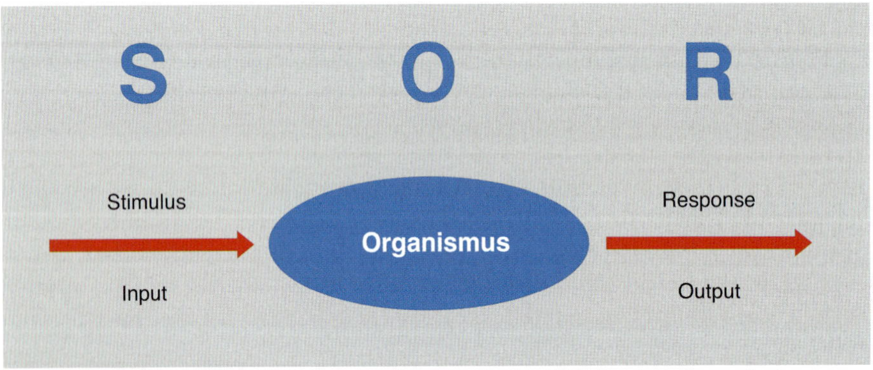

Hinter dem Reiz-Reaktions-Schema stehen drei Annahmen ❷:

- Kausalität: Zwischen Wirkung und Ursache besteht ein direkter Zusammenhang. Diese Vorstellung ist eng mit dem Denken in den Naturwissenschaften verbunden. Schlägt man beispielsweise mit dem Hammer (Ursache) auf einen Nagel, so wird der Nagel (Wirkung) sich bewegen. Das Denken ist linear und einseitig, es ist ein „Wenn-Dann-Denken“.
- Transitivität: Nach dieser Annahme beruht das Reiz-Reaktions-Schema auf einem Vorgang wie der Kraftübertragung zwischen zwei Körpern.
- Proportionalität: Nach dieser Annahme erzeugt ein stets gleicher Reiz eine stets gleiche Wirkung. Je intensiver, anhaltender und direkter ein Stimulus kommt, desto größer wird die Wirkung sein.

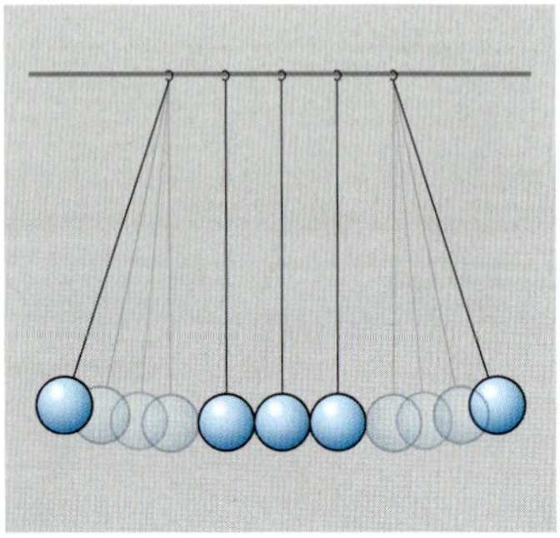

Konstruktivismus

❶ Quelle: Merten, Klaus: Die Wirklichkeit der Medien, Opladen 1994, S. 309ff.

Der Konstruktivismus versteht sich als Antwort auf die beschriebene einseitige und eingeschränkte Sicht des Reiz-Reaktions-Schemas. Er geht von anderen **Annahmen** aus ❶:

- Wirklichkeit ist nicht objektiv gegeben. Jeder Mensch konstruiert sich seine eigene Wirklichkeit subjektiv. Der Mensch ist nicht passiv und hilflos den Medien ausgeliefert, sondern er hat die Möglichkeit, aus den Angeboten auszuwählen (Möglichkeit zu „selektivem Verhalten").
- Die Rezipienten sind sich darüber im Klaren, dass sie diese ihre Wirklichkeit selber konstruieren, und sie versuchen auf alle erdenkliche Weise, für ihre Konstruktion Bestätigungen zu finden.
- Wirklichkeiten werden durch Kommunikation konstruiert.
- Wirklichkeitskonstruktionen und mediale Wirkungen stehen in Verbindung.

❷ Quelle: Merten, Klaus: Die Wirklichkeit der Medien, Opladen 1994, S. 311. Die Goebbels-Rede 1943: Teilnehmer im Sportpalast waren Parteimitglieder. Mit ihnen führte er einen Dialog, indem er von Frage zu Frage mehr fordert und dann die Frage stellt: „Ich frage Euch: Wollt Ihr den totalen Krieg?" Die tosenden Ja-Rufe der eingeschworenen Parteigänger werden reichsweit vom Rundfunk übertragen.

Unter dieser Perspektive ist es notwendig, den Vorgang der **Medienwirkung** anders zu interpretieren. So müssen neben den Botschaften des Kommunikators, die natürlich auch weiterhin eine große Rolle spielen, noch andere „Wirkfaktoren" in Betracht gezogen werden, und vor allem diejenigen, die besonders stark die **Konstruktion der Wirklichkeit** bei den Menschen beeinflussen.

Dies sei am Beispiel der berühmten Goebbels-Rede im Berliner Sportpalast verdeutlicht ❷. Gemäß dem SOR-Denken wird man annehmen, dass die Rede von Goebbels ein maßgeblicher Auslöser (ein medialer Stimulus) dafür war, das deutsche Volk weiter in den Krieg hineinzutreiben (Wirkung). Der Rezipient (das deutsche Volk) war gewissermaßen „schutzlos" den gezielten Attacken des Verführers ausgeliefert.

Konstruktivistisches Denken lehnt diese einseitige Wenn-Dann-Sicht ab und verlangt, auch auf die Randbedingungen zu achten, die eine Wirkung z. B. durch **sich selbst verstärkende Effekte**, „hochschaukeln" können. So war es bei der Goebbels-Rede so, dass zunächst nur die Teilnehmer der Veranstaltung in Begeisterungsstürme ausbrachen. Zu Hause an den Radios nahmen die Hörer wahr, dass die Rede bei anderen Begeisterung auslöste. Der große Effekt entstand erst dadurch, dass die Hörer am Lautsprecher bereit waren, die offensichtlich faszinierende Rede als Modell und Beispiel für die eigene Wirklichkeitskonstruktion heranzuziehen.

In der SOR-Interpretation wird dem Medium Radio als Verbreitungsmittel eine enorme Bedeutung zugemessen. Im Konstruktivismus wird man diese These zwar nicht leugnen, man wird aber zusätzlich auf die anderen Einflüsse verweisen, denen ebenfalls hohe Bedeutung zugemessen werden muss. Das sind vor allem die Erfahrungen, das Wissen und die Einstellungen des Rezipienten (interner Kontext) sowie die Situation und die sozialen Randbedingungen (externer Kontext).

Die Frage der Wirkungstheorie hat viel mit dem **Menschenbild** zu tun, das man zugrunde legt. In Reiz-Reaktions-Kategorien wird der Mensch eher als passiv-rezeptives Wesen verstanden. Geht man einen Schritt weiter, wird man den Menschen eher als ein aktives, sinn- und gestaltgebendes Wesen verstehen, das sich seine eigene Welt aufbaut.

1.4.2 Ein einfacher Modellansatz: Die Lasswell-Formel

Will man einen Vorgang oder ein Phänomen verstehen, benötigt man Erklärungen, wie die Dinge zusammenhängen, wie sie „funktionieren“. Ein Arzt wird nach der Erhebung des Krankheitsbildes (Anamnese) zunächst eine Erklärung der Zusammenhänge suchen (Diagnose), bevor er in die Behandlung (Therapie) einsteigt ❶. Mit der Diagnose erarbeitet der Arzt eine Theorie des Krankheitsgeschehens, zumindest eine theoretische Vorstellung oder einen Modellansatz. Wie man an diesem Beispiel sieht, sind Theorien also von großer Bedeutung. Gelegentlich wird gesagt: „Es gibt nichts Praktischeres als eine gute Theorie“!

❶ Wie geht ein Arzt vor?
1. Anamnese: Beschreibung des Krankheitsbildes
2. Diagnose: Erklärung
3. Therapie: Einflussnahme, Behandlung

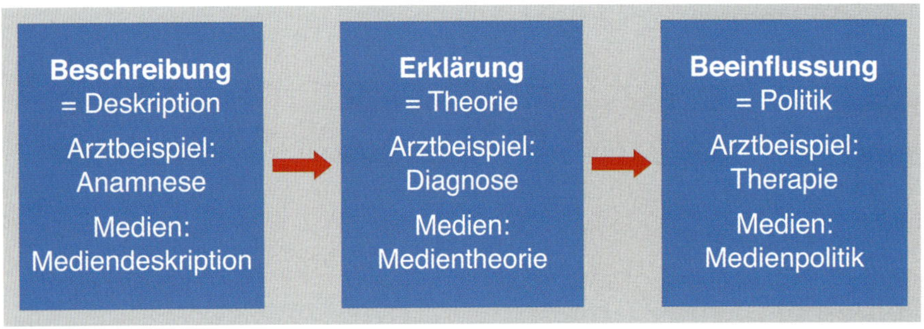

Will man Medien verstehen, benötigt man ebenfalls überzeugende Erklärungen. Über plausible Theorien zu verfügen und gute Modelle zu entwickeln, muss bei diesem wichtigen Thema besonders interessieren ❷. Die **Medientheorie** will die Auswirkungen der Medien und die Zusammenhänge, in denen sie stehen, erkennen und erklären. Einen ersten Einstieg in die Welt der Medienmodelle bietet die sog. **Lasswell-Formel**. Sie lautet:

❷ Maletzke: „Modelle sind Abstraktionsleistungen des menschlichen Denkens“.

➲ **Wer sagt was in welchem Kanal zu wem mit welcher Wirkung?**

Lasswell ❸ hat mit dieser Kurz-Formel grundlegende Themenfelder auf den Punkt gebracht und große Aufmerksamkeit errungen. Diese Formel ist auch heute noch – völlig zu Recht – an Hochschulen und in der Werbe- und Kommunikationspraxis sehr populär. Die Lasswell-Formel schafft es, den recht komplizierten Vorgang der Kommunikation in fünf klar definierte **Bausteine** zu zerlegen. Diese Bausteine sind:

❸ Harold S. **Lasswell**, amerikanischer Politikwissenschaftler, formulierte 1948 seine berühmte Formel.

- Baustein Nr. 1: Kommunikator (wer?)
- Baustein Nr. 2: Aussage (sagt was?)
- Baustein Nr. 3: Medium (in welchem Kanal?)
- Baustein Nr. 4: Rezipient (zu wem?)
- Baustein Nr. 5: Wirkung (mit welcher Wirkung?)

Die Lasswell-Formel ist ein erster Ansatz, der die Medien als einen wesentlichen Baustein im Rahmen des Kommunikationsprozesses positioniert. Es handelt sich um einen „heuristischen Aufhänger“ ❹.

❹ **Heuristisch** heißt, dass die Lasswell-Formel mehr eine Denkhilfe ist als ein ausgearbeites Modell.

Die **Lasswell-Formel** ist wertvoll, weil sie den Kommunikationsprozess verständlich und in einer allgemeingültigen Weise beschreibt. Viele spätere Modellbildungen beruhen auf ihrem Ansatz. Sie ist eine gute Hilfe, die Medien als ein Element der Kommunikation besser zu verstehen und sie sorgt für eine klare **Systematisierung**. Auch Lasswell selbst war bewusst, dass es sich mit seiner Formel eigentlich gar nicht um ein Modell, sondern lediglich um eine Art Navigationshilfe handelte, mit deren Hilfe viele Fragen, die sich im Zusammenhang mit den Medien und mit der Kommunikation stellen, besser bearbeiten lassen.

Nachfolgend soll anhand einer Übersicht noch einmal der **Grundgedanke** der Lasswell-Formel verdeutlicht werden. Die angeführte Liste an Beispielen kann beliebig fortgesetzt werden.

Kommunikator	Aussage	Medium	Rezipient	Wirkung
Sportreporter	Sportbericht	Tageszeitung (Print, Online)	Leser	Information
Autor und Verlag	Roman	Buch (Print, E-Book)	Leser	Unterhaltung
Musikredakteur und Radiosender	Musiksendung	Radio (Kabel, Satellit, UKW, mobil, Internet)	Hörer	Unterhaltung
Show-Redaktion und TV-Sender	Casting-Show	TV (Kabel, Satellit, UKW, mobil, Internet)	Zuschauer	Unterhaltung
Crossmedial arbeitender Nachrichtenreporter	Bericht aus einer Krisenregion	Tageszeitung, Radio, Fernsehen, Online	Leser, Hörer, Zuschauer, User	Information
Autoverkäufer	Web-Shop	Internet	User	Produktwissen
Unternehmen (Werbeabteilung)	Einführung eines neuen Produkts	TV und Zeitschriften	Zuschauer, Leser	Bekanntheit erzeugen
Unternehmen (PR-Abteilung)	Bericht über das Firmenjubiläum	alle erreichbaren Medien	alle erreichbaren Rezipienten	Vertrauen in der Bevölkerung

Im nachfolgenden Kapitel 2 werden die Medien im Hinblick auf den Kommunikationsprozess näher beleuchtet. Dabei dient das Lasswell-Modell als Gliederungsprinzip.

1.4.3 Grundmodelle der Kommunikation

Nachfolgend seien einige **Erklärungsmodelle für Medien und Kommunikation** herausgegriffen, die besondere Aufmerksamkeit erfahren haben und die als besonders aussagekräftig gelten können. Es ist an dieser Stelle nicht möglich, einen Gesamtüberblick über alle Modellvarianten zu geben ❶.

❶ Bei vertieftem Interesse vgl. Maletzke, Gerhard: Kommunikationswissenschaft im Überblick, Opladen, Wiesbaden 1998

Shannon-Weaver-Modell

Im zeitlichen Umfeld der Lasswell-Formel wurde ein Modell entwickelt, das in der Fachwelt einen ähnlich starken Eindruck hinterließ. Es handelt sich um das 1949 von **Shannon und Weaver** vorgestellte Modell der „Mathematischen Theorie der Kommunikation", das als ein **Fundament der modernen Informationstheorie** gilt.

Im Mittelpunkt dieses Modells steht die Vorstellung, dass es sich bei der **Kommunikation** um einen **technischen Vorgang** handelt, wobei von einem Sender zu einem Empfänger ein Vorrat an Zeichen übertragen wird. Damit das auch gelingt, muss man die Zeichen transportfähig machen, indem man sie in technische Signale umwandelt. Das geschieht in Form der sog. **Encodierung** und **Decodierung**. Unter „Encodierung" versteht man die Verschlüsselung der Zeichen beim Kommunikator, und unter „Decodierung" ihre Entschlüsselung beim Rezipienten.

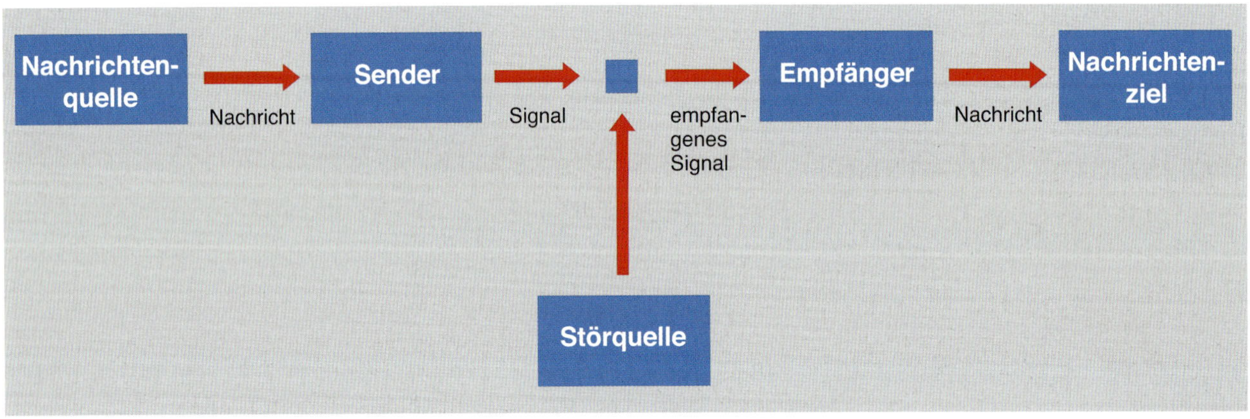

Nach dem vorliegenden Modell ergeben sich Kommunikationsstörungen, wenn die technische Vermittlung nicht funktioniert. **Störquellen** haben also höchste Bedeutung für das Gelingen von Kommunikation, und es geht darum, solche störenden Einflüsse möglichst zu beseitigen. Störungen (technischer Natur) können z. B. wie folgt auftreten:

- Der Übertragungskanal hat eine zu geringe Übertragungskapazität, um eine bestimmte Informationsmenge zu übertragen.
- Es gibt atmosphärische Störungen wie das „Rauschen" im Übertragungskanal (z. B. Kurzwellen-Empfang), die die Signalstärke reduzieren oder den Ton verzerren.
- In einer Gesprächssituation ist Straßenlärm oder ein anderes Umweltgeräusch zu vernehmen.

Badura-Modell

Das Modell von Shannon und Weaver ist oft kritisiert worden, und zwar dahingehend, dass es viel zu einseitig die Realität der Kommunikation aus einem rein technischen Blickwinkel beschreiben würde. Kommunikation, so die Kritiker, könne man nicht auf einen technischen Vorgang verkürzen. Um diesen Mangel zu überwinden, gab es zahlreiche Versuche, das Shannon-Weaver-Modell auf eine allgemeinere Grundlage zu stellen. Ein Beispiel ist das **Badura-Modell**.

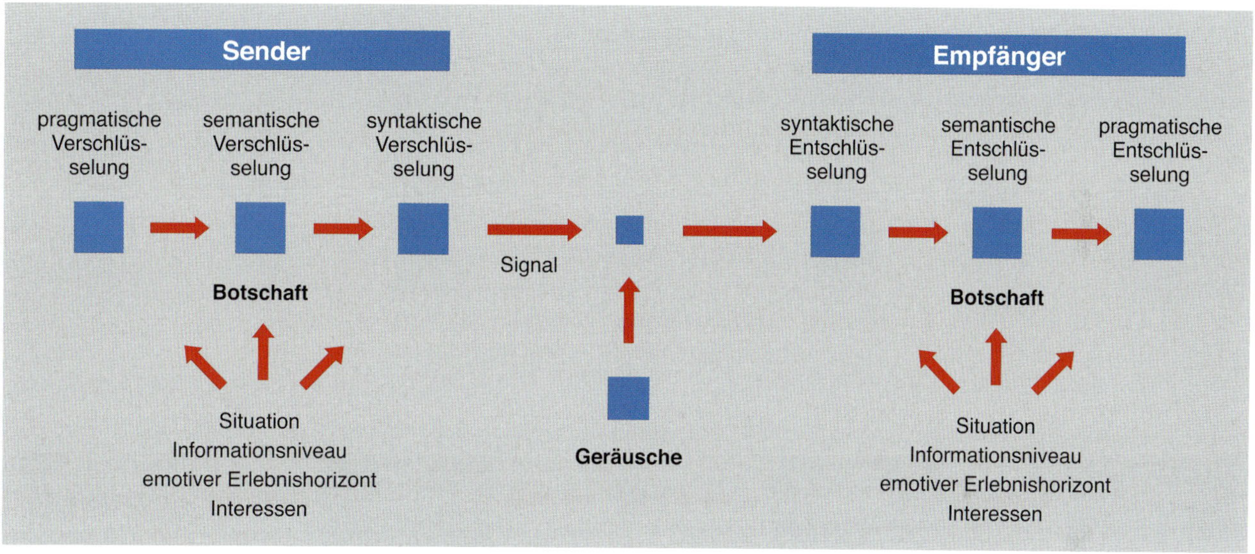

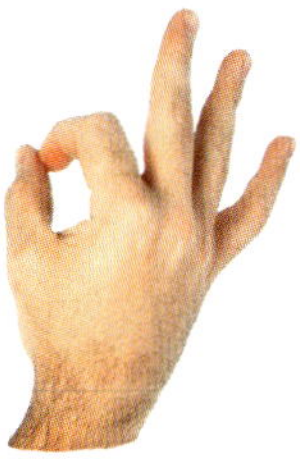

Das Modell erweitert die rein technische Sichtweise des Shannon-Weaver-Modells in Richtung der **menschlichen Komponente**. Es macht deutlich, dass zur **Verständigung** zwischen Menschen mehr gehört als eine perfekte Technik. Für eine wirkliche Verständigung ist es notwendig, dass die übermittelten Zeichen durch den Kommunikator, der die Zeichen verschlüsselt, und den Rezipienten, der sie wieder entschlüsselt, gleich interpretiert werden. **Drei Verständigungsebenen** sind zu unterscheiden:

- Syntaktische Ebene: Die Zeichen werden nach bestimmten grammatischen Regeln zusammengeführt.
- Semantische Ebene: Die Zeichen haben eine Bedeutung bzw. einen Sinngehalt.
- Pragmatische Ebene: Die Zeichen sind auf der Ebene der zwischenmenschlichen Beziehungen zu sehen.

Verständigung bzw. störungsfreie Kommunikation kommt nach dieser Modellvorstellung nur dann zustande, wenn die Kommunikationspartner auf allen drei Ebenen zu gleichen Interpretationen gelangen. Zusätzlich ist es erforderlich, dass nicht noch die sog. „Randbedingungen" einen Strich durch die Rechnung machen. Als Randbedingungen sind zu nennen: die Situation, in der die Kommunikation stattfindet (daheim, unterwegs), das Informationsniveau (Welcher Informationsgehalt? Wie verständlich?), der Erlebnishorizont (Welche Gefühle werden ausgelöst?) und die Interessen der Beteiligten (Wie stark spricht das Thema an?).

Feldschema von Maletzke

Wesentlich differenzierter als in der Lasswell-Formel stellte **Maletzke** 1963 die Beziehungen im Kommunikationsprozess dar ❶. Neu ist die Beschreibung der Kommunikation als ein wechselseitiger Vorgang, nach dem sich alle Bausteine in einer gegenseitigen Abhängigkeit befinden. Bei Lasswell war die Vorstellung vorherrschend, dass Kommunikation ein eher einseitig geprägter Vorgang vom Kommunikator zum Rezipienten sei, eine Art „Einbahnstraße". Diese (zu) enge Sicht wird nun aufgehoben.

❶ Gerhard Maletzke, 1922 – 2010, prominenter Kommunikationswissenschaftler, lebte in Stuttgart

Das Modell bezieht sich vorrangig auf die Massenkommunikation.

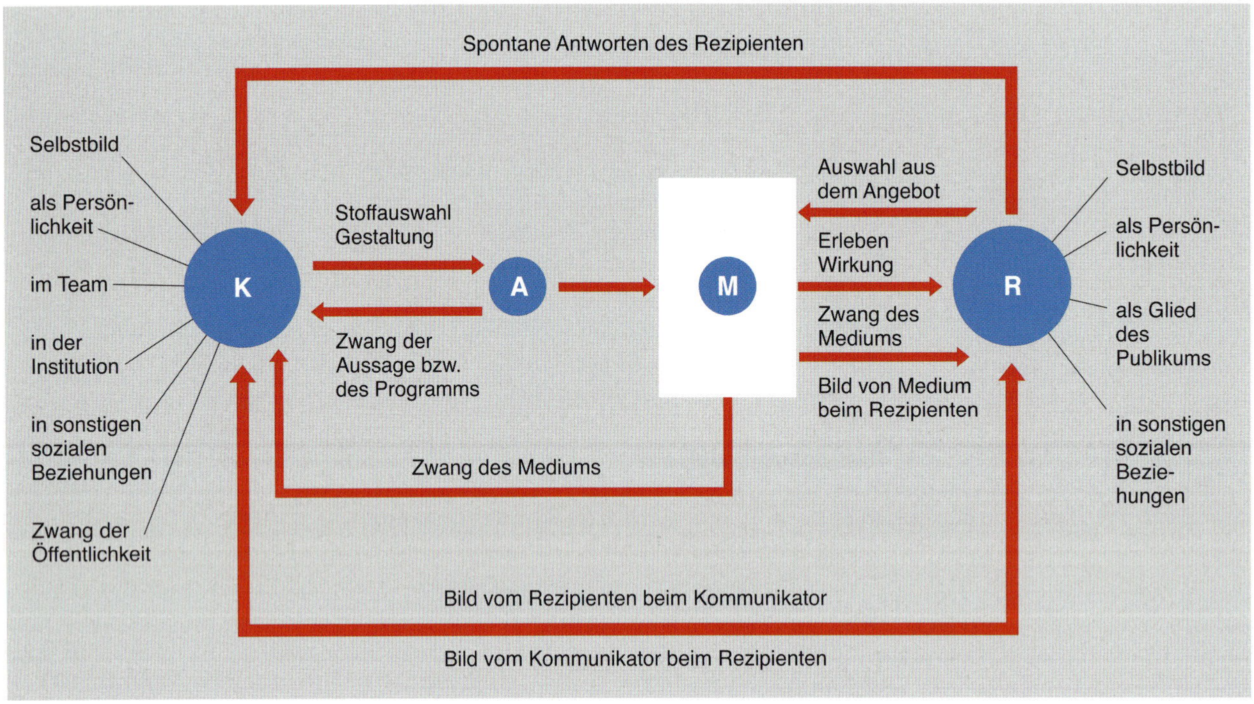

Das Modell führt vor Augen, dass sowohl der Kommunikator als auch der Rezipient keine Einzelwesen sind, sondern in einer **wechselseitigen Beziehung** zueinander stehen. Beide machen sich ein Bild voneinander, und jeder der beiden geht zudem mit ganz bestimmten Vorprägungen (z. B. Bild von sich selbst, Persönlichkeitsmerkmale) in den Kommunikationsvorgang hinein. Das **Zusammenspiel** von **Kommunikator** und **Rezipient** wird dabei von den verschiedensten Zwängen beeinflusst:

- Zwang für den Kommunikator: Er kann unter dem Druck der Öffentlichkeit stehen.
- Zwang der Aussage: Der Kommunikator äußert sich öffentlich und kann im Hinblick auf seine Aussagen beim Wort genommen werden.
- Zwang des Mediums: Es unterliegt ganz bestimmten dramaturgischen und technisch-organisatorischen Voraussetzungen, die das, was produziert und dargestellt werden soll, maßgeblich beeinflussen.
- Zwang für den Rezipienten: Die Art des Mediums bestimmt darüber, in welcher Form das Dargebotene aufgenommen werden muss.

Aufgaben und Übungen, Literaturhinweise

Aufgaben und Übungen

1. Beobachten Sie Ihr eigenes Medienverhalten, indem Sie eine Woche lang über Ihren Medienkonsum Buch führen. Machen Sie dieses in der Form, dass Sie am Ende jedes einzelnen Tages aufzeichnen, wie lange Sie welches Medium genutzt haben. Fertigen Sie eine Übersicht an.
2. Analysieren Sie ein Gespräch zwischen zwei Menschen, das Sie selbst erlebt haben mit dem Konzept der „Vier Seiten einer Nachricht".
3. Analysieren Sie eine Konfliktsituation zwischen zwei Menschen, die Sie selbst erlebt haben, darauf hin, wie die sprachliche Kommunikation abgelaufen ist.
4. Erstellen Sie ein Konzept für eine Kurz-Präsentation vor einer Gruppe, bei der Sie Technik einsetzen sollen.
5. Erstellen Sie einen kurzen Text von wenigen Zeilen über einen interessanten Sachverhalt. Suchen Sie nach einem Bild, mit dem Sie diesen Text möglichst treffend illustrieren können.
6. Erstellen Sie das Konzept für eine Rede, die Sie beim runden Geburtstag Ihres Vaters vor der Verwandtschaft und dem Freundeskreis der Familie halten sollen.
7. Zeigen Sie für ein Wirtschaftsunternehmen Ihrer Wahl, welche Instrumente der Unternehmenskommunikation diese Unternehmen hauptsächlich einsetzt.
8. Sammeln Sie zehn Beispiele zur Lasswell-Formel und fertigen Sie eine Übersicht über die fünf Stufen der Lasswell-Formel an.

Literaturhinweise

Beck, Klaus: Kommunikationswissenschaft, Konstanz 2007 (UVK)

Bentele, Günter/*Brosius*, Hans-Bernd/*Jarren*, Otfried (Hrsg.): Lexikon Kommunikations- und Medienwissenschaft, Wiesbaden 2006 (VS Verlag)

Bruhn, Manfred: Unternehmens- und Marketingkommunikation, München 2005 (Vahlen)

Burkart, Roland: Kommunikationswissenschaft, 4. Aufl., Wien, Köln, Weimar 2002 (Böhlau)

Hartig, Matthias: Erfolgsorientierte Kommunikation, Tübingen, Basel 1997 (A. Francke)

Hartmann, Frank: Medien und Kommunikation, Wien 2008 (Fakultas)

Hasebrook, Joachim: Multimedia-Psychologie, Heidelberg, Berlin, Oxford 1995 (Spektrum)

Hickethier, Knut: Einführung in die Medienwissenschaft, 2. Aufl., Stuttgart 2010 (J. B. Metzler)

Hillebrecht, Steffen: Kommunikation und Medien. Ein Arbeitsbuch für Hochschule und Praxis, Gernsbach 2009 (Deutscher Betriebswirte-Verlag)

Jarren, Otfried/*Bonfadelli*, Heinz (Hrsg.): Einführung in die Publizistikwissenschaft, Bern, Stuttgart, Wien 2001 (Haupt)

Kübler, Hans-Dieter: Mediale Kommunikation, Tübingen 2000 (Niemeyer)

Kübler, Hans-Dieter: Medien und Massenkommunikation, Köln 2003 (LIT)

Kunczik, Michael/*Zipfel*, Astrid: Publizistik, Köln 2001 (Böhlau)

Kroeber-Riel, Werner: Bildkommunikation, München 1993 (Vahlen)

Kroeber-Riel, Werner/*Esch*, Franz-Rudolf: Strategie und Technik der Werbung, 6. Aufl., Stuttgart 2004 (Kohlhammer)
Ludes, Peter: Einführung in die Medienwissenschaft, Berlin 1998 (Erich Schmidt Verlag)
Maletzke, Gerhard: Kommunikationswissenschaft im Überblick, Opladen, Wiesbaden 1998 (Westdeutscher Verlag)
Mast, Claudia (Hrsg.): ABC des Journalismus, 10. Aufl., Konstanz 2004 (UVK)
Mast, Claudia: Unternehmenskommunikation, 3. Aufl., Stuttgart 2008 (Lucius & Lucius)
Merten, Klaus/*Schmidt*, Siegfried J./*Weischenberg*, Siegfried (Hrsg.): Die Wirklichkeit der Medien, Opladen 1994 (Westdeutscher Verlag)
Noelle-Neumann, Elisabeth/*Schulz*, Winfried/*Wilke*, Jürgen (Hrsg.): Fischer Lexikon Publizistik Massenkommunikation, Frankfurt am Main 2009 (Fischer Taschenbuch Verlag)
Ordolff, Martin: Fernsehjournalismus, Konstanz 2005 (UVK)
Paus-Hasebrink, Ingrid/*Woelke*, Jens/*Bichler*, Michelle/*Pluschkowitz*, Alois: Einführung in die Audiovisuelle Kommunikation, München, Wien 2006 (Oldenbourg)
Plake, Klaus: Handbuch Fernsehforschung, Wiesbaden 2004 (VS Verlag)
Rota, Franco P./*Fuchs*, Wolfgang: Lexikon Public Relations, München 2007 (Beck Wirtschaftsberater im dtv)
Schmidt, Siegfried J./*Zurstiege*, Guido: Kommunikationswissenschaft, Reinbek bei Hamburg 2007 (Rowohlt)
Schneider, Wolf/*Raue*, Paul-Josef: Das neue Handbuch des Journalismus und des Online-Journalismus, Reinbek bei Hamburg 2012 (Rowohlt)
Schuhmann, Georg: Rhetorik und Kommunikation, 2. Aufl., Haan-Gruiten 2008 (Europa-Lehrmittel)
Schulz von Thun, Friedemann: Miteinander reden, 3 Bände, Reinbek bei Hamburg 1981, 1992 (Rowohlt)
Schulz von Thun, Friedemann/*Ruppel*, Johannes/*Stratmann*, Roswitha: Miteinander reden: Kommunikationspsychologie für Führungskräfte, Reinbek bei Hamburg 2000 (Rowohlt)
Stöber, Rudolf: Kommunikations- und Medienwissenschaften, München 2008 (C. H. Beck)
Watzlawick, Paul/*Beavin*, Janet H./*Jackson*, Don D.: Menschliche Kommunikation, 12. Aufl., Bern 2011 (Hans Huber)
Wersig, Gernot: Einführung in die Publizistik- und Kommunikationswissenschaft, Baden-Baden 2009 (Nomos)
Weischenberg, Siegfried/*Kleinsteuber*, Hans J./*Pörksen*, Bernhard (Hrsg.): Handbuch Journalismus und Medien, Konstanz 2005 (UVK)
Winter, Carsten/*Hepp*, Andreas/*Krotz*, Friedrich (Hrsg.): Theorien der Kommunikations- und Medienwissenschaft, Wiesbaden 2008 (VS Verlag)

2 Medien im Kommunikationsprozess

Webcode: A0200

Für weitere Infos zu diesem Kapitel mit dem Smartphone einfach QR-Code scannen oder auf www.medien-verstehen.de den Webcode eingeben.

Nach der Lasswell-Formel („Wer sagt was über welchen Kanal zu wem mit welcher Wirkung?") lässt sich der Kommunikationsprozess und damit die Rolle der Medien sehr anschaulich mit den folgenden fünf Bausteinen charakterisieren, die in diesem Kapitel näher beleuchtet werden: (1) Kommunikatoren, (2) Inhalte, (3) Transportwege, (4) Rezipienten und (5) Wirkungen.

2.1 Kommunikatoren

Ein **Kommunikator** ist eine Person, die einer anderen Person, mehreren oder vielen anderen Personen etwas mitteilen will. Diese Mitteilung produziert er selber wie z. B. bei einem Telefongespräch oder er lässt sie in seinem Auftrag produzieren wie z. B. ein Redakteur einer Zeitung durch den Auftrag an einen Reporter. Statt Kommunikator spricht man auch von **Sender**, **Quelle** oder **Produzent**. Das **Erscheinungsbild** eines Kommunikators ist vielschichtig. Ein Kommunikator kann z. B. sein:

- Ein verliebter Mann, der einer Frau im persönlichen Gespräch („face to face") mitteilt, dass er sie hübsch findet.
- Eine junge Mutter, die einer anderen jungen Mutter über das Telefon mitteilt, dass der Kindergarten am nächsten Morgen eine Stunde später beginnt.
- Ein Schüler, der eine Mitschülerin per E-Mail bittet, ihr bei den Hausaufgaben zu helfen.
- Ein E-Commerce-Experte, der vor hundert Leuten einen Fachvortrag zum Thema „Vermarktung von Handwerksleistungen im Internet-Zeitalter" hält.
- Ein Physiklehrer, der die Funktionsweise des elektrischen Stroms erklärt.
- Ein Pfarrer, der am Sonntag im Gottesdienst die Predigt hält.
- Ein Sportjournalist, der über das Fußballspiel in der Lokalzeitung berichtet.
- Ein verärgerter Betroffener, der einen Leserbrief wegen der nicht gebauten Umgehungsstraße schreibt.
- Ein Moderator, der in MTV eine Musiksendung „fährt".
- Ein Reporter, der vom Kirchentag in Stuttgart im Radio berichtet.
- Die Geschäftsleitung von der Daimler AG, die ihren Verkäufern über Business TV vermittelt, welche Chancen mit dem Angebot von Mercedes-Mountain-Bikes verbunden sind.
- Ein Kommentator des WDR, der sich im Fernsehen zur anstehenden Steuerreform äußert.
- Der Bundespräsident, der die Neujahrsansprache hält.

Alle genannten Beispiele gehen davon aus, dass es sich bei einem Kommunikator um eine **Einzelperson** handelt. Der Begriff ist aber weiter zu fassen. In der Massenkommunikation sind normalerweise eine ganze Reihe von Personen damit beschäftigt, Aussagen auszuwählen, zu gestalten, zu produzieren und zu verbreiten. Man denke in diesem Zusammenhang an einen Fernseh- oder Radiosender oder an einen Zeitungsverlag. Als „Kommunikator" ist in diesem Fall das ganze **Team von Personen** anzusehen, die das Medienprodukt auf den Weg gebracht haben ❶.

❶ Die wissenschaftliche Beschäftigung mit dem Bereich Kommunikator nennt man **Kommunikatorforschung**.

Man kann noch weiter gehen und als Kommunikator sogar die ganze **Institution** bezeichnen, die für die Herstellung und Vermittlung von Inhalten (Aussagen, Nachrichten, Botschaften) zuständig ist. In diesem Sinne ist dann eine Fernsehanstalt, eine Radiostation oder ein Zeitungsverlag als Kommunikator zu verstehen.

Es ist zweckmäßig, die Kommunikatoren auch danach zu unterscheiden, ob sie die Kommunikation als ihren **Geschäftszweck** verstehen, wie dies bei den Medienunternehmen der Fall ist, oder ob Kommunikation nur als **Mittel zum Zweck** dient, um andere Ziele zu erreichen, wie es beispielsweise bei Wirtschaftsunternehmen der Fall ist, die Werbung betreiben. Die nachfolgende Übersicht verdeutlicht den Zusammenhang:

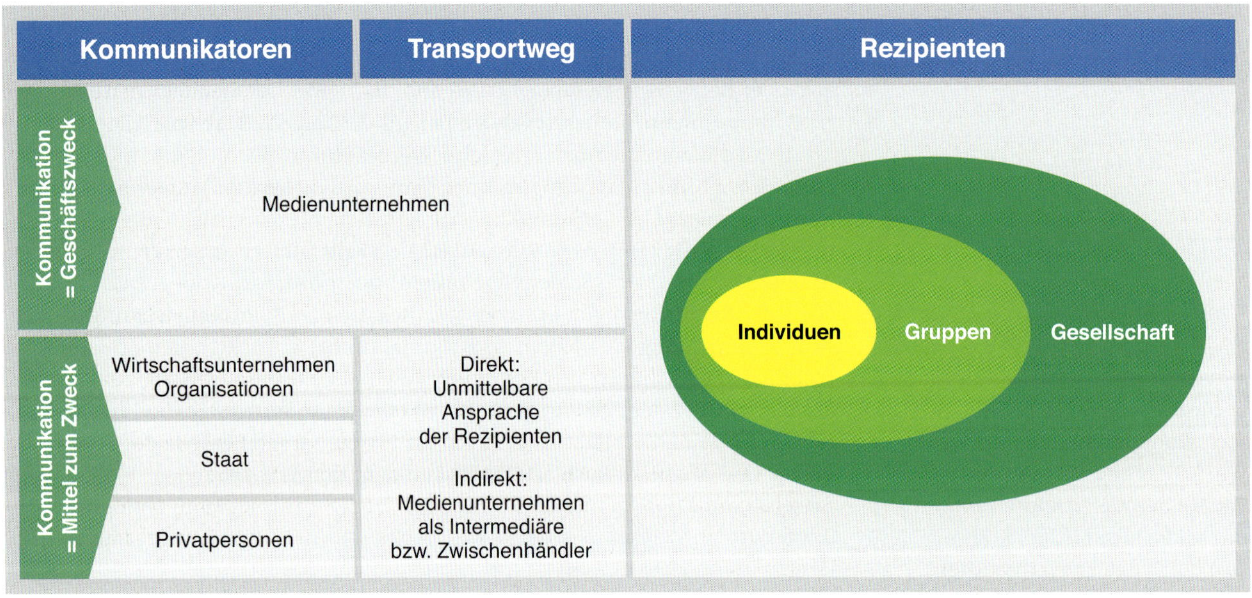

Die **Medienunternehmen** – also Verlage oder Rundfunkunternehmen – betreiben Kommunikation als Geschäftszweck. Ihr erklärtes Ziel ist es, Rezipienten mit Medienprodukten zu bedienen und tun dies unter Einsatz aller dafür notwendiger Technik für Produktion und Transport.

Demgegenüber ist die mediale Ansprache von Rezipienten für **Wirtschaftsunternehmen, Organisationen,** den **Staat** oder für **Privatpersonen** lediglich ein Mittel zum Zweck, etwa um den Absatz der Produkte zu fördern oder dem Staatsbürger die Möglichkeit zu geben, über das Internet Antragsformulare bequem abrufbar zu machen. In diesem Fall fungieren die Medien lediglich als Transporteure, die den genannten Kommunikatoren dabei helfen, ihre Botschaften an die Rezipienten zu überbringen.

Als **Rezipienten** kommen unterschiedliche Adressaten in Frage: es können Einzelpersonen sein, **Gruppen** oder die ganze **Gesellschaft**. Im privaten E-Mail-Verkehr z. B. einsteht eine Verbindung von Individuen und Privatpersonen, eine Fernsehsendung des ZDF richtet sich an die ganze Gesellschaft.

2.1.1 Medienunternehmen

Medienunternehmen sind Einrichtungen, die sich zum Ziel setzen, Inhalte (Botschaften, „**Content**") zu produzieren, zu bündeln (zu „paketieren") und zu verbreiten (zu „publizieren"). Das sind vor allem die Verlage und Rundfunkanstalten als **originäre Medienunternehmen**. Nicht zu vernachlässigen sind aber auch die Zulieferer, Vermittler und Unterstützer wie Produktionsunternehmen, Agenturen, Kabel- und Satellitenbetreiber, Druckereien, Online-Dienste, Kinos oder Markt- und Meinungsforschungsinstitute. Sie sind unverzichtbare Dienstleister und können als **sekundäre Medienunternehmen** bezeichnet werden.

Die vielfältige Welt der Medienunternehmen lässt sich nach unterschiedlichen Aspekten beschreiben:

- Nach der **Betriebsgröße** gibt es große bzw. sehr große Medienunternehmen (z. B. Bertelsmann, Holtzbrinck), mittlere (z. B. Bauer-Verlag) oder kleinere bzw. kleine Medienunternehmen (z. B. eine Werbeagentur mit 10 Beschäftigten).
- Nach dem **räumlichen Bezugsrahmen** kann man international agierende Medienunternehmen (z. B. Springer-Konzern, RTL-Group), nationale Medienunternehmen (z. B. ARD, ZDF), regionale und lokale Medienunternehmen (z. B. Regio TV, Antenne Bayern, Radio Schleswig-Holstein) unterscheiden.
- Nach der **Rechtsform** gibt es Aktiengesellschaften (z. B. ProSiebenSat.1 Media AG), Kommanditgesellschaften (z. B. Burda: GmbH & Co. KG), den öffentlich-rechtlichen gemeinnützigen Rundfunk (ARD, ZDF) u.a.m.
- Nach dem **Grad der Abhängigkeit** gibt es eine breite Spannweite zwischen autonomen Medienunternehmen (z. B. ein Familienunternehmen wie der Europa-Verlag, in dem dieses Buch erscheint) und dem Konzernverbund (z. B. der Bertelsmann-Konzern mit der RTL Group, Gruner+Jahr, Random House und Arvato).

❶ Die Darstellung zeigt die sog. „überbetriebliche mediale Wertschöpfungskette". Den Prozess der Wertschöpfung von der ersten Idee bis zum Konsum durch den Endverbraucher bezeichnet man auch als die **vertikale Richtung** der Wertschöpfung.

Eine besonders wichtige Unterscheidung der Medienunternehmen ergibt sich aus deren **Stellung in der medialen Wertschöpfungskette**. Diese lässt sich durch sieben Stufen charakterisieren (Quelle: Gläser 2010, S. 349) ❶:

Stufe 1	Stufe 2	Stufe 3	Stufe 4	Stufe 5	Stufe 6	Stufe 7
Initiierung	**Beschaffung**	**Herstellung**	**Packaging**	**Vervielfältigung**	**Distribution**	**Nutzung**
Auftraggeber Beauftragung und Veranlassung der Content-Erstellung	Beschaffung von fertigem Content aus internen und externen Archiven	Konzeption Kreation Produktion von neuem Content	Bündelung von Content zu vermarktungsfähigen Produkten	Bereitstellung der Produkte in der vom Markt benötigten Anzahl	Logistik Vertrieb Handel (Groß-, Zwischen- und Einzelhandel) Technische Infrastruktur	Konsum durch Mediennutzer Content im Geschäftsprozess von Unternehmen
Initiierung von Content	**Generierung von Content**			**Vertrieb und Vermarktung von Content**		**Nutzung von Content**

Sortiert man die Medienunternehmen nach den sieben Stufen des medialen Wertschöpfungsprozesses, so ergibt sich folgendes Bild (Quelle: Gläser 2010, S. 74):

Stufe 1: Initiierung	Stufe 2: Beschaffung	Stufe 3: Herstellung	Stufe 4: Packaging	Stufe 5: Vervielfältigung	Stufe 6: Distribution	Stufe 7: Verwendung
Verlage Rundfunk-Unternehmen privat, öffentlich-rechtlich Wirtschaftsunternehmen Öffentliche Institutionen	Beschaffungsabteilungen von Verlagen und Rundfunkunternehmen Archive Programmhändler Akquisition von Werbung	Konzeption: Autoren (fest, frei), Grafiker, Kreativ-Agenturen Produktionsbetriebe von Verlagen und Rundfunkunternehmen Produktionsunternehmen: Tonstudios, Film, Postproduction, Synchronisation, Foto, Werbefilm, Computer, Animation Agenturen: Nachrichten, Bild, Ton, Pressedienste	Redaktionsbetriebe von Verlagen und Rundfunkunternehmen Programmplanungsabteilungen Marketing-Abteilungen, Markt- und Meinungsforschung Consulting	Druckereien, Papierhersteller Vervielfältigung von Bild- und Tonträgern Kopierwerke Technische Abteilungen oder Dienstleister zum Betrieb von Sendern	Buchhandel, Zeitungs- und Zeitschriftenhandel Betreiber von Terrestrik, Kabelnetzen, Satelliten, Internet-Provider Mobilfunk-Anbieter Filmverleiher, Videotheken Media-, PR-Agenturen Messeveranstalter	Konsumenten: Leser, Hörer, Zuschauer, User Wirtschaftsunternehmen, Nutzung für interne Zwecke: Mitarbeiter-Kommunikation Nutzung für externe Zwecke: Marketing Anbieter von technischer Ausstattung, End-User-Geräte, Hardware, Software

Es ist festzustellen, dass verschiedene Unternehmen sich nur auf einer **einzigen Stufe** betätigen, andere aber „breiter aufgestellt" sind und sich auf **zwei oder mehreren Stufen** bewegen. Das Interesse großer Konzerne ist unverkennbar, auf möglichst vielen oder gar auf allen Wertschöpfungsstufen „mitzumischen", sei es direkt und aktiv, sei es über Kooperationen.

Typische „Ein-Stufen-Akteure" sind z. B. Presseagenturen wie die Deutsche Presseagentur „dpa" (Stufe 3), das Film- und TV-Produktionsunternehmen „GrundyUFA" (Stufe 4) oder der Satellitenbetreiber „Astra" (Stufe 6). Beispiele für „Mehr-Stufen-Akteure" sind die großen Verlage wie z. B. die „Verlagsgruppe Georg von Holtzbrinck", die im Grunde auf allen sieben Stufen aktiv ist, oder ein Rundfunk-Unternehmen wie die „RTL Group", die sich auf den Stufen 1 bis 4 – insbesondere den Stufen 3 und 4 – betätigt.

RTL ist Teil des Bertelsmann-Konzerns und ein gutes Beispiel dafür, dass noch erheblich **komplexere Geschäftsmodelle** im Bereich der Medien eine Rolle spielen. So ist Bertelsmann innerhalb der Medien mit dem Verlag Gruner+Jahr (weltweit) vertreten (u. a. mit den Zeitschriften „Stern", „GEO", „Motorpresse", „Brigitte"), mit der RTL Group europaweit im TV- und Radiobereich (Betreiber von 40 TV-Sendern und 33 Radiostationen in Europa), mit Arvato im Bereich von Druck, Medien- und Kommunikationsservice und mit Random House im Buchsegment (Bücher, Hörbücher, E-Books; Random House – „die international führende Publikumsverlagsgruppe").

Verlage

Verlage sind Medienunternehmen, die dafür sorgen, dass die geistigen Leistungen von Urhebern einem breiteren Publikum zugänglich gemacht werden können ❶. Dazu sind verschiedene **Aktivitäten** erforderlich:

❶ „Die Begriffe Verlag und Verleger gehen zurück auf das spätmittelhochdeutsche verlegen im Sinne von Geld auslegen, auf seine Rechnung nehmen. Ein Verleger war demnach ein Unternehmer, der auf Grund seiner Marktkenntnisse und finanziellen Möglichkeiten Geld vorlegen konnte, um andere Handwerker mit der Herstellung von Waren beauftragen zu können" (Breyer-Mayländer 2001, S. 17).

- Akquisition: Suche und Identifikation von interessanten Inhalten
- Lektorat: Betreuung und Förderung von Autoren
- Redaktion: Aufbereitung der Inhalte zu vermarktungsfähigen Produkten
- Gestaltung: Ästhetische und technische Produktgestaltung
- Produktion: Herstellung und Vervielfältigung der Produkte
- Finanzierung: Volle oder teilweise Finanzierung, z. B. durch Gewährung von Vorschüssen an Autoren Vorschüsse oder Zahlung von Gehältern

Traditionell stehen im Zentrum der Verlagsbranche die **Printprodukte**, also Zeitungen, Zeitschriften und Bücher. Angesichts zunehmender Internetnutzung und nachlassendem Konsum von Druckprodukten sind die Verlage aber gezwungen, sich in die elektronischen Geschäftsfelder hinein zu bewegen und ihre bisherigen Grenzen zu überschreiten, was sie auch intensiv tun: So bringen sie ihre Printausgabe der Tageszeitung auch als elektronisches 1:1-Internetangebot (E-Paper), sie bieten eigenständige elektronische „Presse"-Produkte an (z. B. die Netzeitung – eine Zeitung, deren Inhalte sich auf die persönlichen Interessen des Lesers zuschneiden lassen), sie verlegen Hörbücher oder stellen Bewegtbildangebote auf ihre Websites mit dem Ziel, den Lesern einen Zusatznutzen zu bieten und sie „bei der Stange zu halten".

Verlage besonderer Art finden sich im Musikbereich: die **Musikverlage** („Labels"). Sie sind dazu da, Werke der Musik zu verbreiten und werden üblicherweise in Verlage der Unterhaltungsmusik (U-Verlage) und Verlage der ernsten Musik (E-Verlage) unterschieden. Erstere erzielen den Hauptteil ihrer Umsätze aus der Verwertung von Musik in Radio, TV, Werbung, Film und auf der Bühne („Aufführungsrechte") oder durch Abgaben der Tonträgerhersteller („mechanische Rechte"). Auch Umsätze aus neuen Medien wie Klingeltönen, Online-Musik und Musik in Computerspielen wird zunehmend relevant. Im Gegensatz dazu erwirtschaften die E-Musikverlage den Großteil ihrer Umsätze aus Notendruck und Papiergeschäft („**Musikalien**").

Verlage sind **Tendenzbetriebe**. Damit ist gemeint, dass Verlage das Recht haben, ihre publizierten Inhalte in eine bestimmte weltanschaulich-politische Richtung zu bringen, wie es etwa in der Tagespresse geschieht: Die „Süddeutsche Zeitung", die Wochenzeitung „Die Zeit" oder die „taz" gelten als „links", die Zeitungen „Die Welt" oder die „Frankfurter Allgemeine Zeitung" als „rechts". Nach § 118 Betriebsverfassungsgesetz (BetrVG) kann die Verlagsleitung einen solchen Tendenzschutz durchsetzen, ohne dass sich die Mitarbeiter oder die Gewerkschaften dagegen wehren können. Diesen besonderen Schutz der Tendenz genießen neben den Verlagen z. B. auch Parteien, Wirtschaftsverbände, Kirchen, Einrichtungen mit konfessioneller Zielsetzung, Bildungseinrichtungen oder Theater.

Öffentlich-rechtliche Rundfunkanstalten

In Deutschland gibt es das sog. **duale Rundfunksystem**, nach dem neben den öffentlich-rechtlichen Rundfunkanstalten auch private Veranstalter zugelassen sind. Im Hörfunk dominiert deutlich der öffentliche Rundfunk, während im Fernsehen sich öffentliche und private Anbieter in ihrer wirtschaftlichen Bedeutung in etwa die Waage halten.

Die öffentlich-rechtlichen Rundfunkanstalten wurden nach dem 2. Weltkrieg von den Alliierten als eine öffentliche und gemeinnützige Einrichtung gegründet, um sicher zu stellen, dass der Rundfunk nicht noch einmal wie im Dritten Reich in staatliche Hände gelangt und für Propagandazwecke missbraucht werden kann.

Eigentümerin des öffentlichen Rundfunks ist die **Gesellschaft**, die in den Aufsichtsorganen (Rundfunkrat, Verwaltungsrat, Fernsehrat) in Form der sog. gesellschaftlich relevanten Gruppen vertreten. Das heißt, dass sich die Aufsichts- und Kontrollorgane der Sender durch Vertreter aus allen gesellschaftlich wichtigen Gruppen zusammensetzen. Dort sind zwar auch Parteien und staatliche Organe vertreten, aber nur in untergeordnetem Maße.

Um die **Staatsunabhängigkeit** noch zu unterstreichen, erfolgt die **Finanzierung** nicht durch Steuern, sondern durch einen Beitrag, der von allen Gerätebesitzern zu entrichten ist („Rundfunkgebühr"). Es gibt also keine staatlichen Zahlungen (Subventionen) an die öffentlich-rechtlichen Rundfunkanstalten. Sie finanzieren sich völlig außerhalb der staatlichen Budgets. Der öffentlich-rechtliche Rundfunk ist also keine staatliche, sondern eine **öffentliche Einrichtung**. Die **gemeinnützige Konstruktion** hat neben der dargestellten Staatsunabhängigkeit auch das Ziel, den öffentlichen Rundfunk von Einflussnahmen der Wirtschaft und der Verbände unabhängig zu machen. Die Finanzierung aus Werbung macht nur einen kleinen Teil der Gesamteinnahmen aus (ca. 5 %).

➲ **Der öffentlich-rechtliche Rundfunk ist keine staatliche, sondern eine öffentliche Einrichtung! Er ist gemeinnützig und finanziert sich durch Beitragszahlungen der Hörer und Zuschauer.**

Als Fazit kann festgehalten werden, dass der öffentlich-rechtliche Rundfunk als eine unabhängige Einrichtung konstruiert ist, unabhängig von Staat, Wirtschaft und Interessensverbänden.

➲ **Öffentlich-rechtlicher Rundfunk ist freier Rundfunk und erfüllt einen von der Gesellschaft auferlegten Programmauftrag.**

Im übrigen ist in Deutschland die Organisation des Rundfunks gemäß der föderativen Struktur eine Angelegenheit der **Länder**. Alle Fragen, die **ARD** und **ZDF** betreffen, sind in den Länderparlamenten zu lösen und nicht über den Bund. Die Rechtsgrundlagen des öffentlich-rechtlichen Rundfunks sind in zahlreichen Urteilen des Bundesverfassungsgerichts gefestigt worden.

Heute ist das Radio nicht mehr auf das „gute alte“ UKW beschränkt, sondern neue Verteilungswege werden immer wichtiger. Zu nennen sind insbesondere Satelliten und das Internet. Da die Digitalisierung auch im Radio Einzug hält, wird Zug um Zug auch die Übertragung im Digitalstandard DAB+ eingeführt. Eine Übersicht über die in Deutschland verfügbaren Radioangebote gibt die nachfolgende Übersicht:

Private Programme	UKW	Satellit	DAB+[1]	Internet[2]
bundesweite Programme	0	14	4 [6]	188
gesamt 2011	0	14	4 [6]	188

Öffentlich-rechtliche Programme	UKW	Satellit	DAB+[1]	Internet[2]
bundesweite Programme	2	0	1 [2]	0
gesamt 2011	2	0	1 [2]	0

Programme in den Ländern	UKW landesweit	UKW lokal	DAB[1]	gesamt
Baden-Württemberg	1	16	0	17
Bayern	1	64	14 [5]	79
Berlin/Brandenburg[3]	18	6	0 [2]	24
Bremen	2	1	0	3
Hamburg/Schleswig-Holst.	7	0	0	7
Hessen	5	0	0 [1]	5
Mecklenburg-Vorp.	2	2	0	4
Niedersachsen[3]	3	1	0	4
Nordrhein-Westfalen[4]	1	44	0 [1]	45
Rheinland-Pfalz	3	13	0	16
Saarland	1	6	0 [1]	7
Sachsen[3]	4	15	0	19
Sachsen-Anhalt	4	0	0 [4]	4
Thüringen	3	0	0	3
gesamt 2011	55	168	14 [14]	237

Landesrundfunkanstalten	UKW landesweit	DAB[1]	gesamt
BR (Bayern)	5	5 [5]	10
hr (Hessen)	6	0 [6]	6
MDR (SN, ST, TH)	8	1 [5]	9
NDR (HH, MV, SH, NS)	7	2 [6]	9
RB (Bremen)	2	0	2
RBB (BE, BB)	6	0 [7]	6
SR (Saarland)	4	0 [5]	4
SWR (BW, RP)	7	1 [5]	8
WDR (NRW)	5	4 [3]	9
Gemeinschafts-programme[5]	2	1	3
gesamt 2011	52	14 [42]	66

1 Gezählt werden nur terrestrisch originär über DAB/DAB+ verbreitete Programme; in Klammern: Zahl der Programme, mit Simulcastausstrahlung über DAB und UKW.
2 181 Originäre Webradios plus 7 bundesweite Lizenznehmer mit Verbreitung über Internet und in einzelnen Kabelnetzen
3 Bei den landesweiten Sendern in Berlin-Brandenburg sind 3 Auslandsprogramme mitgezählt; zusätzlich über Mittelwelle in Berlin-Brandenburg, Sachsen, Niedersachsen: Stimme Russlands über DVB-T in Berlin-Brandenburg originär 1 simulcast 6 Programme, in Sachsen simulcast 4 Programme
4 landesweit: radio NRW – Mantelprogramm von 44 Lokalradios
5 Gemeinschaftsprogramme über UKW: Funkhaus Europa (WDR, RB, RBB, SWR International, Nordwestradio, (RB, NDR); über DAB: Antenne Saar (SR, SWR)

In mehreren Ländern verbreitete Programme zählen in der Summe nur einfach.

Stand: 31. Dezember 2011, Quelle: Landesmedienanstalten

Agenturen

Agenturen spielen bei den Medien eine große Rolle. Bekanntestes Beispiel sind die **Nachrichtenagenturen** wie die „dpa“, die in Eigenregie Berichte und Reportagen erzeugen, die sie an die Verlage und Rundfunksender verkaufen. Eine Nachrichtenagentur ist insofern ein Zulieferer von Inhalten und unterstützt die Kernaufgaben von (primären) Medienunternehmen.

Die **Agenturlandschaft** im Bereich der Medien ist äußerst bunt und vielfältig ❶. So gibt es z. B. Bildagenturen, Werbeagenturen, Designagenturen, Künstler-Agenturen, PR-Agenturen, Event-Agenturen, Mediaagenturen, Promotion-Agenturen, Model-Agenturen, Casting-Agenturen, Presseagenturen, Nachrichtenagenturen, Messeagenturen, Sponsoring-Agenturen, Pitch-Agenturen. Allen diesen Agenturen ist gemeinsam, dass sie sich als Dienstleister verstehen, die als Auftragnehmer die Interessen von bestimmten Kunden (Auftraggeber) vertreten oder vermitteln. Für diese Arbeit erhalten sie eine zuvor vereinbarte Vergütung.

❶ Agenturen spielen nicht nur im Bereich der Medien eine große Rolle, sondern sind immer dann präsent, wenn es um die Vertretung von Interessen geht. Zum Beispiel werden die Interessen von Arbeitslosen durch die „Agentur für Arbeit“ vertreten, die Interessen von Kapitalanlegern durch „Rating-Agenturen“ oder die Interessen der gesamten Bevölkerung durch die „Europäische Umweltagentur“ oder die „Bundesnetzagentur“.

Besonders hervorzuheben sind **Agenturen**, die im Bereich der **Werbung** tätig sind, wobei **Werbeagenturen** und **Mediaagenturen** zu unterscheiden sind. Diese bieten für Unternehmen, Gewerbetreibende, Handwerker, aber auch für Non-Profit-Organisationen eine Vielzahl von Leistungen an, die diese nicht selbst erbringen können. Werbe- und Mediaagenturen erbringen typischerweise die folgenden Leistungen:

- Marktforschung, Konsumentenforschung, Zielgruppenanalysen
- Entwicklung von Kommunikationsstrategien
- Konzeption, Gestaltung und Produktion von Werbemitteln
- Erarbeitung von Konzepten zum Einsatz der Werbemittel in den Werbeträgern („Mediaplanung“, Festlegung des „Media-Mix“)
- Verhandlung mit den Werbeträgern (Verlage, Sender) über Preise, Leistungen, Rabatte, Sonderkonditionen
- Buchung von Werbung bei den Werbeträgern im eigenen Namen für den Kunden („Mediaeinkauf“)
- Analyse und Kontrolle der Werbewirkung

Der Agenturmarkt für Werbung und Marktkommunikation wird von großen, international tätigen Unternehmensgruppen – **„Werbeholdings“**, **„Agenturnetzwerke“** – beherrscht, die sämtliche kommunikative Leistungen für das werbetreibende Unternehmen erbringen können. Zu den größten Werbeholdings der Welt zählen Omnicom (u. a. mit dem Netzwerk BBDO und den Mediaagenturen OMP und PHD), WPP (mit Ogilvy & Mather) und Publics.

Anders als Werbe- und Mediaagenturen sind **Internetagenturen** („Online-Agenturen“) auf netzbasierte Kommunikationskonzepte spezialisiert. Sie sind Experten für Konzeption, Gestaltung, Design („Webdesign“), Programmierung und Pflege von Websites. Darüber hinaus unterstützen sie das Online-Marketing der Unternehmen, z. B. durch Suchmaschinen-Optimierung. Sie sind fähig, ganze Online-Shops einzurichten oder umfassende Konzepte für das „Social Media“ zu entwickeln.

2.1.2 Wirtschaftsunternehmen und Organisationen

Wirtschaftsunternehmen

Für Wirtschaftsunternehmen ist es von **existenzieller Bedeutung**, dass es Medien gibt. Wirtschaftsunternehmen müssen ständig und viel kommunizieren, um sich bei ihren Kunden bemerkbar zu machen. Sie müssen Werbung betreiben, sie müssen verkaufsfördernde Maßnahmen ergreifen, sie müssen via Public Relations um Vertrauen in der Öffentlichkeit werben. Nur mit einem klugen Medieneinsatz „bleiben sie im Rennen“ ❶.

❶ Der kluge Medieneinsatz kann auch „marktschreierische Kommunikation“ bedeuten. Je heftiger der Wettbewerb, desto mehr muss man sich anstrengen, bei den Interessenten wahrgenommen zu werden. Als **Marktschreier** werden übrigens Händler auf Wochenmärkten bezeichnet, die „unter vollem Einsatz der menschlichen Stimme“ als Werbemittel ihre Ware weithin hörbar feilbieten.

Unternehmen, die nicht kommunizieren, die also kein gezieltes **Corporate Publishing** betreiben, bekommen schnell ein Problem: Sie werden am Markt nicht mehr als Anbieter wahrgenommen, ihre Produkte sind nicht mehr in den Köpfen der aktuellen und potenziellen Zielgruppe präsent, die Produkte sind keine relevante „Persönlichkeit“, die man in der Kaufsituation als mögliche Alternative wahrnimmt. Das Unternehmen läuft Gefahr, irrelevant zu werden und vom Markt zu verschwinden. Es genügt nicht, ein gutes Produkt zu haben, es muss auch in den Köpfen der Zielgruppe wahrgenommen werden.

Die Unternehmen und die Branchen, in denen sie tätig sind, weisen ein **unterschiedliches Kommunikations- und Werbeverhalten** auf. Manche Unternehmen sind z. B. besonders werbeaffin und werbeintensiv, andere halten sich bei der Werbung eher zurück und vertrauen auf andere Kommunikationsinstrumente, z. B. den direkten persönlichen Kontakt oder auf „den guten Ruf der Firma“, den sie immer wieder unter Beweis stellen. In der nachfolgenden Tabelle sind die Top Ten der werbestärksten Branchen in Deutschland für das Jahr 2010 aufgelistet (Quelle: Werbung in Deutschland 2011, S. 25):

	Branche	*Mio. Euro*
1.	Handelsorganisationen	2.949,3
2.	Versandhandel	1.781,0
3.	Pkw	1.485,2
4.	Zeitungen-Werbung	1.318,0
5.	Publikumszeitschriften-Werbung	901,7
6.	Arzneimittel	782,7
7.	Online-Dienstleistungen	777,9
8.	Schokolade und Zuckerwaren	726,4
9.	Sonstige Medien/Verlage	579,0
10.	Mobilnetz	562,1

Hier zeigt sich, dass die Handelsorganisationen mit großem Abstand diejenigen Unternehmen sind, die besonders auf Werbung angewiesen sind. Sehr werbeaktive Handelsorganisationen sind vor allem die Media-Saturn Holding, Aldi, Lidl, Edeka, Penny-Markt, Rewe und Real. Auffällig ist auch der hohe Anteil der Eigenwerbung bei Zeitungen, Zeitschriften und sonstigen Medien (Rang 4, 5 und 9).

Organisationen

Nicht nur die kommerziell ausgerichteten Wirtschaftsunternehmen sind auf eine gute Kommunikation angewiesen, sondern jede Art von **Organisation** muss sich und seine Produkte und Leistungen medial präsentieren. Gerade auch die gemeinnützigen Einrichtungen („Non-Profit-Organisationen") bzw. die „NGOs", die „Non-Governmental Organisations" oder „Nichtregierungsorganisationen" können sich nur halten, wenn sie professionell kommunizieren. Die **NGOs** lassen sich wie folgt unterscheiden:

- Nationale Hilfsorganisationen, z. B. Brot für die Welt, DRK Deutsches Rotes Kreuz, THW Technisches Hilfswerk
- Internationale Hilfsorganisationen, z. B. Ärzte ohne Grenzen, DWHH Deutsche Welthungerhilfe, UNICEF (Weltweite Hilfe für Kinder)
- Menschenrechtsorganisationen, z. B. amnesty international, HRW Human Rights Watch, Internationale Liga für Menschenrechte, Transparency
- Gesellschaftspolitische Organisationen und soziale Einrichtungen, z. B. Paritätischer Wohlfahrtsverband, SOS Kinderdorf
- Arbeitgeberverbände, z. B. Arbeitgeberverband Gesamtmetall, ILO International Labor Organization
- Arbeitnehmerverbände, z. B. DGB Deutscher GewerkschaftsBund, IG Metall, ver.di Vereinigte Dienstleistungsgewerkschaft
- Behindertenorganisationen und Selbsthilfegruppen, z. B. Aktion Mensch, WBU World Blind Union
- Organisationen für Umwelt und Energie, z. B. Greenpeace
- Kirchen, z. B. Katholische, evangelische Kirche
- Sportverbände und -vereine, z. B. DLV Deutscher Leichtathletik Verband, FIFA, UEFA, DFB Deutscher Fußball-Bund, NOK Nationales Olympisches Komitee

Deutsches Rotes Kreuz

Aus Liebe zum Menschen.

GREENPEACE

Bund für Umwelt und Naturschutz Deutschland

BUND

FRIENDS OF THE EARTH GERMANY

Die NGOs setzen sich für ihre Anliegen mit z. T. sehr großen Kampagnen ein und betreiben gezielten Lobbyismus, indem sie versuchen, auf die politischen Entscheidungsträger einzuwirken. Sehr oft geht es um **Fundraising**, also darum, Spendengelder für einen guten Zweck einzusammeln. Anlässe können Naturkatastrophen, Hungersnöte oder kriegerische Auseinandersetzungen sein. Hier gibt es in der Bevölkerung grundsätzlich eine große Hilfsbereitschaft, die aber erst durch richtigen Medieneinsatz in konkretes Spenden „umgemünzt" werden kann.

Im Jahr 2010 betrug die „Bilanz des Helfens" in Deutschland ca. 2,3 Mrd. Euro. Das ist ungefähr so viel, wie die Deutschen für Kino und Musik zusammengenommen ausgegeben haben! Der Deutsche Spendenrat e.V. bemerkt hierzu: „Persönlich adressierte Spendenaufrufe per Post sind immer noch der stärksten Auslöser für Zuwendungen. Insgesamt 28 Prozent der gespendeten Geldsummen lassen sich auf diese Art der Werbung zurückführen. Weitere 21 Prozent kommen durch regelmäßige Spenden zusammen, knapp 9 Prozent werden über Kollekten in Kirchen gesammelt. Deutlich zugelegt hat im letzten Jahr die Wirkung von TV-Beiträgen, TV-Werbung sowie Spendengalas. ... Vor allem Neuspender und Personen unter 60 Jahren lassen sich hierdurch motivieren."

2.1.3 Staat

Großes Landeswappen von Baden-Württemberg

Der Staat mit seinen Organen – das sind die Gebietskörperschaften (Bund, Länder, Gemeinden), die Sozialversicherungen („Parafisci": Renten-, Kranken-, Arbeitslosen- und Unfallversicherung) sowie Sondervermögen (z. B. ehemals Deutsche Bahn) und öffentliche Unternehmen im staatlichen Mehrheitsbesitz – ist **kein gewöhnlicher Kommunikator**, sondern ein Akteur, der an die Interessen der Allgemeinheit gebunden und auf das Gemeinwohl orientiert ist. In ganz besonderer und elementarer Weise ist er auf eine gute **Kommunikation mit den Staatsbürgern** angewiesen. Es geht um Akzeptanz politischer Entscheidungen, um die Legitimation der Entscheidungsträger (Legislative, Exekutive, Judikative) und um den friedlichen Interessenausgleich unterschiedlicher Gruppen und Personen. Zentrale Voraussetzung für das Funktionieren der freiheitlichen Demokratie ist es, dass der Staat in seinem Handeln von den Bürgern verstanden wird. Politikverdrossenheit und Entzug des Vertrauens durch den Bürger sind ein gefährlicher Sprengstoff für das Zusammenleben der Menschen in Frieden und Freiheit!

Weite Bereiche des **kommunikativen staatlichen Handelns** können als unproblematisch eingestuft werden, wie z. B. allgemeine Informationen über die eigene Verwaltungstätigkeit, Informationen im Zusammenhang mit Gesetzgebung und Rechtsanwendung oder Informationen als Teil des Gesetzesvollzugs bzw. der Tätigkeit der Leitungsverwaltung.

Problematisch sind jedoch alle Konstellationen, in denen Interessenkollisionen zwischen Bürgern, zwischen Gruppen von Bürgern und zwischen Bürgern und dem Staat stattfinden ❶. Hier geht es um entgegenstehende öffentliche oder private Interessen, um Kollisionen mit Grundrechten oder um Kollisionen mit politischen Rechten. In allen diesen Situationen ist der Staat als **Kommunikator in der Öffentlichkeit** nachhaltig gefordert, um Frieden zu stiften und Vertrauen zu erhalten. Kommunikation ist hier eine wichtige Ressource, um das staatliche Handeln zu begründen, um sachliche Lösungen zu erläutern, um die Rechtsgrundlagen zu verdeutlichen und um den Blick auf das Gemeinwohl zu schärfen.

❶ Ein recht eindruckvolles Beispiel für eine nicht gelungene Kommunikation zwischen staatlichen Stellen und der Öffentlichkeit ist die Auseinandersetzung um „Stuttgart 21" im Jahr 2010 und 2011. Offensichtlich brachte erst das Schlichtungsverfahren mit offener Kommunikation aller Beteiligten etwas Ruhe in eine extrem aufgeheizte Atmosphäre.

Der Staat wird klugerweise alle zur Verfügung stehenden Kommunikationsinstrumente einsetzen, um den genannten hohen Ansprüchen gerecht zu werden. Insbesondere stehen ihm die folgenden **Instrumente** zur Verfügung:

- Eigene Printmedien: Amtsanzeiger, **Amtsblätter**
- Eigener Internet-Auftritt
- Tages- und Wochenzeitungen: Anzeigen, Zeitungsbeilagen, Broschüren
- Auftritte von Entscheidungsträgern in Radio und TV
- Hintergrundgespräche

Welche Instrumente in der jeweiligen Situation zielführend sind, erweist sich oft erst im Nachhinein. Gute Kommunikationsarbeit von Seiten des Staates darf jedenfalls nicht vorschnell als „hinausgeworfenes Geld" abqualifiziert werden, wenn z. B. die Bundesregierung eine umfangreiche Überzeugungskampagne für die Erhöhung der Mehrwertsteuer für erforderlich hält.

2.1.4 Privatpersonen

Zu wichtigen Kommunikatoren im Mediensystem der Massenkommunikation haben sich inzwischen auch die privaten Einzelpersonen entwickelt. Zwischen ihnen spielt nicht mehr nur der direkte individuelle Kommunikationsaustausch herkömmlicher Art statt wie Telefon oder E-Mail, durch die Bildung von **Communities im Internet** ist es vielmehr möglich geworden, dass auch der Einzelne problemlos mit einer größeren Öffentlichkeit in kommunikativen Kontakt treten kann.

Das diesbezügliche Zauberwort heißt **Social Media**. Social Media ist „ein Sammelbegriff für internet-basierte mediale Angebote, die auf sozialer Interaktion und den technischen Möglichkeiten des sog. Web 2.0 basieren. Dabei stehen Kommunikation und der Austausch nutzergenerierter Inhalte (User-Generated Content) im Vordergrund. Die sozialen Medien gewinnen zunehmend auch kommerzielle Bedeutung, da die vernetzte Struktur der Nutzerschaft großes Potenzial für die wirkungsvolle Übermittlung kommerzieller Nachrichten und Inhalte bildet **(Social Commerce)**" (Gabler Wirtschaftslexikon). Die Social-Media-Anwendungen lassen sich in die folgenden **sechs Gruppen** unterteilen (nach Kaplan/Haenlein 2010):

- Kollektivprojekte (z. B. Wikipedia)
- **Blogs** und Mikroblogs (z. B. Twitter)
- Content Communities (z. B. YouTube)
- **Soziale Netzwerke** (z. B. Facebook)
- **MMORPGs** (Massively Multiplayer Online Role-Playing Game bzw. Massen-Mehrspieler-Online-Rollenspiel, z. B. World of Warcraft)
- Soziale virtuelle Welten (z. B. Second Life)

Aus kommunikationstheoretischer Sicht bedeutet jeder Auftritt in einer dieser Social-Media-Anwendungen, dass neuer **User-Generated Content** (UGC) erzeugt wird. Drei wesentliche Merkmale machen den UGC aus (vgl. Stöckl/Grau/Hess 2006) ❶:

❶ Eine ähnliche Abgrenzung nimmt die OECD-Definition vor, wonach UGC den folgenden Kriterien genügen muss:
1. Die Inhalte müssen publiziert sein.
2. Es muss eine kreative Eigenleistung vorliegen.
3. Die Kreation muss außerhalb von professionellen Routinen erfolgen.

- Konsumenten als Produzenten: Die betreffenden Inhalte werden nicht mehr von professionellen Redakteuren, sondern von Rezipienten erstellt. Der vormals auf die passive Konsumtion beschränkte Kunde nimmt nun zusätzlich eine aktive Rolle ein und wird selbst zum Produzenten von Inhalten.
- Keine unmittelbare Gewinnerzielungsabsicht: Der insofern aktiv gewordene Konsument wird nicht von dem Motiv geleitet, einen kurzfristig und finanziell messbaren Gewinn zu erzielen. Er wird aber die Möglichkeit einer späteren Gratifikation für qualitativ besonders hochwertige Inhalte oder einer Entschädigung für besonders produktionsaufwendige Inhalte nicht ausschließen.
- Massenmediale Ausrichtung: UGC wird im Gegensatz zu den Inhalten der Individualkommunikation für eine unbestimmte Anzahl an Adressaten produziert. Das bedeutet aber nicht, dass jeder selbsterstellte Beitrag ein Massenpublikum auch wirklich erreicht. Ganz im Gegenteil ist oft zu vermuten, dass ein Großteil der von Nutzern produzierten Inhalte nur sehr wenige Rezipienten erreicht.

2.2 Botschaften

2.2.1 Grundbausteine: Inhalt und Form

Wirkungsvolle mediale Gestaltung von Botschaften

Professionelle Medienmacher werden die Wirkung des Medieneinsatzes nicht dem Zufall überlassen. Sie werden intensive Überlegungen darüber anstellen, wie man die Botschaft, die es zu übermitteln gilt, bestmöglich für die Menschen aufbereiten kann, für die sie bestimmt ist. Dabei geht es darum, die unterschiedlichen **Medienbausteine** oder „Modalitäten" in die richtige Mischung zu bringen und in der richtigen Dosierung aufzubereiten. Die folgenden **Modalitäten** stehen zur Verfügung ❶:

❶ Vgl. Bruhn, Manfred: Unternehmens- und Marketingkommunikation, München 2005, S. 453 ff.)

- Text
- Bild
- Ton

Daneben gibt es die Modalitäten Gefühl, Duft und Geschmack, die im Medienbereich eine ergänzende Rolle spielen. Es gilt, die Modalitäten in der Weise zu verschlüsseln, dass die Botschaft in bestmöglicher Form erscheint, sozusagen „auf den Punkt" gebracht ist.

Am besten lässt sich diese Herausforderung der **optimalen Botschaftsgestaltung** am Beispiel der Werbung erklären. Hier geht es darum, die Werbebotschaft (d. h. das „Werbemittel") so zu gestalten, dass die Werbeziele bestmöglich erreicht werden können. Dies ist abhängig von den Faktoren der Werbemittelgestaltung, die nach den Modalitäten geordnet werden können (vgl. Bruhn 2005, S. 457):

Text	Bild	Ton
Generell: • Wortwahl • Satzlänge • Satzart • Argumentationstypik (Eigenargumentation) • Eindeutigkeit/Doppeldeutigkeit • Slogan • Rätselhafte Darstellungen • Hinweiszeichen • Reime • Dialog u. a. m **Speziell für den geschriebenen Text:** • Orthographie • Textform • Schrifttyp, Schriftgrad • Positiv-/Negativschrift u. a. m. **Speziell für den gesprochenen Text:** • Tempo der Sprache (Time Compressing) • Dialekt u. a. m.	**Generell:** • Grundsätzliches Bildmotiv • Zeichnung/Foto • Hinweiszeichen (z. B. Finger) • Farben • Beleuchtung, Helligkeit • Perspektiven (Weitwinkel?) • Rätselhafte Darstellung • Symbolverwendung u. a. m. **Speziell für das ruhende Bild:** • Bildaufteilung • Verzerrung, Vermischung **Speziell für das bewegte Bild:** • Tempo des Szenenwechsels • Zusammenhang der Passagen • Mimik/Gestik der Personen u. a. m.	**Generell:** • Lautstärke u. a. m. **Speziell für die Musik:** • Tonart • Rhythmus • Instrumente • Gesang u. a. m. **Speziell für die Stimme:** • Stimmklang • Sprechdynamik • Stimmkontraste beim Auftritt mehrerer Personen u. a. m. **Speziell für Geräusche:** • Charakteristik u. a. m.

Aus der kreativen Komposition der Faktoren ergibt sich dann das **Format** des jeweiligen Werbemittels, z. B. einer Anzeige, eines TV-Spots oder Werbeartikels.

Aussage

Unter Aussage wird eine **Mitteilung** oder eine **Botschaft** („message") verstanden, die ein Kommunikator von sich gibt. Aussagen können z. B. sein:

- Persönliche Mitteilungen („face to face"), in gesprochener Form, als Mimik, Gestik oder in Form einer Körperbewegung innerhalb eines vertraulichen Gesprächs, eines Statements, einer Präsentation, einer Rede oder einer Kirchenpredigt.
- Künstlerische Darbietungen: Theaterstück, Pantomime (als Ausdruck visueller Kommunikation), Ballett-Aufführung, Oper, Operette, Kleinkunst, Kabarett, Varieté
- Über Telekommunikation vermittelte Botschaften: Telefongespräch, E-Mail, Meldung einer Nachrichtenagentur (aus dem „Ticker")
- Beiträge in Zeitungen und Zeitschriften: Aktueller Bericht, Leitartikel, Kommentar, Reportage, Wandzeitung
- Radiosendungen: Magazinsendung, Interview, Hörspiel, Feature, Musiksendung, Bildungssendung, Reportage, aktueller Beitrag (im Format „1:30" = eine Minute und dreißig Sekunden), Servicesendung
- Fernsehsendungen: Nachrichtensendung (Tagesschau, Heute), Reportage, Kommentar, Dokumentation, Spielfilm, Fernsehfilm, Unterhaltungsshow, Talkshow, Spielshow, Quiz, Serie, Soap-Opera, Live-Übertragung eines Ereignisses (Sport, Musik), Kindersendung, Gottesdienstübertragung, Themenabend, Theater, Kulturmagazin
- Werbebotschaften (die Werbung spricht von „Werbemitteln"): Werbeplakat, Anzeigen in Zeitungen und Zeitschriften, Prospekt, Flugblatt, Fernseh- und Kinowerbespot, Werbesendungen im Radio

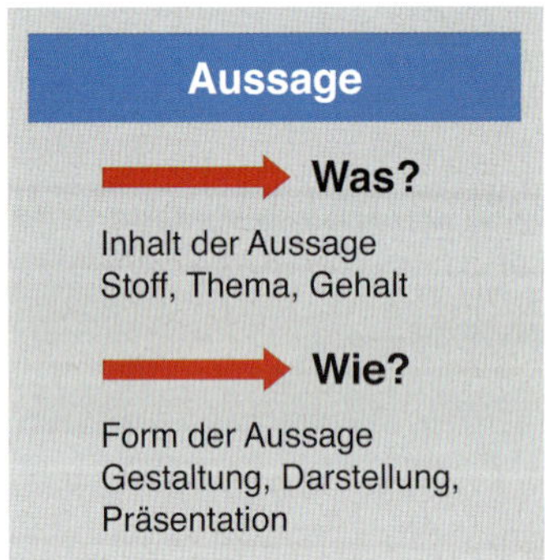

Ob die Aussage so ankommt, wie es der Kommunikator sich vorstellt, hängt z. B. davon ab, wie interessant der **Inhalt** der Aussage aufbereitet ist, welchen Nutzen der Inhalt für den Empfänger hat, aber auch davon, in welcher **Form** der Inhalt vom Kommunikator präsentiert wird. Eine Aussage hat daher immer **zwei Seiten**, die man als das „Grundgesetz der Aussage" bezeichnen kann:

➲ **Es kommt nicht nur darauf an, was mitgeteilt wird, sondern auch wie es mitgeteilt wird.**

Folglich unterscheidet man bei der Aussage immer nach zwei Aspekten, zum einen nach dem „Was", das ist der Inhalt, das Thema, der Stoff, und zum anderen nach dem „Wie", das ist die Form, die Gestaltung, die Präsentation.

Inhalt der Aussage:
Unter dem Inhalt der Aussage ist die Sache zu verstehen, um die es dem Kommunikator geht ❶. Der Inhalt bezeichnet das „Ausgesagte", das er dem Empfänger mitteilen will. Grundsätzlich sind die folgenden Inhaltstypen denkbar:

❶ Um den **Inhalt einer Aussage** zu bezeichnen, wird zunehmend der englische Begriff **Content** verwendet. So ist z. B. ein „Content Management System" eine Software, die aus einem gemeinsamen Datenpool heraus einen Inhalt in den unterschiedlichsten Formen medien- und zielgruppengerecht aufbereiten kann, z. B. gleichzeitig als Zeitungsartikel und als Webangebot.

- Vermittlung von Nachrichten und Informationen
- Interpretation, Kommentierung, Verarbeitung
- Kultur
- Erziehung
- Unterhaltung

❶ Ein bedeutender Kritiker dieser Entwicklung ist **Neil Postman**. Seine 1985 erschienene Veröffentlichung „Wir amüsieren uns zu Tode" hat höchste Beachtung gefunden.

❷ Die wissenschaftliche Befassung mit dem Thema Aussagen nennt man **Aussagenforschung** oder **Inhaltsanalyse**.

Seit einigen Jahren ist festzustellen, dass diese grundlegenden **Aussagentypen** immer mehr **vermischt** werden. Dies ist besonders im Fernsehen der Fall, wo man Mischformen in großer Zahl vorfindet ❶. Das Ziel ist dabei, die Reichweite und Attraktivität von Sendungen zu steigern. Zu nennen sind:

- **Infotainment:** Mischung aus Information und Unterhaltung (entertainment), z. B. in Talkshows, Reality TV, Nachrichtenmagazinen
- **Edutainment:** Mischung aus Erziehung (education) und Unterhaltung, z. B. bei Bildungssendungen und Dokumentationen
- **Advertainment:** Mischung aus Unterhaltung und Werbung (advertising)

Form der Aussage:
Neben dem Inhalt spielt die Form der Aussage für die Wirksamkeit der Botschaft eine große Rolle. Aussagen können je nachdem, wie sie gestaltet sind, eine höchst unterschiedliche Form aufweisen, die wiederum völlig unterschiedlichen Wirkungsgesetzen unterliegt. Eine aktuelle Nachricht wird völlig unterschiedlich aufbereitet sein, je nachdem, welchem Zweck sie dient. Die Ansprachеform hat unterschiedliche Ausprägungen, wenn man die Sachinformation einer Stadtverwaltung mit dem Aufreißer auf der ersten Seite der Bildzeitung vergleicht.

Es ist leicht einzusehen, dass die Form der Aussage von den **Gestaltungselementen** bzw. „Grundbausteinen" abhängt, die dem Kommunikator bei der „Formung" seiner Botschaft grundsätzlich zur Verfügung stehen. Je nach dem, wie er die Bausteine „zusammenmixt", entsteht die Botschaft in der einen oder in der anderen Form ❷.

Grundsätzlich stehen dem Kommunikator die folgenden Bausteine bzw. **Gestaltungselemente** zur Verfügung:

- Medienelemente: Eine Medienproduktion kann sich aus den folgenden sechs Bausteinen (Medienelemente) zusammensetzen: Text, stehendes Realbild (Foto, Dia), stehendes Kunstbild (Grafik), bewegtes Realbild (Film, Video), bewegtes Kunstbild (Computeranimation, Zeichentrick) und/oder Audio. Je nach der Zahl der eingesetzten Medienelemente hat man es mit monomedialen, bimedialen oder multimedialen Aussagen zu tun.
- Darstellungselemente: Bei einem Film sind z. B. die folgenden Darstellungs-elemente von Bedeutung: Farbe, Licht, Einstellungsgröße, Kamera-Perspektive, Kamera-Bewegung, Tiefenschärfe, Ablaufgeschwindigkeit, Art der Montage, Dramaturgie, Schnitt.
- Element Zeit: Eine große Rolle spielt die Reihenfolge, in der ein Inhalt zeitlich präsentiert wird (linearer Ablauf z. B. bei einem Film oder nicht-linearer Ablauf z. B. bei einem Lernprogramm auf CD-ROM).

Am **Beispiel** von **Gewaltdarstellungen in Fernsehfilmen** hat die Kommunikations- und Medienwissenschaft z. B. aufgezeigt, wie einseitig ein Thema dargeboten werden kann. Am Beispiel von Spielfilmen wird dies deutlich ❶:

- Gewalt geht in Spielfilmen regelmäßig von männlichen Erwachsenen aus.
- Es dominiert die Sicht des Angreifers.
- Das Opfer ist überdurchschnittlich häufig eine Frau.
- Gewalt ist oft reiner Selbstzweck und wird nicht näher begründet.
- Erfolgt eine Begründung, dann ist sie ein Mittel, um Konflikte zu lösen.
- Gewalt wird kalt und zynisch ausgeübt. Die unmittelbaren Konsequenzen werden selten gezeigt, und wenn dann aus der Perspektive des Täters, der sich befriedigt zeigt.
- An erster Stelle der Schädigungen rangiert der Tod.
- Ein Viertel aller Gewaltszenen entfällt auf Trickfilme.

Wie wichtig die **Perspektive** ist, aus der ein Thema oder Gegenstand betrachtet wird, zeigt die nachfolgende Übersicht über die sog. **Wahrnehmungseinheiten** ❷, die bei der Darstellung von Bewegtbildprodukten (z. B. Fernsehen) eine Rolle spielen (Quelle: Schaudig 1991, S. 163-183):

❶ Quelle: Groebel, Jo und Gleich, U.: Gewaltprofil im deutschen Fernsehprogramm, Opladen 1993, S. 83ff. Zum Thema Gewaltdarstellungen im Fernsehen vgl. auch: Friedrichsen, Mike und Vowe, Gerhard: Gewaltdarstellungen in den Medien, Opladen 1995; Zeitter, E. / Kapp, F. / Jaiser, F. / Scheltwort, P.: Die „Sprache der Gewalt" und ihre Wirkungen, Villingen-Schwenningen 1996.

❷ Unter einer Wahrnehmungseinheit versteht man die kleinste Gestaltungseinheit, mit der die Festlegung der Perspektive der Wahrnehmung erfolgt.

Einstellung	ohne Unterbrechung aufgenommene Bildfolge; Einheit zwischen zwei Schnitten/Blenden
Sequenz	Einheit aufeinander folgender Einstellungen, die räumlich-zeitlich oder sachlich-logisch zusammenhängen. Der Begriff wird überwiegend für nichtfiktionale Darstellungsformen verwendet (s. Szene).
Szene	räumlich-zeitlich begrenzter, dramaturgisch gestalteter Teil einer Handlung, der in einer Folge von Einstellungen abgebildet wird. Der Begriff wird überwiegend für fiktionale Darstellungsformen verwendet (s. Sequenz).
Motiv	Element innerhalb der Filmhandlung, das über Einstellungs- und Sequenzgrenzen hinweg in den Mittelpunkt der visuellen Wahrnehmung gestellt wird.
Sujet	Gesamtthema, Gegenstand, Stoff des Werkes; als Sujet wird auch ein Beitrag/eine Episode des Gesamtwerkes (Wochenschau, Episodenfilm) bezeichnet.
Bildformat	Normalformat, Breitwandformat, Fernseh-Standardformat
Bildwechselfrequenz	Normalgeschwindigkeit, Zeitlupe, Zeitraffer
Kameraperspektive	Positionierung der Kamera: vertikal/lateral/horizontal
Kamerabewegung	einstellungsinterne Änderung kameraspezifischer Abbildungsvariablen: Schwenk, Kamerafahrt, Zoom
Einstellungsgröße	von der Kamera gewählter Bildausschnitt: Detail, Groß, Nah, Halbnah, Halbtotale, Totale, Panorama
Einstellungsdauer/ -länge	Zeit- oder Längenangaben, Anzahl der Frames
Verbindungs-elemente	Einstellungsverknüpfung, Übergänge zwischen Einstellungen: harter Schnitt, Überblendung (weicher Schnitt), Aufblende, Abblende, Split-Screen.

2.2.2 Information

❶ „In der journalistischen Praxis steht der Begriff Information für alle Formen der Tatsachendarstellung (Objektivität), der Nachricht, des Berichts, der Darlegung von Hintergründen und Wissensbeständen sowie als Verb für den Vorgang ihrer Beschaffung oder Aneignung (sich informieren, Informationssuche, Recherche) und ihrer Erstellung oder Vermittlung (jemanden informieren)" (Weischenberg/Kleinsteuber/ Pörksen 2005, S. 102 f.).

Unter „Information" werden alle jene Botschaften verstanden, die auf die **Darstellung von Tatsachen** ausgerichtet sind ❶. Solchermaßen informierende Botschaften sind dabei nicht auf politische Inhalte und staatliches Handeln beschränkt, sondern können auch mit kulturellen, gesellschaftlichen, wirtschaftlichen und anderen Sachthemen zu tun haben. Sie müssen auch nicht notwendigerweise einen Bezug zum aktuellen Tagesgeschehen haben. Auch historische Inhalte oder wissenschaftliche Beiträge fallen unter den Informationsbegriff.

Journalistische Darstellungsformen

Zur nutzer- und mediengerechten Aufbereitung von Informationen stehen drei **grundlegende journalistische Darstellungsformen** zur Verfügung, die für alle Medien in gleicher Weise gelten (vgl. Mast 2004, S. 237):

Grundformen journalistischer Darstellungsweisen		
Tatsachenbetonte (referierende) Formen	Meinungsbetonte Formen	Fantasiebetonte Formen
Nachricht (als Wortnachricht: Meldung und Bericht, aber auch als Bildnachricht: Foto oder Infografik), Reportage, Feature, Interview, Dokumentation	Leitartikel, Kommentar, Glosse, Kolumne, Portrait, Karikatur, (politisches) Lied, Buch-, Theater-, Musik-, Kunst-, Film-, Fernsehkritik, Essay	Zeitungsroman, Kurzgeschichte, Feuilleton, Spielfilm, Hörspiel, Fernsehspiel, Lied (Schlager), Comics, Witzzeichnungen

Beispiel Information im Fernsehen

Für das Fernsehen kann man vor diesem Hintergrund die folgenden **informierenden TV-Sendungsformen** unterscheiden (vgl. Hickethier 2010, S. 281 f.):

- **Nachrichtensendungen:** Kombination aus verlesenen Meldungen, Live-Berichten von Korrespondenten vor Ort, Filmberichten, Stellungnahmen, Kommentaren.
- Live-Übertragungen von Sportereignissen, Wahlen, wichtigen Geschehnissen wie z. B. Katastrophen. In Unterhaltungsshows finden Simulationen des „Live-Gefühls" statt.
- **Magazinsendungen:** Mischung verschiedener, z. T. sehr unterschiedlicher Einzelbeiträge, zusammengehalten von einem Moderator.
- **Dokumentation**, Feature, Dokumentarfilm: Als Dokumentation wird die Kombination von Material zu einem aktuellen Thema verstanden. Ein Feature ist eine Aufbereitung allgemeiner Art mit künstlerisch-gestalterischen Elementen. Der Dokumentarfilm pflegt die beobachtende Reflexion und basiert auf der filmischen Tradition.
- **Wissenschafts-** und **Bildungssendungen**: Sie zeichnen sich durch eine Bildungsintention mit einem besonderen didaktischen Ansatz aus.

Nachrichtenfaktoren

Im Kontext des informierenden Journalismus ist es eine wichtige Frage, nach welchen Kriterien die Journalisten die Nachrichten auswählen und an das Publikum verbreiten. Die **journalistische Handwerksregel** diesbezüglich lautet, sich an den sinnvollen sog. „Nachrichtenfaktoren" auszurichten.

Nachrichtenfaktoren sind dafür verantwortlich, ob eine Nachricht für den Zuschauer von Wert ist („Nachrichtenwert"). Eine Nachricht ist z. B. von hohem Wert, wenn sie den unmittelbaren Lebensraum eines Menschen betrifft, wenn sie neu ist, wenn sie aktuell ist oder wenn prominente Menschen („große Namen") angesprochen sind. Insbesondere gilt: Je größer die Tragweite eines Ereignisses ist und je mehr es persönliche Betroffenheit auslöst, desto eher wird es zu einer Nachricht.

➲ **Nachrichtenfaktoren sind „Merkmale, die ein Ereignis aufweist und die über seinen Nachrichtenwert (seine Publikationswürdigkeit) bestimmen" (Burkart 2002, S. 279).**

Welches im Einzelnen die Nachrichtenfaktoren sind, die zu einem Nachrichtenwert führen, entscheiden die Journalisten typischerweise nach den folgenden **Kriterien** (Nachrichtenfaktoren nach Schulz, vgl. Burkart 2002, S. 281 ff.):

- Zeit: Ereignisse, die sich über längere Zeit hinziehen, haben einen niedrigen Nachrichtenwert, punktuelle Ereignisse von kurzer Dauer einen hohen. Ferner werden Ereignisse, die bereits zum Thema geworden sind, mit einem höheren Nachrichtenwert versehen als noch nicht etablierte Themen.
- Nähe: Der Wert einer Nachricht ist umso höher, je näher das Ereignis stattfindet. Nähe kann sein: räumliche Nähe, politische Nähe, kulturelle Nähe und Relevanz (als Grad der Betroffenheit und Bedeutung des Ereignisses).
- Status: Angesprochen sind hier der persönliche Status von Personen („Prominenz"), der persönliche Einfluss, die Bedeutung der Region oder des Landes, in der ein Ereignis stattfindet. Je höher der Status, desto eher wird ein Ereignis zu einer Nachricht.
- Dynamik: Als Nachrichtenfaktoren wirken die Überraschung und die Struktur von Ereignissen (Komplexität, Überschaubarkeit).
- Valenz: Der Nachrichtenwert nimmt mit dem Grad der Aggressivität von Ereignissen zu, ebenfalls mit der Kriminalität, dem Schaden oder dem Erfolg, den Personen, Gruppen, Kommunen oder das Land erleiden oder erreichen.
- Identifikation: Je enger der personelle Bezug eines Ereignisses (Personalisierung) oder je direkter der Bezug zur eigenen Bevölkerung (Ethnozentrismus), desto eher wird über das Ereignis berichtet.

Die vielschichtige Welt der Nachrichtenfaktoren führt uns vor Augen, dass man nicht von der laienhaften und naiven Vorstellung ausgehen sollte, die Medien würden die **Wirklichkeit** unverzerrt abbilden. Die Medien und die hier tätigen Journalisten entwerfen ein subjektives Bild von der Wirklichkeit, je nach der zugrunde gelegten Perspektive, z. B. auch durch die Entscheidung über die Nachrichtenfaktoren.

Werbebotschaften

Eine besondere Form der Information ist die **Werbung**. Verlage oder Rundfunksender stellen sich in den Dienst von Wirtschaftsunternehmen und helfen diesen, mit ihren potenziellen oder aktuellen Kunden in kommunikativen Kontakt zu treten.

Die Werbewirtschaft unternimmt enorme Anstrengungen und setzt hohe Summen ein, um mit ihrer Werbung eine maximale **Wirkung** zu erzielen. „Wirkung" heißt vor allem Produktbekanntheit, Image und positives Kaufverhalten den eigenen Produkten gegenüber. Um die Effektivität von Werbung sicherzustellen, muss man die Werbebotschaft durch ein gekonntes Zusammenspiel von gestalterischen und inhaltlichen Variablen professionell „in Szene setzen". In Kapitel 20 dieses Handbuches finden sich einige Beispiele für gelungene Werbekampagnen und vertiefende Informationen über die Gestaltung von Werbebotschaften, im Fachjargon „Werbemittel" genannt.

Es herrscht eine große Vielfalt von Werbeformen, die in klassische und spezielle Formen unterschieden werden kann. Letztere haben nicht selten die Eigenschaft, dass sie versuchen, die Werbung mit dem redaktionellen Inhalt zu vermischen.

Klassische Formen der Werbung

Die **Zeitung** ist ein wichtiger Werbeträger und bietet ein breites Spektrum an Werbemöglichkeiten. Analoges gilt für **Zeitschriften**, insbesondere die Publikumszeitschriften. Klassische Zeitungswerbeformen sind die Anzeigen, die in einer eigenen Rubrik präsentiert werden, aber auch ganze Werbesonderseiten oder ein ganzes Buch ❶. Von hoher Bedeutung sind im Printbereich auch die regionalen Anzeigenblätter, die kostenlos an die Haushalte verteilt werden. Man nennt sie auch Wochenblätter, Wochenzeitungen, Anzeiger, im englischen Sprachraum „Free Papers".

❶ Ein Zeitungsbuch oder kurz Buch ist die Zusammenfassung von Zeitungsseiten, die sich aus den einzelnen gefalzten Druckbögen ergeben. Eine Zeitung besteht aus mehreren Zeitungsbüchern, die hintereinander gelegt und noch einmal gefalzt werden. Einzelne Bücher werden dazu verwendet, um Rubriken abzugrenzen (Sportteil, Wirtschaftsteil, Feuilleton, etc.) aber auch als Sonderbeilagen, als zusätzliches Magazin in der Zeitung oder für PR- und Werbezwecke genutzt.

Die klassische Werbung in **Radio** und **Fernsehen** ist die Spotwerbung, auch „harte Werbung" genannt. Der einzelne Spot dauert standardmäßig 30 Sekunden, wobei allerdings ein Trend zu kürzeren Spots festzustellen ist. Inhaltlich können die Spots höchst unterschiedlich gestaltet sein. So differenziert man nach den folgenden Präsentationsformen: Slice-of-Life, Produkt-Demonstration („Product-is-hero"), Problemlösung, Testimonial, Reminder, Präsentation (Presenter), Jingle, Musik-Spot, Video-Clip, Nachricht, Interview, Tandem-Spot. Neben der harten Spotwerbung sind auch längere Werbesendungen („Dauerwerbesendungen") gebräuchlich, vorzugsweise in diversen TV-Spartenkanälen. Beim Teleshopping stellt sich sogar der ganze Kanal als eine einzige Werbe- und Verkaufslandschaft dar.

Trotz der relativen Neuheit des Mediums haben sich bei der **Internet-Werbung** bereits einige „klassische" Werbeformate herausgebildet. Das bekannteste ist der Banner, eine Werbegrafik im Internet, die man evtl. auch anklicken und vertiefende Werbeinformationen abrufen kann. Werbung im Internet hat lange darunter gelitten, dass es keine einheitliche Sprachregelung bezüglich der unterschiedlichen Werbemöglichkeiten gab. So konnte das Internet nicht systematisch als Werbeträger genutzt werden. Diese Anfangsschwierigkeiten sind inzwischen überwunden.

Spezielle Formen der Werbung

Neben der reinen Anzeigenwerbung bieten die **Zeitungen** inzwischen auch eine breite Palette differenzierter Werbemöglichkeiten an, z. B. Banderolen, „Minenfeldanzeigen", die gezielt und hoch auffällig als „Störer" in den redaktionellen Text eingebaut werden, ein eigenes kommerzielles Buch (d. h. Zeitungsbestandteil) mit 4, 6, 8, 12 oder 16 Seiten oder eine „Flappe", ein halb- oder ganzseitiger Umschlag über die Zeitung, beidseitig bedruckbar.

Auch in **Radio** und **Fernsehen** gibt es eine breite Vielfalt an Sonderwerbeformen. Dies kann als Signal gedeutet werden, dass vor allem die privaten Fernsehanbieter zunehmende Schwierigkeiten haben, sich aus klassischer Werbung zu finanzieren und gezwungen sind, alternative Finanzierungsformen zu suchen. Bekannteste Sonderwerbeformen sind Sponsoring, Product Placement, Gewinnspiele und Game Shows.

Sonderwerbeformen finden sich in besonders vielfältiger Weise im **Internet**. Hier seien nur einige Begriffe genannt: Microsite, Pop-Up-Werbung, Targeting, AdWords, Pixel, Layer Ad, Interstitials, Site Branding, Einbindung von Video usw. Online-Werbung ist für Unternehmen v. a. im crossmedialen Verbund relevant und soll zur Effizienzsteigerung von Werbekampagnen beitragen. Auch im Hinblick auf die Sonderwerbeformen ist das Internet planbar und transparent, nicht zuletzt dank der Standardisierung durch die „**AGOF**", die Arbeitsgemeinschaft Online-Forschung e.V.

Vermischung von Werbung und redaktionellem Inhalt

Werbung besitzt nicht nur in kommerzieller, sondern auch **in publizistischer Hinsicht** einen erheblichen Stellenwert. Dies zeigt sich, wenn journalistische Inhalte und die Werbung aufeinandertreffen und sich **Konflikte** einstellen: Gegenüber stehen sich auf der einen Seite die Redaktion, die ihre Leser, Hörer oder Zuschauer unbeeinflusst informieren und unterhalten will, und auf der anderen Seite die Werbewirtschaft, die bestrebt ist, in der Zeitung mit den Anzeigen oder im Rundfunk mit den TV- und Radiospots in ein attraktives redaktionelles Umfeld hineinzukommen.

Um den Konflikt zwischen Redaktion und Werbung zu entschärfen, verbietet das Wettbewerbsrecht grundsätzlich die gezielte Vermischung von Werbung und Inhalten ❶. Werbung muss jederzeit klar erkennbar sein. Alle Werbeformen, bei denen es zu engen Berührungen oder gar Vermischungen mit dem Programm kommt, gelten als brisant und sind engen rechtlichen Vorschriften unterworfen. Aus systematischer Sicht sind hierbei die folgenden Bereiche zu unterscheiden:

- Werbung neben dem Programm: Anzeigen, Spotwerbung (im Werbeblock)
- Werbung im Programm (programmintegrierte Werbung, „Programming"): Sponsoring, Product Placement
- Werbung als eigenes Programm: eigenes Zeitungsbuch, Teleshopping, Dauerwerbesendungen, PR-Sendungen, Videoclips
- Werbung nach dem Programm: Merchandising (Werbung für Medienmarken durch Merchandising-Artikel wie Plastikfiguren, T-Shirts, Kugelschreiber, Tassen, Schlüsselanhänger etc.)

❶ Es gilt der sog. „Grundsatz der klaren Trennung von Werbung und Programm". Rechtsgrundlage ist das Gesetz gegen den unlauteren Wettbewerb (UWG), nach dem Werbung nicht unwahr, irreführend oder unlauter sein darf. Werbung muss jederzeit klar als solche erkennbar sein.

2.2.3 Unterhaltung

❶ Berühmt wurde das 1985 erschienene Buch von Neil Postman „Wir amüsieren uns zu Tode – Urteilsbildung im Zeitalter der Unterhaltungsindustrie"

Unterhaltung ist ein **zentraler Bereich in der medialen Angebotspalette** und erfreut sich größten Zuspruchs beim Publikum. Traditionell ist z. B. die Nachfrage nach Unterhaltungssendungen im Fernsehen deutlich höher als die nach Informationsangeboten. Spielorientierte TV-Angebote wie Spielshows oder erlebnisorientierte Angebote wie Spielfilme konsumiert der Zuschauer in Massen. Zu denken ist an die Regenbogenpresse, an das Lesen von Unterhaltungsromanen, an Computerspiele oder an den Musikkonsum im Radio. Es fehlt nicht an kritischen Stimmen, die vor einem ausufernden Unterhaltungsangebot warnen ❶.

Den einzelnen Mediengattungen werden **unterschiedliche Qualitäten** im Hinblick auf die Unterhaltung zugeschrieben. Ganz grob kann man festhalten:

- Tages- und Wochenzeitungen zählen zu den informationsorientierten Medien.
- Publikumszeitschriften werden den unterhaltungsorientierten Medien zugerechnet.
- Bücher bieten sowohl Unterhaltung (z. B. Romane) als auch Information (z. B. Fachbücher).
- Das Fernsehen gilt als Unterhaltungs- und Informationsmedium. Als Programmsparte steht die Information in Konkurrenz mit den Sparten Sport, Musik, nonfiktionale Unterhaltung, Kinder- und Jugendsendungen, Fiction und Werbung. Vom gesamten TV-Angebot entfällt auf Informationssendungen fast die Hälfte, während das Publikum deutlich Unterhaltungsangebote bevorzugt (vgl. Hans-Bredow-Institut 2006, S. 150).
- Der Hörfunk gilt wie das Fernsehen als Unterhaltungs- und Informationsmedium, wobei zumeist der Wortanteil mit Information, der Musikanteil am Programm mit Unterhaltung gleichgesetzt wird. Allerdings ist festzustellen, dass die Moderation im Radio zunehmend unterhaltenden Charakter aufweist.
- Direkt der Unterhaltung verschrieben sind das Kino, der Markt für digitale Spiele, interaktive Unterhaltungsmedien, Videos und Musik.
- Das Internet bietet eine unerschöpfliche Fülle von netzbasierten und mobilen Unterhaltungsapplikationen.

Innerhalb der Medienangebote ist die Unterhaltung als eine Gattung zu verstehen, die sich von Informations- und Kulturangeboten abhebt. In diesem Sinne ist Unterhaltung ein Genre, das beim Publikum den Wunsch nach Zerstreuung, Ablenkung, Flucht aus dem Alltag (man nennt dies „Eskapismus" von engl. „to escape" = flüchten), Erheiterung, Freude, Spaß, Vergnügen, Erlebnis, Emotionen erfüllt.

Ein wichtiger Aspekt bei der Beschreibung des Begriffs „Unterhaltung" ist der **Bezug zur Realität**. Hier unterscheidet man zwei Welten:

❷ Reality TV ist ein Sendungsformat, das v. a. Unfälle, menschliche Schicksale, Katastrophen, kriminelle Handlungen, Rettungsaktionen thematisiert.

- Nonfiktionale Unterhaltung (Bezug zur Realität, „dokumentarische Unterhaltung"): z. B. Shows und Spiele (Game- und Unterhaltungs-Shows), Satire, Reality-Formate („Reality TV" ❷)
- Fiktionale Unterhaltung (erfundene Handlung, keine Wirklichkeit, Spielhandlungen): z. B. Spiel- und Fernsehfilme, Serien, Trickfilme („Cartoons"), Bühnenstücke

Beispiel Unterhaltung im Fernsehen

Das Fernsehen als Unterhaltungsmedium par excellence bietet eine breite „Entertainment"-Palette. Die folgenden **unterhaltenden TV-Sendungsformen** lassen sich unterscheiden (vgl. Hickethier 2010, S. 282 ff.):

- **Unterhaltungsshows**: Die Spannbreite reicht von Sendungen mit großen Nummernprogrammen einzelner Musikdarbietungen (Opernabend, Volksmusik, Disco) über Ratespiele, Quizsendungen (Gameshows) bis zu Comedy,
- **Talkshows** sind Diskussionssendungen, bei denen unterschiedliche Personen (meist Prominente) im Studio zu einem Thema diskutieren, geführt durch einen Moderator („Gastgeber").
- Sportsendungen erfahren v. a. bei großen Ereignissen eine besondere Aufmerksamkeit zu und sind als eine der wenigen Formen auch heute noch fähig, sehr hohe Einschaltquoten zu generieren.
- **Fernsehspiel** und **Fernsehfilm** gelten als fiktionale Grundformen des Fernsehens. Das Fernsehspiel entstand als TV-Variante des Theaterspiels und hatte höchste Bedeutung in den 50er Jahren. Heute dominiert der Fernsehfilm, im Privatfernsehen „TV-Movies" genannt.
- **Fernsehserien:** Serien gehören heute zu den wichtigsten Formen der Fernsehunterhaltung. Zu unterscheiden sind insbesondere **Daily Soaps**, **Telenovelas** und **Reality Soaps**.
- **Kinospielfilme** im Fernsehen: Obgleich die Rezeptionsbedingungen von Kinoproduktionen beim TV-Zuschauer deutlich schlechter sind, sind sie hoch erfolgreich: Die meisten Kinofilme erzielen erst in der TV-Verwertung befriedigende Erträge.
- Zielgruppensendungen, z. B. Kindersendungen sind auf ein spezielles Zielpublikum ausgerichtet.

Bild: WDR/Schnitt-Menzel/Reich

Bild: WDR

Was heißt eigentlich **„Qualität im Fernsehen"**? Nachfolgend sei ein Auszug aus einem Fachbeitrag wiedergegeben (Quelle: Blumers, Marianne / Gerstner, Oliver / Tebert, Miriam: Wie Zuschauer die Qualität von Fernsehen beurteilen, in: Media Perspektiven 3/2010, S. 131): „Beim Fernsehen wird oft behauptet, dass die Qualität nicht wirklich messbar sei. Gleichzeitig entbrennen heftige Diskussionen über die Qualität, die nicht selten in einem Schlagabtausch über die mangelnde Qualität von Fernsehen enden, bei dem eine Vielzahl von Qualitätskriterien zum Einsatz kommen, wie zum Beispiel „da werden Menschen bloßgestellt", „das ist oberflächlich", „schlecht recherchiert". Auch wenn Fernsehqualität nicht bis ins kleinste Detail messbar ist, kann man sich ihr über Qualitätskriterien nähern – sowohl aus dem journalistischen Blickwinkel der „Macher" als auch aus dem der Zuschauer. (5) Dabei wird man feststellen, dass beide Gruppen häufig mit ähnlichen Begriffen arbeiten. ... Ausgegangen wird von einem dynamischen Qualitätsbegriff, der dem Wandel der Zeit unterliegt und dessen Relevanz kontinuierlich überprüft wird gemäß der Devise: Über Qualität lässt sich nicht nur streiten, sondern über Qualität muss man streiten!" Der vollständige Artikel ist im Netz abrufbar unter http://www.media-perspektiven.de

Bild: WDR/Klaus Görgen

2.2.4 Kultur, Wissenschaft und Bildung

Die Medien sind wichtige Einrichtungen zur Kulturvermittlung und zur Information über Wissenschaft und Bildung. Mit „Kultur" sind v. a. die klassischen Künste gemeint, also Literatur, Musik, Theater, bildende Kunst und Architektur. Die Verlage und viele Rundfunksender, insbesondere die öffentlich-rechtlichen Rundfunkanstalten, betreiben einen hohen Aufwand zur **Kulturberichterstattung** und haben eigens dafür zuständige Redaktionen eingerichtet. Wegen der breiten Themenpalette, die es abzudecken gilt, ist es eine große Herausforderung, das kulturelle Leben, Wissenschaft und Bildung in Programmangebote zu überführen. Vom Kultur- und Wissenschaftsredakteur wird daher ein besonders hohes Fachwissen und ein sehr breiter Wahrnehmungshorizont verlangt.

Was die **Kulturangebote** anbelangt, so zeigt sich im Hinblick auf die einzelnen Medienbereiche das folgende Bild:

- Tages- und Wochenzeitungen investieren viel Energie in den Kulturteil, „Feuilleton" genannt. Es ist als große Leistung anzusehen, dass täglich und flächendeckend über Deutschland hinweg über Kultur berichtet wird. Die Kulturberichterstattung im Feuilleton-Teil erfolgt hauptsächlich in Form von Reportagen, Kritiken, Interviews und Rezensionen von Büchern und Filmen. Thematisch ist Feuilleton sehr weit gefasst bis hin zu Themen aus Religion und Medienpolitik.
- Zeitschriften: Deutschland weist eine sehr breite Palette an Zeitschriften zu Kultur, Wissenschaft und Bildung auf.
- Radio: Die häufigste Sendeform sind Kulturmagazine und Features. In eigens dafür eingerichteten Kulturkanälen betreiben v. a. die ARD-Anstalten trotz überschaubarer Einschaltzahlen einen hohen Aufwand. Alle öffentlich-rechtlichen Sender unterhalten eigene Sinfonieorchester für klassische und moderne Musik.
- Fernsehen: In den Hauptprogrammen sind kulturelle Angebote nur spärlich festzustellen, sie werden vielmehr in Kultur-Spartenkanäle abgedrängt. Hier aber ist eine beachtliche Vielzahl von Angeboten vorhanden, die sich in Kulturmagazinen, anspruchsvollen Sendungen, Dokumentationen oder in Übertragungen großer Kulturereignisse wie Konzerte und Theateraufführungen ausdrückt.

Nicht zu unterschätzen ist auch der **lokale und regionale Raum** als Bereich der Kulturvermittlung, was das folgende Zitat deutlich macht: „Das Kulturleben einer Stadt oder einer Region ist ein Mosaik unterschiedlicher kreativer Versuche und Aktivitäten. Kulturelle Hauptthemenbereiche sind im Lokaljournalismus: Architektur, Denkmalpflege, Bildende Kunst, Kunsthandwerk, Literatur, Film, Folklore, Erwachsenenbildung, Forschung und Lehre, Musik, Schauspiel, Tanz, Fotografie und Werbung. Neben der Berücksichtigung der kulturellen Aktivitäten kann die Lokalzeitung oder das Lokalradio mit eigenen Aktionen und Initiativen das kulturelle Leben und zugleich den Kulturteil bereichern" (Mast 2004, S. 434).

Ebenso vielfältig werden im Mediensystem Deutschlands Themen aus **Wissenschaft und Bildung** abgebildet. Besonders erwähnenswert ist hierbei die Zeitschriftenlandschaft mit vielen Produkten aus Medizin, Gesundheit oder Naturwissenschaft.

2.2.5 Mischformen

Üblicherweise geht man davon aus, dass **Informationsangebote** das **Denken** ansprechen, informierend und daher nicht emotional erlebt werden, **Unterhaltungsangebote** hingegen unterhaltend und **emotional**. Information und Unterhaltung stehen in dieser Perspektive im schroffen Gegensatz zueinander: Information = Denken, Kognition; Unterhaltung = Erleben, Emotion.

Heute werden die Grenzen zwischen diesen Formen jedoch immer fließender. Information und Unterhaltung werden gezielt miteinander vermischt, so dass es zu **Hybridformen** kommt, die man unter dem Überbegriff „Infotainment" fassen kann, eine Wortkombination aus den englischen Begriffen „information" und „entertainment". Die **Infotainment-Modelle** sind in nachfolgende Übersicht für das Fernsehen systematisiert (Quelle: Krüger 2010, S. 160):

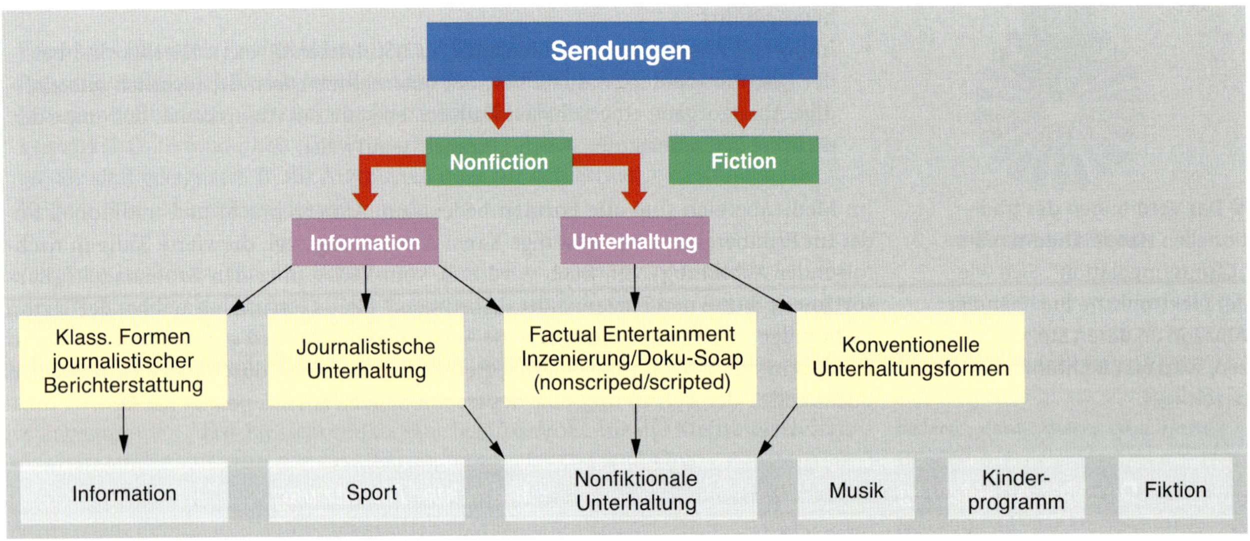

Neben den „reinen" Formen (Klassische Formen journalistischer Berichterstattung, Konventionelle Unterhaltungsformen) unterscheidet man die beiden **Hybridformate** der journalistischen Unterhaltung und des Factual Entertainment. Hybridformate subd „Formate des Reality-TV, die mit dokumentarischen Stilmitteln die Grenzen herkömmlicher Sendungsformen überschreiten, dabei Information mit Unterhaltung und Wirklichkeit mit Fiktion vermischen" (Krüger 2010, S. 158). **Zwei Formen** gibt es:

- **Journalistische Unterhaltung:** Hier werden in journalistische Formen (Magazin, Ratgeber, Reportage, Doku, Talkrunde) gezielt Unterhaltungselemente eingebaut.
- **Factual Entertainment:** Umgekehrt wird hier die Unterhaltung mit Elementen der Information „aufgeladen". So entstehen Dokumentationen, die mit oder ohne **Drehbuch** (Skript) inszeniert sind (**„Doku-Inszenierung"**). Eine **Doku-Soap** ist eine TV-Serie oder Staffel, die in keinem Bezug zu einem journalistischen Ereignis steht, aber als Reportage erscheinen soll, stets mit Affekten und Emotionen von Darstellern aufgeladen, die möglichst natürlich erscheinen sollen.

2.3.2 Netzbasierter Transport

Übersicht über die Plattformen

Die nicht-physische Übertragung von Inhalten zum Endkunden erfolgt über die elektronische Netzinfrastruktur. Dabei sind **sechs Plattformen** zu unterscheiden (vgl. u. a. Holznagel/Dürr/Hildebrand 2008):

❶ von lat. *terra*, die Erde

- **Terrestrik ❶**: Die Botschaften werden über erdgebundene technische Systeme verbreitet. Der Kommunikator gibt die Signale auf den Funksender, der Rezipient empfängt sie – unabhängig von einer Anschlussdose – über eine Antenne (stationär als Haus- oder Zimmerantenne oder portabel und mobil).
- **Kabel:** Das Kabelnetz überträgt die Signale über ein Breitbandkabel zum Endnutzer. Man unterscheidet fünf Netzebenen: (1) Netzebene 1: Überregionaler Signaltransport vom Rundfunkstudio zum zentralen Play-Out-Center des Kabelnetzbetreibers; (2) Netzebene 2: Bündelung der Signale und Transport an regionale „Headends"; (3) Signaltransport über Koaxial- oder Glasfasernetze in den Ortsbereichen bis zu den Grundstücksgrenzen bzw. Hausübergabepunkten; (4) Netzebene 4: Signaltransport innerhalb der Grundstücke und Häuser bis zu Kabelsteckdose innerhalb der Wohnung (Hausverteilung); (5) Netzebene 5: Endgerätebereich.
- **Satellit:** Ein Satellitensystem bietet ein umfassendes Portfolio von Broadcast- und Breitband-Lösungen. SES ASTRA z. B. „versorgt mehr als109 Millionen Satelliten- und Kabelhaushalte in Europa und besteht gegenwärtig aus 13 Satelliten, die 1.864 analoge und digitale Fernseh- und Radiokanäle bzw. Multimedia- und Internetdienste übertragen" (ebd. S. 102).
- **DSL** (Digital Subscriber Line): „Nutzung der Telefonleitung für die Übertragung hoher Bitraten; ADSL (Asymmetrical Digital Subscriber Line) Asymmetrische digitale Teilnehmer-Anschlussleitung; Datenrate im downlink: bis 6 Mbit/s; ADSL2+ bis 20 Mbit/s. VDSL (Very high bitrate Digital Subscriber Line) bis 50 Mbit/s im downlink" (Digitalisierungsbericht 2011, S. 70).
- **Mobil:** Die Botschaften werden mobil auf Endgeräten empfangen, v. a. auf Mobiltelefonen, Handhelds oder mobilen Videoplayern. Die Inhalte werden bislang über die Standards UMTS (Universal Mobile Telecommunications System) und DMB (Digital Multimedia Broadcast) übertragen. In der Entstehung ist LTE (Long-Term-Evolution) als neuer Mobilfunkstandard und UMTS-Nachfolger, der mit bis zu 300 Megabit pro Sekunde deutlich höhere Downloadraten erreichen kann. Das Grundschema von UMTS wird bei LTE beibehalten. „Mobiles Internet" (engl. mobile web) bezeichnet die Möglichkeit, das gesamte oder Teile des Internets, insbesondere das World Wide Web, auf einem Mobilgerät zugänglich zu machen.
- Offenes **Internet**: Das frei zugängliche Internet als technische Plattform ist ein Transportweg für jede Art von Medientypus, seien es Texte, Bilder, Videos, Audioströme oder multimediale Produkte. „Das Internet ist eine genau so grundlegende Infrastruktur wie die Versorgung mit Strom und Verkehrswegen. Es ermöglicht gegenüber den herkömmlichen Kommunikationswegen eine Öffnung, wie das Automobil gegenüber der Eisenbahn" (Digitalisierungsbericht 2011, S. 21).

Bücher, Ton- und Bildträger, Spiele-Software

Bei den nicht-aktuellen Trägermedien wird der Vertrieb der **nicht-körperlichen Version** immer wichtiger. Das (offene) Internet ist eine E-Commerce-Plattform, über die die gesamte Transaktion von der ersten Anbahnung des Geschäfts bis zur Auslieferung abgewickelt wird. Es fungiert also nicht mehr nur als Einrichtung, die den Verkaufsprozess unterstützt und körperlichen Versand des Produkts nur vorbereitet, sondern auch als Lieferant des fertigen Endprodukts – das „Fulfilment" der Transaktion erfolgt nicht-physisch digital. Im Einzelnen kann festgestellt werden:

- **Bücher:** Angeboten werden Downloads von elektronischen Büchern („**E-Books**") oder die Herstellung von digitalen Büchern auf Nachfrage („**Books-on-Demand**"), u. U. nur in der Auflage von einem einzigen Exemplar. Für Verlage eröffnen sich hier neue Möglichkeiten, ihre Produkte direkt über das Internet zu vertreiben und den Handel zu umgehen. Die Antwort des Online-Buchhandels ist freilich schon erfolgt, indem er besondere Lesegeräten auf den Markt gebracht hat, um sich unersetzbar zu machen (z. B. Lesegerät „Kindle" von Amazon).
- **Musik:** Trotz der nach wie vor hohen Zahl illegaler Downloads nimmt der Online-Vertrieb von Musikstücken zu. Es dominiert dabei der indirekte Vertrieb: Haupt-Anbieter sind Musik-Download-Plattformen (z. B. iTunes Music Store von Apple oder Musicload). Ein neues Kaufverhalten entsteht, da nicht mehr ganze CD-Alben gekauft werden müssen, sondern der einzelne Titel erworben werden kann.
- **Filme:** Analog zum Musikbereich nimmt die Zahl legal erworbener Downloads von Filmen zu. Daneben besteht die Möglichkeit zum Verleih von Filmen über Video-on-Demand bzw. Pay-per-View-Angebote.
- **Spiele:** Als Distributionsmodell kommen Hybridformen zur Anwendung: „Der Spieler erwirbt dabei eine Basisversion des Spieletitels in Form einer Hard-Disc im Handel. Spezielle Features, regelmäßige Updates und Service-Patches für das Spiel werden im Internet, zumeist direkt von dem Publisher, bereitgestellt. Die Erlösmodelle dieser Hybridstrategien variieren stark, von kostenlosen Updates über Pay-per-Update bis hin zu periodischen Subscription-Fees" (Wirtz 2011, S. 649).

Fernsehen

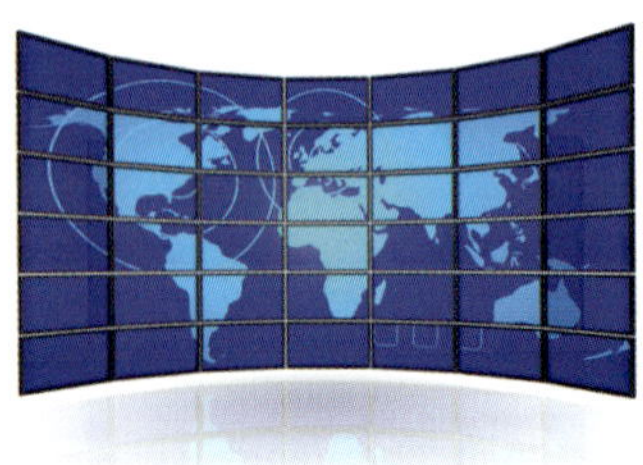

Die Digitalisierung macht es möglich, dass die zur Verfügung stehenden Kanäle viel effizienter genutzt werden können als bei analoger Übertragung. Durch Datenreduktion entstehen deutlich vergrößerte Transportkapazitäten. Der **Übertragungsstandard** im digitalen Fernsehen ist **DVB** (Digital Video Broadcasting), das in die folgenden Arten differenziert werden kann (vgl. Holznagel/Dörr/Hildebrand 2008, S. 93):

- DVB-T: Digitales Fernsehen via Antenne/Terrestrik
- DVB-C: Digitales Fernsehen via Kabel
- DVB-S: Digitales Fernsehen via Satellit
- DVB-H: Digitales Fernsehen via Antenne mit mobilen Empfangsgeräten. Das „H" steht für „Handhelds". Der Standard ist eine Weiterentwicklung von DVB-T.
- DMB (Digital Multimedia Broadcast): Interaktive multimediale Dienste für Mobilgeräte wie Digital-Rundfunk, digitalem Fernsehen und Websites.

❶ HbbTV (Hybrid broadcast broadband TV): „Von dem Europäischen Institut für Telekommunikationsnormen (ET-SI) publizierter Standard zur gleichzeitigen Darstellung von Fernseh- und Internetangeboten auf Fernsehbildschirmen. HbbTV wurde von einem Industriekonsortium und dem Institut für Rundfunktechnik entwickelt und basiert auf einer für die Unterhaltungselektronik entwickelten Variante der Programmiersprache" (Digitalisierungsbericht 2011, S. 71).

Die technische Entwicklung des Fernsehens wird maßgeblich durch das **Zusammenwachsen („Konvergenz")** von **TV und Internet** angetrieben. Beredten Ausdruck findet diese Entwicklung im 2010 eingeführten Standard **HbbTV** ❶, der dafür sorgt, dass der klassische Fernsehbildschirm zu einem „**Smart-TV**-Gerät" wird, das Fernsehen und Internet auf dem großen Bildschirm im Wohnzimmer vereint. Die Ausstrahlung in HD-Qualität ist inzwischen eine Selbstverständlichkeit.

➲ **Das Zusammenwachsen von Fernsehen und Internet wird auch als „Connected TV" bezeichnet.**

Connected TV – das ist die Verbindung von linearem Fernsehen, interaktiven programmbegleitenden Zusatzangeboten (über den sog. „Red Button") und der Onlinewelt. Neben dem hochleistungsfähigen stationären TV-Gerät im Wohnzimmer hat der Endkonsument die Möglichkeit, Fernsehen in höchster Qualität über den PC, das Notebook oder das Handy zu empfangen.

Die Marktanteile der Verbreitungswege im Fernsehen sehen wie folgt aus (Stand: 2011): Kabel 50,2 % / Satellit 44,7 % / Terrestrik 11,8 % / DSL-TV 3,0 %.

Die Entwicklung von **DVB-T** beleuchtet das nachfolgende Zitat: „DVB-T kann auch für Kabel- oder Satellitennutzer eine Ergänzung darstellen, z. B. für Zweit- oder Drittgeräte im Haushalt, für den portablen Empfang innerhalb und außerhalb von Gebäuden oder für zusätzliche regionale und lokale Angebote. Seit 2008 werden die öffentlich-rechtlichen Programme der ARD und des ZDF flächendeckend in ganz Deutschland über DVB-T verbreitet – die analoge Verbreitung von Fernsehprogrammen über Antenne wurde vollständig eingestellt. Laut Digitalisierungsbericht erreicht das digitale Antennenfernsehen einen Marktanteil von rund 11 % der bundesweiten Haushalte (Stand: 06/2010). Die Akzeptanz ist allerdings regional unterschiedlich stark ausgeprägt und lässt sich auf Grundlage der angebotenen Programme einteilen. In Ballungsgebieten mit privatem und öffentlich-rechtlichem Programmangebot liegt der Marktanteil teilweise bei 20 %, in Regionen mit rein öffentlich-rechtlichem Angebot liegt er teilweise unter 5 %." (Quelle: Die Medienanstalten).

❷ Eine Settop-Box ist ein dem Fernsehempfänger vorgeschaltetes Gerät, über das codierte Fernsehsignale, die das Fernsehgerät nicht empfangen kann, in ein Standardsignal decodiert werden. Die Settop-Box kann darüber hinaus diverse Zusatzfunktionen übernehmen wie z. B. die Nutzung von Online-Diensten und interaktive Verteildienste wie Video-on-Demand, Pay-per-View oder Teleshopping.

Der Verbreitungsweg, der noch am wenigsten digitalisiert ist, ist **Kabel-TV**. Nach wie vor hinkt die Digitalisierung im Kabel mit 42,5 % im Jahr 2011 der allgemeinen Entwicklung hinterher. Hauptgrund für diesen Sachverhalt sind die zusätzlichen Kosten, die beim digitalen Empfang für den Zuschauer anfallen: Beim Kabelempfang müssen die Kunden eine monatliche Gebühr an den Kabelnetzbetreiber entrichten. Will er auch die digitalen Programme nutzen, so benötigt er eine besondere Settop-Box für jedes Fernsehgerät ❷. Für den analogen Empfang der Kabelprogramme braucht er keinen Receiver.

Neben dem Kabel ist der **Satellit** Hauptverbreitungsweg für das Fernsehen. Sein Vorteil ist, dass keine laufenden Kosten für den Systemzugang anfallen; lediglich die Start-Investition für die Schüssel ist vom Zuschauer zu tragen. Seit 30. April 2012 ist die analoge Übertragung beendet und damit ein Digitalisierungsgrad von 100 Prozent erreicht, wie schon bei der terrestrischen Übertragung.

Telefongesellschaften bieten an, Fernsehen über das Telefonkabel als **DSL-TV** zu empfangen. Die Nutzung dieses Transportwegs wird als **IP-TV** (bzw. „IPTV") bezeichnet. „Einsatz des Internet-Protokolls bei der Fernsehübertragung führt zu „IP-TV" („Internet Protocol Television"). Aus der Bezeichnung ist nicht ersichtlich, über welches Netz die Übertragung erfolgt, weshalb stets eine zusätzliche Angabe erforderlich ist, z. B. IP-TV via DSL" (vgl. Digitalisierungsbericht 2011, S. 71).

IP-TV ist von **Web-TV** zu unterscheiden. Web-TV ist „Internetfernsehen" über das offene Internet. „Im Unterschied zu DSL-TV handelt es sich nicht um ein an einen bestimmten (Internet-)Provider gebundenes begrenztes Programmangebot, dessen Inhalte vom Infrastrukturanbieter zusammen gestellt werden. Web-TV kann im gesamten world wide web empfangen werden, wenn die Bandbreite eine ausreichende Übertragungskapazität zulässt. Unabhängig von der unbeschränkten Verbreitung über das www kann das Angebot verschlüsselt sein und eine Registrierung bzw. Freischaltung erforderlich sein" (Digitalisierungsbericht 2011, S. 72).

Es ist ein wichtiges Ziel der Medienpolitik, die Bevölkerung flächendeckend mit breitbandigem **Internet** zu versorgen: „Offenes Internet bietet mit dem Breitbandausbau eine annähernd vergleichbare Übertragungsqualität: Es erlaubt die Nutzung von Video sogar in HD-Qualität, mit steigenden Bandbreiten und der Fortentwicklung der Netzstrukturen auch von längeren Fernsehsendungen" (Digitalisierungsbericht 2011, S. 18). Es ist zu erwarten, dass mit dem Ausbau der Breitbandinfrastruktur viele Angebote in das offene Internet abwandern werden.

Immer wichtiger wird **Mobile TV**, also die „Übertragung von Bewegtbildinhalten auf mobile Endgeräte und Handys. Die Übertragung kann auf verschiedenen Wegen erfolgen, bspw. über mobiles Internet oder über Rundfunkinfrastrukturen mit Standards wie DMB (Digital Multimedia Broadcasting) oder DVB-H (Digital Video Broadcasting for Handhelds)" (Digitalisierungsbericht 2011, S. 72).

Radio

Das Radio ist der Bereich, der sich mit dem **UKW-Standard** am längsten als analoges Medium gehalten hat. Erst 2011 hat eine Einigung auf den Standard **DAB+** stattgefunden. Es handelt sich um eine Verbreitungstechnik, für die ein eigenes terrestrisches digitales Broadcastnetz aufgebaut wird. Daneben ist Radio in allen technischen Welten präsent: „Radio kommt via Internetstreaming und mobiler Apps auf webfähige PCs und Handys. Und kaum ein modernes Unterhaltungsgerät von TV bis zum Hifi-Verstärker, das nicht am Netz hängt und somit via Web auch die Radionutzung ermöglicht" (Digitalisierungsbericht 2011, S. 25).

Ein besonderes Augenmerk verdienen die **Web-Radios**. Ihre Zahl beläuft sich in Deutschland bereits auf ca. 3.100 Sender (BLM/Goldmedia: Webradiomonitor 2011). Davon sind rund 80 Prozent reine Webcasts, also Sender mit Programmen, die ausschließlich über das Web verbreitet werden. Hinzu kommen die sog. „Simulcast"-Radios, die 1:1 die Programme von UKW-Sendern übertragen (vgl. Digitalisierungsbericht 2011, S. 26 f.).

2.4 Rezipienten

2.4.1 Rezipienten als Zielgruppen

Ein **Rezipient** ist derjenige, an den die Botschaft eines Kommunikators adressiert ist, der also die Botschaft konsumiert oder empfängt. Ein Rezipient wird auch als **Adressat**, **Konsument**, **Kommunikant** oder **Empfänger** bezeichnet. Sind sehr viele Rezipienten gleichzeitig angesprochen, wie es in der Massenkommunikation der Fall ist, spricht man von einem **Publikum**. Rezipienten können dann beispielsweise folgende **Gruppen** sein:

- Schüler, die dem Lehrer bei der Darstellung des Themas „Die Bedeutung Karls des Großen für Europa" folgen.
- Leser einer Zeitung, einer Zeitschrift oder eines Buches.
- Fernsehzuschauer oder Radiohörer, die eine Sendung verfolgen.
- Zuhörer einer Rede oder einer Präsentation.
- Internet-User, die interessante Beiträge aus dem Netz downloaden.

Für jeden Kommunikator ist es wichtig zu wissen, wie der Rezipient, mit dem er in Kommunikation treten will, eigentlich beschaffen ist ❶. Dass dies notwendig ist, wird am augenfälligsten bei Wirtschaftsunternehmen, die eine Werbebotschaft an ihre Zielgruppe kommunizieren wollen. Erst wenn das Unternehmen genau geklärt hat, welche Zielgruppe als Rezipienten angesprochen werden soll, kann die Werbekampagne sinnvoll konzipiert werden.

❶ Das Forschungsgebiet in der Wissenschaft, das sich mit den Rezipienten befasst, nennt man **Rezipienten- oder Publikumsforschung**.

Zielgruppen (allgemein: Gruppen der Gesellschaft) lassen sich nach unterschiedlichen Kriterien einteilen. Man spricht auch von der Segmentierung von Zielgruppen bzw. von Rezipienten.

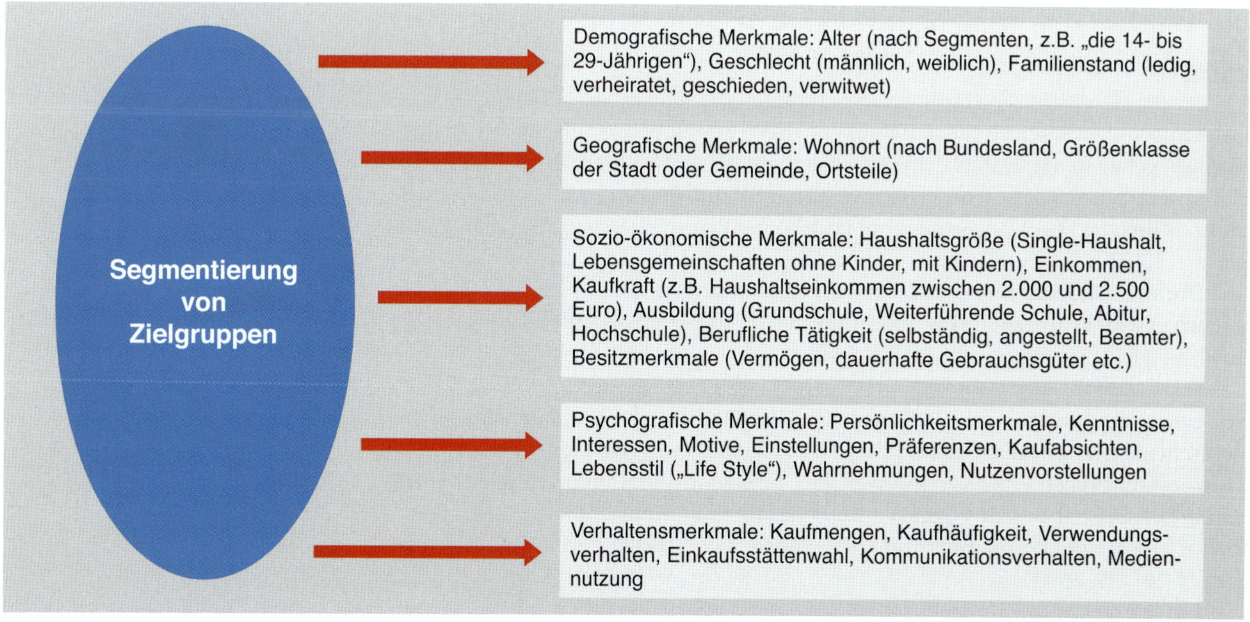

Sinus-Milieus

Von besonderer Relevanz bei der Bestimmung von Zielgruppen sind **psychografische Konzepte** und hier speziell Konzepte, die versuchen, den **Lebensstil** und die **Werthaltungen** der Menschen abzubilden. Sehr bekannt geworden ist dabei das Konzept der Sinus-Milieus. Es „sortiert" die Menschen in der Gesellschaft nach den beiden Kriterien „Soziale Lage" und „Grundorientierung":

- Soziale Lage: 1 = Oberschicht, Obere Mittelschicht, 2 = Mittlere Mittelschicht, 3 = Untere Mittelschicht, Unterschicht).
- Grundorientierung: A = Tradition, B = Modernisierung, Individualisierung, C = Neuorientierung.

Was die Grundorientierung anbelangt, kann man die folgenden langfristige Veränderungstendenzen in unserer Gesellschaft feststellen, die den Hintergrund der vorgenommenen Einteilung bilden (Quelle: Sinus 2010):

Modernisierung und Individualisierung	Überforderung und Regression	Entgrenzung und Segregation
Öffnung des sozialen Raumes durch höhere Bildungsqualifikationen, steigende Mobilität und Kommunikation und dadurch erweiterte Entfaltungsspielräume und Wahlmöglichkeiten	Wachsende Überforderung und Verunsicherung durch den technologischen, soziokulturellen und ökonomischen Wandel, durch die Vielfalt der Möglichkeiten (Multioptionsparalyse) und die Entstandardisierung von Lebensläufen - mit der Folge von Orientierungslosigkeit und Sinnverlust, Suche nach Entlastung, Halt und Vergewisserung (Regrounding)	Durch Globalisierung und Digitalisierung getriebenes Auseinanderdriften der Lebens- und Wertewelten, sozialhierarchische Differenzierung und wachsende soziale Deklassierungsprozesse, Erosion der Mitte, Entstehen einer kosmopolitischen Elite (One-World-Bewusstsein)

Danach sind in der Gesellschaft Deutschlands **zehn große Gruppen** auszumachen, die sich jeweils in Lebensauffassung und Lebensweise ähnlich sind. Diese Gruppierung eignet sich bestens zur Bestimmung der Basis-Zielgruppen im Marketing. Die zehn **Sinus-Milieus** sind auf der nächsten Seite kurz charakterisiert (Quelle: VuMA 2012 II).

➲ **Die Sinus-Milieus segmentieren die Gesellschaft in zehn Gruppen und legen dabei die Kriterien Soziale Lage und Grundorientierung zugrunde.**

Das nachfolgendes **Beispiel** zeigt die Zielgruppen des Radiosenders „MDR Jump" vom Mitteldeutschen Rundfunk (Quelle: ebd.; Stand 02.05.2012). Wie man sieht, ist das Publikum von MDR Jump stark auf die Milieus der Neuorientierung ausgerichtet. Alle vier diesbezüglichen Gruppen sind weit überdurchschnittlich vertreten, gemessen an deren Anteil in der Bevölkerung ❶.

❶ Lesebeispiel: Das Adaptiv-pragmatische Milieu mit einem Indexwert von 183 bedeutet, dass dieses Milieu den Radiosender MDR Jump im Vergleich zu seinem relativen Anteil an der Bevölkerung stark überdurchschnittlich nutzt. Würde die Nutzung dem Anteil an der Bevölkerung entsprechen, wäre der Wert 100.

Beispiel Sinus-Milieus MDR Jump

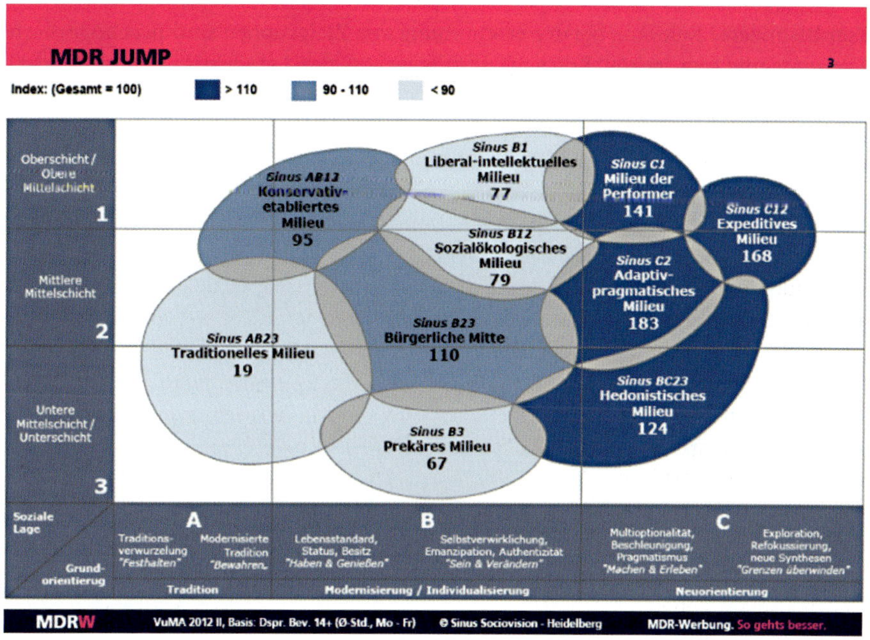

A **Milieus der Tradition**

- Konservativ-etabliertes Milieu: Das klassische Establishment
- Traditionelles Milieu: Die Sicherheit und Ordnung liebende Kriegs- bzw. Nachkriegsgeneration

B **Milieus der Moderne, individualistische Milieus**

- Liberal-intellektuelles Milieu: Die aufgeklärte Bildungselite mit liberaler Grundhaltung
- Sozial-ökologisches Milieu: Idealistisches konsumkritisches bzw. konsumbewusstes Milieu mit ausgeprägtem ökologischen und sozialen Gewissen
- Bürgerliche Mitte: Der leistungs- und anpassungsbereite bürgerliche Mainstream
- Prekäres Milieu: Die Teilhabe und Orientierung suchende Unterschicht mit starken Zukunftsängsten und Ressentiments

C **Milieus der Neuorientierung**

- Milieu der Performer: Die multi-optionale, effizienzorientierte Leistungselite
- Expeditives Milieu: Die extrem individualistisch geprägte digitale Avantgarde
- Adaptiv-pragmatisches Milieu: Die mobile, zielstrebige junge Mitte der Gesellschaft mit ausgeprägtem Lebenspragmatismus und Nutzenkalkül
- Hedonistisches Milieu: Die spaßorientierte moderne Unterschicht/untere Mittelschicht

2.4.2 Massenkommunikation: Publikum

Publikum

Ein „Publikum" war vor der Erfindung des Buchdrucks immer eine Ansammlung von Menschen, die an einem bestimmten Ort zusammenkamen, um z. B. an einer politischen Veranstaltung, einem sportlichen Wettkampf, einem Konzert oder einer Theateraufführung teilzunehmen. Publikum war stets ein **Präsenzpublikum**, das direkte interpersonale Kommunikation betrieben hat.

Das Publikum der **Massenmedien** ist demgegenüber eine undefinierte **Masse** – es ist ein massenhaftes und verstreutes („disperses") Publikum. Dieses **disperse Publikum** lässt sich wie folgt beschreiben: „Die Rezipienten kennen einander nicht und nutzen Massenmedien meist für sich allein oder in der Familie. Während Fernseh- und Radiosendungen immerhin zu einem bestimmten Zeitpunkt ausgestrahlt und deshalb zeitgleich rezipiert werden, ist bei textbasierten Medien (Print, Web) und Medienkonserven (z. B. DVDs, CDs) auch keine Gleichzeitigkeit der Nutzung gegeben. Da schließlich bei den traditionellen Medien kein medienimmanenter Rückkanal existiert, bleiben die Rezipienten auch den Kommunikatoren weitgehend unbekannt und anonym. Das disperse Publikum ist somit keine echte soziale Gruppe, deren Mitglieder untereinander in Kontakt stehen und miteinander interagieren. Es konstituiert sich nur kurzzeitig durch die Nutzung desselben Mediums und löst sich danach wieder auf" (Schweiger 2007, S. 222 f.; vgl. auch Maletzke 1978, S. 28; Bonfadelli 2001, S. 50 f.).

Aus dieser Eigenschaft der Massenmedien (und hier speziell des Fernsehens) folgt ein interessantes Phänomen, das mit dem Begriff **parasoziale Interaktion** belegt wird (vgl. hierzu Plake 2004, S. 210 ff.).

➲ **Parasoziale Interaktion drückt den Sachverhalt aus, dass das Fernsehen so tut, als ob eine direkte („Face-to-Face") Beziehung zwischen dem TV-Vertreter (z. B. Moderator) und dem Zuschauer bestehen würde.**

Der Zuschauer fühlt sich dadurch angesprochen, es entsteht das Gefühl von Nähe, ein wechselseitiges Vertrauensverhältnis wird vorgetäuscht. Der gesamte Kommunikationsvorgang stellt sich als eine Simulation direkter persönlicher Kommunikation dar. Die Interaktion ist nicht sozial, sondern parasozial.

Vor diesem Hintergrund ist es verständlich, dass die Protagonisten des Fernsehens wie Spielleiter, Moderatoren, Schauspieler oder Personen z. B. in Talkshows eine besondere Bedeutung besitzen. Das Publikum nimmt durch die Kamera am Geschehen teil, die Protagonisten sorgen durch den Blick in die Kamera für eine direkte Ansprache des Zuschauers.

Ein starker Effekt wird in diesem Zusammenhang auch durch Wiederholungen ausgelöst. Sie stellen Nähe her, indem in regelmäßigen Abständen immer dieselbe Nachrichtensprecherin, immer derselbe Moderator oder Talkmaster auftritt. Der Zuschauer hat das Gefühl, es mit einem „guten alten Bekannten" zu tun zu haben.

Typen von Mediennutzern

Das oben beschriebene Segmentierungskonzept der Sinus-Milieus hat den Anspruch, ein allgemein geeignetes Analyseinstrument zu sein. Speziell für Fragestellungen der Mediennutzung ist eine Vielzahl anderer Konzepte entwickelt worden (vgl. z. B. die Übersicht bei Meyen 2004, S. 130 ff.).

Ein Konzept aus neuerer Zeit ist die **MedienNutzerTypologie**, die als Version „MNT 2.0" seit 2007 im Rahmen der ARD/ZDF-Onlinestudie Anwendung findet. MNT zieht (wie bei Sinus) das Kriterium der Lebensstile heran, um soziale Gruppen zu bilden. Deren Mediennutzungsverhalten unterscheidet sich erheblich. Die nachfolgende Darstellung zeigt die Befunde (intermediale Nutzungsanteile, Summe 100 %) für 2011 (vgl. Mende/Oehmichen/Schröter 2012, S. 3 f.):

- Junge Wilde: Hedonistisch, materialistisch, konsumorientiert, Selbstbezüglichkeit und -unsicherheit, adoleszentes Verhalten
- Zielstrebige Trendsetter: Pragmatische Idealisten und selbstbewusste Macher, breite Interessen, Erfolgsorientierung, Vollausschöpfung der Möglichkeiten neuer Medien
- Unauffällige: Orientierung am Privaten, wenig Kontakte, passiv, übernehmen ungern Verantwortung, ökonomisch eingeschränkt, starkes Bedürfnis nach Unterhaltung und Ablenkung
- Berufsorientierte: Starke Berufsbezogenheit, wenig Zeit für anderes, nüchtern, rational, Kulturfaible, eher ledig als verheiratet
- Aktiv Familienorientierte: Familienmenschen, bodenständig, selbstbewusst, gut organisiert, clever/findig, dynamisch/lebendig
- Moderne Kulturorientierte: (Ehemalige) kulturelle Avantgarde, unter anderem arrivierte „68er", intellektuellster Typ, hohes Aktivitätsniveau, medienkritisch, weltoffen
- Häusliche: Bedürfnis nach Sicherheit und Kontinuität im Alltag, eher traditionelle Wertvorstellungen und Rollenbilder, relativ enger Aktionsradius, häuslicher Rahmen wichtig
- Vielseitig Interessierte: Sehr breites Interessenspektrum, gesellig, aktiv, erlebnisfreudig, bodenständig
- Kulturorientierte Traditionelle: Eher konservativ und traditionell geprägtes Weltbild, häuslicher Radius ist wichtig, gleichzeitig spielen aber auch (hoch-)kulturelle Aktivitäten eine Rolle
- Zurückgezogene: Traditionell, häuslich, eher passiv, hohe Bedeutung von Sicherheit und Harmonie, gering ausgeprägte Interessen

	Gesamt	Junge Wilde	Zielstrebige Trendsetter	Unauffällige	Berufsorientierte	Aktiv Familienorientierte	Moderne Kulturorientierte	Häusliche	Vielseitig Interessierte	Kulturorientierte Traditionelle	Zurückgezogene
Radio	38,2	30,0	33,6	34,2	34,3	40,7	42,3	40,5	42,3	45,6	28,9
Fernsehen	38,8	27,7	22,3	39,9	27,1	37,9	27,0	50,6	43,8	41,6	60,9
Tageszeitung	6,3	1,9	5,4	2,6	5,9	5,6	11,1	6,8	11,8	10,7	9,5
Internet	16,7	40,4	38,7	23,3	32,8	15,8	19,6	2,1	2,1	2,1	0,6

Beispiel MedienNutzerTypologie MDR Jump

Bei den Sinus-Milieus (s. o.) war der Radiosender MDR Jump vorgestellt worden, wie sich die einzelnen Milieus in der Hörerschaft wiederfinden. Bezogen auf das Konzept der MedienNutzerTypologie ergibt sich das folgende Bild (Quelle: MDR Hörfunk Monitor Jahreswerte 2008):

Die drei Gruppen Junge Wilde, Zielstrebige Trendsetter und Aktiv Familienorientierte sind die stärksten Nutzertypen. Bei Jump-Hörern sind sie fast doppelt so stark wie der Durchschnitt im MDR-Gebiet Sachsen, Sachsen-Anhalt und Thüringen. Die Jungen Wilden stellen mit 18 Prozent den höchsten Anteil der Jump-Hörer.

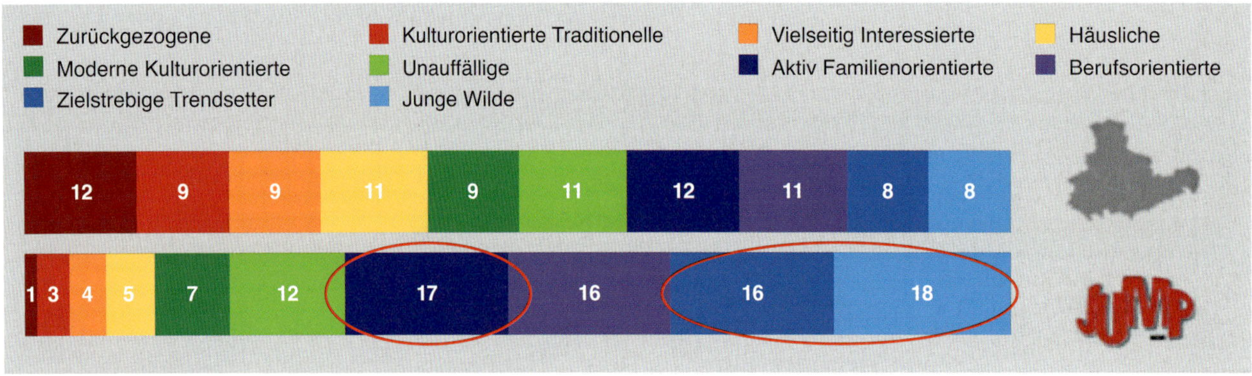

Trends im Nutzungsverhalten

Alle Medienunternehmen stehen vor der wichtigen Frage, welche Zielgruppen ihre Medienangebote in welcher Form nutzen. Sie setzen viel Energie ein, um herauszufinden, wie sich die Rezipienten verhalten und Gründe für die Motive zu finden. Der **Medienforschung** eröffnet sich ein großes Feld!

Ganz generell lassen sich im Hinblick auf die Mediennutzung eine Reihe von **Megatrends** ausmachen, die dafür sorgen, dass sich die Medienlandschaft Stück für Stück verändert. Die wichtigste Konsequenz wird sein, dass die traditionellen Medien Presse und Rundfunk erhebliche Bedeutungsverluste hinnehmen müssen und daher vor der Aufgabe stehen, neue Geschäftsmodelle zu entwickeln. Die Trends:

- Ausweitung des Zeitbudgets
- Zeit- und ortsunabhängige On-Demand-Nutzung
- Parallelnutzung von Medien („Multitasking")
- Reduktion von Komplexität durch Auswahlstrategien: verstärkte, eng auf Interessen abgestimmte Selektion, habituelle Auswahlmuster (v. a. durch Präferenzen für Marken)
- Sinkende Bindung an einzelne Angebote
- Generationsspezifische Nutzungsmuster

2.4.3 Unternehmenskommunikation: Zielgruppen

In der Unternehmenskommunikation sind die Rezipienten die aktuellen oder potenziellen Kunden. Sie gilt es zu erreichen und durch eine gekonnte kommunikative Ansprache für sich zu gewinnen. Der Kunde („customer") und die Beziehung zu ihm („relationship") ist die entscheidende Grundvoraussetzung für den wirtschaftlichen Erfolg eines Unternehmens. Das „Zauberwort" heißt folglich Kundenbeziehung, im Fachjargon „CRM", **Customer Relationship Management**, genannt.

Entscheidende Erfolgsfaktoren im Umgang mit den Kunden sind **Kundenzufriedenheit** und **Kundenbindung**. Frage, wie man das erreichen kann. Interne Faktoren sind wichtig, aber auch externe. Nachfolgende Darstellung zeigt die „Erfolgskette der Kundenorientierung" (Quelle: Meffert/Bruhn 2009, S. 53):

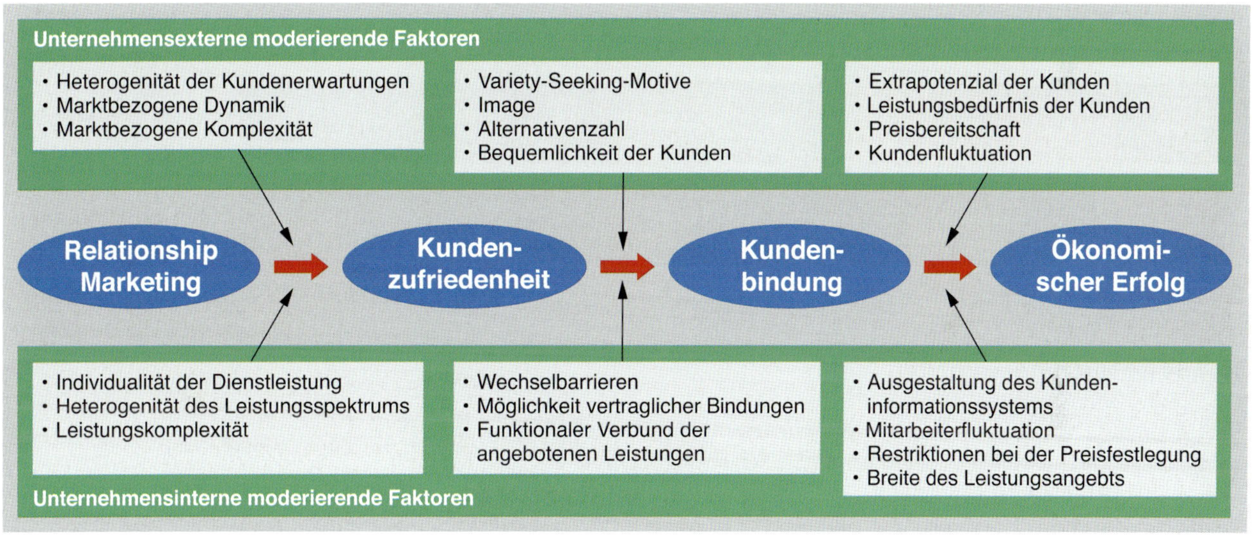

Die Darstellung zeigt, dass **Kundenzufriedenheit** zum einen von den Kundenerwartungen und von der Dynamik und Komplexität des Marktes abhängig ist (externe Faktoren), zum anderen davon, wie individuell das Unternehmen seine Dienstleistung erbringt, aber auch wie vielschichtig (heterogen) und komplex die angebotene Leistung ist (interne Faktoren). Das Unternehmen muss also viel Überzeugungsarbeit leisten, um den Kunden zufrieden stellen zu können!

Was die **Kundenbindung** anbelangt, so wird diese auf der einen Seite (externe Faktoren) durch die Einstellung des Kunden bestimmt: er sucht die Vielfalt („variety seeking"), er ist bequem, er orientiert sich am Image des Unternehmens bzw. der Produktmarken und will bei seinen Kaufentscheidungen möglichst viele Alternativen zur Auswahl haben. Auf der anderen Seite (interne Faktoren) kann das Unternehmen versuchen, sog. Wechselbarrieren aufzubauen, ihn vertraglich zu binden oder ein ganzes Leistungspaket im Verbund anzubieten. Das alles macht es dem Kunden schwer, zu einem anderen Produkt überzuwechseln ❶.

❶ Wechselbarrieren aufbauen und den Kunden „an sich zu fesseln" gelingt z. B. durch technische Standards, z. B. Microsoft-Software. Ein Beispiel für ein Leistungspaket ist z. B. die Apple-Produktfamilie (iPhone, iPad). Eine hohe Kundenbindungswirkung wird auch durch eine starke Marke ausgeübt.

Die Unternehmenskommunikation, insbesondere die Werbung, will beim Rezipienten bzw. Kunden konkrete Ziele erreichen. Vor allem zwei **Ziele der Kommunikation** muss es scharf im Auge behalten:

- Bekanntheit: Zum einen muss sichergestellt werden, dass bei den bestehenden Kunden die Bekanntheit erhalten bleibt, was man durch „Auffrischung" der Werbebotschaft zu erreichen versucht. Zum anderen gilt es, potentielle Kunden mit den Produkten in Berührung zu bringen und sie dazu zu bringen, dass sie die Produkte überhaupt wahrnehmen.
- Image: Ziel muss es sein, die Persönlichkeit der Produkte oder des ganzen Unternehmens positiv erscheinen zu lassen. Ausdruck für die Produktpersönlichkeit ist die Marke, die ein „Vorstellungsbild" im Kopf des Verbrauchers erzeugt.

Um bei einem neuen Produkt ein hohes Maß **Bekanntheit** zu erreichen – und das zudem in relativ kurzer Zeit – bedarf es des Einsatzes von Medien, die in der Zielgruppe schnell und viel **Reichweite** schaffen können ❶. Medien, die diese Fähigkeit aufweisen, sind insbesondere das Fernsehen, das Radio und die Tageszeitung. Die nachfolgende Darstellung zeigt die Leistungsfähigkeit dieser „Mega-Medien" im Hinblick auf die Durchdringung von Zielgruppen (Quelle: Zerdick et al. 2004, S. 24):

❶ „Die Reichweite gibt an, wie viele Personen insgesamt (Grundgesamtheit) bzw. innerhalb einer Bevölkerungsgruppe (Zielgruppe) durch eine Schaltung in einem Werbeträger erreicht werden" (Kloss 2007, S. 261).

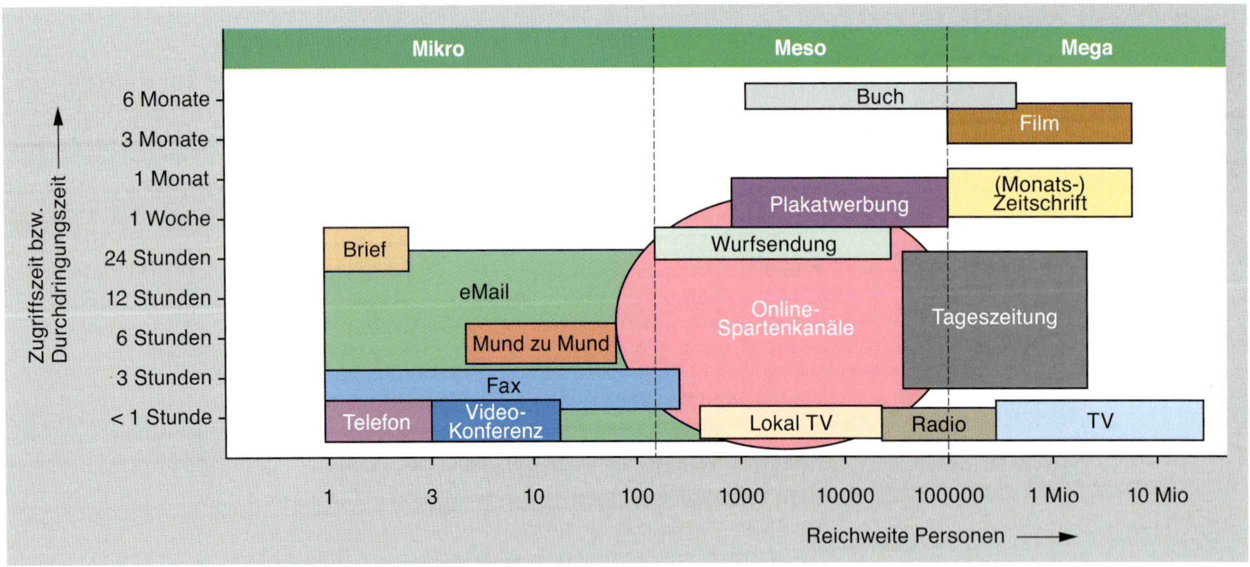

„Mikro-Medien" mit geringer und „Meso-Medien" mit mittelgroßer Reichweite können das Reichweitenziel also deutlich schlechter erreichen.

Um ein Produkt-Image in der Wahrnehmung des Kunden zu formen, bedarf es eines längeren Atems. Es kommt dabei weniger auf die kurzfristige und schnelle Reichweite der Botschaft in der Zielgruppe an, sondern eher darauf, über einen längeren Zeitraum hinweg kontinuierlich die Werbebotschaft bekannt zu machen, m.a.W. es muss die **Kontakthäufigkeit** ❷ ausreichend hoch sein.

❷ Die Kontakthäufigkeit gibt an, wie oft die Zielgruppe Kontakt mit den Werbeträgern hat, in denen die Werbebotschaft eingeschaltet ist.

2.5 Medienwirkungen

❶ In der Wissenschaft nennt man dieses Forschungsgebiet „Wirkungsforschung" oder **Medienwirkungsforschung**.

Das Thema der **Wirkungen** ist der letzte Baustein der Lasswell-Formel. Hier öffnet sich das ganze weite Feld der **Medientheorie**, speziell der **Medienwirkungsforschung**, deren Aufgabe es ist, die Wirkungsweisen von Medien sichtbar und nachvollziehbar zu machen ❶. Bereits hier ist anzumerken, dass die Wissenschaft beim Thema der Medienwirkungen keine einheitliche Sprache spricht und eine große Spannbreite von Erklärungsversuchen, Vermutungen und Modellvorstellungen entwickelt hat. Von einer einheitlichen Theorie der Medienwirkungen kann also nicht die Rede sein. Einig ist sich die Wissenschaft aber darin, dass höchste Vorsicht geboten ist, wenn populäre Vorstellungen über die **Wirkungen von Medien** in den Raum gestellt werden. Häufig sind die Behauptungen schlicht unhaltbar oder zumindest viel zu einseitig. Einige kleine Beispiele:

- Radiohören macht Kinder und Jugendliche bei den Schularbeiten unaufmerksam und nervös.
- Fernsehen macht durch seine Gewaltdarstellungen Kinder aggressiv.
- Fernsehen verleitet den Menschen zu Passivität.
- Die Medien überfluten uns mit Informationen und machen uns orientierungslos.

Auch in der Wissenschaft selbst ist man sich nicht immer einig. Viele der vertretenen Positionen sind bei näherem Hinsehen keineswegs immer überzeugend. Nicht selten stehen sich widersprüchliche Ansichten gegenüber. Allerdings besteht Einigkeit darin, dass den Medien selbstverständlich eine – nicht selten starke – Wirkung beizumessen ist. Einige wenige Beispiele für unmittelbar nachvollziehbare (emotionale) Wirkungen der Medien seien hier dargestellt:

- Bei einer tragischen Kinofilm-Szene brechen drei Viertel der Kinobesucher in Tränen aus.
- Die Familie schaut sich den Urlaubsfilm an und freut sich über die schöne Zeit am Meer.
- Der Schüler arbeitet das vorliegende Lehrbuch über die Medien durch und ist nachher bestens informiert, im Gegensatz zu vorher.
- Die Fernsehberichterstattung über eine Flutkatastrophe in Afrika löst eine Welle von Hilfsbereitschaft aus. Es werden 5 Millionen Euro gespendet.
- Die Besteigung der Eiger-Nordwand wird im Fernsehen live übertragen. Ein Zuschauer vor dem Fernsehgerät erinnert sich an eine brenzliche Situation auf einer Bergwanderung, bei der er beinahe abgestürzt ist, und muss den Fernseher ausmachen.
- Die Hausfrau im Supermarkt ist dabei, Suppenpulver einzukaufen. Sie erinnert sich an die gestrige Fernsehwerbung über „Maggis Suppen-Terrine" und entscheidet sich, diese einmal auszuprobieren.
- In der Mediengeschichte gibt es ein prominentes Beispiel für die Wirksamkeit der Medien, als in den 30er Jahren in den USA nach einer fiktionalen Radiosendung über die Landung von Marsmenschen tausende von Menschen in Furcht auf die Straßen rannten.

2.5.1 Medien und Individuum

Bedeutung des Menschenbildes

Die Beantwortung der Frage, welche Wirkungen die Medien auf den einzelnen Menschen ausüben, hängt entscheidend vom zugrunde gelegten **Menschenbild** ab. Drei unterschiedliche Vorstellungen über die Medienwirkung auf den Menschen stehen sich gegenüber (vgl. Schmidt/Zurstiege 2007, S. 77; Bonfadelli 2001, S. 25 ff.;):

- These von den **starken Medienwirkungen** („Omnipotenz der Medien"): Der Mensch wird als ein direkt beeinflussbares Wesen angesehen und die Annahme unterstellt, dass Kommunikation ein Vorgang der Informationsübertragung ist. Medien üben daher eine starke Wirkung bei den Menschen aus, haben Macht über sie. Die Leitfrage lautet: „Was machen die Medien mit den Menschen?"
- These von den **schwachen Medienwirkungen** („Ohnmacht der Medien"): Hier wird der Mensch als ein autonomes Wesen betrachtet, das in der Kommunikation mit den anderen Menschen eine eigenständige Position einnimmt. Er ist eigenwillig und wählerisch und gesteht den Medien nicht die Oberhoheit in seinem Leben zu. Medien können daher nur eine schwache Wirkung erzeugen. Die Leitfrage lautet nun umgekehrt: „Was macht der Mensch mit den Medien?"
- These von der **differenzierten Medienwirkung:** Noch einmal zu einer anderen Vorstellung kommt man, wenn man den Menschen als ein Wesen versteht, das in ständigem sozialen Austausch mit anderen Menschen steht. Nun stellt sich die Leitfrage: „Wie interagieren Menschen und Medien miteinander?"

Wie man sieht, kommt man zu völlig **entgegengesetzten Aussagen über die Medienwirkungen**, je nachdem, welcher Theorie über den Menschen man folgt. Daher kann es auch nicht überraschen, dass eine große Vielzahl von Modellen „auf dem Markt" ist, die zu teilweise ganz unterschiedlichen Aussagen kommen.

Wie wirken Medien? Einige Anmerkungen

Ein wichtiger Ausgangspunkt der Wirkungsforschung sind die verhaltensorientierten bzw. **behavioristischen Modelle**, wie sie in Kapitel 1 mit den S-R-Modellen und S-O-R-Modellen angesprochen wurden. Bei diesen Modellen wird angenommen, dass die Medien einen Stimulus („S") setzen, z. B. in Form einer Anzeige oder einer Fernsehwerbung, und der Organismus („O"), der Medienkonsument mit einer Antwort, einem „Response" („R") reagiert. Das Verhalten des Menschen ist, so die Annahme, von einem Stimulus abhängig.

Eine große Herausforderung für die verhaltensorientierte Medienwirkungsforschung ist es, die Vorgänge innerhalb des Organismus (des „O") zu erklären. So ist es nicht einfach, die folgenden Fragen zu beantworten: Wie kann man die Wirkung von Medienkonsum auf das Verhalten erklären? Welche Mechanismen löst die Mediennutzung im Menschen aus? Welche Einflussfaktoren kommen in Frage? Woran soll man die Wirkung messen?

❶ Vgl. hierzu Kroeber-Riel, Wolfgang / Weinberg, Peter: Konsumentenverhalten, München 2003, S. 590 ff.)

Eine erste Vorstellung über die Wirkungsmechanismen liefert die Unterscheidung nach den folgenden drei zentralen Wirkungskategorien ❶:

- Informationswirkungen: Vermittlung von Wissen
- Beeinflussungswirkungen: Verstärkung von Meinungen
- Überzeugungswirkungen: Veränderung bestehender Einstellungen

Will man mit Medien eine Vermittlung von Wissen herbeiführen, spricht man von **Informationswirkungen**. Es wird gemeinhin angenommen, dass das Fernsehen mit seinen informativen Sendungen am meisten zur Verbreitung von Informationen in der Bevölkerung beiträgt, – eine Annahme, die als falsch gelten muss. Vielmehr spielen in der Informationsvermittlung eindeutig die gedruckten Medien die Hauptrolle, sie sind dem Fernsehen im Hinblick auf diesen Aspekt überlegen. Ein wichtiger Grund liegt darin, dass das Fernsehen mit seiner ihm eigenen Bildersprache die Aufmerksamkeit auf Aktionen und emotionale Ereignisse lenkt, was die Vermittlung sachlicher Information und von Wissen eher erschwert als fördert. Fernsehen gilt daher als ausgesprochenes Unterhaltungsmedium. Für die Zukunft ist zu erwarten, dass das Internet mit seiner exorbitanten Informationsfülle und im Zuge des Ausbaus des Internets zu einem Hochleistungsnetz, das alle medialen Formen abbilden kann, der Dominanz der Druckmedien heftig zusetzen wird.

Die Wirkungen der Medien auf die Meinungen der Menschen werden als **Beeinflussungswirkungen** bezeichnet. Eine wichtige Erkenntnis der Wissenschaft ist, dass eine Hauptwirkung der Massenkommunikation darin besteht, beim einzelnen Menschen vorhandene Meinungen zu bestätigen und zu verstärken. Der Fernsehzuschauer wählt beispielsweise bevorzugt diejenigen Sendungen aus, die im Einklang mit seinen Meinungen stehen und vermeidet Sendungen, deren Inhalt im Widerspruch zu ihnen stehen. Der Grund für dieses Phänomen liegt darin, dass er die sog. „kognitive Dissonanz" ❷ vermeiden möchte, die entsteht, wenn er Sendungen zur Kenntnis nimmt, die nicht seinen eigenen Meinungen und Einstellungen entsprechen.

❷ **Kognitive Dissonanz** ist ein „Missklang" in der Verstandeswelt eines Menschen, die durch die Konfrontation mit anderen Ansichten ausgelöst wird. Zum Beispiel werden Leser, die sich als konservativ definieren, nicht unbedingt regelmäßig die „taz" lesen wollen, umgekehrt scheuen sich „links" positionierte Leser, die Tageszeitung „Die Welt" zu abonnieren.

Werden durch die Medien bestehende Einstellungen verändert, spricht man von **Überzeugungswirkungen**, ein Aspekt, der besonders für die Werbung von größter Bedeutung ist, geht es dieser doch darum, die Einstellungen der Konsumenten in Richtung des beworbenen Produktes positiv zu verändern und sie zu veranlassen, in der Kaufsituation die richtige Entscheidung zu treffen. Es ist bekannt, dass Überzeugungswirkungen vor allem dadurch ausgelöst werden können, dass systematisch und professionell sog. „Überzeugungstechniken" bzw. „Sozialtechniken" zum Einsatz kommen. Von überragender Bedeutung ist es in diesem Zusammenhang, beim Zuschauer, Zuhörer oder Leser möglichst intensive Emotionen auszulösen, ein Ziel, das am besten durch die Verwendung von Bildern erreicht werden kann. Die Bildkommunikation ist insofern der „Königsweg", wenn es gilt, Überzeugungswirkungen zu erzeugen.

Entscheidender „Knackpunkt" in der behavioristischen Wirkungstheorie ist also die **Einstellung**, die darüber entscheidet, wie ein menschliches Wesen den Medien gegenübertritt. Die Einstellung kann dabei als Tendenz verstanden werden, wie ein Mensch

auf Einflüsse reagiert, und sie kann in drei zentrale Komponenten unterschieden werden (vgl. Burkart 2002, S. 190):

- **Wissen:** Kognitive Komponente. Die Einstellung ist eng und ganz unmittelbar mit den konkreten Vorstellungen oder Wahrnehmungen verknüpft.
- **Gefühl:** Affektive Komponente. Die Einstellung wird immer auch durch die Emotionen geprägt, die mit der Vorstellung oder Wahrnehmung einhergeht.
- **Handlung:** Konative Komponente. Die Einstellung ist mit Verhaltenstendenzen verbunden, die durch die Vorstellung oder Wahrnehmung wachgerufen werden.

Der grundsätzlich starke Einfluss der Medien auf den Menschen begründet man vor diesem Hintergrund also damit, dass der Medienkonsum zu Einstellungsänderungen führt, die unser Wissen, unsere Emotionen und unsere Handlungen beeinflussen.

In einem größeren **Wirkungsmodell** sind von Maletzke (vgl. Maletzke 1981, S. 31) die genannten Einstellungswirkungen noch um die Attitüden und die tiefenpsychologische Reaktionen erweitert worden. In seinem Modell der **„Wirkfaktoren beim Rezipienten"** (vgl. die Abbildung) sind die fünf Wirkungsbereiche auf der letzten Stufe ausgewiesen. Die Brücke zwischen dem Angebot (= Medienkonsum) und den Wirkungen bilden die vier Faktoren (I) Voraussetzungen, Prädispositionen, (II) die Situation, in der sich der Rezipient befindet, (III) die psychischen Prozesse sowie (IV) soziale Faktoren. Diese Faktoren fungieren wie ein Filter zwischen den kommunikativen Angeboten und den beim Rezipienten ausgelösten Wirkungen.

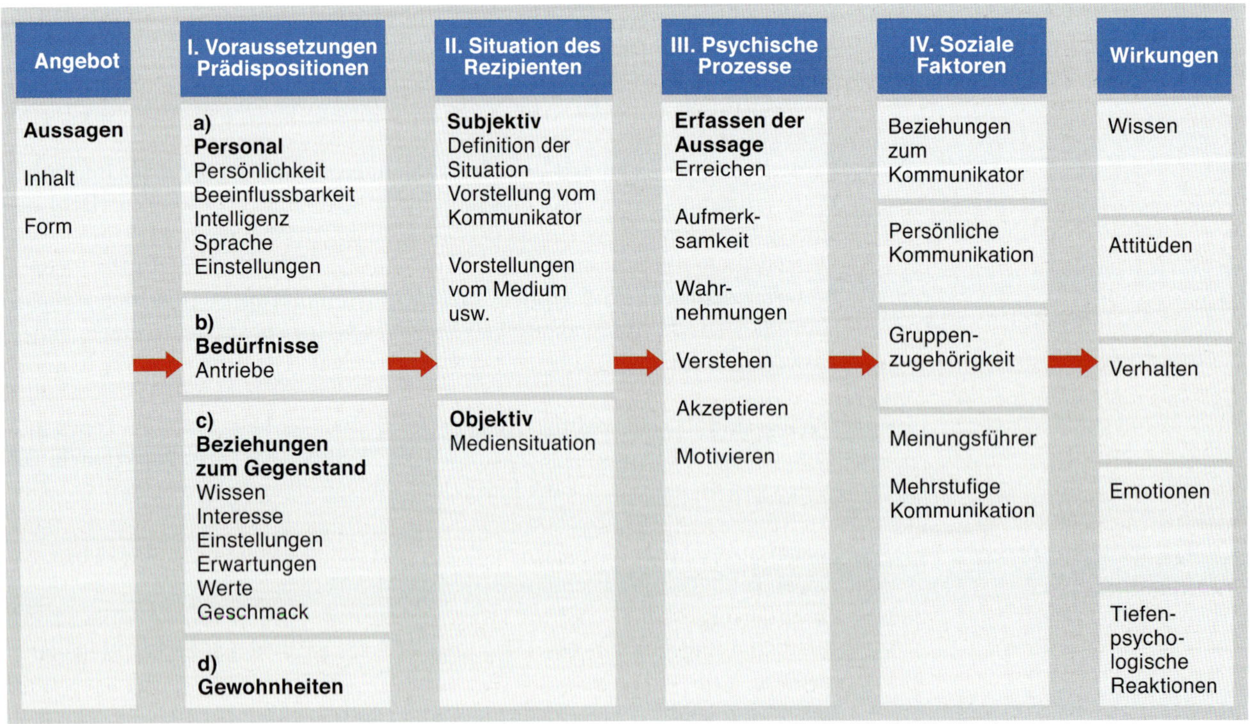

2.5.2 Medien und Gesellschaft

Gesellschaftliche Funktionen der Medien

❶ „Product Placement" spielt in Film und Fernsehen eine große Rolle. Man platziert dabei Markenprodukte ganz gezielt in die Handlung eines Spielfilms und macht dadurch Werbung für das Produkt. Product Placement ist nur in engen Grenzen erlaubt.

Die Medien sind ein wichtiger nicht mehr wegzudenkender **Teil unseres gesellschaftlichen Lebens**. Sie prägen unseren Alltag von morgens bis abends und sind allgegenwärtig. Wenn ein großes Fußballspiel übertragen wird, sitzt die ganze Nation vor dem Fernseher. Viele Stunden eines Tages findet musikalische Beschallung statt. Unser Leben ist geprägt vom Blick auf Bildschirme, im privaten wie auch im beruflichen Bereich. Mit Prospekten, Plakaten, Anzeigen, Werbespots, Trailern oder „Product Placement" ❶ verfolgt uns die Werbung auf Schritt und Tritt. Und auch das Buch ist nach wie vor von hoher Bedeutung. Leitmedium ist und bleibt – trotz Internet – aber immer noch das Fernsehen.

Das **Medium Fernsehen** kann in seiner **Bedeutung** kaum überschätzt werden. Es ist geradezu als ein „Jahrhundertmedium" zu bezeichnen (Burkart), das im Bewusstsein der Bevölkerung größte Beachtung genießt. So kann es nicht verwundern, dass das Fernsehen immer im Gespräch ist, wenn es in unserer Gesellschaft positive oder negative Erscheinungen wie Bildung, Demokratie, Gewaltanwendung oder Kulturverfall zu verhandeln gilt. Die Diagnosen reichen von euphorischer Begeisterung („Fernsehen ist toll") bis zu kulturpessimistischen Angstparolen („Das Fernsehen zerstört die Familien"). Einige **Aussagen**:

- „Das Fernsehen ist – trotz der umfangreicheren Radionutzung und der gewachsenen Bedeutung des Internets – noch immer das Leitmedium der gesellschaftlichen Kommunikation. Es wird von den meisten Menschen als der zentrale Ort des gesellschaftlichen Diskurses angesehen, ihm wird von unterschiedlichen gesellschaftlichen Gruppen eine große Aufmerksamkeit entgegengebracht" (Hickethier, S. 268).
- Fernsehen ist ein „multifunktionales Allroundmedium" und dient der Informationsversorgung, macht Spaß und sorgt für Entspannung, ebenso wie es Denkanstöße gibt und eine Gewohnheit darstellt (Ridder/Engel 2005, S. 431 ff.).
- „Versteht man das Fernsehen als Medium, in dem auf anschaulich-visuelle Weise Probleme der Gesellschaft erörtert, diskutiert und problematisiert werden können, sind eine Vielzahl von Sendungen als Podien zu verstehen, auf denen einem bundesweiten Publikum Meinungen präsentiert werden" (Hickethier, S. 282).

Die Medien sind also ein wichtiger Teil der Gesellschaft. Sie helfen uns, das Leben besser zu bewältigen. Die positiven Leistungen der Medien nennt man **Funktionen**. Die folgenden gesellschaftlichen Funktionen der Medien werden unterschieden:

- **Sozialisation:** Medien erziehen zu Kultur und gedeihlichem Zusammenleben, prägen Leitbilder und beeinflussen den sozialen Wandel.
- **Orientierung:** Medien sind wie Leitsterne, die dazu da sind, Orientierung zu geben und Angebote zur Beantwortung der Frage nach dem Sinn des Lebens zu machen.
- **Rekreation** (= Erholung): Medien decken den Bedarf nach Zerstreuung, Ablenkung und Unterhaltung.

- **Integration:** Medien leisten einen Beitrag dazu, die Gesellschaft zusammen zu halten, die immer komplexer wird und in Gruppen und Grüppchen auseinander zu fallen droht.

Kritik am Fernsehen

Die Medien werden nicht jeder der genannten Funktionen voll gerecht. Es sind auch Mängel zu beklagen, die dem hohen Anspruch nicht gerecht werden. Insbesondere das Fernsehen wird gerne auf die „Anklagebank" gesetzt. Nachfolgend soll eine kurze **Übersicht** über die typischen „Anklagepunkte" aufgelistet werden. Dem Fernsehen wird vorgeworfen:

- Das Fernsehen verwandelt unsere ganze Kultur in eine riesige Arena für das Show-Business. Fernsehen ist nichts als „Show-Biz". Es macht alles zur Unterhaltung. Dadurch nimmt die Urteilsfähigkeit des einzelnen Menschen ab. Der Vertreter dieser kulturpessimistischen These ist Neil Postman, der mit seinem Werk „Wir amüsieren uns zu Tode" größte Beachtung erfahren hat.
- Das Fernsehen vermittelt eine Scheinwelt, in der die Menschen immer wieder Tatsache und Fiktion vermischen oder gar verwechseln. Manche Fernsehsendung wird als Tatsache gewertet, obwohl sie eine reine Fiktion darstellt. Die Fähigkeit der Zuschauer, zwischen den Wirklichkeiten zu unterscheiden, z. B. zwischen **Dokumentation**, **Fiktion** und Werbung, wird vom Fernsehen auf eine extrem harte Probe gestellt. ❶
- Das Fernsehen vermittelt Erfahrungen, die wir nicht unmittelbar aus eigener Anschauung gemacht haben. Man nennt dies das Vorherrschen der Sekundärerfahrung. Wird dem Fernsehen eine hohe Bedeutung in unserem Leben zugemessen, nimmt automatisch die Gefahr des „**Lebens aus zweiter Hand**" zu. Das Fernsehen hindert uns dann daran, die Realität unmittelbar und direkt zu erleben und zu erfahren.
- Das Fernsehen vermittelt ein einseitig negatives Bild von der Welt und trägt dazu bei, die Welt Angst erregender zu empfinden, als sie in Wirklichkeit ist. Dieses als „**Kultivierungsthese**" bezeichnete Phänomen beruht auf der These, dass negative Ereignisse (z. B. Unfälle, Katastrophen, Kriminalität) im Fernsehen deutlich stärker zur Darstellung kommen als positive Aspekte.
- Das Fernsehen trägt dazu bei, dass sich die Ungleichheit zwischen den Teilen der Bevölkerung mit einem hohen Wissen- und Bildungsstand und den Teilen mit wenig Wissen und Bildung verstärkt. Diese „These von der **wachsenden Wissenskluft**" ist insofern überraschend, als man in Zeiten der **Informationsflut** eigentlich eher die Einebnung des Bildungsgefälles annehmen würde.
- Das Fernsehen fördert die Gewaltbereitschaft, insbesondere von Kindern und Jugendlichen. Dabei wird angenommen, dass Gewaltdarstellungen im Fernsehen die Aggressionsbereitschaft und das konkrete aggressive Verhalten der Zuschauer anstacheln (**Stimulationsthese**).

❶ Fernsehen und Scheinwelt: Das mit scheinbar echten Reportage-elementen durchsetzte Hörspiel „Krieg der Welten" von Orson Welles versetzte im Jahr 1938 tausende Amerikaner in Panik.

- Das Fernsehen greift negativ in das Familienleben ein. Das familiäre Gespräch, das gemeinsame Spiel und die gemeinsame Lebensgestaltung werden verhindert. Die einzelnen Familienmitglieder kapseln sich ab, so dass es zur „Einpuppung" **(Cocooning)** kommt. Das Fernsehen bedroht also die Familien.
- Das Fernsehen lässt die öffentliche Auseinandersetzung verkümmern. Auch die Politik verflacht und verkommt zur reinen Unterhaltung.
- Das Fernsehen macht die Menschen passiv. Es gefährdet die persönliche Kommunikation und behindert die Persönlichkeitsentwicklung

Maletzke hat u. a. deutlich gemacht, dass es zu einfach ist, das Fernsehen pauschal als einen „Sündenbock" abzustempeln. Seine Argumente nehmen das Fernsehen zwar nicht in jeder Hinsicht in Schutz, aber er verlangt, das schwierige Thema der Fernsehwirkungen **differenziert** zu behandeln. Mit Recht weist er auf die folgenden Punkte hin (vgl. Maletzke 1988, S. 92 ff.):

- Oft herrscht ein viel zu einfaches Denken vor. Viele stellen sich die Fernsehwirkungen im üblichen Wenn-Dann-Schema vor. Das führt zu einseitigen Behauptungen, die sich nicht aufrecht erhalten lassen.
- Der Untersuchungsgegenstand Fernsehen ist äußerst komplex. Einfache Aussagen führen meist in die Irre.
- Die Medien werden in ihrer Wirkungskraft oft überschätzt. Meistens wird unterstellt, die Medien, insbesondere das Fernsehen hätten eine äußerst starke Wirkung auf unser Leben, ohne zu erkennen, dass die Wirkkraft der Medien auch ihre Grenze hat.
- Die Ergebnisse der wissenschaftlichen Kommunikationsforschung zu den Medienwirkungen sind sehr uneinheitlich, was ein Indiz dafür ist, dass sich einfache „Stammtisch-Erklärungen" verbieten.

Entscheidend bei allem ist jedoch, so Maletzke, „daß wir heute den Menschen nicht mehr als passiv den Medien ausgeliefertes, schutzloses Wesen betrachten, das man beliebig beeinflussen kann, wenn man nur die Medien richtig anzusetzen weiß, sondern dass wir den Menschen in seiner ganzen psychischen und sozialen Fülle verstehen als aktiv in die Welt und das Geschehen eingreifend,, auch in der zunächst einseitig verlaufenden Massenkommunikation" (Maletzke 1988, S. 116). Die Kulturkritik würde es sich zu einfach machen und würde immer noch von einem „simplen mechanistischen **Menschenbild**" ausgehen, von der Vorstellung also, „der Mensch reagiere schematisch nach dem Muster von Reiz und Reaktion".

➲ **Man macht es sich zu einfach, ein Medium, z. B. das Fernsehen oder die Computerspiele, als „Sündenbock" abzustempeln und für alle möglichen Probleme der Gesellschaft verantwortlich zu machen. Die Dinge sind komplizierter. Und die Wissenschaft tut sich auch schwer mit verlässlichen Aussagen.**

Thesen und Theorien

Nachfolgend sollen einige besonders wichtige – teilweise oben schon kurz angerissene – wissenschaftlich-theoretische Vorstellungen über den **Wirkungszusammenhang von Medien und Gesellschaft** wiedergegeben werden ❶.

❶ Viele dieser Theorien beziehen sich explizit auf das Fernsehen als das universale Leitmedium bzw. als „Jahrhundertmedium", wie es Burkart formuliert (S. 316 ff.). Die nachfolgenden Ausführungen stehen im engen Bezug zur Publikation von Burkart 2002.

Existenz-These: McLuhan, Postman, Meyrowitz

Die These besagt, dass die Medien und speziell das Fernsehen allein schon deshalb auf uns einwirken, weil es sie gibt, weil sie existieren. Die berühmte Formel von **Marshall McLuhan** lautet: „Das Medium ist die Botschaft". Damit soll ausgedrückt werden, dass die Medien eine Erweiterung unserer menschlichen Anlagen darstellt, ganz so, wie z. B. das Rad unseren Fuß erweitert, das Buch unser Auge oder die Elektrizität unser Zentralnervensystem. Die Medien verändern uns selbst, unsere Kultur und unsere Umwelt. Mit dem Fernsehen kommt es v. a. zum weltweiten Zusammenwachsen zu einem „globalen Dorf", in dem die ganze Menschheit miteinander verflochten ist. Unter dem Strich bewirkt Fernsehen, dass jeder mit jedem enger verstrickt ist und nicht umhin kann, die Freuden und Leiden des anderen mitzuerleben.

➲ Neil Postman: „Wir amüsieren uns zu Tode!"

Eine (ebenso berühmte) Formel stammt von **Neil Postman**. Sie lautet: „Wir amüsieren uns zu Tode!" und ist eine kulturpessimistische Aussage. Nach Postman strömen mit dem Fernsehen unzählige Informationen auf uns ein, die uns aber nicht automatisch zu sinnvollem Handeln veranlassen, weil sie kontextlos daherkommen. Um diese Informationen gebrauchsfähig zu machen, muss man Kontexte erst erfinden („Pseudokontexte"). Das Fernsehen ist der Inbegriff dieses Pseudokontextes. Es findet seine Nutzanwendung darin, uns zu amüsieren. Es zeigt uns eine amüsante „Guckguck-Welt" ❷. Problematisch ist, dass wir danach trachten, uns in dieser Pseudowelt einzurichten und darin zu wohnen. Das Fernsehen wird zur Hintergrundstrahlung unseres sozialen und intellektuellen Universums und es ist dabei, unsere ganze Kultur in eine riesige Arena für das Showbusiness zu verwandeln. Die schlimmste Folge: Der Mensch verliert seine Urteilsfähigkeit.

Nach **Joshua Meyrowitz** verändert das Fernsehen unseren „Ortssinn". „Viele Menschen wissen heute nicht mehr, ‚wo ihr Ort ist', weil die traditionellen Wesensmerkmale des ‚Ortes' durch die elektronischen Medien aufgespalten worden sind. Die einzigartige Macht des Fernsehens bestehe darin, die Trennung zwischen ‚Hier' und ‚Dort', ‚Live' und ‚Aufgezeichnet', ‚Persönlich' und ‚Öffentlich' aufzuheben. Mehr als jedes andere Medium hat das Fernsehen die Tendenz, uns in Themen einzubeziehen, von denen wir frühen dachten, dass sie uns ‚nichts angehen'; es lässt uns in Gesichter von Mördern und Präsidenten sehen und macht physische Barrieren und Übergänge relativ bedeutungslos, wenn es um den Zugang zu sozialen Informationen geht" (Burkart 2002, S. 321). Die Folgen sind ein tiefgehender gesellschaftlicher Wandel, ausgedrückt z. B. in der Vermischung von Männlichkeit und Weiblichkeit (Trend zum „Androgynen"), in der Vermischung von Kindheit und Erwachsensein, im Prestigeverlust politischer Autoritäten. Fernsehen als das Instrument zur „Entmystifizierung", das Orte zugänglich macht, die früher verschlossen waren.

❷ Für Postman ist das Fernsehen eine Welt, „in der mal dies, mal das in den Blick gerät und sogleich wieder verschwindet. In dieser Welt gibt es kaum Zusammenhänge, kaum Bedeutung; sie fordert uns nicht auf, etwas zu tun, ja, sie lässt es gar nicht zu, wie das Guckguck Spiel der Kinder ruht sie abgeschlossen in sich. Und zugleich ist sie, wie das Guckguck-Spiel, überaus unterhaltsam" (zit. nach Burkart 2002, S. 219).

Das Vermischen von Tatsache und Fiktion

Stark diskutiert wird in der Wissenschaft die Frage, wie die Medien – besonders das Fernsehen – die Wirklichkeit bzw. die **„Realität" abbilden**. Wenn es so sein sollte, dass uns die Medien ein verzerrtes oder gar völlig falsches Bild der Wirklichkeit vermitteln, wäre das von großer Bedeutung für unser gesellschaftliches Zusammenleben.

Es herrscht allgemein die Auffassung, dass das Fernsehen eine **Scheinwelt** vermittelt – Fernsehen ist ein „Simulationsmedium" und „Illusionserzeuger". Wir als Zuschauer sind in seinen Bann gezogen und laufen Gefahr, das audiovisuell Gezeigte für pure Realität zu halten; die im Fernsehen gezeigte Realität vermischt sich mit der Lebenswirklichkeit des einzelnen Rezipienten (vgl. Burkart 2002, S. 325). Nicht selten verschwimmen die Grenzen zwischen der „Welt der Tatsachen" und der „Welt der Fiktion". Es kann zu Verwechslungen dieser beiden Welten kommen, insbesondere bei Kindern, wenn sie Phantasiewelten für bare Münze halten ❶. Aber auch Erwachsene sind nicht gefeit, Fiktion und Realität zu vermengen. Auch sie haben oft Schwierigkeiten gibt, die beiden Welten voneinander abzugrenzen, insbesondere wenn es das Ziel der Macher ist, **dem Zuschauer eine Realität vorzugaukeln**, die in dieser Form gar nicht existiert. Ein Musterbeispiel sind TV-Sendungen, die angebliche Alltagsbegebenheiten in unterhaltsamer und emotionalisierender Form aufbereiten („Reality-TV", z. B. Bauer sucht Frau, Verbrecherjagd durch die Polizei, Big Brother, Super Nanny).

❶ Kinder: „Sie müssen den fundamentalen Unterschied erkennen, der z. B. zwischen dem Zweiten Weltkrieg und den intergalaktischen Kriegen der Science-fiction-Welt oder zwischen den Dinosauriern und King-Kong besteht, obwohl sie über all dies nur über Medien erfahren (Boeckmann 1991, S. 104).

In diesem Zusammenhang ist auch die **Kultivierungsthese** relevant. Sie besagt, dass uns über das Fernsehen ein viel zu negatives Bild von der Realität vermittelt wird ❷. Das Fernsehen trägt dazu bei, die Welt angsterregender zu empfinden, als sie in Wirklichkeit ist. Die Realität wird negativ eingefärbt präsentiert. Dadurch fühlen sich die Zuschauer stärker bedroht als dies bei realistischer Betrachtung nötig wäre.

❷ Die These: Eine Nachricht ist für die Macher dann besonders interessant, wenn über ein „negatives" Ereignis zu berichten ist. „Gute Nachrichten" lohnen sich nicht, bringen vor allem keine Quote und Aufmerksamkeit.

Erfahrung aus zweiter Hand

Medien sind – so eine weitere These – ein nahezu „unendliches **Ersatz-Universum**", in dem wir tief verwurzelt sind. Unmittelbare Erfahrungen („Primärerfahrungen") zu machen, tritt gegenüber der Erfahrung aus zweiter Hand („**Sekundärerfahrung**", „Second-Hand-Erfahrung") in den Hintergrund. Dieses Phänomen gab es zwar auch früher schon, indem man Dinge „vom Hörensagen" erfuhr, heutzutage hat aber diese Rolle die Medienindustrie übernommen, die ungleich schneller und vielfältiger informieren kann (vgl. Burkart 2002, S. 327).

Unser Bild von der Welt wird also stark von den Medien geprägt. Dies muss man nicht unbedingt als negativ verurteilen, haben wir doch durch Fernsehen, Radio und Internet große Chancen, „gute" Informationen zu erlangen und ein viel besseres **Bild von der Welt** zu bekommen als ohne diese Medienangebote. Freilich sind die Gefahren nicht wegzudiskutieren und mit Recht wird „auf die Kehrseite dieser Entwicklung verwiesen, dass selbst durch die optimalste Gestaltung einer Sendung die eigene Erfahrung nicht ersetzt werden kann, weil es eben noch nur um Bilder von der Wirklichkeit handle …, was nicht zuletzt wieder als Gefahr für die Kinder erscheint: gerade Kindern fehlt infolge mangelnder Lebenserfahrung eine angemessene Rezeptionskompetenz, um den Fernsehbildern kritisch gegenüberzutreten (Burkart 2002, S. 328).

Wirkungen von Gewaltdarstellungen

Wie schwierig es ist, plausible Aussagen zu treffen, zeigt z. B. die Frage der **Gewaltdarstellungen im Fernsehen** ❶. Hier gibt es eine breite Palette von Erklärungsansätzen; unter den Fachleuten besteht keine Einigkeit. Immerhin hat sich die Erkenntnis durchgesetzt, dass von einer völligen Wirkungslosigkeit nicht ausgegangen werden darf und dass Gewaltdarstellungen kurzfristig durchaus emotionale Erregungen hervorrufen können. Auch gibt es kaum jemanden, der noch ernsthaft die Katharsisthese vertritt, nach der über das Anschauen von Gewaltszenen das Aggressionspotential beim einzelnen Zuschauer abgebaut wird.

❶ Die Zahl der Studien zur Fernsehgewalt wird heute auf weit über 5.000 geschätzt, die sich in vielerlei Hinsicht unterscheiden.

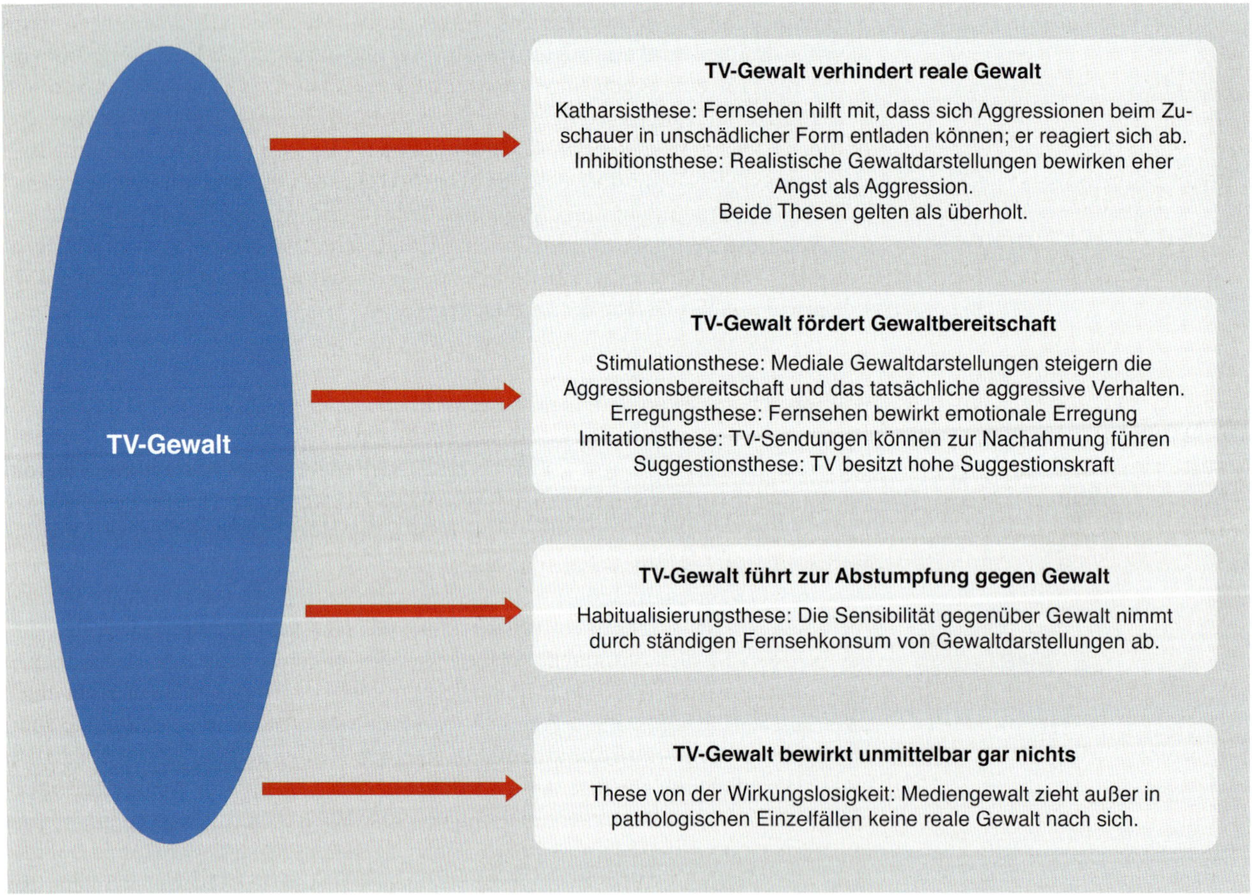

Es besteht in der Wissenschaft weitgehende Einigkeit, dass die erstgenannte These (**Katharsisthese**, **Inhibitionsthese**) nicht realistisch ist. Welche der anderen Thesen greift, kann nur im Zusammenhang mit der Situation beurteilt werden: So ist medialer Gewaltkonsum von Kindern in einer intakten Familie völlig anders zu beurteilen als in zerrütteten Verhältnissen. In jedem Falle darf man sich nicht verleiten lassen, die möglichen negativen Wirkungen von Gewaltdarstellungen undifferenziert herauf zu spielen, aber auch nicht herab zu spielen. Unbestritten ist, dass Fernsehgewalt und emotionale Erregung in engem Zusammenhang stehen.

Eingriff in die Familie: Lagerfeuer-Funktion, Cocooning

Der These, dass die Medien, insbesondere das Fernsehen, in das **Familienleben** eingreifen, kann nicht widersprochen werden. Die Frage ist nur, in welcher Form dies geschieht. Betrachtet man den Zusammenhang zwischen den Medien und den familiären interpersonalen Kommunikationsstrukturen näher, werden sowohl **positive** als auch **negative Aspekte** aufgeführt (vgl. Burkart 2002, S. 352 ff.):

- Positiv wird gewürdigt, dass die Medien dazu beitragen können, das häusliche Familienleben zu stärken. Das Fernsehen kann einen „heimeligen" Effekt auslösen, es kann wie ein „telefunktionales Kaminfeuer" oder ein „Lagerfeuer" die Familienmitglieder vereinen und Gemeinsamkeit schaffen. Auch dem Radio wird eine ähnliche Funktion zugeschrieben, wenn z. B. die Musikbeschallung früh am Morgen für eine angenehme Atmosphäre sorgt.
- Negative Wirkungen werden unterstellt, wenn das Fernsehen – und mit den neuen Medien insbesondere auch das Internet – als „negativer Fluchtpunkt" der Familie dient. Befürchtet wird, dass viel Fernsehkonsum das familiäre Gespräch oder das gemeinsame Spiel verhindert. Selbst gestaltetes Familienleben wird „durch schweigendes Glotzen" ersetzt. Zweit- oder Drittgeräte („jedem sein Fernseher") zersplittern die Familie. Die Familienmitglieder „igeln sich ein", man spricht von der Gefahr der Einpuppung („Cocooning"). Viele Familien bieten ein „Bild der progressiven Introvertiertheit".

Bildung: These der wachsenden Wissenskluft

Die Wissenskluft-Hypothese („Knowledge-Gap-Hypothese") steht im krassen Gegensatz zu der Vorstellung, die Medien – und wieder insbesondere das Fernsehen sowie das Internet – seien ein Instrument, mit dem man sich spielend Wissen aneignen könne – Fernsehen als „Schule der Nation"; die hoch erfreuliche Folge sei, dass Bildungsprivilegien quasi automatisch abgebaut würden (vgl. Burkart 2002, S. 344 ff.). Die These von der **wachsenden Wissenskluft** geht ganz im Gegenteil davon aus, dass das von den Medien vermittelte Wissen von den bildungsmäßig unterschiedlichen Teilen der Bevölkerung unterschiedlich genutzt, und zwar in der Weise, dass die Kluft zwischen den Bevölkerungssegmenten tendenziell immer mehr zu- statt abnimmt. Begründet wird diese Annahme damit, dass Personen mit besserer Bildung es deutlich besser verstehen, die von den Medien bereitgestellten Angebote an Wissen und Information zu nutzen als Personen mit geringerer Bildung. Es kommt quasi zu einem sich selbst verstärkenden Effekt („Matthäus-Effekt" nach dem neutestamentlichen Evangelium des Matthäus): „Wer da hat, dem soll gegeben werden, und wer da nicht hat, dem soll genommen werden".

Einen ähnlich pessimistischen Befund hat auch Neil Postman (s. o. „Wir amüsieren uns zu Tode!") artikuliert: Das Fernsehen sei als ein einziger Angriff auf die Schriftkultur zu sehen, „weil es eine bruchstückhafte, zerstückelte Welt aus Diskontinuitäten präsentiere, während der Buchdruck fast alle jene Eigenschaften verstärkt habe, die für einen entfalteten Diskurs nötig seien" – dies seien v. a. begriffliches, deduktiv folgerichtiges Denken, Wertschätzung von Vernunft und Ordnung, Fähigkeit zur Distanz und zur Objektivität (Burkart 2002, S. 347).

2.5.3 Medien und Politik

Politische Funktionen der Medien

Neben den Auswirkungen auf die Gesellschaft kommt den Medien eine hohe Bedeutung für die Politik zu. Hier gilt es die Leistungen der (Massen-)Medien für die Herstellung, Sicherung und Stabilisierung eines demokratisch organisierten politischen Systems zu hinterfragen. Die folgenden politischen Funktionen sollen die Medien bestmöglich erfüllen:

- Herstellen von **Öffentlichkeit**: Die Medien stellen einen „Raum" her, im dem Öffentlichkeit erzeugt wird. Über die Medien machen die politischen Entscheidungsträger ihre Programme, Absichten, Ziele und Forderungen bekannt. Alle, die am politischen Prozess beteiligt sind, treten über Medien mit- und untereinander in Kommunikation. Die Medien sind ein „Forum" für die Meinungsbildung.
- Artikulationsfunktion: Die Medien helfen den Menschen, den Gruppen von Menschen, den Organisationen, ihre Interessen und Meinungen zu artikulieren. Die Medien sorgen als wichtiges „Sprachrohr" dafür, dass alle Gehör finden.
- Politische Sozialisation und Bildung: Die Medien bringen Licht in das politische Dunkel. Sie machen die politischen Rollen (Wähler, Parteimitglieder, Opponenten, Demonstranten usw.) transparent. Sie tragen dazu bei, dass der einzelne Bürger zu einem politisch denkenden und verantwortlich handelnden Staatbürger heranwächst.
- Kritik und Kontrolle: Die Medien geben den Bürgern die Chance, Kritik an den politischen Machtträgern zu üben und diese zu kontrollieren. Gerade diese Kritik der Medien ist es, was eine funktionierende **Demokratie** ausmacht. Medien sind dazu da, die Demokratie als das einzig legitime politische System zu stützen.

Thesen und Theorien

Aus politischer Sicht gibt es eine Reihe wichtiger theoretischer Erklärungsversuche, die nachfolgend dargestellt werden.

Modell des Zwei-Stufen-Flusses der Kommunikation

Der Zwei-Stufen-Fluss der Kommunikation – auch bekannt als „Two-Step Flow of Communication" – geht davon aus, dass die Massenmedien den Großteil der Bevölkerung nicht direkt erreichen, sondern auf einer ersten Stufe zunächst die Meinungsführer bzw. Meinungsbildner („opinion leaders") und über diese dann die weniger aktiven Rezipienten (vgl. Burkart 2002, S. 209).

➲ **Politische Meinungsbildung geschieht nicht direkt von den Medien zum Bürger, sondern indirekt über Meinungsführer, denen dadurch eine große Macht zuwächst.**

Es ist offenkundig, dass den Meinungsführern eine hohe Macht zuwächst, denn sie haben bei der politischen Meinungsbildung eine bevorzugte Position. Sie haben in politischen Fragen einen großen Einfluss auf andere Personen.

Theorie der Schweigespirale

❶ Prof. Dr. Elisabeth Noelle-Neumann (1916-2010) war eine der bedeutendsten Figuren der deutschen Publizistik- und Kommunikationswissenschaft. Sie gründete das Institut für Demoskopie in Allensbach – das erste deutsche Meinungsforschungsinstitut – und leistete damit wertvolle Pionierarbeit.

Die „Theorie der Schweigespirale" wurde von Elisabeth Noelle-Neumann ❶ vorgelegt. Sie besagt, dass die **„öffentliche Meinung"** eine zentrale Rolle bei der Bildung der eigenen Meinung spiele. Aus Furcht vor sozialer Isolation und weil der Mensch ein tiefes **Bedürfnis nach Zugehörigkeit** habe, sei es wahrscheinlich, „dass Menschen ihre eigene Meinung dann eher verschweigen, wenn sie die Mehrheitsmeinung gegen sich glauben. Im Gegensatz dazu wird angenommen, dass sie ihre Überzeugungen auch öffentlich zeigen, wenn sie glauben, der Mehrheitsmeinung anzugehören" (Burkart 2002, S. 263). Der Mensch besitze ein feines Sensorium für das, was in seiner Umwelt passiert – er verfüge über ein „quasi-statistisches Wahrnehmungsorgan" – und reagiere daher „seismografisch" auf das politische Meinungsklima.

Für den politischen Meinungsbildungsprozess hat das Phänomen der Schweigespirale die dramatische Konsequenz, dass die wirklichen **Mehrheits- und Stärkeverhältnisse** in der Gesellschaft nicht klar zum Ausdruck kommen. Vielmehr muss man mit Täuschungen und Verzerrungen rechnen. Es kann sogar so sein, dass eine Meinung zum Untergang verurteilt ist und damit politisch nicht mehr auf der Tagesordnung steht, weil sie in die Falle der Schweigespirale geraten ist.

Konstruktion politischer Wirklichkeit

Die Frage, in welcher Form die Medien die Wirklichkeit abbilden, war im Kontext der gesellschaftlichen Wirkungen der Medien bereits thematisiert worden. Im Hinblick auf die politischen Wirkungen spielt sie ebenfalls eine wichtige Rolle. **Drei Thesen** bzw. Modelle sind in diesem Zusammenhang besonders relevant: (1) Agenda-Setting-Hypothese, (2) Journalisten als „Gatekeeper", (3) Kepplinger-Modell.

Die **Agenda-Setting-Hypothese** – auch **Thematisierungsansatz** genannt – besagt, dass die die Massenmedien die Macht haben, die Themen zu bestimmen, über die in der Gesellschaft diskutiert wird. Sie haben die Macht, Themen auf die Tagesordnung („Agenda") zu setzen oder sie wieder zu entfernen. Überspitzt ausgedrückt: Wenn es den Medien gefällt, diskutieren wir tage- und wochenlang über die Frage der Endlagerung von Atommüll oder den Ruhestand eines Moderators (z. B. Thomas Gottschalk mit der TV-Sendung „Wetten dass ...?"), wenn es ihnen nicht gefällt, werden u. U. wichtigste Fragen nicht aufgeworfen. Die These nimmt also an, „dass die Massenmedien nicht so sehr beeinflussen, *was* wir denken sollen, sondern eher bestimmen, *worüber* wir nachzudenken haben" (Burkart 2002, S: 248).

➲ **Medien haben die Macht, die öffentliche Diskussion zu beeinflussen.**

Der Ansatz der sog. **„Gatekeeper-Forschung"** sieht **Journalisten als Schleusenwärter**, die durch die Auswahl der Themen, über die sie berichten, großen Einfluss auf den öffentlichen – v. a. auch politischen – Diskurs ausüben (vgl. Burkart 2002, S. 276 ff.). Die Journalisten selbst sind in ihrer Gatekeeper-Funktion von Nachrichtenagenturen abhängig, sie sind meist Teil einer Redaktion und damit im Austausch mit der Chefredaktion und dem Herausgeber und orientieren sich selbst nicht selten auch an Leit- und Meinungsführermedien (vgl. Schenk 2007, S. 444).

Ausgangspunkt des **Kepplinger-Modells** ist die Vorstellung, dass Nachrichten als Mittel zum Zweck eingesetzt werden können. Man kann nicht darauf vertrauen, dass die Journalisten und das Mediensystem die Geschehnisse der Welt (die „genuinen Ereignisse") quasi als „Treuhänder der Wirklichkeit" – als neutrale Beobachter – abbilden. Kepplinger ❶ geht vielmehr davon aus, dass Ereignisse gezielt für bestimmte Interessen benutzt werden. Drei unterschiedliche **Typen von Ereignissen** sind zu unterscheiden (vgl. hier und im Folgenden Kepplinger 1989):

❶ Prof. Dr. Hans Mathias Kepplinger von der Universität Mainz ist eine wichtige Stimme in der Diskussion um die politische Bedeutung der Medien.

- **Genuine Ereignisse:** Geschehnisse, die unabhängig von der Berichterstattung durch Medien passieren (z. B. Erdbeben, Atomkraftwerk-Unfall).
- **Mediatisierte Ereignisse:** Geschehnisse, die auch ohne die Medien stattfinden würden, die jedoch wegen der Medienpräsenz anders ablaufen (z. B. Parteitage).
- **Pseudo-Ereignisse:** Geschehnisse, die eigens für eine Medienberichterstattung herbeigeführt werden (z. B. Pressekonferenzen, TV-Duell von Politikern).

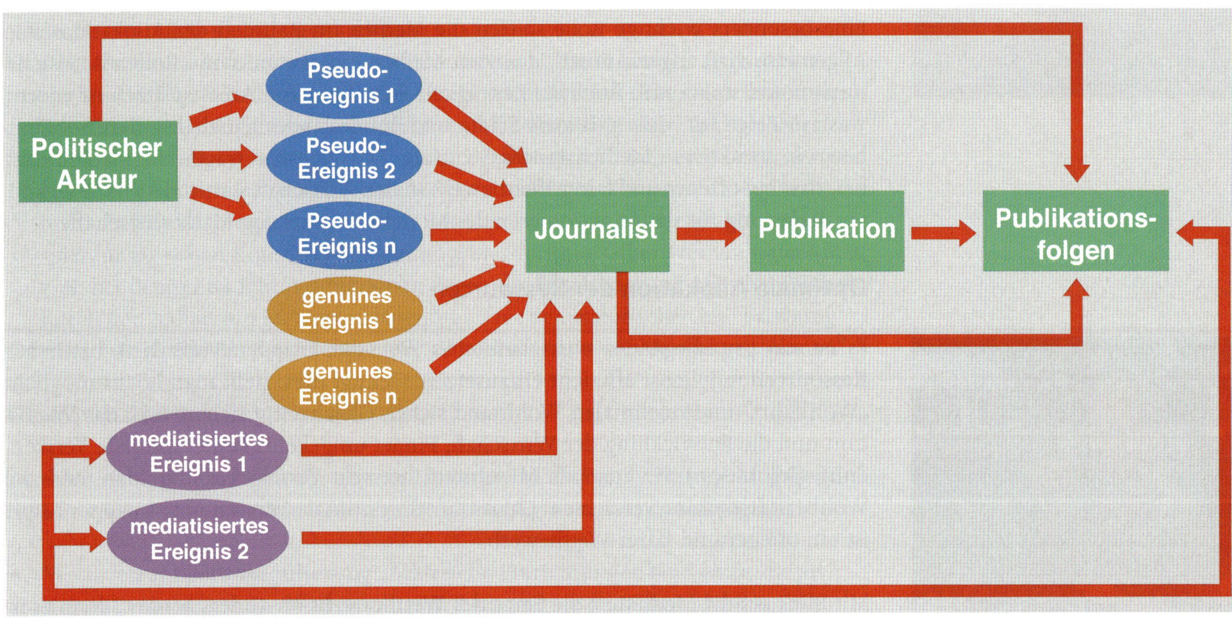

Die Grafik zeigt, dass verschiedene Verzerrungen der Wirklichkeit geschehen können. Bei den **Pseudo-Ereignissen** ist die Triebfeder der Berichterstattung das Interesse eines politischen Akteurs, die Journalisten dazu zu bringen, über von ihm veranstaltetes Ereignis zu berichten. Es geschieht eine **„instrumentelle Inszenierung"**, um eine bestimmte Publikationsfolge zu erreichen.

Desweiteren können es die Journalisten selbst sein, die mit der Berichterstattung einen bestimmten Zweck verfolgen, z. B. eine Partei zu unterstützen. Sie betreiben dann eine **„instrumentelle Aktualisierung"** und sorgen entweder für eine Umbewertung, Betonung oder Abschwächung der genuinen Ereignisse in der Berichterstattung.

Bei **mediatisierten Ereignissen** sorgt die Anwesenheit der Medien dafür, dass das Ereignis (z. B. ein Parteitag) bewusst mediengerecht gestaltet wird.

Zu dieser Theorie gehören folgende Grundannahmen:

- Es existiert eine reale objektive Ausgangssituation, sie lässt sich jedoch in ihrer Existenz weder beweisen noch widerlegen.
- Es gibt subjektive Erkenntnisleistungen.
- Selektivität ist ein wesentliches Merkmal des Erkenntnisprozesses auf der Ebene WII und WIII.

Die Möglichkeit besteht nun, dass es zwischen den Ebenen einen Informationssprung, eine Informationsveränderung bzw. einen zeitlichen Versatz geben kann. Hier besteht die Möglichkeit der Manipulation. Viele Eingriffe in der politischen Vergangenheit in den Medienbereich zielten darauf ab, Informationen zu filtern oder zu verändern, diese vollständig zu negieren oder sie zeitlich verspätet zu übermitteln. Nachfolgend sollen einige Beispiele aus der jüngeren Geschichte, an das negative Einwirken politischer Kreise auf die mediale Welt erinnern:

- Mit der Entwicklung des Buchdrucks im Mittelalter bestand die Möglichkeit, dass prinzipiell jeder Bürger nun zu Informationen kommen konnte. Die Möglichkeit, mehr Bildung zu erlangen wuchs. Klerus und Adel verhinderten jede unkontrollierte Veröffentlichung durch eine entsprechende Zensur und kontrollierten auch die Verbreitung aus Angst vor Machtzerfall. Es durften nur bestimmte Bürgerkreise Bücher käuflich erwerben.
- Der deutsche Kaiser unterstützte Ende des 19. Jh. die Entwicklung der Funktechnik mit großem finanziellen Einsatz aus politischen Gesichtspunkten, um sich vom englischen Nachrichtenmonopol zu befreien. Das Funkwesen wurde der Reichspost unterstellt und war damit unter staatlicher Kontrolle. Dadurch waren alle Bereiche wie Militärfunk, Schiffsfunk sowie Weltfunk mit Kolonialfunkverkehr in staatlicher Hand.
- Im „Dritten Reich" wurden die ca. 1000 Filme, von Heimatfilmen bis zu Propagandafilmen, auf der Basis nationalsozialistischem Gedankenguts gedreht. Die Filmindustrie unterstand dem Propagandaministerium Goebbels. Für Drehbücher und Produktionen bestand eine Vorzensur, Filmkritiken waren verboten und viele Schauspieler durften ihren Beruf nicht weiter ausüben. 1942 wurde die Filmindustrie verstaatlicht. In Filmen zur Kriegsberichterstattung wurde die Sichtweise der Nationalsozialisten dargestellt.
- Der Aufbau der Rundfunkanstalten und der journalistische Neustart nach dem Krieg ist ein Verdienst der Alliierten. In der Ostzone nahm der Mitteldeutsche Rundfunk die Übertragung wieder auf. Der MDR wird in der Folge (nach 1951) einem Komitee des Ministerrats unterstellt. Alle Übertragungen und Produktionen unterlagen bis 1989 einer strikten Zensur.
- Der Irakkrieg der Vereinigten Staaten und einer Anzahl verbündeter Staaten im Jahr 2003 war mit der Existenz von Massenvernichtungswaffen sowie einer angeblichen Verbindung mit der Terrorgruppe Al-Qaida begründet worden. Für beides gibt es bis heute keine Belege. Außenminister Powell wollte den Weltsicherheitsrat mit später als falsch erkannten Behauptungen von der Notwendigkeit des Irak-Kriegs überzeugen. In den USA selbst wurden dabei die von der Regierung veröffentlichten Kriegsgründe von den amerikanischen Massenmedien

weitgehend übernommen und kaum anders lautende Begründungen veröffentlicht. Trotz des Beweises des Gegenteils glaubten 2004 immerhin ca. 55% der Amerikaner, dass der Irak das Netzwerk von Al-Quaida unterstützt und ein Programm zur Erlangung von Massenvernichtungswaffen gehabt hätte.
- Nach dem zweiten Weltkrieg wurde die Tagespresse Zug um Zug wieder aufgebaut. Es entstand eine facettenreiche Zeitungslandschaft. Mitte der 70er Jahre folgte eine Konzentration des Pressewesens in nationalen und internationalen Medienkonzernen. Durch die Reduzierung des Informationsangebots verringert sich zwangsläufig die Möglichkeit einer offenen demokratischen Meinungs- und Willensbildung. Durch die Konzentration ergaben sich für Kritiker viele machtpolitische Fragen. Wem gehört welcher Verlag? Welche politische Ausrichtung hat der Verleger / die Verlagsgruppe? Welche Verbindung gibt es zwischen Medienunternehmen und Parteien bzw. Institutionen? Wie frei ist die redaktionelle Arbeit der Journalisten?

Auf der anderen Seite besitzen die Medien als vierte Macht im Staat eine wichtige Regulierungsfunktion für das gesellschaftliche Handeln und eine Kontrollfunktion über das politische Handeln. Die Medien in ihrer heutigen Form entsprangen dem Drang der Menschen nach Freiheit und einer demokratischen Lebensform und können im Wirken für die Demokratie nicht in Frage gestellt werden.

❶ investigativer Journalismus: investigare = genauestens untersuchen

Der freie Journalismus hat in vielen Fällen dafür gesorgt, dass brisante politische Themen aufgedeckt, Politiker gestürzt und wirtschaftliche Missstände ans Tageslicht gelangten. Diese auch als investigativer Journalismus ❶ bezeichnete Recherche und Veröffentlichung wird oft abwertend als Enthüllungsjournalismus bezeichnet, erhält sie jedoch gerade durch ihre Hartnäckigkeit die demokratischen Formen unserer Gesellschaft (Checks and Balances). Die Basis für diesen Wirkmechanismus der Informationsaufbereitung und Verbreitung ist und bleibt die Festschreibung der Pressefreiheit im 19. Jh.. Diese Errungenschaft konnten auch Politiker und Monarchen nur bedingt einschränken, zu weit verzweigt ist das journalistische und mediale Netzwerk in alle Ecken der Erde.

Beispiele:
Flick Spendenaffäre 1980
Hitlertagebücher von Konrad Kujau 1983
CDU Spendenaffäre 1999
Abfindungen für Manager nach der Übernahme von Mannesmann durch Vodafone 2000

Zukünftig könnten wir vielleicht neue Wege in der Informationsgesellschaft gehen, hin zu einem offenen Austausch ohne finanzielle Abhängigkeiten. Die Bewegung **Open Culture** arbeitet an Konzepten, um den freien Zugang zu Informationen, Kultur, Technik, Software u. a. zu ermöglichen. Open Culture verbindet Schaffende, die nicht aus rein kommerziellen Gründen tätig sind, mit Nutzern, denen aus ökonomischen Gründen proprietäres geistiges Eigentum, Kultur und Produkte schwer zugänglich sind. Darüber hinaus soll das Schaffen frei und nicht durch die Interessen aus Wirtschaft und Politik beschränkt sein. Beispiel dafür sind das freie Publizieren mit Hilfe des Internets, die Verbreitung freier Bild- und Tonwerke, der freie Zugang zu Bildung und offenen Datenbanken (Open Access), im EDV-Bereich die Entwicklung kostenloser Programme mit offenem Programmcode (Freie Software, Open Source), die Schaffung frei verfügbare Spezifikationen (Offene Standards), die unter anderem in freien Formaten und standardisierten Schnittstellen genutzt werden, im technischen Bereich freie Hardware und im Gesundheitswesen Open Medicine mit dem Zugriff auf freie Datenbanken.

Konferenz *OPEN CULTURES - Free Flows of Information and the Politics of Commons, 5. bis 6. Juni 2003 in Wien*

3.1.3 Gesellschaftlich-kulturelle Perspektive

In jeder zeitlichen Epoche spiegelt das Entwicklungsstadium der Medien den Entwicklungsstand der Gesellschaft wider. Dies lässt sich beispielsweise an der Nutzung der Computertechnik erkennen, im Vergleich zwischen Industriestaaten und Entwicklungsländern.

Im Mittelalter steht die Informationsvermittlung ganz im Dienste weltlicher und kirchlicher Bedürfnisse. Adel und Kirchenvertreter nutzten die medialen Möglichkeiten des Buchdruckes, um sich zu den Themen Bildung, Religion und Naturwissenschaften einen Vorsprung gegenüber dem Bürgertum und der Unterschicht zu verschaffen. Wachsende Bildung und Alphabetisierung der Bevölkerung und das Interesse an kulturellen und politischen Themen sorgen für eine stetige Entwicklung von Zeitungen und Zeitschriften ab Ende 17. Jh.. Gleichzeitig entwickelte sich nach der Erfindung des Buchdrucks von Gutenberg das Buch zu einem Kulturmedium, mit der Entstehung von Lesegemeinschaften, sogenannten Büchergilden. Ende des 19. Jh. wurde die Buchpreisbindung eingeführt, nachdem Verleger und Buchhändler 1825 den **Börsenverein** als gemeinsame Dachorganisation gründeten. Das Massenprodukt konnte billig produziert werden (Taschenbuch) und war als Fachbuch für die berufliche Entwicklung der Menschen ein wichtiger Begleiter und besaß auf der anderen Seite als Publikumsliteratur einen hohen Unterhaltungswert. Mit dem Aufkommen des Rundfunks gab das Buch den Anteil der Unterhaltung ab, später übernahm den Unterhaltungsbereich dann das Fernsehen. Mit den Bildungssendungen wie Telekolleg war auch ein Teil der Fachliteratur gefährdet, doch sieht man gerade auf dem Bildungssektor in den letzten Jahren wieder ansteigende Tendenz bei der Produktion von Büchern.

Decretum Gratiani, Veroneser Malerei, 14. Jahrhundert

Mit dem Siegeszug der elektronischen Medien und den heutigen Möglichkeiten, ein Buch und die Tageszeitung nicht nur in gedruckter, sondern auch elektronischer Form zu nutzen, war das Buch und die Zeitung endgültig schwer angeschlagen. Es hat sich aber bis heute gezeigt, dass das gedruckte Produkt ein kulturelles Erbe darstellt und in allen gesellschaftlichen Schichten seinen Platz hat. Je nach soziokulturellem Umfeld wird es nach wie vor mehr oder weniger als alternativer Zeitvertreib und als Informationsmedium eingesetzt.

Der Aufstieg des Rundfunks wurde durchweg euphorisch betrachtet, als Möglichkeit, kulturelle, gesellschaftliche und politische Ereignisse in alle Haushalte zu fördern. Das Radiohören wurde neben den alltäglichen Hausarbeiten und im Beruf als schmückendes Beiwerk gesehen und als familiäre Freizeitbeschäftigung. Der Kulturfaktor Radio erlangte durch Bildungs-, Wissenschafts- und Kunstbeiträge sowie die Übertragung von Musik- und Sportveranstaltungen einen hohen Stellenwert in der Gesellschaft. Kritiker des Rundfunks meinten, dass die Kultur einer Gesellschaft durch ihn zerstört würde. Die aufkeimende Angst entstand vor dem Hintergrund eines sich ausbreitenden Massenmediums. Dasselbe erlebte man mit dem Medium Fernsehen und heute mit dem Medium Internet.

Mit der fortschreitenden Nutzung automatisierter Technologien und der wachsenden Mobilität hat der Mensch mehr Zeit und besitzt mehr Möglichkeiten für ein vielseitiges Freizeitprogramm. Neben dem wachsenden Fitnesstrend spielen Computerspiele, Internetnutzung und Fernsehen eine tragende Rolle im Leben der meisten Familien. Mit einem Mausklick fliegen wir seit ein paar Jahren um die ganze Welt ❶, per Fernsteuerung holen wir uns Menschen ins Wohnzimmer, die wir uns sonst wahrscheinlich nie einladen würden und durch das Handy sind wir so gut wie überall ansprechbar. Die technologischen Entwicklungen zum Ende des 20. Jh. hin können guten Gewissens als dritte industrielle Revolution bezeichnet werden, haben sie doch nicht nur unser gesamtes mediales Verhalten verändert, sondern auch gleichzeitig die Globalisierung und damit auch die Öffnung der Staaten vorangetrieben. Einen ersten Abschluss fand diese Entwicklung mit der Gründung der EU und der Einführung des Euro als gemeinsame Währung.

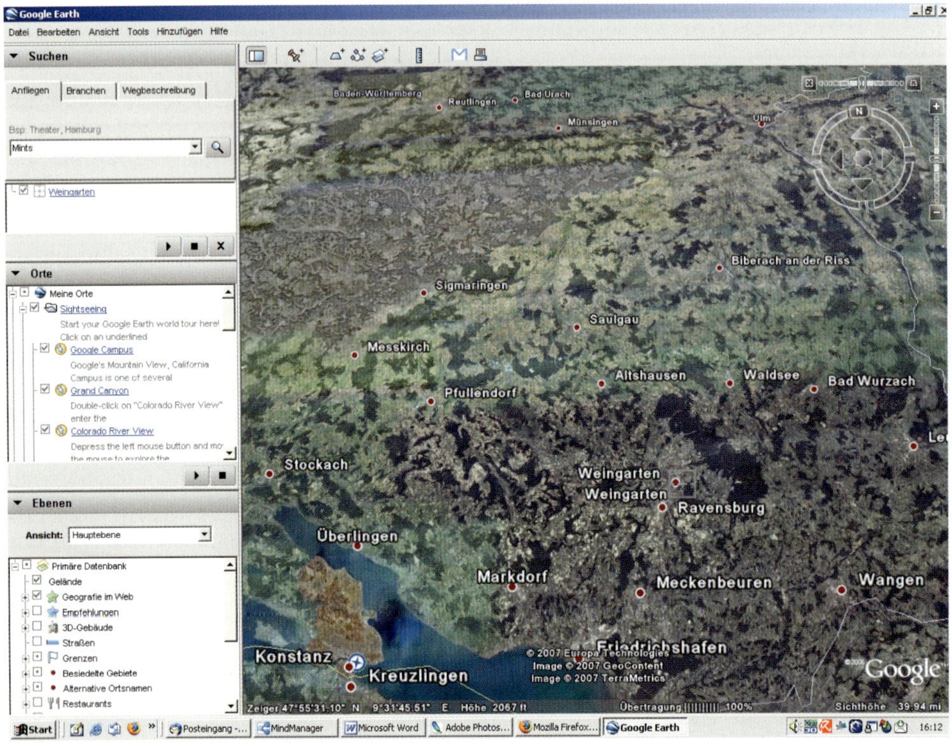

❶

3.1.4 Wirtschaftliche Perspektive

Bereits Anfang des 18. Jh. wurden neben den Nachrichten auch Anzeigen in den Zeitungen gedruckt. Zunächst einmal waren das amtliche Bekanntmachungen, aber auch bezahlte private Anzeigen, die jedoch keine politischen Inhalte enthalten durften. Mit der **Industrialisierung** wuchs die Kaufkraft, expandierten die Arbeitsmärkte, stieg das Interesse nach Informationen. Mit der stärkeren Verbreitung der Zeitungen und Zeitschriften ergaben sich größere Absatzmöglichkeiten durch Anzeigenwerbung.

Mit der Gründung des **öffentlich-rechtlichen Rundfunks** nach dem Krieg wuchs die Verbreitung von Informationen und gleichzeitig auch die Möglichkeit, Werbung flächendeckend zu platzieren. Durch interessante tontechnische Entwicklungen und Audioproduktion wurde die Produktwerbung zur einer wichtigen Einnahmequelle des Hörfunks.

Die Zeitungen kämpften untereinander im direkten Wettbewerb um Anzeigenkunden, die vor allem im Bereich der regionalen Werbung, im Stellenmarkt oder auch Dienstleistungsbereich angesiedelt waren. Die Entwicklung Mitte des 20. Jh. zeigte, dass die Finanzierung eines Zeitungsverlag mindestens gleichrangig aus dem Anzeigenerlös und nicht mehr ganz überwiegend aus dem Vertriebserlös wie in den Anfangszeiten erfolgen konnte. Gegen Ende des 20. Jh. gehen die Anzeigenerlöse der Zeitungen stark zurück, dafür wächst die Zahl der Publikums- und Fachzeitschriften überdurchschnittlich und damit auch das Anzeigenvolumen.

Das Fernsehen und der Film- und Kinomarkt erlebten ein kontinuierliches Wachstum. Zu Beginn des 21. Jahrhunderts haben sie das Umsatzvolumen des Zeitungs- und Zeitschriftenmarktes erreicht. Der stärkste Medienmarkt in Deutschland ist inzwischen das Fernsehen mit mehr als 11 Mrd. Euro, wobei ca. die Hälfte davon allein auf die öffentlich-rechtlichen Sender ARD und ZDF entfallen, der den bislang führenden Zeitungsmarkt mit ca. neun Mrd. Euro von der führenden Position abgelöst hat. Die Fernsehwerbung hat im Programm einen starken Zuwachs erfahren. So hat sich die Zahl der Fernsehwerbespots in den letzten zehn Jahren auf über vier Mio. Spots verdreifacht. Die Einnahmen beim Film kommen vor allem aus dem Verkauf und Verleih sowie aus Lizenzrechten. Beide Bereiche stagnieren in der technischen als auch wirtschaftlichen Entwicklung.

Dafür entwickelt sich seit den 90er-Jahren der **Video- und Computerspielemarkt** zu einem bedeutenden medialen Wirtschaftszweig. Er hat umsatzmäßig inzwischen den Film- und Kinomarkt überflügelt. Bedeutend dabei ist unter anderem, dass die Spielesoftware an entsprechende Spielehardware gekoppelt ist. Zielgruppen sind nicht nur Kinder und Jugendliche, sondern die ganze Familie. Video- und Computerspiele werden zukünftig immer mehr zu einer ernst zu nehmenden Alternative von Film und Fernsehen.

In der historischen Betrachtung ist die **wirtschaftliche Relevanz der Medien** von einer Randerscheinung zu einer beachtlichen Größe herangereift. Sie können heute als ein bedeutender volkswirtschaftlicher Produktivfaktor bezeichnet werden, die mit mehr als 60 Mrd. Euro in Deutschland einen bemerkenswerten Beitrag zum Bruttoinlandsprodukt leisten sowie ein hohes Maß an Beschäftigung bieten.

Erweitert man den Blick vom engeren Mediensektor auf die sog. TIME-Branche, werden die Zahlen noch eindrucksvoller. Die TIME-Branche setzt sich aus den folgenden Teilbranchen zusammen, die sich immer mehr in einem konvergenten Prozess aufeinander zu bewegen:

- Telekommunikation
- IT-Branche, also Computer (Hardware und Software)
- Medien
- Consumer Electronics, d. h. Endgeräte im Konsumentenbereich

Die TIME-Branche generiert ein Umsatzvolumen von über 200 Mrd. Euro und kann sich insoweit „locker“ mit der Automobilindustrie messen – mit Blick auf die Beschäftigung schafft sie sogar erheblich mehr Arbeitsplätze als diese!

Freilich war es ein langer Weg, bis sich die Medien- und TIME-Branche diese starke Position erringen konnten. Lange war Unterhaltung, Film, Fernsehen, Radio eher eine gesellschaftliche Randerscheinung und wirtschaftlich gegenüber der Industrie hoffnungslos unterlegen. Erst mit dem Wandel zur Dienstleistungs- und Informationsgesellschaft wurden „die Karten neu gemischt“.

Einige Hinweise zur Literatur

Abschließend seien einige Literaturhinweise zur Mediengeschichte gegeben, die eine vertiefende Befassung mit der Thematik bestens ermöglichen. Hervorgehoben sei insbesondere das Werk von Wilke.

Böhm, Andreas; *Seidler*, Andreas: Mediengeschichte, Tübingen 2008 (Narr Francke Attempto)
Dussel, Konrad: Deutsche Rundfunkgeschichte, 2. Aufl., Konstanz 2004 (UVK)
Faulstich, Werner: Geschichte der Medien, 4 Bände, Göttingen 1997-2002 (Vandenhoeck & Ruprecht)
Kerlen, Dietrich: Einführung in die Medienkunde, Stuttgart 2003 (Reclam)
Wilke, Jürgen: Grundzüge der Medien- und Kommunikationsgeschichte, Köln, Weimar, Wien 2008 (UTB Böhlau)
Schanze, Helmut (Hrsg.): Handbuch der Mediengeschichte, Stuttgart 2001 (Kröner)
Stöber, Rudolf: Deutsche Pressegeschichte, 2. Aufl., Konstanz 2005 (UVK)

3.1.5 Die Medien: Eine Zeitreise

Wie sich die Medien aus technologischer Sicht im Einzelnen entwickelt haben lässt sich in einer Zeitreise gegliedert nach den Bereichen Schrift und Buchdruck, Presse, Fotografie und Film, Telegrafie und Telefon, Funk und Rundfunk, Fernsehen sowie Computer mit den jeweils anhängenden Technologien darstellen.

Entwicklung Schrift und Buchdruck

3500 v. Chr.	Ägypter entwickeln frühe Schriften
100 n. Chr.	In China wird das Papier erfunden
ca. 900 n. Chr.	In China wird mit Druckstöcken eine Schriftrolle gedruckt
1100 – 1300	In Asien werden die ersten beweglichen Lettern aus Holz gefertigt
ab 1400	Feinpapier wird in einer Papiermühle in Nürnberg aus Lumpen hergestellt, vorher aus Pergament
1440	Johannes Gutenberg erfand den Buchdruck mit beweglichen Bleilettern und einer Handpresse, erstes Werk die 42zeilige Gutenbergbibe
1480	Erstes Fachbuch wird gedruckt
1775	Didot führt ein einheitliches Größensystem für Druckbuchstaben ein, der typografische Punkt (1 Didot-Punkt = 0,3750 mm)
um 1800	Senefelder erfindet in München die Lithografie, den Flachdruck mit Steinplatten Erfindung der Tiegeldruckpresse, später wurde der Tiegel durch eine Walze ersetzt
1840	Erste Rotationsdruckmaschine druckt im Flachdruckverfahren (Offsetdruck)
um 1880	Erste Schriftsetzmaschine von Mergenthaler ersetzt das Zusammensetzen der Buchstaben von Hand
1950	Fotosatzverfahren löst Bleisatz ab
1967	Fotoelektronischer Lichtsatz durch Computer gesteuert (Digiset)
1977	Drucker mit Lasertechnik, Nadeldrucker, Tintenstrahldrucker
1982	PostScript als unabhängige Seitenbeschreibungssprache (Adobe)
1985	Computergesteuerte Desktop Publishing-Systeme
1990	Einführung von PDF (Adobe)
1993	Computer-to-Plate (Offset)
1994	Book-on-Demand
2008	Computer-to-Press

Entwicklung Presse (Zeitschrift, Zeitung)

1609	Erste Wochenzeitungen in Wolfenbüttel und in Straßburg
1650	Gründung der ersten Tageszeitung „Einkommende Zeitung" in Leipzig
1690	Erste amerikanische Zeitung in Boston erscheint
1695	Erste Schritte zur Abschaffung der Zensur in Großbritannien, „LIcensing Act"
Ende 17. Jh.	Unterhaltungszeitschriften aus England, Blütezeit Mitte 18. Jh. in Deutschland mit „Der Weltbürger", „Der Biedermann".
1702	Erste englische Tageszeitung „The Daily Courant".
1776	Pressefreiheit in Amerika in den Bill of Rights festgeschrieben

1789	Die Pressefreiheit wird in Frankreich in der Erklärung der Menschen- und Bürgerrechte festgelegt
1848	Die Tageszeitung „Times“ wird erstmals in London auf einer Rotationsmaschine gedruckt
1848	Pressefreiheit im Grundrecht Deutschlands festgeschrieben, zunächst bis die Sozialistengesetze Ende des 19. Jh. diese wieder teilweise beschränkten
1922	Zeitschrift „Reader's Digest“ erscheint erstmals in den USA
1923	Erstes Nachrichtenmagazin „Time“ erscheint in den USA
1933	Einschränkung der Pressefreiheit durch die NSDAP im Deutschen Reich
1935	Taschenbücher im Paperback als Massenpublikation
Ende 1944	Lizenzierung der Presse in Deutschland durch die Alliierten
1946	Das Nachrichtenmagazin „Der Spiegel“ erscheint erstmalig
1949	Lizenzfreigabe durch die Alliierten in der BRD
1949	Gründung der Frankfurter Allgemeinen Zeitung
1952	Gründung der Bildzeitung durch Axel Springer
seit 1995	Ergänzung der Print-Ausgaben von Zeitungen und Zeitschriften durch Internet-Präsenzen
seit 2000	Eigenständiger Online-Journalismus (Gründung reiner Internetzeitungen)
seit ca. 2007	Entwicklung von personalisierten Zeitungsangeboten

Entwicklung Fotografie und Film

ca 900 n. Chr.	Entdeckung des Grundprinzips der Optik mit der „camera obscura“
Ende 18. Jh.	Niepce erfindet die Fotografie
1837	Daguerre entdeckt die Kochsalzlösung zum Fixieren belichteter Platten. Daguerreotypie als Verfahren veröffentlicht.
1840	Erstes Negativverfahren von Talbot vorgestellt. Er unternimmt erste fotografische Versuch auf Papier.
1878	Zelluloidrollfilm als Trägermaterial für Bildfolgen
1890	Erste Kamera der Fa. Kodak
1895	Die Brüder Lumière führen erstmals öffentlich in Paris einen Kinofilm vor
1902	Erste Linsensysteme (Tessar, Voigtländer)
1912	Edison stellt sein Kinetophon vor, Kombination von Filmkamera und Phonograph (früher Tonfilm)
1916	Erste Farbfilme von Agfa
1917	Erster Spielfilm in Farbe in den USA
1917	Gründung der UFA
1924	Leitz, Wetzlar, baut die erste Kleinbildkamera in Großserie (Leica)
1927	Erste Tonfilme in den USA, Warner und Fox
1932	Erste Spiegelreflexkamera
1936	Mehrschichtfarbfilm nach dem subtraktiven Farbsystem, AGFA-Color-Farbfilm
1947	Erfindung des Polaroidverfahrens, Sofortbild-Fotografie
1982	Mavica (Magnetic Video Camera) war die erste digitale Fotokamera, die die Bilder auf einer 3,5´´-Diskette speicherte
1988	Erste Digitalkamera mit wechselbaren Speicherkarten (Fuji)

1995	„Toy Story" ist der erste computergenerierte Film
1998	Film kann erstmals vollständig auf DVD gespeichert werden.
1998	MPEG-4, Verfahren zur Video- und Audiodatenkompression
seit 2000	Aufblühen des Genres Fantasy (z. B. Der Herr der Ringe, Harry Potter, Star Wars)
2002	Blu-ray Disc als Nachfolgeformat zur DVD wird entwickelt
seit ca. 2005	Mobiltelefone mit eingebauter Digitalkamera (Smartphones)
seit ca. 2006	Sukzessive Umstellung der Kinosäle von Film auf digitale Projektion und Digitalisierung der gesamten Produktionskette von den Filmaufnahmen über die Postproduktion bis hin zur Archivierung, Distribution und Vorführung
seit ca. 2010	3D-Kino erfährt einen Aufschwung

Entwicklung Telegrafie und Telefon

1. Jh. n. Chr.	Im Römischen Reich werden Rauchtelegrafen zum Übermitteln von Nachrichten eingesetzt
17. Jh.	Seeleute verständigen sich durch Flaggensignale
1791	Der Chappe'sche Telegraf (Sémaphore) arbeitete mit 196 Zeichen. Über 22 Stationen wurde von Paris nach Lille (200 km) optisch telegrafiert.
um 1800	Elektrischer Telegraf von Salva benötigt für jeden Buchstaben eine eigene Leitung
1809	Sömmering überträgt in München mit einem elektrischen Telegrafen Nachrichten über einige Kilometer.
1833	Gauß und Weber entwickeln einen elektromagnetischen Telegrafen mit zwei Leitungen
1838	Erfindung des Morsealphabets (Strich und Punkt), Telegraf mit einem Draht und Fernschreiber
1844	Erste Telegrafenverbindung zwischen zwei Städten (Washington und Baltimore)
nach 1850	Telegrafenverbindung Frankfurt – Berlin, Tiefseekabel Dover – Calais, Unterseekabel England – Kanada (3475 km)
1870	Philip Reis erfindet das erste Telefon
1876	Graham Bell baut die ersten marktfähigen Telefone
1890	Einführung der drahtlosen Telegrafie (Funktelegrafie)
1908	Erste automatische Telefonzentrale zur Vermittlung von Gesprächen in Hildesheim
1960	Telefongesellschaften entwickeln elektronische Wählverfahren
1962	Erste transatlantische Bildübertragung über den Satelliten Telstar
1965	Erster geostationärer Nachrichtensatellit
1970	Erste Direktwahl zwischen Europa und USA möglich
1977	Glasfaserkabel-Verbindung in Berlin
1983	Breitbandkommunikation möglich, C-Netz
seit 1990	Digitaler Mobilfunk
2001	Mit einem einzigen Glasfaserkabel können mehr als 10 TeraBits pro Sekunde übertragen werden (15 Mio. ISDN-Kanäle parallel)

Entwicklung Funk und Radio

1886	Experimenteller Nachweis des elektromagnetischen Feldes und der entsprechenden Wellen durch Maxwell und Hertz
um 1900	Erfindung eines Hörers durch Braun und Slaby
seit 1905	Gründung von Gesellschaften für Radioelektronik: Marconi, Telefunken, Sociéte francaise de radioélectricité
1907	Einrichten eines drahtlosen Telegrammdienst zwischen London und New York durch Marconi
1911	Großfunkstationen in deutsche Kolonien, Aufbau einer Funkverbindung in die USA
1919	Vorführung eines Röhrensenders durch Bredow
1923	Erstes deutsches Musikprogramm wird in Berlin auf Mittelwelle ausgestrahlt
1935	Erste Tonbandgeräte werden durch AEG entwickelt
1939	Entwicklung der Frequenzmodulation (FM) durch Armstrong
1948	Die Langspielplatte mit Mikrorillen speichert Musik
1961	Radiosendungen werden in den USA in Stereofonie ausgestrahlt, zwei Jahre später auch in Deutschland.
1965	Das erste Kassettengerät (Philips) kommt auf den Markt.
1971	Musik wird durch Quadrophonie zum Tonerlebnis
1980	Die Industrie bringt die ersten Compact Disk und CDs mit Musik auf den Markt
ab 1980	HIFI-Rundfunkgeräte bieten klangtreuen Klang, Geräte mit elektronischen Bauteilen
seit 1995	Sony bietet die Mini-CD als bespielbare Speichermedien
seit 1992	MPEG1-Standard zur Codierung von Audiodaten
seit 1995	MPEG3-Standard nutzt psychoakustische Effekte der Wahrnehmung des Menschen zur Codierung von Audiodaten
2011	DAB+ als digitaler Übertragungsstandard für terrestrischen Empfang von Digitalradio in Deutschland festgelegt

Entwicklung Fernsehen

1884	Nipkow erfand eine Scheibe zur Bildabtastung und –zerlegung, sowie Übertragung und Wiedergabe, bei sehr kleiner Bildgröße
1898	Braun erfindet die sog. Braunsche Röhre, die zur Bildaufnahme und Bildwiedergabe genutzt wurde
1935	Erste Fernsehsendung in Berlin als regelmäßiger Fernsehbetrieb
1936	Höhepunkt der Propaganda der NSDAP durch die Übertragung der Olympischen Spiele in Berlin, Einrichtung von öffentlichen Fernsehstuben, BBC strahlt erstmals ein Fernsehprogramm mit scharfen Bildern aus.
1945	Übergabe der Sender in deutsche Hände, erste Ausstrahlung des NWDR; Gründung der Landesanstalten MDR in ostdeutscher Verwaltung
1950	Gründung der ARD, erster öffentlich-rechtlicher Sender
1951	Auflösung der Landessender durch den Ministerrat und Zentralisierung des Fernsehens in der DDR
1953	Erste Eurovisionsübertragung der Krönung von Queen Elisabeth II.
1954	Einführung des Farbfernsehens in den USA, Gründung der Eurovision als Länderzusammenschluss mit Sitz in Brüssel
1957	In Frankreich wird das SECAM-System eingeführt
1960	Fernsehdirektübertragung der amerikanischen Präsidentschaftskandidatur zwischen Nixon und J.F.Kennedy
1961	Entwicklung des PAL-Fernsehsystems durch Walter Bruch
1963	ZDF sendet als zweiter öffentlich-rechtlicher Sender
1967	Einführung des Farbfernsehen
1969	Die Mondlandung im Fernsehen
1980	Satelliten-Pilot-Projekt TV-SAT; Bildschirmtext (BTX) und Videotext (VTX) und das Kabelfernsehen.
1981	Stereofonie im Fernsehen
1988	HDTV, hochauflösendes Fernsehen, erstmals zu den Olympischen Spielen in Seoul
bis 2010	Flächendeckende Einführung des terrestrischen digitalen Fernsehens (DVB-T)
2007	Begründung von Internet Protocol Television (IPTV) in Deutschland; Nutzung des Übertragungsweges Internet für Fernsehprogramme im Gegensatz zu klassischem Rundfunk, Kabel oder Satellit
2012	Satellitenempfang von TV-Programmen in Deutschland nur noch digital

Entwicklung Computer

1672	Leibniz entwickelte eine Rechenmaschine, die multiplizieren, dividieren und die Quadratwurzel ziehen konnte. Leibniz entwarf die Devise: „Ohne Gott ist nichts", woraus er schlussfolgerte, dass unser Denken ein Rechenvorgang sei und Gott „1" ist und Nichts „0". Das binäre Zahlensystem oder Dualsystem war erfunden.
1818	Rechenmaschine von Thomas, Colmar, die Wurzelziehen, Potenzieren und Winkelfunktionen berechnen konnte
1847	Boole entwickelte die logischen Verknüpfungen in algebraischen Gleichungen
1886	Hollerith erfand die elektromechanische Sortier- und Zählmaschine zum Auslesen von Lochkartendaten
1930	Am MIT in Cambridge geht der erste elektromechanische Großanalogrechner in Betrieb
1941	Konrad Zuse stellt seinen digitalen Rechenautomaten „Zuse Z 3" vor, der erste programmgesteuerte Rechner
1944	Aiken und IBM konstruieren den elektromechanischen Rechenautomaten „Mark I"
1946	Erste Großrechenanlage „ENIAC" an der Uni von Pennsylvania
1948	IBM baut den ersten lochkartengesteuerten Großrechner „IBM 604"
1952	MIT in Cambridge stellt erstmals eine NC-gesteuerte Werkzeugmaschine vor.
1960	Verfahren zur Herstellung von integrierten Halbleiterbauteilen (IC) werden entwickelt
1963	IBM baut Computer mit Transistortechnik im Miniformat, gleichzeitig kommt die elektrische Schreibmaschine mit Zwischenspeicher auf den Markt.
1968	Elektronikkonzerne stellen Computer mit integrierten Schaltkreisen her.
1971	Erster Mikroprozessor und erster Taschenrechner von Texas Instruments, Hoffmann LaRoche stellt die erste Flüssigkristallanzeige (LCD) her.
1972	Erstes elektronisches Spiel am Computer von Bushnell
1974	Erster programmierbarer Taschenrechner
1978	Intel 8086, erster 16-Bit-Prozessor
1979	VisiCalc-Tabellenkalkulation von Apple
seit 1980	akademische Nutzung des Internets
1980	IBM-PC erhalten Microsoft-DOS als Betriebssystem
1982	IBM präsentiert den Personalcomputer „PC XT", Bürorechner mit Festplatte
1983	Apple stellt den „Macintosh" vor; Intel bringt den 80286-Prozessor für IBM-AT-PC
1984	Sony und Philips entwickeln die CD-ROM
1985	Intel 386-Prozessor verarbeitet 32-Bit
1990	Windows Version 3.0 wird Betriebssystem mit GUI auf den PCs
ab 1990	mit Abschaltung von Arpanet wird das Internet kommerzialisiert (www)
1990	Truetype-Font-Technologie von Microsoft
1994	Netscape-Browser bringt die Benutzer ins Internet
1995	Java als plattformunabhängige Sprache
1996	Nintendo bringt Spielekonsole auf den Markt
1997	Pentium II kommt auf den Markt
1998	DVD-Laufwerke erweitern CD-ROM Speichermöglichkeiten, erste Flachbildschirme
...	Netzwerke, Servertechnologie, USB, Firewire, drahtlose Bedienung, Spielekonsolen, expandierender Spielesektor, Touch Screen-Technologie, iPhone, iPad

3.2 Die Medien im Überblick

3.2.1 Mediennutzung

❶ Quelle: ARD/ZDF-Langzeitstudie Massenkommunikation; BRD gesamt (bis 1990 nur alte Bundesländer), Mo-So, 5.00-24.00 Uhr, Pers. Ab 14 J. in min./Tag (brutto)

Welch hohe Bedeutung den Medien in unserer Gesellschaft zukommt, kann man an der Zeit ablesen, die wir für Fernsehschauen, Zeitunglesen, Computerspielen oder für das Internet verwenden: Im Durchschnitt stehen wir fast 10 Stunden lang (genauer: 584 Minuten) jeden Tag mit Medien in Verbindung! Die nachfolgende Tabelle legt ein beredtes Zeugnis über die Nutzungsgewohnheiten der Menschen in Deutschland seit 1980 bis heute ab ❶:

Medium	1980	1990	1995	2000	2005	2010
Printmedien						
Tageszeitung	38	28	30	30	28	23
Zeitschriften	11	11	11	10	12	6
Bücher	22	18	15	18	25	22
Elektronische Medien						
Fernsehen	125	135	158	185	220	220
Hörfunk	135	170	162	206	221	187
Video/DVD	-	4	3	4	5	5
CD/LP/MC/MP3	15	14	14	36	45	35
Internet	-	-	-	13	44	83
gesamt	**346**	**380**	**393**	**502**	**600**	**584**
Printmedien	71	57	56	58	65	54
Elektronische Medien	275	323	337	444	535	530
Anteile in Prozent:						
Printmedien	20,5	15,0	14,2	11,6	10,8	9,2
Elektronische Medien	79,5	85,0	85,8	88,4	89,2	90,8

Der Medienmarkt im Überblick – Mediennutzung (in min./Tag)

Die vielen Stunden, die wir für die Mediennutzung verwenden, weisen allerdings etwas in die Irre, weil in dieser Statistik die Parallelnutzung von Medien jeweils gesondert gerechnet wird und die Zahl dadurch künstlich aufgebläht ist. Dennoch dürfte sie überaus beeindruckend sein.

Festzustellen ist insbesondere, dass sich die **Mediennutzung** innerhalb eines Vierteljahrhunderts beinahe **verdoppelt** hat. Waren es 1980, also kurz vor dem „medienpolitischen Urknall“ (der Einführung des privaten Hörfunks und Fernsehens in Deutschland im Jahr 1984), noch 346 Minuten, die sich der Bürger in Deutschland (damals nur West) den Medien widmete, erhöhte sich diese Zahl bis 2005 auf 600 Minuten und hält sich im Jahr 2010 mit 584 Minuten in etwa auf diesem Niveau.

Schaut man sich die Nutzungszeiten daraufhin an, wie sie sich auf die **einzelnen Medien** verteilen, sticht sofort der hohe Anteil der elektronischen Medien ins Auge: 90,8 Prozent der Gesamtnutzungszeit zieht der elektronische Bereich auf sich, und nur noch 9,2 Prozent ihres „**Medienbudgets**" widmen sich die Menschen den Printmedien! Der Trend der Abnahme der Nutzungszeiten der Printmedien scheint ungebrochen zu sein, obwohl das Buchsegment mit nach wie vor mehr als 20 Minuten täglich ein bemerkenswerter „Leuchtturm" im Printbereich darstellt.

Ein geradezu dramatisches Wachstum hat die Nutzung des **Internet** erfahren: Zur Jahrtausendwende noch kaum präsent, machte die Nutzung im Jahr 2005 schon 44 Minuten aus und ist bis 2010 bereits auf 83 Minuten angewachsen. Im Durchschnitt widmen die Menschen ab 14 Jahren in Deutschland dem Internet also bereits ca. eineinhalb Stunden täglich.

Interessant ist der Blick darauf, wie sich die **Nutzungsgewohnheiten nach dem Lebensalter** unterscheiden. Jugendliche und junge Erwachsene (14-29 Jahre) zeigen ein gegenüber der Gesamtheit (alle Personen ab 14 Jahre) völlig entgegengesetztes Verhalten: Sie schauen deutlich weniger fern und hören weniger Radio, dafür sind sie viel länger im Internet und nutzen öfter Trägermedien (CD, MP3 usw.). Die nachfolgende Übersicht über die Nutzungsdauer der Medien für 2010 zeigt diesen deutlichen Gegensatz (Quelle: ARD/ZDF-Langzeitstudie Massenkommunikation).

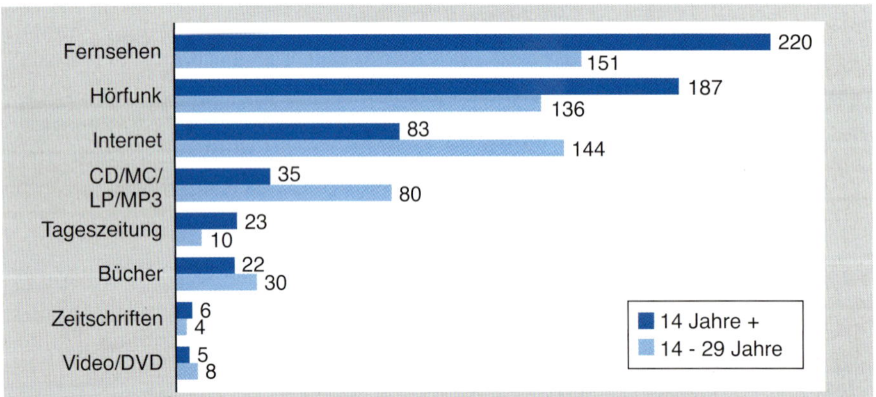

Nutzungsdauer der Medien 2010; Mo - So, 5:00 - 24:00 Uhr, Personen ab 14 Jahre, in Min./Tag; Basis: alle Befragten n = 4503 gewichtet

So wenig schmeichelhaft die Nutzungszeiten für den Printsektor erscheinen, so eindrucksvoll sind die Zahlen für seine wirtschaftliche Bedeutung. Hier zeigen sich völlig umgekehrte Verhältnisse, denn der Printbereich generiert mit 30 Mrd. Euro mehr Umsatz als der elektronische Medienbereich mit lediglich ca. 27 Mrd. Euro. Dieser Sachverhalt wird im nächsten Abschnitt aufgezeigt.

3.2.2 Umsätze und Beschäftigung

❶ Quelle: Zusammenstellung nach den verfügbaren Datenquellen von statistischen Ämtern, Verbänden und Organisationen des Medienbereichs. Vgl. Gläser, Martin: Medienmanagement, 2. Aufl., München 2010, Kap. 6. Wenn nicht anders vermerkt, wird nachfolgend auf diese Quelle Bezug genommen. Alle Angaben beziehen sich auf das Jahr 2008, wenn nicht anders vermerkt.

Die Ausführungen in Kapitel 1 und 2 machen deutlich, dass den Medien in unserer Gesellschaft ein extrem hoher Stellenwert beizumessen ist. Überraschenderweise sind sie aber in wirtschaftlicher Hinsicht eher von nachgeordneter Bedeutung. Einen Überblick über die **Umsätze des Medienmarktes und seiner Teilmärkte** gibt die nachfolgende Tabelle ❶:

Medien-Teilmärkte	Erlöse gesamt	Erlöse Rezipienten	Erlöse Werbung	Erlose Gebühren
Printmedien				
Zeitungen	9,10	4,37	4,73	
Zeitschriften	6,36	3,64	2,72	
Anzeigen-/Offertenblätter	2,01		2,01	
Buch	9,61	9,61		
Außenwerbung	0,80		0,80	
Werbung per Post	3,29		3,29	
Verzeichnismedien	1,22		1,22	
Elektronische Medien				
Fernsehen	11,92	3,38	4,04	4,50
Hörfunk	3,42		0,71	2,71
Kino (Filmtheater)	0,87	0,79	0,08	
Heim-Video	1,56	1,56		
Musik	1,58	1,58		
Video-/Computerspiele	1,80	1,80		
Internet	6,82	6,07	0,75	
Summe Medienmarkt	**60,36**	**32,80**	**20,35**	**7,21**
Printmedien	32,39			
Elektronische Medien	27,97			
Anteile in Prozent	**100**	**54,34**	**33,71**	**11,95**

❷ Die volkswirtschaftliche Gesamtleistung misst man anhand des sog. „Bruttoinlandsprodukts". Es betrug im Jahr 2010 für Deutschland gemäß den amtlichen Zahlen des Statistischen Bundesamtes 2.477 Mrd. Euro.

Der gesamte **Medienmarkt** in Deutschland umfasst also eine Größenordnung von ca. 60 Mrd. Euro. Die volkswirtschaftliche Gesamtleistung Deutschlands pro Jahr liegt bei ca. 2,5 Billionen Euro ❷, was bedeutet, dass der Mediensektor lediglich mit 2,4 Prozent zur Gesamtsumme aller in Deutschland produzierten Güter beiträgt.

Besonders interessant ist es, dass die **Teilmärkte**, die dem Printbereich zuzuordnen sind (Zeitungen, Zeitschriften, Buch, Anzeigenblätter usw.), mit ca. 32 Mrd. Euro nach wie vor ein deutliches Übergewicht gegenüber dem elektronischen Mediensektor mit seinen knapp 28 Mrd. Euro (Radio, TV, Kino, Trägermedien und Internet zusammen genommen) aufweisen. Von einem „Verschwinden" der Druckprodukte kann also keine Rede sein!

Die wirtschaftliche Bedeutung der Medien wird allerdings in eine anderes Licht gerückt, stellt man sie in den größeren Zusammenhang des sogenannten **TIME-Sektors** ❶. Die Zahlen sehen dann anders aus: Dieser TIME-Sektor, dessen vier Teilbranchen untereinander eng verflochten sind, kommt nämlich auf eine Größenordnung von 207 Mrd. Euro und damit bereits auf fast zehn Prozent des deutschen Bruttoinlandsprodukts. Rechnet man noch die Druck- und Papierbranche mit ihren 37,9 Mrd. Euro hinzu, die ja eine große Affinität zu den Printmedien besitzt, kommt man sogar auf 244,9 Mrd. Euro. Das ist eine Größenordnung, die nicht weit vom Automobilsektor (Straßenfahrzeugbau) mit seinen 290 Mrd. Euro entfernt ist, aber den Bereich Elektrotechnik und Elektronik (182 Mrd. Euro) oder der Chemie (140 Mrd. Euro) klar überflügelt hat.

Im Hinblick auf die **Beschäftigung** weist die TIME-Branche und mit ihr der Mediensektor eine vergleichsweise beachtliche Größenordnung auf. Allein in der Medienbranche (inkl. der Druck- und Papierindustrie) sind knapp 650 Tsd. Menschen beschäftigt, wobei bemerkenswert ist, dass auf den Printbereich mehr als doppelt so viele Beschäftigungsverhältnisse wie auf den elektronischen Bereich fallen. Der so charakterisierte Mediensektor ist im Hinblick auf die Beschäftigtenzahl allein schon so groß wie die Automobilindustrie. Die TIME-Branche insgesamt kommt sogar auf fast 1,5 Mio. Beschäftigte.

Deutschland 2010	Beschäftigte in Tsd.
Print	**467**
Verlage (Zeitung, Zeitschriften, Buch)	216
Buchhandel	35
Druckindustrie	173
Papierindustrie	43
Elektronische Medien	**180**
Radio	27
Fernsehen	31
Film, Kino	37
Musik	25
Internet	50
Video- und Computerspiele (freie Schätzung)	10
ITK, Consumer Electronics	**829**
ITK (Telekommunikation und IT-Sektor)	806
Consumer Electronics	23
TIME-Branche insgesamt	**1.476**

Beschäftigte in der Medien- und TIME-Branche in Deutschland

❶ „TIME" liest sich so:

- T Telekommunikation;
- I Informationstechnik (Computer: Hardware, Software);
- M Medien;
- E Consumer Electronics (= CE, Endgeräte der Unterhaltungselektronik)

Die Bereiche Telekommunikation und Informationstechnik werden auch zum „ITK-Sektor" bzw. „IKT-Sektor" zusammengefasst.

3.3 Printmedien

3.3.1 Zeitungen

Definition

Zeitungen sind periodische Veröffentlichungen, die in kurzen Abständen erscheinen. Ihr Hauptzweck ist die **Übermittlung aktueller Nachrichten** aus den verschiedensten Bereichen, vor allem aus Politik, Wirtschaft, Unterhaltung, Kultur, Gesellschaft und Sport. „Die Zeitung ist ein in kurzer, regelmäßiger Folge erscheinendes, grundsätzlich jedermann zugängliches Medium, das aktuelle Informationen aus allen Lebensbereichen verbreitet. In kurzer Folge heißt, Tageszeitungen müssen mindestens zweimal wöchentlich erscheinen, wenn sie ihren Namen zu Recht tragen wollen" (Bremenfeld et al. 1998 S. 8).

Wirtschaftliche Bedeutung

Die ökonomische Bedeutung der Zeitungsmarktes ist mit einem **Marktvolumen** von ca. neun Mrd. Euro nach wie vor sehr hoch, er ist auch als **Werbeträger** von größter Bedeutung. In der mittelfristigen Vergangenheit ist er aber vom Fernsehen mit heute ca. zwölf Mrd. Euro von seinem langjährig angestammten Spitzenplatz verdrängt worden. Seit 2000 büßte der Zeitungsmarkt im Übrigen sogar ca. ein Fünftel seines Gesamtumsatzes in absoluten Zahlen ein. Vor diesem Hintergrund wird der Zeitungsmarkt gelegentlich sogar als eine „Krisenindustrie" bezeichnet. Fest steht, dass das Internet und die Digitalisierung der medialen Wertschöpfungskette die Verlage vor existentielle, historisch einmalige Herausforderungen stellen.

Publizistische Bedeutung

„Die Zeitung ist ein unentbehrliches Mittel der Kommunikation in der Gesellschaft; sie dient der Information, der Meinungsbildung und der Unterhaltung ihrer Leser. Sie trägt in der Industrie- und Dienstleistungsgesellschaft dazu bei, den Menschen die immer komplizierter werdenden Vorgänge der Umwelt zu erschließen und dadurch Verhaltenssicherheit im Zusammenleben mit den Mitmenschen zu geben" (Bremenfeld et al. 1998 S. 8). Zeitungen weisen eine Gegenwartsbezogenheit des Inhalts auf (**Aktualität**), sind zugänglich für jedermann (**Publizität**), offen nach allen Lebensbereichen (Universalität) und erscheinen regelmäßig (**Periodizität**).

Zeitungen konkurrieren im Hinblick auf die Breite der Berichterstattung mit Radio und Fernsehen. Sowohl die auf den nationalen Raum ausgerichteten Zeitungen wie die Frankfurter Allgemeine Zeitung, Die Welt, die Frankfurter Rundschau oder die Süddeutsche Zeitung als auch die regionalen und lokalen Tageszeitungen sind publizistisch von höchster Bedeutung. Zeitungen sind auch heute noch als ein **Basismedium** ❶ anzusehen. Zeitungen zeichnen sich auch dadurch aus, dass sich ihre Leser während der Nutzung *aktiv* dem Medium widmen. Dadurch unterscheiden sie sich vom Radio, das als ausgesprochenes „Nebenbei-Medium" bzw. **„Begleit-Medium"** ❷ gilt. Die Nutzung findet ferner ortsunabhängig statt, also zu Hause, in öffentlichen Verkehrsmitteln oder am Arbeitsplatz. Grund ist die leichte Transportmöglichkeit.

❶ Unter **Basismedium** versteht man ein Medium, das einen maßgeblichen Beitrag zur Meinungsbildung und grundlegenden Beitrag zum Informationsstand der Bevölkerung liefert.

❷ Beim **Nebenbei-Medium** erfolgt die Nutzung zeitgleich mit anderen Medien oder anderen Betätigungen.

Zeitungen

Kommunikatoren, Anbieter

- Haupt-Kommunikatoren: (1) Die großen Verlagsgruppen: Axel Springer AG, WAZ-Mediengruppe, Südwestdeutsche Medien Holding. (2) Andere: z. B. M. DuMont Schauberg, Frankfurter Allgemeine Zeitung, Madsack.
- Regionale und lokale Zeitungsmärkte: Breites Engagement von Großverlagen (z. B. WAZ), daneben Struktur eigenständiger mittlerer und kleiner Verleger.

Produkte, Inhalte

- Typen: Tageszeitungen („Tagespresse"), Wochenzeitungen, Sonntagszeitungen, Sonderformen, Anzeigenblätter, Online-Zeitungen.
- Tageszeitungen: 354 Titel; 135 Publizistische Einheiten (Trend: seit Jahren sinkend, Index 86 auf Basis 1991 = 100; 1954 noch 225 publizistische Einheiten), 20,4 Mio. verkaufte Auflage. Inhaltliche Struktur: Umfassender Inhalt („Vollprogramm"), Schwerpunkt aktuelle Informationen aus allen Bereichen. Zeitungsformate: Rheinisches Format 365 × 510 mm, Halbes Rheinisches Format 255 × 365, Berliner Format 315 × 470, Nordisches Format 400 × 570. Versuche mit Kompaktformat („Tabloid").
- Tageszeitungen: (1) Teilsegment überregionale Tageszeitungen: Anzahl: 10 Titel (Beispiele: FAZ, Die Welt, Handelsblatt), 1,6 Mio. verkaufte Auflage. (2) Lokale und regionale Abonnementzeitungen: Anzahl 333 Titel (z. B. WAZ, Münchner Merkur), 14,5 Mio. verkaufte Auflage, Detailinformationen aus der Region und der lokalen Welt. (3) Kaufzeitungen: 8 Titel (überregional v. a. Bild, lokal-regional z. B. Hamburger Morgenpost), 4,5 Mio. verkaufte Auflage.
- Wochenzeitungen: 28 Titel (z. B. Die Zeit), 2,0 Mio. verkaufte Auflage.
- Sonntagszeitungen: 6 Titel (überregional z. B. FAS, Welt am Sonntag, regional z. B. Sonntag Aktuell), 3,6 Mio. verkaufte Auflage.
- Sonderformen: Konfessionelle Zeitungen, Heimatzeitungen, Kommunale Wochenzeitungen.
- Anzeigenblätter: 1.393 Titel, 90,8 Mio. verbreitete Auflage.
- Online: (1) Internet-Nachrichtenportale (Erweiterung oder Ergänzung der gedruckten Ausgabe); überwiegend kostenfrei bzw. durch Werbung finanziert. (2) Elektronische Zeitungen (E-Paper) mit zwei Ausprägungen: (a) Internet-Angebot als Ergänzung zum Printprodukt, (b) eigens aufbereitete Inhalte.
- Zeitungen als Werbeträger: Anteil am Gesamtinhalt ca. 20 %, Beitrag zur Finanzierung mehr als die Hälfte. Abnehmender Anteil an Werbung.

Transportwege

- Straßenverkauf: Kiosk, Supermärkte, Bäckereien.
- Abonnement: Träger, Post.
- Gelegenheitsangebote in Hotels, Arztpraxen usw.
- Internet als Vertriebskanal nimmt an Bedeutung zu.
- Sonderform: Videotext (Teletext) als textbasiertes Medium im Fernsehen.

Rezipienten

- Reichweite Tageszeitungen gesamt: 71,4 % der Gesamtbevölkerung ab 14 Jahren (Frauen: 69,4 %; Männer: 73,5 %). Durchschnitt-lich nehmen 46,3 Mio. Deutsche über 14 Jahren pro Tag eine Zeitung in die Hand.
- Zeitbudget: Mediennutzungsdauer 23 Min. (2010)
- Nutzer-Schwerpunkt: (1) 40 Jahre und älter; bis 39 Jahre unterdurchschnittlich; (2) gemäß Sinus-Milieus: Etablierte, Traditionsver-wurzelte, Konservative, Postmaterielle.

Gattungen von Tageszeitungen

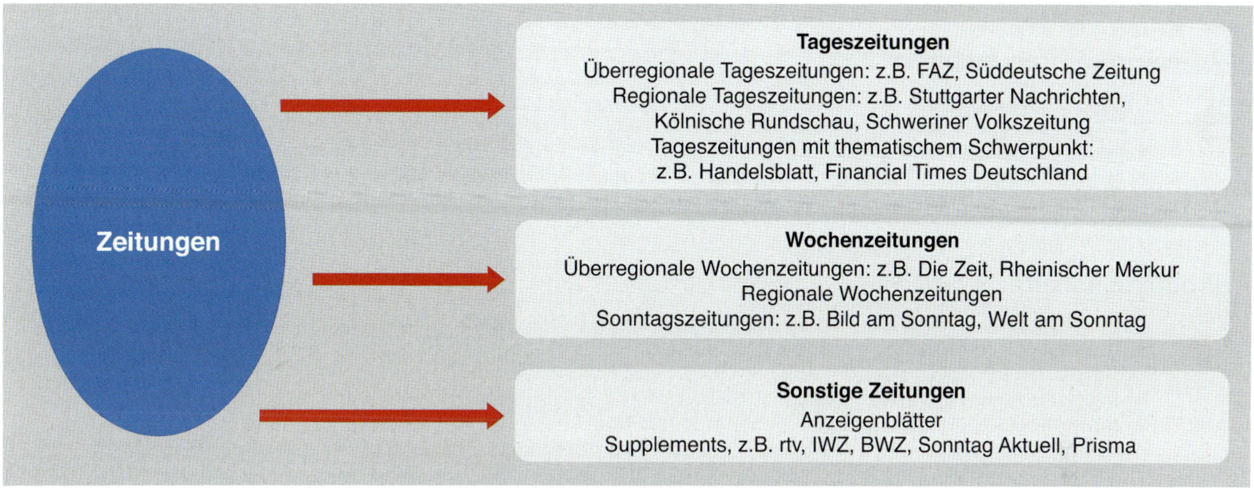

Frankfurter Allgemeine
Neue Zürcher Zeitung
DIE WELT
Süddeutsche Zeitung

Überregionale Tageszeitungen zeichnen sich durch einen hohen redaktionellen Anspruch aus, bei denen die vertiefende Hintergrundinformation eine Rolle spielt. Sie erreichen Angehörige der höheren sozialen Schichten, insbesondere Führungskräfte aus Wirtschaft, Politik und Gesellschaft. Daher sind sie vor allem für die Werbung interessant, wenn es um gehobene Freizeitangebote, um hochwertige langlebige Konsumgüter (z. B. Autos), um wirtschaftsorientierte Produkte (z. B. Software) oder um Stellenanzeigen mittlerer oder oberer Führungspositionen geht.

Regionale Tageszeitungen sind auf ein bestimmtes Verbreitungsgebiet abgestimmt und weisen eine entsprechende inhaltliche Gestaltung auf, bei dem das regionale Geschehen ausführlich vermittelt wird.

Stuttgarter Wochenblatt

Eine Sonderstellung im Zeitungsbereich nehmen die **sonstigen Zeitungen** ein. So sind die für die Werbewirtschaft wichtigen Anzeigenblätter nicht zu unterschätzen, da sie auch für den Nutzer eine Reihe von interessanten Merkmalen aufweisen:

- Sie werden kostenlos verteilt.
- Die Finanzierung erfolgt ausschließlich aus Werbegeldern.
- Beliefert werden fast alle Privat- und Geschäftshaushalte.
- Sie erscheinen regelmäßig, überwiegend wöchentlich.
- Sie beinhalten eine Vielzahl redaktioneller Beiträge, in der Regel von stark ausgeprägtem lokalen Bezug.

Es gibt Zeitungen, die praktisch ausschließlich am Kiosk gekauft werden. Eine solche **Kaufzeitung** ist z. B. „Bild". Sie sind durch den Zwang geprägt, täglich neue Kaufanreize bieten zu müssen und setzen auf Sensationsberichterstattung. Die Aufmachung und die Schlagzeilen sind auffällig und reißerisch. Im Gegensatz zu den **überregionalen Zeitungen** sind die Kaufzeitungen auf die mittleren sozialen Schichten, insbesondere auf qualifizierte Arbeiter und Angestellte ausgerichtet.

Zentrale Trends im Zeitungsmarkt

- Alle klassisch herkömmlichen Zeitungsmärkte sind gesättigt bzw. übersättigt.
- Es findet seit einiger Zeit ein Rückgang von Auflagenhöhe und Reichweiten statt. Besonders starke Einbrüche sind in der Altersgruppe der 14-25-Jährigen zu beklagen.
- Die auf Zeitungen verwendete Nutzungszeit nimmt ab.
- Die Kundenbindung (Leserbindung) nimmt ab.
- Die Lesefähigkeit, der Wortschatz und die Konzentrationsfähigkeit nehmen ab, ein Trend, der sich trotz formal steigender Bildungsabschlüsse verstärkt.
- Die Nutzungshäufigkeit der Online-Medien steigt, während die der Printmedien sinkt. Besonders bei jungen Zielgruppen ist eine hohe Affinität für die Nutzung nicht nur eines, sondern ganz verschiedener Informationskanäle festzustellen.
- Damit einhergehend sinken die Werbeeinnahmen (seit 1999 erhebliche Schrumpfung der Werbeeinnahmen um ca. ein Viertel). Besonders bei den Rubrikenmärkten (Stellen-, Kfz-, Immobilienanzeigen) erfolgt eine deutliche Verlagerung weg von gedruckten Zeitungen hin zum Internet. Als Perspektive droht langfristig die vollständige Verlagerung.
- Dies führt zu einer sich öffnenden Schere zwischen ständig steigenden Kosten und den erzielbaren Einnahmen aus Vertrieb und Werbung.

Konzepte der Zeitungsverlage

- Für die Zukunft des Mediums Zeitung wird es entscheidend sein, inwieweit es den Verlagen gelingt, die elektronischen Verbreitungswege für das Zeitungsgeschäft zu nutzen. Aufgrund geringer Druck- und Distributionskosten ist die elektronische Ausgabe der Zeitung im Internet ❶ von der Produktionsseite her gesehen hoch attraktiv.
- Stark in der Diskussion ist das Konzept der Gratiszeitungen. Diese sind leicht lesbar, dennoch qualitativ ansprechend und dem Stil nach auf junge Berufstätige und Schüler ausgerichtet.
- Eine Reihe von Zeitungen erzielen große Erfolge mit Nebengeschäften. Vom Geschäft mit Nebenprodukten profitieren v. a. die überregionalen Zeitungstitel (v. a. Süddeutsche Zeitung, Die Zeit).
- Interessant ist die Postzustellung als neue Dienstleistung, die nach dem Fall des Postmonopols in Deutschland (zum 1.1.2011) auch für Zeitungsverlage möglich wird. Bereits jetzt erwerben zahlreiche Verlage Lizenzen für das Postgeschäft. Regionalzeitungen arbeiten daran, leistungsfähige Kooperationen zu bilden, um auch größere Gebiete mit privater Briefzustellung versorgen zu können.
- Umsatzzuwächse lassen sich vor allem durch eine Marktausdehnung in das Ausland realisieren, wobei multinationale – also auf das einzelne Land zugeschnittene – Konzepte dominieren (z. B. WAZ in Bulgarien).
- Viel beachtet sind Zeitungsneugründungen im handlichen Tabloid-Format (Kompaktzeitungen), die als Antwort auf die zunehmende Mobilität und den Bedarf an Bequemlichkeit zu sehen sind.

❶ Die elektronische Ausgabe wird auch **E-Paper** genannt.

3.3.2 Zeitschriften

Definition

Zeitschriften können als eine **Zwischenform** zwischen **Zeitungen** und **Büchern** verstanden werden, da sie wie Zeitungen periodisch erscheinen, aber in der Regel nicht so häufig. Sie sind aktueller als Bücher, nicht jedoch so aktuell wie Zeitungen. Ihre Aufmachung im Hinblick auf Format und Druckqualität ist den Büchern ähnlicher als den Zeitungen, und sie werden länger als Zeitungen aufbewahrt, allerdings nicht so lange wie Bücher. Es gibt freilich auch Billigzeitschriften, die ähnlich wie Zeitungen zum Teil nur flüchtig „konsumiert" werden. „Zeitschriften sind periodisch erscheinende Druckerzeugnisse, die wöchentlich, monatlich oder auch in größeren Zeitabständen veröffentlicht werden. Sie sind geklammert oder geleimt und drucktechnisch aufwendiger verarbeitet als Zeitungen" (Bremenfeld et al. 1998, S. 18).

Wirtschaftliche Bedeutung

Der **Zeitschriftenmarkt Deutschland** ist einer der höchst entwickelten der Welt. Sein Volumen beträgt 6,36 Mrd. Euro und verteilt sich zu zwei Dritteln auf **Publikumszeitschriften** und zu einem Drittel auf **Fachzeitschriften**. Nicht in dieser Zahl erfasst sind Verbands- und Vereinszeitschriften, Kunden- und Firmenzeitschriften sowie konfessionelle Zeitschriften. Bei **Publikumszeitschriften** Zahl der Titel in den letzten 25 Jahren stark angestiegen, d. h. verdreifacht (von 1980 mit 271 Titeln zum Jahr 2004 mit 850 IVW-geprüften Titeln). Insgesamt sind 2.340 Objekte auf dem Markt bei im Schnitt ca. 120 bis 130 Neugründungen pro Jahr. Die verkaufte Auflage hat in den letzten zehn Jahren – wie schon in den vierzig Jahren zuvor – zugenommen, aber nur moderat. Veränderungen im Markt rühren von einer starken Zunahme der Titel her, nicht von der Auflagenhöhe. Neueinführungen und Relaunches stehen also im Vordergrund.

Publizistische Bedeutung

Deutschland ist das Land mit der weltweit höchsten Zeitschriftendichte. Das Interesse an Zeitschriften ist sehr groß, die publizistische Bedeutung der Zeitschriften ist hoch: „Die Welt der Zeitschrift übt auf fast jeden eine außergewöhnliche Faszination aus. Kein Wunder: Die verschiedensten Hefte buhlen mit schillernden Titelbildern und reißerischen Schlagzeilen um die Aufmerksamkeit der Leser. Es gibt kaum ein Themengebiet, dem sich nicht ein Heft ausführlich widmen würde: Die trendbewusste Frau kann sich zwischen Dutzenden von Modezeitschriften entscheiden, politisch Interessierte werden von Nachrichtenmagazinen auf dem Laufenden gehalten, für den Bodybuilder gibt es eine spezielle Zeitschrift, ebenso für den passionierten Sportfischer" (Menhard/Trede 2004, S. 15).

Die Zeitschrift ist im Gegensatz zur Zeitung nicht tagesaktuell, sondern aktuell im Hinblick auf **Fachthemen**, ihr Themenspektrum ist auf wenige Sachgebiete beschränkt, das Publikum ist in der Regel auf **kleinere Zielgruppen** zugeschnitten und die Erscheinungsfolge ist nicht so häufig wie bei Zeitungen.

Zeitschriften

Kommunikatoren, Anbieter

- Die vier größten Verlage bei den Publikumszeitschriften (Marktanteile gesamt in %): Bauer 19,5; Burda 16,5; Springer 15,1; Bertelsmann/Gruner + Jahr 10,8 %.
- Fast 500 Fachverlage. Die 10 größten Fachverlage (2006): Springer Science + Business Media, Holtzbrinck, WEKA, Süddeutscher Verlag, Wolters Kluwer, Reed Elsevier, Haufe, Vogel, DSV-Gruppe, Verlag C. H. Beck.

Produkte, Inhalte

- Typen: Publikums-, Fach-, Kunden- und Konfessionelle Zeitschriften.
- Publikumszeitschriften: (1) 842 IVW-geprüfte Titel (insgesamt ca. 2.500 Titel) (Deutschland 2008, in der Langfristperspektive stark steigend, Vervierfachung seit 1975). (2) Top 10: ADAC Motorwelt, Stern, Spiegel, Bild der Frau, Focus, Computer Bild, Bunte, Sport Bild, Brigitte, Geo. (3) Inhaltliche Struktur: Breite Themenvielfalt sowie spezielle Interessen. (4) Erscheinungsintervalle: Wochentitel, 14-Tages-Titel, Monatstitel.
- Fachzeitschriften: gesamt 3.907 Titel (davon 1.222 IVW-geprüft). Jahresauflage 525 Mio. Exemplare, davon verkauft: 45 %.
- Kundenzeitschriften: mehr als 1.800 aktive Titel (national und international); Auflage mehr als 900 Mio. Exemplare.
- Konfessionelle Zeitschriften: 58 Titel, insgesamt 2,21 Mio. verbreitete Auflage.
- Internet-Angebote: als Ergänzung zum Printprodukt, aber mit eigens aufbereiteten, erheblich erweiterten Inhalten, z. B. Focus, Spiegel.
- Werbung: (1) Publikumszeitschriften: Werbung nimmt einen Anteil von ca. 23 % am Gesamtumfang ein. Top 10 der werbestärksten Publikumszeitschriften: Stern, Spiegel, Focus, Bild am Sonntag (BamS), Brigitte, Freundin, Bunte, TV Movie, Bild der Frau, TV Spielfilm. (2) Fachzeitschriften: Werbeanteil ca. 30 %, aber insgesamt 50 % Erlösanteil; Werbevolumen (brutto): ca. 0,9 Mrd. Euro. Top 10 der werbestärksten Fachzeitschriften: Deutsches Ärzteblatt, Lebensmittel Zeitung, Textilwirtschaft, Werben und Verkaufen, Ärztezeitung, Computerwoche, MM Maschinenmarkt, Horizont, DVZ Deutsche Logistik-Zeitung, Markt und Technik.

Transportwege

- Vertrieb Publikumszeitschriften: Abonnement (45 %), Kiosk (40 %) zumeist zweistufiger Vertrieb über Pressegrossisten, Lesezirkel (4 %), Sonstiger Verkauf (11 %); Gelegenheitsnutzung in Arztpraxen, Hotels, Gaststätten usw. Trend: relative Abnahme Abonnement, Zunahme sonstiger Verkauf.
- Vertrieb Fachzeitschriften: Abonnement (90 %), Kiosk (10 %). Stabiler Trend.
- Internet als Zusatzangebot und Vertriebskanal, insbesondere bei Fachzeitschriften.

Rezipienten

- Reichweite Zeitschriften gesamt: 60,63 Mio. Leser . 93,5 % der Personen ab 14 Jahren nutzen Zeitschriften. 50 % der Gesamtbevölkerung ab 14 Jahren liest mehrmals in der Woche Zeitschriften.
- Zeitbudget: Mediennutzung 6 Min. (2010).
- Nutzer-Schwerpunkt Publikumszeitschriften: 30 Jahre und älter.
- Nutzer-Schwerpunkt Fachzeitschriften: 30 Jahre und älter.
- Nutzer-Schwerpunkt: starke Ausdifferenzierung des Zeitschriftenmarktes, alle Milieus werden erreicht.

Gattungen von Zeitschriften

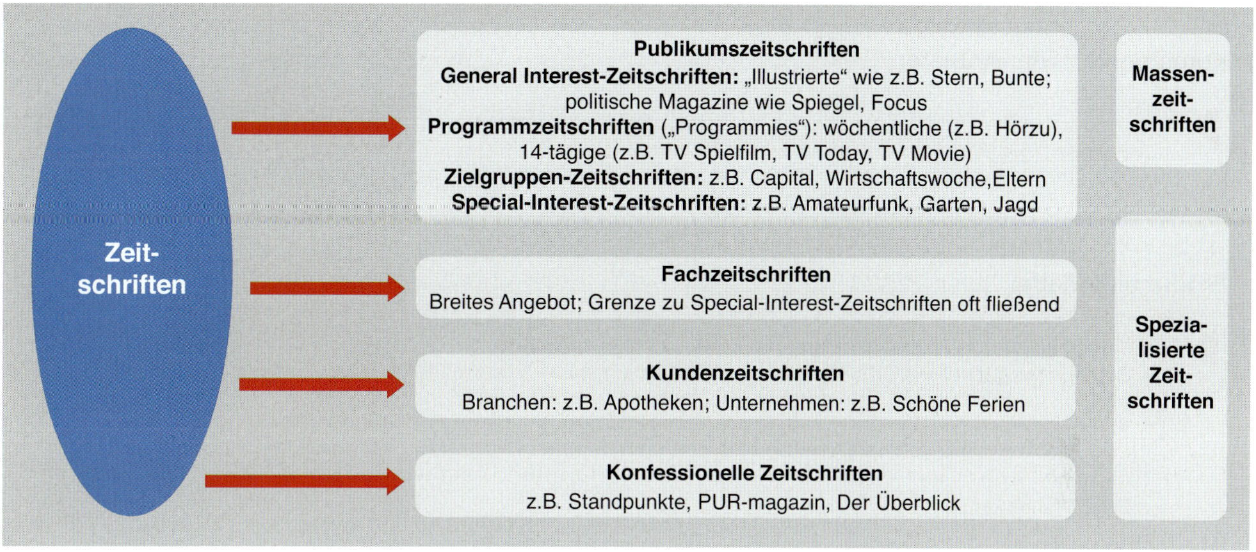

Bei den **Publikumszeitschriften** können die General-Interest-Zeitschriften und die Programmzeitschriften zu den sog. Massenzeitschriften zusammen gefasst werden. Alle anderen Zeitschriften sind sog. Spezialisierte Zeitschriften. Massenzeitschriften bieten eine breite, allgemein interessierenden Themenpalette an. Sie erreichen hohe Reichweiten, die noch durch Lesezirkel und Weiterreichen der Zeitschriften zusätzlich ausgedehnt werden. Das Werbevolumen der Massenzeitschriften ist in den letzten Jahren gesunken, und zwar durch die starke Zunahme der Fernsehwerbung, das mit der Zulassung privater TV-Anbieter Werbegelder auf sich gezogen hat. Auch sind die Auflagen der Massenzeitschriften gesunken.

Zudem werden Massenzeitschriften neben dem Fernsehen immer mehr von den **Zielgruppen-Zeitschriften** und den Special-Interest-Zeitschriften bedrängt. Bei letzteren haben die Computer-Zeitschriften eine große Bedeutung erlangt. Sie haben die anderen Bereiche mit ihrer breiten Themenvielfalt (z. B. Garten, Familie, Segeln, Reiten, Jagd) überflügelt. Für die Werbung sind die Zielgruppen- und Special-Interest-Zeitschriften ein wichtiger Werbeträger, da hier genau definierte Zielgruppen zielgenau erreicht werden können (sog. „Streuverlust“ ist gering).

Fachzeitschriften sind auf die Bedürfnisse von Experten ausgerichtet. Oft sind sie die Plattform für Dokumentationen und Diskussionen unter Spezialisten. Auch in der Aus- und Weiterbildung spielen sie eine prominente Rolle. Fachzeitschriften werden häufig in gebundener Form aufbewahrt. Es ist zu erwarten, dass den Fachzeitschriften über die Online-Dienste eine beachtliche Konkurrenz erwächst.

NEUE APOTHEKEN ILLUSTRIERTE

Kundenzeitschriften werden von Handels- und Dienstleistungsunternehmen herausgebracht und kostenlos an Kunden abgegeben. Sie sollen denn Verkauf unterstützen und bieten Neuigkeiten aus der betreffenden Branche. Besonders stark sind Kundenzeitschriften der Apotheken vertreten.

Zentrale Trends im Zeitschriftenmarkt

- Der Markt für Publikumszeitschriften ist gesättigt bzw. übersättigt. Es findet ein heftiger Umverteilungs- und Verdrängungswettbewerb statt, da neue Zeitschriften stets zu Lasten von etablierten gehen.
- Die Auflagenzahlen bei Publikumszeitschriften sinken, und zwar sowohl in absoluten Größen als auch im Hinblick auf die durchschnittliche Auflage.
- Zuwächse sind meist nur durch Einführung neuer Titel möglich, nicht durch höhere Auflagen der im Markt befindlichen Titel
- Der Zeitschriftenmarkt ist durch einen hohen Grad an Fragmentierung (Zersplitterung) und Diversifikation (Aufteilung) gekennzeichnet. Er besetzt immer weitere Nischen, was die Spezialisierung nach Zielgruppen vorantreibt.
- Massenzeitschriften werden zunehmend von Zielgruppenzeitschriften und Special-Interest-Zeitschriften verdrängt.
- Wissenschaftliche Fachinformationen sind stark von den Etats öffentlicher Bibliotheken abhängig, die zumeist heruntergefahren werden.
- Die demografische Entwicklung, nach der die Hauptzielgruppe der 14-44-Jährigen kontinuierlich zurückgeht, schadet den Publikumszeitschriften.
- Die Markentreue nimmt generell ab, so dass die Zeitschriften immer öfter und immer schneller einem Relaunch unterzogen werden.
- Die Werbeerträge sind seit Jahren bei den Publikumszeitschriften stark schrumpfend, noch stärker bei den Fachzeitschriften.

Konzepte der Zeitschriftenverlage

- Verlage sind bemüht, durch die ständige Gründung neuer Titel den Erfolg zu sichern. So wurde jede zweite Publikumszeitschrift innerhalb der letzten zehn Jahre gegründet.
- Das Phänomen, dass im Zeitschriftenmarkt die verkaufte Auflage bei wachsender Zahl von Titeln stagniert, wird sich weiter verstärken.
- Getrieben wird die „Titel-Flut" durch das Interesse der Anzeigenabteilungen, neue Titel buchen zu können, bei denen die Zielgruppen einen überdurchschnittlichen Ertrag für das Anzeigengeschäft abzuwerfen versprechen.
- Der Ausbau von Online-Angeboten, die zudem eng mit den Print-Ausgaben vernetzt sind, wird vorangetrieben.
- Als Reaktion auf die veränderten Käuferströme im Lebensmittelbereich ist mit den Lebensmittel-Discountern die Erschließung neuer Absatzkanäle für Publikumszeitschriften geplant: So sollen die Discounter (z. B. Penny) mit der Zeit evtl. sogar Vollsortimente mit 150 bis 200 Zeitschriften anbieten können. Dies ist als Reaktion auf die seit Jahren sinkenden Umsätze im Pressefachhandel zu verstehen.
- Bei Fachzeitschriften nimmt die Konkurrenz durch Firmen- und Kundenzeitschriften („Corporate Publishing") stark zu. Im Business-Bereich herrscht im Hinblick auf viele Fachinformationen unverkennbar ein Trend zu kostenlosem Content.

3.3.3 Bücher

Definition

Eine Definition von 1912 lautet: „Das Buch ist eine Vereinigung von Bogen eines geeigneten Stoffes zu einem geschlossenen Ganzen, auf denen ein geistiges Erzeugnis durch Worte und zwar vermittels der herkömmlichen Schriftzeichen wiedergegeben wird" (Kerlen 2003, S. 2). Allerdings können in Büchern auch Fotos erscheinen, so dass man besser der UNESCO-Definition folgt, die besagt: „Alles, was gedruckt über drei Druckbogen (mit je 16 Seiten) hinausgeht, darf Buch genannt werden". In der digitalen Welt ist die Definition von „Buch" schwierig: „Der traditionelle Träger war Papier, auf das die zuvor gesetzten Lettern gedruckt wurden, die Druckbogen in einen Buchblock gefalzt, mit einem Einband aus Pappe versehen und als Objekt per Post verschickt: Papier/Pappe/Post – das „3-P-Szenario". Neue Träger seit zwei Jahrzehnten sind offline CD-ROMs oder online das Internet: In beiden Fällen werden die Buchstaben digitalisiert, d. h. im binären Code als Mikroform fixiert, gespeichert, übermittelt" (Kerlen 2003, S. 1).

Wirtschaftliche Bedeutung

Deutschland ist ein Land mit relativ hoher Buchproduktion und liegt mit jährlich ca. 80.000 neuen Büchern im Weltmaßstab weit vorn. Die ökonomische Bedeutung des Buchmarktes drückt sich in einem Marktvolumen von ca. neun Mrd. Euro aus und übertrifft damit den Zeitungsmarkt. Der deutsche **Buchmarkt** ist damit wertmäßig der **führende Printmedien-Sektor**. Es ist zu erwarten, dass die wirtschaftliche Bedeutung des Buches in Zukunft abnehmen wird, und dies nicht nur relativ, sondern auch in absoluten Umsatzzahlen. Die Einbußen dürften jedoch nicht so groß sein, um die „Schreckensvision" vom Verschwinden der Bücher Wirklichkeit werden zu lassen. Ein fundamentaler Einbruch des Marktes wird nicht erwartet. Festzustellen ist freilich eine seit zehn Jahren anhaltende Umsatzstagnation des deutschen Buchhandels auf Höhe der genannten neun Mrd. Euro.

Publizistische Bedeutung

❶ Laut der Verbraucheranalyse der Bauer Media KG aus dem Jahr 2009 belegt das Bücherlesen in der Rangfolge der beliebtesten Hobbys der Deutschen einen erfreulichen 7. Platz.

Die publizistische Bedeutung des Buches besteht darin, das es für eine umfassende Vermittlung von **Wissen**, **Bildung**, **Kultur** und **Unterhaltung** sorgt. Das Medium Buch ist einer der ältesten Informationsspeicher und Kulturträger. Dem Bücherlesen wird nach wie vor ein hoher Stellenwert in der Gesellschaft beigemessen ❶. Die Dauer der Buchlektüre hat in den letzten zehn Jahren sogar wieder zugenommen und liegt heute bei 22 Minuten täglich. Bedenkt man, dass die Lektüre eines Buches aktive Aufmerksamkeit erfordert, ist diese Zahl durchaus auch im Vergleich zum Fernsehkonsum mit seinen dreieinhalb Stunden Nutzungszeit beachtlich.

Jedenfalls hat das Buch trotz übermächtiger Konkurrenz von Zeitungen, Zeitschriften und der elektronischen Medien seinen Reiz nicht verloren. Es hat grundsätzliche Vorteile und bleibt für den Menschen Quelle und Speicher von Wissen und Unterhaltung über Raum und Zeit hinweg.

Buch

Kommunikatoren, Anbieter

- Anzahl der „buchhändlerischen Betriebe“ (Mitglieder des Börsenvereins): 5.812; davon 1.777 Verlage („Herstellender Buchhandel“), 3.925 Betriebe des „verbreitenden Buchhandels“, 80 Zwischenbuchhandel (klassischer Großhandel), 30 Verlagsvertreter.
- 10 größte Buchverlage: Springer Science + Business, Klett-Gruppe, Cornelsen, Random House, Westermann, Haufe, Weka, Mair-Dumont, Wolters Kluwer Deutschland, Weltbild
- Sehr breites Spektrum mittlerer und kleiner Verlage.

Produkte, Inhalte

- Titelproduktion: 94.276 Neuerscheinungen, davon 83.381 Erst-Auflage und 10.895 Neu-Auflage. Verhältnis Erstauflage zu Neuauflage = 88:12 (bis ca. 2000 jahrelang fast identisch, danach kontinuierliche Verschiebung zugunsten der Erstauflage).
- Titelproduktion (Erstauflagen) nach Sachgruppen: Belletristik 17,7 %, Deutsche Literatur 12,6 %, Kinder- und Jugendbuch 8,8 %, Schulbücher 5,9 %, Medizin, Gesundheit 5,1 %, Theologie, Christentum 4,6 %, Recht 5,5 %, Management 3,9 %, Wirtschaft 3,4 %, Sozialwissenschaften, Soziologie 3,3 %, Geografie, Reisen 3,2 %, Informatik 2,9 %, Übrige Sachgebiete 24,1 %.
- Taschenbuchanteil an der Erst-Auflage: 10,3 %.
- Hörbücher: 600 Verlage; 20.000 Titel. 2000 Neuerscheinungen p.a.; 15.000 Titel als Download.
- Inhaltliche Struktur: Alle Themen vertreten. Werbung spielt keine nennenswerte Rolle.

Transportwege

- Vertriebswege: Sortimentsbuchhandel, Sonstige Verkaufsstellen, Warenhäuser, Reise- und Versandbuchhandel, Verlage direkt, Buchgemeinschaften.
- Sortimentsbuchhandlungen: Anteil am Gesamtumsatz der Branche 53,6 % (entspricht ca. 5,1 Mrd. Euro). Top 10 der Buchhandlungen (2007): Thalia, DBH (u.a. Weltbild, Hugendubel), Mayersche Aachen, Schweitzer München, Libro, Kaufhof, Orell Füssli, Lehmanns, Karstadt, Morawa.
- Verlagsdirektvertrieb: Umsatzanteil 18,0 % (1,7 Mrd. Euro).
- Versandbuchhandel (einschl. Internet): Umsatzanteil 12,6 % (1,2 Mrd. Euro).
- Buchabteilungen der Warenhäuser: Umsatzanteil 3,7 % (0,4 Mrd. Euro).
- Buchgemeinschaften: Umsatzanteil 3,0 % (0,3 Mrd. Euro).
- Sonstige Verkaufsstellen (Bahnhofsbuchhandlungen, Super- und Verbrauchermärkte, Kioske): Umsatzanteil 9,1 % (0,9 Mrd. Euro).
- Große Vertriebsdichte in Deutschland: hohe „Buchhandlungsdichte“.

Rezipienten

- Buchkauf: 59 % der Bundesbürger hat innerhalb eines Jahres Bücher gekauft, davon ca. die Hälfte mehr als 5 Bücher. Überdurchschnittlich: Frauen; 20-59 Jahre. Ansteigend mit Einkommen, Schulbildung und Wohnortgröße.
- Nutzung von Büchern: 37 % der Gesamtbevölkerung ab 14 Jahren liest täglich bzw. mehrmals in der Woche Bücher; Frauen: 45 %; Männer 29 %.
- Nutzung nach Altersgruppen (täglich/mehrmals in der Woche: 14-19 Jahre 42 %; 60 Jahre und älter 40 %; die geringste Nutzung weit die Altersgruppe 20–29 Jahre auf.
- Ein Drittel der Bevölkerung liest keine Bücher.
- 12 Mio. Deutsche hören Hörbücher inkl. Hörspiele
- Zeitbudget (2010): durchschn. Lesedauer pro Tag: 22 Min.
- Bücherkonsumenten verbringen weniger Zeit vor dem Fernsehgerät. Erhebliche Unterschiede nach Alters- u. soziodemograf. Gruppen. Trend zum „Lesezapping“: Selektives Lesen, paralleles Lesen mehrerer Bücher, Überfliegen von Büchern, vorzeitiger Abbruch des Lesens.

3.3.4 Druck- und Papierindustrie

In Ergänzung zur Darstellung der Printmedien soll an dieser Stelle in Kurzform die Druck- und Papierindustrie dargestellt werden. Dieser Bereich ist nicht unmittelbar zum Medienbereich zu rechnen, wenn man mit „Medien" die Entwicklung der Inhalte im Auge hat. Sehr wohl besitzt die Druckindustrie aber eine wichtige Stellung in der medialen Wertschöpfungskette von Printprodukten. Die folgenden **Trendaussagen** können für den Druck gelten (vgl. v. a. Matt, in Friedrichsen 2004, S. 17 ff.):

- Die Entwicklung auf den Druckmärkten wird stark von der Werbewirtschaft bestimmt. So weisen gedruckte Werbeträger und Werbemittel trotz wachsender Bedeutung der audiovisuellen und elektronischen Medien den weitaus größten Anteil am Werbemarkt auf. Die wertmäßig bedeutsamste Produktgruppe sind und bleiben Werbedrucke und Kataloge. Ein Begleiteffekt der starken Ausrichtung der Druckindustrie auf die Werbung ist, dass sie wie die Werbebranche stark konjunkturabhängig ist.
- Unersetzlich wird das Bedrucken von Verpackungen für diejenigen Produkte bleiben, die nicht immaterialisiert werden können.
- Durch die technologischen Entwicklungen kommt es zu grundlegenden Veränderungen der Ausgestaltung der Endprodukte. So steigt die Bedeutung von Farbigkeit, ein Mehr an speziellen Effekten wird möglich, der Aufwand für Verarbeitung und Veredelung steigt, es erfolgt eine zunehmende Personalisierung und Kundengruppen-Orientierung bei den Werbemitteln.
- Künftig werden kleinere Auflagen mit sinkenden Seitenzahlen, aber bei höherer Erscheinungsfrequenz die Regel werden.
- Da die Individualisierung weiter zunimmt, wird der Markt für Direct Mails ❶ weiter wachsen.
- Eine Zunahme ist bei der Zahl der Beihefter und Beikleber in Zeitschriften zu erwarten. Die selektive Bindung wird hierbei eine zunehmende Bedeutung gewinnen.
- Was Zeitungen und Zeitschriften anbelangt, ist von einer eher sinkenden Nachfrage nach Druckprodukten auszugehen.
- Im Buchmarkt ist eine sinkende Zahl der Auflagen je Titel zu erwarten, allerdings bei einer steigenden Titel-Anzahl.

❶ Unter **Direct Mailing** versteht man alle Kommunikationsmaßnahmen eines Unternehmens, die darauf abzielen, den einzelnen Menschen direkt anzusprechen und dadurch einen direkten Kontakt zu dieser Person herzustellen und in einen unmittelbaren Dialog mit ihr einzutreten. Ein Beispiel ist eine adressierte Werbesendung, bestehend aus einem Werbebrief, einem Prospekt, einer Rückantwortkarte und einem Versandkouvert (sog. „Mail Order Package"). Im Zeichen des Internet haben Direct Mails in Form von E-Mails eine hohe Bedeutung erlangt.

Inwieweit die Einflussfaktoren zur Schrumpfung des Marktes beitragen, bewahrende Effekte auslösen oder das Wachstum der Druckbranche antreiben, muss offen bleiben. Festzustehen scheint, dass künftige **Marktpotenziale** mit einem erhöhten Produktionswert nicht mehr über Masse, sondern nur noch über Qualitätssteigerungen und veränderte Geschäftsmodelle erreichbar sind.

Gesamthaft kann gesagt werden, dass sich die Entwicklung der Drucktechnologie auf höchstem Niveau befindet und Rationalisierungs- und Kosteneinsparungspotenziale in nie gekannter Weise besitzt, z. B. durch die Verkürzung der Durchlaufzeiten oder die Verringerung des Materialeinsatzes durch Makulatur-Reduzierung.

Die Druck- und Papierbranche im Überblick

Marktvolumen Druckindustrie

- Gesamt-Umsatz der deutschen Druckindustrie 2008: ca. 23 Mrd. Euro, davon 14,5 Mrd. Euro von Betrieben mit 50 und mehr Beschäftigten (= 62 %)
- davon Auslandsumsatz: 2,1 Mrd. Euro, d. h. Exportquote: 14,6 %.
- Starke Abhängigkeit der Druckindustrie von der Werbung.
- Verteilung des Umsatzes der Druckindustrie auf Druck-Erzeugnisse (in Mrd. Euro): Werbedrucke/ Kataloge: 6,1; Geschäftsdrucksachen: 2,1; Zeitschriften: 1,8; Zeitungen/Anzeigenblätter: 1,8; Bücher/kartografische Erzeugnisse: 1,1; Bedruckte Etiketten: 1,1; Kalender/Karten: 0,2; Sonstige Druck-Erzeugnisse: 1,9.
- Verteilung des Umsatzes der Druckindustrie auf Druck-Erzeugnisse (Anteile in %): Werbedrucke/ Kataloge: 37,9; Geschäftsdrucksachen: 13,3; Zeitschriften: 11,3; Zeitungen/Anzeigenblätter: 11,4; Bücher/kartografische Erzeugnisse: 6,6; Bedruckte Etiketten: 6,9; Kalender/Karten: 1,0; Sonstige Druck-Erzeugnisse: 11,6.

Druckunternehmen

- Anzahl der Industrie- und Handwerksbetriebe: 10.710; Anzahl der Betriebe mit 20 und mehr Beschäftigten: 1.823; d. h.: 83 % aller Betriebe haben weniger als 20 Beschäftigte.
- Die deutsche Druckindustrie ist ein von Klein- und Mittelbetrieben geprägter Industriezweig: Ein Drittel aller Betriebe gehören zum Handwerk.
- Konzentrationsgrad gering, starke Prägung durch kleine und mittlere Unternehmen (KMU). Nur 3 Betriebe mit mehr als 1.000 Mitarbeitern, nur 15 Betriebe mit 500 - 999 Mitarbeitern, alle anderen haben weniger als 500 Mitarbeiter.
- Beschäftigte: 172.710 sozialversicherungspflichtig Beschäftigte, davon: 129.684 in Betrieben mit 20 und mehr Beschäftigten.
- Lehrlinge: Mediengestaltung/Druckvorstufe (u. a. Mediengestalter, Schriftsetzer): 10.919; Drucktechnik (u. a. Drucker, Siebdrucker): 4.586; Druckweiterverarbeitung (Buchbinder, Verpackungsmittelmechnaniker): 3.033.
- Umsatz je Beschäftigten: 138.829 Euro.
- Dominanz der auftragsbezogenen Einzelfertigung.

Marktvolumen Papierindustrie

- Umsatz der deutschen Zellstoff- und Papierindustrie 2008: 14,9 Mrd. Euro.
- Produktion: 22,8 Mio. Tonnen Papier, Karton und Pappe. Gesamtabsatz: 23,0 Mio. Tonnen, davon Inlandsabsatz: 57 %.
- Verteilung der Produktion auf Sorten (Mio. Tonnen): Grafische Papiere: 10,7; Papier, Karton u. Pappe für Verpackung: 9,4; Hygiene-Papiere: 1,4; Techn./Spezialpapiere: 1,5.
- Herstellung von rund 3.000 verschiedenen Papiersorten
- Import: 19,6 Mio. Tonnen; davon: 11,7 Mio. Tonnen Papier, Karton und Pappe; 3,9 Zellstoff; 3,7 Altpapier.
- Export 19,3 Mio. Tonnen; davon: Papier und Pappe: 14,0 Mio. Tonnen (davon entfallen 78 % auf die Staaten der EU 27); Zellstoff 0,9; Altpapier 4,3 Mio. Tonnen. Starke Zunahme der Exporte in die neuen EU-Beitrittsländer.
- Die Papierindustrie in Deutschland ist die Nr. 1 in Europa. Im weltweiten Vergleich lieg sie an vierter Stelle hinter den USA, China und Japan.

Unternehmen der Papierindustrie

- Betriebe (Produktionsstandorte): 178
- Konzentrationsgrad: Globaler Markt ohne regionale Differenzierung – zahlreiche Marktakteure, d. h. fragmentierter Markt.
- Beschäftigte: 43.400

3.4 Elektronische Medien

3.4.1 Fernsehen

Definition

Gemäß dem ABC der ARD ist Fernsehen „in Abgrenzung vom Hörfunk audiovisueller Teil des Rundfunks, in Deutschland regelmäßiger Programmbetrieb ab 22. 3. 1935, zunächst für den Gemeinschaftsempfang in so genannten Fernsehstuben, am 25. 12. 1952 Neubeginn für den Individualempfang durch den Nordwestdeutschen Rundfunk (NWDR), seit 1. 11. 1954 – hervorgegangen aus dem NWDR-Programm – das gemeinsam von den Landesrundfunkanstalten der ARD betriebene (Erste) Deutsche Fernsehen/ Das Erste, seit 1. 4. 1963 zusätzlich das Zweite Deutsche Fernsehen, seit 22. 9. 1964 nach und nach die Dritten Programme der Landesrundfunkanstalten, seit 1984 auch Programmangebote des Privaten Rundfunks, später zusätzliche öffentlich-rechtliche Programme wie 3sat (1984), EINS PLUS (1986–1993), ARTE (1992), Der Kinderkanal/KIKA und PHOENIX (1997) sowie BR-alpha (1998), seit 1997 zusätzliche Angebote im Rahmen digitaler Programmpakete wie ARD Digital".

Wirtschaftliche Bedeutung

Die **ökonomische Bedeutung** des Fernsehens im Kontext von Medien- und TIME-Märkten ist mit mehr als elf Mrd. Euro **sehr hoch**. Er ist inzwischen der umsatzmäßig führende Teilsektor. Der deutsche Fernsehmarkt ist zudem der größte TV-Markt in Europa. Die **Finanzierung** erfolgt – ganz grob – zu etwa gleichen Teilen aus Zuschauer-Erlösen (Kabelgebühren, **Pay-TV**, **Call-Ins**), Werbeerlösen und der Fernsehgebühr.

Publizistische Bedeutung

Das Fernsehen nimmt in der Medienlandschaft eine **Schlüsselrolle** ein: Es ist aus dem Alltag der Menschen nicht wegzudenken, und es übt große publizistische und gesellschaftliche Wirkungen aus. Kein anderes technisches Gerät (außer vielleicht das Auto) prägt unser Leben so nachhaltig wie „der Fernseher". Fernsehen ist ein Phänomen, das zu Recht als das gesellschaftliche Leitmedium bezeichnet wird. Das **Medium Fernsehen** hat gegenüber Radio und Print eine Reihe von Vorzügen, die z. B. auch für die Werbung interessant sind:

- Die Botschaften werden nicht nur akustisch, sondern auch bildlich geliefert. Fernsehen ist ein audiovisuelles Medium.
- Dabei sind die Bilder nicht wie bei Printprodukten statisch, sondern bewegt. Fernsehen ist ein dynamisches Medium, allerdings ein lineares, da die Sendungen nur abgespielt werden und keine Interaktion stattfindet.
- Die Aktualität entspricht der des Hörfunks, ist aber deutlich höher als bei Print.
- Die Reichweite liegt in der Primetime etwa so hoch wie bei den großen Zeitschriften. Fernsehen ist ein leistungsstarkes Medium.
- Die Technik ist weit fortgeschritten: Gute Farbqualität, Stereofunktion, vielfältige Trickmöglichkeiten. Fernsehen ist technisch anspruchsvoll.
- Schließlich ist Fernsehen ein lebendiges, emotionalisierendes Medium.

Fernsehen

Kommunikatoren, Anbieter

- Im TV-Markt gibt es drei große Senderfamilien: (1) Öffentlich-rechtliche Rundfunkanstalten. (2) Bertelsmann (RTL Group). (3) ProSiebenSat1. Daneben zahlreiche mittlere und kleine Anbieter sowie ausländische Anbieter (insbesondere SRG/Schweiz, ORF/Österreich sowie US-amerikanische Anbieter).
- Öffentlich-rechtliche Rundfunkanstalten: gesamt 13. Aufteilung: ARD (9 Landesrundfunkanstalten: davon Mehrländeranstalten MDR, NDR, RBB, SWR; Einländeranstalten BR, SR, RB, WDR; plus Deutsche Welle), ZDF, ARD-ZDF-Einrichtungen (DeutschlandRadio, ARTE). Besonderheit: 3Sat als ARD/ZDF/SRG/ORF-Einrichtung.
- Privat-kommerzielle Veranstalter: Bundesweite Veranstalter: 42. (2) Veranstalter von Landesfenstern: 10. (3) Veranstalter von Ballungsraumprogrammen („City TV") oder Landesprogrammen: 13. (4) Veranstalter von Lokalprogrammen: 38.
- Private nicht-kommerzielle Anbieter: Spendenfinanzierte Anbieter (z. B. Bibel-TV), Bürgerrundfunk (Offene Kanäle).
- Neben dem Fernsehen – in klassischer Weise definiert als Rundfunk – sind zunehmend Bewegtbild-Anbieter im Internet relevant (Telemedien, Web-TV). Infrage kommen: (1) Wirtschaftsunternehmen, Organisationen: Corporate Publishing. (2) Privatpersonen: User Generated Content.

Produkte, Inhalte

- Rechtsform: (1) Öffentlich-rechtliche TV-Angebote: 22. Davon ausschließlich digitale Angebote: 7. (2) Private Angebote gesamt: 365, davon Vollprogramme 16; Spartensender 43; Fernsehfenster 3; Pay-TV-Sender 68; landesweites/regionales/lokales TV 235.
- Finanzierung der Privatprogramme: (1) Free-TV: 297. (2) Pay-TV: 68.
- Zeit-Volumen: (1) Zeitliche Vollprogramme, (2) Fensterprogramme. 24-Stunden-Programme vorherrschend, teilweise Kanal-Sharing im Kabel.
- Inhaltliche Reichweite: (1) Inhaltliche Vollprogramme: Gesamtangebot der öffentlich-rechtlichen Rundfunkanstalten, umfassende Abdeckung aller Themen und Genres, (2) Spartenprogramme: vorherrschend bei Privatanbietern, entweder direkt als Spartenprogramme konzipiert (z. B. Nachrichtenkanal) oder Betonung von Unterhaltung (v.a. Spielfilm, Serien, Shows). (3) Videotext: Angebot von allen Veranstaltern.
- TV als Werbeträger: (1) im öffentlich-rechtlichen Fernsehen: Anteil an der Sendezeit ca. 1,5 % (Begrenzung auf das Vorabendprogramm werktäglich), Beitrag zur Finanzierung ca. 5 %, (2) im privaten Fernsehen: Anteil ca. 15 % am Gesamtinhalt, Finanzierung: 100 %, Ausnahme Pay-TV.
- TV als Verkaufsinstrument (Teleshopping, „T-Commerce"): Anzahl Teleshoppingprogramme: 20.
- Internet-Angebote: (1) bei ARD/ZDF als programmbegleitende Information, (2) bei privaten Veranstaltern auch eigenständige Produktwelten.

Transportwege

- Empfangsebenen: (1) Terrestrik (ausschließlich): 2,6 Mio. Haushalte 6,9 % aller Haushalte, Übertragung digital als DVB-T (Ballungsgebiete versorgt). (2) Kabel: als DVB-C, Anteil 48,8 % aller Haushalte. (3) Satellit: als DVB-S, Anteil 43,0 % aller Haushalte. (5) DSL: IPTV-Haushalte: 0,5 Mio. / 1,4 % aller Haushalte
- Digitalisierungsgrad der Verbreitungswege (analog vs. digital): (1) Kabel: 69,3 % analog; 30,7 % digital. (2) Satellit: 29,3 % analog; 70,7 % digital. (3) Terrestrik: 0,5 % analog; 99,5 % digital.
- Pay-TV-Haushalte: 4,2 Mio. / Anteil der Pay-TV-Haushalte: 11,1 %
- Mobiler Empfang: DVB-T-Empfang, DVB-H (Handheld).

Rezipienten

- Geräteausstattung: 99 %. 23 % der Haushalte besitzen zwei oder mehr Fernsehgeräte.
- Reichweite: 89,2 % der Bevölkerung ab 14 Jahren sieht mehrmals in der Woche fern.
- Zeitbudget: Durchschnittliche Sehdauer Erwachsene ab 14 Jahre 221 Min. täglich (deutliche Zunahme seit 1985); Kinder 3-13 Jahre: 86 Min. Zunahme des Fernsehkonsums mit zunehmendem Lebensalter.
- Nutzung: intensiv, aber mit Neigungen zum Begleit-Medium (vor allem tagsüber)
- Nutzung im Tagesablauf: Hauptnutzung 20:00 bis 22:00 Uhr (Primetime).
- Überdurchschnittliche Nutzung (1) nach Alter: 30 Jahre und älter (2) gemäß Sinus-Milieus: Etablierte, Bürgerliche Mitte.

Konsequenzen der Digitalisierung

Geordnet nach der bekannten Lasswell-Formel („Wer sagt was über welchen Kanal zu wem mit welcher Wirkung?") lassen sich eine Reihe von **Konsequenzen** konstatieren, die sich aus der Digitalisierung des Fernsehens ergeben.

- Neue Akteure: Der TV-Markt bleibt für die derzeitigen Akteure interessant, indem er eine Fülle neuer Möglichkeiten der Produktgestaltung und Erlösgenerierung bietet. Zunehmend ist er aber auch für Anbieter der TIME-Branche interessant, die bislang über keine fernsehspezifischen Kompetenzen verfügen, also die Kabelnetzbetreiber, Unternehmen der Telekommunikation sowie IT-Unternehmen. Analog zum Radio („Podcasting") werden zudem auch im Fernsehen zunehmend die privaten Nutzer selbst zu Inhalte-Generatoren. Insgesamt gesehen erweitert sich der Fernsehmarkt erheblich.
- Neue Inhalte: Mit der Digitalisierung können neue Dienste wie Video on Demand, Pay-TV und interaktive Anwendungen realisiert werden. Eine besondere Rolle spielt das internetbasiertes Fernsehen. Zu erwarten ist eine stark vergrößerte Programmvielfalt und das Angebot von Zusatzdiensten. Insbesondere nimmt auch das Programmangebot in hochqualitativer Technik zu, wie das HDTV-Angebot zur Fußball-WM 2006 in Deutschland gezeigt hat. Besonders zu beachten sind neue Konvergenzprodukte, die alle technischen Möglichkeiten ausnutzen, zumindest die Bereiche Fernsehen, Internet und Telefonie zusammenführen, eine Entwicklung, die als „Triple Play" (im Kontext von IPTV) bezeichnet wird ❶.
- Neue technische Plattformen und Verbreitungswege für TV-Content: Die herkömmlichen Übertragungstechniken Kabel, Satellit und Terrestrik werden zunächst ergänzt, dann aber zunehmend durch die beiden neuen Verbreitungswege des High-Speed-Internet und der Telefonie substituiert. In welcher Dynamik die Entwicklung voranschreitet, hängt maßgeblich von der Verbreitung breitbandiger Übertragungsmöglichkeiten und multimedialer Endgeräte ab.
- Veränderte Nutzungsbedingungen bei den Zuschauern: Im Hinblick auf die Endgeräte-Technik geschieht eine enge Verbindung von Fernsehgerät und Computer, was zu einer Verzahnung bzw. Verschmelzung von TV und Internet führt. Zwei unterschiedliche Nutzungsbedingungen sind dabei zu unterscheiden:
  a) Stationäre Nutzung: Zu erwarten ist, dass sich eine „Home Entertainment Platform" entwickeln wird, die dank vorhandener Schnittstellen in der Lage ist, alle relevanten digitalen Anwendungen abzubilden (vgl. Friedrichsen/Jenzowsky/Dietl/Ratzer 2006, S. 79). Möglich werden integriert wirkende Funktionalitäten wie Festplatte, DVD-Brenner und Internet-Browser, was zu größerer Programmvielfalt beiträgt und z. B. den Download von Filmen, Musik und Spielen, personalisierte exklusive Angebote wie Video-on-Demand und interaktive Lösungen ermöglicht. Das Endgerät der Zukunft ist insofern ein multifunktionales „Home Media Center" oder eine „Multimedia Home Platform", bei der das „Heimkino" eine prominente Rolle spielt.
  b) Mobile Nutzung: Fernsehen in mobiler Nutzung kann erstens über Broadcast-Netzwerke realisiert werden (v. a. DVB-T und DVB-H), zweitens über Mobilfunknetzwerke (v. a. UMTS) und drittens schließlich über das Internet. Das mobile Endgerät der Zukunft dürfte über kurz oder lang einer Hybridlösung folgen, bei der alle Nutzungswege gangbar sind.

❶ Ein Beispiel für ein **Triple-Play-Angebot** ist z. B. das von der Deutschen Telekom im Oktober 2006 gelaunchte Produkt „T-Home". Es bietet Fernsehen, Telefonieren und Internet-Nutzung über eine einzige Verbindung. Für ca. 90 Euro ist ein Bündelangebot erhältlich, das den folgenden Leistungsumfang aufweist: (a) TV: 100 Programme (60 Free-TV und 40 Pay-TV; im Angebot sind Fußball-Bundesliga, Premiere-Pakete, Fremdsprachenpakete etc.), Video on Demand (gegen gesonderte Zahlung), persönlicher Programmführer (EPG), digitaler Videorekorder, Timeshift-Funktion; (b) High-Speed-Internetverbindung; (c) DSL-Telefonie.
T-Home ist in der Startphase nur im neuen Hochgeschwindigkeitsnetz VDSL verfügbar, das bisher in zehn deutschen Ballungsgebieten gebaut wurde. Das Angebot T-Home gilt als wichtiger Hoffnungsträger der Telekom, die unter dem schwindenden Festnetzgeschäft leidet. Den Anbietern von Triple-Play-Angeboten werden gute Wachstumschancen eingeräumt. Neben der Telekom drängen auch die deutschen TV-Kabelnetzbetreiber in das noch junge Geschäftsfeld.

Ein besonders hohes Interesse an **mobiler TV-Nutzung** haben vor allem jüngere Menschen. Die TV-Branche ist offensichtlich bereit, große Summen zu investieren, wobei entscheidende Voraussetzungen für mobiles Fernsehen die einfache Bedienung, eine hochwertige technische Qualität und eine transparente Kostenstruktur sind.

Von zunehmender Bedeutung für den Transport von Video-Inhalten ist das Internet. Zu unterscheiden ist hierbei IPTV von Web-TV. Abspielgerät bei **IPTV** ❶ ist das Fernsehgerät: Fernsehprogramme und Video-on-Demand-Angebote werden für geschlossene Nutzergruppen und gegen Entgelt im Abonnement angeboten, als Alternative für den Kabel-, Satelliten- oder terrestrischen Empfang. IPTV ist Rundfunk. Demgegenüber liefert **Web-TV** am PC über die offene Plattform Internet abrufbare Fernseh- und Videoinhalte, die nur im Falle von Livestreams klassischer Fernsehprogramme als alternativer Empfangsweg zu verstehen sind. Vor allem handelt es sich um Video- und Videoclipportale, die mehrheitlich kostenlos sind. Web-TV ist nicht Rundfunk, sondern wird den Telemedien zugerechnet. ❷

Die derzeitige **Marktsituation** auf dem Fernsehmarkt zeigt die nachfolgende Übersicht:

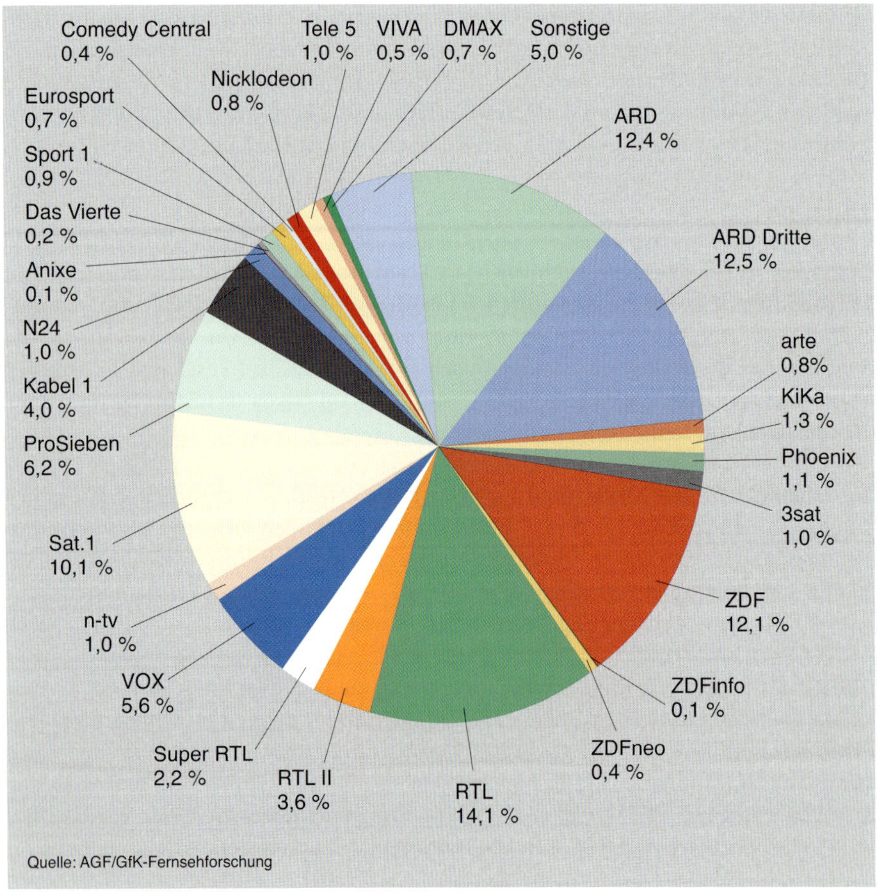

Zuschauermarktanteile 2011

❶ „Unter IPTV („Internet Protocol Television", zu Deutsch: Internet-Protokoll Fernsehen) versteht man die digitale Übertragung von Bild und Ton zu einem Fernsehgerät über einen breitbandigen DSL-Anschluss. Das Internet-Protokoll dient dabei als Übermittler, mit dessen Hilfe die Inhalte (TV, Radio) innerhalb des Telefonnetzes an den richtigen Empfänger geliefert werden. Benötigt wird neben einem schnellen DSL-Anschluss eine Set-Top-Box, die man vom IPTV-Anbieter erhält oder einen IPTV-Player für den PC." (Quelle: ARD Digital, FAQ).

❷ Web-TV bietet im Vergleich zum klassischen Fernsehen einen Mehrwert, indem entweder Fernsehinhalte zur zeitlich unabhängigen Nutzung bereitgehalten werden (z. B. ZDFmediathek, ARD Mediathek, RTL Now!) oder (auch) Inhalte verbreitet werden, die das klassische Fernsehen nicht abdeckt (z. B. MyVideo, Clipfish, YouTube).

Programmformen

Die **Programmangebote** der TV-Sender kann man grob in die folgenden **Bereiche** einteilen:

- Informationssendungen: (1) Nachrichten, Wetter; (2) Magazine, Dokumentationen, Reportagen; (3) Regionalinformationen; (4) Service, Alltag, Lebensbewältigung; (5) Sport
- Unterhaltung: (1) Fiction: Serien, Spielfilme, Fernsehspiele, Cartoons; (2) Moderierte Showprogramme: Talkshows, Unterhaltungsshows, Gameshows, Kindershows, Musikshows
- Kultur, Bildung: (1) Kultur; (2) Wissenschaft, Technik; (3) Schauspiel, Konzert, Kleinkunst
- Werbung

Öffentlich-rechtliche Rundfunkanstalten sind verpflichtet, mit ihrem Gesamtangebot sämtliche Programmformen und Themen abzudecken und damit ein umfassendes Grundangebot zu bieten („volles Programm"). Man nennt dies die Verpflichtung zur Grundversorgung. Die **privaten Veranstalter** hingegen können es sich erlauben, ihr Angebot thematisch enger zu gestalten, bis hin zum Angebot sog. Spartenprogramme. Dies sind Angebote, die z. B. auf Sport (DSF) oder Nachrichten (n-tv) ausgerichtet sind. Die Hauptprogramme der Privaten (RTL, SAT1, ProSieben) sind meist in einer bestimmten Richtung ausgelegt, z. B. ProSieben auf aktuelle Kino-Action-Filme.

Nutzung

Fernsehen wird überdurchschnittlich stark am Abend genutzt, und dort intensiv. Während des Tages gerät das Fernsehen allerdings – ähnlich wie das Radio – zunehmend in die Rolle eines Hintergrund- oder Begleitmediums. Vor allem während der Werbezeiten beschäftigen sich inzwischen vier Fünftel aller Zuschauer neben dem Fernsehen auch mit anderen Dingen. Der Effekt wird durch das **Zapping** (Hin- und Herspringen von Kanal zu Kanal) verstärkt.

❶ Reichweite vs. Marktanteil: Unter **Reichweite** versteht man die Anzahl von Personen, die innerhalb eines Zeitraums von einem Medium erreicht wird. **Marktanteil** ist der Anteil der einzelnen TV-Sender an der gesamten Einschaltzeit der Zuschauer.

Im Hinblick auf den **Marktanteil** halten sich die öffentlich-rechtlichen und die privaten Anbieter in etwa die Waage. Beide kommen mit allen Programmen zusammen genommen auf etwa 50 %. Die Marktführerschaft wechselt immer wieder zwischen dem Ersten Deutschen Fernsehen, dem ZDF, RTL und den Dritten Fernsehprogramme der ARD, die jeweils in der Gegend zwischen 13 und 14 Prozent Marktanteil erzielen ❶.

2005 war die Sendung mit dem höchsten Marktanteil im deutschen Fernsehen – wie schon die Jahre vorher – „Wetten, dass ...?" vom ZDF mit einem exorbitanten Marktanteil von 41,8 Prozent, das waren 13,2 Mio. Zuschauer (ab 3 Jahre). Auf den beiden nächsten Plätzen folgten „Mainz bleibt Mainz" (ARD) mit 29,5 Prozent und „Domino Day – Der Rekord" (RTL) mit 26,0 Prozent. Quizsendungen wie „Wer wird Millionär?" (RTL) bringen es meist auf über 20 Prozent, was als äußerst erfolgreich gilt.

Zentrale Trends

- Die Bedeutung von Entertainment im Fernsehen nimmt weiter zu und bleibt ein hoch attraktiver Medieninhalt. Zu erwarten ist daher eher noch eine Zunahme von Serien, Telenovelas oder Quiz-Shows, auch weil sie günstig zu produzieren sind und einen regen Zuspruch seitens der Zuschauer erfahren.
- Im Zuge der Digitalisierung findet eine nachhaltige Flexibilisierung des Fernsehkonsums statt, und zwar sowohl in räumlicher Hinsicht („Überall-Fernsehen") als auch in zeitlicher Hinsicht („Video on Demand").
- Der Fernsehzuschauer wird zunehmend zum „Channel-Portfoliomanager", der viel stärker aktiv in das Medienangebot und die Mediennutzung eingreift. Er wird zunehmend zu seinem eigenen Programmdirektor.
- Es besteht die Gefahr, dass das Fernsehen in seiner bisherigen Form seine Rolle als Primärmedium der Mediennutzung einbüßt und die Führungsrolle an das Internet abgibt. Das Fernsehen würde dann auch das Schicksal eines Nebenbei-Mediums ereilen. Dass diese These nicht aus der Luft gegriffen ist, zeigt die Tatsache, dass schon heute das Fernsehen in jüngeren Zielgruppen nicht mehr als unumstrittenes Leitmedium verstanden wird, sondern vielmehr vom Internet als meinungsmachendes Medium abgelöst wird. Inwieweit diese Entwicklung Platz greift, hängt davon ab, ob die bislang eher passive Nutzung beim traditionellen Fernsehen weiterhin Gültigkeit haben wird oder ob sich das Nutzungsverhalten in eine aktive, suchende Haltung wandelt.
- Die Fernsehzuschauer stehen – unabhängig davon, ob sie ein aktives oder passives Nutzungsverhalten an den Tag legen – bei einer zunehmenden Programmvielfalt vor einem Informationsproblem und bewerten wirksame Navigationshilfen (EPG ❶, Programmzeitschriften) grundsätzlich als positiv.
- Die **Zahlungsbereitschaft** für interessante TV-Angebote könnte vor dem Hintergrund einer steigenden Bedeutung der Interaktion, also des möglichen kommunikativen Austausches mit dem Sender, merklich zunehmen.
- Im Hinblick auf den TV-Werbemarkt, ist festzustellen, dass nach mehr als einer Dekade konstanten Wachstums seit dem Jahr 2000 ein deutlicher Rückgang der Werbeerlöse erfolgt ist. Für die Zukunft ist zu erwarten, dass die Bedeutung der Werbung durch Fernsehspots („harte Werbung") kontinuierlich abnehmen wird. Gleichzeitig werden Sonderwerbeformen, vor allem diejenigen, die vom Konsumenten besser akzeptiert werden, immer wichtiger, wie z. B. Sponsoring oder Produktplatzierung. Dies führt zu einer Entwicklung, das Trennungsgebot von Werbung und Programm aufzuweichen, eine Entwicklung, die mit dem Begriff „Programming" ❷ bezeichnet wird.
- Die **Fragmentierung** (bzw. Zerstückelung) des TV-Marktes hat einen hohen Grad erreicht. Die Bedeutung von Zielgruppen-Fernsehen ist hoch und nimmt weiter zu. Gleichzeitig wird es schwieriger, für die einzelnen Angebote eine wirtschaftlich tragfähige Basis sicher zu stellen.
- Die Intensität des Wettbewerbs auf dem Fernsehmarkt steigt weiter.

❶ **EPG** = Elektronischer Programmführer (Electronic Program Guide)

❷ **Programming** = die gezielte Vermischung von Werbung und Programm, d. h. die bewusste Aufweichung des Trennungsgrundsatzes von Werbung und Programm.

3.4.2 Film und Kino

Definition

❶ Die Definition stammt von Hartlieb, H. v.: Handbuch des Film-, Fernseh- und Videorechts, 3. Aufl., München, S. 203.

Für den **Begriff Film** existiert die folgende juristische Definition: „Unter Film versteht man ein Produkt, das sich als Aufnahme eines Ausschnitts der Wirklichkeit meist unter Fixierung auf einen Bildträger oder einen Bild- und Tonträger mit der Möglichkeit der Konservierung und/oder der Wiedergabe bzw. Verwendung durch Vervielfältigung, Verbreitung und öffentliche Vorführung oder Funksendung darstellt (vgl. § 94 UrhG)“ ❶. Ein **Kino** ist der Abspielort für Filme. Es wird auch Lichtspieltheater, Lichtspielhaus oder Filmtheater genannt.

Wirtschaftliche Bedeutung

Zur Abschätzung der ökonomischen Bedeutung kann entsprechend nach der **Film-Wertschöpfungskette** nach **vier Stufen** unterschieden werden:

- Vorbereitung, Konzeption, Inhalte: Drehbuch-Autoren
- Herstellung: (a) Kinofilm-Produzenten, (b) TV-Produzenten, (c) Videofilm-Produzenten, (d) Industriefilm-Produzenten, (e) Werbefilm-Produzenten
- Handel: Rechtehändler (nur Rechte)
- Distribution: (a) Distributionskanal Filmtheater (Kino): Filmverleih (Inland), Filmtheater (Kinos), (b) Distributionskanal Kauf und Verleih: Videoprogramm-Anbieter, Videotheken, (c) Distributionskanal Fernsehen: TV-Sender (Pay-TV, Free-TV), (d) Distributionskanal Ausland: Filmvertrieb.

Nach dieser Einteilung lässt sich der Film- und Kinomarkt unterschiedlich abgrenzen, zum einen in einem umfassenden Sinne als die Summe der Wertschöpfungen aller vier Stufen, hier wird das enorme Umsatzvolumen von 18 Mrd. Euro geschätzt, zum anderen im engeren Sinne als die Erlöse aus der Kino-, Video- und DVD-Verwertung (Punkte (a) und (b) der Stufe der Distribution). Das **Umsatzvolumen** beläuft sich hierbei auf die immer noch beachtliche Größe von 2,64 Mrd. Euro im Jahr 2004.

Publizistische Bedeutung

Das Kino hat sich vom Massenmedium in den 50er Jahren zum ausgeprägten Zielgruppenmedium für die Jugend entwickelt. Hatte es früher die breite Bevölkerung angesprochen, sank die Bedeutung mit der Einführung des Fernsehens.

Die publizistische Bedeutung des Kinos ist daher als eingeschränkt zu bezeichnen. Das **Kino** ist im Gegensatz zum Fernsehen **kein Basismedium**. Das Fernsehen erreicht einen großen Teil der Bevölkerung (große Reichweite) und wird sehr häufig eingeschaltet (hohe Kontaktfrequenz in der Bevölkerung). Demgegenüber spricht das Kino vor allem die Bevölkerungsgruppe der 14- bis 30-Jährigen an und ist daher auf eine begrenzte Zielgruppe ausgerichtet. Das macht das Kino für die Werbung aber zu einem ausgesprochen interessanten Medium.

Film und Kino

Kommunikatoren, Anbieter

- Filmunternehmen: (1) Unternehmen, die auf die Abdeckung der gesamten Wertschöpfungskette ausgerichtet sind: insbesondere große US-amerikanische Medien-„Imperien" (Majors); (2) Spezialisierte Nischenanbieter, weniger große Firmen (Independents).
- Die wichtigsten US-Major Studios: Columbia, Disney, MGM/UA, Paramount, Twentieth Century Fox, Universal, Warner Bros.
- Deutsche Produktionsfirmen: 6.830. Hoher Fragmentierungsgrad. Die größten Unternehmen: Bavaria, Constantin, Odeon, Senator, Tele München, UFA Film & TV Produktion, Unitel.
- Spezifika deutscher Produktionen: Fernsehsender als Auftraggeber und Filmförderung von Bund und Ländern spielen eine große Rolle.
- Verleihfirmen: Warner Bros., Universal Pictures, Walt Disney Studios, Twentieth Century Fox, Sony Pictures, Constantin Film Verleih, Senator Film Verleih, Tobis Film.

Produkte, Inhalte

- International: Anzahl der Spielfilmproduktionen: EU-27 (geschätzt) 969; USA 520; Japan 418.
- Deutschland: Anzahl erstaufgeführter deutscher Filmproduktionen: Langfilme gesamt: 185; davon Spielfilme: 125 (davon deutsche Eigenproduktionen: 81, Koproduktionen: 44), Dokumentarfilme: 60. Tendenz: vor 2004 seit Jahren stagnierend; seit 2004 steigend; zum Vergleich 2004 121 Filme.
- DVD-Kaufmarkt Top 7: Kleinohrhasen, Mamma Mia!, Ratatouille, Die Simpsons – Der Film, Harry Potter und der Orden der Phoenix (2 DVDs), The Dark Knight, Der Goldene Kompass.

Transportwege

- Anzahl der Filmtheater-Spielstätten: 1.793. Zahl der Leinwände: 4.810 mit ca. 832.000 Sitzplätzen; digitale Leinwände 164.
- Kino-Typen: Standard-Kino, Multiplexe, Imax-Theater, Programmkino. Spezielle Abspielorte: Open-Air-Kino, Cityplexe. Spartenkinos: Filmkunstkino, Studiotheater, Action-Kino, Familienkino.
- Multiplexe haben Anteil von 30 % aller Leinwände. Einrichtung von Multiplex-Kinocentern auch in Mittelstädten.
- Digitalisierung: Umstieg auf digitale Signale (transportiert über Satellit und Breitbandkabel) erfolgt laufend
- Zunehmende Konkurrenz durch qualitativ verbessertes „Heimkino" (BlueRay, HDTV).

Rezipienten

- Reichweite: 3,4 % der Erwachsenen über 14 Jahren gehen mindestens einmal pro Woche ins Kino.
- Kinobesucher: 129,4 Mio.; Kinobesuche pro Einwohner: 1,58 (zum Vergleich: USA/Kanada ca. 5).
- Home-Video-Nutzung: überdurchschnittlich nach Sinus: Moderne Performer, Konsum-Materialisten, Experimentalisten, Hedonisten.
- Hauptnutzung in der Bevölkerung nach Alter: 14 bis 29 Jahre.

Film-Wertschöpfungskette

Das **Medium Kino** ist in einem größeren Zusammenhang zu sehen. Der Kinomarkt ist eine Art „Aufbereitungsanlage für das Fernsehen": Die großen Spielfilme werden vor ihrer Fernsehausstrahlung zuerst im Kino gezeigt. Sie stehen am Anfang der sogenannten Verwertungskette von Spielfilmen ❶. Das Anliegen der Filmindustrie ist es, die Ware Kinofilm wirtschaftlich möglichst optimal „auszuschlachten". Danach wird ein Spielfilm im Sinne eines **„Wasserfall-Modells"** (auch **„Windowing"** genannt) zunächst exklusiv im Kino gezeigt. Kein anderes Medium kommt in dieser ersten Phase der Verwertungskette zum Zuge. Nach einer Schutzfrist von mehreren Monaten bis zu eineinhalb Jahren erfolgt dann die Videoverwertung mit dem Verkauf und Verleih des Films auf Videocassetten oder DVD. Im Anschluss daran wird der Film im Pay-TV gezeigt und dann erst im Free-TV gezeigt. Eine nicht zu unterschätzende Rolle spielt das Merchandising, d. h. die Verwertung von Fan-Artikeln, der Betrieb von Studio-Stores (z. B. Universal) bis zur Einrichtung von Themenparks (z. B. Disneyland). So ist die maximale wirtschaftliche Ausbeute des produzierten Spielfilms gewährleistet.

❶ Die Verwertungskette von Spielfilmen im **Wasserfallmodell** bzw. **Windowing**:
Stufe 1: Kino
Stufe 2: Videocassette, DVD
Stufe 3: Pay TV (Abo-Kanal oder Pay Per View)
Stufe 4: Freie Ausstrahlung bei öffentlich-rechtliche Rundfunkanstalten oder bei den Privatsendern
Stufe 5: Merchandising

Spielfilmproduktionen sind wirtschaftlich gesehen **riskante Angelegenheiten**: Einem hohen Aufwand steht ein im voraus nicht abschätzbarer Erfolg beim Publikum gegenüber. Manche Filme sind ein Flop, andere die großen Renner. Das Geheimnis des Erfolgs großer US-Produktionen liegt in der mit großem Mitteleinsatz betriebenen Vermarktung, die stets einen großen Anteil am Gesamtbudget ausmacht. So hat der Film „Batman" einschließlich der Vermarktungskosten 85 Mio. Dollar gekostet. Er spielte bis heute nahezu eine Milliarde Dollar ein ❷.

❷ Die Budgets großer US-amerikanischer Spielfilme liegen mittlerweile deutlich über 100 Mio. Dollar, so z. B. Jurassic Park (1993), Independance Day (1996), Titanic (1998)

Der Kinofilm ist untrennbar mit dem Namen Hollywood verbunden, der stellvertretend für die erfolgreiche **amerikanische Filmproduktion** steht. Bis heute beherrschen die US-Filmfirmen den Markt sowohl auf der Produktions- als auch auf der Vermarktungsseite. Im Zentrum stehen die sog. **Majors**, das sind die großen „Spieler" (Big Players) am Filmmarkt wie Time-Warner oder Disney. Daneben gibt es kleinere Firmen, die sog. **Independants**, die im deutschen Film eine Rolle spielen. Die Majors dominieren Produktion und Vertrieb und sind auch an den Kinoketten beteiligt.

Der **Werbeträger Kino** hat gegenüber dem Fernsehen die folgenden Vorzüge:

- Die Qualität des Bildes und die Tontechnik sind überlegen.
- Die Bildgröße ist überlebensgroß. Daher ist das Medium viel eindrucksvoller als das Fernsehen.
- Ein beachtlicher Teil des Fernsehpublikums steht der Werbung ablehnend gegenüber, während im Kino ein voll aufnahmebereites Publikum im abgedunkelten Raum sitzt, das auch Werbefilme aufmerksam betrachtet.
- Der Gang ins Kino ist mit einer positiven Erwartungshaltung verbunden. Kinogänger suchen Entspannung und Unterhaltung und gehen häufig zu zweit oder in der Gruppe ins Kino.
- Das Kino kann vom Werbetreibenden im Gegensatz zum Fernsehen gezielt eingesetzt werden, sowohl lokal also auch regional und national.
- Kinowerbung kann kurzfristig geschaltet werden.

Zentrale Trends im Bereich Film und Kino

- Die Dominanz der ausländischen Akteure, insbesondere aus den USA, wird auch in Zukunft Bestand haben.
- Im Hinblick auf den End-Konsumenten ist festzustellen, dass sich in der für den Film- und Kinomarkt besonders wichtigen Gruppe der unter 40-Jährigen ein deutlicher Trend zur Reduktion des Kinobesuchs und eine gewisse Erlahmung der Kaufbereitschaft von Video-Produktionen abzeichnet. Die Kinos haben daher zunehmend das Problem einer zu geringen Auslastung ihrer Filmtheater („Over-Screening"), die sie seit 1990 in Richtung von Großkinos mit Erlebnischarakter („Multiplexe") ausgebaut hatten.
- Verschärft wird diese Entwicklung durch die rückläufige Bevölkerungsentwicklung.
- Die Entwicklung des Film- und Kinomarktes ist durch Stagnation, rückläufigen Kinobesuch und stagnierende DVD-Verkaufszahlen gekennzeichnet. Das Marktpotenzial ist daher – aktuell, aber auch in mittelfristiger Hinsicht – als eher schwach zu beurteilen. Der Markt weist einen hohen Sättigungsgrad auf und kann nur durch neue Produkte in Bewegung gebracht werden.
- Als besonders kritisch ist die zunehmende Filmpiraterie zu bewerten, die sich verstärken wird, wenn über das Internet in großem Stil Filme zum Download zugänglich sind. Analog zu den Problemen des Musikmarktes werden dann auch **illegale Tauschbörsen** ❶ entstehen, die sogar zu einer nachhaltigen und dauerhaften Schrumpfung des Film- und Kinomarktes führen könnten.
- Die Rolle der Rechtehändler schwächt sich ab: Mit der Digitalisierung wird das traditionelle Geschäftsmodell in Frage gestellt, nach dem alle Filmware über Zwischeninstanzen geschleust werden. Diese Rolle der Händler als sog. intermediäre Instanzen könnte sich zugunsten einer Direktverbindung zwischen den großen Studios und den Konsumenten abschwächen.

❶ Im Fachjargon **Peer-to-Peer-Systeme** genannt bzw. kurz: P-to-P (oder noch kürzer: P2P). Vgl. auch 3.4.4

Konzepte der Film- und Kino-Unternehmen

- Die deutschen Kinofilm-Produzenten müssen versuchen, mit ihren Produktionen der ausländischen Konkurrenz standzuhalten.
- Die TV-Produzenten müssen versuchen, mit schlagkräftigen Wirtschaftsunternehmen dem hohen Grad der Zersplitterung zu begegnen.
- Die Filmtheater-Betreiber stehen vor der Herausforderung, die digitale Kino-Präsentation über Play-Out-Service-Center einzuführen. Hierbei erhalten die Kinobetriebe die Filme nicht mehr als Zelluloid-Kopie, sondern in digitaler Form auf einem Datenträger, per Satellit oder über Breitbandkabel. Die Umstellung der Wertschöpfungskette auf die digitale Plattform führt zu erheblichen Zusatzkosten. Zusätzlich stehen die Kinos vor dem Problem, dass in Zukunft möglicherweise Filme bereits zum Kinostart auf DVD veröffentlicht werden, womit sich die klassische Verwertungskette drastisch ändern würde. Erste Versuche in dieser Richtung werden bereits unternommen. Kinobetreiber sind daher geradezu dazu verurteilt, neue Formen der Kinonutzung zu entwickeln, um der Abwanderung von Zuschauern entgegen zu wirken.

3.4.3 Radio

Definition

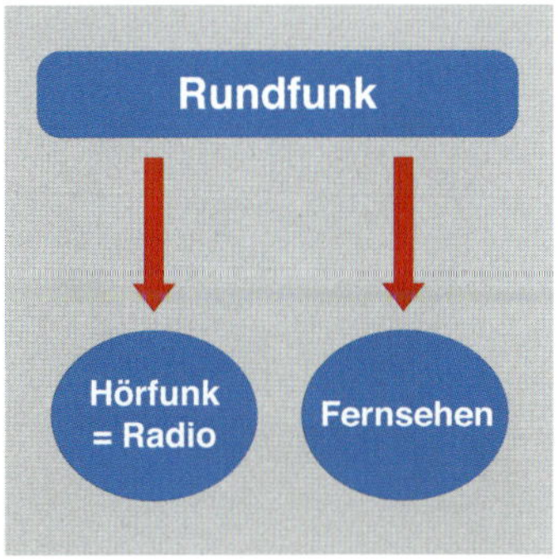

Im ABC der ARD heißt es: „Hörfunk = Erstes elektronisches Massenmedium, anfangs gleichbedeutend mit Rundfunk, dann in Abgrenzung zum Fernsehen von Technikern als Tonrundfunk gekennzeichnet. In Deutschland regelmäßiger Programmbetrieb seit 29. 10. 1923, anfangs durch halbstaatliche, dann voll verstaatlichte, überwiegend regional orientierte Sendegesellschaften, ab 1945 durch Besatzungssender, seit 1948/49 durch Anstalten des öffentlichen Rechts, seit Anfang der 80er Jahre zusätzlich durch privatrechtliche, zumeist kommerzielle Veranstalter, seit 1994 auf nationaler Ebene durch die Körperschaft des öffentlichen Rechts Deutschlandradio".

Wirtschaftliche Bedeutung

Die medienökonomische Bedeutung des Radios ist mit etwas mehr als drei Mrd. Euro gegenüber der Presse und dem Fernsehen als nachrangig zu bezeichnen, Radio ist gleichwohl – ebenso wie das Fernsehen eine Nutzungszeit von ca. dreieinhalb Stunden täglich aufweisend – das am meisten genutzte Medium. Es steht vor großen Veränderungen.

Das **Marktpotenzial** des Hörfunks erscheint vor dem Hintergrund der mittelfristigen Vergangenheit als **eher bescheiden**. So hat sich das Marktvolumen in den letzten fünf Jahren auf gleichem absoluten Niveau erhalten, was nur deshalb möglich gewesen ist, weil die Erlöse aus Rundfunkgebühren einen massiven Rückgang der Werbeerlöse überkompensiert haben. Dies verdeutlicht, dass privates Radio offensichtlich immer schwerer zu finanzieren ist. Verschärfend kommt hinzu, dass die Rolle von Radio als lediglich **begleitendes Medium** eher noch zunehmen wird.

Der Radiomarkt steht vor signifikanten Veränderungen. Eine wichtige Rolle spielen die technischen Entwicklungen, die mit der **Digitalisierung** des analogen Hörfunks einhergehen. Es wird angestrebt, den Hörfunk bis 2010 vollständig auf digitale Technologien umzustellen und nach einer Übergangszeit, in der die analoge und digitale Übertragung parallel erfolgt („Simulcast"), das analoge Signal vollständig abzuschalten.

❶ Die **erste Rundfunkansage in Deutschland** am 29.10.1923 in Berlin: „Achtung, Achtung, hier ist Berlin auf Welle 400 Meter. Meine Damen und Herren, wir machen Ihnen davon Mitteilung, dass am heutigen Tage der Unterhaltungsrundfunkdienst mit Verbreitung von Musikvorführungen auf drahtlos-elektronischem Wege beginnt. Die Benutzung ist genehmigungspflichtig."

Publizistische Bedeutung

Die erste Radiosendung in Deutschland wurde am 29. Oktober 1923 aus dem Vox-Haus in Berlin ausgestrahlt ❶. Seine publizistische Bedeutung war sowohl in der Gründerzeit (1923-1933) als auch im Dritten Reich und in den 50er und 60er Jahren enorm. Privatradios wurden in Deutschland ab dem Jahr 1984 zugelassen. Heute ist das Radio eher ein **Nebenbei-** und **Hintergrundmedium**. Allerdings verwendet die Bevölkerung etwa gleich viel Zeit für das Radiohören wie für das Fernsehen. Radio nimmt bei der aktuellen Information und bei der mobilen Nutzung (vor allem im Auto) eine außergewöhnliche Stellung ein.

Radio

Kommunikatoren, Anbieter

- Öffentlich-rechtliche Rundfunkanstalten: gesamt 11. Aufteilung: ARD (9 Landesrundfunkanstalten: davon Mehrländeranstalten MDR, NDR, RBB, SWR; Einländeranstalten BR, HR, RB, SR, WDR; plus Deutsche Welle), ARD-ZDF-Einrichtung: Deutschlandradio (3 Programme: Deutschlandfunk, Deutschlandradio Kultur, Deutschlandradio Wissen).
- Privat-kommerzielle Veranstalter: Hauptakteure: RTL Group (Bertelsmann), Axel Springer Verlag. Daneben viele kleine und mittlere Anbieter.
- Private nicht-kommerzielle Anbieter: (1) Bürgerradio: Offene Kanäle. (2) Hochschulen: Campus-Radios, Ausbildungsradios. (3) Nicht-kommerzielle Lokalradio-Betreiber.
- Internet-Radios (Webradios): weltweit ca. 15.000 (grobe Schätzung). Deutschland: ca. 1.600 Sender. Veranstalter: Institutionen, Unternehmen, Privatpersonen, Medienunternehmen mit eigenständigen (exklusiven) Angeboten.

Produkte, Inhalte

- Produkte nach Rechtsform: (1) Öffentlich-rechtliche Angebote: 66 Hörfunk-Programme (davon 10: Deutsche Welle und reine Digitalangebote sowie 2 für bundesweite Programme). (2) Private Angebote gesamt: 210 (davon bundesweit: 14; landesweit und regional 57; lokal 131).
- Zeit-Volumen: (1) Zeitliche Vollprogramme vorherrschend. (2) Fensterprogramme bei Lokal- und Regionalradios (Fremdbezug des Mantelprogramms: Syndication).
- Programmleistung und Programmstrukturen: (1) Gesamtes Hörfunksystem: alle Formen (Formate). Dominanz von austauschbaren AC-Einheits-Formaten (Adult-Contemporary „Dudelfunk"). (2) Öffentlich-rechtlicher Rundfunk (ARD): (a) Wortanteile 36,7 %; Musikanteile 62,5 %; Werbung 0,8 %. (b) Information und Service 29,3 %; Kultur/Bildung 7,6 %; Unterhaltung 5,9 %; Rock-/Popmusik 27,6 %; Unterhaltungsmusik 15,9 %; Klassik 12,9 %; Werbung 0,8 %. (3) Private Radioveranstalter, z. B. landesweiter Hörfunk (2002): Musik 72 %, Wort 20 %, Werbung 0,8 %. Dominanz von Unterhaltungsmusik.
- Radio als Werbeträger: (1) Öffentlich-rechtlicher Hörfunk: Anteil Sendezeit 0,8 %, Beitrag zur Finanzierung ca. 5 %. (2) Private: Anteil 5-15 %; Finanzierung: 100 %.
- Internet-Angebote: (1) ARD/ZDF: programmbegleitende Information. (2) Privatveranstalter: auch eigenständige Produktwelten.

Transportwege

- 2011: DAB+ als Digitaler Standard eingeführt.
- Empfangsebenen: (1) Terrestrik (ausschließlich): 7,1 % aller Haushalte, davon: (a) analog/UKW, (b) digital als DVB-T (zahlreiche Ballungsgebiete): 4,6 % (2008). (2) Kabel: als DVB-C, Anteil 51,2 % aller TV-Haushalte (gesamt: 35,3 Mio.). (3) Satellit: als DVB-S, Anteil 44,1 % aller TV-Haushalte. (4) PC: Internet-Radio, Podcasting. (5) Mobiler Empfang. Endgeräte: (a) Tragbare Radiogeräte analog („Kofferradio"). (b) Autoradio: analog, digital. (c) Mobiltelefon. (d) MP3-Player: Podcasting.

Rezipienten

- Erreichbarkeit (technische Reichweite): 100 %.
- Geräteausstattung: 99 %, angemeldete Geräte: 43,1 Mio., 525 Geräte je Tsd. Einw., 85 % besitzen ein Autoradio.
- Reichweite: Weitester Hörerkreis 93,1 %.
- Zeitbudget: Durchschnittliche Hördauer 187 Min. täglich (2010)
- Nutzung betr. Aufmerksamkeitsgrad: meist wenig intensiv, typisches Begleit-Medium.
- Nutzung im Tagesablauf: Hauptnutzung 6:00 bis 8:00 Uhr.
- Nutzer-Schwerpunkt: alle Bevölkerungsschichten nach Alter, Geschlecht und Lebensstil. Aber Leitfunktion bei Jugendlichen. Männer hören etwas mehr, Frauen etwas weniger Radio.
- Überdurchschnittliche Nutzung bei Bürgerlicher Mitte und Konservativen.
- Nutzung nach Hörertypen (2005): Vielhörer 13 %, Frühhörer 23 %, Vormittagshörer 17 %, Späthörer 14 %, Gelegenheitshörer 25 %, Wenighörer 8 %.

❶ **Journalistische Formen** im Radio:

- Nachrichten
- Bericht
- Kommentar
- Interview
- Diskussion
- Feature
- Presseschau
- Programm mit Hörerbeteiligung
- Jingles und Trailer
- Moderation

❷ Wichtige **Formen von Werbespots** in Radio und Fernsehen:

- Problemlöser-Spot
- Präsentation durch Sprecher
- Interview-Technik
- Produkt-Demonstration
- Testimonial
- Slice-of-Life
- Musik-Jingle

Programmformen

Die Programmformen nennt man auch Formate. Es hat sich gezeigt, dass die Akzeptanz der massenattraktiven Hörfunkprogramme vorrangig über die Musikfarbe bestimmt wird. Die folgenden **Formate** werden unterschieden:

- Format 1: Internationale Popmusik, englischsprachig, melodiös, wenig rhythmusbetont. Service und aktuelle Information in knapper Form integriert. Zielpublikum: 25 bis 49 Jahre.
- Format 2: Deutsch-orientiert, melodiös („DOM“); aktuelle Schlager, Schlager-Klassiker, volkstümliche Musik, gemächlicher Programmfluss ohne Hektik, liebenswerte, verständnisvolle Ansprache. Zielpublikum: vor allem ältere Zielgruppen.
- Format 3: Aktuelle Hits aller Gattungen („Contemporary Hit Radio“) von Pop, Rock, Techno, Rap bis House; wenige Titel aus dem letzten Jahrzehnt, sehr schnelle, moderne Anmutung, jugendliche Ansprache, Hörer werden meist geduzt, äußerst knapp gehaltene Nachrichten und Informationen. Zielpublikum: Jugendliche Zielgruppen.
- Format 4: Klassische Musik von Evergreens bis zu weniger eingängigen Werken, auch Weltmusik und Folklore, seriöse Ansprache, Kulturinformationen, Hörspiele. Zielpublikum: Klassik- und Kulturinteressierte aller Altersschichten.
- Format 5: Überwiegender Wortanteil, weitgehendes Fehlen von Musik, Schwerpunkt liegt auf ausführlicher Information aus allen Bereichen, Hintergrundinformationen, Features, Gesprächssendungen. Zielpublikum: Alle an umfassender Information Interessierten, die das Radio nicht wegen der Musik einschalten.

Neben diesen Programmformen sind für die Definition der Inhalte auch die journalistischen Formen ❶ sowie die Werbeformen ❷ von Bedeutung.

Nutzung

Radio wird überdurchschnittlich stark am Morgen zwischen 6:00 und 8:00 Uhr genutzt, auch dort schon – wie den ganzen Tag über – eher als Nebenbeimedium genutzt. Über den Tag hinweg fällt die Nutzungskurve ab, allerdings mit zwei Spitzen als Ausnahme, zum einen einem relativ starken „Hoch“ um die Mittagszeit, zum anderen mit einer Spitze in der Zeit um 16:00 Uhr. Die Radionutzung flacht am Abend stark ab und tritt gegenüber dem Fernsehen völlig in den Hintergrund.

Der **Marktanteil** der öffentlich-rechtlichen Rundfunkanstalten ist gegenüber den Privatradios deutlich höher. Insofern unterscheidet sich die Situation auf dem Radiomarkt von der des Fernsehmarktes. Eine Ausnahme bildet allerdings Berlin, wo in einem heiß umkämpften Markt die privaten Programme dominieren.

Im Hörfunk herrscht zwischen den Sendern eine **starke Konkurrenzsituation**. Dies resultiert aus der Tatsache, dass sich die Sendegebiete nicht selten stark überlappen, aber auch aus der Einspeisung in Kabel- und Satellitensysteme.

Zentrale Trends im Radiomarkt

- Radio nimmt seit jeher die Rolle eines klassischen Begleit-Mediums ein, das passiv zur Unterhaltung und Entspannung hauptsächlich durch Musik genutzt wird. Diese Art der Nutzung zeigt sich in allen soziodemografischen Gruppen als sehr stabil. Hauptnutzungszeit des Radios im Tagesverlauf ist der Morgen.
- Relevante Veränderungen in der Radionutzung zeigen sich nur bei den 14- bis 29-Jährigen, wo eine gewisse Reduktion in der Radionutzung erkennbar ist.
- Als neue Nutzungsformen verdienen Audio-Produktionen, die von Privatpersonen erzeugt und verbreitet werden („User-Generated Content"), höchste Aufmerksamkeit. Besonders wichtig wird dabei das Podcasting ❶.
- Die mobile Nutzung wird zunehmend zu einer wichtigen Säule des Konsums von Radioprogrammen und -elementen.
- Eine steigende Bedeutung erfährt die Personalisierung der Radionutzung. Hier erfolgt eine Anpassung des Radioprogramms an persönliche Vorlieben, z. B. durch Auswahl von Lieblingsmusikrichtungen oder Interpreten, die in einer individuellen Playlist über einen personalisierten Radioservice aus einem Tableau unterschiedlicher Stationen zusammengestellt werden.
- Die völlige Abkehr vom Echtzeit-Konsum der Angebote der Broadcast-Dienstleister schließlich vollzieht „Radio on Demand". Hierbei werden Archive mit hochwertigen Inhalten (O-Töne, Mitschnitt-Dienste oder zu festen Zeitpunkten konservierte Nachrichten) immer wichtiger.
- Zur künftigen technischen Verbreitung in der digitalen Welt: Prinzipiell findet ein Wettbewerb zwischen zwei unterschiedlichen Systemen statt: (a) Monodirektionale Kommunikation über Terrestrik, Kabel und Satellit. Als Technologie steht Digital Audio Broadcasting (DAB) zur Verfügung, die bereits von über 80 % der Bevölkerung genutzt werden kann und eine CD-nahe Tonqualität liefert, allerdings bei mäßigen Mobilempfangseigenschaften. DAB steht in der Kritik wegen hoher Kosten, mangelnder Akzeptanz, fehlender Synergien zum digitalen Fernsehen und alternativer Technologien wie Digital Multimedia Broadcasting (DMB) und Digital Video Broadcasting – Handheld (DVB-H), die DAB als Standard überflüssig machen könnten. (b) Bidirektionale Kommunikation: Radio wird über IP-basierte Netze übertragen, eine Technik, die in direkter Konkurrenz zu den herkömmlichen Übertragungswegen steht und den Vorteil der Rückkanalfähigkeit bietet, sowohl im stationären als auch im mobilen Umfeld. Bereits heute ist die notwendige Bandbreite gegeben, um Audio-Dienste wie Internet-Radio in ausreichender Qualität zu übertragen.

❶ Die Bezeichnung **Podcasting** setzt sich aus den Begriffen „iPod" (Audio-Player) und „Broadcast" (engl. Rundfunk) zusammen. Podcasting macht es möglich, Radio-, aber auch TV-Sendungen zeitversetzt auf den PC oder auf einen beliebigen Audio-Player (z. B. MP3-Player) aus dem Internet herunter zu laden. Die gewünschten Dateien müssen nicht erst mühevoll einzeln abgerufen werden, sondern werden dem Hörer auf Basis eines selbst zusammengestellten Abonnements (Newsfeed) zugespielt. Bei Einwahl in das Internet erfolgt automatisch die Überspielung der aktuellen Ausgaben der gewünschten Sendungen.

Konzepte der Radio-Unternehmen

Angesichts der aktuellen Veränderungen, die im krassen Gegensatz zur bisher sehr stabilen Entwicklung der letzten 30 Jahre stehen, sind die Anbieter auf dem Radiomarkt gezwungen, zukunftsfähige strategische Konzepte zu entwickeln, mit denen sie bestehen können. Grundsätzlich geht es dabei auch um die Frage, welche Perspektive das Radio im Zeichen von Fernsehen und Internet in Zukunft überhaupt haben kann.

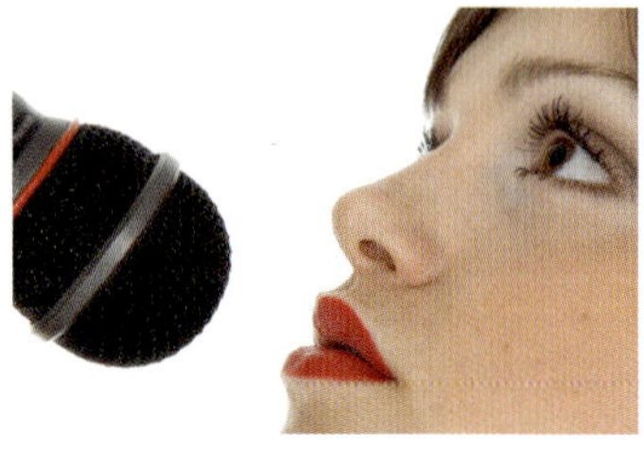

3.4.4 Musik

Definition

In der Musikpsychologie definiert man Musik als „produzierte Schallmuster unterschiedlicher Tonhöhe und -länge, die zu emotionalen, sozialen, kulturellen oder kognitiven Zwecken erzeugt werden" (P. Gray).

Wirtschaftliche Bedeutung

Der Musikmarkt weist ein **Marktvolumen** von knapp zwei Mrd. Euro auf. Damit ist er fast doppelt so groß wie der Kinomarkt. Sein **Marktpotenzial** für die Zukunft abzuschätzen, erscheint schwierig. Eher düstere Aussichten ergeben sich, wenn man auf die technologischen Veränderungen blickt. Bis zum Ende des letzten Jahrhunderts wies der Musikmarkt – im Zeitalter der analogen Technik – eine sehr stabile Marktsituation auf, die sich ab 2000 im Zuge der Digitalisierung der Wertschöpfungskette völlig umkehrte. So ist seitdem ein stetiger Umsatzrückgang festzustellen, der den traditionellen Tonträgermarkt geradezu einbrechen ließ. Musik erscheint insofern derzeit als ein Verlustgeschäft. Als Gründe für die wenig erfreuliche Entwicklung wird von den Verantwortlichen im Musik-Business die Konkurrenz durch **illegale Raubkopien** herausgestellt. Man schätzt, dass 2005 über 500 Mio. Titel mit einem Gesamtwert von ca. 600 Mio. Euro – das entspricht fast einem Drittel des gesamten Musikmarkt-Volumens – illegal über Peer-to-Peer-Filesharing herunter geladen wurden. Andere Quellen gehen von einer Mrd. Euro aus. Allerdings hat der Musikmarkt Antworten gegeben, indem er legale Musik-Download-Angebote offeriert. Ein Drittel der Konsumenten wurden dadurch veranlasst, vom illegalen Download abzusehen. Legale Musik-Downloads sind ebenso wie die Mobilmusik (Musik für Mobiltelefone wie Klingeltöne, ganze Musiktitel oder Musikvideos) starke Wachstumstreiber. Allerdings weisen sie noch keine zehn Prozent Anteil am Gesamtmarkt auf.

Publizistische Bedeutung

Musik ist tief im Leben der Menschen verwurzelt. Sowohl als Hochkultur-Musik als auch als populäre Musik stellt sie eines der **tragenden Fundamente** unserer heutigen **Kultur** dar. Musik wurde in Deutschland stets als ein wichtiges Kulturgut sowohl der Hochkultur als auch der Alltagskultur verstanden und kann auf eine lange Geschichte zurück blicken. Diese Rolle dürfte sie prinzipiell beibehalten.

Nach unserem heutigen Verständnis ist ein Leben ohne Musik schlichtweg nicht vorstellbar: Musik begleitet uns auf Schritt und Tritt und sei es nur als permanente Musikberieselung. Wir bewegen uns unter einer permanenten akustischen Glocke, ein Phänomen, das in der Fachliteratur als „gnadenloser, kollektiver Walkman" oder als „Vertreibung der Stille" bezeichnet wird. Von der „Droge" Musik können und wollen wir uns freilich nicht lösen und erleben immer wieder berauschende Momente, in denen wir tief ergriffen einem Musikstück lauschen.

Musik

Kommunikatoren, Anbieter

- Musik- und Unterhaltungsindustrie („Entertainment“)
- Musikunternehmen (Musikverlage, Musikproduzenten): (1) Große Musikverlage „Majors“ (2005 ca. 72 % des Umsatzes am weltweiten Musikmarkt für Tonträger): Sony BMG 21,5 %, Universal Music 25,5 %, EMI 13,4 %, Warner Music 11,3 %. (2) Unabhängige „Independents“ bzw. „Independent Labels“ (zusammen ca. 28 % des Umsatzes).
- Tonstudio und Produzenten
- Medienunternehmen: Radio, Fernsehen.
- Filmindustrie: Musik als Bestandteil von Filmen, Musikfilme.
- Privatpersonen: Private Mitschnitte, eigene Musikaufnahmen.

Produkte, Inhalte

- Musik: Unterhaltungsmusik (U-Musik), Klassik (Ernste Musik, E-Musik). Verhältnis U- zu E-Musik beim Tonträgerabsatz ca. 90:10.
- Digitale Musik: inkl. Komplette Musiktitel, die auf Mobiltelefone heruntergeladen werden.
- Mobile Musik: Musik, die auf Mobiltelefone geladen werden kann: Klingeltöne, Freizeichentöne (Ringback Tunes, bei denen der Anrufer anstelle eines Freizeichens Musik hört).
- Tonträgerhersteller in Deutschland: ca. 1.000.
- Neue Geschäftsfelder: Musikveranstaltungen, Ticketing, Merchandising.

Transportwege

- Musikdistribution /Handel: (1) Einzelhandel: Verkaufsläden, Supermärkte. (2) Versandhandel, Online-Versand. (3) Direktversand vom Hersteller. (4) Buch-Clubs. (5) Internet.
- Internet: (1) Legale Downloads: 10 Mio. Songs online. (2) Illegale Downloads (Tauschbörsen, Peer-to-Peer – „P2P“).
- Internet: User generated content (auf Video-Plattformen z. B. You Tube, myspace.com).
- Mobil-Telefone.

Rezipienten

- Vielfalt an Endgeräten für Musik: Plattenspieler, Tape-Deck, CD-/DVD-Player, PC, Spielekonsole, Radio-Tuner, TV, Videorecorder, Mobiltelefon.
- Geräteausstattung (Personen aus Haushalten mit ...): Radiogerät 98,2 %, Autoradio 82,4 %, Plattenspieler (2006) 25,6 %, Kassettenrekorder (2006) 55,8 %, MP3-Player ohne Radio 38,9 %, Geräte ohne Radio: Kassettenrekorder 24,9 % / Tragbarer CD-Player 26,4 % / Walkman 21,1 %; Videorekorder 57,5 %, DVD-Player (nur Abspielgerät) 64,1 %, DVD-Rekorder 18,8 %, Festplattenrekorder 8,1 %, PC 61,1 %, Laptop/Notebook 32,3 %, Internet (Modem, ISDN-Anschluss etc.) 68,2 %.
- Zeitbudget Tonträgernutzung (Altersgruppe in Min. pro Tag): (1) 10-19: 79 (2) 14-19: 97. (3) 20-29: 69. (4) 30-39: 35. (5) 40-49: 27. (6) 50-59: 20. (7) 60-69: 14. (7) > 70: 9.
- Tonträgernutzung (nach Geschlecht in Min. pro Tag): (1) Männer: 67. (2) Frauen: 34.
- Nutzerschwerpunkt nach Lebensalter: 14-29-Jährige.
- Nutzer-Schwerpunkt nach Sinus-Milieus: (1) Schallplatten/CDs/Kassetten hören: Postmaterielle, Moderne Performer. (2) Videos/DVDs ansehen: Moderne Performer, Konsum-Materialisten, Experimentalisten, Hedonisten.

Musik-Wertschöpfungskette

Produkte

❶ **iTunes** ist eine Software der Firma Apple, über das Musiktitel aus dem Internet legal herunter geladen, genutzt und in begrenztem Umfang weiterverbreitet werden dürfen. Als Abspielgerät steht der **iPod** zur Verfügung, ein tragbarer MP3-Player, der auch Videos wiedergeben kann.

Die Produkte des Musikmarktes lassen sich in **drei Gruppen** unterscheiden:

- Traditionelle Tonträger (Alben): (a) Alben, Singles, (b) Musikvideos
- Legale Downloaddienste, z. B. iTunes ❶
- Mobilmusik, z. B. Klingeltöne

Die Verkaufszahlen für **traditionelle Tonträger** sind in den letzten Jahren ständig gesunken, sie machen aber immer noch fast 160 Mio. Stück pro Jahr aus (zum Vergleich: 2001 waren es noch fast 250 Mio. Stück). (a) Bei den Alben sind vier Typen zu unterscheiden: CD, Kassette, LP und DVD-Audio. Die CD dominiert dabei mit über 120 Mio. Stück komplett den Markt, die DVD-Audio bringt es nur auf einige Hunderttausend Exemplare. Die stärksten Einbrüche der letzten Jahre haben die Kassetten erlebt, von denen aber immer noch einige Mio. Stück verkauft werden. (b) Die Musikvideos erfreuen sich steigender Beliebtheit, was in einer Absatzzahl von ca. 10 Mio. Stück zum Ausdruck kommt. Als Format hat sich fast vollständig die DVD durchgesetzt. Der Durchschnittspreis pro Stück liegt dabei bei etwa 15 Euro.

❷ **P2P-Filesharing** = „Peer-to-Peer-Systeme", kurz: P-to-P (oder noch kürzer P2P). Nach der Bedeutung des Wortes „peer" (engl. gleichrangig) bezeichnet ein **Peer-to-Peer-Netzwerk** ein Netzwerk, das Gleichrangige mit anderen Gleichrangigen verbindet. Fachbezeichnung für die Tauschbörsen von Musik- und Filmdateien der Verlage im Internet, an denen sich Privatpersonen (illegal) beteiligen.

Mit der Einführung **legaler Downloaddienste** im Jahr 2004 gibt es eine Alternative zum illegalen Tausch von Musikdateien über die P2P-Filesharing-Netze ❷ im Internet. Allerdings wurden bisher nur vergleichsweise geringe Umsätze generiert (ca. neun Mio. Euro), man rechnet aber in den nächsten Jahren mit einer starken Zunahme. Sehr erfolgreich zeigt sich **Mobilmusik** mit einem Umsatz von 225 Mio. Euro. Dies sind Musikangebote für das Handy, v. a. als Klingeltöne.

Akteure

Die **Wertschöpfungskette des Musikmarktes** verläuft in **drei Stufen** und umfasst die folgenden Akteure:

- Stufe 1: Entwicklung. Künstlerische Akteure: Autoren (Komponisten, Textdichter), Interpreten; Musikverlage („Verleger", „music publisher": Verwalter und Vermarkter der Urheberrechte von Komponisten und Musikern).
- Stufe 2: Produktion. Akteure: Musikproduzenten (klassische „Plattenproduzenten"), Ton- und Videostudios, Tonträger- und Video-Hersteller.
- Stufe 3: Verwertung. Akteure: (a) Verkauf von Ton- und Bildträgern: Musikdistribution/-handel (Unterstützung durch Musikproduzenten); (b) Sendung, Kino-Vorführung: Radio-/Fernseh-/Filmindustrie; (c) Aufführung: Konzertveranstalter; (d) Werbung: Musikalische Untermalung von Werbespots; (e) Akteure der Randnutzung (Mechandising, Licensing).

Auf allen diesen Stufen wird das Marktgeschehen von vier großen „Global Playern" beherrscht, den sog. **Majors**. Es sind dies die Universal Music Group, Sony BMG, Warner Music Group und EMI.

Zentrale Trends im Musikmarkt

- Der Musikmarkt ist stark von jugendlichen Zielgruppen abhängig. Eine klare Verknüpfung mit soziodemografischen Kriterien und Musikgenres kann dabei nicht vorgenommen werden.
- Musik ist ein klassisches hedonisches ❶ Produkt, das typischerweise experimenteller Natur ist und Spaß und Vergnügen erzeugt. Zentrale Motivation des Musikkonsums ist die emotionale Komponente. Er steht damit in einer Reihe mit dem Konsum von Filmen, Konzerten oder Musicals. Musik spielt bei jüngeren Konsumenten als ein wichtiges Instrument der sozialen Positionierung eine große Rolle.
- Musik ist starken Modeströmungen unterworfen, woraus sich dynamische Prozesse entwickeln können, die das Konsumentenverhalten stark beeinflussen. Die hohe Schwankungsbreite (man könnte von „Volatilität" sprechen) im Hinblick auf das Konsumverhalten machen Voraussagen und Konzept-Entwicklungen schwierig.
- Musik-Downloads sind in der jungen Generation („Download-Generation") selbstverständliche Formen der Musikbeschaffung.

❶ **Hedonismus** = Leben nach dem Lustprinzip, Freude, Spaß

Konzepte der Musik-Unternehmen

- Umsätze aus dem Verkauf von Alben: Die Branche versucht über Preisanhebungen den Rückgang der Verkaufszahlen bei den physischen Tonträgern mehr als wettzumachen. Dies kann gelingen, ist allerdings insofern eine riskante Strategie, als sie die Wechselbereitschaft der Konsumenten zur digitalen Alternative beschleunigen könnte. Umgekehrt wäre ein Preiskampf für die Anbieter möglicherweise ruinös. Entscheidende Erkenntnis dürfte aber sein, dass die CD den Höhepunkt ihres Produktlebenszyklus überschritten hat und als eine überholte Technologie gelten muss, so dass das Verkaufspotenzial ohnehin ausgereizt erscheint und ein Umstieg auf die leistungsfähigere DVD bzw. auf das MP3-Format vorgezeichnet ist.
- Bekämpfung der illegalen Musik-Downloads: Seitens der Politik wird die Verschärfung des Urheberrechts verfolgt. Ergänzend gibt es Forderungen der Musikindustrie, ihnen einen Auskunftsanspruch über persönliche Daten von Nutzern von P2P-Filesharing-Netzen einzuräumen.
- Für die traditionellen Anbieter auf dem Musikmarkt stellt sich die Frage, inwieweit sie in das Geschäft mit legalen Download-Angeboten einsteigen müssen. Dieser Weg wird bislang eher zaghaft beschritten.
- Zu denken ist an völlig neue Geschäftsmodelle wie z. B. Musik-Abonnements, die analog zu Pay-TV die Buchung eines ganzen Programmpakets ermöglichen. Die wäre eine Erweiterung des iTunes-Modells, das lediglich ein einfaches Pay-per-Song-Modell darstellt.
- Ein beträchtliches Marktpotenzial könnte sich ergeben, wenn Musiktonträger zunehmend als Werbemittel eingesetzt werden.
- Erfolg kann auch die Strategie gezielten Verfolgung von Konzepten der Mehrfachverwertung bringen.

3.4.5 Video- und Computerspiele

Definition

Das Institut für angewandte Kindermedienforschung, Stuttgart, führt aus (siehe www.ifak.de): „Ein Computerspiel ist ein Programm auf einem Computer, das einem oder mehreren Benutzern ermöglicht, ein durch implementierte Regeln beschriebenes Spiel zu spielen. Videospiele sind im allgemeinen alle Arten elektronischer Spiele, die auf einem visuellen Ausgabegerät (z. B.: Fernseher, Monitor etc.) dargestellt werden. Der Spielverlauf kann dabei vom Benutzer mit speziellen Eingabegeräten (z. B. Tastatur, Maus, Joystick etc.) gesteuert werden. Im Speziellen werden damit Computerspiele bezeichnet, die auf Spielkonsolen laufen (Konsolen-Spiele). Spielkonsolen sind Computer oder computerähnliche Geräte, die ursprünglich für Videospiele entwickelt wurden. Man kann zwischen stationären Standgeräten (in der Regel an einen Fernseher angeschlossen) und tragbaren Spielkonsolen mit eingebautem Monitor (Handheld-Konsolen) unterscheiden."

Wirtschaftliche Bedeutung

Der Markt für Video- und Computerspiele ist seit dem Ende der 90er Jahre zu einem zunehmend **bedeutenden Wirtschaftszweig** geworden und bewegt sich derzeit in der Größenordnung von 1,3 Mrd. Euro. Das Wachstum ist hoch.

Elektronische Spiele haben sich zu einer weit verbreiteten und gängigen Unterhaltungsform entwickelt. In den USA übertraf schon 2001 der Umsatz der Video- und Computerspiele-Industrie mit seinerzeit 9,4 Mrd. US-Dollar den Umsatz der US-Filmindustrie mit 8,1 Mrd. US-Dollar. Diese Situation trat in Deutschland im Jahr 2005 ein. Dennoch wird die Video- und Computerspiele-Industrie erst langsam als ernst zu nehmender Teil der Medienindustrie anerkannt.

Publizistische Bedeutung

Die publizistische Bedeutung von Video- und Computerspielen darf nicht mehr unterschätzt werden. Im Gegenteil: „Die globale Computer- und Videospielindustrie hat sich in den letzten 35 Jahren zu einer der umsatzstärksten Medienbranchen entwickelt. Über 25 Millionen Bundesbürger spielen heute mehr oder weniger regelmäßig Computer- und Videospiele. Mit über einer Million E-Sportler in Deutschland hat sich sogar ein wettkampfmäßiger Spielbetrieb etabliert. Und im Zuge fortschreitender Konvergenz verwischen die Grenzen moderner Spiele mit interaktiven Unterhaltungsangeboten aus Film und Fernsehen" (Müller-Lietzkow et al., Vorwort).

Anzumerken ist, dass bei Video- und Computerspielen die **Gefahr jugendgefährdender Produkte** besonders hoch ist. Obgleich in Deutschland relativ strenge gesetzliche Regelungen gelten, was die Hersteller oft veranlasst, auf den deutschen Markt spezielle, „entschärfte" Versionen zu bringen, steht die Gesellschaft hier vor einem Medienbereich, der als besonders kritisch zu betrachten ist.

Video- und Computerspiele

Kommunikatoren, Anbieter

- Entwicklung und Produktion im Weltmaßstab: Dominanz USA und Asien.
- Haupt-Kommunikatoren USA (Spiele-Software-Anbieter), USA Top 5 mit Marktanteilen (2003): Electronic Arts 20,0 %; Nintendo 11,8 %; Sega 7,3 %; Atari 6,2 %, THQ 6,0 %.
- Haupt-Kommunikatoren Deutschland, Top 5 mit Marktanteilen (2010): Electronic Arts 30 %, Koch Media 11 %, Ubisoft 8 %, Take 2 Interactive 6 %, Activision 6 %.
- Nur sehr wenige deutsche Entwickler und Produzenten spielen eine Rolle. Im Gegensatz zu Frankreich (z. B. Atari) und Großbritannien (z. B. Eidos).

Produkte, Inhalte

- Weltmarkt-Volumen für Spiele-Software (2008): 54 Mrd. US-Dollar.
- Spiele nach Genres: (1) Arcade (actionreiche Geschicklichkeitsspiele, Tanzspiele, Party-Games, Rennspiele mit Phantasiefahrzeugen). (2) Familienunterhaltung (Gesellschafts-spiele, Knobel-, Denk- und Geschicklichkeits-spiele, Kinder-Kreativ-Programme, Edutainmentsoftware. (3) Strategiespiele („Aufbau"-Spiele, z. B. Besiedlung eines Landes im Mittelalter, militärische Strategiespiele, Management-Spiele. (4) Rollenspiele (insbes. Online). (5) Sportspiele (actionreiche Mannschaftssportarten wie Fußball und Eishockey, Auto-Rennspiele, kontemplativ-sportliche Betätigungen wie Angeln oder Golf. (6) Shooter (einfache „Ballerspiele", raffinierte Team-Taktik-Spiele). (7) Simulation (Flugsimulatoren, virtuellen Eisenbahnen, virtuelles Lebens-Spiel).
- Spiele verwenden häufig bekannte, populäre Contents und reale Charaktere aus der Film- und Sportindustrie (z. B. Star Wars, FIFA Fußball). Starke Zunahme von „Serious Games".

Transportwege

- Plattformen: (1) Stationäre Konsolen (über das TV-Gerät; seit 2007 in der 7. Generation): Sony PlayStation 3, Microsoft Xbox 360, Nintendo Wii. (2) Tragbare Konsolen (Handheldkonsole): Nintendo DS, Sony PSP. (3) Computerspiele. (4) Internet: Online-Spiele. (5) Mobil („Mobile Gaming"): Spiele auf Mobiltelefonen.
- Verkaufsorte: (1) Fachhandel 40 % (2) Warenhäuser 17 % (3) Verbrauchermärkte 15 % (4) Internet 10 % (5) Lebensmittel-Discounter 4 % (6) Klassischer Versandhandel 2 % (7) Sonstige (Buchladen, Kaffeeröster, Möbelhäuser, Bekleidungsgeschäfte, Baumärkte, Cash & Carry) 12 %.

Rezipienten

- Reichweite: Video-/ Computerspiele spielen im Alltag von Kindern und Jugendlichen (v.a. männlich) eine bedeutsame Rolle. Über 60 % der Jungen und rund 25 % der Mädchen spielen mehrmals pro Woche.
- Zeitbudget: (1) Kinder 6-13 Jahre (KIM-Studie 2010): 19 % bis 30 Min. täglich; 38 % zw. 30 und 60 Min.; 37 % mehr als eine Stunde pro Tag. (2) Jugendliche 12-19 Jahre (JIM-Studie 2011): 34 % bis zu einer Stunde täglich; 26 % eine bis zwei Stunden täglich; 17 % zwei bis vier Stunden täglich; 3 % mehr als vier Stunden täglich; 21 % spielt nie. Jungen spielen deutlich mehr als Mädchen.
- Nutzungsformen: Einzelpersonen („Single Player") vs. Gruppen („Multi Player", z. B. LAN-Partys); mobil vs. stationär; Offline vs. Online. Online: MMOG (Massive Multiplayer Online Games), z. B. World of Warcraft mit ca. 11 Mio. Abos.
- Nutzung nach Genres: (1) Management-Spiele: ein Drittel. (2) Action-Unterhaltung: ein Drittel. (3) Simulationen: 7 %. (4) Renn- und Sportspiele: 6 %.

Nutzungsformen und Kosten

Im Hinblick auf die **Nutzung elektronischer Spiele** ist festzustellen, dass die Ansicht, der Markt für Video- und Computerspiele sei ein nicht massentauglicher Nischenmarkt, der bevorzugt auf die Zielgruppen der Kinder und Jugendlichen, bei den Erwachsenen auf die „Freaks" ausgerichtet sei, der Vergangenheit angehört. So interessiert sich das Alterssegment der Generation über 40 Jahren inzwischen zunehmend für Spiele.

Der Markt für Video- und Computerspiele ist ein Teilmarkt des gesamten Spielemarktes und versammelt alle Produkte, die in digitaler Form vorliegen. Der so definierte **Markt für Video- und Computerspiele** lässt sich wie folgt differenzieren:

- Konsolenspiele: Spiele, die auf eigens dafür geschaffenen Konsolengeräten in Verbindung mit einem Fernsehgerät gespielt werden.
- Computerspiele: Spiele, die auf dem Computer gespielt werden.
- Onlinespiele: Spiele, bei denen Konsolen- oder Computerspiele online genutzt werden.
- Mobilspiele: Spiele, die auf Mobiltelefonen oder anderen Mobilgeräten gespielt werden.

❶ Das Beispiel des Musikangebots von Apple beleuchtet den Systemcharakter: Dieses besteht aus den beiden folgenden **Systemelementen**:

1. Abspielgerät für digitale Musikstücke (iPod)
2. Online-Portal mit entsprechender Software zum Download der Musikstücke (iTunes)

Bei der Video- und Computerspiele-Branche handelt es sich um eine „Systembranche" (vgl. Wirtz, S. 500 f.): Der Spieler kann die Inhalte nur nutzen, wenn er sich in einen Systemverbund aus Spiele-Hardware und Spiele-Software begibt. Spiele sind damit typische **Systemprodukte**. Sie sind analog z. B. zu Musikprodukten zu sehen, bei denen ebenfalls ein technisches System vorhanden sein muss, um das Produkt nutzen zu können ❶.

Der Markt für Video- und Computerspiele in Deutschland ist ein ausgesprochener **Wachstumsmarkt**. Besonders starke Wachstumstreiber sind dabei die Online- und Mobilspiele, die aber zusammen genommen noch keine 20 Prozent des Gesamtmarktes ausmachen. Das Marktpotenzial des Gesamtmarktes ist als ausgesprochen groß zu bezeichnen. Mittelfristig ist eine Wachstumsrate von über zehn Prozent jährlich zu erwarten, womit der elektronische Spielemarkt zu einem der am schnellsten wachsenden Medienmärkte geworden ist (vgl. PwC 2006, S. 117, Wirtz, S. 500, 521).

Bemerkenswert ist, dass Video- und Computerspiele in der Herstellung zumeist extrem teuer sind. Unterscheidet man in A-, B- und C-Titel, so ist festzustellen, dass die beiden letzteren kurze Entwicklungszeiten (C-Titel: ca. 1 Monat; B-Titel: ca. 6 Monate) und niedrige Budgets (C: 10.000 Euro, B: 50.000 Euro) verzeichnen, bei den A-Titeln dem gegenüber hohe bis sehr hohe Entwicklungs- und Produktionskosten anfallen, bedingt durch Entwicklungszeiten von 12 bis 24 Monaten; Kosten von 10 Mio. US-Dollar sind daher normal (vgl. Ernst & Young 2005, S. 265). Sie können ohne weiteres aber auch bis zu 25 Mio. US-Dollar reichen (vgl. Müller-Lietzkow/Bouncken, S. 13). Diese hohen Kosten können so gravierend sein, dass sich Publisher auf internationaler Ebene zusammenschließen, um das Produkt erstellen zu können.

Zentrale Trends im Video- und Computerspielemarkt

- Immer mehr Haushalte verfügen über Breitband-Internetanschlüsse. Dies facht die Nachfrage nach Onlinespielen an.
- Netzwerkbasierte Spiele haben den größten Marktzuwachs in der Branche. Eine zunehmende Popularität erfahren dabei „Massive Multiplayer Online Games" (MMOG), bei denen Tausende von Spielern weltweit gleichzeitig via Internet dasselbe Spiel spielen.
- Die Bedeutung von Spiele-Communities nimmt zu.
- Die Nachfrage nach mobilen Nutzungen nimmt zu, was die Industrie mit einer besseren Gerätetechnik beantwortet. Hierdurch erfahren Mobilspiele einen zusätzlichen Antrieb.
- Mit ihrer zunehmenden Verbreitung sind elektronische Spiele zunehmend für die Werbewirtschaft interessant. Zu denken ist an Werbeunterbrechungen des Spielflusses und an Product Placement.
- Der Video- und Computerspielemarkt gewinnt weiter an Bedeutung. Sein Produktionswert wird sich mittelfristig verdoppeln.
- Video- und Computerspiele sind im Kontext der crossmedialen Verwertung von Medieninhalten ein zunehmend wichtiger Baustein. Dabei verschmelzen einst getrennte Bereiche der Musik-, Spiele- und Filmindustrie zu einer neuen Unterhaltungsbranche, die völlig neue, innovative Produkte erzeugen kann.
- Die Weiterentwicklung der technischen Voraussetzungen schreitet massiv voran. Dadurch wird auch die Entwicklung von Video- und Computerspielen technisch immer anspruchsvoller und aufwändiger.
- Treibende Kraft technologischer Innovationen ist vor allem eine verbesserte Netzfähigkeit. So findet zunehmend eine Anbindung der Geräte an das Internet statt. Aber auch neue Speicherformate, also HD-DVD und BluRay Discs, sind relevant. Wichtiger wird die Verbindung mit Online-Portalen, z. B. für Serviceangebote.
- Auf der Geräteebene ist eine Konvergenz der technischen Entwicklungen zu erwarten.
- Eine starke Veränderung der Marktstrukturen ist zu erwarten, insbesondere zugunsten mobiler Nutzungen.
- Spiele mit dem Zweck des Wissenserwerbs (z. B. Rollenspiele) gewinnen an Bedeutung.

Konzepte der Spiele-Unternehmen

Angesichts des Entwicklungspotenzials im Bereich der Video- und Computerspiele ergeben sich für neue Spieleentwicklung („Developer") und Verlage („Publisher") große Chancen. Es ist darauf hingewiesen worden, dass Deutschland hier einen gewissen Nachholbedarf hat, der angesichts der Tatsache, dass es sich bei elektronischen Spielen um Hochtechnologie handelt, unverständlich ist (vgl. Müller-Lietzkow et al., S. 173 ff.). Lohnend ist auch das Engagement zur Qualitätsverbesserung und Förderung von Spielen mit erzieherischem Wert (z. B. spielerische Lernprogramme).

3.5 Internet und die TIME-Branche

3.5.1 Internet

Definition

Das Internet ist ein globales dezentrales Netzwerk von einzelnen Rechnern bzw. von lokalen, nationalen oder internationalen Netzwerken. Durch eine einheitliche Adressierungssystematik der angeschlossenen Rechner sowie ein gemeinsames Datenübertragungsprotokoll ermöglicht das Internet den Austausch digitaler Informationen zwischen den Nutzern. M. a. W.: Das Internet ist ein weltumspannendes digitales Netzwerk, das eine Vielzahl von institutionellen und privaten Informationsanbietern und Informationsnachfragern auf digitaler Basis miteinander verbindet.

Wirtschaftliche Bedeutung

Das **Medium Internet** hat eine enorme Entwicklung genommen und ist zum **globalen Informationssystem** geworden. Es ist heute im privaten und geschäftlichen Bereich nicht mehr wegzudenken. Das Internet ist ein hoch leistungsfähiges „**Hypermedium**", das eine Reihe von Diensten ermöglicht, die von der Individualkommunikation (E-Mail) bis zur Massenkommunikation reichen (Informationsangebote im World Wide Web). Seine ökonomische Bedeutung ist heute kaum hoch genug einzuschätzen. Diese hohe Bedeutung in Zahlen auszudrücken, macht große Schwierigkeiten. Als Ausgangsgröße, mit der man den „Internet-Markt" beschreiben kann, bietet sich die Summe aus den Ausgaben zum Internetzugang (Erlöse der Internet-Service-Provider), die den Löwenanteil ausmachen, und der Werbeerlöse im Internet an. Diese Summe bewegt sich inzwischen in die Richtung von sieben Mrd. Euro. mit starken Wachstumsaussichten. Damit ist der **Internet-Markt** wertmäßig schon größer als der Zeitschriftenmarkt, und die Zahlungen z. B. für Downloads sind noch nicht einmal berücksichtigt. Die Internetwerbung liegt wertmäßig mit lediglich ca. 330 Mio. Euro noch im Dornröschenschlaf.

Publizistische Bedeutung

Die publizistische und kommunikative Bedeutung des Internet ist enorm und kann nur mit dem Gutenberg'schen „Quantensprung" verglichen werden. Es führte und führt zu einer **grundlegenden Umwälzung** und zum **Strukturbruch**, aus dem sich eine neue Gesellschafts- und Wirtschaftswelt entwickelt. Das Internet hat als neues Medium inzwischen voll umfänglich Einzug gehalten. Hauptgründe für diese in seiner Dramatik kaum zu überschätzenden Entwicklung sind die unvergleichlichen medialen Eigenschaften des Internet, hier insbesondere die Möglichkeit zur Interaktion sowohl in der Individual als auch in der Massenkommunikation, zum Transport und zur Speicherung großer Informationsmengen und zur Erzeugung hochqualitativer multimedialer Dokumente. Für den Nutzer eröffnen sich damit faszinierende und nahezu unbegrenzte Möglichkeiten des Umgangs mit Informationen. Kehrseite der Medaille ist freilich, dass vom Konsumenten eine vergleichsweise hohe Medienkompetenz und eine aktive Grundhaltung abgefordert wird, die seiner bisher eher passiven Medienkonsumhaltung entgegensteht.

Internet

Kommunikatoren, Anbieter

- Content (Kompilierung, Darstellung, Bereitstellung digitaler Inhalte über das Internet): (1) Spezielle Inhalteanbieter („Content Provider"): Medien- und Informationsunternehmen, Wirtschaftsunternehmen, Organisationen, Privatpersonen. (2) Informationshändler („Broker").
- Context (Angebote zur Klassifikation und Systematisierung von Informationen): (1) Suchmaschinen: Google, Yahoo! (2) Web-Verzeichnisse.
- Connection (Herstellung der Möglichkeit von Informationsaustausch in Netzwerken): (1) Zugangsanbieter zu physischen Netzwerken. (2) Anbieter von kommunikativen Dienstleistungen.
- Commerce (Anbahnung, Aushandlung und/oder Abwicklung von Transaktionen im Internet): (1) Wirtschaftsunternehmen: praktisch alle kommerziell agierenden Unternehmen sind mit eigenen Internetauftritten im Netz. (2) Marktplätze (Betreiber von Plattformen).
- Integration: (1) Komplettanbieter (integriertes Geschäftsmodell): z.B. Deutsche Telekom, Yahoo! / Tendenz zu Branchenkonvergenz und Integration. (2) Plattformanbieter (nach RStV). Werbung im Internet

Produkte, Inhalte

- Typen: (1) Content-Angebote: Entertainment, Information, Education, Infotainment. (2) Context-Angebote: Suchmaschinen, Web-Kataloge. (3) Connection: Inter-Connection: z. B. T-Online, Intra-Connection: z. B. Facebook. (3) Commerce: Attraction, Bargai-ning, Negotiation, Auction (eBay), Price Seeking (preisauskunft.de), Transaction, Payment (paypal.com), Delivery (dhl.de), Tailing (otto.de).
- Online Publishing von Medienunternehmen: programmbegleitende und ergänzende Text- und Bildinformationen, Internet Radio, Web-TV, Videoportale, Datenbestände (Download-Angebote), Informationsprodukte, Unterhaltungsprodukte (Musik, Filme), Software.
- E-Commerce und E-Business: Werbung und Public Relations von Wirtschaftsunternehmen und Organisationen, Geschäftsabwicklung über das Netz, Online-Shopping.
- Unternehmensinterne Netzwerke auf der Grundlage des Internet: Intranet, Extranet.
- Private Inhalte: Private Websites, E-Mail-Verkehr, private Informationsbörsen, Gesprächsforen, Chats, Newsgroups, Communities, Internet-Telefonie (Voice over IP), Homebanking, Computerspiele, Weblogs, zielloses Surfen.

Transportwege

- Festnetz breitbandig (DSL, VDSL) über 90 %.
- Kabel, Satellit, Mobile (Handy, Notebook, iPhone etc.), andere Transportwege: Powerline, WiMAX (drahtloser Zugang zum Breitband-Internet).

Rezipienten

- Reichweite: 74 % der Bevölkerung greift mindestens einmal pro Woche auf das Internet zu (2010, BITKOM).
- Zeitbudget, Mediennutzung Internet 2010: 83 Min. (ARD/ZDF Langzeitstudie). Durchschnittliche Verweildauer 2009 nach Selbsteinschätzung (ARD/ZDF-Onlinestudie 2009): 136 Min., davon Männer 148 Min., Frauen 122 Min; 14-29 J. 180 Min., 30-49 Min. 130 Min., ab 50 J. 97 Min.
- Nutzung (ARD/ZDF-Onlinestudie 2009): (1) Die demografische Struktur der Internet-Nutzerschaft nähert sich der Struktur der Gesamtbevölkerung immer mehr an. (2) Nutzungs-Schwerpunkte: Suchmaschinen-Nutzung, E-Mails, zielgerichtete Suche bestimmter Angebote, Surfen im Internet, Homebanking, Instant Messaging, Gesprächsforen/Newsgroups/Chats, Online-Communities, Dateien-Download, Onlinespiele. (3) Tagesablauf: Hauptnutzungszeit 14:00-22:00 Uhr, v. a. 19:00-20:00 Uhr. Damit zunehmende Konkurrenz zur Fernseh-Primetime. (4) Online-Nutzung nach dem Ort: 94,4 % von zu Hause; 31,8 % am Arbeits- bzw. Ausbildungsplatz; 30,0 % bei Freunden und Verwandten.

Funktionen und Nutzungsformen

❶ Eine Übersicht über mögliche **Online-Nutzungen**:

- Versenden und Empfangen von E-Mails
- Zielloses Surfen im Internet
- Downloaden von Dateien
- Reiseinfos, Zug-/Flugpläne
- Infos über PCs und Software
- Aktuelle Infos aus der Region
- Newsletter von Organisationen
- Gesprächsforen, Newsgroups, Chatten
- Wetterinformationen
- Homebanking
- Computerspiele
- Kleinanzeigen
- Online-Shopping
- Radio
- Fernsehen (IP-TV)
- Buchbestellungen
- Sex-/Erotikangebote
- Multiuser-Spiele
- Telefonieren (Voice over IP)
- Web-Cam
- Bildtelefon
- Videoconferencing

Der Siegeszug des Internet ist in erster Linie Folge der **hohen Funktionalität** des World Wide Web, dessen Spektrum der Möglichkeiten immens ist ❶. Das Internet besitzt die folgenden **Leistungsmerkmale** (vgl. Bruhn 2006, S. 1117 ff.):

- **Interaktivität**, bidirektionale Kommunikation, **Rückkanalfähigkeit**
- Konnektivität, Vernetzung, Vernetztheit („connectivity")
- Zeitliche Unmittelbarkeit („immediacy"), **Aktualität**
- **Multimedialität** („media richness")
- **Ubiquität**, grenzenlose räumliche Verfügbarkeit („pervasiveness")
- Vollumfängliche zeitliche Verfügbarkeit
- Informationsvielfalt („information richness")
- Einfache Handhabung („easy-of-use")
- Individualisierung („**Customization**")

Hinzu kommen Funktionen, die das Internet insbesondere auch für die Geschäftswelt hoch interessant werden lassen. Dabei spielt insbesondere die **Konnektivität** eine große Rolle, also dass mit der Anbindung an das Netz der Kommunikator ein extrem hohes Ausmaß an Verbindung („Konnektion") zu anderen Unternehmen oder Personen erreichen kann:

- Transaktionsfähigkeit: Das Internet bietet die Möglichkeit, Servicefunktionen wie z. B. Beratung, Bestellung, Beschwerdenbearbeitung in den Dialog mit dem Kunden zu integrieren. Zahlreiche Informationsprodukte können über das Netz heute sogar schon ausgeliefert werden (z. B. Software, Informationsdienste, Musikstücke).
- Geringer Distributionsaufwand: Die Verbreitung der Informationen ist zu extrem niedrigen Kosten möglich.
- Hohe Internationalität: Die Anwendungen können ohne großen Aufwand einem weltweiten Publikum angeboten werden.
- Intranet-Fähigkeit: Durch Passwortschutz können geschlossene Benutzergruppen erzeugt werden, z. B. die Mitarbeiterschaft eines Unternehmens.

Die **Nutzung des Internets** hat sich in den vergangenen Jahren stürmisch entwickelt und bewegt sich in Richtung von einer Stunde täglich im Durchschnitt. Damit hat es längst die Nutzungszeiten der Printmedien hinter sich gelassen. Es ist verständlich, dass die Verantwortlichen der klassischen Printmedien dieser Entwicklung mit Sorge entgegensehen und große Anstrengungen unternehmen, mit der Entwicklung Schritt zu halten, z. B. durch attraktive Angebote im Internet (z. B.: elektronische Zeitung – „**E-Paper**") oder anderer elektronischer Produkte (z. B.: Hörbücher).

Das Internet steht im Grunde erst am Anfang der Entwicklung. Insbesondere im Hinblick auf die **Multimedialität des Netzes** wird sich eine Entwicklung von der momentan eher statischen Darstellung der Inhalte (Text, Bild) in Richtung Bewegtbild, Audio und 3-D-Welten einstellen. Dadurch wird das Internet zur multimedialen Plattform, auf der grundsätzlich alle Medien, auch das Fernsehen, transportiert werden können.

Zentrale Trends im Internetmarkt

- Das Internet ist inzwischen erfolgreich in allen Bevölkerungsschichten etabliert. Seine Nutzung erfolgt gleichermaßen als Informations-, Unterhaltungs- und Kommunikationsmedium. Es entwickelt sich mehr und mehr zum normalen Medium, bei dem sich die Struktur der Nutzerschaft immer mehr der Gesamtbevölkerung angleicht.
- Die heimische Nutzung sowie die berufliche Online-Nutzung am Arbeits- und Ausbildungsplatz wird selbstverständlich.
- Das Internet spielt im Einkaufsverhalten der Menschen eine zunehmend wichtige Rolle. Fast alle Internetnutzer haben sich schon einmal über Produkte im Internet informiert. Drei Viertel haben im Internet eingekauft.
- Das Internet wird sich immer mehr als zentrales Informationsmedium für tagesaktuelle Informationen etablieren. Dabei werden vor allem die Internet-Auftritte der etablierten Medienunternehmen genutzt.
- Mit der zunehmenden Internet-Präsenz der deutschen Bevölkerung wird die Werbewirtschaft zunehmend im Internet aktiv, womit sich das Medium zum normalen und professionellen Werbemedium entwickelt.
- Nicht von der Hand zu weisen sind allerdings zunehmende Sättigungserscheinungen bei den Konsumenten, die von der Fülle der Informationen und dem Zwang zur aktiven Suchhaltung überfordert sein könnten. Immer wichtiger werden daher leistungsfähige Navigationssysteme.
- Zunehmend wichtig werden Communities und Plattformen, auf denen sich große Menschenmengen begegnen. Als besonderes interessant empfindet der (junge) Nutzer die Möglichkeit, selbst erstellte Inhalte einer großen Öffentlichkeit zu präsentieren ❶.
- Das Internet wird sich zu einem „**Hypernet**" und „Überall-Medium" entwickeln, das ein immer und überall verfügbares Netz darstellt, das alle erdenklichen Inhalte zugänglich macht und über hochqualitative Endgeräte voll mobil sein wird.

❶ Dieses Phänomen wird als **user generated content** bezeichnet, ein Phänomen, das mit dem Begriff **Web 2.0** belegt wird. Beispiele sind Online-Lexika (z. B. wikipedia), Foto-Communities (z. B. flickr.com), Internet-Communities (z. B. myspace.com), Blogging-Dienste (z. B. blogger.com), Videoclip-Börsen (z. B. youtube.com) oder Business-Kontakt-Plattformen (z. B. xing.de)

Konzepte der Internetunternehmen

- Alle Unternehmen, so auch die Medienunternehmen, die sich im Internet bewegen, stehen in einer extremen Wettbewerbssituation. Die Märkte sind transparent (z. B. Preisvergleiche), die Eintrittsbarrieren für neue Unternehmen sind niedrig. Das Kundenverhalten verändert sich durch den höheren Informationsstand und eine steigende Nachfragermacht nachhaltig, vor allem nimmt die Kundenloyalität und die Kundenbindung immer mehr ab.
- Damit verbunden steigt die Komplexität und Innovationsgeschwindigkeit. Die Märkte zersplittern in immer kleinere Teile („**Fragmentierung**").
- Notwendig sind Geschäftsmodelle, die langfristig tragfähig sind. Dabei kann man z. B. eine Integrationsstrategie verfolgen, bei der das Unternehmen die horizontale oder vertikale Integration durch Kooperation oder Fusion anstrebt. Exemplarisch hierfür können große Medienunternehmen wie Microsoft, Google oder Time Warner gelten. Alle diese Unternehmen versuchen, auch im Internet stark vertreten zu sein.

3.5.2 TIME-Branche

Definition

❶ Telekommunikation (T) und Informationstechnik (I) werden auch zum „ITK-Markt" zusammen gefasst.

Typisches Kennzeichen der Medienentwicklung in der digitalen Welt ist das Zusammenwachsen bzw. die Konvergenz des Mediensektors mit denjenigen Industrien, die im Hinblick auf die Erzeugung von Medienprodukten in einem logischen **Wertschöpfungsverbund** stehen. Diese Industrien werden unter dem **Dachbegriff TIME-Branche** zusammengefasst. Im Einzelnen ist darunter zu verstehen ❶:

- T = **Telekommunikation**:(1) Hersteller von nachrichtentechnischen Geräten. (2) Bereitstellung der Netzinfrastruktur: Telefon, Kabel, Satellit, Terrestrik. (3) Fernmelde- und Telekommunikationsdienste: Netzbetreiber (Festnetz und Mobilnetz), Anbieter von Dienstleistungen im Telekommunikationsbereich. Internet-, Online- und Datendienste.
- I = **Informationstechnik**: (1) Hardware: Computertechnik, PC, Workstations, Notebooks, Büromaschinen, Datenverarbeitungsgeräten. Hersteller: z. B. HP, IBM, Dell. (2) Software: Hersteller z. B. Microsoft, SAP, Oracle. (3) IT-Dienstleistungen: z. B., Accenture, T-Systems (4) Zulieferindustrie: vor allem elektronische Bauelemente, Hersteller z. B. Infinion, AMD.
- M = **Medien**: Gestaltung von inhaltlichen Angeboten (1) monomedial: TV, Radio, Kino, Spiele, Musik, Zeitungen, Zeitschriften, Bücher; (2) multimedial aufbereitete Inhalte.
- E = **Unterhaltungselektronik** (Entertainment): TV- und Radiogeräte, Rekorder, MP3-Geräte, DVD-Player, Spielekonsolen etc.

Wirtschaftliche Bedeutung

❷ „Prognosen für Deutschland gehen davon aus, dass im Jahr 2010 55 Prozent der Arbeitsplätze im Bereich Informationstechnologie – inklusive Medien – bestehen werden. Waren um die Jahrhundertwende noch rund 40 Prozent der Bevölkerung mit Ackerbau und Viehzucht beschäftigt, gefolgt von industrieller Produktion, ist nun das Zeitalter der TIME-Industrie Realität" (Scholz/Stein/Eisenbeis, S. 183).

Die TIME-Branche wies 2004 ein **Umsatzvolumen** von 200 Mrd. Euro auf. Es verteilte sich auf die Teilbranchen wie folgt:

- Medien: 57 Mrd.
- IT: 131 Mrd.
- Unterhaltungselektronik: 12 Mrd. Euro

Damit trägt dieser Sektor ca. zehn Prozent zur Wertschöpfung der Volkswirtschaft bei. Immer mehr Beschäftigte werden dort arbeiten ❷.

Publizistische Bedeutung

Die Medien können in der digitalen Welt der Zukunft nicht mehr ohne den Bezug zur TIME-Branche erklärt werden. Wichtigstes Merkmal ist das Entstehen neuer Medienprodukte, die das **kommunikative Verhalten** der Menschen **nachhaltig verändern**. Durch technische Unterstützung der Telekommunikation, der Informationstechnik und der Unterhaltungselektronik findet eine dramatische Erweiterung – man könnte sagen: „Entgrenzung" – der bisherigen Nutzungsformen der Medien statt.

TIME-Branche

Telekommunikation („T")

- Marktvolumen: Gesamtumsatz (BITKOM 2010): 66,1 Mrd. Euro. Tendenz: kontinuierlich mäßig fallend. Umsatzverteilung: (1) TK-Infrastruktur 5,8 Mrd. Euro. (2) TK-Endgeräte 4,9 Mrd. Euro. (3) TK-Dienste 55,4 Mrd. Euro.
- Konzernumsatz der Deutschen Telekom 61,7 Mrd. Euro; davon in Deutschland 26,4 Mrd. Euro.
- Netzinfrastruktur: Telefonanschlüsse 38,91 Mio., davon Analoganschlüsse 21,65 Mio.
- Beschäftigte 2007: 204.900, davon Deutsche Telekom AG 148.900
- Verkehrsvolumen über klassische Telefon-, Kabel- und IP-basierte Netze: 186,7 Mrd. Minuten, davon Deutsche Telekom 95 Mrd. Minuten. Tendenz: kontinuierlich leicht steigend.
- Teilnehmer in deutschen Mobilfunknetzen 107,25 Mio. Penetration 130,8 % (d. h. auf jeden Einwohner entfallen etwa 1,3 SIM-Karten). Sprachverkehrsvolumen (aus Mobilfunknetzen abgehender Verkehr) 86,14 Mrd. Minuten. Anzahl der versendeten SMS: 27,8 Mrd.
- Hohe Konkurrenz sorgt für geringe Preismargen.

IT-Branche („I")

- Gesamtumsatz 67,1 Mrd. Euro. Verteilung: (1) IT-Hardware 19,1 Mrd. Euro. (2) Software 15,0 Mrd. Euro. (3) IT-Services 33,0 Mrd. Euro.
- IT-Hardware (PCs, Server, Storage und Druckersysteme etc.): Große Hardware- Produzenten: Fujitsu, Hewlett-Packard.
- Software: Standard-Software-Unternehmen Deutschland Top 3 (2003): SAP, Microsoft Deutschland, Oracle Deutschland.
- Microsoft Deutschland Umsatz 2008: 60,42 Mrd. Dollar.
- IT-Services: Wichtige IT-Service-Unternehmen: T-Systems, IBM Deutschland, Siemens Business Services, Accenture.
- Beschäftigung: 556.000, davon (1) IT-Hardware 38.000; (2) Software und IT-Services 518.000.
- Hohe Nachfrage nach IT-Projekten.
- Starker Wettbewerb sorgt für geringe Preismargen.

Consumer Electronics („E")

- Umsatzvolumen Deutschland: 13,4 Mrd. Euro. Davon digitale CE: 12,7 Mrd. Euro.
- Verteilung Absatz und Umsatz ausgewählter CE-Bereiche: (1) TV-Geräte 7,6 Mio. Stück / 6,0 Mrd. Euro; (2) DVD Player und Recorder 3,8 Mio. Stück / 0,5 Mrd. Euro; (3) Set-Top-Boxen 4,3 Mio. Stück / 0,4 Mrd. Euro; (4) Digitale Fotoapparate 9,3 Mio. Stück / 2,2 Mrd. Euro; (5) MP3 Player und portable Videoplayer (MPEG4) 7,8 Mio. Stück / 0,6 Mrd. Euro; (6) Spielekonsolen 4,6 Mio. Stück / 1,0 Mrd. Euro (7) Auto-Navigationssysteme 4,3 Mio. Stück / 0,9 Mrd. Euro.
- Produktsegmente mit deutlich-positiver Umsatzentwicklung seit 2005: TV-Geräte, digitale Fotoapparate, Spielekonsolen, Auto-Navigationsgeräte. Produktsegmente mit deutlich-negativer Umsatzentwicklung seit 2005: DVD Player und Recorder, MP3 Player und portable Videoplayer (MPEG4).
- Hersteller von Unterhaltungselektronik, Marktführer Deutschland: Philips, Samsung, Panasonic, Sony
- Einzelhandel (2004): 10.300 Unternehmen (traditioneller Facheinzelhandel, Fachmarktunternehmen, Handwerksbetriebe).
- Beschäftigte in der Herstellung von elektronischen Gebrauchsgütern (incl. Elektrohaushaltsgeräte): 106.000.
- Ausstattungsgrad der privaten Haushalte mit Geräten der Unterhaltungselektronik: Fernsehgeräte 97,0 %; Pay-TV-Decoder/d-box 35,7 %; MP3-Player ohne Radio 38,9 %; DVD-Player (nur Abspielgerät) 64,1 %; PC 61,1 %; Notebook 32,2 %.
- Hohe Konkurrenz sorgt für geringe Preismargen. 2005 bis 2010 in den meisten Produktsegmenten deutlicher Preisverfall.

In der Nacht vom 14. auf den 15. April 1912 sinkt das „unsinkbare" Luxuspassagierschiff Titanic im Nordatlantik. Ein junger Funker nimmt schwache Signale auf: „S.S. Titanic auf Eisberg gelaufen. Sinken schnell."

Bedeutung des Telefons

Von größter Bedeutung für die Menschheit war die Erfindung der Fernübertragung von Signalen, die Telekommunikation. Nach dem Start im Jahre 1880 verbreitete sich das **Telefon** rasant. Das Telefon war ursprünglich nur zur Übertragung von Sprache und Texten geeignet, heute kann es im Grunde alle medialen Formen übertragen: Bild, Daten oder Video.

In den Jahren seit 1880 hat das **Medium Telefon** eine enorme Bedeutung erlangt: Es wurde binnen weniger Jahrzehnte zum wichtigsten technischen Kommunikationsmedium in Hinblick auf die Verbindung von Mensch zu Mensch. Damit wurde das menschliche Zusammenleben auf eine neue Stufe gestellt, das Telefon ist heute überall im Einsatz, v. a. dank moderner Mobiltechnik. Mit der **Digitalisierung** wird das Telefon mehr und mehr zu einem **Multifunktionsgerät**.

Konvergenz

Entscheidendes Merkmal der TIME-Branche ist „das auf dem universalen Netzwerkprotokoll TCP/IP basierende Internet, das erstmals die Möglichkeit der digitalen Übertragung von Informationen zwischen dem Telekommunikations-, Informationstechnologie- und Mediensektor eröffnet" (Keuper/Hans, S. 42). Damit sind vernetzte Wege vorhanden bzw. im Entstehen, über die rechnergestützt Informationen sowohl im Hinblick auf die Anwendungen als auch auf den Ort flexibel und vor allem multimedial übertragen werden können. Erforderlich sind allerdings Endgeräte, die fähig sind, die technologische Integration aller Medienquellen sicher zu stellen.

Die TIME-Branche wächst zusammen, ein Phänomen, das man als **Konvergenz** bezeichnet. Konvergenz ist dadurch gekennzeichnet, dass es zu einer strukturellen Verbindung bislang getrennter Märkte kommt, was zu neuen Produkten und Systemen führt. Konvergenz bringt die starke Annäherung und wechselseitige Durchdringung des Medienmarktes mit den Märkten der Telekommunikation, Informationstechnologie und Unterhaltungselektronik. Es entsteht ein neuer gemeinsamer Markt, den man im Verbund sehen muss, da sich die Grenzen zwischen den ehemals getrennten Sektoren auflösen.

Ein hervorstechendes Merkmal der Konvergenz ist das Entstehen **neuer innovativer Produkte**, die ohne Medienbruch – also ohne dass man beim Wechsel von einer Anwendung in die andere mit neuer Technik arbeiten muss – gehandhabt werden können, wie z. B. Fernsehen über das Internet oder Video on Demand. Ein solchermaßen zusammenwachsender TIME-Markt erbringt alle Informations-, Kommunikations- und Unterhaltungsleistungen in integrierter Form und macht Multimedia möglich. Es entsteht ein neuer „Multimedia-Markt", der die bisherige mediale Produktlandschaft revolutioniert.

Zentrale Trends der TIME-Branche

- Was die Marktpotenziale anbelangt, gibt es gegenläufige Entwicklungen. Teilbereichen mit fulminanten Wachstumschancen stehen andere Bereiche mit u. U. starken Schrumpfungstendenzen gegenüber. So ist im Teilmarkt der Telekommunikation mittelfristig eine deutlich Umsatz-Schrumpfung bei Festnetzgesprächen festzustellen, eine Stagnation in der individuellen Mobilkommunikation, während mobile Daten- und Multimediadienste als treibende Kraft im Markt wirken. In der Summe zeigt der Markt für Telekommunikationsdienste eine Stagnationstendenz. Ein echter Umsatz-Boom ist demgegenüber bei Festnetz-Datendiensten durch die Zunahme der DSL-Anschlüsse zu verzeichnen.
- Der zentrale treibende Faktor für alle Teilbereiche ist der weitere Ausbau der Netze zu einem hoch leistungsfähigen Breitbandnetz.
- Die Festnetz-Telefonie nimmt zugunsten der Mobiltelefonie ab. Langfristig wird nur Mobiltelefonie übrig bleiben. Das Mobiltelefon entwickelt sich dabei zu einem herausragenden Multimedia-Produkt, das zahlreiche Funktionen wie Telefonie, Organizer, MP3, Mailing, Foto und Video in sich vereinigt.
- Führende IT-Konzerne wie Intel, Dell, HP oder Microsoft dringen mit ihren Produkten immer stärker in benachbarte Märkte ein, insbesondere in den attraktiven Markt der Unterhaltungselektronik.
- Der heimische PC entwickelt sich zur Empfangs-, Speicher- und Steuerzentrale für die digitale Unterhaltung.
- Neue Speicherformate (HD-DVD, Blu-Ray) spielen eine große Rolle für die Entfaltung weiterer Konvergenzpotenziale.
- IPTV ist ein Wachstumsmarkt, wobei die Dynamik von der DSL-/VDSL-Verbreitung abhängt. Ein schneller Durchbruch ist nicht zu erwarten.
- Ein sehr großes Potenzial hat Handy-TV. Hemmnisse sind fehlende Entscheidungen über die Vergabe der Sendefrequenzen und mangelnde Kooperation der Beteiligten (Netzbetreiber, Sender).
- In der Unterhaltungselektronik dauert der Wechsel von der analogen zur digitalen Technik noch längere Zeit. Die Umrüstung der Endgeräte hat einen hohen Zeitbedarf.
- In der Unterhaltungselektronik, aber auch bei Computern, ist der Trend besonders interessant, dass sich als neuer Vertriebsweg mittlerweile die Discounter wie Aldi oder Tchibo etabliert haben.

Konzepte der TIME-Unternehmen

Vor diesem Hintergrund ist es für alle Akteure reizvoll, **Allianzen** und **Netzwerke** bis hin zu Fusionen mit Akteuren in anderen Segmenten der TIME-Branche einzugehen. Dies ist insbesondere im Zuge des Trends zur **Globalisierung** wichtig und notwendig. Insofern gibt es einen starken Anreiz, große internationale Konzerne zu bilden und auszubauen. Die **Internationalisierung** ist insofern eine zentrale Begleiterscheinung der Konvergenz in der TIME-Branche. Ziel des Zusammenwachsens ist es, Kosten einzusparen und die Leistung durch Schaffung internationaler Netzwerke zu steigern. Für alle Akteure ist es attraktiv, sich entweder selbst zu Multimedia-Unternehmen weiter zu entwickeln oder in entsprechenden Netzwerken mitzuwirken.

Aufgaben und Übungen, Literaturhinweise

Aufgaben und Übungen zur Geschichte der Medien

1. Beschreiben Sie Aufgaben und Kennzeichen des Nachrichtenwesens in der Antike, im Mittelalter, in der Industrialisierung und in der Moderne.
2. Stellen Sie die Entwicklung der Schrift in einer Präsentation dar.
3. Weshalb hat die Erfindung Gutenbergs die Buchherstellung revolutioniert? Welche kulturellen und gesellschaftlichen Auswirkungen waren damit verbunden?
4. Erläutern Sie die wichtigsten Verfahrensschritte zur Buchherstellung von Gutenberg bis zur heutigen Satz- und Drucktechnik.
5. Suchen Sie nach Beispielen für Staaten, in denen die Pressefreiheit abgeschafft wurde.
6. Erstellen Sie eine Übersicht zur Entwicklung des Rundfunks und des Fernsehens im 20. Jahrhundert.
7. Wie konnte eine Verringerung der benötigten Übertragungsleitungen in der elektrischen Telegrafie erreicht werden?
8. Beschreiben Sie die Funktion des Glasfaserkabels.
9. Stellen Sie Daten zusammen, welche die Entwicklung der Filmindustrie als bedeutenden Wirtschaftsfaktor dokumentieren.

Aufgaben und Übungen zu den einzelnen Medienmärkten

1. Erstellen Sie eine Informationsgrafik, aus der die Anteile der Erlöse der einzelnen Medien-Teilmärkte ersichtlich sind.
2. Überprüfen Sie, inwieweit Ihre persönliche Mediennutzung vom Durchschnitt der Bevölkerung abweicht.
3. Listen Sie zu jedem Mediensegment (Tageszeitungen, Wochenzeitungen, Publikumszeitschriften, Fernsehen, Radio etc.) drei Beispiele für Werbeträger auf.
4. Erstellen Sie ein Text-Dokument zum Thema „E-Paper".
5. Suchen Sie nach Argumenten, warum die Internationalisierung im Zeitschriftenmarkt eine zentrale Marketingstrategie darstellt.
6. Überprüfen Sie, wie Ihre eigene Einstellung zur Nutzung von Hörbüchern aussieht. Begründen Sie Ihr Verhalten.
7. Nehmen Sie Stellung zum Thema „Entwicklung des Buches im digitalen Zeitalter".
8. Ermitteln Sie für eine Gruppe von Gleichaltrigen das Spektrum des Musikgeschmacks durch eine Befragung. Beurteilen Sie das Ergebnis vor dem Hintergrund der gängigen Musikformate im Radio.
9. Erstellen Sie einen Aufsatz zum Thema „Die gesellschaftlichen Funktionen des öffentlich-rechtlichen Rundfunks".
10. Analysieren Sie einen Kino- oder TV-Film, den Sie gerade gesehen haben, und zwar darauf hin, aus welcher Perspektive das dort Gezeigte dargestellt wurde.
11. Stellen Sie die Vor- und Nachteile von legalen Musik-Downloads dar.
12. Machen Sie eine Umfrage unter Gleichaltrigen und fragen Sie danach, wie flexibel die Befragten auf Preissenkungen für Musik-Produkte (CD, DVD, Download) reagieren würden.
13. Stellen Sie die Vorteile des Internet dar und geben für jeden Punkt ein Anwendungsbeispiel aus der Praxis.

Literaturhinweise

Gläser, Martin: Medienmanagement, 2. Aufl., München 2010 (Vahlen). Dort finden sich auch alle statistischen Nachweise zu den Zahlenangaben sowie weitere ausführliche Literaturhinweise zu den einzelnen Medien. Zum Markt für Video- und Computerspiele vgl. v. a. auch Wirtz (s. u.).

Bremenfeld, Eckhard/*Kapalla*, Ralf/*Knapp*, Holger/*Tohermes*, Kurt/*Veeh*, Winfried: Fachwissen Zeitungs- und Zeitschriftenverlag, 2. Aufl., Düsseldorf 1998 (Springer-VDI)

Breyer-Mayländer, Thomas/*Seeger*, Christof: Verlage vor neuen Herausforderungen, Berlin 2004 (ZV)

Bruhn, Manfred: Unternehmens- und Marketingkommunikation, München 2005 (Vahlen)

Burckhardt, Martin: Metamorphosen von Raum und Zeit, 2. Aufl., Frankfurt/M. 1997 (Campus)

Burckhardt, Martin: Vom Geist der Maschine, Frankfurt/M., New York 1999 (Campus)

Faßler, Manfred/*Halbach*, Wulf R. (Hrsg.): Geschichte der Medien, München 1998 (W. Fink)

Godau, Marion/*Polster*, Bernd: Design Lexikon Deutschland, 2. Aufl., Köln 2002 (DuMont)

Heinold, Ehrhardt F./*Spiller*, Ulrich (2004): Der Buchhandel in der Informationsgesellschaft, in: Aus Politik und Zeitgeschichte, 15. März 2004, B 12/13, S. 30-38

Hiebel, Hans H./*Hiebler*, Heinz/*Kogler*, Karl/*Walitsch*, Herwig: Große Medienchronik, München 1999 (W. Fink)

Kerlen, Dietrich: Lehrbuch der Buchverlagswirtschaft, Stuttgart 2003 (Hauswedell)

Matt, Bernd Jürgen: Printtechniken im Wandel, in: Friedrichsen, Mike (Hrsg.): Printmanagement, Baden-Baden 2004, S. 17-26 (Nomos)

Menhard, E./*Treede*, T.: Die Zeitschrift, Konstanz 2004 (UVK)

Müller-Lietzkow, Jörg./*Bouncken*, Ricarda B./*Seufert*, Wolfgang: Gegenwart und Zukunft der Computer- und Videospielindustrie in Deutschland, Dornach 2006 (Entertainment Media)

PwC - PriceWaterhouseCoopers: German Entertainment and Media Outlook: 2011-2015, Frankfurt am Main 2011 (Fachverlag Moderne Wirtschaft)

Schanze, Helmut (Hrsg.): Handbuch der Mediengeschichte, Stuttgart 2001 (Kröner)

Scholz, Christian/*Stein*, Volker/*Eisenbeis*, Uwe: Die TIME-Branche, München, Mering 2001 (Rainer Hampp)

Sjurts, Insa (Hrsg.): Gabler Lexikon Medienwirtschaft, 2. Aufl., Wiesbaden 2011 (Gabler)

Wilke, Jürgen: Grundzüge der Medien- und Kommunikationsgeschichte. Von den Anfängen bis ins 20. Jahrhundert, Köln, Weimar, Wien 2000 (Böhlau)

Wirtz, Bernd W.: Medien- und Internetmanagement, 7. Aufl., Wiesbaden 2011 (Gabler).

Zerdick, Axel et al.: Die InternetÖkonomie, 3. Aufl., Berlin, Heidelberg 2001 (Springer)

B

4 Elementares Gestalten. 192
5 Typografie 228
6 Bild 276
7 Grafik. 324
8 Bewegtbild. 350
9 Animation 384
10 Audio. 404
11 Druck. 454
12 Multimedia 484
13 Internet 514
14 Medieninformatik 572

Gestaltung und Produktion

Medien tauchen heute selten isoliert auf – sie bilden vielmehr einen Verbund einzelner Elemente. Zeitungs- und Internetseiten enthalten Text und Bild, das Fernsehen zeigt Informationen in Bild-, Grafik und vielen anderen Formaten.

Im zweiten Teil dieses Lehrbuches sollen die in den Medien verwendeten Bausteine näher betrachtet werden. Die Gestaltungsregeln und -spielräume sind entscheidend für eine erfolgreiche Medienproduktion.

In den Kapiteln 4 und 5 werden gestalterische Grundlagen gelegt, die für die verschiedensten Medienbausteine von Bedeutung sind. Ebensolche Bausteine sind das Bild und die Grafik, beschrieben in den Kapiteln 6 und 7. Werden Bild und Grafik bewegt, ergeben sich Bewegtbild und Animation, in Kapitel 8 und 9. Analog hierzu werden Töne, deren Produktion und Bearbeitung in Kapitel 10 behandelt.

Diese zunächst isoliert zu sehenden Medienbausteine finden in Druck- und Multimediaproduktionen Ihre Anwendung. In Kapitel 11 und 12 werden dann die Bausteine zusammengefügt. In unserem modernen Kommunikationszeitalter nehmen darüber hinaus noch das Internet in Kapitel 13 und die damit verbundene Medieninformatik in Kapitel 14 einen hohen Stellenwert ein.

Webcode:
B0400

Für weitere Infos zu diesem Kapitel mit dem Smartphone einfach QR-Code scannen oder auf www.medien-verstehen.de den Webcode eingeben.

4 Elementares Gestalten

Gestaltung hat etwas mit der Gestalt zu tun und ein wesentliches Element der **Gestalt** ist die **Form**. Die elementare Gestaltungslehre beschäftigt sich mit Formen, Formelementen, deren Anordnung, sowie deren Beziehung zueinander und der damit verbundenen Wirkung auf den Betrachter. So wird aus dem elementaren, dem grundsätzlichen Gestalten, ein Gestalten mit Elementen.

Mit Hilfe verschiedener Parameter bekommen wir schließlich einen Einblick in das Regelwerk der Gestaltung. Zu diesen Parametern gehören neben den Formen auch die Farben und Buchstaben, sowie die Schrift – einige der wichtigsten visuellen Hilfsmittel, mit denen wir unsere Nachrichten und Botschaften verbreiten.

In diesem Zusammenhang verweisen wir auf Kapitel 5 Typografie (Gestalten mit Schrift), dem wir aufgrund seiner Wichtigkeit ein eigenes Kapitel gewidmet haben.

4.1 Grundsätze der Gestaltung

Jeder Mensch gestaltet täglich sein persönliches Umfeld. Lehrer gestalten ihren Unterricht, Architekten konstruieren Gebäude und Onkel Franz entwirft mal eben eine Glückwunschkarte am heimischen Computer. Nicht vergessen sollte man die gestaltenden Konditoren, die Friseure und Modeschöpfer, die Schreiner und viele mehr.

Bei der Gestaltung handelt es sich um einen **Schaffensprozess**, einen Prozess, welcher im Idealfall am Ende ein Ergebnis zum Vorschein bringt.
Im Mittelpunkt des Schaffens steht jedoch nicht nur das Ergebnis, sondern vor allem auch der Weg dort hin. Diesen Weg bezeichnet man auch als den **Gestaltungsprozess** oder den **Entwurfsprozess**.

Doch wie funktioniert Gestaltung? Wie macht man sich auf den Weg, eine interessante Glückwunschkarte, ein spannendes Plakat oder eine fesselnde Internetseite zu entwickeln?

➲ **Gestaltung braucht Regeln!**

Vor allem in einer Zeit, in der immer schnellere Computer in die Büros und heimischen Wohnzimmer einziehen, wird ein gestalterisches Regelwerk immer wichtiger! Die Tatsache, daß sich auch die technischen Geräte permanent verändern (Smartphones, Tablett-PCs) verleihen diesem Anspruch Nachdruck.

- Warum verwendet Onkel Franz für die Glückwunschkarte als Hintergrundfarbe ein helles Grün mit dunkler Schrift darauf?
- Welche Farben passen zueinander?
- Welche Formen erzeugen Spannung?
- Welche Schrift sieht interessant aus?

Hierbei gilt allein der Grundsatz: „Der Zweck heiligt die Mittel!"
Aber er „heiligt nicht nur die Mittel", sondern auch das gesamte Erscheinungsbild eines Medienproduktes. Dies bedeutet, dass die Gestaltung durch den Verwendungszweck bestimmt wird. Das Aussehen hat sich der **Funktion** unterzuordnen ❶.

Oftmals wird die Gestaltung aber mit der Kunst verwechselt – man gestaltet „schöne Dinge". Die Kunst jedoch definiert sich durch ein freies, emotional gesteuertes Schaffen ❷.

Die folgenden Kapitel sollen einen Einblick in das Regelwerk der elementaren Gestaltungslehre geben.

❶ **Form follows function:**
„Die Form eines Gebäudes oder eines Gegenstandes leitet sich von seiner Funktion ab."
Gestaltungsgrundsatz aus dem 18. Jahrhundert, erstmals schriftlich vom US-amerikanischen Architekten Louis Sullivan formuliert.

❷ Gestaltung ist zweckorientiert, Kunst ist zweckfrei!

4.2 Sehen und wahrnehmen

Wer die Regeln der elementaren Gestaltungslehre verstehen will, muss sich zunächst mit den Gesetzmäßigkeiten der **Wahrnehmung** auseinandersetzen.

➲ **Die Wahrnehmung bezeichnet im Allgemeinen eine bewusste Informationsaufnahme. Einen Vorgang, bei dem wir eine Sache gedanklich, seelisch oder physisch verinnerlichen, nachdem wir ihn mit unseren Sinnesorganen aufgenommen haben.**

Ein Beispiel:
Bei einem Waldspaziergang kann man das Gezwitscher der Vögel hören, man riecht den Duft der Fichten und Tannen, man fühlt den Wind, der über das Gesicht streicht und man sieht, wenn man Glück hat, Füchse und Rehe auf ihrer Pirsch.

Der Eindruck vom Hören, Riechen, Fühlen und Sehen wird von unserem Gehirn verarbeitet und einem Ergebnis zugeordnet: Der Waldspaziergang vermittelt ein positives Gefühl. Man nimmt seine eigene Umgebung als angenehm wahr.

4.2.1 Wahrnehmungskette

Den oben geschilderten Wahrnehmungsvorgang bezeichnet man im Allgemeinen als **Wahrnehmungskette**. Diese beschreibt sechs miteinander verknüpfte Aktionen, welche sich nacheinander direkt beeinflussen und zu einem Wahrnehmungsergebnis führen.

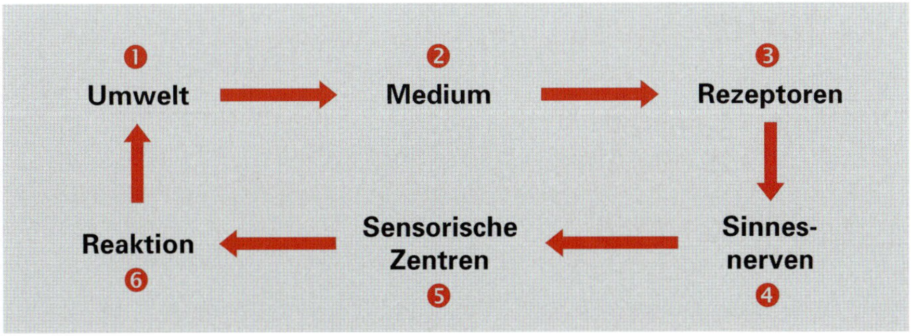

Die Stationen der Wahrnehmungskette im Einzelnen:

1. Die **Umwelt** ist der Ausgangspunkt jeder Wahrnehmung (Aufenthaltsort: Wald).
2. Das **Medium** überträgt die Eigenschaften der Umwelt an den Menschen (der Wind oder die Schallwellen des Vogelgezwitschers).
3. Die **Rezeptoren** sind Sinneszellen des Körpers, welche vom Medium direkt gereizt werden und die Information weitergeben an das Sinnesorgan (das Medium Licht reizt die Sinneszellen des Auges).
4. Die **Sinnesnerven** leiten die Reize der Sinnesorgane gebündelt weiter an das Gehirn.
5. In die **sensorischen Zentren** im Gehirn münden die Sinnesnerven der Sinnesorgane ein. Hier werden direkte Assoziationen hergestellt, Prozesse wie Erinnern, Erkennen und Kombinieren führen vom Sinneseindruck zur Wahrnehmung (der Waldspaziergang erzeugt bei positiver Grundstimmung zum Wald im Allgemeinen eine positive Wahrnehmung).
6. Das Wahrnehmungsgefühl führt zu einer **Reaktion**, die wiederum die Umwelt beeinflussen und einen neuen Kreislauf auslösen kann.

Für die elementare Gestaltungslehre bedeutet dies, dass die Wahrnehmung keinesfalls isoliert unter dem Aspekt der **Sinnesorgane** betrachtet werden kann. Der Gestalter versucht vielmehr, sich mit Hilfe des Regelwerkes der elementaren Gestaltungslehre in die Wahrnehmungskette einzuklinken und diese an geeigneten Stellen zu beeinflussen. So kann man auf die Umwelt und das Medium einwirken, um schlussendlich eine gewünschte Reaktion, einen Eindruck hervorzurufen.

Ein Beispiel:
Die Einladungskarte zu einem Kindergeburtstagsfest soll Fröhlichkeit und gute Laune zum Ausdruck bringen. Dies gelingt, wenn Gestaltungsregeln hinsichtlich der verwendeten Elemente beachtet werden. Die Wahrnehmungskette wird in Gang gesetzt und erzeugt beim Betrachter der Einladungskarte eine Reaktion (Freude).
Wendet der Gestalter jedoch „falsche Regeln" an, wird die Reaktion eine Andere sein!

Die für den Gesamteindruck der Einladungskarte verantwortlichen Elemente sind:

Die Schriftart
Die Farbigkeit
Die Grundelemente
Die Platzierung

So kann aus der Einladungskarte schnell eine Trauerkarte werden!

4.2.2 Wahrnehmungsarten

Man unterscheidet, ausgehend von den Sinnesorganen, sieben Wahrnehmungsarten:

- Visuelle Wahrnehmung: Sehen (Augen)
- Auditive Wahrnehmung: Hören (Ohren)
- Taktile Wahrnehmung: Tasten, Fühlen (Haut, Hand und Mund)
- Olfaktorische Wahrnehmung: Riechen (Nase)
- Gustatorische Wahrnehmung: Schmecken (Mund, Gaumen und Zunge)
- Kinästhetische Wahrnehmung: Bewegungsempfindung (Sehnen, Muskeln und Gelenke)
- Vestibuläre Wahrnehmung: Gleichgewichtsregulation (Vestibulärapparat)

Von besonderem Interesse ist die **visuelle Wahrnehmung**, da der Mensch die meisten seiner alltäglichen Informationen über das Auge erfasst. Jedoch:

➲ **„Nur" Sehen ist nicht Wahrnehmen!**

Durch das Sehen wird die Wahrnehmungskette in Gang gesetzt und veranlasst uns zu immer neuen Aktionen und Reaktionen. Eine besondere Bedeutung bei jedem Wahrnehmungsvorgang muss man der individuellen Erfahrung des Betrachters zuordnen!

Ein Beispiel:
Wir sehen täglich auf der Armatur unseres Wasserhahnes im Badezimmer die Farben Rot und Blau. Unsere Wahrnehmung verknüpft aufgrund unserer Erfahrung die Farbe Rot mit warmem Wasser und die Farbe Blau mit kaltem Wasser!

4.2.3 Gestaltgesetze

Das Regelwerk der elementaren Gestaltungslehre geht von der visuellen Wahrnehmung als eigentliche Basis aus. Die Grundlage hierzu sind die **Gestaltgesetze**.

➲ **Gestaltgesetze sind Gesetzmäßigkeiten, welche die menschliche Wahrnehmung lenken, beeinflussen oder auch täuschen können(positiv wie negativ).**

Ihren Ursprung haben diese Gesetzmäßigkeiten in der **Gestaltpsychologie** ❶.
Ein guter Gestalter versteht es, die verschiedenen Gestaltgesetze für seine Ziele auszunutzen, ja sogar zu manipulieren.

Optische Täuschungen:
Die Wahrnehmung kann durch Unregelmäßigkeiten im Zusammenspiel von Auge und Gehirn getäuscht werden!

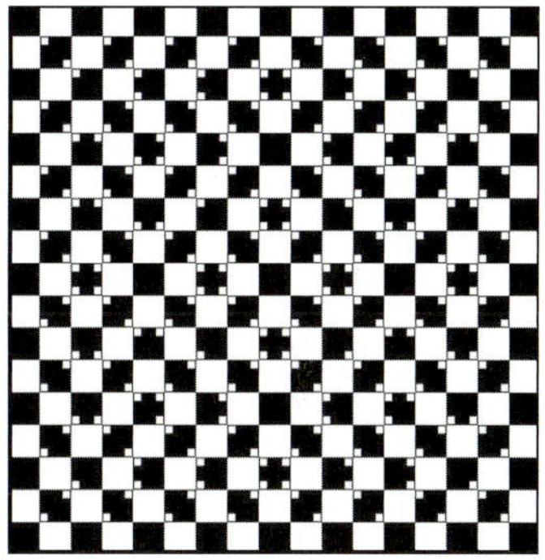

Das Quadrat besteht aus schachbrettartig angeordneten dunklen und hellen Teilquadraten. In einigen der dunklen Teilquadrate sind die Ecken durch kleine helle Quadrate gestört.
Es entsteht der Eindruck, als seien die – nachweislich geraden – Trennlinien zwischen den Teilquadraten wellenförmig gekrümmt.

❶ Gestaltpsychologie:
Wurde zu Beginn des 20. Jahrhunderts von dem Psychologen Max Wertheimer (1880-1943) begründet. Er bezog sich dabei auf eine Begriffsbildung von Christian von Ehrenfels (1859-1932), der 1890 den Aufsatz „Über Gestaltqualitäten" veröffentlicht hatte.
Die Gestaltpsychologie widmet sich der Erforschung des Vorganges, wie der Mensch „Figuren", „Ganzheiten" und „Sinneinheiten" wahrnimmt. In den Gestaltgesetzen kommt die Gestaltpsychologie zur Anwendung.

Figur-Grund-Beziehung

Handelt es sich hier um den liegenden Buchstaben H oder um zwei weiße Rechtecke auf einer schwarzen Fläche?

Die menschliche Wahrnehmung nimmt bei einer Zusammenstellung von Elementen entweder Figurenelemente oder Grundelemente (auch Hintergrundelemente) wahr. Die Figurenelemente sind immer Blickpunktelemente, sollten immer im Mittelpunkt des Betrachters stehen, während die Grundelemente immer einen undifferenzierten Eindruck hinterlassen sollten.

Kann sich unsere Wahrnehmung nicht entscheiden, ob wir eine Figur oder deren Hintergrund sehen, entsteht der unerwünschte Effekt einer Kippfigur. Dies ist meistens bei zielgerichteter Gestaltung ein Hindernis, wenn es darum geht, einen Sachverhalt klar darzustellen.

- **Der Grund (auch Hintergrund) sollte von der eigentlichen Aussage der Figur nicht ablenken!**
- **Kippfiguren und unerwünschte Nebeneffekte sollten vermieden werden!**

Das Gesetz der Nähe

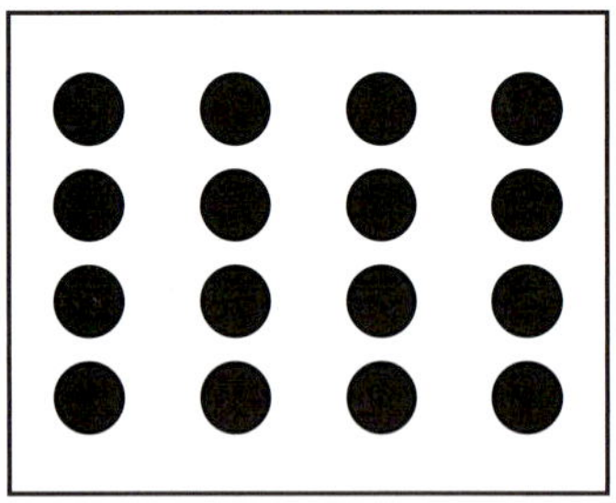

Die Punkte werden als senkrecht angeordnete Reihen wahrgenommen.

Nahe beieinander liegende Elemente werden leichter als Einheit wahrgenommen, als solche, die weit voneinander entfernt sind. Elemente, die nach dem Gesetz der Nähe zueinander angeordnet sind, reduzieren die Komplexität der Gestaltungsobjekte und verstärken die Beziehung der jeweiligen Elemente untereinander. Ein Fehlen der Nähe unterstreicht im Gegensatz dazu die Verschiedenartigkeit der Elemente.

- **Zueinander gehörende Elemente sollten nahe beieinander liegend dargestellt werden!**
- **Nicht zueinander gehörende Elemente sollten in einem ausreichenden Abstand dargestellt werden!**

Das Gesetz der Geschlossenheit

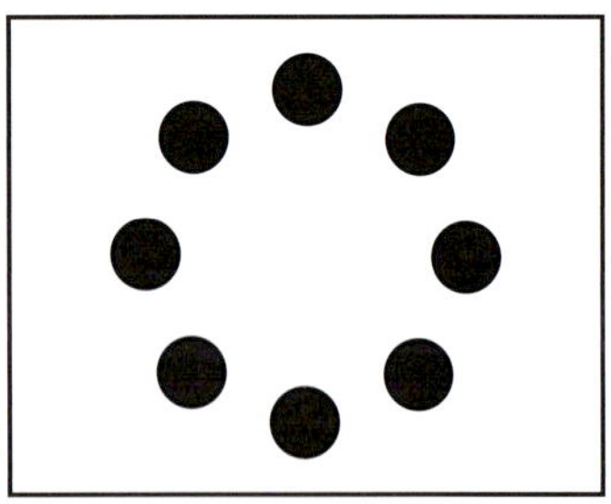

Die Punkte werden zuerst als Kreis wahrgenommen, dann erst als einzelne Elemente.

Einzelne Elemente werden nicht mehr als einzelne Elemente wahrgenommen, sondern als zusammengehöriges, erkennbares Muster. Wir verfügen über eine sehr starke Neigung, Muster wahrzunehmen. Dabei schließen wir bei Bedarf Lücken in vorhandenen Mustern und ergänzen so die Formen zu einem Ganzen. Elemente, die diese Eigenschaft nutzen, wirken in der Regel besser strukturiert, als Elemente, die einer wahllosen Anordnung folgen.

- **Zusammengehörende Elemente können durch ihre Anordnung neue Formen und Zugehörigkeiten erzeugen!**
- **Die wahllose Anordnung von Elementen sollte grundsätzlich vermieden werden!**

Das Gesetz der Kontinuität

Elemente lassen sich sehr gut dadurch gruppieren, dass man Ihnen einen fortlaufenden Charakter verleiht. Werden die Elemente daher auf Linien oder Kurven angeordnet, empfinden wir diese als zusammengehörig.

Wie bereits beim Gesetz der Geschlossenheit bringt auch das Gesetz der Kontinuität das Auge dazu, nicht sichtbare Teilstücke von Linien oder Kurven zu ergänzen. Bei der Anordnung der Elemente ist daher auf einen entsprechend passenden Abstand der Elemente zueinander zu achten.
Das Gesetz ist auch bekannt unter dem Gesetz der guten Fortsetzung.

- **Zueinander gehörende Elemente sollten auf einer Linie oder Kurve liegen. Man nennt dies die Platzierung auf einem Anordnungspfad.**
- **Nicht zueinander gehörende Elemente sollten verschiedene Anordnungspfade haben.**

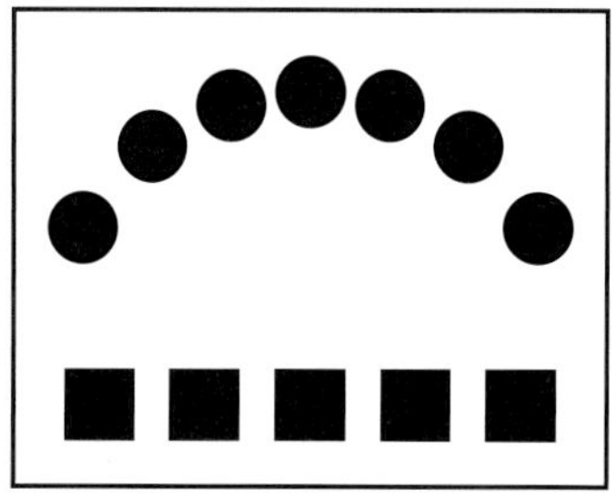

Die Zusammengehörigkeit der Punkte und Quadrate ist aufgrund des jeweiligen Anordnungspfades sehr deutlich erkennbar.

Das Gesetz der Ähnlichkeit

Elemente, die sich ähnlich sind, werden besser als Gruppe erkannt, als Elemente, die sich völlig unterscheiden.

Auch hier finden die zuvor dargestellten Gestaltgesetze Anwendung und werden durch verschiedene Parameter erweitert. So können die Elemente sich nicht nur in der Form ähnlich sein, sondern zum Beispiel auch in Farbe und Größe.

- **Elemente sollten so angeordnet werden, dass ihre Ähnlichkeit auch deren Zusammenghörigkeit entspricht.**
- **Für Elemente, die nicht zusammen gehören, sollten verschiedene Farben, Formen und Größen verwendet werden.**

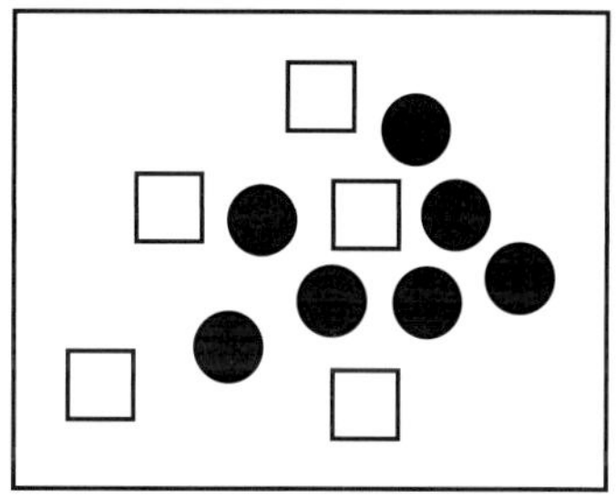

Unsere Wahrnehmung kann sofort die entsprechenden Gruppen erkennen.

Das Gesetz der Prägnanz

Dieses Gesetz besagt, dass einfache Formen besser wahrgenommen werden, als komplexe Gebilde.

Wird unsere Wahrnehmung mit einer Reihe nicht eindeutiger Elemente konfrontiert, entscheiden wir uns immer für die einfachste Zusammenstellungsvariante. Dabei gilt außerdem, dass symetrische Formen schneller erkannt werden.
Bei der Gestaltung von Logos ist dieses Gesetz sehr wichtig, da sich unser Gehirn einfache Formen besser einprägen kann, als komplizierte Formen.
Das Gesetz ist auch bekannt unter dem Gesetz der guten Gestalt oder dem Gesetz der Einfachheit.

- **Die Gestaltungselemente sollten auf ein Minimum beschränkt werden.**
- **Einfache, eventuell sogar symmetrische Formen sind komplexen Gebilden vorzuziehen.**

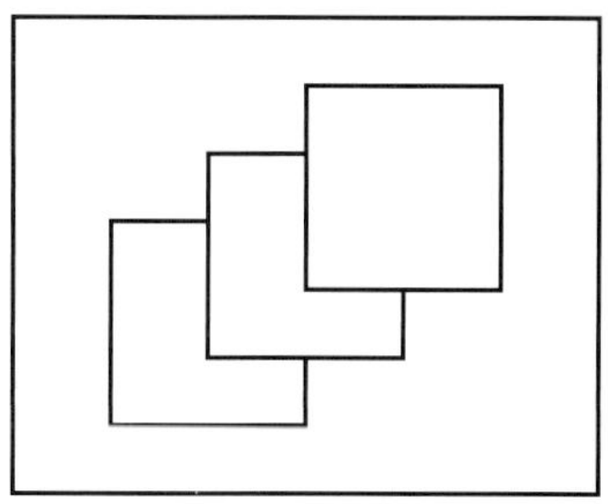

Diese Figuren werden als sich überschneidende Quadrate wahrgenommen. Eine andere Deutung (die hinteren Quadrate könnten auch als „L" gesehen werden) ist sehr unwahrscheinlich.

Das Gesetz der Erfahrung

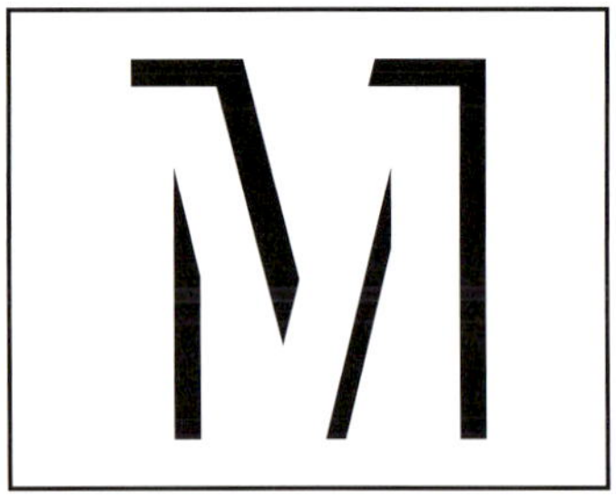

Unsere Wahrnehmung erkennt hier sofort den Buchstaben „M", obwohl Konturlinien fehlen.

Neben den optischen Eigenschaften eines Elementes spielt vor allem unsere individuelle Erfahrung bei der Einordnung ins **Gedächtnis** eine große Rolle.

Die zuvor erläuterten Gestaltgesetze zeigen die Fähigkeit unserer Wahrnehmung, fehlende Elemente und Linien zu ergänzen. Ob die Ergänzung nun korrekt ist, hängt von unserer individuellen Erfahrung und vor allem von unserem Lebensraum ab.

Ein Beispiel:
Chinesen können im Allgemeinen mit dem lateinischen Alphabet, das der deutschen Sprache zugrunde liegt, nicht viel anfangen. Sie kennen die Formen der Buchstaben nicht; sie haben keine Erfahrung im Umgang mit diesen Buchstaben.
Chinesen werden daher das abgebildete „M" nicht erkennen können.

Das Gesetz der **Erfahrung** ist ein sehr wichtiges Gestaltgesetz, da es verantwortlich dafür ist, ob das visuell Wahrgenommene aufgrund unserer individuellen Erfahrung im Gehirn gespeichert wird!

Beispiel Internetauftritt

Die Gestaltung von Medienprodukten aller Art lehnt sich bewusst und unbewusst an die Gestaltgesetze an. Egal, ob Internetauftritt, Plakat oder Postkarte, die Gestaltgesetze sollten erkennbar sein!

❶ Figur-Grund-Beziehung:
Der zurückhaltende Hintergrund der Internetseite lenkt nicht vom Inhalt ab.

❷ Gesetz der Geschlossenheit:
Die Linien und grauen Flächengrenzen einzelne Inhalte auf der Internetseite vom Rest ab.
Diese Inhalte werden daher als Einheit wahrgenommen.

❸ Gesetz der Nähe:
Die einzelnen Rubriken im Navigationsmenü sind räumlich nahe beieinander.
Dadurch zeigt sich das Menü einheitlich und aufgeräumt.

Internetauftritt der Traumpalast-Kinos (www.traumpalast.de)

Beispiel Plakat einer Ausstellung

Ausstellungsplakat eines Schülerwettbewerbes mit dem Motto: „Ich sehe was, was Du nicht siehst"

❶ Gesetz der Kontinuität:
Uns bekannte Buchstaben werden durch ihre sinngemäße Abfolge zu einer Einheit verbunden.
Der Untertitel „Schüler-Kunst in Ausstellung" wird somit trotzdem gut verständlich dargestellt, obwohl die Leserichtung nicht unserem gewohnten Lese-Pfad von links oben nach rechts unten folgt.

❷ Gesetz der Ähnlichkeit:
Die farbigen Kreise sind räumlich weit auf dem Plakat verteilt. Dennoch empfinden wir die Kreise als zusammenghörig, da es keine weiteren Grundformen auf dem Plakat mehr gibt. Die Kreise sind ähnliche Elemente.

❸ Gesetz der Prägnanz:
Wichtige Grundelemente auf dem Plakat sind die farbigen Kreise und der rote Balken auf der linken Seite.
Die Wirkung dieser Elemente ist sehr stark, da es sich um einfachste Grundelemente handelt. Diese werden besser wahrgenommen, als kompliziertere Elemente.

❹ Gesetz der Erfahrung:
„Ich sehe was, was Du nicht siehst" lautet das Motto der Ausstellung.
Das Wort „nicht" wurde auf dem Plakat gespiegelt dargestellt. Unsere Erfahrung mit dem deutschen Wortschatz macht das Wort für uns dennoch leicht verständlich, obwohl es eigentlich in der gewohnten Leserichtung schwer lesbar ist.

4.3 Formelemente der Gestaltung

❶ Aristoteles:
Griechischer Naturwissenschaftler, Philosoph und einflussreicher Denker der abendländischen Geistesgeschichte, 384 - 322 v. Chr.

Aristoteles ❶ hat vor langer Zeit einen Gedanken in Worte gefasst, der meistens der heutigen **Gestaltpsychologie** zugesprochen wird:

➲ **„Das Ganze ist mehr als die Summe seiner Teile."**

Dieser Gedanke lässt sich sehr gut auf die elementare Gestaltungslehre übertragen! Jedes „Ganze" wird zwar aus vielen „Teilen" zusammengesetzt, dabei ergibt das Ganze aber eben mehr, als nur eine Ansammlung von Teilen:

➲ **Das Ganze hat eine Wirkung!**

Ein Beispiel:
Das auf der Seite zuvor abgebildete Plakat soll auf eine Ausstellung aufmerksam machen. Das Plakat wurde aus vielen Teilen zusammengesetzt. Bilder, Texte und so weiter sollen den Betrachter anregen, sich die Ausstellung anzusehen. Dabei darf das Plakat weder traurig noch ausladend wirken. Es soll vielmehr das Thema der Ausstellung präsentieren und eine positive Wirkung auf den Betrachter haben.

Um ein solches Plakat gestalten zu können, ist es daher notwendig, Kenntnisse über die „Teile" zu haben, damit ein wirkungsvolles „Ganzes" am Ende des Entwurfsprozesses steht!

Betrachten wir im Folgenden die „Teile" der elementaren Gestaltungslehre, die sogenannten **Formelemente**.

❷ Mediengestaltung:
Befasst sich mit der Gestaltung von Medien, d.h. neben den alltäglichen Publikationskanälen Radio, Fernsehen, Internet auch Zeitungen, Plakate, Magazine u. a.

❸ Produktgestaltung:
Befasst sich mit der Gestaltung von Produkten des täglichen Gebrauchs, unterscheidbar in Konsumgüter (Rasierapparate, Kaffeemaschinen, Mixer) und Investitionsgüter (Maschinen, die ihrerseits andere Dinge herstellen können, zum Beispiel Verpackungsmaschinen, Druckmaschinen).

Der **Punkt** ist das kleinste Formelement der elementaren Gestaltungslehre. Wird der Punkt fortgesetzt, in die Länge gezogen, entsteht die **Linie**. Die Linie wiederum wird durch deren Breite zur **Fläche**. Durch das Volumen von Flächen entstehen letztlich **Körper**.

In der elementaren Gestaltungslehre werden nach dieser Definition folgende Formelemente unterschieden:

- Der Punkt (dimensionslos)
- Die Linie (eindimensional)
- Die Fläche (zweidimensional)
- Der Körper (dreidimensional)

Punkt, Linie und Fläche werden als allgemeingültige Form- und **Grundelemente** aller Gestaltungsdisziplinen (insbesondere jedoch der **Mediengestaltung** ❷) bezeichnet, während die sehr komplexen Körper eine eigene Betrachtung im Rahmen der **Produktgestaltung** ❸ benötigen. Auf die Körper werden wir daher in den folgenden Abschnitten nicht eingehen.

4.3.1 Der Punkt

In der Mathematik wird der Punkt als nulldimensionales Objekt ohne jede Ausdehnung verstanden. An der Börse steigen oder fallen unsere Aktien um einen Punkt.

Aus dem Spätlateinischen:
punctus = Einstich
Ursprünglich das von einem Schreibgriffel in eine Wachstafel gestochene Satzzeichen.

In der elementaren Gestaltungslehre ist der Punkt als Ursprung der visuellen Gestaltung zu verstehen, das kleinste Element. Im Gegensatz zur Mathematik jedoch hat der gestalterische Punkt eine Ausdehnung, da er sonst nicht sichtbar wäre. Der Punkt ist daher mit Vorsicht als Punkt zu genießen, da er durch die Ausdehnung auch als Fläche gesehen werden kann. Durch Darstellungen mit dem Punkt können die gestalterischen Mittel auf ein absolutes Minimum beschränkt werden.

Anhaltspunkt
Anknüpfungspunkt
Ausgangspunkt
Aussichtspunkt
Berührungspunkt
Blickpunkt
Brennpunkt
Fixpunkt
Gefrierpunkt
Höhepunkt
Kernpunkt
Minuspunkt
Mittelpunkt
Notenpunkt
Nullpunkt
Orientierungspunkt
Pluspunkt
Punkt für Punkt
Punkte sammeln
Schnittpunkt
Schwerpunkt
Standpunkt
Strafpunkt
Tiefpunkt
Treffpunkt
Wendepunkt
Zeitpunkt
...

Die Parameter des Punktes sind:

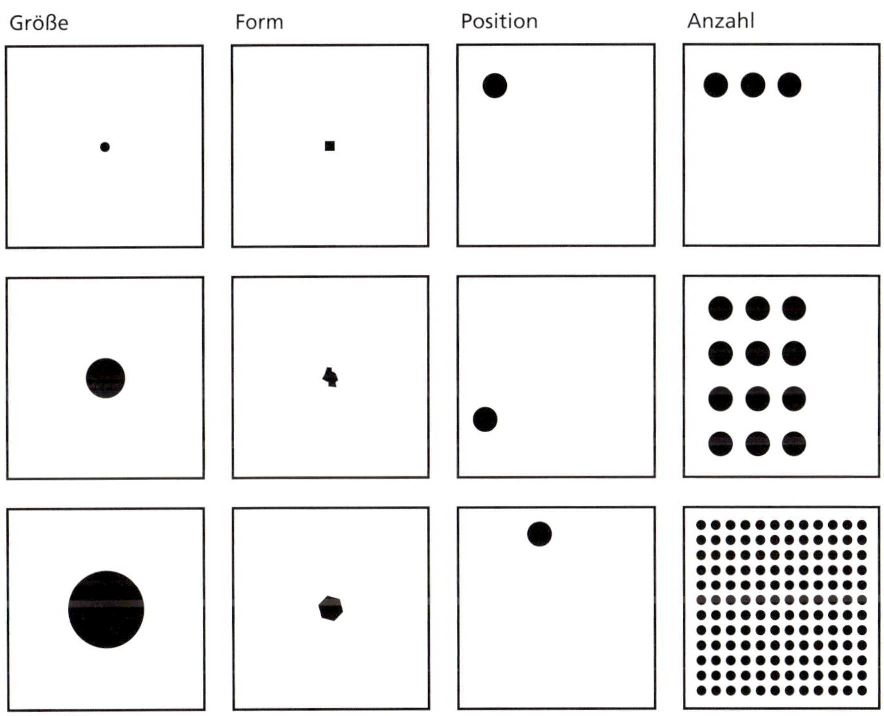

Durch die Kombination der Parameter untereinander entstehen in der Verwendung der Elemente unterschiedliche Interpretationen.

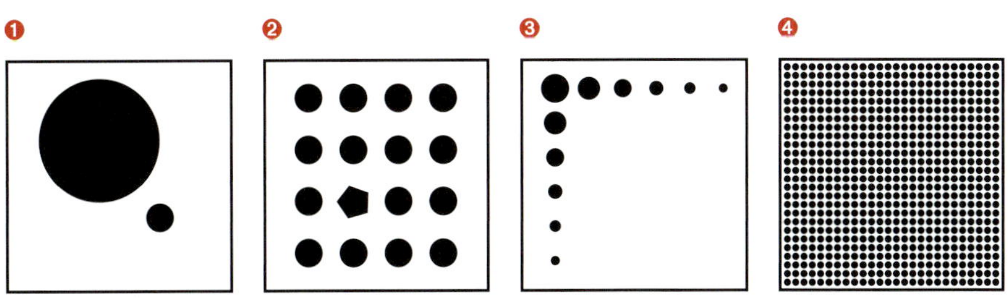

❶ Großer Punkt, kleiner Punkt
❷ Auffallender Unterschied eines Punktes in der Menge
❸ Variierte Größe, Form und Position ergeben eine interessante Reihung
❹ Viele Punkte erzeugen ein Muster

4.3.2 Die Linie

Aus dem spätlateinischen:
linea = Strich
Ursprünglich der mit einem Griffel gezeichnete Strich, später auch die mit einem Leinfaden gespannte Linie.

Außenlinie
Buslinie
Fluglinie
geradlinig
Innenlinie
Leitlinie
Lineal
linientreu
liniert
Luftlinie
Markierungslinie
Mittellinie
Schifffahrtslinie
Schlangenlinie
seine Linie finden
Seitenlinie
Sichtlinie
Startlinie
Straßenbahnlinie
Ziellinie
…

Verbindet man zwei Punkte miteinander, ensteht eine gerade Linie.

Fügt man auf der Linie einen weiteren Punkt hinzu, kann die Linie an diesem Punkt knicken. Wird an den Enden einer Linie auf diese Druck ausgeübt, entsteht eine gebogene Linie.

Die Parameter der Linie sind:

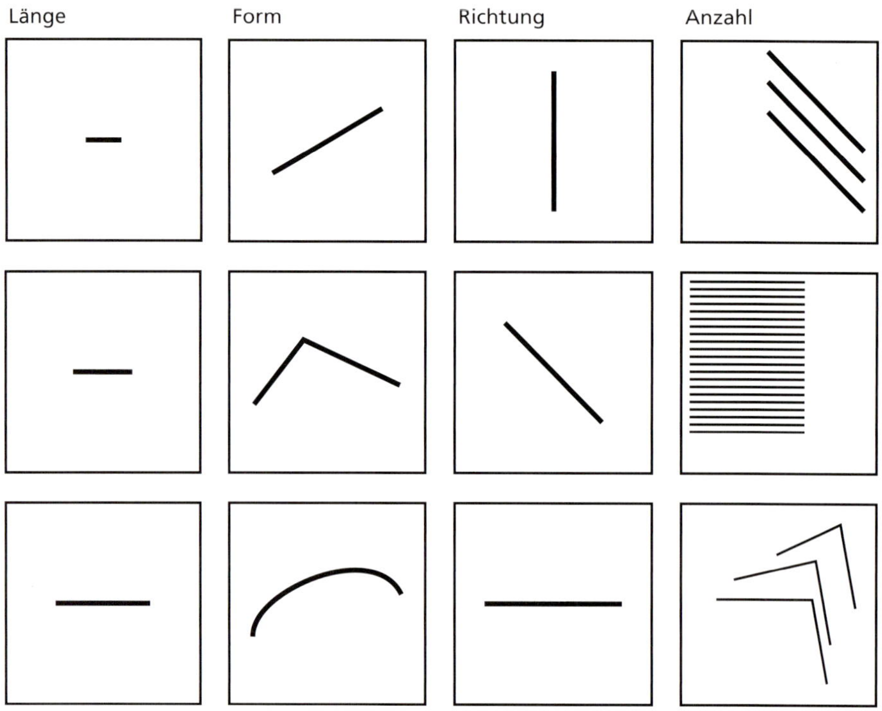

Im Gegensatz zum Punkt, der noch keine Ausdehnung besitzt, kommt der Linie bei der Gestaltung eine besondere Bedeutung durch deren Länge und der damit verbundenen Richtung bei.

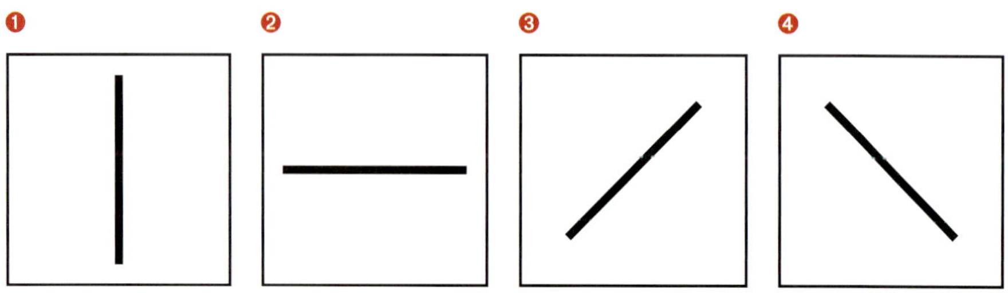

❶ Senkrechte Linien stehen für Statik und Aktivität
❷ Waagerechte Linien stehen für Ruhe und Passivität
❸ Die steigende Linie hat eine positive Wirkung, es geht aufwärts
❹ Die fallende Linie hat eine negative Wirkung, es geht abwärts

4.3.3 Die Fläche

Die Fläche ist ein sehr komplexes Formelement der elementaren Gestaltungslehre. Gebildet wird sie durch die Linie, die hierbei als Begrenzung einer zunächst noch offenen Fläche fungiert.

So grenzt eine gekrümmte Linie, welche an den Endpunkten geschlossen ist, eine runde Fläche ein. Drei gerade Linien bilden eine dreieckige Fläche, vier gerade Linien eine viereckige Fläche. Die Fläche ist also eine Begrenzung mit Hilfe von Linien.

Aus der Seemanns-Sprache überliefert: **das Flach**
Seichte, nicht tiefe Stelle im Meer oder Fluß, ein ausgedehntes Flach soll zum Durchqueren benutzt werden.

abflachen
Außenfläche
flach
Flachheit
Flachland
großflächig
Häuserfläche
Innenfläche
Oberfläche
oberflächlich
Seitenfläche
...

Die Parameter der Fläche sind:

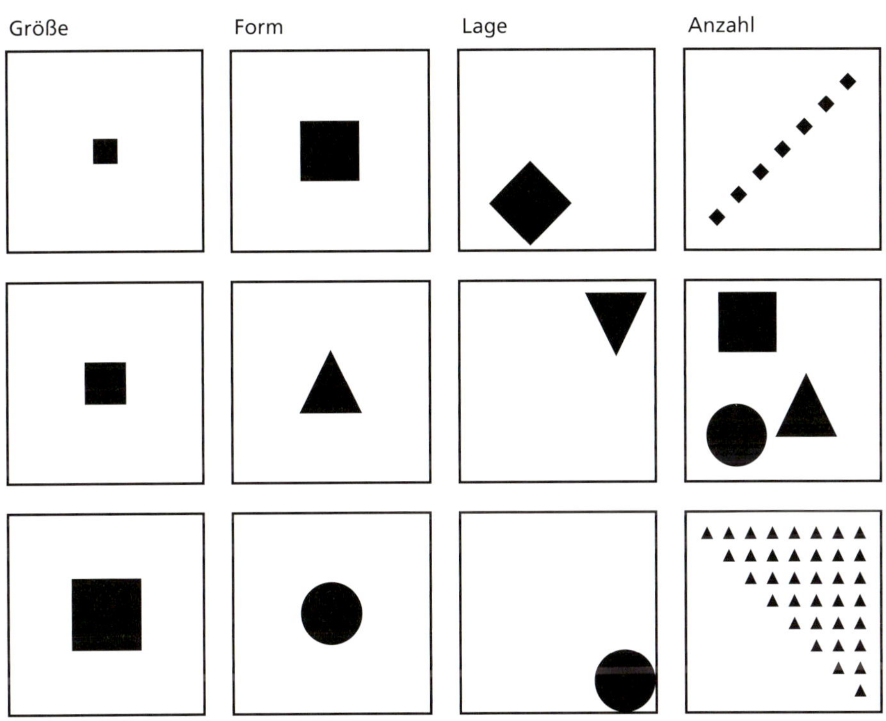

Auf der Basis des Formparameters unterscheidet man in der elementaren Gestaltungslehre drei Grundelemente: Quadrat, Dreieck und Kreis.

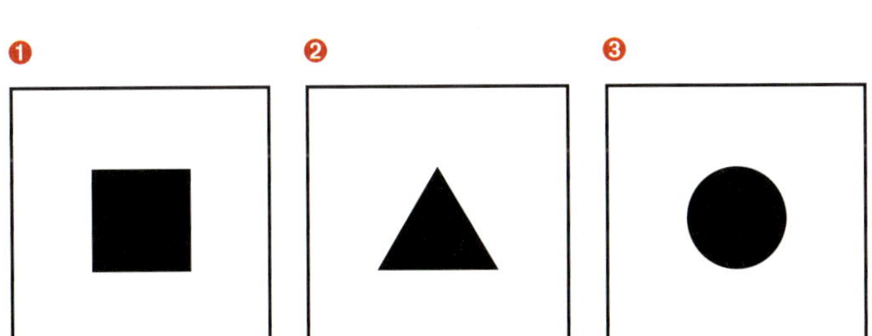

❶ Das Quadrat steht für Stabilität, Sicherheit und Männlichkeit
❷ Das Dreieck steht für Aggression, Warnung, Neutralität
❸ Der Kreis steht für Harmonie, Vollkommenheit, Weiblichkeit

❶ Eine Transformationsreihe bezeichnet allgemein die Veränderung der Form in eine andere.

Ein Beispiel für Formanordnungen nach dem kombinatorischen Prinzip stellen **Transformationsreihen** ❶ von Grundelementen dar. Solche Reihen werden in mehreren Schritten entwickelt. Zuerst wird eine Art „Startreihe“ gestaltet: Hier verändert ein schwarzes Dreieck seine Aussenform und seine Füllung in neun Schritten zu einem weißen Kreis.

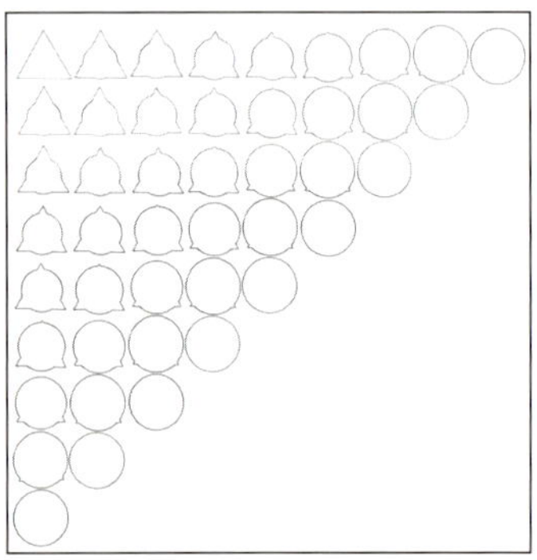

Die so erstellte Reihe wird nun noch um 90 Grad im Uhrzeigersinn dupliziert. Durch das Auffüllen der Lücken entsteht eine Matrix voller Platzhalter. Der weiße Kreis bildet die Diagonale einer späteren quadratischen Fläche. In der Ecke, die dem schwarzen Dreieck gegenüberliegt, wurde ein schwarzes Quadrat platziert. Dies bedeutet, dass noch eine Transformationsreihe vom weißen Kreis zum schwarzen Quadrat erfolgen muss. So entsteht schließlich eine spannende Kombination, welche von Hand oder mit Hilfe des Computers gezeichnet werden kann.

4.4.2 Formbeziehung

In der elementaren Gestaltungslehre kann man die Formbeziehungen wie folgt unterscheiden:

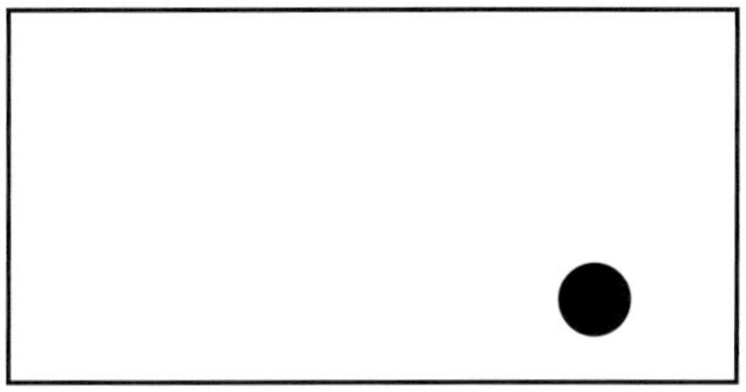

Schwerpunktbildung:
Wird ein Formelement auf einer Grundfläche angeordnet, entsteht durch den direkten Zusammenhang ein neuer Schwerpunkt der gesamten Konstellation, man spricht von der Schwerpunktbildung.

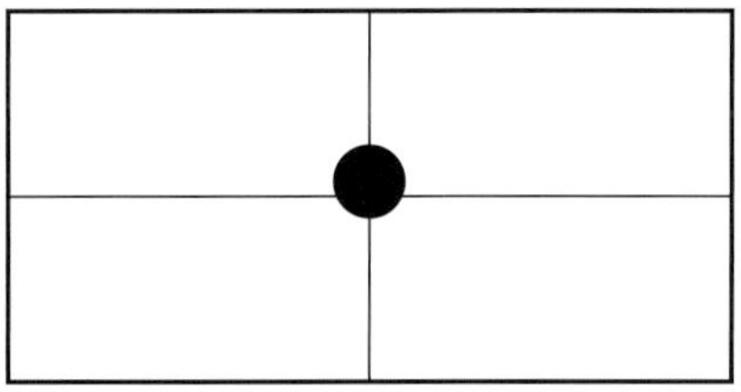

Optische Mitte:
Die konstruierte, geometrische Mitte einer Fläche wird von vielen Menschen als zu tief empfunden. Wird das Element etwas höher angesetzt, spricht man von der optischen Mitte. Diese ist oft als bessere Mitte sichtbar.

Proportionen:
Unter Proportionen versteht man Verhältnisse einzelner Teile zu einem Ganzen. Bei Flächen kann durch deren Einteilung die Wirkung untereinander definiert oder verändert werden.

Kontrast:
Kontrast ist der Gegensatz einzelner Elemente untereinander. Durch Kontraste entstehen meistens spannungsreiche und aktive Zusammenstellungen. Je größer der Kontrast, umso größer ist die Wirkung.

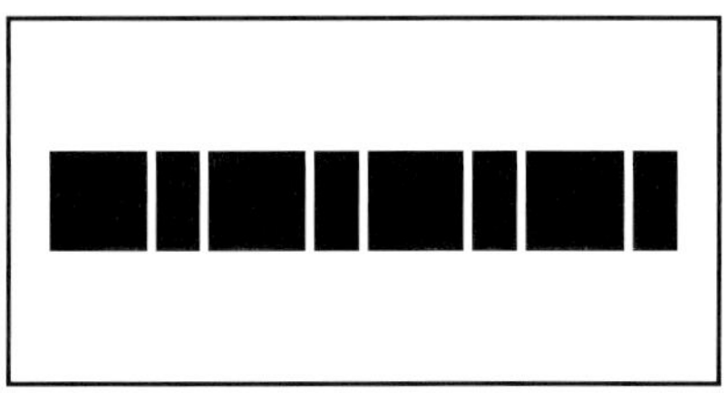

Rhythmus:
Durch die Wiederholung von Formelementen in gleichmäßig wiederkehrenden Anordnungen entsteht der Rhythmus. Dieser hat immer etwas mit Bewegung zu tun.

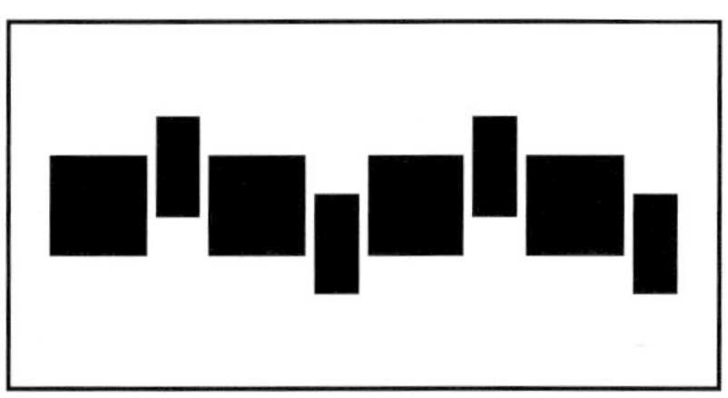

Dynamik:
Wird der gleichmäßige Rhythmus variiert, enstehen neue Bewegungsmuster. Diese sind oft dynamischer und spannungsreicher, als reine Wiederholungen. Dynamik hat etwas mit „Aus-der-Reihe-tanzen“ zu tun.

Kontrast

❶ Kontrast:
Starker Gegensatz, auffallender Unterschied.
„Der Kontrast ist das fundamentale visuelle Darstellungsprinzip schlechthin. Ohne Form kein Kontrast, kein Kontrast ohne Form.“ (Anton Stankowski)

Die in den Formbeziehungen dargestellten Möglichkeiten bezeichnet man auch als **Gestaltungsmittel**. Eines dieser Gestaltungsmittel ist der Einsatz von Kontrasten. ❶

Die verschiedenen Kontrast-Arten der elementaren Gestaltungslehre lassen sich von den Parametern der Formelemente ableiten:

- Größenkontrast (groß / klein)
- Formkontrast (rund / eckig)
- Positionskontrast (links / rechts)
- Richtungskontrast (oben / unten)
- Mengenkontrast (wenig / viel)
- Längenkontrast (kurz / lang)
- ...

Die Kontrastpaarungen sind mit den oben genannten natürlich noch lange nicht vollständig! Eine eigene Betrachtungsweise der Farbkontraste erfolgt innerhalb dieses Kapitels im Abschnitt 4.6 (Gestalten mit Farbe).

Aber alle diese und weitere Kontrastarten haben Eines gemeinsam:

➲ **Kontraste sind das Salz in der Suppe der Gestaltung!**
➲ **Ohne Kontraste ist Gestaltung langweilig!**

Oliver Hardy (1892 – 1957) und Stan Laurel (1890 – 1965) drehten zwischen 1926 und 1951 als US-amerikanisches Duo über 100 Filme. Sie gelten als eines der berühmtesten und erfolgreichsten Film-Duos aller Zeiten.

Ein Beispiel:
Warum haben sich einige Generationen mit Dick & Doof amüsiert? Dick ist dick. Und Doof ist doof. Das ist aber eigentlich noch nicht lustig. Erst die weiteren Gegensätze der beiden scheinbaren Freunde machen das Ganze interessant. Dick, alias Oliver Hardy, scheint ein Denker zu sein. Ein schlauer Kerl, handwerklich begabt. Doof, alias Stan Laurel, ist im Gegensatz dazu etwas einfältig und naiv. Ihm scheint nichts zu gelingen, was er in die Hand nimmt. Darüber hinaus ist er sehr schlank, geradezu dünn! Dick und dünn, klug und doof, begabt und naiv sind interessante und kontrastreiche Paarungen!

Rhythmus und Dynamik

Zwei weitere **Gestaltungsmittel** sind Rhythmus und Dynamik.

Bei der Anordnung von Formelementen kann man, bestimmt durch den Parameter Position, viele Variationen entwickeln. Eine Variation ist die Anordnung nach rhythmischen Gesichtspunkten. Der Rhythmus bezeichnet die periodische Wiederkehr von Vorgängen verschiedenster Art. Rhythmische Anordnungen sind jedoch in der Regel monotone Anordnungen.

Die Dynamik ist eine besondere Erscheinung des Rhythmus und bietet hierzu eine gelungene Abwechslung! Sie entsteht daher als rhythmische Störung und ist ein „Aus-der-Reihe-tanzen“.

Beispiel Kontrast, Rhythmus und Dynamik

Diese Abbildungen zeigen zwei Postkartenentwürfe, von Hand gestaltet und geklebt, zum Thema „Zeit“. Die obere Postkarte wurde gezielt mit Hilfe des Gestaltungsmittels Kontrast entworfen, die untere Postkarte nach den Gesichtspunkten des Rhythmus und der Dynamik.

Kontrast:
Der Kontrast entsteht hierbei durch die Verwendung der schwarzen Flächenelemente auf einem weißen Hintergrund. Die Schriften variieren in der Größe, der Richtung und der Schriftstärke.

Man erkennt daher die Kontrast-Arten:
hell / dunkel
groß / klein
horizontal / vertikal
dick / dünn

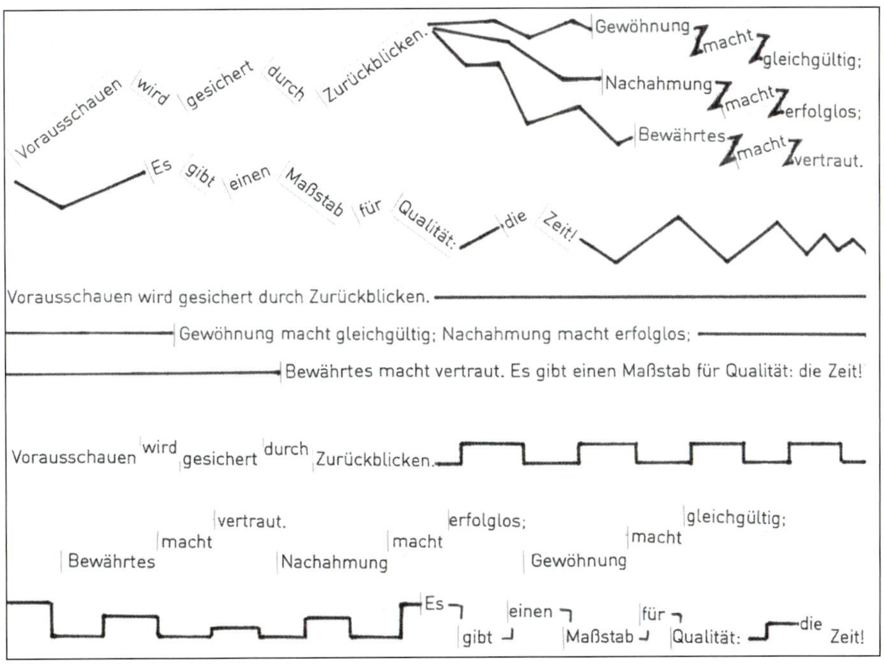

Rhythmus:
In der Mitte der Karte sind die Schriftlinien sehr regelmäßig dargestellt. Der Abstand von Linie zu Linie ist gleich, wodurch eine rhythmische Anordnung entsteht.

Dynamik:
Interessant wird die Postkarte dadurch, dass es Zickzack-Linien oberhalb und „Aufundab“-Linien unterhalb der rhythmischen Linien in der Mitte gibt.

4.4.3 Formwirkung

In der elementaren Gestaltungslehre kann man die Wirkung von Formen wie folgt unterscheiden:

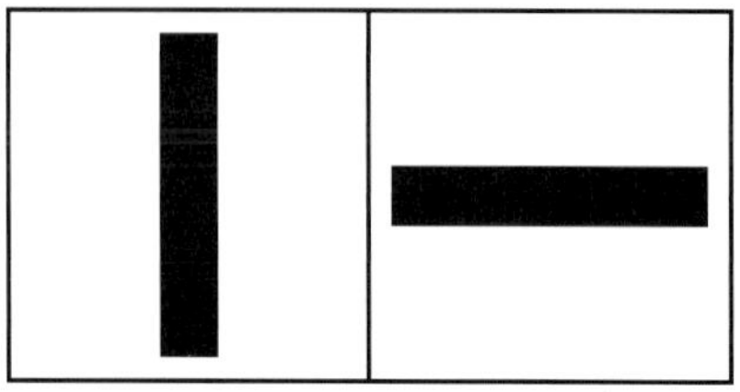

Emporstrebend / Ruhend:
Linien und linienhaft geformte Flächen wirken kraftvoll und aktiv bei einer vertikalen Anordnung. Die horizontale Anordnung hingegen erzeugt eine ruhige und ausgeglichene Wirkung.

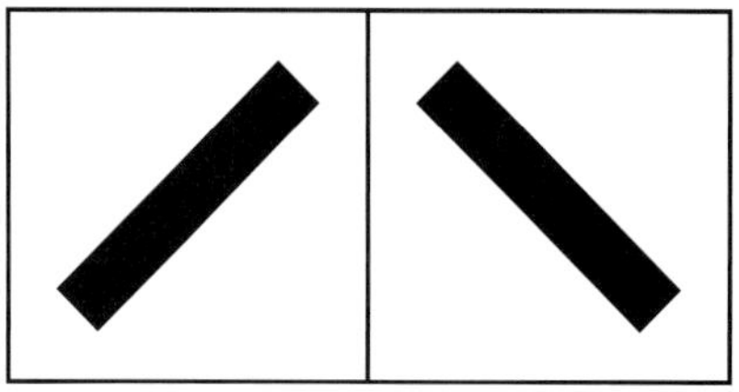

Steigend / Fallend:
Die Anordnung von links unten nach rechts oben symbolisiert eine Aufwärtsbewegung, einen positiven Trend. Die Anordnung von links oben nach rechts unten drückt einen negativen Trend aus, eine Abwärtsbewegung.

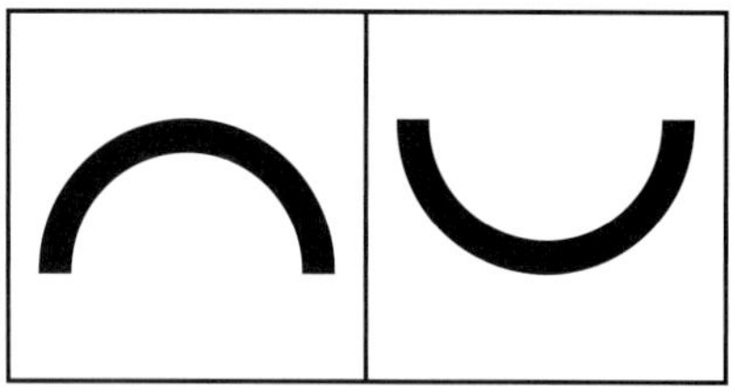

Schützend / Empfangend:
Bei gebogenen Formen spielt die Richtung der Öffnung eine große Rolle. So hat eine auf den Kopf gestellte „Schüssel“ eine schützende Wirkung, während die Kehrseite eine empfangende Wirkung zeigt.

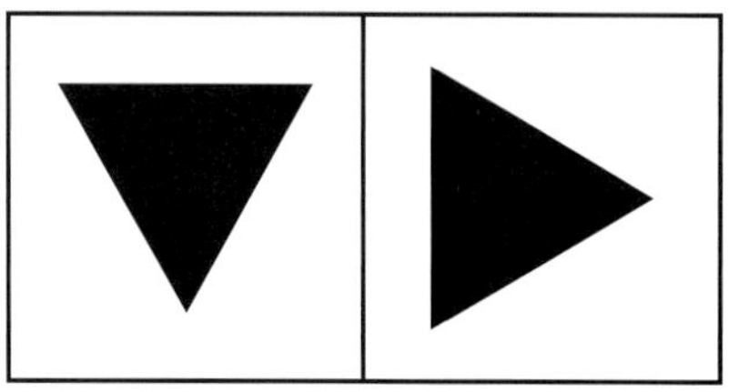

Dynamisch / Richtungsweisend:
Formen mit Spitzen und Ecken haben eine sehr dynamisierende Wirkung, da Formen, die auf der Spitze stehen, immer umzukippen drohen. Diese Spitze kann aber auch gezielt auf eine Richtung hinweisen.

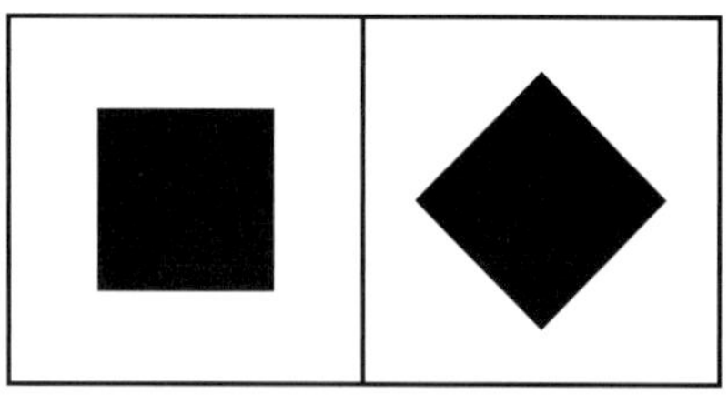

Statisch / Instabil:
Flächige Formen stehen sicher auf einer Ebene und wirken damit sehr statisch. Beim Kippen auf eine Spitze drohen diese Formen jedoch auf eine Seite umzukippen. Die Wirkung kehrt sich in eine instabile Position.

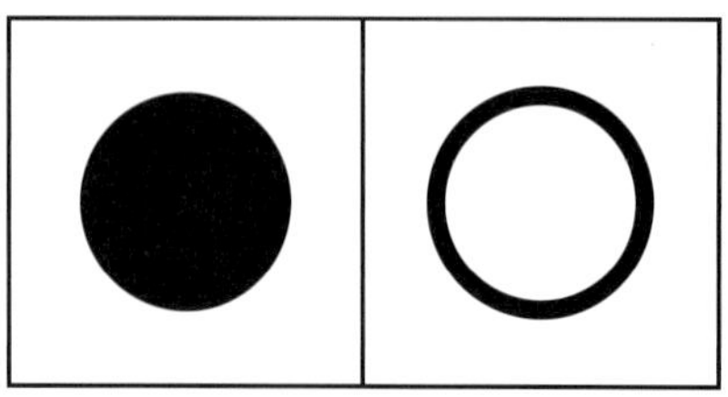

Geschlossen / Umschlossen:
Alle Flächen zeigen eine in sich abgeschlossene Wirkung, wenn die Flächen als solche gefüllt sind. Flächen können aber ebenso gut dazu dienen, in sich weitere Elemente zu vereinen, zu umschließen.

Beispiel Plakat

Die Erkenntnisse aus Formanordnung, Formbeziehung und Formwirkung lassen sich anhand eines Beispieles nochmals nachvollziehen.

Plakat (Schülerarbeit) zum Thema: „Sehen und Wahrnehmen"

Es werden auf dem Plakat die 26 Buchstaben des lateinischen Alphabetes abgebildet.
Die Buchstabenformen wurden in der Natur entdeckt.

Formelemente:
Alle Quadrate (hauptsächliches Flächenelement) sind gleich groß. Damit wird erreicht, dass einige Buchstaben nicht wichtiger erscheinen als andere.
Weitere Elemente sind Schriftzeilen, die durch deren Anordnung auch als Linienelemente gesehen werden können.

Formanordnung:
Die Quadrate werden teilweise in einer Reihe, teilweise gestreut auf der Fläche angeordnet.
So entsteht eine interessante Kombination der Elemente unter den Aspekten der Formbeziehung und -wirkung.

Formbeziehung:
Durch die Verwendung von freien Flächen (Weißraum) gelingt es, einen hohen Kontrast zu den sehr rhythmisch erscheinenden Quadraten herzustellen. Das einzelne nach rechts geneigte Quadrat stellt eine dynamische Variante zur Platzierung der restlichen Elemente dar.

Formwirkung:
Die Quadrate wirken ruhig und ausgeglichen. Sie lenken die Aufmerksamkeit des Betrachters auf das Wesentliche, den Inhalt des Plakates.

4.5 Gestalten mit Farbe

❶ **Farbeindruck:**
Bezeichnet die im Gehirn gebildete Sinneswahrnehmung einer Farbe. Diese lassen sich in bunte und unbunte Farben einteilen. Unbunte Farben sind Schwarz, Weiß und alle dazwischen liegenden Grautöne. Bunte Farben sind alle Anderen.

Die **Gestaltungsmittel** der elementaren Gestaltungslehre werden nun um ein weiteres erweitert: Die Farbe.

Farbe hat auf unsere Stimmungslage einen direkten Einfluß! Wir werden grün und blau vor Ärger, wir sehen nur noch rot vor Zorn und frisch Verliebte blicken durch eine rosarote Brille. Wir sehen Farbe, wir fühlen Farbe, wir gestalten mit Farbe. Unsere Welt ist farbig! Wir empfinden beim Betrachten von Farbe drei grundlegende Eigenschaften.

➲ **Jede Farbnuance wird definiert durch den Farbton, die Farbhelligkeit und die Farbsättigung.**

Der **Farbton** bezeichnet die Eigenschaft, nach der man Farbempfindungen z. B. nach rot, gelb oder grün unterscheidet.

Der Begriff **Helligkeit** bezeichnet die Intensität der auf einen Betrachter wirkenden Strahlung. Man kann davon ausgehen, dass dunkle Farben einen Menschen eher müde machen, während helle Farben eher aufmunternd wirken. Dunkle Farben wirken also mit weniger Intensität auf den Betrachter, als Helle.

Der Begriff **Farbsättigung** beschreibt, wie stark sich ein farbiger Eindruck von einem unfarbigen Eindruck ❶ unterscheidet. Gesättigte Farben, auch reine Farben genannt, wirken anregend und dynamisch, entsättigte Farben meistens eher dezent.

4.5.1 Farbensehen

❷ **Schnitt durch das Auge:**

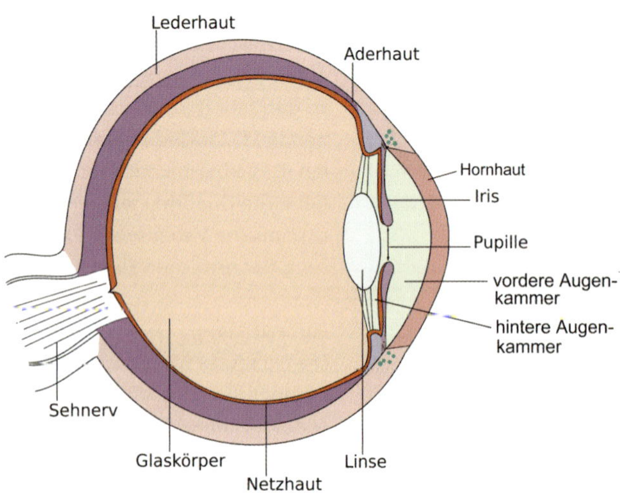

Um etwas sehen zu können, wird **Licht** benötigt. Das Licht gehört physikalisch betrachtet zu den elektromagentischen Wellen, die uns ständig umgeben (weitere Wellen sind zum Beispiel Radiowellen und Infrarotwellen). Diese **Lichtwellen** gelangen durch die Pupillenöffnung in unser Auge ❷. Die Linse projiziert das Licht nun auf unsere **Netzhaut**. Dort sind die eigentlichen **Sinneszellen (Rezeptoren)** für das Farbensehen angebracht: **Stäbchen** und **Zapfen**. Durch die unterschiedlichen Wellenlängen des Lichtes werden die Zapfen unterschiedlich stark angeregt.

Es gibt drei Zapfenarten. Die erste reagiert hauptsächlich auf die längeren Wellen des Lichtes (im Rot-Bereich), die zweite reagiert hauptsächlich auf die mittleren Wellen des Lichtes (im Grün-Bereich) und die dritte reagiert hauptsächlich auf kurze Wellenlängen (im Blauviolett-Bereich). Alle drei Zapfenarten analysieren also gemeinsam die Zusammensetzung des Lichtes. Im Gehirn entsteht dann schließlich, angeregt durch die Wahrnehmungskette (siehe Kapitel 4.2), der Farbeindruck.

Bei nachlassendem Umgebungslicht verlieren die Zapfen aber nach und nach ihre Aufnahmefähigkeit. Die Stäbchen sind lichtempfindlicher und senden weiterhin Signale ans Gehirn. Jedoch können die Stäbchen nicht zwischen den Farbnuancen unterscheiden sondern sind ausschließlich für die Intensität der Lichtstärke, also der Helligkeit zuständig. Unser Farbsehen lässt deshalb bei eintretender Dunkelheit langsam nach. Das Nachtsehen ist meist nur noch ein Differenzieren von Helligkeitswerten ohne Farbeindruck. Nachts sind eben alle Katzen grau!

Wellenlängen des Lichtes (im sichtbaren Spektrum):

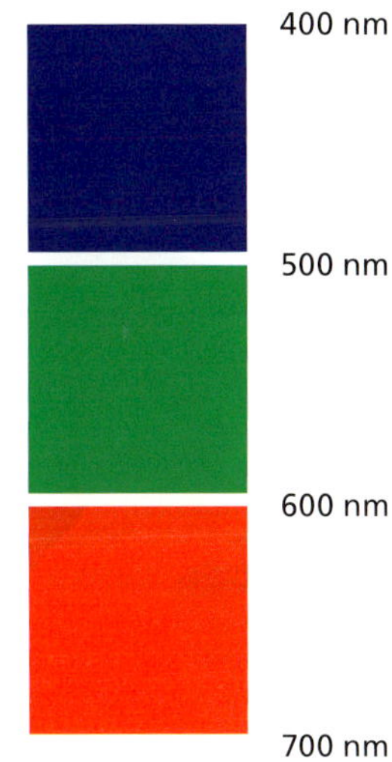

4.5.2 Farbwahrnehmung

Alle Gegenstände und Lebewesen unserer Umwelt sind farbig. Oder besser gesagt: Durch das Betrachten dieser Gegenstände und Lebewesen entsteht in unserem Gehirn ein Farbeindruck. Diesen Eindruck nennt man auch die Farbwahrnehmung.

Ein für die **Farbwahrnehmung** wichtiges Prinzip ist die Unterscheidung der Farben in **Lichtfarben** und **Körperfarben**:

- **Die Farben von nicht-selbstleuchtenden Gegenständen und färbende Substanzen wie Druck- und Malfarben werden zusammenfassend als Körperfarben bezeichnet.**

- **Die von Selbstleuchtern ausgesandte Farbe (Lampen, Sonne, ...) oder von Körperfarben reflektierte Farben werden zusammenfassend als Lichtfarben bezeichnet.**

Der Vorgang der Farbwahrnehmung lässt sich nun wie folgt darstellen: Trägt ein Körper eine Farbsubstanz, ist also eine Körperfarbe, so wird ein Teil des einfallenden Lichtes von dieser Substanz absorbiert ❶. Es wird sozusagen vom einfallenden Licht subtrahiert. Die Zusammensetzung des Restlichtes wird reflektiert ❷. Diese kommt auf der Netzhaut an und bestimmt so den Farbeindruck. Der gesamte Vorgang dieses Teiles der Farbwahrnehmung wird Remission ❸ genannnt.

❶ Absorption:
Aus dem lateinischen: absorptio = Aufsaugung bezeichnet im Allgemeinen das Aufsaugen, das In-sich-Aufnehmen von etwas.

❷ Reflexion:
Aus dem lateinischen: reflectere = zurückbeugen wenn ein Lichtstrahl, eine elektromagnetische Welle, oder ganz allgemein, eine Welle von einer Oberfläche zurückgeworfen wird.

❸ Remission:
Ein Gegenstand oder Körper absorbiert einen Teil des auftreffenden Lichtes und reflektiert einen anderen Teil des Lichtes. Remission = Absorption + Reflexion

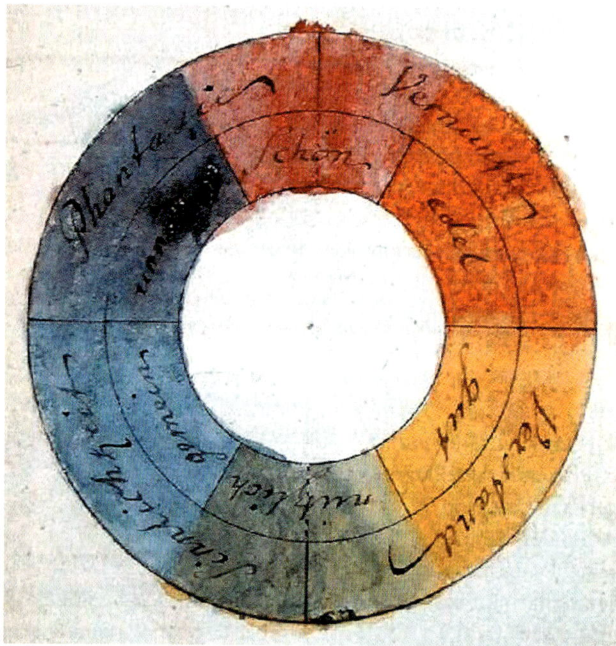

Goethes Farbtheorie baut auf einem polaren Gegensatz von Hell und Dunkel auf. Er bezeichnet Farben als Grenzphänomene zwischen Licht und Finsternis. Gelb liegt an der Grenze zur Helligkeit und Blau an der Grenze zum Dunklen. Seine Farbenlehre geht daher nur von zwei reinen Farben aus, Gelb und Blau, er betont jedoch, dass das Purpur in seinem Farbkreis nicht aus anderen Farben mischbar ist, das Rot hingegen schon.

Den vom Gelb zum Rot übergehenden Teil seines Farbkreises sieht Goethe als Plusseite und die andere Hälfte zum Blau hin als Minusseite. Dabei bringt er das Gelb mit Wirkung, Licht, Helligkeit, Kraft und Wärme in Verbindung und das Blau mit Beraubung, Schatten, Dunkelheit, Schwäche und Kälte.

Damit zeigt sich, dass Goethe den Schwerpunkt auf die **psychologische Wirkung von Farben** legte. Diese Erkenntnisse haben bis heute Gültigkeit!

Die Wirkung von Farbe auf den Betrachter ist eine sehr subjektive Angelegenheit. Bei genauerer Betrachtung lassen sich jedoch drei grundsätzliche Merkmale feststellen:

➲ **Die Wirkung von Farbe hat biologische, kulturelle und individuelle Merkmale!**

Auf der Netzhaut unseres Auges befinden sich wesentlich mehr **Rezeptoren** für die Grundfarbe Rot, als für die anderen Farben. Dadurch fallen uns Farben mit Rotanteilen mehr auf, als Farben mit zum Beispiel Grünanteilen. Rot, Orange und Gelb gelten deshalb als Signalfarben.

Die Auslegung einer Farbe ist sehr stark durch den **Kulturkreis** eines Lebensraumes geprägt. Während die Farbe schwarz zum Beispiel im westlichen Kulturkreis den Tod und das Böse symbolisiert, steht sie im ägyptischen Kulturkreis für die Wiedergeburt und die Auferstehung.

Dennoch hat jeder Mensch auch bestimmte Vorlieben, wodurch der Farbwirkung ein hohes Maß an Individualismus zukommt. Die Mode ihrerseits beeinflusst ganz besonders unseren Geschmack und Zeitgeist.

➲ **Farbe wirkt nie neutral!**

Bei der Farbwirkung kann man zwei Arten erkennen:

➲ **Farbe kann Assoziationen herstellen!**
➲ **Farbe kann Gefühle und Stimmungen auslösen!**

Assoziationen sind Vorstellungen, gedankliche Verknüfungen, gebildet auf der Basis von Erinnerungen an Dinge wie zum Beispiel das Feuer (Rot), das Gras (Grün) oder die Zitrone (Gelb). Gefühle und Stimmungen kommen vor allem dann gut zum Ausdruck, wenn man Substantive in Eigenschaftswörter verwandelt oder von vornherein Eigenschaftswörter verwendet, die am ehesten Gefühle auszudrücken vermögen wie zum Beispiel gefährlich (Rot), giftig (Grün) oder frisch (Gelb).

Bevor man einzelne Farbtöne genauer betrachtet, lassen sich diese in ihrer Wirkung in bestimmte Gruppen einteilen. So wirken hellere Farben im allgemeinen freundlicher, dunklere Farben eher düster. Farben mit viel Rotanteilen wirken wärmer, Farben mit viel Blauanteilen wirken kälter!

Ein Gestalter muss versuchen, die Farbwirkung möglichst genau zu analysieren, um mit der Farbanwendung einen möglichst großen Personenkreis anzusprechen. Im Folgenden sind einige Farben mit Begriffen belegt worden. Diese erheben keinen Anspruch auf Vollständigkeit!

Die Marke Coca-Cola hat eine exklusive Hausfarbe, die ihre Einzigartigkeit sichert:
Die Sonderfarbe Coca-Cola Rot 2000.
Sie kann nicht im Zusammendruck der vier Grund-Druckfarben hergestellt werden, sondern bedarf der separaten Anmischung.

WEISS

- Sauberkeit
- Reinheit
- Klarheit
- Vollkommenheit
- Unschuld
- Sterilität

GELB

- Wärme
- Helligkeit
- Optimismus
- Heiterkeit
- Freundlichkeit
- Veränderung

BLAU

- Unendlichkeit
- Weite
- Harmonie
- Kälte
- Passivität
- Seriösität

GRAU

- Neutralität
- Nüchternheit
- Langeweile
- Nachdenklichkeit
- Schlichtheit
- Eleganz

ORANGE

- Wärme
- Lebhaftigkeit
- Spaß
- Aktivität
- Wildheit
- Aufmerksamkeit

GRÜN

- Wachstum
- Frische
- Leben
- Hoffnung
- Entspannung
- Ruhe

SCHWARZ

- Eleganz
- Würde
- Trauer
- Einengung
- Schwere
- Hoffnungslosigkeit

ROT

- Aktivität
- Dynamik
- Hitze
- Kraft
- Temperament
- Aggression

VIOLETT

- Emanzipation
- Mystik
- Geheimnis
- Würde
- Spiritualität
- Kreativität

4.5.5 Farbkontraste

Man spricht von einem **Farbkontrast**, wenn zwischen zwei nebeneinander liegenden Farben deutliche Unterschiede bestehen. Die Farbkontraste sind, wie schon die Kontraste im Allgemeinen, ein sehr wichtiges Gestaltungsmittel.
Nach Johannes Itten gibt es sieben Farbkontraste:

Farbe-an-sich-Kontrast:
Jeder Farbton unterscheidet sich zunächst von einem Anderen. Ittens Grundfarben Gelb, Rot und Blau zum Beispiel bilden den einfachsten und stärksten Kontrast. Auch die Unterscheidung von Schwarz und Weiß kann dazu gezählt werden.

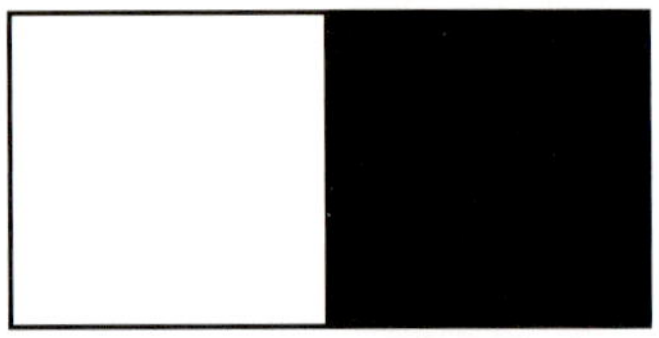

Hell-Dunkel-Kontrast:
Farben mit helleren Farbanteilen unterscheiden sich von Farben mit dunkleren Farbanteilen. Dabei bilden Weiß und Schwarz natürlich den größten Kontrast.

Kalt-Warm-Kontrast:
Farbempfindungen werden subjektiv wahrgenommen und unterscheiden sich dadurch individuell. Durch die Assoziation mit Feuer und Sonne wird jedoch ein roter Farbton als warm wahrgenommen. Ein blauer Farbton wird als kalt wahrgenommen, da dieser mit Wasser und Eis verknüpft wird.

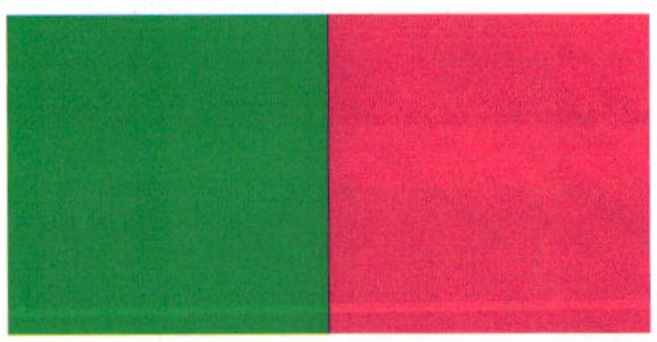

Komplementär-Kontrast:
Komplementär bedeutet Ergänzung. Komplementäre Farben liegen sich im Farbkreis oder Farbsechseck gegenüber und sollten sich in ihrer Mischung zu Grau ergänzen (je nach Farbmischprinzip). Komplementäre Farben haben somit einen der stärksten Kontraste zu bieten.

Simultan-Kontrast:
Der Eindruck eines Farbtones wird durch seine Umgebung beeinflusst. Betrachtet man eine Farbe, zum Beispiel ein helles Grau, auf verschiedenen Hintergründen, so wirkt das Grau zweimal ganz anders!

Qualitäts-Kontrast:
Aus dem Gegensatz von gesättigten, leuchtenden Farben zu stumpfen, getrübten Farben entsteht der Qualitäts-Kontrast. Man spricht hierbei von der Qualität einer Farbe, wenn diese farblich möglichst rein ist, sich also wenig Schwarz- oder Weißanteile darin befinden.

Quantitäts-Kontrast:
Hierbei geht es um die Verhältnisse „viel und wenig" oder „groß und klein". Es geht um die Menge einer Farbe im Vergleich zur Menge einer anderen. Die Leuchtkraft und die Flächengröße bestimmen somit die Wirkung der Farbe.

Beispiel Farbwürfel

Modell eines Würfels, Transformation durch Raum und Farbe mit Kalt-Warm-Kontrast in verschiedenen Entwicklungsschritten.

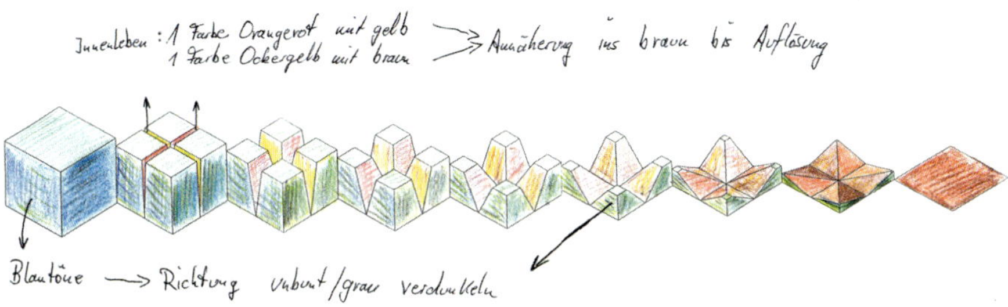

Entwurfsprozess:
In der Skizzenphase wird die Transformation der Konturen und der Farben mit einem Kalt-Warm-Kontrast entwickelt. Anschließend werden die Formen gezeichnet und die Farben von Hand oder am Computer gemischt.
Durch ein Stapeln der Transformationsreihe kann ein Kubus erstellt werden, der in verschiedenen Variationen modifiziert wird. Gestaltung mit System!

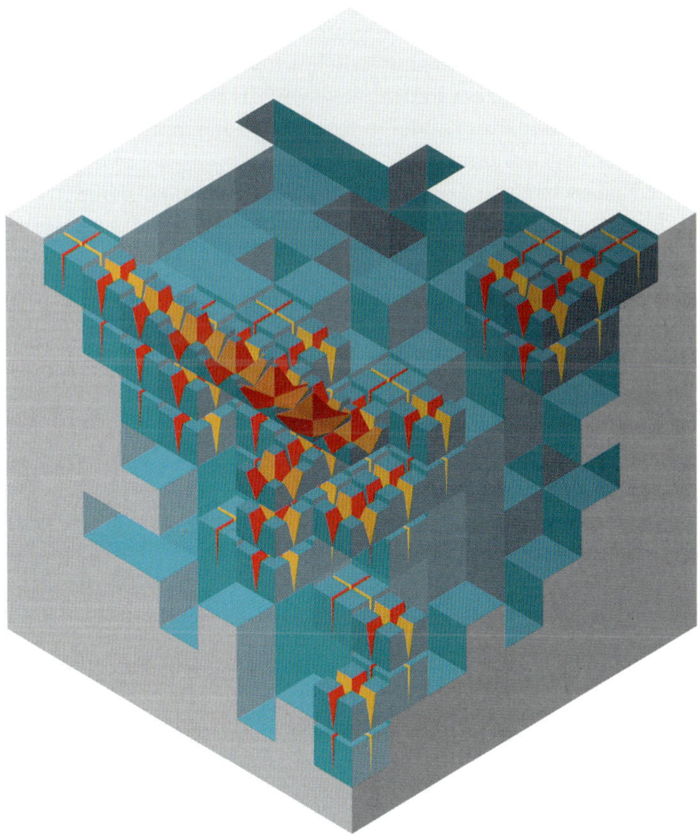

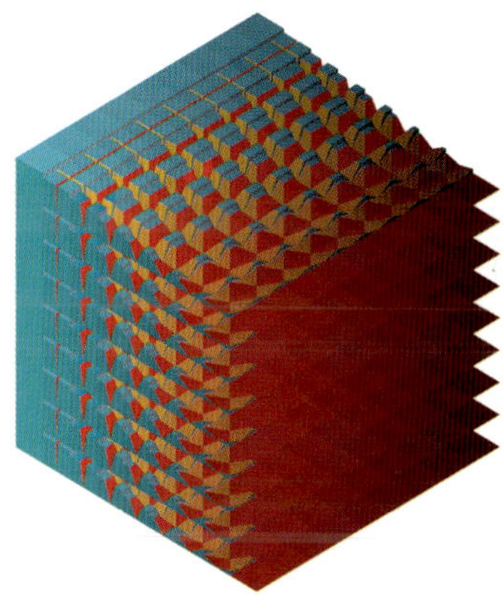

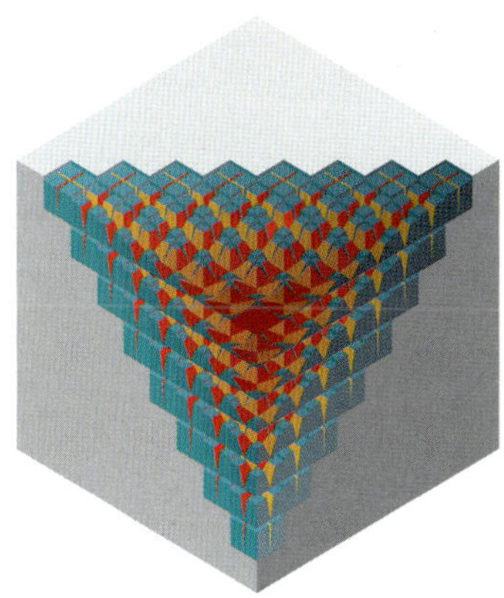

4.5.6 Farbharmonie

Griechisch: harmonia (Zusammen)fügung.
Indogermanische Herkunft: Vereinigung von Entgegengesetztem zu einem Ganzen.

Harmonie bedeutet Wohlbefinden. Wir können uns wohl fühlen, wenn wir Musik hören oder ein Bild betrachten. Das Gegenteil der Harmonie ist die Disharmonie. Diese tritt auf, wenn wir uns im Gegensatz zur Harmonie nicht wohl fühlen.

In der elementaren Gestaltungslehre tauchen Harmonien immer dort auf, wo zwei oder mehr Elemente im Verbund gemeinsam für eine positve Grundstimmung sorgen. Hier stellt der Einsatz von Farben eine der besten Möglichkeiten dar.

Eine Farbe allein ist in der Regel langweilig, erst im Zusammenspiel mit anderen Farben oder Formen entfaltet sie ihre Wirkung. Farben müssen sich ergänzen und steigern sich im Idealfall gegenseitig. Aber je mehr Farben dazu kommen, um so schwieriger wird es, eine Harmonie herzustellen. Harmonie entsteht bei Farben nur dann, wenn gewisse Regeln und Gesetzmäßigkeiten beachtet werden!

- **Farbkombinationen sind im Allgemeinen dann harmonisch, wenn der Kontrast nicht ganz so stark ist.**
- **Farbtöne mit gleicher Helligkeit harmonieren in der Regel besser, als Farbtöne mit ganz unterschiedlichen Helligkeitswerten.**
- **Farbtöne mit ähnlichen Sättigungswerten harmonieren in der Regel besser, als Farbtöne unterschiedlicher Sättigung.**
- **Harmonieren zwei Farben grundsätzlich miteinander, lässt sich aus deren Mischung eine dritte finden, die ebenfalls harmonieren wird.**
- **Auf dem Farbsechseck und anderen Farbkreisen harmonieren benachbarte Farben in der Regel miteinander.**
- **Unbunte Farben harmonieren mit bunten Farben immer dann, wenn der Sättigungsgrad und die Helligkeit der Farbtöne angepasst werden.**

Ein Beispiel:
Der Westdeutsche Rundfunk hat ein konsequent durchgestaltetes Erscheinungsbild. Auszug aus dem Corporate Design Manual:
„Die Hausfarbe Blau im Logo vermittelt die kommunikative und servicefreundliche Grundhaltung des WDR. Die Akzentfarbe Gelb bringt das Blau zum Leuchten und unterstreicht die positive Stimmung des visuellen Auftritts. Weitere zehn Grundfarben ergänzen die Hausfarben zum wdr-Farbklima."
Die Farbtöne weisen alle in etwa die gleichen Sättigungs- und Helligkeitswerte auf und liegen jeweils in zwei Kombinationen benachbart auf dem Farbsechseck.

Blau:
Pantone 293
100% Cyan, 60% Magenta

Gelb:
Pantone 108
10% Magenta, 100% Gelb

Beispiel Internetauftritt zum Thema Überraschungs-Ei-Figuren

Bei diesem Beispiel handelt sich um einen von Schülern erstellten Internetauftritt zum Thema „Überraschungs-Ei-Figuren".
Die verwendeten Farbtöne auf den einzelnen Seiten folgen allen den in diesem Kapitel dargestellten Gesetzmäßigkeiten. Sie sind von gleicher Helligkeit, der Kontrast ist schwach. Ebenso ist die Farbsättigung jeweils immer die Gleiche. Obwohl also fünf sehr unterschiedliche Farben verwendet werden, sind diese alle harmonisch aufeinander abgestimmt.

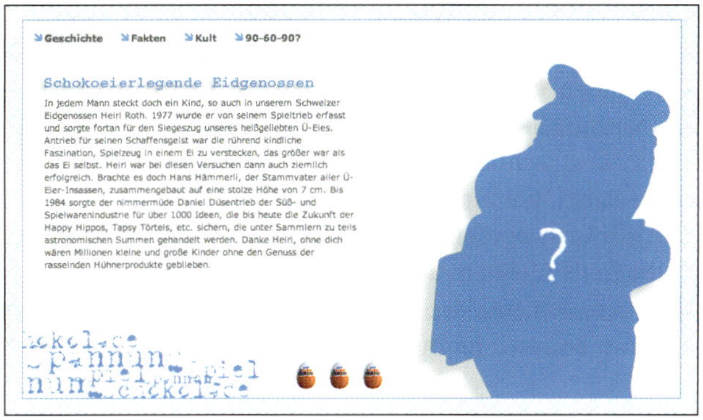

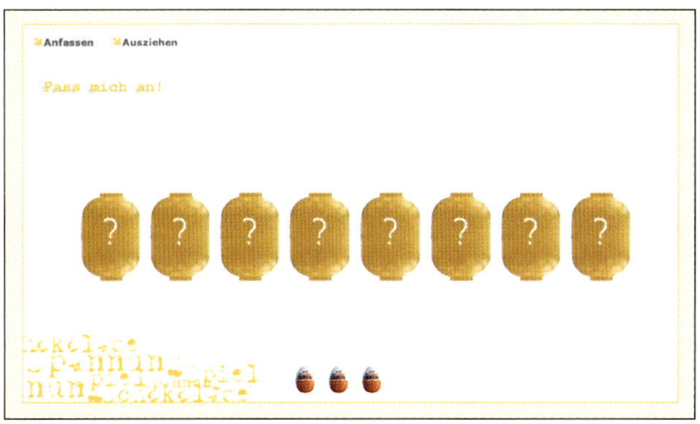

5 Typografie

Webcode: B0500

Für weitere Infos zu diesem Kapitel mit dem Smartphone einfach QR-Code scannen oder auf www.medien-verstehen.de den Webcode eingeben.

Die Typografie ❶ bedeutet im engeren Sinne das **Gestalten mit Schrift**. Es genügt aber nicht, für diese Art der Gestaltung die Schrift isoliert zu betrachten!

Der Mensch beginnt seinen schulischen Werdegang damit, dass er das Alphabet lernt, Großbuchstaben von Kleinbuchstaben unterscheidet und in sein erstes Schulheft Wörter und Sätze niederschreibt. Zusätzlich werden noch eine Menge Bilder eingefügt. So wird das Heft nach und nach mit Schrift und Bildern gefüllt, die Elemente Schrift, Bild und Fläche (das Heft) gehören also untrennbar zusammen.

Die Typografie bedeutet daher im weiteren Sinne nicht nur das Gestalten mit Schrift, sondern das **Gestalten mit Text und Bild**. Mit dieser Erkenntnis kann man die Typografie nach Mikro- und die Makrotypografie unterscheiden:

- **Mikrotypografie beschäftigt sich mit dem Aufbau der Buchstaben, den Zeichen, Wörtern und Sätzen.**
- **Makrotypografie beschäftigt sich mit dem gesamten gestalterischen Werk, also der Gestaltung von Text und Bild und dem Umgang damit auf einer Fläche.**

❶ Aus dem Griechischen: **tipografía (típos = Schlag, Abdruck, Figur, Typ und gráphein = malen, schreiben, ritzen)** Ursprünglich das Malen und Schreiben von Figuren und Typen.

Um sich mit der Mikro- und Makrotypografie auseinandersetzen zu können bedarf es noch einiger Hintergrundinformationen vorneweg, die im Folgenden dargestellt werden.

5.1 Grundsätze der Typografie

5.1.1 Kommunikationsaspekt

Das Schreiben dient nicht dem Selbstzweck. Es dient der **Kommunikation** wie das Gespräch. Die Worte, die ein Mensch spricht, werden von der Sprache, dem Dialekt, dem Tonfall und dem Auftreten des Sprechers beeinflusst und spielen bei der Übertragung der Information eine große Rolle. Wer schreibt, kann aber nicht selbst auftreten oder sprechen. Vergleicht man das geschriebene mit dem gesprochenen Wort, gelangt man von der Sprache zum Satzbau, vom Tonfall zur Formulierung und vom Auftreten auf die Gestaltung ganzer Medienprodukte.

Somit wird der Typografie eine besondere Rolle zuteil: Sie ist dafür verantwortlich, dass eine Information an einen Informationssempfänger (einen Leser) übermittelt wird. Einfach formuliert kann man so auch gute von schlechter Typografie unterscheiden:

- **Gute Typografie ist in der Lage, Informationen zu übermitteln.**
- **Schlechte Typografie übermittelt Informationen nicht oder missverständlich.**

Die Information kann dabei ganz unterschiedlicher Art sein! Ob es sich dabei um eine Einladungskarte handelt, einen Großstadtplan mit der Übersicht der S-Bahnen oder einem Faltblatt mit dem aktuellen Kinoprogramm: Verständlich muss es sein!

Ein Beispiel:
Wird in dieser Kleinanzeige ein Garten gesucht? Oder ein Balkon? Oder Möbel?
So missverständlich kann schlechte Typografie sein!

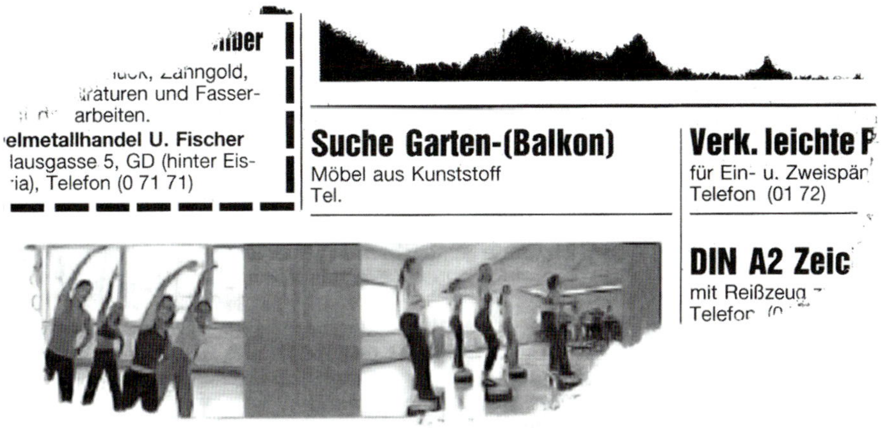

5.1.2 Aufgaben der Typografie

Die Medien überfluten uns täglich mit neuen Informationen. Doch welche Informationen sind wichtig? Welche kann und darf man übersehen? Kaum einer, der etwas zu sagen hat, wird behaupten, es sei nicht wichtig! Typografie steht daher auch im engen Zusammenhang mit Themen der **Wahrnehmung** (vgl. Kapitel 4.2.1 Wahrnehmungskette).

Der Gestalter einer **Werbeanzeige** zum Beispiel wird versuchen, die ganze Aufmerksamkeit des Lesers auf die Anzeige zu lenken. Dies kann entweder durch einen pfiffigen Slogan erfolgen oder durch ein markantes Bild! Oder aber durch eine entsprechende Platzierung der einzelnen Elemente auf der leeren Fläche.

Die Aufgaben der Typografie sind also stets zweckorientiert! Sie sollen:

- Informationen zielgruppenorientiert kommunizieren.
- Informationen strukturieren und ordnen.
- Emotionen und Stimmungen erzeugen.
- Aufmerksamkeit erregen (oder auch von einer Sache ablenken).
- Trendig und nicht ganz alltäglich sein.

Eine Ausnahme kann man im Bereich der Kunst machen. Es gibt Künstler, die mit Buchstaben und Zeichen mehr experimentieren, als Informationen vermitteln zu wollen.

Zwischen der Typografie und dem elementaren Gestalten (vgl. Kapitel 4) gibt es große Gemeinsamkeiten! Im Prinzip können die Buchstaben als Formelement der elementaren Gestaltungslehre gesehen werden. Im Folgenden wird auf solche Gemeinsamkeiten, vor allem im Rahmen der geschichtlichen Entwicklung, hingewiesen.

5.2 Geschichte der Typografie

Die Geschichte der Typografie steht in engem Zusammenhang mit der Entwicklung der Menschheit und deren Bedürfnis nach Kommunikation!

Seit Jahrtausenden schon versuchen Menschen, sich einander mitzuteilen. Steht keine Sprache zur Verfügung, greift man auf **Zeichen** zurück. Ob Rauch-, Morse- oder Handzeichen, so geht es bei allen darum, Informationen und Botschaften zu übermitteln und sich mitzuteilen.

5.2.1 Ursprünge der Schrift

Sumerische Keilschrift

Die Ursprünge der Schrift gehen geschichtlich weit zurück. In Mesopotamien (dem Gebiet des heutigen Irak) entwickelten die Sumerer etwa 4000 vor Christus die erste Form einer Schriftart, die sogenannte **Keilschrift**. Man nimmt an, dass die Entwicklung dieser Schrift im Zusammenhang mit der dortigen Buchführung stand. Die Form dieser Schriftzeichen entstand dadurch, dass angespitzte Schilfrohre in Tontafeln gedrückt wurden. Die daraus resultierende Keilform gab der Schrift ihren Namen. Sie bestand aus etwa 800 verschiedenen Schriftzeichen und wurde von oben nach unten geschrieben.

Ägyptische Hieroglyphen

Aus dem Altgriechischen: **hieroglyphikà grámmata (hierós = heilig und glýph = (in Stein) gravieren, ritzen)** Hieroglyphen werden somit auch als heilige Schriftzeichen bezeichnet.

Etwas jünger und auch deutlich bekannter als die Keilschrift sind die **ägyptischen Hieroglyphen**. Die ältesten Funde verzeichnete man um etwa 3000 vor Christus. Im Allgemeinen werden die Hieroglyphen auch als **Bilderschrift** bezeichnet. Bestimmte grafische Figuren stehen dabei für das Objekt, das dargestellt werden soll. Für die Ägypter selbst waren die Hieroglyphen offensichtlich etwas heiliges. Die alten Funde belegen dies dadurch, dass sich an Grabkammern und Kellergewölben sehr viele Götterverehrungen gefunden haben. Königliche Geschichten wurden ebenso aufgezeichnet, Kriege und Schlachten wurden dokumentiert. Die Ägypter verwendeten als Schriftmedium Steine oder Ton sowie Rollen aus Leder, Leinen oder Papyrus, der Zeichenvorrat zählte über 1000 Elemente.

Inschrift im unteren Teil der Stele (Inschriften- oder Grabstein) des Anchefenchons im Totentempel der Königin Hatschepsut in Ägypten.
Die Stele steht heute im Ägyptischen Museum in Kairo.

Chinesische Wortschrift

Im fernen Osten wurde etwa 2600 vor Christus die **chinesische Wortschrift** entwickelt, der Überlieferung nach gab es auch andernorts Tendenzen zur Entwicklung eigener Zeichensysteme. Der größte historisch überlieferte Umfang des Zeichenvorrates der chinesischen Wortschrift liegt bei rund 87.000 Zeichen, von denen heute aber etwa 85% nicht mehr in Gebrauch sind. Ein Durchnittswörterbuch listet rund 10000 Zeichen auf, rund 3000 reichen für das Lesen einer Tageszeitung aus.

Die Zeichen aller bildhaften Systeme lassen wie folgt unterscheiden:

- **Piktogramme:** Stilisierte Bildzeichen für Objekte oder Lebewesen
- **Phonogramme:** Zeichen, die Laute charakterisierten (ähnlich der Lautschrift in einem Rechtschreib-Lexikon)
- **Ideogramme:** Abstrakte Begriffe (zum Beispiel: Das Zuhalten der Augen für den Begriff „blind")

5.2.2 Entwicklung des Alphabetes

Phönizisches Alphabet

Etwa 2000 vor Christus entstand das erste **Alphabet** in Ägypten. Es war als Weiterentwicklung der Hieroglyphen zu verstehen und wurde von semitischen Arbeitern in Zentralägypten verwendet. Das Alphabet verfügte über 22 Zeichen, die die Konsonanten der ägyptischen Sprache wiedergaben sowie ein weiteres Zeichen, welches am Anfang und Ende eines Wortes für einen Vokal stand. Somit dienten diese Zeichen als Aussprachehilfe für die Piktogramme.

Im Laufe der folgenden Jahrhunderte erweiterten die Semiten den Zeichenvorrat auf rund 30 Zeichen. Das Alphabet, welches sich zu diesem Zeitpunkt immer mehr zu einem reinen „Laut"-Alphabet entwickelte, verbreitete sich in weiten Teilen des Mittelmeerraumes. Einer der Staaten, der das Alphabet regelmäßig verwendete, war Phönizien, weshalb man die weitere Entwicklung des Alphabetes diesem Volk zuschreibt. Dieses Alphabet bezeichnet man daher auch als **Phönizisches Alphabet**.

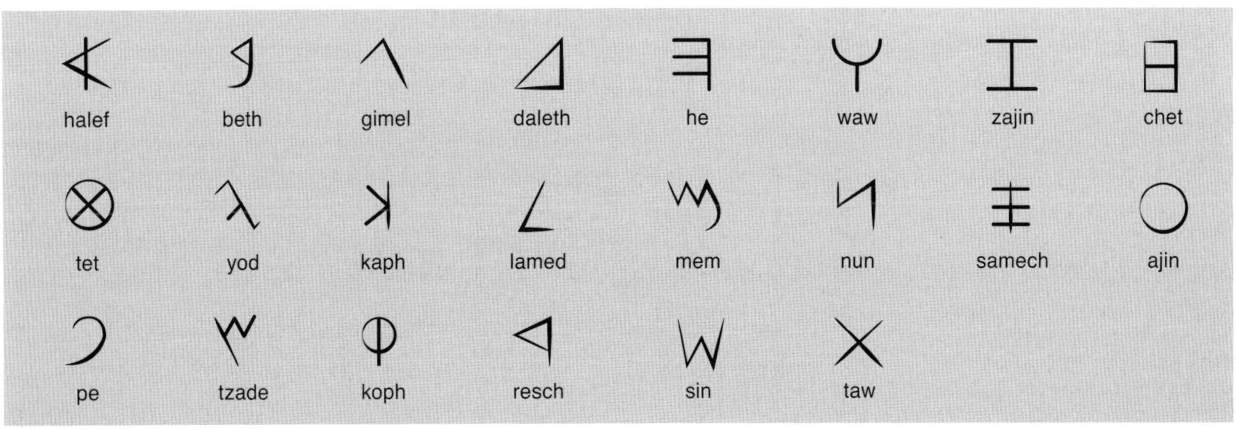

Griechisches Alphabet

Im Laufe der Geschichte verdrängten die Griechen im Mittelmeerraum zunehmend den Handel der Phönizier, somit auch deren Sprache und deren Schriftzeichen. Um 1000 vor Christus tauchte das erste **griechische Alphabet** auf. Es enthielt 24 Schriftzeichen, welche alle auf einfachen geometrischen Grundformen aufgebaut waren. Das Lesen gestaltete sich jedoch noch recht schwierig, da es im Schreibfluss noch keine Worttrennungen gab. Dennoch wurde dieses Schriftsystem die Basis für alle weiteren Entwicklungen in der slawischen und abendländischen Schriftentwicklung.

Römisches Alphabet

❶ Als Serifen bezeichnet man die Linien, die einen Buchstabenstrich am Ende, quer zu seiner Grundrichtung abschließen.

Die Römer übernahmen die Schriftzeichen von den Etruskern in Zentralitalien und entwickelten daraus ihr eigenes Alphabet, welches dem heute von uns verwendeten, lateinischen Alphabet sehr ähnlich ist. Etwa 100 nach Christus entstand die **Capitalis Monumentalis**, die klassische römische Steinschrift, in der das lateinische Alphabet seine Vollendung erfuhr. Mit einem pinselartigen Werkzeug wurden die Buchstabenformen vorgegeben, mit einem Meißel wurden die Formen aus Stein herausgemeißelt. Man vermutet heute, dass durch die Formen des Flachpinsels und der Meißeltechnik die Abstriche an den Buchstabenenden und -anfängen entstanden sind. Diese Abstriche werden als **Serifen** ❶ bezeichnet.

Der Lesefluss hatte sich mit der Weiterenwicklung dieses Alphabetes sehr gesteigert, zur Satz- und Worttrennung wurden feine Interpunktionen eingeführt, die Serifen unterstützten die Führung des Auges bei den Schriftzeilen.
Mit der **Capitalis Monumentalis** gilt die frühe Schriftentwicklung als abgeschlossen.

Grabdenkmal für den aus der Gefangenschaft freigelassenen Brutius Acutus, Mitte des 1. Jahrhunderts nach Christus, Römisch-Germanisches Museum in Köln

Die Römer entwickelten die in Stein gemeißelte Schrift im Laufe der Zeit kontinuierlich weiter. Der noch aufstrebende römische Staat organisierte sein Wachstum mit Hilfe eines mächtigen Verwaltungsapparates. Die damaligen Gelehrten hatten den Anspruch, schneller und lesbarer zu schreiben. So entwickelte sich aus der Capitalis Monumentalis etwa 400 nach Christus die **Capitalis Quadrata** ❶, parallel dazu die **Capitalis Rustica** und die daraus resultierende **römische Kursive** als schnelle Gebrauchsschreibschrift.

❶ Kapitalis Quadrata

5.2.3 Mittelalterliche Handschriften

Unziale

Mit dem Niedergang der römischen Kaiserzeit 476 nach Christus begann die Reise in das frühe Mittelalter. Es entwickelten sich in Europa eine ganze Reihe christlich geprägter Feudalstaaten. Viele neu errichtete Gebäude waren mit Rundbögen und Kuppelbauten versehen, Formen, die sich auch bei den weiterentwickelten Schreibschriften wieder fanden. Die **Unziale** (eine **Majuskelschrift** ❷) war geboren. Die deutlich gerundeten Buchstaben liesen sich schneller schreiben, als die quadratisch anmutenden römischen Schriften. Bei der **Halbunziale** etwa 800 nach Christus stehen die Buchstaben noch enger zueinander. Die weitere Verbreitung des Christentums sorgte schließlich dafür, dass Latein als einheitliche Sprache eingeführt wurde.

❷ Majuskel = Großbuchstabe, Versalie

❸ Minuskel = Kleinbuchstabe, Gemeine

Minuskel

In den Schreibklöstern Karls des Großen wurde um 800 nach Christus die **Karolingische Minuskel** ❸ entwickelt. Durch einen gleichmäßigen Rhythmus im gesamten Schriftbild war die Schrift sehr gut lesbar und hat sich zum Vorbild für ein einheitliches Kleinbuchstaben-Alphabet entwickelt.

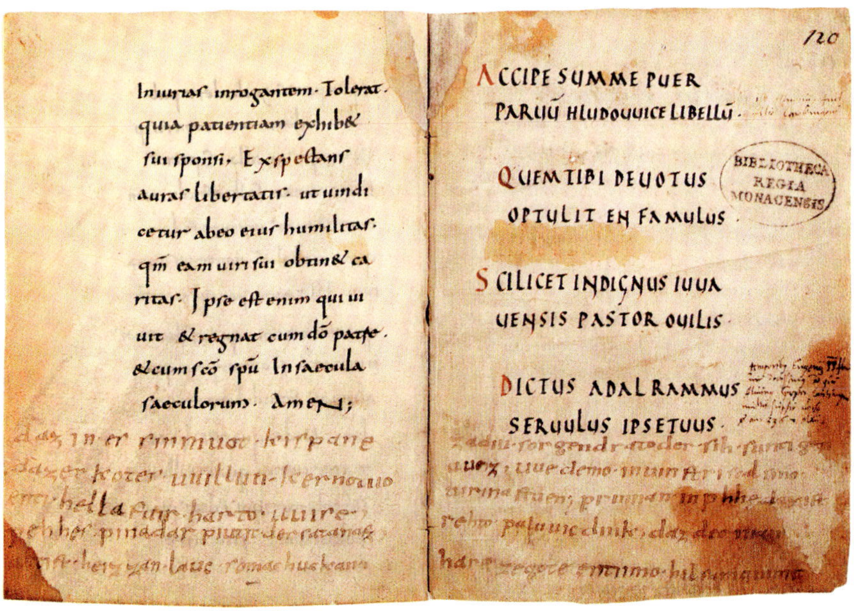

Handschrift aus dem Besitz König Ludwigs des Deutschen, um 830 nach Christus

Gebrochene Schriften

Im Hochmittelalter wurde 1163 mit dem Beginn der Kathedrale Notre-Dame in Paris begonnen. Es entwickelte sich ein neues Stilempfinden, das von Spitzen, schlanken Formen geprägt war. Das Zeitalter der **Gotik** hatte begonnen.

Die Schriften wurden wieder strenger, die Buchstaben rückten noch enger zueinander, die Rundungen der Buchstaben wurden begradigt und somit „gebrochen“, Als Hauptzweck stand somit nicht mehr die Lesbarkeit im Vordergrund, sondern die feierliche Anmutung!

Links:
Auszug aus der Gutenberg-Bibel

Rechts:
Ulmer Münster, höchster Kirchturm der Welt, erbaut nach gotischem Baustil, Titel in gebrochener Schriftart geschrieben

Einzig in Italien konnte sich die gotische Stilepoche nicht richtig durchsetzen. Zusätzlich fand dort gegen 1400 eine Abkehr der kirchlichen Machtansprüche statt, eine geistige Neuorientierung wurde eingeleitet und die Werte der alten Antike wieder entdeckt. Die Schriftgelehrten kombinierten das Großbuchstabenalphabet der Capitalis Monumentalis mit dem Kleinbuchstabenalphabet der Karolinger Minuskel. Diese Buchstaben haben dann zusätzlich noch Serifen bekommen, was zu einer deutlich besseren Lesbarkeit der Schrift geführt hat. Die Renaissance hatte begonnen, das Mittelalter war beendet.

5.2.4 Druckschriften

Johannes Gensfleisch zu Gutenberg, Kupferstich um 1600

Mit der Erfindung der beweglichen Lettern von **Johannes Gensfleisch zu Gutenberg** 1452 konnte plötzlich ein einheitliches Schriftbild erzeugt werden. Die zuvor von der Handschrift geprägten Bücher und Zeitungen konnten in einem einheitlichen, sauberen Erscheinungsbild gedruckt werden.

Gutenbergs Erfindung war in Europa revolutionär, obwohl es bereits in Asien einige hundert Jahre zuvor entsprechende Einsätze gab. So wurden der Überlieferung nach in China bereits um 700 nach Christus Holztafeldrucke angefertigt. Hierbei wurden die zu druckenden Bilder spiegelverkehrt in Holztafeln geschnitten. Andere Quellen sprechen ähnliche Erfindungen Korea zu.

Doch: Geschmäcker sind ja bekanntlich verschieden und so entwickelte sich fortan ein Trend, welcher stark an die Entwicklung der Kulturepochen geknüpft war: Schriftentwickler unterschiedlichster Herkunft gingen ans Werk und veränderten die Schriften von Zeit zu Zeit, neue Schriftarten sind entstanden.

Renaissance (1400 - 1600)

Die **Renaissance** bezeichnet eine Kunst- und Kulturepoche, bei der sich die Menschen an Werten und Formen der römischen und griechischen Antike orientierten. Die Gebäude waren geprägt vom Bau antiker Säulentempel, zu den bekanntesten Wissenschaftlern und Künstlern dieser Zeit zählen das italienische Universaltalent **Leonardo da Vinci** und der deutsche Mathematiker **Albrecht Dürer**.

Aldus Manutius, Kupferstich um 1600

Die Renaissance brachte gleich zwei unterschiedliche Schriftarten hervor, bedingt durch die verschiedenen kulturellen Strömungen aus Italien und Frankreich:
Die **Venzianische Renaissance-Antiqua** gilt als die erste Weiterentwicklung von noch verschiedenen mittelalterlichen Schriften, kommt jedoch heute aufgrund eines noch mittelalterlich wirkenden Erscheinungsbildes eher seltener zum Einsatz.
Eine heute noch gültige Form entwickelte der venezianische Verleger **Aldus Manutius** mit seiner um 1495 entstandenen **Bembo**. Obwohl viele dieser Schriften noch in Italien entwickelt wurden, werden diese bereits der kurz danach in Frankreich entstehenden **Französischen Renaissance-Antiqua** zugeordnet.
Der Pariser Stempelschneider **Claude Garamond** gilt heute als der bekannteste Vertreter dieser Schriftarten mit seiner um 1532 entstandenen gleichnamigen Schrift **Garamond**. Die Schrift ist außerordentlich gut entwickelt und zeichnet sich durch ein harmonisches Schriftbild aus.

Barock (1600 - 1760)

Der **Barock** löste die auf Ruhe und Einheit zielende Denkweise der Renaissance ab. Die Menschen strebten nach Reichtum und Bewegtheit, der Baustil entwickelte sich zu einer Überzeichnung der von der Renaissance geprägten Formen. Ein Beispiel hierfür stellt die St. Paul's Cathedral in London dar, die zwischen 1675 und 1710 erbaut wurde.

Mit dem Beginn des Barockzeitalters verlagerte sich die Schriftentwicklung zunehmend in die Niederlande. Bei Garamond angestellte Mitarbeiter trugen dazu bei, das diverses technische Material von Frankreich in die Niederlande transportiert wurde. Man verzeichnete jedoch keine schnellen Formänderungen, vielmehr wurde über einen relativ langen Zeitraum kontinuierlich an neuen Formen gearbeitet, diese fanden schließlich auch ihren Weg nach England.

Um 1722 veröffentlichte der noch in England unbekannte Schriftgießer **William Caslon** seine gleichnamige Schrift. 1734 brachte er ein Schriftmusterblatt mit insgesamt 47 von ihm hergestellten Schriftschnitten heraus und konnte somit die englischen Drucker endgültig zur Einführung der **Barock-Antiqua** bewegen.

A SPECIMEN
By WILLIAM CASLON, Letter-Founder, in Chiswell-Street, LONDON.

ABCD
ABCDE
ABCDEFG
ABCDEFGHI
ABCDEFGHIJK
ABCDEFGHIJKL
ABCDEFGHIKLMN

Quousque tandem abutere, Catilina, pati-
Quousque tandem abutere, Catilina, patientia nostra?

Two Lines Great Primer.
Quousque tandem abutere, Catilina, patientia nostra? quamdiu nos etiam
Quousque tandem abutere, Catilina, patientia nostra? quamdiu nos etiam furor

Two Lines English.
Quousque tandem abutere, Catilina, patientia nostra? quamdiu nos etiam furor iste tuus elu-
Quousque tandem abutere, Catilina, patientia nostra? quamdiu nos etiam furor

Double Pica Roman.
Quousque tandem abutere, Catilina, patientia nostra? quamdiu nos etiam furor iste tuus eludet? quem ad finem sese effrenata jactabit audacia?
ABCDEFGHJIKLMNOP

Double Pica Italick.
Quousque tandem abutere, Catilina, patientia nostra? quamdiu nos etiam furor iste tuus eludet? quem ad finem sese effrenata jac-
ABCDEFGHJIKLMNO

Great Primer Roman.

Great Primer Italick.

Klassizismus (1760 - 1830)

Giambattista Bodoni

Der **Klassizismus** tritt als künstlerisches Gegenprogramm zum Barock auf und löste diese Kulturepoche ab. Die noch hier feudal geprägten Gebäude wurden stark vereinfacht und basierten erneut auf Formen des griechischen Tempelbaus.

Mit dem Zeitalter des Klassizismus erreichte die Entwicklung der **Antiqua-Schriften** ❶ einen vorläufigen Endpunkt. Die Schriftentwickler konstruierten die Schriften mit Lineal und Zirkel um somit dem Anspruch nach Klarheit und Perfektion zu genügen. Die bedeutendsten Schriftentwerfer dieser Zeit waren der Italiener **Giambattista Bodoni**, sowie der deutsche Stempelschneider **Walbaum**. Beide haben Schriften entworfen, die ebenfalls nach ihnen benannt sind.

Industrialisierung (1830 - 1890)

Mit der **Industrialisierung** rückte der technische Fortschritt der Gesellschaft in den Vordergrund. So wurden auch die Druckmaschinen immer ausgefeilter und die Druckprodukte konnten immer schneller gefertigt werden. Stilistisch gab es daher in dieser Zeit kaum noch Innovationen in der weiteren Schriftentwicklung.

❶ Als Antiqua-Schriften oder Serif-Schriften werden Schriftarten bezeichnet, die auf dem lateinischen Alphabet basieren und sich ursprünglich auf Vorbilder der römischen Antike bezogen. Sie besitzen Serifen.

1850 schuf der Londoner Schriftgießer **Benjamin Fox** eine Schrift mit dem Namen **Clarendon**. Diese Schrift zeigt eine enge Verwandtschaft zu den Schriften aus der Zeit des Klassizismus. Die Schrift zeichnet sich dadurch aus, dass die Serifen sehr stark ausgeprägt sind. Schriften dieser Art wurden zum einen aufgrund des stärkeren Bedarfs nach Werbe- und Plakatschriften entwickelt, zum anderen konnten die stärker ausgeprägten Serifen von den Druckmaschinen feiner gedruckt werden, die Ränder brachen weniger aus.

Moderne (seit 1890)

❷ Als Grotesk-Schriften oder Sans Serif-Schriften werden Schriftarten bezeichnet, bei denen die Strichstärken der Buchstaben (nahezu) gleichmäßig sind und die keine Serifen besitzen.

Mit dem Beginn des 20. Jahrhunderts kann man die Sternstunde der bis heute sehr wichtigen Schriftarten definieren: Die Gruppe der **serifenlosen Schriften** oder auch **Grotesk-Schriften** ❷ genannt. Durch einen gestiegenen Bedarf an Werbeschriften entwickelte zwar bereits 1816 der Urgroßenkel von William Caslon eine gleichnamige Schrift ohne Serifen, dieser fand jedoch vorerst keine Abnehmer. Erst etwa ab 1832 verbreiteten sich verschiedene abgewandelte Formen in England.

1896 brachte die **Berthold AG** die Schrifttype **Akzidenz-Grotesk** heraus. Diese gilt als Meilenstein der modernen Schriftgestaltung und fand in der weiteren Schriftentwicklung unzählige Nachahmer.

Den Eingang in die **Moderne** läutete 1919 die Gründung des **Bauhauses** ein. Die von dem Architekten **Walter Gropius** 1919 gegründete Kunstschule in Weimar vereinte unterschiedliche Ansätze aus Industriedesign, Grafikdesign, Kunst und Architektur. Hier lehrten heute noch sehr bekannte Künstler und Grafiker wie **Johannes Itten** oder **Wassily Kandinsky**.

Zunächst war das Bauhaus eigentlich wie ein Werkstudium aufgebaut. Die im Gebäude untergebrachten Werkstätten wurden von den Künstlern und von verschiedenen Handwerksmeistern geleitet, jeder Student musste zunächst eine handwerkliche Lehre absolvieren, bevor er sich zum Formdesigner ausbilden lassen konnte. Diese Ausbildung wurde dem Anspruch des Bauhauses gerecht, dass jeder gute Designer erst dann ein „Meister der Form" werden konnte, wenn er über ein handwerklich-technisches Grundwissen verfügte.

Die Entwicklung von Schriften gehörte ebenso zur Lehre des Bauhauses dazu. Im Wesentlichen wurden Groteskschriften entwickelt, die auf geometrischen Grundformen basierten. 1925 führte das Bauhaus in allen seinen Publikationen die **radikale Kleinschrift** ein und verbannte alle Großbuchstaben.

Der deutsche Typograf **Jan Tschichold** lancierte in den folgenden Jahren zum Verfechter einer neuen Typografie der Einfachkeit. Stark von Tschicholds Lehren wurde zum Beispiel auch die 1928 entstandene Schrift **Futura** von **Paul Renner** beeinflusst, die sich zu einer der meistverkauften Schriften aller Zeiten entwickelte.

Durch die Machtergreifung der Nationalsozialisten 1933 wurde das Wirken der Bauhausgeneration beendet und die Schule musste schließen.

Nach Ende des zweiten Weltkrieges begründete der ehemalige Bauhausstudent **Max Bill** gemeinsam mit **Otl Aicher** und seiner Frau **Inge Aicher-Scholl** in Ulm die **Hochschule für Gestaltung**, welche nach dem Vorbild des Bauhausprinzipes wirken sollte.

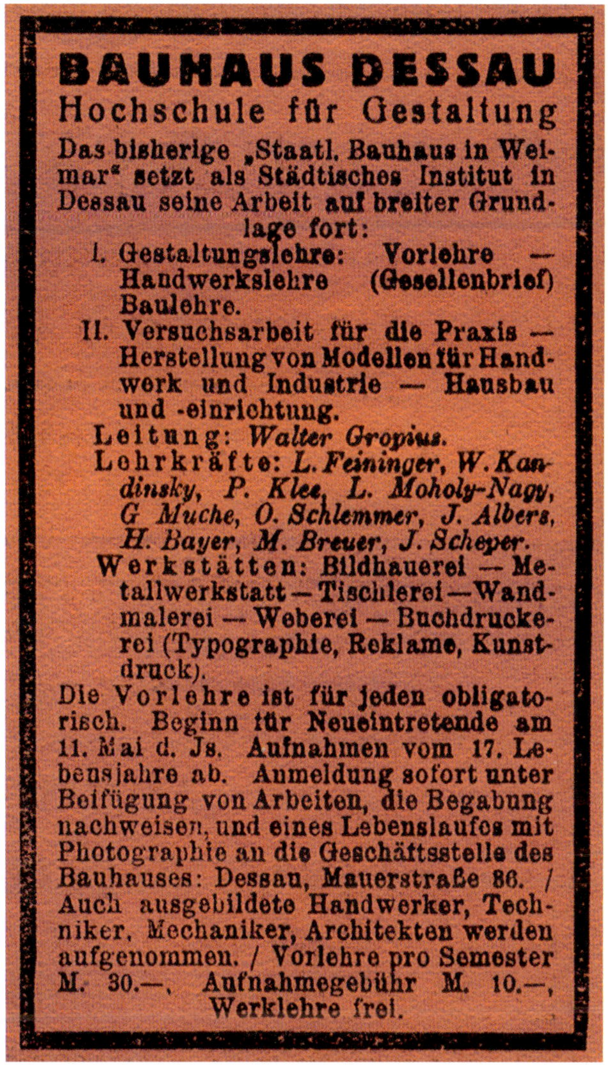

BAUHAUS DESSAU
Hochschule für Gestaltung
Das bisherige „Staatl. Bauhaus in Weimar" setzt als Städtisches Institut in Dessau seine Arbeit auf breiter Grundlage fort:
I. Gestaltungslehre: Vorlehre — Handwerkslehre (Gesellenbrief) Baulehre.
II. Versuchsarbeit für die Praxis — Herstellung von Modellen für Handwerk und Industrie — Hausbau und -einrichtung.
Leitung: *Walter Gropius.*
Lehrkräfte: *L. Feininger, W. Kandinsky, P. Klee, L. Moholy-Nagy, G. Muche, O. Schlemmer, J. Albers, H. Bayer, M. Breuer, J. Scheper.*
Werkstätten: Bildhauerei — Metallwerkstatt — Tischlerei — Wandmalerei — Weberei — Buchdruckerei (Typographie, Reklame, Kunstdruck).
Die Vorlehre ist für jeden obligatorisch. Beginn für Neueintretende am 11. Mai d. Js. Aufnahmen vom 17. Lebensjahre ab. Anmeldung sofort unter Beifügung von Arbeiten, die Begabung nachweisen, und eines Lebenslaufes mit Photographie an die Geschäftsstelle des Bauhauses: Dessau, Mauerstraße 86. / Auch ausgebildete Handwerker, Techniker, Mechaniker, Architekten werden aufgenommen. / Vorlehre pro Semester M. 30.—, Aufnahmegebühr M. 10.—, Werklehre frei.

Eigenwerbung des Bauhauses in der Zeitschrift „Die Weltbühne" vom 28. April 1925

Die bereits im Bauhaus vorherrschende **Schweizer Typografie** wurde auch hier das Markenzeichen einer neuen Moderne. Kennzeichnend für die Schriftentwicklung war eine asymmetrische, sachliche Darstellung der Schriften, die extreme Weißräume verzeichnete und auf jede Art Schmuckelemente zerzichtete. Aufgrund interner Streitigkeiten über das Lehrkonzept der Schule musste diese 1969 schließen. 20 Jahre danach veröffentlichte der Mitbegründer Otl Aicher seine nach seinem Wohnort benannte Schrift **Rotis**, die heute als eine der bedeutendsten Industrie- und Gebrauchsschriften gilt.

Die heutige Typografie ist geprägt vom Fortschreiten der technischen Entwicklungen. Mit der Erfindung des Computers mussten die Schriften vom Papier auf ein anderes Medium, den Bildschirm, transportiert werden. Auf diese Aspekte wird im Kapitel 5.5.3 eingegangen.

5.3 Gestalten mit Schrift

5.3.1 Schriften bezeichnen

Es gibt heute eine Unmenge verschiedener **Druckschriften**. ❶ Diese Vielzahl bringt automatisch die Qual der Wahl, für einen bestimmten Gestaltungszweck eine entsprechende Schrift auszuwählen. Bevor wir uns gezielt mit dieser Wahl beschäftigen können, wollen wir im Folgenden einige Grundbegriffe zur Thematik Schrift darstellen.

❶ Unter einer **Druckschrift** versteht man heute eine mit dem Computer oder anderen professionellen Herstellungsverfahren druck- oder darstellbare Schrift. Man vermutet heute etwa rund 100.000 solcher Schriften auf der Basis des lateinischen Alphabets.

Schriftfamilie und Schriftschnitt

Schriften werden in **Schriftfamilien** zusammengefasst, wie zum Beispiel die Univers, die Frutiger oder die Times New Roman. In ihr sind alle Varianten einer Schrift, die sogenannten **Schriftschnitte**, zusammengefasst. Die Schnitte einer Schrift werden gekennzeichnet von der **Schriftstärke**, der **Schriftbreite** und der **Schriftlage**.
Die gängigsten Bezeichnungen sind:

- Schriftstärken: Fein, Thin, Ultralight
  Leicht, Light, Mager
  Normal, Buch, Roman, Regular, Medium, Book
  Halbfett, Semibold, Demi, Heavy, Bold
  Fett, Black, Extrabold, Ultrablack, Poster
- Schriftbreiten: Eng, Ultra Condensed
  Schmal, Condensed
  Normal
  Breit, Extended
- Schriftlagen: Normal (gerade)
  Kursiv, Italic, Oblique

❷ Adrian Frutiger, in der Schweiz 1928 geboren, gilt als einer der bedeutendsten Typografen des 20. Jahrhunderts. Die gleichnamige Schrift Frutiger wurde die Hausschrift des Pariser Flughafens Charles de Gaulle. Frutiger entwarf noch weitere Schriften, allen voran auch die Univers und eine Machinenschrift, die OCR-B.

Bildquelle:
DVZ Druckmarkt Verlag
Zürich GmbH

So ergibt sich für eine Schriftfamilie je nach Schrift eine mehr oder weniger große Anzahl von Schnitten. Zum Beispiel einige Schnitte der von **Adrian Frutiger** ❷ 1975 entworfenen gleichnamigen Schrift Frutiger in der Schriftgröße von 10 Punkt:

Frutiger 45 Light
Frutiger 46 Light Italic
Frutiger 47 Light Condensed
Frutiger 55 Roman
Frutiger 56 Italic
Frutiger 57 Condensed
Frutiger 65 Bold
Frutiger 67 Bold Condensed
Frutiger 77 Black Condensed
Frutiger 87 Extra Black Condensed
Frutiger 95 Ultra Black

Einsatz der Schriften und Schriftschnitte

Je mehr Schriftschnitte eine Schrift besitzt, um so gezielter und damit auch universeller ist eine Schrift einsetzbar! Dabei muss allerdings beachtet werden, dass insbesondere die Schriftlage und meistens auch die Schriftstärke von allen Anwendungsprogrammen am Computer einstellbar ist, viele Schriften aber gar keinen echten Schriftschnitt mit einer entsprechenden Schriftlage oder Schriftstärke besitzen. In diesem Fall täuscht (= emuliert) das Anwendungsprogramm durch eine Verfettung der Schriftstärke oder durch einfaches Schrägstellen der Buchstaben entsprechende Schriftschnitte vor.

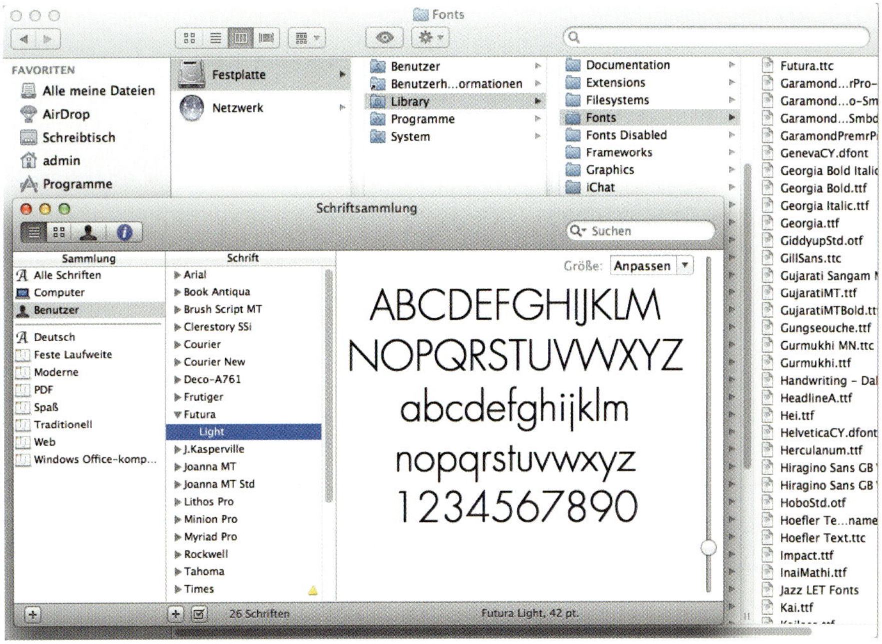

Echte Schriftschnitte einer Schriftfamilie sind im Ordner Schriftarten oder Fonts im Betriebssystem ❶ zu finden! Sind Sie dort nicht vorhanden, emuliert das Anwendungsprogramm den entsprechenden Schriftschnitt. Dies sollte jedoch grundsätzlich vermieden werden!

5.3.2 Klassifikation der Druckschriften nach DIN 16518

Die wachsende Anzahl an Schriften zwang die Typografen zu einem **Ordnungsprinzip**, einer Art System, um die Schriften unterscheiden zu können. Dieses Ordnungsprinzip wurde 1964 in einer DIN-Norm verabschiedet, der **DIN 16518 zur Klassifikation der Druckschriften**. Die Schriften werden in dieser Norm in 11 Gruppen eingeteilt.

Unter Schriftexperten ist diese Klassifikation umstritten. Ihr wird vor allem vorgeworfen, dass sich die Schriftentwicklungen der letzten Jahre in das historisch eingeteilte Schema nicht gut einordnen lassen. Außerdem wird eine zentrale Frage nicht geklärt: Welche Schrift für welchen Zweck? Die Norm wird daher immer wieder von verschiedenen Typografen überarbeitet, es entstehen andere Ordnungsalternativen.

Schrifteinstellung im Anwendungsprogramm Word:

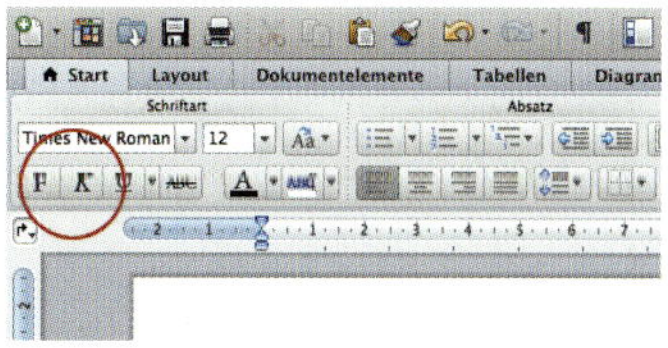

Mit Klick auf das dicke **F** wird ein fetter Schriftschnitt emuliert. Mit Klick auf das schräge **K** wird ein kursiver Schriftschnitt emuliert.

❶ Je nach Computerplattform an unterschiedlichen Orten erreichbar:

Windows-Systeme:
Start > Einstellungen > Systemsteuerung > Schriftarten
MAC OS-Systeme:
Festplatte > Library > Fonts

Unter MAC OS-Systemen ist ein Zugriff auch über das mitgelieferte Hilfsprogramm Schriftsammlung möglich.

Centaur
Zwölf Boxkämpfer jagen Viktor quer über den großen Sylter Deich

Ceg

Gruppe I: Venezianische Renaissance-Antiqua (seit ca. 1470)
- Kräftige Serifen
- Übergang zu den Serifen deutlich ausgerundet
- Achse der Rundungen deutlich nach links geneigt
- Querstrich des kleinen e liegt fast immer schräg
- Großbuchstaben basieren auf der römischen Capitalis
- Beispiele: Centaur, Stempel Schneidler

Bembo
Zwölf Boxkämpfer jagen Viktor quer über den großen Sylter Deich

Ceg

Gruppe II: Französische Renaissance-Antiqua (seit ca. 1532)
- Kräftige Serifen
- Übergang zu den Serifen deutlich ausgerundet
- Achse der Rundungen nach links geneigt
- Querstrich des kleinen e liegt immer waagerecht
- Strichstärke differenziert
- Beispiele: Bembo, Garamond, Palatino

Baskerville
Zwölf Boxkämpfer jagen Viktor quer über den großen Sylter Deich

Ceg

Gruppe III: Barock-Antiqua (seit ca. 1722)
- Serifen nicht so kräftig ausgeprägt
- Übergang zu den Serifen schwach ausgerundet
- Achse der Rundungen leicht nach links geneigt oder senkrecht
- Querstrich des kleinen e liegt immer waagerecht
- Strichstärke deutlich differenziert
- Beispiele: Baskerville, Caslon, Times New Roman

Bodoni
Zwölf Boxkämpfer jagen Viktor quer über den großen Sylter Deich

Ceg

Gruppe IV: Klassizistische Antiqua (seit ca. 1789)
- Dünne Serifen
- Kein (oder kaum wahrnehmbarer) Übergang zu den Serifen
- Achse der Rundungen immer senkrecht
- Querstrich des kleinen e liegt immer waagerecht
- Strichstärke deutlich differenziert
- Beispiele: Bodoni, Utopia, Walbaum

Rockwell
Zwölf Boxkämpfer jagen Viktor quer über den großen Sylter Deich

Ceg

Gruppe V: Serifenbetonte Linear-Antiqua (seit ca. 1815)
- Stark betonte Serifen
- Unterscheidung nach
- a - Egyptienne (Serifen rechteckig ohne Übergang)
- b - Clarendon (Serifen zum Stamm ausgerundet, enden rechteckig)
- c - Italienne (Serifen stärker als der Grundstrich)
- Beispiele: Rockwell, Clarendon, Zirkus

Helvetica
Zwölf Boxkämpfer jagen Viktor quer über den großen Sylter Deich

Ceg

Gruppe VI: Serifenlose Linear-Antiqua (seit ca. 1816)
- Keine Serifen
- Schriften ohne Serifen werden auch Groteskschriften genannt
- Strichstärke annähernd gleich
- Grundformen auf Basis geometrischer Formen
  oder Grundformen auf Basis der Antiqua-Schriften
- Beispiele: Helvetica, Frutiger, Univers

Gruppe VII: Antiqua-Varianten

- Antiqua-Varianten, die nicht in die Gruppen I bis III, VIII und IX passen
- Mit oder ohne Serifen
- Strichführung weicht vom Charakter der oben genannten Gruppen ab
- Meist Versalschriften für Werbezwecke (dekorativ und monumental)
- Beispiele: Codex, Optima, Copperplate

Codex
Zwölf Boxkämpfer jagen Viktor quer über den großen Sylter Deich
Ceg

Gruppe VIII: Schreibschriften

- Ahmen die Wirkung heutiger Handschriften nach (mit der Feder geschrieben)
- Manchmal verbundene Buchstaben
- Schon zu Bleisatzzeiten vorhanden
- Mit dem Zeitalter des Computers sehr in Mode gekommen
- Beispiele: Mistral, Brush Script, Wiesbaden Swing

Mistral
Zwölf Boxkämpfer jagen Viktor quer über den großen Sylter Deich
Ceg

Gruppe IX: Handschriftliche Antiqua

- Basieren auf der Antiqua oder der Kursiva
- Buchstaben sind handschriftlich abgewandelt
- Ahmen die Wirkung heutiger Handschriften nach (mit der Feder geschrieben)
- Buchstaben nicht verbunden
- Beispiele: Post-Antiqua, Omnia, Hobo

Post-Antiqua
Zwölf Boxkämpfer jagen Viktor quer über den großen Sylter Deich
Ceg

Gruppe X: Gebrochene Schriften (seit ca. 1445)

- Basieren auf der Schreibweise mit einer Breitfeder
- Rundungen und Ecken sind gebrochen
- Unterscheidung nach
  a: Gotisch
  b: Rundgotisch
  c: Schwabacher
  d: Fraktur
  e: Frakturvarianten
- Beispiele: Wilhelm Klingspor, Fette Fraktur, Old English

Gotisch
Rundgotisch
Schwabacher
Ceg

Gruppe XI: Fremde Schriften

- Alle Schriften, die nicht lateinischen Ursprunges sind
- Lassen sich nicht in die Gruppen I bis X einsortieren
- Beispiele: Chinesisch, Japanisch, Kyrillisch

Яа Яа Гг
山田太郎
Χεγ

Die Gruppen I bis IV sind streng genommen nach **Kulturepochen** eingeteilt (vgl. Kapitel 5.2 Geschichte der Typografie). Diese haben vor allem einen zeitlichen und geschichtlichen Bezug. Ab Gruppe V (mit Ausnahme der Gruppe X) erfolgt die Einteilung nicht mehr nach zeitlichen sondern nach **Formmerkmalen**. Die Schriften sind teilweise geometrisch konstruiert und weisen gewisse Ähnlichkeiten zu den Formelementen der elementaren Gestaltungslehre auf.

Bei näherer Betrachtung dieser Schriften kann ein gezielter Vergleich von Formmerkmalen und deren Wirkung auf den Betrachter erfolgen!

Bei diesem Beispiel wurde ein Faltblatt eines Pizza-Express-Lieferservice so verändert, dass der gleichnamige Schriftzug in vier verschiedenen Schriftarten vorliegt, aus jeder der im vorangegangenen Abschnitt geschilderten Gruppen eine.

Beispiel Faltblatt Pizza-Express Lieferservice

Welche Schrift passt am Besten? Nun, es gibt hier kein absolutes „Richtig“ oder „Falsch“, vielleicht eher ein „Sehr passend“ und ein „Weniger passend“.

Welche **Assoziationen** verbinden Sie mit Pizza? Ein Glas Rotwein an einem lauen Sommerabend, den Sonnenuntergang genießen. Lust auf Pizza? Für Freunde der Romantik ist sicherlich eine Variante in einer Schreibschrift ❸ sehr gelungen!
Oder bedeutet die Pizza für Sie doch eher den schnellen Imbiss zwischendurch? Dann ist wahrscheinlich die schnörkellose Variante einer Grotesk-Schrift ❶ besser geeignet. Ganz bestimmt nicht funktioniert die gebrochene Schrift ❹. Die Assoziationen zur traditionellen, gut bürgerlichen, einheimischen Küche sind hier doch sehr weit weg.

5.3.5 Schriften mischen

Bedingt durch die Vielzahl der erhältlichen Druckschriften werden diese natürlich häufig miteinander gemischt. Hierbei haben sich zwei Grundsätze unter den führenden Typografen entwickelt:

- **Schriften sollten nur miteinander gemischt werden, um einen Kontrast zu erzeugen!**
- **Die Mischung von mehr als zwei Schriften ist im Regelfall nicht indiziert.**

Beim vorliegenden Buch zum Beispiel wurden die Schriften wohl dosiert ausgewählt. Als Schrift des Buchtextes wird die 1930 von **Eric Gill** entworfene Schrift **Joanna** verwendet, eine Barock-Antiqua, die von der Fontshop AG aus Berlin 2008 zu einer der besten 100 Schriften gewählt wurde. Sie ist leicht zu handhaben und sehr gut lesbar. Für die Überschriften und den Text in den Marginalspalten wurde die **Frutiger** ausgewählt, eine serifenlose Linear-Antiqua, die 1975 von **Adrian Frutiger** entworfen und von der deutschen Schriftgießerei D. Stempel veröffentlicht wurde. Die Frutiger zählt ebenfalls zu den 100 besten Schriften im Katalog der Fontshop AG.
Die beiden Schriften kontrastieren sich deutlich hinsichtlich der Strichstärke und der Schriftlage. Dadurch werden die Überschriften und die Texte in der Marginalspalte besser wahr genommen, bilden aber ein ausgewogenes, harmonisches Gesamtbild miteinander.

Lebensgefühl

Frühlingsgefühle – ein Gefühl

Wenn die ersten warmen Sonnenstrahlen des Jahres unsere Haut berühren, läuft unser Körper zu neuen Höchstformen auf, unsere tiefen Winterdepressionen scheinen flott dahinzuschmelzen, und nicht nur die geraten ins Schwitzen. Nein, auch das jeweils andere Geschlecht wird zum Kochen gebracht: Die Tage werden wieder länger, die Kleidung kürzer, die Flirtwütigen strotzen vor lauter Tatendrang.

Das Phänomen der Frühlingsgefühle kehrt wieder ein in unsere Welt.

Sowohl die bekannten Glückshormone, in der Fachsprache auch Endorphine genannt, als auch sämtliche Sexualhormone bringen unser Blut – pünktlich zum Frühjahr – in Wallungen. Der Winterschlaf ist also endgültig vorbei und keine Frage: Jeder Single würde gerne einen Partner an seiner Seite haben, um gemeinsam in Richtung Sommer zu gehen, denn die Einsamkeit der kalten Tage konnte ja nicht mal mehr durch die künstlichen Endorphine aus der Schokolade geheilt werden. Ab jetzt lautet nun das Motto: „Ich will keine Schokolade, ich will lieber einen Mann bzw eine Frau!"

Verliebtsein ist eines der schönsten Gefühle, die jemand in seinem Leben erfahren kann. Rauschartig kann das ganze Bewusstsein eine rasante Achterbahnfahrt durchleben. Und weil diese Gefühle süchtig machen, können manche Menschen einfach nicht anders als immer jemanden an ihrer Seite haben zu wollen. Und das ist schon eines von zwei Extremen: Die „BAN- Beziehung". BAN steht für besser als nichts. Besser gesagt: Eben einen Partner haben, nur um nicht allein zu sein. So wie bei Katharina* und Manuel*. Fragt man Katharina nach Dingen, die sie an Manuel mag, so bekommt man etwa Folgendes zu hören: „Seine Tapete im Wohnzimmer", oder „dass er einen Führerschein hat". Gar nichts anderes? Stille.

Jeder normale Mensch fragt sich jetzt, wieso die beiden dennoch ein Paar sind und eine „Beziehung" führen. Die Antwort ist einfach: Manuel liebt Katharina, Katharina hasst das Alleinsein.

Welche Gründe führen noch zu typischen BAN- Beziehungen? Da wäre zum einen mangelndes Selbstbewusstsein. BAN- Typen empfinden das Single- Dasein als Dilemma und bevor sie in den von ihnen so gefürchteten Zustand geraten, ziehen sie den Nächstbesten vor um damit dem Alleinsein quasi zu entfliehen. Sie können einfach keine Zeit mit sich selbst verbringen. Außerdem empfinden diese Menschen einen gewaltigen Druck aus ihrem Umfeld, für sie scheint die ganze Welt nur aus Paaren zu bestehen. Ob glücklich oder nicht, egal, Single sein ist out. Ohne Rücksicht auf Gefühle oder Verluste. Denn ein Partner wird immer um seine Gefühle betrogen, da dieser meist mit 100% Gefühl und Herz dabei ist. Katharina ist ein Paradebeispiel für einen typischen BAN- Beziehungstyp. Sie lernte Manuel erst vor kurzem kennen. Zuerst war es für sie nur eine einmalige Sache, doch er hatte ernsthafte Absichten. Sie hatte schon seit einer Zeit keine „feste" Beziehung mehr, da kam Manuel ihr gerade recht. Sie überlegt immer wieder, welchen Sinn ihre Liebschaft eigentlich macht, denn eigentlich gäbe es ja noch weitere Männer, mit denen sie doch lieber zusammen wäre, aber dann sagt sie wiederum auch, dass es ja doch eine Chance gäbe, dass sich noch wirkliche Gefühle entwickeln. Vielleicht, irgendwann.

zwei Extreme

Der Frühling hat ja gerade erst angefangen. Und Gelegenheit macht ja bekanntlich Liebe. Vielleicht auch in Katharinas Fall.

Als Gegenteil zu dem schändlichen Betrug an dem wunderbaren Gefühl der Liebe von BAN- Typen gibt es aber die Paare, die sich wahrhaftig lieben. Natalie* und Mario* zum Beispiel. Ein Bilderbuchpaar. Sie sind schon eine ganze Weile zusammen. Im Mai 2004 hat es zwischen den beiden gefunkt, mit den berühmten Schmetterlingen und allem drum und dran. Der Wonnemonat hat ihnen also bis heute Glück gebracht, denn sie sind immer noch genauso unzertrennlich wie am Anfang ihrer Beziehung. Fragt man Natalie nach Dingen, die sie an Mario liebt, sagt sie mit ganz verträumten Augen: „Alles".

Aber wieso funktioniert es bei den beiden so gut und bei anderen nicht? Was macht eine Liebe beständig? Darüber streiten sich bestimmt selbst die Experten. Es gibt wohl kein Rezept à la 1 Prise Vertrauen und 2 Teelöffel Treue.

Auf jeden Fall sollte man sich seine Eigenständigkeit auch in einer Beziehung bewahren, man sollte sich selbst treu bleiben und seinen Freundeskreis nicht zu sehr vernachlässigen.

Es gibt bestimmt viele Tipps für eine gut geführte Beziehung und das, was sie langanhaltend macht. Das wichtigste ist und bleibt aber das Gefühl des Verliebtseins.

Liebe – wie wird die eigentlich definert? Im Wörterbuch steht: „Bezeichnung für die stärkste Zuneigung, die ein Mensch einem anderen Menschen zu empfinden fähig ist". Aber da Gefühle sowieso von jedem anders empfunden werden ist eine rationale Erklärung unmöglich. Deswegen führen sowohl Natalie als auch Katharina eine „normale" Beziehung, jede auf ihre (eigen-) Art.

Geleitet vom Phänomen Frühlingsgefühl, oder eher gesagt vom Phänomen Hormone und persönlicher Einstellung.

Magazinseite eines Schülermagazines. Hier wurde nicht nur mit einer geschickten Farbwahl ein Kontrast geschaffen, sondern auch mit dem Einsatz zweier völlig unterschiedlicher Schriftarten.

5.4 Mikrotypografie

Die **Mikrotypografie** beschäftigt sich mit dem Aufbau der Buchstaben, den Zeichen, Wörtern und Sätzen. Vereinfacht ausgedrückt kann man auch sagen: Sie beschäftigt sich mit dem, was sich rund um und zwischen den Buchstaben abspielt. Die Mikrotypografie umfasst danach sowohl den Entwurf von Schriften, also die optische Konstruktion der Buchstaben und Figuren selbst, als auch deren Anwendung.

5.4.1 Buchstabe und Wort

Wenn man sich mit den Details einer Schrift befasst, ist es sehr wichtig, eine einheitliche Sprache zu sprechen – man spricht von der **Typologie** der Schrift! Damit sind die Fachbegriffe gemeint, die man benutzt, wenn man sich mit anderen Gestaltern und Typografen über die Merkmale einer Schrift austauscht. Diese Fachbegriffe sind für die gesamte Arbeit an und mit Schrift sehr wichtig. Das Arbeiten an Schriften bezeichnet den Entwurfsprozess einer Schrift, wohingegen das Arbeiten mit Schrift Typografie selbst bedeutet.

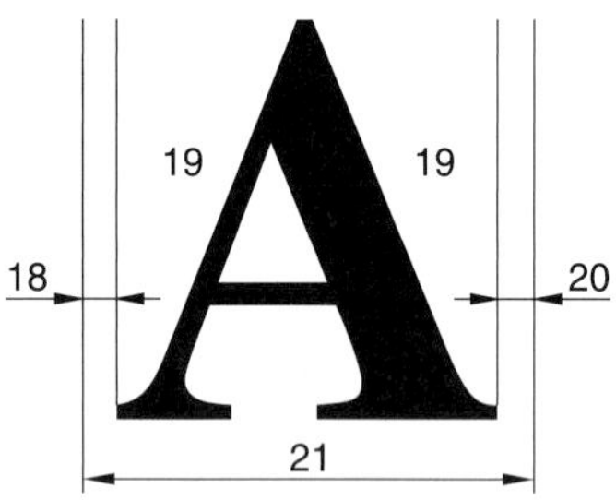

1 Grundstrich, Hauptstrich
2 Haarstrich
3 Serife
4 (Schatten)achse
5 Anstrich
6 Abstrich, Endstrich
7 Scheitel
8 Bauch
9 Schlinge
10 Punzen, Innenform
11 Kehlung
12 Schriftlinie
13 Versalhöhe
14 Oberlänge
15 Mittellänge, x-Höhe
16 Unterlänge
17 Max. Ausdehnung, hp-Höhe
18 Vorbreite
19 Fleisch
20 Nachbreite
21 Dickte

Es genügt bei der Arbeit mit Schrift natürlich nicht, sich nur über die Begrifflichkeiten im Klaren zu sein. Ebenso wichtig sind die Bezugsgrößen, um Schriften miteinander zu vergleichen, um Maß zu nehmen und um Schriften zu messen!

Maßeinheit von Schriften

Die Maßeinheit ❶, um Schriften zu vermessen, ist der **typografische Punkt**. Diese Maßeinheit bildet jedoch kein allgemeingültiges, gesetzlich festgelegtes Längenmaß, sondern ein Maß, welches lediglich im Bereich der Gestaltungs- und Medientechnik Gültigkeit hat. Erschwerend kommt hinzu, dass es mehrere typografische Punkte gibt, die sich aus der geschichtlichen Entwicklung ableiten.

Seit 31.12.1977 darf für die Maßeinheit zur Vermessung von Schriften nach der Ausführungsverordnung des Einheitengesetzes nur noch das metrische System ❷ verwendet werden. Da sich aber bei Einführung dieser Verordnung der typografische Punkt seit einigen Jahrhunderten etabliert hatte, konnte sich bis heute das metrische System in der Gestaltungs- und Medientechnik noch nicht ganz durchsetzen. Obwohl die Branche damit gegen geltendes Recht verstößt, wird es nach der Ausführungsverordnung geduldet.

Seit 1999 existieren in Deutschland zwei gültige DIN-Normen ❸, der Drucktechnik zugeordnet, welche die Maßeinheiten von Schriften festlegen:

- **DIN 16507-1, Ausgabe:1998-09**
  Drucktechnik – Schriftgrößen, Maße und Begriffe – Teil 1: Bleisatz und verwandte Techniken

- **DIN 16507-2, Ausgabe:1999-05**
  Drucktechnik – Schriftgrößen, Maße und Begriffe – Teil 2: Digitaler Satz und verwandte Techniken

Der Hintergrund für die Verwendung dieser zwei Normen liegt in der geschichtlichen Entwicklung begründet: Teil 1 der DIN-Normen 16507 bezeichnet das Maßsystem des **Bleisatzes** ❹, Teil 2 des **digitalen Satzes**.

Geschichtlicher Hintergrund

Der Pariser Schriftgießer **Pierre Simon Fournier** definierte 1737 ein typografisches Maßsystem auf der Grundlage des englisch-amerikanischen Fußes (304,8 mm). Er teilte den Fuß in 12 Teile ein; ein Teil entspricht hier der Größe eines Zolls. Den zwölften Teil eines Zolls nannte er eine Linie, den sechsten Teil einer Linie nannte er den typografischen Punkt.

- **Typografischer Punkt nach Fournier: 0,35277 mm**

Der französische Typograf **François Ambroise Didot** griff die Angaben von Fournier auf, glich aber die Größe des Fußes dem „Pied de Roi" an, dem französischen königlichen Fuß (324,9 mm). Damit ergab sich nach Fourniers Einteilung ein neuer typografischer Punkt:

- **Typografischer Punkt nach Didot: 0,37604 mm**

❶ Die physikalisch technische Bundesanstalt in Braunschweig legt die Maßeinheiten in Deutschland fest.
Diese werden im deutschen Gesetz über Einheiten im Messwesen (Einheitengesetz) vom Bundesministerium für Wirtschaft und Arbeit erlassen.

❷ Metrisches Sytem:
Das metrische System ist ein auf dem Meter basierendes Einheitensystem. Das System ging 1966 im internationalen Einheitensystem, auch einfach SI-System (Système international d'unités) auf. Neben dem metrischen System existiert das angloamerikanische Maßsystem noch in einigen englischsprachigen Regionen der Welt, vor allem in den USA. Die Basiseinheit ist das Zoll (inch).
1 Zoll (inch) = 2,54 cm

❸ Zu beziehen sind die Normen beim Beuth Verlag GmbH, einem Tochterunternehmen des Deutschen Institutes für Normung e.V.

❹ Bleisatz:
Druckmethode, nach der einzelne Bleilettern zu Schriftzeilen zusammengesetzt und nach dem Druck wieder auseinandergenommen werden.

Umrechnungstabelle für den DTP-Punkt (Werte gerundet)

1 DTP-Punkt [pt]	= 0,353 mm
72 DTP-Punkte	= 2,54 cm
	= 1 inch
1 DTP-Cicero	= 12 DTP-Punkte
	= 4,236 mm
	= 1,668 inch

Das Cicero wurde nach dem römischen Schriftsteller Marcus Cicero benannt, da in dieser Schriftgröße erstmals im Jahre 1467 „Ciceros Briefe" in Rom gedruckt wurden.

Dieser von Didot eingeführte typografische Punkt löste in Westeuropa den Fournier-Punkt ab. Die kleinste typografische Maßeinheit war ab diesem Zeitpunkt nur noch der Didot-Punkt.

Im Jahre 1879 stellte die Vereinigung der deutschen Schriftgießereien einen Antrag, den Didot-Punkt auf ein handhabbares Maß nach dem metrischen System abzurunden. Die deutschen Typografen **Herrmann Berthold** und **Wilhelm Foerster** legten den Didot-Punkt so fest, dass 2660 Punkte genau einen Meter ergeben:

➲ **Typografischer Punkt nach Didot ab 1897: 0,376 mm**

In den USA wurde der Fournier-Punkt weiterhin benutzt und verschmolz im Laufe des 19. Jahrhunderts mit einem von **William Caslon** 1720 erstellten englischen Punkt-System zum **Pica-Point**. 1892 wurde der Pica-Point in den USA durch die „American Type Founders Company" offiziell eingeführt (ein Pica-Point ist 0,025 mm kleiner als der Didot-Punkt):

➲ **Typografischer Punkt [P] in den USA (Pica-Point): 0,351 mm**

1979 hat der Bundesverband Druck den Vorschlag gemacht, gerundete Werte (mit 0 und 5) bei der Verwendung des für Deutschland geltenden Didot-Punktes einzuführen. Dieser Wert wurde damit verbindlich festgelegt und gilt nach DIN 16507-1:

➲ **Typografischer Punkt [p] im Bleisatz: 0,375 mm**

Mit der Einführung der EDV-Systeme in der Satztechnik 1985 sollte der Didot-Punkt eine weitere Revolution erfahren.

Die von der Firma Adobe 1984 entwickelte Seitenbeschreibungssprache **PostScript** verwendet einen Punkt anderer Größe, welcher als **DTP-Punkt** bezeichnet wurde. Die Basis für diesen Punkt bildet das Zoll (inch), denn die ersten Apple Macintosh DTP-Computer ❶ verwendeten eine Bildschirmauflösung von 72 Pixeln pro Zoll. Ein Pixel sollte nun einem Punkt entsprechen, um die Schriften möglichst präzise auf dem Bildschirm darstellen zu können. Ein DTP-Punkt ist also der 72. Teil eines Zolls. Heutige Layout-, Grafik- und Textverarbeitungsprogramme greifen in der Regel auf diesen DTP-Punkt zurück:

❶ **DTP = Desktop Publishing:** Englisch für das Publizieren vom Schreibtischcomputer aus. Gemeint ist das computergestützte Setzen hochwertiger Dokumente, die aus Texten und Bildern bestehen und später als Publikationen, wie zum Beispiel Broschüren, Magazinen oder Büchern ihre Verwendung finden. Im Mittelpunkt des DTP steht ein Computer, Software für die Erstellung der Seiten und ein Drucker.

➲ **Typografischer Punkt [pt] im DTP: 0,353 mm**

Die DIN-Norm 16507-2 schlägt nun einen neuen, typographischen Punkt von genau 0,25 mm vor, um dem oben geschilderten Zahlenwirrwarr ein Ende zu setzen. Ob dieser aber je Realität werden wird, erscheint höchst zweifelhaft, da er im internationalen Vergleich aufgrund der beiden unterschiedlichen Maßsysteme (metrisch und angloamerikanisch) nicht standhalten kann. Die Norm, eine ausschließlich deutsche Norm wird zwar international begrüßt, aber es findet keine Umrechnung ins angloamerikanische System statt, weshalb dieses Maßsystem mit der Bezeichnung 0,25 mm nichts anzufangen weiß.

Messen von Schriften

Die Größe einer Schrift wird definiert durch die **Schriftgröße**, auch **Schriftgrad** genannt. Diese Definition stammt noch aus der Zeit des Bleisatzes. Dort waren die Buchstaben auf einem **Bleikegel** montiert. Die Kegel mussten wegen des Zeilensatzes alle gleich hoch sein. So definiert die Schriftgröße das Maß des Kegels, die Kegelgröße. Dies ist auch heute noch die Ursache dafür, dass unterschiedliche Schriften bei gleicher Schriftgröße optisch unterschiedlich ausfallen können, da es keine Regelung gibt, wie die Verteilung der Versalhöhe, der x-Höhe und der Unterlängen auf dem Kegel auszufallen hat.

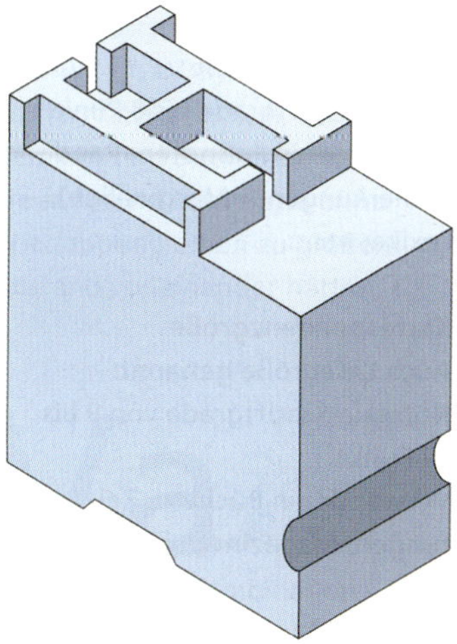

In der Praxis kann man heute die Kegelgröße nicht mehr nachvollziehen. Man kann daher festlegen, dass die maximale vertikale Ausdehnung einer Schrift zur Ermittlung der Schriftgröße geeignet ist.

Um die Schriftgröße und weitere typografische Maße ermitteln zu können, benötigt man ein **Typometer** ❶. Dies ist ein aus transparentem Kunststoff bestehendes Lineal von etwa 10 Zentimeter Breite und 32 Zentimeter Länge. Es gibt verschiedene Hersteller, die verschiedene Messmethoden anbieten, üblich ist es jedoch in ein vorgegebenes Feld die maximal vertikale Ausdehnung einer Schrift einzupassen ❷. Dann kann der Wert der Schriftgröße direkt abgelesen werden.

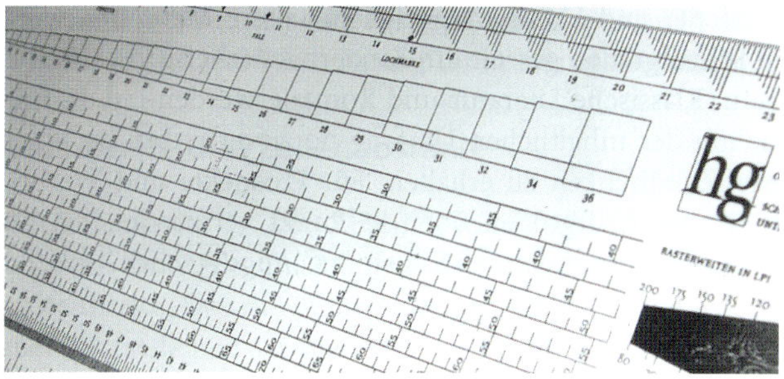

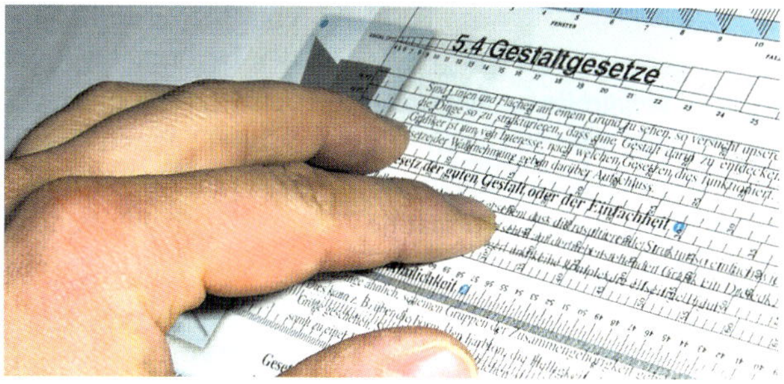

5.4.2 Vom Buchstaben zur Schrift

Schrift taucht immer in einer bestimmten Größe und in der Regel zeilenweise auf. Kommen mehrere Zeilen Schrift zusammen, haben diese meistens einen Abstand zueinander, den Zeilenabstand. Auch die Buchstaben eines Wortes haben einen Abstand zueinander, den Buchstaben- oder Zeichenabstand. Wörter haben einen Wortabstand und die Buchstaben und Wörter im Verbund haben eine Laufweite.

Diese Eigenschaften haben Einfluss auf die **Leserlichkeit** ❸ eines Textes. Die Leserlichkeit ist ein Maß für die **Lesegeschwindigkeit**. Danach lässt sich ein Text mit guter Leserlichkeit schneller lesen, als ein Text mit schlechter Leserlichkeit.

➲ **Das Einstellen einer optimalen Leserlichkeit ist Aufgabe der Mikrotypografie!**

❸ Leserlichkeit von Schrift:
Für lange, gedruckte Texte sind in der Regel Antiqua-Schriften leserlicher als Grotesk-Schriften. Für den Einsatz am Bildschirm gibt es jedoch spezielle Grotesk-Schriften, die hier deutlich leserlicher sind als Antiqua-Schriften. Für den Gestalter besteht bei der Schriftwahl eine Herausforderung!

5.5 Makrotypografie

Im Gegensatz zur Mikrotypografie beschäftigt sich die Makrotypografie mit dem gesamten gestalterischen Werk, also der Gestaltung von Text und Bild. Hierzu gehören insbesondere das Format, der Satzspiegel, der Aufbau und die Gliederung der Seite im Verhältnis von Text und Bild.

5.5.1 Lesefreundlichkeit

Die **Lesefreundlichkeit** eines Medienproduktes bestimmt dessen Erfolg oder Misserfolg. Unter der Lesefreundlichkeit ist im weitesten Sinne daher der „Mehrwert" für den Leser zu verstehen. Ist ein Konzept mikrotypografisch gut aufgestellt sind dies schon gute Voraussetzungen, um ein lesefreundliches Produkt zu gestalten. Hinzu kommen aber Gesetzmäßigkeiten der **visuellen Kommunikation**; die Hauptfrage hierbei:

➲ **Kommt die Botschaft beim Leser an?**

Lesefreundlichkeit ist daher in die beiden Bereiche aufzuteilen:

- **Leserlichkeit** (mikrotypografische Gesetzmäßigkeiten)
- **Lesbarkeit** im Sinne der visuellen Kommunikation

Linke Seite:
Doppelseite aus einem Filmmagazin, lesefreundlich zum informierenden Lesen gestaltet. Die obere Textkante der Spalten ist gleichmäßig angeordnet, Bild und Texttitel sparsam eingesetzt. Das Auge wird gut geführt.

Rechte Seite:
Gleiche Doppelseite, anders verteilt. Die Lesefreundlichkeit leidet.

THE LIVERPOOL GOALIE

ODER: WIE MAN DIE SCHULZEIT ÜBERLEBT!

„FUßBALL IST NICHT GERADE DIE SICHERSTE SPORTART. ES STERBEN MENSCHEN AUF NORWEGISCHEN FUßBALLFELDERN. JAHR FÜR JAHR."

Liebe Leser, in der letzten Ausgabe unseres Kinomagazins Abspann stellten wir Ihnen an dieser Stelle mit *„Bela Kiss"* ein neues Projekt aus Heinz Lochmanns „drei-freunde"-Filmverleih vor. Doch damit nicht genug – im Jahr 2012 dürfen Sie sich auf weitere filmische Highlights aus unserem Verleih freuen! Nach der Millennium-Trilogie von Stieg Larsson präsentieren wir Ihnen ab 15. März 2012 einen weiteren Filmhöhepunkt aus Skandinavien: Die norwegische Jugendkomödie *„The Liverpool Goalie"* verspricht witzige Unterhaltung mit Tiefgang für Jung und Alt!

Hochspannung mit *„Das Kind"* und Grusel pur mit *„Bela Kiss"* werden 2012 im Portfolio des drei-freunde Filmverleihs stehen – doch auch für erfrischende Kinounterhaltung der jungen Besucher ist gesorgt: Wenn der 13-jährige Jo sich in spektakulären Tagträumen die Konsequenzen seiner Entscheidungen ausmalt, während er eigentlich nur die hübsche Mari beeindrucken möchte, können Kinder und Jugendliche mitfühlen und auch die Erwachsenen geraten schnell ins Schmunzeln…

Jo Idstadt (Ask van der Hagen) ist 13 Jahre alt, ein fleißiger Schüler, sein Leben aber ist eine einzige Problemzone!

Jo´s übervorsichtige Mutter (Andrine Saether) nervt ihn mit ihren ständigen Warnungen vor den Gefahren des Alltags. In der Schule zwingt ihn sein streitlustiger Klassenkamerad Tom Erik (Jostein Sranes Brox), die Hausaufgaben für ihn zu erledigen, eine Pflicht, die Jo´s Freizeit bedeutend verringert. Und Mädchen geht er am liebsten aus dem Weg. Zu allem Übel ist Jo noch so ziemlich der schlechteste Torwart, den man sich nur vorstellen kann. Indem er all diese Probleme konsequent meidet, schlägt sich Jo durch sein Schulleben. Und schließlich gibt es neben dem Lösen mathematischer Gleichungen auch noch ein Hobby, das sein Leben bestimmt: Wie alle seiner Freunde sammelt Jo Fußballkarten und wie alle jagt er nach der einen, seltenen und damit wertvollen Karte, die den Torwart des FC Liverpool zeigt.

Als eines Tages Mari (Susanne Boucher) in Jo´s Klasse kommt, ist nichts mehr so, wie es war: Mari ist nicht nur hübsch, sondern auch noch die Zweitbeste der Klasse in Mathe – und sie spielt Fußball! Jo muss feststellen, dass Mari das Mädchen seiner Träume ist. Doch um sie zu beeindrucken, muss er einige Risiken auf sich nehmen. Plötzlich beginnen die Dinge, schief zu gehen, und bald steckt Jo richtig in der Klemme…

Es gibt nur ein Objekt, das alle seine Probleme auf einen Schlag lösen und ihn zum Siegertypen machen könnte: Eine Fußballsammelkarte mit dem LIVERPOOL GOALIE!

Nach der Romanvorlage „Keepern til Tunisia" von Lars Mæhle hat Arild Andresen mit *„The Liverpool Goalie"* eine amüsante Coming-of-Age-Komödie abgeliefert, bei der Groß und Klein sofort mit dem Schicksal des Protagonisten Jo mitfiebern können.

Mit Ask van der Hagen (Jo), Andrine Saether (Else), Susanne Boucher (Mari) und Jostein Sranes Brox (Tom Erik) konnte er einen authentischen, sehr sympathischen Cast verpflichten, der das Publikum ab der ersten Minute mitreißt. Denn wer könnte nicht mit Jo mitfiebern, wenn er sich in spektakulären Tagträumen ausmalt, wie sein Konflikt mit dem rüpelhaften Tom Erik schließlich so eskaliert, dass er mit seiner Mutter in einem Zeugenschutzprogramm am Ende der Welt hausen muss…?

Und das alles nur, weil er sich nicht gegen Tom-Eriks ständige Forderung, seine Hausaufgaben für ihn zu erledigen, wehren kann!

„Die frische Aufmachung und der packende Humor haben mich gleich mitgerissen", berichtet auch drei-freunde-Geschäftsführer Heinz Lochmann. „Nach verschiedenen Thrillern aus dem skandinavischen Raum freuen wir uns sehr, nun auch eine Komödie in unserem Programm präsentieren zu können – dieser lustige Film macht einfach nur fröhlich!"

Das finden nicht nur Heinz Lochmann und der drei-freunde Filmverleih, sondern auch die Jurys verschiedener großer (Kinderfilm-)Festivals in Deutschland! Bereits im Februar 2011 wurde THE LIVERPOOL GOALIE auf der Berlinale mit dem Gläsernen Bären in der Sektion „Generation KPlus" ausgezeichnet. Im September gewann er auf dem internationalen Kinderfilmfestival LUCAS in Frankfurt den Don Quijote Preis der internationalen Fachjury. Das LUCAS hat den Anspruch, künstlerisch und thematisch wertvolle Filme auf Augenhöher seiner jungen Besucher zu zeigen; so sahen in zwei Aufführungen neben der Jury fast 500 Besucher den Film. Und das Kinopublikum war beigeistert: „Los Jo!", „Sag ja, Jo", großer Lacher und Jubelausrufe, als Jo sich zum ersten Mal gegen Tom Erik wehrt – die Stimmung im Kinosaal kochte! Auch die älteren Zuschauer schlossen den Film ins Herz, denn Nebenstränge wie die Affäre von Jo´s Mutter Else mit dem sympathischen Nachbarn Einar, die sie auf sehr komische Art und Weise zu verbergen versucht, erreichen auch die erwachsenen Besucher mit ihrem subtilen Humor und regen an zum Nachdenken über den Wahrheitsgehalt. So begründete die Jury: „Der Film ist zum einen herzerwärmend, zum anderen so anspruchsvoll, dass das Schauen des Films zu einer zum Nachdenken anregenden Erfahrung wird. Wir sind der Meinung, dass das Publikum in eine enge Beziehung zu den Charakteren und der Geschichte tritt und die hohe cineastische Qualität des Films und der Produktion wahrnimmt. Die Kinder können in die Geschichte eintauchen, von ihr lernen, können sie hinterfragen und über sie sprechen!"

Pünktlich zur Einstimmung auf die Fußball Europameisterschaft 2012 kommt die Komödie am 15. März 2012 in die deutschen Kinos!

Lesbarkeit

Hans-Peter Willberg ❶ unterscheidet die Medienprodukte nach **Lesearten** ❷. Im Folgenden werden jeweils zwei Beispiele genannt:

- Romane, Geschichten > lineares lesen
- Zeitungen, Sachbücher > informierendes / selektives lesen
- Aufsätze, Diplomarbeiten > wissenschaftliches lesen
- Lexika, Telefonbücher > konsultierendes lesen
- Werbefaltblätter, TV-Werbung > aktivierendes / inszenierendes lesen
- Internet, mobile Geräte > vernetztes lesen

Nach dieser Unterscheidung können die verschiedenen Medienprodukte daher keinesfalls gleich gestellt werden. Jedes Medium hat seine eigenen Anforderungen zu erfüllen. Dennoch gibt es eine Gesetzmäßigkeit, die für alle Medienprodukte gilt: Die Lesefreundlichkeit! Man sollte beim Betrachten einer Werbeanzeige Lust bekommen, das beworbene Produkt zu kaufen. Man sollte ein Magazin gerne aufschlagen, um darin zu schmökern. Man sollte sich durch die morgendliche Tageszeitung nicht „durchquälen" müssen. Nein, das Lesen soll Freude bereiten! Dabei muss das Lesen als ganzheitlicher Wahrnehmungsprozess verstanden werden!

❶ Hans Peter Willberg lebte von 1930 bis 2003. Er war ein bedeutender deutscher Typograf und galt als einer bedeutendsten Buchgestalter der Nachkriegszeit.

❷ Vergleiche:
Willberg, Hans-Peter:
Lesetypografie, Mainz 2005 (Verlag Hermann Schmidt),
Seite 15 ff.

THE LIVERPOOL GOALIE

ODER: WIE MAN DIE SCHULZEIT ÜBERLEBT!

„FUßBALL IST NICHT GERADE DIE SICHERSTE SPORTART. ES STERBEN MENSCHEN AUF NORWEGISCHEN FUßBALLFELDERN. JAHR FÜR JAHR."

Liebe Leser, in der letzten Ausgabe unseres Kinomagazins Abspann stellten wir Ihnen an dieser Stelle mit *„Bela Kiss"* ein neues Projekt aus Heinz Lochmanns „drei-freunde"-Filmverleih vor. Doch damit nicht genug – im Jahr 2012 dürfen Sie sich auf weitere filmische Highlights aus unserem Verleih freuen! Nach der Millennium-Trilogie von Stieg Larsson präsentieren wir Ihnen ab 15. März 2012 einen weiteren Filmhöhepunkt aus Skandinavien: Die norwegische Jugendkomödie *„The Liverpool Goalie"* verspricht witzige Unterhaltung mit Tiefgang für Jung und Alt!

Hochspannung mit *„Das Kind"* und Grusel pur mit *„Bela Kiss"* werden 2012 im Portfolio des drei-freunde Filmverleihs stehen – doch auch für erfrischende Kinounterhaltung der jungen Besucher ist gesorgt: Wenn der 13-jährige Jo sich in spektakulären Tagträumen die Konsequenzen seiner Entscheidungen ausmalt, während er eigentlich nur die hübsche Mari beeindrucken möchte, können Kinder und Jugendliche mitfühlen und auch die Erwachsenen geraten schnell ins Schmunzeln…

Jo Idstadt (Ask van der Hagen) ist 13 Jahre alt, ein fleißiger Schüler, sein Leben aber ist eine einzige Problemzone!

Jo´s übervorsichtige Mutter (Andrine Saether) nervt ihn mit ihren ständigen Warnungen vor den Gefahren des Alltags. In der Schule zwingt ihn sein streitlustiger Klassenkamerad Tom Erik (Jostein Sranes Brox), die Hausaufgaben für ihn zu erledigen, eine Pflicht, die Jo´s Freizeit bedeutend verringert. Und Mädchen geht er am liebsten aus dem Weg. Zu allem Übel ist Jo noch so ziemlich der schlechteste Torwart, den man sich nur vorstellen kann. Indem er all diese Probleme konsequent meidet, schlägt sich Jo durch sein Schulleben. Und schließlich gibt es neben dem Lösen mathematischer Gleichungen auch noch ein Hobby, das sein Leben bestimmt: Wie alle seiner Freunde sammelt Jo Fußballkarten und wie alle jagt er nach der einen, seltenen und damit wertvollen Karte, die den Torwart des FC Liverpool zeigt.

Als eines Tages Mari (Susanne Boucher) in Jo´s Klasse kommt, ist nichts mehr so, wie es war: Mari ist nicht nur hübsch, sondern auch noch die Zweitbeste der Klasse in Mathe – und sie spielt Fußball! Jo muss feststellen, dass Mari das Mädchen seiner Träume ist. Doch um sie zu beeindrucken, muss er einige Risiken auf sich nehmen. Plötzlich beginnen die Dinge, schief zu gehen, und bald steckt Jo richtig in der Klemme…

Es gibt nur ein Objekt, das alle seine Probleme auf einen Schlag lösen und ihn zum Siegertypen machen könnte: Eine Fußballsammelkarte mit dem LIVERPOOL GOALIE!

Nach der Romanvorlage „Keepern til Tunisia" von Lars Mæhle hat Arild Andresen mit *„The Liverpool Goalie"* eine amüsante Coming-of-Age-Komödie abgeliefert, bei der Groß und Klein sofort mit dem Schicksal des Protagonisten Jo mitfiebern können.

Mit Ask van der Hagen (Jo), Andrine Saether (Else), Susanne Boucher (Mari) und Jostein Sranes Brox (Tom Erik) konnte er einen authentischen, sehr sympathischen Cast verpflichten, der das Publikum ab der ersten Minute mitreißt. Denn wer könnte nicht mit Jo mitfiebern, wenn er sich in spektakulären Tagträumen ausmalt, wie sein Konflikt mit dem rüpelhaften Tom-Erik schließlich so eskaliert, dass er mit seiner Mutter in einem Zeugenschutzprogramm am Ende der Welt hausen muss…?

Und das alles nur, weil er sich nicht gegen Tom-Eriks ständige Forderung, seine Hausaufgaben für ihn zu erledigen, wehren kann!

Das finden nicht nur Heinz Lochmann und der drei-freunde Filmverleih, sondern auch die Jurys verschiedener großer (Kinderfilm-)Festivals in Deutschland! Bereits im Februar 2011 wurde THE LIVERPOOL GOALIE auf der Berlinale mit dem Gläsernen Bären in der Sektion „Generation KPlus" ausgezeichnet. Im September gewann er auf dem internationalen Kinderfilmfestival LUCAS in Frankfurt den Don-Quijote-Preis der internationalen Fachjury. Das LUCAS hat den Anspruch, künstlerisch und thematisch wertvolle Filme auf Augenhöher seiner jungen Besucher zu zeigen; so sahen in zwei Aufführungen neben der Jury fast 500 Besucher den Film.

„Die frische Aufmachung und der packende Humor haben mich gleich mitgerissen", berichtet auch drei-freunde-Geschäftsführer Heinz Lochmann. „Nach verschiedenen Thrillern aus dem skandinavischen Raum freuen wir uns sehr, nun auch eine Komödie in unserem Programm präsentieren zu können – dieser lustige Film macht einfach nur fröhlich!"

Und das Kinopublikum war beigeistert: „Los Jo!", „Sag ja, Jo", großer Lacher und Jubelausrufe, als Jo sich zum ersten Mal gegen Tom Erik wehrt – die Stimmung im Kinosaal kochte! Auch die älteren Zuschauer schlossen den Film ins Herz, denn Nebenstränge wie die Affäre von Jo´s Mutter Else mit dem sympathischen Nachbarn Einar, die sie auf sehr komische Art und Weise zu verbergen versucht, erreichen auch die erwachsenen Besucher mit ihrem subtilen Humor und regen an zum Nachdenken über den Wahrheitsgehalt. So begründete die Jury: „Der Film ist zum einen herzerwärmend, zum anderen so anspruchsvoll, dass das Schauen des Films zu einer zum Nachdenken anregenden Erfahrung wird. Wir sind der Meinung, dass das Publikum in eine enge Beziehung zu den Charakteren und der Geschichte tritt und die hohe cineastische Qualität des Films und der Produktion wahrnimmt. Die Kinder können in die Geschichte eintauchen, von ihr lernen, können sie hinterfragen und über sie sprechen."

Pünktlich zur Einstimmung auf die Fußball Europameisterschaft 2012 kommt die Komödie am 15. März 2012 in die deutschen Kinos!

Der Entwurfsprozess:

1. Am Anfang steht immer eine Idee oder ein Kundenauftrag.

2. Der Auftrag wird von Hand, mit Hilfe von Papier und Bleistift in mehreren Skizzen visualisiert. So entsteht eine Ideenvielfalt! Die Skizzen dürfen „Briefmarken-Größe" haben.

3. Wenn man diese Ideen einem Bekannten oder Kollegen zeigt, hat dieser vielleicht noch weitere Anregungen!

4. Nach der Auswahl einiger weniger Entwürfe sollten diese am Computer umgesetzt werden. Hilfreich ist das stichwortartige notieren der typografischen Vorgaben!

5. Man sollte immer einen Ausdruck seiner Entwürfe machen. Eine Beurteilung der Typografie lässt sich nicht am Bildschirm vornehmen (bei gedruckten Medien).

6. Eine Nacht über die Entwürfe schlafen birgt manchmal Wunder! Am nächsten Tag hat man mehr Distanz und kann objektiver an die Sache herangehen.

7. Im sogenannten Reinlayout wird nach allen Korrekturschritten das Medienprodukt schließlich fertig gestellt.

Beurteilungskriterien

Die Wirkung eines Lesemediums ist nicht allein dem subjektiven Geschmack des Betrachters unterworfen, sondern lässt sich nach objektiven Kriterien beurteilen. Allerdings haben Betrachter, Gestalter und Typografen Präferenzen, nach denen die eigene Kriterienliste in einer Art „Rangfolge" geordnet wird. Das ist durchaus legitim! Im Folgenden werden einige typografische Kriterien genannt:

Visuelle Kommunikation:
- Kommt die Nachricht beim Adressaten an?
- Ist die Nachricht zielgruppengerecht dargestellt?
- Welche Gesamtwirkung hat das Medienprodukt auf den Betrachter?
- Ist die Gestaltung „gewöhnlich" oder „originell"?

Schriftwahl und Schriftwirkung:
- Ist die Schrift passend zum Medium gewählt?
- Wird mit der gewählten Schrift die gewünschte Wirkung erzielt?
- Passen die Schriftmischungen zueinander?
- Sind die Schriftschnitte gezielt eingesetzt und stimmig?

Mikrotypografie und Leserlichkeit:
- Ist eine angemessene Schriftgröße vorhanden?
- Ist die Laufweite korrekt eingestellt?
- Gibt es noch kritische, nicht unterschnittene Buchstabenabstände?
- Ist der Zeilenabstand optisch angepasst?

Elementare Gestaltung:
- Sind die Seiten kontrastreich gestaltet?
- Werden die Gesetzmäßigkeiten der Formwirkung beachtet?
- Stehen die Elemente in den richtigen Beziehungen und Proportionen zueinander?
- Werden die Gestaltgesetze richtig interpretiert?

Farbgebung:
- Passen die Farben zum Produkt?
- Sind die Farbkombinationen harmonisch gewählt?
- Unterstützt der Farbeinsatz die Leserlichkeit?
- Sind die Farben zu penetrant oder halten sie sich dezent im Hintergrund?

Makrotypografie und Lesbarkeit:
- Ist der Satzspiegel richtig eingestellt?
- Gibt es eine Leseführung oder muss der Betrachter seine Inhalte „suchen"?
- Ist eine typografische Gliederung der Lesbarkeit zuträglich?
- Stören Bilder oder sonstige Elemente den Lesefluss?

Inhaltliche Vollständigkeit:
- Sind alle Inhalte korrekt erfasst und dargestellt?
- Wurde der Text oder das Bildmaterial verändert?
- Entstehen durch inhaltliche Veränderungen Missverständnisse?

5.5.2 Seitengestaltung

Zur **Seitengestaltung**, auch **Text-/Bild-Integration** genannt, zählt man die Gestaltung aller Medienprodukte, die als **Ausgangsbasis** eine **leere Fläche** haben. Dies kann ein leeres Blatt Papier ebenso sein, wie ein noch nicht gefüllter Bildschirm einer Internetseite. Im Laufe des Entwurfsprozesses wird diese unbedruckte Fläche zur bedruckten Fläche. Die beiden Flächen stehen in einer engen Wechselwirkung zueinander.

➲ **Die unbedruckte Fläche ist Ausgangsbasis für spannungsreiche Gestaltung!**
➲ **Die bedruckte Fläche wirkt erst bei der Beachtung der Anordnungsregeln für Text und Bild!**

Nach dieser Kennzeichnung umfasst die Seitengestaltung ein- und mehrseitige Produkte. Zu den einseitigen Produkten zählen Visitenkarten, Briefbögen und Plakate. Die Königsdisziplin der Makrotypografie ist jedoch die Gestaltung mehrseitiger Produkte. Hier muss zusätzlich zu den Regeln der Seitengestaltung darauf geachtet werden, dass die einzelnen Seiten auch noch zusammen passen. Im Folgenden wird auf die Seitengestaltung gedruckter Medien eingegangen. Bezüglich der Seitengestaltung von Internetseiten und multimedialen Anwendungen verweisen wir auf die Kapitel 12 (Multimedia) und 13 (Internet).

Proportionen und Formate

Die gängigen **Papierformate** im europäischen Raum entsprechen den Maßen des metrischen Systemes und sind für Deutschland in der DIN-Norm 476 aus dem Jahre 1922 festgelegt. Die deutsche Norm diente als Grundlage für das internationale Äquivalent DIN EN ISO 216, das wiederum in fast allen Ländern Anwendung findet. Unterschiede gibt es meist nur innerhalb erlaubter Toleranzen. Parallel existieren, etwa in den USA und Kanada, auch traditionelle, meist weniger systematisch und praktisch aufgebaute Systeme. Für die Anwendungsprogramme bedeutet dies, dass man meistens neben dem bekannten DIN A 4 Papier auch US-Formate auswählen kann ❶!

Die **DIN-Reihe** weist die Proportion $1:\sqrt{2}$ auf (1:1,414). Diese Proportion ist ausgewogen, dafür aber nicht unbedingt sehr spannend oder harmonisch.

Schwierig zu gestaltende Proportionen sind quadratische und darauf aufbauende Verhältnisse (1:1, 2:1, etc.).

Das Proportionsverhältnis nach dem **goldenen Schnitt** ($(1+\sqrt{5}):2 = 1:1,618$) gilt in der Kunst, der elementaren Gestaltungslehre und vielen anderen wissenschaftlichen Disziplinen als sehr harmonisches Verhältnis. Weitere gängige Formate sind:

- Kleinbildformat: 24 × 36 mm = 1:1,5 (auch harmonisches Buchformat)
- Seitenverhältnis TV: 1,333:1 (entspricht 4:3, auch Doppelseite DIN A-Reihe)
- Seitenverhältnis TV: 1,777:1 (entspricht 16:9)
- Cinemascope (Kino): 2,35:1

Das Referenzformat der DIN A-Reihe ist A0, dessen Flächeninhalt einen Quadratmeter beträgt.

Die DIN A-Reihe von 0 bis 10:

DIN A0	=	841	×	1189	mm
DIN A1	=	594	×	841	mm
DIN A2	=	420	×	594	mm
DIN A3	=	297	×	420	mm
DIN A4	=	210	×	297	mm
DIN A5	=	148	×	210	mm
DIN A6	=	105	×	148	mm
DIN A7	=	74	×	105	mm
DIN A8	=	52	×	74	mm
DIN A9	=	37	×	52	mm
DIN A10	=	26	×	37	mm

Das erstgenannte Maß ist immer das Maß der Breite! So ist immer klar, ob das Papier Hoch oder Quer vor einem liegt.

Satzspiegel

Als **Satzspiegel** wird die Fläche auf einem Papier bezeichnet, die mit Bildern und Texten bestückt werden kann. Die Seitenränder Kopf, Bund, Fuß und Seite begrenzen die nutzbare Fläche.

Theoretisch könnte man nun einen Satzspiegel dadurch erstellen, in dem alle Ränder das gleiche Maß haben und los geht's! Doch in der Praxis hat sich gezeigt, dass solche Einteilungen äußerst langweilig wirken! Man sollte sich also etwas mehr Gedanken bei der Gestaltung seines Satzspiegels machen!

Eine gängige und einfach zu erlernende Methode ist die Diagonalkonstruktion. Diese klassische Konstruktion des Satzspiegels nach dem Goldenen Schnitt teilt die Seite des DIN-Formats im Verhältnis 1:1,414.

Die Diagonalkonstruktion wird wie folgt durchgeführt:
Zunächst zeichnet man zwei Diagonalen durch den Papierbogen sowie zwei Diagonalen durch die einzelne Seite.
Die Schnittpunkte S sind die Ausgangspunkte für den Satzspiegel.
Die Verbindungsstrecken mit dem Punkt A ergeben mit der Seitendiagonalen den Punkt 1.
Die weiteren Begrenzungslinien des Satzspiegels werden über waagerechte und senkrechte Strecken, ausgehend vom Punkt 1, hergestellt.

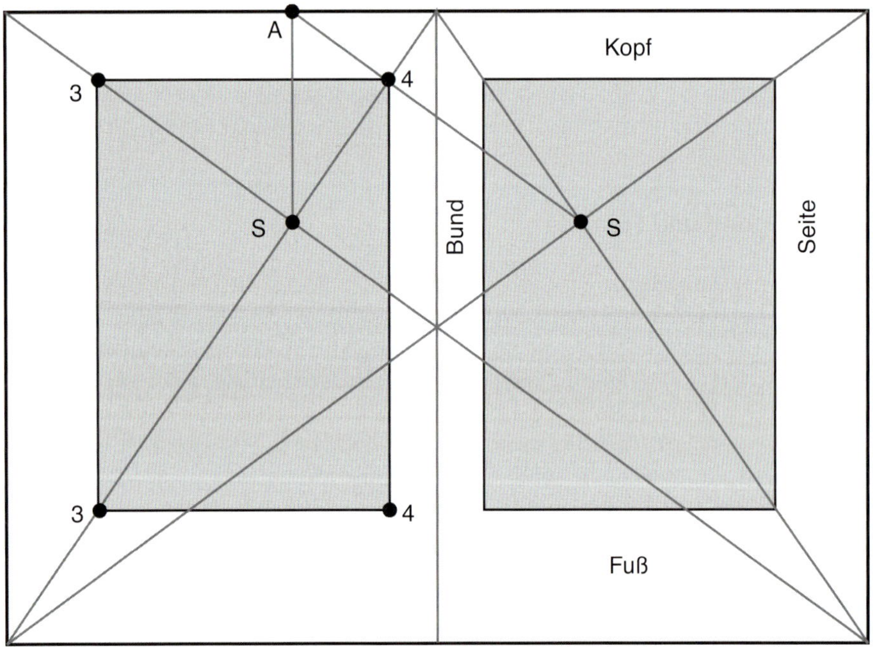

Die so voreingestellte Seite lässt sich nun mit Hilfe eines Seitenrasters weiter einteilen. Dabei werden die Spalten und Zeilen in Segmente zerlegt. So lassen sich Bildformate, Textrahmen, Positionen von Überschriften, Marginalien, Kopf- und Fußzeilen exakt in der Größe über das gesamte Dokument festlegen.

Natürlich kann man Bilder und Texte auch außerhalb des Satzspiegels positionieren! Dies lockert sogar die sonst strenge Anordnung innerhalb eines Rasters auf. Allerdings sollte dieser Effekt nur sparsam und gezielt eingesetzt werden. Die Positionierung von Elementen, die sogar über den Papierrand hinausragen, nennt man **randabfallende Positionierung**. Diese schafft meistens gute Kontraste auf einer Doppelseite.

Beispiel Satzspiegel Handbuch der Medien

Bei der Entwicklung des Satzspiegels zum vorliegenden Handbuch der Medien wurde zuerst in einer Skizzenphase ein zweispaltiger Satzspiegel entwickelt. Aufgrund vorheriger Auflagen war die Seitengröße mit 210 mm x 245 mm jedoch bereits festgelegt worden, die zweispaltige Einteilung konnte nicht richtig überzeugen. Im nächsten Schritt wurde daher versucht, mit drei ungleichen Spalten bzw. fünf gleichen Spalten zu arbeiten, ein vielversprechendes Konzept entwickelte sich.
Die Doppelseite wurde dann mit der zuvor beschriebenen Diagonalkonstruktion aufgebaut, die Maße jedoch anschließend leicht modifiziert. So ergaben sich dabei einige Abweichungen, die jedoch das harmonisch wirkende Gesamtbild nicht weiter beeinträchtigen. Ein Beispiel dafür, dass man nicht automatisch an fixen Werten festhalten darf, sondern das die Gestaltung eines Satzspiegels individuell angepasst werden muss.

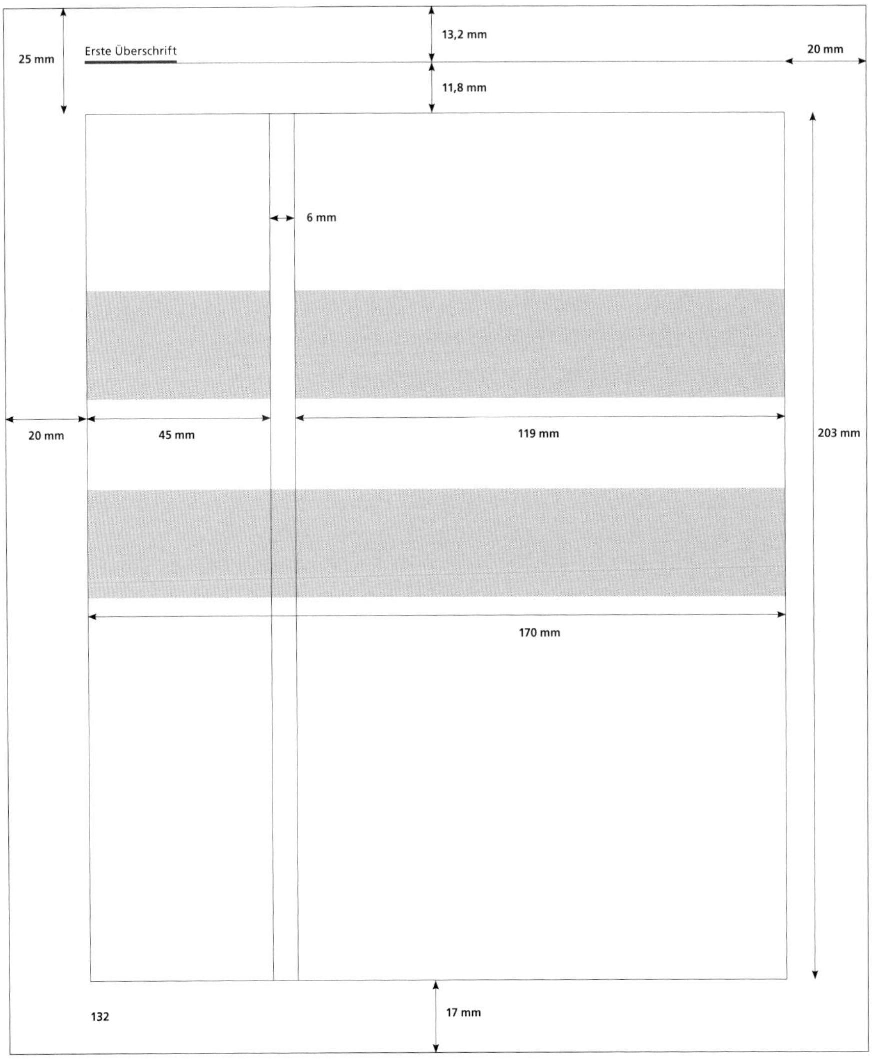

Satzspiegel der linken Seite des vorliegenden Handbuchs der Medien

5.5.3 Satzarten

Zusammenhängende Texte können linksbündig, rechtsbündig, zur Mitte zentriert oder wie im vorliegenden Fachbuch über die gesamte Zeilenbreite blockartig angeordnet sein. Man spricht hierbei von der **Satzart**. Im Folgenden werden diese Satzarten beschrieben.

Blocksatz

UND ES BEGAB SICH

Es begab sich aber zu der Zeit, daß ein Gebot von dem Kaiser Augustus ausging, daß alle Welt geschätzt würde …
Da machte sich auf auch Joseph aus Galiläa, aus der Stadt Nazareth, in das jüdische Land zur Stadt Davids, die da heißt Bethlehem, darum daß er von dem Hause und Geschlechte Davids war, auf daß er sich schätzen ließe mit Maria, seinem vertrauten Weibe, die war schwanger. Und als sie daselbst waren, kam die Zeit, daß sie gebären sollte. Und sie gebar ihren ersten Sohn und wickelte ihn in Windeln und legte ihn in eine Krippe; denn sie hatten sonst keinen Raum in der Herberge.
Und es waren Hirten in derselben Gegend auf dem Felde bei den Hürden, die hüteten des Nachts ihre Herde. Und siehe, des Herrn Engel trat zu ihnen, und die Klarheit des Herrn leuchtete um sie; und sie fürchteten sich sehr. Und der Engel sprach zu ihnen: »Fürchtet Euch nicht! Siehe, ich verkündige Euch große Freude, die allem Volk widerfahren wird; denn Euch ist heute der Heiland geboren, welcher ist Christus, der Herr, in der Stadt Davids. Und das habt zum Zeichen: Ihr werdet finden das Kind in Windeln gewickelt und in einer Krippe liegen.« Und alsbald war da bei dem Engel die Menge der himmlischen Heerscharen, die lobten Gott und sprachen: »Ehre sei Gott in der Höhe und Friede auf Erden und den Menschen ein Wohlgefallen.«

EVANGELIUM NACH LUKAS, KAPITEL 2, VERS 1-14

Wird ein Text über die gesamte Zeilenbreite in einer Art regelmäßigem Block gesetzt, dann bezeichnet man ihn als **Blocksatz**. Der Wortzwischenraum im Blocksatz ist nicht konstant, das Anwendungsprogramm moduliert die Zwischenräume, um bei unterschiedlicher Buchstabenanzahl immer gleiche Zeilenbreiten zu bieten. Aus diesem Grund ist auf eine ausreichende Zeilenbreite zu achten, damit diese Eigenschaft im gesamten Schriftbild nicht ins Gewicht fällt.

Der Blocksatz strahlt durch sein einheitliches und gleichmäßiges Erscheinungsbild Ruhe und Geschlossenheit aus und steigert die Lesbarkeit. Durch Herausstellen von Punkt, Komma und Trennstrich außerhalb der rechten Seitenbegrenzung, wird ein registerhaltiger Blocksatz mit Randausgleich erzeugt. In Gutenbergs Bibel und alten Geschichtsbüchern wurde diese doch aufwendige Satzart angewandt. Aus wirtschaftlichen Gründen lässt sich der Blocksatz mit Randausgleich nicht immer verwirklichen.

➲ **Der durchschnittliche Wortzwischenraum im Blocksatz sollte der Breite des „i" entsprechen.**

Eignung: Lesetexte in Büchern, Zeitungen und Magazinen.

Flattersatz

Ungünstiger Flattersatz: Treppenförmige Abfolge der Zeilen, mit wiederkehrendem, eher eintönigem Verlauf.

Der dynamische Vertreter der Satzarten ist der **Flattersatz**. In Fließtexten wird der
linksbündige Flattersatz angewandt. Damit das rechte Zeilenende einen
günstigen **Zeilenfall** erhält, muss in der Regel manuell umgebrochen
werden. In diesem Fall sind meist 3 bis 4 Zeilen betroffen, die
nachfolgend kürzer werden. Dieser Eingriff eignet sich nur bei kleinen Textmengen.

Mit der Einrichtung einer Flatterzone wird auch die Silbentrennung beeinflusst. Dabei kann es zu unerwünschten Trennungen wie „Tex-te" kommen. Solche zweibuchstabigen Trennungen sollten wiederum von Hand nachgebessert werden.

➲ **Die Flatterzone darf etwa 25 % der Spaltenbreite ausmachen!**
➲ **Die Trennungen sollten zuerst nach den Kriterien der Leserlichkeit erfolgen, dann nach der Ästhetik des Grauwertes der Spalte!**

Eignung: Aufzählungen und Texte mit kürzeren Zeilen.

Der rechtsbündige Flattersatz ist für längere Lesetxte nicht geeignet. Er kann aber in Ausnahmefällen für schmale Textspalten und im Kontrast zum restlichen Text eingesetzt werden.

Wird der Flattersatz nicht von Hand nachgebessert, sondern so belassen, wie das Anwendungsprogramm die Trennungen vornimmt, nennt man diese Art Flattersatz auch **Rausatz**. Dieser hat eine kürzere Flatterzone und ist meistens ästhetisch nicht so hochwertig.

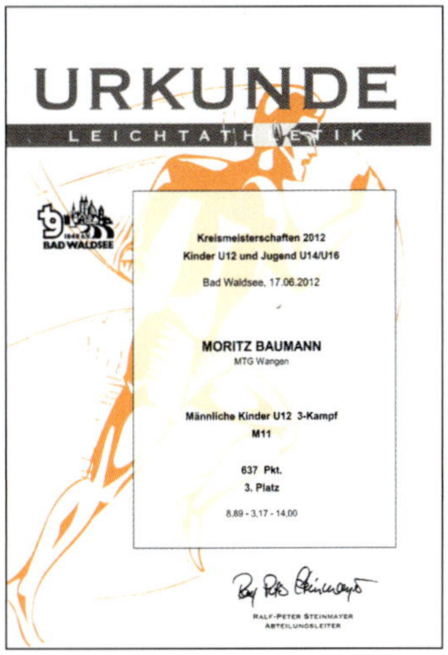

Mittelachsensatz

Beim **Mittelachsensatz** werden die Textzeilen in der Mitte zentriert.
Die Definition der Mitte bezieht sich wie im vorliegenden Fall
auf die rechts und links vorliegenden Abstände.

Positive Auswirkung auf die Gesamtgestaltung
hat auch im Mittelachsensatz das dynamische Zeilenende
von oben nach unten.

Der Mittelachsensatz muss unbedingt ein dynamisches Zeilenende besitzen, schon um sich vom Blocksatz abzuheben. Der mangelhafte Umbruch in diesem Absatz erzeugt wenig Spannung und ist dem Blocksatz sehr ähnlich. Die axiale Anordnung des Textes soll natürlich durch den Zeilenwechsel einen Leserhythmus erzwingen und auch Satzteile, beispielsweise in Gedichten besonders hervorheben.

Den Mittelachsensatz trifft man häufig in Titelblättern und Drucksachen für Anlässe an, wobei hier die Raumaufteilung und die Wahl der Schriftgröße eine große Rolle spielen. Dynamik erhält das Schriftbild dann durch Verstärken und Abschwächen der Schriftgröße und eine ungleichmäßige Aufteilung der Seite.

➲ **Der Mittelachsensatz ist für längere Lesetexte nicht geeignet!**

Eignung: Familiendrucksachen, Titelblätter, Urkunden, Gedichte.

Formsatz

Der **Formsatz** folgt, wie der Name schon sagt, mit der Schriftlinie einer Form.

In gedruckten Medien eignet sich diese Satzart nur für Überschriften oder herausgestellte Botschaften, die dem Leser ins Auge springen sollen. Allerdings hat der Formsatz mit der Einführung der interaktiven Medien eine große Bedeutung im Bereich der Animationen bekommen, wenn es gilt, eine Überschrift zum Beispiel von links nach rechts durch den Bildschirm laufen zu lassen (vgl. Kapitel 9 Animation).

➲ **Der Formsatz ist für längere Lesetexte nicht geeignet!**

Eignung: Überschriften, Werbebotschaften, Interaktive Medien, Animationen.

5.5.4 Typografische Gliederung

Schnitt
Das Filmmagazin,
Gestaltung: Oktober
Kommunikationsdesign GmbH

Die **typografische Gliederung** eines Medienproduktes ist eine der Hauptaufgaben der Makrotypografie. Die Gliederung gewährleistet, dass der Leser nicht „suchend“ auf der Seite umherirrt, sondern zielgerichtet geführt wird. Erst durch eine geschickte Gliederung kann der Gestalter sicher sein, dass die Nachricht des Produktes beim Leser ankommt! Zu den Gliederungselementen gehören:

Inhaltliche Elemente:
- Haupttitel ①
- Untertitel, Spitzmarke ②
- Rubriktitel ③
- Zwischentitel ④
- Pagina, Seitennummerierung ⑤

Lese-Elemente:
- Lesetext oder Grundtext ⑥
- Enleitungstext ⑦

Doppelseite Ausgabe 3 / 2000

...denn sie haben nichts zu tun

Heute ein König

Handlung ist überflüssiger Ballast. Das richtige Leben hat auch keine Handlung. Und Matthias Lehmanns Film ist ganz nah dran am richtigen Leben. Seine Helden, die Pilstrinker Hoffi und Lehmi, lassen sich 88 Minuten sinnlos durch Dortmund und den Tag treiben. Sie besuchen den Zoo, machen ein Paßfoto, kaufen eine Postkarte, wandern durch den Park: „Wir sind die Könige des Westparks."

Die wohl auf realen Personen beruhenden Ralf „Hoffi" Hoffmann und Matthias „Lehmi" Lehmann, von Markus Knüfken und Eckhard Preuß gespielt, tauchten zuerst vor drei Jahren auf, im Kurzfilm *Pas de deux*. Seitdem hat sich wenig verändert. Lehmi ist jetzt Student. Aber beide sind weiter Ignoranten der Leistungsgesellschaft geblieben. Solange sie ausreichend Bier dabei haben, nehmen sie das Leben, wie es kommt. Manches, was ihnen begegnet, während sie die Trinkhallen, also die Schönheiten Dortmunds abklappern, taucht sogar wieder auf. Wie Horst, der Werbung für ein mittelalterliches Punkkonzert macht, oder wie die Ananas vom Hawaiitoast von heute morgen. Anderes eben nicht, zum Beispiel der kleine „Pimmelkopp" mit seinem Frisbee.

Die Leichtigkeit, die schon *Pas de deux* ausmachte und die auch diesen Film trägt, verdankt er zu einem guten Stück Preuß und Knüfken, aber auch Nickel, Völker, Tremsal und Zapatka in den Nebenrollen. Die von ihnen dargestellten Charaktere wirken ungekünstelt, das sind Menschen, denen man – zumindest im Ruhrgebiet – jeden Tag auf der Straße begegnet. Was aber *DoppelPack* zum eigentlichen Genuß macht, ist die scheinbare Systemlosigkeit, mit der nicht nur die beiden Hauptfiguren vorgehen, sondern mit der auch Regisseur Lehmann herkömmliche Erzählmodelle ignoriert. Insgesamt wirkt sogar der Film selbst nicht wie das Ergebnis harter Arbeit, sondern wie an einem Tag abgedreht und fertig geschnitten aus der Kamera gefallen. Die meisten Filmemacher bemühen sich, Geschichten bedingungslos auf einen Punkt hin zu erzählen. Oder zwängen sie, wenn sie keinen Punkt haben, zumindest in eine aufgesetzt wirkende Rahmenhandlung. Lehmann verweigert sich dem, schaut lieber nach links und rechts, und kaum einmal geradeaus. Er reiht Szenen und Momente aneinander, die wohl von jedem anderen als unwichtig herausgeschnitten würden. Dabei sind es gerade diese Augenblicke, die das Leben lebenswert machen, Augenblicke, die man vielleicht bald schon vergessen haben wird, die man aber im Jetzt genießt. Es gibt keine straight story, und deshalb ist auch nie vorhersehbar, wie es weitergeht oder ob überhaupt noch was passiert. Wie im richtigen Leben. Das ist nicht dümmlicher Proloklamauk à la *Bang Boom Bang*, dessen Charaktere Idioten sind und der Lächerlichkeit preisgegeben werden; es gelingt *DoppelPack* vielmehr, auf unterhaltsamste Weise eine Lebenseinstellung darzustellen, die auch auf den Zuschauer ansteckend wirken wird. Folglich wäre es Unsinn, dem Film vorzuwerfen, er habe kein System. Lehmi sagt bereits zu Filmbeginn (und *DoppelPack* hält sich zum Glück konsequent an diese Worte): „Ich habe schon ein System. Das ist bloß nicht das System der anderen Leute." *Carsten Tritt*

Doppelpack
D 2000. R.B: Matthias Lehmann. B: Eckhard Preuß. K: Jo Heim. S: Edith Eisenstecken, Evi Oberkofler. M: Attila the Stockbroker u.a. P: Catapult/Prokino. D: Eckhard Preuß, Markus Knüfken, Jochen Nickel, Margret Völker, Edgar Selge, Jeanne Tremsal, Manfred Zapatka u.a. 88 Min. Prokino ab 17.8.00

Letzte Ausfahrt Dorstfeld

Slacken in Dortmund: Schnapsverkostung bei Feinkost Köhler, im Westpark unter den Bäumen liegen, im Schatten, ausruhen vom Nichtstun. Ein Film über Körperöffnungen. In die obere wird Dosenbier geschüttet. Aus der anderen, weiter unten, kommt alles wieder raus. Im besten Fall – manchmal dauert es etwas länger. Hoffi und Lehmi sind wieder da – Matthias Lehmann gibt den beiden Figuren seines Kurzfilms *Pas de deux* diesmal die knappe Spielfilmlänge. Ein dezentes, liebevoll gezeichnetes Buddy Movie ist dabei entstanden, mit allem, was dazugehört: gemeinschaftlichem Herumgehänge, Reden, Trinken. Vor allem: Bier trinken. Und „das Kokoszeug", zwischendurch, mehr versehentlich, weil Lehmi nicht schnell genug reagiert. Lehmi, bei Geburt: Steißlage, heute, bei Frauen: Scheißlage. Er ist einfach zu langsam. Und zu schweigsam, klar. Nach eigener Meinung, im inneren Monolog, so, wie es zuletzt modisch geworden zu sein scheint, wird das von der Figur selbst vorgetragen. Wenn Lehmi nur hin und wieder mal was sagt, redet Hoffi die ganze Zeit. Markus Knüfken spielt ihn mit einer Mischung aus entschlossener Naivität und infantiler Ausgelassenheit. An manchen Stellen gerät ihm das unfreiwillig zum Tom-Gerhard-Imitat: die albernen Gesten, das überdrehte Gehabe beim Anprobieren einer Jacke, das ist schon ziemlich hanswurstig und ja auch: unnötig. Eckhard Preuß, der am Drehbuch mitgeschrieben hat, bleibt mimisch ganz zurückhaltend. Schade, daß es dem Film nicht gelingt, der mittlerweile schon oft gesehenen Industrielandschaft des Ruhrgebietes neue Seiten abzugewinnen: Soviel Gasometer war wohl noch nie da, und der Linienbus, in dem sich die beiden Helden fortbewegen, fährt alle klischeehaften Wahrzeichen der Stadt ab. Immerhin: So poetisch, so relaxt, so cool ist der öffentliche Personennahverkehr in Deutschland noch nicht dargestellt worden. In langen Einstellungen und mit einer gemütlichen Steadycam paßt sich Jo Heims unaufdringliche Fotographie dem Erzählrhythmus des Films an: Lehmann läßt sich Zeit, für seine Figuren und für seine Geschichte. Manchmal, wenn die Handlung ganz reduziert ist, bei Null anzukommen scheint, bleibt nur noch die wundervolle Leichtigkeit des Nichtstuns. „Wir haben keine Termine", sagt Lehmi einmal, „und wir brauchen auch keine." In solchen Momenten stört allein der unattraktive Popsoundtrack. Das Konzert am Ende des Films bestreitet eine Pogoband, die Punk und Mittelalter in einer ungewollt komischen Synthese zusammenführt. Ist das Parodie oder ist das ernst gemeint? Hoffen wir entgegen aller Symptome Ersteres. Aber so recht übel nehmen mag ich diesem Film selbst das nicht. *Thomas Waitz*

Dortmund Downtown

„Downtown", tönt es verheißungsvoll in der Punkversion, wenn unsere beiden Helden der Arbeitslosigkeit im Bus Richtung City fahren, dabei ist jede Erwartungshaltung fehl am Platz: denn auch wenn sich Hoffi und Lehmi mal in Bewegung setzen, es passiert nichts. Und das ist unwahrscheinlich unterhaltsam, wie schon Kaurismäki beweist, der sich bei soviel Lakonie aufdrängt. Doch hier wird nicht das finnische Vorbild kopiert wie in *Zugvögel*. Matthias Lehmann und Jo Heim lassen sich die Bilder vom Lauf der Dinge bestimmen, immer auf Augenhöhe mit ihren Helden; jede Einstellung spricht für sich. Bei solchem Minimalismus in den Ausdrucksmitteln genügt für eine gelungene Pointe dann schon ein einfacher Gegenschuß, und unsere Helden sehen sich von einer Herde Antilopen umgeben. Überhaupt, es braucht eben keine große Geschichte, um von Liebe und Freundschaft, von Heimat und Familie zu erzählen, *DopppelPack* beweist es. Hoffi und Lehmi bewältigen die Widrigkeiten des Alltags mit stoischem Gleichmut, sprich, sie sorgen für einen konstant bleibenden Alkoholpegel. Und Regisseur Lehmann widersteht standhaft allen Versuchungen, in eine Säufer- und Fäkalposse abzugleiten. Dafür ist er sich seiner Sache zu sicher, durchweg behält der Film sein Tempo, nimmt sich liebevoll viel Zeit für Pointen als auch für die ausnahmslos gut geführten Darsteller. Und wenn die Kamera den bierseligen Freunden folgend einmal in Schräglage gerät, ist das eben die angemessene Visualisierung eines berauschten Streifzugs durch die Einkaufszone. Stuhlgang ist zwar auch ein Problem – Nickel kann es nur zu Hause, Knüfken hat es einmal besonders eilig – doch erspart der Film sich und uns jegliche akustische Ausschweifung. Unsere Helden haben gewichtigere Prüfungen zu bestehen. Tante Christas Geburtstag etwa, dessen immergleiches Ritual mit Sahnetorte und Personenraten genug Fallstricke bietet.

DopppelPack ist ein gelungenes Loblied auf faule Gelassenheit und gelassene Faulheit, wie es im deutschen Kino seit *Zur Sache, Schätzchen* nicht mehr zu sehen war. Und wie damals Werner Enke im sonnenbeschienenen Schwabing vor lauter Nichtstun *Außer Atem* war, so taumeln jetzt Markus Knüfken und Eckhard Preuß dem Schwermut der westfälischen Ruhrmetropole davon. Lebensfreude sieht im Ruhrpott eben anders aus als in München. Hier leuchtet wie eine Fackel der flammende Schlot einer Kokerei den Weg durch Nacht zum Licht. *Thomas Warnecke*

24

25

Erklärende Elemente: Autorenhinweis ❶
Legende ❷
Zitat ❸
Bildunterschrift ❹
Randbemerkung, Marginalie ❺
Fußnote

Schmuck-Elemente: Initiale ❻

Grafische Elemente: Linie ❼
Farbe ❽
Kasten, Fläche ❾
Stopper
Hintergrund

Gliederungselement Bild:
„Bilder sind schnelle Schüsse ins Gehirn“ und eignen sich zur Gliederung makrotypografischer Aufgaben ganz besonders!
Sie können bei entsprechender Größe und Platzierung Blickfang sein und den Lesefluss ganz gezielt steuern.
Bilder lassen nach der Imagery-Theorie Aktivierungspotentiale im Bereich der emotionalen, gedanklichen und physischen Reize entstehen!

Hervorhebungen durch Änderungen der Schriftbreite, -stärke oder -lage im Lesetext werden **Auszeichnungen** genannt und sind ein weiteres Gliederungselement!

Doppelseite Ausgabe 4 / 2006

❽ 16

Anhand spezifischer Ansprecheformen und sechs möglicher Erzählmodi kann man dokumentarische Kindersendungen genretheoretisch einordnen. Dadurch gewinnt man einen Ausblick auf Chancen und Perspektiven des Kinderdokumentarfilms hinsichtlich einer Dramaturgie, die offene (Deutungs-)Räume und Platz läßt für eine eigenständige Reflektion des Gesehenen durch die Kinder. ⑦

AUTORIN ¦ CLAUDIA TÖPPER ❶

THEMA
DEUTUNGSRÄUME ÖFFNEN ❼

→ »WILLI WILLS WISSEN«, FOLGE: »WANN IST KRIEG UND WANN IST FRIEDEN?« © BR ❷ ❹

AUSGABE # 44 04 ¦ 2006 — SCHNITT DAS FILMMAGAZIN — THEMA KINDERDOKUMENTARFILM — 17

i ❻

nsbesondere in den letzten Jahren wurden viele erfolgreiche dokumentarische Fernsehformate für Kinder entwickelt, die dokumentarische Elemente vor allem zur Wissensvermittlung einsetzen. Diese eher knappen Stücke sind vorrangig im Fernsehen zu sehen, entweder als kurze Beiträge in Magazinsendungen oder als Reihen- beziehungsweise Serienformate. Im Unterschied zu fiktionalen Narrationen, die sich hauptsächlich auf die Motivation der Charaktere und die Plausibilität ihrer Aktionen konzentrieren, nutzen sie unterschiedliche Erzählweisen und argumentative Strukturen, um glaubhaft Authentizität zu vermitteln. Eine nähere Betrachtung der dokumentarischen Kindersendungen zeigt, daß sich diese narrativen Strukturen und Formen der Adressierung in sechs Erzählmodi unterscheiden lassen.

Die am häufigsten vorzufindenden Formen sind der beschreibende und der fiktionale Modus.

1. DER BESCHREIBENDE MODUS

Beschreibende dokumentarische Filme und Fernsehsendungen (z.B. *Wissen macht Ah!*, *Die Sendung mit der Maus*, *logo!* oder *Fortsetzung folgt*) zeichnen sich durch die starke Präsenz eines verbalen Off-Kommentars aus. Der Erzähler ist zwar nicht im Bild, aber durch seine expressive Art deutlich spürbar. Seine Funktion besteht im Veranschaulichen durch Beschreibungen und Erklärungen. Er bestätigt so entweder die Aussagen der Bilder, oder aber die Bilder dienen als Beleg seiner Ausführungen. Die Montage folgt dabei dem Grundsatz der funktionellen Sachlichkeit. Sie wirkt unterstützend und vermittelt auch auf der Bildebene Objektivität. Diese wechselseitigen Versicherungen bestätigen den Wahrheitsgehalt der Aussagen. Da der Kommentar alle nötigen Erklärungen der Bildebene vorgibt, brauchen die Kinder lediglich seiner Argumentation zu folgen, die die Deutungsmöglichkeiten des Gesehenen vorgibt.

2. DER FIKTIONALE MODUS

Ebenso beliebt ist die an den Unterhaltungsbedürfnissen der Kinder orientierte

»Während bei der beschreibenden Form der Deutungsspielraum durch den Kommentar vorgegeben ist, übernimmt dies im fiktiven Modus die Perspektivierung.«

→ ZITAT ❸

fiktionale Form des dokumentarischen Erzählens (z.B. *Anja und Anton*, *Löwenzahn*, *Siebenstein*, *Teletubbies*). Dabei werden authentische Darstellungen teilweise nahezu unerkennbar in eine fiktionale Spielhandlung eingebettet. Die starke Durchmischung dokumentarischer und fiktionaler Darstellungsweisen soll Spannung und Aufmerksamkeit schaffen. Die zu vermittelnden Inhalte werden anhand der Figuren konkret und veräußerlicht beschrieben. Durch die fiktionale Form entsteht eine größere (identifikatorische) Nähe zu den Figuren. Die verinnerlichte und lebendige, persönliche Perspektive spricht die Zuschauer emotional an und betont das Ausprobieren und Erlebbarmachen. Die referentielle Qualität der dokumentarischen Aufnahmen, die in der beschreibenden Form eher vorherrschend ist, weicht hier einer expressiven Qualität.

Doch auch bei dieser Form wird die eigenständige Interpretationsleistung der Zuschauer vorweggenommen. Während bei der beschreibenden Form der Deutungsspielraum durch den Kommentar vorgegeben ist, übernimmt dies im fiktionalen Modus die Perspektivierung. Der Interpretationsspielraum durch die Kinder ist zwar größer als bei der beschreibenden Form, aber immer noch vorgegeben durch den Deutungsrahmen, den die Figuren festlegen. Sowohl im beschreibenden als auch im fiktionalen Modus dient die Narration damit vor allem dem Argumentationsaufbau. Indem die Erzählerfiguren die Interpretation der Ereignisse im fiktionalen Modus übernehmen, sollen die dokumentarischen Aussagen von den Kindern scheinbar besser aufgenommen und überzeugender wahrgenommen werden. Außerdem dient die Simulation einer direkten Ansprache der Erzeugung von emotionaler Nähe. Dabei stellt insbesondere die Anwesenheit von Erzählerfiguren eine Form der unmittelbaren Kommunikation her. Fehlt die Erzählerfigur, ist die starke Präsenz einer Kommentarstimme kennzeichnend.

3. DER INTERAKTIVE MODUS

Eine weitere Form dokumentarischen Erzählens für Kinder ist der interaktive Modus (z.B. *Felix und die wilden Tiere*, *Tigerentenclub* oder *Tabaluga tivi*). Hier nimmt der Erzähler oder Moderator die Rolle eines sozialen Akteurs ein. Die Aussagen des Films entstehen durch das Zusammentreffen des Erzählers mit seinem Objekt. Der Erzähler tritt als Figur vor die Kamera und ist als eine ganz bestimmte Person identifizierbar. Er begibt sich an den Ort des Geschehens, nimmt aber an diesem selbst nicht unmittelbar teil, sondern präsentiert sich als Interviewpartner und fungiert so als verbindendes Element zwischen den Gesprächspartnern und/oder dokumentarischen Einspielern. Dabei wendet er sich an die Figuren im Bild und adressiert die Zuschauer direkt. Er berichtet in einer scheinbar objektiven Form von den Ereignissen. Hierarchisch steht die Erzählerfigur über den am Geschehen Beteiligten. Sie behält das letzte Wort. Die Ansprecheform des interaktiven Modus macht die dargestellten Ereignisse indirekt erlebbar. Dabei wird der Zuschauer jedoch eher als teilnehmender Beobachter statt als Teilnehmer positioniert.

4. DER PARTIZIPATIVE MODUS

Dies wiederum ist eher der Fall bei partizipativen Formen, wie beispielsweise *Willi wills wissen* oder *loggo TV*. Der Erzähler nimmt direkt an den Ereignissen teil, macht sie für die Zuschauer erfahrbar und spricht den Rezipienten als Teilnehmer an. Die Kinder erleben die Ereignisse aus der Perspektive der Figur. Die Darstellung ihrer Ängste und Bedenken, ihr Nachfragen bei Dingen, die sie angeblich nicht versteht, machen die Ereignisse für die Zuschauer auf eine direktere und emotionalere Art und Weise erlebbar als dies dem Erzähler im beschreibenden oder interaktiven Modus möglich ist. Die Kinder werden dadurch nicht als Beobachter oder

5.6 Typografisches Erscheinungsbild

In einem **typografischen Erscheinungsbild** kommen alle Grundkenntnisse der Mikro- und Makrotypografie zum Einsatz. Dieses wird als Teil des gesamten **visuellen Erscheinungsbildes** betrachtet, welches auch als **Corporate Design** bezeichnet wird. Auf dieses wird im nächsten Kapitel eingegangen.

Beispiel Gestaltung eines Faltblattes zur Image-Darstellung

Bei einem Faltblatt zur Image-Darstellung kommt es darauf an, mit einem soliden typografischen Konzept auf wenigen Seiten für ein Unternehmen oder eine Institution zu werben. Beim hier gezeigten Beispiel handelt es sich um ein schulisches Projekt, den Entwurf eines Faltblattes für das „Staatliche Seminar für Didaktik und Lehrerbildung in Weingarten". Das Faltblatt hat im Original das Format DIN A 5.
Die Typografie, sowie die grundsätzliche Gestaltung ist durch die grafischen Gestaltungsrichtlinien des Landes Baden-Württemberg vorgegeben. Es gelang somit, ein durchgängig solides Faltblatt zu entwerfen. Die Gestaltungsrichtlinien werden auf den folgenden Seiten näher erläutert.

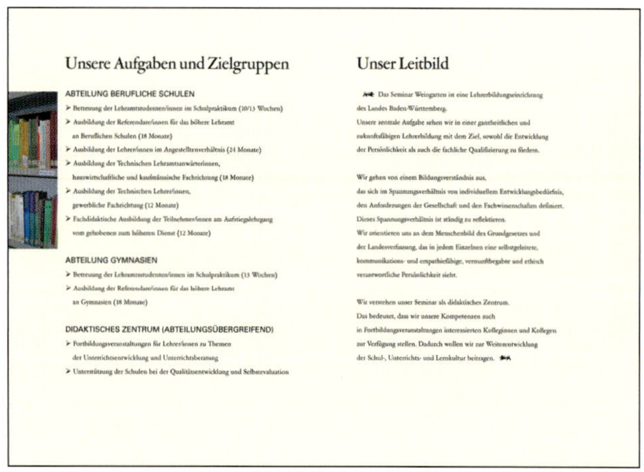

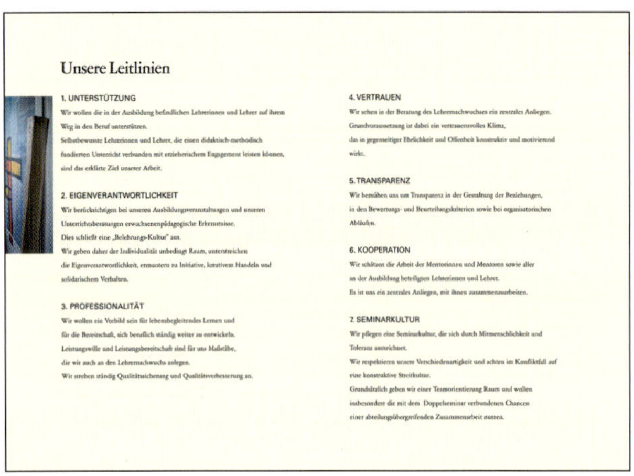

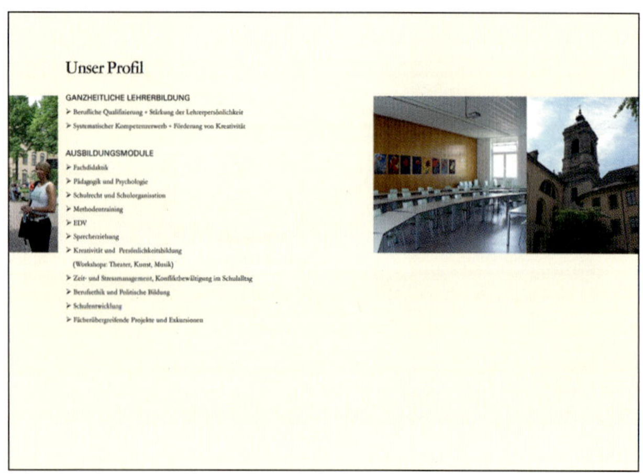

Beispiel Grafische Gestaltungsrichtlinien für Baden-Württemberg

Unter dem Titel „Ein Bild von einem Land“ hat das Staatsministerium des Landes Baden-Württemberg einen über 100-seitigen Leitfaden veröffentlicht.
Im folgenden werden anhand von fünf Seiten beispielhaft die Elemente Typografie und Layout besprochen, sowie auf die Gestaltung von Titel- und Innenseiten einer Broschüre eingegangen.

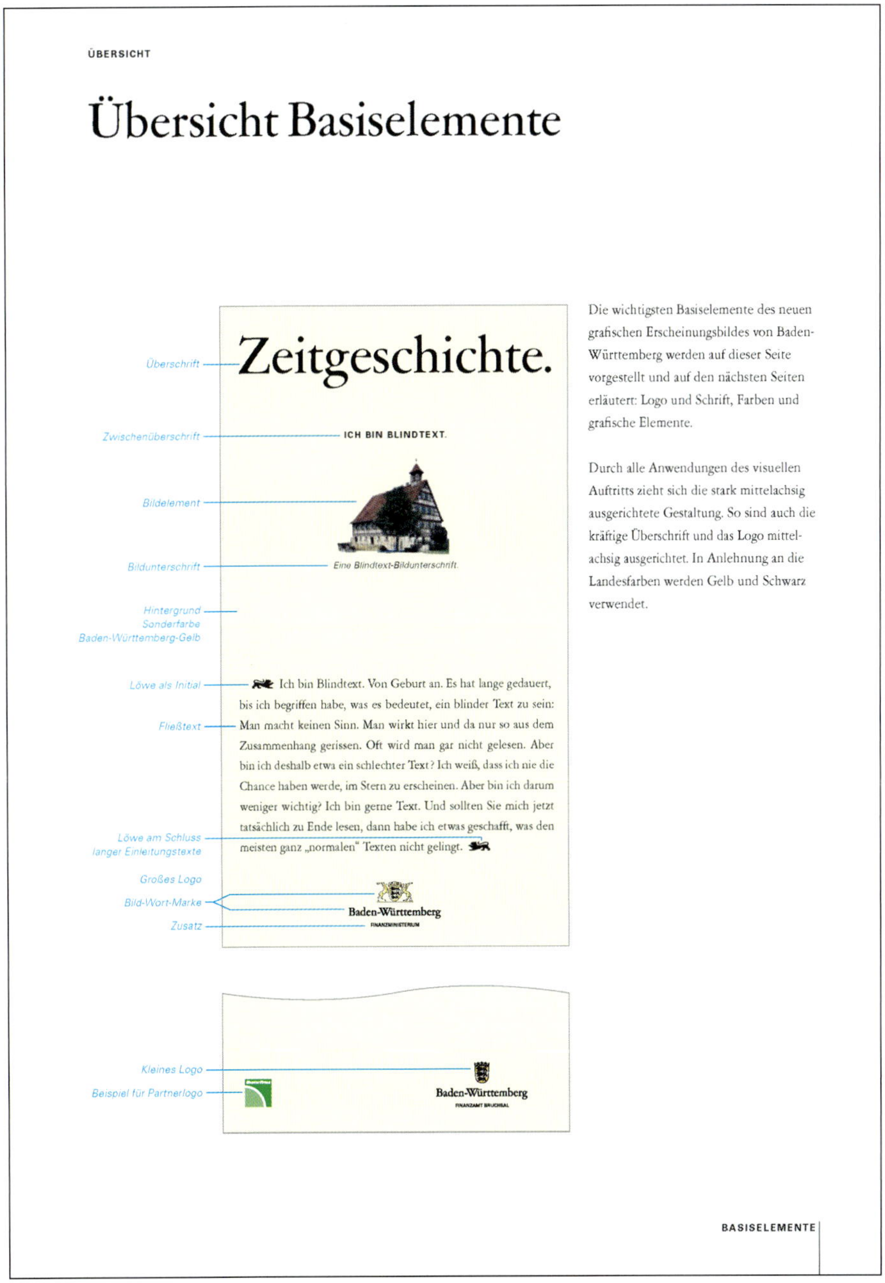
ÜBERSICHT

Übersicht Basiselemente

Die wichtigsten Basiselemente des neuen grafischen Erscheinungsbildes von Baden-Württemberg werden auf dieser Seite vorgestellt und auf den nächsten Seiten erläutert: Logo und Schrift, Farben und grafische Elemente.

Durch alle Anwendungen des visuellen Auftritts zieht sich die stark mittelachsig ausgerichtete Gestaltung. So sind auch die kräftige Überschrift und das Logo mittelachsig ausgerichtet. In Anlehnung an die Landesfarben werden Gelb und Schwarz verwendet.

BASISELEMENTE

Seite 6 des Leitfadens: „Ein Bild von einem Land“ des Staatsministeriums von Baden-Württemberg

Eine der verwendeten Hausschriften des Landes Baden-Württemberg ist die Garamont Amsterdam.
Die Definition der Hausschrift ist wichtigstes Element eines typografischen Erscheinungsbildes. Sie ist das Aushängeschild eines Unternehmens, einer Institution oder eines Medienproduktes. Eine Hausschrift sollte einen guten Wiedererkennungswert besitzen, gut lesbar sein und überall eingesetzt werden. Ebenso sollte diese Schrift die Unternehmenskultur wiederspiegeln, sowie zum Produktangebot passen.

Schriftcharakter:
Die gesamten Garamond-Schriftfamilien besitzen einen edlen, traditionellen Touch. Die hier verwendete Garamont wurde später als die Grundtype entwickelt. Sie wirkt wesentlich dynamischer und trotz ihres konservativen Einschlags sehr modern. Man könnte daher den Schriftcharakter bezeichnen als: Traditionell modern.

2 SCHRIFT UND TYPOGRAFIE

2.1 Hausschrift 1: Garamont Amsterdam

Garamont Amsterdam SH

ABÇDEFGHIJKLMÑOPQRSTÜVWXZ
äbcdefghijklmnpqrstuvwxyß„!?“«1234567890»
Garamont Amsterdam SH medium

Garamont Amsterdam SB

A B Ç D E F G H I J K L M
Ñ O P Q R S T Ü V W X Y Z
ä b c d e fi fl g h i j k l m n œ p q r s t u v
w x y z ß „ ! ? “ « 1 2 3 4 5 6 7 8 9 0 »
Garamont Amsterdam SB roman

A B Ç D E F G H I J K L M
Ñ O P Q R S T Ü V W X Y Z
ä b c d e fi fl g h i j k l m n œ p q r s t u v
w x y z ß „ ! ? “ « 1 2 3 4 5 6 7 8 9 0 »
Garamont Amsterdam SB medium

A B Ç D E F G H I J K L M
Ñ O P Q R S T Ü V W X Y Z
ä b c d e fi fl g h i j k l m n œ p q r s t u v
w x y z ß „ ! ? “ « 1 2 3 4 5 6 7 8 9 0 »
Garamont Amsterdam SB italic

A B Ç D E F G H I J K L M
Ñ O P Q R S T Ü V W X Y Z
ä b c d e fi fl g h i j k l m n œ p q r s t u v
w x y z ß „ ! ? “ « 1 2 3 4 5 6 7 8 9 0 »
Garamont Amsterdam SB medium italic

SCHRIFT
Claude Garamond (um 1480–1561) gab der Schrift nicht nur seinen Namen, sondern auch ihre klassisch-dynamische Form. Namhafte Schrifthersteller wie Stempel, Linotype, Berthold und ITC beauftragten berühmte Schriftdesigner, die Bandbreite von Schriftschnitten und Schmuckbuchstaben zu erweitern und zu optimieren. Die für Baden-Württemberg verwendete Schrift hat den gleichen Duktus, aber einen anderen Namen:
GARAMONT (MIT „T“) AMSTERDAM.
Im Gegensatz zu den anderen weist diese 1917 von Benton und Cleland für die Firma Lettergieterij Amsterdam entwickelte Version bewusst rauere Strichführungen auf und ähnelt von der Anmutung her einer Venezianischen Früh-Antiqua.

Diese charaktervolle Schrift – eine der beiden Hauptschriften Baden-Württembergs – kommt besonders gut in großen Schriftgraden zur Geltung. Für Überschriften wird der etwas schmalere Schriftschnitt Garamont Amsterdam SH medium eingesetzt. Fließtext wird in der Garamont Amsterdam SB roman bzw. für Hervorhebungen im Fließtext in Medium, Italic und Medium italic gesetzt (*SH* – Headline, *SB* – Bodytext).

Garamont Amsterdam ist die Hausschrift 1 für alle gedruckten Medien, *siehe Kapitel 2 Schrift und Typografie.*

BASISELEMENTE | 2.1(1)

Seite 17 des Leitfadens: „Ein Bild von einem Land“ des Staatsministeriums von Baden-Württemberg

Broschüren jeder Art verfügen über eine Titelseite, die erste und somit eventuell auch wichtigste Seite eines Medienproduktes.
Auf dieser Seite wird die Vermaßung einer Titelseite dargestellt und die wichtigsten Elemente werden beschrieben. Selbst wenn nur wenige Elemente vorkommen, so ist es doch sehr wichtig, diese einheitlich zu platzieren. Dies erhöht die Wiedererkennbarkeit neben den weiterhin zu verwendenden Parametern wie zum Beispiel die Farbe, die Verwendung der Schriftart und der Einsatz von Bildern.

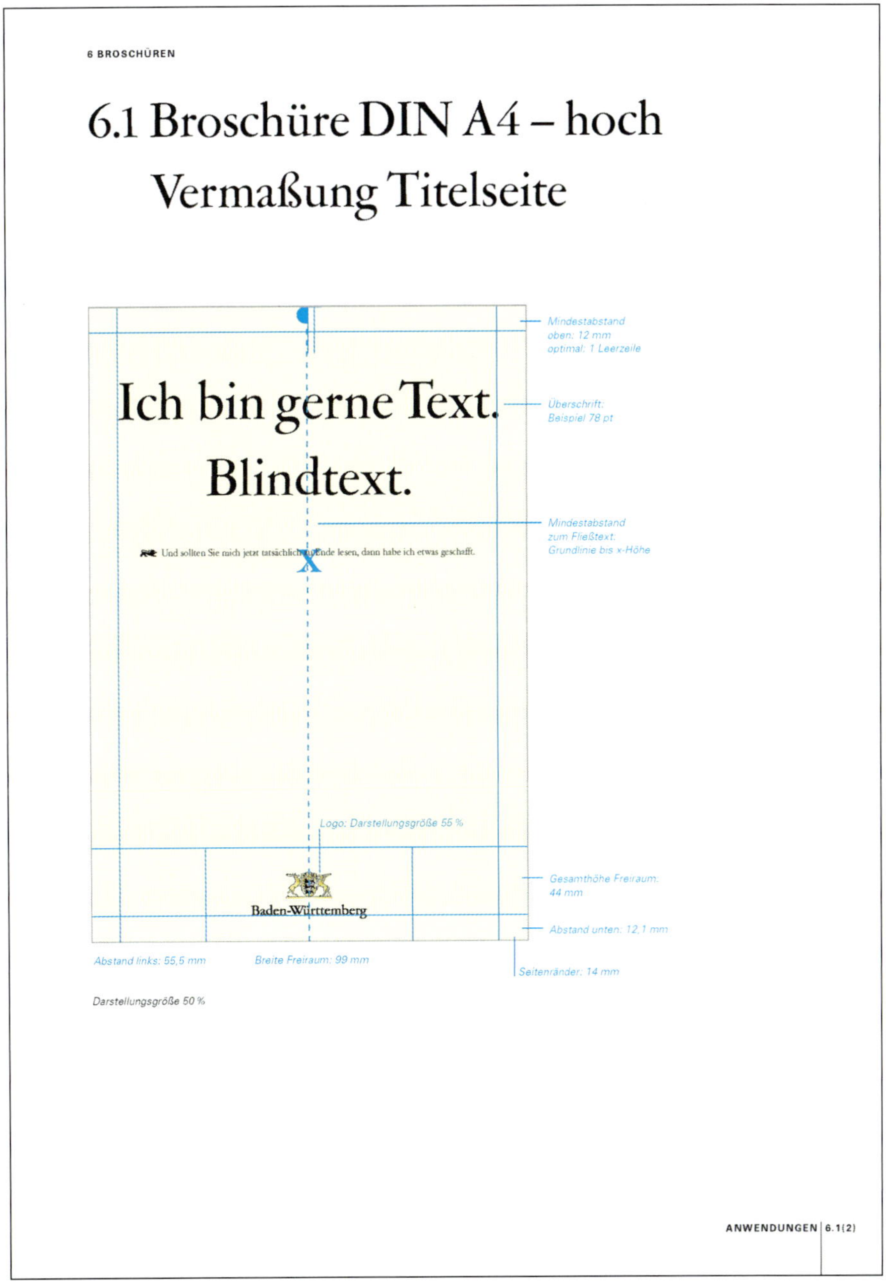

Mittelachsensatz:
Eines der zentralen Merkmale bei der Textverwendung ist der Mittelachsensatz. Normalerweise wirkt dieser eher nicht besonders interessant. Durch den geschickten Einsatz verschiedener Schriftgrößen jedoch gelingt es, äußerst spannende Kompositionen zu gestalten.

Seite 60 des Leitfadens: „Ein Bild von einem Land" des Staatsministeriums von Baden-Württemberg

Auf dieser Seite des Leitfadens wird auf die Vermaßung und somit auf die Gestaltung der Innenseiten eingegangen.
Bei Medienprodukten aller Art ist es hilfreich, auf ein Gestaltungsraster zurück zu greifen. Im Rahmen eines Leitfadens geht es weniger um die Erstellung eines Raster, als viel mehr um die Beschreibung der Vorgaben und deren Verwendung. Somit können Medienprodukte von der Stange produziert werden, die alle den Eindruck erwecken, aus dem gleichen Hause zu stammen.

Grundlinienraster:
Zeilenraster, auf dem die Grundlinien der Schriftzeilen positioniert sind. Das Zeilenraster hat somit das gleiche Maß wie der Zeilenabstand des Fließtextes.

6 BROSCHÜREN

6.1 Broschüre DIN A4 – hoch
Vermaßung Innenseite

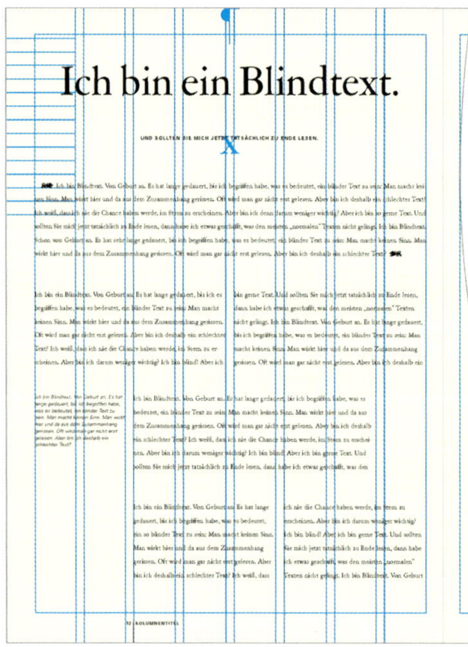

Darstellungsgröße 50 %

INNENSEITEN

Broschüren in DIN A4 sollen großzügig gestaltet sein, Marginalspalten dienen der Platzierung von Grafiken und kleineren Tabellen. Einleitungstexte können einspaltig (ca. zwei Drittel der Satzspiegelbreite) oder zweispaltig, Fließtext zwei- oder dreispaltig mit Marginalspalte gesetzt werden.

Satzspiegel	188 x 271 mm
Spalten	Anzahl 8, Abstand 4 mm, Breite 20
Ränder (mindestens)	oben 12, unten 14, innen 8, außen 14 mm
Grundlinienraster	(optimiert für Fließtext 10 pt, ZAB 18 pt) Start 14,2 mm, Schrittweite 18 pt (mind. 16 pt, max. 20 pt)
Fließtext	10 pt, LW 0, ZAB 18 pt (mind. 9 pt, max. 11 pt)
Zwischenüberschrift	6,6 pt, LW +20, ZAB 18 pt (mind. 6 pt, max. 7,3 pt)
Bildunterschrift	6,6 pt, LW +4, ZAB 9 pt

Angaben für QuarkXPress, LW = Laufweite, ZAB = Zeilenabstand

Weitere Angaben *siehe Kapitel 2 Schrift und Typografie, Kapitel 3 Farben und Kapitel 4 Bilder, Grafiken und Tabellen.*

ANWENDUNGEN | 6.1(4)

Seite 62 des Leitfadens: „Ein Bild von einem Land" des Staatsministeriums von Baden-Württemberg

Erst die Verwendung von Bildern macht eine Broschüre richtig interessant und kann auch die verwendete Schrift in Ihrer Aussage unterstützen.
Die Verwendung von Bildern gehört streng genommen nicht mehr zum typografischen Erscheinungsbild, sondern wagt nun den Sprung zum gesamten, visuellen Erscheinungsbild, dem Corporate Design. Im Rahmen der Regeln der Makrotypografie jedoch (siehe Kapitel 5.5) bildet die Verwendung von Bildern, um aus dem typografischen Werk ein Gesamtwerk zu machen, einen wichtigen Baustein.

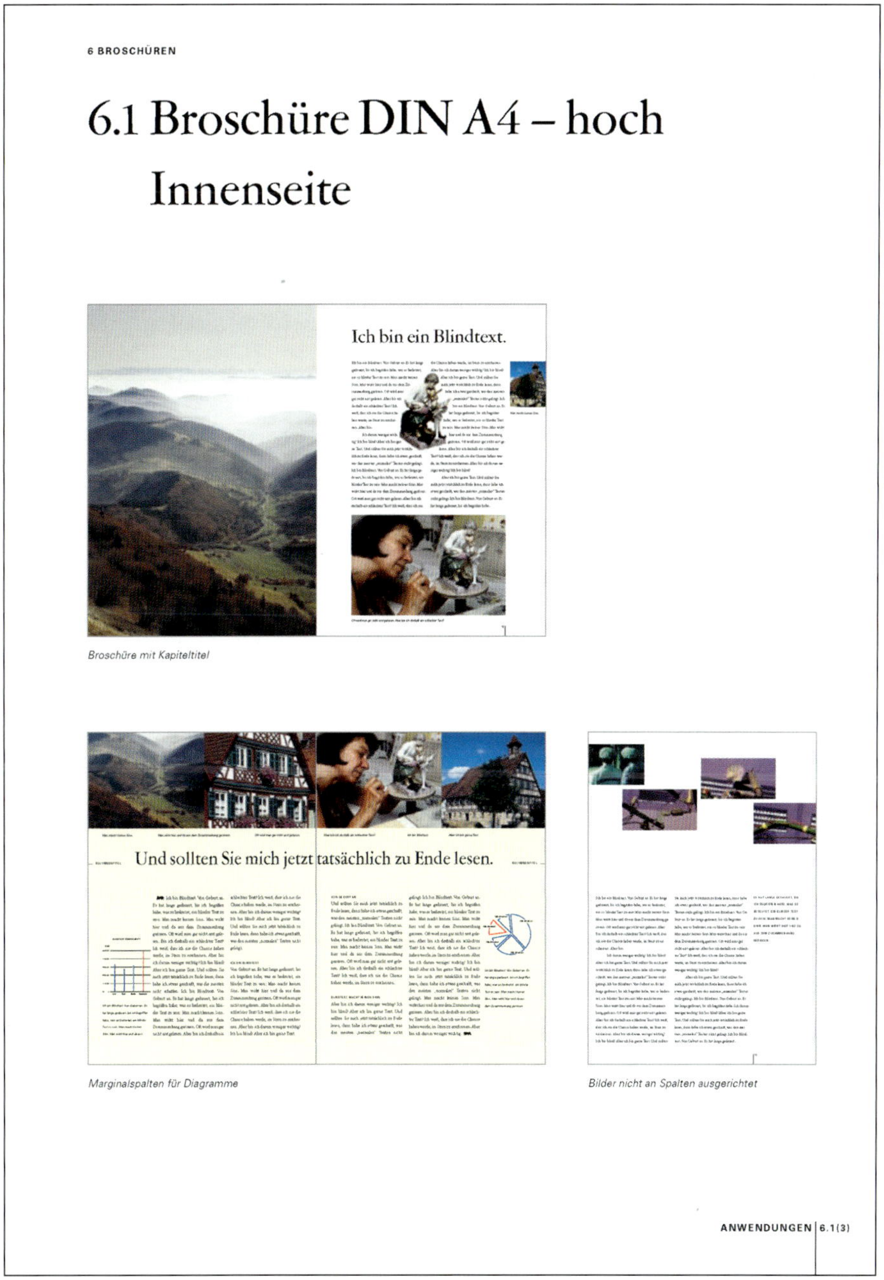
6 BROSCHÜREN

6.1 Broschüre DIN A4 – hoch
Innenseite

Broschüre mit Kapiteltitel

Marginalspalten für Diagramme

Bilder nicht an Spalten ausgerichtet

ANWENDUNGEN | 6.1(3)

Bildpositionierung:
Man merkt deutlich, dass mehr Kontraste entstehen, wenn die verwendeten Bilder größer sind. Das Gestaltungsraster gibt eine großzügige Verwendung problemlos her.

Seite 61 des Leitfadens: „Ein Bild von einem Land" des Staatsministeriums von Baden-Württemberg

5.7 Visuelles Erscheinungsbild

Das **visuelle Erscheinungsbild** eines Unternehmens, einer Institution oder eines Medienproduktes wird auch als **Corporate Design** bezeichnet. Es handelt sich dabei um ein formales Konzept, welches sämtliche Designaspekte zu einem starken, wiedererkennbaren Auftritt vereinigt. Neben allem „sichtbaren“ gehört hier auch alles Tast-, Hör- und Riechbare dazu (wie zum Beispiel die Architektur eines Unternehmens, der Wandschmuck in der Lobby oder eine eventuell zu verwendende Arbeitskleidung der Angestellten).

Beispiel Gestaltung mehrerer Medien der Traumpalast-Kinos

Die Traumpalast-Kinos bringen mehrere Medien, teilweise regelmäßig, teilweise unregelmäßig auf den Markt. Im Rahmen des Corporate Design wird auf folgende Aspekte wert gelegt: Verwendung einer **Wortmarke**, einer **Hausschrift** in allen Medien und Festlegungen der **Farben**. Wichtig sind ebenso einige prägnante **grafische Elemente** (Linien, Sterne und Filmstreifen) und die Einbindung eines **Themenschwerpunktes** in allen Medien (hier der Film: „Der Lorax“).

Doppelseite aus dem Kinomagazin Abspann

TOP-FILM

Der LORAX

Ab 19. Juli im Kino

Die Macher von *„Ich – Einfach unverbesserlich“* und *„Hop – Osterhase oder Superstar?“* schöpfen im phantastischen Kosmos von Dr. Seuss aus dem Vollen: *„Der Lorax“* ist eine 3D-Adaption der beliebten Geschichte über einen Schutzgeist des Waldes und die immerwährende Kraft der Hoffnung.

Thneedville ist eine Stadt, aus der jegliche Natur vertrieben wurde. Die Pflanzen sind aus Kunststoff und der gerissene Geschäftsmann Aloysius O'Hare (Rob Riggle) scheffelt Millionen damit, in Plastikflaschen abgefüllte Frischluft zu verkaufen.

Hier lebt auch der zwölfjährige Ted (Zac Efron), der das Herz seiner Angebeteten Audrey (Taylor Swift) für sich erobern will – indem er ihren größten Wunsch erfüllt: Sie möchte unbedingt einmal einen echten Baum sehen, denn die existieren in Thneedville nicht mehr.

Also macht sich Ted mit einer Hacke auf, um in der davorliegenden Brachlandschaft nach dem geheimnisvollen Once-ler (Ed Helms) Ausschau zu halten. Denn dieser soll angeblich wissen, was mit all den Bäumen geschehen ist.

Und tatsächlich erzählt der zunächst zögerliche Once-ler dann Ted seine Geschichte: Als junger Mann machte er eine Erfindung, die sich schnell zu einem unerreichten Verkaufsschlager entwickelte. Doch um die Erfindung herzustellen, musste er immer mehr Truffula-Bäume abholzen.

Die idyllische Landschaft des Truffula-Tals ist der Lebensraum für eine vielfältige Fauna. Besonders niedlich sind die kleinen, bärchenartigen Bar-ba-loots, die unter den Truffula-Bäumen umhertollen. Und der Lorax ist ein amüsanter und liebenswerter „Waldmeister“, der über sich hinauswächst, um die Bäume und die im Wald lebenden Tiere zu beschützen.

Sobald der Once-ler also einen Baum fällt, taucht der Lorax (Danny DeVito) auf – doch selbst die eindringlichen Warnungen konnten den Once-ler nicht davon abhalten, seinen ehrgeizigen Plan voranzutreiben.

Von ihrem ersten Treffen an stehen der Lorax und der Once-ler auf entgegengesetzten Seiten. Jeder der beiden will den anderen loswerden, doch im Laufe der Zeit wachsen sie einander ans Herz. Letztendlich kann der Lorax sich dem skrupellosen Ehrgeiz und der Gier nicht widersetzen, die den Once-ler umtreiben – denn der lässt sich einfach nicht aufhalten. Auch wenn das bedeutet, auch den letzten Baum zu fällen und das gesamte Tal zu zerstören.

Jahre später, in einer baumlosen Welt, wagt sich Ted aus seiner perfekt industrialisierten Stadt Thneedville hinaus und macht sich auf die Suche nach dem Once-ler. Denn Ted will wissen, wie er für Audrey, das Mädchen seiner Träume, einen Baum beschaffen kann.

Der Once-ler ist zunächst gar nicht zugänglich, doch dann sieht er in Ted etwas, das ihn dazu inspiriert, von seiner früheren Begegnung mit dem Lorax zu berichten. Das wiederum inspiriert Ted zu der Mission, Thneedville wieder ins Gleichgewicht zu bringen – indem er der ganzen Stadt Truffula-Bäume bringen will.

Bundesstart: 19. Juli 2012
Genre: Animation
Regie: Chris Renaud
Bilder und Pressetext: Universal Pictures

10 11

Publikationen der Traumpalast-Kinos im einheitlichen Erscheinungsbild: Abspann – Das Magazin, Abspännle – Ihr Wochenprogramm und Abspann for kids. Titelmotive mit freundlicher Genehmigung von Universal Pictures Germany.

Mit einem soliden Gestaltungskonzept soll erreicht werden, dass alle Medien ansprechend aussehen und vor allem einen hohen Wiedererkennungswert haben.
Das Corporate Design ist ein Teilaspekt einer Gesamtheit, dem sogenannten **Corporate Identity**. Über das visuelle Konzept hinaus wird bei der Corporate Identity vor allem auch die gesamte Konzeption eines Unternehmens definiert. Hierzu gehören auch bestimmte Arbeitsabläufe, gemeinsame Unternehmungen der Mitarbeiter oder die festgelegten Arbeitszeiten.

6 Bild

Webcode: **B0600**

Für weitere Infos zu diesem Kapitel mit dem Smartphone einfach QR-Code scannen oder auf www.medien-verstehen.de den Webcode eingeben.

Dieses Kapitel gibt einen Einblick in die gestalterischen Möglichkeiten beim visuellen, statischen Medium – dem Bild. Dies kann zum Beispiel bei einem Web-Aufritt, einem Videofilm oder einer multimedialen Produktion der Fall sein. Dabei steht nicht nur die Gestaltung im Mittelpunkt, sondern auch die dazu benötigte Technik und deren Werkzeuge. Visuell Gestaltetes soll optisch ansprechen, auffallen, „ins Auge springen", provozieren, eine Harmonie für die visuellen Sinne bieten, Gefühle wecken, Assoziationen hervorrufen oder einfach nur gefallen – keine leichte Aufgabe für den Gestalter, der dies erreichen soll. Die Wirkung der Gestaltung ist subjektiv, emotional und dem Zeitgeist unterworfen. Trotzdem ist es möglich, Regeln aufzustellen, die das Gestalten begleiten und unterstützen. Diese Regeln basieren auf optischen Gesetzen und den Eigenschaften der Medien. Gestalten nach Regeln – kann das kreativ sein? Warum nicht, denn Gestalten erfüllt selten nur einen Selbstzweck. Der Betrachter soll schließlich animiert, provoziert, fasziniert sein! Um dies zu erreichen, muss der Gestalter sein Handwerk verstehen. Er muss wissen, wie und wann er seine Medien einsetzt, und welche Gestaltungstechniken er benutzen kann. Außerdem sollte er über Kenntnisse der Medieneigenschaften verfügen..

6.1 Fotografie

6.1.1 Camera Obscura

❶ Die **Camera Obscura** bestand in den Anfängen aus einem großen Raum, in den über ein Loch ein „punktgespiegeltes" Bild projiziert wurde. Daher die Bezeichnung „Camera" für Zimmer und „Obscura" für das obskure Bild, welches sich durch die Projektion abzeichnete.

Die Ursprünge der **Fotografie** gehen bis auf die berühmte **Camera Obscura** ❶ zurück, deren Anfänge nicht mehr exakt nachzuverfolgen sind. Schon der griechische Philosoph Aristoteles (384-332 v. Chr.) soll die Camera Obscura verwendet haben, um die Sonnenfinsternis besser beobachten zu können.

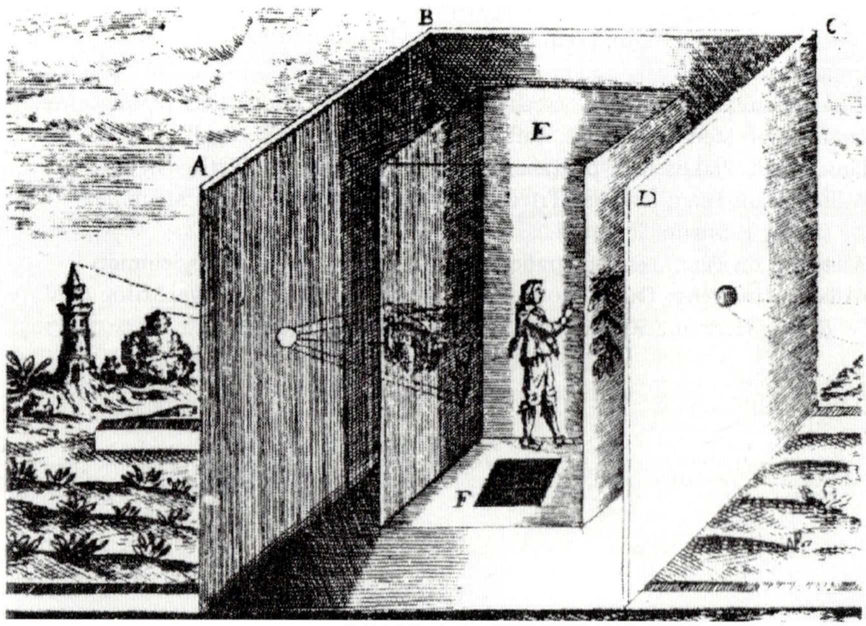

Transportable, begehbare Camera Obscura nach Athanasius Kircher um 1646.

Ab dem 17. Jahrhundert wurde sie in transportabler Form konstruiert und durch eine Sammellinse in ihrer Abbildungsleistung verbessert. Aber erst um 1826 begann man, das projizierte Bild mit Hilfe chemischer Verfahren zu konservieren. Anfang des 20. Jahrhunderts, begleitet durch wesentliche Fortschritte im chemischen Bereich, wurde mit dem ersten Rollfilm und kleinen transportablen Kameras die kommerzielle Ära der Fotografie eingeläutet.

6.1.2 Fotografischer Prozess

Zeit und Blende

Bei der Fotografie spricht man von ‚Belichten von Bildern', ob auf Filmmaterial oder auf einen elektronischen Chip. Voraussetzung für eine korrekte **Belichtung** ist, dass die richtige Menge Licht auf den Bildträger (Filmmaterial oder Chip) fällt.

Dies wird durch ein Zusammenspiel aus Zeit und Blende erreicht. Die beiden Faktoren bestimmen, in welcher Zeit (= **Belichtungszeit**) welche Lichtmenge (bestimmt durch die Größe der **Blendenöffnung**) durch das Objektiv auf den Bildträger fällt. Wie hoch die richtige Menge Licht für den Bildträger ist, hängt von dessen Lichtempfindlichkeit ab.

Wie kann sichergestellt werden, dass für jede Aufnahmesituation mit der richtigen Lichtmenge belichtet wird? Dies kann durch das Steuern der Belichtungsdauer und /oder Steuern der Blendenöffnung in Abhängigkeit mit Empfindlichkeitswerten des Bildträgers erreicht werden.

❶ Belichtungsvorgang bei einem **Zentralverschluss**.

Es wird prinzipiell zwischen dem Zentralverschluss und dem Schlitzverschluss unterschieden. Beim **Zentralverschluss** ❶ wird die Lichtöffnung durch mehrere dünne Lamellen aus Stahlfolie abgedeckt, die beim Auslösen des Verschlusses um einen festen Drehpunkt geschwenkt werden. Damit geben sie, von der Mitte her beginnend, kurzzeitig die Lichtöffnung zur Belichtung frei.

❷ Belichtungsvorgang bei einem **Schlitzverschluss**.

Beim **Schlitzverschluss** ❷, der horizontal wie auch vertikal angeordnet sein kann, laufen während des Belichtungsvorganges zwei Rollos, die aus Folie oder Metallstreifen bestehen können, über die Lichtöffnung hinweg. Während der Belichtung gibt das erste Rollo die Lichtöffnung frei und das zweite deckt es nachfolgend wieder ab. Dabei wird

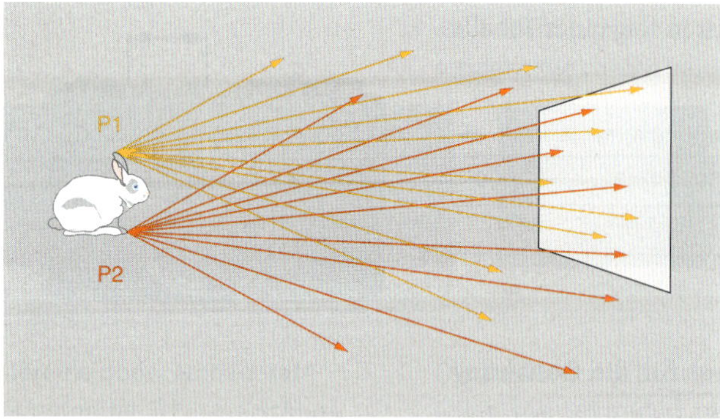

❶ Ungebündeltes Licht

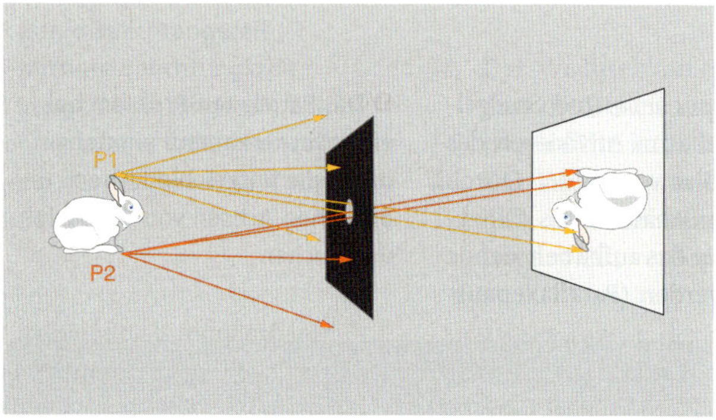

❷ Camera Obscura

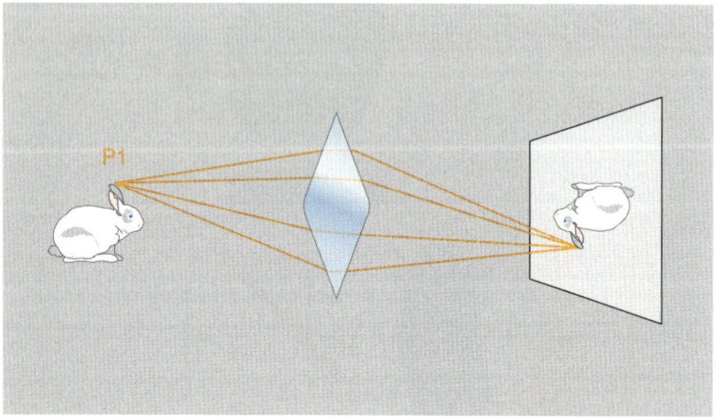

❸ Konvexlinse

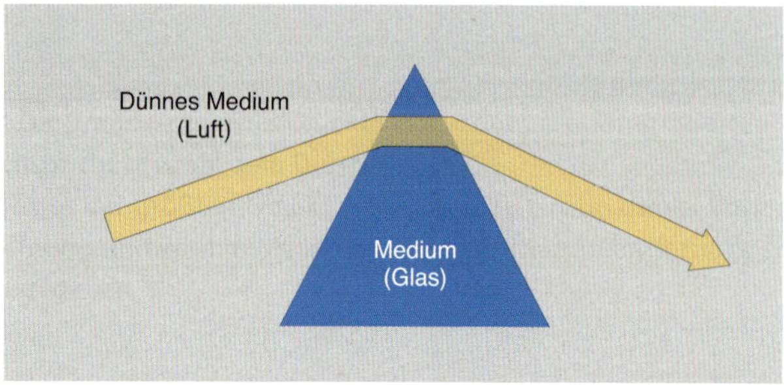

Objektive

Um ein Bild auf die Mattscheibe und damit auch auf den Bildträger zu bekommen, muss man eine Lichtlenkungs-Einrichtung benutzen – etwas, das die Lichtstrahlen sammelt und so bündelt, dass sie als scharfes Bild auf den Film gelangen. Sonst würden die unregelmäßigen Lichtstrahlen nur ein gleichmäßig belichtetes Stück Film erzeugen. Beispiel: Das reflektierende Licht von den Gegenstands-Punkten P1 und P2 treffen auf alle Flächenpunkte des Bildträgers ❶.

Wie kann man nun Lichtstrahlen bündeln? Nimmt man eine Lochblende mit einer sehr kleinen Öffnung, werden nur ganz wenige Lichtstrahlen eines Gegenstandspunktes auf den Bildträger geworfen. Es entsteht ein auf dem Kopf stehendes, seitenverkehrtes Abbild. Da aber nur eine relativ kleine Öffnung benutzt werden kann, da sonst das Abbild wieder unscharf wird, muss eine sehr lange Belichtungszeit verwendet werden. Mit diesem Verfahren, bekannt als ‚Camera Obscura' ❷, begann die Fotografie.

Eine effektive Bündelung des Lichts erreicht man mit einer Linse. Mit einer Konvexlinse ❸, auch auf Grund ihrer Eigenschaft als Sammellinse bezeichnet, werden viele Strahlen, die von einem einzelnen Punkt reflektiert werden, gesammelt und auf der Bildebene zu einem einzigen Punkt vereinigt. So entsteht ein scharfes, lichtstarkes Abbild des Gegenstandes. Aber wie kann eine Linse das Licht lenken?

Trifft ein Lichtstrahl aus einem optisch dünneren Medium (Luft) in einem schrägem Winkel auf ein optisch dichteres Medium (Linse), ändert sich die Fortbewegungsrichtung des Lichts. Verursacht wird dieser Effekt durch die vom Medium abhängige Fortbewegungsgeschwindigkeit. Tritt der Lichtstrahl wieder aus dem dichten Medium in das dünne Medium aus, erfolgt auch an dieser Schnittstelle wieder eine Änderung der Fortbewegungsrichtung.

➲ **Durch Strahlenbrechung regeln und lenken Linsen das Licht.**

Eine Linse in der einfachsten Form ist die bikonvexe Sammellinse, die man von der Lupe her kennt. Linsen mit konvexer Form ❶ sammeln das Licht (Sammellinse) und Linsen mit konkaver Form ❷ zerstreuen das Licht. Für die Verwendung einer Linse als Objektiv würde zwar prinzipiell eine Sammellinse genügen, da sich aber nicht alle Lichtstrahlen gleich verhalten, treten Abbildungsfehler und Unschärfen auf. Diese Fehler werden korrigiert, indem man Linsen verschiedener Glassorten und Krümmung zu einem Objektiv aneinanderreiht.

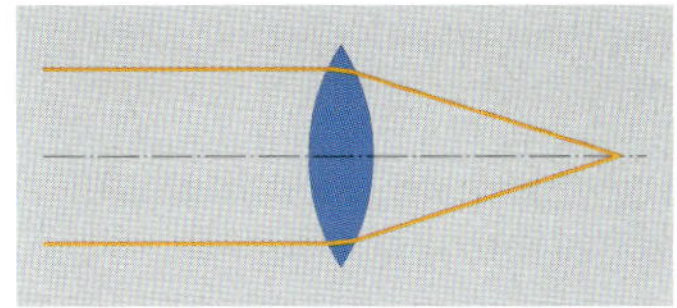

❶ **Sammellinse** (positive Linse). Parallele Strahlen werden von einer konvexen Linse so abgelenkt, dass sie sich in einem Punkt sammeln.

Die sechs wichtigsten Linsenformen sind:

1 Bikonvex
2 Plankonvex
3 Konkavkonvex
4 Bikonkav
5 Plankonkav
6 Konvexkonkav

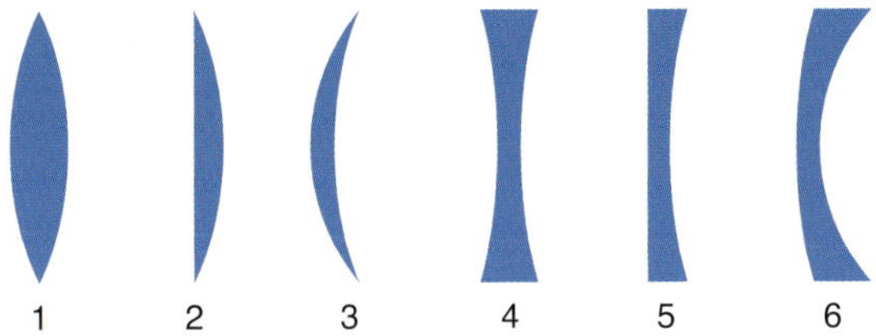

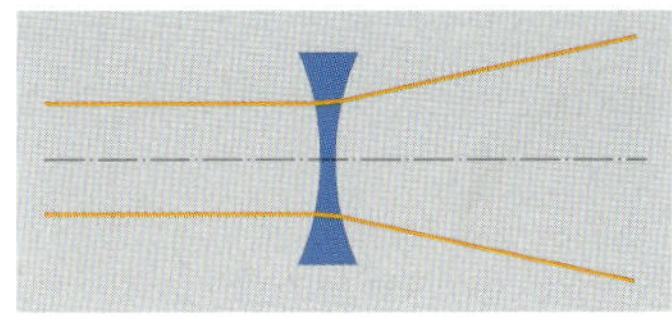

❷ **Zerstreuungslinse** (negative Linse). Parallele Strahlen werden von einer konkaven Linse so abgelenkt, dass sie sich nicht in einem Punkt sammeln.

Betrachtet man parallele Lichtstrahlen (etwa von der Sonne), die auf eine Sammellinse fallen, werden sie durch die konvexe Form der Linse dahingehend abgelenkt, dass sie alle durch den gleichen Punkt (Brennpunkt) laufen. Den Abstand des Brennpunktes zur Linsenmitte bezeichnet man als Brennweite.
Liegt das Objekt der Lichtstrahlen „unendlich" weit entfernt, also ist die **Gegenstandsweite** ❸ gleich unendlich, so gilt **Bildweite** ❹ gleich Brennweite.

❸ Die **Gegenstandsweite** ist die Distanz vom abzubildenden Gegenstand zum Objektiv.

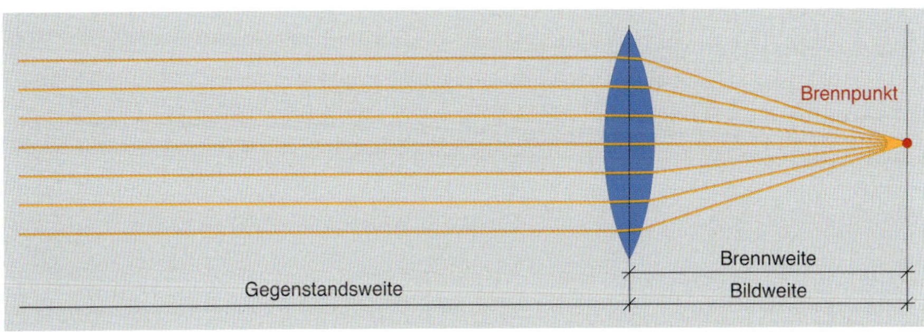

❹ Die **Bildweite** beschreibt den Abstand zwischen Linsenmitte und der Bildebene (Filmschicht bzw. Digitalsensor).

Die **Brennweite** bestimmt die Größe des Bildes auf dem Bildträger. Da ein Objektiv aber nur auf eine Distanz scharf darstellt und die Bildweite größer wird, je näher der Gegenstand an das Objektiv heranrückt, muss das Objektiv über eine Fokussierung verfügen.

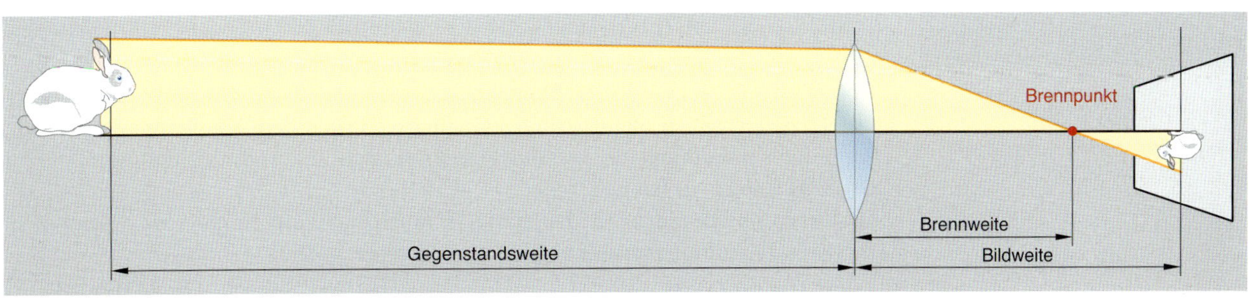

Mit **Weitwinkelobjektiven** können Objekte in einem großem Bildwinkel eingefangen werden. Die Abbildung enspricht jedoch einem kleinerem Maßstab.

Ein **Normalobjektiv** verfügt über einen Bildwinkel von 45° und einer Brennweite von 50 mm bei einem Bildträgerformat von 24 x 36 mm. Es kommt dem menschlichen Augeneindruck am nächsten.

Mit dem **Teleobjektiv** können von einem entfernten Standort aus Objekte in größerer Abbildung eingefangen werden. Wegen der Verwacklungsgefahr möglichst kurze Belichtungszeit oder Stativ verwenden.

Wird das Objekt im Verhältnis 1:1 aufgenommen, ist Bildweite = Gegenstandsweite. Damit ist das abgebildete Objekt auf dem Bildträger gleich dem realen Objekt (Abbildungsgröße 1:1).

In der Praxis möchte man in der Gegenstandsweite möglichst flexibel sein, um unabhängig vom Aufnahmestandort unterschiedliche Abbildungsgrößen zu erreichen. Dazu benötigt man Objektive mit unterschiedlichen Brennweiten.

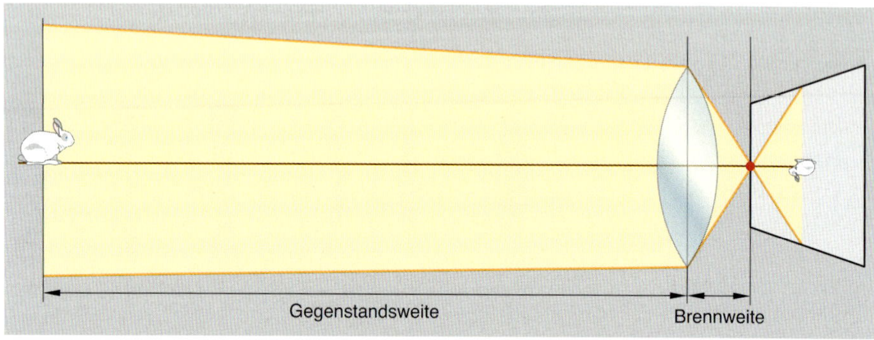

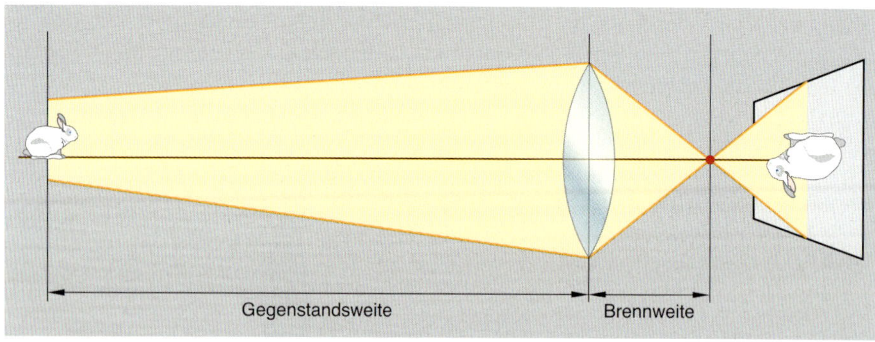

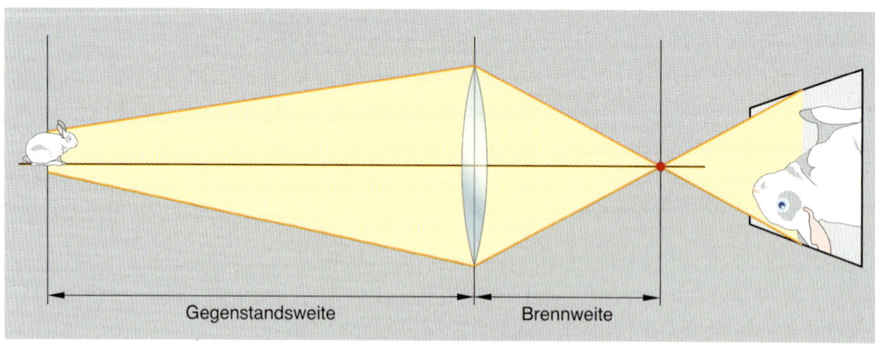

Objektive mit veränderlicher Brennweite, sogenannte Vario-Objektive oder Zoom-Objektive, bieten bei meist geringen Qualitätsverlusten dem Fotografen den Vorteil, von einem Standpunkt aus verschiedene Bildausschnitte und Abbildungsgrößen des Objektes wählen zu können.

Mit Makroobjektiven kann der Fotograf Aufnahmen im Nahbereich vornehmen. Dabei sind Abbildungsmaßstäbe bis 1:1 realisierbar.

Teleobjektive und Makroobjektive verfügen bei offener Blende über eine sehr geringe **Schärfentiefe** ❶. Nur durch Abblenden (Wahl einer kleineren Blendenöffnung) kann die Schärfentiefe vergrößert werden.

❶ Unter **Schärfentiefe** versteht man den Entfernungsbereich, innerhalb dem die abgebildeten Objekte scharf erscheinen.
Je kleiner der Bildträger (bei digitalen Kameras der Bildsensor) ist, desto größer ist die generelle Schärfentiefe.
Beispiel der jeweiligen Schärfentiefe bei Blende 5,6 und einer Entfernung von 3 m:
Kleinbild = 1,15 m
4/3 Zoll Bildsensor = 2,22 m
2/3 Zoll Bildsensor = 4,57 m

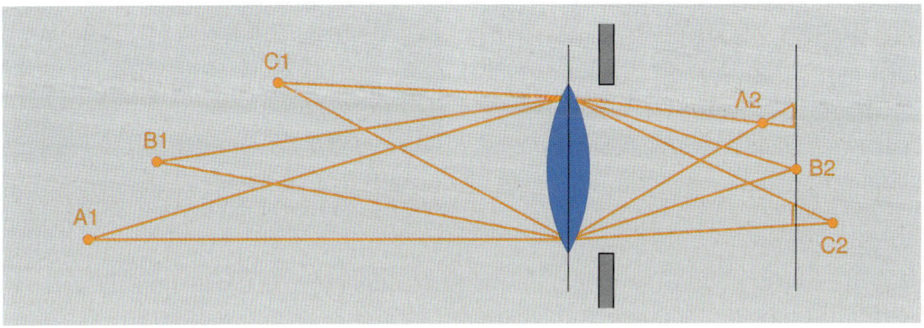

Geringe Schärfentiefe bei offener Blende. Punkt A und C werden sehr unscharf auf dem Bildträger abgebildet.

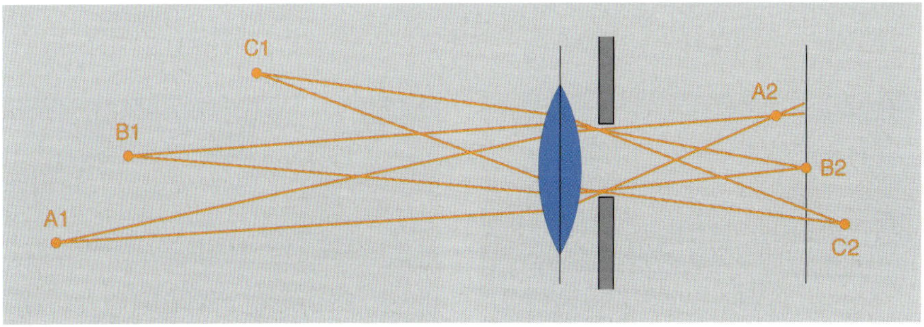

Größere Schärfentiefe bei kleiner Blendenöffnung. Punkt A und C werden nun schärfer auf dem Bildträger abgebildet.

Ein weiteres Kriterium bei Objektiven ist die **Lichtstärke**. Sie ist ein Maß für die Lichtmenge, die auf den Bildträger gelangen kann. Man bezeichnet sie auch als „relative Öffnung". Sie wird als Verhältnis ❷ von Durchmesser der Frontlinse des Objektivs zu Brennweite des Objektivs angegeben.

❷ Beispiel:

Linsen Ø	35 mm
Brennweite	50 mm

Lichtstärke = 1 : 1,4

Filter

Durch Verwenden eines Filters kann der Fotograf in die Wirkung der Aufnahmeoptik eingreifen. Dabei können Filter zur Korrektur verwendet werden oder zum Erzielen eines speziellen Trickeffektes.

Mit UV-Filtern werden ultraviolette Strahlen zurückgehalten. Eine hohe Konzentration von UV-Strahlen, wie sie oft im Hochgebirge anzutreffen ist, erzeugt eine Bildunschärfe auf dem Bildträger.

❶ Die **Farbtemperatur** des Lichts beschreibt die spektrale Leistungsverteilung (Farbverteilung) einer Lichtquelle. Die Farbtemperatur wird in Kelvin (K) ausgedrückt. Um in der Fotografie farbechte Ergebnisse zu bekommen, muss die Filmemulsion an die Farbverteilung des Lichts angepasst werden. Farbemulsionen gibt es für Kunstlicht und Tageslicht.
Unter Kunstlicht versteht man künstliche Lichtquellen (Glühlampen, Scheinwerfer etc.), die eine Farbtemperatur von ca. 2000 K bis 5000 K aufweisen. Tageslicht bezeichnet vorwiegend natürliches Licht (Sonnenlicht) mit einer Farbtemperatur von etwa 6500 K.

Beispiel: Aufnahme mit einem Tageslichtfilm bei Kunstlicht.

Beispiel: Aufnahme mit einem Tageslichtfilm bei Kunstlicht mit Korrekturfilter.

Mithilfe von Korrekturfiltern können die **Farbtemperatur** ❶ der Lichtquelle mit der Sensibilisierung des Bildträgers in Übereinstimmung gebracht werden.

Polarisationsfilter dienen zum Einen zur Kontraststeigerung in der Farbfotografie – zum Beispiel, um die Wirkung des blauen Himmels bei Landschaftsaufnahmen zu verstärken – und zum Anderen, um Spiegelungen auf nichtmetallischen Oberflächen ganz oder teilweise zu beseitigen.

Beispiel: Landschaftsaufnahme ohne Pol-Filter

Beispiel: Landschaftsaufnahme mit Pol-Filter

Spezielle Trickfilter kommen in der Effektfotografie zum Einsatz. Dies können Weichzeichner, Sternfilter, Prismenfilter oder Farbfilter sein.

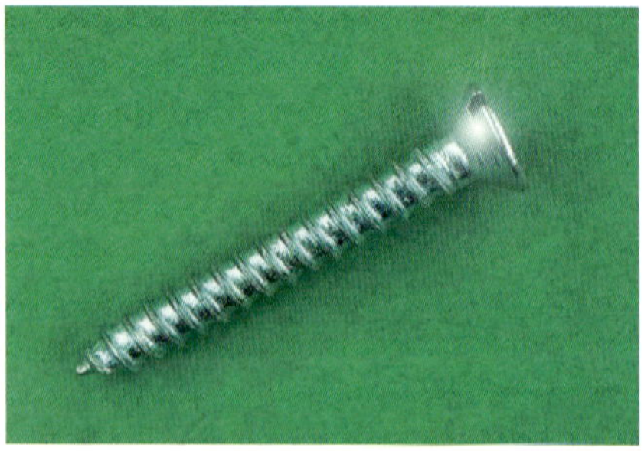

Beispiel: Objektfoto ohne Trickfilter

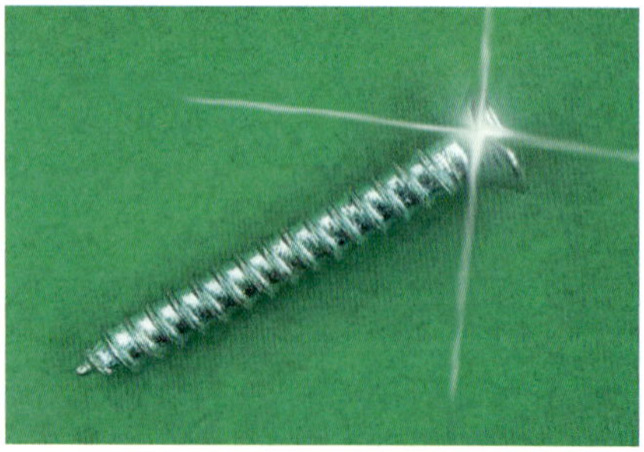

Beispiel: Objektfoto mit Sternfilter

Kontrastfilter werden in der Schwarzweiß-Fotografie verwendet, um bewusst Kontraste zu erhöhen oder zu verändern. Dabei werden Farbkontraste in Hell-Dunkel-Kontraste umgesetzt.

Spezialfilter, wie ein Infrarotfilter, lassen nur ein ganz spezifisches Lichtspektrum durch. Bei einem Infrarotfilter wird das sichtbare Licht (bis ca. 700 nm) gesperrt. Wird als Bildträger ein Infrarotfilmmaterial verwendet, kann der Fotograf zum Beispiel die faszinierende Stimmung einer Landschaft, gesehen mit Infrarot-Augen, aufnehmen.

Zubehör

Zusätzlich zu unterschiedlichen Objektiven und Filtern kommen in der Fotografie Zusatzgeräte und spezielles Kamerazubehör zum Einsatz.

Ein zusätzlicher Belichtungsmesser, der außerhalb der Kameramesseinrichtung das richtige Verhältnis von Blendenöffnung zu Belichtungszeit ermittelt, kann zur Objektmessung oder Lichtmessung eingesetzt werden.

Augenmuscheln dienen als Anlagefläche für das Auge des Fotografen und halten beim Blick durch das Okular das störende Fremdlicht fern.

❶ Beispiel bei Verwendung einer falschen Gegenlichtblende. Die Bildränder werden abgeschnitten.

Gegenlichtblenden am Objektiv dienen als Sonnenschutzblenden, um störende Gegenlichtreflexe auf der vordersten Linse zu vermeiden. Sie müssen immer speziell an das Objektiv angepasst sein, um nicht das Bildfeld abzuschneiden ❶ und trotzdem genügende Blendwirkung zu erreichen.

Mit einem **Stativ** kann der Fotograf trotz langer Belichtungszeiten, zum Beispiel bei Teleobjektiven, verwacklungsfreie Aufnahmen realisieren.

Für Langzeitbelichtungen auf einem Stativ, muss die Belichtung der Kamera erschütterungsfrei ausgelöst werden. Dies kann entweder mit einem eingebautem Selbstauslöser oder externen Auslöser in Form eines Drahtauslösers, bzw. eines elektrischen Auslösers erfolgen.

❷ Computer-Blitzgerät

Bei ungenügenden Lichtverhältnissen kommt das **Blitzgerät** zum Einsatz. Tragbare Blitzgeräte gehören zum unentbehrlichen Handwerkszeug eines Fotografen – nicht nur als Lichtergänzung, sondern auch zur Beleuchtung schattiger Motive oder als Hintergrundbeleuchtung.

Die einfachsten Blitzgeräte ❶ erzeugen einen Blitz unveränderlicher Intensität, zu dem die Blendeneinstellung entsprechend der Filmempfindlichkeit und Motiventfernung berechnet werden muss. Bei Computer-Blitzgeräten ❷ misst das interne Messsystem des Blitzgerätes durch einen eingebauten Sensor die erforderliche Blitzleuchtdauer und regelt dann den Blitz. Eine noch etwas elegantere Methode ist die TTL-Belichtungsmessung (TTL = Through The Lens) ❸. Dabei wird die Blitzdauer über den kameraeigenen Belichtungsmesser gesteuert.

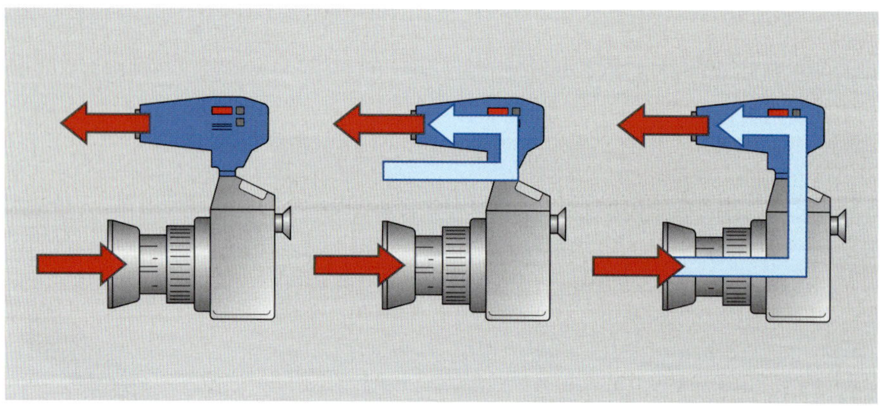

❶ ❷ ❸

❹ Beispiel eines Balkengeräts mit Tilt- und Shift-Funktion. Quelle: Nikon

Bei Kamerasystemen mit Mattscheiben können, je nach Typ, die Einstellscheiben ausgewechselt werden. Spezielle Einstellscheiben für spezifische Anwendungen, wie der Architekturfotografie, der Mikro- und Makrofotografie, verfügen über besondere Einstellhilfen für die Fokussierung und für die Auswahl des Bildausschnittes.

Speziell für die Mikro- und Makrofotografie kommen Balgengeräte ❹ und/oder Zwischenringe zum Einsatz, die es dem Fotografen erlauben, die Bildweite zu verlängern und damit die für die Nahfotografie notwendigen Abbildungsmaßstäbe zu erreichen. Bei speziellen Balkengeräten kann zusätzlich über eine Tilt- und Shift-Funktion die Bildebene relativ zur Linse gekippt werden. Damit sind größere Tiefenschärfe-Bereiche erreichbar (Tilt-Funktion) und/oder optische Verzerrungen, z. B. in der Architektur-Fotografie, korrigiert werden (Shift-Funktion).

6.1.3 Analoge Fotografie

Mittlerweile wurde die analoge Fotografie im Amateur- wie auch im proffesionellen Bereich durch die digitale Fotografie ersetzt und spielt nur noch für Liebhaber und in Ausnahmefällen eine Rolle.

Unter analoger Fotografie versteht man das Fotografieren mit Filmmaterial. Dabei muss das Filmmaterial nach der Belichtung mit Hilfe von chemischen Prozessen entwickelt werden.

Kameras

Kameras für die analoge Fotografie können generell in Kleinbildkameras, Mittelformatkameras, Großformatkameras und Spezialkameras eingeteilt werden.

❶ Beispiel einer analogen Kleinbild-Spiegelreflexkamera

❷ Beispiel einer analogen Kleinbild-Sucherkamera

❸ Beispiel einer Mittelformat-Spiegelreflexkamera

Die **Kleinbildkameras** arbeiten mit einem Bildfeld von 24 × 36 mm. Sie sind die verbreitetsten Kameras der Welt und werden vom Hobby-Fotografen wie vom professionellen Fotografen eingesetzt. Das verwendete 35 mm Kleinbildformat liefert Farbdias für anspruchsvolle Projektionen und Negative, die Vergrößerungen im begrenzten Umfang zulassen. Kleinbildkameras als Spiegelreflexkameras ❶ überzeugen als Systemkameras durch ihre Flexibilität und das große Systemzubehör. Kleinbildkameras als Sucherkameras ❷ eignen sich durch ihre Kompaktheit besonders für den mobilen Einsatz, zum Beispiel für Schnappschussaufnahmen.

Mittelformatkameras sind üblicherweise für Rollfilme im Format 6 × 4,5 cm, 6 × 6 cm oder 6 × 9 cm ausgelegt. Durch das größere Filmformat sind Vergrößerungen bis zum Posterformat und Detailausschnitte problemlos machbar. Sie sind als einäugige Spiegelreflexkameras (SLR = Single Lens Reflexe) ❸ und als zweiäugige Sucherkameras ❹ verbreitet. Mittelformatkameras finden ihre Verwendung in der professionellen Fotografie, zum Beispiel für Produkt- und Modeaufnahmen. Auf Grund der Vorteile des SLR-Prinzips kommen heute nur noch Spiegelreflexkameras zum Einsatz. Das Standardobjektiv einer Mittelformatkamera hat eine Brennweite von etwa 80 mm, was einem 50 mm-Objektiv in einer Kleinbildkamera entspricht.

❹ Beispiel einer zweiäugigen Mittelformatkamera. Sie verfügt über ein Aufnahmeobjektiv und einem Sucherobjektiv.

❶ Beispiel einer historischen Großformatkamera

Bei **Großformatkameras** ❶ sind die Formate 9 × 12 cm, 13 × 18 cm und 18 × 24 cm am weitesten verbreitet. Großformatkameras zeichnen sich durch die komplette Verstellbarkeit der optischen Achse von Objektiv zur Filmebene aus. Das kann nur mit unabhängigen Halterungen für Objektiv und Film erreicht werden, die beide über einen lichtundurchlässigen Balgen miteinander verbunden sind. Auf Grund der Komplexität in der Handhabung, aber auch auf Grund der Möglichkeiten in der Bildbeeinflussung, eignen sich Großfor-matkameras besonders als Studiokameras oder für Landschaftsaufnahmen, wenn hohe Bildauflösungen gebraucht werden.

Besondere Anwendungen erfordern zusätzlich **Spezialkameras**, wie zum Beispiel Sofortbildkameras, Kleinstbildkameras, Hochgeschwindigkeitskameras, Panorama- oder Stereokameras.

Sofortbildkameras ❷ nach dem Polaroidverfahren erlauben dem Fotografen, das Ergebnis seiner Fotografie nach wenigen Minuten zu betrachten. Dieser zeitliche Vorteil führte vor der Verbreitung der digitalen Fotografie zur Entwicklung von einfachen Sofortbildkameras für die Schnappschuss-Fotografie oder für dokumentarische Anwendungen. Auch als Kamerarückteil für viele Groß- und Mittelformatkameras brachte das Polaroidverfahren große Vorteile, um Belichtung und Bildeinstellung zu testen.

❷ Beispiel einer einfachen Sofortbildkamera

Kleinstbildkameras, wie die berühmte Minox, mit speziell kleinen Filmformaten, finden auch in der Schnappschuss- oder dokumentarischen Fotografie ihren Einsatz.

Zum fotografischen Festhalten und Analysieren von schnell bewegten Objekten werden spezielle **Hochgeschwindigkeitskameras** eingesetzt. Sie zeichnen sich durch besonders kurze Verschlusszeiten und filmkameraähnlichen Mechanismen für den Filmtransport aus.

❸ **Panoramakameras** basieren auf einem Schwenkmechanismus, bei dem das Objektiv über das Bildfeld geschwenkt wird, während synchron dazu der Film langsam vortransportiert wird.

In der Landschaftsfotografie können spezielle **Panorama- und Weitwinkelkameras** ❸ eingesetzt werden, wenn es um Aufnahmen mit möglichst großem Bildwinkel geht und wenn möglichst keine optischen Verzerrungen vorkommen sollen.

Auch zum Herstellen von Stereobildern sind Spezialkameras notwendig. Mit speziellen **Stereokameras** wird durch das gleichzeitige Belichten von zwei durch den Augenabstand getrennten Objektiven ein Stereobild erreicht.

Filmmaterial

❶ **Filmemulsionen** können für Tages- oder Kunstlicht sensibilisiert sein. Tageslichtfilme sind auf eine Farbtemperatur von 5500 Grad Kelvin geeicht, Kunstlichtfilme auf 3200 Grad Kelvin.

In der analogen Fotografie unterscheidet man grundsätzlich zwischen Schwarzweiß- und Farb- und Filmmaterial und zwischen positiven und negativen Filmmaterialien. Die Filmmaterialien gibt es mit Filmemulsionen ❶ für verschiedene Farbtemperaturen.

Farbumkehrfilme sind positive Filmmaterialien. Nach dem Entwicklungsprozess erhält man sogenannte Farbdiapositive. Diese Farbdias können dann unmittelbar betrachtet ❷ und mit einem **Diaprojektor** ❸ auf eine große Leinwand projiziert werden.

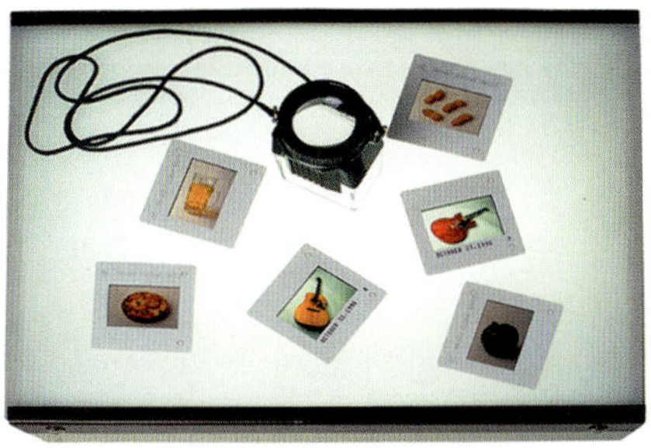

❷ Leuchtpult zum Betrachten, Auswählen und Sortieren von Dias.

❸ Der Diaprojektor projiziert Dias auf eine große Leinwand.

Bei Farbdias werden die subtraktiven Farben, die das endgültige Bild bestimmen, während des Vergrößerungsprozesses selbst gebildet, so dass es hier keine Gelegenheit zu Bildgestaltung gibt. Diapositive haben ihre Stärken beim Kopieren, für Projektionen und als Druckvorlage.

Farbnegativfilme ergeben bei der Entwicklung ein Negativbild des Motivs in Komplementärfarben, von dem dann Positive (Papierbilder) hergestellt werden können. Beim Herstellen im Vergrößerer bietet dieser Prozess die Gelegenheit zur Korrektur von Unter- und Überbelichtungen und zur Farbabstimmung, also eine letzte Möglichkeit der direkten Bildgestaltung. Die Negative werden üblicherweise als Filmstreifen in transparenten Filmtaschen ❹ aufbewahrt.

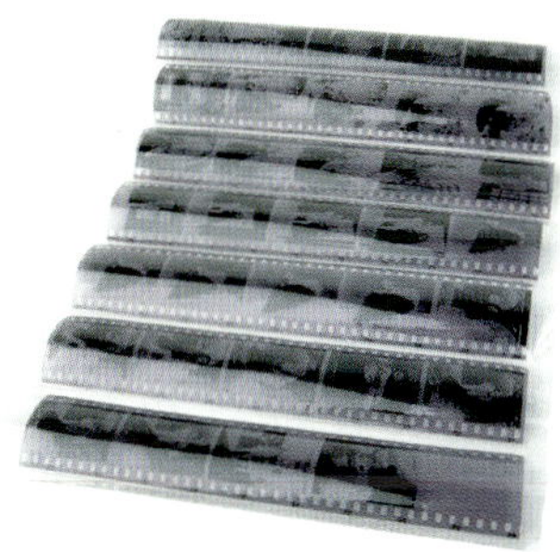

❹ Transparente Filmtaschen für die Archivierung von Negativen.

Filmmaterialien gibt es mit unterschiedlichen Filmempfindlichkeiten. Angegeben wird die Filmempfindlichkeit in DIN (Deutsches Institut für Normung e. V.)- oder ASA (American Standard Association)- Werten.

Vergleichstabelle:

DIN	10	11	12	13	14	15	16	17	18	19	20	21	22
ASA	8	10	12	16	20	25	32	40	50	64	80	100	125

DIN	23	24	25	26	27	28	29	30	31	32	33	34	35
ASA	160	200	250	320	400	500	650	800	1000	1250	1600	2000	2500

Entwicklung und Verarbeitung

Das Entstehen eines Bildes beruht auf chemischen Prozessen. Der prinzipielle chemische Entwicklungsprozess ist bei der Film- und Papierentwicklung gleich.

Ein Film (A) besteht aus einem Trägermaterial, auf dem die Filmemulsion aufgebracht ist. Die Emulsion besteht aus lichtempfindlichen Kristallen, sogenannten Silberhalogenidsalzen.

Während der Belichtung (B) fällt Licht auf die Emulsion, die Silberhalogenidsalze zersetzen sich, und reines, metallisches Silber lagert sich in der Schicht ab.

Diese Silberpartikel dienen als Entwicklungskeime für den anschließenden Entwicklungsprozess (C), bei dem mit Hilfe von Chemikalien die Silberhalogenide zu reinem Silber reduziert werden. Dabei schwärzen sich die belichteten Stellen schneller als die unbelichteten. Der Entwicklungsprozess wird mit Hilfe eines Stoppbades abgeschlossen, sonst würden sich allmählich alle Stellen verschwärzen.

Im Fixierungsprozess (D) werden durch Chemikalien alle restlichen Silberhalogenide aus der Schicht entfernt und der Film haltbar gemacht.

Eine anschließende Wässerung entfernt die verschiedenen Chemikalienlösungen aus dem fotografischen Material. Nach dem Trocknungsprozess kann das fertige Filmnegativ ❶ (E) verwendet werden.

Zur Herstellung eines positiven Papierbildes wird mit Hilfe eines Vergrößerungsapparates oder eines Kontaktkopierers das Filmnegativ auf **Fotopapier** belichtet (F). Anschließend wird das Fotopapier entwickelt (G), fixiert, gewässert und getrocknet, damit man ein haltbares Papierpositiv ❷ (H) erhält.

❶ Beispiel eines Filmnegativs

❷ Beispiel eines Papierpositivs

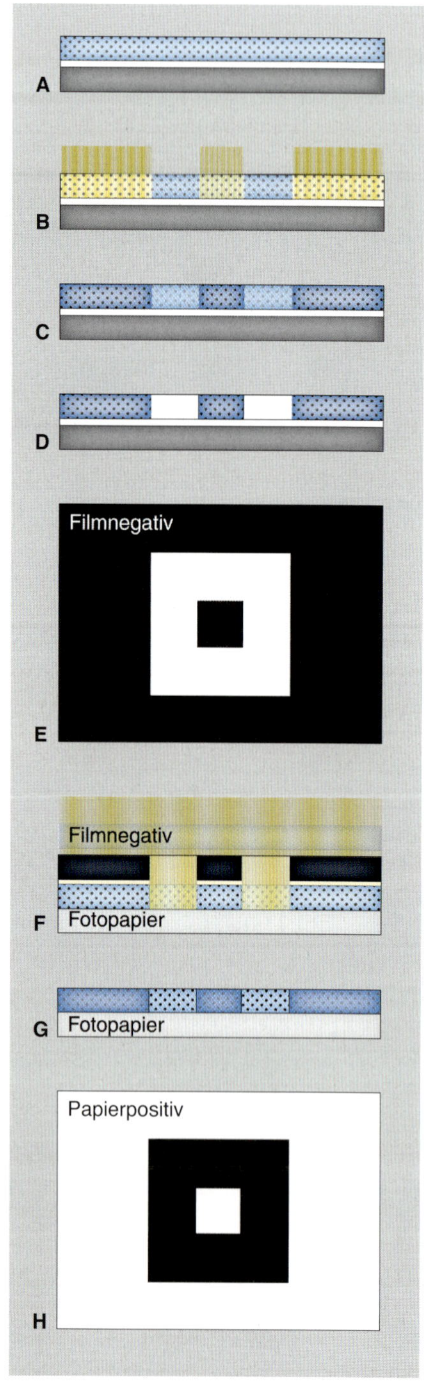

6.1.4 Digitale Fotografie

Im Gegensatz zur analogen Fotografie, bei der auf Filmmaterial aufgezeichnet wird, benutzt die digitale Fotografie zur Aufzeichnung ein elektronisches Medium. Dieses Medium besteht aus einem **CCD-Chip** (Charge Coupled Device).

CCD-Sensor

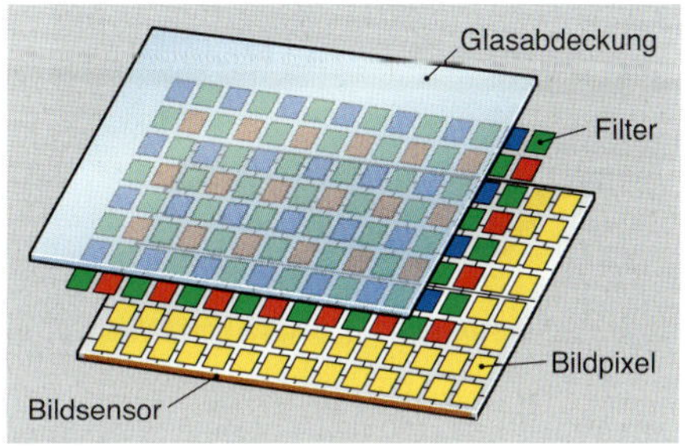

Prinzip eines CCD-Chips

Bei Lichteinfall laden sich die Pixel auf dem Chip elektronisch auf. Diese Ladungen werden mit Hilfe eines Mikroprozessors und einer speziellen Software ausgewertet, umgerechnet und an ein in der Kamera befindliches Speichermedium weitergegeben.

❶ LCD-Displays zeigen bei Sucherkameras immer das effektive Bild. Über das LCD-Display können die Aufnahmen nachträglich betrachtet werden.

Kameras

Wie bei den analogen Kameras gibt innerhalb der digitalen Fotografie Sucherkameras und Spiegelreflexkameras. Desweiteren gibt es auch Datenrückteile für professionelle Mittelformat- und Studiokameras, die hier aber nicht weiter betrachtet werden sollen. **Sucherkameras** verfügen in der Regel über einen optischen Sucher, zusätzlich aber auch über ein LCD-Display ❶, welches das über den CCD-Chip empfangene Bild darstellt. Dieser Monitor übernimmt somit die Aufgabe eines Spiegelreflexsuchers.

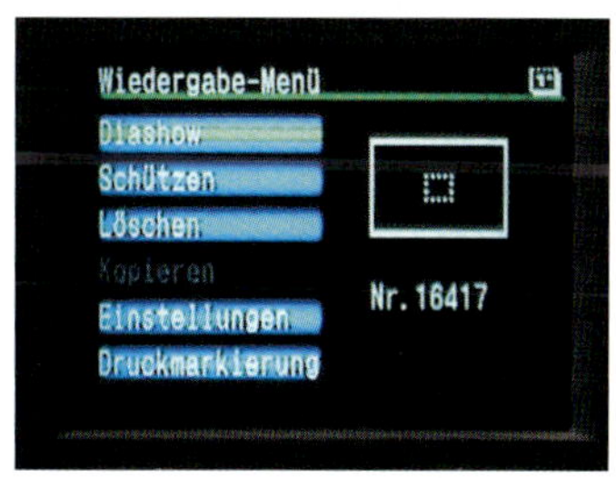

LCD-Displays dienen gleichzeitig zur Steuerung der Bildverwaltung.

❷ Kompakte Sucherkamera mit optischen Sucher und LCD-Display.

❸ Sucherkamera mit elektronischem Sucher und schwenkbarem LCD-Display.

Den größten Teil der Sucherkameras machen die **digitalen Kompaktkameras** ❷ aus. Sie verfügen meist über einen optischen Sucher, ein LCD-Display und ein versenkbares Objektiv – alles optimiert für den unkomplizierten und mobilen Einsatz. Semiprofessionelle Sucherkameras ❸ sind größer, verfügen aber über ein Objektiv mit großem Brennweitenbereich und viele weiter Funktionen, wie z. B. einem schwenkbarem LCD-Sucher.

Digitale Spiegelreflexkamera mit Wechselobjektiv (Quelle: Canon).

Wechselobjektiv mit Image Stabilisator, speziell für digitale SLR-Kameras mit Crop-Faktor (Quelle: Canon).

Spiegelreflexkameras (Single Lens Reflex = SLR) gibt es mit fest eingebautem Zoomobjektiv und mit Wechselobjektiven. Letztere stellen für den professionellen Fotografen das flexibelste digitale Aufnahmewerkzeug dar. Das Spiegelreflex-Sucherokular erlaubt eine präzise, optische Beurteilung der Aufnahmesituation. Systembedingt ist dadurch keine Sucher-Funktion auf dem LCD-Display möglich. Wechselobjektive aus der analogen Fotografie können bei digitalen SLRs ebenso verwendet werden, wie spezielle digitale Wechselobjektive. Jedoch ist der Brennweitenangabe zum dargestellten Blickwinkel von der Sensorgröße abhängig. Bei SLRs mit vollformatigem Sensor entspricht der Sensor genau der Kleinbildgröße von 35 mm und bietet für die verwendeten Objektive den gleichen Blickwinkel wie bei analogen SLRs. Digitale SLRs mit einem sogenannten „Crop-Faktor" verfügen über Sensoren, die kleiner sind als die Kleinbildgröße. Dadurch werden die Ränder des Objektiv-Bildrahmens beschnitten und erscheinen um den Crop-Faktor vergrößert. Diese Kameras erfordern Objektive mit kürzerer Brennweite, um denselben Blickwinkel zu ergeben, wie bei einer analogen SLR, bzw. einer digitalen SLR mit vollformatigen Sensor.

Vollformat (35 mm und digital)	Normaler Blickwinkel (horizontal)	Digitalkamera mit 1,5-facher Vergrößerung	Effektiver Blickwinkel (horizontal)
14 mm	104‘ 15‘	21 mm	80‘ 29‘
17 mm	93‘ 16‘	26 mm	69‘ 45‘
20 mm	83‘ 58‘	30 mm	61‘ 17‘
24 mm	73‘ 44‘	37 mm	52‘ 33‘
28 mm	65‘ 28‘	43 mm	45‘ 52‘
35 mm	54‘ 25‘	53 mm	37‘ 24‘
50 mm	39‘ 35‘	76 mm	26‘ 39‘
85 mm	23‘ 54‘	130 mm	15‘ 52‘
105 mm	19‘ 27‘	160 mm	12‘ 52‘
135 mm	15‘ 11‘	206 mm	10‘ 01‘
180 mm	11‘ 25‘	274 mm	7‘ 31‘
200 mm	10‘ 17‘	305 mm	6‘ 46‘
300 mm	6‘ 52‘	457 mm	4‘ 31‘

Brennweiten und Blickwinkelvergleich zwischen Vollformat- und Crop-Faktor-SLRs

Speichermedien

Zum Speichern der großen Datenmengen, die bei der digitalen Fotografie anfallen, kommen in der Regel **Speicherkarten** zum Einsatz. Das Spektrum an Speicherkarten ist recht groß und unterliegt einer ständigen Weiterentwicklung. Dabei sind Größe, Robustheit, Datenspeicherkapazität und die Datentransferrate die bestimmenden Kriterien für die Leistungsfähigkeit und die Auswahl der einzelnen Kartentypen. Einige Kartentypen haben bereits das Ende der Entwicklung erreicht. Dazu gehört die Smartmedia-Karte, welche mit einer Kapazität von 128 MByte am Systemlimit ist. Alle derzeit erhältliche Speicherkarten verwenden Flash-Speicher zur Datenspeicherung. Eine Ausnahme stellen *Microdrives* dar, die aus einer elektromechanischen Festplatte in der CompactFlash (CF)-Bauform bestehen und die Daten magnetisch speichern. Bei einem Flash-Speicher hingegen werden die Daten auf „nicht flüchtige" Speicherzellen geschrieben, die ihre Information auch ohne Versorgungsspannung behalten. Dazu sind keine beweglichen Teile notwendig – dies macht Flash-Speicher äußerst unempfindlich gegenüber mechanischen Stößen. Die derzeit meist verwendeten **Flash-Kartenformate** sind:

❶ Beispiel einer CompactFlash-Karte. Quelle: SanDisk

- **CompactFlash** (CF) Typ I und Typ II
- **MultimediaCard** (MMC) und **Secure Digital** (SD)
- Extreme Digital (xD-PictureCard)
- SmartMedia (SMC)
- Memory Stick

❷ Beispiel einer MultimediaCard für den mobilen Einsatz in Kleinsgeräten. Quelle: SanDisk

CompactFlash ❶ oder kurz CF-Karten genannt, sind sehr verbreitet und bieten hohe Leistungswerte. Es gibt sie in der Bauform Typ I mit 3,3 mm Stärke und Typ II mit 5 mm Stärke. Typ II kommt momentan nur als *Microdrive* zum Einsatz. Microdrives sind kleine Festplatten, die zum Einsatz kamen, als die Flash-Speicherkapazität noch kleiner als 1 GByte war.

❸ Beispiel einer Secure Digital HC Speicherkarte. Quelle: SanDisk

Die **MultimediaCard** (MMC) ❷ gibt es in vielen Ausprägungen. Angefangen bei der MMC, über die leistungsfähigere MMC Plus und diversen kleinen Varianten, speziell für Mobilgeräte, z. B. der MMC RS. Mittlerweile geht die Verbreitung der MMC zurück. Sie wird sich aber noch längere Zeit am Markt halten, da MMC-Karten auch in die weit verbreiteten SD-Kartenslots passen.

Secure Digital (SD) ❸ ähnelt den MMC-Speichermedien, besitzen jedoch einen mechanischen Schreibschutzschalter zum Verhindern von unbeabsichtigtem Löschen der Bildinformationen. Mit SD High Capacity (SDHC) sind auch Kapazitäten über 2 GByte möglich. SDHC benötigen SDHC-kompatible SD-Lesegeräte. Für Kleinstgeräte, z. B. im Mobilfunkbereich, kommen kleine Baugrößen der SD-Karte zum Einsatz: Die miniSD bzw. miniSDHC und die noch kleinere microSD bzw. microSDHC.

❹ Beispiel von xD-PictureCards. Quelle: Fuji und Olympus

Extreme Digital (xD-PictureCard) ❹ werden primär von Fuji und Olympus verwendet, sind sehr kompakt, besitzen aber keinen eigenen Controller auf der Speicherkarte. Die Controller-Funktion muss hierbei über die Kamera erfolgen. Dieses proprietäre Verhalten sorgt dafür, dass Universal-Kartenlesegeräte mit der xD-PictureCard in der Regel nicht kompatibel sind.

Diese Drucktechnik zeichnet sich durch höchste Qualität aus, ist jedoch mit höherem Aufwand für die Gerätewartung und auch Umweltproblemen verbunden. Toner als solcher ist giftig, man sollte ihn nicht einatmen. Ältere Laserdrucker erzeugen hohe Mengen von Ozon, welches ein Nervengift ist. Bei heutigen Geräten wird diese Emission meist gut gefiltert und gilt deshalb als unbedenklich.

Thermotransferdrucker sind Farbdrucker, welche das Druckbild aus den Grundfarben Cyan, Magenta und Gelb zusammenstellen. Jede Farbe liegt in Form einer Folie vor. Soll eine Farbe gedruckt werden, wird diese mittels Wärme auf das darunter liegende Papier übertragen. Diese einfach erscheinende Technik bietet eine sehr gute Farbwiedergabe (satte, kontrastreiche Farben), ist leise und die gedruckten Werke sind von sehr guter Haltbarkeit. Der Nachteil: Teure Druckfolien heben den Preis pro Seite erheblich. Da bei vielen Systemen pro gedruckte Seite jeweils eine Farbfolie pro Farbe verbraucht wird, sind Probe- und Fehldrucke sehr teuer.

❶ Thermosublimationsdrucker

❷ Digitalfotoprinter

Thermosublimationsdrucker ❶ bieten höchstmögliche Farbqualität. Bei dem aufwändigen Druckprozess werden aus einer Trägerfolie Farbpartikel verdampft, die dann als Gas in das Druckpapier eindringen. Es entsteht ein Farbbild mit einer rasterlosen Farbschicht mit kontinuierlicher Intensität. Da die Farben beim Thermosublimationsdruck nicht gerastert werden, sondern in das Spezialpapier eindringen, bleiben – trotz der teils geringen Detailauflösung – keine störenden Strukturen zurück. Mit speziellen **Digitalfotoprintern** ❷, die auf Basis des Thermosublimationsverfahrens arbeiten, kann ohne den Umweg über den Computer direkt von CompactFlash-Karten oder PCMCIA-Karten der Fotoabzug ausgedruckt werden. Als Standardausgabe ist das Postkartenformat 10 × 14 cm und das Format 10 × 24,5 cm möglich. Darüber hinaus können Indexbilder mit bis zu 25 Verkleinerungen auf einem Einzelabzug untergebracht werden.

6.2 Gestalten von Bildern

6.2.1 Funktion des Standbildes

Die Dokumentarische Beschreibung

Soll ein Gegenstand bildlich so beschrieben werden, dass der Betrachter eine klare Vorstellung von ihm bekommt, dann spricht man von einer dokumentarischen Beschreibung. Dabei können Bildelemente, wie Fotos, Grafiken oder Illustrationen verwendet werden. Ziel ist dabei immer, den Gegenstand möglichst klar zu beschreiben.

Die Situationsbeschreibung

Steht nicht nur ein Gegenstand im Vordergrund, sondern eine bestimmte Situation von Gegenständen und deren Konstellationen, spricht man von einer **Situationsbeschreibung**. Ist dem Betrachter diese Situation aus dem Alltag bekannt, erreicht das Bild eine bestimmte emotionale Wirkung. Ob und wie stark diese Wirkung erzielt wird, hängt von den persönlichen Erfahrungen des Betrachters ab.

Die Funktionsbeschreibung

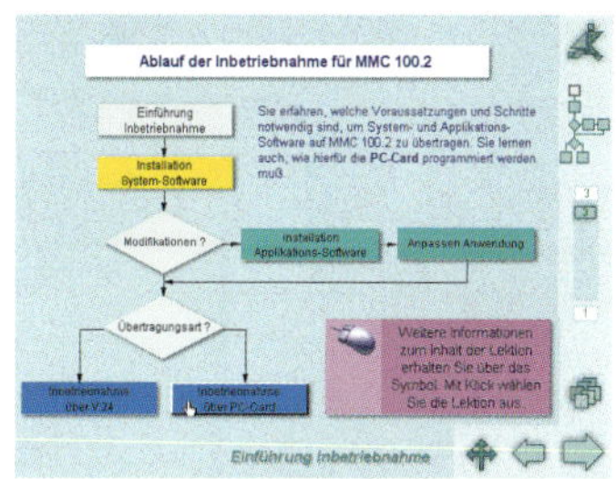

Soll der Ablauf eines Vorganges beschrieben werden, damit der Betrachter die funktionalen Zusammenhänge des Prozesses versteht, spricht man von einer **Funktionsbeschreibung**. Dabei können auch sehr abstrakte Zusammenhänge visualisiert werden.

Da das Standbild in diesem Verwendungsbereich sehr rasch an die Grenze der Visualisierungsfähigkeit stößt, setzt man das Standbild gern im Verbund mit anderen Medien, wie Ton, Animationen und Video, ein.

Für jede Anwendung und für jede Zielgruppe muss die Bildsprache entsprechend angepasst werden. Bilder zur Unterhaltung verfügen über eine andere Bildsprache als Bilder zum Lernen, Dokumentieren oder Werben.

Kinder reagieren auf bildliche Beschreibungen anders als Erwachsene, Fachleute erkennen die Bildinhalte anders als Laien. Der Anspruch für den Gestalter ist hoch, wenn er sichergehen möchte, dass er mit seinem Bild die gewünschte Reaktion beim Betrachter erreicht. Eine Zielgruppenanalyse und ein gutes Einfühlvermögen sind dabei wichtige Voraussetzungen für eine wirkungsorientierte Gestaltung.

Welche Gestaltungsformen sollte der Gestalter für seinen Bildaufbau beachten?

Dazu gehören die **Einstellung**, die **Perspektive**, die **Raumtiefe**, die **Farbgestaltung**, die Gestaltung von **Strukturen**, das Gestalten mit **Licht** und das Gestalten mit **Schärfe** und **Unschärfe**.

6.2.2 Einstellungen

❶ Detail

❷ Groß

❸ Nah

❹ Amerikanisch

Die Einstellung, beschrieben durch die **Einstellgröße**, ist die klassische Einheit für die Bildgestaltung. Sie definiert die Distanz zum abzubildenden Objekt. In der Fotografie, wie auch in der Filmkameratechnik, werden die möglichen Bildausschnitte in acht Einstellgrößen unterteilt, die von der Größe des menschlichen Körpers abgeleitet sind.

Einstellung: Detail
Die Detaileinstellung ❶ ist die extreme Großeinstellung. Sie zeigt z. B. nur Körperteile, wie Hände, Augen, Mund etc. Objekte, so im Detail dargestellt, wirken offen und enthüllend und deshalb äußerst emotional in ihrer Bildwirkung.

Einstellung: Groß
Die Großaufnahme ❷ zeigt einen kleinen Ausschnitt des Ganzen. Dieser Bildausschnitt verdichtet auf Einzelheiten des Objektes, die sonst nicht stark wahrgenommen werden würden. Bei der Darstellung von Personen zeigt die Großaufnahme beispielsweise bildfüllend den Kopf.

Einstellung: Nah
Die Naheinstellung ❸ zeigt bei Personen etwa ein Drittel seiner Körpergröße. Diese Einstellung ist stark subjektiv und wählt bewusst einen Teil des Objektes aus. Auch diese Einstellung hat noch emotionalen Charakter in der Bildwirkung.

Einstellung: Amerikanisch
Die amerikanische Einstellung ❹, bekannt aus amerikanischen Western-Filme zeigt Personen im Mittelpunkt vom Scheitel bis zum Knie. Das besondere Augenmerk ist dabei die mögliche Darstellung eines Revolvers als Machtmittel. Sie liegt etwa zwischen den Einstellgrößen Nah und Halbnah.

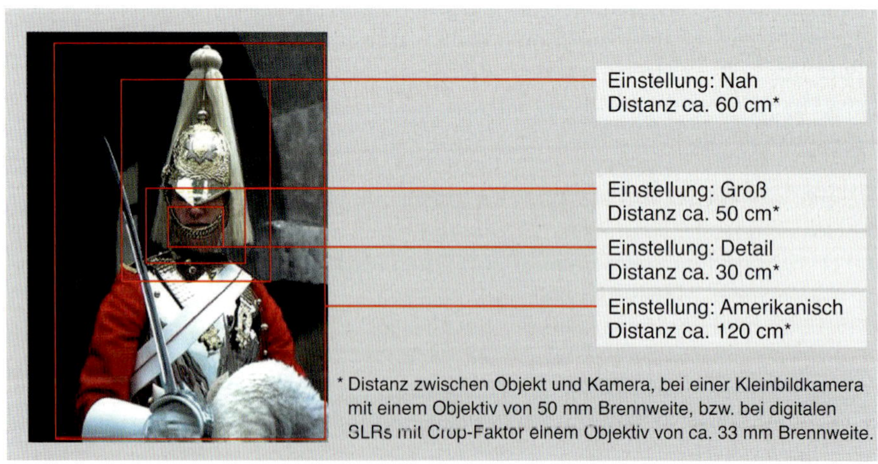

Die Einstellgröße ist abhängig von der Brennweite des verwendeten Objektivs und des Bildaufnahmeformats.

Einstellung: Halbnah
Bei der Einstellgröße Halbnah ❶ handelt es sich um einen Teilausschnitt, bei dem noch die unmittelbare Umgebung zu erkennen ist. Bei Personen oder Personengruppen sind dabei etwa zwei Drittel ihrer Körpergröße zu erkennen. Diese Betrachtungsweise lässt schon eine objektivere Bildwirkung zu.

❶ Halbnah

Einstellung: Halbtotale
Bei der Halbtotalen ❷ sind die Objekte ganz zu erkennen und füllen den Bildausschnitt aus. Dabei ist das Blickfeld noch etwas eingeschränkt und lässt nicht so viel von der Umgebung erkennen. Die Bildwirkung ist vorwiegend objektiv und weniger emotional.

❷ Halbtotale

Einstellung: Totale
Die Totale ❸ erlaubt einen Überblick über das gesamte Geschehen. Diese Einstellung übernimmt die Funktion des distanzierten Beobachters mit objektiver Bildwirkung. Da die Totale eine Fülle von Einzelobjekten enthalten kann, benötigt der Betrachter mehr Zeit, um einen klaren Eindruck des Bildausschnittes zu bekommen.

❸ Totale

Einstellung: Weite
Die Einstellung „Weite“ ❹ bietet gegenüber der Totalen einen noch größeren Raum, bei dem mögliche Personen eine völlig untergeordnete Rolle als Detail darstellen. Diese Einstellgröße vermittelt „Weite“ und wird daher gern bei Landschaftsdarstellungen verwendet.

❹ Weite

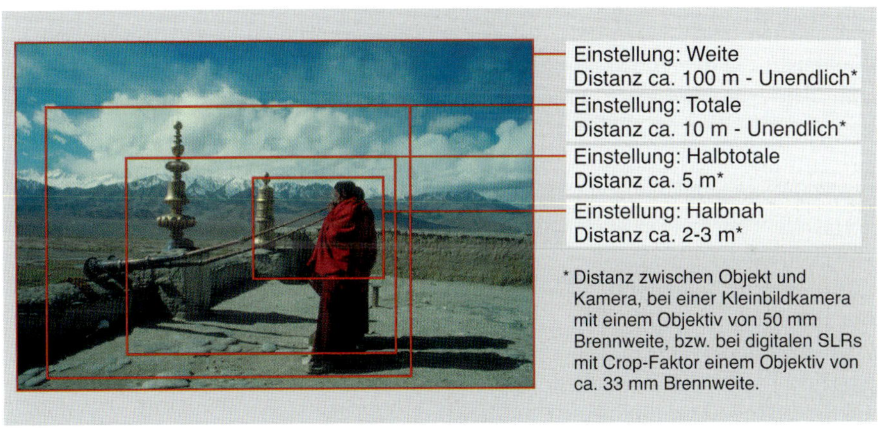

Die Einstellgrößen, die dem Betrachter den Überblick verschaffen, sind die Weite, die Totale, die Halbtotale und Halbnah.

➲ Die Einstellgröße definiert den relativen Abstand des Betrachters zum Objekt. Sie ist gleichzeitig die erste Vorselektion in Bezug auf „Was soll der Betrachter sehen und was nicht“.

6.2.3 Perspektive

Neben den unterschiedlichen Einstellgrößen beeinflusst die Wahl der **Perspektive** maßgeblich die Wirkung des Bildausschnittes. Unter Perspektive versteht man den Standpunkt des Betrachters, wie „normal", „oben", „unten" oder „schräg". Zusammen mit der Blickrichtung, wie „von vorn", „von hinten", „seitlich", und der variablen Einstellgröße, formt die Perspektive die innere Beziehung zwischen dem Betrachter und dem Objekt. Das macht die Faszination der Medien aus, dass je nach Standpunkt des Betrachters und dessen Bildausschnitt die Bildwirkung sehr unterschiedlich sein kann. Durch Verzerrung der gewohnten Betrachtungsweise von ganz normalen Objekten können völlig neue und ungewohnte Eindrücke entstehen. Objekte können dabei bewusst übertrieben, verzeichnet oder entstellt dargestellt werden.

➲ **Rein fotografisch verleiht die Perspektive den visuellen Medien eine dritte Dimension – die Raumtiefe.**

Die Perspektive lässt sich auf Grund der vier Standpunkte primär in die **Normalperspektive**, die **Froschperspektive**, die **Vogelperspektive** und die Perspektive auf Basis eines **schrägen Standpunktes** einteilen.

Die Normalperspektive ❶
Darunter versteht man die Normalansicht aus der gewohnten Augenhöhe des Betrachters. Diese Perspektive lässt Gegenstände und Personen bewusst vertraut erscheinen.

Die Froschperspektive ❷
Nimmt man einen Standpunkt ein, der den Blick von unten nach oben ermöglicht, erscheinen alle dargestellten Gegenstände, Objekte und Personen selbstbewusst, erhaben, überlegen oder sogar unheimlich. Durch gezielten Einsatz dieses Standpunktes kann bewusst eine visuelle Faszination erreicht werden.

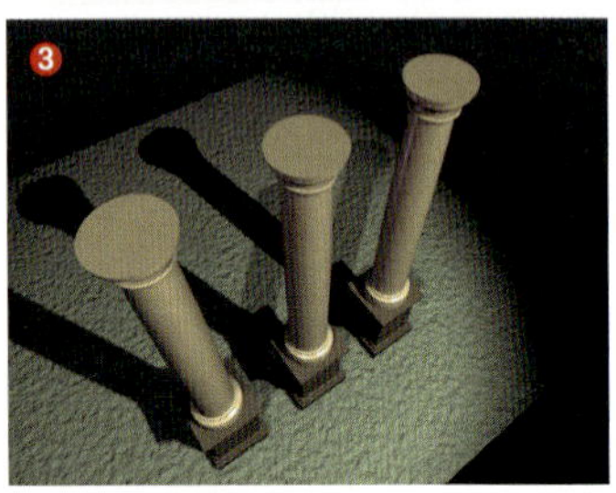

Die Vogelperspektive ❸
Von oben betrachtete Gegenstände und Personen wirken eher erniedrigt, einsam oder unterwürfig.

Der schräge Standpunkt ❹
Wird zusätzlich zu einem Oben- oder Unten-Standpunkt die optische Achse gedreht, so erreicht man stark irreale Eindrücke. Bewusst eingesetzt kann damit eine stark dramaturgische Bildwirkung erzielt werden.

6.2.4 Raumtiefe

Die Illusion von Tiefe auf zweidimensionalen **Bildkompositionen** ist eine traditionelle Herausforderung an den Gestalter.

Raumtiefe entsteht durch den Größenunterschied zwischen den Objekten im Vordergrund und denen im Hintergrund. Dabei kann die lineare Perspektive mit Hilfe von geometrischen Regeln auf die richtigen Proportionen der Objekte hinweisen, die mit wachsendem Abstand kleiner werden. In der Natur vorkommende parallele Geraden lässt sie zusammenlaufen, um damit Tiefe zu vermitteln.

6.2.5 Denken in Schwarzweiß

Formen, Linien und Muster von Objekten lassen sich mit reinen **Schwarzweiß**-Bildkompositionen auf das Wesentliche konzentrieren. Durch das Fehlen der **Farbkomponente** führt man das Auge des Betrachters unwillkürlich auf die elementaren Eigenschaften von **Form**, **Tonwert** und **Licht**.

In der Fotografie ist der Blick durch den Sucher farbig. Der Gestalter muss deshalb das Ausblenden der **Farbkomponente** im Kopf üben, damit das Ergebnis seiner Erwartung entspricht.

6.2.6 Denken in Farbe

Farbe ist in der **Bildkomposition** ein sehr starkes Element. Farbe spricht die Gefühle des Betrachters sehr direkt an. Manche Farbkompositionen wirken freundlich und harmonisch, andere lebendig, dramatisch oder sogar störend. Farben, die im Farbkreis einander gegenüberliegen, wie Rot und Grün, oder Gelb und Blauviolett, werden **Komplementärfarben** genannt.

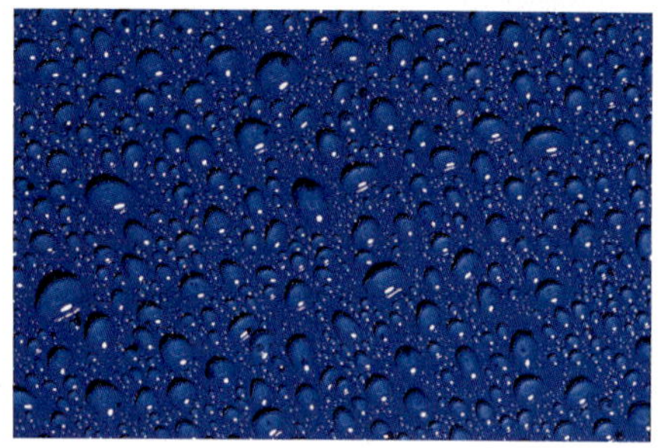

In eine **Bildkomposition** umgesetzt, erreichen sie starke und lebendige Kontraste. Nebeneinanderliegende Farben, wie Rot, Orange und Gelb harmonieren in einer Bildkomposition und bewirken eine ausgewogene Stimmung. Farben unterscheiden sich auch in ihrer Helligkeit. So wirkt Gelb heller als Blau. Auch wird die Wirkung einer Farbe durch die Nachbarfarbe beeinflusst. Eine für sich allein stehende Farbe auf neutralem Hintergrund wirkt besonders lebhaft. Steht sie hingegen zusammen mit vielen anderen Farben in einer Komposition, so wird sie abgeschwächt.

6.2.7 Kontur und Umriss

Hat der Gestalter das Ziel, ein Objekt in seiner **Form und Gestalt** klar herauszustellen, und sollen dabei andere Eigenschaften des Objektes ausgeblendet werden, so stellt er nur die Kontur bzw. den Umriss des Objektes dar. Der **Umriss** ist das sparsamste Gestaltungselement.

Umrisse lassen sich besonders gut im **Gegenlicht** darstellen. Dabei wird das Objekt als Silhouette im Gegenlicht aufgenommen. Es lässt sich sehr einfach durch Verwendung von Filmmaterial mit geringem Tonwertumfang, z. B. Diafilm, erzielen.

6.2.8 Muster und Struktur

Muster tragen zur Harmonie einer **Bildkomposition** bei. Muster entwickeln sich aus der Wiederholung eines Grundmusters. Jede erkennbare Form lässt sich zu einem Muster verwandeln. Ein charakteristisches Merkmal für Muster in der Fotografie ist, dass solche Bildkompositionen immer flach wirken und keine Raumtiefe besitzen.

6.2.9 Licht und Schatten

Durch Licht ❶ und Schatten entsteht Räumlichkeit. Durch Setzen von Licht erreicht man verschiedenartige Ausleuchtungen und damit verschiedene Bildwirkungen beim Betrachter. Damit der Gestalter die Möglichkeiten von Licht und Schatten einsetzen kann, muss ihm bewusst sein, dass Licht verschiedenartige Qualität haben kann. Es kann hart oder weich, diffus oder gebündelt sein. Es kann variieren in seiner Stärke, der Entfernung zum Objekt und in der Farbzusammensetzung. Durch Gegenlicht oder starkes Seitenlicht hebt man die plastische Wirkung von Objekten an. Durch direktes Licht wirken Objekte flacher.

Das Licht erzeugt Schatten durch die angestrahlten Objekte. Die Qualität der Schatten hängt von der Lichtquelle und deren Abstand zum Objekt ab. Schräg einfallendes Licht erzeugt lange Schatten und direktes Licht von oben erzeugt weniger Schatten.

❶ Atmosphäre mit Licht

6.2.10 Schärfe und Unschärfe

Durch bewussten Einsatz von Schärfe und Unschärfe ❷ lassen sich Elemente eines Gesamtbildes voneinander trennen. Bildwichtige Teile können hervorgehoben und unwichtige Teile verdrängt werden. Da diese Technik durch Wahl geeigneter Objektive und Blendeneinstellungen ❸ erreicht wird, kann sie auch nur bei der fotografischen Aufnahme durch besondere Handhabung der Kamera eingesetzt werden.

❷ Bewusstes Spiel mit der Schärfe und Unschärfe von Objekten.

❸ Setzt auch einen ausreichend großen Bildsensor bzw. Bildträger voraus. Digitalkameras mit kleinem Bildsensor haben eine große Schärfentiefe, die eine bewusste Unschärfe zur Gestaltung nicht erlaubt.

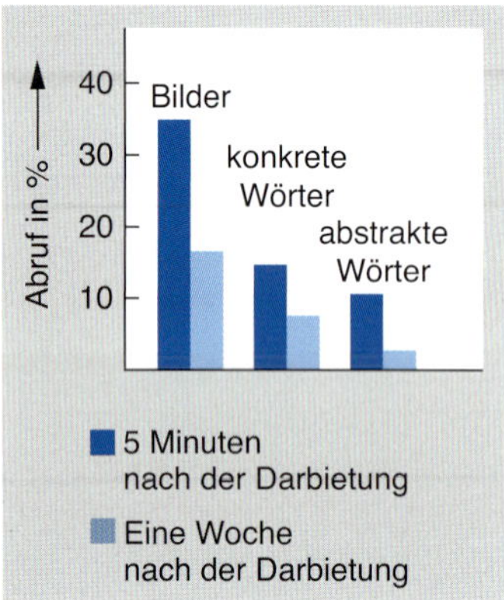

❶ Gedächtnisleistung für Bilder und Wörter, nach einem klassischen Experiment von Paivio, 1971

❷ Beispiel: Das Bild einer Anzeige zeigt einen jeansgekleideten, dynamischen jungen Mann neben einem Geländewagen stehen, einen Fuß auf dem Kotflügel. Auto und Mann bilden eine Einheit und das Objekt Auto wirkt kraftvoll, aber auch jugendlich und erfolgreich. Die durch das Bild erzeugte Assoziation wäre durch eine sprachliche Umschreibung nicht zu erzielen, wie „ein Mann steht neben einem Geländewagen und hat einen Fuß auf dem Kotflügel".

Semiotik: Wissenschaft von den Zeichen, hier von den bildhaften Zeichen.
Syntaktik: beschäftigt sich mit den Eigenschaften und formalen Beziehungen der Zeichen.
Semantik: beschäftigt sich mit dem Inhalt und der Bedeutung von Zeichen.
Pragmatik: beschäftigt sich mit den Wirkungen der Zeichen auf Sender und Empfänger.

6.2.11 Bildkommunikation

Im menschlichen Kommunikationsprozess spielen **Bilder** eine wichtige Rolle bei der Übertragung von Informationen. Die **Imageryforschung** beschäftigt sich mit der Wirkung von Bildern auf den Menschen. Dabei unterscheidet man das Bild, das von außen auf den Betrachter einwirkt und das Bild, das daraufhin als „inneres" Bild erzeugt wird und zu Verhaltensänderungen führen kann, wie es durch Werbemaßnahmen geschieht. Das Bild von außen ist häufig die Abbildung eines real existierenden Gegenstandes, das „innere" Bild eine subjektivierte Vorstellung desselben. Fragen wir beispielsweise einen Menschen danach, welche Gegenstände sich bei ihm auf dem Schreibtisch befinden, dann versucht er sich eine bildhafte Vorstellung von dem gesamten Schreibtisch und den darauf befindlichen Dingen zu machen. Der Mensch erstellt sich von dem Sachverhalt ein „inneres" Bild, um mit seinen „inneren" Augen den Schreibtisch zu betrachten und ihn im Anschluss beschreiben zu können. Dabei kann es durchaus vorkommen, dass die Beschreibung des „inneren" Bildes mit der momentanen Wirklichkeit, dem realen Abbild, nicht übereinstimmt.

Bildinformationen können im Gehirn sprachlich verschlüsselt (Schlüsselbegriffe) werden, in der gleichen Weise, wie Sprachinformationen bildlich verschlüsselt werden. Betrachtet man komplexe Zusammenhänge, so lässt sich feststellen, dass das Bild vielschichtiger und tiefer abrufbar ist als das Wort. Man spricht auch von der **Bildüberlegenheitswirkung** ❶. Dabei verarbeitet das Gedächtnis das Bild ganzheitlich-analog (rechte Gehirnhälfte), den Text hingegen in sequentieller Folge logisch-analytisch (linke Gehirnhälfte) ❷.

Bildsemiotik

Um die Wirkungsweise von Bildern zu erforschen, werden in der **Semiotik** drei Teilgebiete, die Syntaktik, die Semantik und die Pragmatik, untersucht. Beispielsweise wird das Produkt Armbanduhr nicht zufällig gekauft, sondern ist auf der einen Seite ein Schmuckstück und auf der anderen gleichzeitig ein Objekt mit kommunikativer Wirkung.

Für die Armbanduhr kann eine **semiotische Analyse** folgendermaßen aussehen:

- Syntaktik: Unter syntaktischen Gesichtspunkten werden die Merkmale und Gemeinsamkeiten unter den verschiedenen Armbanduhren betrachtet. Dabei geht es beispielsweise um das Zusammenwirken von Werkstoff, Farbe und Gestaltung des Gehäuses und die Frage nach der Rolle, die diese Eigenschaft im Kommunikationsprozess besitzt.
- Semantik: Welche Bedeutung hat eine bestimmte Armbanduhr in der Gesellschaft? Wie stellt sich der Mensch dar, der diese Armbanduhr trägt? Wie wird das Erscheinungsbild des Uhrenträgers von der Umwelt aufgenommen?
- Pragmatik: Die Armbanduhr hat auf Sender (Uhrenträger) und Rezipient (Beobachter) unterschiedliche Verhaltenswirkungen. Wird der Mensch aufgrund seiner Uhr anerkannt oder abgelehnt? Stärkt das Tragen dieser Art von Schmuckstück seine berufliche Position? Welche Personenkreise fühlen sich zu diesem Typus hingezogen?

Bild als Abbildung der Wirklichkeit

Das Bild ist die Aufzeichnung eines realen oder fiktiven ❶ Gegenstandes. Bilder sind Fotografien, Gemälde, Zeichnungen, animierte und gefilmte Szenen. Die Abbildungen können einen konkreten Sachverhalt wiedergeben oder abstrakte Darstellungen sein, die eine Beziehung zu einem Produkt oder einer Firma aufbauen sollen.

❶

Reale wie auch fiktive Sachverhalte werden durch das **Gedächtnis** in ein **inneres Bild** verwandelt. Die dabei entstehende **fiktive Wirklichkeit** kann zu Veränderungen der Bildinterpretation führen. Emotionale Aspekte führen beim Übergang von der Objektebene auf die Abbildungsebene zu Veränderungen der Informationen und der Gefühle. Ein Schwein, das in einer Darstellung ein Kleeblatt im Maul hält, wird als Glücksbringer betrachtet, dasselbe Schwein im Schlamm liegend abgebildet, wird zum schmutzigen und hässlichen Tier. Durch textuelle Ergänzungen kann die Übertragung zusätzliche Veränderung bzw. Intensivierung erfahren.

In unserem Gedächtnis entsteht im Augenblick der Betrachtung eines Objektes ein **Wahrnehmungsbild**. Haben wir das Objekt nicht vor Augen oder denken wir sehr viel später über das Auftreten und Aussehen eines Gegenstandes nach, so versuchen wir ein Gedächtnisbild vom Objekt aufzubauen bzw. abzurufen. **Gedächtnisbilder** (memory images) beeinflussen unser Verhalten in starkem Maße und werden zum Aufbau von Marketingstrategien genutzt. Diese **inneren Bilder** haben eine kognitive und eine emotionale Wirkung auf das Verhalten des Menschen.

Bei der **kognitiven Wirkung** geht es speziell um sachliche und räumliche Zusammenhänge und dem damit verbundenen Wissen. Beipielsweise erzeugt die raketenähnliche Form einer Motorenölflasche auf der sachlichen Ebene beim Menschen die Vorstellung von Dynamik, Kraft und Beschleunigung, welche das Motorenöl im Fahrzeug verbessert. Das räumliche Wissen bezieht sich beispielsweise auf das Wiederfinden von Produktbereichen beim Einkaufen in einem Supermarkt oder das Einordnen und Aneignen umfangreicher Lerngebiete mit Hilfe von **Mindmaps**. Mit einer Mindmap skizziert man ein räumliches Gebilde von den zu lernenden Inhalten und erzeugt dadurch wesentlich nachhaltiger ein inneres Bild (cognitive map) von der Abbildung im Gedächtnis.

Die **emotionale Wirkung** und die bildliche Vorstellung sind schon durch die Verarbeitung in der rechten Gehirnhälfte eng miteinander verbunden. Die Ausprägung der inneren Bilder, ihre „Gestaltung" im Gedächtnis, sind Ausdruck von Gefühlen. Diese Gefühle können aus visuellen, akustischen, geruchsintensiven oder auch haptischen Eindrücken entstehen.

Bildwirkung durch Wahrnehmung

❶ vgl.: Kroeber-Riel, Werner: Bildkommunikation, 1996; S. 55f.

Der Mensch ist in der Lage, innerhalb 1/100 Sekunde das Thema eines Bildes wahrzunehmen. Möchte man darüber hinaus die Inhalte eines Bildes aufnehmen, so werden schon ein bis zwei Sekunden für ein Bild mittlerer Komplexität benötigt. Diese Zeit ist notwendig, um die Inhalte des Bildes so zu speichern, so dass sie später wieder erinnert werden. In der gleichen Zeit, wie das Bild wahrgenommen wird, können jedoch nur fünf bis zehn Wörter eines leicht strukturierten Textes wahrgenommen werden. Das ist nur ein Bruchteil des Informationsgehaltes eines Bildes.

Damit die Wahrnehmung so schnell ablaufen kann, sind **Schemata** notwendig, nach denen die Informationen aufgenommen und verarbeitet werden. Jeder Mensch bildet unterschiedliche Wahrnehmungsstrukturen aus, die nach entsprechender Verfestigung automatisch ablaufen. Die visuellen Eigenschaften des wahrgenommenen Bildes werden mit den Attributen des gespeicherten Schemas verglichen. Entspricht das Bild weitgehend dem Schema, so wird es schneller erkannt und abgespeichert.

❷

Quelle: Fiona Bennett; Scholz & Friends

Mit einer Aufnahme des **Blickverlaufs** lassen sich Bereiche eines Bildes und die einzelnen Elemente festhalten und zeitlich einordnen, die von den Augen des Betrachters erfasst werden. Punkte, auf denen der Blick verharrt, werden als **Fixationen** bezeichnet, Sprünge im Blickverlauf als **Saccaden** ❶. Für einen ersten Überblick und um das Thema zu erfassen, benötigt der Betrachter eine oder zwei kurze Fixationen. Mit den längeren Fixationen, im Durchschnitt 0,2 s, werden die Inhalte selektiv erfasst, so dass in einer Sekunde ca. 3–5 Informationseinheiten gespeichert werden können. Nach Durchwandern des Bildes kann man feststellen, dass nicht alle Elemente erfasst wurden, manche jedoch durchaus mehrmals. Die Mehrfachfixationen werden dabei verstärkt gespeichert. Die einzelnen erfassten Elemente genügen häufig, um im Gedächtnis durch gedankliche Ergänzung ein komplexes Bild entstehen zu lassen. Der Blickverlauf gibt Auskunft über die wahrgenommenen Bilder und einzelner Elemente und dient in der Werbung als Mittel zur Feststellung der Wirkung einzelner Bildteile.

❸

Quelle: Prinz Myshkin, Vegetarisches Restaurant; Xynias, Wetzel, von Büren

Damit der Blick ein Bildelement erfasst und dieses auch gegenüber unterschiedlichen Einflüssen dauerhaft abspeichert, müssen inhaltliche oder visuelle Ereignisse geschaffen werden. Dies kann durch das Bildmotiv, die inhaltliche oder formale Gestaltung geschehen. Der gezielte Einsatz von Farbe, Kontrast, Konturen, von Interaktion und Bewegung können zu einem nachhaltigen, visuellen Auftritt beitragen. Schafft es der Bildgestalter, einen oder mehrere aktivierende Reize zu setzen, wird die Aufmerksamkeit verstärkt auf das Bild gezogen. Eine **Aktivierung** kann durch physische, emotionale oder spontane, überraschende Reize geschehen:

- **Physische Reize** ❷: Große und farbige Bildelemente erzeugen physische Reaktionen, mit Farben, die als wohltuend oder belastend empfunden werden.
- **Emotionale Reize:** Personenabbildungen, sowie Detailaufnahmen von Gesichtern, Augen, Beinen und Händen besitzen meist eine emotionale Wirkung.
- **Überraschende Reize** ❸: Verstößt das Bild gegen die Erwartungen der Wahrnehmung, dann veranlasst dieser aktivierende Reiz den Betrachter mehrmals hinzuschauen, um den unbekannten Sachverhalt, der vom Schema im Gedächtnis abweicht, aufzunehmen.

Bild als Transportmittel

Bild und Text sind die **Träger von Informationen**. In der Werbung versucht man mit diesen Medien Produkteigenschaften, Produktwirkungen, das Produkt selbst, die Gestaltung eines Fahrzeuges und die Funktion, Reiseziele u. a. benutzerorientiert darzustellen. Das Bild zeigt diese konkreten Gegenstände direkt. Abstrakte Begriffe, wie Gesundheit, Geldanlage, „entspannt reisen" oder die Leistungen, die ein Dienstleister anbietet, können ohne das Bild als Brücke nicht aussagekräftig umgesetzt werden. Was wird beispielsweise unter „entspannt reisen" verstanden? Ist es das Fliegen im geräumigen Flugzeug, wobei die Füße des Fluggastes nicht bis zur nächsten Sitzreihe reichen, oder ist es, wie auf einem Werbeplakat abgebildet, der im Liegestuhl liegende Mensch auf und neben einem Zug. Mit beiden Beschreibungen wird der Leser sicher kein entspanntes Reisegefühl bekommen. Werden die Beschreibungen in einem Bild umgesetzt, kann dem Betrachter das Gefühl vom „entspannten Reisen" durchaus bewusst werden.

Quelle: Bürgel Wirtschaftsinformationen; Claus Peter Dudek

Es lassen sich nun **zwei Wege** zur **Visualisierung** einschlagen: Für konkrete, auch greifbare Gegenstände und Sachverhalte, kann das Bild direkt eine Vorstellung bewirken. Für die abstrakten Attribute müssen indirekte Wege mit Bild und Text durch Auslösen einer Bildvorstellung gewählt werden.

„Groß, stark und brummt leise. Der ML270 CDI"; Quelle: Daimler Chrysler AG; Springer & Jacobi; Foto: F. A. Cesar / Hamburg Stand 2000, CI nicht mehr aktuell

Direkte Bildumsetzung

Der konkrete Sachverhalt bzw. Gegenstand wird durch eine wahrheitsgetreue Abbildung direkt dargestellt. Mit gestalterischer Kreativität werden Spannungen im Bild erzeugt, die es von Bildern konkurrierender Produkte abheben. Durch textliche Ergänzungen wird das Bildverständnis zusätzlich gelenkt und verstärkt.

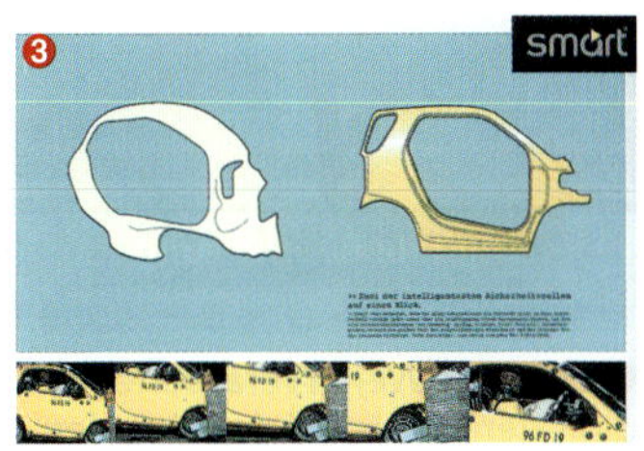

„Zwei der intelligentesten Sicherheitszellen auf einen Blick"; Quelle: Daimler Chrysler AG; Springer & Jacobi; Illustration: Tina Berning / Berlin, Stand 2000, CI nicht mehr aktuell

Indirekte Bildumsetzung

- Freie **Bildassoziation**: Beinhaltet eine Werbeanzeige für ein Produkt oder eine Dienstleistung ein Bild ohne direkte Beziehung zum beworbenen Sachverhalt, dann wird zur Informationsvermittlung eine freie Vorstellung vom Sachverhalt, eine freie Bildassoziation, vermittelt. Durch entsprechende räumliche Anordnung können dabei unabhängige Bilder zu neuen Sinneinheiten verbunden werden. Beispiel ❶: In diesem Paket bekommt der Kunde „gut geschnürte" Wirtschaftsinformationen.
- **Bildanalogien:** In der Werbung findet man oft Bilder, in denen ein Gegenstand, ein Tier, ein Mensch u. a. die Eigenschaften eines Produkts oder einer Dienstleistung besitzen und beide Darstellungen räumlich eng zusammenrücken. Beispiel ❷: Das Auto ist so stark und kräftig wie der Bärenpapa und brummt leise.
- **Bildmetapher:** Die Metapher hat ähnlich wie in der Literatur symbolische Bedeutung und soll die Eigenschaften eines Produktes durch Vergleich stärker hervorheben. Dabei werden direkte Aussagen auch direkt im Bild umgesetzt. Beispiel ❸: Die Karosserie des Autos wird mit dem menschlichen Kopf verglichen.

❶ Be
mit [
Quel

6.3.3 Bildoptimierung

Eine Aufnahme kann aus den verschiedensten Gründen Mängel aufweisen. Vorausgesetzt, die Mängel sind nicht bewusst als gestalterisches Element eingesetzt worden, können über die Bildbearbeitung im elektronischen Fotolabor immer noch sehr brauchbare Ergebnisse erzielt werden. Die klassischen Methoden zum Optimieren und Verbessern eines digitalen Bildes sind:

- Tonwertkorrektur
- Farbkorrekturen
- **Gradationskurve**
- Partielle **Aufhellungen** und Abdunkelungen

Und danach entsprechend der Bildverwendung:

- Tiefen und Lichter anpassen
- **Ausschnittvergrößerung**
- **Skalierung**
- Scharfzeichnen und Weichzeichnen

Tonwertkorrektur

Bei der Tonwertkorrektur werden die hellsten und dunkelsten Pixel des Bildes als Weiß- und Schwarzwerte definiert und die dazwischenliegenden Pixel proportional verteilt.

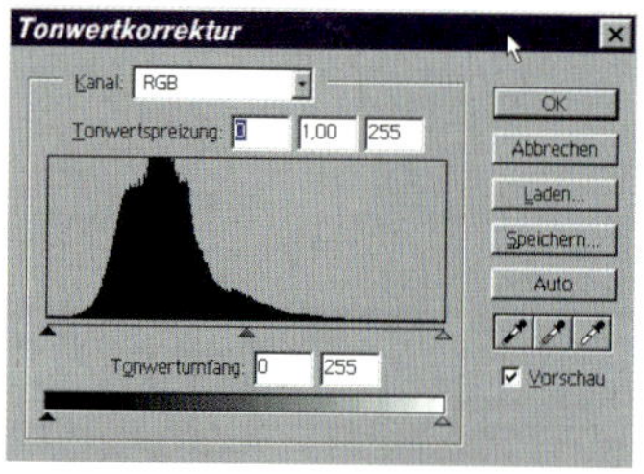

Tonwertkorrektureinstellung in einer Bildbearbeitungssoftware.

Originalbild

Bild mit Tonwertkorrektur

Farbkorrekturen

Farbkorrekturen sind immer dann notwendig, wenn die Aufnahme zu flau erscheint oder aber die Aufnahme bei ungünstigen Lichtverhältnissen die Farben verfälscht erscheinen, zum Beispiel bei Kunstlichtaufnahmen mit einem Tageslichtfilm.

Originalbild

Bild mit Farbkorrektur

Zur Farbkorrektur kann zum Einen die **Farbbalance**, das heißt das Verhältnis der Farben Cyan, Magenta und Gelb zueinander, verändert werden. Zum Anderen ist die Einstellung des Farbtons und der **Sättigung** ❶ maßgeblich am Farbeindruck des Bildes beteiligt.

Originalbild

Bild mit Farbkorrektur

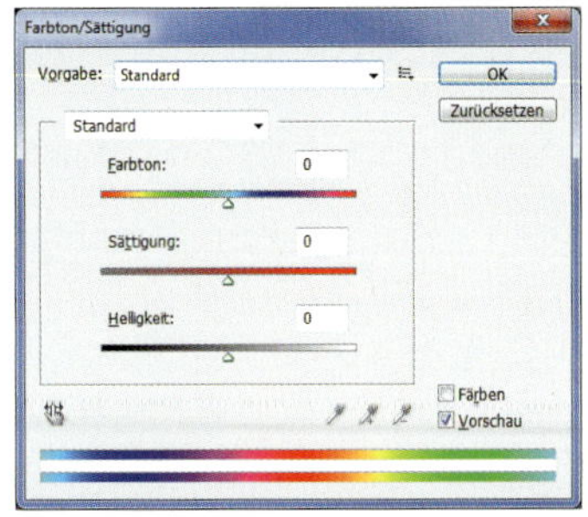

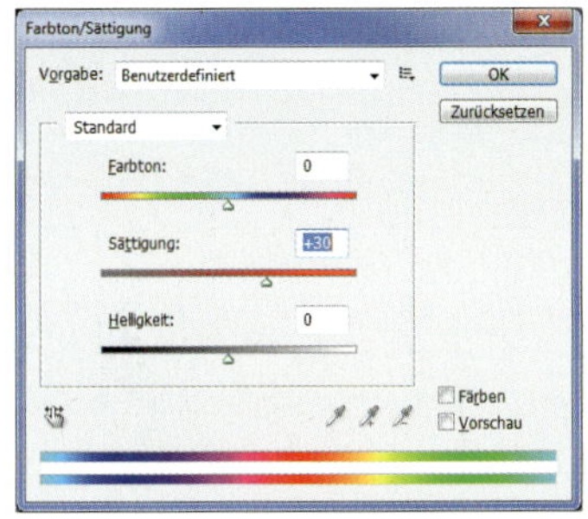

❶ Einstellen der Sättigung.

Gradationskurve

Als Ergänzung zur Tonwertkorrektur können über das Verändern der **Gradationskurve** ❷ ausgewählte Tonwertzonen, zum Beispiel nur die dunklen Bildpunkte, angehoben bzw. gesenkt werden.

Originalbild

Bild mit veränderter Gradationskurve

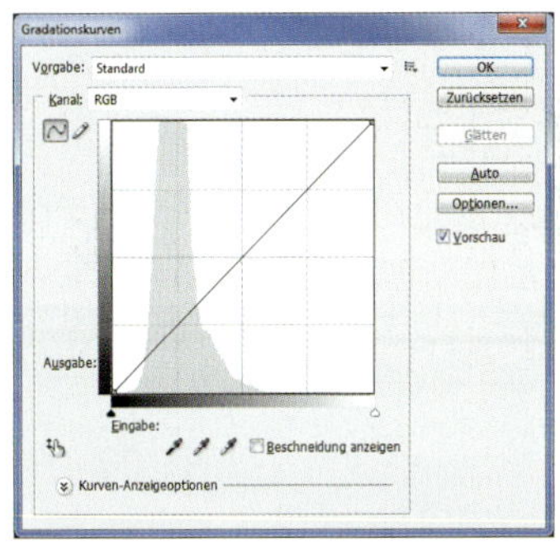

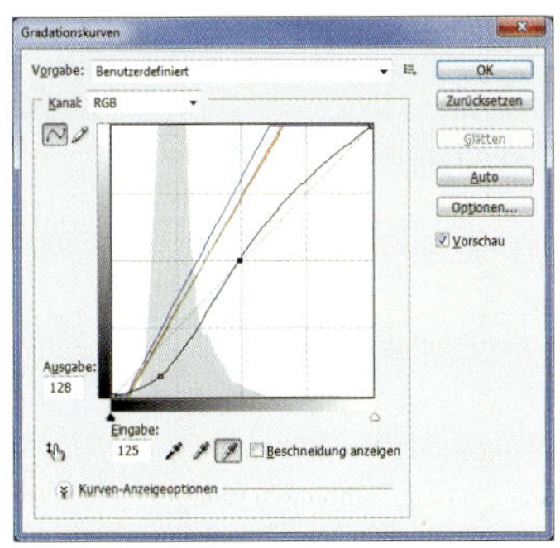

❷ Einstellen der Gradationskurve.

Partielle Korrekturen

Nicht immer sind Unter- und Überbelichtungen oder Farbfehler auf die gesamte Aufnahme anzuwenden. Beispiel: Ein Motiv ist vor hellem Hintergrund, eventuell sogar noch bei Gegenlicht, aufgenommen worden. Das Resultat ist meist ein zu dunkles Motiv bei zu hellem Hintergrund. In solchen Fällen müssen Aufhellungen bzw. Abdunkelungen partiell, das heißt begrenzt auf die notwendigen Bildelemente, vorgenommen werden.

Originalbild

Bild mit partiellen Aufhellungen

Tiefen und Lichter anpassen

Bei starken Kontrastverhältnissen kann die Funktion zum Anheben der Helligkeit speziell in dunklen Bildteilen und zusätzlich das Abschwächen von Lichter-Partien hilfreich sein. Hierbei werden Schatten (Tiefen) aufgehellt, ohne bereits vorhandene helle Flächen noch weiter aufzuhellen. Im Gegenzug können helle Flächen (Lichter) verdunkelt werden, ohne bereits vorhandene dunkle Flächen noch dunkler zu machen.

Originalbild

Bild nach der Tiefen- und Lichterkorrektur

Ausschnittvergrößerung

Die nachträgliche Bestimmung des Bildausschnittes und die Vergrößerung eines Bilddetails sind in der digitalen Bildverarbeitung ebenfalls möglich. Eine Ausschnittvergrößerung aus einem digitalen Bild reduziert jedoch gleichzeitig die Auflösung. Jedes digitale Bild verfügt über eine genau definierte Anzahl von Pixeln. Nimmt man bei einer Ausschnittvergrößerung nur einen Teil des Bildes, so erhält man auch nur diesen Anteil der Pixel.

Originalbild

Großer Ausschnitt

Kleiner Ausschnitt

Skalierung

Das Verkleinern eines Bildes auf die gewünschte Zielgröße sollte mit dem noch ungeschärften Bild erfolgen, da sonst Qualitätsverluste auf Grund der harten Kantenübergänge entstehen können. Beim Neuberechnen von Bildern werden neu erstellten Pixeln Farbwerte zugewiesen, die auf den Farbwerten vorhandener Pixel im Bild basieren. Die verwendete Interpolationsmethode, z. B. bikubisch, sorgt dafür, dass Qualität und Detailgenauigkeit der Originalbilder beim Neuberechnen erhalten bleiben. Derartige Interpolationsmethoden kommen auch zum Einsatz, falls das Bild hochskaliert, also vergrößert, werden muss, was aber, auf Grund der begrenzten Bildinformationen, nur begrenzt möglich ist.
Beim Erstellen von Bildern für Print-Medien empfiehlt es sich, die Bildgröße anhand der Ausgabegröße und Bildauflösung festzulegen. Diese beiden Maße werden als

Dokumentgröße bezeichnet und bestimmen die Gesamtzahl der Pixel und somit die Dateigröße des Bildes. Beim Erstellen von Bildern für Non-Print-Medien hingegen ist die Aulösung auf 72 dpi, der Bildschirmauflösung, festgelegt und die Bildgröße, z. B. 800 × 600 Pixel, von der gewünschten Größe innerhalb der Anwendung abhängig.

Scharfzeichnen

Das Schärfen sollte immer die letzte Korrekturmaßnahme sein, bevor das Bild endgültig verwendet wird – egal, ob im Print-Bereich oder Non-Print-Bereich. Durch das Scharfzeichnen kann ein leicht unscharfes Bild nachträglich aufgebessert werden. Das Anheben der Bildschärfe ist aber nur begrenzt möglich, da es nicht mehr Details in das Bild bringen kann, sondern nur die Konturen und Übergänge in den Bildelementen verstärkt und somit einen subjektiven Eindruck von Schärfe erzeugt.

Leicht unscharfe Aufnahme

Nachträglich scharfgezeichnetes Bild

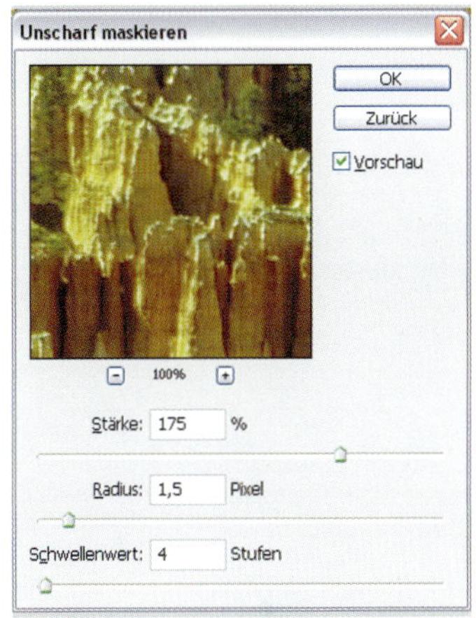

❶ Mit den Einstellwerten beim **Unscharf maskieren** kann das Scharfzeichnen sehr individuell vorgenommen werden. Quelle: PhotoShop CS2

Das professionelle Werkzeug zum Schärfen ist das **Unscharf maskieren** ❶. Dabei sorgen die drei Standard-Einstellwerte **Stärke**, **Radius** und **Schwellenwert** für eine Kontrolle über die Schärfe. Die „Stärke" beschreibt, in Prozent ausgedrückt, die Intensität des Schärfens. Bei Bildern in hoher Auflösung können das zwischen 150-200% sein. Der „Radius" definiert den Bereich der Pixel, die zur Schärfung herangezogen werden. Je größer der Radius gewählt wird, desto breiter erscheinen die Kanten der Schärfung. Bei hochaufgelösten Bildern sind in der Regel 1-2 Pixel sinnvoll. Der „Schwellenwert" gibt in Tonwertschritten an, wie groß der Unterschied der angrenzenden Pixel dargestellt werden soll. Bei der Stufe 0 wird alles geschärft und bei Stufe 10 nur die Kanten, die einen Tonwertunterschied von mindestens 10, also z. B. jene mit 162 und 178, aufweisen. Bei hochauflösenden Bildern liegt der Wert zwischen 2 und 20.

Weichzeichnen

In bestimmten Situationen möchte man den genau umgekehrten Effekt erzielen. Das Bild soll bewusst weich erscheinen. Durch das Weichzeichnen kann eine sanfte oder auch romantische Stimmung hervorgerufen werden. Dieser Effekt wird fast ausschließlich in der Porträt- und Aktfotografie verwendet. Bei einem Porträt wirkt das Gesicht weicher und die Haut glatter.

ohne Weichzeichner

mit Weichzeichner

6.3.4 Verfremdungen

Verschiedene Motive eignen sich auch zu besonderen **Bildverfremdungen**. Die folgenden Beispiele zeigen, jeweils im Vergleich zum Ausgangsbild, wie moderne Bildbearbeitungswerkzeuge durch Effektfilter interessante Bildverfremdungen produzieren können.

Kunst- und Malfilter-Effekte

Originalbild

Filter mit Ölfarbbild-Effekt

Originalbild

Filter mit Buntstift-Effekt

Originalbild

Filter mit Farbcollagen-Effekt

Originalbild

Filter mit Kohlezeichnungs-Effekt

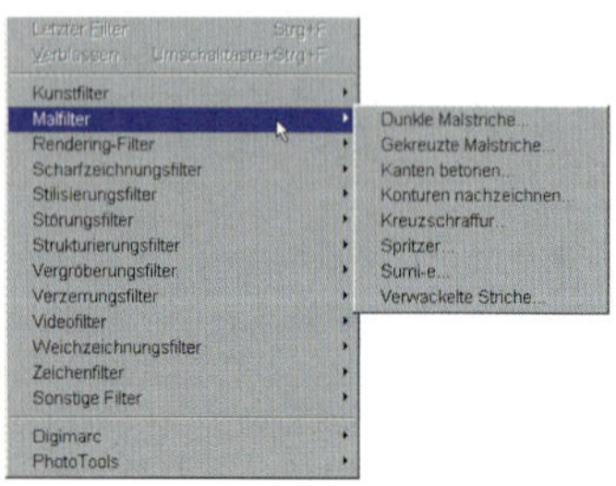

Die modernen Bildbearbeitungswerkzeuge verfügen über eine Vielzahl von Filtern, die zur Bildverfremdung eingesetzt werden können.

Originalbild

Filter mit Kornstruktur-Effekt

Originalbild

Filter mit Glasstruktur-Effekt

Über das interaktive Verändern der Filterparameter kann der Gestalter den Effekt direkt am Bildschirm kontrollieren.

Verzerrungs- und Vergröberungseffekte

Originalbild

Filter mit Strudel-Effekt

Originalbild

Filter mit Vergröberungs-Effekt

Jede Menge Filter für Bildverfremdungen sind für professionelle Bildbearbeitungsprogramme im Handel erhältlich und können als Plug-In hinzugeladen werden.

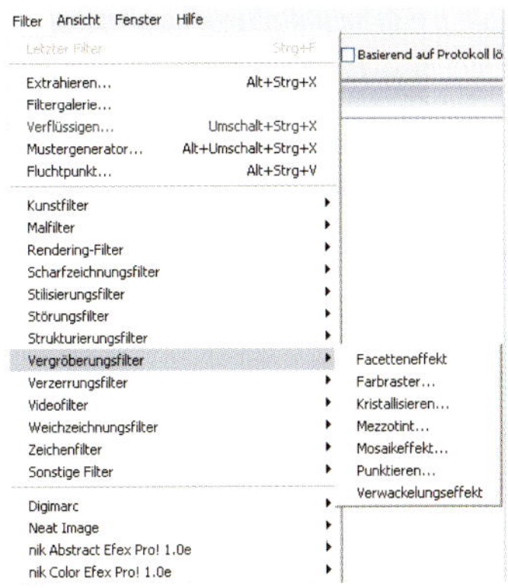

Filter und Zusatzfunktionen können als Plug-in direkt in das Bildbearbeitungsprogramm geladen werden und stehen dann dem Gestalter für seine Kreativität zur Verfügung.

7 Grafik

Webcode: B0700

Für weitere Infos zu diesem Kapitel mit dem Smartphone einfach QR-Code scannen oder auf www.medien-verstehen.de den Webcode eingeben.

Das bekannte Sprichwort „Ein Bild sagt mehr als tausend Worte" ❶ bezieht sich darauf, dass man komplizierte Sachverhalte mit einem Bild oftmals schneller und präziser erklären kann als mit einem langen Text. Diesen Umstand versucht man sich insbesondere bei der Vermittlung von betriebswirtschaftlichen Zahlen und Statistiken zunutze zu machen. Mit Bildern sind dann aber **Grafiken** ❷ gemeint. Man könnte sinngemäß das oben dargestellte Sprichwort umtaufen in „Eine Grafik sagt mehr als tausend Zahlen".

❶ Das Sprichwort tauchte erstmals in gedruckter Form im Jahre 1921 in einer Fachzeitschrift der Werbebranche auf.
Bilder drücken nach diesem Sprichwort also nicht nur Emotionen aus, sie werden verwendet, um Sachverhalte zu erklären.

❷ Aus dem griechischen: **gráphein = malen, schreiben**
Ursprünglich war das Malen und Schreiben gemeint.
Heute im Zusammenhang mit Grafik zu verstehen im Sinne von „be"-schreiben.

Doch Grafiken lassen sich nicht nur auf Zahlen oder **Statistiken** beschränken. Immer dann, wenn wir mit einer Fotografie eine Sache nicht erklären können, wir aber bildhaft arbeiten wollen, müssen wir unser Bild künstlich erzeugen, indem wir zeichnen, malen oder am Computer illustrieren.

In den verschiedenen Gestaltungsdisziplinen wird der Begriff der Grafik vielschichtig verwendet. Die folgenden Abschnitte sollen die Verwendung von Grafiken, deren Erstellung und den Einsatz in der Medienpraxis darstellen.

7.1 Technische Merkmale

Am Bildschirm werden alle Bilder mit Pixeln (picture elements = Bildpunkte) angezeigt. Die Art der Beschreibung der Darstellungen kann jedoch unterschiedlich sein. Um zum Beispiel ein Dreieck am Bildschirm reproduzieren zu können, gibt es zwei verschiedene Möglichkeiten: **Vektor**- oder **Pixelgrafik**.

Als Standard am Bildschirm gelten immer noch 72 pixel per inch (ppi), obwohl die Geräte in den letzten Jahren deutlich leistungsfähiger geworden sind. 1 Zoll setzt sich in diesem Fall aus 72 Punkten zusammen. Die Maßeinheit dots per inch (dpi) gilt in Zusammenhang mit Druckern, wird aber häufig gleichgesetzt.

7.1.1 Vektorgrafik

In einer **Vektorgrafik** werden nur wenige Daten über Eigenschaften benötigt um eine Grafik eindeutig reproduzieren zu können. Zum Beispiel die Koordinaten der Ecken, die Breite und Farbe der Umrisslinie und die Füllfarbe des Dreiecks. Diese Eigenschaften bezieht die Grafik aus mathematischen Beschreibungen in Form von Vektoren.

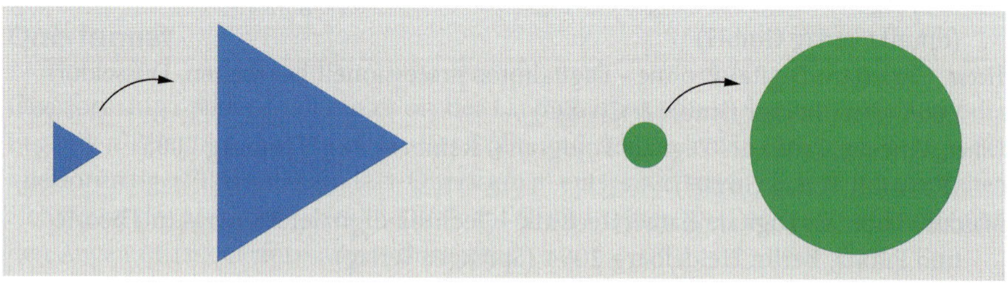

Vektorgrafiken sind geeignet, um mit einfachen Elementen zu gestalten. Der besondere Vorteil liegt darin, dass die erstellten Abbildungen **ohne Qualitätsverlust skalierbar** sind. Das bedeutet, dass sie in ihrer Größe verändert werden können, ohne dass dabei störende Effekte wie „Treppenstufen" auftreten. Die Linienkonturen bleiben glatt.

Die Vektorgrafiken müssen vor der Ausgabe am Bildschirm umgewandelt werden. Diesen Umwandlungsprozess nennt man Rasterung. Die mathematischen Vektoren werden in Pixel zerlegt.

Vektorgrafiken werden mit **Vektorgrafikprogrammen** oder auch **Illustrationsprogrammen** erstellt. Diese wiederum werden in Anwendungen ❶ unterschieden, die zwei- oder dreidimensionale Grafiken erzeugen können. Verwendung finden diese Grafiken im Planungs- und Entwurfsprozess von Produkten aller Art. Immer dann, wenn ein Produkt noch nicht existiert, der Gestalter sich dieses jedoch vorstellen und anderen zeigen möchte, kann eine Vektorgrafik erstellt werden. Im Entwurfsprozess können Vektorgrafiken schnell und unkompliziert Farb- und Formgebung in verschiedenen Ansichten visualisieren.

❶ Anwendungsprogramme zur Erstellung von Vektorgrafiken sind zum Beispiel für zweidimensionale Grafiken:
- Adobe Illustrator
- CorelDraw

dreidimensionale Grafiken:
- Maxon Cinema 4D
- Autodesk 3ds Max

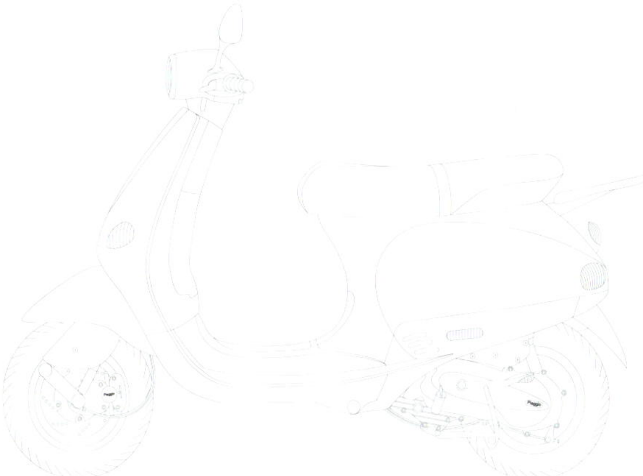

7.1.2 Pixelgrafik

In einer **Pixelgrafik** werden im Gegensatz zur Vektorgrafik sehr viele Informationen benötigt, um die Eigenschaften einer Abbildung zu speichern. Jedes Pixel benötigt einen Farbwert und eine genaue Koordinatenposition, an der es sich befindet.

Die Bezeichnung Pixelgrafik wird immer dann verwendet, wenn eine zuvor erstellte Vektorgrafik so umgewandelt wurde, dass sie am Bildschirm ausgegeben werden kann. Dabei ist zu beachten: Eine Pixelgrafik kann nur mit großer Mühe in eine Vektorgrafik verwandelt werden, eine Vektorgrafik aber leicht und jederzeit in eine Pixelgrafik. **Pixelgrafiken** können im Gegensatz zu Vektorgrafiken **nicht ohne Qualitätsverlust** vergrößert werden! Es entstehen beim Vergrößern „Treppenstufen“.

➲ **Die Mediengestaltung bezeichnet Abbildungen aus der Realität (Fotografien) nicht als Pixelgrafiken, sondern als Bilder (siehe vorhergehendes Kapitel)!**

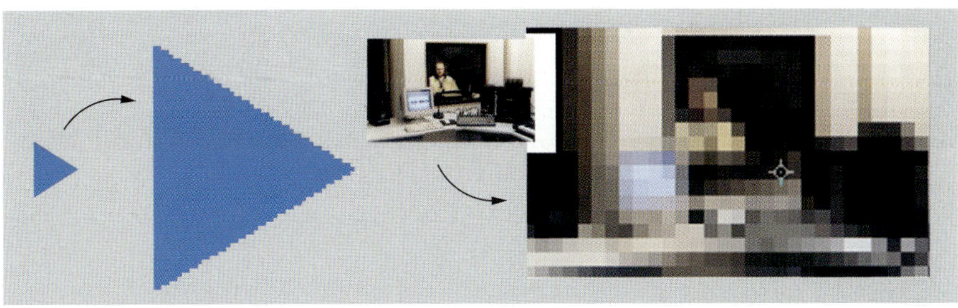

Die Abbildung zeigt die Veränderung beim Skalieren einer Pixelgrafik.

7.2 Darstellungsmethoden

Heutzutage arbeiten Designagenturen und Unternehmen in **Entwurf** und **Konstruktion** eng zusammen. Das Produkt entwickelt sich über mehrere Phasen hinweg. Dabei entstehen Darstellungen in Form von Vektorgrafiken, Illustrationen oder Zeichnungen von Hand, welche nach unterschiedlichen Methoden ausgeführt werden. Welche Bedeutung die einzelnen Darstellungsmethoden in der Praxis haben und wie sie eingesetzt werden, wird in den folgenden Abschnitten erläutert.

7.2.1 Entwurfszeichnung

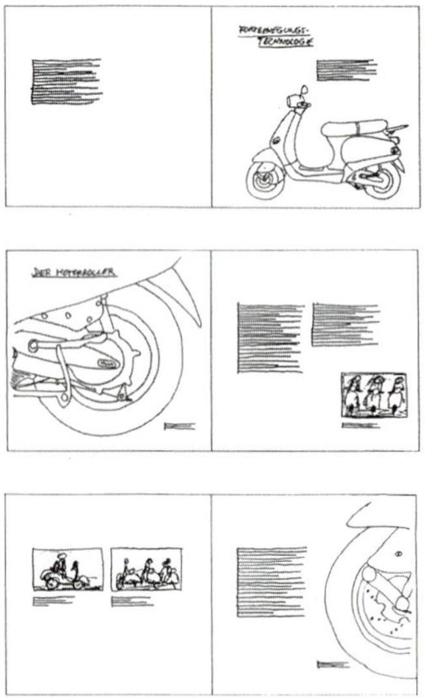

Scribbles einer Broschüre zum Thema Motorroller

Die **Entwurfszeichnung** ist eine Zeichnung, meist von Hand angefertigt, welche zu unterschiedlichen Zeitpunkten im Entwurfsprozess den aktuellen Entwicklungsstand visualisiert. Die Qualitätsanforderungen einer solchen Entwurfszeichnung legen deren Bezeichnung und Größe fest.

Die einfachste zeichnerische Umsetzung einer Idee wird als **Scribble** (Mediengestaltung) oder **Ideenskizze** (Produktgestaltung) bezeichnet. Es handelt sich hierbei um eine kleinformatige Umsetzung der Idee in Briefmarken-, maximal Postkartengröße. Bemaßungen am Objekt sind meistens noch nicht notwendig.

In Form des **Layouts** werden Scribble oder Skizze konkretisiert. Die Darstellungsgröße muss annähernd genau und proportional gezeichnet sein. Maßeintragungen sollten vorhanden sein.

Das **Reinlayout** ist eine 1:1-Umsetzung in Originalgröße und dient als Produktionsvorlage in der Mediengestaltung für die Reinzeichnung, die Fertigstellung eines Medienproduktes mit Hilfe des Computers. Das Reinlayout entspricht in der Produktgestaltung den entsprechenden Darstellungsmethoden in den folgenden Abschnitten.

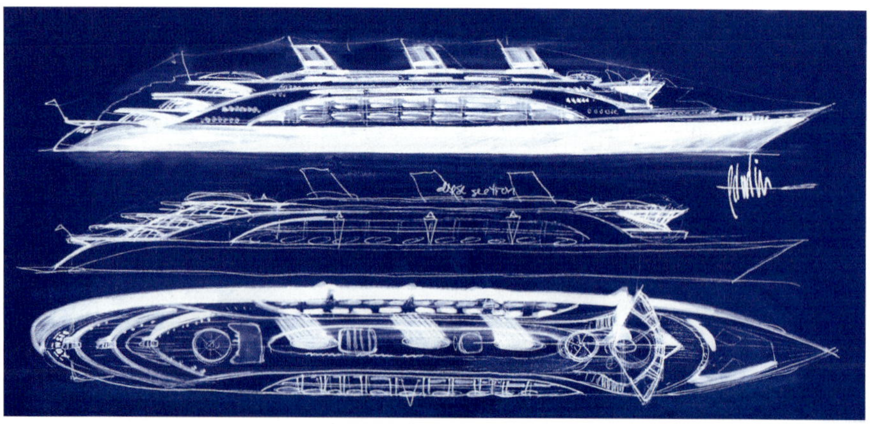

Ideenskizzen für das Kreuzfahrtschiff „Disney Magic". In seinen Entwürfen orientierte sich die international agierende Designagentur „frogdesign" an der Raumfahrt und an Science-Fiction-Filmen.

7.2.2 Prinzipdarstellung

Die Prinzipdarstellung stellt das Funktionsprinzip dar, zeigt Bewegungsmöglichkeiten eines Gegenstands, Handhabungsabläufe oder auch das Gebrauchsprinzip auf.

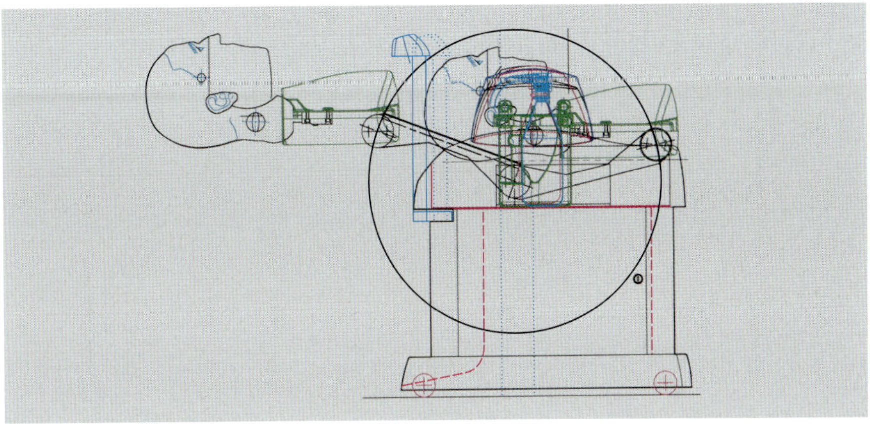

Darstellung der Bewegungsmöglichkeiten eines dentalen Patienten-Simulators, Fa. Kavo Dentaltechnik. Der Kopf kann in verschiedene Arbeitspositionen gebracht werden.

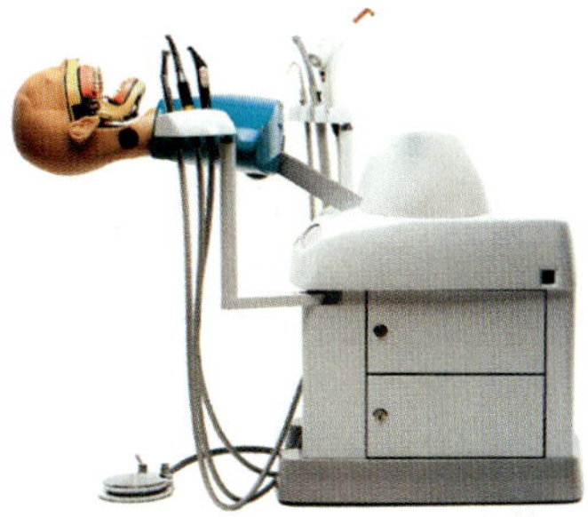

7.2.3 Ergonomische Darstellung

Die Darstellungsmethode findet dort ihren Einsatz, wo die Arbeitsbedingungen für den Menschen untersucht und optimiert werden müssen. Dies betrifft beispielsweise die Gestaltung von Computer-, Schreib- und Montagearbeitsplätzen, Sportgeräte sowie Möbel. Für die Festlegung der Maße für Möbel, Geräte und Maschinen werden normierte Personen zugrunde gelegt.

Ergonomie: Wissenschaft von den Leistungsmöglichkeiten und -grenzen des arbeitenden Menschen und von der Anpassung der Arbeitsbedingungen an den Menschen.

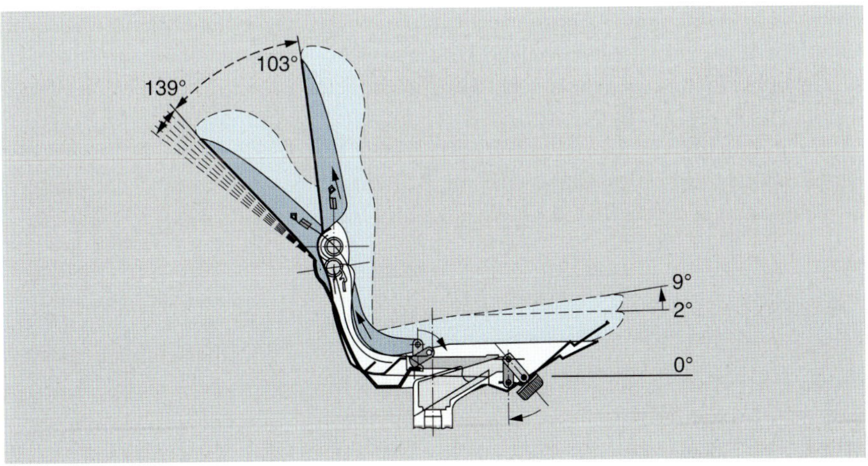

Dynamisches Sitzen: Schreibtischstühle werden heute so gestaltet, dass der Mensch sich jederzeit darauf bewegen kann und dadurch ständig seine Sitzposition verändert. Hierbei wird die Rückenlehne in Abhängigkeit von der Sitzflächenneigung um einen bestimmten Winkel mitgeschwenkt.

7.2.4 Schematische Darstellung

Hier wurde eine neuartige Schlittschuhkufe entwickelt, die nach Abnutzung ausgetauscht werden kann. Die drei konstruktiv entscheidenden Teile sind der Systemträger, der Stabilisator und das Kufenmesser.

Die schematische Darstellung ist eine auf wesentliche Merkmale des abzubildenden Objekts reduzierte eher „schemenhafte" Zeichnung oder Computergrafik. Dabei können durchaus verschiedene Bauteile detailliert dargestellt werden. Damit können beispielsweise Anzeigeinstrumente eines KFZ-Armaturenbretts im Bild hervorgehoben oder auch die Anordnung von Schaltflächen an einem Fernseher vorgenommen werden.

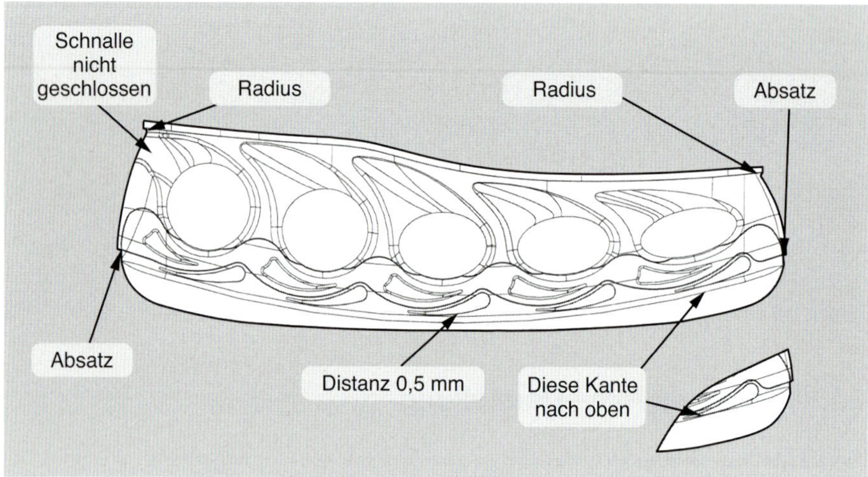

7.2.5 Dimensionsdarstellung

Sind sich Entwickler und Designer über die Gestaltung des Produktes einig, werden die besonderen Merkmale, normierten Bauteile, Normvorgaben und Werkstoffe sowie Oberflächenbeschaffenheit festgelegt. Diese Angaben werden in einer Art Pflichtenheft festgehalten und dienen dem Designer für die Feinbearbeitung des Projekts. Dann werden die maßgenauen Darstellungen in Form einer Zusammenbau- oder Baugruppenzeichnung und die Darstellungen von Einzelheiten des Gegenstands, Geräts oder der Maschine angefertigt. Damit sind die Grundlagen für die Einzelteilzeichnungen der Konstruktion geschaffen, nach denen dann gefertigt werden kann.

Konstruktionen und Entwürfe zum Kufensystem eines Schlittschuhes: Der Entwurf des Schuhs mit dem Trägersystem für die Kufe muss so gestaltet sein, dass unterschiedliche Fußgeometrien mit dem Systemträger kombiniert werden können.

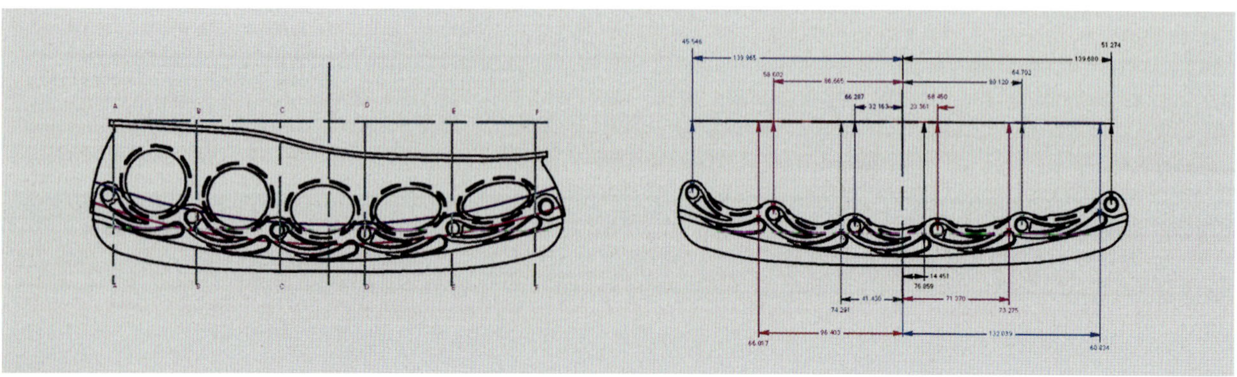

7.2.6 Explosionsdarstellung

In der Explosionsdarstellung werden die einzelnen Bauteile eines Gerätes räumlich abgebildet und so geordnet, wie sie zusammengebaut werden müssen. Diese Art des Bildes zeigt auch komplexe Bauteile, wie Getriebe und Motoren in Teilschnitten, um die Funktionen kenntlich zu machen. Die Explosionsdarstellung kommt vor allem in Ersatzteillisten und Montageanleitungen zum Einsatz.

❶ Montage des Kufenmessers am Trägersystem des Schlittschuhs als gerenderte 3D-Darstellung.

❷ Funktionsdarstellung einer Messuhr, durch Abheben der einzelnen Elemente aus der Ebene heraus.

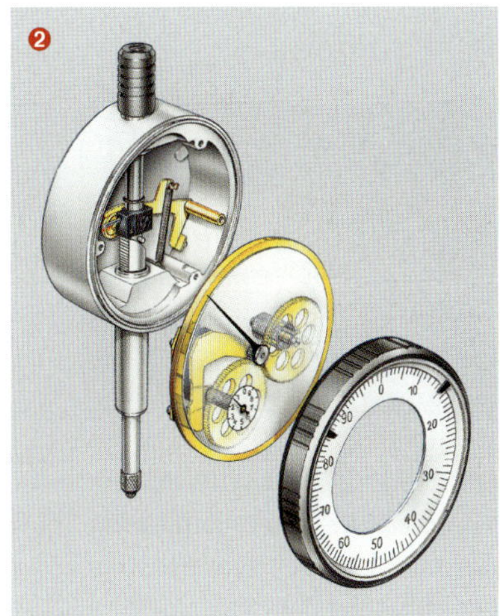

7.2.7 Gerenderte Darstellung

Sollen Designlösungen präsentiert werden, können sie durch eine Rendering-Zeichnung ❸ oder durch eine gerenderte dreidimensionale Darstellung am Rechner dem Betrachter so realitätsnah wie möglich vorgeführt werden. Mit Hilfe einer Kamerafunktion in den dreidimensionalen Programmen lassen sich auch „Flüge" in und um das Produkt simulieren. Darüberhinaus ist es möglich, beliebige Ansichten des Objekts „einzufrieren".

❸ **Rendern**: Projektion einer drei-dimensionalen Objektdarstellung in die zweidimensionale Ebene der Bildschirmdarstellung mit einer entsprechenden Nachbearbeitung des entstehenden Bildes durch Licht, Schatten, Reflexionen und Farben.

Auf der Basis von Vektor-Daten wird in einem Anwendungsprogramm das Kufensystem als Gitterdarstellung erzeugt. Mit Materialeigenschaften und Oberflächentexturen wird die Darstellung zu einer wirklichkeitsgetreuen Abbildung und lässt sich von allen Seiten betrachten.

7.3 Räumliche Darstellung

Werden Körper auf einem Papier gezeichnet, so erhält man eine Darstellung auf einer Ebene. Die Dreidimensionalität der Gegenstände kann durch Veränderung der Linienstärken, Schatten, Hell-Dunkel-Effekte und Perspektiven auf dem Papier erzeugt werden. Körper und umgebender Raum können mit Hilfe der **perspektivischen** oder **axonometrischen Darstellung** räumlich dargestellt werden. Eine weitere Möglichkeit ist die **Darstellung in Ansichten** als Flächendarstellung.

7.3.1 Perspektivische Darstellung

❶ Albrecht Dürer veröffentlichte 1525 die erste Zusammenfassung der mathematisch-geometrischen Verfahren der Zentralperspektive. Die Bildebene wird daher auch als Dürer-Ebene bezeichnet.

Wesentliches Element der perspektivischen Darstellung ist die perspektivische Verkürzung. So wirken Gegenstände, die auf einem Tisch weiter hinten stehen kleiner als der gleiche Gegenstand, der vor dem Betrachter steht!

Zur perspektivischen Darstellung müssen einige Dinge beachtet werden:
Die **Horizontlinie** ist die Linie, die sich in horizontaler Richtung in Höhe der Augen des Menschen ziehen lässt. Der Blick des Betrachters fokusiert sich in einem Fluchtpunkt oder Augpunkt. Der Betrachter steht auf dem Boden. Dieser Boden wird Grundebene genannt. Senkrecht unter den Augen des Betrachters befindet sich die Grundlinie. Der Weg, auf dem der Betrachter steht, verjüngt sich zum Fluchtpunkt hin (perspektivische Verkürzung). Will der Betrachter nun einen Körper, den er vor sich sieht, abbilden, verhält sich dies, als wenn der Betrachter durch ein Fenster hindurch schaut und auf die Scheibe des Fensters zeichnet, was er vor sich sieht. Dieses „Fenster" wird **Bildebene** ❶ genannt.

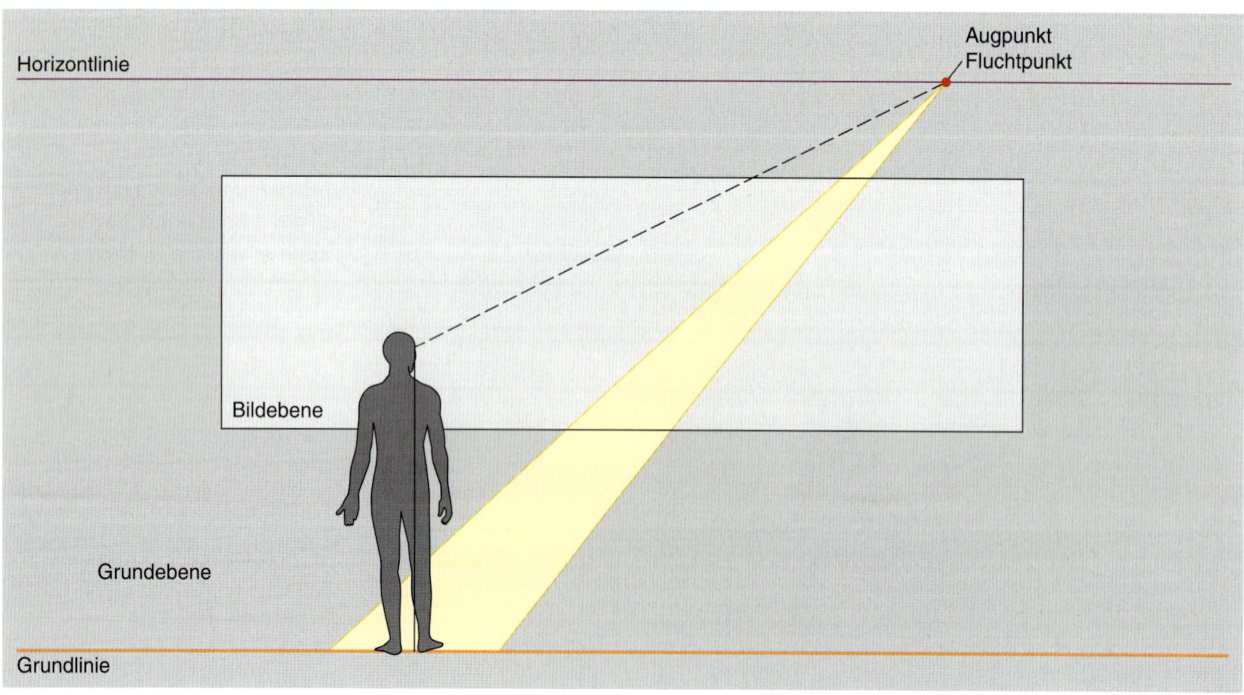

Möchte man nun mit diesen Erkenntnissen ein Schachbrett zeichnen, ergibt sich folgende Vorgehensweise: Zuerst zeichnet man die Horizontlinie; dann wird der Flucht- oder Augpunkt festgelegt. Die Grundlinie wird parallel zur Horizontlinie gezeichnet (der Abstand der beiden Linien zueinander bildet den Abstand des Betrachters zur Bildebene). Nun wird im Auge ein rechtwinkliges Dreieck errichtet. Die Schnittpunkte der beiden Schenkel bilden mit der Horizontlinie zwei weitere Fluchtpunkte (für die Diagonalen). Jetzt zeichnet man parallel zur Horizontlinie die vordere Kante des Schachbrettes. Diese Kante wird in acht gleiche Teile aufgeteilt. Jede Kante eines Teiles wird mit dem Fluchtpunkt verbunden. Die Tiefe des Schachbrettes definiert sich durch die Diagonalen. Zum Schluss werden die Teilstücke mit den jeweiligen Fluchtpunkten verbunden.

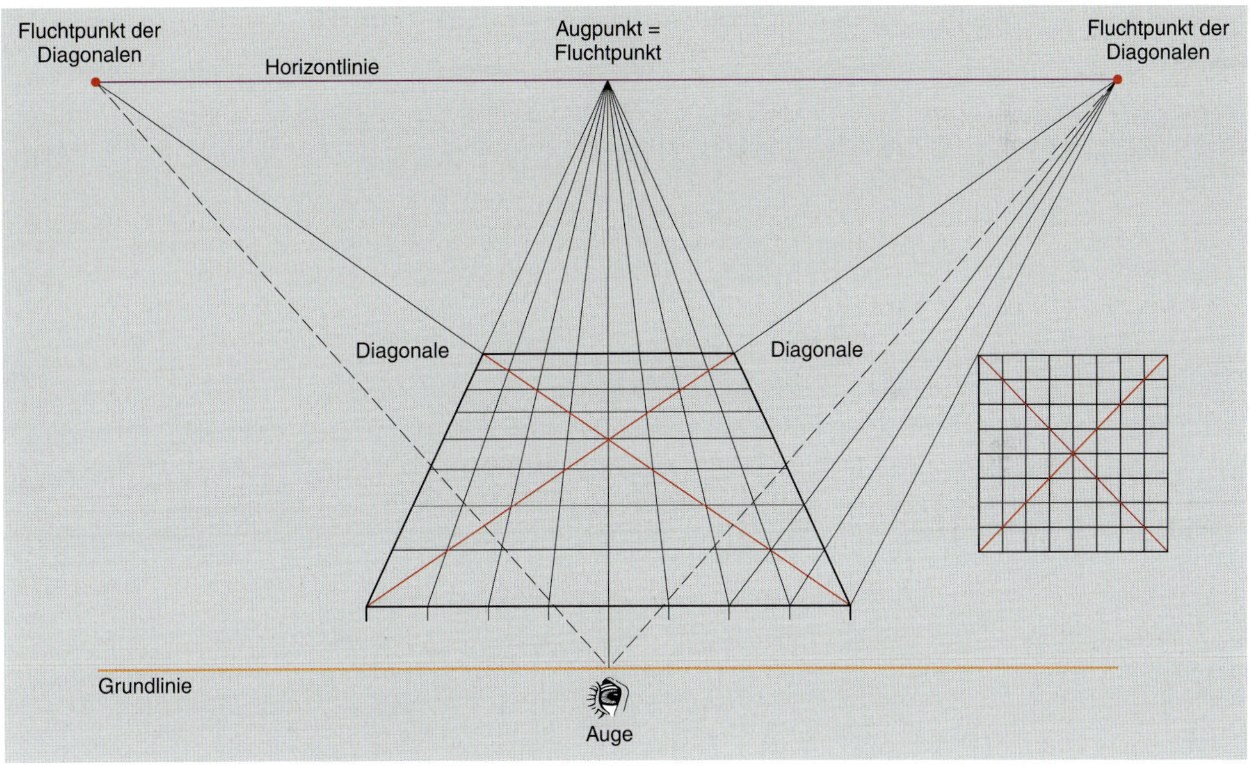

➲ **Die perspektivische Darstellung von Gegenständen mit einer nach vorne gerichteten Seite nennt man Zentralperspektive oder Einfluchtpunktperspektive.**

Schaut man bei einem Körper aber nicht frontal auf eine Seite, sondern auf eine Kante ergeben sich zwei Fluchtpunkte.

➲ **Die perspektivische Darstellung von Gegenständen mit einer nach vorne gerichteten Kante nennt man Übereckperspektive oder Zweifluchtpunktperspektive.**

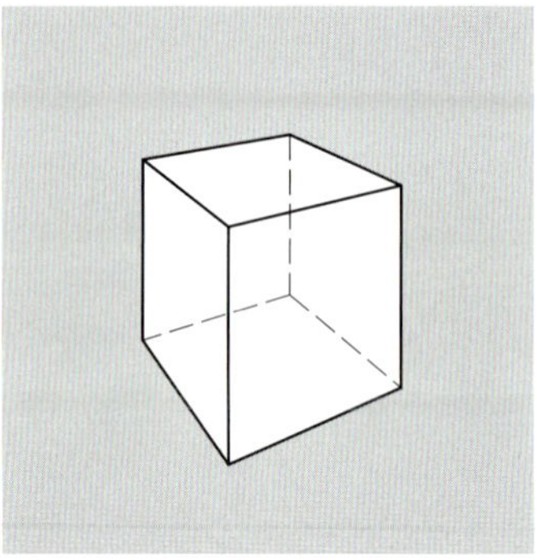

Die zeichnerische Darstellung eines Würfels lässt sich wie folgt realisieren: Zuerst zeichnet man wie bei der Zentralperspektive die Horizontlinie. Dann werden zwei nicht zu nahe beieinander liegende Fluchtpunkte gewählt. Die Grundlinie wird parallel zur Horizontlinie gezeichnet (der Abstand der beiden Linien zueinander bildet den Abstand des Betrachters zur Bildebene). Nun zeichnet man das Auge ein. Es bildet den Eckpunkt eines über den Fluchtpunkten errichteten rechtwinkligen Dreieckes. Um die zwei Messpunkte zu finden trägt man die Schenkellänge auf die Horizontlinie ab. Die Schnittpunkte ergeben die Messpunkte. Anschließend kann die vordere Kante des Würfels auf der Grundlinie errichtet werden. Die Kante kann beliebig hoch sein. Die Enden der Kante werden mit den Fluchtpunkten verbunden. Nun wird die nach vorne gerichtete Kante rechts und links auf die Grundlinie projeziert und die Schnittpunkte mit der Grundlinie mit den Messpunkten verbunden. Die restlichen Kanten ergeben sich durch die Kreuzungspunkte der Fluchtlinien.

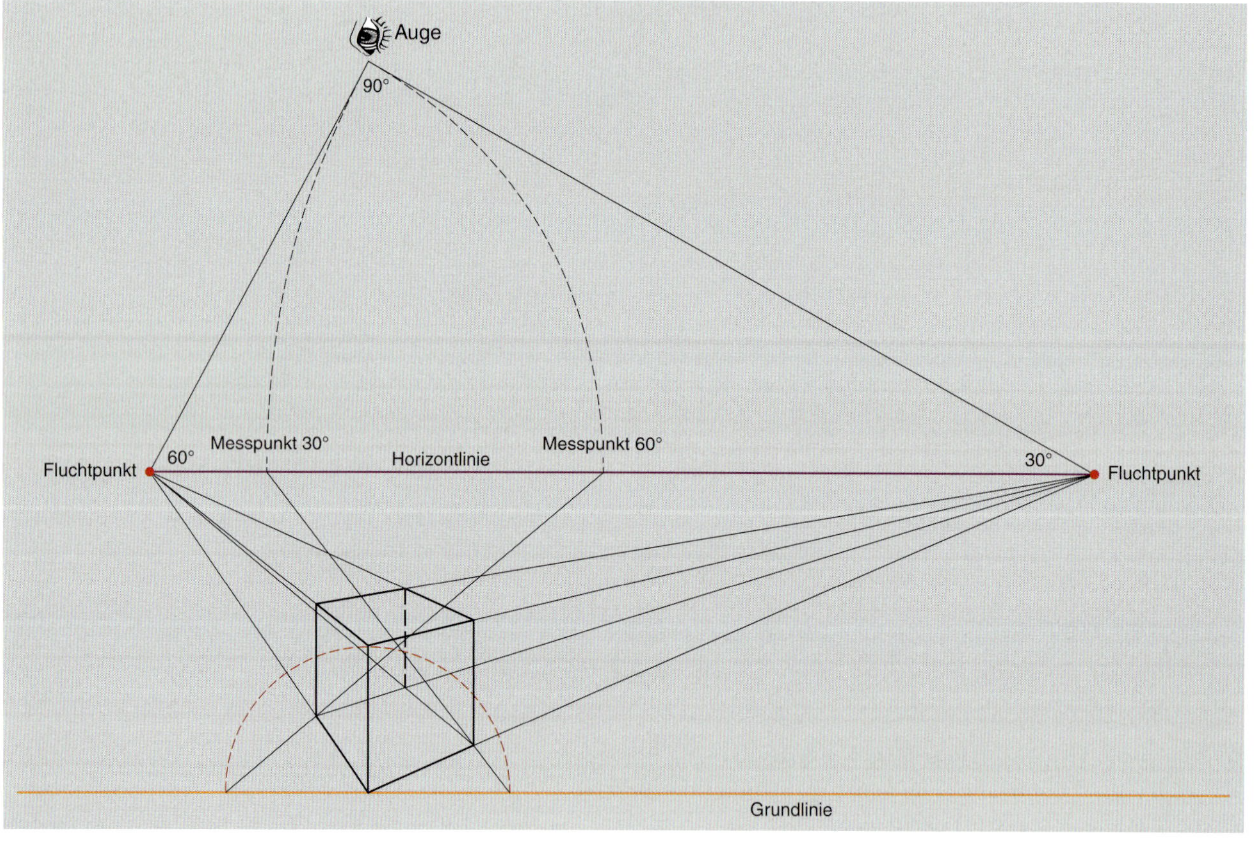

Die perspektivische Darstellung mit zwei Fluchtpunkten kommt unserem räumlichen Sehen sehr nahe. Sie wird daher auch als **Normalperspektive** bezeichnet. Liegt die Augenhöhe oberhalb eines Körpers spricht man von der **Vogelperspektive**. Liegt die Augenhöhe unterhalb eines Körpers spricht man von der **Froschperspektive**.

➲ **Die perspektivische Darstellung von Gegenständen mit einer nach vorne gerichteten Ecke nennt man Dreifluchtpunktperspektive (Vogel- oder Froschperspektive).**

❶

❷
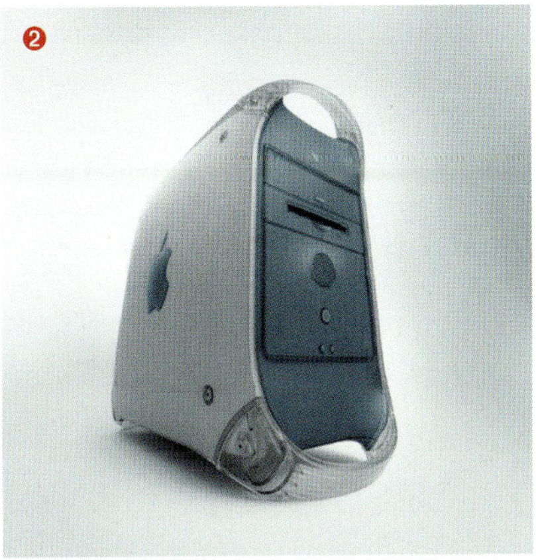
❸
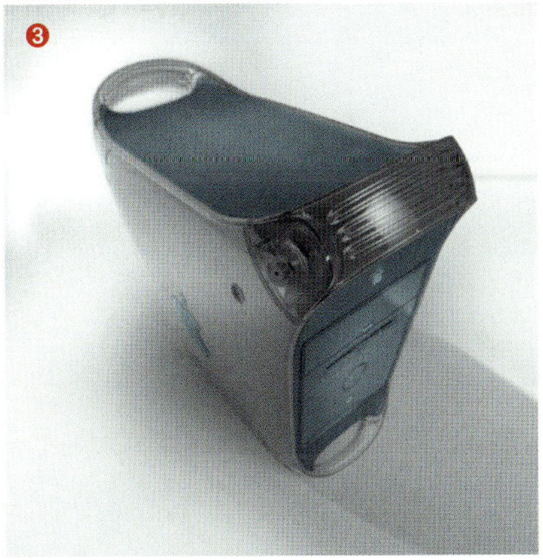

Abbildungen eines Computers in der Normalperspektive ❶ (zwei Fluchtpunkte), der Froschperspektive ❷ (drei Fluchtpunkte) und der Vogelperspektive ❸ (ebenfalls drei Fluchtpunkte). Die Fluchtpunkte ergeben sich jeweils aus der Verlängerung paralleler Objektkanten.

7.3.2 Axonometrische Darstellung

Die axonometrischen Darstellungen zeigen den Körper wie er ist und nicht aus einem entsprechenden menschlichen Blickwinkel. Die Merkmale Horizont, Fluchtpunkt und Entfernung haben hier keine Bedeutung. Das planparallele Projektionsverfahren stellt den Körper mit drei Seiten in einem bestimmten Maßverhältnis und unter einem vorgegebenen Winkel dar.

Wegen ihrer Einfachheit wird die **Axonometrie** gerne für schnell zu erstellende und maßhaltige Skizzen verwendet, aber auch in der Architektur und in weiteren Sparten der Technik. Ebenso beliebt ist die Axonometrie in der EDV, weil sie zum Beispiel für Blockdiagramme einfach programmierbar ist und eine gute räumliche Visualisierung erlaubt.

Seit 1998 existiert eine gültige DIN-ISO-Norm ❹, dem Technischen Zeichnen zugeordnet, welche die axonometrischen Darstellungen festlegt:

❹ Zu beziehen sind die Normen beim Beuth Verlag GmbH, einem Tochterunternehmen des Deutschen Institutes für Normung e.V.

➲ **DIN ISO 5456-3**
Technische Zeichnungen – Projektionsmethoden – Teil 3: Axonometrische Darstellungen

Bei der axonometrischen Darstellung unterscheidet man die **Isometrie** mit gleichem Seitenverhältnis und die **Dimetrie** mit unterschiedlichem Seitenverhältnis.

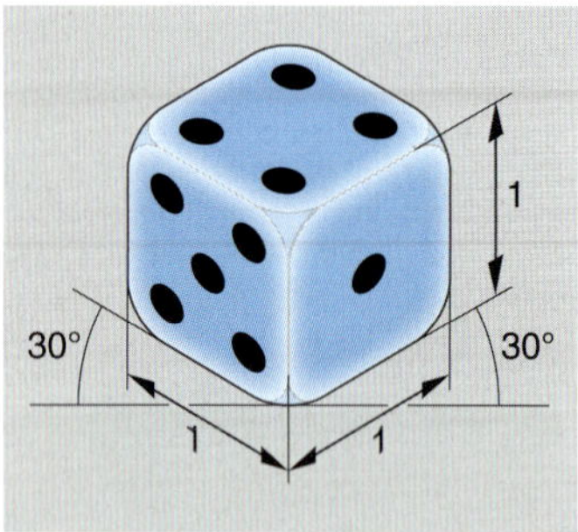

Isometrie

Der Begriff Isometrie kommt aus dem Lateinischen und lässt sich in die Worte „iso = gleich" und „metrie = Länge" aufteilen. Breite, Höhe und Tiefe werden im gleichen Verhältnis 1:1:1 abgebildet. Ein Würfel wird dabei mit gleichlangen Kantenlängen gezeichnet.

Die Winkel zur Horizontalen stehen unter 30°/30°. In älteren Darstellungsformen findet man noch Erhebungswinkel von 45°/45°. Diese entsprechen jedoch nicht der gültigen DIN-ISO-Norm.

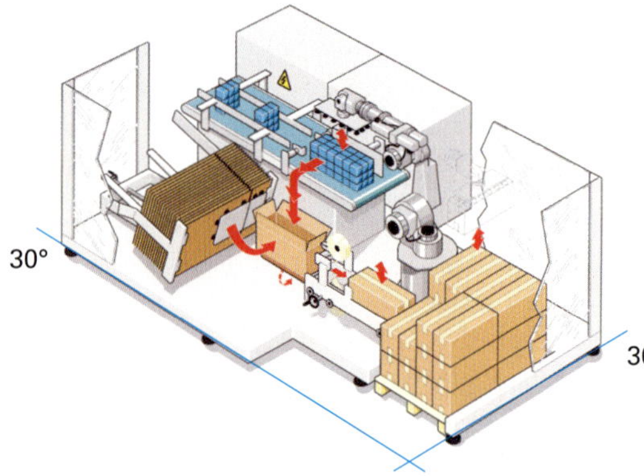

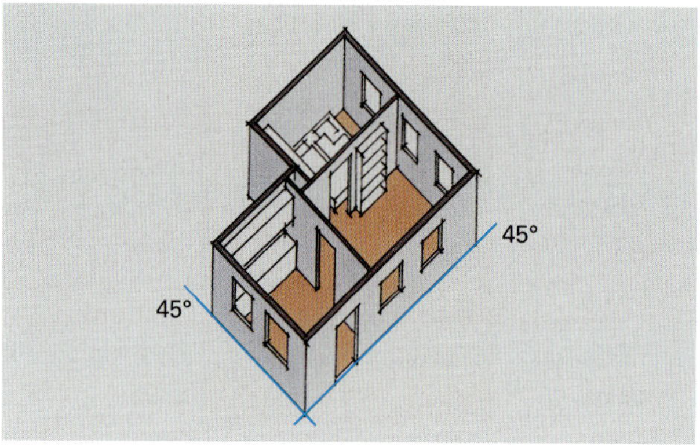

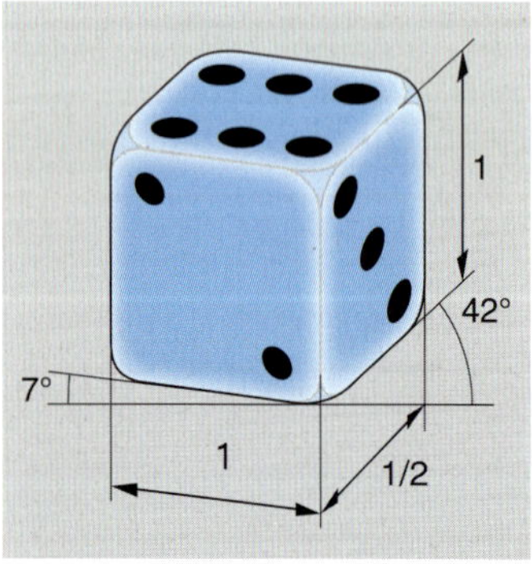

Dimetrie

In der dimetrischen Darstellung wird die Vorderseite des Körpers hervorgehoben. Die Darstellung wird durch die Winkelung von 7°/42° erzeugt. Die Dimetrie beinhaltet zwei unterschiedliche Längenmaßstäbe, wie schon der Begriff „Di = zwei" sagt. Breite, Höhe und Tiefe verhalten sich wie 1:1:1/2. Das bedeutet, dass der Körper in der Tiefe um die Hälfte verkürzt dargestellt wird.

Die Darstellung in der dimetrischen Projektion wirkt realistischer, da die Verkürzung des Körpers in der Tiefe dem räumlichen Empfinden des Menschen näher kommt als die Isometrie.

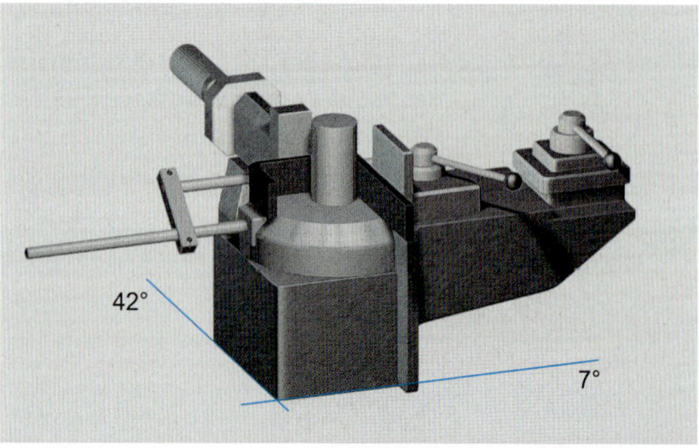

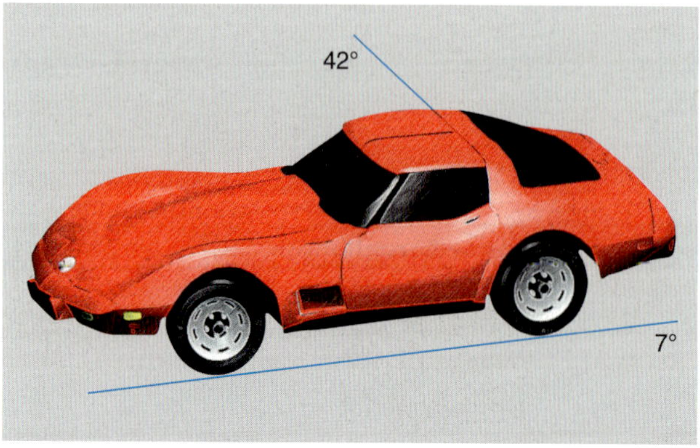

7.3.3 Darstellung in Ansichten

Die Darstellung in Ansichten wird vor allem in technischen Einzelteilzeichnungen oder in der Architektur verwendet, wenn die Proportionen und Maße eines Körpers oder von Räumen im Vordergrund stehen. Der Körper wird dabei in der Ebene ohne räumliche Tiefe dargestellt. Dadurch besteht die Zeichnung immer aus zwei Dimensionen in der x/y-, x/z-, y/z-Ebene. Man benötigt zur Darstellung der Tiefe mindestens eine zweite Ansichtsdarstellung. Die Anzahl der zu zeichnenden Ansichten richtet sich nach der Komplexität des Körpers. Insgesamt stehen bis zu 6 Ansichten zur Verfügung, die durch Umklappen aus der Vorderansicht erzeugt werden.

In den meisten Fällen werden die Vorderansicht, eine ❶ oder zwei Seitenansichten und eine Draufsicht gezeichnet ❷. Seit 1998 existiert eine gültige DIN-ISO-Norm, dem Technischen Zeichnen zugeordnet, welche die Darstellung in Ansichten festlegt:

➲ DIN ISO 5456-2
Technische Zeichnungen – Projektionsmethoden – Teil 2: Orthogonale Darstellungen

Eine Variante der Ansichtsdarstellung stellt die plastisch wirkende Zeichnung ❸ dar, die auch zu Präsentationszwecken oder für Werbeprospekte verwendet wird. Diese Zeichnungen erzeugen beim Betrachter durch Lichter und Schatten in den Konturen des Körpers und durch Einfärben eine räumliche Vorstellung.

❶
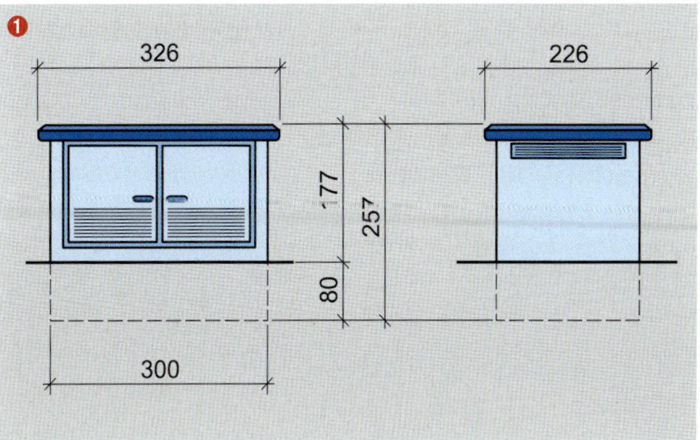

❷
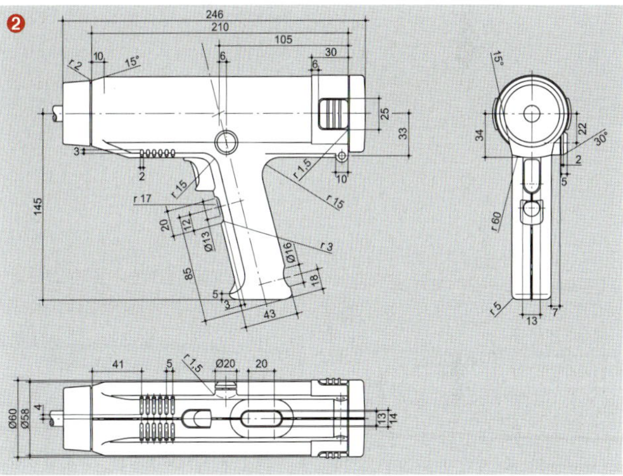

❸

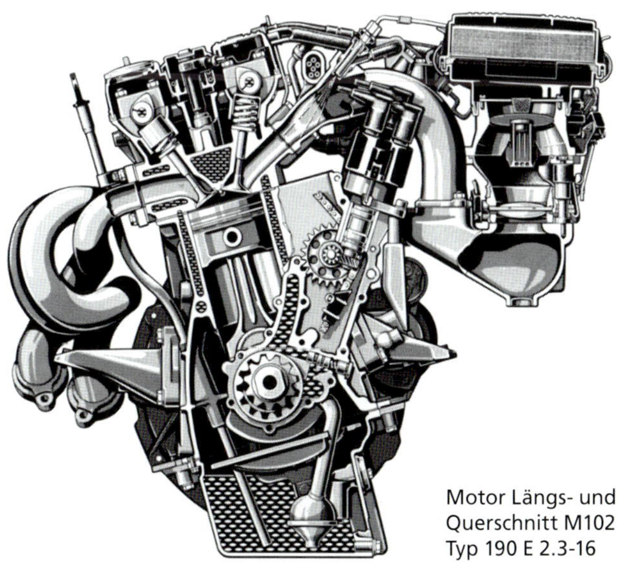

Motor Längs- und Querschnitt M102 Typ 190 E 2.3-16

7.3.4 Steigerung der räumlichen Wirkung

Licht und Schatten

Darstellungstechniken, Schattenkonstruktionen. Vergleiche: Holder, Eberhard: Design – Darstellungstechniken

Zur Steigerung des plastischen Eindrucks wird in der Darstellung von Gegenständen mit Licht und Schatten gearbeitet. In den meisten Darstellungen wird eine Lichtquelle von links oben angenommen. Diese strahlt paralleles Licht aus, womit die Lichtstrahlen zur Konstruktion des Schattens verwendet werden können.

Beleuchtet man einen Körper, dann werden die dem Licht zugewandten Kanten heller dargestellt, die dem Licht abgewandten Kanten dunkler. Zeichnerisch erzielt man diesen Verdunkelungseffekt durch unterschiedliche Strichstärken der Körperkanten. Durch Verteilung der Helligkeit auf der Fläche, erzeugen eines **Körperschattens**, wird ebenso eine räumliche Wirkung erzielt.

Dabei besitzt ein Kubus drei unterschiedliche Körperschatten, die je nach Größe des Körpers auch als Hell-Dunkel-Verlauf auftreten können. Bei zylindrischen Körpern verläuft der Körperschatten aufgrund der Wölbung in jedem Fall von Dunkel nach Hell und wieder nach Dunkel.

Licht und Schatten lassen sich besonders durch Körperteile wie Rohre, Vertiefungen, Rippen, Mulden, Schlitze, Ringe oder Gitter erzielen. Dadurch wird auch eine verstärkte Tiefenwirkung erzielt.

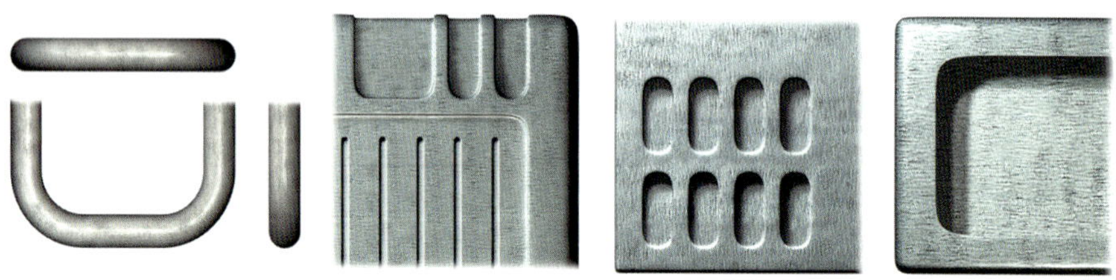

Durch die Möglichkeiten der Fotografie und der 3-D-Animation können auch Schatten durch mehrere Lichtquellen gestaltet werden. Dadurch werden interessante Schattenspiele, Effekte und Betonungen von bestimmten Elementen erzielt.

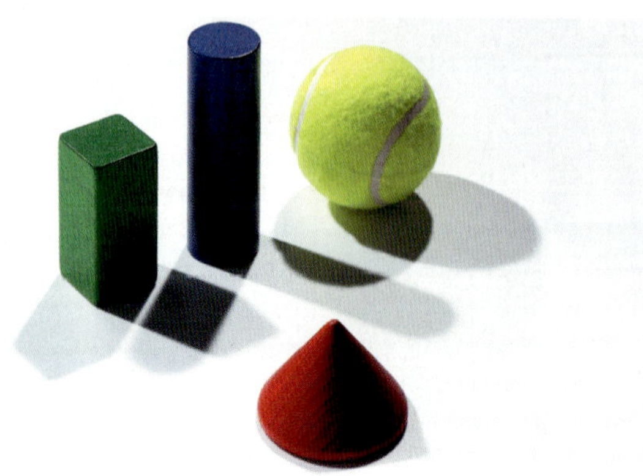

Farbe

Durch Farbe im Bild werden Objekte räumlich verstärkt oder getrennt oder auch von ihrem Hintergrund abgehoben. Zum Zwecke stärkerer räumlicher Wirkung und zum Hervorheben von Gegenständen kann eine Schwarz-Weiß-Grau-Darstellungen mit farbigen Hintergründen ❹ versehen werden und umgekehrt farbige Gegenstände mit Grauverläufen hinterlegt werden. Durch einen **Komplementärkontrast** ❶ kann die Farbwirkung gesteigert und dadurch eine intensivere Betonung des Körpers erzielt werden.

Komplementärkontrast: Polare Farben, z. B. rot und grün, liegen sich auf dem Farbkreis ❶ gegenüber.

Bei der Farbwahl ist zu beachten, dass z. B. die orangefarbenen Töne ❷ am wärmsten wirken und die Farbtöne im blauen und grünen Bereich ❸ am kältesten sind. Weiterhin hat man festgestellt, dass z. B. graue Gegenstände stärker hervortreten und gelbe Flächen eher zurücktreten ❹.

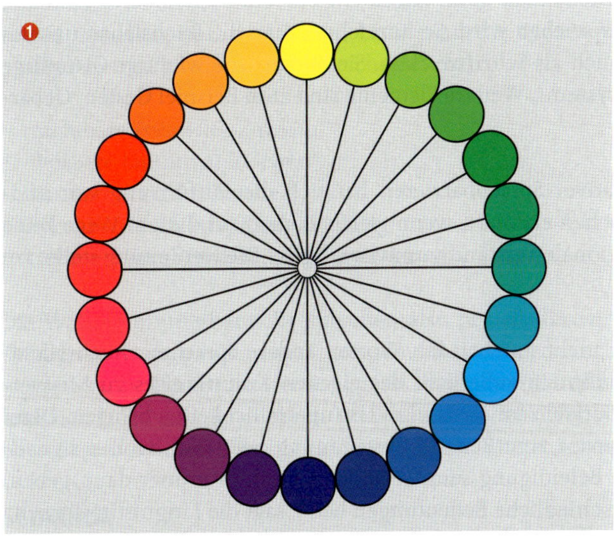

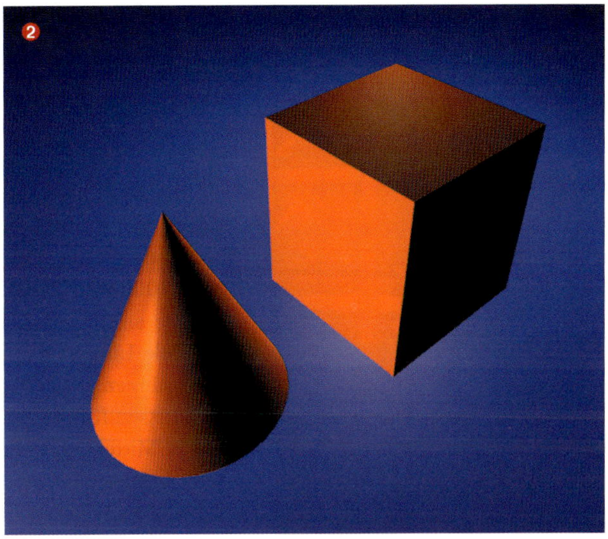

Beispiel „tagesschau.de" Wahlmonitor

Der Wahlmonitor aus Baden-Württemberg bildet die Ergebnisse der Landtagswahl 2011 mit allen gängigen Diagrammarten ab.

Der Internetauftritt **tagesschau.de** fungiert als zentrales Nachrichtenportal der ARD. Die im August 1996 veröffentlichte Seite bot früher lediglich begleitende Informationen zum Fernsehangebot der gleichnamigen Nachrichtensendung. Heute ist sie jedoch ein eigenständiges Telemedienangebot und steht in Konkurrenz mit einigen anderen namhaften Anbietern.
Der Wahlmonitor bildet die gesamte statistische Landschaft Deutschlands mit allen Ergebnissen aller Land- und Bundestagswahlen ab.

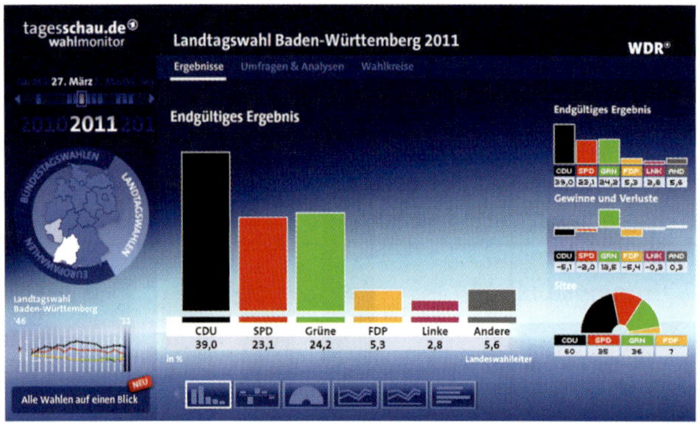

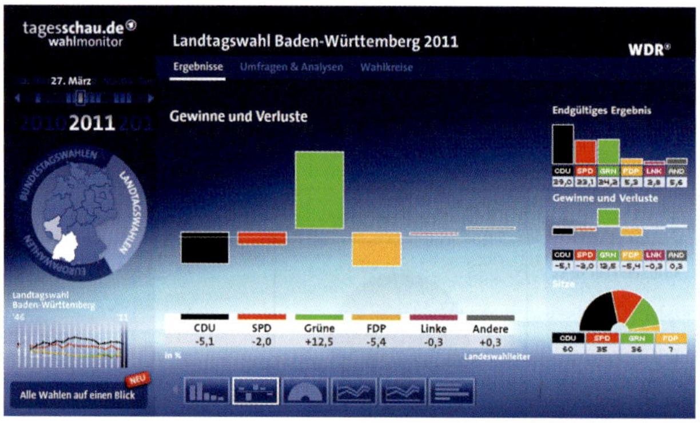

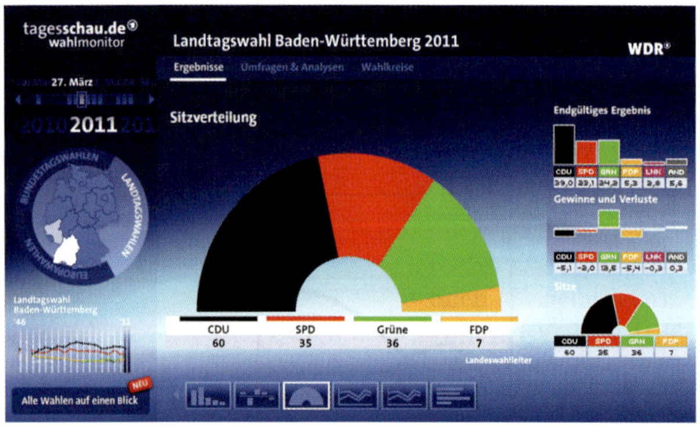

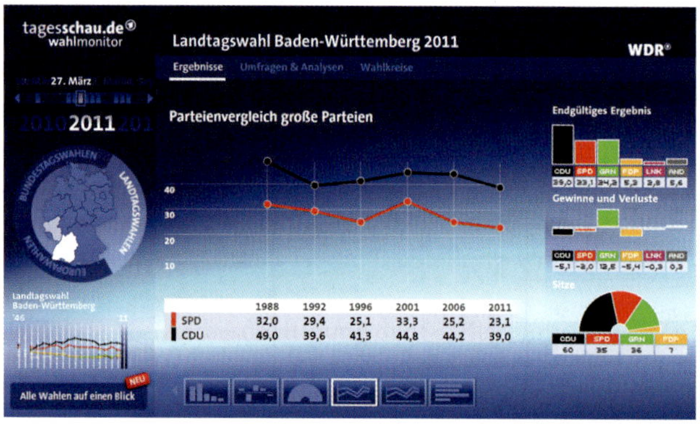

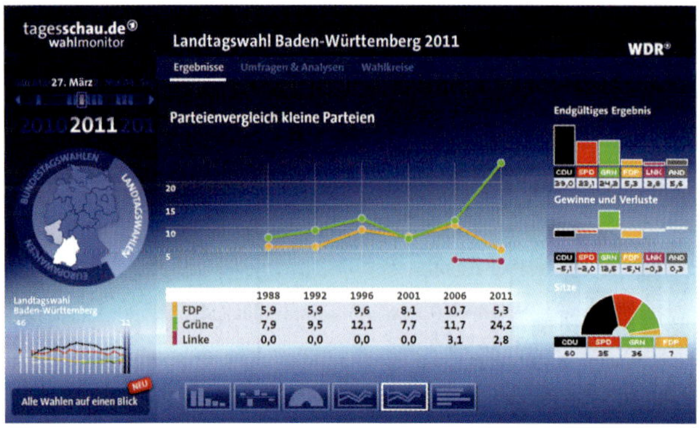

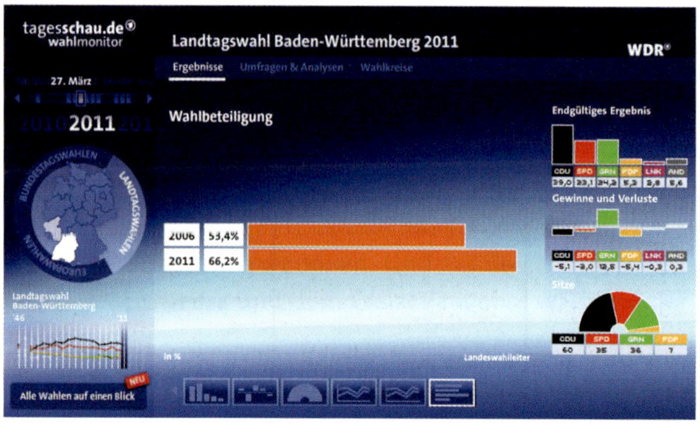

Beispiel Digitaler Recherchearbeitsplatz „global access"

Für die EXPO 2000, der Weltausstellung in Hannover, wurde im Rahmen einer Diplomarbeit ein digitaler Recherchearbeitsplatz entwickelt, mit dem die Komponenten aus Wirtschaft, Ökologie und Gesellschaft datengrafisch und multimedial aufbereitet werden können.
Im Zuge zunehmender Globalisierung und immer stärker werdender Bindungen der einzelnen Länder untereinander auf wirtschaftlicher, ökologischer und sozialer Ebene ist es für alle Menschen von großer Bedeutung, diese Zusammenhänge zu erkennen und zu erschließen. Die Medienlandschaft beschränkt sich meistens immer nur auf Teilsequenzen dieses Geflechtes. Die Aufgabe von „global access" ist es, Daten visuell einfach und dennoch vergleichbar darzustellen.

Daten zur Geburtenrate des Landes China, der EU und den USA im Vergleich aufbereitet von der ❶ Tabellenform, zum ❷ Balkendiagramm, hin zum ❸ Trend über mehrere Jahre und als örtliche Organisationsform auf einer ❹ Weltkarte.

❶

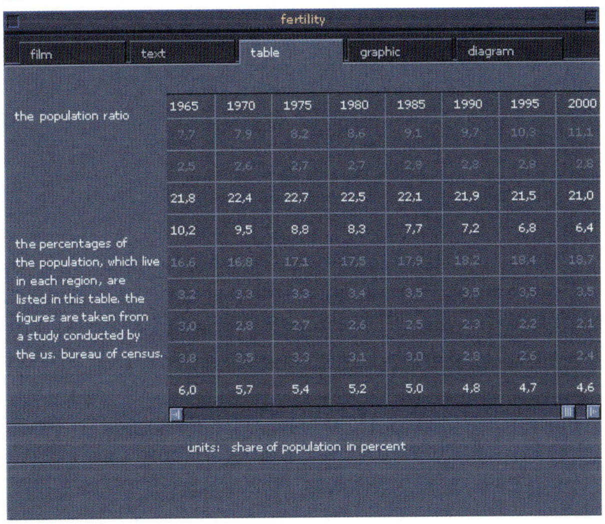

❷

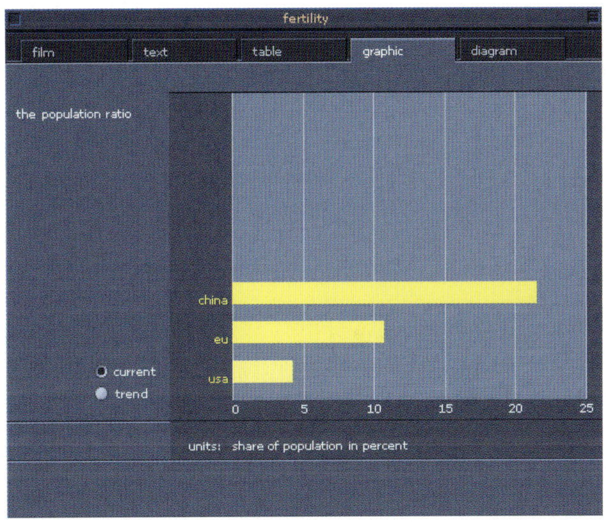

❸

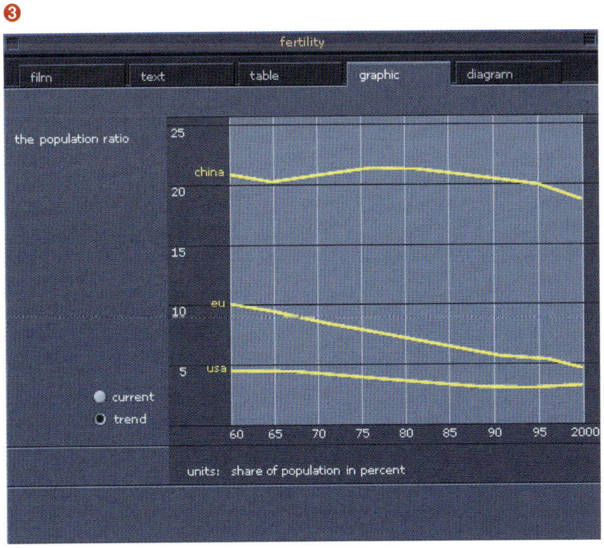

❹

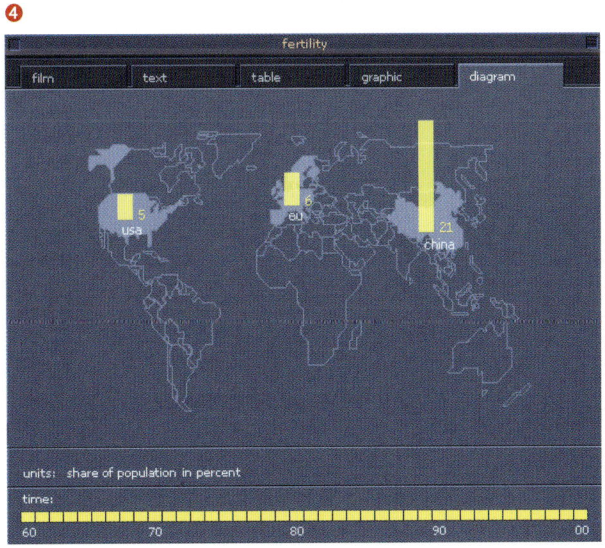

Aufgaben und Übungen, Literaturhinweise

Aufgaben und Übungen

1. Erstellen Sie in einem Illustrationsprogramm das Abbild eines Autos. Vereinfachen Sie soweit wie möglich und lassen Sie unwichtige Teile weg.
2. Suchen Sie in Bedienungs- und Aufbauanleitungen (zum Beispiel für Möbel) nach verschiedenen Darstellungsmethoden und ordnen Sie diese ein!
3. Erstellen Sie eine Übereckperspektive eines bekannten städtischen Gebäudes. Die Zeichnung kann freihand, mit Lineal oder mit einem Illustrationsprogramm ausgeführt werden.
4. Erstellen Sie eine Zentralperspektive des Raumes, in dem Sie sich gerade aufhalten. Die Zeichnung kann freihand, mit Lineal oder mit einem Illustrationsprogramm ausgeführt werden.
5. Zeichnen Sie eine Kaffee- oder ähnliche Verpackung in axonometrischer Darstellung (isometrisch und dimetrisch). Die Zeichnung kann freihand, mit Lineal oder mit einem Illustrationsprogramm ausgeführt werden.
6. Definieren Sie die Syntax, die Semantik und die Pragmatik von folgenden Zeichen: Rote Ampel, Toilettenpiktogramm (männlich / weiblich) und Emoticon „Smiley".
7. Recherchieren Sie nach den fünf Höchsten Türmen eines beliebigen Landes. Ordnen Sie diese nach den Prinzipien der Informationsorganisation.
8. Erheben Sie Zahlen, indem Sie einige Ihrer Bekannten nach folgenden Sachverhalten befragen: Einkommen, Wohnort, Körpergröße, Religionszugehörigkeit und Lieblingshobby. Erstellen Sie geeignete Informationsgrafiken.
9. Suchen Sie verschiedene Informationsgrafiken in der Tagespresse. Bestimmen Sie die Diagrammart und bewerten Sie die grafische Aufbereitung.
10. Erstellen Sie Piktogramme für die folgenden Begriffe: Kinderspielplatz, Bibliothek, Kino und Supermarkt.
    Setzen Sie die Piktogramme anschließend mit einem Illustrationsprogramm um.

Literaturhinweise

Aicher, Otl; Krampen, Martin: Zeichensysteme der visuellen Kommunikation, Neuausgabe, Stuttgart 1996 (Ernst & Sohn Verlag)

Berlin, Katja; Grünlich, Peter: Was wir tun, wenn der Aufzug nicht kommt, 4. Auflage, München 2012 (Wilhelm Heyne Verlag)

Böhringer, Joachim; Bühler, Peter; Schlaich, Patrick: Kompendium der Mediengestaltung für Digital- und Printmedien, 5. Auflage, Berlin 2011 (Springer Verlag)

Erco: Lichtbericht, Lüdenscheid 1977 (Selbstverlag)

Doelker, Christian: Ein Bild ist mehr als ein Bild, Visuelle Kompetenz in der Multimedia-Gesellschaft, Stuttgart 2002 (Verlag Klett-Cotta)

Grandt, Anke: Visualisierte Kommunikation, Haan-Gruiten 2012 (Verlag Europa-Lehrmittel)

Holder, Eberhard: Design – Darstellungstechniken, Augsburg 1994 (Augustus Verlag)

Klein, Klaus: Grundlagen der Gestaltung, 4. Auflage, Bad Homburg vor der Höhe 1997 (Verlag Gehlen)

Krisztian, Gregor; Schlempp-Ülker, Nesrin: Ideen visualisieren, 6. Auflage, Mainz 2011 (Verlag Hermann Schmidt)

Lidwell, William; Holden, Kritina; Butler, Jill: Design. Die 100 Prinzipien für erfolgreiche Gestaltung, München 2004 (Stiebner Verlag)

Lewandowsky, Pina; Zeischegg, Francis: Visuelles Gestalten mit dem Computer, 5. Auflage, Reinbek bei Hamburg 2002 (Rowohlt Verlag)

Paasch, Ulrich: Farbe in Druck und Medien, Itzehoe 2001 (Verlag Beruf und Schule)

Paasch, Ulrich; Moritz, Christian; Ottersbach, Jochem; Kieslinger, Klemens; Mörsberger, Annette: Informationen verbreiten, 5. Auflage, Itzehoe 2010 (Verlag Beruf und Schule)

Prenzel, Rudolph: Bauzeichnung und Darstellungstechnik, 3. Auflage, Stuttgart 1994 (Krämer Verlag)

Radtke, Susanne; Pisani, Patricia; Wolters, Walburga: Handbuch Visuelle Mediengestaltung, 3. Auflage, Berlin 2006 (Cornelsen Verlag)

Rathgeb, Markus: Otl Aicher, Berlin 2006 (Phaidon Verlag)

Siegle, Michael: Logo. Grundlagen der visuellen Zeichengestaltung, 4. Auflage, Itzehoe 2005 (Verlag Beruf und Schule)

Turtschi, Ralf: Mediendesign, 2. Auflage, Zürich 2000 (Verlag Niggli)

Turtschi, Ralf: Praktische Typografie, 5. Auflage, Zürich 2003 (Verlag Niggli)

Wäger, Markus: Grafik und Gestaltung, Bonn 2010 (Verlag Galileo Press)

8 Bewegtbild

Webcode: **B0800**

Für weitere Infos zu diesem Kapitel mit dem Smartphone einfach QR-Code scannen oder auf www.medien-verstehen.de den Webcode eingeben.

In diesem Kapitel geht es um das bewegte reelle Bild. Angefangen beim dynamischen Wechsel von Gesamtbild zu Gesamtbild (Überblendungen) bis hin zur Gestaltung von kompletten Filmsequenzen (Videos) werden die notwendigen Elemente und Techniken beschrieben, die der Gestalter für seine Arbeit kennen sollte.

Schon das Flimmern der ersten Stummfilme löste bei den Zuschauern eine enorme Faszination für die „bewegten Bilder" aus. Heutzutage ist das bewegte Bild ein selbstverständliches Element in vielen Medien, mit denen wir täglich konfrontiert werden. Zum Einen sind es die dynamischen Bildwechsel, die heute möglich sind, und zum Anderen die realitätsnahe Simulation von kontinuierlichen Bewegungsabläufen einzelner Objekte, die den bewegten Bildern quasi Leben einhauchen können.

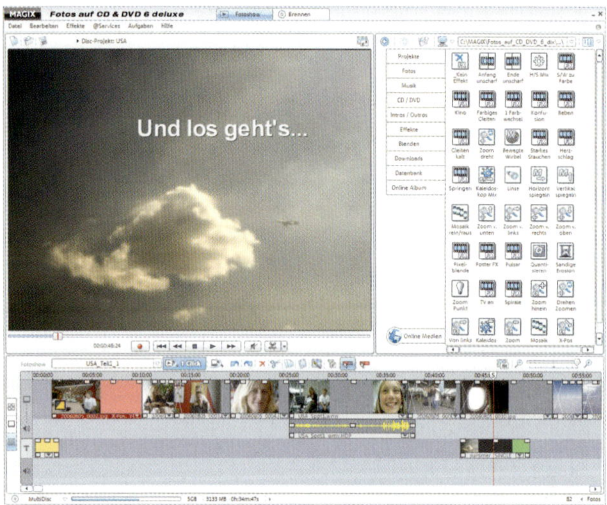

❶ Dynamische Bildwechsel durch Überblenden von Einzelbildern oder Einblenden von Titeln. Beispiel: Diashow-Programm Magix Fotos auf CD & DVD 6.

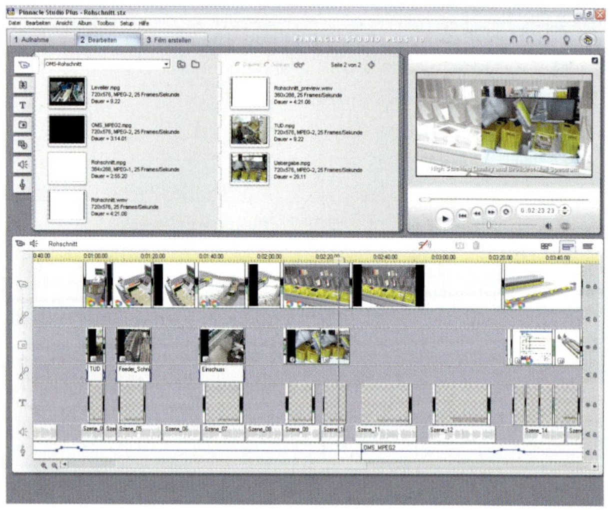

❷ Gestalten von Videosequenzen mit einem digitalen Schnittsystem. Beispiel: Pinnacle Studio 10 Plus.

Dynamische Bildwechsel entstehen zum Beispiel bei Diashows ❶ durch gegenseitiges Auf- und Abblenden der Einzelbilder, beim Überblenden von Filmszene zu Filmszene bei einer Film- bzw. Videoproduktion oder bei einer Multimedia-Anwendung beim Wechsel von einem Bildschirminhalt zum nächsten Bildschirminhalt. Man spricht dabei von einer visuellen Blende.

Bei dynamisch bewegten Bildern hingegen wird die sich kontinuierlich verändernde Bewegung von Objekten mit dem schnellen Ablauf einzelner Bilder einer Bewegungsphase simuliert. So entsteht Bewegung in den Bewegtbildmedien, wie der Animation, dem klassischen Film oder in der Videotechnik ❷.

8.1 Dynamische Bildwechsel

8.1.1 Visuelle Blende

Wie kann ein statisches Bild in Bewegung gesetzt und zu einem dynamischen Bild werden?

Durch Mischen von statischen Bildern erreicht man auf einfache Weise neue Bildkompositionen, die ohne echte Bewegungsabläufe beeindruckende Bildeffekte hervorrufen können. Diese sogenannten Blenden erleben wir alle tagtäglich in den Medien, wie Film, Video oder Fernsehen. Angefangen bei einfachen Bildüberblendungen mit zwei Diaprojektoren bis hin zu komplexen digitalen Überblendungen bei Multimedia -Anwendungen, erreicht man mit visuellen Blenden einen zeitlich gedehnten Übergang von einer Bildkomposition zur nächsten Bildkomposition.

❶

❷

❸

❹

❺

❻

❼

❽

Beispiel von Überblendeffekten:
❶ Ausgangsbild
❷ Endbild
❸ Einfache Wischblende
❹ Irisblende
❺ Runde Irisblende
❻ Schachbrettblende
❼ Jalousieblende
❽ Kreuzblende

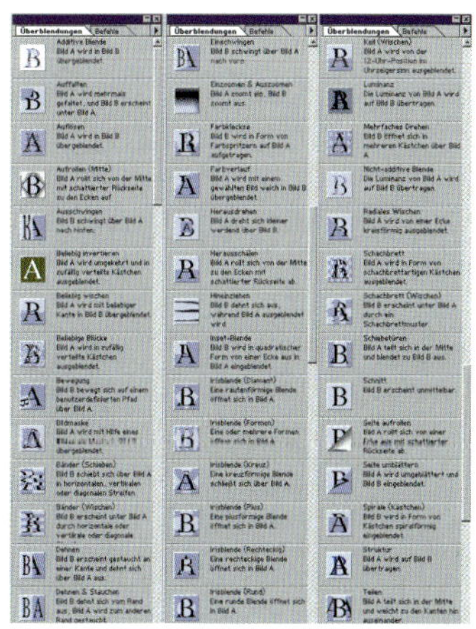

Moderne Schneidesoftware, z. B. Adobe Premiere, verfügt über eine Vielzahl von Überblendeffekten.

❶ Klappblende
❷ Würfelblende
❸ Weiche Überblendung
❹ Blätterblende

❶ ❷ ❸ ❹

Die Frage ist nur, welche Blende nimmt man für welchen Zweck?

Entscheidend für die Beantwortung der Frage ist die angestrebte dramaturgische Wirkung beim Betrachter, die die Wahl der Effekte bestimmt.

8.1.2 Auf- und Abblenden

Mit diesem dramaturgischem Mittel lassen sich Themen optisch gut voneinander trennen. Dabei kann auf jede beliebige Farbe geblendet werden. Mit Schwarzblenden erreicht man Themenabgrenzungen. Dabei wird die vorherige Bildkomposition komplett auf Schwarz geblendet und erst danach die nächste Bildkomposition möglichst mit dem umgekehrten Effekt wieder eingeblendet.

Beispiel: Schwarzblende

8.1.3 Einblendungen

Um in ein bestehendes Bild weitere Bild-, Text- oder Grafikelemente zu integrieren, benutzt man sogenannte **Einblendungen**. Bei Titeleinblendungen wird eine Schrift zusätzlich in ein Gesamtbild eingeblendet. Die Lesbarkeit der Schriftinformation wird dabei sehr stark von den verwendeten Farben und der Kontraste beeinflusst.

Durch Einblendungen von ganzen Bildteilen, die aus Realbild oder Grafik bestehen, können ganz neue Bildkompositionen erzielt werden. Diese Technik erlaubt das Gestalten ganzer Bildcollagen.

Bei allen Blenden fällt der Blendcharakteristik ❶ eine besondere Bedeutung zu.

❶ Je nach Geschwindigkeit des Ein-, Aus- bzw. Überblendens einzelner Bildelemente kann die Dramaturgie und die gewünschte Bildwirkung sehr stark variieren. Bei Überblendungen kann die Blendgeschwindigkeit und die resultierende Lichtintensität synchron erfolgen, das heißt beide Bilder ergeben zum gleichen Zeitpunkt immer die Lichtintensität von 100 %, oder asynchron erfolgen, dass heißt, die gesamte Bildhelligkeit schwankt.

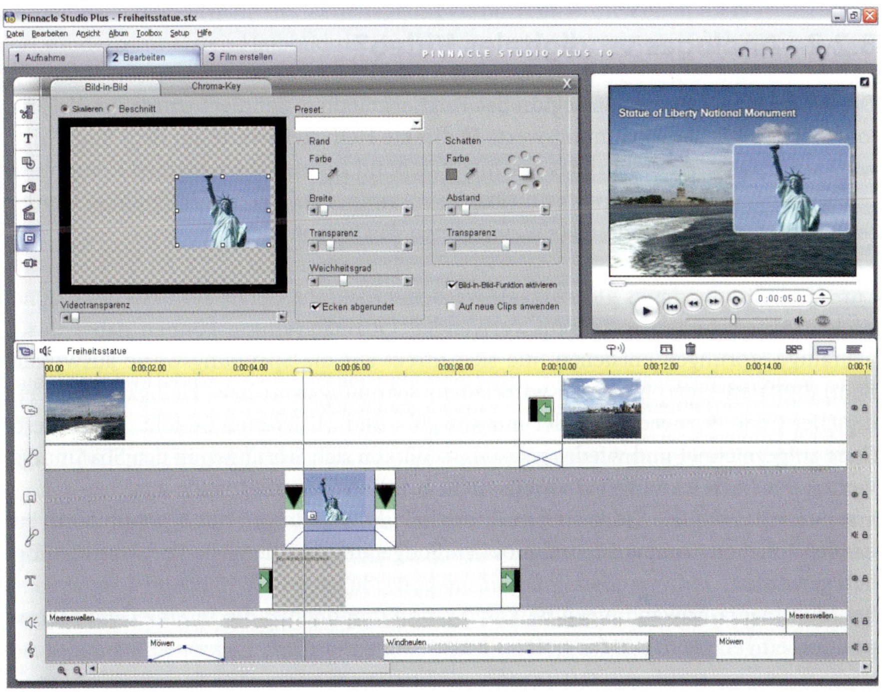

Beispiel einer „Bild in Bild"-Komposition. Realisiert mit der Videoschnitt-Software Pinnacle Studio Plus.

Das Prinzip der elektronischen Bildübertragung auf Basis der analogen Video- bzw. Fernsehtechnik funktioniert folgendermaßen: Als Aufnahmeeinheit dient eine Videokamera mit elektronischem Chip oder die Videokamera mit Aufnahmeröhre. Über die Ablenkschaltung wird eine zeilenweise Bildabtastung auf der Sender-Seite vorgenommen. Der Sender verknüpft das Bildsignal mit den Bild- und Zeileninformationen zu einem Videosignal und überträgt es zum Empfänger, der diese Informationen wieder in ein Bildsignal und die Synchronsignale für die Ablenkschaltung trennt. In der Bildröhre wird aus diesen Signalen zeilenweise das Bild aufgebaut.

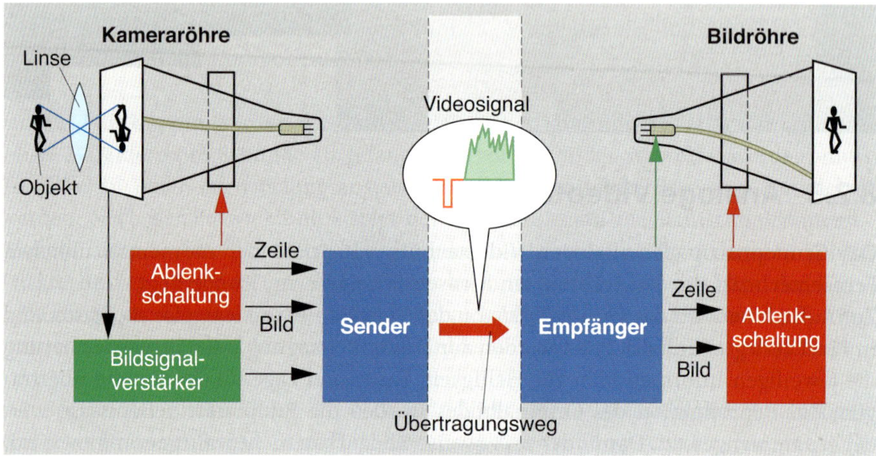

Prinzip der elektronischen Bildübertragung bei der analogen Videotechnik.

Analoge Video-Formate

Für die Speicherung der Helligkeitsinformation (Luminanz; Y) und Farbinformation (Chrominanz; C) bei analogen Videosignalen wurden verschiedene Prinzipien entwickelt:

Composite-Video	FBAS (Farb-Bild-Austast-Synchronsignal)	Farb- und Helligkeitsinformationen werden in einem Signal geführt
Component-Video	S-Video oder Y/C-Video	Getrennte Übertragung der Farb- und Helligkeitsinformationen
Component-Video	YUV-Video	Getrennte Übertragung des Farbtons, der Farbsättigung und der Helligkeitsinformation
(Computertechnik)	RGB-Video (Rot, Grün, Blau)	Große Bandbreite notwendig, deshalb nicht als Video-Aufzeichnungsprinzip praktikabel

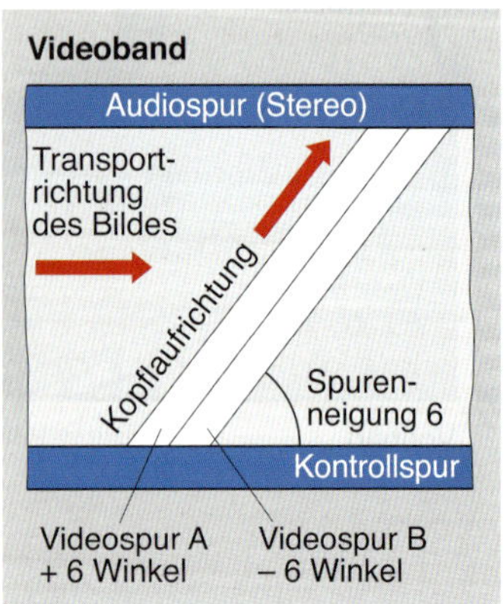

❶ Aufzeichnung von analogem Video nach dem VHS-Videoband-Format.

Die Speicherung analoger Videosignale erfolgt üblicherweise auf Magnetband. Im Laufe der Zeit haben sich mehrere Formate etabliert:

- **VHS** ❶, ein im Heimbereich, insbesondere im Austausch und Verkauf von Spielfilmen, weit verbreitetes Format. Es arbeitet mit dem FBAS-Signal. Als VHS-C in kleinerer Kassettenform auch im Camcorder-Bereich eingesetzt.
- **Video-8**, ähnlich dem VHS-Format, aber mit kleineren Kassetten
- **S-VHS**, die Weiterentwicklung von VHS, arbeitet mit dem Y/C-Video
- **Hi-8** arbeitet mit dem Y/C-Video und wird semiprofessionell eingesetzt.
- Betacam und **Betacam SP** kommen im professionellen Bereich zum Einsatz. Sie verwenden das hochwertige YUV-Videosignal.

Für das bildgenaue Bearbeiten der auf Magnetband gespeicherten analogen Videosignale muss jedes Bild mit einer Adresse – dem Timecode ❶ – versehen werden. Damit wird jedem Bild eine eindeutige Position zugewiesen und andere Audio- und Videoelemente können damit synchronisiert werden.

❶ Der verbreitetste Timecode ist der SMPTE-Timecode der Society of Motion Picture and Television Engineers.

Fernseh-Standards

Für die analoge Video- und Fernsehtechnik haben sich weltweit mehrere Standards bzw. Normen durchgesetzt:

- **PAL** (Phase Alternation Line), ein in Deutschland und anderen Europäischen Ländern verwendeter Standard mit einer Bildwiederholfrequenz von 50 Halbbildern pro Sekunde und 625 Zeilen, davon 576 sichtbare Zeilen. Die Auflösung beträgt 768 Bildpunkte × 576 Zeilen. Die Erweiterung PAL-Plus bietet zusätzlich das 16:9-Breitbildformat bei voller Kompatibilität zum PAL-Format.
- **NTSC** (National Television Systems Commitee), ein in der USA eingeführter Fernseh-Standard mit 60 Halbbildern pro Sekunde und 525 Zeilen, davon 480 sichtbare Zeilen. Die Auflösung beträgt 640 Bildpunkt × 480 Zeilen. Gegenüber dem PAL keine zuverlässige Farbübertragung.
- **SECAM** (Sequentiel Couleur à Mémoire), ein in Frankreich und Osteuropa verwendeter Fernseh-Standard. Unterscheidet sich gegenüber des PAL in seiner Farbübertragung.

Ein weiterer Standard mit höherer Auflösung ist **HDTV** (High Definition Television) und bedeutet soviel wie „Fernsehen mit hoher Auflösung". HDTV arbeitet mit einer deutlich höheren Bildauflösung von bis zu 1920 × 1080 Pixeln (2,1 Megapixel) bei einem Seitenverhältnis von 16:9. HDTV gibt es in der Ausprägung „1080i" mit der vollen Bildauflösung und in einer geringeren Auflösung „720p" von nur 1280 × 720 Pixeln (0,9 Megapixel). Die Unterschiede zwischen PAL und HDTV liegt nicht nur in der Bildqualität, sondern auch in der Übertragungstechnik. Beim HDTV-Format gibt es zwei Standards: 1080i und 720p. Die HDTV-Version „1080i" baut das Bild ebenfalls im Halbbildverfahren auf und erreicht die volle Bildauflösung von 1920 × 1080 Pixeln. Dagegen erzeugt 720p die Fernsehbilder im sogenannten Vollbildverfahren (progressive) mit einer etwas geringeren Auflösung von nur 1280 × 720 Pixeln (0,9 Megapixel). Hier wird jede Zeile sequentiell beschrieben.

	PAL	720p	1080i
Auflösung	576 × 768	720 × 1.280	1.080 × 1.920
Bildpunkte gesamt	442.368	921.600	2.073.600
Bildpunkte pro Sek.	11.059.200	46.080.000	51.840.000
Bilddarstellung	Halbbild (interlaced)	Vollbild (progressive)	Halbbild (interlaced)
Frequenz	50 Hz	50 Hz	50 Hz
Format	4:3	16:9	16:9

Vergleich Fernseh-Standard PAL mit HDTV

Als Gütesiegel für Geräte, die HDTV in ganzer Qualität darstellen kann, wird das Logo „HD ready" verwendet. Die werbeträchtigen Slogans „HD-fähig" oder „HDTV-kompatibel" definieren generell nur die Kompatibilität zum Empfang des HD-Signals, können dieses aber nicht in der vollen Qualität darstellen.

HD ready

8.2.4 Digitale Videotechnik

Analog-digital-Wandlung

Das Prinzip der Analog-digital-Wandlung:

1. Die Ausgangsbasis ist ein analoges Signal.
2. In festen Zeitabständen wird das analoge Signal abgetastet (Sampling).
3. Die abgetasteten Amplitudenwerte werden digitalen Werten zugeordnet (Quantisierung)
4. Die digitalen Abtastwerte werden binär kodiert.

Jedes aufzunehmende Bild muss mit einem A/D-Wandler (Analog-digital-Wandler) digitalisiert werden. Dies geschieht entweder direkt im Aufnahmegerät (Digitalkamera) oder mit einer speziellen Digitalisierungskarte (Video Capture Card) im Computer.

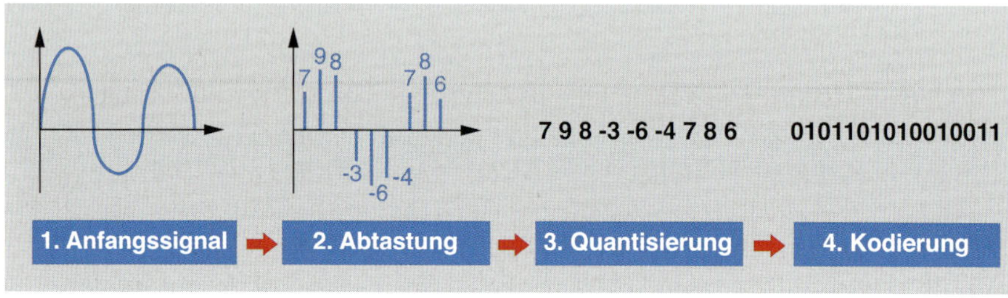

Das Endprodukt sind digitale Videodateien, gespeichert auf der Festplatte des Computers. Sollen die Dateien wieder auf analoge Bänder zurückgespielt werden, ist dafür eine D/A-Wandlung notwendig. Ein maßgebliches Kriterium für den weiteren Gestaltungsprozess ist die Videoqualität nach dem Digitalisierungsprozess.

❶ Video in Broadcast-Qualität dient primär als analoges Ausgangsmaterial für die Digitalisierung.

❷ Die digitalisierten Datenmengen müssen oft begrenzt werden. Über eine eingeschränkte Farbpalette (die Bildpixel des Videos können nur eine begrenzte Anzahl von Farben annehmen) kann eine Datenreduzierung vorgenommen werden.

❸ Eine starke Reduzierung der Auflösung des Videos und eine nachträgliche Vergrößerung des Bildes hat immer Informationsverluste zur Folge.

❶ Video-Quelle

❷ Reduzierte Farbpalette

❸ Reduzierte Auflösung

Die Qualität des digitalisierten Videos hängt zum einen von der Hard- und Software der Digitalisierungsausrüstung ab, und zum anderen von dem gewünschten späteren Einsatzumfeld des Videofilms. Das Einsatzumfeld ist die Hard- und Softwareausrüstung der Zielgruppe zum Abspielen des Videofilmes. Diese Ausrüstung erfordert oft eine bewusste Reduzierung der Video-Datenmenge mit einer Begrenzung der Pixelauflösung, einer Begrenzung der Farbauflösung (Farbtiefe) und einer Begrenzung der Bilder pro Sekunde.

Digitale Video-Formate

Für die Bandaufzeichnung kommen folgende Formate zum Einsatz:

- **ITU 601**, ein Komponenten-Video-Format, das durch Digitalisierung analoger Videoformate in der Komponenten-Repräsentation entsteht. Das Abtastratenverhältnis Y:U:V von Luminanz (Y) und zwei Grundfarben (U, V) ist 4:2:2 bei einer Grundabtastrate von 3,374 MHz und einer Auflösung von 720 × 568 Pixel.
- **D1, D2, D3** sind Videoformate im Komponenten-Format von 4:2:2 für den professionellen Bereich mit sehr hohen Datenströmen bis zu 27 Mbyte/s.
- **Digital-Betacam**, ein Komponenten-Video-Format mit 4 digitalen Tonspuren
- **Mini-DV** ❶ im YUV-Format 4:2:0. Ton wird mit 44,1 KHz/16 Bit oder 32 KHz/12 Bit aufgezeichnet. Die Gesamtdatenrate beträgt 41 Mbit/s. Mini-DV wird bei digitalen Camcordern verwendet.
- **DV** ist aufgebaut wie das Mini-DV-Format, verwendet jedoch größere Kassetten. Es verwendet zwei Tonspuren mit 48 KHz/16 Bit oder vier mit 32 KHz/12 Bit.
- **DVCAM** und **DVCPro**, sind professionelle Varianten des DV, nur mit vergrößerter Spurbreite.
- **Digital 8**, verwendet das Mini-DV-Format mit der Kassette des analogen Hi8.

❶ Beim **Mini-DV-Format** wird das RGB-Signal (Rot, Grün, Blau) in ein YUV-Signal (Signal mit getrennter Übertragung des Farbtons, der Farbsättigung und der Helligkeit) umgewandelt, digitalisiert und komprimiert. Zum Einsatz kommen dabei spezielle Mini-DV-Kassetten.

Für die Verwendung am Computer bzw. für die Verbreitung in Datennetzen kommen folgende Formate zum Einsatz:

- **CIF**, das Common Intermediate Format. Ein digitaler Standard für Videokonferenzsysteme mit einem Abtastratenverhältnis von 4:1:1 bei einer Auflösung von 352 × 288 Pixel.
- **QCIF**, das Quarter Common Intermediate Format. Entspricht dem CIF, jedoch mit einer Auflösung von 180 × 144 Pixeln.
- **H.261**, ist der Standard für die Bewegtbildkomponente bei audiovisuellen Diensten, z. B. der Videotelefonie. Es arbeitet mit einem YUV-Signal nach dem QCIF bzw. CIF. Die Bildrate liegt zwischen 10 und 30 Bildern/s.
- **MJPEG**, das Motion-JPEG-Format. Es beruht auf dem Einzelbild-Kompressionsstandard JPEG. Durch die Intraframe-Technik wird jedes Bild einzeln komprimiert.
- **MPEG-1**, das Format der Moving Pictures Expert Group. Ein Videostandard, der Interframe- und DCT-Technologie (Discrete Cosinus Transformation) benutzt. MPEG-1 erreicht eine Datenrate von 1 Mbit/s (VHS-Qualität) bei einer Auflösung von 352 × 266 Pixeln.
- **MPEG-2** hat Datenraten zwischen 2 und 60 Mbit/s (Fernsehqualität), wird als Videoformat für DVDs (720 × 576 Pixel) verwendet und ist in der Auflösung variabel bis zu 1920 × 1080 Pixel.
- **MPEG-4** ist für die Übertragung in Datennetzen gedacht und ermöglicht eine hohe Komprimierung. MPEG-4, auch als AVC oder H.264 bekannt, kommt u. a. bei HDTV, bei DVB-S2, bei Apples iTunes und bei Adobe Flash ab Version 10 um Einsatz.
- **WMV** steht für „Windows Media Video" und umfasst mehrere Audio- und Video-Codecs für verschiedene Anwendungszwecke (u. a. Streaming, Screencapturing, HD, 5.1 Audio und ein DRM (Digital Rights Managment) System.

- **AVI** steht für „Audio Video Inter leaved" und ist ein Video-Dateiformat für Windows. Die Dateiendung *.AVI sagt dabei noch nichts über die Kompressionsmethode des Videos aus, sondern ist als „Container-Format" zu verstehen, welches verschiedene Codecs beinhalten kann. Sehr verbreitete Codecs sind der „Cinepac", der „Indeo",„Microsoft 1", **„DivX"** und **„Xvid"**.
- **MOV**, das Quicktime-Format ist eine universelles Format für Multimedia-Daten und ist als „Container-Format" in der Qualität und im Abspielverhalten vom verwendeten Codec abhängig.
- Real Media Video ist ein Videoformat für Streaming Video über das Internet.
- Sorenson, ein Video-Codec der Firma Sorenson Media, der in frühen Apple Quicktime (Version 4) und Adobe Flash (Version 6) verwendet wurde.
- VP6, ein propietärer Video-Codec von On2 Trumotion, der als Standard-Videoformat in Adobe Flash (ab Version 8) u. a. auch für das Flash-Video-Containerformat **FLV** verwendet wird.
- VP7, als Nachfolger von VP6, findet u. a. Einsatz bei der IP-Telefonie, insbesondere bei Skype.
- **AVCHD** (Advanced Video Codec High Definition), wird als Aufzeichnungsformat für digitale Datenträger (z. B. SD-Karten, Memory Sticks, Festplatten) bei Camcordern verwendet. Als Codec kommt der H.264 bzw. MPEG-4 zum Einsatz.

Für die Video-Containerformate sind die verschiedensten Codecs verfügbar. Zum Erreichen von sehr hohen Komprimierungsverhältnissen bei guter Bildqualität werden neben den standardisierten Formaten auch Codecs verwendet, die nicht standardisiert und ständig weiterentwickelt werden. Typischerweise definiert ein Containerformat nur die Art und Struktur, wie der Inhalt aufzubewahren ist. Container ermöglichen so zum Beispiel das synchrone Wiedergeben von Audio- und Videospuren. Der verbreitete AVI-Container kann beispielsweise eine mit dem XviD-Codec erstellte MPEG-4-Videospur und eine mit LAME erstellte MP3-Audiospur enthalten. Einige Containerformate können darüber hinaus weitere Daten wie Untertitel, Menüstrukturen oder zusätzliche Audiospuren enthalten. Das Zusammenführen der Audio- und Videospuren in einen Video-Container übernimmt ein Multiplexer. Beim Abspielen werden die Spuren entsprechend durch einen Demultiplexer bzw. Splitter wieder getrennt, um dann vom Codec dekodiert werden zu können.

➲ **Wenn Dateien anderen Anwendern zugänglich gemacht werden sollen, muss darauf geachtet werden, dass nicht jeder Codec auf allen PCs installiert ist. Der richtige Codec ist aber zwingende Voraussetzung für das Abspielen des damit verpackten Videos. Im Zweifelsfall lieber die etwas ältere Version eines Codecs bei der Komprimierung der Video- oder Audio-Dateien verwenden.**

❶ **Firewire**, auch als **IEEE 1394-Schnittstelle** bezeichnet, ist ein plattformübergreifendes Protokoll für Hochgeschwindigkeitsübertragungen.

Zur Übertragung der auf Band aufgezeichneten Daten von der Kamera zum digitalen Schnittsystem hat sich die **Firewire-Schnittstelle** ❶ durchgesetzt.
Im Konsumer-Bereich setzen sich mittlerweile immer mehr Videokamera durch, die nicht mehr auf Band aufzeichnen, sondern direkt auf eine Speicherkarte oder eine DVD schreiben. Diese Datenträger können dann direkt am PC gelesen werden und benötigen somit keine serielle Übertragung per Kabel.

Videokompression

Setzt man beispielsweise eine normale CD-ROM als Datenträger für den digitalen Videofilm ein, so stünden bei Broadcast-Qualität ❶ ohne spezielle Datenkompression nur 20 Sekunden Spielzeit zur Verfügung. Aber auch die Datengeschwindigkeit zwischen den Computerkomponenten würde für diese enormen Datenmengen, die pro Sekunde auftreten, nicht ausreichen.

❶ Unter **Broadcast-Qualität** versteht man sendefähiges Videomaterial mit 25 Bildern pro Sekunde und einer Datenmenge von ungefähr 1 MB pro Einzelbild.

Damit Video auf handelsüblichen Personalcomputern abgespielt werden kann, muss der Videofilm auf eine praktikable Größe komprimiert werden. Ziel ist dabei immer: möglichst hohe visuelle Qualität bei gleichzeitiger Sicherstellung, dass die zur Verfügung stehende Abspielhardware nicht überlastet wird.

Die am weitesten verbreiteten Kompressionsverfahren für die Hardware-unabhängige Wiedergabe digitaler Videofilme sind Microsoft's Video für Windows und das Windows Media Video, Apple's QuickTime, Adobe Flash oder das MPEG-Verfahren in verschiedenen Varianten. Diese Verfahren arbeiten in Bezug auf Kompressions- und Dekompressionsverhältnis asynchron, das heißt, obwohl für die Kompression eine hohe Prozessorleistung benötigt wird, kommt man auf der Wiedergabeseite mit relativ geringer Leistung für die Dekompression aus. In den meisten Fällen kann eine solche Kompression bis zu 95% der analogen Originaldaten eines Videos entfernen, ohne die visuelle Bildqualität stark einzuschränken.

Dazu werden komplexe mathematische Algorithmen benutzt, die das Video hinsichtlich redundanter Informationsinhalte untersucht und diese dann ausblendet. Diese sogenannte **Redundanzreduktion** ❷ nutzt statische Eigenschaften, wie die Beziehung zwischen zeitlich und räumlich benachbarter Bildpunkte, um möglichst eine kompakte Kodierung zu erreichen.

❷ Bei der **Redundanzreduktion** werden häufigere auftretende bzw. wahrscheinlichere Bildpunkte mit kürzeren Codewörtern beschrieben als selten vorkommende Bildpunkte. Dabei gehen keine Informationen verloren (verlustfreie Kodierung).

Zusätzlich berücksichtigt man, dass im gesamten Spektrum des Videosignals auch Informationen dabei sind, die für den menschlichen Betrachter wenig relevant sind und deshalb entfernt werden können. Mit dieser sogenannten **Irrelevanzreduktion** ❸ erreicht man eine hohe Kompression mit vertretbaren Störungen.

❸ Bei der **Irrelevanzreduktion** wird die menschliche Wahrnehmung optimal ausgenutzt. Dabei gehen aber Informationen verloren (verlustbehaftete Kodierung).

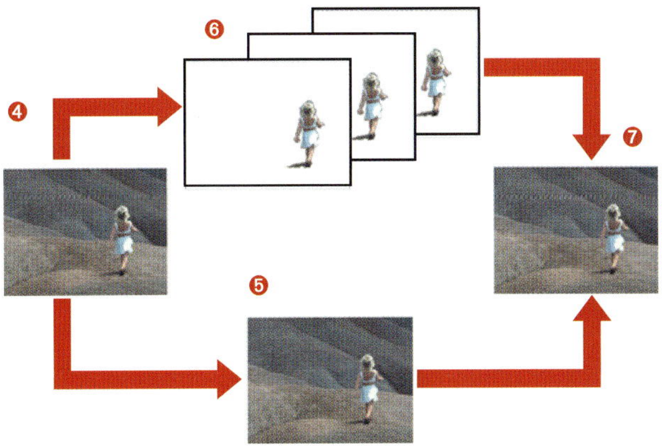

❹ Komplettes Video mit allen Daten jedes Einzelbildes.

❺ Gesamtbild (I-frame) – komplett mit statischen Daten. I-frames müssen nur wenige übertragen werden.

❻ B-frames und P-frames beinhalten nur die sich ändernden Bildinformationen, z. B. Bewegungen eines Objektes, in festgelegten Rasterblöcken.

❼ Das Ergebnis nach der Dekompression: I-frames, B-frames und P-frames wurden wieder zusammengeführt.

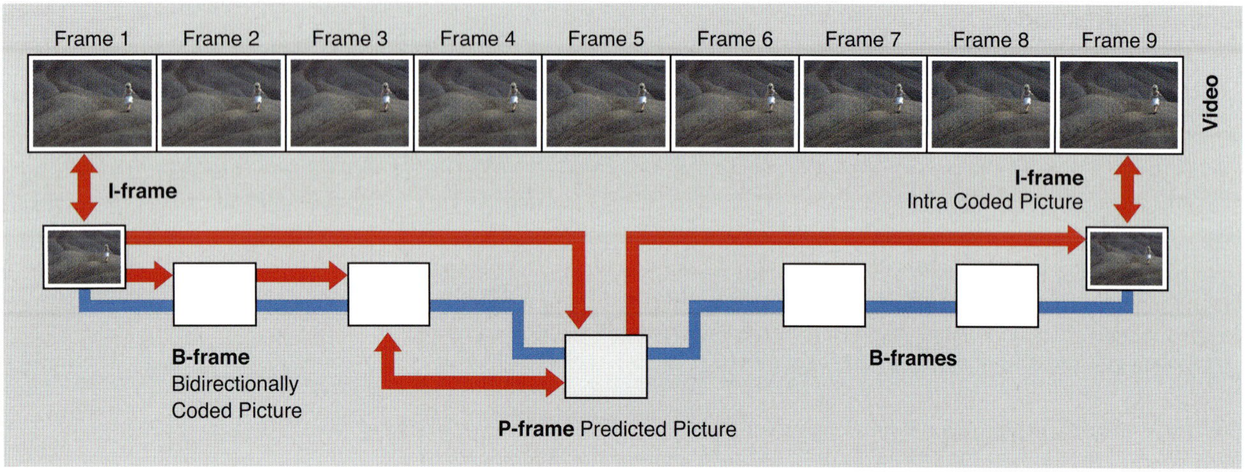

Prinzip des MPEG-Verfahrens.

Das **Grundprinzip** lässt sich am Beispiel des MPEG-Verfahrens erklären:
Aus den gesamten Videoeinzelbildern (Frames) werden wenige Bilder vollständig im JPEG-Verfahren als Intraframe-Bild (I-frame) komprimiert. Zwischen den I-frames nehmen spezielle Zwischenbilder (P-frames) die Bildinformationen auf, die sich von einem I-frame zum nächsten I-frame ändern. Zusätzliche Zwischenbilder (B-frames), die immer die Bildinformationen beinhalten, die sich von Frame zu Frame ändern, komplettieren den Datenstrom. Zum Erzeugen der Zwischenbilder wird jedes Bild in festgelegte Rasterblöcke unterteilt. Dabei wird vorausberechnet, ob und wie sich der Bildinhalt jedes Blocks über die Zeit verändert. Die Daten der sich nicht verändernden Blöcke werden von Bild zu Bild nicht gespeichert, sondern nur die Daten der Blöcke, die sich von Bild zu Bild unterscheiden, werden neu kodiert und gespeichert.

Die MPEG (Moving Picture Experts Group) hat diverse Komprimierungsformate zu einem ISO-Standard geführt. Dazu zählen u. a. MPEG-2, das Videoformat bei Standard Video-DVDs und **MP3** (MPEG-1 Layer 3), welches sich als dominierendes Verfahren zur Speicherung von Musik auf Computern und im Internet verbreitet hat.

Beim Gestalten von digitalen Videosequenzen, die komprimiert werden sollen, muss darauf geachtet werden, dass möglichst nicht die gesamte Bildfläche verändert wird, sondern nur begrenzte Bildteile. Sonst werden die durch die Kompression erzeugten B-frames und P-frames zu groß. Dies trifft insbesondere bei Schwenks und Zooms zu. Da die Kompressionsalgorithmen üblicherweise auf eine konstante Datentransferrate eingestellt sind, kompensieren die Systeme eine solche Erhöhung der Datenmenge durch eine Reduktion in der Pixelauflösung, die sich jedoch negativ auf die Bildqualität auswirkt.

8.3 Filmgestaltung

In der **Filmgestaltung** gelten auch die Grundsätze der Bildgestaltung, wie Einstellungen und Perspektive (siehe Kapitel 6). Hinzu kommen noch mehrere Parameter, die sich erst beim bewegten Bild zeigen.

8.3.1 Bewegung

Bewegung kann durch den Wechsel des Betrachtungsstandpunktes erreicht werden. Verändert der Gestalter den Bildausschnitt, in dem er die Kameraposition oder die Brennweite der Kamera verändert, so kommt Bewegung ins Bild. Dies kann durch verschiedene Bewegungsarten realisiert werden.

Bewegung von Ort zu Ort

Die Bewegung in Bewegtbildmedien beruht hauptsächlich auf der Eigenbewegung ❶ der dargestellten Objekte oder der Bewegung des Betrachtungsstandpunktes ❷.

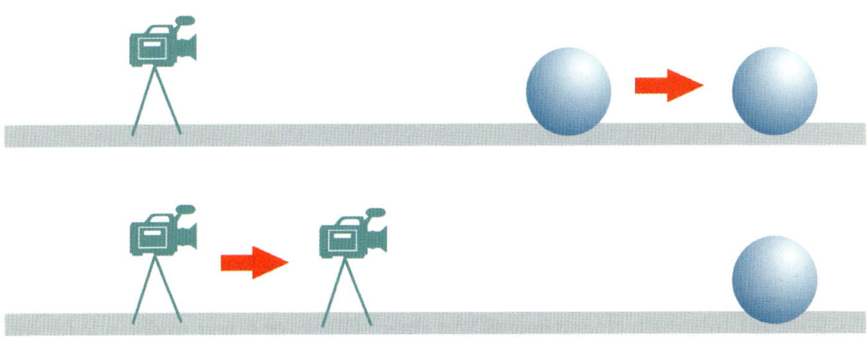

❶ Unter **Eigenbewegung** der Objekte versteht man das örtliche Verändern der dargestellten Objekte, sowie die Veränderung der Objekte in ihrer Gestalt.

❷ Bei der **Bewegung des Betrachtungsstandpunktes** wird dynamisch die Einstellgröße des Bildausschnittes verändert. Die klassische Kamerafahrt ist ein typisches Beispiel für diese Gestaltungsform.

8.3.3 Beleuchtung

Wie in der Bildgestaltung ist beim Gestalten einer Filmeinstellung das Aufnahmeobjekt, je nach gewünschter dramaturgischer Wirkung, richtig auszuleuchten. Dies ist nicht nur in lichtschwachen Innenräumen notwendig, sondern auch in freier Umgebung, bei der genügend Tages- oder Sonnenlicht vorhanden ist.

Bei Außenaufnahmen und strahlender Sonne ist der entstehende große Beleuchtungskontrast nicht immer erwünscht. Mit Aufhellschirmen, Aufhellspiegeln und Reflektoren können einzelne Bildbereiche bewusst aufgehellt werden.

Bei Dämmerung, Nachts oder in Mischlichtsituationen muss auch im Freien zusätzliches künstliches Licht eingesetzt werden.

In Innenräumen und in Filmstudios kommt die künstliche Beleuchtung im vollen Umfang zum Einsatz. Sie wird in folgende Arten eingeteilt:

- **Hauptlicht** ❶ leuchtet die Szene und all ihre Objekte fast ohne Schatten aus.
- **Führungslicht** ist ein starkes, auf das Objekt gerichtetes Licht.
- **Füll-Licht** als Aufhellung mindert Schatten und gleicht Kontraste durch eine weiche Ausleuchtung aus.
- **Gegenlicht** befindet sich hinter dem Objekt und schafft einen Lichtkranz um das Objekt. Es darf nicht in die Kamera fallen.
- **Hintergrundlicht** leuchtet nur den Hintergrund aus, unabhängig von der Hauptbeleuchtung.
- **Kamera-Licht** wird als kleine Lichtquelle auf die Kamera montiert, wirkt ähnlich einer „Grubenlampe".

❶ Je nach Anordnung und Intensität des Hauptlichtes erreicht man unterschiedliche Lichteffekte:

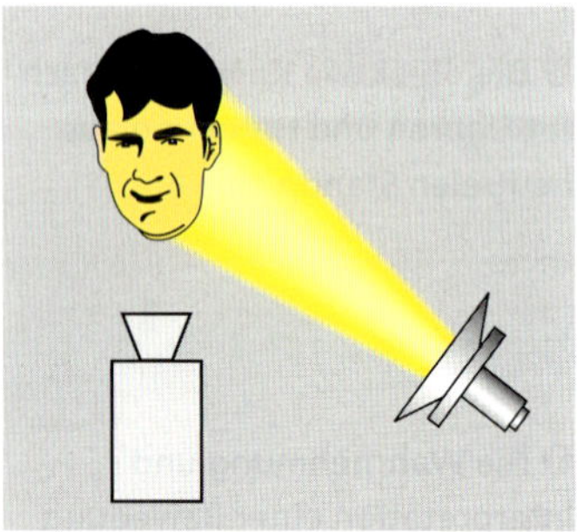

Voll-Licht

Schlank-Licht

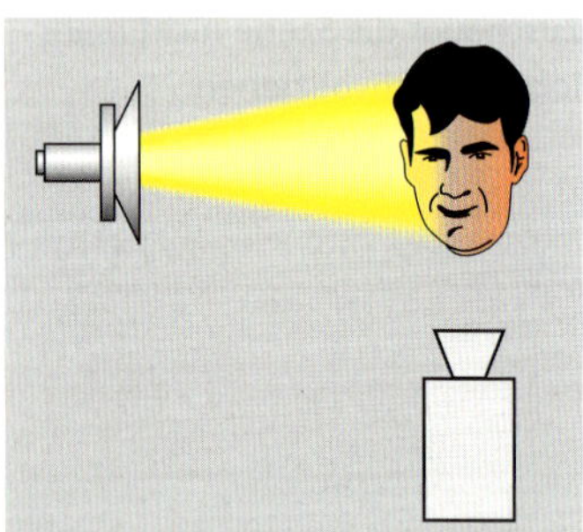

Teilungslicht

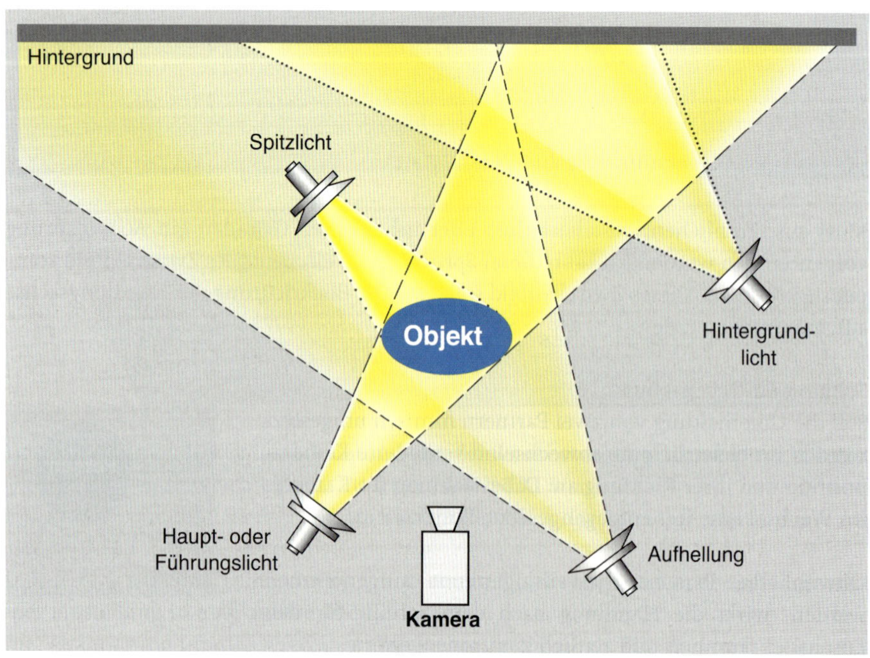

Prinzipielle Studiobeleuchtung mit Hauptlicht, Spitzlicht, Hintergrundbeleuchtung und einer Aufhellung.

8.3.4 Aufnahmetechniken

Die Gestaltungsmöglichkeiten während der Videoaufnahmen eröffnen zur Gestaltung des einzelnen Bildausschnittes auch zusätzliche Tricktechniken.

Dies kann sich zum Beispiel auf die Manipulation der Filmzeit beziehen. Filmzeit und Wirklichkeit stimmen innerhalb einer Einstellung im Allgemeinen überein. Es gibt jedoch immer wieder Situationen, in denen durch bewusste Veränderung dieser Über-einstimmung Handlungen und Objekte in einer ganz neuen Betrachtungsweise gesehen werden können.

Zeitlupe
Soll eine Zeitdehnung vorgenommen werden, kann der Gestalter die Zeitlupe (Slow Motion) einsetzen.
Dabei ist die Aufnahmefrequenz höher als die Wiedergabefrequenz. Bei der Wiedergabe mit normaler Bildfrequenz wird der Bewegungsablauf somit verlangsamt.

Die **Zeitlupe** ermöglicht eine Zeitdehnung von Momentaufnahmen bei Sportereignissen (Beispiel: Startprozess beim 100 m-Lauf).

Wie durch ein Vergrößerungsglas kann plötzlich mehr erkannt werden. Beispielsweise beim Start eines 100 m-Laufes zeigt Slow Motion den genauen Startprozess der Sprinter und lässt genaue zeitliche Einzelheiten erkennen. Wer zuerst vom Startblock losgekommen ist, bleibt somit kein Geheimnis mehr.

Zeitraffer
Soll dagegen die Aufnahmezeit komprimiert werden, so kommt der Zeitraffer (Quick Motion) zum Einsatz.
Beim Zeitraffer ist die Aufnahmefrequenz niedriger als die Wiedergabefrequenz. Somit werden Bewegungsvorgänge bei der Wiedergabe mit größerer Geschwindigkeit dargestellt.

Der **Zeitraffer** komprimiert alle Bewegungen eines langen Zeitraumes zu einer kurzen Szene (Beispiel: Sonnenaufgang).

Besonders interessante Effekte lassen sich mit Hilfe der Einzelbildschaltung erzielen. Dadurch besteht die Möglichkeit, zwischen die Belichtungen der Einzelbilder lange Wartepausen einzuschieben. Mit einer derartigen Aufnahmemethode lassen sich zum Beispiel Landschaften über einen Tagesablauf darstellen oder das Auffalten von Blüten und andere normalerweise nicht als Bewegung erkennbare Wachstumsvorgänge.

❶ Blue Box Technik bei Nachrichtensendungen.

Blue-Screen-Technik

Eine weitere sehr populäre Gestaltungstechnik bei der Videoaufnahme ist die sogenannte Blue-Screen-Technik oder auch **Blue Box** genannt. Ein Projektionsverfahren, mit dem es möglich ist, einzelne Objekte separat aufzunehmen und direkt im Aufnahmestudio vor einen beliebigen Hintergrund einzublenden. Diese Technik erlaubt zum Beispiel das Agieren eines Schauspielers vor einem fiktivem Hintergrund.
Ein bekanntes Beispiel ist der Flug des Drachens Fuchur bei der Verfilmung von Michael Endes ‚Die unendliche Geschichte'. Aufgenommen mit der Blue Box Technik lässt der Regisseur den Drachen mit dem Darsteller Bastian für den Zuschauer über weite Landschaften fliegen. Aber auch aus den täglichen Nachrichten ❶ ist die Blue Box Technik bekannt. Themenbezogene Bilder werden in den Hintergrund des Nachrichtensprechers eingeblendet und unterstreichen damit bildlich die Meldungen, ohne den Sprecher auszublenden. Ein anderes Beispiel ist Rüdiger Nehberg als Survival-Führer ❷ oder Peter Lustig bei der Multimedia-Anwendung ‚Löwenzahn' ❸, bei der er als Darsteller auf einem grafischen Hintergrund durch die interaktive CD-ROM führt.

❷ Rüdiger Nehberg, einkopiert in eine fiktive Survival-Landschaft (Rüdiger Nehberg - SURVIVAL).

❸ Peter Lustig agiert in voller Größe auf dem Screen (Löwenzahn - Terzio-Verlag)

Wie funktioniert nun die Blue-Screen-Technik? Möchte man zum Beispiel das Küken mit dem Ei in eine Wüste versetzen ohne es wirklich an diesen heißen Ort zu bringen, so wird einfach das Küken vor einer einfarbigen (am Besten einer blauen) Leinwand aufgenommen.

Alle Teile der Vollfarbe Blau werden auf elektronische Weise aus den Aufnahmen ausgeblendet. Das so freigestellte Objekt kann auf einem beliebigen Hintergrundfilm eingestanzt werden.

Um keine unschönen Nebeneffekte zu produzieren, muss darauf geachtet werden, dass das Vordergrundobjekt keine Stellen mit blauer Vollfarbe ❶ besitzt, sonst würden diese selbstverständlich auch entfernt. Alternativ zur Farbe blau können auch andere Vollfarben verwendet werden, die sich mit ausreichendem Kontrast vom Vordergrundobjekt abheben.

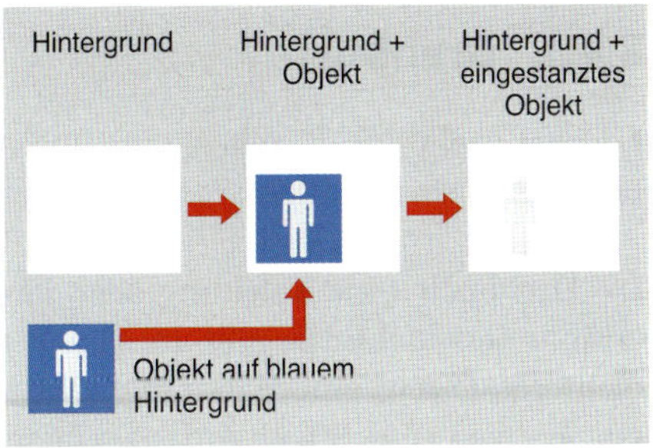

❶ Die Farbe Blau als Hintergrundfarbe war der Namensgeber für die Stanztechnik „Blue Screen" bzw. „Blue Box".

8.4 Video-Produktion

Das Produzieren von Videofilmen ist ein sehr umfangreicher Prozess. Er beginnt bei der Ideenfindung und geht bis hin zur Integration des Films in die Präsentationsumgebung.

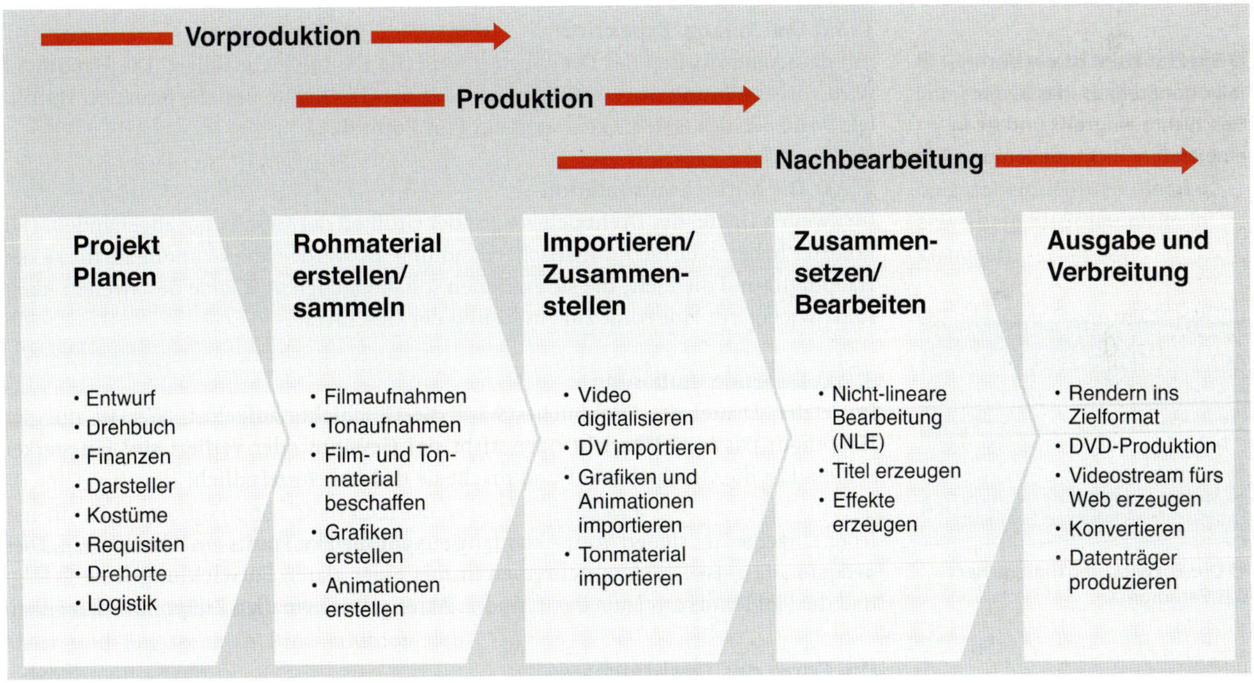

Prinzipielle Vorgehensweise bei einer Videoproduktion

Schon bei den ersten konzeptionellen Schritten sollte der Gestalter von Filmsequenzen bei seiner Arbeit in kontinuierlichen Zeitabläufen denken, in der Aneinanderreihung von Filmszenen.

➲ **Eine Szene gilt im Allgemeinen als kleinste Einheit einer Filmerzählung, die aus einer oder mehreren Einstellungen besteht, welche durch Ort oder Handlung miteinander verbunden sind.**

Die Gestaltung des einzelnen Bildausschnittes reicht für die Gestaltung eines Filmes noch lange nicht aus.

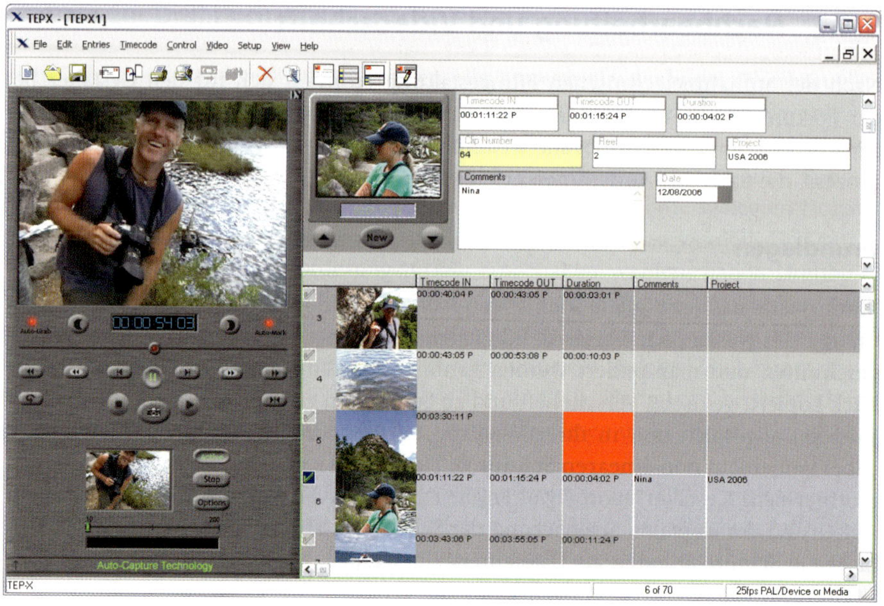

Logging-Programme helfen beim Sichten des Rohmaterials und sorgen für eine effiziente Verwaltung der Videoszenen für das Schnittsystem. Beispiel Imagine TEPX.

❶ Der **SMPTE-Timecode** ist ein von der Society of Motion Picture and Television Engineers eingeführter Standard im Fernseh-, Rundfunk- und Studiobereich, der Geräte unterschiedlicher Hersteller und beliebiger Video- und Audiotechniken miteinander synchronisiert.

Zur Definition der In- und Out-Punkte und generell für ein bildgenaues Verarbeiten wird der **SMPTE-Timecode** ❶ als Standard im professionellen Videoschnitt verwendet. Er stellt für jede Position im Videomaterial eine Art Adresse mit der Form Stunden:Minuten:Sekunden:Frames zur Verfügung.

Das Vorschaufenster zum Testen.

Aufbau der Schnittsystem-Oberflächen

Die Benutzeroberflächen der Schnittsysteme ähneln sich hinsichtlich des Aufbaus. Sie bestehen in der Regel aus den Fensterbereichen „Archiv", „Vorschaufenster" und „Zeitleiste". Im Archiv werden alle Video-Clips, dargestellt durch „Thumbnails" aufgelistet. Im Vorschaufenster kann der ausgewählte Clip oder die aktuelle Schnitt-Sequenz abgespielt werden. In der Zeitleiste erfolgt die eigentliche Schnittarbeit. Hier werden Clips und zusätzliche Medienelemente, wie Geräusche, Sprache und Titel, zeitlich angeordnet und aufeinander abgestimmt.

Im Archiv-Bereich werden die Clips mit Thumbnails übersichtlich dargestellt.

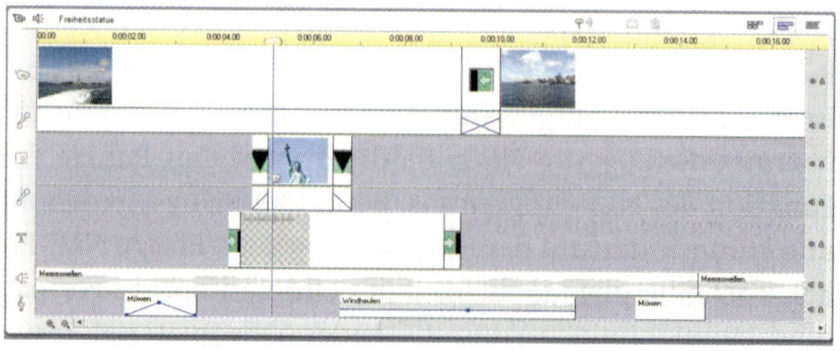

In der Zeitleiste erfolgt die „Schnittarbeit" mit den Medienelementen.

Die Zeitleiste ist die grafische Darstellung des Inhalts eines Films. Sie kann in unterschiedlichen Maßstäben dargestellt werden. Damit ist eine übersichtliche Darstellung vieler Sequenzen, wie auch eine detaillierte Sicht in kurzen Zeitabschnitten zum präzisen Anlegen der Clips und Effekte möglich. Die meisten NLE-Programme bieten verschiede Zeitleistendarstellungen an.

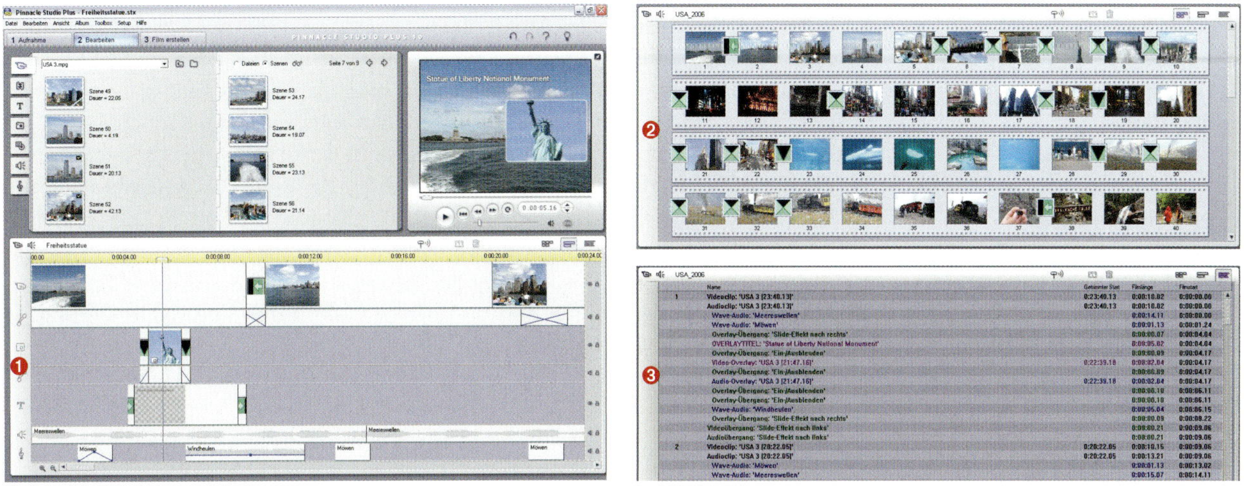

Verschiedene Zeitleistendarstellungen: Die proportionale „**Timeline-Darstellung**" ❶ und die „**Storyboard-Ansicht**" ❷ sind die maßgebenden Schnitt-Umgebungen. Einige Programme bieten auch weitere Darstellungen, wie „**Listen-Ansicht** ❸ (Beispiel Pinnacle Studio 10 Plus).

NLE-Programme im Konsumer-Bereich verfügen in der Regel über eine begrenzte Anzahl von **Tracks** ❹, die über die Zeitleiste bearbeitet und miteinander kombiniert werden können. Zum Beispiel beim Pinnacle Studio Plus ist man auf zwei Video-Tracks begrenzt. Bei professionellen Programmen können eine Vielzahl von Video- und Audio-Tracks verwendet werden.

❹ Ein **Track** ist ein Informationskanal der Zeitleiste, der Video-, Audio- oder Titelmaterial beinhaltet und diese dem Video-Schnitt zuordnet.

Professionelle Schnittsysteme bieten umfangreiche Darstellungsmöglichkeiten für die notwendigen Fensterbereiche (Beispiel: Pinnacle Liquid Silver).

Professionelle NLE-Programme erlauben es, diese Bereiche über mehrere Monitore zu verteilen. Dies verbessert die Übersicht und erlaubt den direkten Zugang zu den wichtigsten Funktionen, ohne langwieriges Auswählen über mehrstufige Menüs.

Aufbau einer Schnittfolge

- Zuerst werden die Clips im Archiv-Bereich ausgewählt. Hierzu können die Clips über das Vorschaufenster beurteilt werden.
- Dann nimmt man ein **Trimmen** ❶ der Clips vor, damit später auf der Zeitleiste nur der Teil des Clips aufgebaut wird, den man auch verwenden möchte.
- Per ‚Drag and Drop' setzt man dann die Clips in der gewünschten Reihenfolge auf die Zeitleiste ein. Zur besseren Übersicht für diese auch als **Assemble-Schnitt** ❷ bezeichnete Vorgehensweise bietet sich die „Storyboard-Ansicht" der Zeitleiste an.
- Zur weiteren Optimierung des Schnitts verwendet man die „Timeline-Darstellung" der Zeitleiste, um eine genaue Übersicht über Länge und Positionierung der einzelnen Clips zu bekommen.
- Jetzt können die einzelnen Clips in der Zeitleiste einzelbildgenau angeordnet werden. Falls erforderlich, können längere Clips in kleinere Clips geteilt werden.
- Dann können mit Hilfe des **Insert-Schnitts** ❸ die Clips neu geordnet, bzw. weitere Clips hinzugefügt werden.
- Sollen Clips durch andere ersetzt werden, so wendet man die **Overwrite-Schnitt-Technik** ❹ an. Im Gegensatz zum Insert-Schnitt wird die bestehende Sequenz in diesem Teil überschrieben. Dies eignet sich zum Beispiel dazu, um zusätzliches Material, das aus einer anderen Perspektive aufgenommen wurde, in die ursprüngliche Film-Sequenz zu integrieren.
- Lässt man dabei die Tonspur der ursprünglichen Film-Sequenz unangetastet, spricht man von einer B-Rollen-Technik, bei der durch den ununterbrochenen Ton beim Zuschauer der Eindruck von Gleichzeitigkeit entsteht. Dieses Verfahren wird gerne bei Interviews verwendet, um bei gleichbleibendem Ton ein Wechsel zwischen den beteiligten Personen vorzunehmen.
- Dann werden die Clips hinsichtlich des Anfangs und Endes nochmals „getrimmt" und, falls gewünscht, mit entsprechenden Überblendeffekten (siehe auch „Dynamische Bildwechsel" in diesem Kapitel) versehen.

❶ Unter **Trimmen** versteht man das genaue Festlegen von Anfang und Ende des einzusetzenden Clips.

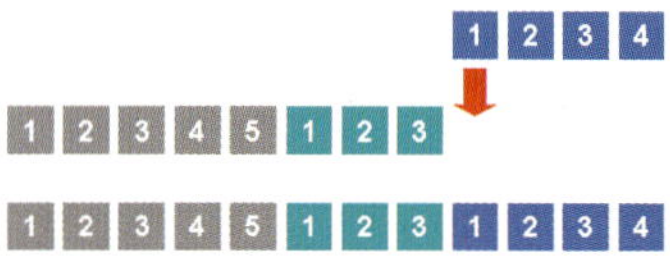

❷ Beim **Assemble-Schnitt** werden die Clips ohne Zwischenraum sequentiell aneinandergereiht.

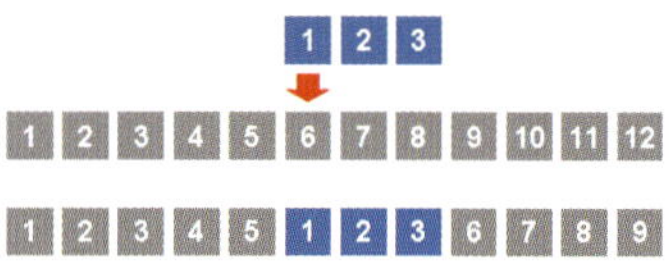

❸ Beim **Insert-Schnitt** wird der einzufügende Clip in die vorhandene Sequenz eingesetzt und die Sequenz wird entsprechend verlängert.

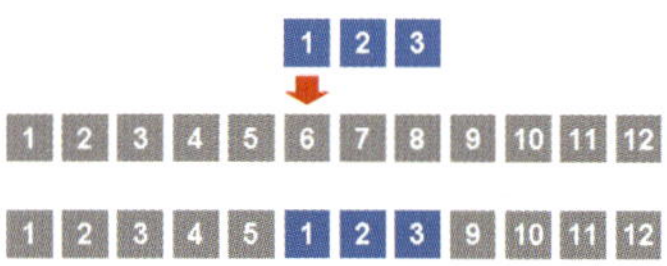

❹ Beim **Overwrite-Schnitt** wird der Teil der alten Sequenz in der Länge des neuen Clips überschrieben. Die Länge der gesamten Film-Sequenz ändert sich dabei nicht.

Bei allen Clip-Bearbeitungen über Trimmen, Teilen und Schnitt-Techniken bleiben die Original-Videodateien der Clips unberührt. Es wird lediglich eine Aufgabenliste mit allen Bearbeitungsschritten erzeugt. Diese Schnitt-Information ist bei professionellen NLE-Programmen als elektronische Schnittliste, die EDL (Edit Decision List), systemübergreifend austauschbar.

Erst beim Ausspielen der Film-Sequenz, dem sogenannten Rendern, werden entsprechend der Schnittliste die Original-Videodateien herangezogen. Sie werden dabei mit allen digitalen Effekten, wie Titeleinblendungen, Szenen-Überblendungen und den Tönen zu einem neuen Videofilm im Zielformat produziert. Dazu muss vom NLE-Programm jedes Einzelbild (Frame) errechnet werden. Dieser Render-Prozess stellt, je nach Komplexität der Effekte, enorme Anforderungen an die Rechenleistung des Schnittsystems.

Besondere Schnitttechniken

Dank der digitalen Schnitttechnik lassen sich auch außergewöhnliche Anforderungen sehr einfach umsetzen. Zum Beispiel gibt es aufnahmetechnische Situationen, die in umgekehrter Richtung einfacher zu realisieren sind. Mit dem NLE-Programm lässt sich diese Szene dann durch **Umkehren der Laufrichtung** ❶ wieder richtigstellen.

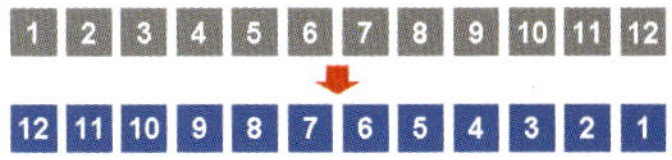

❶ Rückwärtslauf durch **Umkehren der Frame-Folge**.

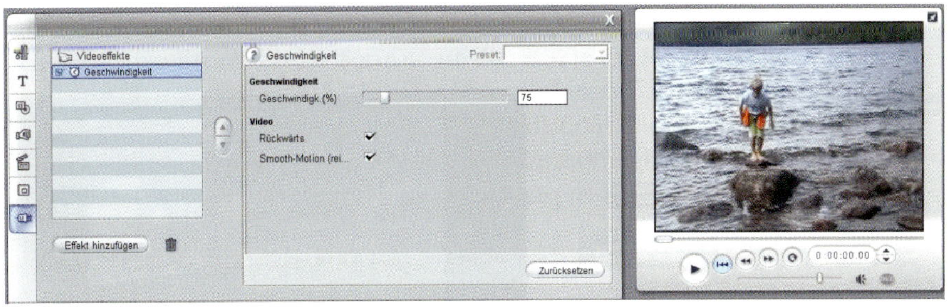

Der Laufrichtungswechsel und das Verändern der Ablaufgeschwindigkeit ist für einen Clip jederzeit möglich und eröffnet kreativen Spielraum. Beispiel Pinnacle Studio.

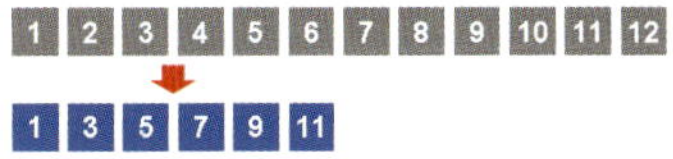

❷ **Zeitraffer-Effekt** durch Weglassen von Frames.

Durch Ändern der Clip-Geschwindigkeit kann ein **Zeitraffer-Effekt** ❷ produziert werde. Das NLE-Programm lässt dabei Frames wegfallen, der Clip läuft dadurch schneller ab. In einem begrenzten Rahmen ist auch ein **Zeitlupen-Effekt** ❸ möglich. Da für diese Zeitdehnung aber zusätzliche Frames notwendig sind, werden sie durch Duplizieren erzeugt. Dies ergibt einen etwas „holprigen" Effekt, da die Informationen der Zwischenbilder fehlen.

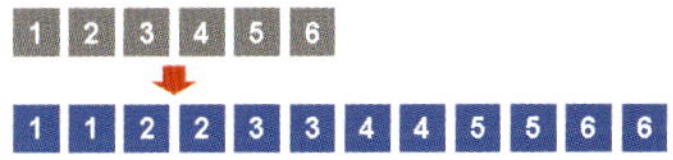

❸ **Zeitlupen-Effekt** durch Duplizieren von Frames.

Mit der **Freeze-Frame-Technik** ❹ kann ein Clip angehalten, sozusagen „eingefroren" werden. Dabei wird aus dem Clip ein Standbild erzeugt und dieses für eine bestimmte Zeit in der Film-Sequenz dargestellt. Zur Verstärkung des Effekts kann es Sinn machen, über die Standbilddauer den Bildausschnitt in der Darstellungsgröße zu verändern.

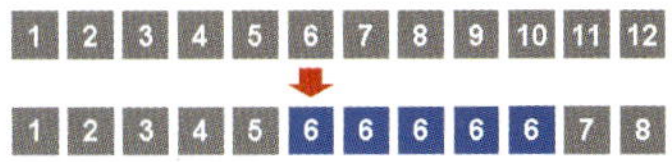

❹ Bei der **Freeze-Frame-Technik** wird ein Frame als Standbild dupliziert.

Bild-Optimierung

Die meisten NLE-Programme ermöglichen nachträgliche Belichtungs- und Farbkorrekturen der einzelnen Clips. Damit können Clips besser aufeinander abgestimmt werden. Die Bandbreite der Möglichkeiten zieht sich dabei vom nachträglichen Weißabgleich, der Kontrast- und Helligkeitsanpassung, einer Rauschunterdrückungs-Funktion für Aufnahmen bei schwachem Licht bis hin zur Kompensation verwackelter Clips durch eine Image-Stabilisation.

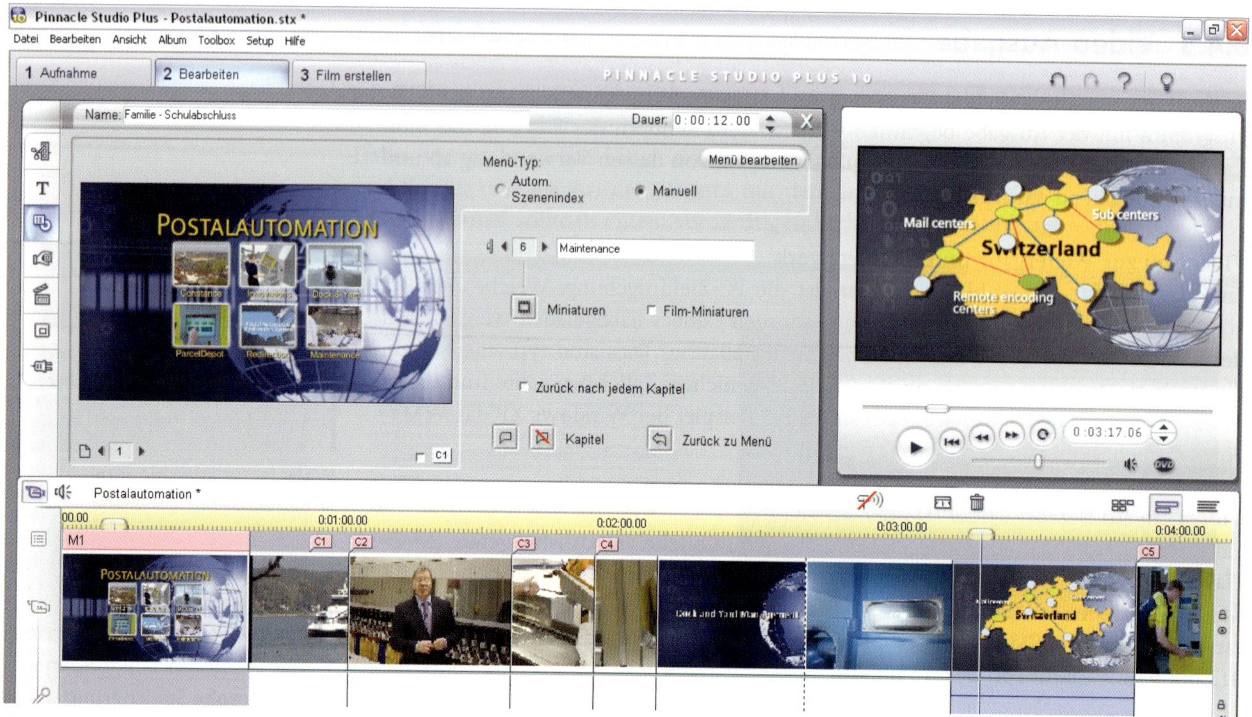

Über Marker werden Kapiteleinsprünge für das DVD-Menü gesetzt.
Beispiel Pinnacle Studio 10 Plus.

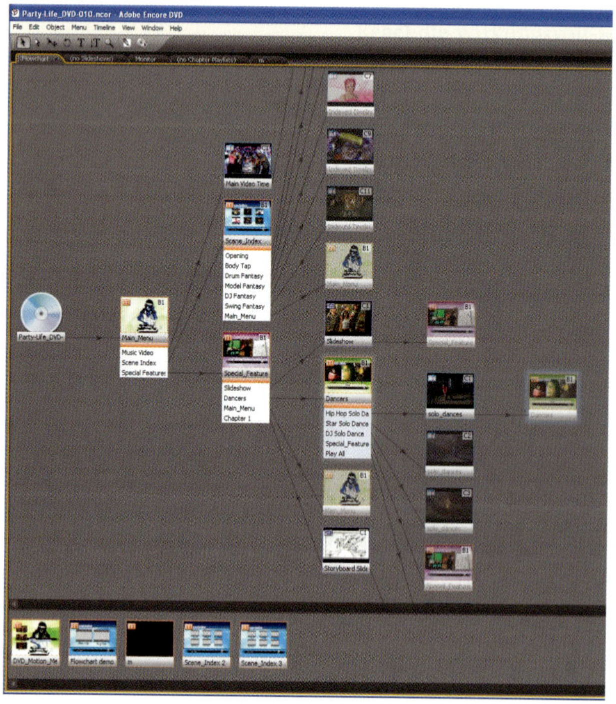

Vorgehensweise zur Erstellung von einfachen Menüs im NLE-Programm:

- Im Menü werden für jede anzusteuernde Videosequenz Kapitelaufrufe erstellt. Dazu können auch mehrere Menüseiten verwendet werden.
- Als Hintergrund sind Standbilder, aber auch kurze Videosequenzen einsetzbar.
- Im Film werden dann die Einsprungstellen mit Markern versehen und mit den interaktiven Schaltflächen verknüpft.
- Die Schaltflächen können dann ein inhaltstypisches Thumbnail als visuelle Orientierung zugeordnet bekommen.

Visuelle Strukturdarstellung umfangreicher DVD-Menüs.
Beispiel Adobe Encore.

Videosequenz für interaktive Anwendungen
Soll eine Videosequenz im Rahmen einer interaktiven Anwendung für den PC, zum Beispiel in einer Präsentation oder in einem Lernprogramm, verwendet werden, gibt es dazu zwei unterschiedliche Vorgehensweisen:

- Das Video wird mit eigenen Videotreibern oder mit den Betriebssystem-eigenen Treibern aufgerufen und innerhalb der Anwendung dargestellt. Hier muss ebenfalls die PC-Zielumgebung berücksichtigt werden. Anwendungsbeispiel Microsoft Powerpoint: WMV oder AVI mit Cinepac-Codec.
- Das Video wird in ein internes Format der Anwendung konvertiert und dort eingebettet (embedded). Die Anwendung übernimmt dann die Videodarstellung mit eigenem Decoder. Anwendungsbeispiel Adobe Flash: Video wird in das eigene Format FLV (Abk. für Flash Video), zum Beispiel mit dem VP6-Codec, konvertiert und kann dann komplett in eine Flash SWF-Datei eingebettet werden.

Schon beim Erstellen der Streaming-Videodateien ist die Internet-Anbindung der Zielgruppe zu beachten.

Videofilm zur Veröffentlichung im Internet
Da Videosequenzen als normale Internet-Downloads in der Regel sehr zeitintensiv sind, verwendet man hierfür **Video-Streaming** ❶. Dazu ist auf der Empfängerseite eine spezielle Abspiel-Software erforderlich.
Dies kann ein im Web-Browser integriertes Plug-In oder ein eigenständiges Wiedergabeprogramm sein. Um das „Streamen" zu ermöglichen, muss gleichzeitig auf dem Web-Server ein spezieller Streaming-Server installiert sein, der die synchrone Kommunikation gewährleistet. Es existieren eine Vielzahl verschiedener konkurrierender Technologien für das Video-Streaming:

❶ **Video-Streaming**: Durch dieses Verfahren wird der Film geladen und gleichzeitig schon abgespielt.

- **Windows Media Video** (WMV) ist das proprietäre Codec-Format von Microsoft. Auf Grund der weiten Verbreitung des in Windows integrierten Windows Media Players sind WMV-Videostreams sehr beliebt, da in den meisten Fällen kein extra Player benötigt wird. Zum Bereitstellen der Videostreams auf dem Web-Server wird der Windows Media Server benötigt.
- **RealVideo** (RV oder RM) ist das proprietäre Videoformat von RealMedia. Die Qualität ist vergleichbar mit MPEG-4-Videocodecs wie XviD oder DivX, sowie Windows Media Video 9.
- **QuickTime** (MOV) ist das Format von Apple, das aber auch in der Windows-Welt weit verbreitet ist. Auf dem Server wird der QuickTime Streaming Server zum Bereitstellen der Live-Streams über das Internet benötigt.
- **Flash Video** (FLV) ist das Video-Dateiformat von Adobe Flash. Flash zeichnet sich dadurch aus, dass es plattformübergreifend genutzt werden kann und neben dem Flash Player, der in vielen Internet-Browsern schon vorhanden ist, keine Codecs zum Abspielen installiert werden müssen.

Die für die Übertragung zur Verfügung stehende Datenübertragungsrate muss größer sein, als die für das Streaming verwendete Datenübertragungsrate. Deshalb ist die Qualität noch entsprechend niedrig, um bei den heute üblichen Datenübertragungsraten eine flüssige Übertragung zu ermöglichen. Um unterschiedliche Laufzeiten der Daten-Pakete im Internet auszugleichen und damit verbundene Stockungen zu verhindern, wird in der Abspiel-Software ein Puffer verwendet, der die Wiedergabe um einige Sekunden leicht verzögert, aber dann den Abspielfluss sicherstellt.

Videofilm zur Verwendung auf tragbaren Mediengeräten

Seit der Verbreitung der mobilen Medien-Abspielgeräte, die auch Videosequenzen abspielen können, steigt der Bedarf an speziell für diese Plattformen angepasste Videoausgabe-Möglichkeiten. Dabei sind es nicht vorwiegend Spielfilme, die den Weg auf die mobilen Abspielgeräte finden, sondern kleinere Videosequenzen, zum Beispiel in Form von sogenannten Video-Podcasts, den kleinen individuellen Videobeiträgen, die sich einer immer größeren Beliebtheit erfreuen. Bietet das NLE-Programm eine solche Ausgabemöglichkeit nicht direkt, wird erst ein Standardformat, wie zum Beispiel MPEG2 oder MPEG4 gerendert und dann durch einen nachgeschalteten Konvertierprozess mit einem speziellen Videokonverter der Film in das Zielformat gewandelt.

Konvertierte Videosequenz auf dem videofähigen einfachen mobilen Endgerät (iPOD MP3-Player von Apple).

Videokonverter für mobile Endgeräte (Filme für Unterwegs von Magix).

Je nach mobilen Endgerät ist ein kompatibles Videoformat mit Codec und möglichst in der nativen Auflösung des Bildschirms zu wählen. Bei einfachen Geräten, z. B. einem MP3-Player mit Videofunktion kann das eine sehr begrenzte Auflösung sein. Trotz der sehr kleinen Bildschirmgröße und der begrenzten Speicherkapazität, soll der Film qualitativ gut wirken.

Smartphone mit hochauflösendem Bildschirm. Kompatibel mit HD-Videomaterial (Galaxy von Samsung).

Gebräuchliche mobile Videoformate sind:

- MP4, ein Containerformat mit **H.264-Codec**
- WMV, das Videoformat von Microsoft
- MOV, Quicktime-Containerformat von Apple
- FLV, das Flash-Videoformat mit VP6-Codec
- **3GP**, ein Containerformat mit Codecs wie MPEG-4 oder H.263

Aufgaben und Übungen, Literaturhinweise

Aufgaben und Übungen

1. Blue Screen Technik: Nehmen Sie Beispiele auf Video auf, die die Blue Screen Technik aus bekannten Film- und Fernsehproduktionen zeigen.
2. Visuelle Blende: Beschreiben Sie an Hand einer Nachrichtensendung die verwendeten Überblendeffekte mit der Einstellung davor und der Einstellung danach.
3. Beleuchtung: Bauen Sie die Beleuchtungssituation für eine Portrait-Aufnahme auf. Variieren Sie die Hauptlichtanordnung zwischen Voll-, Schlank und Teilungslicht. Beschreiben Sie die Änderung der dramaturgischen Wirkung. Wie verändert sich die Wirkung bei zusätzlichem Spitz- oder Hintergrundlicht?
4. Drehbuch: Schreiben Sie ein Drehbuch im klassischen Stil für eine Kurzgeschichte.
   Welche Vorteile bietet eine spezielle Drehbuch-Software gegenüber einem einfachen Textverarbeitungsprogramm?
5. Aufnahmetechnik: Erstellen Sie Videosequenzen ohne Schwenk, für ein von zwei Personen geführtes Interview. Erstellen Sie dazu bewusst ausreichend Material in Schuss- und Gegenschuss-Perspektive.
6. Schnitttechnik: Fügen Sie das Material von Aufgabe 5 zu einem abwechslungsreichen Schnitt zusammen. Benutzen Sie dazu die B-Rollen-Technik.
7. Digitale Video-Formate: Rendern Sie den fertigen Schnitt aus Aufgabe 6 in die verschiedensten Formate und vergleichen dann Dateigröße, Auflösung und Qualität der Formate.

Literaturhinweise

Ang, Tom: Digitales Video. Ausrüstung, Techniken, Projekte, Nachbearbeitung, London 2005 (Dorling Kindersley)

Büchele, Fridhelm: Digitales Filmen. Einfach gute Videofilme drehen und nachbearbeiten, Bonn 2005 (Galileo Press)

Burder, John: Postproduction für Film & Video.Handbuch zur Film- und Videonachbearbeitung, Stein-Bockenheim 2001 (Mediabook-Verlag Reil)

Gabathuler, Simon: Video Digital, München 2006 (Markt & Technik)

Kandorfer, Pierre: Lehrbuch der Filmgestaltung. Theoretisch-technische Grundlagen der Filmkunde, Stein-Bockenheim 2003 (Mediabook-Verlag Reil)

Petrasch, Thomas; *Zinke*, Joachim: Einführung in die Videofilmproduktion, München 2003 (Carl Hanser Verlag GmbH & CO. KG)

Rogge, Axel: Die Videoschnitt-Schule. Tipps und Tricks für spannendere und überzeugendere Filme, Bonn 2006 (Galileo Press)

Saalfeld, Stefan: Grundlagen der Fernseh- und Videotechnik, Stein-Bockenheim 2006 (Mediabook-Verlag Reil)

Schiemann, Bernd u. a.: Informationstechnik und Kommunikationstechnik. Fachwissen IT-Berufe, Haan-Gruiten 2011 (Europa Lehrmittel-Verlag)

Schmidt, Ulrich: Digitale Film- und Videotechnik, München 2002 (Hanser Fachbuchverlag)

9 Animation

Webcode:
B0900

Für weitere Infos zu diesem Kapitel mit dem Smartphone einfach QR-Code scannen oder auf www.medien-verstehen.de den Webcode eingeben.

Dieses Kapitel gibt einen Einblick in die Welt der bewegten Grafik – der **Animation**. Es werden die grundsätzlichen Prinzipien, nach denen Animationen aufgebaut sind, vorgestellt. Man erfährt, wie komplexe Animationen mit 3D-Objekten aufgebaut werden, welche Werkzeuge dafür eingesetzt werden und wie über virtuelle Realität die Animation interaktiv wird.

Mit Überblendungen, Ein- und Ausblendungen, wie sie im letzten Kapitel dargestellt wurden, sind nur sehr begrenzte Effekte realisierbar. Um Objekte richtig in Bewegung zu setzen, sind Animationen notwendig.

Animationen werden typischerweise durch Film- oder Videoformate, also durch eine kontinuierliche Abfolge von einzelnen Bildern, dargestellt. Die Bewegungswahrnehmung wird damit wie in der Film- und Videotechnik durch die Trägheit des menschlichen Auges sichergestellt, die diese Abfolge als Bewegung interpretiert.

Eine Animation beschreibt hierbei alle Änderungen, die einen visuellen Effekt bedingen. Visuelle Effekte können dabei verschiedener Natur sein:

- Bewegungsdynamik, bei der die Position eines Objektes über einen Zeitraum hinweg verändert wird
- Änderungsdynamik, bei der Form, Farbe, Transparenz, Struktur und Musterung eines Objektes über die Zeit verändert wird
- Änderung der Beleuchtung, der Kameraposition und des Fokus über einen Zeitraum hinweg.

Diese Effekte können bei Präsentationen als Blickfang oder zur Veranschaulichung von komplexen Inhalten dienen. Die Bandbreite der Animationen geht von einfachen Veränderungseffekten von Objekten, zum Beispiel als Visualisierung einer Schaltfläche für verschiedene Zustände, bis hin zu komplexen 3D-Animationen.

9.1 Prinzip der Animation

9.1.1 Bewegungswahrnehmung

❶ Ab 18 Einzelbildern pro Sekunde werden die einzelnen Phasenbilder als kontinuierliche **Bewegung** wahrgenommen.

Ab 72 Einzelbildern pro Sekunde ist das Flimmern für das menschliche Auge unsichtbar.

Animationen sind nur möglich auf Grund eines biologischen Phänomens, bekannt als ‚Persitence of Vision'. Das Abbild eines durch das menschliche Auge gesehenen Objekts bleibt auch nach dem Abbilden auf der Netzhaut für einen kurzen Moment erhalten. Dadurch ist die visuelle Illusion einer **Bewegung** ❶ durch eine Serie von schnell aufeinander folgenden Bildern möglich. Schon das allgemein bekannte Daumenkino basiert auf diesem Effekt.

Am Beispiel einer Uhr mit mehreren aufeinander folgenden Zeigerstellungen kann man diesen Effekt gut darstellen. Wenn die Einzelbilder in schneller Abfolge gezeigt werden, verwischen die statischen Zeigerstellungen zu einer kreisenden Bewegung der Uhrzeit. Führt man die Einzelbildserie bis zu 12 Stunden weiter, wird ein kontinuierlicher Bewegungsprozess erreicht, der durch ständige Wiederholungen permanent dargestellt werden kann.

9.1.2 Bildraten in der Animation

Für den Animationseffekt sind primär zwei Arten von **Bildraten** ❶ verantwortlich. Die eine spiegelt die dargestellte Anzahl der Bilder pro Sekunde wieder, während die andere die Anzahl der verschiedenen Bilder, die pro Sekunde vorkommen, darstellt. Die Erstgenannte ist die sogenannte **Playback Rate** (Bildwiederholungsrate), und die Zweite ist die **Sampling Rate**. Im Fernsehen werden 25 Bilder pro Sekunde dargestellt, während alte Comicsendungen zum Beispiel aber nur 5 verschiedene Bilder pro Sekunde enthalten. Um nicht den Geschwindigkeitseindruck zu verändern, muss somit jedes Bild fünfmal wiederholt werden, damit die Bildwiederholungsrate von 25 Bildern pro Sekunde eingehalten wird. Tut man dies nicht, läuft der Film zu schnell ab (Zeitraffer-Effekt).

❶ Unter **Bildrate** versteht man die Anzahl von Einzelbildern pro Sekunde.

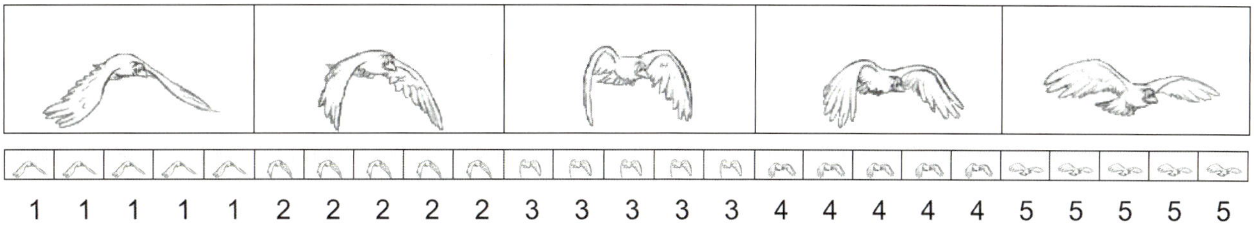

Durch Bildwiederholungen wird ein Trickfilm, der eine geringe Frame Rate besitzt, an einen Film mit höherer Bildwiederholungsrate angepasst. Beispiel: Trickfilm (5 Bilder/Sekunde) für das Fernsehen (25 Bilder/Sekunde).

9.1.3 Phasenanimation

Die meisten Animationen bauen auf einfachen Zeichnungen von **Einzelphasen** ❷ auf, wie man sie aus dem klassischen Zeichentrickfilm kennt. Für einfache Bewegungsanimationen reichen oft auch schon wenige Phasenzeichnungen aus.

❷ Bei der **Einzelphasenanimation**, auch **„Frame-by-Frame-Technik"** genannt, wird jedes Einzelbild gezeichnet.

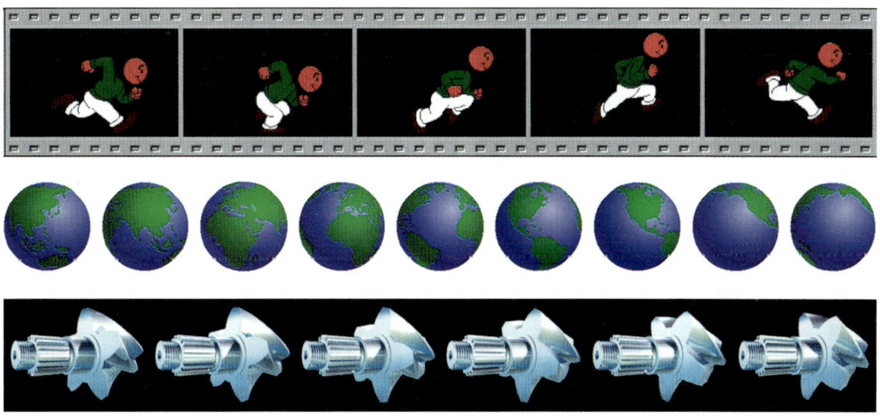

Phasenanimationsbeispiele: Springende Zeichentrickfigur (oben), kontinuierlich drehende Weltkugel (mitte) und drehender Fräseinsatz (unten).

9.2 Techniken der Bewegungsanimation

Da es verschiedene Arten von Animationen gibt, haben sich auch für die jeweilige Animation passende Erstellungstechniken etabliert, die auf unterschiedlichen Ansätzen basieren. Im Folgenden werden Techniken beschrieben, bei denen der Entwickler auf viele Einzelheiten der Animation Zugriff hat und somit das Resultat direkt beeinflussen kann.

9.2.1 Schlüsselbildtechnik

Die **Schlüsselbildtechnik** kommt aus der traditionellen Zeichentrick-Animationstechnik. An markanten Schlüsselpunkten der Aktion oder der Handlung werden aussagekräftige Komplett-Bilder erstellt. Diese sogenannten **Schlüsselbilder** oder **Key Frames**, stellen den roten Faden durch die Handlung der zu erstellenden Animation dar.

Zur Komplettierung der Animationssequenz werden zwischen diesen Key Frames Zwischenbilder eingesetzt, die den Übergang von Key Frame zu Key Frame realisieren. Dieser Prozess wird In-Betweening oder auch Tweening genannt und wird vom Animationsprogramm durch automatisches Interpolieren des Objektes in den Zwischenbildern erreicht. Der Interpolationsalgorithmus ist dabei ein entscheidender Faktor für das Erscheinungsbild der endgültigen Animation.

Diese Schlüsselbildtechnik veranschaulichen wir an Hand eines kleinen Beispiels mit vier Key Frames.

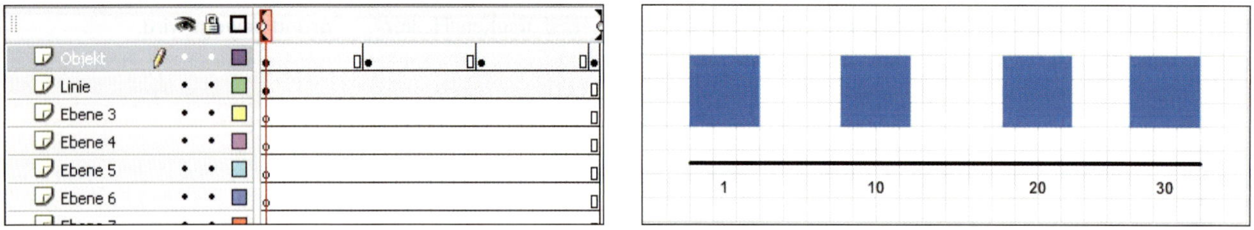

Beispiel eines Animationsaufbaus nach der **Schlüsselbildtechnik**. Auf einer Zeitleiste sind an den Positionen 1, 10, 20 und 30 für das Objekt „Blaues Quadrat" sogenannte Key Frames erstellt worden. Darstellung im Animationsprogramm Adobe Flash.

9.2.2 Positions-Interpolation

Ohne eine Interpolation gibt es nur die vier unterschiedlichen Positionen des Objektes an den Key Frames. Durch ein **Bewegungs-Tweening** werden neue Einzelbilder zwischen den Key Frames durch Interpolation vom Animationsprogramm errechnet.

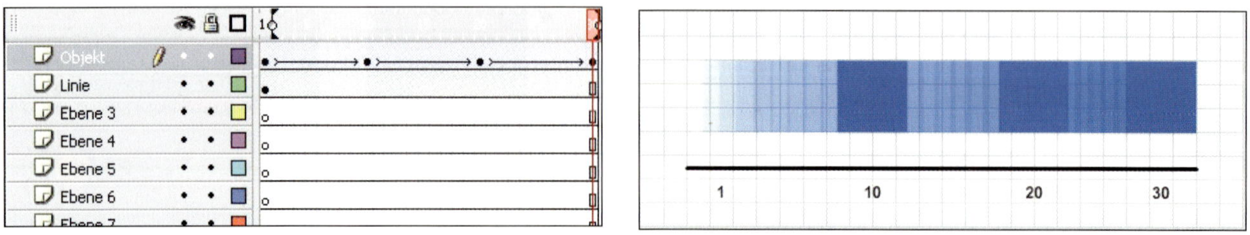

Zwischen den Key Frames sind durch ein **Bewegungs-Tweening** Zwischenbilder erzeugt worden.

9.2.3 Form-Interpolation

Erfolgt die Veränderung von Key Frame zu Key Frame nicht nur über die Position des Objektes, sondern auch in der Darstellung des Objektes, können über die Form-Interpolation alle notwendigen Zwischenbilder erzeugt werden. Die Veränderung kann sich dabei auf Skalierung und Position (**lineare Transformation**), Form (**Warping** und **Morphing**) und Objekt-Attribute, wie Farbe, auswirken. Die Zwischenbilder zeigen dann die einzelnen Übergangsphasen der Objekt-Veränderung.

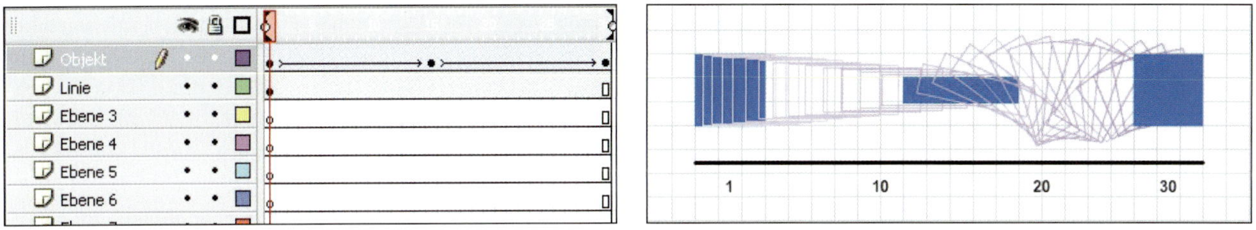

Rotationen und nicht-einheitliche Skalierungen durch **lineare Transformation** verändern die Form des Objekts. Beispiel mit drei Key Frames: Vom Quadrat (Position 1), über ein Rechteck (Position 15) rotiert wieder zum Quadrat (Position 30).

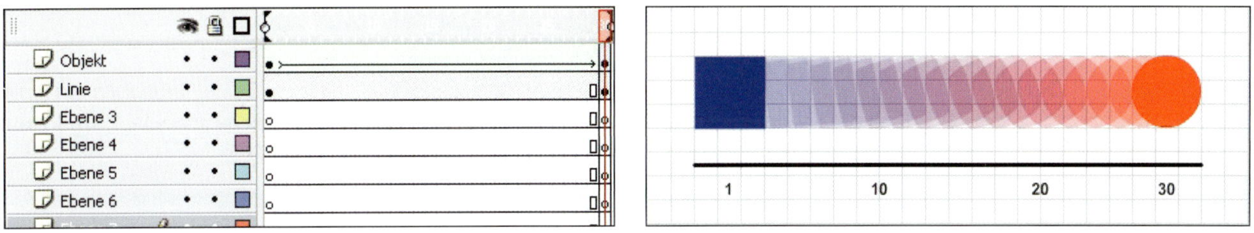

Morphing interpoliert zwischen Form und Attributen von zwei Objekten und sorgt für eine Formüberblendung. Beispiel mit zwei Key Frames: Vom blauen Quadrat (Position 1) zum roten Kreis (Position 30).

Warping und Morphing verändern die Form graphischer Objekte. Beim Warping werden einzelne Objekte deformiert, während beim Morphing immer zwischen zwei graphischen Objekten interpoliert wird.

9.3 3D-Animation

Animationen mit dreidimensionalen Darstellungen von Objekten eröffnen beim Visualisieren sehr beeindruckende und realitätsnahe Effekte. 3D-Animationen finden mittlerweile in allen digitalen Medien ihre Verwendung. Über Werbespots und Filmproduktionen erreichen sie heutzutage fast jeden Haushalt und tragen zu einem automatischen Selbstverständnis des Machbaren bei.

Aber auch im Bereich der Technik, Architektur und Naturwissenschaft bieten sich interessante Möglichkeiten der realitätsnahen und anschaulichen Dokumentation. So sind z. B. Simulationen und Konstruktionen visualisierbar, die in der Realität noch nicht verfügbar sind. Der Zielgruppe gibt man somit eine neue Dimension der Vorstellungskraft in die Hand.

Mit den heutigen Werkzeugen zur 3D-Animationserstellung ist es nur noch eine Frage des Aufwandes, und damit von Zeit und Geld, auf welche Weise mehr oder weniger realistisch wirkende virtuelle Gegenstände und virtuelle Welten dargestellt werden. Beispiele des aktuell Machbaren können wir meist auf der Kinoleinwand bei verschiedenen Filmproduktionen bewundern, da hier, dank der kräftigen finanziellen Grundlage, die heutigen Systeme zur 3D-Animationserstellung voll ausgespielt werden können.

Komplexe realitätsnahe Animationen, wie zum Beispiel natürlich wirkende dreidimensionale Simulation menschlicher Bewegungsabläufe erfordern eine sehr teure Hard- und Softwareausstattung. Auch die Macher dieser Animationen müssen über ein entsprechendes Know-how verfügen, da diese Systeme in der Regel nicht sehr intuitiv zu bedienen sind.

Der Arbeitsablauf einer Animationserstellung im 3D-Raum kann je nach Komplexität in verschiedene Bereiche gegliedert werden:

- **Modellierung**, das Konstruieren der Objekte
- **Rigging**, dem Hinzufügen der Bewegungseigenschaften
- **Mapping** und **Shading**, Oberflächen definieren und beleuchten
- **Animation**, dem zeitlichen Verhalten der Objekte
- **Rendering**, dem Errechnen des End-Resultates

Professionelle 3D-Animationsprogramme, welche diese Bereiche abdecken, sind zum Beispiel 3D Studio Max, Soft Image 3D, Maya und Blender 3D.

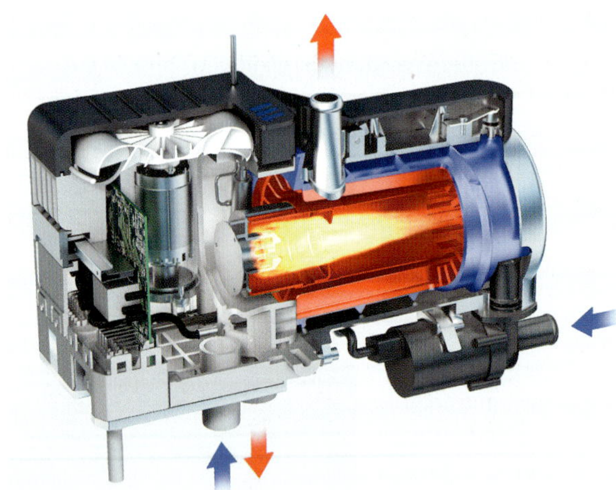

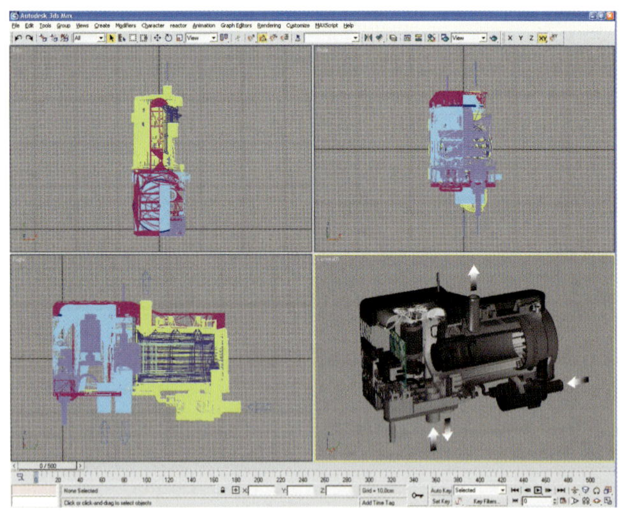

3D-Visualisierung für technische Produkte am Beispiel einer Hydronic Standheizung. Konstruiert in 3D Studio Max.
Quelle: Image Affairs für Firma Eberspächer GmbH & Co. KG.

9.3.1 Modellierung

Um dreidimensionale Animationen erstellen zu können, müssen zuerst die Objekte als 3D-Modell konstruiert und im dreidimensionalen Raum festgelegt werden. Hierzu gibt es verschiedene Ansätze, die je nach umzusetzendem Modell ihre Vorzüge haben.

Einsatz vordefinierter Primitive

Einfach, vorgefertigte Objekte, wie Kugel, Quader, Zylinder, Rohr usw. lassen sich durch Eingabe bestimmter Parameter automatisch generieren. Diese Grundkörper, auch **Primitive** ❶ genannt, dienen als Bausteine für komplexere Modelle. Über die Methode der **Constructive Solid Geometry (CSG)** ❷ können die Primitive miteinander kombiniert werden. Durch boolesche Operatoren, das sind mathematische Aktionen, wie Addition, Subtraktion und deren Kombinationen, entstehen somit zusammengesetzte, neue Objekte. Diese neuen Objekte können dann wiederum mit andern Primitiven kombiniert werden. So lassen sich zunehmend komplexere Körper konstruieren.

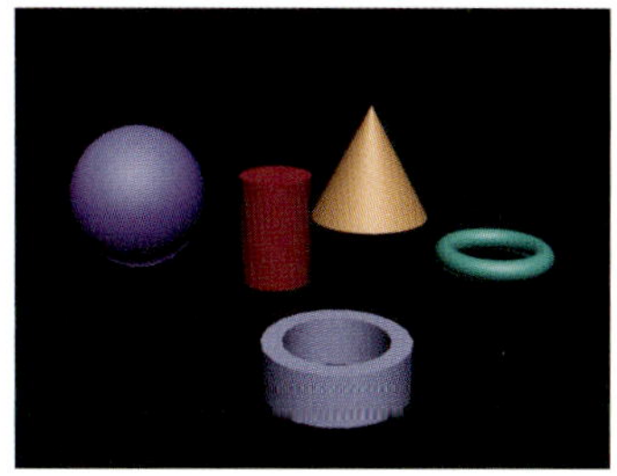

❶ Beispiele von **Primitive**.

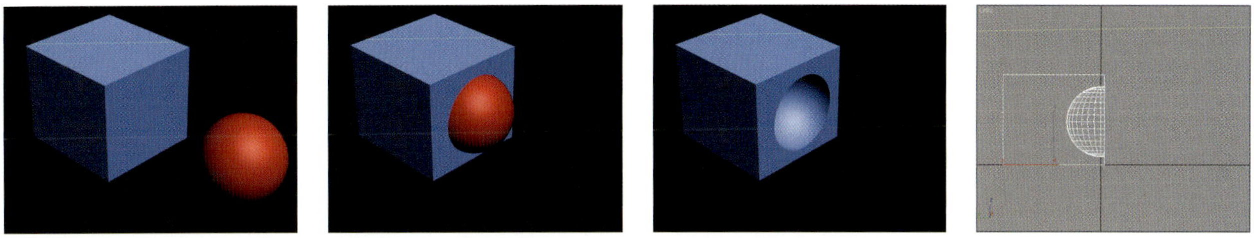

❷ Beispiel der Erstellung eines neuen Objektes mit Hilfe der **Constructive Solid Geometry**. Mit einem Quader und einer Kugel wird ein neues Objekt kombiniert, indem vom Quader-Volumen ein Teil des Kreis-Volumens subtrahiert wird.

Freiform-Modellierung

Diese Methode definiert ein Objekt anhand seiner Oberflächen. Dabei unterscheidet man hinsichtlich der Arbeitsweise und der Konstruktionsmethode generell zwischen dem Polygon-Verfahren und dem Spline-Verfahren.

Beim **Polygon-Verfahren** ❸ setzt man Objekte aus einer Vielzahl kleiner Flächen (Polygone) zu Netzen (Meshes) zusammen. Polygone sind im Computer leicht zu verarbeiten und die Speicherung und Berechnung einer Grafik aus Polygondaten ist sehr effizient. Jedoch werden runde Formen wie bei Kugeln nur näherungsweise dargestellt. Deshalb können diese Körper nicht beliebig vergrößert und verformt werden.

❸ In den 3D-Programmen besteht ein **Polygon** aus einer Fläche mit 3 Punkten.

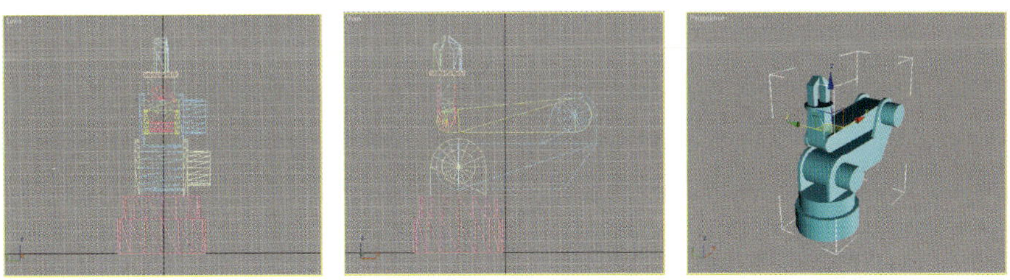

Beispiel eines zusammengesetzten Körpers, der aus Polygon-Netzen besteht.
In den Drahtgitteransichten sind die Polygon-Dreiecke klar zu erkennen.

Über Methoden, wie dem Sub-Division-Surfaces, bei dem die Polygon-Flächen weiter unterteilt und abgerundet werden, lässt sich die Auflösung verbessern. Nur wird das Modellieren dadurch schwieriger.

➲ **Polygone eignen sich für einfache Objektmodelle mit überschaubaren Datenmengen, zum Beispiel Objekte in Computerspielen.**

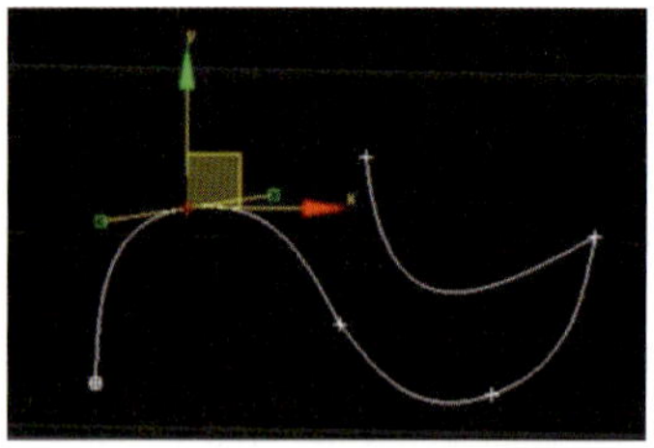

❶ **Splines** bestehen aus einer Linie zwischen zwei oder mehreren Punkten. Der Verlauf der Linie kann über sogenannte Anfasser verändert werden, welche die Steigung der Kurve bestimmen.

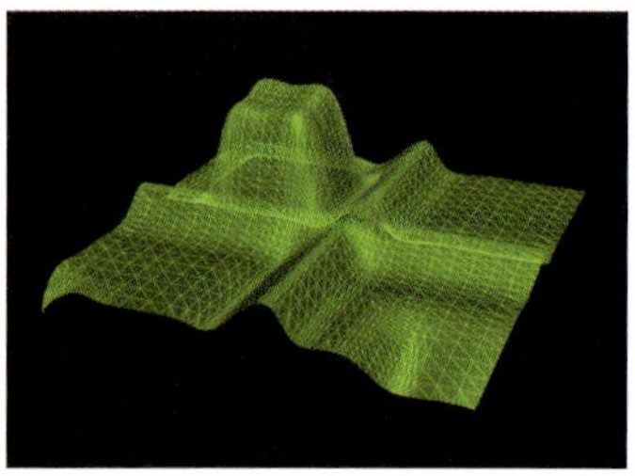

❷ **NURBS** (Non Uniform Rational B-Splines) ist eine Methode, um Flächen und Körper mit Splines zu modellieren. NURBS eignen sich besonders für weiche, organische Flächen. Sie stellen jedoch höhere Anforderungen an die Rechenleistung des 3D-Grafiksystems.

Beim **Spline-Verfahren** ❶ werden die Körper anhand komplexer mathematischer Beschreibungen der geometrischen Form definiert. Splines berechnen Kurven aus zwei Endpunkten und zwei Kontrollpunkten, die die Stärke der Auslenkung eines Kurvenabschnitts bestimmen. Die Modellierung kann auflösungsunabhängig ohne Qualitätsverlust erfolgen. Um Flächen und Körper mit Splines aufzubauen, gibt es verschiedene Verfahren. Beim Patch-Verfahren wird eine drei- oder viereckige Oberfläche, die in Einzelflächen unterteilt ist, an den Kanten durch Splines modelliert. Beim **NURBS-Verfahren** ❷ kann jeder dieser Punkte mit einem Gewichtsfaktor belegt werden, sodass ihr Einfluss auf die Form unterschiedlich wird.

Modellierung über Rotation und Extrusion

Eine effiziente Methode, dreidimensionale Modelle zu entwerfen, ist das Zeichnen von Querschnitten mit Splines. Für Rotationskörper wird die Splinekurve um eine Achse im Raum gedreht und mehrmals dupliziert. Für Extrusionskörper wird ein Splineprofil entlang einer Achse verschoben und dabei kopiert. Die kopierten Splines werden zu einer Oberfläche verbunden, damit ein Körper entsteht.

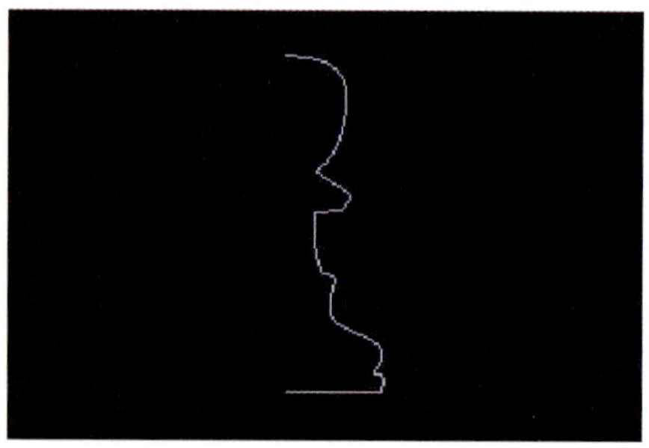

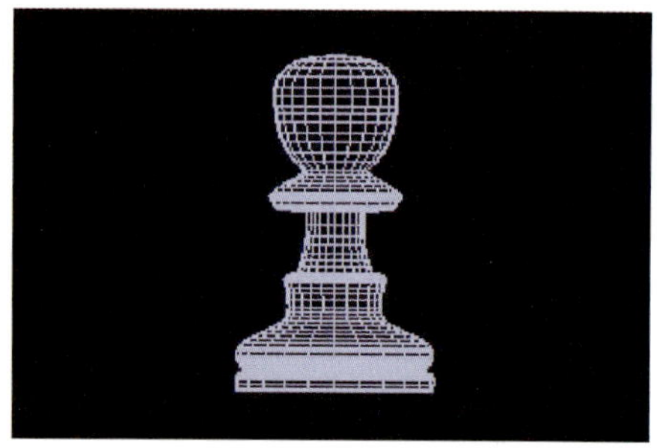

Beispiel der Erstellung eines Rotationskörpers. Die gezeichnete Splinekurve wird im Raum dupliziert und so zu einem Körper geformt.

Extrusion am Beispiel eines Textobjektes. Das Splineprofil wird entlang einer Achse dupliziert und so zu einem Körper geformt.

Weitere Modelliermethoden

Zur Übertragung von reellen Objekten in 3D-Grafiksysteme können auch 3D-Scanner eingesetzt werden, die das reelle Objekt mit umkreisenden Laserstrahlen abtasten und Oberflächenpunkte mit exakter Lage berechnen. Auch aus Fotos sind 3D-Informationen errechenbar, vorausgesetzt, die zu bestimmenden Eckpunkte des Objekts sind auf mindestens zwei Fotos zu erkennen. Mit einer speziellen Software müssen dann die Eckpunkte miteinander synchronisiert werden, damit daraus das 3D-Modell berechnet werden kann. Diese Methoden erfordern in der Regel eine Nachbearbeitung im 3D-Grafiksystem.

9.3.2 Rigging

Für komplexe Objektanimationen, zum Beispiel mit bewegten Figuren, müssen die Objekte mit Bewegungseigenschaften versehen werden. Dabei wird definiert, wie die hierarchische Verknüpfung der zu bewegenden Objekte zueinander ist und welche Bewegungsbeschränkungen notwendig sind. Fragen wie: „Soll sich Objekt 2 immer bewegen, wenn sich Objekt 1 bewegt, aber umgekehrt nicht", gehören zu diesen Eigenschaften.

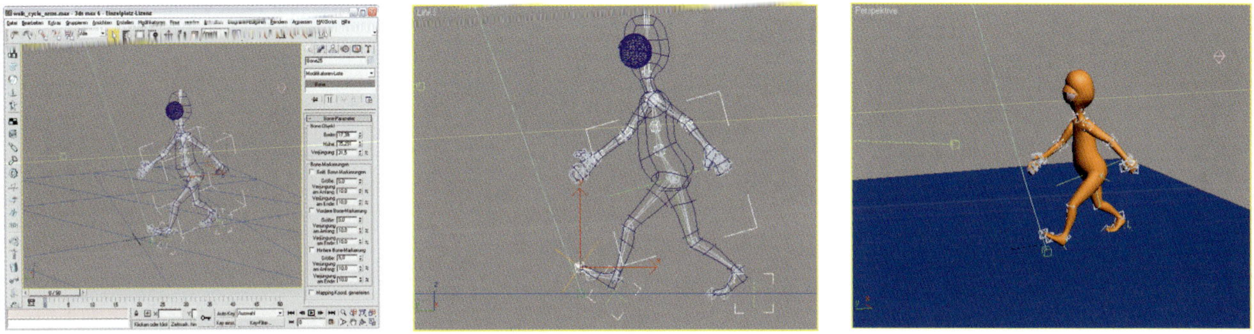

Beim Rigging, dem Vorbereiten der Modelle für die Animation, werden die zu bewegenden Teilobjekte als Skelettsystem miteinander verbunden. Zur Animation muss dann nur noch das Skelettsystem bewegt werden.

Dazu können spezielle Techniken zum Einsatz kommen, wie z. B. das Motion Capturing oder die Inverse Kinematik.

Beim **Motion Capturing** werden menschliche Bewegungen eines Akteurs mit speziellen Sensoren an den Gelenken in Echtzeit auf virtuelle Figuren in ein 3D-System übertragen. Die Koordinaten werden als Key Frames des Skelettsystems verwendet.

Die **Inverse Kinematik** bezieht sich auf die Position und Geschwindigkeit von Massepunkten. Jedes einzelne Teilobjekt des dreidimensionalen Objektes, z. B. ein Arm der Figur, besitzt eine Vielzahl von physikalischen Parametern. Setzt man die Teilobjekte zu einer Gesamtfigur zusammen, bekommen die Teilobjekte einen begrenzten Spielraum in ihrer Bewegung, z. B. ein Unterarm kann nicht nach hinten gebogen werden. Da alle Teilobjekte in einer bestimmten Abhängigkeit zueinander stehen, ergeben sich bei äußeren Einwirkungen auf die Gesamtfigur ganz spezifische Reaktionen.

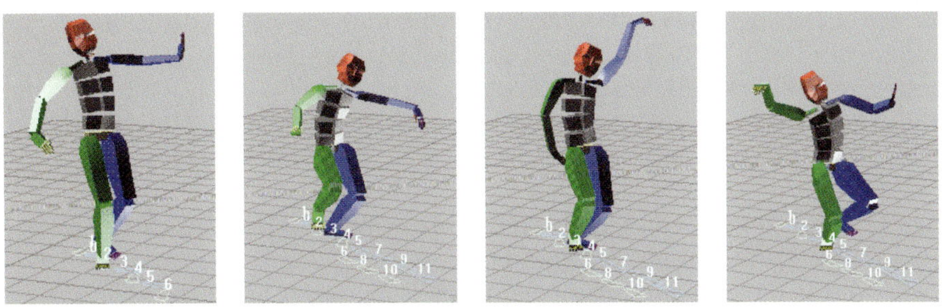

Beispiel eines Schrittablaufes. Die Schritte werden vorgegeben. Die durch inverse Kinematik verknüpften Teilobjekte ziehen in der Animation mit.

9.3.3 Mapping und Shading

❶ Texturen (Maps) bestehen aus Bilddaten.

Beim Mapping können die Modelle mit verschiedenen Oberflächen, sogenannten **Texturen** ❶, versehen werden. Die 3D-Programme verfügen hierzu über Materialbibliotheken mit realistisch aussehenden Oberflächenstrukturen. Für die Beleuchtungswirkung kann das Mapping ganz selektiv Oberflächeneigenschaften kontrollieren. Beispielsweise kann in Abhängigkeit von der Textur die Farbe, Leuchtstärke oder Transparenz beeinflusst werden.

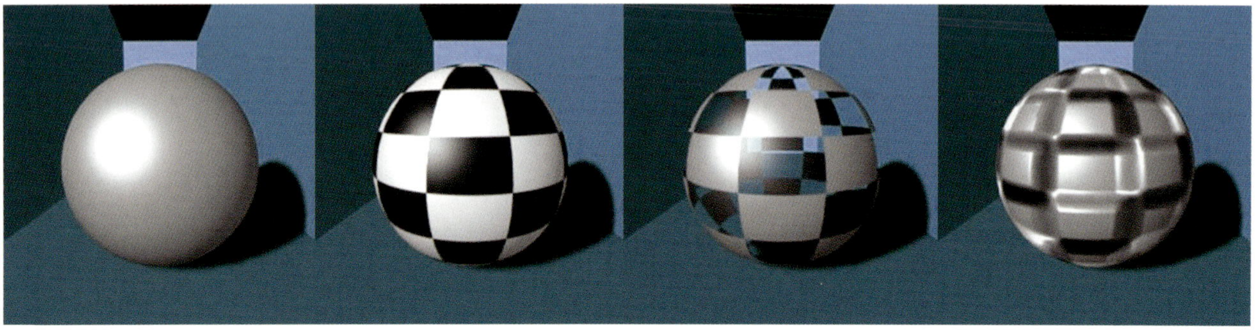

Kugel ohne Mapping

Beim Farb-Mapping wird die Farbe der Oberfläche durch eine Textur ersetzt.

Beim Transparent-Mapping bestimmt die Textur die Transparenz.

Bump-Mapping simuliert eine Oberflächenstruktur

❷ Shading bedeutet in der Computer-Animation „Gestalten mit Farbverläufen“. Es wird durch Beleuchtungsmodelle (Shader) mit deren komplexen Algorithmen realisiert.

Beim **Shading** ❷ wird festgelegt, wie die Oberflächen auf das einfallende Licht reagieren. Man unterscheidet zwischen spiegelndem und diffusem Reflexionsverhalten.

Sind die Oberflächen definiert, wird durch Setzen der Lichtquellen und der Kamerapositionen die virtuelle Beleuchtungssituation aufgebaut. Das Modellieren der Lichtquellen besteht aus dem Einrichten ihrer Position und Definition der Lichtfarbe und der Lichtform (beispielsweise Punktlicht, Spotlicht und Umgebungslicht). Zum Einrichten der Kamera wird deren Position und Einstellung bestimmt.

Eine erweiterte Form der Beleuchtungsverfahren ist das **Ray Tracing** und das Radiosity. Hierbei handelt es sich um komplexe Algorithmen für eine möglichst realitätsnahe Wiedergabe einer Szene. Diese Verfahren berücksichtigen stets auch Phänomene wie Schattenwurf, Transparenz und Reflexion im Zusammenspiel mit anderen Objekten.

Beim Ray Tracing, dem Strahlverfolgungsverfahren, werden neben der Reflexion von Lichtstrahlen auch die Refraktion und die Schattenbildung bei spiegelnden und transparenten Objekt-Oberflächen berücksichtigt. Beim Rendervorgang wird dabei von jedem Pixel des Bildes ein Strahl in die Szene geschickt. Dieser wird hinsichtlich der Räumlichkeit ausgewertet und die Farbe des Pixels kann berechnet werden.

Beispiel: Zwei nebeneinander liegende Kugeln mit Chrom-Mapping über Ray Tracing gerendert, erzeugen gegenseitig mehrfache Lichtspiegelungen.

Beim **Radiosity**, dem Lichtenergiekalkül, wird zu Grunde gelegt, dass die Summe der ausgestrahlten und reflektierten Energie der gesamten Menge der von einer Oberfläche abgestrahlten Energie entspricht. Damit kann unabhängig vom Betrachtungsstandpunkt die Farbe jedes Pixels des Bildes berechnet werden. Diese Art der Berechnung ist sehr zeitintensiv, liefert aber eine realitätsnahe Beleuchtung.

9.3.4 Animation

Sind die Objekte erst einmal konstruiert, hat jetzt der Gestalter alle Möglichkeiten, die Objekteigenschaften über einen Zeitraum zu verändern. Dazu verfügen die Programme über die Schlüsselbildtechnik mit Key Frames und Zwischenbildanimationen, sowie über die Möglichkeit der Pfadanimation.

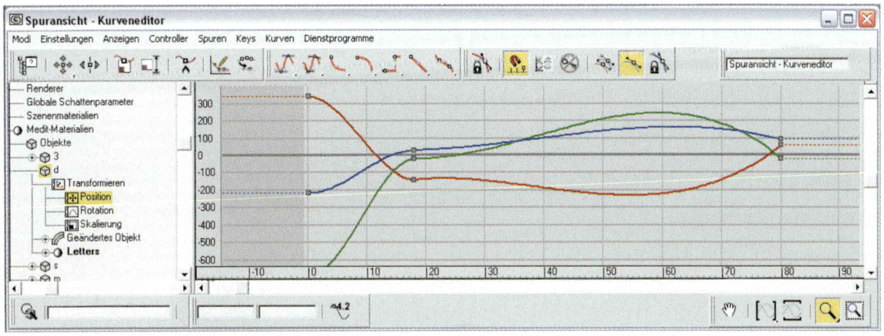

Jede Eigenschaft der Objekte kann zeitlich präzise animiert werden.
Beispiel: Kurveneditor des 3D-Programms 3DStudio Max.

Bei der Erstellung einer Animation müssen generell die Positionierungen der Beleuchtung, der Kamera und der Objekte beachtet werden. Bei der Kamera gehören Schwenks und Fahrten durch die Szene zu den Bewegungsanimationen.
Für jeden Key Frame kann der Zustand und die Position der Objekte, der Kamera und der Beleuchtung verändert werden. Dazu zählen auch Skalierungen und Formveränderungen der Objekte.

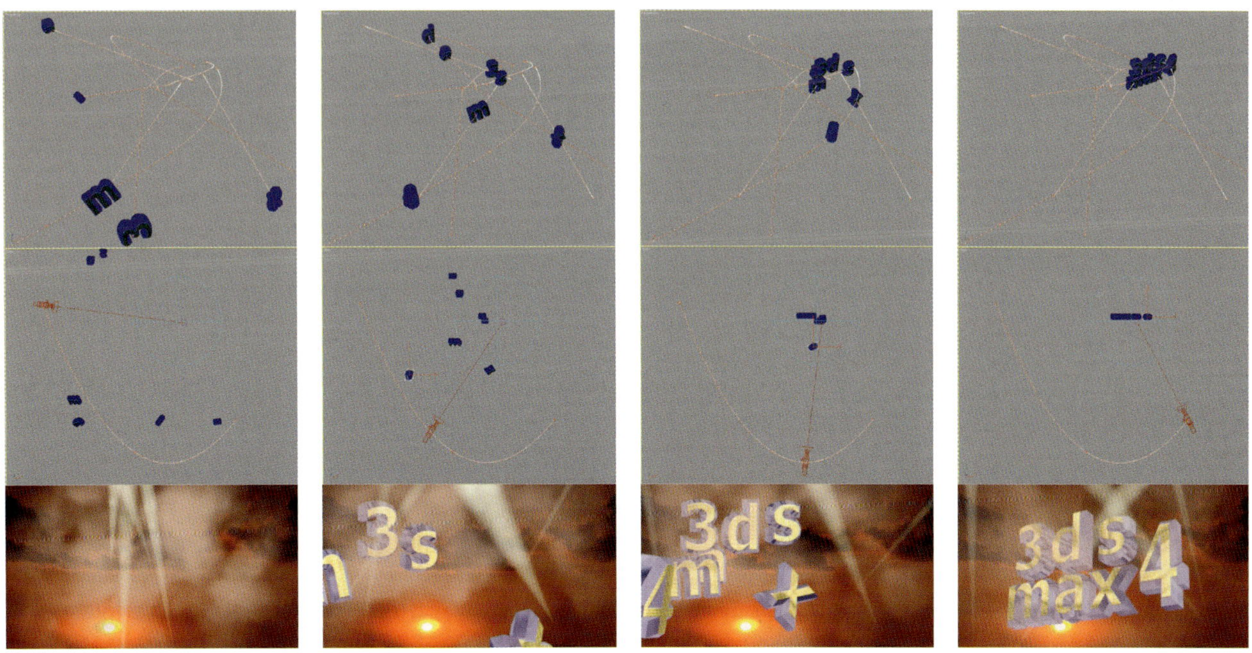

Beispiel einer 3D-Animation mit einem sich aufbauenden Buchstaben-Logo. Die obere Reihe zeigt die Pfadanimation, die mittlere Reihe den Kameraschwenk von oben und die untere Reihe die gerenderte Sequenz aus der Kameraperspektive.

9.3.5 Rendering

Beim Rendering berechnet das 3D-Programm alle Einzelphasenbilder mit allen Veränderungen des Objektes, der Lichtwirkung und der Kamerafahrt. Je nach verwendetem Renderverfahren werden Schattenwurf der Objekte, Reflexion und Transparenz der Oberflächen berücksichtigt. Entscheidend für die Qualität einer realitätsnahen Darstellung ist neben der exakten Modellierung der Szene in erster Linie die genaue Bestimmung der Lichtverteilung auf den Oberflächen der Objekte, welche sich aus der Beleuchtung durch direkte und indirekte Lichtquellen und der Interaktion mit anderen Körpern (Schatten und Reflexionen) ergibt. Dies kann, insbesondere bei komplexen Beleuchtungsverfahren wie dem Radiosity, zu sehr zeitintensiven Berechnungen führen.

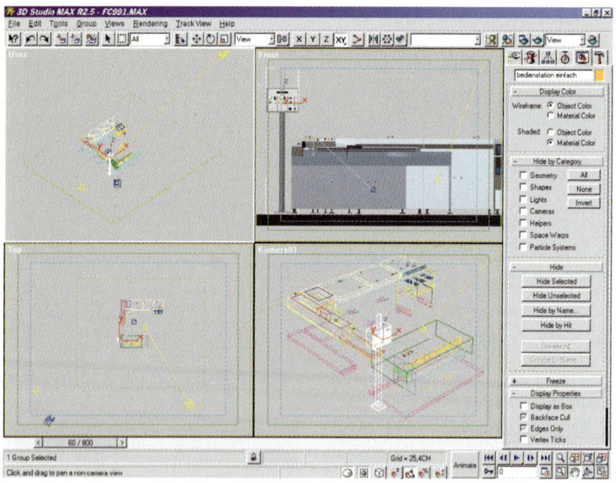

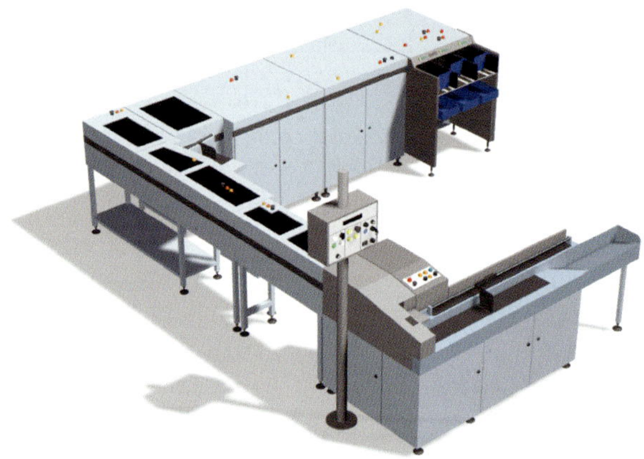

Komplexe technische Maschine aus der Automatisierungstechnik. Das linke Bild zeigt das Objekt, konstruiert und mit Beleuchtung versehen im 3D-Programm und das rechte Bild zeigt ein daraus gerendertes Einzelbild für eine Filmsequenz.
Quelle: Siemens AG.

Bei der Wahl des Render-Verfahrens ist dabei immer Qualität gegenüber dem Zeitaufwand zu optimieren. Dazu werden im professionellen Bereich Renderaufgaben auf mehrere Rechner, sogenannte **Render-Farmen**, verteilt. Damit kann die rechenintensive Aufgabe beim Rendern durch einen Parallelbetrieb von mehreren Rechnern beschleunigt werden. Viele 3D-Grafikprogramme verfügen bereits im Standardumfang oder als Modul über die Möglichkeit, eine eigene Render-Farm aufzubauen. Eine Render-Farm besteht meist aus handelsüblichen PCs, die miteinander vernetzt sind. Dabei kommuniziert ein Render-Manager mit einer festgelegten Gruppe von Render-PCs, um Aufträge zuzuweisen und den Fortgang des Renderns zu überwachen. In der Regel erfolgt die Auftragsvergabe auf Einzelbildbasis. Ein Render-PC erhält den Auftrag, ein Einzelbild zu rendern. Nachdem er das Bild errechnet hat, schickt er es zum Render-Manager zurück und erhält dann den nächsten Auftrag, wieder ein Einzelbild zu rendern usw. Wenn ein einzelner Render-PC ausfällt, rechnen die anderen PCs weiter. Steht nicht genügend Rechenkapazität zur Verfügung, kann die Render-Farm durch weitere PCs erweitert werden.
Umfangreiche Render-Farmen kamen unter anderem bei aufwendigen 3D-Animationen für Kinofilme, wie zum Beispiel „Herr der Ringe“ oder „Titanic“ zum Einsatz.

9.4 Virtual Reality

Virtual Reality (VR), die virtuelle Realität, ist heutzutage wohl die faszinierendste Bildkomponente bei Multimedia-Anwendungen. Im Wesentlichen ist es eine Technik, die dem Benutzer erlaubt, sich interaktiv in einer computergenerierten, oft dreidimensionalen, Umgebung zu bewegen. Das Besondere an VR-Komponenten ist die Interaktivität. Einfach per Mausklick ändert der Benutzer den Betrachtungsstandpunkt und bekommt ein neues Bild präsentiert. Man unterscheidet bei Virtual Reality-Systemen zweidimensionale (2D) und dreidimensionale (3D) Systeme.

9.4.1 2D-VR-Systeme

Zweidimensionale VR-Anwendungen bieten auf einem Computerbildschirm äußerst interessante Möglichkeiten. Speziell zusammengesetzte Raumbilder können durch einfaches Steuern mit der Maus verändert werden. Dabei kann der Betrachter die Blickrichtung um 360° drehen und mit Hilfe einer Zoomfunktion den Bildausschnitt verändern. Hinsichtlich der Betrachtungsweise unterscheidet man hierbei zwischen **Panoramen** ❶ und **Objekt-Movies** ❷.

Für das Darstellen der Panoramen und Objekt-Movies wird eine eigene Viewer-Software benötigt. Für Publikationen im Internet werden proprietäre Viewer-Programme verwendet, die sich entweder in Form von Plug-ins in den Internet-Browser integrieren oder als Java-Applets durch die Java-Funktionalität des Browsers dargestellt werden. Verbreitete Plug-ins sind dabei das QuickTime Virtual Reality (QTVR) von Apple oder das iPIX-Plug-in von IPIX-Software.

❶ Giraffen als interaktives Panorama im iPIX-Viewer.

❷ Uhr als **Object-Movie** im QTVR-Viewer.

Interaktive VR-Panoramen

Diese Anwendungen verwenden Panoramabilder, die aus Einzelbildern zusammengesetzt wurden. Die Einzelbilder können anhand von Fotografien oder computergenerierten Bildern erstellt werden. Das Zusammenfügen der Einzelbilder erfolgt durch das **Stitching-Modul** ❸ der Panorama-Erstellungssoftware. Für das realitätsnahe Darstellen im Viewer ist es erforderlich, dass eine Raumkrümmung durch Projektion erzeugt wird. Je nach Projektionsform unterscheidet man zwischen Zylindrischen Panoramen, Sphärischen Panoramen und Kubischen Panoramen.

❸ Der Begriff **Stitchen** kommt aus dem Englischen und bedeutet wörtlich übersetzt „Nähen". Man bezeichnet damit das nahtlose Zusammenfügen von Einzelbildern.

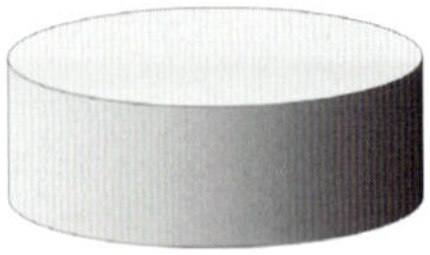

❶ Zylindrische Projektion

❷ Sphärische Projektion

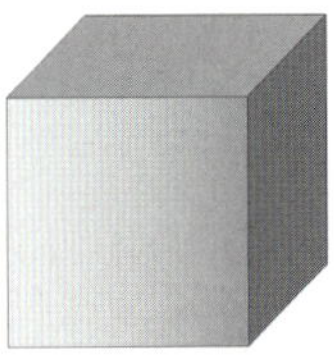

❸ Kubische Projektion

Bei der **zylindrischen Projektion** ❶ wird das Panoramabild quasi um einen Zylinder gewickelt, in dessen Mitte sich der Betrachter befindet. Durch eine leichte Wölbung bekommt das Bild die notwendige realistische Anmutung. Bei dieser Art der Projektion können Panoramen mit einem vertikalen Bildwinkel bis zu 120° erstellt werden. Im Gegensatz zur zylindrischen Projektion ist bei der **sphärischen Projektion** ❷ der vertikale Bildwinkel nicht begrenzt, reicht also komplett von unten nach oben und erreicht deshalb 180°. Dabei werden die Bilder kugelförmig projiziert und der Betrachter befindet sich optisch im Zentrum der Kugel.

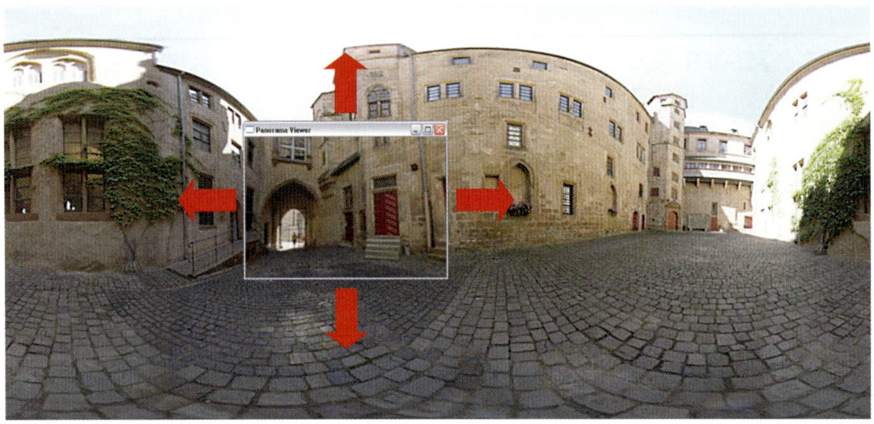

Beispiel eines Panoramas in sphärischer Projektion. Mit dem Viewer kann der Benutzer das komplette Raumbild, horizontal 360° und vertikal 180°, erkunden.

Die **kubische Projektion** ❸ projiziert die Bilder in Form eines Würfels. Die Speicherung des Panoramabildes erfolgt über sechs Teilbilder. Um bei der Projektion eine kantenlose Darstellung zu erreichen, werden die Teilbilder bei der Projektion je nach Betrachtungsposition entsprechend verzerrt.

Virtuelle Rundgänge mit Hotspots

Diese Technik eignet sich besonders zum eigenen Erkunden innerhalb eines virtuellen Raumes, zum Beispiel im Innern eines Gebäudes. Aber auch als Benutzerschnittstelle kann VR dem Benutzer einen völlig neuen Zugang zu Informationen eröffnen. Technisch werden **virtuelle Rundgänge** ❹ so realisiert, dass mehrere Einzelpanoramen mittels so genannter **Hotspots** miteinander verlinkt sind. Klickt man auf einen Hotspot im Panorama, so gelangt man zur nächsten Stelle des Rundgangs und kann auf diesem Panorama den Rundgang fortsetzen.

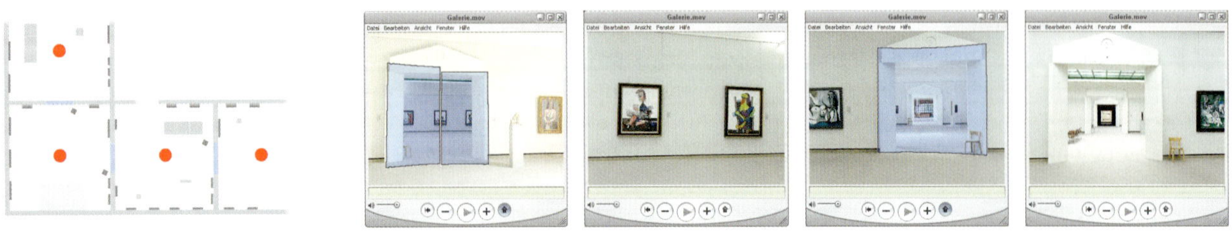

❹ Beispiel eines virtuellen Galerie-Rundganges. Die Einzel-Panoramen (rot) sind über Hotspots (blau) miteinander verbunden.

Interaktive VR-Object Movies

Ein Objekt-Movie ist ein umgekehrtes Panorama. Hier wandert der Betrachtungswinkel sozusagen um das fotografierte Objekt. Es entsteht der virtuelle Eindruck, dass sich das Objekt um die eigene Achse dreht. Im Gegensatz zu VR-Panoramen sind Object-Movies aus einer größeren Anzahl von Bildern zusammengesetzt.

Um in einem **Object-Movie** das Produkt fließend darzustellen, sollten für eine 360° Umrundung möglichst viele Einzelbilder (> 36) verwendet werden.

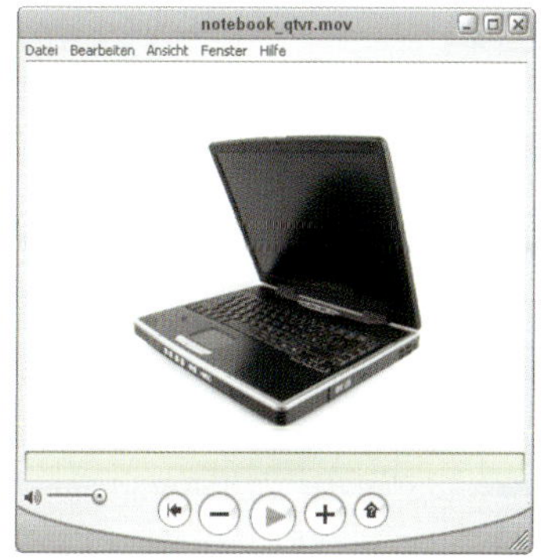

Object-Movie mit QuickTimeVR

Jedes Bild zeigt das Objekt von einem sich gering unterscheidenden Winkel. Wenn der Benutzer das Objekt nach links oder rechts bzw. hoch oder herunter bewegt, wird die entsprechende Bildfolge als Film abgespielt. Mit anderen Worten sind VR-Object Movies navigierbare Filme von Objekten.

❶ Bei der **Singlerow-Technik** wird eine Reihe von Einzelbildern aufgenommen. Diese Technik eignet sich für **zylindrische Projektionen.**

Produktion der VR-Panoramen und VR-Object Movies

Zur Produktion dieser VR-Anwendungen muss zuerst für die richtige Aufnahmetechnik gesorgt werden. Man erfasst dazu die komplette 360°-Umgebung durch eine Vielzahl von Einzelbildern mit handelsüblichen Fotokameras.

❷ Bei der **Multirow-Technik** werden mehrere sich überlappende horizontale Bildreihen aufgenommen. Durch diese Technik kann der für die **sphärische** und **kubische Projektion** notwendige vertikale Bildwinkel von 180° erreicht werden.

Die Vorgehensweise ist dabei Folgende: Die Kamera wird auf ein Stativ gestellt und das erste Einzelbild wird fotografiert. Dann wird die Kamera um einen bestimmten Winkel weitergedreht, dort wird das nächste Bild aufgenommen, bis die kompletten 360° erfasst sind. Dabei müssen die Einzelbilder im Winkel eine Überlappung aufweisen, damit sie später sauber zusammengefügt werden können.

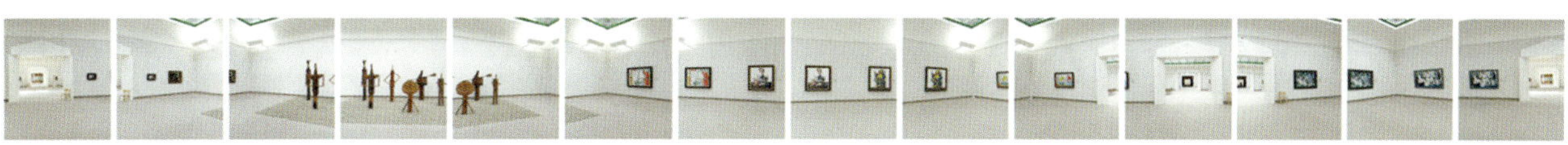

❶ Einzelbilder eines Singlerow-Panoramas.

Je nach Projektionsform des Panoramas ist entweder die **Singlerow Technik** ❶ oder die **Multirow-Technik** ❷ zu verwenden. Für sphärische Panoramen muss auf Grund des großen vertikalen Bildwinkels die Multirow-Technik verwendet werden.

Die Belichtung sollte auf einen für alle Einzelbilder gültigen Mittelwert konstant eingestellt sein. Um Parallaxefehler zwischen Bildvordergrund und -hintergrund zu vermeiden sollten Spezialstative Verwendung finden, die um den **Nodalpunkt** ❸ drehen können.

❸ Der **Nodalpunkt** bezeichnet das optische Zentrum einer Kamera- und Objektivkombination.

Einzelbilder eines Multirow-Panoramas.

❶ Die **Stitching-Software** ist ein Bestandteil der VR-Programme. Beispiele für VR-Programme sind: REALVIZ Stitcher, VR Worx, PTools, HotMedia, iPIX Builder und QTVR Edit.

Mit einer **Stitching-Software** ❶ werden die Einzelbilder dann zu dem 360° Panoramabild zusammengefügt. Dabei wird mit Hilfe der sich überlappenden Bereiche der Einzelbilder das Komplettbild zusammengefügt.

9.4.2 3D-VR-Systeme

Eine weitere Stufe zur virtuellen Realität ist die **Virtual Reality Modeling Language** (VRML), ein Format zur dreidimensionalen VR-Darstellung. Über VRML ist es möglich, nicht nur die Ansichten interaktiv zu bestimmen, sondern VRML erlaubt zusätzlich eine komplette 3D-Navigation in vom Computer erzeugten virtuellen Räumen. Im Gegensatz zu image-orientierten VR-Formaten, wie z. B. QTVR, ist VRML ein vektor -orientiertes Grafikformat. Alle Informationen des 3D-Raumes werden dabei erst bei Bedarf errechnet. Die eigentliche Informationsmenge ist dabei gegenüber reiner Image-Formate sehr gering. Zur Wiedergabe im Internet-Browser wird eine Programmerweiterung (Plug-in), ein sogenannten VRML-Viewer, benötigt. Das individuelle Bild ruft der Anwender mit Hilfe der interaktiven Steuerung ab.

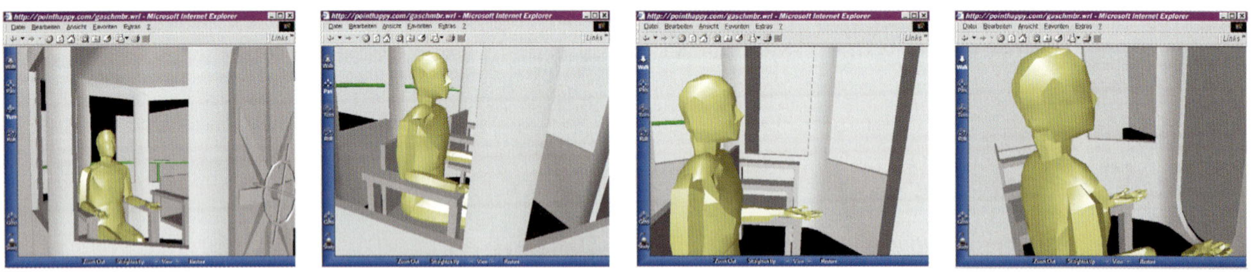

Virtual Reality mit VRML erlaubt interaktiv ein freies Bewegen in einem virtuellen Raum.

9.4.3 3D-VR-Simulatoren

Spezielle VR-Simulationseinrichtungen erlauben mit Hilfe zusätzlicher Hardwarekomponenten verblüffend wirklichkeitsnah, in computergenerierten 3D-Welten zu navigieren. Spezielle Monitorbrillen, die beiden Augen leicht versetzte Bilder vorspielen, lassen beim Anwender einen räumlichen Eindruck entstehen.

Die interaktive Steuerung durch den Anwender kann durch den **Datenhandschuh** ❶ erfolgen, der die Handposition und Handgestik in Steuerungsbefehle umsetzt. Abhängig von der Steuerung des Anwenders wird mit Hilfe eines enormen Rechenaufwands in Echtzeit das jeweilige dreidimensionale Bild der virtuellen Umgebung errechnet. Über die **Monitorbrille** ❷ sieht der Anwender zu jeder Zeit dann genau das Bild, das der virtuellen Umgebung entspricht. Eine weitere Stufe der virtuellen Realität ist z. B. CyberstageTM der GMD oder CAVETM. Beim System CAVE ❸ handelt es sich um einen zimmergroßen Raum, der von allen Seiten durch Rückprojektionen beleuchtet wird. Darin können mehrere Personen, ausgerüstet mit **Shutter-Brillen** ❹ faszinierende virtuelle Welten erleben. Gebäude, die noch nicht existieren, werden begehbar, Ärzte können Operationen am genau nachgebildeten Computermodell eines Patienten durchführen, um sich auf schwierige Operationen vorzubereiten. Dies stellt eine vielversprechende Technologie für die Zukunft dar.

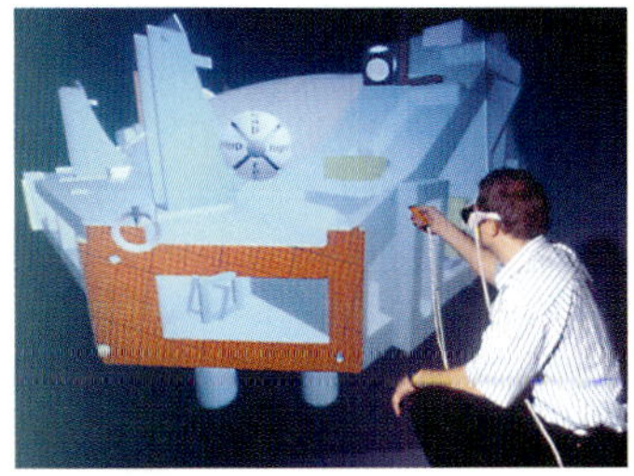

Virtual Reality Anwendung „Personal Immersion System" des Fraunhofer-Instituts.

❶ **Datenhandschuh** für die interaktive Navigation in der virtuellen Welt.

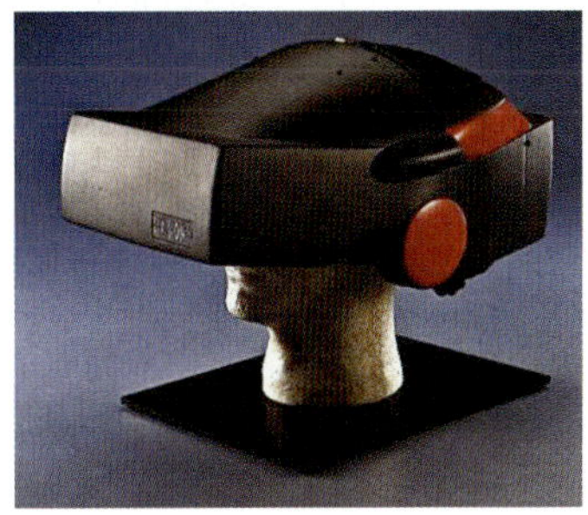

❷ Head-Mounted Displays (HMD) als **Monitorbrille** für VR-Anwendungen.

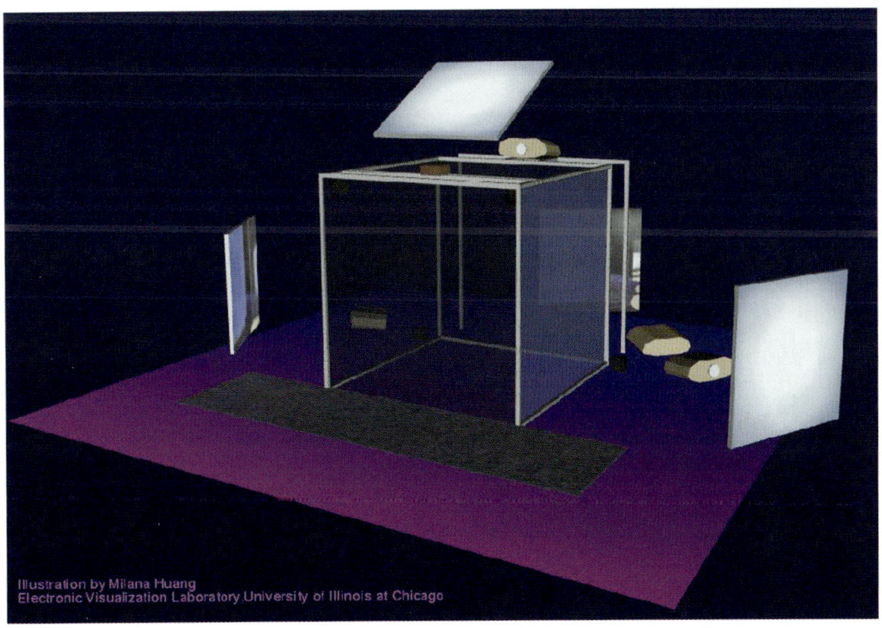

❸ **CAVE** – Cave Automatic Virtual Envirement (Electronic Visualisation Laboratory, University of Illinois).

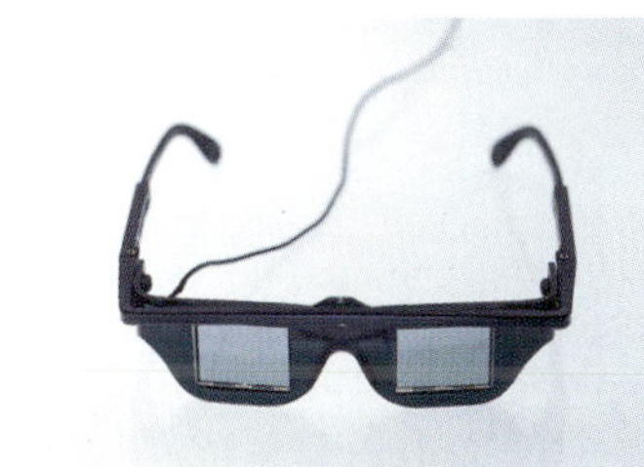

❹ **Shutter-Brillen** blenden, synchron zur Bildwiederholfrequenz des zu betrachtenden Bildes, im Wechsel immer ein Auge zu und erlauben dadurch das Betrachten von virtuellen 3D-Bildern. Quelle: 3D Revelator von Elsa.

9.4.4 Augmented Reality

❶ **AR-Systemkomponenten**: Tragbarer Computer, Monitorbrille, Kamera und Sensoren. Quelle: Rockwell.

Augmented Reality (AR) steht für „erweiterte Realität" und bezeichnet eine Weiterentwicklung der Technologien der 3D-Visualisierung und der Virtual Reality.
In der AR wird nicht versucht, die reale Welt komplett nachzubilden, sondern die Umgebung wird integriert. Der Anwender nutzt dabei einen tragbaren Computer ❶ mit spezieller Monitorbrille, der mit unterschiedlichen Sensoren ausgestattet ist.

Ein AR-System funktioniert prinzipiell folgendermaßen:
- Das AR-System erkennt und analysiert die Umgebung.
- In Abhängigkeit der analysierten Umgebungsinformationen generiert das System Bilder und Daten.
- Mit Hilfe eines Tracking-Verfahrens werden die generierten Bilder mit den realen Bildern in Deckung ❷ gebracht.
- Über Spezialmonitore, z. B. Monitorbrille, werden die kombinierten Bilder direkt in das reale Sichtfeld des Anwenders eingeblendet.

AR zur Auto-Navigation. Der Navigations-Bildschirm zeigt landschaftliche Details fast fotorealistisch. Navigationshinweise werden direkt auf der Windschutzscheibe abgebildet. Quelle: Siemens VDO.

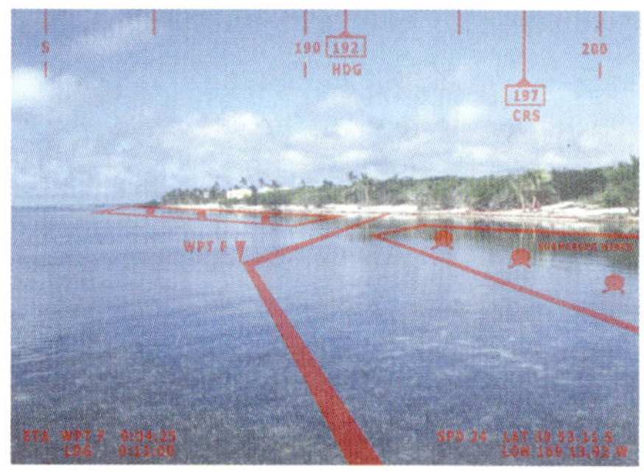

AR Minenfeld-Navigation in einer Küstenzone. Beispiel aus dem militärischen Bereich. Quelle: Information in Place, USA.

❷ Beispiel von Realbild und 3D-Bild- Überlagerung. Quelle: Mars Outdoor AR, Columbia University.

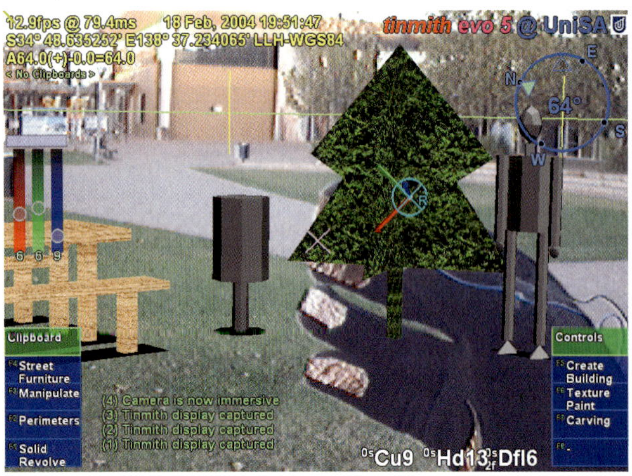

Dazu muss das System über aufwändige Algorithmen für die Bilderkennung verfügen, ein schnelles Rendern der generierten Computerbilder ermöglichen und in Echtzeit (Realtime) Realbild und Computerbild deckungsgleich zur Anzeige bringen.
Die dafür notwendige Echtzeit-Systemleistung (Realtime-System) sprengt heute noch handelsübliche IT-Systeme. AR ist eine Technologie, die sich weltweit noch im Pionierstadium befindet, sich aber durch die fortschreitende Miniaturisierung der Gerätetechnologie und der zunehmenden Leistungsfähigkeit in vielfältigen Anwendungen weiterentwickeln wird.
Beispiele für zukünftige Anwendungsbereiche finden sich bei der Unterstützung in der Industrie von Entwicklung bis Service, der Architektur, dem Tourismus, dem Medizinbereich, dem Militär und der Archäologie.

Aufgaben und Übungen, Literaturhinweise

Aufgaben und Übungen

1. Phasenanimation
   Erstellen Sie in einem MS Powerpoint eine Figur mit separat angelegten Elementen „Körper“, „Beine“, „Füße“, „Arme“ und „Kopf“. Duplizieren Sie diese Figur 10 mal und verändern Sie die Position der Elemente so, dass Einzelphasenbilder entstehen. Die Einzelphasenbilder können Sie nun über „Automatische Folienübergänge“ zu einer Phasenanimation ablaufen lassen.
2. Button-Animation
   Erstellen Sie wie in Aufgabe 1 insgesamt drei Einzelphasenbilder eines Buttons (Schaltfläche) für die Zustände „Aktiv“, „Mouse-over“ und „Deaktiv“. Verknüpfen Sie über „Aktionseinstellungen“ die Einzelphasen-Elementen untereinander.
3. Schlüsselbildtechnik
   Erstellen Sie in einem 2D-Animationsprogramm, z. B. Adobe Flash, mit der Schlüsselbildtechnik eine Interpolations-Animation mit Form- und Bewegungs-Tweening.
4. 3D-Modellierung
   Entwickeln Sie eine Vorgehensweise in Skizzen, wie Sie die Objekte „Flasche“, „Golfball“ und „Eierbecher“ in einem 3D-Programm modellieren würden. Verwenden Sie dabei unterschiedliche Modellierungsmethoden.
5. VR-Panorama
   Fotografieren Sie die notwendigen Einzelbilder für ein zylindrisches VR-Panorama in Singlerow-Technik. Verwenden Sie dazu ein Stativ und eine manuelle Belichtung. Verknüpfen Sie die Einzelbilder mit einer Stitching-Software und exportieren das Panorama in ein Viewer-fähiges Format (z. B. QTVR oder Java).

Literaturhinweise

Friedrich, Wolfgang: ARVIKA. Augmented Reality für Entwicklung, Produktion und Service, München u. a. 2004 (Publicis Corporate Publishing)

Jackel, Dietmar; *Neunreither*, Stephan; *Wagner*, Friedrich: Methoden der Computeranimation, Berlin 2006 (Springer Verlag)

Jacobs, Corinna: Digitale Panoramen. Tipps, Tricks und Techniken für die Panoramafotografie, Berlin u. a. 2004 (Springer Verlag)

Kohlmann, Klaus: Der computeranimierte Spielfilm. Bielefeld 2007 (Transcript-Verlag)

Lama, Toni: 3D-Welten. Professionelle Animationen und fotorealistische Grafiken mit Raytracing, München u. a. 2004 (Carl Hanser Verlag)

Parent, Rick: Computer Animation. Algorithms and Techniques, San Francisco 2001 (Morgan-Kaufmann)

Schäffer, Florian: Das große Buch Webdesign. Design, Navigation, Grafik, Animation, Düsseldorf 2001 (Data Becker)

Weishar, Peter: Blue Sky: The Art of Computer Animation. Algorithms and Techniques, New York 2002 (Harry N. Abrahamas)

Velsz, Istvan: Grundlagen und Praxis der 3D-Visualisierung und –animation, München u. a. 2002 (Addison Wesley)

10 Audio

Webcode: B1000

Für weitere Infos zu diesem Kapitel mit dem Smartphone einfach QR-Code scannen oder auf www.medien-verstehen.de den Webcode eingeben.

Dieses Kapitel soll einen Einblick in die Welt der Töne geben, Möglichkeiten der Gestaltung mit Tönen in den Neuen Medien aufzeigen und Grundlagen der dabei erforderlichen Tontechnik vermitteln.

Fast jeder kennt die Kinofilme „2001- Odyssee im Weltraum", „E.T.", „Jurassic Park" und „Titanic". Es sind nur einige wenige Beispiele hervorragender Vertreter ihres Genres. Wie wirkungsvoll verwoben das bewegte Bild, Sprache, Musik und Geräusch ist, lässt sich erahnen, wenn wir diese Filme ohne Ton betrachten.

Auch in interaktiven Anwendungen, wie zum Beispiel „SimCity 3000" oder „Die Sims 2", wird der Ton vorteilhaft in das Programm integriert. Musik und Geräusche ertönen und sogleich glaubt der Betrachter die Handlung nicht mehr nur auf einem flachen Bildschirm zu erleben, sondern in einem Raum, der sich von der Mattscheibe zu lösen scheint. Sprecher führen den Nutzer durch die Anwendung, stellen Aufgaben oder geben Hinweise. Der Ton wird ein Teil des Dialogs zwischen Mensch und Maschine. Diese Produkte stehen am Ende einer intensiven und spannenden Arbeit am Ton.

Oft bleiben dem Hörer die Vorarbeiten zur Tonaufnahme verborgen. So müssen Tonquellen für eine Nachvertonung ausfindig gemacht und daraufhin möglicherweise Verwertungsrechte an Tonmaterialien geklärt werden.

Seit es interaktive Anwendungen gibt, spielt der Programmierer eine wichtige Rolle im Produktionsteam. Mit ihm werden die Möglichkeiten der programmiertechnischen Einbindung von Ton in die interaktive Anwendung erörtert und gegebenenfalls Standards für das Produkt definiert. In der Arbeit am Ton finden wir sowohl Musiker, wie Komponisten, Sounddesigner und Geräuschemacher, Sprecher und Synchronsprecher, Multimedia-Autoren, -Produzenten und Regisseure, Mischtonmeister und Sound Editoren.

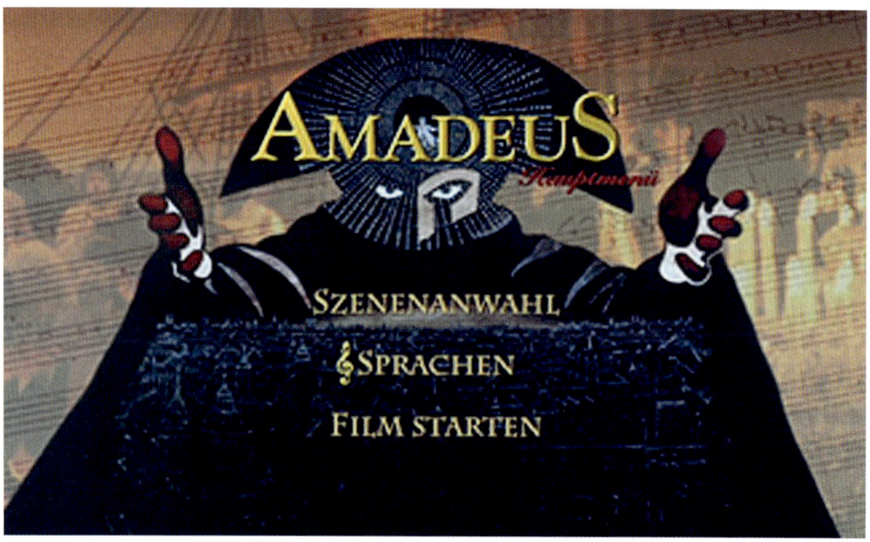

DVD-Menu zum Film „Amadeus" von Milos Forman. The Saul Zaentz Company 1984, Time Warner Entertainment Gesellschaft.

10.1 Töne

Auf dem Bahnhof, im Cafe, auf dem Flughafen, in der Sporthalle beim Basketballspiel, im Schwimmbad, auf der Straße sind unsere Ohren stets offen, für das, was auf sie einströmt; es sei denn, wir halten uns die Ohren zu. Da dies jedoch selten der Fall ist, müssen wir davon ausgehen, dass unsere Ohren ständig für alles auf Empfang stehen, was uns umgibt, sogar im Schlaf.

Im alltäglichen Leben steht der visuelle Sinn stark im Vordergrund der Wahrnehmung. Man denke an die vielen Schilder, die im Straßenverkehr zu beachten sind. Oder gar an das Informationsleitsystem auf einem Flughafen, das in überwiegendem Maße auf den visuellen Sinn ausgerichtet ist.

Im Gegensatz zur visuellen Wahrnehmung über die Augen verrät uns das Gehör zusätzlich etwas über den Raum, der außerhalb unseres Gesichtsfeldes liegt. Dabei muss etwas an die Ohren dringen, was sie in ihrer Funktion als Empfänger aufnehmen können: der Schall. Er ist begrifflich der Physik zuzuordnen und geht von Schallerzeugern aus, von Menschen, Musikinstrumenten oder anderen Gegenständen. Sprechen, Singen, Schreien, Musizieren, Knallen. Auditive Ereignisse werden in drei Kategorien unterteilt: Sprache, Musik und Geräusch. Spätestens seit der Musique concrète des Franzosen Pierre Schaeffer verschwimmt beispielsweise die Definition von Musik und Geräusch. In seiner Musik hat er Straßenlärm, Maschinengeräusche und vieles mehr verarbeitet. Er wäre sicherlich hoch erfreut gewesen, hätte er Ende der vierziger Jahre die Sample-Maschinen der Techno-Musiker als Werkzeuge für seine Musik einsetzen können. Hiermit sei lediglich angedeutet, dass es uns nicht um musikwissenschaftlich eindeutige Definitionen oder gar um das Verwerfen der drei Kategorien Sprache, Musik und Geräusch geht. Wir verwenden sie im alltäglichen Sinn.

Schallereignis, Hörereignis

Es ist heiß. Das Fenster steht offen, um ein wenig frische Luft hereinzulassen. Draußen lärmt der Straßenverkehr. Die Tür geht auf. Jemand tritt ein und beginnt ein Gespräch. Im ersten Moment ist kaum etwas zu verstehen. Das Fenster wird besser wieder geschlossen.

Schallereignis = objektiv
Hörereignis = subjektiv

Sprache kann sich mit Hilfe von Schallwellen ausbreiten. Ob jedoch die Sprache ins Bewusstsein des Zuhörers dringen kann, ist eine andere Sache. Deshalb wird zwischen dem objektiven Schallereignis und dem subjektiven Hörereignis unterschieden. Dabei ist das Schallereignis der messbare, physikalische Vorgang und das Hörereignis das, was der Wahrnehmungsvorgang daraus macht.

Schallereignis

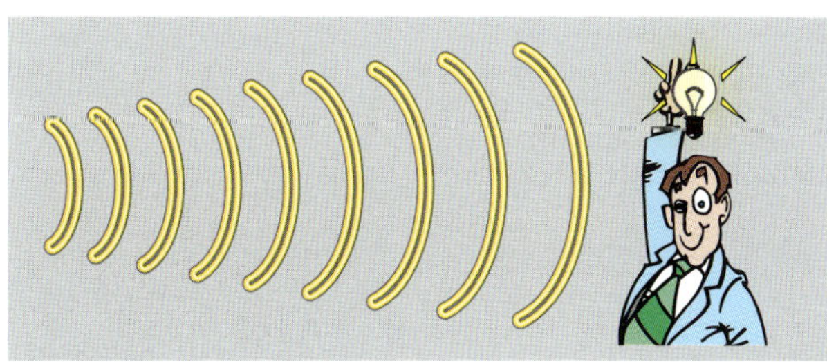

Hörereignis

10.1.1 Physik der Töne

Ton oder Ton?

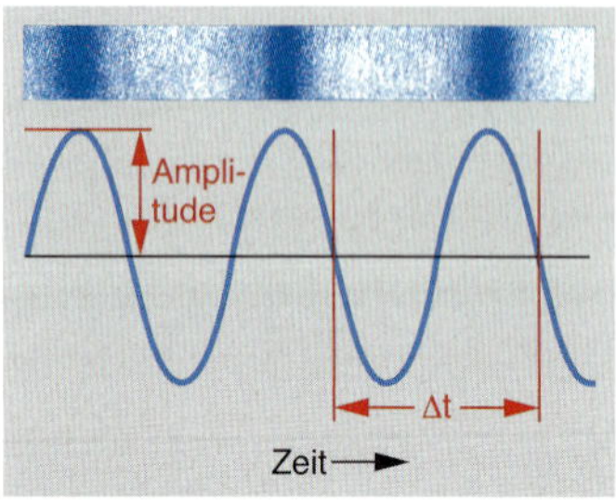

Sinuston

Was ist allen Schallereignissen gemeinsam? Hierfür müssen wir die Physik bemühen. Für den Physiker ist das kleinste Element des Schalls der Ton. Er wird beschrieben von einer sinusförmigen Druckschwankung der Luft an einem festen Ort, z. B. dem Trommelfell oder einer Mikrofonmembran. Diese sinusförmige Druckschwankung hat eine Frequenz $f = 1/\Delta t$ und eine Amplitude.
Spricht jedoch der (klassische) Musiker von einem Ton, so meint er im Sinne der Physik bereits einen Klang oder ein Tongemisch, denn natürliche Schallquellen können nur annähernd reine Sinustöne abgeben.

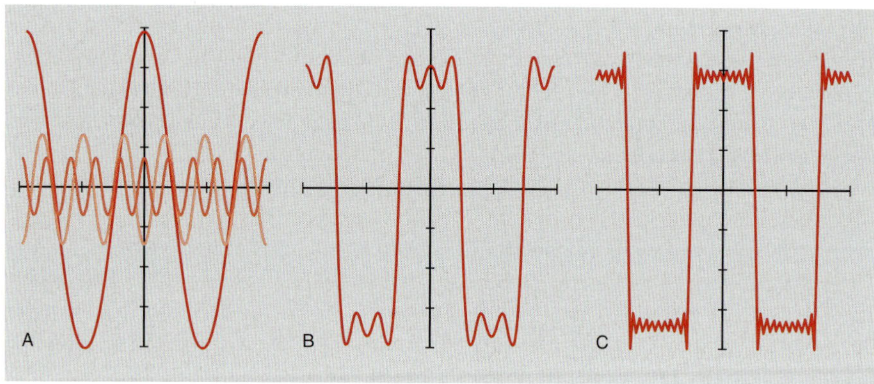

A: Darstellung dreier Schwingungen. Das Verhältnis der Frequenzen der hohen Töne zum tiefsten Ton (Grundton) ist ungeradzahlig.

B: Zeigt das Ergebnis ihrer Überlagerung, wenn sie gleichzeitig ertönen.

C: Überlagerung von mehr als drei Schwingungen mit ungeradzahligem Verhältnis der Frequenzen zur Frequenz des tiefsten Tones (Grundton).

Klangverlauf

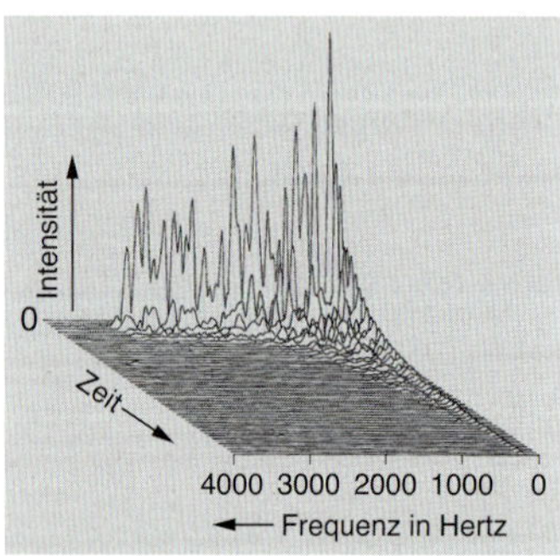

Quelle: J. R. Pierce, Klang. Mit den Ohren der Physik, 1999, S. 44.
Klangverlauf: Veränderung des Tonfrequenzspektrums eines Instrumentes über der Zeit t

Der Klang einer natürlichen Schallquelle durchläuft die Einschwing-, die quasistationäre- und die **Ausschwingphase**.

Einschwingphase:
In der **Einschwingphase** formieren sich sozusagen die spektralen Bestandteile des Klanges. Neben Grundton und harmonischen **Obertönen** bilden auch nichtharmonische Bestandteile den Klang. Sie sind abhängig von der Art der Schallquelle. Bei einem Instrument, wie z. B. dem Vibraphon, überwiegen in der Einschwingphase zunächst die nichtharmonischen spektralen Bestandteile. Sie verleihen dem Klang seine metallische Färbung. Einschwingvorgänge haben bei Schlaginstrumenten eine Dauer von einigen Millisekunden, bei großen Orgelpfeifen und Bassinstrumenten bis zu einer halben Sekunde. Im anschließenden Ausschwingvorgang des Vibraphons bestimmen die harmonischen Obertöne die Klangfarbe, der Ton klingt im Verlauf zunehmend weicher. Bei diesem Instrument ebenso wie bei allen anderen Schlag- und Zupfinstrumenten setzt der Ausschwingvorgang bereits nach dem Einschwingvorgang ein.

Quasistätionäre Phase:
Anders ist dies bei Schallquellen, die für ihre Tonbildung eine permanente Anregung erfordern. Das ist bei allen Blasinstrumenten, einer Orgel, einer Sirene oder beim Singen der Fall. Hier sorgt der Luftstrom für eine permanente Anregung. Bei ihnen

schließt sich nach der Einschwingphase deshalb eine quasistationären Phase des Klangverlaufes an. Quasistationär, weil sich der Klang auch in dieser Phase noch ändert, also nicht exakt stationär ist, messtechnisch jedoch als stationär betrachtet werden kann. So ist diese Phase durch dauernde leichte Veränderungen von Frequenz und Amplitude der Teiltöne gekennzeichnet, was zu Schwebungen, Vibrato und Tremolo führen kann. In dieser Phase bestimmen der Grundton und seine Obertöne das Klanggeschehen. Deren Frequenzen stehen im Mittel in einem ganzzahligen Verhältnis zur Frequenz des Grundtons. Das ist nicht so bei Schallquellen, die einen starken Anteil an Rauschhaftem im Klang haben, wie zum Beispiel dem Becken. Schwebungen treten auch auf, wenn sich reine Töne mit geringfügig unterschiedlicher Frequenz überlagern, dann entsteht ein Klang mit langsam periodisch schwankender Amplitude.

Vibrato = periodische Schwankung der Tonhöhe
Tremolo = periodische Schwankung der Lautstärke

Teile von Schallquellen schwingen um für sie typische Mittenfrequenzen herum besonders gut. Beispielsweise der Boden, die Decke und das eingeschlossene Luftvolumen einer Geige werden in **Resonanz** versetzt. Sie wirken dabei wie Klangfilter. Sie filtern das Frequenzspektrum der schwingenden Saite. Die Frequenzbereiche, die auf diese Weise durch Resonanz entstehen, werden Formanten genannt. Auch bei sich ändernder **Tonhöhe** der Saitenschwingung bleiben sie unverändert. Sie stehen für die Schallquelle fest, denn die Größe der resonierenden Teile oder Hohlräume sind unveränderlich. Deshalb prägen sie einen Teil des charakteristischen Klangbildes.

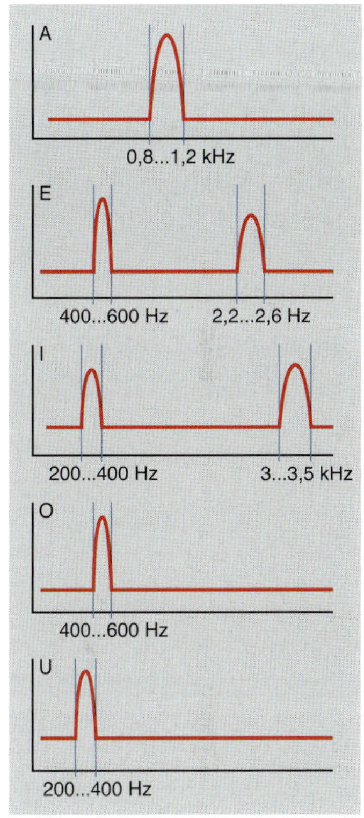

Formantbereiche der deutschen Sprache

Die Mundhöhle lässt sich jedoch in ihrer Größe variieren. Das Ergebnis sind unterschiedliche Formantbereiche, die Grundlage der Vokale. Ohne diese wäre unsere menschliche Sprache undenkbar.

Weiterhin ist auch in der quasistationären Phase ebenso wie in der Einschwingphase Rauschhaftes im Klang vertreten, was z. B. bei Blasinstrumenten vom Anblasen oder bei Streichinstrumenten vom Streichen der Saite mit dem Bogen herrührt.

Ausschwingphase:
Die Ausschwingphase beendet den Klangverlauf. Sie setzt ein, sobald die Anregung des Instrumentes beendet ist. Nimmt z. B. ein Geiger in der Bewegung den Bogen von der Saite, so ist in dem Resonanzsystem der Geige noch Energie gespeichert. Sie wird großenteils im Ausschwingvorgang über die Schallwellen abgegeben.

10.1.2 Empfindung von Tönen

Tonhöhe

Die Empfindung der Tonhöhe eines musikalischen Tones wird durch die Frequenz seines Grundtones bestimmt. Je höher seine Frequenz, desto höher wird der Ton empfunden. Das Tonhöhenempfinden ändert sich mit dem Logarithmus der Frequenz. Das Intervall einer Oktave beispielsweise besteht aus zwei Tönen deren Frequenzen im Verhältnis 1:2 stehen.

Beispiel: 20 Hz zu 40 Hz; 500 Hz zu 1000 Hz; 8000 Hz zu 16000 Hz. Der Tonfrequenzbereich des menschlichen Gehörs umfasst etwa 10 Oktaven.

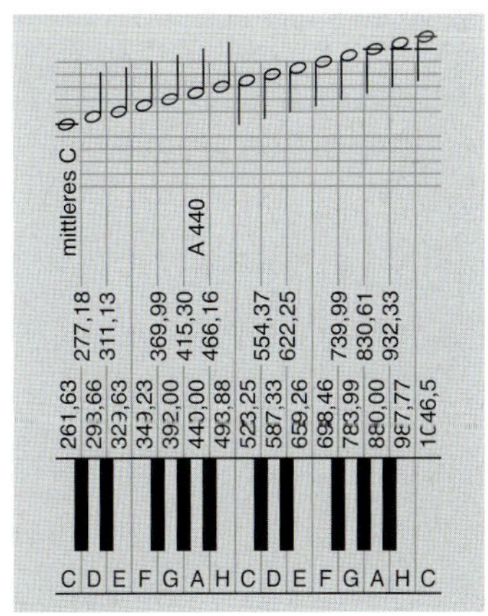

Zwei Oktaven

startender Düsenjet (Schmerzschwelle)	140
startendes Propellerflugzeug	120
U-Bahn-Express	100
laute Radiomusik/ lauter Straßenlärm	80
normales Gespräch	60
ruhiges Wohngebiet	40
Blätterrascheln	20
kaum hörbares Geräusch (Schwelle)	0

Lautstärkevergleich in dB

Lautstärke

Die Empfindung der Lautstärke eines musikalischen Tones ist dagegen komplexer. Vom Gebrauch der Stereoanlage ist uns das bekannt. Hören wir beispielsweise Musik leise im Hintergrund, so entsteht der Eindruck, die Musikaufnahme klänge flach, habe keine Bässe und keine Höhen. Eine Korrektur des Klangbildes mit dem Loudness-Schalter verstärkt die spektralen Bestandteile der tiefen und hohen Frequenzen. Drehen wir den Lautstärkeregler danach jedoch wieder auf, beginnt es zu dröhnen und das Klangbild wird aufdringlich höhenreich und spitz. Das legt die Vermutung nahe, dass die Empfindung der Lautstärke eines Tones auch von seiner Frequenz, und bei Klängen von ihrer spektralen Zusammensetzung abhängig ist.

Dies belegen Untersuchungen, die mit vielen Testhörern durchgeführt worden sind. Als Ergebnis ergaben sich die Kurven gleicher Lautstärkepegel von Fletcher und Munson.

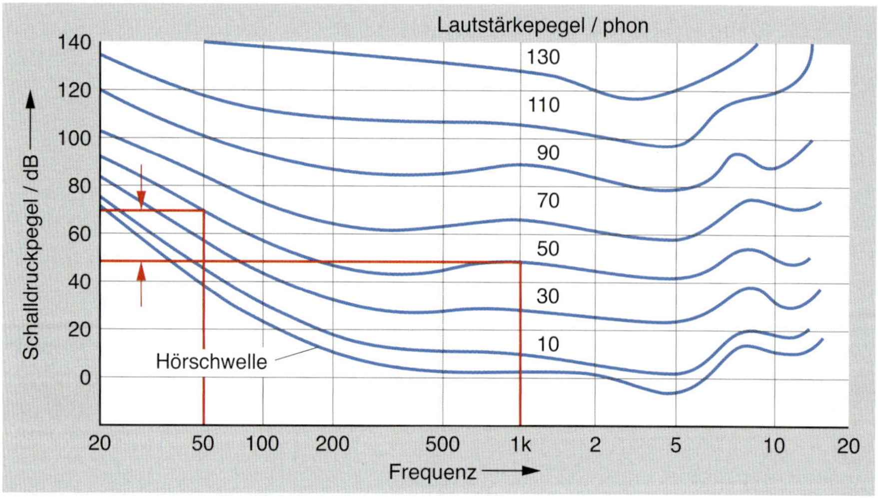

Kurven gleicher Lautstärkepegel

Die obigen Kurven gleicher Lautstärkepegel sind entstanden durch den Vergleich von Tönen mit einer Frequenz von 1000 Hz und benachbarten Tönen höherer oder tieferer Frequenz. Dabei hat sich gezeigt, dass Töne unterschiedlicher Frequenz mit dem selben **Schalldruckpegel** unterschiedlich laut empfunden werden. Wie groß der Schalldruckpegel eines Tones im Vergleich zu einem Ton von 1000 Hz sein muss, um gleich laut empfunden zu werden, zeigen die Kurven. Ein Ton mit 1000 Hz und einen Lautstärkepegel von 50 Phon wird gleich laut empfunden, wie ein tiefer Ton mit der Frequenz von 50 Hz mit einem Schalldruckpegel von 70 dB. Der tiefe Ton muss demnach einen Schalldruckpegel haben, der um 20 dB höher ist als der Ton mit 1000 Hz, um gleich laut empfunden zu werden. Lautstärkepegel und Schalldruckpegel haben für einen Ton mit der Frequenz von 1000 Hz den gleichen Betrag.

Das Gehör scheint im Bereich mittlerer Frequenzen am empfindlichsten zu sein. Menschliche Rufe oder Schreie sind deshalb besonders gut auch über große Entfernung wahrzunehmen. Dies ist vermutlich eine überlebensbegünstigende Entwicklung der menschlichen Evolution.

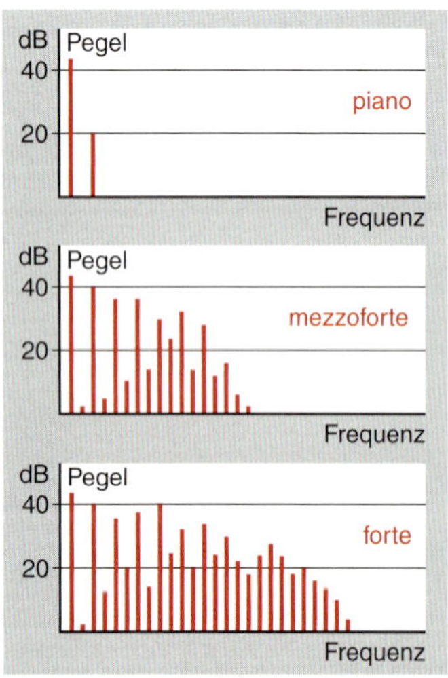

Spektrum verschiedener Dynamikstufen

Klangfarbe

Im musikalischen Ton liegt wie bereits beschrieben nicht nur die Amplitude eines einzelnen „physikalischen" (reinen) Tones vor, sondern die Amplituden der Teiltöne, des Grundtones und seiner Obertöne. Die Klangfarbe eines musikalischen Tones wird von der Zusammensetzung genau dieser Teiltöne charakterisiert. Wird ein Ton laut gespielt, so treten seine Obertöne gegenüber dem Grundton deutlich stärker hervor, als wenn er leise ertönt. Deshalb wird hier anschaulich klar, dass die Empfindung der Lautstärke eines musikalischen Tones davon abhängt, wie stark die einzelnen Obertöne gegenüber dem Grundton vertreten sind und wie sich der musikalische Ton aus eben diesen Teiltönen zusammensetzt. Es wirkt sich also auf die Empfindung der Lautstärke aus. Flüstern wird nicht zum Schreien, nur weil es elektrisch verstärkt wird! Obenstehende Grafik des Spektrums für verschiedene Dynamikstufen zeigt dies deutlich.

Werden die Amplituden der Teiltöne mit dem Grundton gleichmäßig in gewissen Grenzen erhöht, so empfinden wir dies selbstverständlich auch als Erhöhung der Lautstärke.

Der Grundton ist der Ton mit der niedrigsten Frequenz im Spektrum eines Klanges. Obertöne sind weitere reine Töne (Sinusschwingungen) höherer Frequenzen im Klang.
Die Beziehung von Oberton zu Grundton heißt harmonisch, wenn deren Frequenzen in einem ganzzahligen Verhältnis stehen.

Hinweis: In der Filmvertonung müssen auch im nachhinein Klänge an das Geschehen angepasst werden. Das erfordert auch die nachträgliche Veränderung der Lautstärke von Tönen. Durch eine elektroakustische Verstärkung eines Tones lässt sich nur bedingt der Eindruck erwecken, er sei auch laut erzeugt worden! Das Wesentliche ist in diesem Zusammenhang die Beschaffenheit seines Spektrums. Soll also ein Ton laut klingen, so muss das Ereignis bereits entsprechend eingespielt worden sein, oder die betreffenden Obertöne müssen mit geeigneten Mitteln entsprechend verstärkt werden.
Jedoch führt dies häufig nur zu einem begrenzten Erfolg!

Dauer

Eine Fotografie ist eine Momentaufnahme eines Ereignisses in einem Vorgang, fängt ein Portrait oder ein Stillleben ein. Es ist ein kurzer Moment, den der Fotograf mit dem Foto als Zeitscheibe aus einem Vorgang herauslöst. Der Faktor Dauer spielt hierbei keine Rolle. Nicht so im Ton.

Ein auditives Ereignis ist ohne den Faktor Zeit bei Aufnahme und Wiedergabe nicht vorstellbar.

Richtung und Entfernung

Neben **Tonhöhe**, **Klangfarbe** und Dauer wird auch die Richtung und Entfernung als Teil eines Hörereignisses empfunden.
Dabei ist es besonders wirkungsvoll, die Ereignisse im Raum so zu platzieren, dass sie dem Geschehen auf der visuellen Ebene entsprechen. Besonders eindrucksvoll wird der Ton mit Surround-Sound-Systemen wiedergegeben. Sie arbeiten mit mehr als nur zwei Lautsprechern und lassen den Ton gezielt aus mehreren Richtungen im Raum auf den Zuschauer einströmen. Auch in Hörspielen entstehen neue Welten durch die auditive Abbildung virtueller Räume. Um diese technischen Möglichkeiten nutzen zu können, brauchen wir ein Grundverständnis für die Wahrnehmung von Richtung und Entfernung.

Richtung

Zunächst teilen wir den uns umgebenden Raum in eine horizontale und eine vertikale Ebene.

Horizontalebene:
Die Empfindung der Richtung auf der horizontalen Ebene beruht auf der Auswertung der Unterschiede des Schalls zwischen linkem und rechtem Ohr.

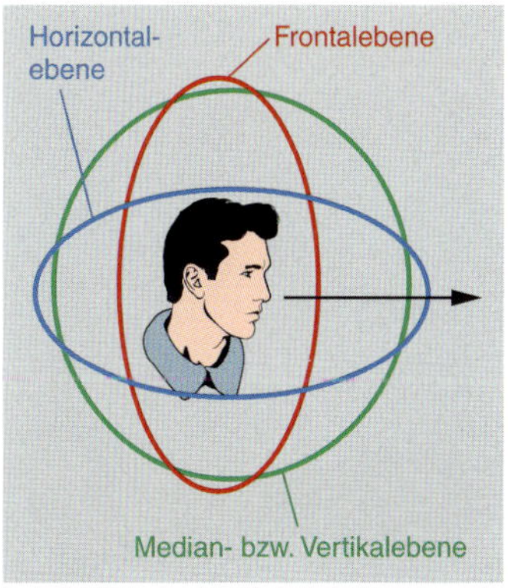

Koordinatensystem zur Beschreibung der Richtungswahrnehmung

Hinweis: Richtungsinformationen in der Tonproduktion sind am einfachsten mit Intensitätsstereofonie realisierbar. Am Mischpult finden wir den Regler Panorama. Mit ihm weisen wir dem linken und rechten Kanal einen entsprechenden Pegel der gleichen Tonquelle zu. Und platzieren somit die Tonquelle auf der Verbindungslinie zwischen den beiden vorderen Lautsprechern.

Intensität und Klangfarbe:

Der Kopf schattet den Schall bei seitlicher Schalleinfallsrichtung ab. Der Schall ist deshalb auf einem Ohr leiser als auf dem anderen. Dieser Effekt ist jedoch erst wirksam oberhalb von etwa 500 Hz und nimmt mit steigender Frequenz zu. Bei breitbandigem Schall verändert sich dadurch sein Frequenzspektrum auf dem Ohr der abgewandten Seite des Kopfes. Unterhalb von etwa 500 Hz wird der Schall um den Kopf gebeugt.

Laufzeit:

Bei seitlichen Einfallsrichtungen braucht der Schall zum abgewandten Ohr eine geringfügig längere Zeit als zum zugewandten. Die Differenzen liegen deutlich unter 1 ms. Auch aus dieser Differenz leitet unser auditives Wahrnehmungssystem die Richtung ab.

Beide Abbildungen zeigen die Abhängigkeit der Laufzeitdifferenz Δt von dem Schalleinfallswinkel Ψ

0°=	Einfallsrichtung aus der Mitte von vorne
90°=	Einfallsrichtung von links, hier erreicht die Laufzeit ihr Maximum
180°=	Einfallsrichtung aus der Mitte von hinten

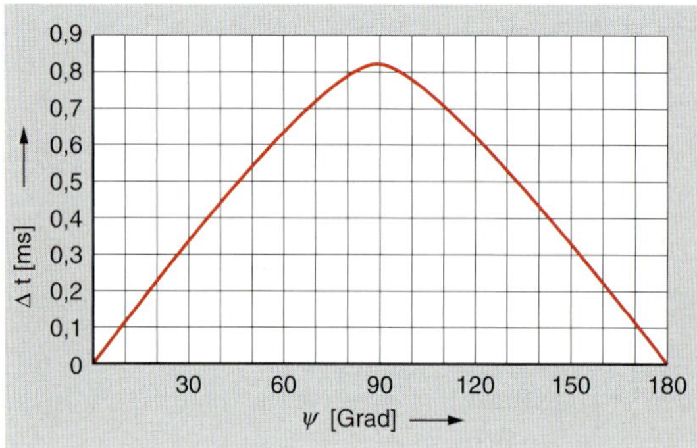

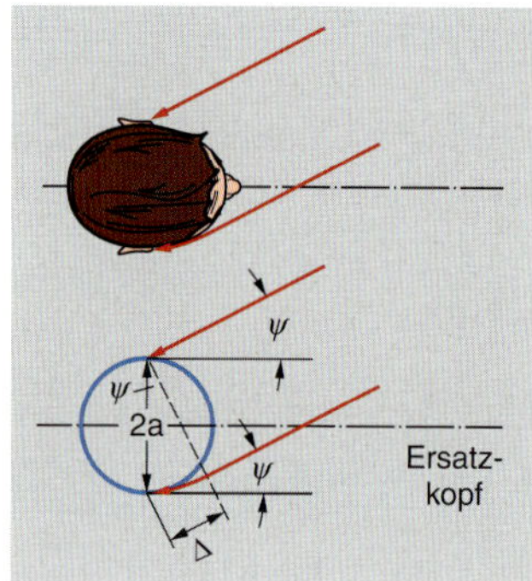

Hinweis: Wie aus den beiden obenstehenden Grafiken ersichtlich ist, sind die Laufzeiten für vorn und hinten gleich. Hier wird bereits deutlich, dass die Richtung des einfallenden Schalls in der auditiven Wahrnehmung aus mehreren zusammenspielenden Verfahren ermittelt wird.

Vertikalebene:

Aber was ist mit der Richtung auf der vertikalen Ebene? Der Schall, der auf beide Ohren trifft, ist in diesem Fall gleich! Form und Beschaffenheit von Kopf und Ohrmuscheln wirken wie ein akustisches Filter in Abhängigkeit von der Schalleinfallsrichtung. Bei unterschiedlichen Schalleinfallswinkeln auf der Vertikalebene werden entsprechende richtungbestimmende Frequenzbänder angehoben. Diese Beziehung zwischen Schalleinfallsrichtung und Klangfarbe wird für die Empfindung der Richtung ausgewertet.

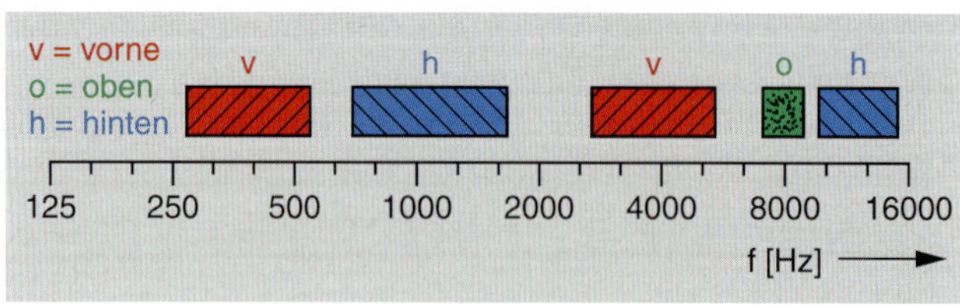

Frequenzbänder für die Ortung des Schalls auf der Vertikalebene

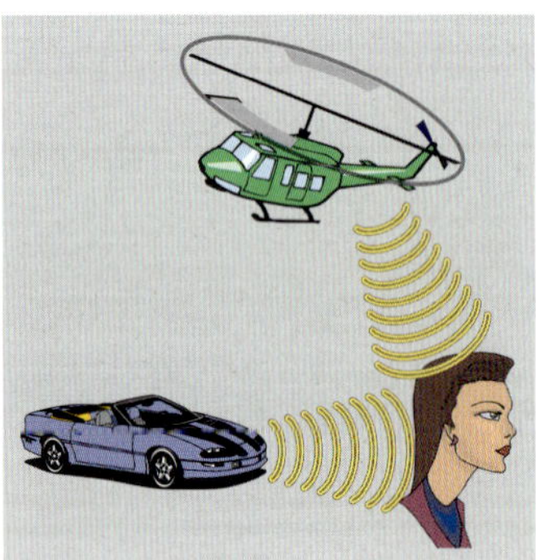

Fliegt ein Hubschrauber über uns hinweg, so trifft der Schall von oben auf den Kopf. Der Frequenzbereich um 8000 Hz im Schall des Flugzeuges wird angehoben. Werden wir von einem hinter uns fahrenden PKW angehupt, so wird das Frequenzband von etwa 700-1800 Hz und das von etwa 10-15 kHz im Schall der Hupe angehoben.

Raumakustik und Richtungswahrnehmung:
Wie wir im Kapitel Raumakustik ebenfalls erfahren, trifft in geschlossenen Räumen der Schall einer punktförmig gedachten Schallquelle nach dessen Reflexionen an den Begrenzungsflächen des Raumes von allen Seiten beim Hörer ein. Die zuerst beim Hörer eintreffende Wellenfront bestimmt dabei die Richtung des Hörereignisses. Bedingung ist, dass die 2. Wellenfront mindestens etwa 1 ms später eintreffen muss. Dies nennt man das Gesetz der ersten Wellenfront (Haas- oder Präzedenzeffekt). Treffen die Wellenfronten mit einem Zeitversatz von mehr als etwa 60 ms ein, so wird die 2. Wellenfront als Echo wahrgenommen. Der Einfachheit halber nehmen wir an, der Schall von erster und folgender Wellenfront habe den gleichen Pegel.

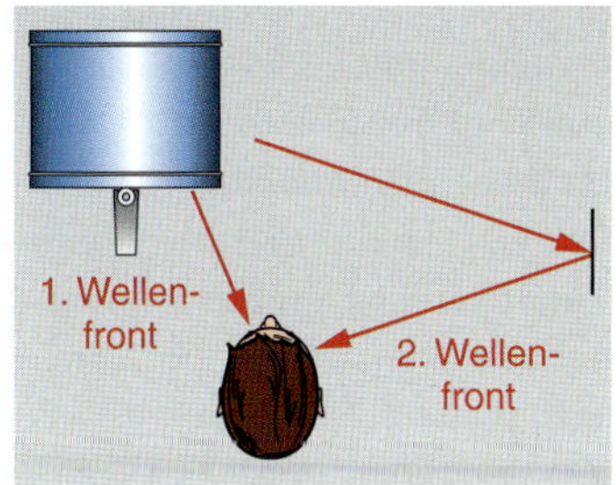

Haas-Effekt

Entfernung

Warum können wir mit geschlossenen Augen feststellen, ob jemand aus nächster Nähe mit uns spricht, oder uns aus großer Entfernung zuruft?

Schallereignis
Wenn ein **Schallereignis** in der Mitte vor mir stattfindet, so besteht kein Unterschied zwischen dem Schall an linkem und rechtem Ohr. Das legt die Vermutung nahe, dass sich die Entfernung auch mit lediglich einem Ohr wahrnehmen lässt. Sobald jedoch der visuelle Eindruck fehlt, ist dies nur noch eingeschränkt möglich. Die Entfernung des Hörereignisses stimmt nicht exakt mit der wirklichen überein, wird jedoch mit kleiner werdendem Abstand zwischen Schallquelle und Hörer genauer abgeschätzt.

Ein Park. Eine Wiese. Eine Person spricht unverändert und nähert sich Ihnen. Der Klang ihrer Stimme ändert sich. Auch ihre Lautstärke nimmt zu. Je näher sie kommt, desto voller klingt die Stimme. Die **Lautstärke** der tiefen Frequenzen im Frequenzspektrum der Stimme nimmt in größerem Maße zu.

Hinweis: Vergleich mit Off-Stimmen in der Werbung und im Rundfunk. Durch die Betonung der tiefen Frequenzen wird Nähe in jeglicher Beziehung erzeugt.

Sowohl die Klangfarbe als auch die Lautheit des Hörereignisses ändern sich also mit der Entfernung des Hörers zur Schallquelle. Wodurch kommt das? Wir beschränken uns auf die Betrachtung eines Schallereignisses in einem (annähernd) freien Schallfeld, eben z. B. eine Wiese. Aus der Wellenlehre ist bekannt, dass sich tieffrequenter Schall (halb-) kugelförmig von der Schallquelle ausbreitet. Voraussetzung ist jedoch, dass deren Wellenlänge groß gegenüber den Dimensionen der Schallquelle ist. Unterschreitet die Wellenlänge die Größe der Abmessung der Quelle, so werden sie zunehmend gebündelt abgestrahlt. Die abgegebene Energie konzentriert sich sozusagen auf den Strahl, während sie sich im Falle der kugelförmigen Ausbreitung auf den gesamten umliegenden Raum verteilt. Aus der Anschauung wird somit klar, dass die Tiefen im Frequenzspektrum mit größer werdender Entfernung mit einem geringeren Pegel vertreten sind als die Höhen. Das Hörereignis verliert deshalb an „Fülle". Trotz gebündelter Abstrahlung wird die Energie der hochfrequenten Schallanteile mit steigender Entfernung auf einen größer werdenden Raum verteilt. Deshalb verändert sich selbstverständlich die empfundene Lautstärke auch insgesamt. Hierbei wirkt sich zusätzlich die Frequenzabhängigkeit der Empfindung der Lautstärke aus, die mit den Kurven gleicher Lautstärke beschrieben wird (vgl. Abschnitt Lautstärke). Bei größer werdender Entfernung nimmt die Lautstärke ab, wobei wir die Abnahme der Lautstärke der tiefen Frequenzen als größer empfinden als die der mittleren und hohen Frequenzen.

Hinweis: Um den Eindruck der Entfernung zu unterstützen hilft es, die Tiefen im Klangspektrum (des direkten Schalls) der Tonquelle mit dem Klangfilter am Mischpult oder der Tonbearbeitungssoftware zu dämpfen.

Hinweis: Raumsimulationsprogramme (oder auch Hallprogramme) sind in externen Geräten, als Teil von Multieffektgeräten und als Softwarebestandteile/Plug-Ins von Tonbearbeitungsprogrammen erhältlich (siehe unten). Das Mischungsverhältnis aus dem originalen und bearbeiteten Ton bestimmt dabei den Eindruck der Entfernung der Tonquelle im künstlich erzeugten akustischen Raum (synthetisches Schallfeld) zum Hörer.

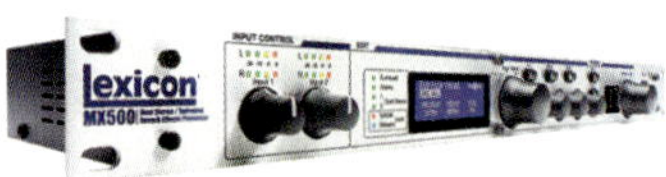

Externes Effektgerät
Quelle: Lexicon, Inc., Bedford USA

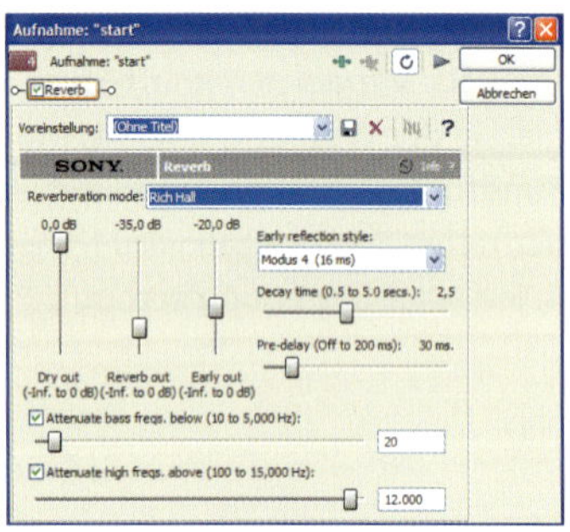

Plug-In eines Hallgerätes

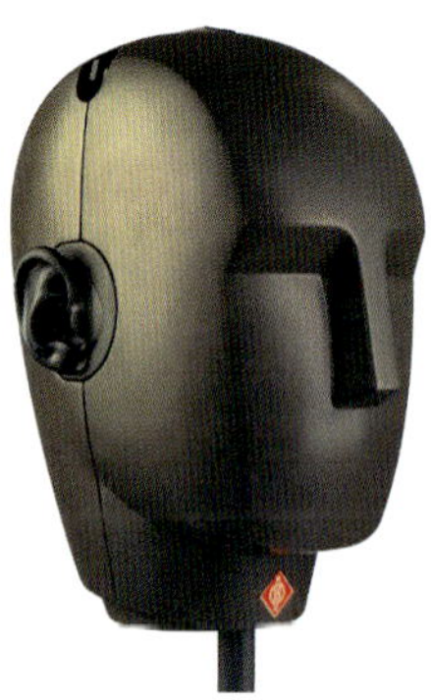

Kunstkopf
Quelle: Georg Neumann GmbH, Berlin

Wie klingen Schallquellen aus nächster Nähe und welcher Abstand ist welchem Klang zuzuordnen? Hierfür ist natürliche, alltägliche Hörerfahrung notwendig.

Raumakustik und Entfernungswahrnehmung:
Finden Schallereignisse in einem geschlossenen Raum statt, so hören wir keinesfalls nur das, was direkt von der Schallquelle stammt, sondern auch das, was der umgebende Raum daraus macht. Das wird Hall genannt (vgl. Abschnitt Raumakustik). Eine Sporthalle. Der Basketball schlägt vor Ihnen auf. Der Anteil des Schalls, der direkt von der Schallquelle kommt, ist hoch im Gegensatz zum diffusen Schall (Hall) der Sporthalle. Der Basketball schlägt weit entfernt unter dem gegnerischen Korb auf. Der Anteil des direkten Schalls ist niedrig im Gegensatz zum diffusen Schall der Sporthalle. Ein Vergleich von direktem zu indirektem Schall ist eine zusätzliche Informationsquelle für die Wahrnehmung von Entfernung. Auch für diesen Vergleich ist eine gewisse Hörerfahrung notwendig, denn es müssen Kenntnisse beim Hörer darüber vorliegen, wie Räume unterschiedlicher Größe und Beschaffenheit klingen und welchen Abständen von Hörer zu Schallquelle welchen Verhältnissen von direktem zu indirektem Schall zuzuordnen sind.

Mit Hörerfahrung ist jedoch nicht diejenige von Audio-Profis gemeint, sondern das Ergebnis eines Prozesses, der bereits nach der Geburt beginnt. Ein Prozess des ständigen Zuordnens der Empfindung von Klängen und Lautstärken von Stimmen, Instrumenten, Geräuschen zu deren Positionen in ihrerseits „klingenden" Räumen.

Für das Erkennen von Richtung und Entfernung setzt unser auditives Wahrnehmungssystem alle angesprochenen Verfahren gleichzeitig ein. Mit unterschiedlichem Erfolg. Denn die Qualität der Beiträge an der Wahrnehmung durch die verschiedenen Verfahren, einzeln und in ihrer Gesamtheit, hängt nicht nur von der Leistungsfähigkeit unseres Wahrnehmungssystems ab, sondern auch von der Beschaffenheit des Schallereignisses! Beispielsweise lassen sich Töne tiefer Frequenz nur sehr schlecht bis gar nicht oder Dauertöne schlechter als impulshafter Schall (ähnlich der Sprache) orten.

Tonaufnahmen, die mit einem Kunstkopf gemacht werden, enthalten all die für unsere auditive Wahrnehmung wichtigen Informationen. Leider sind diese Aufnahmen an die Wiedergabe mittels eines Kopfhörers gebunden. Da diese Aufnahmen jedoch bereits Rauminformationen enthalten, wären sie z. B. in der Vertonungsarbeit nicht für alle Situationen einsetzbar. Schallereignisse werden zum Zwecke der Vertonung in der Regel mit möglichst geringem Anteil an Rauminformationen aufgezeichnet. Das eröffnet die Möglichkeit, dass Rauminformationen nachträglich künstlich entsprechend der im bewegten Bild sichtbaren Räume mit Hall- (Raumsimulatoren) und Verzögerungsgeräten erzeugt und dem Original zugemischt werden (vgl. Abschnitt Raumakustik) können.

Die Empfindung der Schallereignisse unterscheiden sich also in ihrer Tonhöhe, Lautstärke, Dauer, Klangfarbe und der Richtung, aus der sie einfallen. Diese elementaren Eigenschaften finden sich deshalb in allen drei auditiven Kategorien Sprache, Musik und Geräusch wieder. Sie werden uns deshalb in der Gestaltung mit Tönen ständig begegnen.

10.1.3 Raumakustik

Im Film wie auch in interaktiven Anwendungen werden Umgebungen innerhalb und außerhalb geschlossener Räume visuell abgebildet. In der Regel soll der Ton diesem Eindruck folgen. Beim Filmton machen manchmal unerwünschte Umgebungsgeräusche während der Dreharbeiten, zum Beispiel von den Generatoren für die Stromversorgung, eine Nachvertonung unumgänglich. Aber auch Computeranimationen für Filme oder multimediale Anwendungen erhalten ihren Ton häufig erst nach ihrer Fertigstellung. Dann müssen Tonaufnahmen nachträglich in Räumen ähnlich der abgebildeten erstellt oder Tonaufnahmen mit einem künstlich erzeugten Raumanteil versehen werden.

Quelle: Camgaroo AG, München camgaroo - digitale video-produktion, Heft 02/2001, S. 36. Zu sehen sind die Arbeitsgegenstände und die Projektionsleinwand im Tonstudio Meloton des Geräuschemachers Mel Kutbay. Wenn nötig, so werden die hier entstehenden Geräusche mit einem Hall versehen, spätestens aber vom Mischtonmeister mit einem Raumsimulator in den auf der Leinwand sichtbaren Raum akustisch eingebettet. Deshalb müssen sich solche Aufnahmeräume „klangneutral" verhalten.

In der Filmtonmischung wird schon seit geraumer Zeit für die mehrkanalige Wiedergabe auf Surround-Sound-Systemen gemischt. Mit interaktiven Anwendungen und Filmen auf DVD hält der Mehrkanalton auch Einzug in die Wohnzimmer. Deshalb ist es für die Tonproduktion von Nutzen, den Einfluss des Raumes auf den Schall und auf das **Hörereignis** zu kennen (vgl. Abschnitt Richtung und Entfernung).

- Wie verhält sich ein Raum?
- Wie baut sich sein Schallfeld auf?
- Welchen Einfluss nimmt ein Raum auf ein **Schallereignis**?
- Was verändert er am Schall, der von einer Quelle in den Raum abgestrahlt wird?

Wenn Aufnahmen mit dem Mikrofon in geschlossenen Räumen statt finden, tritt auch die Akustik des Raumes in Erscheinung. Gleichgültig, ob es sich um Sprachaufnahmen in einer kleinen Kabine oder eine Choraufnahme in einer Kirche handelt. Das Mikrofon nimmt immer sowohl den direkten Schall, wie auch den Schall auf, der an den Begrenzungsflächen des Raumes oder an Gegenständen reflektiert, gebeugt, gebündelt oder zerstreut wird.

Bevor ein Raum nachzuhallen beginnen kann, muss er sich erst einmal mit Schallenergie „voll saugen". Nach dem Eintreffen von direktem Schall und den ersten **Reflexionen** von Decke, Boden und Wänden beim Hörer, vermehren sich die Reflexionen und verdichten sich rasch zu dem, was Hall genannt wird (vgl. Abschnitt Geometrische Raumakustik).

Der Hall hat ebenso wie der **Direktschall** charakteristische Klangeigenschaften. Seine Zusammensetzung hängt davon ab, wie die Oberflächen von Decke, Fußboden und Wänden beschaffen sind, welche Geometrie der Raum besitzt, ob der Raum bestuhlt ist und welche übrigen Gegenstände an welchem Ort im Raum versammelt sind usw. Direkter und indirekter (diffuser) Schall sind also verschieden.

Hinzu kommt, dass das Abstrahlverhalten von Schallquellen sehr komplex ist. Nicht alle Töne unterschiedlicher Frequenz werden kugelförmig oder in gleicher Richtung von der Schallquelle abgestrahlt. So übernimmt der Hall sozusagen den Transport der Schallanteile unterschiedlicher spektraler Zusammensetzung, die nicht auf direktem

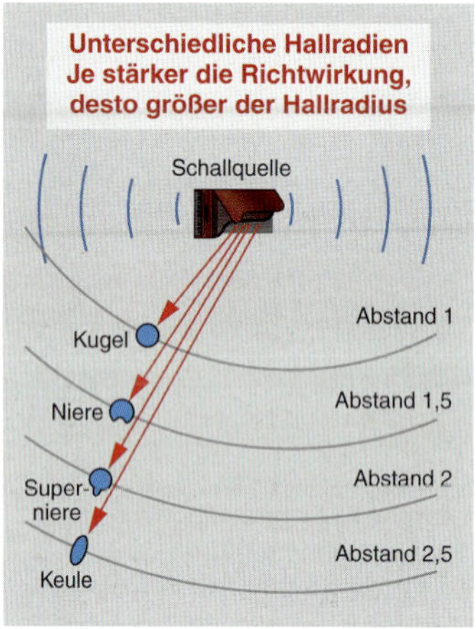

Richtwirkung und Hallradius

Wege zum Hörer gelangen. Er färbt sie dabei ein. Beim Hörer verschmelzen direkter und indirekter Schall zu einem einzigen Hörereignis! Somit bestimmen immer die Schallquelle und ihre Umgebung den Gesamteindruck. Das entspricht unserer Hörerfahrung und -erwartung.

Beispiel: Direkter und indirekter Schallanteil werden bei einer Tonaufnahme dadurch voneinander (näherungsweise) getrennt, indem das Mikrofon weit innerhalb des Hallradius in sehr geringem Abstand zum Instrument aufgestellt wird. Damit werden die ersten Reflexionen und der Nachhall des Raumes sozusagen nahezu ausgeblendet. Das kann dazu führen, dass das Instrument seinen natürlichen Klangcharakter einbüßt, da der resultierende Klang des Instruments bei der Wiedergabe nicht der Erwartung des Instrumentenklanges aufgrund der Hörerfahrung entspricht. Dieser setzt sich zusammen aus dem Gesamteindruck von direktem und diffusem Schall am Ort des Hörers.

Aufnahmen im Freien finden selbstverständlich auch in der Nähe von Gegenständen oder Begrenzungsflächen statt.
Eine Filmszene: Eine Kutsche fährt auf altem Kopfsteinpflaster in einer Gasse. Häuserwände reflektieren den Schall der schlagenden Pferdehufe. Es kommt zu typischen Klangverfärbungen und Echos. Bedingungen, die für Musikaufnahmen oder gar Sprachübertragungen unvorteilhaft wären, führen hier zu einem authentischen Gesamteindruck von auditiver und visueller Ebene. Selbst ein Wald hat akustische Eigenschaften, denn auch dieser würde z. B. den Schall der Kutsche an seinen Baumstämmen reflektieren (streuen) und beugen.

Die geometrische **Raumakustik** betrachtet ähnlich der Strahlenoptik u. a. die Richtung und die Veränderung der Richtung des Schalls. Dies hat jedoch seine Grenzen genau dann, wenn sich die Reflexionen der Schallwellen bereits so stark vermehrt und „durchmischt" haben, dass sie nur noch als diffuser Schall ohne Richtungsinformation betrachtet werden können. Dies ist das Gebiet der statistischen Raumakustik.

Geometrische Raumakustik

Es hat sich gezeigt, dass ein Raum besonders angenehm klingt, wenn er möglichst homogen mit Schall „durchmischt" ist. Die Schallausbreitungsrichtungen der Reflexionen verlaufen dann nicht parallel und der Schall wird an Begrenzungsflächen gestreut.

Die Abbildungen zeigen, wie sich der Schall ausbreitet.

Links: Nicht parallel laufende Strahlen der Ausbreitungsrichtungen von Schallreflexionen

Rechts: Der Schall wird an einem Gegenstand gestreut.

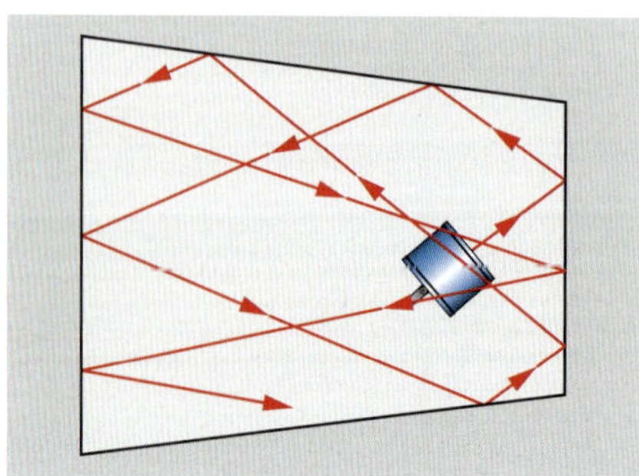

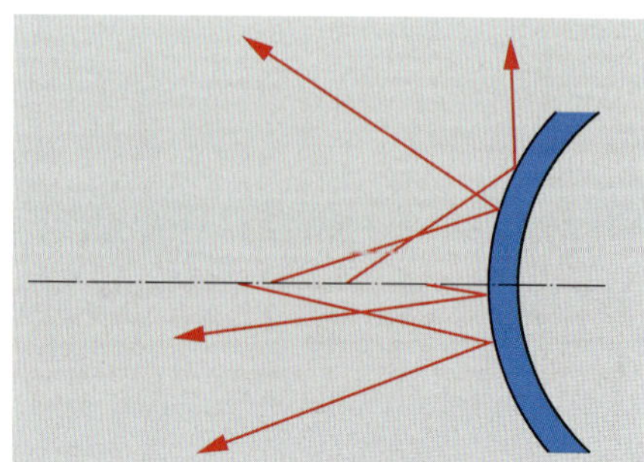

Zwischen planparallel angeordneten Wänden kommt es mit größer werdendem Abstand der Wände zueinander erst zu einem Schnarren und dann zu Flatterechos. Bei letzteren müssen die Verzögerungen der Wellenfronten der einzelnen Reflexionen zueinander mit mehr als etwa 30 ms am Ohr des Hörers eintreffen. Das tritt bei einer Wegdifferenz ab etwa 10 m ein und ist bereits in leerstehenden Räumen normaler Wohnungen zu beobachten.

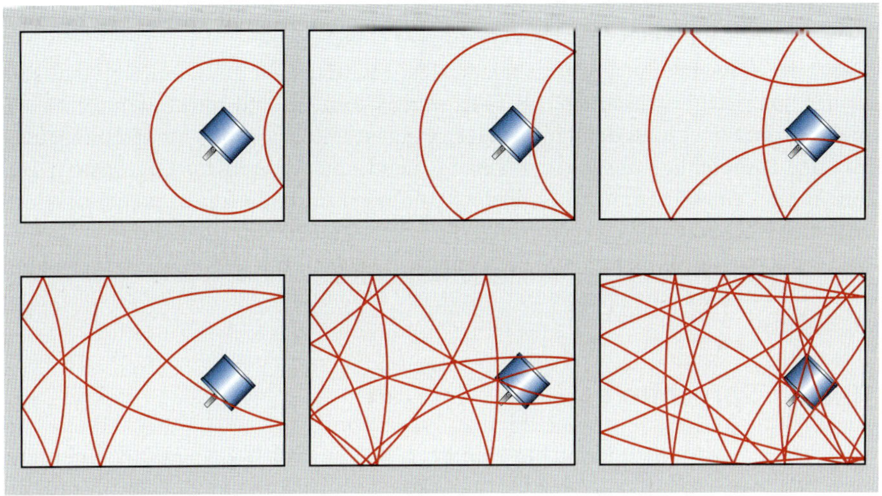

Die Abbildung zeigt von links nach rechts verschiedene Phasen der Schallausbreitung in einem Raum mit planparallelen Begrenzungsflächen. Die Linien zeigen die Wellenfronten der Reflexionen an den Begrenzungsflächen des Raumes. Im Punkt befindet sich die Schallquelle. Von ihr geht ein impulsartiger Schall (Knall) aus. Die Phasen zeigen auch, wie sich die Reflexionen zu einem Hall verdichten.

Statistische Raumakustik

Sie gibt uns Aufschluss darüber, wie groß die Dauer des Nachhalls eines Raumes ist. Die Nachhallzeit ist definiert als die Zeit, in der der Schalldruckpegel nach Abschalten der Schallquelle um 60 dB sinkt. Anzumerken ist dabei, dass die Nachhallzeit frequenzabhängig ist und auf diese Weise den Klangeindruck eines Hörereignisse entscheidend prägt. Das Frequenzverhalten des Halles wird beeinflusst durch die Materialien der Begrenzungsflächen und der Gegenstände im Raum und durch seine Geometrie. Am angenehmsten wird ein Hall empfunden, wenn er in seinem Spektrum gleichmäßig abnimmt.

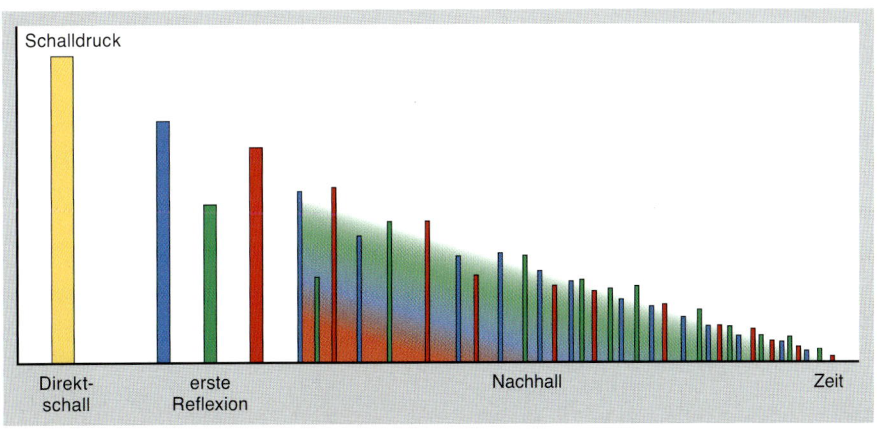

Die Abbildung zeigt die zeitliche Abfolge von Direktschall, ersten Reflexionen und Nachhall am Ort eines Hörers.

ARD Tagesschau

10.2 Funktion von Tönen

Bis hierher haben wir erfahren, welche elementaren Eigenschaften allen Tönen zu eigen sind und wie wir Töne empfinden. Im Weiteren soll es darum gehen, welche Funktionen Sprechtext, Musik und Geräusch einnehmen können. Gestalteter Ton findet sich in vielen Bereichen: Rundfunk, Theater und Konzert, Film und Video und natürlich interaktive Anwendungen im Multimedia-Bereich. Wir beschränken uns auf die Betrachtung des Tons im Zusammenspiel mit dem (bewegten) Bild, wobei ein Fokus besonders auf interaktive Anwendungen gelenkt wird.
Interaktive Anwendungen unterscheiden sich untereinander zum Teil sehr stark. Sie reichen von „Blättermaschinen“ bis zu Expertensystemen, sind zum Teil mit Simulationen, Animationen und digitalen Videos versehen oder auch nur mit geschriebenem Text und Standbildern ausgestattet. Entsprechend unterschiedlich ist der Einsatz von Ton. Es folgt eine Zusammenfassung der vielfältigen funktionalen Verwendungsmöglichkeiten von Ton zu bewegtem Bild. Sie erhebt keinen Anspruch auf Vollständigkeit, sondern will in erster Linie die Bandbreite zeigen, mit der Musik, Sprache und Geräusch genutzt werden können. Und sie soll motivieren, mit Ton zu Bild zu experimentieren.

10.2.1 Sprechtext

Im Gegensatz zu Musik und Geräusch ist Sprechtext besonders gut geeignet, um Informationen möglichst eindeutig zu transportieren und Sinnzusammenhänge herzustellen. Beispiel: Gesprochener Text im Lehrfilm oder einem interaktiven Lernprogramm. Deshalb ist es besonders wichtig, darauf zu achten, dass genau diese Eigenschaft des gesprochenen Textes zum Tragen kommt. Gesprochener Text muss verständlich sein. Es ist zu bedenken, dass der Ton immer in der Zeit abläuft und sich im Gegensatz zum geschriebenen Text schlecht rekapitulieren lässt. Besonders schwierig wird es, wenn es sich um einen Reproduktionsvorgang handelt, der sich für den Anwender nicht anhalten und zurückstellen lässt. Als Beispiel lassen sich hier Rundfunk, Kino und Theater nennen (siehe auch Abschnitt 9.1.4 Umsetzung). Für die Verständlichkeit des gesprochenen Textes ist wichtig, dass

- der Wortschatz der Zielgruppe bekannt ist. Fremdwörter sind zu vermeiden ❶.
- kurze Sätze (keine Schachtel- oder Kettensätze) gebildet werden ❷.
- nach Möglichkeit die Hauptaussage am Anfang des Satzes steht ❸.
- Substantivierungen vermieden werden ❹.
- sich der Text auf das gezeigte Bild direkt bezieht (Bild-Text-Schere).
- die Sprechgeschwindigkeit angemessen ist (nicht zu schnell).
- der Sprecher den Inhalt des Textes verstanden hat und den Text beim Lesen in Sinnzusammenhänge gliedern kann.

Das Procedere dieses Probanden darf generalisiert werden.
Besser:
Die Vorgehensweise der Testperson darf verallgemeinert werden.

❶

Die Spannvorrichtung, die... sitzt, an dem... zu beachten ist, wenn...
Besser:
Die Spannvorrichtung sitzt... .
Wenn..., dann ist... zu beachten.

❷

Da das Risiko..., sollten Sie sich vor Sonnenstrahlen schützen.
Besser:
Sie sollten sich vor Sonnenstrahlen schützen, da das Risiko ... .

❸

Ich führte eine Reparatur an meinem Mountain-Bike aus.
Besser:
Ich reparierte mein Mountain-Bike.

❹

Insbesondere für kommentierende Texte wird ein mediengerechter, gepflegter umgangssprachlicher Stil gewählt. Der Anwender muss die Möglichkeit haben, die angebotene Information gedanklich nachvollziehen zu können! Deshalb erfolgen Beschreibungen in kurzen Sätzen. Die Häufigkeit und Dauer von Pausen sind angemessen und orientieren sich am Rhythmus der Folge von Szenen. Szenen und Sprechtext sollten sich inhaltlich und in ihrer Dauer entsprechen und ergänzen.

10.2.2 Musik

Musik wird der emotionalen Ebene zugeordnet. Sie „färbt“ die übrigen Informationen emotional ein und kann somit die Bedeutung der Informationen ändern.

Musik zu Vorspann und Abspann

Es entsteht eine Erwartungshaltung durch den Einsatz von Musik oder Geräusch im Vorspann. Da Musik bei den meisten Menschen hauptsächlich die Emotionen anspricht, ist es hier möglich, den Nutzer auf die interaktive Anwendung einzustimmen. Hilfreich sind die musikalische Verarbeitung einfacher Klänge und musikalischer Motive, die in der Anwendung wiederzufinden sind. Auch komplette Musikstücke/Songs eignen sich dazu, sofern sie einen Bezug zu den Inhalten des Programms widerspiegeln. Im Abspann kann auf Tonmaterial zurückgegriffen werden, dass dem Anwender bereits aus der Anwendung bekannt ist. Es kann somit gelingen, den Gesamteindruck der Anwendung im Nutzer nachklingen zu lassen.

Dramaturgische Funktionen von Filmmusik

Musik kann sich sehr stark an dem orientieren, was parallel auf der visuellen Ebene geschieht. Ein Beispiel ist das Mickey-Mousing. Hier werden die Vorgänge mit Musik auf extreme Weise illustriert. Auch ohne Bilder glaubt man das Geschehen nur durch das Hören der Musik nachvollziehen zu können.
Sie kann aber auch kommentieren und interpretieren, sozusagen eine eigene Auffassung von dem mitteilen, was gerade auf der Leinwand oder dem Bildschirm zu sehen ist. Dem Betrachter wird somit eine Interpretationshilfe über die Musik angeboten für das, was Bilder zeigen. Zwischen diesen beiden Polen bewegt sich die Funktion der Musik zum bewegten Bild.

So ist es möglich, Klänge mit unterschiedlichen Bedeutungen zu schichten. Dabei entsteht eine komplexe Atmosphäre mit vielen Gefühlsebenen. Eine Polyphonie musikalischer Schichten.

❶ pp < ff > pp

Wie bereits erwähnt, kann Musik strukturbildend wirken. Insbesondere kann sie in interaktiven Anwendungen z. B. Kapitel, Themenbereiche, Übergänge, Vor- und Abspann markieren. In Filmen wird sie zusätzlich an „Plot-Points“ und an dramaturgischen Höhepunkten eingesetzt und lässt somit die Großform des Filmes erkennen.
Ähnlich wie mit Geräuschen lassen sich Abschnitte im Geschehen mit Musik unterstreichen. Das wirkt dann wie das Ausrufezeichen ❶ am Ende eines Satzes.
In interaktiven Anwendungen wird unter Umständen Bild- oder Filmmaterial unterschiedlicher Herkunft verwendet und in einer Anwendung integriert. Mit der Unterlegung einer Musik lassen sich so die qualitativen und stilistischen Unterschiede teilweise ausgleichen.
Musik kann das Befinden der Handelnden vermitteln ❷. Sie gewährt damit einen Einblick in ihr Gefühlsleben, ihre Wahrnehmung und Erinnerung. Aber nicht nur das Befinden kann vermittelt werden, sondern auch die Handlung selbst kann Musik interpretieren. Ein klassisches Beispiel sind die tiefen Töne der Kontrabässe, die in uns die Erwartung eines nahenden Unglücks schüren und damit Ereignisse in Teilen vorwegnehmen können.

❷

Geht es um eine Dokumentation eines gesellschaftlichen Problems aus der Zeitgeschichte, bietet es sich an, die Musik der damaligen Zeit und insbesondere der betroffenen Bevölkerungsgruppen zu recherchieren und zu verwenden. Auf diese Weise lassen sich gesellschaftliche und historische Zusammenhänge unterstreichen.

Wenn wir unsere Musik hören, dann fühlen wir uns Wohl und sind dazu bereit, Dinge wohlwollend zu betrachten, die mit dieser Musik in Beziehung gebracht werden. Es gibt Menschen, mit denen wir die Vorliebe zu dieser Musik teilen. Das erzeugt ein angenehmes Gruppengefühl. Wird diese Musik im Film oder einer interaktiven Anwendung eingesetzt, so sind zumindest wir als Zielgruppe positiv auf die Aussagen des Filmes eingestimmt.

Ein Beispiel: Eine Familie ist im Gleichschritt auf dem Weg zum Strandbad. Durch die Überzeichnung mit unterlegter Marschmusik lässt sich ihr Aufenthalt im Strandbad als stabsmäßig geplantes Ausflugsvorhaben karikieren.

Spezifische Musiken können Handelnden zugeordnet werden. Durch die entsprechende Wahl von Musik können sie in ihrer Größe ❶ oder generell in ihrer Wirkung beeinflusst werden. Die „Größe“ der Musik sollte mit der „Größe“ der Handelnden übereinstimmen. Damit ist nicht nur ihre physische Größe gemeint. In Stanley Kubricks Film „2001 – Odyssee im Weltraum“ wird Musik aus „Also sprach Zarathustra“ von Richard Strauss, einer Szene mit dem Zerstörungsrausch eines Affenmenschen an der Schwelle zum Aufbruch der Menschheit unterlegt.

Atmo = Atmosphäre
Die Atmo ist ein gleichförmiges Hintergrundgeräusch z. B. der Wellenschlag am Strand, das Rauschen der Blätter im Park, der Straßenlärm einer Großstadt.

Mit einer **Atmo** oder dem Eigenklang eines Raumes lässt sich relativ genau seine Beschaffenheit oder eine räumliche Umgebung akustisch darstellen. Mit Musik gelingt das nicht so präzise. Es gibt einen Tonraum mit hohen und tiefen Tönen, die in einem physikalischen Raum mit oben und unten eine Entsprechung findet. Doch gibt es auch hier in gewissen Grenzen eine Entsprechung. Ertönt beispielsweise beim Anblick eines Sees in einem Park eine sinfonische Musik, so erscheint die Umgebung groß. Musik beeinflusst die Wahrnehmung von Räumen ❷.

10.2.3 Geräusch

Für eine wirklichkeitsnahe Gestaltung braucht es für die visuellen Eindrücke eine Bestätigung durch begleitende auditive Ereignisse. Eine zufallende Tür verursacht einen Knall, ein Luftstrom verursacht ein Windgeräusch, ein Automotor verursacht im Betrieb ein Brummen.

Das Bild auf dem Computerschirm oder auf der Kino-Leinwand ist zweidimensional. Eine Zunahme der Wirkung des Bildes in der dritten Dimension lässt sich neben der Gestaltung der visuellen auch mit der auditiven Ebene erreichen. So zum Beispiel ist eine Tiefenstaffelung mit einer deutlichen Aufteilung in Vordergrund und Hintergrund mit Lautstärke und Klangfarbe von Tönen sehr wirkungsvoll. Große Lautstärke für Vordergrund, kleinere Lautstärke für Hintergrund. Dabei ist diese Wirkung um so größer, je größer die Dynamik des Mediums ist. Im Kino ist die Dynamik größer als im Fernsehen.

Die Filmsprache bedient sich vieler hintereinandergeschnittener Einstellungen. Handeln sie an einem Ort, so können sie insbesondere durch Atmos räumlich verschmolzen werden. Dies fördert die Kontinuität der Bild- oder Einstellungsfolgen.

➲ **Der Realitätseindruck kann verstärkt werden, indem visualisierte Vorgänge akustisch bestätigt werden, die Dreidimensionalität des Bildes gesteigert wird und die Kontinuität über Bild- bzw. Einstellungswechsel hinweg gewahrt bleibt.**

Insbesondere Atmos vermitteln einen guten Eindruck von der Umgebung. Zumeist werden Atmos aus **Geräuscharchiven** entnommen oder „Nur-Ton"-Aufnahmen am Drehort erstellt und in der Postproduction zum Film angelegt.

Hinweis: Es ist sinnvoll das Ruhegeräusch eines Raumes aufzunehmen, damit es kopiert und in Dialogpausen eingesetzt werden kann.

Weiterhin sind Orientierungslaute sehr nützlich. Dies sind typische Laute ❶ eines Ortes (wie die Figur zum Grund). Jeder Raum verfügt über einen typischen Eigenklang, auch dann, wenn in ihm völlige Stille zu herrschen scheint. Wenn mit O-Ton gearbeitet wird und Dialogpausen im Film eintreten, ist nur noch das Ruhegeräusch des Raumes zu hören.

Nicht nur der Ort, sondern auch die Zeit lässt sich mit dem Ton festlegen. Zum Beispiel steht das Geräusch einer schlagenden Uhr für die entsprechende Uhrzeit.

Dinosaurier in Steven Spielbergs Film „Jurassic Park"

So wie es Geräusche gibt, die einem Ort zuzuordnen sind, gibt es auch Geräusche, die typisch für eine Epoche oder eine Zeitspanne sind. Die Laute von Dinosauriern ❷ sind dieser Zeit eindeutig zugeordnet, weil die Tiere heute ausgestorben sind, selbst, wenn sie aus der Soundmaschine von Sounddesignern stammen. Das Fahrtgeräusch einer Dampflokomotive ist der Vergangenheit zuzuordnen.

➲ **Geräusche können Ort und Zeitpunkt einer Handlung festlegen.**

Die Vergrößerung der Lautstärke und die Änderung der Klangfarbe bis hin zur Verfremdung lässt den Ton mit der Absicht in den Vordergrund treten, eine größere Anteilnahme vom Zuschauer zu erlangen.

Tönende Flugobjekte in George Lucas „Krieg der Sterne"

Damit lässt sich Aufmerksamkeit erzeugen und lenken. Insbesondere in der Werbung werden diese Maßnahmen dazu verwendet, um die Zuschauer und Hörer wieder in ihrer Aufmerksamkeit zurückzuholen. Aus der Menge an visuellen Objekten, die im Bild angeboten werden, wird auf diese Weise die Aufmerksamkeit auf bestimmte Objekte gelenkt.

Die Wirkung des Zaubertrankes an Asterix von Goscinny und Uderzo

Es gibt viele Vorgänge die sehr leise, oder sogar unhörbar verlaufen. Wird Unhörbares hörbar gemacht, so nimmt die Intensität des audiovisuellen Gesamterlebnisses zu. Beispiel: Es werden Fluggeräusche zu Bewegungen von Raumgleitern angelegt, obwohl sich bekanntlich im luftleeren Raum kein Schall entwickeln kann ❸. Zeichentrickfiguren, die bis über einen Abgrund laufen, kurze Zeit in der Luft auf der Stelle verharren, dabei wild mit Armen und Beinen kreisen und schließlich abstürzen. Auf dem Bild ist es Asterix, der Gallier, kurz nachdem er einen Schluck Zaubertrank zu sich genommen hat ❹.

In der Werbung tragen diese Effekte zur Imagebildung bei. Beispiel: Die Reflexionen an strahlend sauberem Geschirr, die mit einem „Glöckchen-Klang" unterlegt sind.

- **Geräusche können visuelle Eindrücke verstärken.**

„Innere" Bilder dienen dem Zuhörer als Bildersatz für einen Vorgang oder ein Objekt. Beispiel: Auf einer Bühne wird ein Instrumental-Solist beklatscht. Der Zuschauer hört jedoch nur den Applaus und zu sehen ist nur das Gesicht des Solisten, die Klatschenden jedoch nicht. Der Zuschauer macht sich sein eigenes Bild vom applaudierenden Publikum.

- **Geräusche können Bilder ersetzen, indem sie „innere" Bilder beim Hörer erzeugen.**

10.2.4 Töne in interaktiven Anwendungen

Erinnern wir uns an die Definition von Multimedia: Integration von mehreren Medien, nämlich Bild, Ton, bewegtes Bild, Text. Sie müssen unabhängig voneinander abrufbar sein. Die Anwendung läuft auf einem Computer und ist interaktiv. Das eröffnet der Anwendung von Ton neue Dimensionen, stellt jedoch auch höhere Anforderungen an die Konzeption.

Im Gegensatz zu linear zu nutzenden Medien, wie Film und Video, lebt die interaktive Anwendung von der Dateneingabe und Beteiligung des Anwenders.

Software-Ergonomie und Interaktion

Viele haben schon einmal eine „leidige" Erfahrung gemacht, als sie einem Videorekorder „beibringen" wollten, eine bestimmte Sendung aufzuzeichnen. Die Ergebnisse können äußerst deprimierend sein. Am Besten kommen wir mit einer Benutzerführung zurecht, die eine Fehlbedienung sofort aufdeckt.

Gute Benutzerführungen leiten deshalb den Anwender mit intelligenten Rückmeldungen und einsehbaren Anweisungen von einem Programmschritt zum Nächsten.

Ein Videorekorder lässt sich anschauen, anfassen und beim Drücken einer Taste oder beim Einlegen einer Kassette gibt er Geräusche von sich. Das sind unmittelbare Rückmeldungen der Maschine, die uns über das Gehör signalisieren, wie die Maschine auf unsere Eingaben reagiert. Der Computer lässt sich zwar anfassen, die Anwendung selbst jedoch nicht. Deshalb muss eine Schnittstelle (Interface) zwischen Anwender und Anwendung gestaltet werden, die Rückmeldungen und Anweisungen über den Bildschirm wie auch über die Lautsprecher erlauben. Beim Screen- und **Sounddesign** müssen Inhalte und Corporate Design didaktisch angemessen umgesetzt werden. Navigation und Benutzerführung müssen intuitiv zugänglich gestaltet werden. Die Beachtung dieser software-ergonomischen Gesichtspunkte spielt eine entscheidende Rolle bei der erfolgreichen Nutzung und damit für die Akzeptanz der multimedialen Anwendung.

Beispiel: Der Nutzer eines Spieles wird vom Programm aufgefordert, mit dem Mauszeiger eine Taste auf dem Bildschirm zu drücken. Als Rückmeldung an den Nutzer verändert sich die Taste. Sie erscheint hineingedrückt. Gleichzeitig ertönt ein Klick-Geräusch, und signalisiert, dass die Taste mit dem Mauszeiger getroffen wurde. Im Anschluss daran springt das Programm an eine andere Stelle. Das wiederum braucht Zeit, denn es müssen Bilder und Texte in den Arbeitsspeicher geladen werden. Gleichzeitig ertönt bereits eine Musik, ein Flächensound oder eine (Geräusch-) **Atmo**. Der Ton leitet zum neuen Thema des Spieles über und signalisiert zusammen mit einem grafischen Fortschrittsanzeiger, dass das Programm mit einem Ladevorgang „beschäftigt" und keineswegs „abgestürzt" ist.

Musikunterlegter Fortschrittsanzeiger beim Simulieren der Dritten Dimension

Strukturieren einer Anwendung

Ein Nutzer soll sich möglichst einfach und intuitiv in der Anwendung orientieren können. Die auditive Ebene lässt sich für die Orientierung in interaktiven Anwendungen sehr gut nutzen. So ist es denkbar, (Geräusch-) Atmos, themenbezogene Musik oder Flächensounds den verschiedenen inhaltlichen Abschnitten (Kapitel, Umgebung, Menü, schriftlicher Dialog etc.) zuzuordnen. Wichtig dabei ist, dass entsprechend der Gestaltungsrichtlinien der interaktiven Anwendung die Zuordnung des Tones zu den Abschnitten stets eindeutig ist.

Hinweis: Es ist nützlich, Tonereignisse in Schleifen (loops) laufen zu lassen. So werden die Audio-Dateien möglichst klein gehalten und beanspruchen daher relativ wenig Speicherplatz. Die Gefahr besteht jedoch, dass Tonschleifen den Zuhörer nach kurzer Zeit wegen ihrer Eintönigkeit stören. Deswegen muss bei der Auswahl des Tonmaterials und der Erstellung größte Sorgfalt verwendet werden.

Freie Auswahl durch den Anwender

Manche Menschen mögen es, während einer Beschäftigung nebenbei das Radio laufen zu lassen oder eigene CDs abzuspielen. Interaktive Anwendungen geben die Möglichkeit, eine Auswahl an Musikstücken anzubieten. Diese können vom Anwender zusammengestellt und in eine entsprechende Reihenfolge gesetzt werden. Diese laufen dann im Hintergrund der Anwendung ab. Die Lautstärke kann vom Anwender eingeben werden. Wenn neben der Musik noch andere Tonquellen zu hören sind, ist häufig dem Anwender die Möglichkeit gegeben, das Mischungsverhältnis zwischen den Quellen selbst zu regeln.

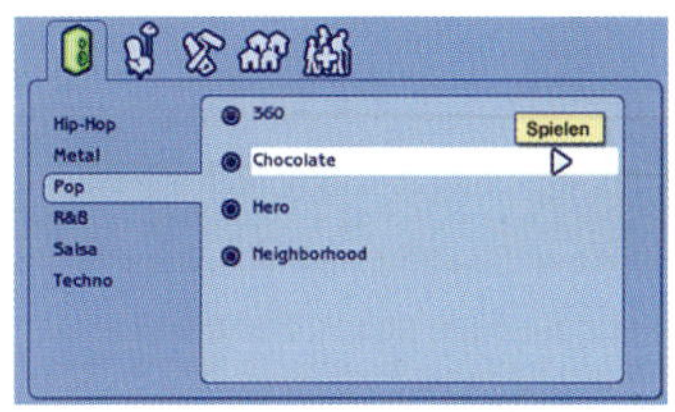

Musikauswahl in „Die SIMS 2"

Zusammenstellen per Zufall

Um die Aufmerksamkeit zu halten, kann es von Vorteil sein, die Musik in Abhängigkeit der Aktivitäten des Nutzers vom Zufall auswählen zulassen. In diesem Fall sollte die gesamte Anwendung jedoch einen spielerischen Charakter haben, vom Reiz des Unbekannten oder des Unerwarteten geprägt sein und eine vom Anwender durchschaubare Struktur und Navigation aufweisen.

Veränderung in Abhängigkeit der Nutzeraktivitäten

Besonders interessant wird die Möglichkeit, insbesondere Musik in Abhängigkeit der Nutzereingaben zu steuern.
Beispiel: Ein Anwender kämpft sich durch den Fragendschungel eines interaktiven Quiz-Spieles. Je mehr Fragen er beantwortet, desto mehr Zeit verstreicht. Die Spannung steigt. Bei jeder weiteren Schwierigkeitsstufe wird die Tonart der Musik einen halben Ton höher gerückt.

10.3 Tonaufnahme

Sprachaufnahmen in der Synchronisation: Andreas von der Meden leiht David Hasselhoff seine Stimme.
Quelle: Studio Hamburg GmbH

Im vorangegangenen Kapitel haben wir Funktionen von Musik, Sprache und Geräusch kennen gelernt. Musik- und Geräuschaufnahmen können häufig aus Archiven entnommen werden, Sprachaufnahmen müssen jedoch individuell hergestellt werden. Deswegen soll anhand einer Sprachaufnahme gezeigt werden, wie prinzipiell eine Tonaufnahme stattfindet, welche Hard- und Software grundsätzlich erforderlich sind und was insbesondere für die Verwendung in interaktiven Anwendungen dabei zu berücksichtigen ist. Wie kommt der Ton in den Computer? Was für Möglichkeiten der Bearbeitung sind gegeben? Welche Bearbeitungen sind für interaktive Anwendungen notwendig? Zunächst soll es aber um konzeptionelle Vorüberlegungen zur Tonproduktion gehen.

10.3.1 Konzeptionelle Vorüberlegungen

Soll der Ton optimal auf die interaktive Anwendung abgestimmt sein, dann muss er in der Regel eigens dafür produziert werden. Am Anfang der Überlegungen zum Ton einer interaktiven Anwendung steht deshalb die Frage nach dem Budget. Danach entscheidet sich, welcher Aufwand in der Vertonung getrieben werden kann. Während die Produktion von Filmmusik mit Orchester in der Regel der Filmindustrie im Stile Hollywoods vorbehalten bleibt, so ist doch die Vergabe eines Auftrages für die Produktion von Musik mithilfe von **MIDI-Instrumenten** denkbar. Wenn neben der Musik auch Geräusche eigens für die Anwendung produziert werden sollen, so gibt es dabei verschiedene Möglichkeiten. So wäre es denkbar, zunächst Sounds von geeigneten Geräusch-CDs zu nehmen, zu verändern und miteinander zu mischen. Sollte das nicht zum gewünschten Erfolg führen, so bietet es sich an, mit einem DAT-Recorder, Mikrofonen und einem Kopfhörer geeignete Geräusche bei Außenaufnahmen einzufangen.

Raptoren in Steven Spielbergs Film „Jurassic Park"

So ist beispielsweise der grauenhafte Schrei eines angreifenden Raptoren in Jurassic Park eine Mischung aus dem hohen Unterwasser-Schrei eines Delphins und dem tiefen Brüllen eines Walrosses. Ein anderes Beispiel sind die Laserhandfeuerwaffen in George Lucas „Krieg der Sterne". Ihr Sound ist entstanden, indem der Toningenieur gegen die Kabelstränge einer Funkstation schlug. Science-Fiction Geschichten sind ein dankbares Genre für eifrige Sounddesigner und Geräuschemacher. Selbst wenn die Geräusche nicht ganz den Lauten der Tiere der Vergangenheit oder der Gegenstände der Zukunft entsprechen, so unterstützen sie das bewegte Bild und lassen es realistischer und eindrucksvoller erscheinen. Und da wären wir bereits mitten im Tätigkeitsbereich der Sounddesigner.

Peitschende Geräusche der Laserwaffen in George Lucas „Star Wars" (Krieg der Sterne)

Zunehmend wird die Gestaltung der gesamten Tonebene (Musik, Geräusch, Sprechtext) einer interaktiven Anwendung als Teil eines ganzheitlichen Prozesses in Abstimmung mit der Gestaltung der visuellen, didaktischen und ergonomischen Ebene als Sounddesign bezeichnet. Auf den Begriff Sounddesign stößt man nicht nur im audiovisuellen Bereich oder in der Filmproduktion. Zum Beispiel überlassen es Automobilhersteller nicht immer dem Zufall, wie die Türen ihrer Autos klingen, wenn sie ins Schloss fallen. Auch das ist das Ergebnis von Sounddesign.

Musik- und Geräuscharchiv

Musikarchive bieten häufig eine Alternative, wenn Musik nicht in Auftrag gegeben oder selbst produziert werden soll. Sie bieten Musik aus jeder Stilrichtung passend zu jedem Genre. Musikarchive erleichtern den Umgang mit Urheber- und Verwertungsrechten, um die Musik juristisch einwandfrei nutzen zu können. Denn grundsätzlich muss sich ein Nutzer um mehrere Rechte kümmern, um die von ihm gewünschte Musik verwerten zu dürfen. Dazu gehören das Vervielfältigungs- und Verbreitungsrecht, das Recht zur Nutzung eines Musikwerkes bzw. Werkteiles und das Recht der öffentlichen Wiedergabe. Will ein Nutzer also Musik von einem GEMA-Mitglied (Urheber und Verlag) verwerten, so übernimmt die GEMA das Inkasso und wacht darüber, dass die Musikstücke ordnungsgemäß vom Nutzer angemeldet werden.

Musik- und Geräusch-Archive

www.sonoton.com
www.sound-ideas.com
www.hollywoodedge.com
www.bestservice.de
www.masterbits.de

Nur Nichtmitglieder dürfen ihre Musik ohne die GEMA frei zur Verwertung anbieten. Das ist die sogenannte GEMA-freie Musik. Diese Musik wird also von Komponisten hergestellt, die sich durch keine Verwertungsgesellschaft vertreten lassen. Die Musik wird auf eigenes Risiko produziert und an die Kunden in Lizenz zur Verwertung freigegeben. Dieser darf die Musik, wie jeder Andere nutzen. Der Kunde kann sich das Recht der Verwertung der Musik jedoch auch exklusiv sichern. D. h. die Musik darf dann nur von ihm für einen vereinbarten Zeitraum oder zeitlich unbegrenzt genutzt werden. Tantiemen sind also nur an den Anbieter der Musik abzuführen. Sie decken in der Regel nicht nur die Nutzung der „Noten" ab sondern auch der Musikaufnahme auf Tonträger.

Interessante Links zum Thema Filmmusik (Film Scores) und Geräusche (Sound FX, Foley)

www.skysound.com
www.marblehead.net/foley
www.filmsound.org/starwars
www.scorereviews.com/horner.shtml
www.johnwilliams.org

Eine andere Kategorie bilden Musikverlage, die Musik auf Tonträger anbieten, für deren Nutzung GEMA-Gebühren für die Urheber anfallen. Das Recht der Verwertung der Tonaufnahmen auf vom Verlag überlassenem Tonträger wird mit einer Lizenz erworben und die verwendete Musik bei der GEMA angemeldet. Diese verlangt dann ebenfalls einen Obulus für die Urheber der Kompositionen, Bearbeitungen und Texte. Die Rechte an den Tonaufnahmen selbst liegen jedoch im Allgemeinen nicht zwangsläufig beim Komponisten, sondern möglicherweise beim Produzenten, dem Tonträgerhersteller, dem Verlag und den Interpreten. Diese Musikverlage haben sich jedoch die Rechte an den Musikaufnahmen bei den Beteiligten bereits gesichert, so dass für den Nutzer keinerlei juristische Probleme zu erwarten sind.

GEMA: Gesellschaft für musikalische Aufführungs- und mechanische Vervielfältigungsrechte, vertritt die Rechte von Komponisten, Musikern und Verlegern an ihren Musikwerken.

Bei Musik, deren zugehörige Verwertungsrechte ausschließlich von der GEMA wahrgenommen werden, muss direkt dort angefragt werden, ob eine Komposition zur Verwertung freigegeben werden kann. Die GEMA wird ihrerseits dem Nutzer dabei behilflich sein, die Erlaubnis bei den Urhebern einzuholen, um die Musik in dem zu erwartenden Rahmen und zu dem gewünschten Zweck verwenden zu dürfen. Liegt die Musik bereits auf Tonträger vor, so sind die Rechte an den Tonaufnahmen darüber hinaus zusätzlich zu klären.

Geräusche werden meistens aus einem **Geräuscharchiv** auf CD oder CD-ROM entnommen. Gedruckte Schlagwortkataloge oder Datenbanken erleichtern den Zugriff auf die gesuchten Geräusche. Mit den Ton- oder Datenträgern wird in der Regel auch das Recht der Nutzung der Geräusche erworben. CD-ROMs sind besonders für die computergestützte Tonproduktion geeignet.

Audio-Grabbing: Bei diesem Vorgang werden die tonrelevanten Daten einer Audio-CD digital kopiert und aus dem Format des Red Book-Standards in ein PC-übliches Format konvertiert. (Vgl. Abschnitt Überspielung von Ton einer Audio-CD).

Hinweis: Die Sprecherkabine und der Regierraum sind akustisch voneinander getrennt. Der Sprecher kann deshalb nicht hören, was im Regieraum geschieht. Deshalb kann der Sprecher unbeabsichtigt vom Geschehen abgeschnitten werden. Um dies unbedingt zu vermeiden, sollte der Sprecher mittels Gegensprechanlage darüber informiert werden, was sich im Regieraum zuträgt.

Hinweis: Erst nach dem alle Vorbereitungen technischer Art getroffen wurden, darf die Aufnahmesitzung beginnen.

Aus diesem Grund lassen sich damit insbesondere für interaktive Anwendungen bereits fertig „konfektionierte" Geräusch- oder Musik-„Schnipsel" nutzen. Sie liegen als Audio-Datei häufig in einem **WAVE- oder AIFF-Dateiformat** vor. Das hat den Vorteil, dass sie ohne Formatumwandlung verwendet werden können. Eine Alternative der digitalen verlustfreien Übertragung ist natürlich auch das Audio-Grabbing von Geräuschen einer käuflich erworbenen Audio-CD.

Sprechtext

Sprechtext nimmt in der Regel den größten Teil des Tones in interaktiven Anwendungen ein. Hier übernimmt er Funktionen, die vom Filmton bekannt sind und zusätzlich Aufgaben der Benutzerführung und der Navigation. Sprachaufnahmen müssen also neu und individuell für die Anwendung erstellt werden.

Aus der konzeptionellen Arbeit geht hervor, welche „Sorten" von Text es geben wird. Damit ist klar, welche Texte z. B. emotional oder eher sachlich gesprochen werden sollen. Der Text wird auf weibliche und männliche Stimmen verteilt.
Dann erfolgt die Auswahl von geeigneten Sprechern. Tonstudios oder Agenturen verfügen häufig über Sprecherkarteien mit entsprechenden Sprechproben / Demonstrationsmaterial professioneller Sprecher. Soll mit eigenen Mitteln (in der Schule, Fachhochschule, Universität, etc. mangels Budget) und eigenen Tonstudiogeräten gearbeitet werden, so kann in jedem Fall die eigene Stimme erprobt werden. Jedoch sollte eine „unabhängige" geschulte Person die Aufnahmen bewerten. Im Normalfall ist wenigstens darauf zu achten, dass die Stimme akzentfrei ist. Die Wirkung der Stimme und ihre Auswirkung auf die Glaubwürdigkeit des gesamten multimedialen Produktes ist nicht zu unterschätzen! Sie ist hier ebenso tragend, wie die Off-Stimme in einem Dokumentarfilm oder einer Werbung im Rundfunk. Im Zweifelsfall sollte für professionelle Produkte immer ein Budget für einen medienerfahrenen Sprecher eingeplant werden. In einem ständigen Dialog zwischen Regie und Sprecher wird während der Aufnahmesitzung die Interpretation des Textes erarbeitet.

Abschließend folgen zwei Beispiele für die Einbindung von Ton in interaktiven Anwendungen und eine Checkliste.

Einstellungsmöglichkeiten der auditiven Ebene in der interaktiven Anwendung „Herr der Ringe – Die Rückkehr des Königs". In dem Menu Audio wird angeboten,

- Soundqualität,
- Musik,
- Sprache,
- Effekte,

mittels abgebildeter beschrifteter Tasten (Buttons) und Schiebereglern den Wünschen des Anwenders anzupassen.

Das Mischungsverhältnis der drei Tonebenen zueinander kann mit den Schiebereglern auf der rechten Seite des Sound- und Musik-Menues eingestellt werden.

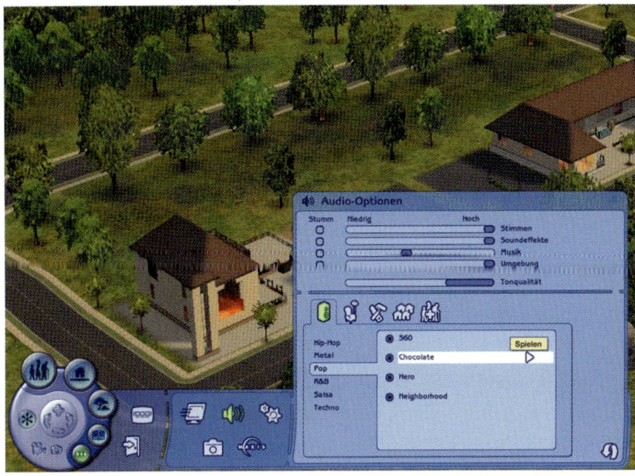

Einstellungsmöglichkeiten der auditiven Ebene in der interaktiven Anwendung „Die SIMS 2".

In der oberen Hälfte des Menüs werden Audio-Optionen angeboten.

- Stimmen,
- Soundeffekte,
- Musik und
- Umgebung (Hintergrund)

mittels kleiner Check-Boxen ein oder auszuschalten und in ihrer Lautstärke zueinander festzulegen. Hierzu dienen die oben abgebildeten Schieberegler (Fader). Die Musik lässt sich aus einem Angebot von vielen Stücken zusammen stellen. Um die Auswahl zu erleichtern, lassen sich die Stücke zuvor markieren und abspielen.

Hier sind einige weitere Fragen, die zu Beginn der Produktion einer interaktiven Anwendung geklärt werden sollten:

Checkliste:

- Welchen Stellenwert besitzt der Ton?
- Wie viel Speicherplatz steht zur Verfügung?
- Wie hoch ist die Datentransferrate?
- Müssen Systemvoraussetzungen eigens für die Wiedergabe des Tones definiert werden?
- Welche Tonqualität muss/darf der Ton haben?
- Soll es Atmos und Feedback-Geräusche geben?
- Sollen mehrere Geräuschebenen im Sinne einer Tiefenstaffelung (vorne, Mitte, hinten) mit Atmos und Geräuschen (auch für Feedback) erzeugt werden?
- Können alle Geräusche aus einem Archiv entnommen oder müssen einige eigens für die Anwendung erzeugt werden (Sounddesign)?
- Muss Musik eigens für die Anwendung komponiert und produziert werden?
- Sollen Ton-Kanäle für Musik, Geräusch und Sprache einzeln abschaltbar und/oder in ihrer Lautstärke regelbar sein?
- Können einzelne Audio-Dateien im Autorensystem (Programmierwerkzeug) bei der Wiedergabe mit individueller Lautstärke versehen werden?
- Lassen sich mit dem Autorensystem (Programmierwerkzeug) Töne ein-, aus- und überblenden?
- Wie viele Ton-Kanäle lassen sich mit einem Autorensystem (Programmierwerkzeug), Betriebssystem und Hardware realisieren?
- Welche Dateiformate werden benötigt?
- Ist die Anwendung für CD-ROM oder/und Internet geplant?
- Ist Datenkompression erforderlich?
- Lassen sich komprimierte Dateien mit dem Programmierwerkzeug (Autorensystem) verwenden und beim Anwender wiedergeben?

Diese Checkliste dient der konzeptionellen Planung des Tones für interaktive Anwendungen. Hiermit lässt sich im Vorfeld prüfen, welche technischen Voraussetzungen beim Produzenten und Anwender vorhanden und welche gestalterischen Anforderungen an die Planung und Umsetzung gestellt werden.

10.3.2 Technik

In der Kette von Aufnahme, Speicherung, Bearbeitung und Wiedergabe von Ton steht zunächst ganz vorn das **Mikrofon**. Über einen Mikrofonvorverstärker oder ein **Mischpult** gelangt das Tonsignal an die **Soundkarte** mit ihren AD- und DA-Wandlern. Ist der Ton erst einmal mit ihrer Hilfe in eine digitale Form gebracht, so lässt er sich im RAM oder auf Festplatte speichern und mit geeigneter Software im Computer bearbeiten. Schließlich folgt am Schluss der Übertragungskette eine Monitoranlage im Studio, eine Hifi-Anlage oder kleine PC-Lautsprecher neben dem Bildschirm für die Wiedergabe des Tones.

Tonstudios sind für die unterschiedlichsten Zwecke eingerichtet. So unterscheidet sich z. B. die Arbeitsweise und die Ausstattung an Hard- und Software für den Filmton gravierend von denen bei der Produktion von klassischer Musik.

Tonstudio: Sprecherkabine, Lautsprechermonitore, PC mit Aufnahme- und Bearbeitungssoftware, Gegensprechanlage, analoges Mischpult, Peripheriegeräte im 19"- und 9,5"-Einbaumaß, MIDI-Masterkeyboard

Deshalb beschränken wir uns auf die Betrachtung einer Sprachaufnahme für interaktive Anwendungen und hierbei nur auf die wesentlichen Schritte. In interaktiven Anwendungen werden häufig Stimmen aus dem Off eingesetzt. Sie geben z. B. Hilfen zur Navigation und führen den Anwender durch das Programm. Der Ort der Stimmen aus dem Off entspricht keinem abgebildeten Raum oder einer abgebildeten Umgebung. Deshalb sollten sie in einer reflexionsarmen **Raumakustik** aufgenommen werden. Es sei denn, es wird bewusst ein Raumeindruck zu erwecken versucht, der dem visuellen Eindruck auf dem Bildschirm entspricht. Selbst in diesem Fall ist es jedoch ratsam, die Aufnahme möglichst „trocken" zu halten. Auf diese Weise sind die Nachbearbeitungsmöglichkeiten flexibler zu handhaben.

Beispiel: Sprachaufnahmen sollen nachträglich mit dem künstlichen Hall einer Betonröhre versehen werden, der einem auf dem Screen abgebildeten Raum entspricht. Dabei würde sich der Hall, der bereits zusammen mit der Sprache aufgenommen worden ist, mit dem künstlichen überlagern und möglicherweise stören.

Um Tonaufnahmen durchführen, bearbeiten und verteilen zu können, wird eine Vielzahl von Geräten benötigt. Die Hard- und Software eines kleinen Tonstudios ist auf den Abbildungen zu sehen.

Mikrofonhalterung mit „Spinne" und Mikrofon. Gummibänder halten das Mikrofon und schützen es vor Erschütterungen, die ein tieffrequentes Geräusch verursachen würden.

❶ Mikrofonvorverstärker
❷ Multieffektgerät
❸ Stereo-Kompressor/Expander
❹ CD-Player
❺ Vollverstärker
❻ Doppelcassettendeck
❼ MIDI-Klangerzeuger

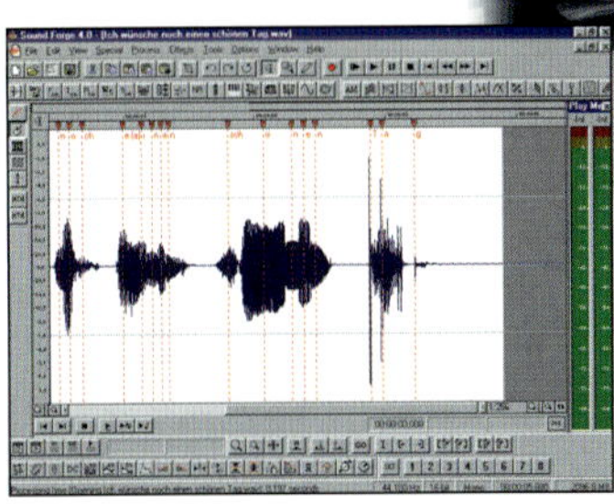

Tonaufnahme- und -bearbeitungssoftware

Steckverbindungen
❶ XLR
❷ Stereo-Klinke 6,3 mm
❸ Mono-Klinke 6,3 mm
❹ Cinch
❺ Stecker nach DIN, 180°-Variante (Teil des MIDI Standards)
❻ Stereo-Klinke 3,5 mm
❼ Adapterkabel: Stereo-Klinke 3,5 mm auf 2 x Cinch (links und rechts)

Plan eines einfachen Tonstudios mit PC

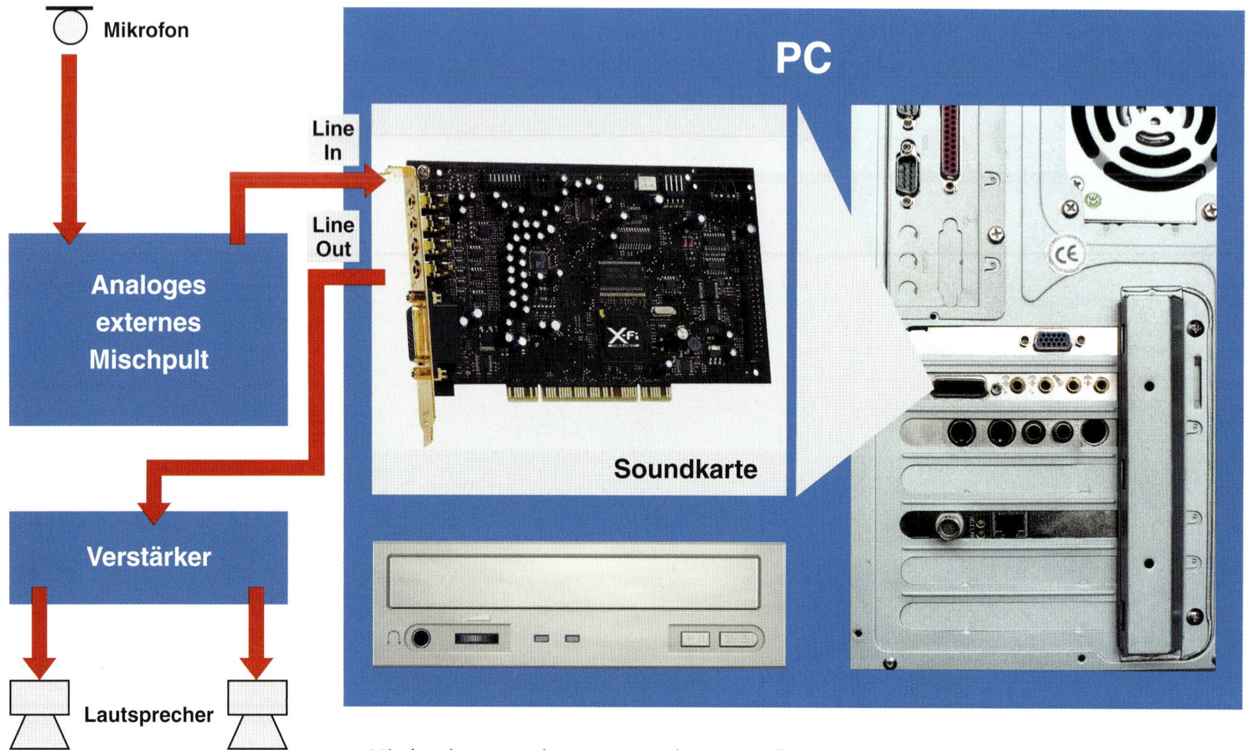

Mischpult, Verstärker, Lautsprecher, Soundkarte, Ausschnitt der Rückansicht eines PCs und internes DVD-ROM-Laufwerk

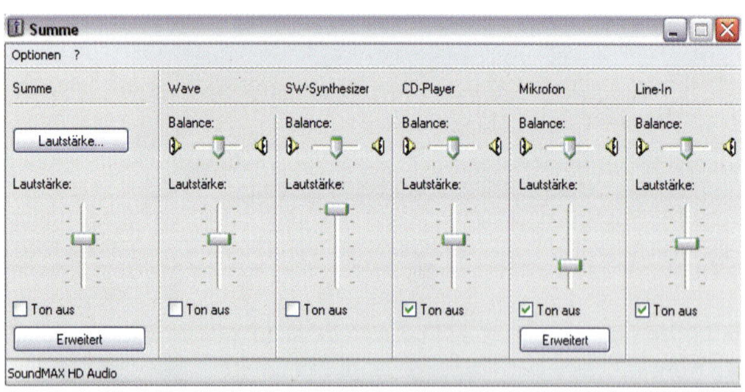

Mischpult für die *Tonwiedergabe* (Volume Control) unter Windows. Es wird nach einem Doppelklick auf das Lautsprechersymbol in der Symbolleiste sichtbar. Hier können die Quellen ausgewählt (oder stummgeschaltet) werden, die der Anwender hören möchte. Auch das Mischungsverhältnis lässt sich mit den Schiebereglern einstellen.

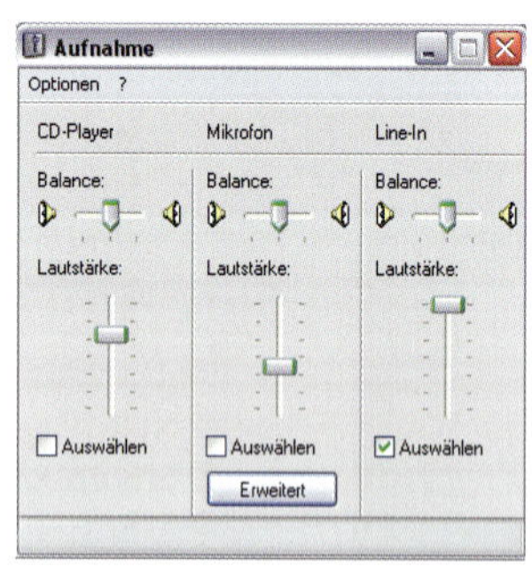

Mischpult für die Tonaufnahme (Recording Control) unter Windows. Unter *Optionen > Eigenschaften > Aufnahme* des Mischpultes für die *Tonwiedergabe* lässt es sich aufrufen. Auch hier lassen sich die Ton-Quellen auswählen und für die Aufnahme mit der Soundkarte vorbereiten.
Hinweis: Vor der Aufnahme alle nicht benötigten Quellen, insbesondere den Mikrofoneingang, ausschalten. Dadurch wird unnötiges Rauschen vermieden!

Verkabelung

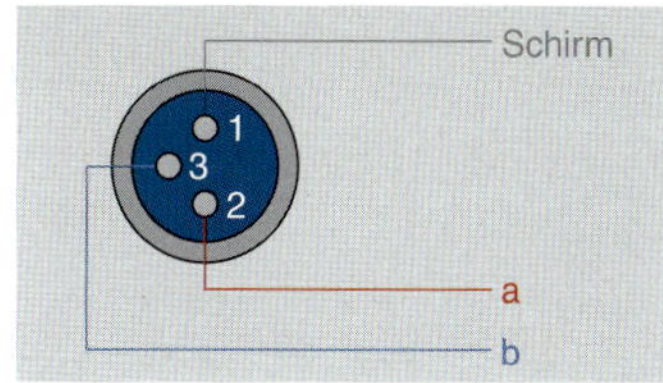

Belegung der Stifte eines XLR Steckers für symmetrische Leitungen

Im Tonstudio werden viele verschiedene Geräte miteinander verbunden. Dabei wird bei der Übertragung von Tonsignalen im Wesentlichen zwischen analogen und digitalen Signalen unterschieden.

Analog:
Mikrofone geben Signale mit kleinem Spannungspegel ab. Sie werden über eine Mikrofonleitung zum Mischpult oder Vorverstärker übertragen. Die übrigen Geräte werden mit Leitungen verbunden, die einen höheren Pegel übertragen müssen.
Die niedrigen Ausgangspegel von Mikrofonen müssen mit einem externen Mikrofonvorverstärker oder einem in das Mischpult integrierten Vorverstärker verstärkt werden. Der Verstärkungsfaktor liegt häufig zwischen 50 und 1000. Wegen der kleinen Ausgangsspannung der Mikrofone und der hohen Verstärkung wirken sich deshalb selbst kleinste Störungen auf extreme Weise aus, denn diese werden ebenfalls um diesen Faktor angehoben. Deshalb brauchen ihre Signale einen besonderen Schutz. Das wird durch die Verwendung symmetrischer Leitungen erreicht. Im Allgemeinen verbinden sie Geräte, die mit Trennübertragern und/oder Symmetrierstufen an Eingang oder Ausgang bestückt sind.

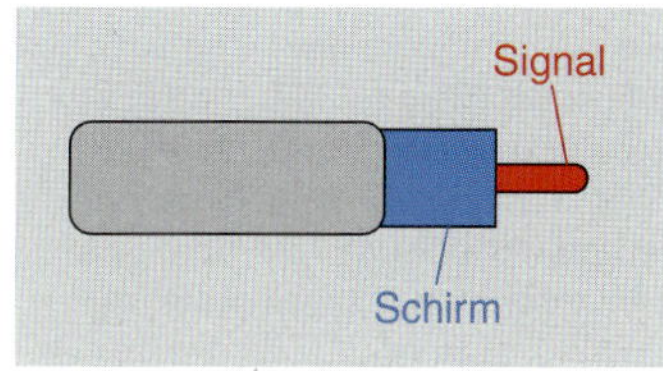

Belegung der Stifte eines Cinch-Steckers für asymmetrische Leitungen

Elektromagnetische Wechselfelder Φ_{Fremd} streuen in das Kabel und induzieren eine schwache Spannung U_{Fremd}. Da diese induzierte Störspannung U_{Fremd} jedoch in der oberen Ader a, wie in der unteren b gleich groß ist, heben sich beide in ihrer Summe zu null auf. In der Regel tragen die Kabel der symmetrischen Leitungen an ihren Enden **XLR-Stecker**. Für rechten und linken Kanal (L, R) wird jeweils eine Leitung gebraucht.

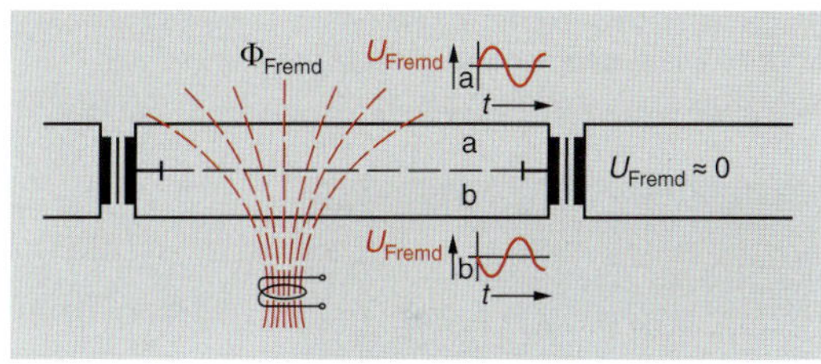

Wirkungsprinzip bei der Übertragung eines Tonsignals auf einer symmetrischen Leitung

Zwischen Geräten mit hochpegeligen Ein- und Ausgängen genügen in Studios mit kurzen Signalwegen ebenso wie bei der Verkabelung von Heim-Video/HiFi-Anlagen asymmetrische Leitungen. Dies reduziert zudem den Kostenaufwand erheblich. Der hohe Pegel wird auch Line-Level oder Line-Pegel genannt. Auf diese Weise werden niederpreisige Soundkarten und Effektgeräte, Mischpulte mit Line-Ein- und Ausgängen und CD-Player, DAT-Rekorder und Mini Disk-Rekorder mit analogen Ein- und/ oder Ausgängen verbunden. Die Kabel tragen häufig **Cinch-Stecker** oder 6,3 mm Mono-Klinkenstecker. Auch hier benötigt man pro Kanal (L, R) eine Leitung. Soundkarten tragen häufig kleine 3,5 mm Stereo-Klinken Buchsen für den Line-Ein- und Ausgang. Hier werden für den linken und rechten Kanal (L, R) zwei asymmetrische Leitungen auf drei Adern geführt.

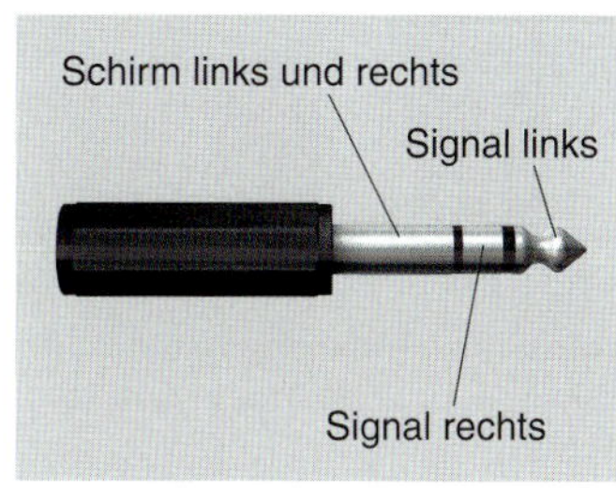

3,5 mm Stereo Klinke
Zwei asymmetrische Leitungen auf drei Adern

Digital:
Digitale stereofone Tonsignale werden jedoch bei S/P-DIF und AES/EBU pro Leitung mit zwei Känalen (L, R) übertragen! Bei geeigneter Hardware können mit der Consumer-Schnittstelle S/P-DIF auch Geräte mit Lichtwellenleiterkabeln (Toslink) verbunden werden. Ansonsten wird ein koaxiales Kabel mit einem Wellenwiderstand von 75 Ohm und einer maximalen Länge von 10 m mit Cinch-Steckern genutzt. Die Verbindungen nach dem professionellen AES/EBU-Standard verwendet symmetrische Leitungen und Kabel mit XLR-Steckern.

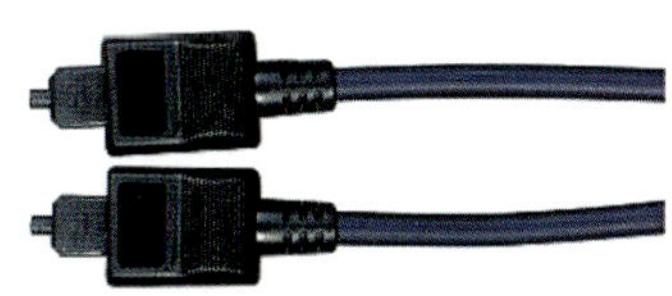

Lichtwellenleiter

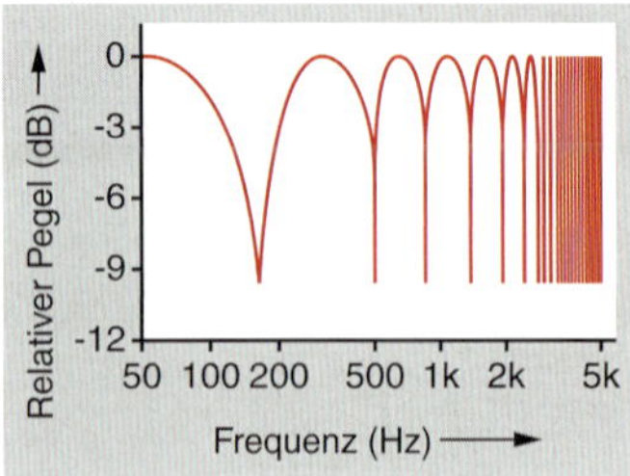

Quelle: Shure Europe GmbH, Heilbronn

Der **Kammfiltereffekt** tritt auf, wenn sich Originalklang und sein zeitverzögertes Signal (an einem Ort) überlagern. Das zeitverzögerte ist gegenüber dem Original phasenverschoben. Dadurch werden im Spektrum des Klanges in regelmäßigen Abständen auf der Frequenzskala Frequenzen verstärkt und andere bis zur Auslöschung abgeschwächt. Der Originalklang wird demzufolge klanglich verändert. Die entsprechende Filterkurve sieht aus wie ein Kamm.

Raumakustik und Sprachaufnahmen

Wie bei Aufnahmen im allgemeinen, so ist auch bei Sprachaufnahmen besonders darauf zu achten, dass keine störenden **Reflexionen** an das Mikrofon dringen können. Das ist besonders der Fall bei **Laufzeitunterschieden** zwischen direktem und indirektem Schall bis etwa 10 ms. Hierbei treten Kammfiltereffekte mit unangenehmen Klangfärbungen auf. Aus diesem Grund wird nach der Modellvorstellung der geometrischen Raumakustik versucht, den Schall so zu lenken, dass sich dessen direkter und indirekter Anteil nicht zu früh am Ort des Mikrofons überlagert.

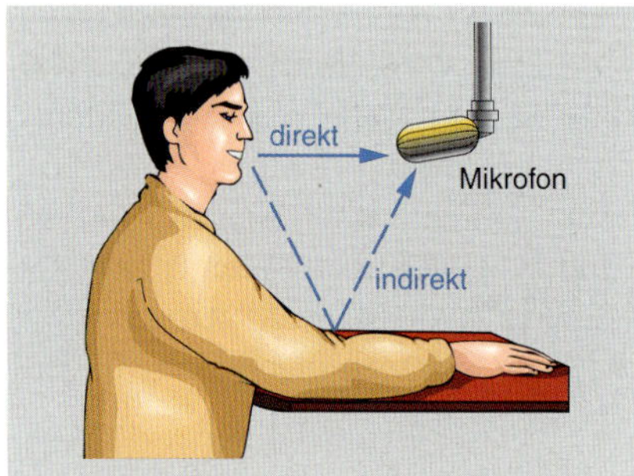

Klangfärbung durch Überlagerung von direktem Schall und Reflexionen beim Mikrofon

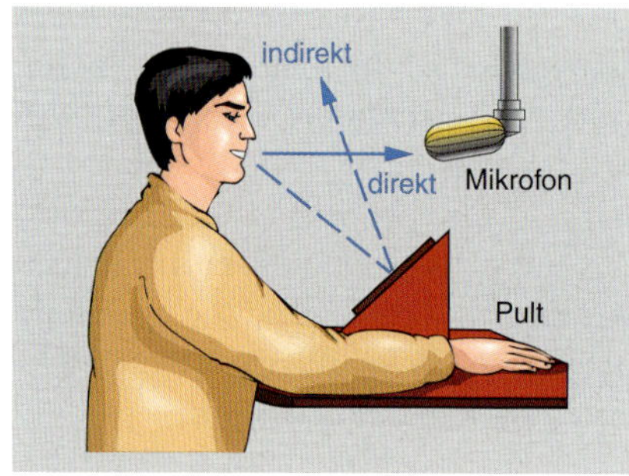

Vermeidung von unerwünschten Reflexionen und damit verbundenen Klangfärbungen

Mikrofone

Das Mikrofon wandelt mechanische in elektrische Energie. Besonders relevant für die Praxis im Tonstudio oder bei Außenaufnahmen sind deshalb die Unterscheidungsmerkmale im Wandlungsprinzip und zusätzlich in der Richtcharakteristik. Dies schlägt sich in der Bauart nieder und zieht viele weitere Eigenschaften der unterschiedlichen Mikrofone nach sich.

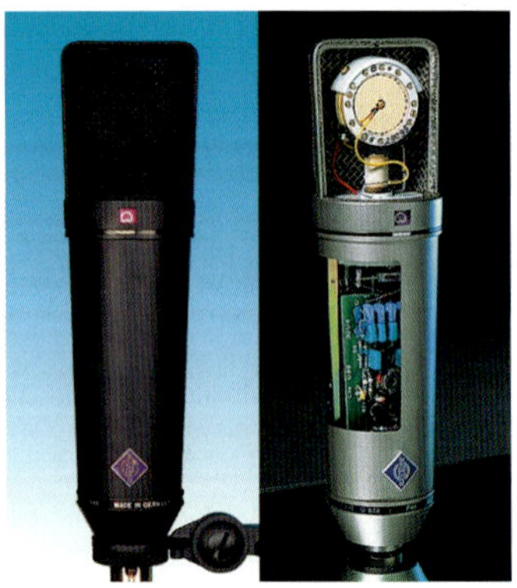

Kondensatormikrofon U 87
Quelle: Georg Neumann GmbH, Berlin

Wandlungsprinzip

Von besonderer Bedeutung für die Aufnahmepraxis sind das elektrostatische und das elektrodynamische Wandlungsprinzip.

Prinzip eines Kondensatormikrofons (Schnittzeichnung)

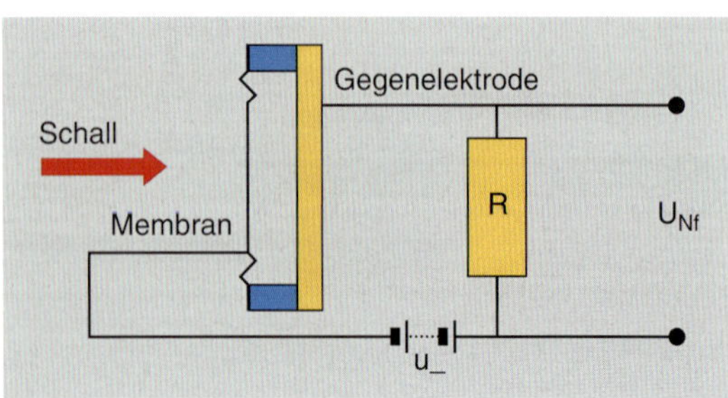

Elektrostatisch: Verändert sich der Abstand der Platten eines Plattenkondensators, so verändert sich dessen Kapazität. Ist eine Spannungsquelle am Kondensator angeschlossen, so findet dann ein Ladungsausgleich statt und es fließt ein kleiner elektrischer Strom.

Im Kondensatormikrofon stehen sich sozusagen auch zwei „Platten" gegenüber. Eine „Platte" ist eine etwa 1-10 µm dünne den elektrischen Strom leitende schwingungsfähige Membran. Sie ist planparallel gegenüber einer feststehenden Gegenelektrode eingespannt. Der Abstand beträgt etwa 5-10 µm. Die zweite „Platte" des Plattenkondensators ist die Gegenelektrode. Trifft Schall auf die schwingungs-

Quelle: Georg Neumann GmbH, Berlin

Das elektrostatische Wandlungsprinzip erlaubt auch die technische Umsetzung einer veränderbaren Richtcharakteristik (vgl. Abschnitt Richtcharakteristik) ohne die Kapseln zu tauschen. So ist es möglich, mit einem Handgriff die Richtcharakteristik des Mikrofons an veränderte Aufnahmebedingungen anzupassen. Auch das ferngesteuerte Umschalten der Charakteristik aus dem Regieraum ist bei einigen Mikrofonen möglich. Auf diese Weise lässt sich während des Hörens der Einfluss des Raumes auf die Aufnahme variieren.

Kondensatormikrofon mit Verstärkerteil (unten) und auswechselbaren Mikrofonkapselaufsätzen für unterschiedliche Richtcharakteristiken (links Kugel, Mitte Keule), rechts ein Popp-/Windschutz. Sie lassen sich mit einem Gewinde verschrauben.

fähige Membran, so verändert sich die Kapazität dieser Anordnung mit der Frequenz der Schallschwingung am Ort der Mikrofonmembran. Es pulsiert ein schwacher Strom im Rhythmus dieser Frequenz.

Das Kondensatormikrofon ist der Hauptvertreter für das elektrostatische Wandlungsprinzip. Es kann sehr hohe Tonqualität mit sehr gutem **Frequenzgang** bieten, benötigt aber eine zusätzliche Betriebsspannung. Kondensatormikrofonkapseln lassen sich mit sehr kleinen Abmessungen herstellen. Deshalb sind sie gut geeignet überall dort, wo Mikrofone unauffällig zum Einsatz kommen sollen.

Unauffälliger Einsatz von Kondensatormikrofonen in der Tagesschau

Elektrodynamisch:
Bewegt sich ein elektrischen Leiter senkrecht zur Richtung eines magnetischen Feldes, so wird in ihm eine elektrische Spannung induziert. Auf ähnliche Weise funktioniert auch ein Dynamo am Fahrrad. Für den Bau eines Mikrofons lässt sich dieses Prinzip ebenfalls nutzen. Beispiel: Eine Membran ist schwingungsfähig mit einer Spule verbunden. Trifft eine Schallwelle auf die Membran, so bewegt sie die mit ihr verbundene Spule im Rhythmus der Schallschwingung im Luftspalt eines Topfmagneten. Dabei wird in der Spule eine Spannung mit der Frequenz der Schwingung induziert.

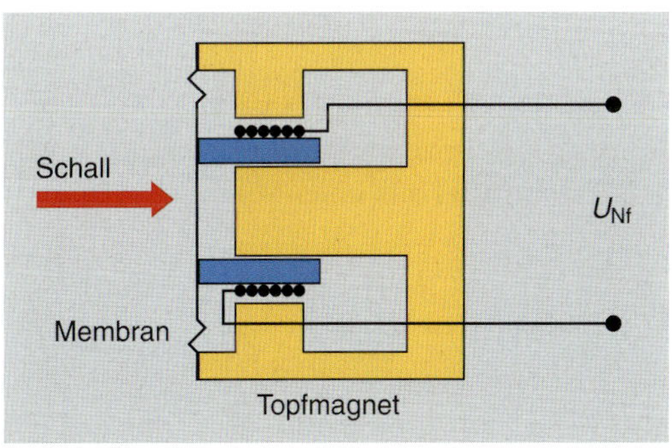

Prinzip eines Tauchspulenmikrofons (Schnittzeichnung)

Ganz rechts das dynamische Mikrofon SM58
Quelle: Shure Europe GmbH, Heilbronn

Das Tauchspulenmikrofon ist der Hauptvertreter des elektrodynamischen Wandlungsprinzips. Es ist sehr robust, benötigt keine Speisespannung (Phantomspeisung) und arbeitet auch noch bei hohen Lautstärken einwandfrei. Jedoch ist sein Frequenzgang im Vergleich zum Kondensatormikrofon unregelmäßiger. Es färbt den Originalklang stärker als ein vergleichbares Kondensatormikrofon.

Frequenzgang

Der Frequenzgang gibt an, wie sich das Übertragungsmaß in Abhängigkeit von der Frequenz verhält. Häufig wird dabei nur eine Schalleinfallsrichtung berücksichtigt. Sie zeigt dabei von vorn senkrecht auf die Mikrofonmembran. Ist die Linie linealglatt, so deutet dies darauf hin, dass das Mikrofon dem Originalklang der Schallquelle weder etwas hinzufügt noch wegnimmt. Das Mikrofon verhält sich klangneutral. Ist die Linie jedoch wellig, so beeinflusst das Mikrofon den Klang, wobei dies jedoch erwünscht sein kann. Mikrofone werden dann gezielt zu diesem Zweck eingesetzt. Messtechnisch ist dies ein Makel, gestalterisch jedoch beabsichtigt.

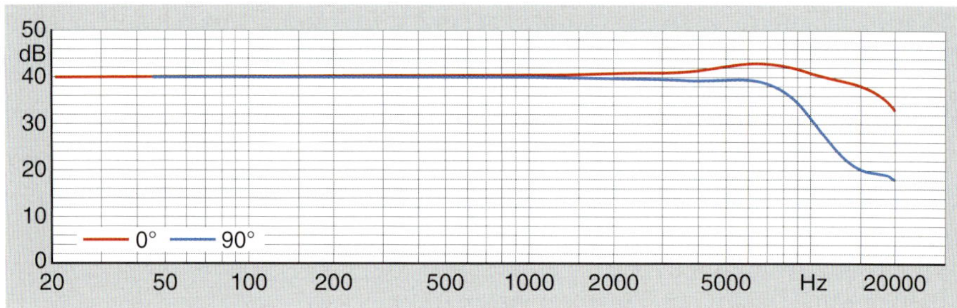

Frequenzgang eines Elektret-Kondensatormikrofons mit Kugelcharakteristik. Violette Linie: Schalleinfallsrichtung von 90°. Da die violette Linie von der Roten abweicht, lässt sich vermuten, dass Mikrofone ihre Richtcharakteristik nur näherungsweise einhalten!

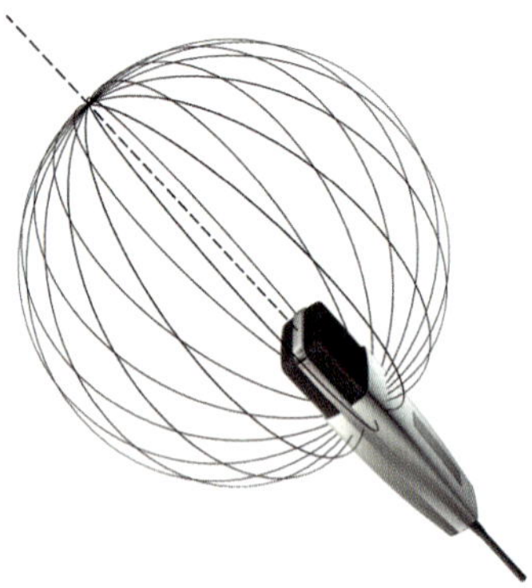

Quelle: Sennheiser electronic GmbH & Co. KG, Wedemark
Räumliche Darstellung der Richtcharakteristik eines Mikrofons. Hier ist es eine Niere.

Richtcharakteristik

Die Richtcharakteristik gibt an, wie sich das Richtungsmaß in Abhängigkeit von der Schalleinfallsrichtung und der Frequenz verhält. Welche Bedeutung hat das für die Praxis? Um den Einfluss der Umgebung bei der Aufnahme zu reduzieren, werden Mikrofone mit Richtwirkung benutzt. Die Richtwirkung ist umso größer, je „unempfindlicher" das Mikrofon gegenüber dem Schall von den Seiten oder von hinten ist. Verglichen wird dabei mit dem Schall, dessen Richtung senkrecht auf der Mikrofonmembran steht und deshalb aus der Mitte von vorn auf das Mikrofon trifft. Um dies für den Anwender zu verdeutlichen, wird eine Darstellung in einem Polardiagramm gewählt.

Um die Frequenzabhängigkeit der Richtwirkung bei möglichst vielen Frequenzen darstellen zu können, werden die Diagramme in eine linke und eine rechte Hälfte unterteilt. Das ist deshalb möglich, weil die Richtcharakteristik eines Mikrofons rotationssymmetrisch ist.

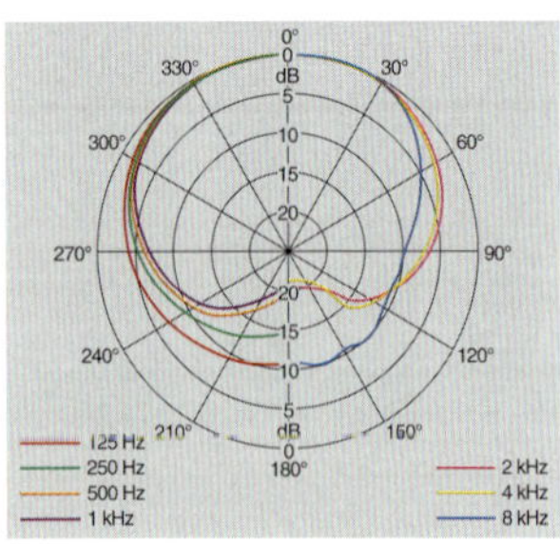

a: Richtcharakteristik: Niere, Schwache Richtwirkung

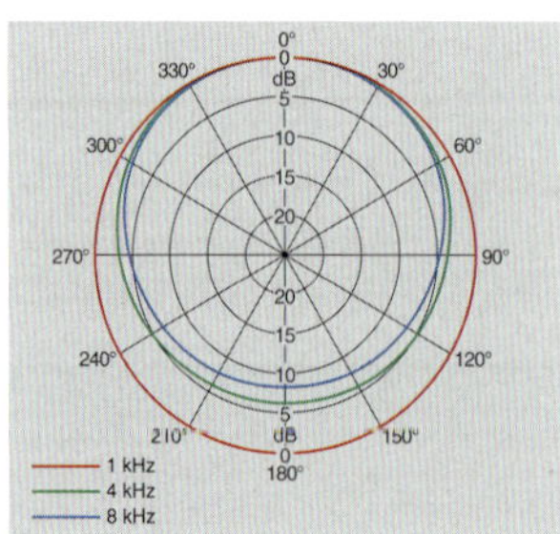

b: Richtcharakteristik: Kugel, Im Idealfall keine Richtwirkung

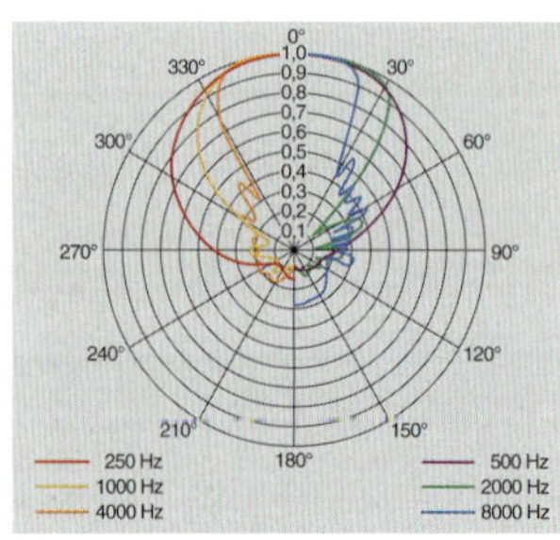

c: Richtcharakteristik: Keule, Starke Richtwirkung

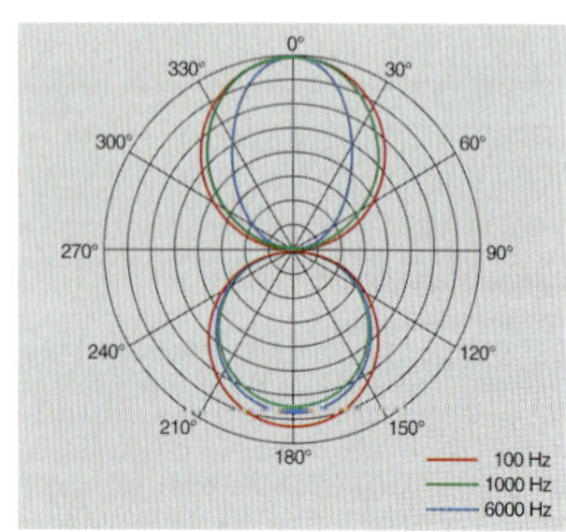

d: Richtcharakteristik: Acht, Richtwirkung von vorn und hinten

Nach dem Grad der Richtwirkung abgestuft gibt es folgende Charakteristiken: Kugel, Niere, Superniere, Hyperniere und Keule. Die Acht nimmt eine Sonderstellung ein, weil sie den Schall von vorne wie von hinten gleichermaßen aufnimmt und von der Seite im Idealfall nicht.

„Angeln" von Ton
Quelle: The Making Of Jurassic Park, Universal City Studios

Niere und Superniere sind Standardcharakteristiken. Atmos (typische Umgebungsgeräusche) lassen sich mit einer Kugelcharakteristik gut einfangen. Ein Mikrofon mit Kugelcharakteristik erfordert jedoch im Einsatz bei Instrumental-, Gesangs- und Sprachaufnahmen eine gute Raumakustik und eine störungsfreie Umgebung. Deshalb werden bei Reportageeinsätzen mit ungünstigen störenden Umgebungsgeräuschen oder beim „Angeln" von O(riginal)-Ton beim Film gerne Mikrofone mit Hypernieren- oder Keulencharakteristik verwendet.

Analog-digital-Wandlung

Die **Luftschwingungen** werden am Ort der Mikrofon-Membran in elektrische Schwingungen gewandelt. Diese werden elektrisch verstärkt und einem Analog-Digital -Wandler zugeführt. Dort wird zum zweiten mal gewandelt. Aus einem analogen Signal entsteht ein digitales. Dieser Vorgang wird Digitalisieren oder auch Quantisieren genannt. Bedingung für diesen Wandlungsvorgang ist, dass sich das ursprüngliche analoge Signal möglichst exakt reproduzieren lassen soll.

Zu diesem Zweck werden am analogen elektrischen Signal in regelmäßigen zeitlichen Abständen (Spannungs-) Proben, engl. Samples, abgelesen.
Diese Proben von Spannungswerten werden mit Werten aus einem Wertevorrat verglichen. Er ist über die Digitalisierungshard- und -software vorgegeben. Die Größe des Vorrates entspricht der zur Verfügung gestellten Wortbreite in Bit.

Hinweis: Musiker verstehen unter Samples digitalisierte Klänge, die z. B. per MIDI-Befehle mit einem Sampler (Musikinstrument) oder mit einem Harddisk-Recorder wiedergegeben werden (auch Kombinationen möglich). Nicht verwechseln mit Samples beim Digitalisierungsvorgang!

Beispiel: 2^8 = 256 verschiedene Werte: entspricht 8 Bit
2^{16} = 65.536 verschiedene Werte: entspricht 16 Bit
2^{24} = 16.777.216 verschiedene Werte: entspricht 24 Bit

Diese Werte bilden ein Spannungsraster, welches eine zu digitalisierende Spannung maximal überstreichen kann. Der Wert, der der Spannungsprobe am nächsten kommt, wird genommen und vom **Wandler** ausgegeben. Je mehr Werte zur Verfügung stehen, desto feiner ist das Raster und desto genauer kann ein Wert aus dem Wertevorrat eine abgelesene Spannungsprobe repräsentieren. Diese Genauigkeit steht in einem direkten Verhältnis zum Rauschen, das dem ursprünglichen analogen Signal über den Wandlungsvorgang hinzugefügt wird. Je feiner das Raster, desto geringer das Rauschen. D. h.: Je größer die zur Verfügung gestellte Wortbreite in Bit, desto geringer das Rauschen.

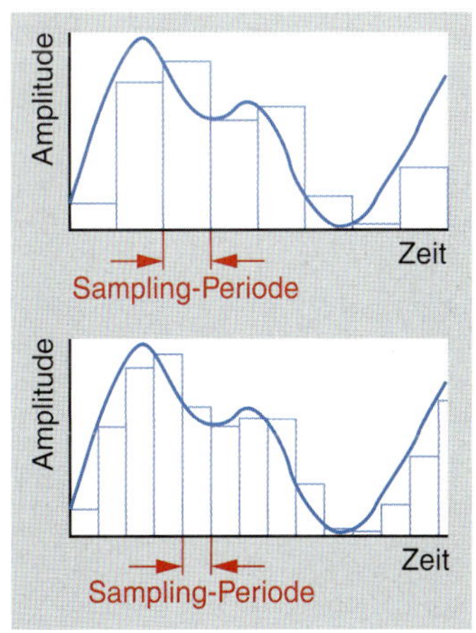

Sampling mit verschiedenen Abtastfrequenzen

Die Rasterung der Zeit (Abtastfrequenz):
Nicht nur die Spannung wird gerastert, sondern auch die Zeit. Um Spannungsproben (Samples) ablesen zu können, muss das elektrische Tonsignal im Analog-Digital-Wandler abgetastet werden. Die Häufigkeit, mit der dies pro Sekunde geschehen soll, wird mit der Abtastfrequenz festgelegt. Wie häufig muss ein Tonsignal abgetastet werden? Auch in diesem Fall ist das menschliche Gehör wieder das Maß der Dinge. Es hat einen Frequenzumfang von maximal 16 Hz-20 kHz. Der höchste zu reproduzierende

physikalische Ton hat also eine Frequenz von 20 kHz. Um diesen Ton exakt reproduzieren zu können, muss er mindestens mit dem doppelten seiner Frequenz abgetastet werden. Das entspricht nach dem Abtasttheorem von Shannon in diesem Fall einer **Abtastfrequenz** von 40 kHz.

Diese Betrachtungen sind idealisiert. In der Praxis würde unser Ton entsprechend einer technischen Festlegung mit 44.1 kHz oder 48 kHz abgetastet werden. Geringere Abtastfrequenzen vermindern die Tonqualität gegenüber dem Original. Insbesondere leidet der Anteil der Höhen im Frequenzspektrum darunter.

Datenmenge:
Anhand eines Beispiels rechnen wir aus, wie groß die Datenrate, die dabei anfallende Datenmenge pro Zeiteinheit, ist. Pro Abtastung fällt ein Wert in Form eines digitalen Wortes mit einer Wortbreite in Bit an. Die Wortbreite sei 8 Bit. Die Abtastfrequenz sei 44.100 Hz. Das bedeutet, dass pro Sekunde die analoge Spannungskurve 44.100 mal abgetastet wird. Demnach fallen in einer Sekunde 44.100 digitale Worte mit einer Wortbreite von 8 Bit an.

Die Datenrate:	*Abtastfrequenz [Hz]*	× *Wortbreite [Bit]*	
besser:	*Abtastfrequenz [1/sec]*	× *Wortbreite [Bit]*	
	44.100 [1/sec]	× 8 [Bit]	= 352.800 [Bit/sec]

Da 8 Bit zu einem 1 Byte zusammengefasst werden, vereinfacht sich die Sache zu:

44.100 [1/sec]	× 1 [Byte]	= 44.100 [Byte/sec]

Als nächstes wollen wir untersuchen, wie groß die Datenrate einer Tonaufnahme ist, die der Qualität einer Audio-CD entspricht. Wobei lediglich die Daten gemeint sind, die für unser Beispiel relevant sind. Keine zusätzlichen Kodierungsdaten!
Die Wortbreite der digitalisierten Tondaten einer Audio-CD beträgt 16 Bit, entsprechend 2 Byte. Also:

44.100 [1/sec]	× 2 [Byte]	= 88.200 [Byte/sec]

Berücksichtigen wir noch, dass zwei Kanäle, links und rechts, vorliegen, dann ergibt sich für die Datenrate:

Abtastfrequenz [1/sec]	× *Wortbreite [Byte]*	× *Anzahl d. Kanäle*
44.100 [1/sec]	× 2 [Byte]	× 2
		= 176.400 [Byte/sec]

In der Minute sind dies also:

176.400 [Byte/sec]	× 60 [sec]	= 10.584.000 [Byte/min]

➲ **Eine Datei, die für eine Minute unkomprimierten „Ton in CD-Qualität" enthält, ist ca. 10 MByte groß!**

Hier deutet sich bereits an, dass sich durch geeignete Maßnahmen die Datenmenge reduzieren lässt. Zu Beginn eines Projektes einer interaktiven Anwendung werden Standards für die zu erstellenden medialen Bestandteile festgelegt. Die gewünschte Qualität ist hier das Maß dafür, wieweit die Reduzierung der Datenmenge gehen darf. Um hier zum gewünschten Erfolg zu kommen, ist ein Vergleich mit dem Original unumgänglich.

Aussteuerung

Im Übertragungsweg der elektrischen Signale befinden sich elektrische Bauteile. Sie enthalten Widerstände, Kondensatoren, Halbleiterelemente oder auch Elektronenröhren. Die thermische Bewegung der Atome und Moleküle verursacht Spannungsschwankungen. Sie sind statistisch gleichmäßig über der Zeit verteilt und ergeben deshalb eine Rauschspannung. Wie wir bereits erfahren haben, entsteht auch Rauschen durch den Wandlungsvorgang digitaler Wandler.

Die Schaltungen aus Halbleiter oder Elektronenröhren (in Mikrofonvorverstärkern sehr beliebt) arbeiten nur in gewissen Spannungs- (oder Strom-) Grenzen annähernd verzerrungsfrei. Werden diese Grenzen deutlich überschritten, so kommt es zu hörbaren Verzerrungen des Nutzsignals.

Werden Signale quantisiert, d. h. von der analogen Signalform in eine digitale überführt, so treten genau dann starke Verzerrungen auf, wenn die größtmögliche Spannung, die der Analog-Digital-Wandler digitalisieren kann, überschritten wird. Dann reicht der Wertevorrat zu größeren Werten hin nicht mehr aus, um den überschreitenden Spannungswert zu repräsentieren. Der Analog-Digital-Wandler wird übersteuert. Das Tonsignal, welches die Information trägt, das Nutzsignal, darf diesen Wert nicht überschreiten. Andererseits soll es aber auch nicht in die Nähe der Größe der Rauschspannung kommen, damit das Rauschen das Nutzsignal nicht zu stark beeinträchtigt. Der Abstand zwischen Nutzsignalspannung und Rauschspannung soll also möglichst groß sein, ohne dass jedoch das Nutzsignal verzerrt wird. Den dafür notwendigen Regelvorgang nennt man Aussteuern.

Hinweis: Um Übersteuerungen zu vermeiden, ist eine Aussteuerungsreserve einzuplanen.

Bei der Betrachtung dieses Vorgangs ist jedoch zu berücksichtigen, dass ein grundsätzlicher Unterschied zwischen analogen und digitalen Systemen besteht. Analoge Systeme fügen dem Nutzsignal bei größer werdender Signalspannung eine größer werdende Verzerrung zu. Bei digitalen Systemen ist die Verzerrung knapp unterhalb der Übersteuerungsgrenze am geringsten, oberhalb nimmt sie jedoch sprunghaft zu.

Um Übersteuerungen zu vermeiden, werden Aussteuerungsmessinstrumente eingesetzt. Sie tragen eine dB-Skala und sind geeignet, um Spannungsspitzen oder/und einen „gemittelten" Spannungswert anzuzeigen.

Hinweis: Tonaufnahmen sollten zunächst maximal ausgesteuert werden, unabhängig davon, in welchem Lautstärkeverhältnis zueinander sie später in der interaktiven Anwendung wiedergegeben werden sollen.

Spitzenspannungsmessinstrumente (auch Peak-Meter genannt) sind geeignet, um Spannungsimpulse anzuzeigen, die insbesondere bei digitalen Systemen bei Übersteuerung zu hörbaren Verzerrungen führen können. Bei gleicher Amplitude werden kurze Impulse leiser empfunden als Dauertöne. Peak-Meter zeigen kurze Impulse jedoch deutlich an. Deshalb sind sie nur bedingt geeignet, um Lautheit zu kontrollieren. Generell ist es in der Tontechnik ein Problem, geeignete Instrumente für die Beurteilung der Lautstärke zu finden. VU-Meter (Volume Unit) sind der Empfindung der Lautstärke angenähert. Deshalb soll ein VU-Meter tendenziell besser für die Beurteilung von Lautstärke/Lautheit geeignet sein als ein Peak-Meter. Über die Anwendbarkeit gibt es jedoch unter Praktikern unterschiedliche Auffassungen. Heute werden in der Tonstudiopraxis auch Messinstrumente eingesetzt, die eine Kombination der Eigenschaften beider Aussteuerungsmessinstrumente in sich vereinen. Letztendlich entscheidet jedoch das Gehör!

Hinweis: Werden (Pop-) Musik und Sprache gemeinsam in einer Anwendung verwendet, so ist bei der Empfindung gleicher Lautstärke die Musik tendenziell mit niedrigerem Pegel wiederzugeben als die Sprache! Bei „klassischer" Musik ist dies eher umgekehrt.

Aussteuern ist nicht nur ein technischer, sondern auch ein gestalterischer Vorgang. Geht es darum, dass Tonereignisse z. B. Sprachbeiträge und Musik von der Lautstärke her gleich groß sein sollen, dann ist dies nur bedingt am Aussteuerungsinstrument ablesbar. Die Empfindung der Lautstärke ist nicht identisch mit der Arbeitsweise eines Aussteuerungsmessinstrumentes. Hier hilft nur die Beurteilung mit dem Gehör.

In der Tonmischung ist ein guter Kompromiss zu suchen zwischen einem im Sinne der Messtechnik maximal möglichen und einem gestalterisch sinnvollen Aussteuerungspegel.

Überspielung von Ton einer Audio-CD

Red Book bezeichnet einen in einem roten Buch veröffentlichten Standard für die von Philips und Sony Ende der 70er Jahre entwickelte Audio-CD. Er gibt die Garantie, dass CDs aller Hersteller auf jedem CD-Player abgespielt werden können.

Ob Musik oder Geräusch, häufig liegt der Ton bereits digitalisiert auf CD vor. Wie kommt der Ton von der CD in den PC? Am besten über das eingebaute CD-ROM-Laufwerk. Denn dann gibt es mehrere Möglichkeiten der Übertragung.

Übertragung auf dem analogen Weg:
Das CD-ROM-Laufwerk muss zu diesem Zweck mit seinem analogen Ausgang mit der eingebauten Soundkarte verbunden sein. Das geschieht zumeist mit einem kurzen Kabel im Inneren des PCs. Jetzt ist nur noch das Softwaremischpult des Soundkartenherstellers für die Tonaufnahme oder das mitgelieferte Mischpult (Aufnahmeweg!) des Betriebssystems und die Tonaufnahmesoftware aufzurufen. Die Aufnahme kann hiermit ausgesteuert werden.

Hinweis: Bei stark verkratzten Audio-CDs und durch Jitter verursachten fehlerhaften Bitstrom besteht die Gefahr, die Daten nicht vollständig auslesen zu können. Das führt zu Knacksern und Aussetzern in den konvertierten Ton-Dateien.

Übertragung mit der digitalen Audio-Schnittstelle:
Der Vorgang ähnelt der analogen Übertragung. Der Ton verlässt jedoch nicht die digitale Ebene und die Aufnahme muss nicht noch einmal ausgesteuert werden. Erforderlich ist ein CD-ROM- oder DVD-Laufwerk mit einer digitalen Consumer-Audio-Schnittstelle namens S/P-DIF (Sony/ Philips Digital Interface oder auch Interconnect Format). Auch hier findet sich ein kurzes Kabel im Inneren des PCs zwischen Laufwerk und Soundkarte.

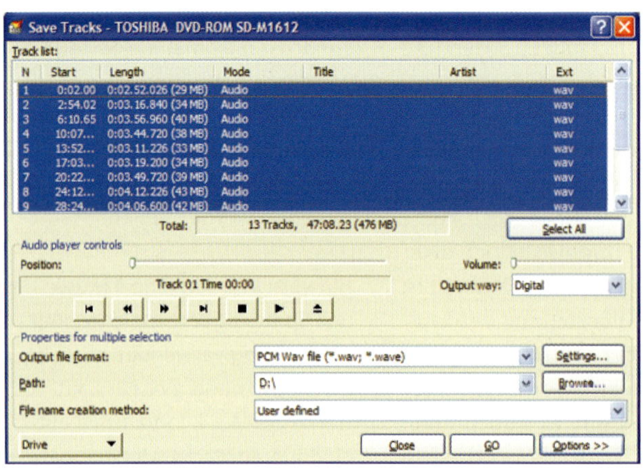

Funktionen eines Audio-Grabbers bei einer käuflich erworbenen und nicht kopiergeschützten Audio-CD.

Übertragung mit dem Datenbus:
Ton-Dateien auf CD-ROM (z. B. Yellow-Book-Standard) liegen im Normalfall im WAVE-, AIFF- oder MP3-Format vor. Sie können ohne große Anstrengung auf Festplatte kopiert und mit einem Autorensystem in eine Anwendung integriert werden.

Etwas aufwändiger ist der digitale Kopiervorgang von Ton-Daten einer normalen Audio-CD (CD-DA). Hier liegt der Ton in einer Form vor, die ihrem Red Book-Standard entspricht. Sie werden von speziellen Programmen ausgelesen (Audio-Grabbing) und in das entsprechende Format, zumeist WAVE, AIFF oder MP3, konvertiert.

10.3.3 Soundkarte

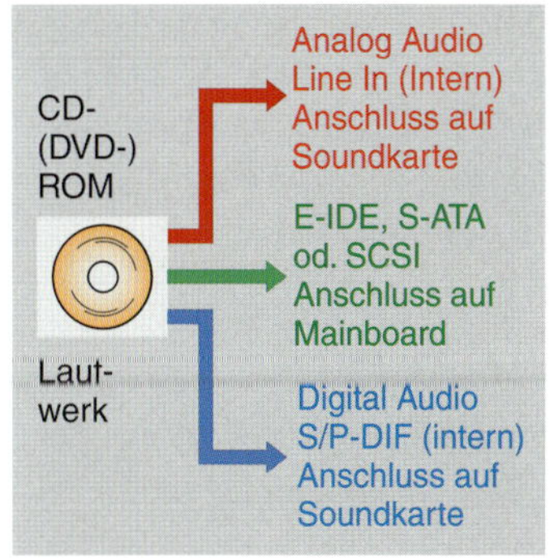

Um Ton mit dem Computer aufnehmen, speichern, bearbeiten und wiedergeben zu können, muss der Computer mit geeigneten Anschlüssen und Schnittstellen ausgestattet sein. Diese Funktion übernimmt in der Regel eine Soundkarte. Die Tondateien werden von CD-ROM oder Festplatte gelesen und über den PC-Bus an die Soundkarte übergeben. Für die Wiedergabe von Ton ist also eine Soundkarte erforderlich, die das digitale Tonsignal wieder in eine analoge Spannung zurückwandeln. Diese wird dann außerhalb oder mit einem Verstärker auf der Karte verstärkt und Lautsprechern oder einem Kopfhörer zugeführt. Viele Computerlautsprecher enthalten einen Verstärker, so dass der Ton unabhängig von einer Hifi-Anlage ohne viel Aufwand direkt am Computer abgehört werden kann.

MIC In ❶
LINE In ❷
LINE OUT FRONT ❸
LINE OUT REAR ❹
S/PDIF OUT ❺
MIDI / JOYSTICK INTERFACE ❻
WAVETABLE EXTENSION ❼

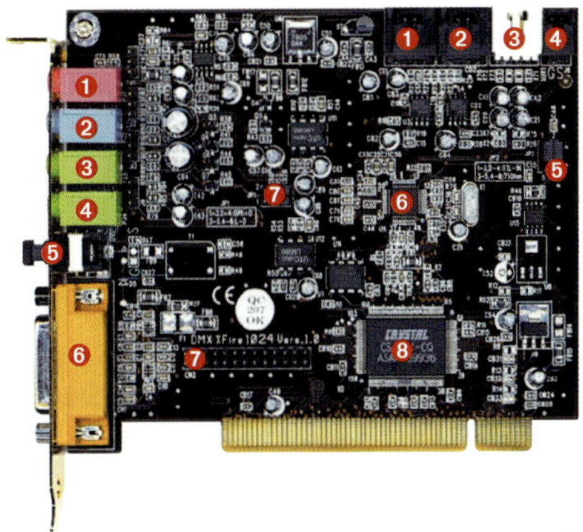

❶ CD1 In (intern)
❷ CD2 In (intern)
❸ AUX In (intern)
❹ S/PDIF In (intern)
❺ Jumper2: TTL (CD-IN) S/PDIF OUT
❻ CS4294 FOUR CHANNEL AC97 AUDIO CODEC
❼ Jumper1: LINE OUT / HEADPHONE
❽ CS4624 PCI AUDIO CONTROLLER

Quelle: TerraTec Electronic GmbH, Nettetal

Je nach Verwendungszweck ist die Bestückung einer Soundkarte recht unterschiedlich. Was auf einer Soundkarte im Wesentlichen untergebracht sein kann ist hier kurz dargestellt:

Anschlüsse und Audio-Schnittstellen

Der Mikrofoneingang ist für kleine Pegel im Bereich von einigen Millivolt vorgesehen. Da einige Hersteller Mikrofone mit einer eigenen speziellen Beschaltung der Anschlussstecker versehen, um hauseigene Mikrofone daran betreiben und mit einer Speisespannung versorgen zu können, ist hier bei der Nutzung mit anderen Mikrofonen oder Quellen Vorsicht geboten. Der Line-Eingang ist für hochpegelige Eingangsspannungen gedacht. Hier können die analogen Ausgänge von CD-Playern, externen Mikrofon-Vorverstärkern, Mischpulten und u. ä. angeschlossen werden. S/P-DIF oder AES/EBU bezeichnen digitale Audioschnittstellen. S/P-DIF bezeichnet eine Schnittstelle von Sony und Philips für den Consumer-Bereich, während die Schnittstelle für professionelle Ansprüche kurz mit AES/EBU bezeichnet wird.

Hinweis: Die Lautsprecher sollten geschirmt sein, damit sie auch in unmittelbarer Nähe des Computermonitors aufgestellt werden können, ohne die Bildwiedergabe zu beeinträchtigen.

Hinweis: Zum Abhören in der Ton-Produktion sollten gute Studio-Monitore, deren Klangverhalten Sie kennen und durchschnittliche, kleine Computerlautsprecher zum Einsatz kommen. Schalten Sie regelmäßig zur Kontrolle von einem Lautsprecherpaar zum anderen.

Neben den Ausgängen, die mit Buchsen von außen zugängig sind, gibt es auch Anschlüsse, die nur nach Öffnen des Rechners direkt auf der Soundkarte erreichbar sind. Hier können z. B. die Audio-Ausgänge von DVD-ROM-Laufwerken, Videoschnittkarten oder MPEG-Decoder-Karten angeschlossen werden.

Der Ausgang für den Anschluss von aktiven Computerlautsprechern ist ebenso wie der Line-Eingang hochpegelig. Lautsprecher sind im Klang sehr unterschiedlich. Sie sind in der Übertragungskette das Glied, welches den Originalklang am stärksten beeinträchtigt. Deshalb hört der Toningenieur insbesondere beim Mischen mit unterschiedlichen Lautsprechern ab, um sich dabei einem Klangideal zu nähern, das sowohl auf durchschnittlichen wie auch hochwertigen Lautsprechern angemessen gut klingt.

Wandler

Der Analog-Digital-Wandler übernimmt die Quantisierung der analogen Eingangsspannung (vgl. Abschnitt Analog-Digital-Wandlung). In der Regel werden die Signale, die am Line-Eingang oder am Mikrofon-Eingang anliegen, zuvor mit einem Verstärker an den Wandler angepasst. Der Digital-Analog-Wandler führt den digitalen Datenstrom zurück in ein analoges Signal.

MIDI-Schnittstelle

MIDI ist ein Standard und bedeutet Musical Instrument Digital Interface. Hier können MIDI-Masterkeyboards, MIDI-Musik-Instrumente oder generell alles, was sich mit MIDI steuern lässt angeschlossen werden.

Soundchip

In den Soundchips liegen digitalisierte Musikinstrumentenklänge auf Abruf bereit. Nach dem General-MIDI-Standard muss dies eine festgelegte Auswahl von mindestens 128 Klängen sein. Sie sind nach diesem Standard nummeriert. Per MIDI-Befehl können die Klänge dann eindeutig aufgerufen und über einen DA-Wandler ausgegeben werden. Mittels **FM-Synthese** können ebenfalls Klänge erzeugt werden. Diese Art der Tonerzeugung spielt jedoch zunehmend eine untergeordnete Rolle.

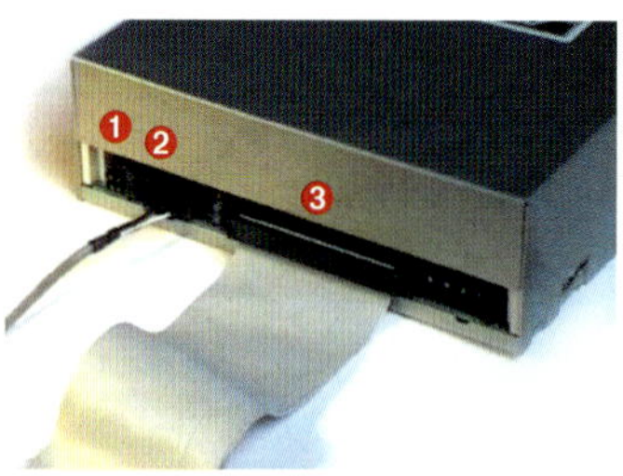

❶ S/P-DIF Digitaler Audioausgang
❷ Analoger Audioausgang
❸ EIDE Anschlusskabel

Schnittstellen am DVD-Laufwerk

Ein IDE-DVD-Laufwerk wird in der Regel mit einem Flachbandkabel direkt auf dem Mainboard angeschlossen. SCSI-DVD-Laufwerke benötigen in der Regel eine eigene Schnittstellenkarte im Rechner. DVD-Laufwerke verfügen über einen eigenen Digital -Analog-Wandler, so dass beim Einlegen einer Audio-CD (CD-DA) der Ton mittels einer analogen Signalspannung zur Soundkarte geführt werden kann. Häufig lässt sich ein Kopfhörer auf der Vorderseite des DVD-Laufwerks anschließen. Mit geeigneten Programmen und Laufwerken lassen sich die Audio-Daten auch in digitaler Form von der Audio-CD auslesen (Audio-Grabbing) und z. B. in den Formaten WAVE, AIFF oder auch MP3 speichern.

10.3.4 Harddisk-Recording

Was unterscheidet einen Harddisk-Recorder von einer Soundkarte mit Software? Der Begriff Harddisk-Recorder stammt aus einer Zeit, in der der Personal Computer den Anforderungen an Zuverlässigkeit und Technik für die Tonaufzeichnung auf Festplatte nicht gerecht werden konnte. Aus diesem Grunde basierten die Harddisk-Recorder auf eigenen Betriebssystemen und ihre Hard- und Software wurde auf die vom Anwender erwarteten Leistungen abgestimmt. Aufgrund der hohen Kosten waren diese Systeme ausschließlich professionellen Anwendern vorbehalten.

Aus den Anfängen des Soundsampling und Harddiskrecording: Synclavier von New England Digital (Direct-To-Disk im Bild nicht zu sehen)

Workstation – All-In-One

Wie bereits erwähnt, ist es von Vorteil, wenn der Ton digitalisiert vorliegt. Alle Bearbeitungsschritte lassen sich dann an einer Arbeitsstation abwickeln. Zu den Bearbeitungsschritten zählt auch das Mischen der Töne. Das ist häufig das Konzept von Harddisk-Recordern. Dann werden sie deshalb treffender Arbeitsstationen oder Workstations genannt und lassen genaugenommen einen Vergleich mit den analogen und digitalen Magnetband-Aufzeichnungsgeräten nicht mehr zu.

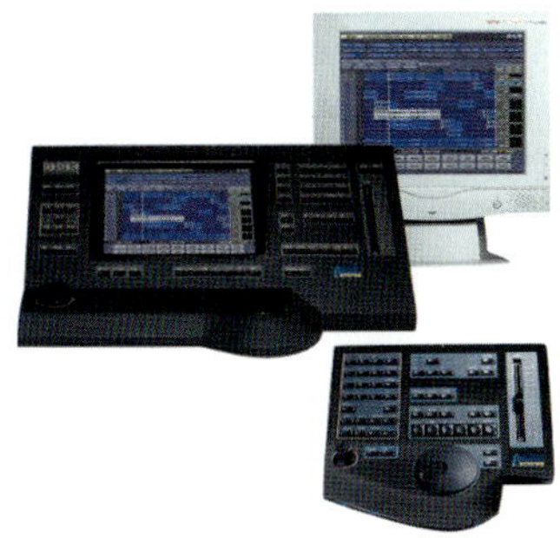

Professionelle Tonbearbeitung mit Soundstation von Digital Audio Research

Eine normale Soundkarte mit geeigneter Tonbearbeitungssoftware nutzt die gesamte „Infrastruktur" des Personal Computers. Die damit zu erzielende Arbeitsgeschwindigkeit hängt deshalb ganz entscheidend von der Leistungsfähigkeit der einzelnen Komponenten, deren Zusammenspiel und der Software ab. Um diese Abhängigkeit zu reduzieren bieten Hersteller PC-Steckkarten an, die einige der Funktionen eines PCs übernehmen, jedoch speziell auf die erforderlichen Zwecke abgestimmt sind und die CPU des PCs entlasten. Der Übergang von der einfachen Soundkarte zum professionellen High-End-System ist fließend.

Recording mit Digi 002 Factory von Digidesign

Nach einer **Analog-digital-Wandlung** speichern Harddisk-Recording-Systeme den Ton auf Festplatte oder einem geeigneten Wechselmedium. Im Gegensatz zu beispielsweise den DAT-Recordern, die ihre digitalen Tondaten linear auf Magnetband ablegen, bieten Harddisk-Recorder die Möglichkeit des wahlfreien Zugriffs und der exakten Reproduzierbarkeit von zusätzlichen Ton- und Bearbeitungsdaten. Was bedeutet das für die Praxis? Beim Tonschnitt lassen sich ähnlich wie in einem Textverarbeitungsprogramm Bestandteile ausschneiden und nach Belieben verschieben oder kopieren. Dabei wird zunächst nichts an den Originaldaten manipuliert, sondern lediglich zusätzliche Daten angelegt, aus denen hervorgeht, in welcher Reihenfolge die Tonbestandteile erklingen sollen. Auf diese Weise lassen sich die Bearbeitungsschritte beliebig oft ungeschehen machen und wiederholen. Dies gilt auch für alle anderen Bearbeitungsmöglichkeiten, von denen einige in Abschnitt Tonbearbeitung aufgeführt sind. Dies nennt man „Non-destructive Editing". Für die Verwendung in interaktiven Anwendungen sind die auf diese Weise entstandenen Dateien unbrauchbar. Deshalb werden am Schluss der Bearbeitungskette Tondateien erzeugt, die die Wirkungen, aller Bearbeitungsschritte hineingerechnet, enthalten. Einige Harddisk-Recorder tun dies bereits von sich aus nach jedem Bearbeitungsvorgang.

Sound Blaster Xtreme Gamer von Creative Labs

Liegt der Ton nach einer Analog-Digital-Wandlung erst einmal in Form von digitalen Signalen vor, so lassen sich nicht nur Bearbeitungen des Tons durchführen, sondern

DSP = Digital Signal Processor
Hochspezialisierte Bausteine zur kontinuierlichen, extrem schnellen und rechenintensiven Bearbeitung einer eng begrenzten Menge von Eingangssignalen. Dabei sind die Befehlssätze des DSPs für die Aufgaben optimiert.

Hinweis: Echtzeitfähigkeit wirkt sich direkt auf die Kosten eines digitalen Audio-Systems aus. Sowohl bei den Investitionen, wie auch bei den damit ausgeführten Dienstleistungen.

Hinweis: Die Wirtschaftlichkeit und Brauchbarkeit hängt sehr stark von den Arbeitsabläufen und dem Einsatzgebiet ab.

auch Analysen: Beispielsweise kann nach einer Stunde unbeaufsichtigter Tondigitalisierung überprüft werden, ob, wann und wie oft eine Übersteuerung vorgelegen hat. Selbstverständlich erscheint uns mittlerweile die grafische Darstellung des Tones auf dem Bildschirm und die durch Transformation gewonnene Visualisierung des Frequenzspektrums.

Für die Archivierung lassen sich den digitalen Toninformationen zusätzliche Daten hinzufügen. Über ein Netzwerk können die Daten aus einem Archiv von einem Server abgerufen oder von Arbeitsstation zu Arbeitsstation übertragen werden.

Echtzeitfähigkeit

Wird an der Hifi-Anlage ein Regler gedreht, so erwarten wir, das Ergebnis sogleich hören zu können. Im Gegensatz zu analogen Geräten ist das bei digitalen nicht selbstverständlich. Veränderungen an digitalisierten Tondaten erfordern immer eine Rechenzeit, auch wenn sie noch so klein ist. Nehmen wir diese Rechenzeit während der Bearbeitung nicht mehr wahr, so laufen die Bearbeitungsprozesse in Echtzeit. Je mehr Prozesse simultan laufen, desto mehr sind DSP und CPU gefordert. Je größer die Performance des Gesamtsystems, desto mehr Prozesse lassen sich pro Zeiteinheit durchführen.

10.3.5 Software für Ton und Bild

Professionelle Systeme verfügen über umfangreiche Synchronisationsmöglichkeiten. So ist es möglich Videorecorder zu steuern und den Ton mit dem Bild zu verkoppeln. Die Spulzeiten der Videorecorder jedoch hemmen den Arbeitsablauf. Es liegt also nahe, eine Software zu entwickeln, die sowohl den Ton, wie das dazugehörige Bild verarbeiten können.

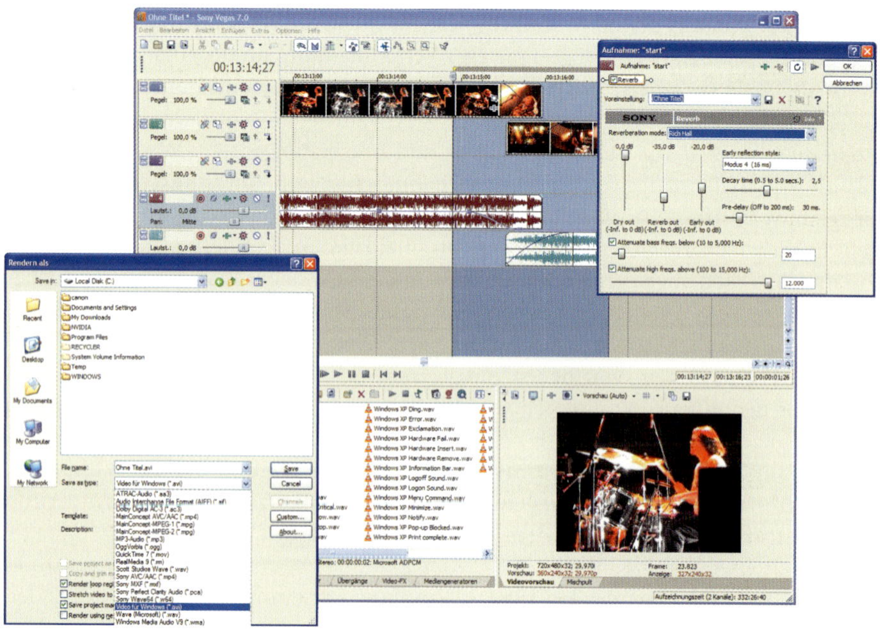

Beschreibung der Hauptseite von Vegas Video von ehemals Sonic Foundry, jetzt Sony:
- Bild-/Videospur
- Audiospuren
- Tonbearbeitungsfunktionen
- Besonderheiten für das Anlegen des Tones an das Bild
- Import und Export Formate

10.4 Tonbearbeitung

Mit geeigneter Tonbearbeitungssoftware und -hardware lassen sich auf dem Computer die aufgenommen Töne nicht nur abhören, sondern auch anschauen.

Das erleichtert das Auffinden geeigneter Stellen für die Tonbearbeitung, z. B. den Tonschnitt erheblich. Anhand der abgebildeten Wellenform lassen sich sogar Schlüsse auf das Tonmaterial ableiten. Dabei ist die Wellenform nichts anderes, als die Darstellung des Tonsignals über der Zeit.

❶ Die Wellenformgrafik beschreibt den Verlauf der Spannung über der Zeit. Schön zu sehen sind die Sprechpausen. An diesen Stellen ist die Spannung nahezu Null bzw. -Inf. und die Grafik zeigt einen horizontalen Strich.

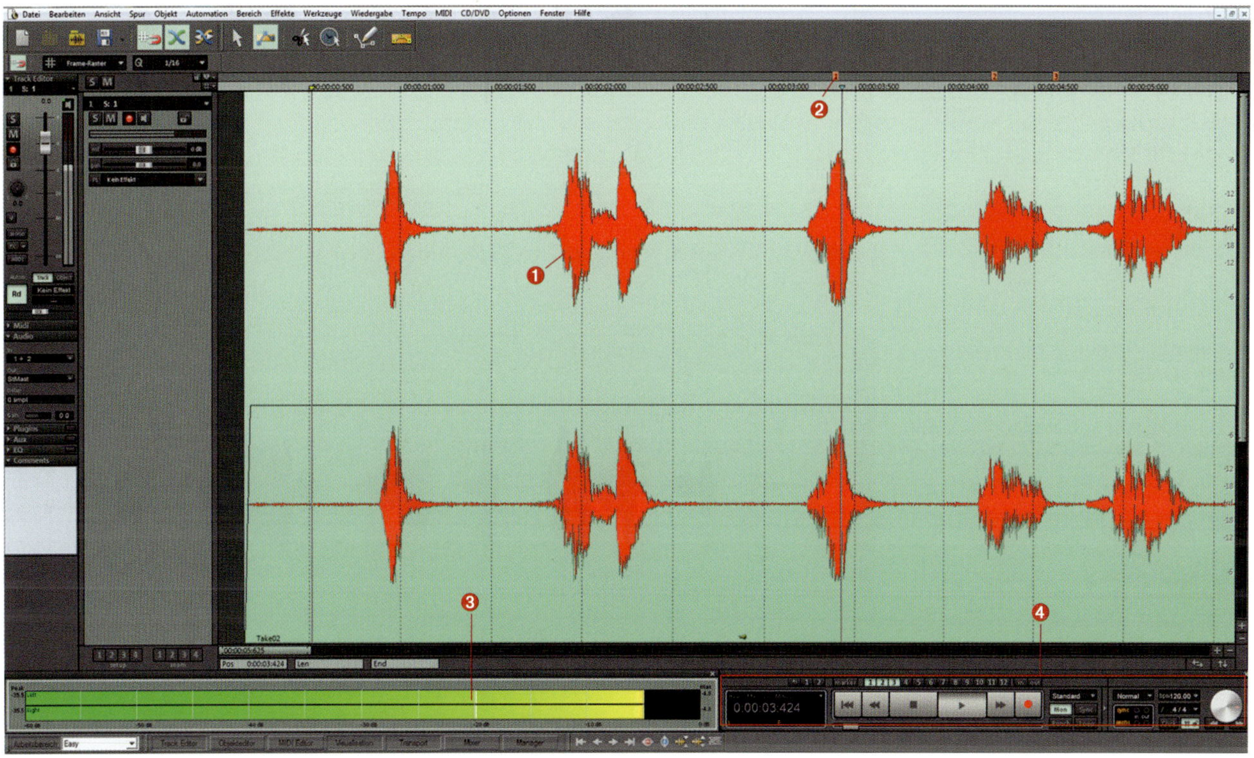

Sollte ein verlustfreier Bearbeitungsschritt einmal misslingen, so lässt er sich mit entsprechender Software beliebig oft wiederholen.

Ein Teil der aufgeführten Bearbeitungsfunktionen können von Geräten vorgenommen werden, die eigens für diesen Zweck meist in 19“- Einschubtechnik hergestellt worden sind. Häufig liegen sie aber auch als feste Bestandteile von oder als **Plug-Ins** für Tonbearbeitungs-Software vor. Siehe Abschnitt „All-In-One“.

❷ In der Wellenformgrafik können Markierungen während der Aufnahme gesetzt werden. Diese lassen sich benennen und jederzeit leicht auffinden. Auf diese Weise können auch umfangreiche Aufnahmen strukturiert werden.

❸ Aussteuerungsmessinstrument

❹ Mit der Transport-Steuerung lässt sich der Ton aufnehmen, wiedergeben, anhalten an den Anfang springen, usw.

10.4.1 Bearbeitungsschritte

In diesem Abschnitt sind einige typische Schritte für die Bearbeitung von Sprache für interaktive Anwendungen auf dem Computer aufgeführt. Dazu dient nach einem Mundgeräusch und einmaligem Einatmen der Satz *„Ich wünsche noch einen schönen Tag.“*

DC-Offset – Tonsignal symmetrieren

Ein Gleichspannungsanteil kann einem Nutzsignal überlagert sein. Ursache hierfür können Ungenauigkeiten des Analog-Digital-Wandlers sein. Oder die Überlagerung ist bereits auf der Übertragung zum Wandler geschehen.

In diesem Screenshot ist die Achse der Wellenformgrafik nach oben verschoben. Das deutet auf einen positiven Gleichspannungsanteil hin.

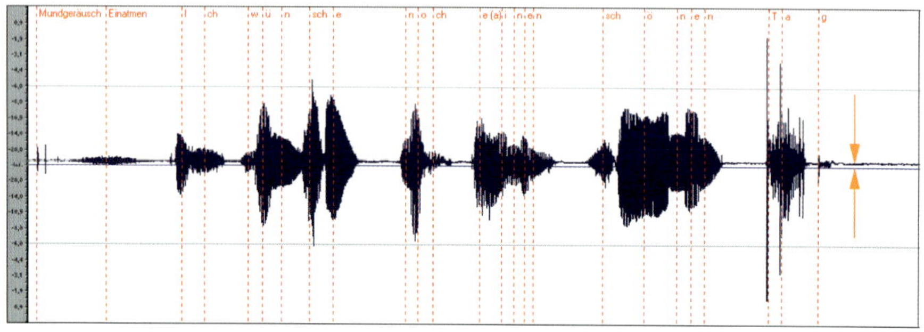

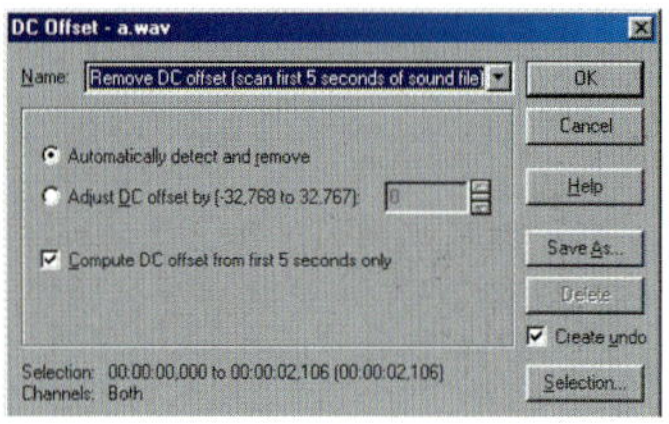

Beim Symmetrieren wird der Gleichspannungsanteil wieder aus dem Signal herausgerechnet.

Die beiden Achsen liegen wieder übereinander.

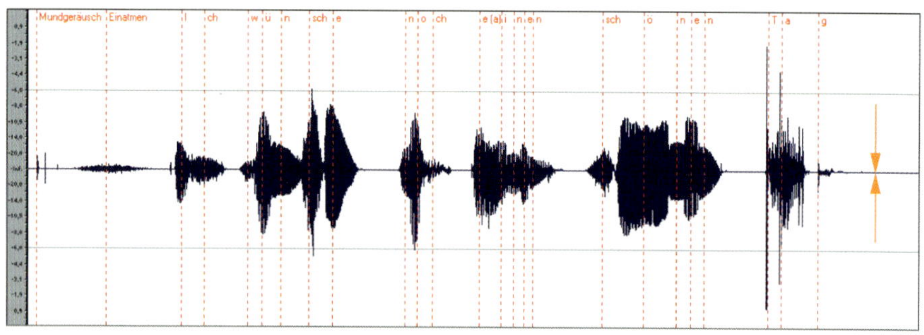

De-Esser-Zischlaute reduzieren

Ein Exciter fügt einem Klang Obertöne hinzu und verhilft ihm dadurch zu mehr Lebendigkeit. Die Sprachverständlichkeit steigt. Durch weitere Verfahren lässt sich das gesamte Frequenzspektrum erweitern.

Um einer Stimme die nötige Brillanz zu verleihen, werden Mikrofone mit entsprechender Klangcharakteristik verwendet oder die Stimme mit Klangregelung oder Exciter bearbeitet. Dabei nimmt der Pegel hoher Frequenzbestandteile der Sprechstimmen zu. Ein Übriges bewirkt ein kleiner Abstand von Sprecher zum Mikrofon. Die genannten Verfahren verleihen einer Stimme einen runden sonoren Klang. Die Folge ist jedoch häufig, dass die Zisch- und Explosivlaute danach zu stark im Klangspektrum vertreten sind. Wie stark diese Laute bei Sprechern vertreten sind, ist von Natur aus unterschiedlich. Um jedoch ein ausgewogenes Klangbild der Stimme zu erreichen, ist es deshalb nötig, diese Zisch- und Explosivlaute abzuschwächen. Der De-Esser leistet dabei gute Dienste. Er komprimiert den Pegel frequenzabhängig.

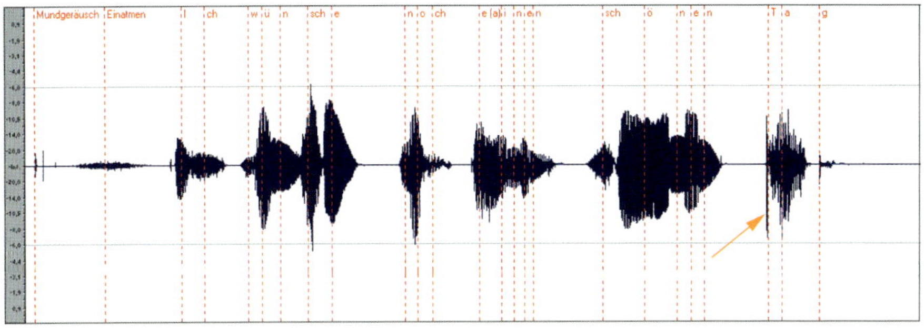

An dieser Stelle ist der Laut „T" vom Wort Tag in seinem Pegel reduziert worden. Das ist durch einen Vergleich mit der vorangehenden obigen Wellenformgrafik deutlich sichtbar.

Kompressor – Aufnahme komprimieren

Der Kompressor hat die Aufgabe, das Verhältnis zwischen laut und leise zu verkleinern. Die Dynamik einer Aufnahme wird damit verringert. D. h. laute und leise Stellen rücken in ihrer Lautstärke dichter zusammen. Auf diese Weise werden die Auswirkungen von Schwankungen des Abstandes von Sprecher zum Mikrofon ausgeglichen, soweit dies unter klanglichen Aspekten vertretbar ist. Die Aufnahme kann dann insgesamt in ihrem Pegel angehoben werden. Das erhöht die durchschnittliche Lautstärke der Sprachaufnahme. Dieser Effekt stellt sich auch bei gleichbleibendem Abstand des Sprechers zum Mikrofon ein. Das Klangbild verdichtet sich. Die Folge ist eine Erhöhung der Durchsetzungskraft der Stimme. Auch die Systemdynamik wird dabei besser genutzt. Damit ist sowohl einem gestalterischen, als auch dem technischen Anspruch an eine gelungene Aufnahme Genüge getan.

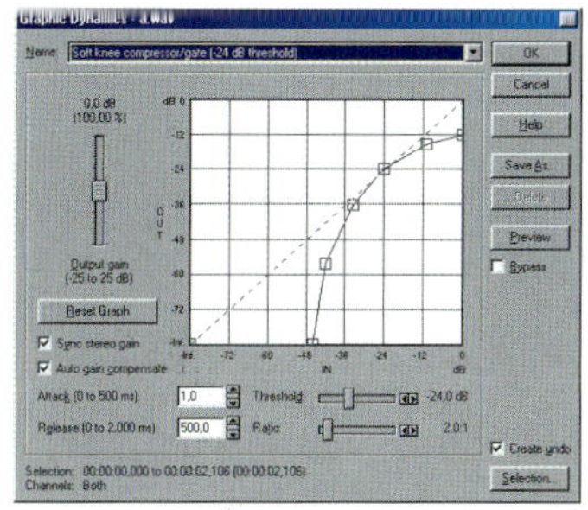

Hinweis: Komprimieren und Normalisieren sollten unbedingt vor einer Konvertierung von 16 auf 8 Bit durchgeführt werden, um die verbleibende Dynamik des Audio-Systems voll auszuschöpfen.

Normalize – Systemdynamik nutzen

In Tonbearbeitungssoftware lässt häufig die Bearbeitungsfunktion „Normalize" finden. Mit dieser Funktion wird die Aufnahme auf einen maximalen Spannungspegel gebracht. Auch dabei lässt sich bei einigen Programmen mit einer Variante der Normalize-Funktion auch zusätzlich der durchschnittliche Pegel erhöhen und damit ähnliche Wirkungen wie die eines Kompressors erzielen.

Hinweis: Beim Normalisieren den Pegel nicht zu hoch anheben, weil Soundkarten bei der Wiedergabeeventuell verzerren. Eine Sicherheitsreserve von 1 dB bis zum Aussteuerungsmaximum ist deshalb sinnvoll!

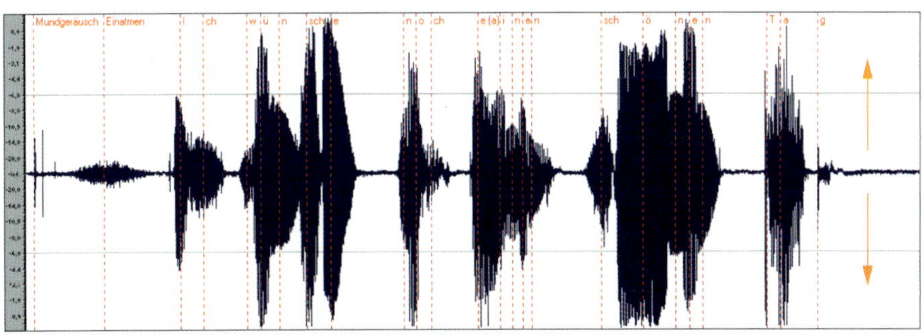

Die Wellenformgrafik ist gegenüber der vorangegangene obigen entlang der Pegel-Achse gespreizt. Der Spannungspegel hat sich also deutlich erhöht.

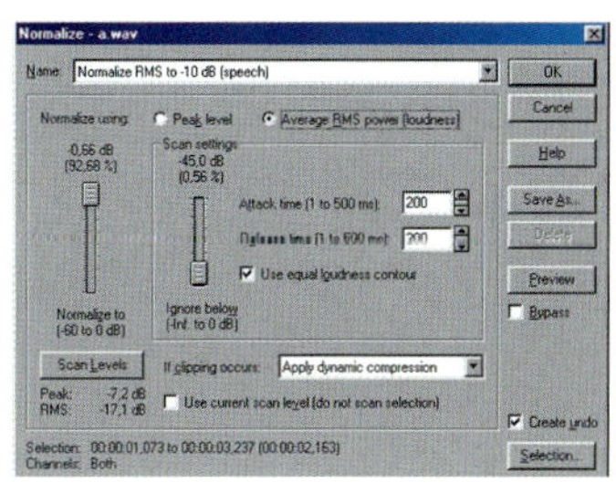

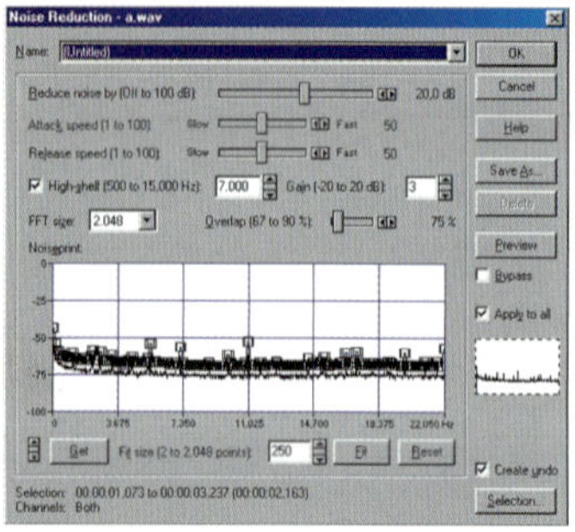

Gegenüber der vorangegangen Wellenformgrafik fehlen hier die rauschhaften Anteile. Das Rauschen wurde vermindert. Ganz besonders gut zu sehen in den Sprechpausen. Der schwarz markierte Teil der Grafik enthält unerwünschte Atem- und Mundgeräusche. Er wird im nächsten Schritt herausgeschnitten.

De-Noiser – Aufnahmen entrauschen

Liegen Tonaufnahmen in digitalisierter Form vor, so lassen sich ihre Daten durch entsprechende Algorithmen manipulieren. Beispielsweise wird bei einigen Programmen ein Noiseprint ähnlich eines Fingerprint (Fingerabdrucks) von einer Stelle abgenommen, die lediglich das für die Aufnahme typische Rauschen enthält. Dies wird analysiert. Das Ergebnis dient als Grundlage für den Vorgang des Entrauschens. Das Rauschen wird aus der gesamten Aufnahme heraus gerechnet.

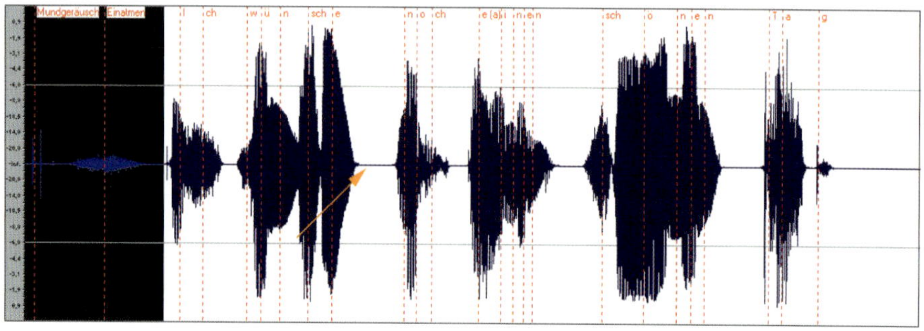

Cut, Copy, Paste – Sprechtext durch Schneiden für die Anwendung vorbereiten

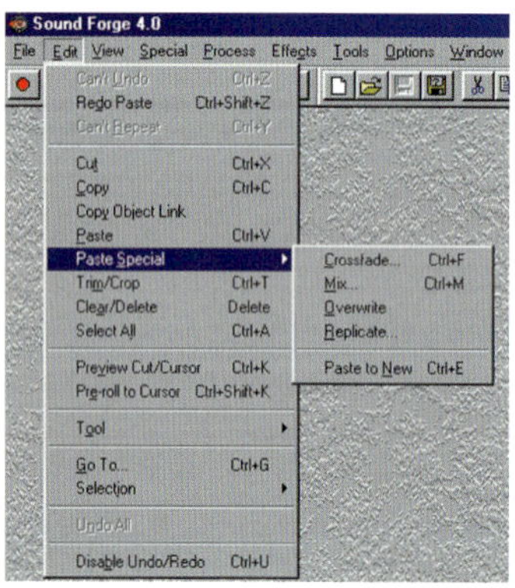

Der in der vorangegangen Wellenformgrafik schwarz markierte Abschnitt fehlt hier, ist also aus der Aufnahme herausgeschnitten worden. Im Normalfall bleibt das entfernte Daten-Stück bei vielen Tonbearbeitungsprogrammen physikalisch im Speicher (z. B. Festplatte) erhalten, um den Vorgang rückgängig machen zu können (Non-destructive Editing).

Geräusche, die durch Mundbewegungen und Luftholen entstehen und die besonders laut aufgenommen werden, wenn der Sprecher nahe am Mikrofon spricht, werden in ihrem Pegel verringert oder gar herausgeschnitten. Ebenso verschwinden unnötige Pausen am Anfang und Ende von Textpassagen.

Gesprochene Texte werden in interaktiven Anwendungen zum Teil interaktiv abgerufen. Deshalb müssen die gesprochenen Texte in Abschnitte zerlegt und als voneinander getrennte Ton-Dateien vorliegen. Auch dies lässt sich mit den Funktionen Cut, Copy und Paste unterstützt von der Wellenformgrafik hervorragend meistern. Dabei lassen sich in der Regel Shortcuts und Cursorsteuerungen nutzen, die aus dem Bereich der Textbearbeitungssoftware bekannt sind.

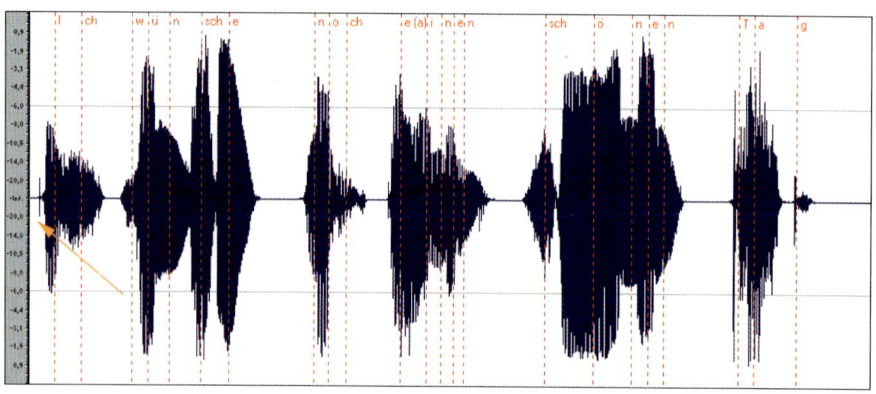

Fade in/out – Ein- und Ausblenden

Um sicher zu gehen, dass die Aufnahme nicht mit „knacksenden" Spannungssprüngen beginnt und endet, können kurze Blenden im Bereich von Millisekunden am Anfang und Ende in die Aufnahme gerechnet werden.

Schließlich werden die einzelnen Sprechtextbestandteile als Audio-Dateien in einem Format gespeichert, das für die Programmierung der Anwendung erforderlich ist. Die gängigsten Formate sind das WAVE-Format mit der Datei-Endung WAV und AIFF (Audio Interchange File Format) mit der Datei-Endung AIF. Die Eigenschaften dieser Formate sind recht ähnlich. So lassen sie sich auch an das Maximum für interaktive Anwendungen auf CD-ROM von 44.1 kHz und 16 Bit anpassen. Das entspricht der Abtastfrequenz und Auflösung und damit der Tonqualität einer Audio-CD.

Hinweis: Möglichst keine Zwischengrößen bei der Abtastfrequenz, wie z. B. 32 kHz nehmen, weil einige Soundkarten diese nicht unterstützen und es deshalb zu Klangeinbußen bei der Umrechnung in ein entsprechendes Format kommen kann (Microsoft Soundmapper mit Audio Compression Manager).

Am Ende dieser Bearbeitungsvorgänge liegen oft sehr viele Audio-Dateien vor. Um auch noch in diesem Bearbeitungsstadium an allen Dateien die gleichen Veränderungen mit einem vertretbaren Arbeitsaufwand vornehmen zu können, werden Batch-(Converter)-Programme (Stapelverarbeitungsprogramme) eingesetzt. Beispiel: Die Audio-Dateien einer Anwendung auf CD-ROM sollen zukünftig auch im Internet verfügbar sein. Alle Dateien müssen vom WAVE-Format in das MP3-Format konvertiert werden.

Hinweis: Die Sprachaufnahmen sollten zunächst in möglichst guter Qualität mit hoher Auflösung erstellt werden. Es ist Voraussetzung dafür, dass an dieser Stelle der Bearbeitungskette die Aufnahmen in die unterschiedlichsten Formate mit hoher oder niedriger Tonqualität konvertiert werden können. Die unterschiedlichsten Auflösungen und Formate in den unterschiedlichsten Qualitätsstufen stehen hierfür zur Verfügung. Datenreduzierende Formate nach dem ADPCM-Verfahren zählen ebenso dazu, wie das durch Internetanwendungen bekannt gewordene MP3-Format.

10.4.2 Datenreduktion

Ganz allgemein ist Datenreduktion von Nutzen bei der Datenarchivierung oder Speicherung, der Verkürzung von Übertragungszeiten und Verringerung von Datenmengen bei begrenzter Übertragungskanalkapazität.

Im Speziellen gibt die Speicherkapazität von CD-ROMs und die **Datenübertragungsrate** von CD-ROM-Laufwerken Anlass, bereits bei der Konzeption zu überlegen, wie viel Speicher dem Ton in etwa zur Verfügung zu stellen ist. Abhängig von der Menge des Sprechtextes, der notwendigen Musik und der Geräusche muss dann überlegt werden, wie viele Daten pro Zeiteinheit der Ton haben darf. Davon abhängig ist jedoch die Tonqualität.

Läuft die Anwendung im Internet, so entscheidet ganz besonders die Datenübertragungsrate, in welcher Tonqualität die Übertragung stattfindet.
Falls nötig, gibt es mehrere Möglichkeiten, die Menge an Daten zu reduzieren.

Beispiel: Eine Minute Ton in CD-Qualität (44.1 kHz und 16 Bit) braucht ohne reduzierte Datenmenge ca. 10 MByte. Die Datenmenge soll schrittweise reduziert werden, um die Tonqualität zu testen:

Hinweis: Für Sprache lässt sich eine Verminderung der Qualität auf 22.05 kHz und 16 Bit gegenüber den 44.1 kHz und 16 Bit einer Audio-CD zugunsten einer geringeren Datenmenge gut vertreten. Bei gleicher Reduzierung der Datenmenge ist das Ergebnis besser als mit 44.1 kHz und 8 Bit!

Dann kann hintereinander konvertiert werden von

1. Stufe: Stereo nach Mono	ca.5,00 MByte	1/2 vom Original
2. Stufe: 44.1 kHz nach 22.05 kHz	ca.2,50 MByte	1/4 vom Original
3. Stufe: 16 Bit nach 8 Bit	ca.1,25 MByte	1/8 vom Original

Wie leicht zu erkennen ist, verringert sich der Speicherbedarf von Stufe zu Stufe um den Faktor 0,5 (Vgl. Abschnitt Datenmenge).

➲ Alle Änderungen am Ton in Form von Effekten, wie Raumsimulation, Tonhöhenverschiebung usw., und Klangfilter müssen im Normalfall in die Tondateien hineingerechnet werden! Sie stehen in Autorensystemen als Echtzeit-Effekte bei der Wiedergabe in der Regel nicht zur Verfügung!

10.5.2 Anwenderbezug

Hinweis: Autorensysteme und PC-Hardware sind meist nur in der Lage, mehrere Tondateien der selben Abtastfrequenz gleichzeitig wiederzugeben! Andernfalls ist bei einem Teil der Dateien eine unfreiwillige Verschiebung der Tonhöhe die Folge.

In Autoren-, Animations- und Filmschnittprogrammen können zum Teil

- bis zu 8 Tonkanäle für Stereoton gleichzeitig voneinander unabhängig genutzt,
- Lautstärken für die Tonkanäle eingestellt,
- Ein- und Ausblendungen (Fade in/out) auf allen Kanälen vorgenommen,
- die Richtung der Töne mit dem Panorama festgelegt,
- datenkomprimierte Tondateien auf allen Kanälen abgespielt werden.

Die aufgelisteten Features sind auch von der Hardware und deren Konfiguration beim Anwender abhängig!

Hinweis: Wie bereits angedeutet muss der Hersteller der interaktiven Anwendung sich vergewissern, was die Zielgruppe an Hard- und Software zur Verfügung hat, um die Anwendung nutzen zu können.

Um einen zeitlichen Bezug zu Aktionen auf der visuellen Ebene herstellen zu können, werden den Tondateien Markierungen mit Tonbearbeitungsprogrammen zugefügt. Mit Hilfe dieser Markierungen können dann Ereignisse, z. B. Seiten- oder Bildwechsel, gesteuert werden. In der Regel werden Töne als Folge von Aktionen und Ereignissen ausgelöst.

An dieser Stelle wird deutlich, dass die programmiertechnischen und anwenderseitigen Voraussetzungen an Hard- und Software bei der Konzeptionierung des Einsatzes von Ton in einer interaktiven Anwendung eine entscheidende Rolle spielen.

Vergleich zwischen Filmtonproduktion und Ton in interaktiven Anwendungen. In beiden Fällen liegen die Tondateien auf einem Datenträger mit wahlfreiem Zugriff. Nachdem der Ton im Film zum Bild angelegt worden ist, hat er immer einen festen Bezug zur Zeitachse. Im Gegensatz dazu ist in interaktiven Anwendung sein Einsatz von den Aktionen des Anwenders abhängig!

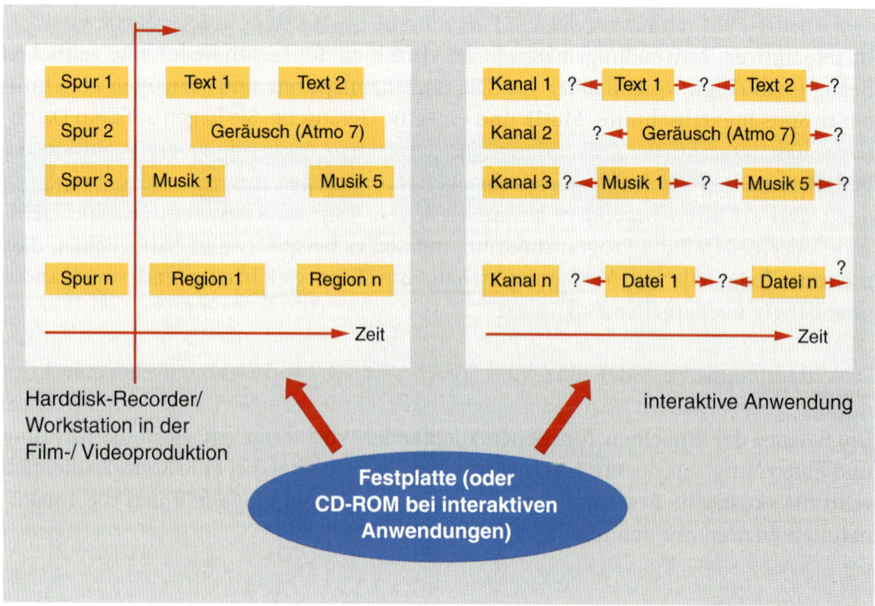

10.6 Ton und Internet

Alles, was bis hierher im Kapitel Ton behandelt worden ist, behält auch im Abschnitt Ton und Internet seine Gültigkeit. Heute ist ein Zugang zum Internet sowohl über das Telefon- und Fernsehkabelnetz wie auch über Satellit möglich. Die meisten Anwender nutzen den Zugang über das Telefonnetz, aber noch nicht alle verfügen über DSL. Deshalb nimmt auch heute noch der technische Aspekt bei der Konzeptionierung von Internet-Seiten in Bezug auf den Ton einen besonderen Stellenwert ein. Hervorzuheben ist dabei wie in jedem Netzwerk die Kombination von Client-/Server-Software, Dateiformat und Übertragungsprotokoll.

Download und Streaming

Beim Download wird eine Datei zunächst in voller Größe auf einen Rechner übertragen. Erst nachdem die Datei restlos übertragen worden ist, kann mit der Wiedergabe begonnen werden. Im Gegensatz dazu kann die Wiedergabe beim Streaming einer Datei bereits beginnen, nachdem die ersten Daten in einem Puffer zwischengespeichert worden sind.

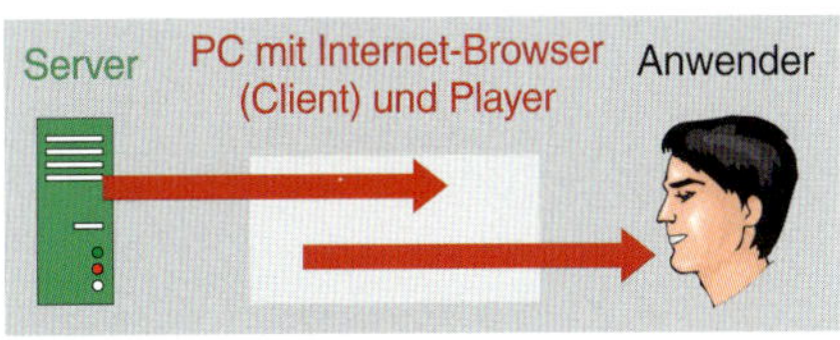

Herunterladen (Download) und anschließende Wiedergabe einer Datei

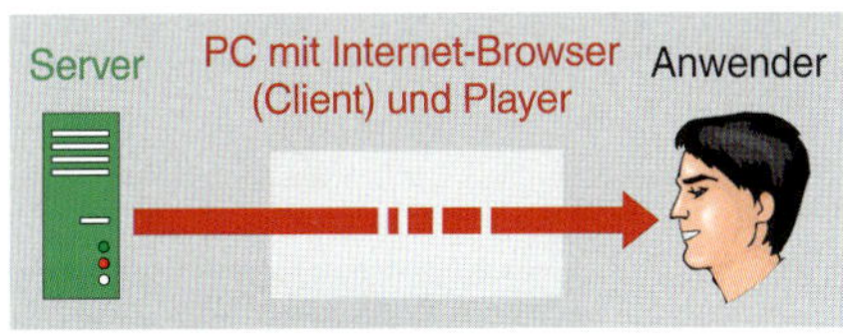

Streaming einer Datei

Die uns bekannten WAVE-, AIFF- und MP3-Dateien können mittels Standard HTTP-Server mit einem Download übertragen werden. Von den dreien eignet sich jedoch nur das MP3-Format für das Streaming im Internet.

Player

Mit den heutigen **Browsern** (Clients) können die gängigsten Formate für Ton und Bewegtbild wiedergegeben werden, sei es, dass die Funktionalität bereits fester Bestandteil der Browser ist, oder beim Installationsvorgang der Browser entsprechende Plug-Ins zusätzlich installiert werden. Die gebräuchlichsten Player sind der RealPlayer von RealNetworks, der Windows Media Player von Microsoft und der QuickTime Player von Apple. Sind bewegte Bilder, Grafiken, Ton und interaktive Elemente mit Flash oder Shockwave von Adobe erstellt worden, so benötigen wir das entsprechende **Plug-In** für Flash oder Shockwave zusätzlich zu unserem Browser. Werden streamingfähige Dateien durch den Browser von einem Server angefordert, so öffnet sich derjenige installierte Player, der dem eingetroffenen Dateiformat durch den Browser zugeordnet ist. Mit dem Player stehen typische (Laufwerks-) Funktionen, wie Stop, Wiedergabe, Pause, Vor- und Zurückspulen zur Verfügung.

Das Erscheinungsbild eines Players kann durch die Wahl aus verschiedenen Skins, vorgegebene und frei wählbare grafische Benutzeroberflächen, den eigenen Wünschen angepasst werden.

Infos zum Thema Streaming Media:
www.streamingmedia.com
www.streamingmediaworld.com

Quicktime von Apple:
http://www.apple.com/quicktime/ download/
RealPlayer von RealNetworks:
http://www.real.com/player/index.html
Shockwave- und Flash-Player von Adobe:
http://www.adobe.com/downloads
Media Player von Microsoft:
http://www.microsoft.com/germany/ms/windowsmedia

Quicktime Player von Apple, Voreinstellung für Anbieter von Internet-TV

Windows Media Player von Microsoft

Anhand des RealPlayers und des RealServers von RealNetworks soll gezeigt werden, wie eine Ton-Datei von einem Anwender abgerufen und mit einem Player im Streaming wiedergegeben wird:

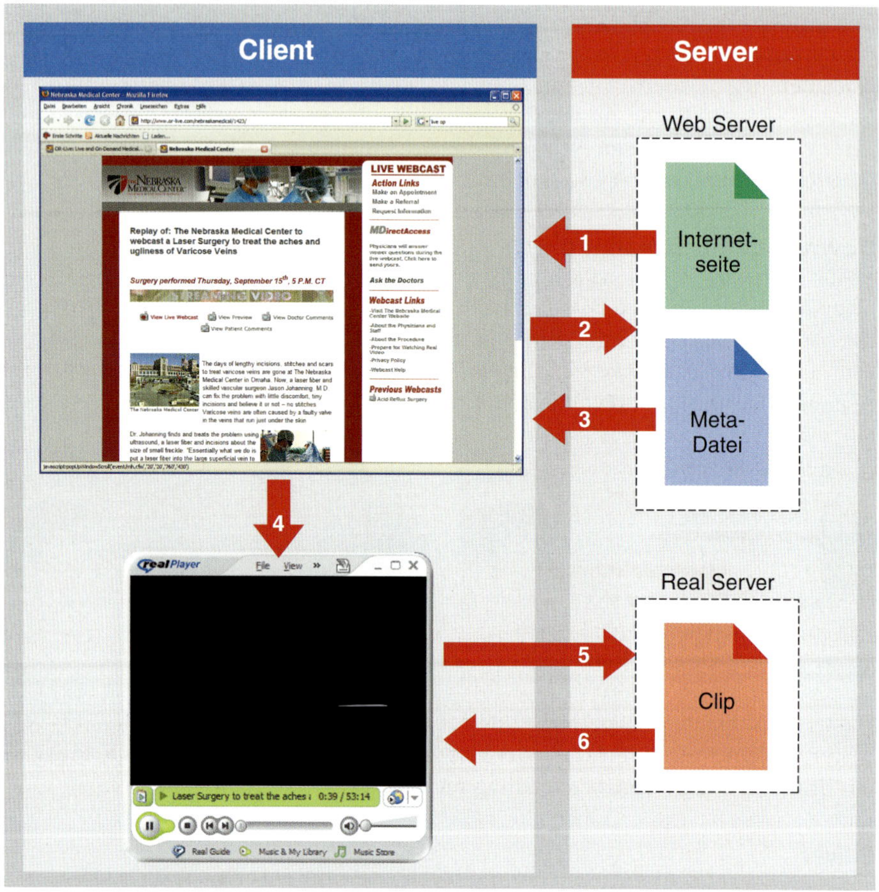

1. Der Browser zeigt eine Internetseite. Sie enthält einen Link zu einer RealAudio-Meta-Datei.
2. Der Anwender klickt auf den Link. Der Browser fordert die Meta-Datei vom Webserver an.
3. Der **Webserver** übergibt die RealAudio-Meta-Datei an den Browser. Für Dateien mit der Datei-Erweiterung .ram setzt der Webserver den MIME-Typ der Datei auf audio/x-pn-realaudio. Für Dateien mit der Erweiterung .rpm (RealPlayer Plug-In) setzt der Webserver den MIME-Typ der Datei auf audio/x-pn-realaudio-plugin.
4. Der Browser erkennt den MIME-Typ der RealAudio-Meta-Datei. In Abhängigkeit des MIME-Typs startet der Browser z. B. den RealPlayer als Anwendung und stellt eine Verbindung zur Meta-Datei her.
5. Der RealPlayer liest die erste URL der Meta-Datei und fordert den RealAudio-Clip vom RealServer an.
6. Der **RealServer** beginnt den angeforderten RealAudio-Clip zum RealPlayer zu streamen.

MIME = Multipurpose Internet Mail Extension

Quelle: nach Beggs/Thede, Designing Web Audio, 2001, S. 115

Protokolle

In den Anfängen des Internets ging es darum, Textdokumente über das Internet zugängig zu machen. Hierfür leistete das **HTTP** und das **TCP/IP** gute Dienste. Kommt es im Internet zu Engpässen oder gar zum Verlust von Daten, so stellt das TCP sicher, dass alle Datenpakete fehlerfrei, vollständig und in der richtigen Reihenfolge beim Anwender eintreffen. Hierfür ist es jedoch notwendig, dass Daten wiederholt beim Server angefordert werden müssen. Es ist deshalb langsam und nicht für das Streaming geeignet

Hier schaffen das **RTP** und das **UDP** Abhilfe. Das UDP ist schnell, weil es auf Fehlererkennung und -korrektur verzichtet. Diese Funktionen müssen aber von den darauf aufsetzenden Protokollen wie RTP oder **RTSP** und den folgenden Anwendungen mit Ihren entsprechenden Dateiformaten übernommen werden! Hier liegt die Priorität bei Kapazitätsengpässen im Internet darauf, dass ein kontinuierlicher Datenstrom mit höchstmöglicher Ton- und Bewegtbildqualität beim Anwender erhalten bleibt, anstatt Dateien bitgenau zu übermitteln. So lassen sich Daten mit geeigneten Servern, die die entsprechenden Protokolle nutzen, live im Internet übertragen. Im Unterschied dazu wird eine Datei On Demand (Auf Verlangen) abgerufen, wenn sich die Datei zunächst auf einem streamingfähigen Server befindet und schließlich zum Anwender gestreamt wird.

HTTP =
HyperText Transfer Protocol

TCP =
Transmission Control Protocol
Es ist ein verbindungsorientiertes Transportprotokoll. Im Vergleich zu UDP gilt TCP als langsam aber zuverlässig. Deshalb wird TCP dort verwendet, wo viele Daten sicher übertragen werden müssen.

IP = Internet Protocol

RTP = Real Time Protocol

RTSP =
Real Time Streaming Protocol

UDP = User Datagram Protocol

Dateiformate

Neben Quicktime von Apple und dem Advanced oder Active Streaming Format (ASF) von Microsoft werden in der Praxis weitere streamingfähige Dateiformate eingesetzt.

So sind Shockwave und Flash von Macromedia besonders gut geeignet, um Interaktionen zwischen Anwender und Anwendung zu unterstützen. Hier sind als Anwendungen Spiele, Präsentationen und eLearning-Module zu nennen. Diese Dateiformate eignen sich nicht für niedrigste Datentransferraten im Internet. MP3-codierte Töne können in Flash-Anwendungen eingebunden werden.

Werden größte Mengen an zeitgleichen Zugriffen erwartet, etwa auf die Filmmusiken von weltweit angekündigten Kinofilmen, so werden besonders hohe Anforderungen an die Technologie der Server gestellt. Datenströme können von einem zum anderen Server weitergeleitet werden (Splitting). Zudem können Server sozusagen verkoppelt werden (Clustering) und arbeiten wie eine Multiprozessor-Maschine. Um besonders bei Live-Übertragungen (z. B. **Internet-Radio**) die Zugriffe auf einen einzigen Server zu verringern, werden die Daten innerhalb des Internet-Netzwerkes live auf andere Server verteilt. Von dort können sich die Nutzer dann den aus einer Live-Datenquelle entstehenden Datenstrom streamen (IP Multicasting). Dies alles wird mit dem RealServer und dem Dateiformat RealAudio von RealNetworks unterstützt.

Die Einstellung der Datenübertragungsrate eines Players wird vom Server abgefragt und es kann möglicherweise dynamisch auf Veränderungen der Datenübertragungsraten im Internet mit einer Änderung der Qualitätsstufe der zu streamenden Datei reagiert werden (Bandwith Negotiation). Je niedriger die Datentransferrate ist, um so geringer fällt die Qualität des zu übertragenden Tones aus. Wie hoch die Tonqualität nach subjektiver Einschätzung ist, zeigt die Tabelle in Abschnitt 10.4.2 Datenreduktion.

Hinweis: Flash und Director Shockwave von Adobe, Beatnik mit Rich Music Format (RMF) von Headspace, QuickTime von Apple und MIDI sind Formate, die auch ohne die Unterstützung der Protokolle UDP und RTSP bzw. RTP für die Übertragungen auskommen. Sie lassen sich auch von einem Standard HTTP Webserver mit Funktionseinschränkungen streamen (Pseudo-Streaming). Jedoch besteht hier die Gefahr, dass die Übertragung von „Aussetzern" begleitet wird.

Hinweis: Mit RealFlash von RealNetworks lassen sich Flash-Anwendungen mit dem RealServer streamen.

Datenübertragungsraten des Übertragungskanals	Datenübertragungsraten für das Streaming
64 Kbps ISDN	45 Kbps
112 Kbps Dual ISDN	80 Kbps
Corporate LAN	150 Kbps
256 Kbps DSL/Cable Modem	225 Kbps
384 Kbps DSL/Cable Modem	350 Kbps
512 Kbps DSL/Cable Modem	450 Kbps

Mögliche Datenübertragungsraten für das Streaming von Dateien im Internet bei gegebenen Datenübertragungsraten des Übertragungskanals

Vor der Produktion von Internetauftritten brauchen wir einen Anhaltspunkt für die zu erwartende maximale Datenübertragungsrate für die zu streamenden Dateien.

In der Tabelle ist zu sehen, dass sie etwa 60% - 90% der Datenübertragungsrate des Übertragungskanals (z. B. das Telefonnetz mit Modem) entspricht. Das Verhältnis verbessert sich zunehmens, je größer die Raten sind (z. B. xDSL). Zu beachten ist, dass hier jeweils die maximalen Größen angegeben sind. Im Internet sind die Datenübertragungsraten jedoch nicht immer stabil. Um auch noch eine Übertragung bei geringeren Raten zu gewährleisten, kann mit entsprechenden Dateiformaten, wie oben beschrieben, auf eine niedrigere Tonqualitätsstufe umgeschaltet werden. Die für die Tonübertragung im Internet gebräuchlichen Dateiformate und Protokolle unterliegen einer raschen Entwicklung. Für eingehende Betrachtungen sei deshalb auf die entsprechende Fachliteratur verwiesen.

Als Hilfestellung sind hier jedoch einige grundlegende Fragen für die Konzeptionierung eines Internetprojektes zusammengestellt, mit denen man auf die Suche nach geeigneten Dateiformaten und Übertragungsprotokollen für den Ton gehen kann:

- Hat die Internet-Anwendung einen hohen Grad an Interaktivität?
- Gibt es Vorgaben für die Qualität des Tones beim Anwender?
- Wie hoch ist der Verbreitungsgrad der erforderlichen Plug-Ins für die Browser. Hat die Zielgruppe das Know How und ist sie gewillt, sich bei Bedarf ein für die Wiedergabe des Tones erforderliches Plug-In selbst herunterzuladen und zu installieren?
- Wie störungsfrei soll die Übertragung selbst bei erheblich schwankenden und niedrigsten Datenübertragungsraten sein?
- Soll lediglich Sprache oder auch Musik (größeres Tonfrequenzspektrum) übertragen werden?
- Wie viele Teilnehmer sollen gleichzeitig auf die Tondateien zugreifen können?
- Soll es eine Beschränkung der Zugriffsrechte geben?
- Soll der Server Daten für eine Statistik aus den Zugriffen auf die Tondateien generieren können?
- Ist die Nutzung der Tondateien entgeltlich? Wird es ein Server gestütztes Abrechnungssystem geben müssen?
- Ist es erforderlich, dass der Tondatei aus Gründen des Urheber- und Verwertungsrechtes ein digitales Wasserzeichen mitgegeben werden muss?
- Genügt es, dem Anwender einen Download anzubieten, oder muss der Ton möglichst sofort hörbar sein?
- Sind die Mittel für das Einrichten eines weiteren Servers für das Streaming von Tondateien vorhanden?

Codec = Kunstwort aus dem Englischen. Setzt sich zusammen aus den Wörtern **Co**der und **Deco**der. Bezeichnet die aufeinander abgestimmten Funktionen für das Kodieren und das Dekodieren von Signalen.

➲ **Ausreichende Zugriffskapazitäten und Datenübertragungsraten, geeignete Übertragungsprotokolle und effiziente Codecs für die Datenkompression sind Voraussetzungen für technisch sinnvolle Anwendungen von Streaming Media!**

Aufgaben und Übungen, Literaturhinweise

Aufgaben und Übungen

Eine interaktive Anwendung soll entwickelt und hergestellt werden. Das kann eine Anwendung für einen Messestand, eine verkaufsunterstützende Produktpräsentation für den Außendienstmitarbeiter oder eine Anwendung nach Ihren Vorstellungen sein.

1. Bestimmen Sie Zielgruppe und Einsatzzweck der interaktiven Anwendung.
2. Bringen Sie in Erfahrung, in wieweit die programmiertechnischen Eigenschaften des zu verwendenden Autorensystems Ihre gestalterischen Wünsche unterstützt.
3. Finden Sie heraus, welche typischen Funktionen von Musik und Geräusch Sie für Ihren Ton nutzen können.
4. Legen Sie fest, in welchem Umfang Sie Sprechtext, Musik und Geräusch benötigen.
5. Überlegen Sie sich, auf wie vielen Ebenen der Ton abgebildet werden soll/kann.
6. Finden Sie heraus, welche Räume es mit dem Ton nachzubilden gilt.
7. Legen Sie eine Liste der zu erstellenden Tondateien an und achten Sie dabei auf eine eindeutige nachvollziehbare Benennung der Dateien für eine reibungslose Programmierung.
8. Recherchieren Sie die Quellen für Ihre Musik und Sounds und achten Sie dabei auf Verwertungsrechte.

Literaturhinweise

Arnold, Bernd-Peter: ABC des Hörfunks, 2. Aufl., Konstanz 1999 (UVK)

Beggs, Josh; *Thede*, Dylan: Designing Web Audio, Beijing, Cambridge, Farnham, Köln, Paris, Sebastopol, Taipei, Tokyo 2001 (O'Reilly & Associates)

Dickreiter, Michael: Handbuch der Tonstudiotechnik, 2 Bände, 7. Aufl., München, New York, London, Paris 2008 (Verlag K.G. Saur)

Pierce, John R.: Klang, 2. Aufl., Heidelberg, Berlin, Oxford 1999 (Spektrum)

Schneider, Enjott: Handbuch Filmmusik I, 2. Aufl., Konstanz 1990 (UVK)

Simpson, Ron: Cutting Edge Web Audio, New York u. a. 1998 (Prentice Hall)

Webers, Johannes: Tonstudiotechnik, 7. Aufl., Feldkirchen 1999 (Franzis-Verlag)

Wolff, Harald: Geräusche und Film, Frankfurt am Main u. a. 1996 (Peter Lang)

Zander, Horst: Das PC-Tonstudio, Feldkirchen 1998 (Franzis-Verlag)

Webcode:
B1100

Für weitere Infos zu diesem Kapitel mit dem Smartphone einfach QR-Code scannen oder auf www.medien-verstehen.de den Webcode eingeben.

11 Druck

Die Erfindung der Drucktechnik geht zurück auf die Holztafeldrucke in China und Japan im 8. Jahrhundert n. Chr., wobei Bilder spiegelverkehrt in Holzplatten geschnitten wurden. In Europa wurde mit Beginn des 15. Jahrhunderts diese Technik eingesetzt. Mit den beweglichen Lettern von **Johannes Gensfleisch zu Gutenberg** begann dann 1452 der Buchdruck. Gutenberg erfand jedoch nicht nur die wiederverwendbaren Metalllettern, sondern auch eine hölzerne Druckpresse, mit deren Hilfe kostengünstige Vervielfältigungen der Druckwerke produziert werden konnten. Als Druckfarbe diente eine Mischung aus Ruß und Leinölfirnis, die mit Lederballen aufgetragen wurde. In kürzester Zeit wurden in Europa Druckereien gegründet und die Druckkunst fand rasche Verbreitung. Informationen konnten jetzt in größerer Stückzahl zu Papier gebracht und verteilt werden.

Die Drucktechnik entwickelte sich stetig weiter mit dem Steindruck, der sogenannten **Lithografie**, der ersten Zylinderdruckpresse Anfang des 19. Jahrhunderts über den Tiefdruck Ende des 19. Jahrhunderts bis zum **Offsetdruck** und dem **Siebdruck** zu Beginn des letzten Jahrhunderts. Mit der Entwicklung neuer Technologien wie Lasertechnik und **Digitaltechnik** sind die Wege und Produktionszeiten der Druckerzeugnisse kürzer geworden. Unterschiedliche Auflagen, individuell gestaltete Drucke sind möglich. Darüberhinaus können durch Datenfernübertragung (DFÜ) Druckdaten an jeden beliebigen Ort zur Weiterverarbeitung in einer Druckerei gesandt werden. In diesem Kapitel soll gezeigt werden, wie ein Druckprodukt entsteht und wie die unterschiedlichen Verfahren eingesetzt werden.

Der Workflow

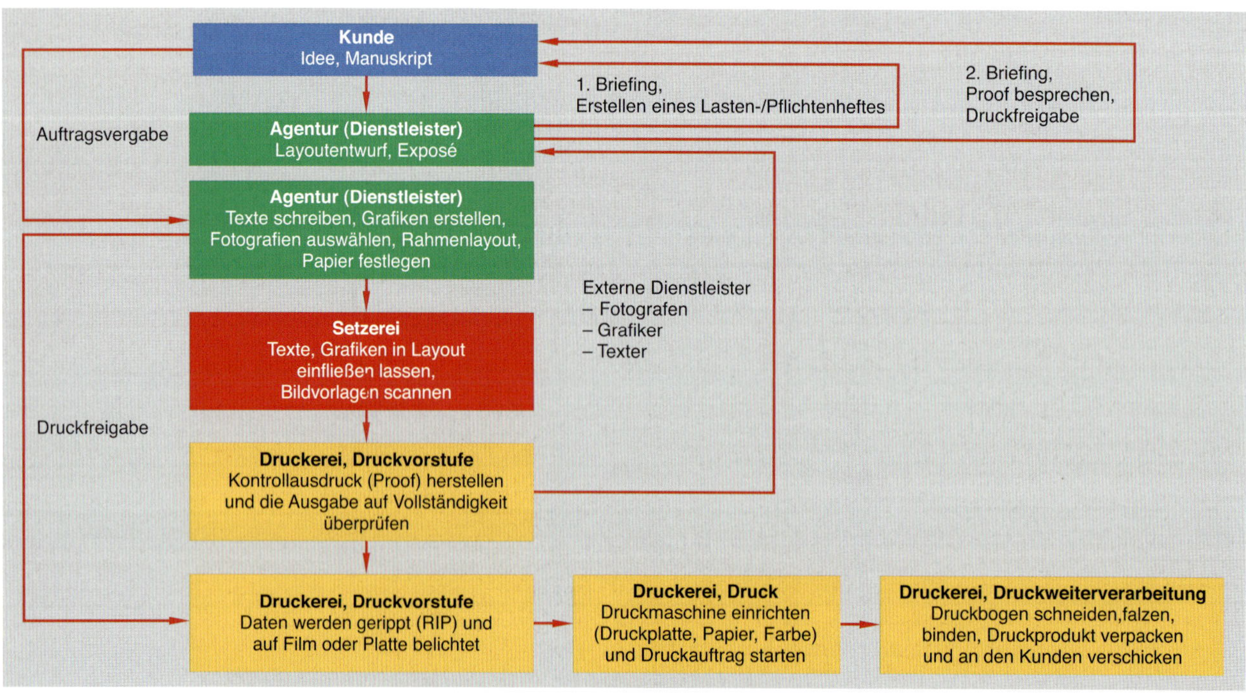

11.1 Bildvorlagen

11.1.1 Druckqualität

Mit dem Entwickeln einer Idee stellt sich gleichzeitig die Frage nach der Umsetzung und dem Ausgabegerät für das Druckprodukt. Die Inhalte der Druckseiten werden durch Texte, Bilder und Grafiken wiedergegeben. Die Vorlagen liegen entweder analog als Ausdruck vor, wie Halbtonvorlagen ❶ oder Strichvorlagen ❷ oder in digitaler Form als digitale Fotografie, Screenshot oder Vektorgrafik aus einem Grafikprogramm. Früher wurden Halbtonvorlagen und Strichzeichnungen durch fotografische Reproduktion in Filmmaterial verwandelt. Mit der Erfindung des Scanners konnten die analogen Vorlagen digitalisiert werden. Hochwertige Scanner können sofort das digitale Ergebnis als separierte Dateien ❸ im CMYK-Modus ausgeben.

Das Druckprodukt weist in der Regel ein Qualitätsmerkmal auf: die Schärfe der Bilder, sofern die Druckseite nicht nach den Vorgaben der Gestalter beispielsweise mit weichgezeichneten oder bewegungsunscharfen Bildern bestückt werden soll. Die Bildschärfe wird durch die Auflösung beim Scannen oder bei der Bildbearbeitung des digital vorliegenden Bildmaterials bestimmt. Mit der Auflösung wird die Feinheit der Abtastung des Bildes bestimmt, und damit die Anzahl der **Tonwertstufen** oder auch Graustufen für jeden Farbkanal Rot, Grün und Blauviolett. Damit man die kleinste Eingabefrequenz festlegen kann, d. h. die Anzahl der Pixel pro Zentimeter (ppcm) oder Pixel pro Inch (ppi), mit welcher der Scanner das Bild abtastet oder die Datei aus einem Bildbearbeitungsprogramm abgespeichert werden soll, muss zunächst ein Blick auf die Ausgabe des Druckprodukts geworfen werden.

❶ **Halbtonvorlage**: Fotografische Abbildung oder Dia, das über theoretisch unendlich viele Grautöne oder Farbabstufungen verfügt.

❷ **Strichvorlagen**: Handskizze, Tuschezeichnung, Text, Gemälde

❸ **Separierte Dateien**: Die Tonwerte eines Farbkanals, wie beispielsweise bei der Vierfarbseparation, werden in einer eigenen Auszugsdatei abgelegt.

Auflösung der Graustufen: Im einfachsten Fall liegt die Information in Schwarz und Weiß vor, d. h. Farbe ist vorhanden oder nicht vorhanden. Die Graustufenauflösung beträgt dann 1 Bit = 21 = 2 Graustufen.

1 inch = 2,54 cm

Pixel und Dots

Spricht man beim Scannen von **Pixeln** (Eingabepixel) als das kleinste Element des Bildes, so ist es beim Druckvorgang der **Druckpunkt** (Dot). So ein Dot ist ein 1-Bit-Element das zwei Zustände, Schwarz und Weiß, darstellen kann. Damit die Tonwertstufung eines Halbtonbildes im Druck wiedergegeben werden kann, benötigt man eine variable Anzahl von Druckpunkten, die in einer **Rasterzelle** zusammengefasst werden. Die Rasterzelle kann man sich als eine quadratische Matrix vorstellen , die über eine bestimmte Anzahl von Gitterplätzen verfügt, welche mit den einzelnen Druckpunkten besetzt werden.

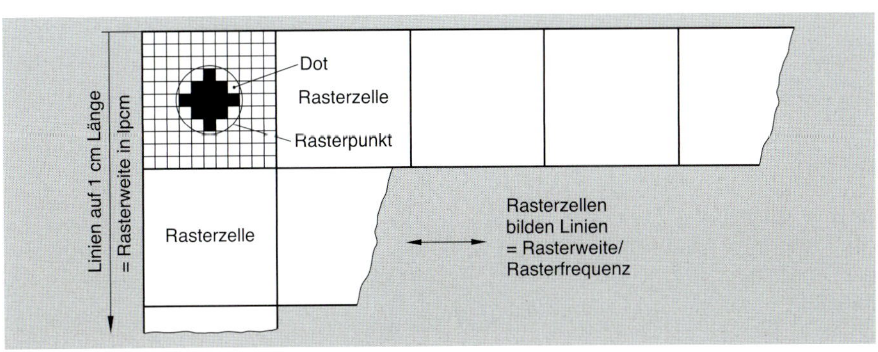

Betrachten wir beispielsweise ein Quadratgitter 8 × 8, dann erhalten wir 64 Gitterplätze. Damit wir einen 50%-Rastertonwert abbilden können, benötigen wir einen Rasterpunkt mit 32 Dots innerhalb der Rasterzelle 8 × 8. Diese 32 Druckpunkte werden bei Laserbelichtern und Laserdruckern in sogenannten Belichterelementen innerhalb der Rasterzelle bebildert.

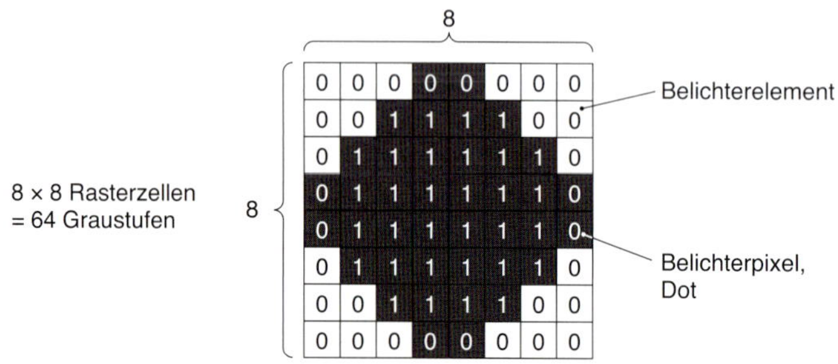

32 Dots, 50% Tonwert

Der kleinste Druckpunkt (Dot) tritt beim Offsetdruck auf und hat einen Durchmesser von 20 µm. Damit hat beispielsweise eine Rasterzelle mit 8 × 8 Belichterelementen und 64 + 1 Tonwerten eine Kantenlänge von 160 µm.

Rasterfrequenz

Reiht man nun eine Vielzahl von Rasterzellen aneinander, dann erhält man eine Linie. Mehrere Linien aneinandergereiht stellen die **Rasterweite** oder **Rasterfrequenz** des Druckverfahrens dar. Die Rasterfrequenz wird in Linien pro cm (lpcm) oder in Linien pro inch (lpi) angegeben. Je nach angewandtem Druckverfahren und dem verwendeten Bedruckstoff variiert die Rasterfrequenz.

Akzidenzdrucksachen: Druckerzeugnisse, die nur gelegentlich produziert werden, wie Visitenkarten, Briefpapier, Prospekte, Broschüren, Kataloge.

Im Gegensatz zu **Periodika**, Drucksachen die regelmäßig erscheinen, wie Zeitungen, Zeitschriften.

Druckverfahren	Rasterfrequenzwerte
Siebdruck (Durchdruck)	20 lpcm – 40 lpcm / 50 lpi – 101 lpi
Flexodruck (flexible, weiche Druckform, Hochdruck)	40 lpcm – 60 lpcm / 101 lpi – 152 lpi
Tiefdruck	70 lpcm / 178 lpi
Zeitungsdruck (Rollenoffsetdruck)	34 lpcm – 48 lpcm / 86 lpi – 122 lpi
Akzidenz-Offsetdruck	60 lpcm / 152 lpi

Die verschiedenen Graustufen, z. B. 256 bei einem Halbtonbild mit 8-Bit-Farbtiefe oder auch eine Tonwertstufung von 0% bis 100% müssen gerastert werden, um sie im Druck wiederzugeben. Das menschliche Auge ist bei der Aufnahme gestufter Tonwerte lediglich in der Lage, 100 Tonwertstufen bewusst zu unterscheiden. Das würde einer Rasterzelle mit 10 × 10 Gitterplätzen entsprechen. In einem solchen Gitter können die Farbwerte in 1%-Schritten gestuft abgebildet werden.

Adressierbarkeit oder Auflösung A (dpcm bzw. dpi), kennzeichnet die Anzahl der möglichen belegbaren Gitterplätze des Ausgabegerätes

Die Anzahl der Graustufen ist abhängig von der Größe der Rasterzelle und damit von der Anzahl der Gitterplätze, in der ein Tonwert simuliert wird. Das Maß für die Größe des Gitters und die Größe des Druckpunktes wird durch die Adressierbarkeit A (dots pro cm) ausgedrückt. Durch den Einsatz des entsprechenden Druckverfahrens wird die Rasterweite L (Linien pro cm) definiert. Aus den Werten für die Rasterweite oder Rasterfrequenz (lpi, lpcm) und der Auflösung (dpi, dpcm) berechnet sich die Anzahl der **Graustufen** wie folgt:

$$\text{Graustufen N} = \left(\frac{\text{Ausgabeauflösung } A}{\text{Rasterweite L}}\right)^2 + 1$$

In der Formelbeziehung wird 1 dazugezählt für den Zustand, dass in der Rasterzelle kein Dot geschwärzt wird.

Beispiel: Auflösung im Druck 600 dpi und Rasterweite 50 lpi

$$\text{Graustufen} = \left(\frac{600 \text{ dpi}}{50 \text{ lpi}}\right)^2 + 1 = 12^2 + 1$$

$$\text{Graustufen} = 144 + 1$$

Bei der Ermittlung der Graustufen wurde vorausgesetzt, dass die einzelnen Gitterplätze vollständig mit geschwärzten Rasterpunkten bedeckt sind. Nun ist es heute möglich Rasterpunkte mit einer unterschiedlichen Farbschichtdicke zu drucken, so dass pro Rasterzelle mehrere Grauwerte ❶ wiedergegeben werden können. Je höher die Anzahl der möglichen Graustufen ist, um so weicher und gleichmäßiger werden Übergänge und Verläufe im Bild.

Auflösung von Bildern in verschiedenen Druckprodukten:

Zeitungsdruck, Strich . . . . 150 dpi
bis Halbtonvorlage . . . . . 1270 dpi
Buch . . . . > 150 dpi
Plakat, Flyer DIN A4 . . 300–600 dpi
Siebdruck, Flexodruck . . . > 80 dpi

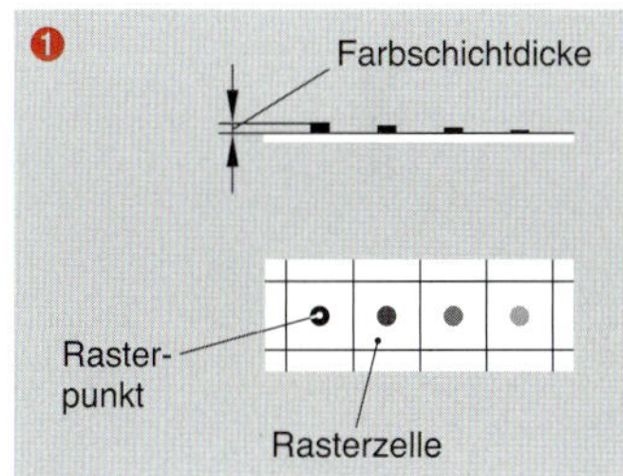

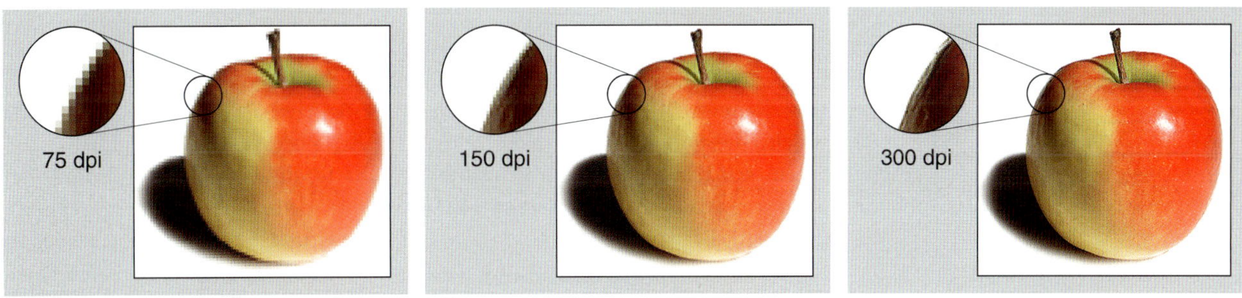

Die nachfolgende Tabelle beinhaltet die maximal mögliche Anzahl der Tonwertstufen für eine bestimmte Rasterweite und **Auflösung** (Ausgabefrequenz). Unter einem Tonwert von 100 muss man mit einer geringeren Druckqualität rechnen.

Tonwertstufen	Auflösung			
Rasterweite	600 dpi	1200 dpi	2400 dpi	3200 dpi
50 lpi	145	577	2305	4097
86 lpi	50	196	780	1385
100 lpi	37	145	576	1025
120 lpi	26	101	401	712
150 lpi	17	65	256	456

Rasterung und Moiré-Effekt

Bei einer **periodischen Rasterung, AM- oder auch autotypische Rasterung genannt,** sind die Rasterpunkte nach einem festgelegten Muster in der Rasterzelle angeordnet. Die Punktform kann kreisförmig, elliptisch oder quadratisch sein. Werden nun die einzelnen Farben Cyan, Magenta, Gelb und Schwarz zusammengedruckt, so entstehen regelmäßige Muster mit Rosetten, die man auch als Moiré bezeichnet. Dieser Effekt ist vor allem auf älteren Fotografien und Drucken zu erkennen. Bei periodischer Rasterung lässt sich der **Moiré-Effekt** dadurch vermindern, dass die Rasterstruktur um einen bestimmten Winkel gedreht wird. Im Vierfarbdruck haben sich folgende Winkel als praktikabel erwiesen: Gelb 0°, Magenta 15°, Cyan 75° und Schwarz unter 135°.

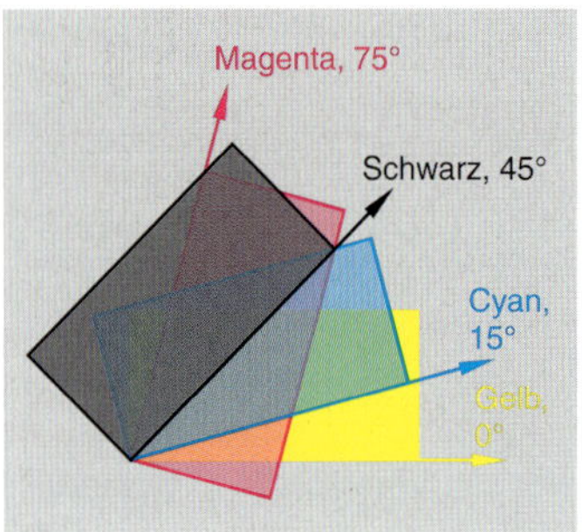

Bei nichtperiodischer oder **frequenzmodulierter Rasterung** (FM-Rasterung) gibt es keine festgelegten Rasterpunkte, Rasterweiten und Rasterwinkel. Die gleichgroßen Rasterpunkte werden nur nach der Helligkeit des Bildes verteilt. Helle Bildflächen erhalten weniger zufällig angeordnete Druckpunkte, dunkle Bildflächen mehr Druckpunkte. Dadurch erhält man beim FM-Raster keinen Moiré-Effekt.

Heute lassen sich mit der digitalen Rasterung die Vorteile der FM-Rasterung voll ausschöpfen. Die Simulation von Tonwerten in Bildern geschieht durch die Nachbildung der Bildinformation mit Hilfe kleiner Bildelemente, engl. picture elements oder pixel, die in unterschiedlicher Anzahl und Form zu Gruppen (Cluster) zusammengefasst werden.

11.1.2 Eingabeauflösug, Datenvolumen bei Bildern

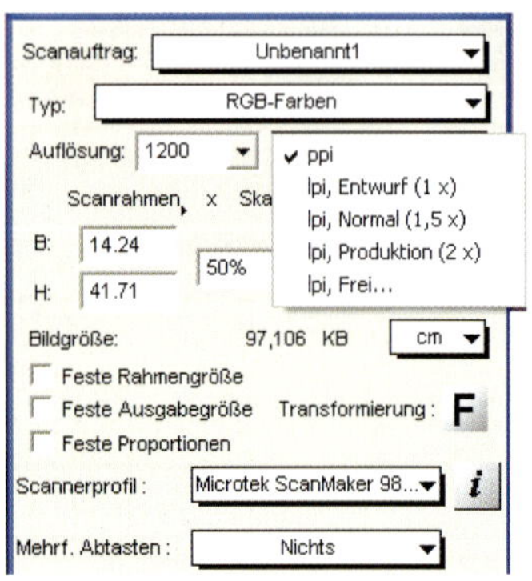

Abtastfrequenz oder auch Eingabefrequenz kennzeichnen die Auflösung beim Scannen. Die Auflösung wird beim Scannen und in der digitalen Fotografie in ppi oder ppcm angegeben.

Die Rasterfrequenz des Druckverfahrens und der Bedruckstoff stellen die Kriterien dar, welche die Qualität des Druckprodukts auf der Ausgabeseite beeinflussen und begrenzen. Auf der Eingabeseite ist es die Bildschärfe, die durch die Auflösung bei der Aufnahme analog auf Film oder digital sowie durch die Auflösung beim Scannen begrenzt wird. Die spätere Verwendung im Zeitungsdruck, Hochglanzdruck oder in einer Bildschirmanwendung bestimmt die Höhe der Auflösung eines digitalen Fotos bzw. die Auflösung beim Abtasten des Originals im Scanprozess.

Digitale Bilder werden heute im RAW-Format von der Kamera in die Bildbearbeitung übernommen und dort mit allen Ebenen und Berarbeitungsaktionen (z. B. psd-Format) bis zur endgültigen Ausgabe im TIF-Format gehandhabt.

Beim Abtastvorgang werden eine Vielzahl von Bildpixeln erfasst und gespeichert. Die Anzahl der Pixel pro Zentimeter (ppcm) ist ein Maß für die Abtastfeinheit oder auch **Abtastauflösung**. Mit der Größe der Auflösung wächst auch die Dateigröße an. Die Auflösung in ppcm oder ppi sollte daher nur so groß als nötig gewählt werden. Als Grundregel zur Bestimmung der **Abtastfrequenz** (Eingabefrequenz) gilt:

Abtastfrequenz (Eingabeauflösung) =
Rasterfrequenz (Ausgabe im Druck) × Skalierungsfaktor × Qualitätsfaktor

Um eine möglichst gute Detailzeichnung des Bildes zu erhalten, wird in den meisten Fällen mit einem **Qualitätsfaktor** QF = 2 gearbeitet. Um Speicherplatz zu sparen kann auch ein Wert zwischen QF 2 und QF 1,4 gewählt werden. Unter QF 1,4 ist wieder mit Qualitätseinbußen zu rechnen.

Der Skalierungsfaktor wird in den meisten Fällen auf 100% gesetzt, d. h. man scannt das Bild im Maßstab 1:1. Anpassungen der Bildgröße werden erst in der nachfolgenden Bildbearbeitung vorgenommen

Beispiel Apfelbild:

Bildgröße 82,5 × 82,5 mm,
Rasterfrequenz 60 lpcm, Maßstab 1:1, Qualitätsfaktor 2

Abtastfrequenz = 60 lpcm × 1 × 2

Abtastfrequenz = **120 ppcm = 304 ppi**

Dateigröße für das Apfelbild:

Anzahl der Bildpixel = (120 ppcm × 8,25 cm)2
= 990 × 990 = **980.100 Bildpixel**

RGB Farbinformation pro Bildpixel bei einer
8-Bit-Graustufenauflösung (256) = 3 × 8 Bit oder 3 × 1 Byte
Speicherbedarf in verschiedenen Ausgabemodi:

Farbbild RGB: 3 × 980.100 Byte = 2.940.300 Byte = **2,94 MB**
Graustufenbild: 980.100 Byte = **0,98 MB**
Strichzeichnung: 2,94 MB : 24 × (3 × 8 Bit) = **122,5 kB**

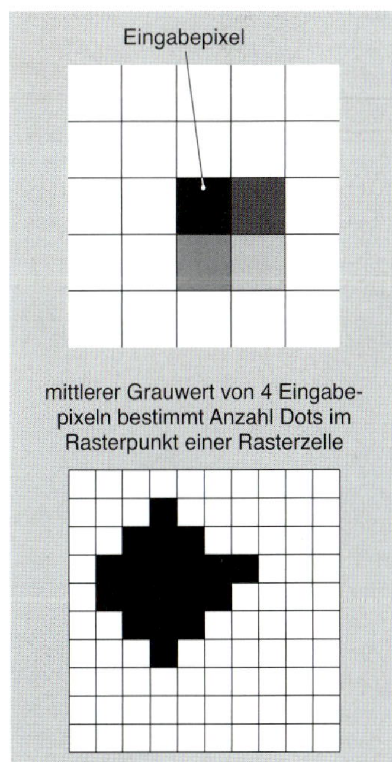

Mit dem Qualitätsfaktor, oder auch **Samplingrate** genannt, steht fest, wie die Bildpixel in Verbindung zum Rasterpunkt beim Drucken stehen. Jeder Rasterzelle auf der Ausgabeseite werden vier Bildpixel zugeordnet. Mit dem Qualitätsfaktor 2 wird das Längenverhältnis zwischen zwei Bildpixeln im Scan und der Kante der Rasterzelle beschrieben. Die Tonwerte der vier Bildpixel der Bildvorlage wird gemittelt und das Ergebnis gespeichert. Mit diesem Mittelwert wird dann der Rastertonwert in Prozent bestimmt und daraus wiederum die Anzahl der Dots für einen Rasterpunkt berechnet.

Die Bildvorlagen für das Scannen sind in der Regel ein Druckprodukt, das gerastert ist und mit einer bestimmten Rasterfrequenz hergestellt wurde. Um die bestmögliche Qualität beim Scannen zu erzielen, kann man bei vielen Scannergeräten mit der Funktion **„Entrastern“** arbeiten. Dabei wird die Rasterweite der Vorlage berücksichtigt und beim Scanvorgang eingesetzt.

11.2 Colormanagement

ICC, International Color Consortium

CIE, Commission Internationale de l´Eclairage

HSB, **H**ue (Farbton), **S**aturation (Sättigung), **B**rightness (Helligkeit)

Betrachtet man den Weg des Bildes vom Scan über die Bildbearbeitung, das Layoutprogramm bis zum Druck, dann findet vor der Ausgabe des Bildes eine Umwandlung des Farbmodus statt. Eine Bildvorlage wird im **RGB-Modus** gescannt und im gleichen Modus am Bildschirm dargestellt und bearbeitet. Die drei Lichtfarben Rot, Grün und Blau finden Anwendung in der Scantechnik und Bildbearbeitung, aber nicht im Druckvorgang. Da die Farbräume nicht deckungsgleich und die Farbwerte unterschiedlich definiert sind, benötigt man ein Hilfsmittel zur Umrechnung und Umwandlung der Farbräume. Mit Hilfe einer Software, ein sogenanntes **Color-Management-Modul** (**CMM**), wird Farbprofil erstellt, das eine zahlenmäßige Verknüpfung der Werte zwischen den in der Ein- und Ausgabe verwendeten Farbräumen herstellt. Mit einem solchen **ICC-Profile** werden zunächst die Farbwerte RGB in Farbkoordinaten im Raum umgewandelt.

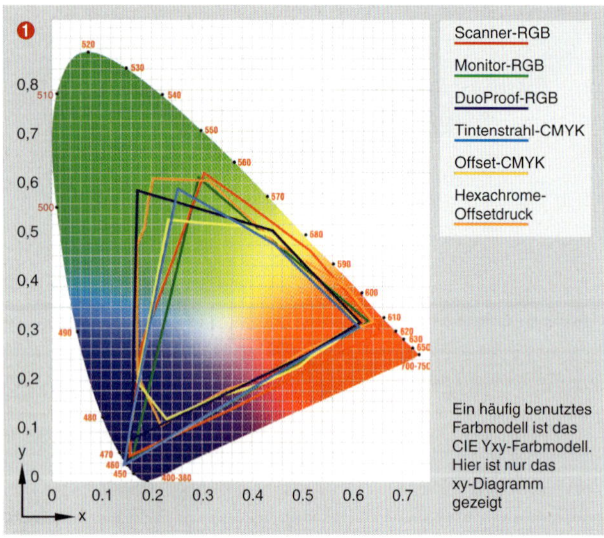

Ein häufig benutztes Farbmodell ist das CIE Yxy-Farbmodell. Hier ist nur das xy-Diagramm gezeigt

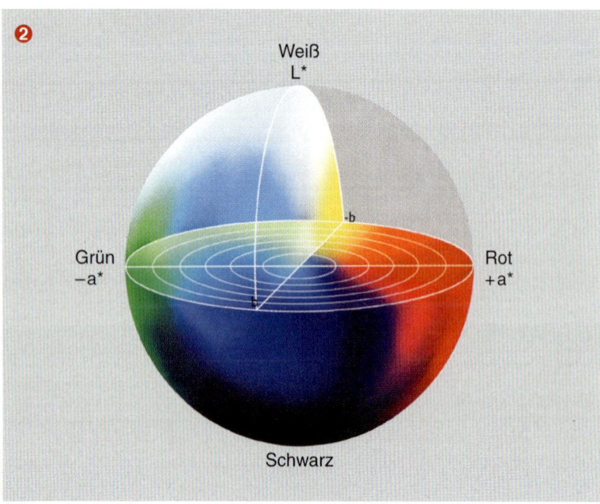

Die Umsetzung in Koordinaten erfolgt wie im CIE Yxy-Farbmodell der Hufeisenform ❶ oder wie im CIELAB-Farbmodell ❷ in der Kugelform dargestellt. In dieser Form können die Bilddaten für beliebige Ausgabeverfahren und -geräte weitergegeben werden.

Benennung der Achsen im CIE Yxy-Modell:
Y-Achse (senkrecht zur Bildebene) – Helligkeit
x/y-Ebene – Farbtöne und Sättigung

Benennungen der Achsen im CIELAB-Modell:
L – Helligkeit
a – Rot bis Grün-Werte
b – Gelb bis Blau-Werte.

Das LAB-Modell entspricht auch den plattformunabhängigen HSB- oder FSH-Modellen, die in vielen Grafikprogrammen eingesetzt werden. Diese Modelle teilen die Farben in der Ebene in die verschiedene Farbtöne ein, von innen nach außen nimmt die Sättigung und in der Vertikalen die Helligkeit zu. Alle Farben gleicher Helligkeit liegen auf einer Ebene.

Mit einem Farbprofil wird eine stets gleichbleibende Farbwiedergabe gewährleistet, unabhängig vom Eingabegerät, dem Monitor und dem Ausgabegerät.

Nach der Bildbearbeitung und der Umsetzung im Layoutprogramm werden die Farben für den Druck im Allgemeinen in Cyan, Magenta, Gelb und Schwarz, also die Körperfarben CMYK oder im Sechsfarbdruck zusätzlich in die Farben Orange und Grün umgewandelt. Neben den Eingabeprofilen kommen auch geräte- und verfahrensspezifische Ausgabeprofile zum Einsatz.

Ein wichtiges Kontrollinstrument für den richtigen Farbwert stellt der Monitor dar. Er bildet die Schnittstelle zwischen Scanner und Ausgabegerät. Der **Gammawert** des Monitors ❶ soll so eingestellt sein, dass die Bildschirmdarstellung die Bildvorlage möglichst exakt wiedergibt. Die Einstellung lässt sich in der Systemdatei Monitoreinstellungen vornehmen. Dort findet man einen Kalibrierassistenten zur Bestimmung der passenden Parameter. Ein genaueres Verfahren stellt die Kalibrierung des Bildschirms mit Hilfe eines Kalibriergerätes und Kalibriersoftware dar. Mit einem Sensor ❷, der direkt auf der Glasscheibe des Bildschirms befestigt wird, misst man den Weißpunkt des Bildschirms. Dann werden softwareabhängig die Farben Rot, Grün und Blau schrittweise auf die Intensität 100% erhöht und die Farbwerte über die Farbtemperatur bestimmt.

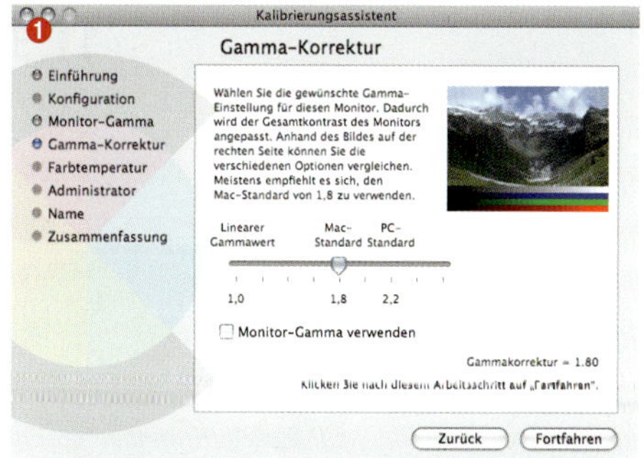

Nach dem Kalibrieren liegt ein Farbprofil fest, das zum Bearbeiten von Farben in Grafikprogrammen ausgewählt werden kann und die Farbwerte auf dem jeweiligen Bildschirm richtig anzeigt und umwandelt. Um den CMYK-Farbraum zu erweitern, lassen sich Prozessfarben aus weiteren Farbsystemen wie Trumatch und Focoltone auswählen. Prozessfarben sind Farben, die immer durch Farbmischungen aus Primärfarben entstehen.

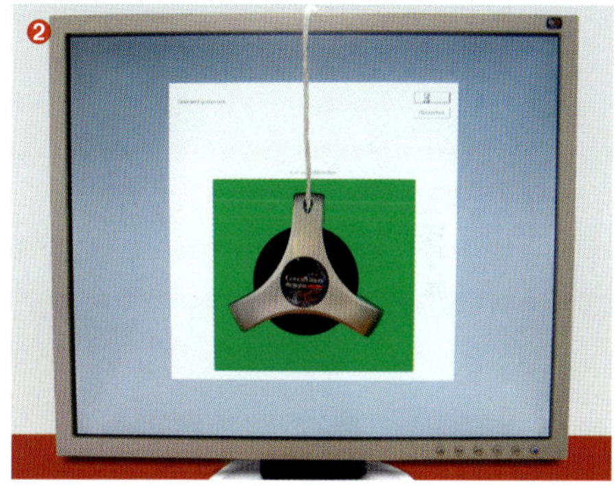

Sonderfarben wie Gold, Silber, Neonfarben oder andere spezielle Farben werden aus einem System wie Pantone oder HKS ❸ gewählt und stellen Volltonfarben dar. Die Farbabstufungen für diese Sonderfarben lassen sich aus den Farbfächern oder Farbmusterbüchern der Hersteller bestimmen.

Neben den drei bunten Druckfarben Cyan, Magenta, Gelb kommt der unbunten Farbe Schwarz (K = **Key-Color**) eine besondere Bedeutung zu. Der technologische und finanzielle Aufwand aus drei Buntfarben ein Schwarz oder einen Grauwert zu erzeugen ist nicht praktikabel. Zudem lässt sich aus den drei Buntfarben lediglich ein dunkles Braun erzeugen. Schwarz trägt bei Farbmischungen dazu bei, Schwankungen der Einzelfarben zu minimieren. Beim Buntaufbau von Farben aus den drei Buntfarben CMY ist die Flächendeckung zur Erzeugung dunkler Bildteile sehr hoch. Im Farbfeld wird ein Violett gemischt. Die Flächendeckung ❹ der drei Buntfarben beträgt 200%. In dieser Mischfarbe ist ein Grauwert mit 50% enthalten, der aus den drei Buntfarben zu 50 % ❺ gemischt wird. Würde man diesen Grauwert durch Schwarz ersetzen, dann besteht der Rest des Farbwertes aus 20% Cyan und 30% Magenta. Dadurch kann auf eine kostenintensive Mischung dunkler und gesättigter Farbtöne durch die Farben CMY verzichtet werden.

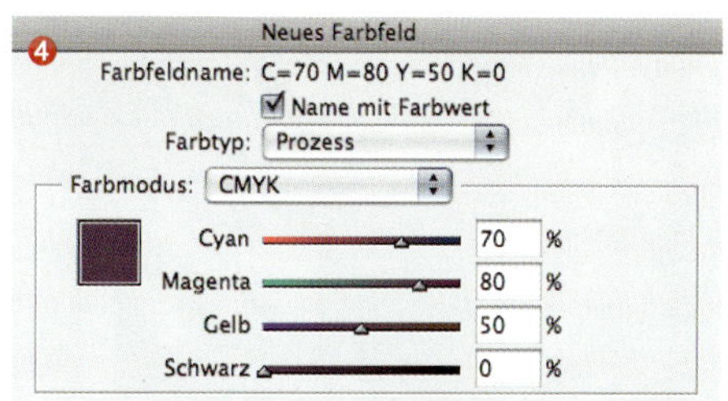

Für den Ersatz von Farben durch Schwarz werden in der Praxis zwei Verfahren unterschieden. Beim Buntaufbau mit **Unterfarbenreduzierung** (UCR) wird die Druckfarbe Schwarz verwendet, um wie oben beschrieben die bunten Prozessfarben in dunklen Bildteilen und Neutraltönen zu ersetzen. Beim **Unbuntaufbau** (GCR) werden grundsätzlich in allen Farbbereichen die Mischergebnisse der Buntfarben durch Schwarz ersetzt und die Farbdeckung auf 100% reduziert.

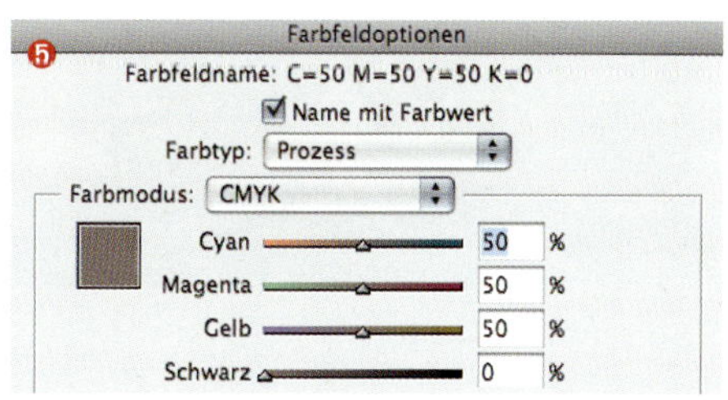

11.3 Kontrolle des Druckjobs

Verwendung von Schriften

Sind beispielsweise Schriften in einem Dokument geändert worden und werden nicht mehr verwendet, dann sollten sie gelöscht werden. Die nicht benötigten Schriften hängen oft noch mit Leerzeichen oder Absatzmarken zusammen. Im Proof sind diese Schriften natürlich nicht zu erkennen.

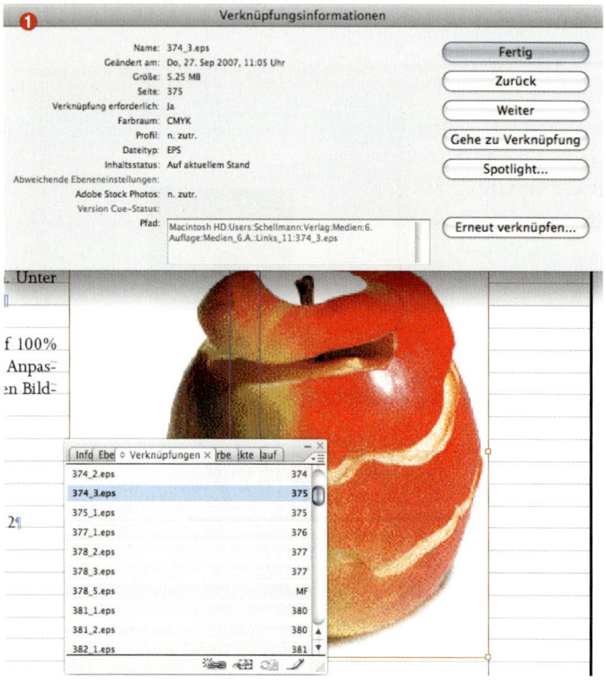

Verknüpfung der Grafikdateien ❶

In Layout-Programmen besteht die Möglichkeit, die Aktualität und das Verzeichnis verknüpfter Objekte zu kontrollieren. Hier lässt sich auch überprüfen, ob die Dateien nach einer Änderung aktualisiert wurden und ob sie das gewünschte Format haben. Wichtig wird die Kontrolle der Grafikdateien, wenn mit dem **OPI-Bildaustausch** (Open Prepress Interface) gearbeitet wird. Hierbei werden im Arbeitsprozess niedrigauflösende Grafikplatzhalter (LowRes) verwendet, die vor dem Druck durch die hochauflösenden Bilder (HiRes) ersetzt werden.

Überflüssige Objekte

Während der Arbeit in einem Layout-Programm werden viele Objekte auf der Montagefläche platziert. Diese Elemente können unter Umständen in der fertigen Ausgabe erscheinen. Ebenso verhält es sich mit Objekten, die hinter anderen Objekten auf dem Seitenlayout liegen und übersehen wurden. Diese können über das Verknüpfungsmenü erkannt und beseitigt werden.

Farbseparation ❷

Ein häufiger Fehler tritt bei der Umwandlung der Farben für den Druck auf. Bei der Farbseparation vor dem Belichten tauchen dann plötzlich Fotografien und Grafiken im RGB-Modus auf und die Farben würden beim Belichten völlig falsch umgesetzt. Es müssen alle Grafiken darauf konrolliert werden, ob sie im CMYK-Modus oder als Schmuckfarbe mit Namen definiert sind. Der **Farbproof** deckt Fehler bei der Farbenfestlegung nochmals auf.

Trapping

Ein Korrekturabzug hilft auch beim **Überfüllen** und **Unterfüllen**, das man als **Trapping** bezeichnet. Durch die hohen Geschwindigkeiten mit denen das Papier durch die Druckmaschine läuft, kommt es zu Verschiebungen des Papiers und dadurch zu Passerdifferenzen beim Auftrag der Einzelfarben. Aneinanderliegende Farben werden dann mit einem Versatz gedruckt. Eine Lücke am Übergang ist die Folge und die Papierfarbe scheint als schmaler

Streifen, auch Blitzer genannt, durch. Um diesem Effekt vorzubeugen, werden aneinanderstoßende Farbflächen durch einen Farbrand größer gemacht, man spricht auch vom **Überfüllen**. Je nach Rasterweite liegt die Randstärke zwischen 0,1 und 0,4 mm.

Trapping: Angrenzende Farben werden im Druck etwas überlappt.

Das **Unterfüllen** findet Anwendung, wenn auf einem hellen Hintergrund eine dunkle Farbfläche platziert wird, die durch Hinterlegen einer zusätzlichen Cyan-Fläche kräftiger erscheinen soll. Wird nun beispielsweise eine weißer Text auf dem dunklen Hintergrund gesetzt, dann wird die Farbe an dieser Stelle ausgespart. Damit die cyanfarbige Zusatzfläche nicht durchscheint muss diese dann verkleinert, d. h. unterfüllt, werden.

Überfüllen: Eine Farbe wird über eine andere Farbe gedruckt, wie beispielsweise bei einer Linie in einer Fläche. Dadurch kann es zu unerwünschten Farbmischungen kommen.

Raster Image Processor

Mit der Übergabe des Druckjobs an den **RIP** endet die Bearbeitung. Der RIP trennt die Druckdatei in vier neue Dateien, für die Farbwerte Cyan, Magenta, Gelb und Schwarz. Diese Bitmapdateien sind gerastert und nach dem Bitmuster 1 oder 0, geschwärzt oder nicht geschwärzt, aufgebaut. Neben der Herstellung der Bitmapdatei prüft der RIP die Veränderung der Punktgröße und die Registerhaltigkeit.

RIP, Raster Image Processor

Bei der Übergabe des Rasterpunktes von der Druckplatte über das Drucktuch auf das Papier, kann es zu einer Vergrößerung des Rasterpunktes (Punktzuwachs) kommen. Dadurch erscheinen Bildteile auf dem Papier dunkler als vorgesehen. Diese Erscheinung ist auf die Qualität des Papiers, die Saugfähigkeit, die Eigenschaften der Druckfarben und die Einstellung der Druckmaschine zurückzuführen. Im Proof lassen sich diese Veränderungen erkennen, so dass der **Punktzuwachs** im Farbmanagement noch entsprechend berücksichtigt werden kann.

Datenvolumen im Workflow

Speziell Grafiken und Fotografien beeinflussen den Zeitaufwand in der Druckvorstufe. Durch die optimale Bereitstellung der Bilddaten wird der Aufwand zur Weiterverarbeitung auf das notwendige Maß reduziert. Dazu lassen sich folgende Hinweise geben:

- Auflösung beim Scannen beachten und auf die Endgröße des zu druckenden Bildes einstellen. Wird das Bild im Anschluss verkleinert, dann vergrößert sich dadurch die effektive Auflösung.
- Bilder und Grafiken sollten bevorzugt im Grafikprogramm skaliert, beschnitten und gedreht werden. Erst danach wird die Bilddatei in das Layout-Programm importiert. So verknüpft man nur den bearbeiteten Teil des Bildes im Dokument, der wirklich gebraucht wird.
- Komplexe und sehr detaillierte Pfade können im Druck eventuell gar nicht wiedergegeben werden. Diese werden vorher im Grafikprogramm auf die notwendige Anzahl reduziert.
- Die Schriften müssen immer überprüft und eventuell nicht vorhandene Fonts oder TrueType-Fonts in EPS-Grafiken konvertiert werden. Der Vorgang lässt sich in Grafikprogrammen durch den Befehl „Text in Pfad umwandeln" durchführen.

11.4 Druckvorstufe

11.4.1 EPS oder PDF erzeugen

PDF: Portable Document Format, plattform- und programmübergreifendes Dokumentenformat

EPS: Encapsulated PostScript, Dateiformat, das Text- und Bildinformationen geräteunabhängig speichert und ein Vorschaubild bereitstellt.

Wenn die Texte geschrieben und korrigiert sind, die Bilder in der richtigen Größe in der gewünschten Qualtität an ihrem Platz stehen, der Satz abgeschlossen ist, dann kann es eigentlich losgehen mit der drucktechnischen Umsetzung. Zunächst wird die zu druckende Datei im PDF- oder EPS-Format gespeichert. **PostScript** stellt eine Programmiersprache dar, die es ermöglicht Text, Grafik und Bilder für den Druckprozess zu codieren. Das Dokumentenaustauschformat PDF ist auf PostScript aufgebaut und ist als Datenformat vergleichbar mit EPS. Es kann, wie PostScript, eine Dokumentseite beschreiben, besitzt darüberhinaus viel umfangreichere Möglichkeiten. So kann man Inhalte verlinken, Such- und Indexfunktionen nutzen, Job Tickets verwalten und beispielsweise Hyperlinks und Videos integrieren. Eine PDF-Datei lässt sich nicht nur drucken, sondern genauso als Bildschirmpräsentation oder im Web nutzen.

PostScript (PS) von Adobe ist eine Seitenbeschreibungssprache, die Druckseiten in einer Datei so ablegt, dass sie von beliebigen Ausgabegeräten umgesetzt werden können.
PostScript Level 1:
Farbtiefe 8 Bit = 256 Graustufen
PostScript Level 2:
Farbtiefe 12 Bit = 4096 Graustufen
PostScript Level 3: Verbesserter RIP-Workflow (JDF), Unterstützung von neuen Formaten, z. B. JPEG 2000

PostScript-Dateien lassen sich über den Adobe Distiller in PDF-Dateien verwandeln. Danach können sie angesehen und beispielsweise für eine Bildschirmdarstellung aufbereitet werden. Das Erstellen von PDF-Daten aus Programmen wie Photoshop und InDesign läuft über Speicher- bzw. Exportfunktionen ab. Mit dem Speichern des Dokuments kann gleichzeitig die Schriftart eingebettet werden.

11.4.2 Der Proof in der Druckvorstufe

Ein wenig Unsicherheit schwingt trotz allem mit, und die Frage nach der farbgetreuen Wiedergabe lässt einen nicht schlafen. An dieser Stelle hilft ein **Proof**, das ist ein Andruck, der das spätere Druckprodukt nahezu identisch wiedergibt. Die Druckdatei wird zur Beurteilung am besten auf dem Originalpapier ausgegeben. Mit dem Andruck kann festgestellt werden, ob das Layout passt, ob die Farben, Schriften und Linien in Grafiken vorhanden und nicht deformiert sind oder treppenartige Erscheinungen aufweisen. Die Probleme können dann noch behoben werden.

Analoge Farbproofverfahren:
- Matchprint (Imation)
- Color-Key (Imation)
- Color-Art System (Fuji)
- Cromalin-StudioSprint
- Cromalin-Tonerproof
- Maschinenproof mit Offset-Andruckmaschine

Bei analogen Farbproofverfahren wird der Korrekturabzug auf der Basis von belichteten Folien oder mit Druckplatten im Offsetandruck erstellt. Vielfach wird heute aus Kostengründen eine digitale Lösung mit dem **Thermosublimationsverfahren** oder dem Laserdruckverfahren eingesetzt, bei der die Filmbelichtung entfällt. Durch den Einsatz von Farbmanagementsystemen wird eine recht gute Übereinstimmung mit den Druckfarben erzielt. Abweichungen können immer auftreten, haben ihre Ursache aber vor allem in der Wahl des Bedruckstoffes und den zur Verfügung stehenden Farbpigmenten beim Andruck.

Bei den digitalen Proofverfahren gibt es, neben der Möglichkeit, einen Korrekturabzug in Papierform (**Hardproof**) zu erstellen, den Softproof. Hierbei wird der Druckjob auf einem kalibrierten Bildschirm dargestellt. Ein Farbmanagementsystem analysiert das Bild und stellt Abweichungen fest. Der **Softproof** eignet sich vor allem zur Korrektur von Farben und bietet eine plattformunabhängige Beurteilung der Daten an beliebigen Orten.

Beim Hardproof unterscheidet man grundsätzlich fünf Arten:

- **Blaupause (Blueprint):** Der Datenbestand kann kontrolliert werden auf Vollständigkeit und inhaltliche Übereinstimmung. Der Ausdruck ist einfarbig.
- **Standproof (Layout- oder Imposition-Proof):** Der Ausdruck ist in Farbe, jedoch nicht farbverbindlich. Eine kostengünstige Möglichkeit den Bestand der Bildelemente und den Inhalt zu prüfen.
- **Halbtonproof (Color-Proof):** Der Color-Proof stellt einen farbverbindlichen Korrekturabzug dar. Voraussetzung ist dabei der Einsatz eines Color-Management-Systems.
- **Rasterproof (True-Proof):** Farbe und Raster werden wie im späteren Druckprozess simuliert. Der Punktaufbau und die Einflüsse von Rasterpunkt, -winkel und -frequenz können geprüft werden. Tonwertverläufe, Moiré und Rosetten werden hier im Vorfeld der Druckproduktion erkannt.
- **Maschinenproof:** Der Andruck des Datenbestands erfolgt auf einer der Seriendruckmaschine vergleichbaren Maschine. Neben dem Proof werden auf diesen Maschinen häufig Kleinauflagen hergestellt.

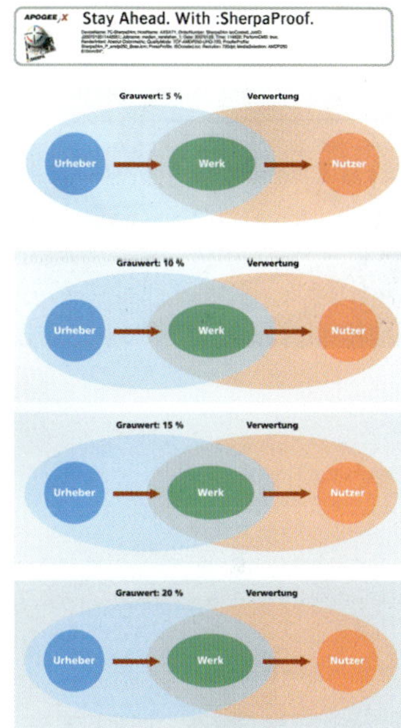

11.4.3 Belichten und Bebildern

Der Datenbestand für ein zu druckendes Dokument liegt als PostScript-Datei mit Bildpixeln vor. Die Dateien werden an einen **Raster Image Processor** (RIP) weitergegeben. Der RIP sorgt dafür, dass die digitalisierten Daten für den Druck gerastert werden. Dies geschieht heute meist durch eine Software, einen Software-RIP. Seltener werden die hardwaretechnischen Lösungen mit Computerbausteinen zum elektronischen Aufrastern der Bildvorlagen. Der Software-RIP wird von verschiedenen Herstellern angeboten und auf leistungsfähigen Rechnern installiert. Neben der Aufgabe der Rasterung übernehmen diese Programme unter anderem auch die Bogenmontage mit dem entsprechenden Ausschießschema.

Raster Image Processor (RIP): Der RIP rastert die fertige Seite und stellt für jede Farbe eines Vierfarbsatzes C-M-Y-K ein Bitmap her.

Computer to Film:
Mit einem Laserbelichter werden vier Filme für die vier Farben belichtet. Diese werden dann entwickelt, montiert und auf Druckplatten kopiert. Der Film beinhaltet das Bild in unterschiedlichen Grautönen. Diese bilden die jeweilige Farbe und ihre Farbabstufungen ab.

Computer to Plate:
Mit Hilfe von digitalen Plattenbelichtern (CtP-Anlage) können die Druckplatten direkt, ohne den Einsatz von Film, belichtet werden. Die zu druckenden Bereiche sind farbaufnehmend aufkopiert.

Computer to Press:
Die Druckplatten sind bei einer Digitaldruckmaschine durch einen Plattenzylinder mit Folienmagazin ersetzt. Die Druckfolie mit Silikonschicht wird vor Gebrauch auf den Plattenzylinder gezogen. Ein präziser Laserstrahl „bebildert" die Druckfolie, da an den bestrahlten Stellen die Silikonschicht abgelöst wird und diese Stellen dadurch Farbe aufnehmen können.

11.4.4 Ausschießen

In der manuellen **Bogenmontage** werden auf einem Leuchttisch belichtete Filmabschnitte auf Umbruchbögen positionsgerecht (standgerecht) gelegt, fixiert und anschließend auf die Druckplatten kopiert. Die manuelle Bogenmontage kommt noch bei Nachbearbeitungen und kurzfrisiigen Änderungen vor dem Andruck zum Einsatz. Aus dem fertig montierte Standbogen wird dann im Anschluss entweder mit Hilfe eines belichteten Films die Druckplatte hergestellt oder die Daten direkt auf die Druckplatte kopiert.

Die Anordnung der Seiten auf Vor- und Rückseite des Druckbogens ist von verschiedenen Kriterien abhängig, wie dem Druckverfahren, der Druckmaschinenart mit Greifervorrichtung, der Bogenwendeart, der Falz- und Bindeart, der Papierlaufrichtung und der Falzmaschine. Den gesamten Vorgang nennt man Ausschießen.

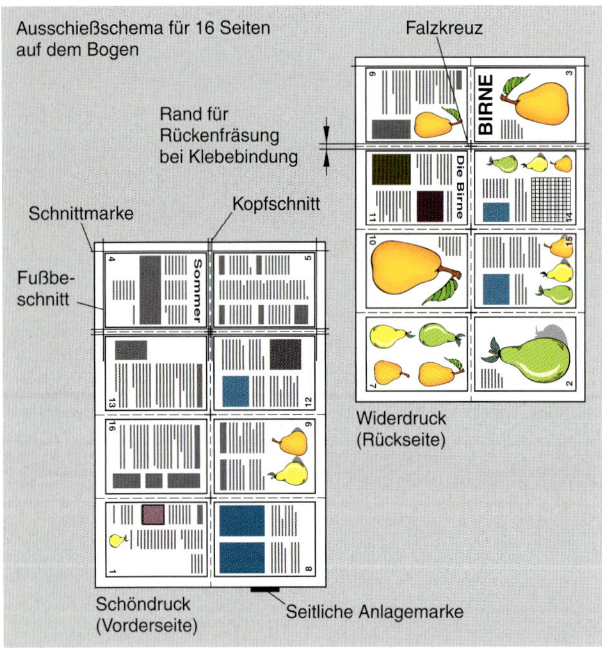

Die **elektronische Bogenmontage** vereinfacht die bisher manuellen Tätigkeiten des Ausschießens. Mit Hilfe einer Software werden die Seiten automatisch richtig positioniert und können noch mit Schneide- und Falzmarken, Farbkontrollstreifen und Passkreuzen versehen werden. Durch die Nachbearbeitung mit Falzen, Beschnitt der Ränder und Heftung entsteht eine fertig gebundene Broschüre.

Mit einem **Ausschießschema** werden die Seiten auf dem Bogen so angeordnet, dass wie beim abgebildeten Beispiel nach dreimaligem Falzen (Kreuzbruch) die Seiten von 1 bis 16 in der richtigen Reihenfolge vorliegen. Man bezeichnet diesen Bogen auch als Dreibruchbogen. Die acht Seiten stehen „Kopf-an-Kopf", d. h. sie sind so angeordnet, dass sich die Oberkanten sowie der Kopf der Seite, im Bund gegenüberstehen.

Nutzen: Druckt man auf einem Druckbogen 16 Seiten im Schön- und Widerdruck (Buchbinderbogen), dann wird der Druckbogen einmal genutzt, es wird zu einem Nutzen gedruckt. Stehen 32 Seiten im Schön- und Widerdruck auf einem Druckbogen, dann wird der Druckbogen zweimal genutzt, es wird zu zwei Nutzen gedruckt. Durch Auseinanderschneiden des Bogens erhält man dann zwei sogenannte Buchbinderbogen.

Beim Drucken von Vor- und Rückseite mit Bogendruckmaschinen muss der Druckbogen gewendet werden. Dabei unterscheidet man in der Praxis folgende Verfahren:

- **Umschlagen**: Ist die Hälfte der Druckauflage auf der einen Seite gedruckt, dann wird der Druckbogen um die senkrechte Mittelachse, in Druckrichtung gewendet und von der gleichen Druckform bedruckt.
- **Umstülpen**: Gedruckt wird mit einer Druckform wie beim Umschlagen. Gewendet wird der Druckbogen jedoch über die Querachse, d. h. quer zur Druckrichtung. Mit Umschlagen und Umstülpen können pro Druckbogen jeweils zwei doppelseitige Drucksachen hergestellt werden.
- **Schön- und Widerdruck**: Das Papier der gesamten Druckauflage wird auf einer Seite von einer Druckform bedruckt (Schöndruck). Anschließend wird das Papier nach dem Ausschießschema gewendet und von einer zweiten Druckform auf der Rückseite bedruckt (Widerdruck).

11.5 Druckverfahren

11.5.1 Einteilung der Druckverfahren

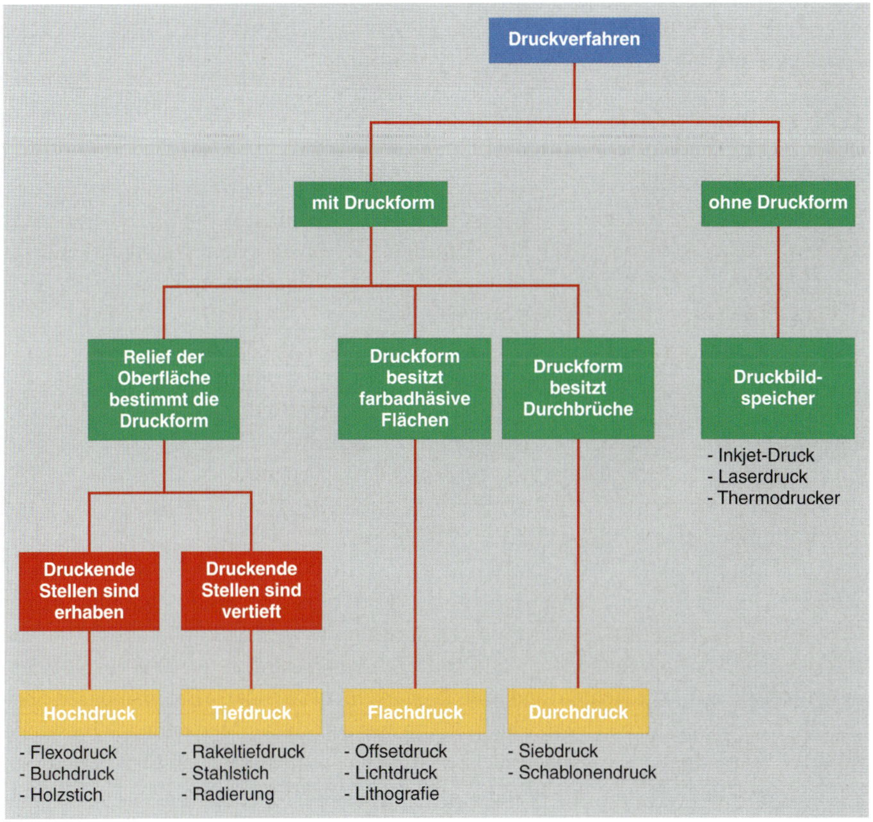

11.5.2 Hochdruck

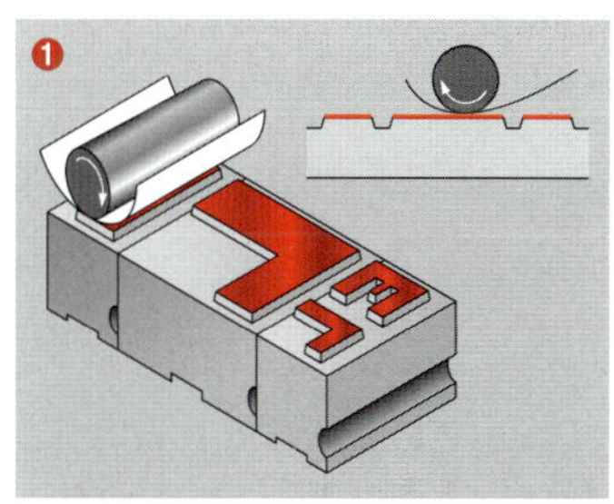

Der Hochdruck beruht auf dem Prinzip von Kraft und Gegenkraft und ist ein mechanisches Verfahren. Ähnlich wie bei einem Stempel liegen die zu druckenden Teile erhaben, d. h. hoch auf dem Druckträger. Die nicht druckenden Teile werden vertieft. Der klassische Vertreter der Druckträger ist die Bleisatzschrift, wie sie von Gutenberg im Buchdruck des 15. Jahrhunderts eingesetzt wurde, oder die Holzschnitte. Im Buchdruck kommen die Druckprinzipien Fläche-Fläche (Tiegeldruck), Fläche-Zylinder (Flachform-Zylinderdruck) und Zylinder-Zylinder (Rotationsdruck) zur Anwendung. Bei diesem direkten Verfahren ist das Druckbild spiegelverkehrt auf der Druckform ❶ und wird nach dem Einfärben direkt auf das Papier übertragen. Damit breite Flächen und dunkle Teile einer Halbtonvorlage genau den gleichen Druck bekommen wie dünne Linien oder spitze Teile, wird mit einer reliefartigen Zurichtung gearbeitet, die für gleichen Druck sorgt. Der Hochdruck ist vor allem erkennbar an einem leichten Relief auf der Rückseite des bedruckten Bogens und an den Quetschrändern der Buchstaben, das sind Anhäufungen von Farbe am Rand der Type. Mit dem Hochdruck erzielt man ein sehr scharfes Druckbild. Es lassen sich damit alle Papiere und Kartonagen bedrucken.

Flexodruck

Beim Flexodruck wird eine erhabene Druckfolie aus Weichgummi oder Fotopolymer (z. B. Nyloprint) verwendet, die das Druckbild übertragen. Mit den flexiblen Klischees, die auf Druckzylinder geklebt sind, werden Verpackungen, Folien, Aluminiumfolien, Versandhüllen und Wellpappe gedruckt.

11.5.3 Flachdruck

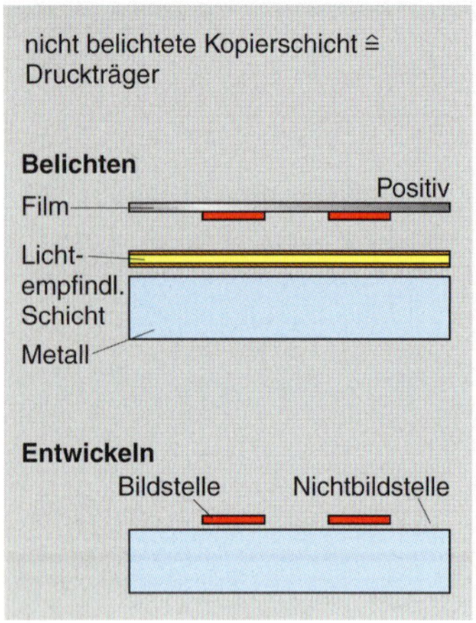

Auflagen im Offsetdruck: Mit Aluminiumplatten ca. 100 000 Auflage, Mit Bi- und Trimetallplatten ca. 300 000 Auflage in bester Qualität

Das Druckverfahren entwickelte sich aus dem Steindruck, nach dem Prinzip, dass sich Fette und Wasser abstoßen. Die Druckplatten sind so behandelt, dass die druckenden Flächen Wasser abweisen (oleophil) und die farbfreien Flächen Wasser annehmen. Der Flachdruck ist ein chemisches Verfahren, wobei druckende und nichtdruckende Teile in einer Ebene flach nebeneinanderliegen.

Die industrielle Form ist der **Offsetdruck** (to set off = absetzen). Dabei wird die Druckfarbe von den eingefärbten Stellen der Druckplatte auf ein Gummituch „abgesetzt“. Diese Art zu drucken bezeichnet man als indirektes Verfahren. Der Zwischenschritt über das Gummituch ist notwendig weil die Druckplatte zu viel Feuchtigkeit auf das Papier übertragen würde. Zudem würde das Papier wie ein Schleifpapier auf der empfindlichen Oberfläche wirken.

Zur Herstellung der Druckplatte wird ein Positivfilm und eine lichtempfindliche Metallplatte benötigt. Die seitenverkehrten Positivfilme werden unter Vakuum auf die beschichtete Druckplatte gepresst und mit UV-Licht bestrahlt. An den zeichnungsfreien Stellen wird die lichtemfindliche Kopierschicht zerstört, an den anderen Stellen bleibt sie erhalten. Nach der Entwicklung werden die verbleibenden Schichtteile gehärtet, die aufgelösten Schichtteile gewaschen, so dass dort das Metall freiliegt. Der Wasser annehmende Teil ist nun das nichtbeschichtete Metall. Beim Drucken wird die Druckplatte zunächst mit Wasser und anschließend mit einer Druckfarbe auf Ölbasis befeuchtet. Die ölhaltige Farbe haftet auf den Stellen, die nicht mit Wasser befeuchtet sind.

Den Flachdruck erkennt man daran, dass er im Gegensatz zum Hochdruck keine Quetschränder hat und keine Reliefs auf der Bogenrückseite. Eine Variante des Offsetdrucks ist der Trockenoffsetdruck der ohne Feuchtwerk auskommt. Beim wasserlosen Druck ist die Oberfläche der Druckplatte, z. B. eine Silikonschicht, grundsätzlich was-

serabweisend. Bei den Druckträgern handelt es sich beispielsweise um eine silikonbeschichtete Trägerfolie, die auf einen **Plattenzylinder** ❶ aufgezogen wird. Digital gesteuerte Laserstrahlen brennen kleine Vertiefungen in die Silikonschicht. Wasserlose Druckfarben füllen diese Vertiefungen, um das Druckbild zu erzeugen, während die nichtdruckenden Stellen durch das Silikon geschützt bleiben. Der Druck erfolgt indirekt über ein Gummituch auf das Papier. Soll eine neue Bebilderung stattfinden, wird die verbrauchte Folie auf eine Leerwalze im Inneren des Plattenzylinders aufgewickelt und gleichzeitig eine neue Folie auf den Druckträger ❷ gespannt. Durch den wasserlosen Druck werden einheitliche und intensive Farben mit geringem Punktzuwachs erzielt.

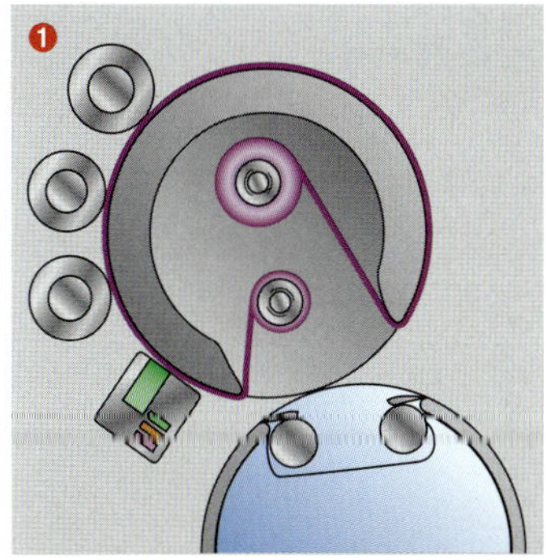
❶

❷

11.5.4 Tiefdruck

Der Vorläufer des heutigen Tiefdrucks ist der Kupferstich. Die zu druckenden Teile liegen dabei vertieft in einem Kupferzylinder. Durch einen Sprühmechanismus oder durch Eintauchen des Druckzylinders in die Farbwanne ❸ füllen sich die Näpfchen mit Farbe. Ein Rakelmesser ❹, ein dünnes Stahllineal, streift die überschüssige Farbe ab. Daher stammt auch der Name Rakeltiefdruck. Für jede Farbe wird ein eigener Formzylinder (Kupferzylinder) benötigt. Durch die unterschiedlich tiefgeätzte Näpfchen wird die gewünschte Farbmenge reguliert. Halbtöne werden nicht durch die Größe des Rasterpunktes festgelegt, sondern über die Farbmengenabgabe aus den Näpfchen. Je nach der Menge der Farbe, die über die Stege in die benachbarten Näpfchen fließt, entsteht der optische Eindruck eines Halbtones.

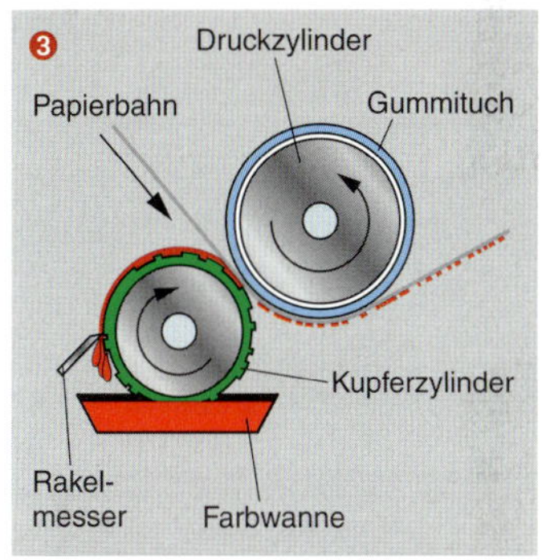

❸

Auf dem Druckträger, einem Kupferzylinder, werden die Näpfchen heutzutage durch eine Gravureinrichtung mit Hilfe eines Elektronenstrahls oder eines Diamantstichels hergestellt. Die Näpfchen können je nach angewandtem Verfahren unterschiedlich groß und unterschiedlich tief sein. Bei der Gravur mit Diamantstichel wird eine Leistung von bis zu 4000 Näpfchen pro Sekunde erzielt, bei der Elektronenstrahlgravur eine Leistung von bis zu 150 000 Näpfchen. Die gleichmäßig über den Druckzylinder angeordneten Stege dienen zur Auflage des Rakelmessers. Die kleinsten Näpfchen haben eine Diagonale von 30 mm. Typische Merkmale des Tiefdrucks sind die gerasterte Schrift und der satte Farbauftrag. Darüber hinaus ergeben sich keine scharfen Rasterpunkte, da die niedrigviskose Druckfarbe auf dem Bedruckstoff ausfließt. Die Stege der Druckform sind dadurch nicht sichtbar. Der Tiefdruck wird für Versandhauskataloge, Zeitschriften, Verpackungsmaterial, Briefmarken und Banknoten sowie im qualitativ hochwertigen Bilderdruck eingesetzt. Durch die hohen Kosten für die Gravur oder Ätzung, sieht man jedoch im Buchdruck von diesem Verfahren ab.

❹

11.5.5 Siebdruck

Beim Siebdruck wird Farb durch ein feinmaschiges Sieb auf den Bedruckstoff gedrückt. Man spricht dabei auch vom Durchdruck. Das Sieb aus Naturseiden-, Kunststoff- oder Metallfäden besteht aus 10 - 200 Fäden pro cm. Die erzielbare Rasterung entspricht etwa 1/3 bis 1/4 der Gewebefeinheit (Fäden pro cm). Dadurch lassen sich zum Teil fein abgestufte Tonwerte erzielen. Damit nur an den Stellen Farbe durchgedrückt wird, wo ein Bildelement sein soll, muss der bildfreie Teil abgedeckt werden. Das Abdecken geschieht durch eine Schablone, deren Fläche und Kontur auf das Sieb aufbelichtet

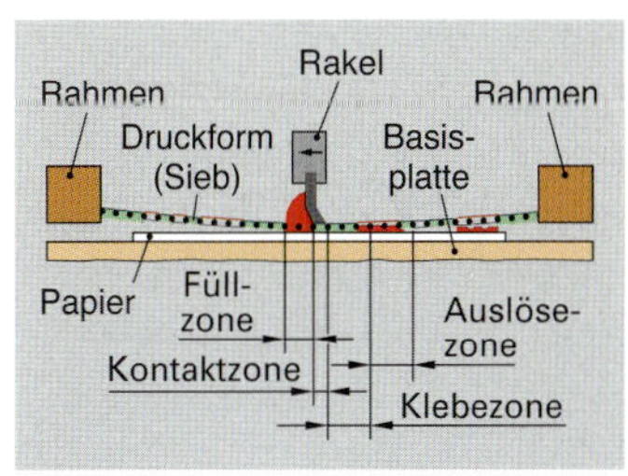

❶

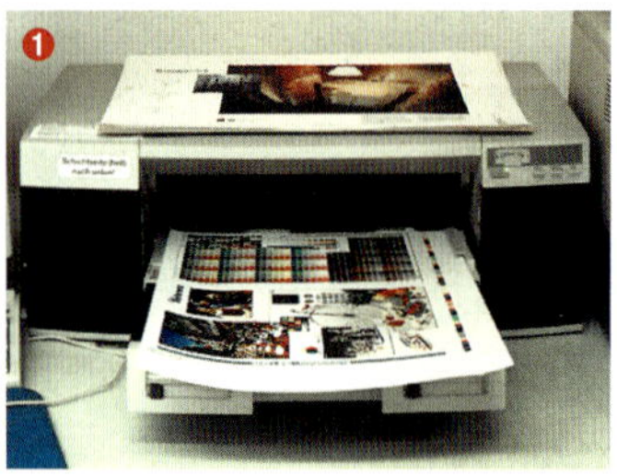

❷

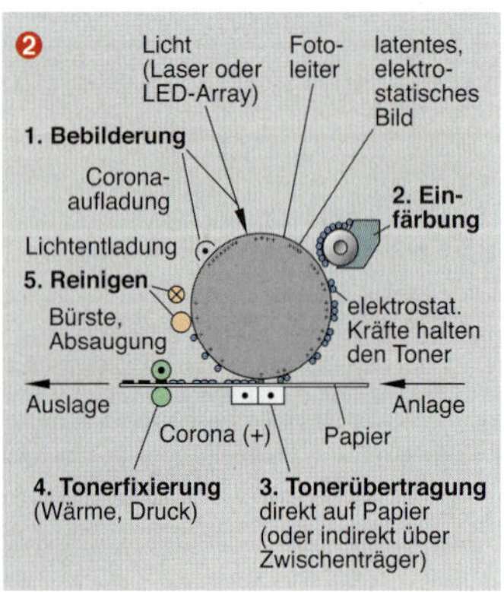

und mit UV-Licht ausgehärtet wird. Die Bildstellen sind unbelichtet und werden mit Wasser abgewaschen. Die Farbe wird entweder mit einem beweglichen Rakel über einer feststehenden Druckform oder mit einer beweglichen Druckform unter stehendem Rakel durch das feinmaschige Sieb auf den Bedruckstoff gedrückt. Der Siebdruck hat einen breiten Einsatzbereich und reicht vom Bedrucken von Textilien, Spielwaren, Kunststoffprodukte, Werbeplakate, Verpackungen bis zu großflächigen Fahnen.

11.5.6 Non-Impact-Printing

Durch den Einzug des Computers im gesamten Workflow von der Erstellung des Druckprodukts bis zum Druck veränderte sich auch die Druckvorstufe und die Bogenmontage. Verfahren wie Computer-to-Film und Computer-to-Plate waren der Anfang einer digitalen Datenweitergabe. Die Techniken werden mittlerweile ergänzt durch die Ausgabesysteme Computer-to-Press und Computer-to-Print.

Unter Computer-to-Print versteht man das Drucken ohne Druckform, das sogenannte **Non-Impact-Printing** (NIP-Verfahren). Dazu zählen die Elektrofotografie sowie Inkjet- und thermografische Verfahren. Grundsätzlich zeichnen sich die Verfahren dadurch aus, dass die Bildinformationen in digitaler Form im Workflow weitergegeben werden. Ein wesentliches Merkmal sogenannter digitaler Druckverfahren ist das Fehlen einer permanenten Druckform.

Bei der **Elektrofotografie** wird mit Hilfe eines Laserlichts oder eine LED die Bild- und Schriftinformationen auf eine fotoleitende Schicht übertragen. Das Druckprinzip wird im **Laserdrucker** ❶ verwendet. Dabei wird die elektrostatische Schicht auf einem Zylinder durch das Licht an den Stellen unterbrochen, die keine Farbe aufnehmen sollen. Durch elektrostatische Kräfte haftet der Toner an den elektrisch geladenen Stellen des Druckzylinders ❷. Das nicht sichtbare, latente Ladungsbild ist dann eingefärbt und wird auf das Papier übertragen. Da die Bildinformation ohne mechanische Einwirkung oder sichtbaren Partikelauftrag auf den Druckzylinder übertragen wird, bezeichnet man dieses Verfahren als Non-Impact-Verfahren (NIP).

Anschließend wird der Zylinder mechanisch und elektrisch gereinigt. Zum einen werden Tonerpartikel entfernt und das Ladungsbild elektrisch neutralisiert, d. h. die Trommel für den nächsten Druckauftrag vollständig elektrostatisch aufgeladen. Soll das Druckbild in einer größeren Auflage gedruckt werden, dann wird nach jedem Druck das Ladungsbild neu erstellt. Das kann zu Positionsabweichungen im Druckbild führen. Auf der anderen Seite ermöglicht das ständig neue Bebildern unterschiedliche Druckjobs, Auflagenhöhen und Seitengrößen variabel und sehr flexibel herzustellen. Wir sprechen dann auch vom **printing on demand**.

Non-Impact-Verfahren (NIP): Anschlagloses Verfahren im Gegensatz zu dem Druckprinzip der früheren Matrixdrucker mit Anschlag (impact) der Type

Das **Inkjetverfahren (Tintenstrahldrucker)** arbeitet ohne Zwischenträger für die Bildinformationen. Die Tintentropfen werden mit Hilfe einer Pumpe über eine Düse durch ein elektrisches Feld geschleudert. Die elektrisch geladenen Farbtröpfchen werden, je nach Ladungszustand, im elektrischen Feld abgelenkt und wieder aufgefangen, oder durchfliegen dieses, bis sie auf dem Papier auftreffen. Die digital vorliegenden Informationen einer Tonwertstufung werden durch mehr oder weniger Tinte auf dem Papier wiedergegeben.

11.5.7 Computer to Press Verfahrensvergleich

Die **Computer to Press**-Verfahren verzichten auf die Zwischenschritte der Film- und/oder Plattenherstellung. Beim Verfahren **Direct Imaging** wird beispielsweise eine silikonbeschichtete Druckform in der Druckmaschine bebildert (s. 11.6.3 Flachdruck). Als **Computer to Print** bezeichnet man die verschiedenen **NIP-Verfahren**. Hierbei wird zwar wie bei der Elektrofotografie ein Druckform in einem Zwischenschritt bebildert, was jedoch ohne Veränderung einer Trägersubstanz stattfindet. Ohne jegliche Zwischenträger kommen Druckmaschinen mit InkJet Systemen aus.

Workflow

Am Beispiel der direkten Bebilderung (Direct Imaging) schauen wir uns den Funktionsablauf eines Computer To Press-Verfahrens näher an. Mit Hilfe einer Layout-Software werden vollständig digitalisierte Text-, Bild- und Grafikdaten auf einem Druckbogen gestaltet und im PDF- oder EPS-Format gespeichert. In der Datenvorbereitung der Druckerei werden die Druckdaten mit Hilfe eines digitalen Proofs auf ihre Vollständigkeit hin kontrolliert und an einen Raster Image Processor (RIP) weitergegeben. Der RIP rastert die Seiten und gibt von jeder zu druckenden Seite ein Bitmap aus, das von einer Bebilderungseinheit Punkt für Punkt auf den silikonbeschichteten Druckträger übertragen wird. Im Druckwerk wird im Offset-Verfahren (Feuchtung, Einfärbung und Druck) das Druckbild vom Druckträger (Plattenzylinder) über ein Gummituch auf das Papier übertragen.

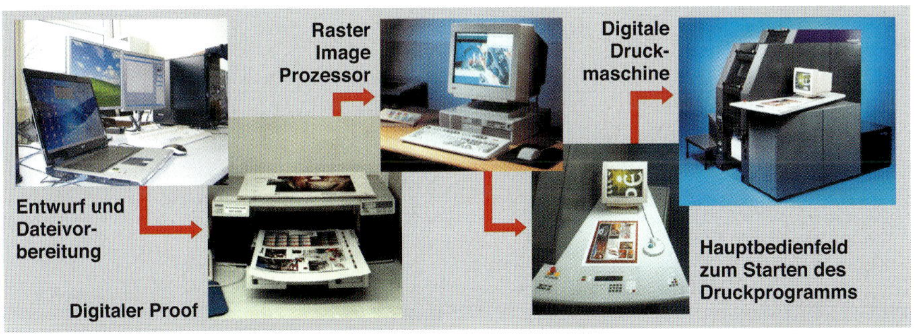

Drucksystem Fa. Xerox nach dem NIP-Verfahren, Daten:
- 35 Blatt pro min.
- bis 250 g Papier
- max. A3-Format
- doppelseitiger Druck
- Heftung und Bindung optional
- Auflösung max. 1200 × 1200 dpi
- Laser Farbe

11.6 Druckmaschinen

Die Druckmaschine hat seit der Erfindung des Drucks eine lange Entwicklung durchgemacht. Zunächst wurde mit Tiegeldruckpressen eine flache Druckform auf einen flachen Bedruckstoff, meist Papier gepresst, später dann mit Zylinderdruckmaschinen auch rund gegen flach. Beide Maschinenarten gehören heute eher zu den Raritäten in den Druckereien, dominieren doch die Bogendruck- und Rollendruckmaschinen, die nach dem Prinzip der Rotation mit einem Plattenzylinder arbeiten.

11.6.1 Bogendruckmaschinen

Bogenoffsetmaschinen werden als Einfarben- oder Mehrfarbenmaschine mit bis zu sechs Farbwerken eingesetzt. Die einzelnen Papierbögen werden von einem Vorratsstapel in die Zufuhreinheit mit einem Greifer einzeln eingezogen.

Für den doppelseitigen Druck muss das Papier durch Umstülpen oder Umschlagen gewendet und wieder zugeführt werden. In einigen Druckmaschinen muss das Wenden manuell durchgeführt werden, in anderen Druckmaschinen wird der Vorgang automatisch ausgeführt. Druckmaschinen, die in einem Durchgang den Bedruckstoff vorn und hinten bedrucken, bezeichnet man als Schön- und Widerdruckmaschinen. Im Mehrfarbendruck wird „nass in nass“ gedruckt, d. h. dass die noch nicht trockenen Farben hintereinander in einem Maschinendurchgang auf den Bedruckstoff gedruckt werden.

Die digitalen Bogendruckmaschinen bieten durch den Einsatz neuer Technik ein hohes Maß an Genauigkeit. Das Papier wird nur einmal über eine Greifereinrichtung auf den vierfachgroßen Druckzylinder geführt und dann ohne Bogenübergabe bis zur Auslage transportiert. Das Papier liegt durch viermaliges Überrollen in den Farbwerken und durch Adhäsion, der Anhangskraft des Papiers, exakt auf dem Druckzylinder auf. Das Auslagegreifersystem entnimmt das Papier und stapelt es nach dem Druck.

Bauweise einer digitalen Vierfarboffsetdruckmaschine:

Greifereinrichtung ❶
Druckzylinder ❷
Farb- oder Druckwerk ❸
Auslagegreifersystem ❹

Am Papierlauf ist auch die Druckreihenfolge Schwarz, Cyan, Magenta und Gelb erkennbar.

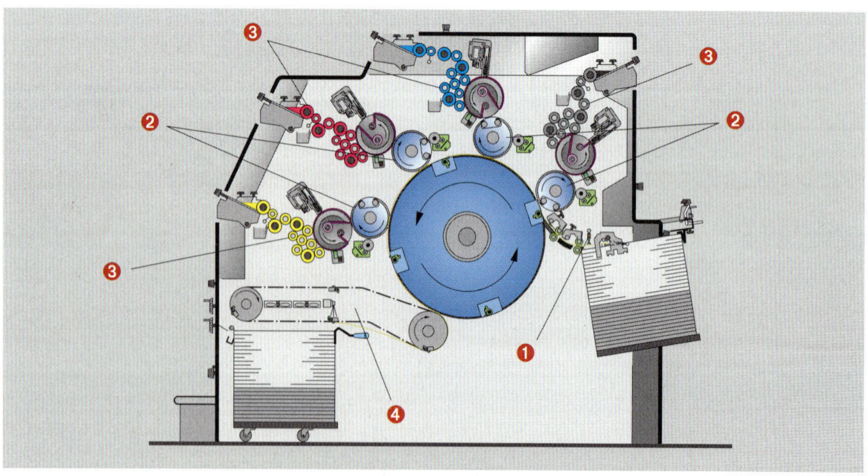

Funktionsprinzip einer Quickmaster DI 46-4, Heidelberger Druckmaschinen AG

Aufbau eines Farbwerks

Das Farbwerk einer Digital-Druckmaschine soll hier näher betrachtet werden. Das Farbwerk besteht aus 12 Walzen mit unterschiedlicher Funktion:

- Farbkasten mit gekühltem Farbduktor ❶
- Farbheber ❷
- Farbreiber, teilweise mit Kühlung ❸
- Übertragwalzen ❹
- Farbauftragwalzen ❺

Die Farbe wird aus dem Farbkasten über den Farbduktor auf den Farbheber abgegeben. Über die Farbreiber und die Übertragwalzen gelangt die Farbe auf die Farbauftragwalzen. Die Farbauftragwalzen übertragen die Farbe auf die silikonbeschichtete Druckfolie auf dem Plattenzylinder ❻. Die silikonfreien Stellen der Trägerfolie nehmen nun die Farbe auf und geben diese während des Druckvorgangs wieder an den Gummituchzylinder ❼ ab.

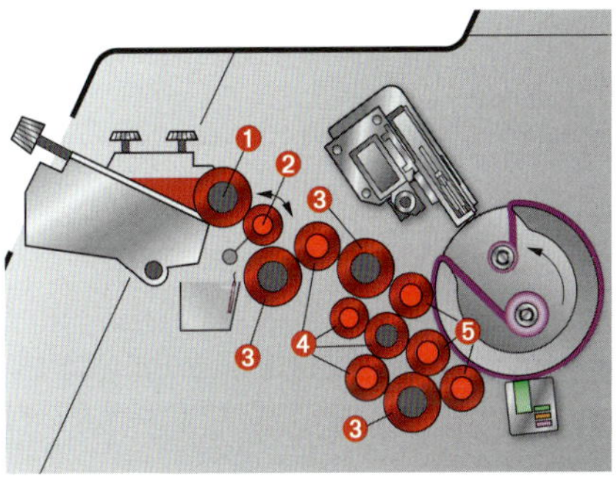

11.6.2 Rollendruckmaschine

Rollendruckmaschinen werden auch als Rotationsmaschinen bezeichnet. Den Druckvorgang bei einer Zeitung bezeichnet man auch als „Rotation".

Für hohe Auflagen speziell im Bereich der Tageszeitungen, Zeitschriften, Magazine und Versandhauskataloge, werden Rollenoffsetmaschinen eingesetzt. Durch das Hintereinanderschalten von Satellitendruckwerken können mehrere Farben in einem Durchgang und gleichzeitig auf beiden Seiten, also im Schön- und Widerdruck, gedruckt werden.

Rollendruckmaschinen sind oft schneller und flexibler in bezug auf Bogenlängen und -formate und haben eine hohe Druckleistung mit bis zu 60 000 Drucken pro Stunde. Durch den Einsatz von Rollenpapier können neben den üblichen acht Seiten auch großformatige Bilder für Poster und Banner gedruckt werden. Eine Beschränkung gibt es dabei nur in der Breite, die für die Rollendruckmaschine passend sein muss.
Eine Schwierigkeit tritt vor allem im Zeitungsdruck auf. Hohe Druckleistung und gleichzeitig niedriges Gewicht des Endprodukts erfordern reißfeste Papiersorten. Heutzutage ist es möglich das Papiergewicht reißfester Papiersorten im Zeitungsbereich auf 30 g/m^2 zu senken und so hohe Druckleistungen mit bis zu 30 000 Zeitungen à 48 Seiten pro Stunde zu erzielen.

Registerhaltigkeit: Einhalten der Einstellungen von Maschinenwerten, wie Greiferrand und Seitenanlage, um beispielsweise einen deckungsgleichen Satzspiegel im Schön- und Widerdruck zu erzielen

Passergenauigkeit: Genauigkeit, mit der die Farben von der Druckmaschine übereinander gedruckt werden. Beim Herstellen der Druckplatten werden die Filme mit Hilfe von Passerkreuzen ausgerichtet.

Die Rollendruckmaschinen im Zeitungsbereich sind im Anschluss an das letzte Druckwerk mit einem Falzaggregat verbunden, aus dem die gefalzten und beschnittenen Zeitungen mit Greifereinrichtungen zu den Einlegestationen für Beilagen und Werbebroschüren gefördert werden.

11.6.3 Drucküberwachung

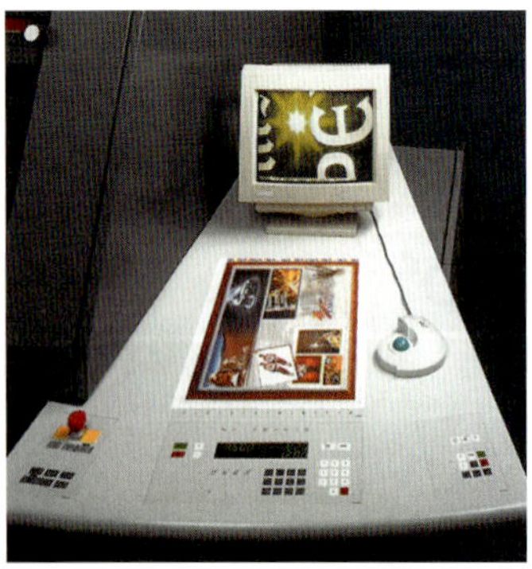

Die Kontrolle über die Farbgebung, die Registerhaltigkeit und die Passergenauigkeit wird bei Bogen- und Rollendruckmaschinen vom Computer übernommen und als **Computer Printing Control (CPC)** bezeichnet.

Die Druckplatten befinden sich auf dem Druckzylinder, das Papier ist eingelegt und die Farbkästen sind mit Farbe gefüllt. Mit dem Starten der Druckmaschine übernimmt das Computer Printing Control-System die Überwachung der Druckergebnisse. Damit dieses System eingreifen kann, müssen dem Programm die Daten über Farben, Formate, Papiersorte u. a. eingegeben werden.

Das Einrichten des Systems findet im Vorfeld mit einem Andruck statt. Die Kontrolle des Andrucks ist notwendig, weil der Druckjob auf unterschiedliche Weise beeinflusst werden kann. Benötigt eine Fläche beispielsweise eine höhere Farbintensität, dann kann sich diese Erhöhung der Farbführung auch auf andere Abbildungen auswirken. Jede zu druckende Seite hat wichtige Bereiche, auf die besonders geachtet werden muss. So sind dies in einem Buch über Fotografie die Schärfe der Abbildungen sowie die Registerhaltigkeit der Farben und in einem Buch über Typografie die Schärfe und die richtige Verwendung der Schriften. In einem Reiseprospekt für ein Segelrevier sind die Farben des Himmels und des Wassers als wichtige Elemente zu betrachten. So muss der Techniker die entsprechenden Werte an der Druckmaschine einstellen und im Andruck überprüfen. Die Intensität und Balance der Farben werden meist nochmals vom Designer zum Zeitpunkt des Andrucks überprüft. Mit der Genehmigung des Proofs erteilt der Auftraggeber dann die Druckfreigabe. Jetzt ist es die Aufgabe des Druckers die Vorgaben zu kontrollieren und für die Einhaltung der Qualität zu sorgen.

Auf dem **Druckbogen** sind wichtige Hinweise zur Drucküberwachung gegeben. Die wichtigen Bereiche sind markiert, die vom Drucker und auch vom Auftraggeber kontrolliert werden sollten.

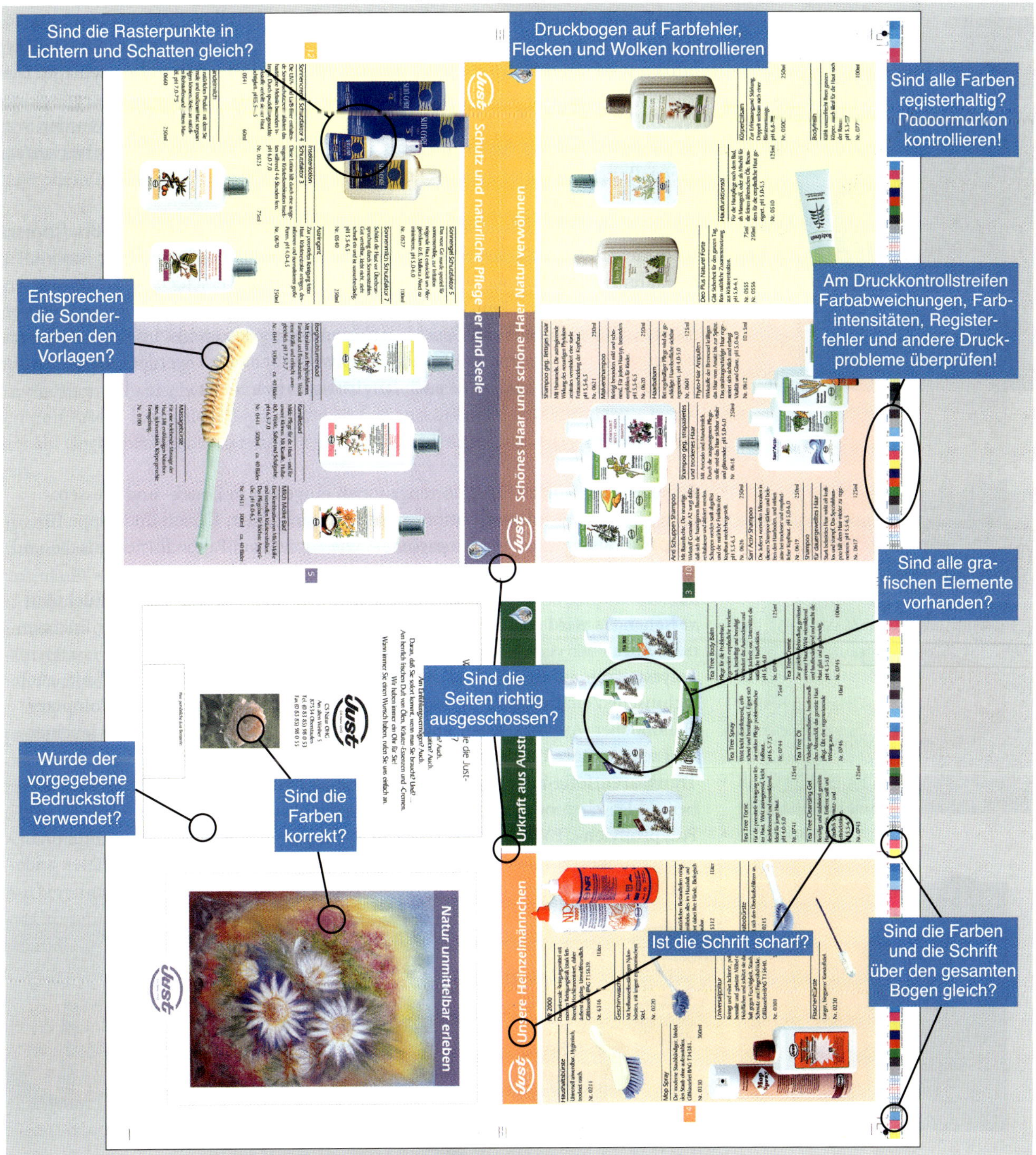

11.7.2 Falzen

In der Druckmaschine werden mit einer Druckplatte mehrere Seiten, in der Regel acht Seiten pro Bogen, gleichzeitig gedruckt. Damit die Buchseiten nach dem Druck in der seitenrichtigen Reihenfolge gebunden werden können, müssen sie schon auf der Druckplatte entsprechend angeordnet sein.

Dies geschieht in der Druckvorstufe durch Ausschießen der Dateien. Das angewandte Ausschießschema hängt von der Falzart ab, die nach dem Druck angewandt wird. Mit Falzmaschinen kann der Falzprozess wirtschaftlich durchgeführt werden. Neben den unten dargestellten Falzarten gibt es einige gebräuchliche wie den Kreuzbruchfalz, den Leporellofalz, der Wickelfalz oder auch Gemischtfalzungen wie Kreuz- und Parallelfalz.

Kreuzbruchfalz:
Der Bogen wird kreuzweise halbiert. Die Falzart wird auch nach der Anzahl der Brüche bezeichnet, z. B. Dreibruch.

Leporellofalz:
Prospekte oder Karten werden im Zickzack-Falz

Wickelfalz:
Beim Wickelfalz werden die Seiten in gleicher Richtung gefalzt oder „eingewickelt".

Für Werbematerial und Firmenpräsentationen werden heute häufig Gemischtfalzungen verwendet, die einzelne Bereiche der Seiten besonders hervorheben und durch die Art des Öffnens der Falzung eine bestimmte Lese- und Betrachtungsabfolge erzwingt.

Beim Falzen sei noch auf einen Effekt hingewiesen, der beim Zusammentragen für eine Rückstichheftung auftritt und mit Hilfe des Ausschießprogramms korrigiert werden kann, der **Bundzuwachs**. Dabei verschieben sich die Seiten in der Mitte des Buches nach außen, wodurch das gesamte Layout nach außen wandert. Durch eine Korrekturfunktion im Ausschießprogramm wird die Position des Satzspiegels jeder Seite verschoben und dadurch entsprechend der Seitenposition im Buch angepasst.

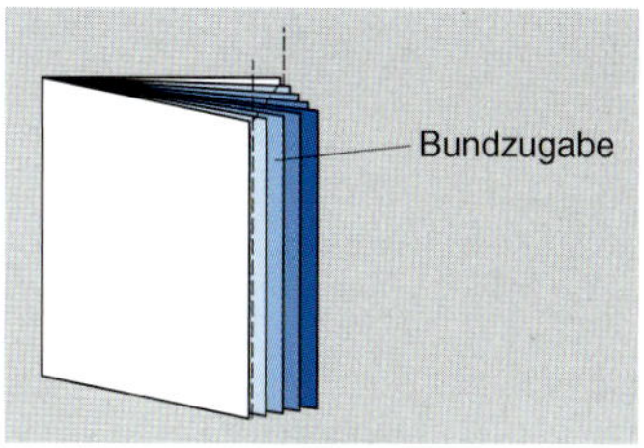

11.7.3 Binden

Alle Druckprodukte außer den Zeitungen werden nach dem Falzen noch gebunden. Die einzelnen Falzbogen eines Buchdrucks stellt man zu Buchblöcken zusammen und beschneidet sie.

Das Buchbinden hat viel Tradition und alte handwerkliche Buchbindeverfahren werden heute noch an wertvollen Büchern gepflegt. In der heutigen Zeit spielt jedoch die Wirtschaftlichkeit bei der Wahl des entsprechenden Buchbindeverfahrens eine große Rolle. Die Wahl der Bindetechnik hängt beispielsweise ab von der Auflagenhöhe und dem Buchpreis, von der Frage der Haltbarkeit hochwertig hergestellter Bücher oder auch davon, wie sich die Bücher und Dokumente aufschlagen lassen müssen. Einfache Firmendrucksachen und Tischvorlagen für Tagungen werden in kurzer Zeit mit klebelosen Bindungen hergestellt. Nachfolgend sind die heute wichtigsten Bindetechniken beschrieben und dargestellt.

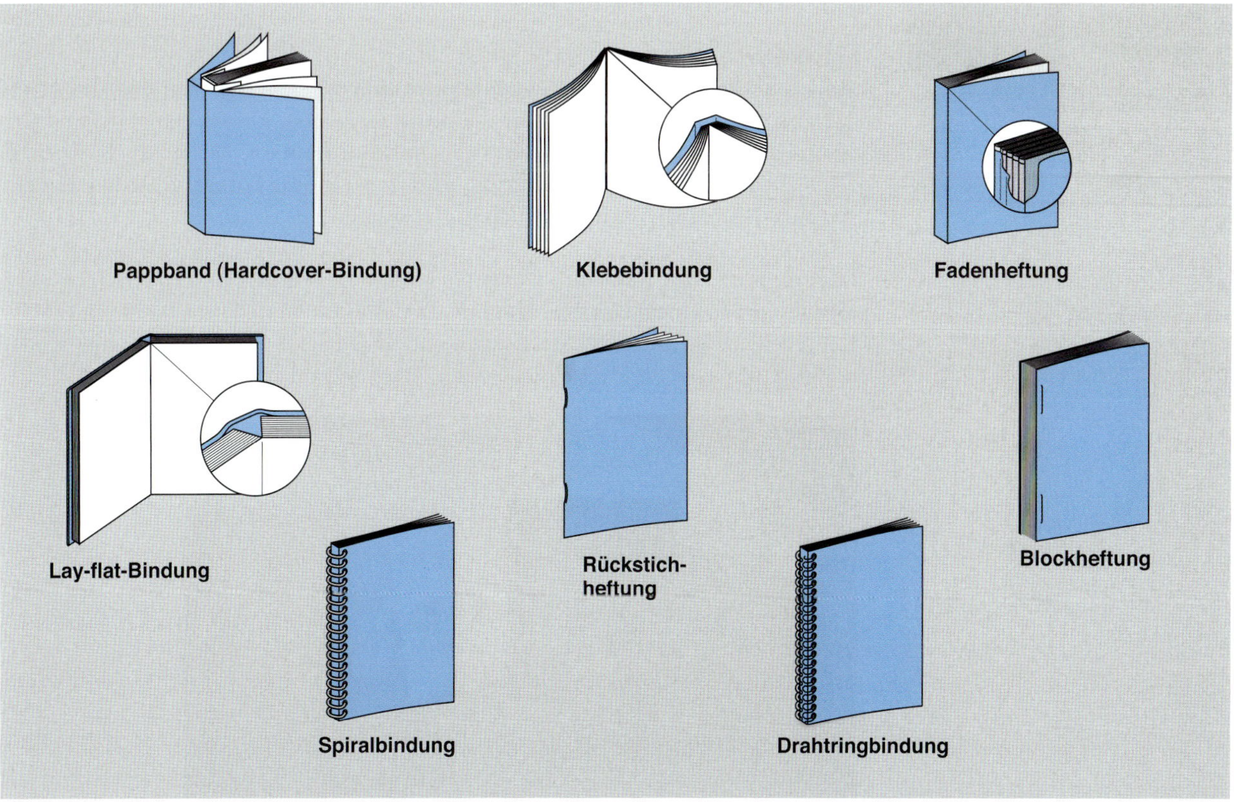

11.8 Praxis

Gestaltung und Herstellung eines Buches

Das Buch vereinigt in bester Weise den gesamten Workflow von der Idee bis zum Produkt im Druckbereich. Aus den drei Bausteinen Text, Bild und grafischen Elementen werden in einem Layoutprogramm Seiten gestaltet. Bei der Gestaltung der Seiten bieten sich verschiedene Möglichkeiten an vom goldenen Schnitt und der daraus abgeleiteten Varianten, über eine streng gerasterte Form bis zum freien Entwurf. Nach der Fertigstellung der Druckdateien, dem Ausschießen, Drucken, Falzen und Binden hält man ein individuelles Produkt in den Händen.

Eckdaten

Das Buch beschreibt und dokumentiert landes- und regionaltypische Merkmale, Charaktere und Besonderheiten, beispielsweise unter dem Titel „Schwäbische Anekdoten, Sprüche und Geschichten". Selbstverständlich lässt sich der Titel auch auf alle anderen Regionen des Landes anwenden.

Das Büchlein soll 16 Seiten beinhalten. Durch die Seitenbeschränkung wird eine inhaltliche Konzentration erreicht. Das Format ist beliebig bis zu einer Größe von DIN A4 frei wählbar, damit auch auf gängigen Bürodruckern gedruckt werden kann. Die Qualität und Farbe des Papiers ist frei wählbar. Das Buch soll in einer stabilen und verschleißfesten Ringbindung hergestellt werden.

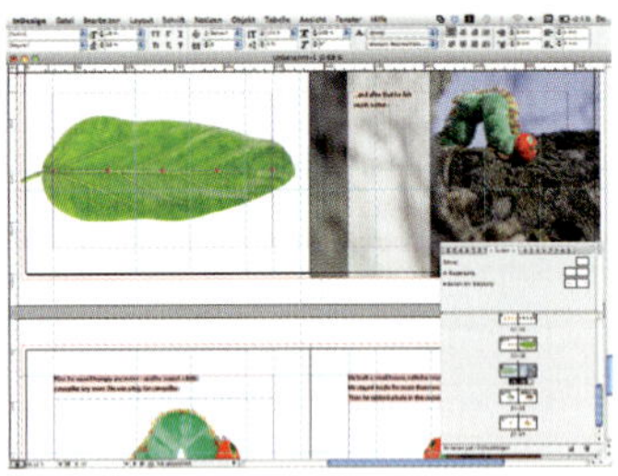

Vorgehensweise

Zunächst werden allgemeine Gestaltungsrichtlinien erstellt, die über den Einsatz von Schriftarten, -familien und -schnitte, eingesetzte Farben, Art der Fotografie und Grafik sowie über Längen- und Größenverhältnisse informiert. Wenn das Büchlein als Kundenauftrag hergestellt werden soll, dann muss ev. das Corporate Design und entsprechende Kundenvorgaben berücksichtigt werden.

Das Layout und die Umsetzung werden in Form von Freihandskizzen (Scribble) vorgearbeitet und in einem Layoutprogramm als Musterseiten mit Formatvorlagen erstellt. Die Seitenabfolge mit Titelblatt, geraden und ungeraden Seiten, Impressum u. a. wird im Entwurf geplant und anschließend die Seiten mit Inhalten gefüllt.

Aufgaben und Übungen, Literaturhinweise

Aufgaben und Übungen

1. Drucken Sie ein Bild mit unterschiedlichen Auflösungswerten bei gleicher Rasterweite aus. Vergleichen Sie die Qualität des Ausdrucks. Testen Sie unterschiedliche Drucker im Haus.
2. Recherchieren Sie in einer nahegelegenen Druckerei nach der praktizierten Umsetzung der Ausgabeverfahren Computer-to-Film, Computer-to-Plate und Computer-to-Press.
3. Stellen Sie den digitalen Workflow vom Entwurf bis zum Computer-to-Print mit einer Bildschirmpräsentation dar.
4. Sie wollen ein Bild mit einem 60er-Raster auf einem Laserdrucker mit 600 dpi oder einem Filmbelichter mit 1270 dpi ausgeben. Wieviele Graustufen (Tonwerte) sind darstellbar?
5. Ein Bild wird im Maßstab 1:1 gescannt. Die Rasterfrequenz des Ausgabeverfahrens ist 150 lpi. Wie hoch muss die Eingabeauflösung sein, bei einer Samplingrate 2?
6. Drucken Sie eine Bilddatei auf verschiedenen Papieren aus und vergleichen Sie die Druckqualität und die Ausgabe der Farben.
7. Stellen Sie am Beispiel eines PDF-Dokuments die Anwendungsmöglichkeiten dar, die sich in Verbindung mit dem Programm Acrobat ergeben.
8. Untersuchen Sie unterschiedliche Bücher hinsichtlich Gestaltung des Titels, Aufbau des Buches, Ordnungsprinzipien und Inhaltsverzeichnisstruktur.
9. Entwerfen Sie für ein Buch den Umschlag. Legen Sie für das Buch ein Format fest und zeichnen Sie einen Aufriss.
10. Stellen Sie auf einem DIN A3-Bogen ein achtseitiges Ausschießschema zusammen. Legen Sie die Falzabfolge fest und schneiden Sie anschließend den Bogen.

Literaturhinweise

Blana, Hubert: Die Herstellung: Ein Handbuch für die Gestaltung, Technik und Kalkulation von Buch, Zeitschrift und Zeitung, München 1998 (Verlag K.G. Saur)
Kipphan, Helmut (Hrsg.): Handbuch der Printmedien, Berlin, Heidelberg 2000 (Springer)
Schönstedt, Eduard: Der Buchverlag, 3. Aufl., Stuttgart 2010 (Metzler)
Teschner, Helmut: Druck- und Medientechnik, 13. Aufl., Konstanz 2010 (Christiani)
Holzki; *Rohloff*: Handinhandbuch, 7. Aufl., Berlin 2006 (satzinform, Berlin)
Martins; *Kobylinska*: PDF Workflow, Kilchberg 2002 (smartbooks)

12 Multimedia

Webcode: B1200

Für weitere Infos zu diesem Kapitel mit dem Smartphone einfach QR-Code scannen oder auf www.medien-verstehen.de den Webcode eingeben.

❶ Unter **Interaktivität** versteht man die Eingriffs- und Steuermöglichkeiten eines Systems durch den Benutzer.

Die Integration verschiedenartiger audiovisueller Medien auf einem Verbreitungsmedium (CD-ROM, Netzwerk, Internet, Diashow) mit einem bestimmten Kommunikationsziel wird im Allgemeinen unter dem Begriff **Multimedia** geführt.

In diesem Kapitel erfahren Sie, wie multimediale Anwendungen aufgebaut sind. Dabei geht es um die Aufbereitung und Strukturierung der Inhalte, der möglichen Interaktionen für den Anwender und die Gestaltung der Benutzeroberfläche.

Schon bei den klassischen audiovisuellen Medien, wie Film oder Dia-AV, werden Ton und Bild miteinander verknüpft, um eine gemeinsame Wirkung beim Betrachter zu erzielen. Erst die Möglichkeit, die verknüpften Einzelmedien auf dem Bildschirm darzustellen und zusätzlich das Dargestellte durch eine **Interaktivität** ❶ vom Betrachter abhängig zu machen, ist die eigentliche Revolution in den Medien, die weit mehr Wirkung beim Betrachter erreichen kann, als eine Gestaltung der Einzelmedien und deren Verknüpfung.

Text und Videosequenz in einem Multimedialen Informationssystem. Quelle: Retrospect, Spiegel Online.

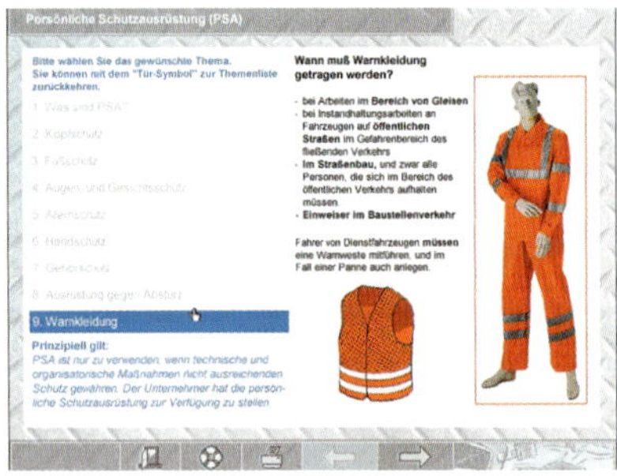

Abarbeiten eines strukturierten Lernpfades in einem multimedialen Lernsystem. Quelle: Interaktive Arbeitssicherheitsunterweisung, Siemens AG.

Interaktiv begehbare virtuelle Landschaft in einem Abenteuerspiel. Quelle: Myst III, Cyan Inc.

Dem Gestalter steht dazu fast die gesamte Palette der audiovisuellen Medien zur Verfügung. Hierzu gehören Text, Fotografie, Grafik, Animation, Film, Sprache, Soundeffekte und Musik sowie deren unterschiedliche Kombinationsmöglichkeiten mit und ohne Interaktivität. Eine multimediale Kombination muss natürlich nicht alle diese Elemente enthalten. Die gewünschte Wirkung beim Betrachter, also das Kommunikationsziel, steht im Vordergrund und sollte aus gestalterischen, didaktischen oder wirtschaftlichen Gründen die Kombination der Einzelmedien bestimmen.

12.1 Multimediale Anwendungen

Multimediale Programme sind interaktive Anwendungen, die aus Inhalten mit multimedialen Komponenten, wie Text, Bild, Video und Ton, bestehen. Je nach Verwendung unterscheidet man zwischen Informations-, Lern-, Präsentations- und Unterhaltungssystemen.

12.1.1 Informationssysteme

Unter Informationssystemen versteht man multimediale Programme, die durch wenige Mausklicks Informationen zu einem oder mehreren Themen anbieten. Die Darstellung der Information kann in Form unterschiedlicher Medien erfolgen.

➲ **Die prägnante Eigenschaft eines Informationssystems ist der schnelle Zugang zur Information.**

Beispiele sind Kiosk-Systeme, Enzyklopädien, multimediale Lexika usw.

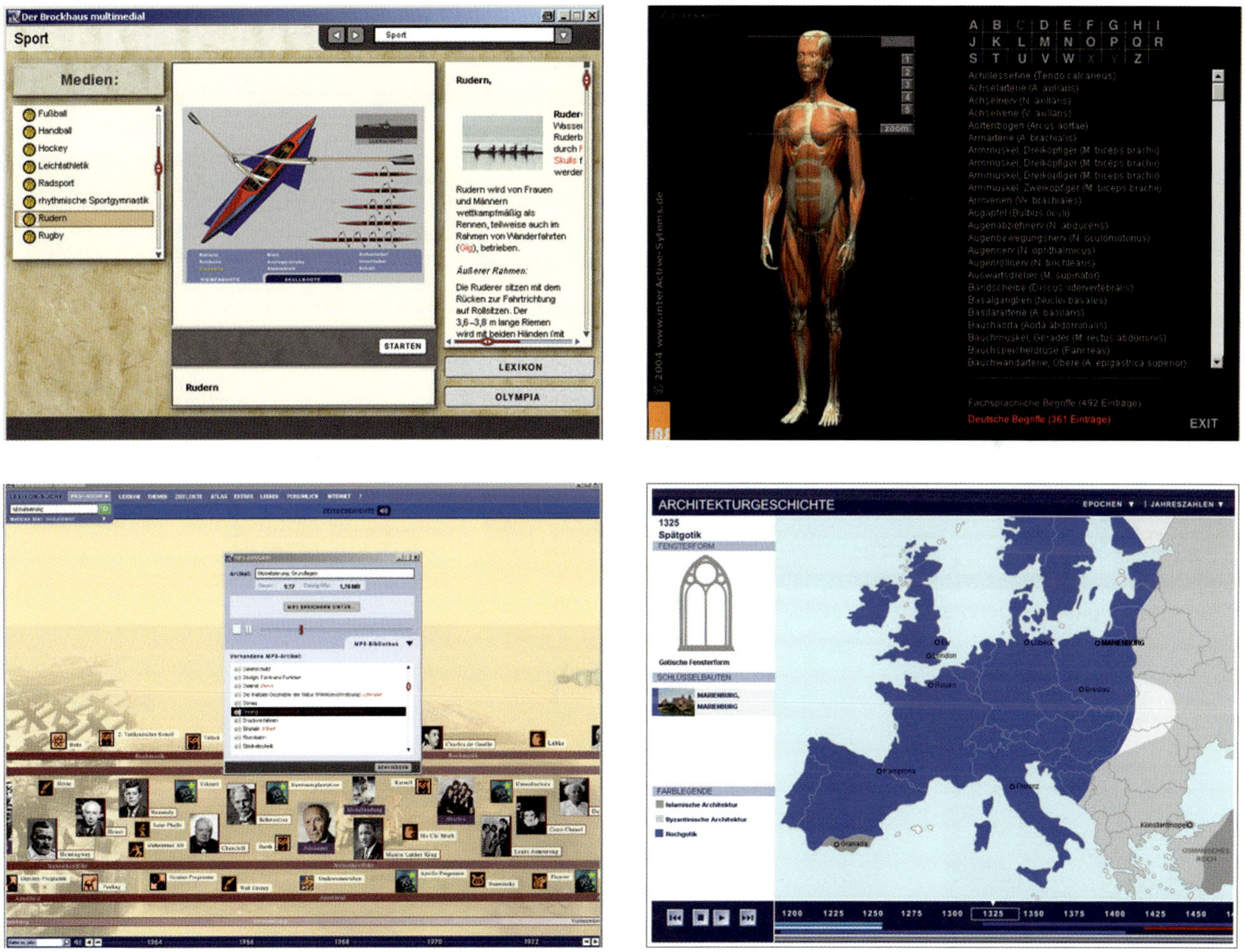

Beispiel eines Multimedialen Informationssystems: Der Brockhaus multimedial 2010. Quelle: F.A. Brockhaus AG.

Technisch realisiert werden Informationssysteme über Programmiersprachen ❶ oder Autorensysteme in der Regel mit Datenbankanbindungen. Bei Online-Informationssystemen kommen serverseitige Script-Sprachen, wie z. B. PHP, zum Einsatz, um Internet-kompatibel zu sein.

❶ Im Kapitel Medieninformatik erfahren Sie mehr über Programmiersprachen und Autorenwerkzeuge zur Erstellung multimedialer Anwendungen.

12.1.2 Lernsysteme

❶ Unter **Computer Based Training** versteht man das Lernen mit Hilfe von lokal gespeicherten Lernprogrammen.
Beim **Web Based Training** erfolgt das Lernen web-basiert über das Internet.

Didaktisch aufbereitete Inhalte zum Selbststudium werden von Lernsystemen angeboten. Hierzu sind die Lernthemen sinnvoll aufeinander aufbauend abgestimmt. Durch einen zielgruppenspezifischen Lernweg und Lernerfolgskontrollen wird sichergestellt, dass das Lernziel erreicht wird.

➲ **Bei Lernsystemen steht das Lernen nach didaktischen Gesichtspunkten im Vordergrund.**

Um das Lernziel zu erreichen, bedarf es neben den multimedialen Inhalten zusätzlich interaktiver Komponenten zur Motivation des Lernenden. Beispiele sind **Computer Based Training (CBT)** und **Web Based Training** (WBT) ❶ über das Internet.

CBT-Beispiel Digitale Fotografie. Quelle: National Geographics.

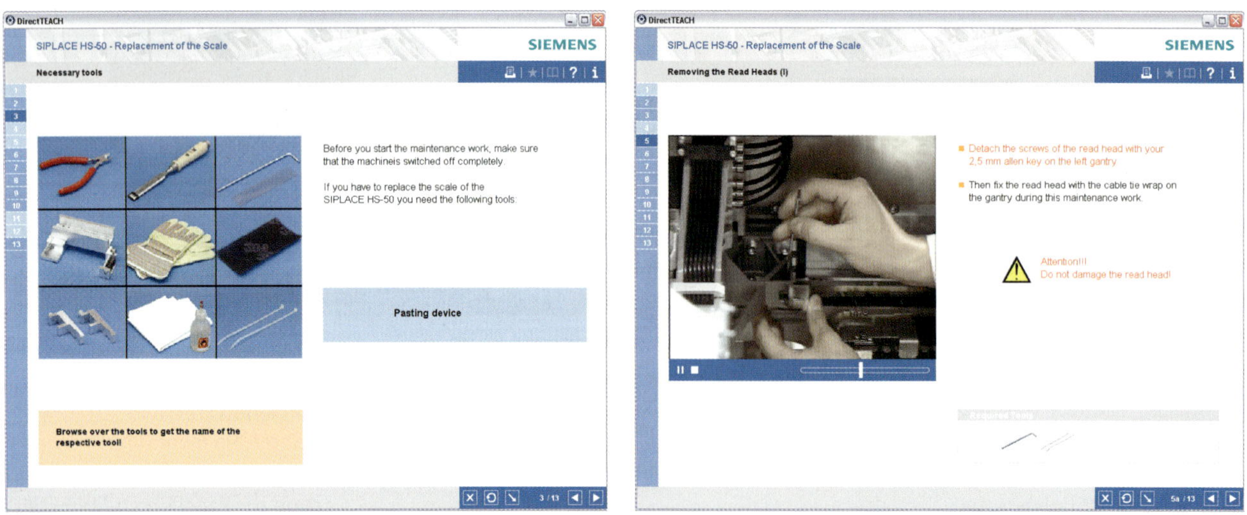

WBT-Beispiel: SIPLACE Scale Replacing. Quelle: Siemens AG.

Technisch realisiert werden Lernsysteme in der Regel mit Autorensystemen, die für die Lernanwendung schon spezifische Funktionen von Haus aus mitbringen.

12.1.3 Präsentationssysteme

Wo mit multimedialen Inhalten neue Themen, Produkte und Sachverhalte vorgestellt und präsentiert werden sollen, findet man Präsentationssysteme. Dies kann sowohl im kommerziellen Bereich, zum Beispiel in der Werbung und Verkaufsförderung, als auch im nicht kommerziellen Bereich, zum Beispiel einer in Expeditions-Präsentation geschehen. Die Führung und Steuerung durch das Thema kann dabei über einen Live-Kommentar des Referenten oder automatisch per Programmsteuerung erfolgen.

❶ **Multivision** (Multidisplay) nutzt mehrere nebeneinander angeordnete Projektionsflächen für die multimediale Präsentation.

Großformatige HDAV-Präsentationen auf mehrere Projektionsflächen.
Quelle: Werner Kenzel bei einem Multivisons-Vortrag mit AV-Systeme von Stumpfl.

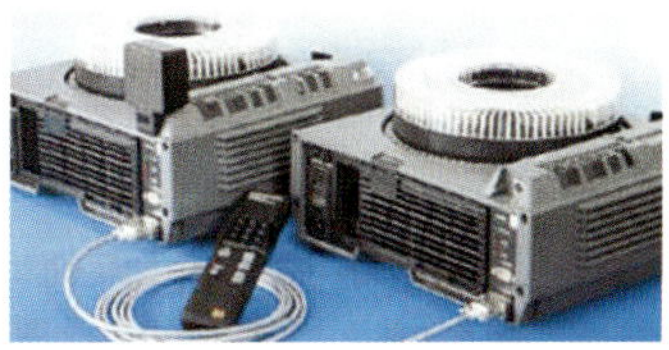

❷ PC-gesteuerte Dia-Projektoren.
Quelle: Kodak

➲ **Bei Präsentationssystemen steht die geführte Vorstellung von Themen im Fokus.**

Technisch realisiert können Präsentationssysteme über Standard-Software-Produkte, angefangen bei Microsoft Powerpoint bis hin zu spezialisierten Software-Produkten für **Multivisionen** ❶ über **HDAV-Präsentationstechnik**.

HDAV steht für „High Definition Audio Vision" und ist ein Qualitätsstandard für digitale Audiovisions-Produktionen. Es unterstützt volle Medienintegration (Bild, Video, Ton) und Multivisions-Projektion über Video-Beamer.

Aber auch über PC-gesteuerte Diaprojektoren ❷ sind Multivisionen möglich. Diese als **Dia-Audiovision** (Dia-AV) bezeichnete Technik, kombiniert Bild und Ton in einer gesteuerten Präsentation.

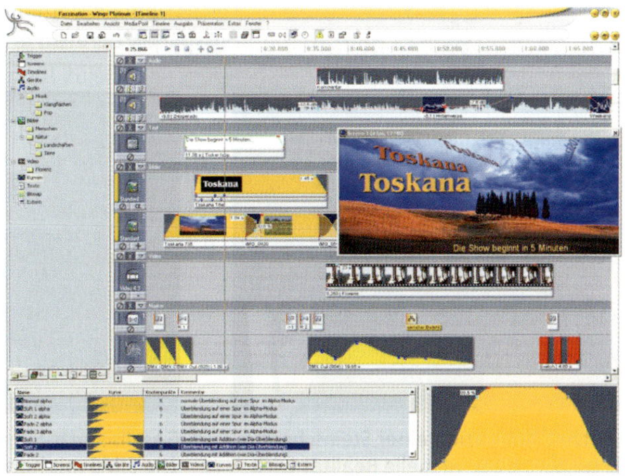

Multivisions Software Wings Platinum
Quelle: AV-Systeme von Stumpfl.

Spannung kann erzeugt werden durch:
- Neugierde
- Überraschung
- Humor
- Erregung
- Kontraste

❶

❷

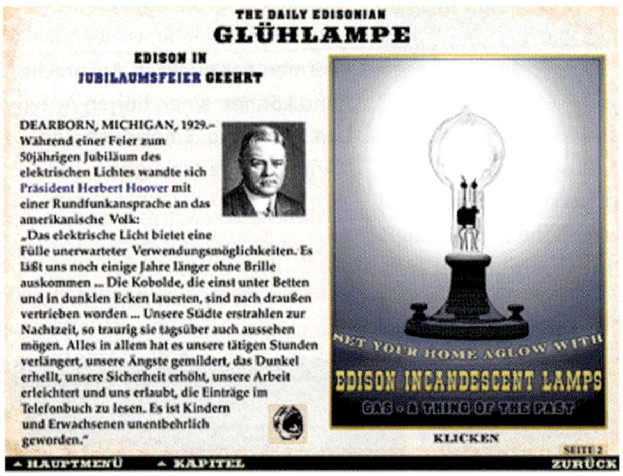

❸

❹

Dramaturgischer Aufbau einer Informations-Anwendung:

❶ Die Auswahl der Themen erfolgt zur Aufmerksamkeitserregung über ein drehendes Themenrad.

❷ Jedes Thema wird über einen ansprechenden Einführungsfilm vorgestellt.

❸, ❹ Jeder einzelne Informationsblock innerhalb eines Themas weist einen eigenen dramaturgischen Bogen auf.

Bildreihe ❶ bis ❹ aus: Edison, der Zauber von Menlo Park, Tewi Verlag GmbH

Der dramaturgische Aufbau besteht immer aus einzelnen Bausteinen, die didaktische Aufgaben übernehmen. Die dramaturgischen Höhen visualisiert man am besten mit Hilfe eines Schemas.

Beispielschema eines Dramas:

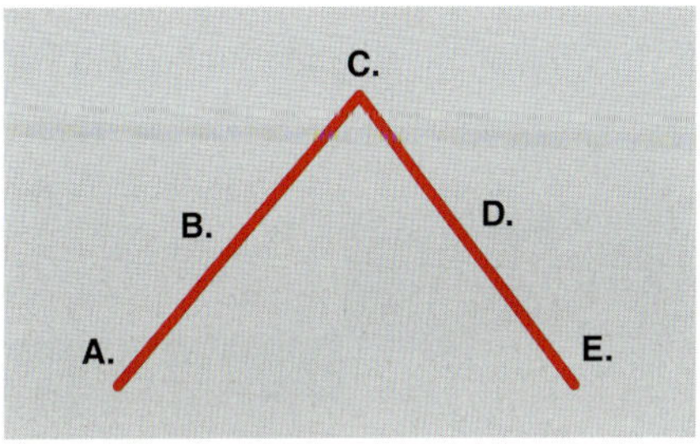

A. Einführung
B. Steigerung
C. Höhepunkt
D. Fallende Handlung
E. Katastrophe und Schluss

Beispielschema einer Promotion-CD:

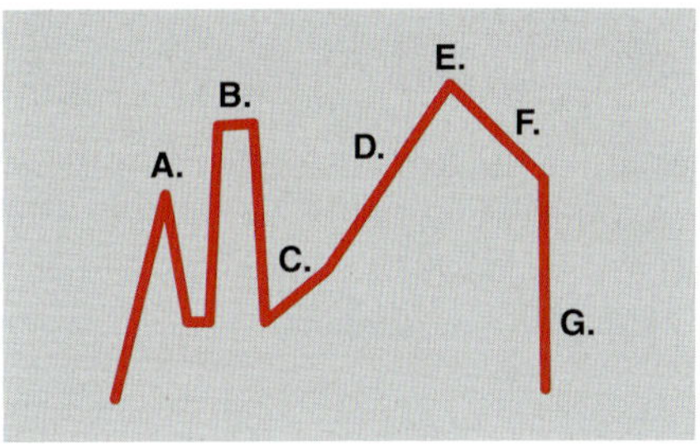

A. Vorstellung / Intro
B. Problemdarstellung
C. Marktanalyse
D. Strategie-Vorstellung
E. Ideen / Lösungspräsentation
F. Fazit
G. Entscheidungsphase

Ein dramaturgischer Spannungsbogen ist auch innerhalb einer Sequenz denkbar – und da befindet man sich wieder auf der Ebene des linearen Films.

➲ **Dramaturgisch geschickt aufgebaute Konstruktionen verfügen über einen großen Bogen, der das Gesamtthema „zusammenhält", sowie über mehrere kleine dramaturgische Einheiten.**

Durch die Interaktivität und die dadurch freie Auswahl der Sequenzen sollte sichergestellt sein, dass dem großen Spannungsbogen keine allzu gewichtige Bedeutung zukommt. Zu leicht könnte sonst das dramaturgische Gesamtziel verfälscht werden, wenn einzelne kleine dramaturgische Einheiten ausgelassen werden.

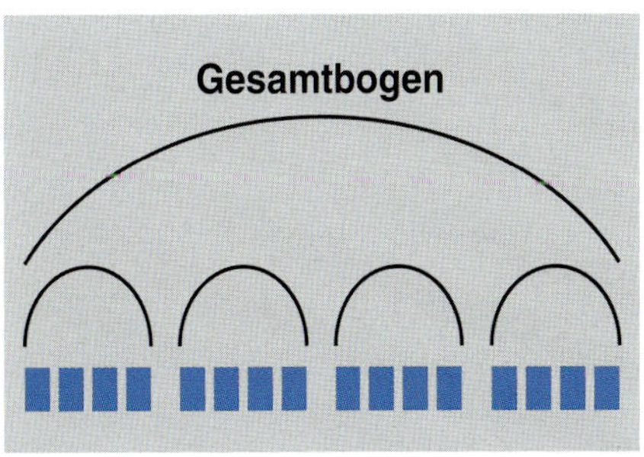

Jede einzelne Sequenz ist für sich abgeschlossen und beinhaltet bei Bedarf einen eigenen Spannungsbogen.

12.2.3 Montage

Die Verknüpfung zwischen Bild und Ton unter dramaturgischen Gesichtspunkten erzielt eine ganzheitlich wirkende Aussage.

Beim Medium Film und Video geschieht dies durch den Schnitt bzw. dem Editieren; in der Dia-AV durch dramaturgisch eingesetzte Überblendtechnik und im Bereich von Multimedia durch eine Vermischung dieser Techniken.

Die Art und Weise, wie diese Verknüpfung aufgebaut werden kann, wird „Montage“ genannt.

➲ **Montage ist eine visuell gewordene Assoziation, die den einzelnen Medienelementen erst ihren endgültigen Sinn verleiht.**

Montage kann nach verschiedenen Ansätzen unterschieden werden:

Montage von Raum und Zeit:
Bei der erzählenden Montage wird der Inhalt einer Einstellung oder eines Bildes als Ursache des Inhalts der folgenden Einstellung bzw. Bilder verstanden und kontinuierlich und damit chronologisch verknüpft. Werden zwei oder mehrere ineinandergreifende Handlungsstränge dramaturgisch zu einem Auflösungspunkt zusammengeführt, spricht man von einer Parallelmontage.

Montage als Ideen-Assoziation:
Hier werden weniger die real abgebildeten Gegenstände miteinander montiert und in Beziehung ❶ gesetzt, sondern vielmehr die gedanklichen Assoziationen und Gefühle, die sie auslösen oder die Bedeutung, auf die die Bilder verweisen.

❶ Bei dieser Montageart gibt es verschiedene dramaturgische Ansätze:

- **Assoziations-Montage**, bei der gedankliche Assoziationen und Gefühle miteinander in Beziehung gesetzt werden.
- **Ersatzmontage**, welche Augenblicke, die nicht gezeigt werden sollen, durch Ersatzbilder abdeckt. Zum Beispiel eine stehengebliebene Uhr für den Tod.
- **Metaphorische Montage**, die sich auf die Symbolkraft der Bildkombinationen stützt.

Montage als Formalprinzip:
Bei der formalen Montage werden nach ästhetischen Gesichtspunkten Objekte nach Form, Farbe und Bewegung verknüpft. Dabei liegen die Kriterien ausschließlich im optisch-grafischen Bereich.

12.2.4 Umsetzung

Die eigentliche Umsetzung der didaktischen und dramaturgischen Konzepte erfolgt hauptsächlich beim Prozess des Drehbuchschreibens. Dies setzt voraus, dass die grundsätzlichen Ideen in Form der Grobkonzeption bzw. des Treatments schon zu Papier gebracht worden sind. Wie setzt der Multimedia-Autor diese Ideen in einem Drehbuch um?

➲ **Ein Drehbuch für eine Multimedia-Produktion wird für Zuschauer, Zuhörer und weniger für Leser verfasst. Literarische Rhetorik ist weniger gefragt, als ausdrucksstarke Bildersprache in Verbindung mit kurzen, prägnanten Text- und Sprachelementen.**

Ein möglicher theoretischer Ansatz für diesen Denkprozess könnte folgendermaßen ausschauen:

1. Stufe
Zunächst formuliert man im Geist den Gedanken, den man mitteilen möchte.

2. Stufe
Man stellt sich eine Folge von Bildern zusammen, die diesen Gedanken veranschaulichen oder illustrieren. Dies können Realbilder, Filmsequenzen oder grafische Darstellungen sein.

3. Stufe
Dann schreibt man einen Teil des Text- bzw. Sprecherkommentars nieder.

Gedanklicher Entwicklungsprozess:

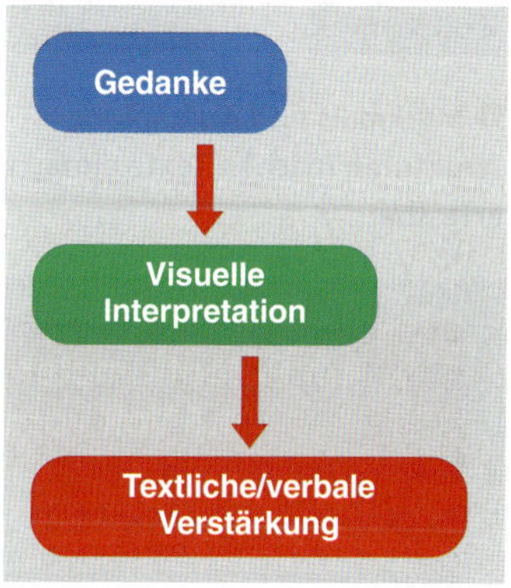

Verständlichkeit

Der Anspruch auf verständliches Schreiben ist nicht neu. Schon seit den Anfängen des Films sind Ausdrucksweise und die Strukturierung und Größe der Inhaltseinheiten gegenüber der Literatur neu definiert worden.

Eine grundsätzliche Regel für Drehbuch-Autoren, die sowohl für Text als auch für Sprachpassagen gilt:

➲ **Man muss in kurzen, klaren, einfach verständlichen Sätzen schreiben. Niemals sollte man lange oder komplizierte Sätze, ungewöhnliche Ausdrücke oder seltene Fremdwörter verwenden – auf keinen Fall einen verschachtelten Satzaufbau.**

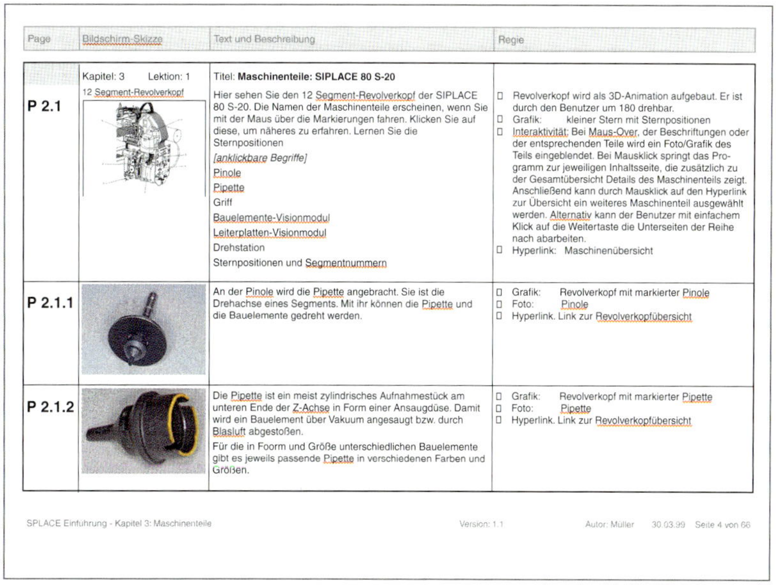

Page	Bildschirm-Skizze	Text und Beschreibung	Regie
P 2.1	Kapitel: 3 Lektion: 1 12 Segment-Revolverkopf	Titel: **Maschinenteile: SIPLACE 80 S-20** Hier sehen Sie den 12 Segment-Revolverkopf der SIPLACE 80 S-20. Die Namen der Maschinenteile erscheinen, wenn Sie mit der Maus über die Markierungen fahren. Klicken Sie auf diese, um näheres zu erfahren. Lernen Sie die Sternpositionen *[anklickbare Begriffe]* Pinole Pipette Griff Bauelemente-Visionmodul Leiterplatten-Visionmodul Drehstation Sternpositionen und Segmentnummern	☐ Revolverkopf wird als 3D-Animation aufgebaut. Er ist durch den Benutzer um 180 drehbar. ☐ Grafik: kleiner Stern mit Sternpositionen ☐ Interaktivität: Bei Maus-Over, der Beschriftungen oder der entsprechenden Teile wird ein Foto/Grafik des Teils eingeblendet. Bei Mausklick springt das Programm zur jeweiligen Inhaltsseite, die zusätzlich zu der Gesamtübersicht Details des Maschinenteils zeigt. Anschließend kann durch Mausklick auf den Hyperlink zur Übersicht ein weiteres Maschinenteil ausgewählt werden. Alternativ kann der Benutzer mit einfachem Klick auf die Weitertaste die Unterseiten der Reihe nach abarbeiten. ☐ Hyperlink: Maschinenübersicht
P 2.1.1		An der Pinole wird die Pipette angebracht. Sie ist die Drehachse eines Segments. Mit ihr können die Pipette und die Bauelemente gedreht werden.	☐ Grafik: Revolverkopf mit markierter Pinole ☐ Foto: Pinole ☐ Hyperlink. Link zur Revolverkopfübersicht
P 2.1.2		Die Pipette ist ein meist zylindrisches Aufnahmestück am unteren Ende der Z-Achse in Form einer Ansaugdüse. Damit wird ein Bauelement über Vakuum angesaugt bzw. durch Blasluft abgestoßen. Für die in Foorm und Größe unterschiedlichen Bauelemente gibt es jeweils passende Pipette in verschiedenen Farben und Größen.	☐ Grafik: Revolverkopf mit markierter Pipette ☐ Foto: Pipette ☐ Hyperlink. Link zur Revolverkopfübersicht

SPLACE Einführung - Kapitel 3: Maschinenteile   Version: 1.1   Autor: Müller   30.03.99   Seite 4 von 66

Beispiel einer Drehbuch-Seite eines technischen CBTs. Kurze und klare Sätze (siehe Textspalte) prägen dieses Medium (Quelle: Siemens AG)

12.3 Struktur

In dieser Lektion geht es um den strukturellen Aufbau von multimedialen Kompositionen. Anders als beim sequentiellen Aufbau der Bildelemente beim Medium Film und Video eröffnen sich bei interaktiven Medien eine Vielzahl von Möglichkeiten, wie Inhalte und Informationszugänge strukturiert werden können.

Welcher strukturelle Ansatz sinnvoll ist, hängt u. a. von der Art, dem Einsatz und der Zielgruppe, also dem Anwender, der Medienproduktion ab.

12.3.1 Strukturwahl

Um eine für den Zweck optimale Struktur zu finden, ist es sinnvoll, zunächst die unterschiedlichen Arten einer multimedialen Komposition zu klassifizieren. Bei der Unterscheidung nach der Klassifizierung, ob die Medien für einen **begrenzten Zeitraum** oder für **permanente Wiederverwendbarkeit** konzipiert worden sind, werden generell zwei Bereiche unterschieden:

- **Multimedia-Systeme**, die produziert und gleichzeitig konsumiert werden. Darunter fallen Videokonferenzen am PC, Online-Teaching, Multimedia-Mail etc.
- Multimedia-Systeme, die zeitversetzt produziert und konsumiert werden. Darunter fallen alle Multimedia-Produktionen, die sich immer wieder benutzen lassen. Das sind z. B. Lernprogramme, Präsentationsprogramme, Informationssysteme etc.

In den weiteren Betrachtungen bezüglich einer Multimedia-Produktion wird nur auf die zuletzt genannten Systeme eingegangen und diese aus praktischen Gründen folgendermaßen klassifiziert:

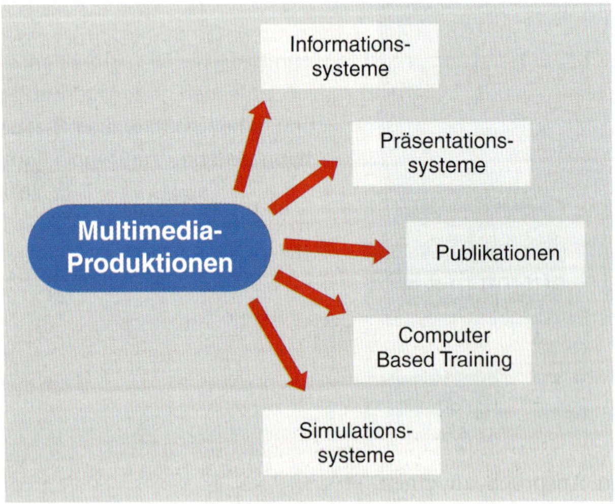

- **Informationssysteme**:
  Kiosk-Systeme, Kataloge, Online-Dokumentation, Lexika, Landkarten/Atlanten, Ausstellungs-Guide
- **Präsentationssysteme**:
  Produktvorstellungen, Firmenpräsentationen
- **Publikationen**:
  Fachmagazine, Multimedia-Zeitschriften
- **Lernsysteme**:
  Computer Based Training (CBT), Web Based Training (WBT)
- **Simulationssysteme**:
  Beratungssysteme für den Vertrieb, Kundendialog-Systeme

Natürlich sind noch weitere Produktarten im Rahmen von Multimedia denkbar, jedoch vom heutigen Standpunkt aus gesehen ist es sinnvoll, sich auf die oben genannten Produktarten zu beschränken. Schon im Rahmen des Grobkonzeptes macht sich das Produktionsteam Gedanken über die richtige Struktur des Multimedia-Programms.

Die grundsätzlichen Programmstrukturen werden über Metaphern ausgedrückt. Strukturelle Metapherszenarien verbildlichen die grundlegenden Bedingungen, nach denen die Informationsaufbereitung und Strukturierung des Lernprogramm-Ablaufes erfolgt. Ein Ablaufdiagramm, auch „**Flowchart**“ genannt, veranschaulicht diese Metapher durch eine symbolorientierte Darstellung von zusammenhängenden Abläufen.

Grundsätzlich lassen sich diese Metaphern in drei verschiedene **Verknüpfungsmodelle**, auch „**Flowdesign**“ genannt, unterteilen, die in der Praxis oft in Kombinationen auftreten:

- Leiter-Metapher
- Baum-Metapher
- Netzwerk-Metapher

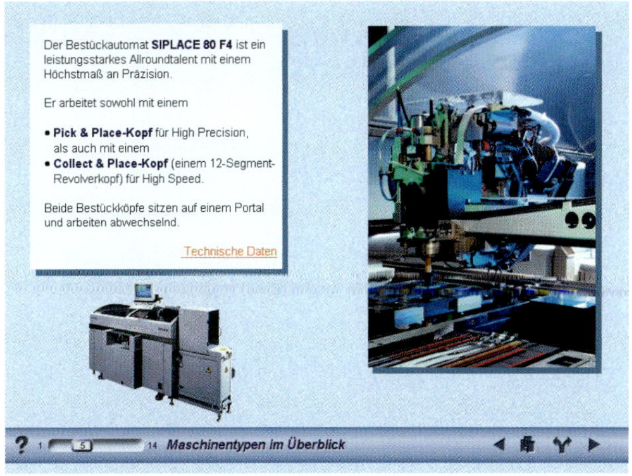

CBT-Lernprogramme mit aufeinander aufbauenden Inhalten weisen oft eine Struktur nach der Leiter-Metapher auf, da der Anwender die Inhalte sequentiell durcharbeiten soll. (Beispiel: CBT für SIPLACE – Siemens AG)

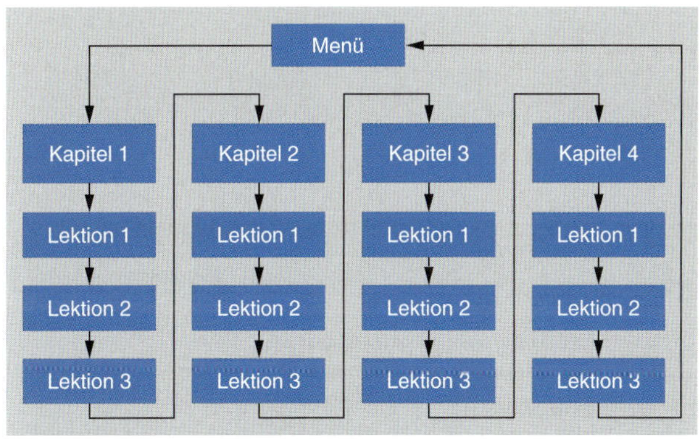

12.3.2 Leiter-Metapher

Ein einfaches Beispiel für die Leiter-Metapher ist die lineare Präsentation (z. B. mit dem Programm Microsoft Powerpoint). Auch für Lernprogramme, die aufeinander aufbauende Inhalte besitzen, eignet sich die Leiter-Metapher als Verknüpfungsmodell. Eine **lineare Abfolge** von aufeinanderfolgenden Informationseinheiten, bzw. Lernabschnitten, kennzeichnet diese Metapher. Diese Struktur bietet eine etwas eingeschränkte Interaktivität, die aber einige didaktische Vorteile für CBT-Programme mitbringt. Sie stellt am besten sicher, dass alle aufeinanderfolgenden Lernabschnitte dem Lerner automatisch angeboten werden und unterstützt so die beabsichtigten Lernziele.

12.3.3 Baum-Metapher

Die Baum-Metapher gliedert die Informations- bzw. Lerneinheiten **hierarchisch** von oben nach unten. Von einem Hauptmenü gelangt man zu mehreren Untermenüs. Die Übersichtlichkeit kann je nach Menütiefe, d. h. wie viel Untermenüs werden verwendet, und je nach Menübreite, d. h. wie viel Untermenüs werden parallel angeboten, stark schwanken. Die betreffende Zielgruppe sollte hierbei als Kriterium für das „Flowdesign“ herangezogen werden. Je weniger die Zielgruppe mit dem Medium vertraut ist, desto weniger sollte in die Menübreite strukturiert werden, sondern eher in die Menütiefe, bei der der Lerner mehr das Gefühl des Geführtwerdens hat.

Informations-Anwendungen sollen dem Anwender die größtmögliche Freiheit geben, sich die Inhalte anzuschauen, für die er sich interessiert. (Beispiel: Präsentation Audi TT – Audi)

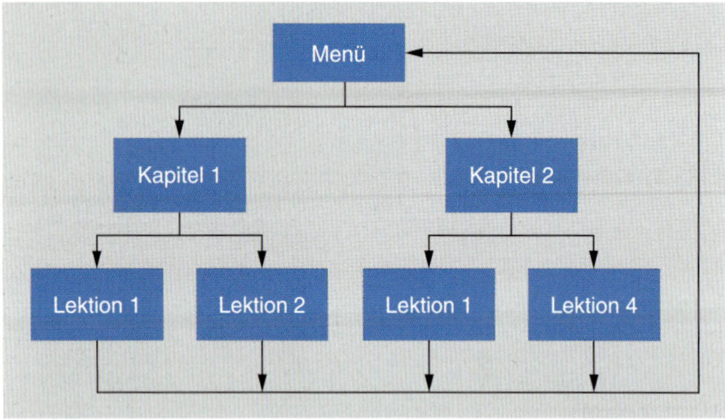

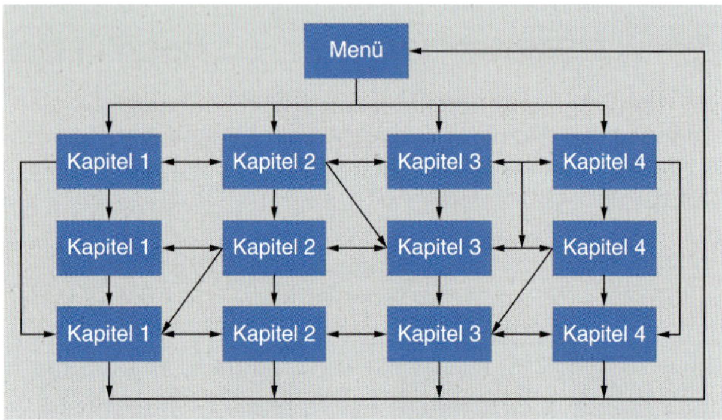

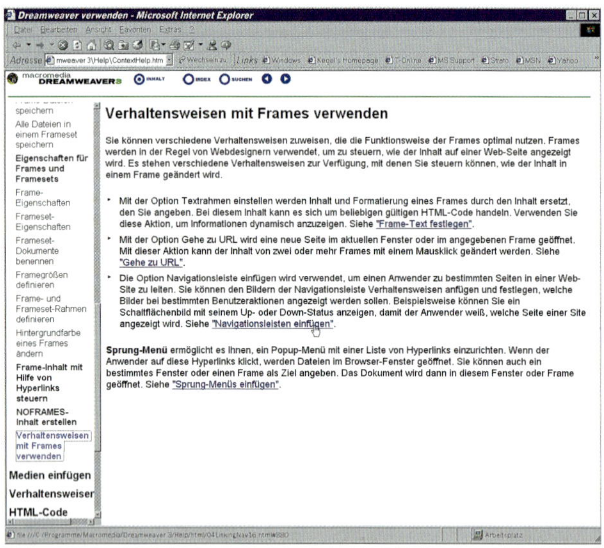

HTML-basierende Lernprogramme weisen oft starke Hypertext-Anteile auf. Damit ist ein schneller kontextbezogener Wechsel zwischen den Inhaltsteilen möglich. (Beispiel: Lernprogramm Dreamweaver – Macromedia).

Ist der Lerner mit dem Medium vertrauter, so erwartet er möglichst rasch, d. h. ohne über viele Menü-Auswahlschritte gehen zu müssen, den gewünschtem Lernstoff präsentiert zu bekommen.

Die Baum-Metapher erfordert im Gegensatz zur Leiter-Metapher eine höhere Gedächtnisleistung vom Lerner, damit er nicht die Orientierung verliert. Sie bietet aber den größten Freiheitsgrad bezüglich der Informationswahl in einem Lernprogramm.

Sie kann zusätzlich durch übergreifende Funktionen wie „Hilfe“, „Drucken“, „Exit“, „Lexikon“ oder Ähnliches ergänzt werden. Solche Sonderfunktionen können trotz Baumstruktur ebenenübergreifend von jeder Informationsseite aus zugänglich gemacht werden.

12.3.4 Netzwerk-Metapher

Die Netzwerk-Metapher eignet sich prinzipiell weniger als „Flowdesign“ für CBT-Lernprogramme. Die Informationsverknüpfungen und Programmverzweigungen lassen zwar vielfältige Bearbeitungswege des Lerners zu, so dass sogar spontane Bewegungen in beinahe **alle Richtungen** möglich sind; eine Lenkung bzw. Führung des Lerners durch die Lernprogrammthematik ist bei dieser Struktur aber nur bedingt möglich. Die Gefahr, dass der Lerner die Orientierung im Programm verliert, ist ziemlich hoch und erfordert von ihm eine gewisse Disziplin bei der Auswahl und Inanspruchnahme der Informationsangebote.

Die Struktur der Netzwerk-Metapher trifft man vorwiegend bei **Hypertext-** und **Hypermediasystemen** an, die primär als Informationssystem konzipiert sind, da hierbei der Benutzer möglichst frei in einer Informationsvielfalt recherchieren soll.

Unter Hypertext versteht man sensitive Textbereiche (dargestellt durch eine Unterstreichung oder eine andere Textfarbe) auf der Bildschirmseite. Durch Klick auf diesen Bereich erfolgt eine Aktion, entweder das Einblenden eines Zusatztextes oder der Sprung (**Hyperlink**) zu einer anderen Seite.

12.4 Interaktionen

In dieser Lektion geht es um die Interaktionen bei multimedialen Kompositionen. Interaktionen sind eine Form der Interaktivität. Die Interaktivität ermöglicht dem Anwender, sein Programm zu steuern, zu kontrollieren und Informationen auszuwählen. Je mehr Möglichkeiten der Anwender hat, in sein Programm einzugreifen und mit ihm zu kommunizieren, desto höher ist der Interaktivitätsgrad.

Interaktivitätsgrad	Beschreibung
1. Lineare Navigation	Der Anwender kann auf festen Pfaden vor- und zurück navigieren.
2. Nonlineare Navigation	Der Anwender kann uneingeschränkt durch die Informationen navigieren.
3. Medienkontrolle	Der Anwender kann Video- und Toneinstellungen vornehmen und Texte nach bestimmten Begriffen durchsuchen.
4. Ein- und Ausgabefunktionen	Der Anwender kann Daten eingeben, ausdrucken oder versenden.
5. Konfigurierbarkeit	Der Anwender kann Spiel- und Lernsituationen selbst bestimmen und in diese eingreifen.
6. Erweiterbarkeit	Der Anwender kann Informationen hinzufügen oder verändern.
7. Integration	Der Anwender wird durch neue Schnittstellen, wie Datenhandschuh, Augenabtastung und Spracherkennung in das System integriert.
8. Anpassung	Die Anwendung ist in der Lage, sich vom Anwender ein Benutzerprofil zu erstellen, und kann seine Funktion dementsprechend einstellen

Das Spektrum der Interaktivität zieht sich von einfachen Anwendungen mit linearer Navigation, über Informations- und Katalogsysteme mit Suchfunktionen und Möglichkeiten, Medien zu steuern, bis hin zu komplexen Lernanwendungen mit Auswertemöglichkeit von Benutzereingaben und der davon abhängigen Funktionalität.

➲ **Das richtige Maß an Interaktivität, bezogen auf den Anwender und der Zielsetzung der multimedialen Komposition, entscheidet oft über die Akzeptanz des Mediums.**

Zuviel Interaktivität kann den Anwender leicht überfordern und führt zur Desorientierung in der Fülle aller angebotenen Informationen und Möglichkeiten. Der Begriff „Lost in Hyperspace" beschreibt den Zustand eines Anwenders, wenn er seinen Standpunkt und seine Herkunft in der Anwendung nicht mehr genau definieren kann.

Interaktionen von einfachen Informationsabrufen bis zu Simulationen von Abläufen. (Beispiel: Das Wetter – Systhema Verlag GmbH).

Der Begriff „**Cognitive Overload**" beschreibt die Situation des Anwenders, wenn er die Fülle der Informationen nicht mehr adäquat verarbeiten kann.

Deshalb übernehmen die Elemente und Ausprägungen der Interaktionen eine sehr wichtige Rolle im Kommunikationsprozess und der Akzeptanz der interaktiven, multimedialen Kompositionen.

12.4.1 Dialog- und Benutzerführung

Aufgabe und Funktion

Damit der Benutzer die Inhalte einer multimedialen Anwendung erschließen kann, bedarf es einer sorgfältig überlegten Benutzerführung. Diese **Benutzerführung** erlaubt dem Benutzer, mit Hilfe von Zeichen, Symbolen und typografischen Elementen eine selbstständige Steuerung des Programms innerhalb der vorhandenen Struktur. Somit stellt sie die Schnittstelle zwischen Medium und Mensch dar. Ihre logische und ergonomische Gestaltung ist sehr entscheidend für eine Akzeptanz des Mediums bei der entsprechenden Zielgruppe. Dabei muss besondere Rücksicht auf die Fähigkeiten und Vorlieben der Zielgruppe genommen werden.

Ein ansprechendes und funktionales Design der Benutzerführung weist eine klare Trennung zwischen Inhalten und Navigationselementen auf.

➲ **Die Benutzerführung sollte nicht Selbstzweck sein, sondern nur den Zugang zu den Inhalten ermöglichen.**

Beispiel einer spielerischen Umsetzung einer Benutzeroberfläche. Themenspezifische Objekte als Metaphern stellen den Zugang zu den Inhalten dar.
(Rüdiger Nehberg – SURVIVAL)

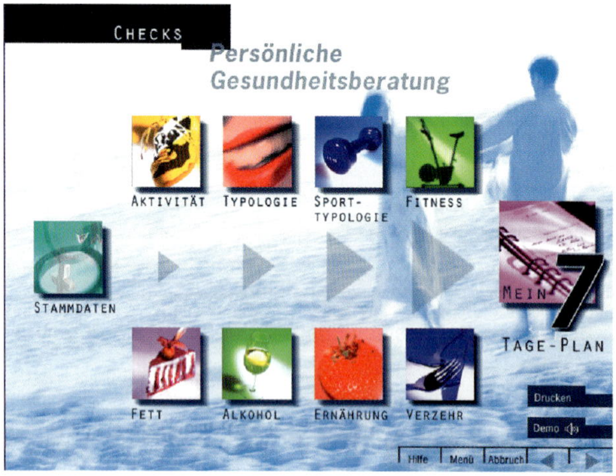

Beispiel einer symbolischen Umsetzung einer Benutzeroberfläche. Symbole stellen den Zugang zu den Inhalten dar.
(fit for more – VITAL & aktiv)

Beispiel eines dem Thema angepassten Menüs (HOBBYTHEK – Betörende Parfüms).

Spielerischer Informationszugang mit Entdeckungscharakter (CLIMATE EFFECTS).

Für fast alle Anwendungsfälle gilt:

➲ **Eine Benutzerführung soll nicht nur gefallen, sondern sie muss auch funktionieren.**

Ob dies im Einzelfall zutrifft, kann man als Benutzer einer Anwendung auf jeder Seite an folgenden Kriterien messen:

- Sehe ich, wo ich mich in der Anwendung befinde?
- Ist zu erkennen, was ich alles auf dieser Seite tun kann?
- Wie geht es weiter im Programm?
- Sehe ich, wohin ich verzweigen kann?
- Ist es klar, von wo aus ich auf diese Seite gekommen bin?
- Gibt es eine Anzeige, wie viel Informationen ich noch zu erwarten habe?
- Ist es klar, wie ich das Programm verlassen kann?

Werden diese Kriterien erfüllt, so ist sichergestellt, dass der Benutzer seine Informationen schnell und problemlos findet und ein transparentes Bild der Anwendungsstruktur erhält. Dies ist besonders bei Informationsanwendungen ❶, wie Lernprogrammen und Kiosksystemen ❷, von Bedeutung. Je mehr Navigationsmöglichkeiten das Programm bietet, umso wichtiger wird der Aspekt der Orientierung innerhalb der Anwendung.

❷ **Kiosksysteme** sind Informationsterminals, die z. B. auf Messen am Point of Information (POI) zum Abrufen von Produktinformationen eingesetzt werden.

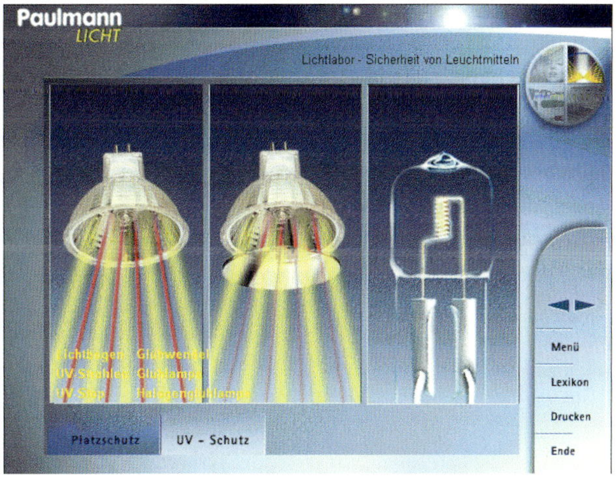

❶ Klar zu erkennende Elemente für die Navigation und Orientierung im Programm dienen der Benutzerführung (Beispiel: Paulmann LICHT – Multimedia CD-ROM).

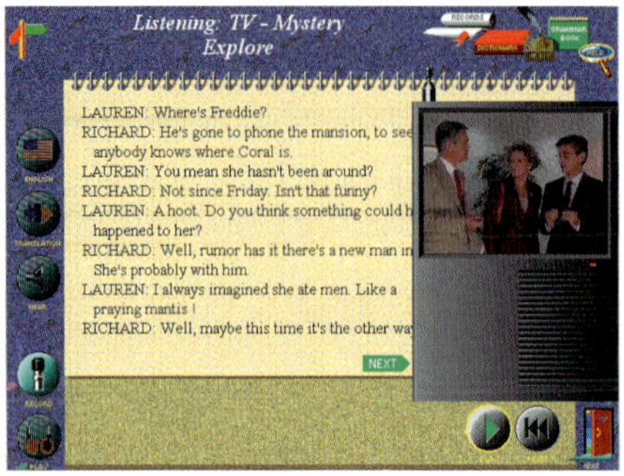

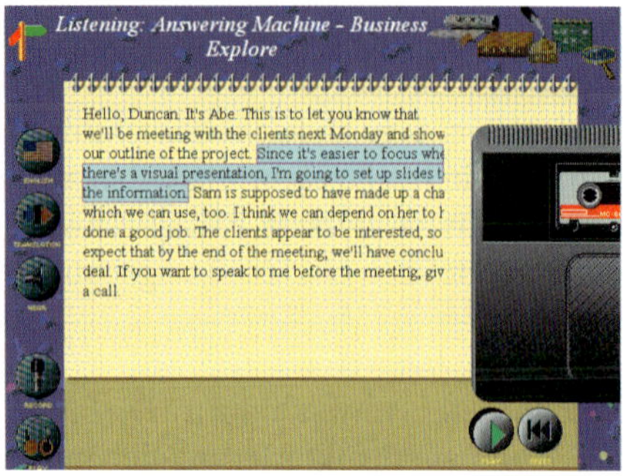

Aufruf zusätzlicher Medien, wie Videofilm und Ton, per Schaltfläche. Geschriebener Text wird multimedial vorgetragen (Beispiel: Language Trainer English – Bertelsmann).

Für zusätzliche Elemente, die nicht per Roll-over aktiviert und deaktiviert werden, müssen zusätzliche Bedienfunktionen zum Deaktivieren ❶ vorgesehen werden.

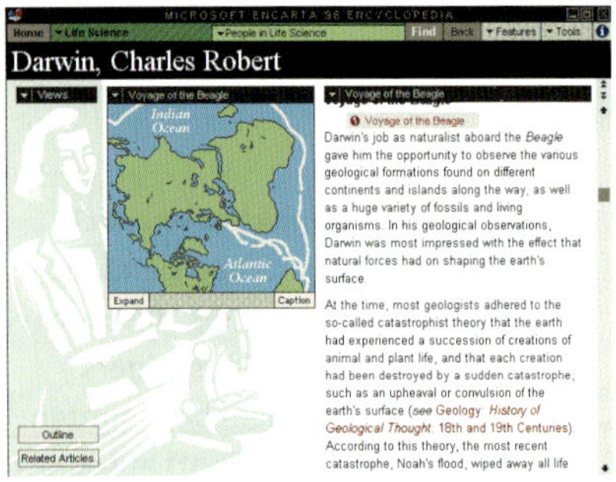

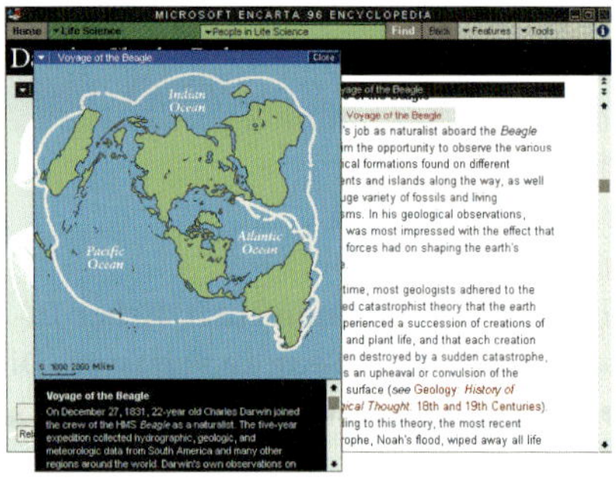

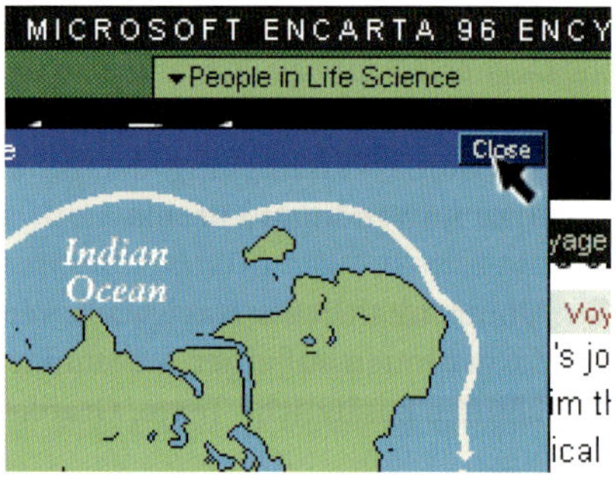

❶ Überlagernde Objekte müssen „abklickbar" sein, entweder durch Anklicken des Objektes oder durch explizite Buttons, die eindeutig sind (Beispiel: MICROSOFT ENCARTA).

Bei informativ angelegten Multimedia-Anwendungen ist es wichtig, dass der Benutzer klar zwischen struktureller und inhaltlicher Navigation unterscheiden kann. Erwartet der Benutzer beim Drücken eines Buttons zusätzliche Informationen auf der Seite, so sollte er nicht durch den Sprung auf eine andere Seite enttäuscht werden. Eine klare Trennung kann durch ein eindeutiges visuelles Erscheinungsbild der aktiven Flächen bzw. Navigationselemente erreicht werden. Dieses Erscheinungsbild sollte in der gesamten Anwendung konsistent seine Verwendung finden.

Konsistente Benutzerführung

Die Auswahlsystematik und ihre visuelle Darstellungsformen für Navigationen und Interaktionen sollten innerhalb einer Anwendung konsistent verwendet werden. Alle Bedienungselemente müssen leicht nachvollziehbar und wiedererkennbar sein.

Alle aktiven Flächen und Elemente sollten als solche auch erkennbar sein. Dazu gehört auch die Änderung des Mauszeigers in ein anders Symbol, während er sich auf dem aktiven Feld befindet.

Auch eine graphische Veränderung des Elements beim Roll-over kann zur Signalisierung von aktiven Schaltflächen benutzt werden.

Eine Änderung des Mauszeigers weist den Benutzer auf ein aktives Element hin, welches durch Anklicken eine Aktion herbeiführt.

Zur Konsistenz in einer multimedialen Anwendung zählen ebenso einheitliche typographische Hervorhebungen bei besonderen Wertigkeiten der Textinhalte wie einheitliche farbige Markierungen bei graphischen Hinweisobjekten.

Eine grafische Veränderung von Objekten beim Roll-over deutet auf aktive Schaltflächen hin.

Technische Vorgaben durch die Hardware

Die visuelle Gestaltung einer Benutzerführung in multimedialen Anwendungen ist auch von den Ein- und Ausgabegeräten abhängig. Die Abspielkonfiguration, bestehend aus Hard- und Software, und der Einsatzort der Anwendung bestimmen die Ein- und Ausgabegeräte. Als Eingabegeräte kommen üblicherweise Tastatur, Maus, Touchscreen oder Spracheingabe zum Einsatz, als Ausgabegeräte Monitor, Display, Videobeamer oder Sprachausgabe.

So müssen unter Anderem die aktiven Flächen, wie Navigationselemente etc., für eine Anwendung, die über einen Touchscreen-Monitor bedient werden soll, ausreichend groß gestaltet sein. Damit ist eine leichte Bedienbarkeit mit den Fingern gewährleistet.

Anwendungen für Touchscreen-Monitore müssen besonders gestaltet werden.

12.4.2 Navigationselemente

Gestaltung von Navigationselementen

Navigation durch das Programm über einen Zeitstrahl (Beispiel: Chronik des 20. Jahrhunderts – Bertelsmann).

Der Gestaltung von Navigationselementen für die Benutzerführung sind kaum Grenzen gesetzt. Von einfachen graphischen und typographischen Objekten bis zu aufwendigen Umsetzungen von thematischen Metaphern reicht die Bandbreite der Navigationselemente. Im Vordergrund steht dabei immer die Funktion. Das visuelle Erscheinungsbild sollte dem Benutzer ohne großen Interpretationsaufwand die Funktion signalisieren und ihn zur Benutzung der Elemente auffordern.

Eine zusätzliche Signalisierung des Zustandes, ob das Element aktiv ist oder nicht, wirkt einer Fehlbenutzung der Navigationselemente entgegen. Jede Schaltfläche (Button) kann dabei verschiedene Zustände einnehmen.

Mögliche Zustände der Schaltflächen sind:

- Button inaktiv ❶, d. h. die Schaltfläche kann nicht betätigt werden.
- Button aktiv ❷, d. h. die Schaltfläche kann betätigt werden.
- Button mit Roll-over ❸, d. h. die Maus befindet sich gerade über der Schaltfläche.
- Button gedrückt ❹, d. h. die Schaltfläche wird gerade mit der Maus betätigt.

❶ ❷ ❸ ❹

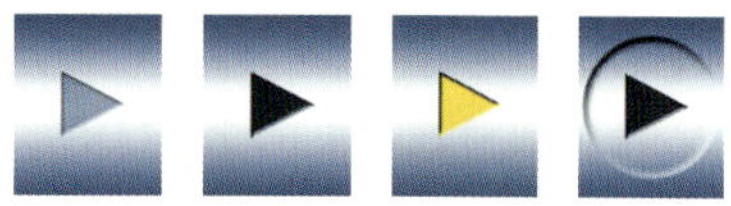

❶ ❷ ❸ ❹

Die Positionierung der Navigationselemente auf der Bildfläche sollte sehr sorgfältig vorgenommen werden. Zum Einen muss die Programmnavigation so klar ins Auge fallen, dass der Benutzer möglichst intuitiv die Bedienung vornehmen kann, und zum Anderen darf sie nicht die Wirkung der eigentlichen Inhalte der Anwendungsseite beeinträchtigen.

Oft werden die Bedienungselemente in Form einer Navigationsleiste am Bildschirmrand untergebracht. Dadurch erhält der Benutzer die Sicherheit, dass er die Navigationselemente immer an der gleichen Stelle aufgeräumt vorfindet. Gleichzeitig reserviert man sich eine im Programm immer gleich große Gestaltungsfläche für die Inhalte der Anwendung.

Ob die Funktion der einzelnen Elemente über Symbolik, über Text oder über eine Symbol-Text-Kombination dargestellt wird, ist nach den zu vermittelnden Inhalten auszurichten!

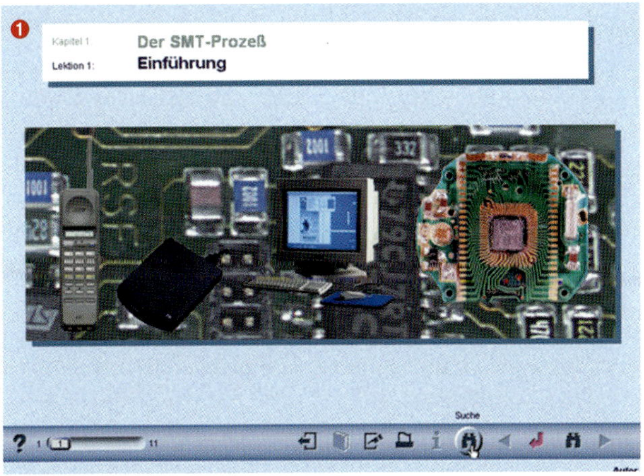

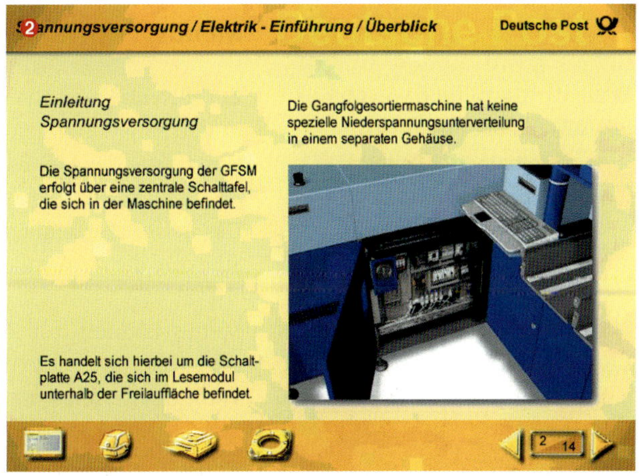

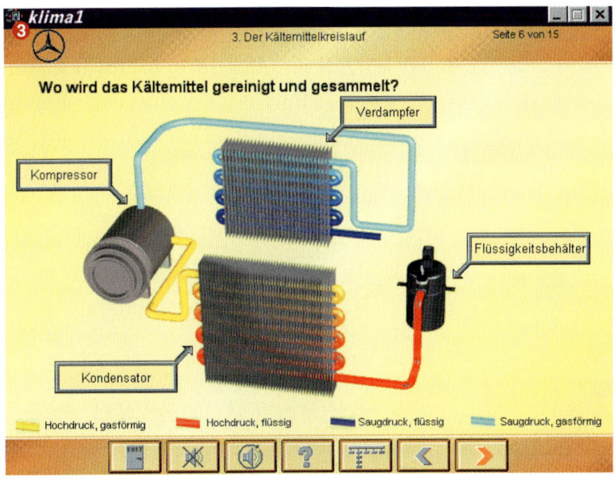

Verschiedenste Navigationselemente, jeweils harmonisch integriert in das Screendesign der jeweiligen multimedialen Anwendung. Beispiele: ❶ SIPLACE – Siemens AG, ❷ Deutsche Post AG / Siemens AG, ❸ Grundlagen der Klimatisierung – Mercedes-Benz AG, ❹ Unternehmenspräsentation – Voith Turbo GmbH, ❺ TIGRA – Opel, ❻ Wälder – Bertelsmann Lexikon Verlag GmbH.

Menüs

❶ Bei der Gestaltung von Menüs gilt, wie bei der Benutzerführung allgemein, der Leitsatz: „form follows function".

Zur Orientierung in einer Anwendung und als primärer Informationszugang werden in den Anwendungen spezielle Strukturseiten, sogenannte Menüs, verwendet. Bei der Gestaltung der Menüs sollte die Funktion ❶ den Vorrang haben.

Das heißt, der Benutzer soll sich schnell zurechtfinden, und dazu gehört, dass er die Struktur der Anwendung überblickt und schnell die Untereinheiten anwählen kann.

❷ **Pull-Down-Menüs** klappen bzw. rollen eine Auswahlliste aus einer Menü- oder Navigationsleiste heraus.

❸ Bei **Pop-up-Menüs** wird ein seperates Menüfenster auf den bestehenden Bildschirm gelegt.

Menüs können mit Ziffern, Text, grafischen Elementen und Realbildern aufgebaut sein. Die Thematik der Anwendung und die Benutzer-Zielgruppe bestimmen die Wahl der Menüelemente und deren Gestaltung.

Je nach Anwendung können auch Unterstrukturen dargestellt werden. Dies kann zum Beispiel über **Pull-down-Menüs** ❷, **Pop-up-Menüs** ❸ oder **Scrollbalken** ❹ erfolgen. Zusätzliche Vorschauinformationen, zum Beispiel kleine **Vorschaubilder** ❺, geben beim Anwählen (per Roll-over) einen kurzen Einblick in den anwählbaren Strukturpfad.

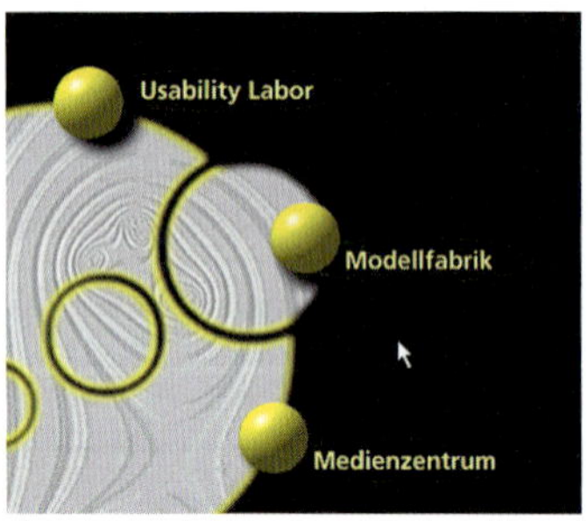

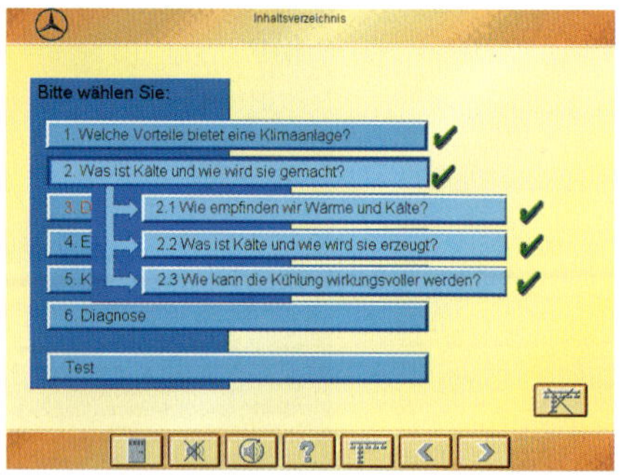

Mit Pull-down- und Pop-up-Menüs können viele Menüpunkte platzsparend gezeigt werden (Beipiel: CBT Klimaanlage – Daimler Chrysler).

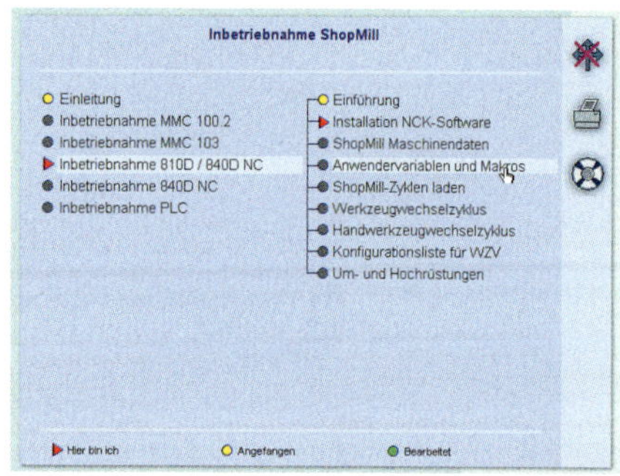

Markierungen an den Menüpunkten zeigen Bearbeitungsstände oder, wo man sich befindet (Beispiel: ShopMill – Siemens AG)

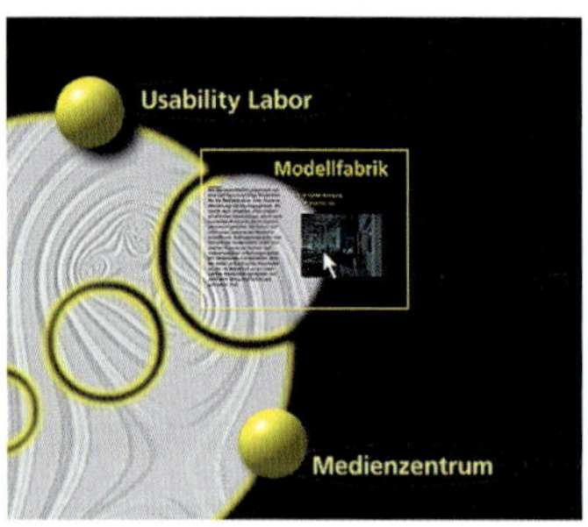

❺ Menü mit **Vorschaubildern** (Beispiel: Technologie Management – Fraunhofer Institut)

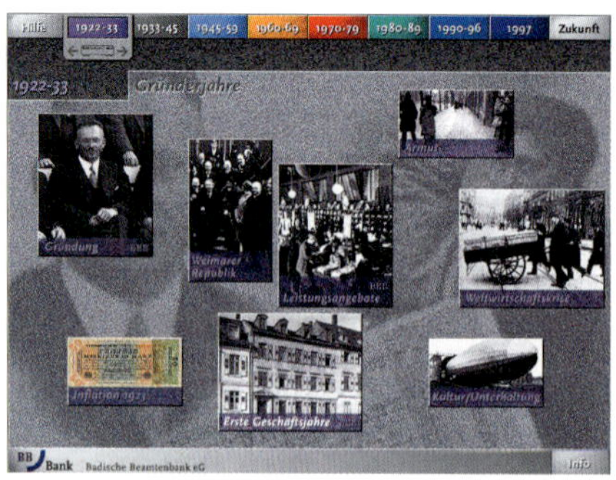

Zeitstrahl als Menüsystem (Beispiel: 75 Jahre Badische Beamtenbank)

❹ Schnelle Informationsanwahl bei flacher Hierarchie durch ein Pull-up-Menü mit **Scrollbalken** (Beispiel: GFSM – Siemens AG für Deutsche Post AG)

Metaphern

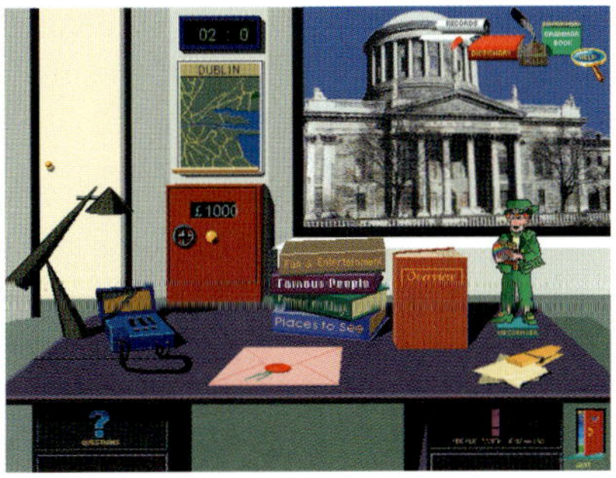

❶

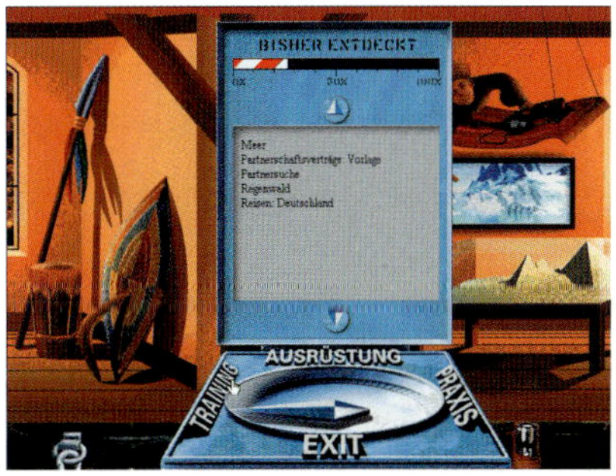

❷

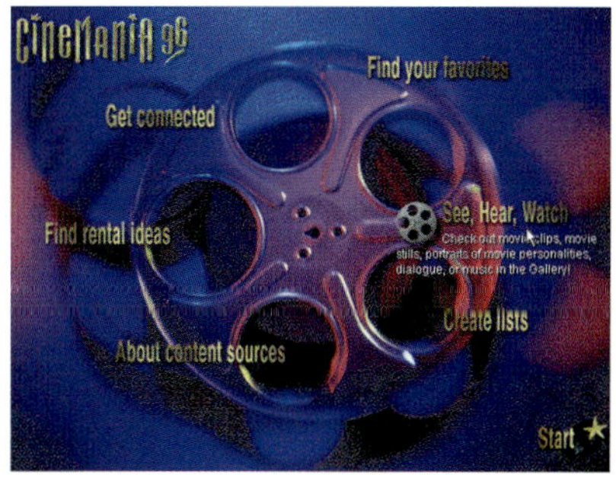

❸

Für spezielle Themen bietet es sich an, Benutzerumgebungen in ganz besonderer Form zu gestalten. Die Identifikation der Zielgruppe mit der Metapher und die spielerische Umsetzung steht bei der Gestaltung derartiger Menü-Umgebungen im Vordergrund. Der rein informative Überblick rückt dabei etwas in den Hintergrund, kann aber durch eine hohe Benutzerakzeptanz kompensiert werden.

❶ Language Trainer English – Bertelsmann

❷ Rüdiger Nehberg, Die Kunst zu überleben – Navigo Multimedia

❸ Cinemania 96 – Microsoft

Aufgaben und Übungen, Literaturhinweise

Aufgaben und Übungen

1. Didaktik: Wenden Sie die Instruktionsmethode an einem beliebigen Lernthema an. Gliedern Sie den gesamten Lernprozess mit Beispielen auf.
2. Dramaturgie: Suchen Sie einen Werbespot, der in Spielfilm-Manier aufgebaut ist. Skizzieren und analysieren Sie den dramaturgischen Aufbau.
3. Verständlichkeit: Nehmen Sie einen beschreibenden technischen Text aus einem Fachbuch und bereiten Sie ihn mediengerecht für ein CBT vor. Benutzen Sie Bildelemente, gliedern und strukturieren Sie den Inhalt des Textes in Sequenzen.
4. Struktur: Suchen Sie eine Multimedia-Anwendung, analysieren und skizzieren Sie die Struktur der Inhaltsseiten.
5. Interaktionen: Beschreiben Sie an Hand von Multimedia-Anwendungen verschiedene Interaktionsformen zur inhaltlichen und strukturellen Navigation.

Literaturhinweise

Clement, Ute; *Kräft*, Klaus: Lernen organisieren: Medien, Module, Konzepte, Berlin u. a. 2001 (Springer-Verlag)

Fröbisch, Dieter; *Lindner*, Holger; *Steffen*, Thomas: MultiMediaDesign, das Handbuch zur Gestaltung interaktiver Medien; Benutzerführung, Text, Bild, Sound & Grafik, München 1997 (Laterna Magica)

Holzinger, Andreas: Basiswissen Multimedia. 3 Bände. Bd. 1: Technik, Bd. 2: Lernen, Bd. 3: Design, Würzburg 2001 (Vogel-Verlag)

Thissen, Frank: Kompendium Screen-Design, Effektiv informieren und kommunizieren mit Multimedia, Berlin u. a. 2003 (Springer Verlag)

13 Internet

Webcode: **B1300**

Für weitere Infos zu diesem Kapitel mit dem Smartphone einfach QR-Code scannen oder auf www.medien-verstehen.de den Webcode eingeben.

In diesem Kapitel dreht sich alles um das Thema **Internet**, dem weltumspannenden Medium. Es werden die Grundlagen für das Verständnis dieses Mediums vermittelt und praktische Anwendungsbeispiele vorgestellt.

Das Internet ist mittlerweile als Informationsmedium nicht mehr wegzudenken. Es hat den erfolgreichen Einzug in fast alle gesellschaftlichen Schichten und Themen gehalten. Das Internet hat nicht nur die Art des Nachrichtenaustauschs verändert, sondern ganz allgemein auch den Umgang mit Informationen. Die Präsenz „im Netz", dem Internet, ist selbstverständlich geworden. Die Angabe der Internetadresse hat teilweise schon einen höheren Stellenwert als die Postadresse erreicht. Fernsehsendungen veranstalten „Chats" während aktueller Sendungen. Bücher und Zeitschriften verweisen auf weiterführende Informationen im Internet. In Communities, Foren und Auktionshäusern im Internet treffen sich Tausende von Gleichgesinnten, fachsimpeln und handeln miteinander. Millionen von Internet-Nutzern tauschen untereinander E-Mails aus. In Sekunden können in einem gigantischen Informationspool Recherchen durchgeführt werden. Ganze Marktsegmente wickeln ein Großteil ihrer Geschäfte „online" ab. Und ein Ende dieses Veränderungsprozesses ist noch lange nicht abzusehen.

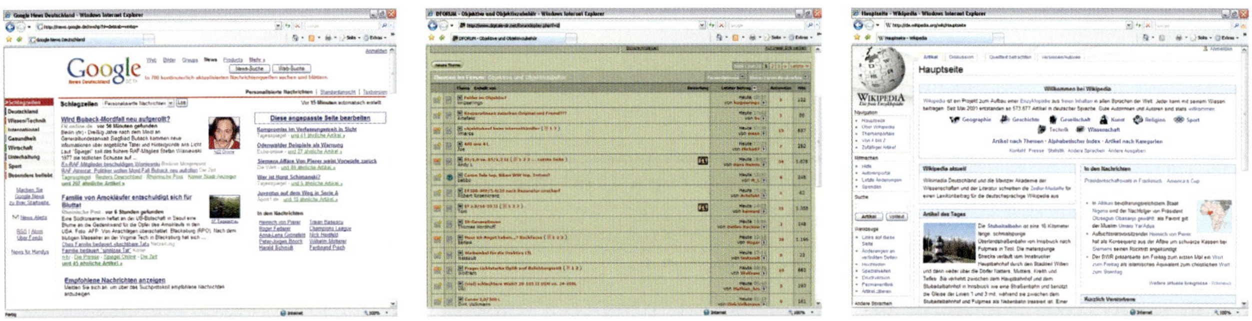

Informationsportale im Internet, Diskussionsforen zum Erfahrungsaustausch, Enzyklopädien an denen jeder mitwirken kann und Weblogs zur gemeinsamen Diskussion sind typische Informationstechnologien, die das Internet von heute prägen. Beispiele von links nach rechts: 1. Portalseite Google; 2. Fotografie-Forum dforum; 3. Enzyklopädie Wikipedia.

Parallel zur ständig weiteren Verbreitung hat sich das Medium Internet von einem reinen Abrufmedium zu einem pro-aktiven Interaktionsmedium entwickelt. Die „neue Generation des Internets", das sogenannte Web 2.0, verändert mittels neuer Informationstechnologie, wie Wikis, Blogs und kollaborativer Softwareplattformen das Zusammenspiel sozialer Entwicklungen und technischer Elemente.

Ein großes Potential liegt auch in der automatisierten Verknüpfung der bestehenden Dienste und Angebote untereinander, um neue, umfangreiche Informations- und Kommunikationsangebote zu generieren. Sei es in der semantischen Verknüpfung von Informationen oder in der personalisierten Aufbereitung und deren individuellen Sichten auf Informationen.

13.1 Grundlagen

13.1.1 Definition Internet

Das Internet ist ein komplexes, sehr dynamisches Medium mit den verschiedensten Auswirkungen auf unser tägliches Leben. Es kann die hauptsächlichen Elemente der Kommunikation (Text, Bild, Sprache, Ton, Video) verwenden und über verschiedenste Interaktionsebenen zu einem Kommunikationsmedium verbinden. Im Internet gibt es eine Reihe verschiedener Anwendungen, sogenannter Dienste, wobei das **WWW (World Wide Web)** im Allgemeinen als „das Internet" bezeichnet wird.

Lexikalische Definition des Begriffs „Internet": „Weltweit zugängliches, unkontrolliertes und nicht zentral verwaltetes Datennetzwerk aus miteinander standardisiert verbundenen Computern."

Technisch ist es als riesiges Netzwerk zu verstehen, das verschiedene Technologien miteinander verbindet. Dabei kann es sich um komplette Datennetze oder auch einzelne Rechner oder Rechnersysteme handeln, die miteinander verbunden sind. Diese Systeme basieren auf unterschiedlicher Hardware und Software, die nur über weltweit allgemein gültige Standards ❶ miteinander in Verbindung treten können. Grundlage sind Protokolle, die einheitliche Standards für den Datenaustausch festlegen. Damit ist eine vom System unabhängige Kommunikation sichergestellt. Eine Besonderheit des Internets ist auch die netzförmige Verknüpfung aller Systeme, die bei Ausfall eines Teilsystems das Internet in seiner Funktion nicht beeinträchtigt.

Keine einzelne Firma oder Organisation betreibt das Internet, sondern das Internet ist eine Sammlung vieler individueller Netzwerke und Organisationen, die über einheitliche Standards und Protokolle miteinander kommunizieren, aber alle werden einzeln betrieben und finanziert. Zur Koordination steuern verschiedene Gruppen das Internet-Wachstum, in dem Standardisierungen vereinbart, Entwicklungen unterstützt und die Internet-Registrierung gepflegt werden. Die Verwaltung der Internet-Adressen übernimmt das **InterNIC** ❷. Die Internet Society (ISOC) veranstaltet Kongresse und unterstützt die Arbeit des Internet Activity Boards (IAB), welches sich mit dem Aufbau des Internets beschäftigt. Das World Wide Web Consortium (W3C) erstellt Standards für die Entwicklung des WWW. Die administrativen Aufgaben, wie Zugang, Nutzungsbeschränkung, Adressenbeschaffung etc., die den Nutzer des Internets betreffen, übernehmen die Dienstleister des Internets (**Provider** ❸).

❶ Unter **Standards** versteht man technische Empfehlungen, die von nationalen oder internationalen Gremien ausgegeben werden. Sie spezifizieren und verabreden technische Prozesse.

❷ **Network Information Center** mit seinen nationalen Ablegern, in Deutschland DENIC, registriert offiziell gemeldete Computer im Internet mit Name und Rechnernummer.

❸ Die **Provider** stellen dem Internet-Nutzer den Zugang zum Internet zur Verfügung. Dies können sowohl kommerzielle Onlinedienste, wie AOL, T-Online, als auch reine Dienstleister für den Internet-Zugang sein.

13.1.2 Entstehungsgeschichte

Die Anfänge des Internets begannen schon im Jahre 1958. Zu dieser Zeit starteten die USA zahlreiche Forschungsprojekte, die nach der Überlegenheit in der Militärtechnologie strebten. Ausgelöst wurde dies auf Grund wissenschaftlicher Erfolge der damaligen Sowjetunion, die erfolgreich die Raumsonde „Sputnik" ins Weltall sandte, und der ständigen Bedrohung durch einen möglichen Atomkrieg. Die kalifornische RAND Corporation ❹ wurde damals beauftragt, ein Konzept für ein militärisches Netzwerk zu entwickeln, dass im Fall einer Notsituation Informationen jederzeit überregional zur Verfügung stellt und gleichzeitig als dezentrale Kommunikationsplattform dienen konnte. Dieses System sollte auch dann noch funktionsfähig bleiben, wenn ein Teil des Netzes zum Beispiel durch einen atomaren Militärschlag vernichtet werden würde. Aufbauend auf dieses Konzept entwickelte die Advanced Research Projects

❹ Research And Development, eine 1948 gegründete , nichtkommerzielle Forschungseinrichtung der Vereinigten Staaten.

❶ Bei der **paketorientierten Datenübertragung** wird die Information in kleine Datenpakete aufgeteilt, die unabhängig voneinander und auch auf verschiedenen Wegen zum Zielort transportiert und dort wieder zusammengesetzt werden.

❷ Bei der **leitungsorientierten Datenübertragung** wird eine feste Leitung zwischen den Rechnern benutzt. Bei dieser Datenübertragung führten etwaige kurzzeitige Unterbrechungen des Datenflusses zum Zusammenbrechen der bestehenden Kommunikationsverbindung.

❸ USENET, ein Netzwerk, über das Newsgroups transportiert werden.

❹ BITNET (Because It's Time Network), ein auf IBM-kompatible Rechner basierendes Netzwerk, welches die akademische Welt miteinander verband.

❺ EUnet (European Unix Network), ein 1982 gegründetes europäisches Forschungsnetz.

❻ Der Name des Internet kommt von „Interconnected sets of networks".

Agency (**ARPA**), eine Abteilung des US-amerikanischen Verteidigungsministeriums, die paketorientierte Datenübertragung ❶, welche die bis dahin übliche leitungsorientierte Datenübertragung ❷ ablöste. 1969 wurde von der ARPA das erste paketorientiert arbeitende Netz (ARPANET) mit dezentralen Netzknoten in Betrieb genommen. Bei diesem ersten überregionalem Netzwerk wurden zuerst vier Computersysteme – an der University of Utah, der University of Santa Barbara, der University in Los Angeles und dem Stanford Research Institute – miteinander verbunden. Drei Jahre später hatten sich 50 militärische und wissenschaftliche Institutionen an das ARPANET angeschlossen. Vorerst konnte ein Datenaustausch von Rechner zu Rechner über den FTP-Service (File Transfer Protocol) vorgenommen werden. Später kam für die angeschlossenen ARPANET-Teilnehmer mit der E-Mail (Electronic Mail) die elektronische Post zur direkten Kommunikation hinzu, dabei wurde das @-Zeichen für die Trennung von Name und Adresse eingeführt. Um an das ARPANET verschiedene andere paketorientierte Netze anschließen zu können und eine sichere Datenübertragung zu gewährleisten, schrieb 1974 der US-Amerikaner Robert Kahn das **TCP/IP** (Transmission Control Protocol/Internet Protocol), welches 1983 zum einheitlichen Protokoll auch im ARPANET wurde. In diesem Jahr schlossen sich weitere Netze an. Dazu gehörten das USENET ❸, das BITNET ❹ und das europäische EUnet ❺. Das damit entstandene „Netz der Netze" erhielt den Namen „Internet" ❻.

Durch den rasanten Zuwachs an angeschlossenen Rechnern und Angeboten bestand der Bedarf, die Namensgebung im Internet zu standardisieren. 1984 wurde das **DNS** (Domain Name System) vorgestellt, nach dem bis heute alle Rechner im Internet über Internet-Namen identifizierbar sind. Im Jahre 1986 spaltete sich das Netz in ein nichtöffentliches, rein militärisches Netz (MILNET) und dem öffentlichen, forschungsorientierten ARPANET. Am Europäischen Forschungszentrum für Teilchenphysik CERN in Genf entstand 1990 das World Wide Web (WWW) auf Basis des neuen Internet-Protokolls HTTP (Hypertext Transfer Protocol). Ziel des WWW war es, weltweit Dokumente mit eingebundenen Grafiken und Hypertextfunktionalität zur Verfügung zu stellen, die eine direkte Verknüpfung von Dokument zu Dokument erlauben. Im Jahre 1993 waren schon über 1,3 Millionen Nutzer im Internet. Die explosionsartige kommerzielle Nutzung des Internets wurde durch die Entwicklung benutzerfreundlicher Web-Browser für PCs und Macintosh vorangetrieben. 1994 entstanden die ersten Internet-Shops und 1995 waren die ersten Ton- und Filmsequenzen über das Internet abrufbar. Immer mehr Internetbasierte Dienste, welche die Internet-Wirtschaft geradezu beflügelten, kamen hinzu. Relativ kleine Internet-Firmen, wie Yahoo!, Intershop oder Amazon gingen an die Börse und schlugen in kurzer Zeit etablierte Großkonzerne in ihren Aktienwerten.

Der nahezu euphorisch umjubelte „Goldrush" vieler Internet-Firmen brach Mitte 2000 nach dem Platzen einiger hochspekulierter Aktienwerte zusammen. Manche Werte sanken regelrecht ins Bodenlose und verunsicherten viele spekulationsfreudige Anleger. Die Zeit der Konsolidierung im Internet-Business war angebrochen.
Aber neue soziale Netzwerke und eine Entwicklung von neuen, portalen Endgeräten treibt die Verbreitung des Internets stetig voran.
Die Anzahl der Internet-Nutzer überschritt im Jahre 2011 die 2-Milliarden-Grenze.

13.1.3 Grundprinzip

Datenaustausch über TCP/IP

Der Informationsaustausch im Internet geschieht mit einheitlichen Verfahrens- und Ablaufvorschriften über viele Ebenen von Netzwerken, Computern und Kommunikationsverbindungen. Die wichtigsten Protokolle im Internet sind das Transmission Control Protocol (TCP) und das Internet Protocol (IP), kurz **TCP/IP** ❶ genannt. Zunächst werden die Informationen vom TCP in einzelne Pakete aufgeteilt. Mit Hilfe des IP werden diese Pakete an ihren Bestimmungsort gebracht und dort mit dem TCP wieder zusammengesetzt. Dabei können die Pakete, je nach Verkehrsaufkommen (traffic) auch unterschiedliche Pfade einschlagen. Unterwegs können die Informationen über verschiedenste Hardwarekomponenten, z. B. **Hubs** ❷, **Bridges** ❸, **Gateways** ❹, **Repeater** ❺ und **Router** ❻, transportiert werden, welche die unterschiedlichen Netze und Systeme miteinander verbinden.

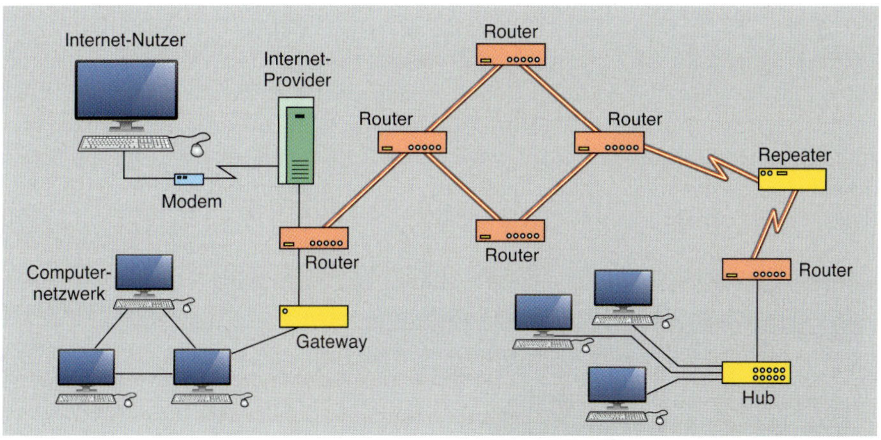

Damit die Datenpakete auch immer den richtigen Adressaten in dem komplexen Netzwerk erreichen, werden sie von Router zu Router auf dem schnellsten Wege weitergegeben. Sind sie dann entgültig beim Adressaten angekommen werden sie in der richtigen Reihenfolge zusammengesetzt und auf Vollständigkeit und Fehlerfreiheit geprüft. Fehlende oder fehlerhafte Datenpakete werden vom Sender nachgefordert. Zusätzlich zu den Protokollen des TCP/IP werden für die Internet-Dienste weitere Protokolle verwendet. Der gesamte komplexe Datenübertragungsprozess lässt sich in Form eines **Schichtenmodells** ❼ darstellen.

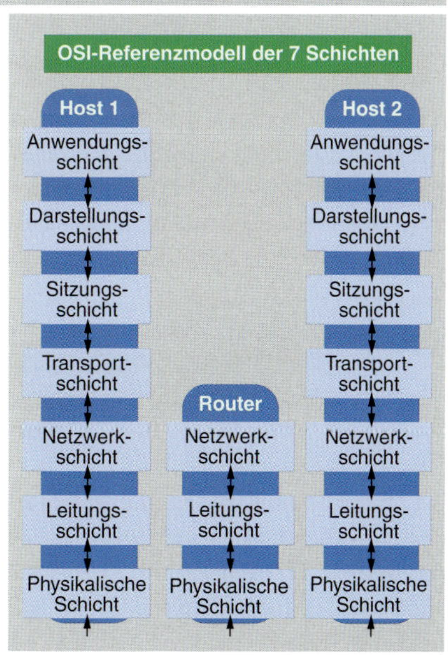

❶ **TCP/IP** ist das Internet-Standard-Protokoll. Es besteht aus dem TCP, dem Protokoll für den paket-orientierten Datentransport, und dem für die Adressierung zuständigen IP.

❷ **Hubs** verbinden einzelne Computer zu Gruppen.

❸ **Bridges** verbinden örtliche Netzwerke miteinander. Sie lassen Daten für andere Netze passieren, lokale Daten halten sie zurück.

❹ **Gateways** verbinden unterschiedliche Netzwerke miteinander, in dem die Daten übersetzt werden.

❺ **Repeater** verstärken die Signale, um größere Entfernungen überbrücken zu können.

❻ **Router** verbinden Netze mit gleichen Protokollen und übernehmen die Datenpaketvermittlung im Internet. Sie geben die Datenpakete entsprechend der Zieladresse zum nächsten Router weiter.

❼ Das **Schichtenmodell** nach dem OSI-Referenzmodell definiert 7 Schichten. Die reine Bitübertragung erfolgt in der untersten Schicht. Höhere Schichten küm-mern sich um die fehlerfreie Datenübertragung und auf der obersten Schicht werden die plattformunabhängigen Internet-Dienste angeboten. Somit ist die eigentliche Anwendung von der Aufgabe des Datentransportes entkoppelt.

Adressen im Internet

Damit auch immer die richtige Adresse im Internet gefunden werden kann, benutzt das Internet Protocol (IP) eine aus Zahlengruppen bestehende eindeutige Internet-Adresse (**IP-Adresse**) ❶. Sie besteht in der Version IPv4 aus einer Zahlenfolge mit vier Nummernblöcken, die durch Punkte voneinander getrennt sind, z. B. „132.51.131.71". Jeder dieser vier Zahlen kann Werte von 0 bis 255 annehmen. Da diese Zahlengruppen schlecht zu merken sind, wurde das **Domain-Name-System (DNS)** entwickelt. Dieses System gibt jedem Computer im Internet einen **Domain-Namen** ❷ (Host-Namen) mit leicht verständlichen Wörtern und Buchstaben. Jeder Domain-Name ist einer eindeutigen IP-Adresse zugeordnet. Spezielle „Name-Server" führen Listen der Domain-Namen und vermitteln zwischen IP- und Domain-Adresse.

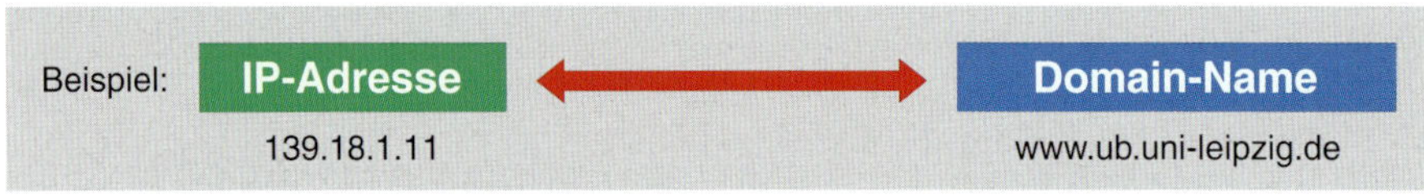

Nach dem Domain-Name-System sind Domain-Namen hierarchisch aufgebaut und durch die einzelnen Ebenen durch Punkte voneinander getrennt. Beginnend mit dem Rechnernamen, über eventuelle Sub-Domains (Rechnergruppen), der Domain und zum Schluss die Top Level-Domain, wird der Domain-Name gebildet. Die Top Level-Domains sind entweder geografisch ❸ nach Ländern organisiert oder nach Zugehörigkeit zu einer bestimmten Nutzergruppe ❹.

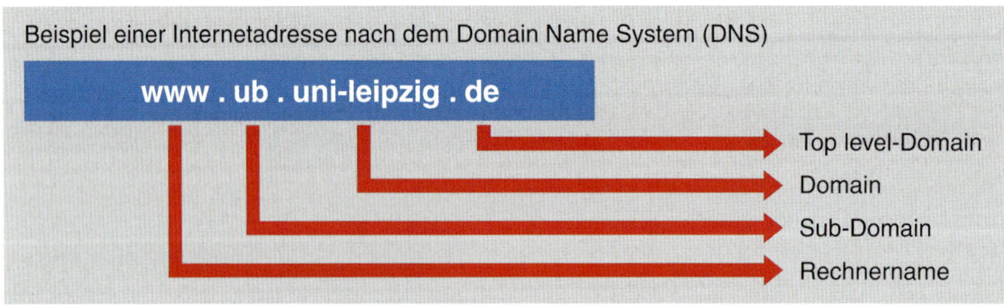

Die Second Level-Domain (oder einfach Domain genannt) wird über DeNIC vergeben. Die Sub-Domain und den Rechnernamen vergibt der Systemadministrator des jeweiligen Rechners. So hat auch jedes Dokument, auf das im Internet zugegriffen werden kann, seine eigene Adresse, die sogenannte **URL** (**Uniform Resource Locator**).

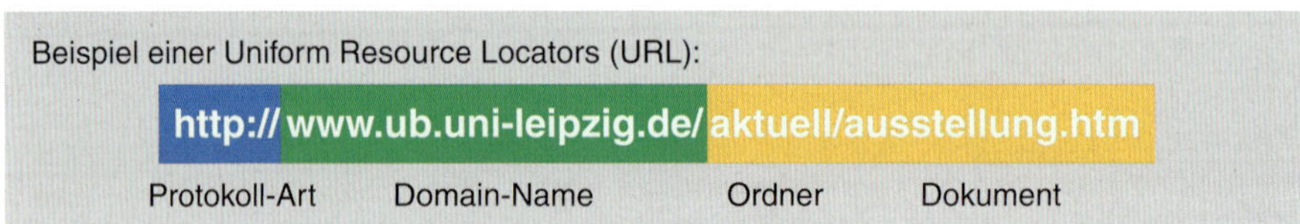

Bei einer URL wird zusätzlich das notwendige Protokoll angegeben, welches zum Lesen des Dokumentes benötigt wird. Im WWW werden hauptsächlich Daten im **HTTP** (**Hypertext Transfer Protocol**) ausgetauscht. Aber auch **FTP** (**File Transfer Protocol**) zum Datei-Transfer wird im **WWW** verwendet. Das eigentliche Dokument wird dann über den Pfad (Ordner und evtl. Unterordner) und dem Dokumentennamen gefunden.

❶ Eine **IP-Adresse** nach der Version IPv4 besteht aus 32 Bits. Da der mögliche IP-Adressraum damit nicht ausreicht, wurde im Jahre 2012 das IPv6 mit 128 Bits eingeführt.

❷ Die **Domain-Namen** können – sofern noch nicht belegt – weitgehend frei ausgesucht werden. In Deutschland ist dafür das Deutsche Network Information Center (DeNIC) für die Vergabe zuständig. Die Beantragung einer Domain kann auch über einen Internet-Provider erfolgen. Mittlerweile werden schon interessante Domain-Namen in verschiedenen Auktionen versteigert. Welche Namen von wem registriert sind, erfährt man über die WHOIS-Datenbank (www.whois-service.de).

.eu	Europa
.at	Österreich
.be	Belgien
.ch	Schweiz
.cz	Tschechische Republik
.de	Deutschland
.dk	Dänemark
.es	Spanien
.fi	Finnland
.fr	Frankreich
.is	Island
.it	Italien
.uk	Großbritannien
...	...

❸ Beispiele für geografische Top Level-Domains.

.com	Kommerzieller Anbieter
.edu	Bildungseinrichtung
.gov	Regierungsbehörde
.mil	Militäreinrichtung
.net	Netzanbieter / Provider
.int	Internationale Organisation
.mobi	Mobile Endgeräte
...	...

❹ Beispiele für Top Level-Domains nach Nutzergruppen.

13.2 Dienste im Internet

Im Internet kommen verschiedene Anwendungen, sogenannte Dienste, zum Einsatz. Alle Dienste basieren auf dem Client-Server-Prinzip, das heißt, ein Rechner (der sogenannte Server) stellt eine Dienstleistung im Internet zur Verfügung, die von anderen Rechnern (den sogenannten Clients) in Anspruch genommen werden können.

❶ **Browser** kommt vom englischen Wort „to browse", was soviel bedeutet wie das flüchtige Durchblättern eines Buches.

13.2.1 World Wide Web

Das World Wide Web (WWW) wird im Allgemeinen als „das Internet" bezeichnet, da hier die meisten Online-Aktivitäten, im Volksmund auch gerne „Surfen" genannt, ablaufen. Das WWW ist der momentan spannendste, innovativste und am schnellsten wachsende Teil des Internets. Es ist als global vernetztes gigantisches Informationssystem zu verstehen, wie auch schon durch die Bezeichnung „Web" (engl. = Spinnennetz) zu erkennen ist. Das WWW arbeitet mit dem Hypertext Transfer Protocol (HTTP) und erlaubt die weltweite Verknüpfung von Hypertext-Dokumenten.

Beispiel eines Browsers: Der Internet Explorer von Microsoft.

Zur Anzeige der Dokumente wird ein sogenannter **Browser** ❶ verwendet. Da dies der meistgenutzte Internet-Dienst ist, wird in der nächsten Lektion dieses Kapitels die Funktionsweise des WWW noch genauer behandelt.

13.2.2 E-Mail

E-Mail, aus dem englischen Begriff „Electronic Mail" abgeleitet, ist die elektronische Post im Internet. Jeden Tag verschicken und empfangen Millionen Internet-Nutzer E-Mails zum schnellen Informationsaustausch.

➲ **E-Mail arbeitet zeitversetzt, das heißt, die Sender und Empfänger müssen nicht gleichzeitig im Internet anwesend sein.**

Der E-Mail-Versand erfolgt nicht direkt von Computer zu Computer, sondern über sogenannte Mail-Server, an denen sich die Benutzer mit einer **E-Mail-Software** ❷ anmelden und E-Mails zum Versand abgeben bzw. erhaltene E-Mails abrufen. Der Mail-Server übernimmt die Aufgabe eines Postamtes mit individuellen Postfächern.

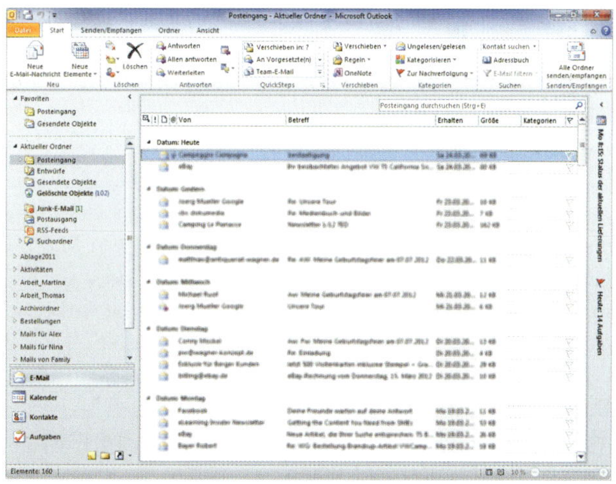

❷ Die **E-Mail Software**, auch Mail-Client genannt, ist für den E-Mail-Benutzer die Kommunikationszentrale auf dem PC. Damit werden Nachrichten vom Mail-Server auf den eigenen Computer geholt. Anschließend können die Nachrichten gelesen, gespeichert, gelöscht oder beantwortet werden. (Beispiel: Microsoft Outlook)

Für den Transport der E-Mails werden mehrere Protokolle verwendet. Das Senden der E-Mail vom Mail-Client zum Mail-Server übernimmt das seit 1982 eingeführte SMPT-Protokoll (Simple Mail Transfer Protocol).

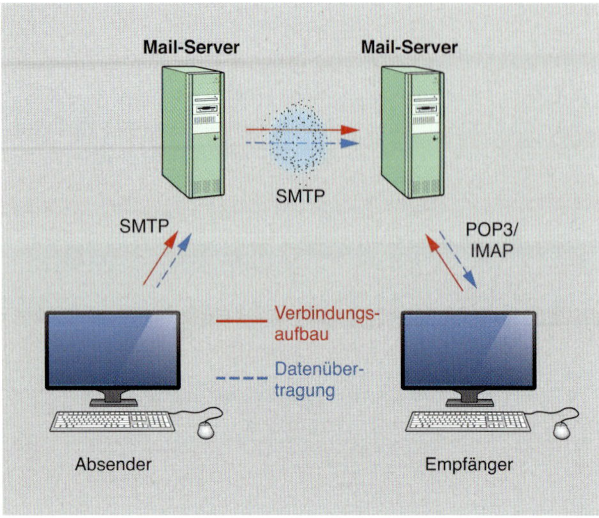

SMPT ist ein einfach gehaltenes Protokoll, das einige Probleme und Risiken mit sich bringt: SMPT kann nur ungeschützte Textnachrichten übertragen und erfordert vom Mail-Server eine ständige Empfangsbereitschaft. Da man dies für das Empfangen von Mails mit dem Mail-Client nicht voraussetzen kann, kommt für das Abholen der Mails vom Mail-Server das weit verbreitete **POP3** (Post Office Protocol) oder das **IMAP4** (Internet Message Access Protocol) zum Einsatz. Das IMAP4 bietet für den mobilen Internet-Benutzer mehr Flexibilität, da er zum Beispiel Eingangspost auf dem Mail-Server lagern kann. So kann von unterschiedlichen Orten mit mehreren unabhängigen PCs auf das gleiche Postfach zugegriffen werden. Der eigentliche Datenaustausch von Mail-Server zu Mail-Server erfolgt meist in wenigen Sekunden. Wie lange die E-Mail wirklich unterwegs ist, hängt von der Distanz, den Router-Verbindungen und der Netzauslastung ab.

E-Mails mit Anhang

Mit E-Mails können nicht nur Nachrichten in Form von Text verschickt werden, sondern auch Bilder, Grafiken, Sound-Dateien und andere binäre Daten, z. B. Programm-Dateien. Da das SMPT-Protokoll nur reine Textnachrichten mit den Zeichen des amerikanischen 7-Bit-**ASCII-Standards** ❶ übertragen kann, haben sich die Mehrzweck-Erweiterungen MIME (Multi Purpose Mail Extensions) durchgesetzt. Durch MIME können in E-Mails beliebige Sonderzeichen verwendet und binäre Daten können als sogenannte Anhänge (Attachments) mitgeschickt werden. Für den Transport im Internet werden die binären Daten mit dem Mail-Client in den ASCII-Code ❷ umgewandelt und müssen beim Empfänger wieder in binäre Daten rückgewandelt werden.

Die meisten Mail-Clients erlauben dem Sender, die Mails entweder als reine Textnachrichten (ASCII), als HTML-Datei, oder sogar in einem proprietären Format ❸, wie z. B. dem Microsoft Outlook-Rich-Text-Format, zu verschicken. In proprietären Formaten oder im HTML-Format lassen sich Textinformationen durch Gestaltungselemente, wie Farbe, Schriftformatierungen, Verknüpfungen und sogar integrierte Bilder aufwerten. Doch Vorsicht: Es gibt keine Gewähr dafür, dass diese Formatierungen beim Adressaten auch wirklich ankommen.

❶ **ASCII** (American Standard Code for Information Interchange) ist der Standard für den Austausch von Texten. Dabei steht für jedes Zeichen ein Zahlencode.

❷ Die Umwandlung der binären Dateien erfolgt innerhalb von **MIME** z. B. mit der Base64-Codierung. Alternativ wird auch die UUEncode-Kodierung verwendet. Beide Seiten, Sender und Empfänger, müssen über die gleichen Verfahren verfügen, sonst können die Datei-Anhänge nicht gelesen werden.

❸ Proprietäre Formate sind nicht offiziell standardisierte Formate, die jedoch auf Grund der starken Verbreitung eines Software-Produktes sehr oft verfügbar sind. Werden solche Formate vorwiegend eingesetzt, spricht man von einem „Quasi-Standard".

Aufbau der E-Mail

Eine **E-Mail** besteht immer aus dem E-Mail-Kopf (E-Mail-Header) und der Textnachricht (Body). Eventuell kann eine elektronische Unterschrift (Signatur) am Ende der Textnachricht integriert und zusätzliche Dateien angehängt werden. Der E-Mail-Header besteht hauptsächlich aus der Adresszeile mit der E-Mail-Adresse des Empfängers (An- oder To-Zeile), den möglichen Empfängern einer Kopie (CC-Zeile, auch Carbon Copy genannt), der E-Mail-Adresse des Senders, dem Datum und der Betreff-Zeile (Subject).

E-Mail-Adresse

Eine E-Mail-Adresse ist im Internet die Post-Adresse des Benutzers. Nur, dass im Internet ein Benutzer auch über mehrere E-Mail-Adressen verfügen kann und dass über die E-Mail-Adresse nicht auf den eigentlichen Wohnort und Namen des Benutzers zu schließen ist. Sie ist prinzipiell nach dem Muster IhrName@IhrProvider.de aufgebaut. Das „@“-Zeichen trennt dabei den persönlichen, selbstdefinierten Namen vom Namen des Internet Service Providers ❶, der das E-Mail-Konto und den Mail-Server anbietet und der Top Level-Domain. Auch E-Mail-Adressen mit eigener Domain ❷ sind möglich.

❶ Beispiel einer E-Mail-Adresse über den Internet-Provider T-Online: HansMuster@t-online.de.

❷ Beispiel einer E-Mail-Adresse mit eigenem Domain-Namen: info@medien-verstehen.de

Fast alle **Provider** bieten webbasierte E-Mail-Konten ❸ an, die über den Browser bedient werden. Anbieter kostenloser E-Mail-Konten sind z. B. MSN Hotmail, Yahoo!, GMX und FreeMail.

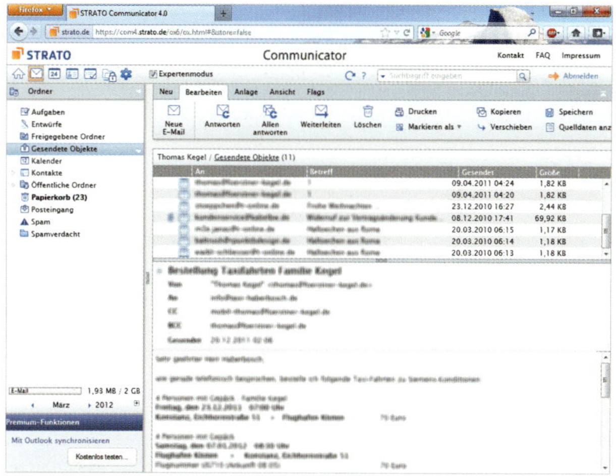

❸ Einige Provider bieten auch ein webbasiertes Interface für das E-Mail-Konto an.

Mit der weiten Verbreitung des E-Mail-Dienstes steigt auch das Problem der Werbe-E-Mails. Dies sind in der Regel Werbesendungen von Firmen, von denen man häufig noch nie etwas gehört hat. Diese unerwünschten Nachrichten werden als Spam oder Junk-Mail bezeichnet. Die Bezeichnung Spam stammt ursprünglich von einem Monty-Python-Sketch, bei dem mit jedem Gericht das Spam-Frühstücksfleisch (Abkürzung für Spice and Ham) serviert wurde. Die Versender derartiger Mails kaufen E-Mail-Adressen oder erstellen E-Mail-Listen über Roboter-Software, die z. B. Newsgroups nach E-Mail-Adressen durchsuchen. Um den eigentlichen Sender zu verbergen, sind die Sender-Adressen oft verfälscht und bieten keine Möglichkeit der Streichung von der entsprechenden Spam-Liste. Um sich dennoch vor der Überflutung von Spam-Mails zu schützen, gibt es entweder beim E-Mail-Provider oder in der verwendeten E-Mail-Software Spam-Filter, die derartige Werbe-Mails blockieren. Leider bedienen sich die Versender der Spam-Mails immer mehr der Methode der Verfälschung des Adressen-Headers und können deshalb nicht immer ausgefiltert werden. Mittlerweile gibt es eine Reihe von Gesetzesvorschlägen, die Spam-Mails regulieren bzw. verbieten wollen.

Newsletter

Im Gegensatz zu unerwünschten Werbe-Mails können über sogenannte **Newsletter** neue Informationen als regel mäßig versendete E-Mails abonniert werden. Firmen und professionelle Redaktionen geben Newsletter heraus, um über Aktionen, neue Produkte oder sonstige Neuigkeiten zu informieren. Es gibt kostenlosen und kostenpflichtigen Bezug von Newslettern. Die Bestellung erfolgt in der Regel über die Homepage des Herausgebers.

Beispiel einer E-Mail als Newsletter (interAir GmbH).

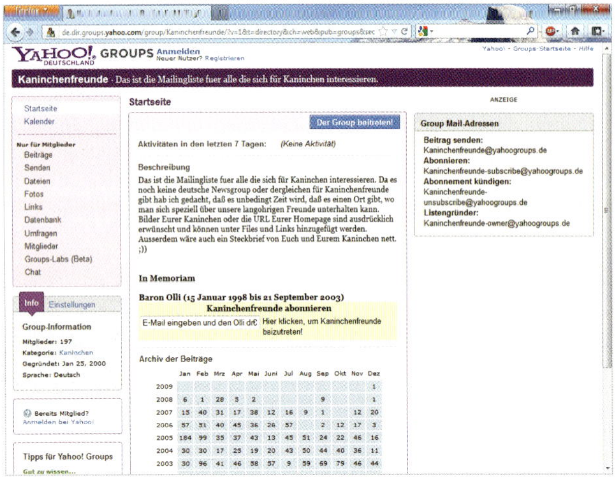

Über Mailinglisten werden Diskussionen geführt und neue Informationen per E-Mails verbreitet (Beispiel: Mailingliste „Kanichenfreunde" über Yahoo.com).

Mailinglisten

Anders als bei Newslettern, bei denen nur ein Sender die Informationen verschickt und viele diese empfangen können, erfolgt die Kommunikation bei sogenannten **Mailinglisten** öffentlich, das heißt, jeder kann Informationen verbreiten.

➲ **Die einzelnen Beiträge werden von den Teilnehmern an die Mailingliste geschickt und dann automatisch als E-Mail den anderen Abonnenten zugeschickt.**

Sehr aktive Mailinglisten erreichen problemlos 50 oder mehr Beiträge am Tag. Solche E-Mail-Mengen sind üblicherweise nur noch mit entsprechenden Mail-Eingangsassistenten zu bewältigen.

Bei moderierten Mailinglisten werden die Beiträge von einem Moderator daraufhin untersucht, ob dieser Beitrag zum Mailinglisten-Thema gehört und von allgemeinem Interesse ist. Mailinglisten werden vorwiegend als Medium zur Diskussion und zum Informationsaustausch innerhalb einer überschaubaren Interessensgruppe eingesetzt.

13.2.3 Newsgroups

❶ Das USENET wurde 1979 an der Universität von Duke in North Carolina entwickelt und integrierte 1983 in das Internet.

Eine weitere Möglichkeit, über das Internet Informationen auszutauschen und Diskussionen zu führen, bietet das USENET ❶. Dieser News-Dienst, dessen Diskussionsforen **Newsgroups** genannt werden, ist als ein globales „Schwarzes Brett" zu verstehen. Das Prinzip ist einfach: Ein Teilnehmer stellt ein Frage oder veröffentlicht seine Meinung in einem der Diskussionsforen. Das Absenden eines Beitrages wird im News-Jargon „Posting" genannt. Die anderen Teilnehmer können diese Nachricht lesen und ihrerseits darauf antworten.

➲ **Newsgroups sind vergleichbar mit Mailinglisten, nur dass die Nachrichten nicht über E-Mails verteilt, sondern auf sogenannten News Servern gespeichert werden.**

Der Newsgroups-Teilnehmer tritt mit Hilfe eines News Readers mit einem News Server in Verbindung. Als News Reader kann eine spezielle Client-Software eingesetzt weren oder der Newsgroups-Teilnehmer nutzt den integrierten Reader seines Internet-Browsers. Aber auch große Internet-Provider, wie z.B. Google, haben Web-Interfaces entwickelt, um Newsgroups einfach über Web-Seiten bedienen zu können.

Dabei reicht es meistens, nur mit einem News Server Kontakt aufzunehmen, da die News Server untereinander in Verbindung stehen und in regelmäßigen Abständen die Diskussionsbeiträge über das NNTP-Protokoll (Network News Transfer Protocol) untereinander austauschen. Im **USENET** sind die mehr als 10 000 Diskussionsforen nach Themen hierarchisch gegliedert. Die Struktur beginnt von links nach rechts mit der Hauptkategorie ❶ und geht über mehrere Unterkategorien bis hin zum Forumthema. Ein kompletter Forum-Name kann dann zum Beispiel so aussehen: „de.rec.reisen.camping".

alt	Sonstige Themen
at	Österreichische Foren
comp	Computerthemen
de	Deutsche Foren
microsoft	Rund um Microsoft-Produkte
misc	Vermischtes
news	Mailboxen
rec	Freizeit und Unterhaltung
sci	Wissenschaftliches
soc	Kultur, Politik und Soziales
talk	Klatsch und Tratsch
...	...

❶ Beispiel von Hauptkategorien

Informationsfilter

Die meisten News Reader unterstützen den Anwender mit praktischen Suchfunktionen, die das umfangreiche Angebot der News Server durchforsten. Hat man interessante Foren gefunden, so können diese „abonniert" werden. Mit dieser Funktion werden dann in Zukunft mit dem News Reader immer die neuesten Nachrichten der abonnierten Foren auf den Client-Computer geladen. Somit kann der Anwender die Diskussionen seiner ausgewählten Newsgroups auf einfache Weise mitverfolgen. Man unterscheidet zwischen moderierten und unmoderierten Newsgroups. Bei moderierten Newsgroups überprüft der jeweilige Moderator der Group, ob dieser Beitrag zum Thema der Group passt und gibt die Nachricht frei bzw. lehnt sie ab. Bei unmoderierten Newsgroups hingegen gelangt der neue Nachrichten-Beitrag ungefiltert auf den News Server und wird veröffentlicht.

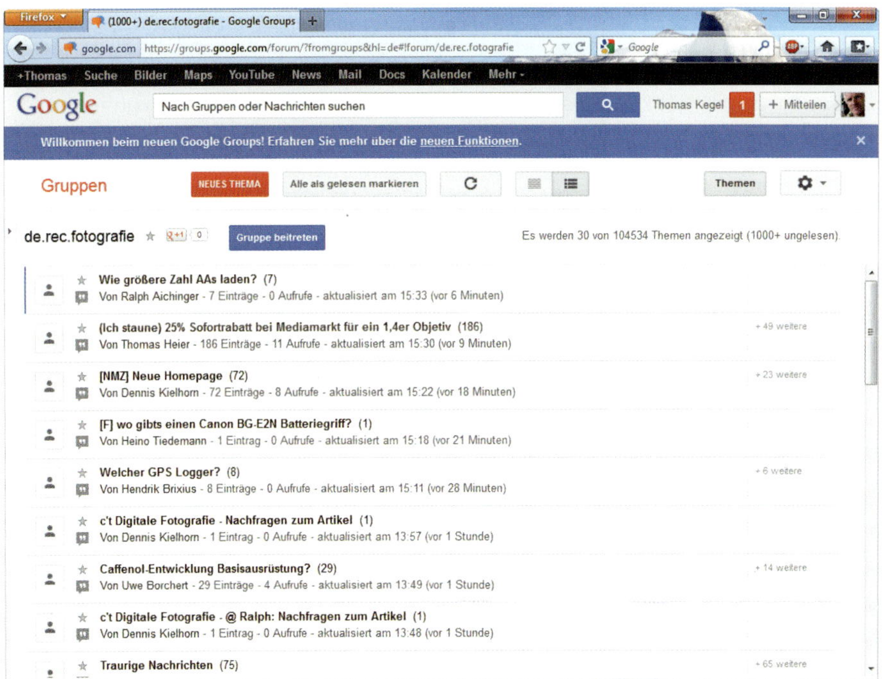

Über Spezialservices z. B. Google.de kann auch ohne einen News Reader auf die Newsgroups des USENET zugegriffen werden (Beispiel: Newsgroup de.rec.fotografie).

13.2.4 Foren

Eine weitere Möglichkeit Informationen zielgerichtet auszutauschen, ist das Internet-**Forum**. Auch hier findet die Kommunikation asynchron statt, das heißt, Fragen, Antworten, Meinungen und Erfahrungen werden online gestellt und können jederzeit wieder aufgerufen werden. Die Diskussionsbeiträge, auch **Postings** genannt, werden in der Regel nach Rubriken strukturiert. Eröffnet ein Beitrag ein neues Thema, dann werden Beiträge zum selben Thema als Diskussionsstränge, als sogenannter **Threads** (engl. für Faden) zusammengefasst.

➲ **Foren sind Diskussions-Plattformen für spezielle Interessensgruppen.**

Anwendung finden sie vorwiegend in Form von Hilfe-Foren für Nutzer eines Produktes, einer Software oder generell eines gemeinsamen Interessensbereichs. Über Internet-Foren haben sich aber auch komerzielle Bewertungs-Communities für Produkte und Dienstleistungen etabliert, die sich primär durch werbung finanzieren (Beispiel: Idealo, Ciao).

Eigene Foren lassen sich durch die Website-Betreiber durch Installieren von Foren-Software einfach realisieren.

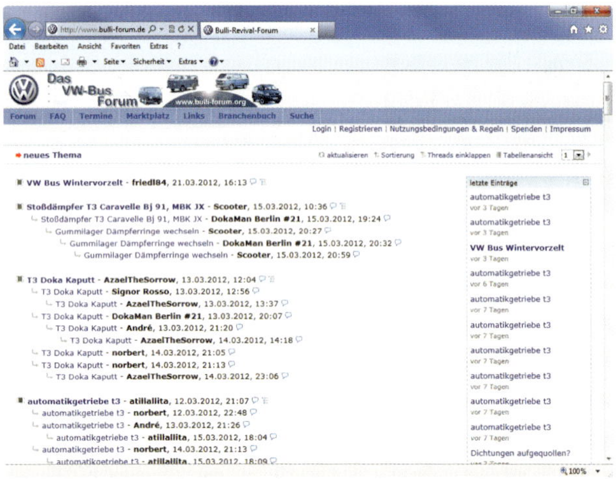

Klassisches Forum mit hierarchischer Darstellung der Themen- und Antwort-Beiträgen eines Threads.
(Beispiel: Das VW-Bus Forum, www.bulli-forum.de).

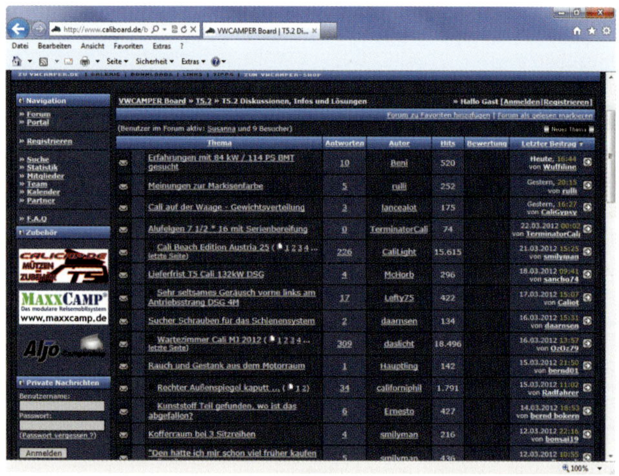

Forum im Stil eines Bulletin Boards mit einer Übersichtsseite der jeweiligen Titel der Threads.
(Beispiel: VWCAMPER Board, www.caliboard.de).

Im klassischen Forum sind die Diskussionsstränge in Form eines Baumes dargestellt. Sortiert sind sie sowohl chronologisch als auch in Bezug zum betreffenden Beitrag. In **Bulletin Boards** hingegen sind alle Themen auf einer Übersichtsseite aufgelistet. Dabei wird immer der Titel des ersten Beitrages eines Diskussionsstranges dargestellt. Erst nach Anklicken eines Themas werden alle Postings chronologisch auf einer bzw. auf Folgeseiten aufgeführt.

13.2.5 Chat

Ein weitere Form des Informationsaustausches ist der **Chat**. Im Gegensatz zu den Newsgroups und den Mailinglisten handelt es sich beim Chat um eine Form der synchronen Online-Interaktion, bei der Menschen sich aus aller Welt in einem virtuellen Raum treffen und in Echtzeit – oder mit geringer Verzögerung – kurze Textnachrichten austauschen. Chat kommt von „plaudern“ und hat im Internet eine eigene Kulturform angenommen. Das Besondere am „Chatten“ ist der Kontakt und die Gespräche nicht nur mit Bekannten, sondern auch mit völlig fremden Menschen. Dabei kann jeder Teilnehmer des Chats eine Identität seiner Wahl annehmen, sei es als weiblicher oder männlicher Chatter, indem er sich nur mit einem **Nicknamen** ❶ zu erkennen gibt. Mit diesem Deckmantel der Anonymität ist es für manche Anwender einfacher und unkomplizierter als im realen Leben, mit Fremden ins Gespräch zu kommen.

❶ **Nickname** ist eine Art Spitzname oder „alias“ des Chat-Teilnehmers. Richtige Namen werden im Chat üblicherweise nicht verwendet.

Die Chatter treffen sich in virtuellen **Chaträumen** (Chatrooms), auch **Kanälen** (Channels) genannt, die es zu allen möglichen Themengebieten gibt. In der Chat-Szene entstehen auch immer mehr sogenannte Online-Communities, bei denen sich Chatter regelmäßig treffen und sogar soziale Beziehungen entwickeln. Grundsätzlich gibt es zwei verschiedene Formen des Chat: den **Internet Relay Chat (IRC)** und den immer populärer werdenden **Webchat**.

Internet Relay Chat

Der **Internet Relay Chat** wurde 1988 als Weiterentwicklung von Unix-Talk, einem Chat-System aus der Unix-Betriebssystemumgebung, entwickelt und gilt als der klassische Chat. Das IRC arbeitet nicht über das WWW und den Browser, sondern es kommuniziert über ein eigenes Netzwerk von IRC-Servern. Auf der Anwenderseite wird eine spezielle Zusatzsoftware, der **IRC-Client** ❷, benötigt. Alternativ zum IRC-Client kann auch über Provider, die ein Web-Interface für den Zugriff auf das IRC anbieten, zugegriffen werden. Bei den über 42 000 IRC-Kanälen kann man leicht den Überblick verlieren. Zur besseren Orientierung sind die Kanäle nach Themen sortiert und bieten dem Chatter zu fast jedem Thema die Möglichkeit, Informationen auszutauschen.

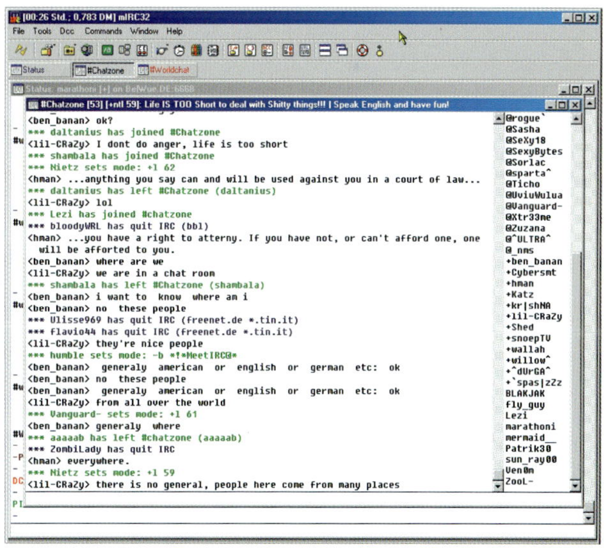

❷ Beispiel einer IRC-Client-Software: mIRC

Der IRC-Chat erfordert vom Chatter die Kenntnisse über IRC-Befehle, die immer mit einem „/“-Zeichen beginnen. Damit steuert der Chatter Aktionen und gibt Informationen aus. Zum Beispiel zeigt der Befehl „/list“ alle verfügbaren Kanäle auf dem Server. Die Kanäle sind keine statischen Einrichtungen, sondern Chatter können Kanäle erzeugen und Kanäle werden bei Nichtbenutzung auch automatisch wieder geschlossen. Deshalb trifft man in den Kanälen häufig auf einen Bot, einen digitalen Roboter, dessen Aufgabe es ist, den Kanal offen zu halten, auch wenn sich kein Chatter mehr in diesem Kanal befindet.

WebChat

Die andere Form des Chats, der **Webchat**, benötigt nur einen aktuellen Internet-Browser und ist im Umgang in der Regel einfacher zu erlernen als der IRC. Viele Portal-Anbieter, Onlineshops und Magazine bieten dezentrale WebChat-Dienste an. Diese sind jedoch untereinander nicht vernetzt und bieten in der Regel branchenspezifische Themen oder lokale Themen zum Chatten an. Zum Beispiel die Web-Auftritte von TV-Reportage-Sendungen wie „maybrit illner Polit-Talk im ZDF“ ❶ oder „WISO“ bieten Webchats zu aktuellen Themen. Dabei sind diese Chat-Veranstaltungen meist direkt an andere Medien-Veranstaltungen, zum Beispiel als nachgeschaltete Diskussionplattform für eine TV-Reportage, gekoppelt.

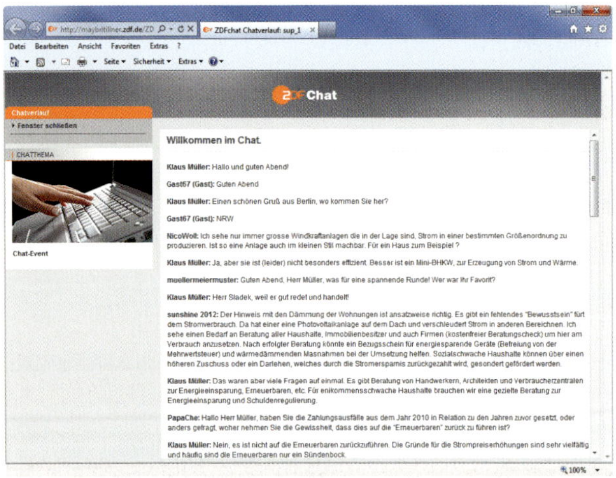

❶ Chat parallel oder im Anschluss an eine TV-Sendung (Beispiel: „maybrit illner Polit-Talk im ZDF “).

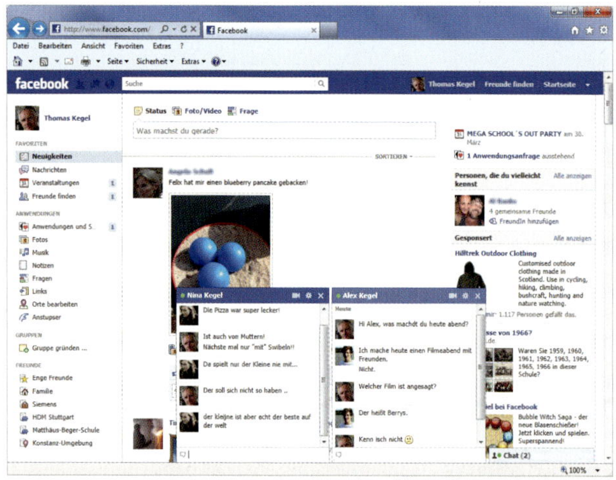

❷ Chat-Raum in der Online-Community „Facebook“.

Auch das Chatten über Online-Communities, wie zum Beispiel „Facebook“ ❷ oder „StudiVZ“ ist ein weit verbreiteter Kommunikationskanal in unserer Gesellschaft geworden. Insbesonder jugendliche Internet-Teilnehmer pflegen darüber soziale Bindungen, treffen spontane Verabredungen und teilen Meinungen aus.

Die Chat-Funktionalität im WebChat wird über zusätzliche Software im Browser realisiert. Dabei kommt z. B. JavaScript, Java oder Flash von Adobe zum Einsatz.

Voice-Chat

Das Chatten ist nicht nur auf den textlichen Onlineplausch begrenzt. In speziellen Sprachchats kann – entsprechende Soundausrüstung, wie Mikrofon, Soundkarte und Boxen vorausgesetzt – der Chatter mit Freunden, Bekannten oder Fremden direkt sprechen. Auf Grund der notwendigen hohen Übertragungsbandbreite für Sprachübertragung sind diese Chat-Räume meist Mischformen aus Text und Sprache.

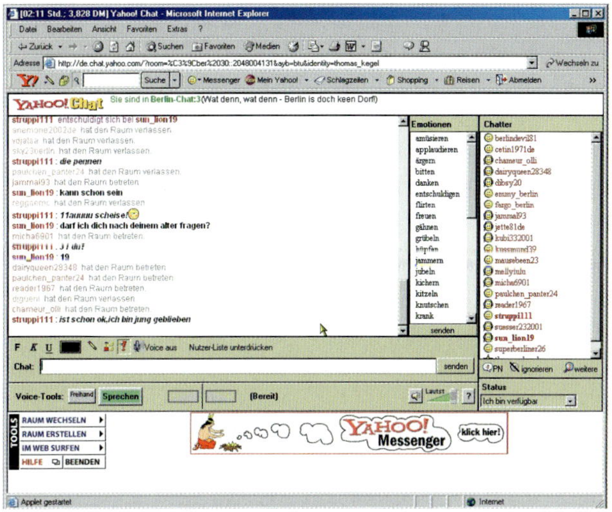

❶ Voice-Unterstützung im Yahoo!-Chat

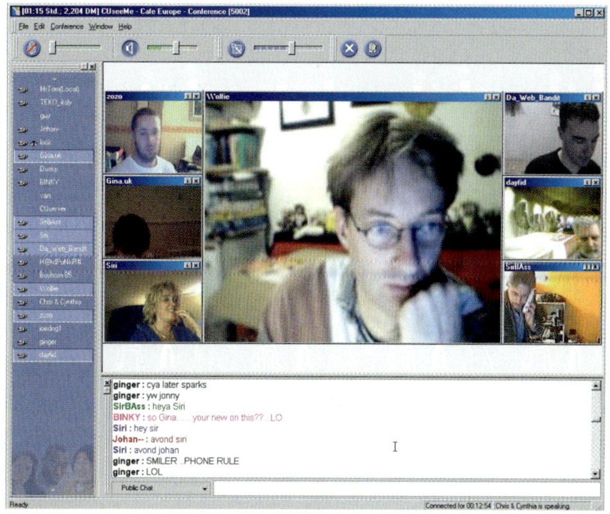

❷ Chatten im Videokonferenzstil mit CUseeMe.

Eine weitere Stufe zur Voice-Unterstützung ❶ ist das visuelle Chatten. Dazu muss eine Webkamera am PC angeschlossen werden und eine spezielle Software, z. B. CUseeMe ❷ von CUseeMe Networks oder Microsoft Netmeeting zum Einsatz kommen. Hat man diese technische Ausstattung, so kann über das Internet regelrecht eine Videokonferenz abgehalten werden.

Instant Messaging

Eine Art „Walkie-Talkie" im Internet ist das sogenannte **Instant Messaging**.

➲ **Beim Instant Messaging handelt es sich nicht um ein eigenständiges Netzwerk, sondern um einen Service größerer Onlinedienste, bei dem kurze Informationen direkt von Teilnehmer zu Teilnehmer ausgetauscht werden können.**

Gleichzeitig wird eine Art Online-Status über Freunde und Bekannte (englisch: **Buddy**), die sich ebenfalls beim Instant Messaging eingetragen haben, gemeldet. Die Buddies müssen dem eigenen System angemeldet werden, damit über ein Telegrammprogramm den Teilnehmern sofort gemeldet wird, ob ein Buddy online gegangen ist oder sich gerade abgemeldet hat. Damit ist man immer über den Online-Status seiner Buddies informiert. Leider handelt es bei diesen Diensten um proprietäre Systeme, die untereinander nur bedingt austauschfähig sind. Im Rahmen der Messaging-Dienste kann über eine Art Mini-Chat direkt mit den Buddy kommuniziert werden.

Verbreitete Systeme sind der MSN Messenger ❸ von Microsoft, der Yahoo! Messenger, der Klassiker ICQ („I seek you" = Ich suche Dich) oder Messenger, die sozusagen Buddy-kompatibel sind, d. h. die Buddies aus unterschiedlichen Messengern integrieren können (z. B. Trillian oder Stern).

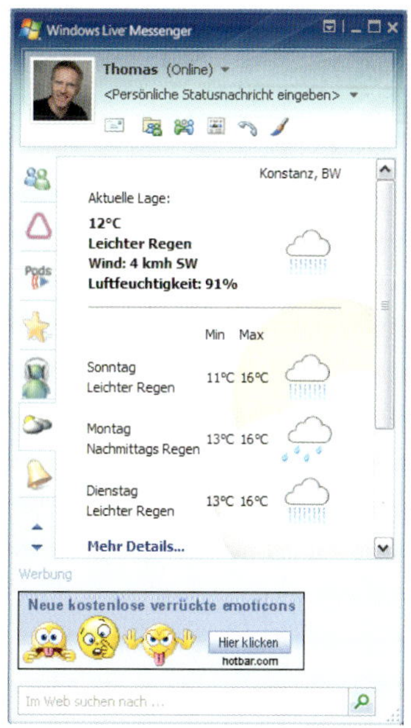

❸

3D-Chat

❶ Das Wort **Avatar** bedeutet soviel wie die „Fleischwerdung" (Inkarnation) eines Geistes. In den digitalen Medien ist darunter die Repräsentation einer Person in einer virtuellen Gemeinschaft in Form einer Figur gemeint.

Eine weitere Stufe im multimedialen Chat stellt der **3D-Chat** dar. Hier agiert der Chatter als bewegliche 3D-Figur in virtuellen Räumen und trifft auf andere Chatter, mit denen er über Text, Mimik und Bewegung kommunizieren kann. Dabei nimmt jeder Chatter die Gestalt eines virtuellen Körpers, den sogenannten **Avatar** ❶, an.

➲ **„Avatare" sind virtuelle Körper, die über Bewegung, Mimik und Kleidung das Chatten in neue Dimensionen bringen.**

Der Chatter kann seinen virtuellen Körper (Avatar) wechseln und aktiv auf die Raumgestaltung einwirken.

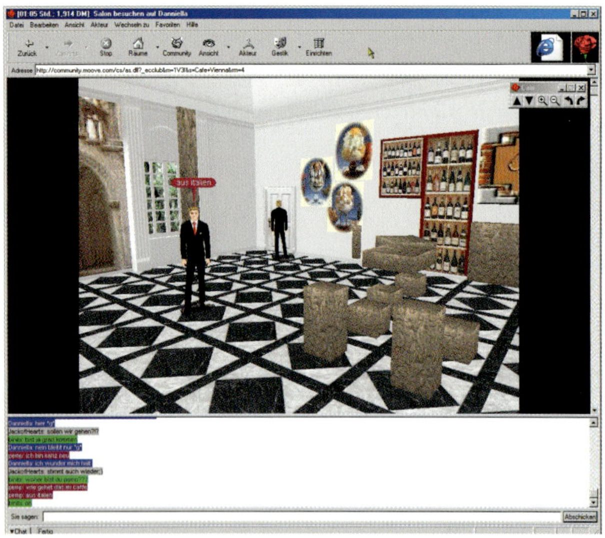

❷ In der **Community** „Moove Online" kann der Chatter die Gestaltung eigener virtueller Räume vornehmen (www.moove.de).

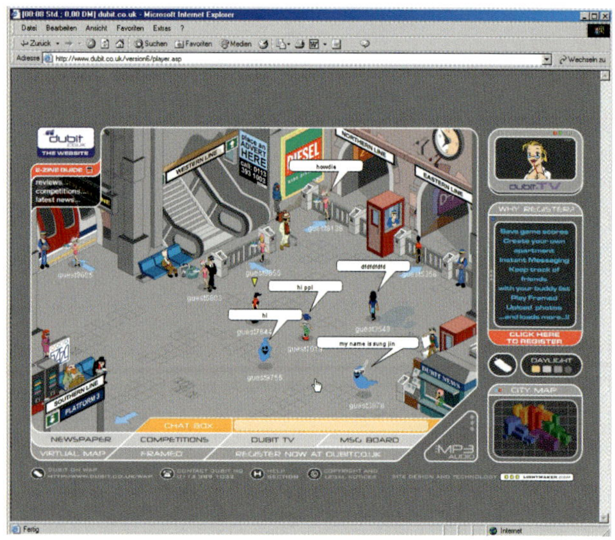

❸ Eine in Flash realisierte virtuelle Stadt als Chatwelt (Dubit-Flash-Chat, www.dubit.co.uk).

Diese Chat-Räume werden auch als **Communities** ❷ bezeichnet und benötigen noch spezielle Browser, die als proprietäre Software miteinander nicht kompatibel sind und zum Chatten vom Anwender vorher über das Internet geladen und installiert werden müssen. Einfacher verhalten sich da 3D-Chats, die in „Flash" von Adobe programmiert sind ❸. Flash ist in aktuellen WWW-Browser-Versionen als Standard-Erweiterung integriert und muss in der Regel nicht gesondert installiert werden.

Eine sehr populäre Variante der 3D-Chat Communitys ist Second Life, das im Jahr 2011 schon über 28 Millionen registrierte Nutzer aufweisen konnte. Second Life vermischt 3D-Chat, Simulation und Online-Spiel. Die Nutzer können kommunizieren, spielen und Handel treiben, in dem sie sich gegenseitig virtuelle Waren und Dienstleistungen anbieten. Dazu existiert sogar eine virtuelle Währung, der sogenannte Linden Dollar, der auch in echte US-Dollars umtauschbar ist.

Die virtuelle Welt existiert dabei in einer großen **Serverfarm** ❶, die von Linden Labs betrieben wird. Zur Darstellung der kontinuierlichen 3D-Animation wird eine Client-Software verwendet, die ein Raumgefühl verleiht und in die zusätzliche Audio- und Videostreams eingebunden werden können.

❶ Eine **Serverfarm** ist eine Gruppe von gleichartigen, vernetzten Servern, welche zu einem logischen System verbunden sind.

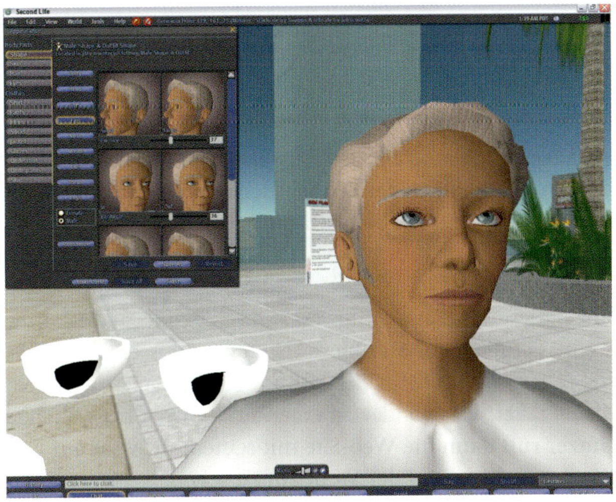

Der Nutzer kann seinen Avatar individuell gestalten.

In Second Life kann Land erworben, Häuser gebaut und Handel betrieben werden.

Da die Nutzer die virtuelle Welt selbst entwickeln können, entstehen immer mehr neue Gegenstände, wie Landgestaltung, Häuser, Wohnungen, Kleider, Accessoires, mit denen auch gehandelt werden kann.

Mittlerweile sind auch Firmen und Institutionen in Second Life vertreten, welche diese Plattform vor allem für PR-Zwecke verwenden. Firmen können hier ohne große Kosten Artikel erstellen und verbreiten, um zu sehen, ob die Produktinformationen oder das Image bei potenziellen Käufern Anklang finden würden.

So nutzen Firmen, wie Apple, Adidas, BMW, Mercedes Benz, Mazda, IBM, Reebok, Sony BMG, Deutsche Post u. a. die virtuelle Welt als Kommunikationsmedium. Zum Beispiel bietet Adidas Schuhe aus der aktuellen Kollektion für den Avatar des Nutzers zum kaufen an.

Neben Firmen sind inzwischen auch verschiedene private und staatliche Organisationen und Institutionen in Second Life präsent. So findet man dort u. a. auch ein Büro von Greenpeace, virtuelle Botschaften sowie eine Repräsentanz des deutschen Bundeslandes Baden-Württemberg.

Szene aus Second Life. Beispiel Apple auf Apfelland.

❶ Die VoIP-Software **Skype** wird inzwischen von mehr als 9 Millionen Benutzern täglich genutzt.

mern zu IP-Adressen besteht und das Endgerät des Anrufers beim Verbindungsaufbau dort immer die aktuelle IP-Adresse des Gesprächsteilnehmers erfragen muss. Als herstellerunabhängiges Signalisierungsprotokoll wird das Session Initiation Protocol (SIP) verwendet. Die Teilnehmer besitzen bei SIP eine SIP-Adresse (ähnlich einer E-Mail-Adresse) im Uniform-Resource-Identifier-Format (URI-Format), wie zum Beispiel „sip:12345@beispiel-server.de“. Die eigentliche Gesprächsübertragung geschieht dann direkt über das Netzwerk von IP-Adresse zu IP-Adresse über das Real Time Transport Protocol (RTP).

Die am meisten verwendete VoIP-Software ist **Skype** ❶. Skypes VoIP-Protokoll ist proprietär und kann nur mit der Original Skype-Software genutzt werden. Mit anderen Protokollen, wie zum Beispiel SIP ist Skype nicht kompatibel. Skype arbeitet nach der Peer-to-Peer-Technologie (P2P) und verursacht auch ohne Telefonie, zum Beispiel für Telefonbuch-Anfragen, einen hohen permanenten Datenverkehr im Netz. Der Funktionsumfang von Skype wird durch Gruppenunterhaltungen und –diskussionen, Chat-Funktionen und Videogespräche kontinuierlich erweitert.

Da das Internet in seiner heutigen Form auf Grund des TCP/IP-Prinzips und der schwankenden Datenübertragungsgeschwindigkeit keine gesicherte Übertragungsqualität zwischen Teilnehmern garantiert, kann es durchaus zu Übertragungsverlusten, störenden Echos oder Aussetzern kommen, so dass die Sprachqualität nicht ganz der von herkömmlichen Telefonnetzen entspricht. Voraussetzung für VoIP ist ein qualitativ hochwertiger Internet-Anschluss mit hohen Down- und Upstream-Geschwindigkeiten.

13.2.7 FTP

FTP

❷ Bei sogenannten „Anonymous-FTP-Servern“ lautet der Anmeldename „anonymous“ und als Passwort wird immer die eigene E-Mail-Adresse eingegeben.

Der Internet-Dienst „**File Transfer Protocol**“ (**FTP**) ermöglicht das Übertragen von Daten auf der Basis des TCP/IP-Protokolls. Er arbeitet nach dem Client-Server-Prinzip und verwendet während der Datenübertragung eine permanente Verbindung zwischen dem FTP-Server und dem FTP-Client. Der FTP ist einer der ältesten Internet-Dienste und wird vorwiegend für den Transport von großen Datenmengen eingesetzt. Dabei schickt der Sender (FTP-Client) die Daten per „Upload“ auf dem FTP-Server, von dem andere Empfänger (FTP-Client) diese Daten per „Download“ abholen können. Der Zugang zu einem FTP-Server kann paßwortgeschützt oder anonym ❷ erfolgen. Zur Bedienung der FTP-Kommandos verwendet man eine FTP-Client-Software ❸, die je nach Ausführung ein einfaches und visuelles Arbeiten, ähnlich dem „Windows-Explorer“, erlaubt. Eine typische Anwendung für den FTP-Dienst ist das im Rahmen eines Website-Betriebes erforderliche „Hochladen“ (Upload) der Homepage-Daten auf einen Web-Server.

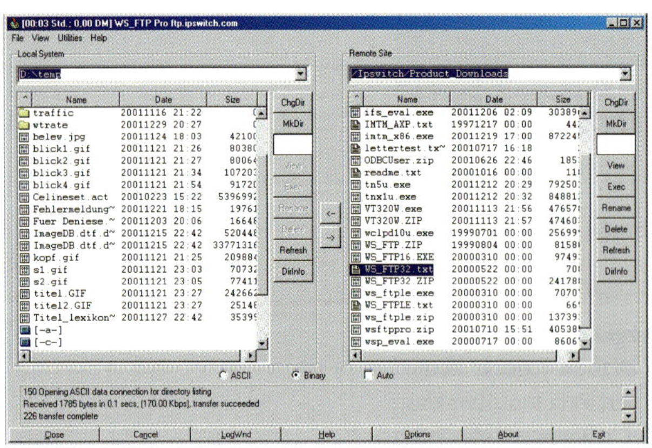

❸ Mit einer FTP-Client-Software wird der Datentransfer bedient. Beispiel: WS_FTP Pro.

13.2.8 Suchdienste und Agenten

Mit der Verbreitung des WWW im Internet stieg das Angebot an Informationen und Dokumenten im Internet enorm. Da das WWW kein organisiertes Informationsnetz ist, scheint es nahezu unmöglich, die Informationen zu finden, die man sucht.
Um trotzdem im Internet fündig zu werden, gibt es eine Reihe von Lösungen: Portale, Webkataloge oder -verzeichnisse, Suchmaschinen und Metasuchmaschinen.

Portale

Namhafte Online-Dienste-Provider bieten „**Portale**" als Zugang zu den Informationen im WWW zur Verfügung. Portale sind aufwändig gestaltete Websites, die den Eindruck vermitteln sollen, dass sie den idealen Zugang zum Internet bieten. Sie versuchen, ein möglichst attraktives und vielfältiges Angebot von Diensten und Links auf weitere Informationen im Internet anzubieten.

❶ Yahoo! war historisch gesehen eines der ersten Portale, als Jerry Yang und David Filo an der Stanford Universität begannen, eine durchsuchbare, nach Kategorien geordnete Linkliste zur Verfügung zu stellen.

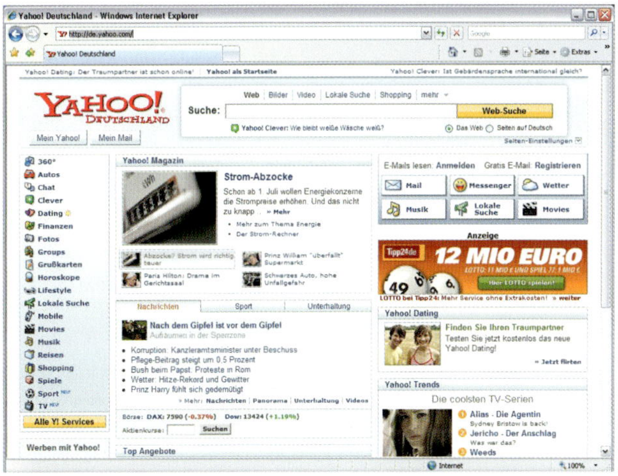

❶ Portale bieten auch vom Benutzer konfigurierbare Bereiche (Beispiel: Yahoo!).

❷ Portale mit Themenschwerpunkten sprechen bestimmte Zielgruppen an (Beispiel: Linux-Knowledge-Portal).

Es gibt Portale, die eher von allgemeinem Interesse sind, wie z. B. Yahoo! ❶, MSN, AOL oder T-Online, und Portale, die mit einem Themenschwerpunkt ❷ auf eine spezielle Zielgruppe gerichtet sind. Das Angebot ist in der Regel kostenlos und wird primär durch Werbebanner auf der Portalseite finanziert.

Zu den üblichen Angeboten auf Portalseiten gehören:

- Nachrichten oder Neuheiten in Form von Schlagzeilen und Links
- Kommunikationsdienste, wie Instant Messager und Chat
- Links zu Lexika, Telefon-, Adress- und E-Mail-Verzeichnissen etc.
- Suchmaschine und Webkatalog
- Individuelle anpassbare Terminkalender, Adressbücher und Bookmark-Manager, die über das Internet von jedem PC aus verwendbar sind
- Bestimmte Bereiche des Portals individuell konfigurierbar, d. h. der Portal-Benutzer kann aus einer Auswahl seine Portalsicht zusammenstellen.

Webkataloge

Bei Webkatalogen oder -verzeichnissen ❶ erstellen Redaktionen eine bewertete Katalogisierung der Informationen im Internet. Sie begutachten unzählige von Webseiten und entscheiden, welche Themen für die Zielgruppe interessant sind. Dabei bilden sie Kategorien und Unterkategorien und legen virtuelle Karteikarten mit Stichwörtern an. Auf Grund dieses sehr zeitaufwändigen Verfahrens bilden Webkataloge nur einen Bruchteil des Internets ab. Durch die Prüfung und Bewertung wirken sie aber sehr aufgeräumt und bieten qualitativ hochwertige Links.
Eine automatisierte **Katalogisierung** ❷ erreicht heute noch nicht das Niveau, welches bei der manuellen Sortierung besteht.

❷ Ein bekanntes Beispiel der automatischen **Katalogisierung** ist die Bildung von Ad-hoc-Kategorien aus Suchbegriffen. Ein Beispiel ist der WiseGuide des Suchdienstes WiseNut.

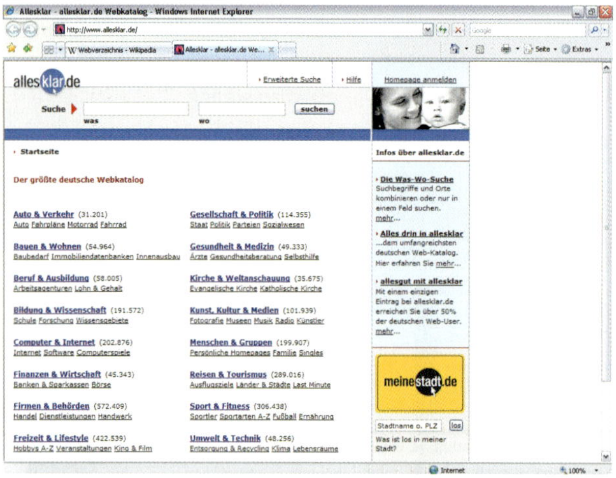

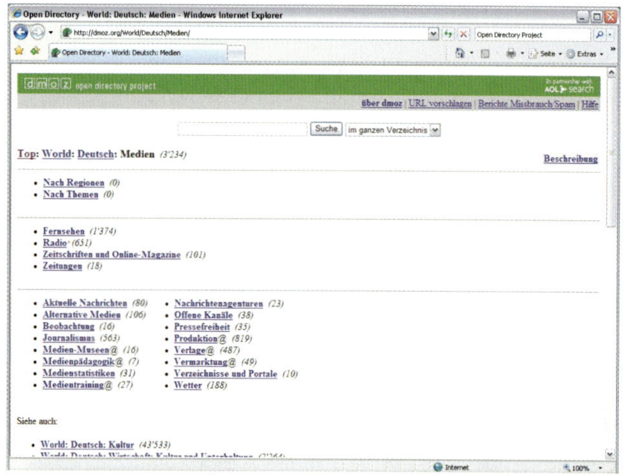

❶ **Webkataloge** bieten eine strukturierte Sicht auf eine Auswahl von Informationen im Internet (Linkes Beispiel: Allesklar.de. Rechtes Beispiel: Open Directory Project).

Suchmaschinen

Einen weitaus unstrukturierteren Such-Dienst stellen die „Suchmaschinen" ❸ dar. Dabei handelt es sich vorwiegend um Hochleistungscomputer mit einer großen Datenbank. Die Suchmaschinen durchforsten rund um die Uhr das Internet nach neuen Webseiten. Dabei hangeln sich spezielle Datensammler, sogenannte **Robots** oder **Spider** genannt, von Link zu Link und melden bei einer neu entdeckten Website einem **Software-Agenten** ❹ der Suchmaschine den Namen der URL. Somit kann der Agent dieses Dokument holen und einer Index-Software übergeben, die aus der Website bestimmte Informationen ausliest, diese indiziert und der großen Suchmaschinen-Datenbank übergibt.

Startet nun ein Internet-Nutzer eine Suche, so gibt er Stichwörter, nach denen gesucht werden soll, in die Suchmaske der Suchmaschine ein. Je nach Suchmaschine bekommt er eine detaillierte Auflistung der Treffer aus der Datenbank mit kurzen Kontexthinweisen und der Angabe der Wahrscheinlichkeit.

Bei zu allgemein formulierten Suchbegriffen wird der Benutzer von der Suchmaschine regelrecht mit scheinbaren Ergebnissen überschüttet.

❸ Die **Suchmaschinen** werden auch WebSpiders bzw. WebCrawler genannt, da sie bei der Suche nach Informationen das Internet durchkrabbeln (englisch: crawl) oder sich von Link zu Link wie eine Spinne (englisch: spider) durchhangeln.

❹ **Software-Agenten** sind Programme, die selbstständig Daten sammeln und ohne zusätzliche Benutzeraktion Daten austauschen. Agenten agieren unbeaufsichtigt durch das Netz, um ihre komplexen Aufträge zu erledigen. Deshalb werden sie auch gerne als „gutartige" Viren betrachtet.

➲ **Je allgemeiner das Suchwort, desto unüberschaubarer das Ergebnis.**

Zur genaueren Eingrenzung der Suche sollte man den Suchbegriff möglichst ausführlich formulieren. Darum bieten die Suchmaschinen mit logischen Verknüpfungen ❶, wie „UND“ und „ODER“ zusätzliche Verknüpfung von Suchbegriffen und besonderen Einschränkungen im Suchbereich. Die Standardeinstellung beim Suchbegriff ist bei den meisten Suchmaschinen die UND-Verknüpfung. Wenn nach Webseiten gesucht wird, bei denen zum Beispiel die Begriffe „Konstanz“ und „Hörnle“ gleichzeitig vorkommen sollen, so müssen nur die Begriffe mit einem Leerzeichen getrennt eingegeben werden. Bei der Suchmaschine Google ❷ können die einzelnen Suchbegriffe auch mit einem „+“ getrennt, oder bei einer ODER-Verknüpfung mit einem „OR“ oder „|“ getrennt eingegeben werden.

❶ Die meisten Suchmaschinen unterstützen **Bool'sche Operatoren**. Damit lassen sich Suchbegriffe mit „und“, „oder“ oder „nicht“ miteinander verknüpfen.

❷ Bei Suchmaschinenanfragen im deutschen Internet besitzt **Google** bereits einen Marktanteil von über 90 Prozent. Das Verb „googeln“, wurde sogar in den Rechtschreib-Duden aufgenommen und steht dabei nicht nur für die Suche mit Google, sondern teilweise schon allgemein als Synonym für Websuche mit beliebigen anderen Suchmaschinen.

Um die Suche weiter einzugrenzen, kann man auch nach exakten Phrasen suchen. Die Suchbegriffe tauchen dann nicht wahllos im Dokument auf, sondern müssen in einer bestimmten Anordnung vorhanden sein. Exakte Suchphrasen werden zum Beispiel bei Google mit Anführungszeichen „„...““ kenntlich gemacht.

Als weiteres Ausschlusskriterium kann zum Beispiel bei Google ein Minuszeichen „-“ Verwendung finden. Suchbeispiel: „Hannibal -Lecter“. Sucht nach einem antiken Feldherrn und schließt aber Seiten aus, in denen der Name in Verbindung mit einer Filmfigur namens „Lecter“ steht.

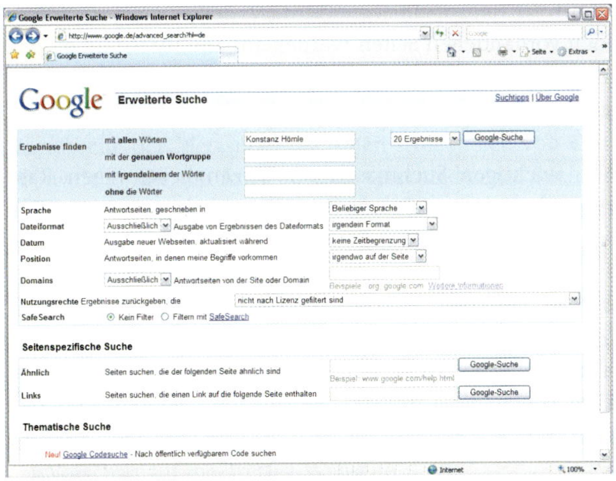

❸ Typische Suchmaske einer Suchmaschine bei einer erweiterten Suche (Beispiel: Google).

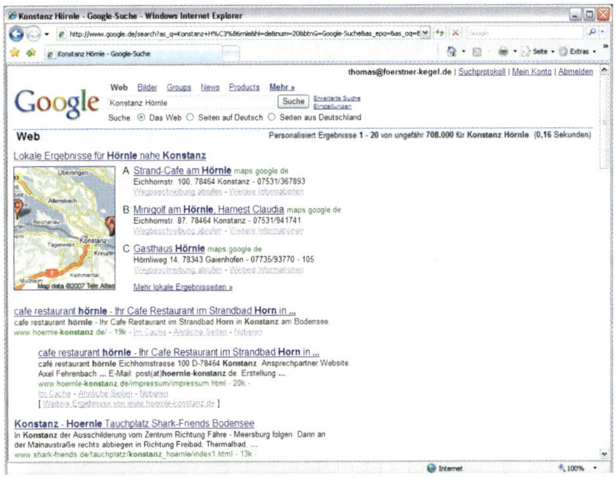

Auflistung der Treffer mit kurzen Kontexthinweisen und teilweise grafischen Ortshinweisen (Beispiel: Google).

Alle diese Funktionen sind über die Erweiterte Suche ❸ über ein Formular zugänglich. Dort finden sich auch darüber hinaus gehende Suchmasken, über welche die Suche zum Beispiel auf spezielle Dateitypen und Suchbereiche eingeschränkt werden kann oder es kann nach Webseiten gesucht werden, die einer anderen Website sehr ähnlich sind.

Agenten

Software-Agenten ❶ werden nicht nur als Vermittler bei Metasuchmaschinen eingesetzt, sondern können als digitale Assistenten weitaus mehr Rechercheaufgaben im Internet übernehmen. Es handelt sich hierbei um gewissermaßen „intelligente“ Robots, die selbstständig Webkataloge, Onlineshops und andere Informationsdienste besuchen und dabei mit diesen Diensten kommunizieren und hochwertige Informationen zusammentragen. Dies beschränkt sich nicht nur auf die Ortsbeschreibung von Suchtreffern, sondern es können Produkt- oder Preisvergleiche sein, das Zusammentragen von personalisierten Informationen für Online-Zeitungen oder das Mitteilen über Informationsveränderungen im Internet. Realisierungsbeispiele findet man zum Beispiel bei AutoBingooo ❷, Copernic Shopper, My Yahoo! und Webplanet.

❶ Als **Software-Agent** bezeichnet man ein Computerprogramm, das weitgehend unabhängig von Benutzereingriffen arbeitet, es löst Aktionen aufgrund eigener Initiative aus (proaktiv), reagiert auf Änderung der Umgebung (reaktiv), es kommuniziert mit anderen Agenten und lernt aufgrund zuvor getätigter Entscheidungen bzw. Beobachtungen.

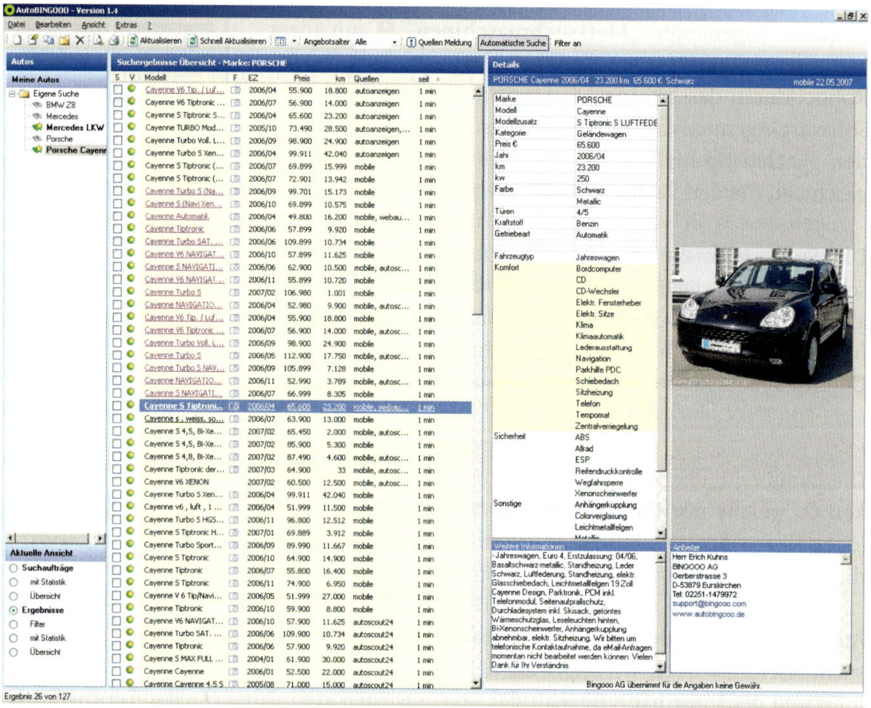

❷ Die Agenten-Software AutoBingooo durchsucht eine Vielzahl von Autobörsen und wertet die Daten der Neu- und Gebrauchtwagen aus. Die Ergebnisse werden einheitlich und übersichtlich mit Foto dargestellt. Zahlreiche weitere Details wie Preis, km-Stand, Motor etc. können als Ordnungs- und Selektionskriterium verwendet werden.

Das Anwendungsspektrum dieser digitalen Helfer ist derzeit noch sehr diffus und es wird an einer ganzen Reihe von Forschungsarbeiten und Projekten an immer spezielleren und umfassenderen Agenten gearbeitet. Eine Informationsplattform für die Entwicklung von Agenten ist die UMBC (University of Maryland Baltimore County).

13.2.9 Mobiles Internet

Der Zugriff von unterwegs auf Informationen im Internet bekommt einen immer höheren Stellenwert. Schnell mal eine Bahnverbindung abfragen, Kinokarten reservieren, E-Mails abrufen, In Facebook schauen was Freunde tun oder ortsspezifische Informationen über den aktuellen Standort erfragen, ist Dank heutiger mobiler Endgeräte und der immer schneller werdenden Mobilfunkstandards kein Problem mehr.

Mobile Endgeräte

Endgeräte für den mobilen Einsatz zeichnen sich durch praktikable Größen und der Nutzungsmöglichkeit von Mobilfunk und/oder WLAN-Tauglichkeit aus.

Dazu gehören

- Mobiltelefone mit WAP-Browsern ❶ (Mittlerweile von Smartphones abgelöst.)
- **PDAs** (Personal Digital Assistants) – PocketPC mit Windows CE oder Palm PDA (Weitgehend von Smartphones abgelöst.)
- **Smartphones** ❷ – das am weitesten verbreitete Endgerät in Telefongröße
- **Tablet-PCs** ❸ – Endgerät in Buchgröße ohne mechanischer Tastatur
- Notebooks, Subnotebooks und Netbooks ❹ – komplette mobile Computer mit richtiger Tastatur.

❶ WAP-fähiges Mobiltelefon

❷ Smartphone mit Betriebssystem Android 4 (Beispiel: HTC One S)

❸ Tablet-PC mit Betriebssystem iOS 5 (Beipiel: iPad von Apple.)

❹ Netbook mit Betriebssystem Microsoft Windows 7 (Beispiel: Samsung Netbook)

WAP

Angefangen hat der mobile Internet-Zugang mit dem **WAP** (**Wireless Application Protocol**, deutsch: Protokoll für drahtlose Anwendungen), einem Internet-Dienst, der sich ausschließlich auf den mobilen Bereich konzentriert.
Die Endgeräte waren dabei Mobiltelefone, die über einen WAP-fähigen Microbrowser verfügen und über ein Mobilfunknetzwerk mit dem Internet in Verbindung treten.

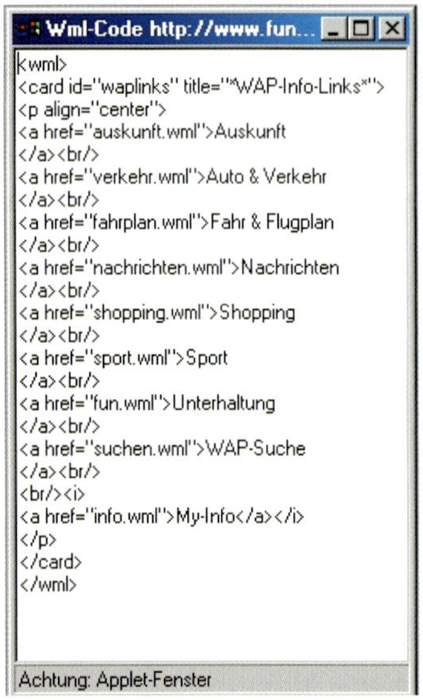

❷ Inhalte für das WAP müssen in **WML** aufbereitet sein.

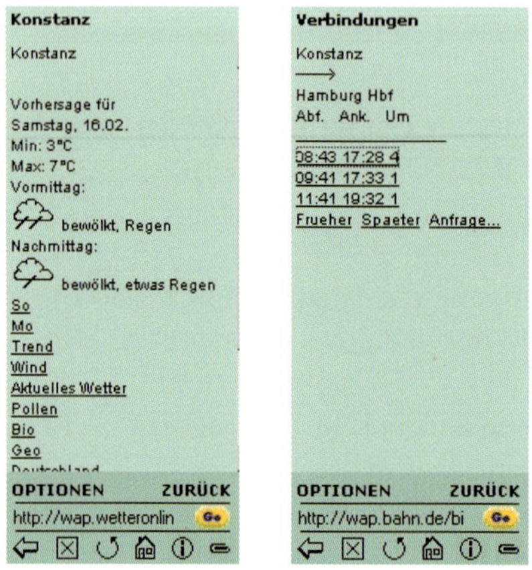

❶ Textbasierte WAP-Anwendungen

Aufgrund der anfänglich geringen Datenübertragungsgeschwindigkeit und der geringen Displaygröße wurden die Inhalte speziell für WAP-Endgeräte angepasst und beinhalteten primär aktuelle Informationen in Textform ❶.

Dazu wurde die offene Sprache WML ❷ (Wireless Markup Language) entwickelt, die HTML (Hypertext Markup Language) sehr ähnlich ist. Der erwartete WAP-Boom nach der Markteinführung blieb jedoch aus.

Mobile-gerechte Websites

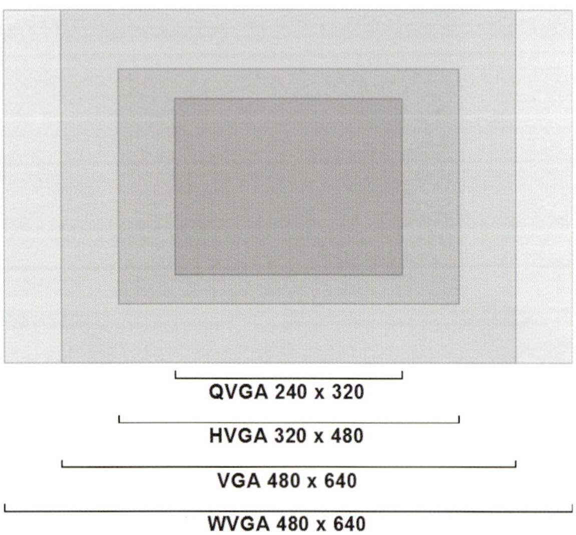

❸ Standardisierte Auflösungen, die sich an VGA orientieren.

Mit Verbreitung der mobilen Endgeräte, die über eine grafische Darstellung in entsprechender Auflösung verfügen, und schnellerer Mobilfunkstandards, übernehmen normale Internet-Browser die Darstellung der Web-Seiten.

Standardisierte Display-Auflösungen ❸, die sich an die Desktop VGA-Größe orientieren, haben sich in der Praxis nicht durchgesetzt. Sie dienen nur als grobe Orientierung. Design, kompakte Bauform und optimale Lesbarkeit sind die Maßstäbe der Smartphone-Hersteller.
Mobile Web-Seiten müssen deshalb mit verschiedensten Auflösungen und Seitenverhältnissen klar kommen. Die Auflösung wird hierbei durch die physikalische Auflösung des Displays definiert aber auch durch die optische Lesbarkeit des Menschen.

Mittlerweile können auch physikalisch kleine Displays über hohe Auflösungen verfügen. Beispiel: Das iPhone 4S von Apple verfügt über ein 3,5 Zoll (Inch) Display mit 960 × 640 Pixeln. Dies ergibt eine physikalische Auflösung von 326 ppi (PPi = Pixel per Inch).

Bei hochauflösenden Desktop-Monitoren hingegen geht man von 120-150 dpi aus. Deshalb erreicht eine für den Desktop optimierte Web-Seite auf einem mobilen Endgerät mit gleicher physikalischer Auflösung nicht die gleiche Lesequalität. Schriften müssen größer dargestellt werden. Die hohe Auflösung sorgt dabei durch Glättungsverfahren für eine optimierte Darstellungsqualität.

Bei einer vergleichbar nutzbaren Auflösung spricht man hierbei von vituellen Pixeln.

➲ **Web-Seiten müssen für mobile Endgeräte angepasst werden.**

Hochformatige Darstellung auf einem Smartphone (Beispiel: Google News auf einem HTC mit Android).

Hochformatige Darstellung auf einem Tablet-PC (Beispiel: Google News auf einem Apple iPad mit iOS).

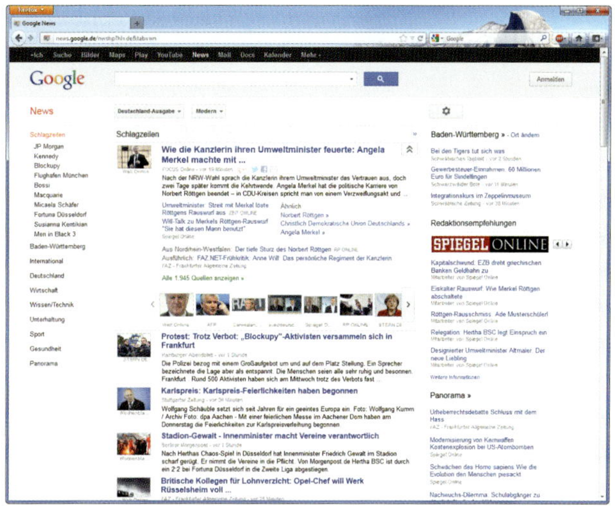

Querformatige Darstellung auf einem Netbook (Beispiel: Google News auf einem Netbook mit Windows).

Kriterien dazu sind:

Effektive Lesbarkeit (virtuelle Pixel)
Auflösungen und Pixelabstände sind bei mobilen Endgeräten nicht von Desktop-Monitoren übertragbar. Der effektive Betrachtungsabstand kann durch Skalieren (Zoomen) durch den Benutzer variiert werden. Dies sollte jedoch nur in Ausnahmefällen in die Seitengestaltung eingeplant weden.

Konzentration auf das Wesentliche
Auf Grund des geringen Platzes ist es besonders wichtig sich auf die wichtigsten Punkte der Web-Seite zu konzentrieren. Typische Fragen dazu sind: Welche Informationen benötigt der Benutzer? Was sind die wichtigsten Inhalte? Wie können die Inhalte klar und übersichtlich präsentiert werden? Auf welche Informationen und Designelemente kann verzichtet werden?

Design-optimiert für Touchscreens
Das Navigieren über Touchscreens erfordert ausreichend große interaktive Schaltflächen, die auch als interaktive Flächen erkennbar sind. Ein Bildlauf (engl. Scrollen) sollte dabei immer nur in eine Richtung notwendig sein. Auch wenn moderne Touch-

screen-Display ein einfaches Zoomen mittels Gestensteuerung über zwei Finger erlauben, ist es nicht lesefreundlich, wenn der Bildschirminhalt in mehrere Richtungen verschoben werden muss.

Unterschiedliche Seiten-Orientierungen

Mobile Endgeräte sind flexibel im Einsatz und können schnell zwischen Hochformat und Querformat umschalten. Dies erfolgt meistens automatisch über einen Lage-Sensor. Deshalb müssen mobile Web-Seiten die Fähigkeit besitzen sich an unterschiedliche Seiten-Orientierungen anzupassen. Dies kann beispielsweise mit sogenannten „Fluid Layouts“ erfolgen. Dabei werden Designelemente, Bilder und eingebettete Videos mit Hilfe relativer Bezüge (Prozent-Angabe zur Seitenbreite) skaliert und somit an das fexible Format angepasst.

❶ Browserweichen (engl. browser sniffing) ermitteln serverseitig mittels Skripting den Browsertyp.

❷ Anwendungs-Programm (engl. Application, kurz „App“) ist ein für mobile Endgeräte optimiertes Software-Programm. Das Programm wird individuell für das Betriebssystem (Android, iOS, Windows Phone) erstellt.

Kompatibilität mit eingeschränkten Browsern

Browsern auf mobilen Endgeräten sind in der Regel gegenüber ihrer Desktop-Varianten im Funktionsumfang eingeschränkt. Dies bezieht sich primär auf die Unterstützng von Skriptsprachen, Stylesheets und Plugins. Beispielsweise unterstützt der Browser Safari auf dem Apple iPhone und dem iPad kein Adobe Flash, welches auf Desktop-Webseiten eine große Verbreitung erreicht hat. Zum Testen der mobilen Web-Seiten für verschiedenste mobile Endgeräte sind Test-Plattformen im Internet verfügbar, die ständig an die wechselnden Endgeräte angepasst werden.

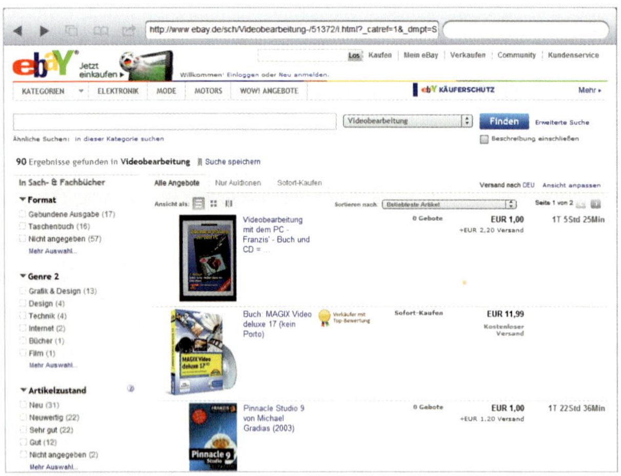

Unterschiedliche Darstellung für unterschiedliche mobile Endgeräte (Beispiel: Internet Auktionshauses eBay).

Oben: Webseiten-basierte Darstellung der Angebote auf einem Apple iPad.

Rechts: Die Darstellung aus der gleichen Informationsquelle über eine App auf einem Smartphone mit Android-Betriebssystem.

Um den Besonderheiten der mobilen Displays gerecht zu werden, gibt es mehrere Möglichkeiten:

1. Mobile Web-Seiten vorhalten

Der Anbieter erzeugt zusätzlich zum Desktop-optimiertem Web ein spezielles Mobile Web. Die Inhalte dazu werden in der Regel einmal in darstellungsneutralen Datenbanken (Content Management System) gepflegt und dann in die Zielumgebungen produziert. Eine Browserweiche ❶ liest den Browsertyp und die Darstellungsgröße aus und verzweigt dann zum geeignetem Web.

2. Einfache „Fluid Layouts“ verwenden

Hierbei verzichtet man auf feste Layouts. Alle Bildschirm-Elemente werden in Abhängigkeit der Displaygröße skaliert und positioniert. Dies ergibt für den Web-Designer eine sehr eingeschränkte Gestaltungsmöglichkeit.

3. Informationen in ein spezielles Darstellungsprogramm (App) packen

Die Informationen der Desktop-Website, zum Beispiel ein Nachrichtenartikel, wird nicht über einen Browser dargestellt, sondern über ein **App** ❷ geladen, mobile-gerecht aufbereitet und dargestellt.

13.2.10 Netiquette

Die Vielfalt von Diensten und neuen Kommunikationsformen im Internet erfordern gewisse Spielregeln im Umgang miteinander. Dort, wo mehrere Personen miteinander in Kontakt treten (im Internet sind das mehrere Millionen Menschen) sind Benimmregeln, an die sich alle halten, unabdingbar. Unter dem Begriff „**Netiquette**" ❶ haben sich Standards für den Umgang der Internet-Teilnehmer in den einzelnen Diensten etabliert. Eigentlich ist die Netiquette eher als ein Ehrenkodex zu verstehen und nicht als bindendes Recht, da es die Nutzer und Betreiber selbst in der Hand haben, negatives Verhalten im Internet zu ahnden.

Beim Schreiben von E-Mails und bei öffentlichen Diskussionen in Newslettern, Mailinglisten oder im Usenet haben sich Vereinfachungen in Form von Abkürzungen und **Emoticons** ❷ verbreitet. Als Abkürzungen werden **Akronyme** ❸ verwendet.

Einige wichtige Emoticons:

:-)	Spaßig
;-)	Scherzhaft, ironisch
:-)))	Sehr fröhlich
:-D	Breites Lächeln
(:-)	Breites Grinsen
:-(	Ziemlich sauer
:-	Herbe Enttäuschung
:-[	Schmollen
:*)	Hicks
:-/	Skeptisch
:-v	Schreiend
:-@	Brüllen
:-I	Ist mir egal
:-x	Ich schweige wie ein Grab
:'-)	Weinen
I-o	Gähnen
:-<	Traurig
:-0	Ruhe!
:->	Bitterböse Bemerkung machen
:-e	Enttäuscht
%-(	Verwirrt

Einige wichtige Akronyme:

<g>	grinsen
<i>	irony (ist ironisch gemeint)
<jk>	just kidding (nur ein Scherz)
<l>	laugh (lachen)
<s>	sigh (Seufz)
< >	no comment (kein Kommentar)
ASAP	as soon as possible (so bald wie möglich)
B4N	bye for now (Tschüss erstmal)
BAK	back at keyboard (bin zurück)
BTW	by the way (nebenbei)
CU	see you (bis später)
FYI	for your information (zu deiner Information)
IC	I see (ich verstehe)
HTH	hope that helps (ich hoffe das hilft)
RQWT	right question, wrong forum (Richtige Frage, falsches Forum)
\V/	live long and prosper (Lass es dir gut gehen!)
...	back in a second (ein Moment, bitte)

Grundsätzlich sollte der Internet-Nutzer

- durch Beobachten Erfahrung sammeln, bevor er aktiv loslegt;
- möglichst kurz und prägnant formulieren;
- Großbuchstaben vermeiden, denn sonst wirkt dies wie schreien;
- niemanden beleidigen;
- keine Schreibfehler oder Ausdrucksweisen anderer kritisieren;
- bei Antworten immer einen textlichen Bezug verwenden;
- Sonderzeichen vermeiden, da sich nicht alle Software-Clients gleich verhalten;
- keine Kettenbriefe oder Mailschleifen produzieren;
- die gewollte Anonymität Anderer respektieren.

❶ **Netiquette** ist ein Kunstwort aus dem englischen Wort „Net" und dem französischen „Etiquette", das die Benimmregeln und die Gepflogenheiten des zwischenmenschlichen Umgangs im Internet beschreibt.

❷ 1979 „erfand" Kevin MacKenzie das Emoticon. **Emoticons** sind aus Satzzeichen bestehende, um 90° nach links gedrehte kleine Gesichter, die Emotionen ausdrücken sollen. Die gleichen Gefühle – textlich ausformuliert – würden oft mehrere Zeilen in Anspruch nehmen.
Mit einer zunehmenden Anzahl von Programmen und Mobiltelefonen werden Emoticons automatisch in eine Grafik, dann **Smiley** genannt, umgewandelt.

❸ **Akronyme** sind Abkürzungen, bei denen jeder Buchstabe für ein einzelnes Wort steht. Die Mehrzahl der Akronyme beruhen auf englischen Abkürzungen und stehen in der Regel für eine konkrete Aussage, die sonst sehr viel mehr Platz einnehmen würde.

Im Internet-Dienst Chat hat sich zusätzlich ein spezieller Chat-Slang etabliert:

aws	Auf Wiedersehen
bsvl	Biegt sich vor lachen
bvid	Bin verliebt in Dich
dbdb	Du bist der Beste
g	Grinsen
gn8	Gute Nacht
hea	Hau endlich ab
ikd	Ich küsse Dich

...

13.3 World Wide Web

13.3.1 Definition WWW

Das **World Wide Web (WWW)**, auch kurz „das Web“ genannt, ist das am weitesten verbreitete und der am schnellsten wachsende Teil des Internets. Es besteht aus einer riesigen Anzahl von weltweit verteilten Websites. Jede Website besteht aus einzelnen, über eine Startseite ❶ miteinander verknüpften Dokumenten ❷, die aus multimedialen Inhalten, wie Texte, Grafiken, Sound und Videos aufgebaut sind.

❶ Als Startseite oder Homepage wird ein HTML-Dokument mit dem Namen „index.htm“ oder „index.html“ vom Browser erwartet.

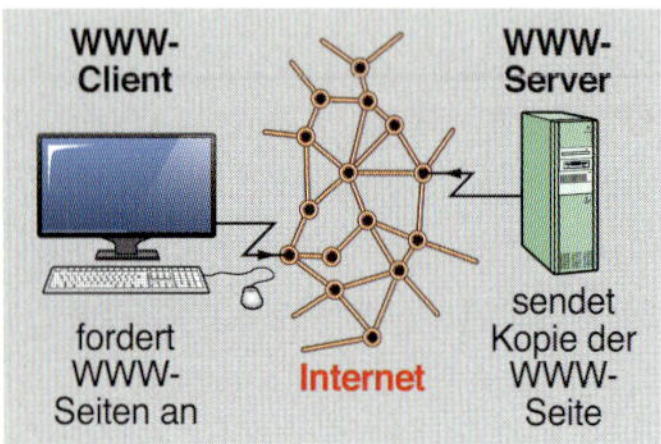

13.3.2 Funktionsweise des WWW

Das WWW arbeitet nach dem Client-/Server-Prinzip. Das heißt, mit einer Client-Software auf einem lokalen Computer, dem sogenannten „WWW-Browser“ oder auch „Web-Browser“, greift man über einen Internet-Zugang auf den „WWW-Server“ zu, auf dem die Dokumente gespeichert sind. Das gewünschte Dokument wird über den Client am WWW-Server, auch Webserver genannt, angefordert. Die Server-Software nimmt die Anfrage entgegen und sendet dann eine Kopie des Dokuments an den Client, wo es mit Hilfe des Web-Browsers dargestellt wird. Zur gegenseitigen Kommunikation wird das HTTP-Protokoll verwendet.

❷ Die Dokumente im WWW sind primär in der Seitenbeschreibungssprache, der Hypertext Markup Language (HTML), codiert und als HTML-Dateien abgelegt. Jede Seite kann Verknüpfungen zu Inhalts-Medien oder zu anderen HTML-Seiten haben.

Hypertext Transfer Protocol (HTTP)

Das HTTP ist der Standard zur Übermittlung von multimedialen Dokumenten im Internet. Es regelt die Kommunikation zwischen den WWW-Servern und den WWW-Clients. Soll ein Dokument im WWW abgerufen werden, so wird die Adresse als URL des gewünschten WWW-Servers, bzw. des Dokumentes, über den Browser eingegeben und an den Rechner des Internet-Providers übergeben. Das Domain-Name-System (DNS) ermittelt aus dem Domain-Namen der URL die IP-Adresse des gewünschten WWW-Servers. Dann wird die Verbindung mit dem WWW-Server aufgebaut. In der Regel erfolgt dies über eine Vielzahl von Rechnern, bis der betreffende Server gefunden wird. Der WWW-Server empfängt die Anfrage über das HTTP-Protokoll und erhält dadurch die Mitteilung, welches Dokument gewünscht wird. Das Dokument wird dann dem Client zugeschickt und im WWW-Browser dargestellt. Wenn nur der Rechnername angefordert wird, so wird der WWW-Server automatisch die Startseite laden. Ist das HTML-Dokument übertragen worden, so werden nach und nach die im Dokument enthaltenen Bilddateien angefordert und übertragen. Ist die Übertragung komplett, dann ist diese Anforderung abgearbeitet und die HTTP-Verbindung zwischen Client und Server bis zur nächsten Daten-Anforderung beendet.

❸ **Hyperlinks** sind im Dokument markierte Wörter, Symbole oder Grafiken, die den Anwender nach Anklicken zu weiteren Informationseinheiten wechseln lassen.

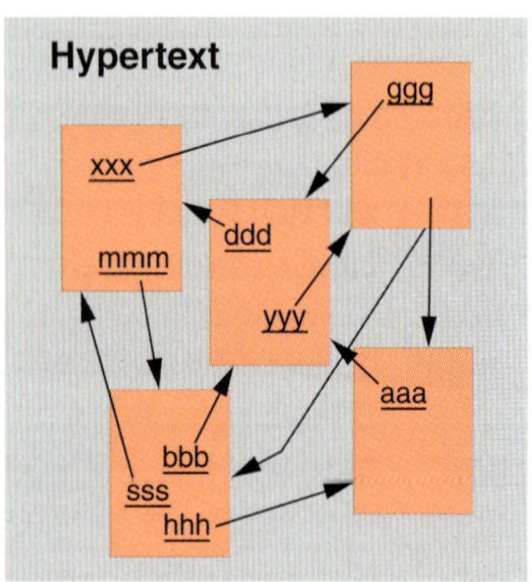

Das WWW ist eine Hypertext-Anwendung.

Hypertext und Hypermedia

Im Gegensatz zu einem traditionellen Buch, bei dem die Informationen in der dargestell-ten Reihenfolge sequentiell von Seite zu Seite gelesen werden, bietet eine Hypertext-Anwendung durch **Hyperlinks** ❸, auch einfach nur „Links“ genannt, den direkten Querverweis von einer Hypertext-Seite auf eine andere oder innerhalb einer Hypertext-Seite von Information zu Information. Diese Hyperlinks sind in den WWW-Dokumenten eingebettet und bestehen aus HTML-Befehlen, die beim Anklicken den WWW-Browser zum Sprung auf die Zieladresse veranlassen. Dabei kann die Zieladresse ein relativer Link oder ein absoluter Link sein. Ein relativer **Link** ❶ ist eine Verknüpfung auf ein anderes Dokument im gleichen Webserver. Ein absoluter Link ❷ hingegen verweist auf Informationen, die auf ganz anderen Webservern gespeichert sind. Damit sind assoziative Informationsverknüpfungen mit Dokumenten möglich, die auf den verschiedensten weltweit verteilten Webservern liegen.

Das jeweilige HTML-Dokument selbst besteht jedoch nur aus Text und HTML-Code. Bilder und Grafiken können über Links eingebettet werden. Der Browser lädt dann automatisch die Elemente und zeigt sie an. Auch andere Multimedia-Elemente wie Sound und Videos können über Links eingebunden werden und erweitern damit den Hypertext zum Hypermedia ❸.

❶ Beispiel für einen **relativen Link**: „/oursite/dokument.htm"

❷ Beispiel für einen **absoluten Link: „http://www.medien-verstehen.de/index.htm"**

❸ **Hypermedia** bezeichnet die Verbindung von Schrift, Grafik, Ton und Video in einem interaktiven Dokument.

13.4 Zugang zum Internet

13.4.1 Hardware

Die Zugangsmöglichkeiten zum Internet sind vielfältig. Grundvoraussetzung ist ein internetfähiges ❹ Endgerät. Der Zugang erfolgt dann entweder über ein lokales Netz, über eine Telefonverbindung oder eine Breitbandverbindung.

Zum Beispiel: Internet-Daten über den Telefonanschluss, über **Satellit** ❺ oder **TV-Kabel** ❻, durch das **Strom-Netz** ❼ oder per Funk. Für den Internet-Zugang am Arbeitsplatz kann auch über ein Firmen-Netzwerk, ein sogenanntes LAN (Local Area Network), welches an das Internet angeschlossen ist, die Verbindung mit dem Internet aufgebaut werden.

Direkte Internet-Zugänge kann man prinzipiell in drei Verfahren unterscheiden:

- Über eine Schmalband-Datenfernübertragung. Dazu zählen analoge Telefonleitung mit Hilfe eines analogen Modems oder eine ISDN-Verbindung mit ensprechender ISDN-Karte
- Über eine Breitband-Datenfernübertragung. In der Regel per DSL- oder Kabelmodem.
- Über eine mobile Verbindung, z. B. GPRS, UMTS oder LTE.

Welches das geeignete Verfahren ist, hängt von den individuellen Leistungsansprüchen des Benutzers ab.

Modem

Beim Anschluss über eine analoge Telefonleitung muss eine Digital-Analog-Wandlung vorgenommen werden, damit die digitalen Informationen zwischen PC und dem Internet übertragen werden können. Diese Aufgabe übernimmt das Modem, welches zwischen PC und der Telefonanschluss-Dose (TAE-Dose) geschaltet wird. Das Modem (Modulator/Demodulator) wandelt digitale Informationen in akustische Signale (Modulation), um sie über eine analoge Leitung übertragen zu können.

❹ Möchte man die volle Bandbreite der Internet-Dienste, insbesondere die Angebote mit multimedialen Inhalten nutzen, so ist ein zeitgemäßer PC mit leistungsfähigem Prozessor, ausreichend Arbeitsspeicher und eine Festplatte notwendig.

❺ Internet-Zugänge über Satellit nehmen in der Regel zwei Wege in Anspruch: Der Upload über den Telefonanschluss und der Download über die Sateliten-Emfangsanlage.

❻ Der Breitband-Internetzugang über das TV-Kabel wird auch **Kabel Internet** bezeichnet. Im Gegensatz zu DSL surft man völlig unabhängig vom Telefonanschluss. Für die Internet-Verbindung über den Kabelanschluss benötigt man ein Kabelmodem und einen rückkanalfähigen Hausverstärker. Im Moment sind Geschwindigkeiten bis zu 100 MBit/s möglich.

❼ **PLC (Powerline Communication)** nennt sich die Daten-Übertragung über das Stromnetz.

Geschwindigkeit verschiedener verfügbarer Internet-Zugänge:
Modem-Datenrate....... < 56 kBit/s
ISDN-Datenrate .... 64 kBit/s
SkyDSL................ bis zu 36 Mbit/s
DSL...................... bis zu 50 Mbit/s
TV-Kabel........... bis zu 100 Mbit/s
Mobil (LTE)....... bis zu 100 Mbit/s

Am anderen Ende wandelt ebenfalls ein Modem die akustischen Signale wieder in digitale Signale um (Demodulation). Bei diesem Verfahren steht dem Nutzer immer nur eine Leitung zur Verfügung.

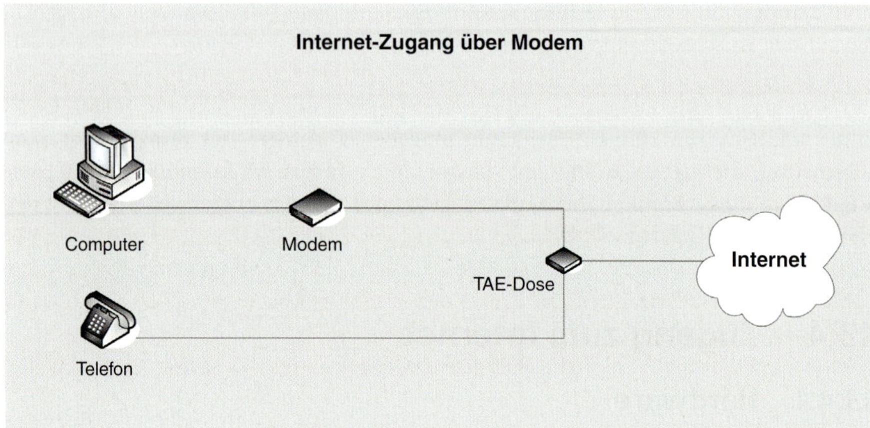

ISDN

Mithilfe der ISDN-Technologie (**Integrated Services Digital Network**) werden die Daten direkt in digitaler Form über die Telefonleitung geschickt und müssen nicht mehr in analoge Signale gewandelt werden. Dadurch können höhere Datenübertragungsraten als bei einer Modemverbindung erzielt werden.

❶ Der NTBA (Network Termination Basic Access) ist der Netzabschluss beim Teilnehmer und übernimmt die Wandlung der ankommenden Signale vom Anschlusskabel auf den S0-Bus des ISDN-Hausnetzes.

❷ Die ISDN-Karte übernimmt die Anbindung des PCs an das ISDN-Netz (S0-Bus). Sie wird als Steckkarte in den PC eingebaut.

❸ Auf einem Nutzkanal, auch B-Kanal genannt, wird normalerweise über das Point-to-Point-Protokoll (PPP) eine Internetverbindung mit einer Datenrate von 64 kBit/s betrieben. Mit einem Multilink-PPP ist es möglich, die beiden B-Kanäle zu bündeln um dadurch eine Datenrate von 128 kBit/s zu erreichen.

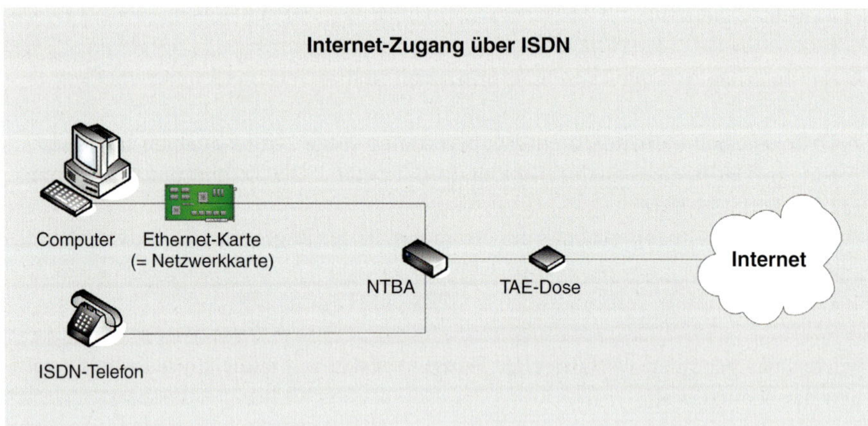

Beim ISDN-Anschluss ist die digitale Endstelle beim Nutzer der **NTBA** ❶. Über eine **ISDN-Karte** ❷ wird der PC mit dem NTBA verbunden. An dem NTBA sind auch alle anderen ISDN-Endgeräte, wie z. B. ein ISDN-Telefon, angeschlossen. Bei einem ISDN-Basisanschluss stehen dem Nutzer gleichzeitig zwei **Nutzkanäle** ❸ mit je 64 kBit/s zur Verfügung. Das heißt er kann z. B. telefonieren und gleichzeitig im Internet surfen.

DSL

Mit der **DSL**-Technologie **(Digital Subscriber Line)** hat man eine Breitband-Datenfernübertragung geschaffen, die weit über die Leistungsfähigkeit von Modem- und ISDN-Verbindungen hinausgehen. Die DSL-Technologie gibt es in verschiedenen Varianten ❶. Die meistverbreitete und momentan auch für den normalen Internet-Nutzer erschwingliche, ist die ADSL-Technologie. Dabei handelt es sich um eine asynchrone Datenübertragung, das heißt, die Geschwindigkeit für den Download und den Upload sind unterschiedlich. **ADSL** ist in der Praxis neun Mal schneller als ISDN. Dies erreicht man zum Einen durch eine Begrenzung der Entfernung von Sender und Empfänger auf 5,5 Kilometer und zum Anderen dadurch, dass die Daten nicht, wie bei Modem- oder ISDN-Verbindungen, in hörbare Töne umgewandelt werden, sondern in unzählige verschiedene, für den Menschen nicht wahrnehmbare Frequenzen. Dadurch lassen sich deutlich mehr Daten über das Kupferkabel verschicken und die Übertragung wird wesentlich schneller.

❶ Die DSL-Familie:
ADSL (Asynchronous DSL)
Datenrate theor. bis zu 8 MBits/s; praktisch:
Download .... 768-6000 kBit/s
Upload .... 128-1000 kBit/s
ADSL2+ (Erweitertes ADSL)
Datenrate theor. bis zu 25 MBits/s; praktisch:
Download...... bis zu 16 000 kBit/s
Upload .... bis zu 3500 kBit/s
HDSL (High Data Rate DSL)
Datenrate .... bis zu 2,3 MBit/s
SDSL (Symmetrical DSL)
Datenrate ....bis zu 3 MBits/s
VDSL2 (Very High Speed DSL)
Datenrate .... bis zu 100 MBit/s

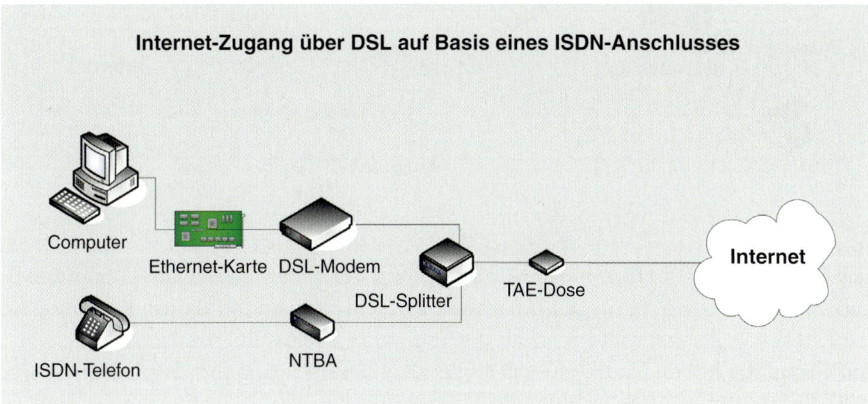

Die Trennung erfolgt durch den **DSL-Splitter** ❷. Der PC ist über eine Ethernet-Netzwerkkarte an das **DSL-Modem** ❸ angeschlossen, welches die Signale an den DSL-Splitter weitergibt.

Auch ist bei DSL dank des Splitter-Verfahrens Datenübertragung und Telefonieren gleichzeitig möglich.

- **Vorteile: Die bestehende Teilnehmeranschlussleitung mit den bereits verlegten Kupfer-Doppelader des Telefonnetzes kann für den Weg vom Teilnehmer bis zur nächsten digitalen Vermittlungsstelle genutzt werden.**
- **Nachteil: Je weiter ein Teilnehmer von der Vermittlungsstelle entfernt ist, desto niedriger ist die maximal erzielbare Datenübertragungsrate.**

In Ballungszentren wird vermehrt die DSL-Weiterentwicklung **VDSL2** angeboten. Diese Datenrate ermöglicht sogenannte **„Triple Play"**-Angebote, welche eine gemeinsame Nutzung von TV inklusive Video-on-Demand, IP-Telefonie und Internet vorsehen.

❷ Die ADSL-Informationen werden beim Anwender mit einem sogenannten **Splitter** aus dem gemeinsamen Daten-/Telefonstrom herausgeholt und zum DSL-Modem weitergeleitet.

❸ Das **DSL-Modem** ist per 10BaseT-Technik an den Computer angeschlossen. Es nimmt nicht, wie man vom Namen her meinen könnte, eine Analog / Digital-Wandlung vor, sondern setzt die digitalen Signale auf unterschiedliche Frequenzen, damit die hohe Bandbreite an Daten übertragen werden kann.

Kabel Internet

❶ Im Gegensatz zu einfachen TV- und Radioanschlüssen, bei denen nur einseitig Informationen empfangen werden, ermöglicht ein Rückkanal die Kommunikation in beide Richtungen. Das ist die Voraussetzung für einen Internetzugang und für interaktive Videoangebote .

Ein weiterer Breitband-Internetzugang ist über das Kabelfernsehnetz möglich. Dazu muss der TV-Kabelanschluss beim Kunden „rückkanalfähig" ❶ sein. Diese Infrastruktur mit speziellen rückkanalfähigen Verstärkern und Frequenzumsetzern nutzt die hohen Bandbreite des Kabelanschlusses und sorgt dafür, dass Signale bidirektional übertragen werden können. Der Anschluss erfolgt über sogenannte Multimediaanschlussdosen, welche zusätzlich zu den TV- und Radio-Buchsen einen Anschluss für ein Kabelmodem besitzen.

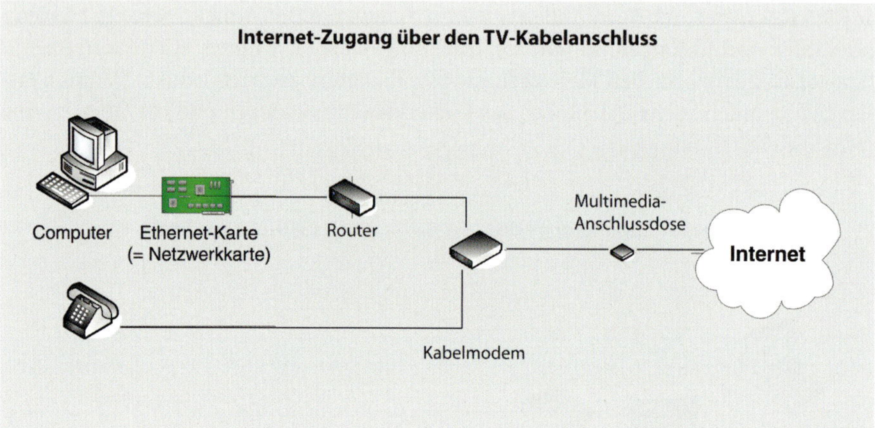

❷ Im Kabel Internet sind durch Verbindung von Frequenzkanälen Datenraten von über 100 MBit/s möglich.

Das Kabelmodem übernimmt die Umwandlung der Daten zwischen PC und Kabelnetz. Ein Splitter wie beim DSL-Anschluss ist nicht notwendig, da das Kabelmodem die Extraktion der Internetdaten und der Telfondaten selbst übernimmt.
Auf Grund der hohen Bandbreiten ❷ eignet sich dieser Zugang für „Triple Play"-Angebote. Ein separater Telefonschluss wird damit überflüssig.

Mobilfunk

❸ Datenraten in 2G-Mobilfunknetzen:

GSM	bis 9,6 kBit/s
HSCSD	bis 57,6 kBit/s
GPRS	bis 171,2 kBit/s
EDGE	bis 384 kBit/s

Als Internetzugang für den mobilen Einsatz kann der Mobilfunkstandard **GSM** (Global System for Mobile Communication) als Datenübertragungskanal genutzt werden. Damit erreicht man eine sehr hohe Netzabdeckung für einen mobilen Zugang ins Internet. GSM nutzt die Infrastruktur der vorhandenen D- und E-Mobilfunknetze. GSM als Datenübertragungsart der sogenannten 2. Generation (2G) ❸ wird auch **Circuit Switched Data (CSD)** genannt und erlaubt nutzbare Datenraten von 9,6 kBit/s. Für viele Internet- und Multimediaanwendungen ist dies zu wenig, so dass einige Mobilfunk-Provider mit Hilfe von Kanalbündelungen den **HSCSD** (High Speed CSD) einsetzen. Verbreiteter ist aber mittlerweile der paketvermittelte Datendienst **GPRS** (General Packet Radio Service). Bei GPRS besteht nur virtuell eine dauerhafte Verbindung zur Gegenstelle. Erst wenn wirklich Daten übertragen werden sollen, werden auch Daten gesendet. Deshalb braucht kein Funkkanal dauerhaft (wie bei HSCSD) für einen Benutzer reserviert zu werden. Die Kostenabrechnungen durch den Provider sind deshalb hauptsächlich von den übertragenen Datenmengen abhängig, und nicht von der Verbindungsdauer. Eine Weiterentwicklung von GPRS ist **EDGE** (Enhanced Data Rates for GSM Evolution), bei der ein effizienteres Modulationsverfahren eingesetzt wird.

Aber erst durch die Einführung einer neuen Netzinfrastruktur der 3. Generation (3G) ❶ mit dem 3G-Standard **UMTS** (Universal Mobile Telecommunications System) und der UMTS-Erweiterung HSDPA (High Speed Download Packet Access) wird parallel zum GSM-Netz ein Netz für hohe Datenraten geschaffen.

❶ Datenraten in 3G-Mobilfunknetz

UMTS	bis 384 kBit/s
HSDPA	bis 7200 kBit/s
WiMAX	bis 2 MBit/s
LTE	bis 100 MBit/s

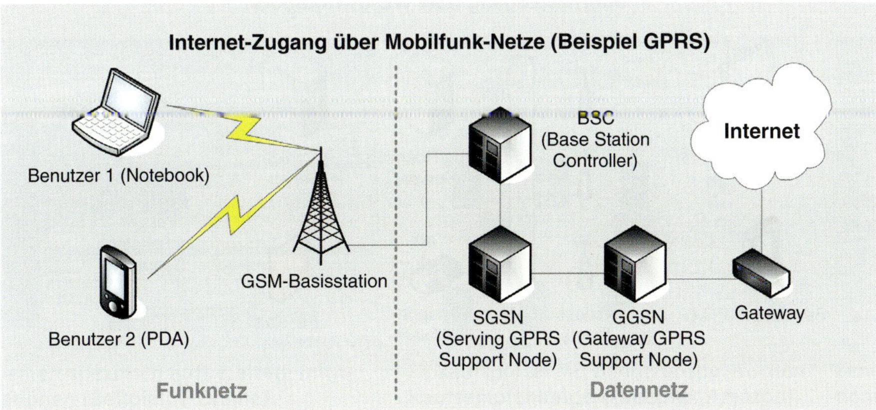

Mit der **WiMAX**-Technologie (Worlwide Interoperability for MicroWave) entstehen breitbandige Internetzugänge über ein Funknetz. Diese nicht mit dem WLAN kompatible Technik erreicht in städtischer Umgebung mit einer Basisstation üblicherweise eine Reichweite zwischen 2 und 3 Kilometer. Im ländlichen Bereich können aber auch größere Reichweiten erreicht werden. Die bisherigen (Stand 2007) WiMAX-Netze arbeiten mit Datenraten von bis zu 2 MBit/s.

Mit dem Mobilfunkstandard **LTE** (Long Term Evolution) wurden skalierbare Bandbreiten eingeführt, die bei einer Kanalbreite von 20 MHz eine Download-Datenrate von bis 100 MBit/s ermöglichen. Mit dem zukünftigen LTE Advanced ❷ sollen noch größere Kanalbreiten genutzt werden.

❷ Datenraten in 4G-Mobilfunknetz
LTE-Advanced .... bis 300 MBit/s

Bei entsprechender Netzabdeckung bietet LTE das Potential als Alternative zu festnetzbasierten DSL-Zugängen zu werden. Jedoch muss die verfügbare Bandbreite pro Funkzelle zwischen den Nutzern geteilt werden. Da LTE keine leitungsgebundene Verbindung ist, sondern IP-basiert funktioniert, wird von den mobilen Endgeräten zur Sprachübermittlung weiterhin GSM oder UMTS verwendet.

WLAN

Einen weiteren mobilen Zugang ins Internet bieten die drahtlosen Internetzugriffspunkte über **WLAN** ❸, auch **Hotspot** genannt, an. Sie sind vorwiegend an öffentlichen Plätzen, wie Flughäfen oder Bahnhöfen vorzufinden, aber auch Hotels und Restaurants bieten diesen Service ihren Kunden an. Mit Hilfe eines eingebauten WLAN-Adapters kann mit einem Internet-fähigen Endgerät, zum Beispiel einem Notebook oder einem PDA, innerhalb des Funkbereiches (Hotspot) auf einen WLAN-**Access-Point** zugegriffen werden. Der Access-Point stellt dabei die Funkverbindung bereit und eine Router-Funktion übernimmt die Schnittstelle zwischen dem öffentlich zugänglichen WLAN und dem Internet.

❸ Bei der **WLAN** (Wireless Local Network)-Technologie wird meist der IEEE802.11b/g-Standard verwendet. Dabei muss der Access-Point wie auch der WLAN-Adapter beim Benutzer über den gleichen Standard verfügen. In der Praxis werden dabei Datenraten von 2 bis 50 MBit/s erreicht. Pro Access-Point können ca. 30-100 Meter Reichweite aufgebaut werden.

Auch die Datenübermittlung ist in der Regel nicht anonym, d. h. mit entsprechenden Maßnahmen kann der Datentransport im Internet von Unbefugten eingesehen werden. Eine Abhilfe bieten gesicherte Verbindungen mit Verschlüsselungstechnologie nach dem SSL-Protokoll (Secure Socket Layer) oder dem SHTTP (Secure-HTTP). Leider kann nur der Anbieter im Internet eine sichere Verbindung veranlassen und nicht der Benutzer allein.

SSL ermöglicht verschlüsselte Verbindungen ❶ und Echtheitsbestätigungen mit Zertifikaten ❷. SSL nutzt das **Public-Key-Verfahren** ❸. Wichtige Größe für die Datensicherheit ist dabei die verwendete Schlüssellänge – je länger, desto sicherer. Empfehlenswert ist eine Schlüssellänge von wenigstens 768 Bit.

Auch für den sicheren Austausch von E-Mails gibt es mittlerweile sichere Verfahren. **PGP** (Pretty Good Privacy, engl. = recht gute Privatsphäre) ❹ und **S/MIME** (Secure Multipurpose Internet Mail Extension) sind dabei gebräuchliche Verfahren. PGP arbeitet ebenfalls nach dem Public-Key-Verfahren.

❶ Bei verschlüsselten Verbindungen wird die Information mit Kryptosystemen kodiert bzw. dekodiert. Eine sichere Verbindung erkennt man an der Protokollart in der Adresszeile (https://) und in der Statuszeile des Browsers durch ein Schloss bzw. einen Schlüssel.

❷ **Zertifikate** für Digitale Signaturen und Schlüssel werden von vertrauenswürdigen Instanzen (**Trustcenter**) ausgestellt und dienen der Authentifizierung von E-Mails und Software-Downloads.

❸ Beim **Public-Key-Verfahren**, auch asymmetrische Verschlüsselung genannt, besitzt jeder immer zwei Schlüssel: Einen öffentlichen Schlüssel (engl: public key), der frei zugänglich ist, und einen privaten Schlüssel (engl.: private key), der nur im Besitz des einen Anwenders ist. Mit dem öffentlichen Schlüssel können Nachrichten kodiert werden, aber nur mit dem dazugehörigen privaten Schlüssel können sie dekodiert werden.

Beispiel eines öffentlichen Schlüssels:

-----BEGIN PGP PUBLIC KEY BLOCK-----
Version: 2.7
mQA9Ai2wD2YAAAEBgJ18cV7rMAFv7P3
eBd/cZayl8EEO6XGYkhEO9SLJOw+DFyH
gPx5o+IiR2A6Fh+HguQAFEbQZZGVtbyA
8ZGVtb0B3ZWxsLnNmLmNhLnVzPokARQ
IFEC2wD4yR2A6Fh+HguQEB3xcBfRTi3D/
2qdU3TosScYMAHfgfUwCelbb6wikSxoF5
ees9DL9QMzPZXCioh42dEUXP0g===sw5W
-----END PGP PUBLIC KEY BLOCK-----

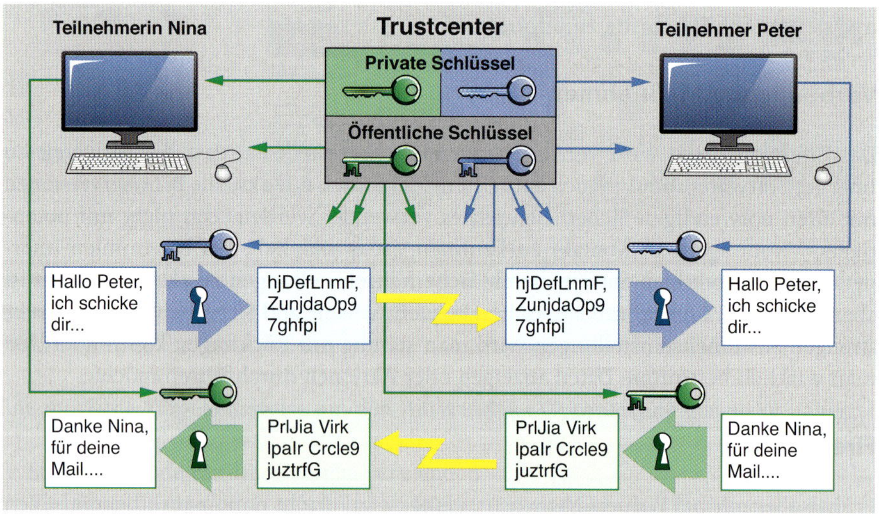

❹ Vereinfachte Darstellung eines gegenseitigen E-Mail-Austausches mit der Verschlüsselungsmethode PGP. Teilnehmerin Nina kodiert mit dem öffentlichen Schlüssel von Teilnehmer Peter ihre Mail und schickt sie über das Internet an Teilnehmer Peter. Er dekodiert diese Mail mit seinem privaten Schlüssel und kann sie lesen. Die Antwort-Mail kodiert Peter dann mit dem öffentlichen Schlüssel von Nina, die diese Mail mit Hilfe ihres privaten Schlüssels lesen kann.

13.4.5 Publizieren im WWW

Wer Informationen verbreiten will, die der ganzen Welt schon nach wenigen Minuten bekannt sein sollen, publiziert im Internet. Grundvoraussetzung für die eigene Website ist ausreichend „Webspace" – Platz auf einem Webserver. Diesen Platz stellen ISPs oder Onlinedienste zur Verfügung. Sie können auch gleichzeitig die Registrierung eines eigenen Domänen-Namens übernehmen. Als Software zum Erstellen der Inhalte kommen spezielle Web-Editoren wie Dreamweaver von Macromedia oder FrontPage von Microsoft zum Einsatz.

Diese Web-Editoren visualisieren die Struktur der Website und erlauben das Setzen von Links per ‚Drag and Drop' (Beispiel: Dreamweaver von Macromedia). Zusätzlich übernehmen sie die Kommunikation mit dem Host – dem Webserver der Website. Das Erstellen geschieht „offline" in einem lokalen Speicherbereich, der jedoch spiegelbildlich zu seiner späteren „online"-Variante auf der Website aufgebaut wird.

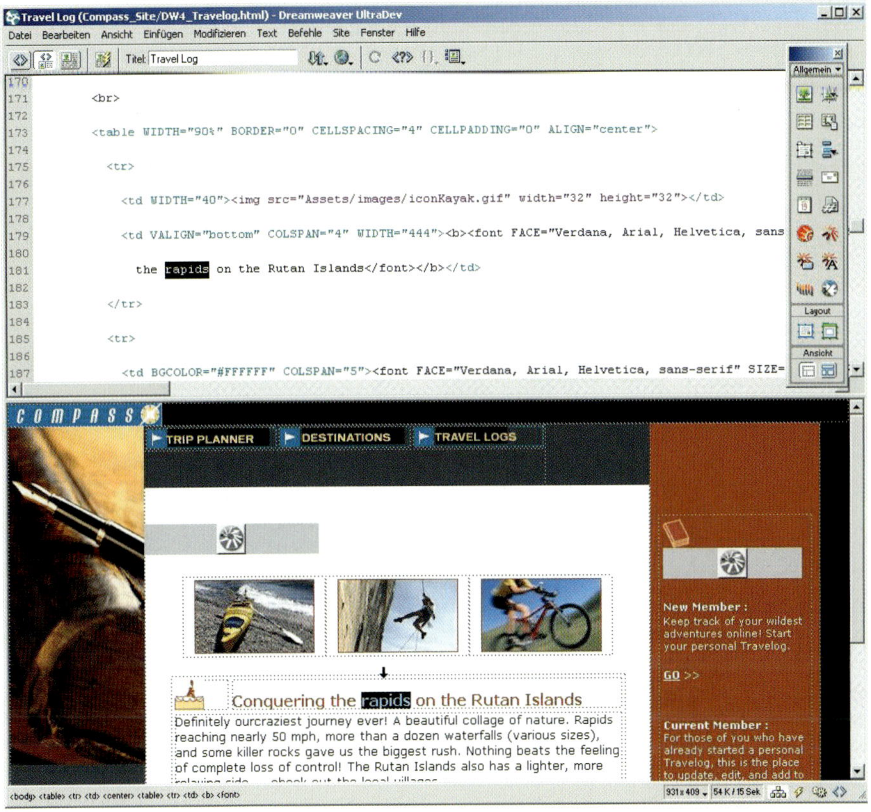

Editieren mit gleichzeitiger HTML-Code- und Layoutansicht (Beispiel: Dreamweaver).

Bevor man jedoch mit dem Eingeben der Inhalte beginnt, ist es ratsam, sich Gedanken über die Struktur der Website und der Navigationsmöglichkeiten zu machen. Dabei geht man immer von der Startseite, der sogenannten „Homepage", aus. Diese heißt in der Regel „index.html" oder „default.html". Dieser Seite kommt eine besondere Bedeutung zu. Sie repräsentiert den ersten visuellen Eindruck der Website. Auch für die Agenten der Suchmaschinen ist diese Seite von besonderer Bedeutung. Deshalb müssen die Metainformationen, wie Site-Beschreibung und Stichwörter, vorhanden sein. Hat man nun die HTML-Seiten, deren Verlinkungen und die eingebundenen Medienelemente erstellt und lokal getestet, so kann mit der Veröffentlichung der Website begonnen werden. Mit einem FTP-Upload im Web-Editor stellt man die lokale Website spiegelbildlich auf den Webserver und testet danach die Website mit einem Browser. Ist die Seite veröffentlicht, heißt das noch lange nicht, dass sie auch von der gewünschten Interessensgruppe gefunden wird. Dazu muss sie erst bei Suchmaschinen angemeldet werden und mit aussagefähigen Beschreibungen, präzisen Stichworten und Kategorien versehen werden.

Tipps für die Praxis:

- Auf kurze Ladezeiten achten, besonders bei der Startseite
- Navigation klar und intuitiv für die Zielgruppe gestalten
- Seiten nicht überfrachten
- Bilder und andere Medienobjekte in Unterverzeichnisse ablegen
- Bilder mit 72 dpi in der darzustellenden Größe einbinden
- Bilder mit Farbflächen im GIF-Format verwenden
- Bilder mit Fotografien im JPG-Format verwenden
- Website mit verschiedenen Browsern und Auflösungen testen.

Für Informationsanbieter, die Inhalte mit hohem Aktualisierungsbedarf veröffentlichen, bedeutet diese Vorgehensweise der Website-Erstellung immer noch einen beträchtlichen Zeitaufwand. Deshalb setzen Online-Redaktionen und vergleichbare Anbieter verstärkt **Redaktionssysteme**, bzw. **Content Management Systeme** (CMS) ❶ ein. Diese Systeme vereinfachen das Aktualisieren einer Website, indem sie mit standardisierten Seitenvorlagen arbeiten und die Inhalte über eine Datenbank pflegen. Beim Besuch auf der Website werden dann die einzelnen HTML-Seiten für den Interessenten „On Demand" aus der Datenbank zusammengestellt. Dazu verwenden die Systeme serverseitige Scriptsprachen, wie z. B. ASP (Active Server Pages) von Microsoft, PHP (Hypertext Preprocessor) oder JSP (JavaServer Pages) von Sun.

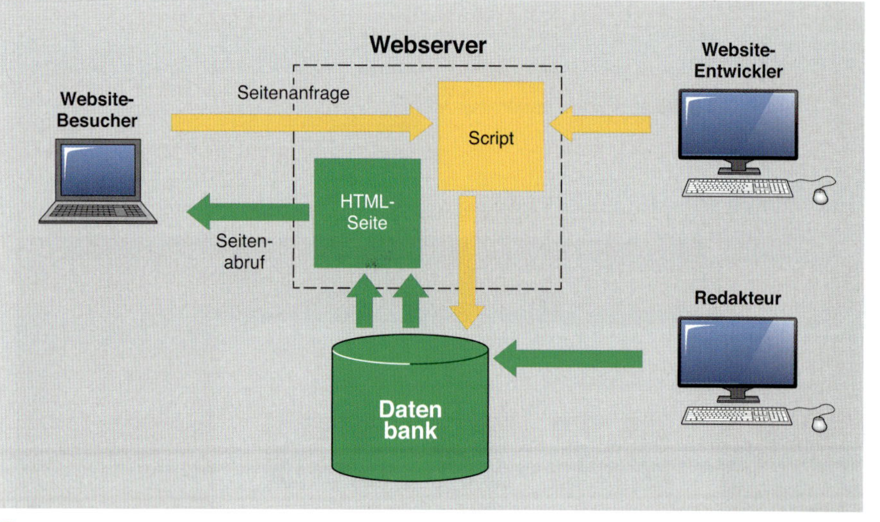

❶ Vereinfachtes Prinzip eines Content Management Systems. Die angeforderten HTML-Seiten werden stets vom System mit den aktuellsten Inhalten aus der Datenbank generiert.

13.5 Anwendungen

13.5.1 Intranet und Extranet

❷ **Intranets** werden als firmeninterne Informations-Plattform eingesetzt, teils mit Schnittstellen zu internen Datenbank-Systemen, wie z. B. ERP-Systemen (Enterprise Ressource Planning) für Produktionsplanung, Finanzbuchhaltung und Personalabrechnung usw.

Als **Intranet** ❷ wird ein geschlossenes Computernetz auf Basis der Internet-Technologie bezeichnet, das nur innerhalb eines Unternehmens für die Mitarbeiter verfügbar ist. Intranets sind von außen nicht erreichbar und erlauben nur Mitgliedern der Organisation den Zugriff.

Extranets sind im Gegensatz zu Intranets auch von außerhalb erreichbar, erlauben aber im Vergleich zum öffentlichen Internet nur registrierten Benutzern, also einer geschlossenen Benutzergruppe, den Zugang. Extranets werden meist für geschlossene Informationsangebote auf einem öffentlichen Webserver eingesetzt. Dieses Konzept wird häufig in der B2B-Kommunikation eingesetzt (B2B – Business to Business). Die externen Netze können über das Internet miteinander verbunden werden und bilden damit Sub-Netze innerhalb des Intranets. Die Anbindung erfolgt dabei über gesicherte IP-Tunnels.

13.5.2 E-Business und E-Commerce

Unter **E-Business** versteht man alle Formen von elektronischen Geschäftsprozessen, unter Anderen auch den **E-Commerce**, den Handel von Waren und Dienstleistungen über das Internet.

Online-Banking und Online-Aktienhandel

Bankgeschäfte per Internet - für viele schon längst die Alternative zum Besuch am Bankschalter. Mittlerweile verfügt nahezu jede Bank über ein entsprechendes Angebot, Überweisungen ❶, Kontostandsabfragen und mehr von zu Hause aus erledigen zu können. Um den virtuellen Bankbesuch so abzusichern, dass kein Fremder Einsicht bzw. Manipulationsmöglichkeiten hat sind momentan zwei Verfahren verbreitet: Die **SSL-Technik** (Secure Socket Layer) ❷ und der **HBCI-Standard** (Homebanking Computer Interface). Beim HBCI-Standard werden alle Daten verschlüsselt gesendet und jeder Auftrag mit der „elektronischen Unterschrift" aus einer Chipkarte bestätigt. Dazu muss ein spezielles Lesegerät am PC verwendet werden.

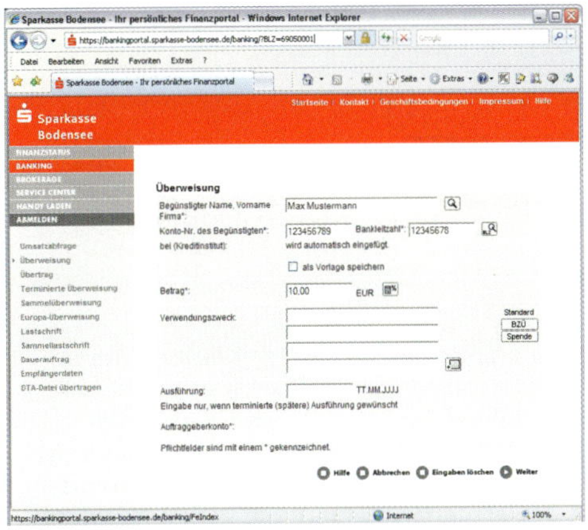

❶ Überweisung mit Online-Banking (Beispiel: Sparkasse Bodensee).

❷ Bei der **SSL-Technik** wird der Transportweg verschlüsselt. Mit einer „Persönlichen Identifikationsnummer" (PIN) weist sich der Kunde aus und mit einer jeweils nur einmal gültigen „Transaktionsnummer" (TAN) „unterschreibt" er sozusagen den Bankauftrag.

Auch im Aktienhandel eröffnet das Internet dem privaten Anleger interessante Möglichkeiten. Es bietet den direkten Zugriff auf aktuelle Börsenkurse und Hintergrundinformationen, unterstützt bei der Depotverwaltung und erlaubt den direkten Online-Aktienhandel, den sogenannten „Brokerage", bei dem Aktien mit Hilfe von PIN und TAN gekauft und verkauft werden können.

Online-Shops und Online-Auktionen

Der Marktplatz im Internet. Das ist Shopping von zu Hause aus, auch außerhalb der Ladenöffnungszeiten. Mittlerweile nutzen viele Firmen diesen Absatzweg für ihr Warenangebot. Die Vorteile liegen in der Vielfalt und Aktualität der Shops. Über Preisagenturen sind auch Preisvergleiche unter verschiedenen Anbietern möglich. Nur können dabei die Produkte noch nicht in der Hand gehalten und getestet werden. Um dies auszugleichen, versuchen die Anbieter, die Produkte multimedial zu präsentieren, z. B. bei Musik-CDs durch Anspielen der Musikstücke ❸.

❸ In Musikstücke hereinschnuppern (Beispiel: Amazon.de).

Eine multimediale Umsetzung finden wir bei Textilien durch virtuelle Anproben ❶, bei denen dreidimensionale Figuren die gewünschten Kleidungsstücke annehmen und dann von allen Seiten betrachtet werden können.

Auch lassen sich Käuferverhalten und Meinungen gezielt in die Produktangebote mit einbeziehen, z. B. in Einkaufsportalen gibt es **Rezensionen** ❷ zu Produkten und Hinweise auf Kaufverhalten von Gleichgesinnten ❸.

❶ Virtuelle Anprobe im Online-Shop (Beispiel: OTTO-Versand).

❷ Leser-Rezensionen bieten potentiellen Käufern interessante Hinweise und Erfahrungen anderer Käufer. Deshalb haben sie einen großen Einfluss auf das Kaufverhalten. Viele Portale erlauben jedoch anonyme Beiträge, das birgt die Gefahr der Manipulation durch geschönte Rezensionen - denn positive Bewertungen steigern die Verkaufszahlen. Schätzungen sagen, das bis zu jede dritte Rezension „gefaked" ist. (Beispiel: Amazon.de).

❸ Was kaufen andere Käufer mit gleichem Interessensgebiet? Online-Shops können es aufzeigen (Beispiel: Amazon.de).

❹ Die Kreditkarten-Daten sollten nur verschlüsselt (per SSL) oder über den SET-Zahlungsverkehr (Secure Electronic Transaction) einer Bank übertragen werden.

Bezahlt werden kann dabei mit klassischen Methoden, wie Rechnung, Nachnahme, Lastschriftverfahren, per Kreditkarte ❹ oder mit einem der elektronischen Bezahlverfahren, wie zum Beispiel Click&Buy oder PayPal.

PayPal ist ein Online-Bezahlverfahren für das Internet. Für Transaktionen müssen beide Geschäftspartner über ein Konto bei PayPal verfügen. Transaktionen sind für beide Partner ohne Zeitverzug wirksam.

Unter dem Begriff „Powershopping" laden virtuelle Marktplätze, wie z. B. „Letsbuyit.com", zu gemeinschaftlichen Einkäufen ein. Bei diesem kollektiven Kauf gilt: Je mehr Käufer, desto billiger wird es für den Einzelnen.

In Online-Auktionen, wie „eBay“ ❶ findet sich fast alles – von Raritäten und Schnäppchen bis hin zu hochwertigen Neuprodukten. Verkäufer finden bei solch einem großen, überregionalen Flohmarkt für fast alles einen Interessierten. Nicht nur Gegenstände werden über das Internet verkauft, sondern auch Dienstleistungen. Zum Beispiel lassen sich im virtuellen Reisebüro Hotels reservieren (Beispiel: www.hrs.de) und nach den billigsten Flügen suchen (Beispiel: www.start.de).

E-Business-Aktivitäten im nicht-kommerziellen Bereich, zum Beispiel in öffentlichen Verwaltungen und in Ämtern, bietet das Internet unter dem Begriff **„E-Government“**. Immer mehr Städte und Gemeinden bieten Dienstleistungen für den Bürger, indem sie Amtsbesuche beschreiben und notwendige Formblätter zum Download anbieten. In Zukunft könnte der Bürger, ein entsprechendes Sicherheitssystem vorausgesetzt, online Steuererklärungen ausfüllen, Wahlen über das Internet durchführen und An- und Abmeldungen vornehmen.

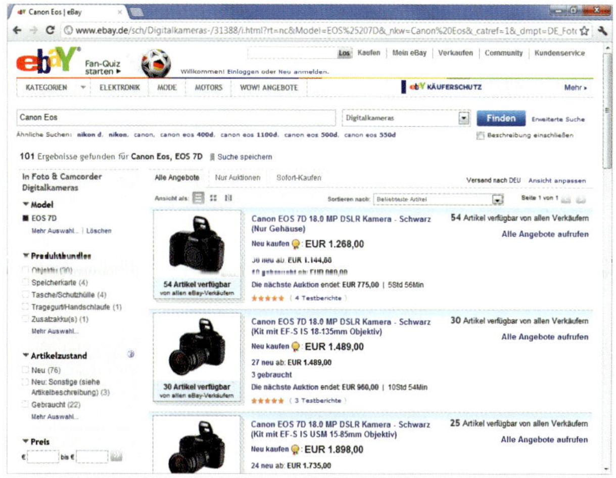

❶ Im Online-Auktionshaus eBay werden durchschnittlich über 50 Millionen Artikel gleichzeitig angeboten.

13.5.3 E-Learning

E-Learning ❷ bedeutet im Allgemeinen computerunterstütztes Lernen. Mit interaktiven Lernprogrammen in Form von **CBT** ❸ und **WBT** ❹ kann unter Verwendung von didaktisch aufbereiteten, multimedialen Inhalten (Rich Media) ein Selbstlernprozess über verschiedene Kommunikationsmedien (Text, Bild, Audio, Animation, Video) aufgebaut werden. Hierbei können Teilnehmer unabhängig von Zeit und Ort selbstgesteuert auf Lerninhalte zugreifen.

Kommunikation (synchron)	Kommunikation (asynchron)
Chat	CBT, WBT
Videokonferenz	E-Mail
Webinar	Foren, Newsgroups
Application Sharing	Newsletter
Whiteboard	Agenda, Gruppen-Kalender

Durch das Internet sind sowohl asynchrone Kommunikationsformen als auch synchrone Kommunikationsformen in den Lernprozess integrierbar.

Die Inhalte (Content) werden primär über WBT-Module vermittelt. Je nach Ausstattung der Lernumgebung, kann der Lernende sich sowohl mit Tutoren als auch mit Lernkollegen über E-Mail, Chats, Blackboards und Foren austauschen. E-Learning kann auch sehr erfolgreich als Bestandteil einer **Blended Learning** ❺ Maßnahme verwendet werden.

❷ **E-Learning** findet statt, wenn Lernprozesse in Szenarien ablaufen, in denen multimediale und (tele)kommunikative Technologien integriert sind.
(Quelle: Seufert/Mayr: Fachlexikon e-le@rning).

❸ **CBT** (Computer Based Training) sind Lernsysteme, die multimedial Lerninhalte vermitteln. In der Regel sind dies eigenständige Programme, die auf Datenträgern, wie CD-ROM oder DVD ausgeliefert werden.

❹ **WBT** (Web Based Training) ist internet-basiertes Lernen mit Unterstützung durch Chats, E-Mail oder Diskussionsforen.

❺ **Blended Learning** (integriertes Lernen) kombiniert die Vorteile von Präsenztraining mit E-Learning.

Der Vorteil gegenüber konventionellen Lernformen liegt im Potential, in kurzer Zeit ortsunabhängig eine große Zielgruppe zu schulen und durch weniger Reise- und Ausfallzeiten die Trainingskosten zu senken.

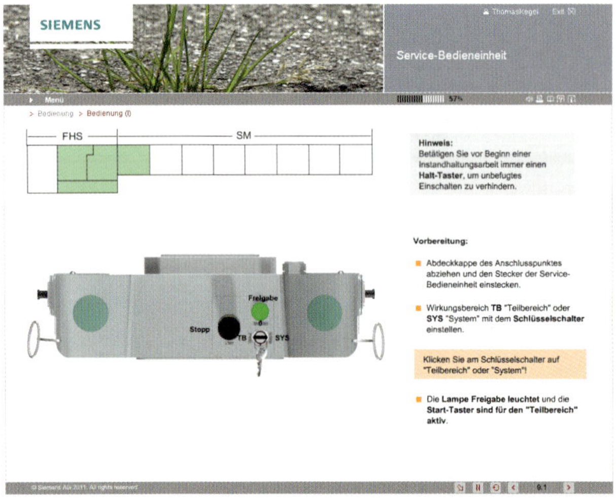

Technisches WBT zur Erläuterung von Bedienung und Funktion mit interaktiven Animationen (Quelle: Siemens AG).

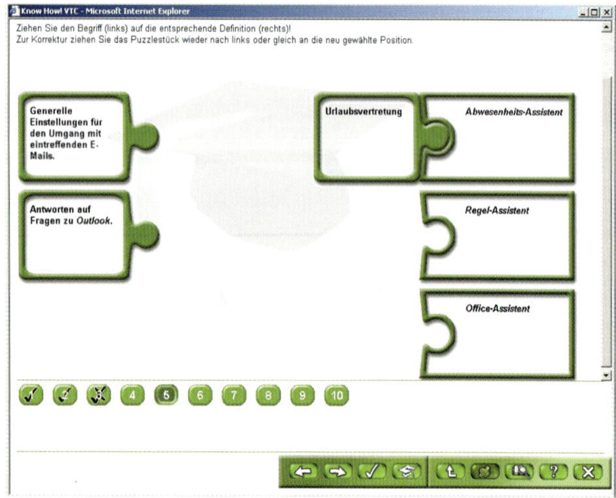

Lernerfolgskontrolle im WBT (Quelle: Know How! AG).

Die Hersteller der E-Learning-Inhalte bedienen sich spezieller Autorensysteme, um die Lernziele mittels Didaktik und der notwendigen Medienelementen wie Text, Bild, Animation und Ton umzusetzen. Dazu gibt es leicht bedienbare Systeme, die auch beispielsweise Dozenten die Möglichkeit bieten, ohne größere Kenntnisse über HTML, XML oder spezieller Programmiersprachen ihre Lernmaterialien in WBTs umzusetzen. Sollen produzierte Lerninhalte für verschiedene Kurse wiederverwendet werden oder werden Varianten und Sprachversionen benötigt, empfehlen sich leistungsfähigere Autorensysteme. Diese können für eine zukunftssichere Weiterverwendung mit XML-Technologien arbeiten und an ein Dokumenten-Management-System (Content Management System CMS) angeschlossen sein.

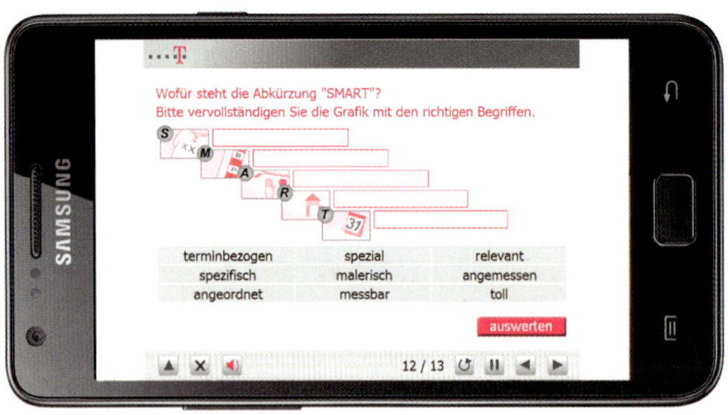

Mobile Learning auf dem Smartphone: Drag'n'Drop-Aufgabe als Lernerfolgskontrolle (Quelle: Know How! AG für Telekom Training).

In der Regel sind die E-Learning-Anwendungen für den Einsatz auf Desktop-PCs oder Notebooks konzipiert. Die Verbreitung von leistungsfähigen mobilen Endgeräten, wie zum Beispiel Smartphones und Tablet-PCs, ermöglichen aber auch den Einsatz von E-Learning im mobilen Umfeld. Diesem Anwendungsbereich, der auch m-Learning oder Mobil Learning bezeichnet wird, steht auf Grund der rasanten Entwicklung im Bereich der mobilen Endgeräte ein hohes Entwicklungspotential bevor. Die verschiedenen mobilen Endgeräte mit unterschiedlichen Betriebssystemen (Android, iOS, Windows Phone) und den unterschiedlichen Displaygrößen setzen jedoch noch individuelle Anpassungen der Lernprogramme voraus.

Durch Mobil Learning können u. a. Warte- und Reisezeiten aktiv in die Aus- und Weiterbildung miteinbezogen werden. Sei es zum Aneignen von neuem Wissen oder zum Festigen von Gelerntem.

Um E-Learning-Inhalte im Internet zur Verfügung zu stellen und den Zugang für die Lernenden zu regeln, bedarf es einer Lernplattform, auch **Learning Management Systems (LMS)** ❶ genannt. Diese Software wird auf einem zentralen Server installiert und über einen lokalen Client, beispielsweise über einen Web-Browser, angesprochen. Die typischen Funktionsbereiche eines LMS umfassen in der Regel die Zugangsverwaltung für die Lernenden, das zur Verfügung stellen der WBT-Lektionen und sonstiger Lernmedien, die Kommunikation (E-Mail, Chat etc.), die Evaluation bzw. Bewertung der Ergebnisse und die Administration der Kurse und Termine.

❶ **LMS** (Learning Management Systems) stellen zum Einen die notwendige Plattform und zum Anderen die Funktionalität zur Verwaltung von Kursen, der Teilnehmer sowie die gesamte Kommunikation zwischen den Teilnehmern zur Verfügung.

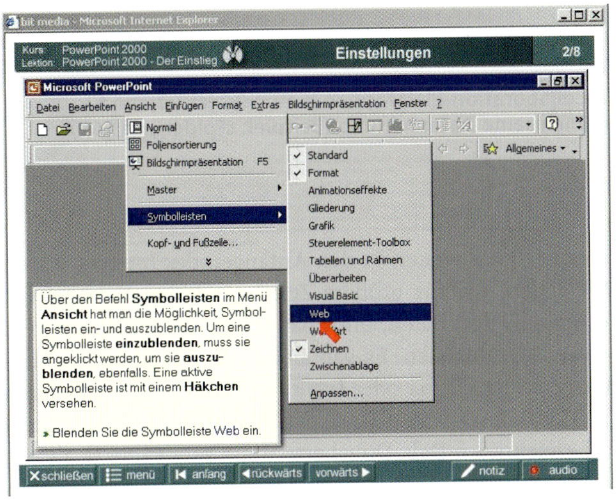

WBT-Lektion über Microsoft Excel (Quelle: bit media).

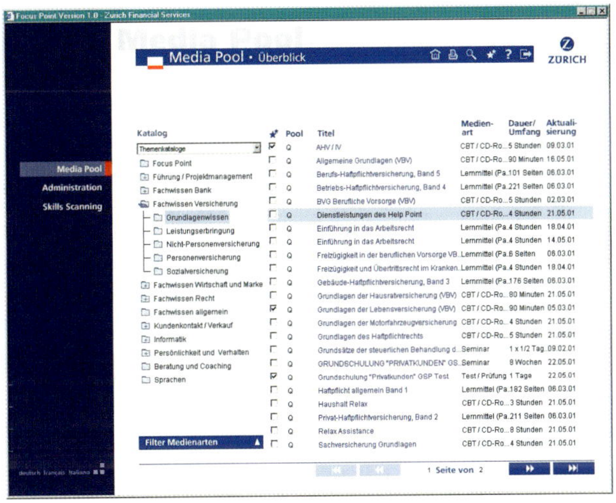

Lernportal mit Learning Management System (Quelle: Zürich Schweiz).

Damit die WBTs und das LMS zusammenarbeiten, müssen beide die gleichen Standards (z. B. **SCORM**, AICC oder IMS) verstehen. Sie definieren die Lernpakete und alle notwendigen Ressourcen und sorgen damit für eine Austauschbarkeit der elektronischen Lerninhalte über verschiedenste Lernplattformen. Gleichzeitig sorgen sie für die Kommunikation zwischen WBT und LMS, damit WBT-Bearbeitungsstände und Lernerfolgsmeldungen im LMS verwaltet werden können.

13.5.4 E-Collaboration

Kollaborative Software Plattformen im Internet unterstützen die Zusammenarbeit von unternehmensübergreifenden Projektgruppen über zeitliche und räumliche Distanzen hinweg. Dieses sogenannte **E-Collaboration** (engl. Zusammenarbeit) hat in der Regel das Ziel, Kostenpotentiale auszuschöpfen, Qualitätsniveaus zu erhöhen und Entwicklungs- und Anpassungsprozesse zu verkürzen. Typische Komponenten dieser Software sind Dokumentenablage, Terminsteuerung, Planung- und Kommunikationstools.

13.6.2 Weblog

❶ Weblog-User werden in der Umgangssprache als **Blogger** bezeichnet.

❷ **Trackback** ist ein System, mit dem ein Hinweis auf einen Beitrag zum gleichen Thema in einem anderen Weblog hinterlassen werden kann.

❸ **Permalinks** sind permanente individuelle Links (URLs). Durch diese stabilen Internet-Adressen können Weblog-Beiträge einfach mit anderen Webseiten verlinkt werden.

Weblog, oder die Kurzform **Blog**, bezeichnet ein digitales Journal im Web, deren Einträge in umgekehrter chronologischer Reihenfolge angeordnet sind. Das heißt, die aktuellen Beiträge erscheinen immer oben auf der Seite.

Blogs sind hinsichtlich ihrer Kommunikation vergleichbar mit Newslettern oder Foren. Sie verfügen in der Regel über eine Kommentarfunktion, die es den Lesern ermöglicht, einen Eintrag zu kommentieren und so mit dem Autor oder anderen Lesern zu diskutieren. **Blogger** ❶ greifen Themen anderer Blogger auf, interpretieren und erweitern das Thema um zusätzliche Informationen. Der ursprüngliche Blogeintrag wird dabei verlinkt. Über **Trackback**-Funktionen ❷ können Hinweise über weitere Einträge sichtbar gemacht werden.
Ein Beispiel: Alex liest bei Nina im Blog einen Beitrag über MP3-Player. Alex schreibt auch einen Beitrag über MP3-Player und bezieht sich auf Ninas Beitrag. Alex will, dass die Leute, die bei Nina den Beitrag lesen, auch seinen Beitrag beachten. Er schickt einen Trackback-Ping an die Trackback-URL, die in Ninas Beitrag angegeben ist. Jetzt erscheint auf Ninas Blog ein Verweis mit einem kurzen Textauszug zu Alex' Blog.
An Blogs können, je nach Berechtigung, auch mehreren Autoren beteiligt sein. Blogeinträge verfügen über stabile URLs, den so genannten **Permalinks** ❸.
Die meisten Blogs sind als so genannte „Private Blogs" im privat persönlichen Umfeld angesiedelt und dienen der Erlebnismitteilung und fördern die Aufmerksamkeit des Bloggers im Internet. Man schätzt, dass mittlerweile weltweit über 50 Millionen Blogs im Internet vertreten sind. Blogs werden aber auch immer mehr im nicht-privaten Bereich, zum Beispiel in Unternehmen und Institutionen eingesetzt. Diese „Corporate Blogs" dienen dabei als Kommunikationsinstrument, um auf einfache Weise ein Erfahrungs- und Wissenstransfer aufzubauen.

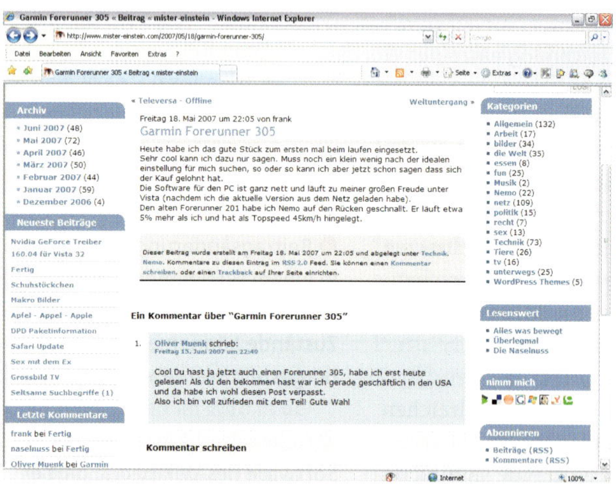

Beispiel eines privaten Blogs (Quelle: www.mister-einstein.com).

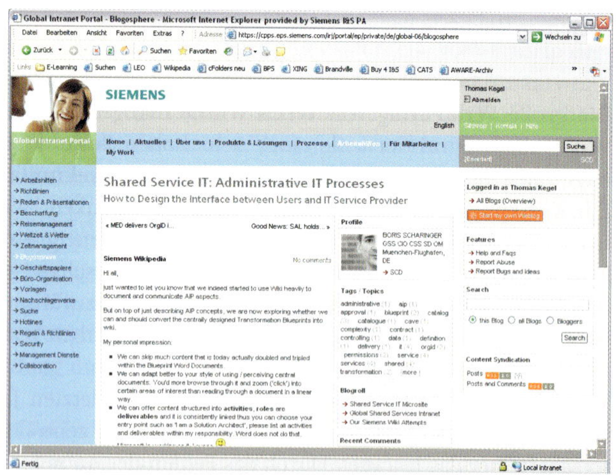

Beispiel eines Corporate Blogs (Quelle: Siemens AG).

Zum Beispiel kann ein Produktmanager in seinem Blog über aktuelle Entwicklungen, Planungen und Ideen für die Weiterentwicklung seines Produktes berichten. Oder ein Entwicklungsleiter schreibt über den aktuellen Stand der Arbeit seines Teams (sofern dies nicht zu vertraulich ist). Die Marketing-Mitarbeiter können damit den Status der Entwicklung verfolgen. Wartungstechniker informieren sich über Verbesserungen der Produkte und können über Kommentare zu den Blog-Einträgen sinnvolle Anregungen geben.

13.6.3 RSS-Feed

Um Artikel einer Website oder eines Weblogs in andere Websites zu integrieren, bedarf es einheitlicher Datenformate, die in maschinenlesbarer Form gespeichert werden. RSS (Really Simple Syndication) ist ein elektronisches Nachrichtenformat, das vom Informationsanbieter über so genannte **RSS-Feeds** ❶ auf der Website angeboten wird. Der RSS-Feed besteht aus einer XML-Datei, welche in strukturierter Form ausschließlich die Nachrichteninformation bereitstellt. Layout oder Formatierungen sind dabei unberücksichtigt. Mit Hilfe von Feed-Readern oder RSS-fähigen Browsern lassen sich die RSS-Feeds nach dem Prinzip des Abonnierens automatisiert herunterladen und in geordneter Form als Nachrichten-Sammlung anzeigen. Ebenso können fremde RSS-Feeds in eigene Webseiten integriert werden.

❶ Angebotene RSS-Feeds (engl. to feed = füttern) werden über ein Logo auf der Webseite visualisiert.

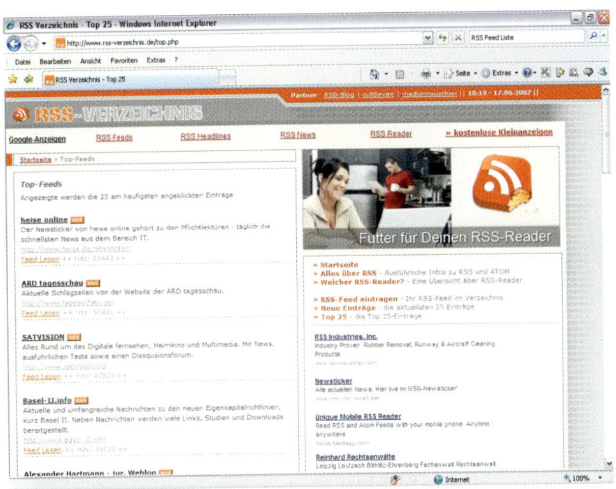

Anbieter von RSS-Feeds werden auch in speziellen Verzeichnissen gelistet (Quelle: www.rss-verzeichnis.de).

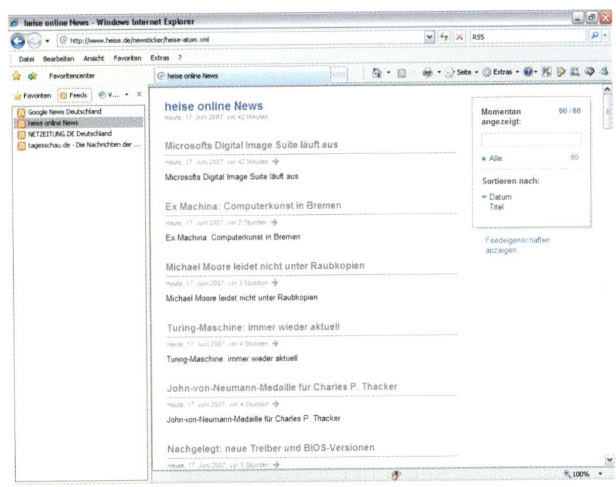

Nachrichtensammlung im RSS-Reader am Beispiel der Microsoft Internet Explorer 7. (Quelle: www.mister-einstein.com).

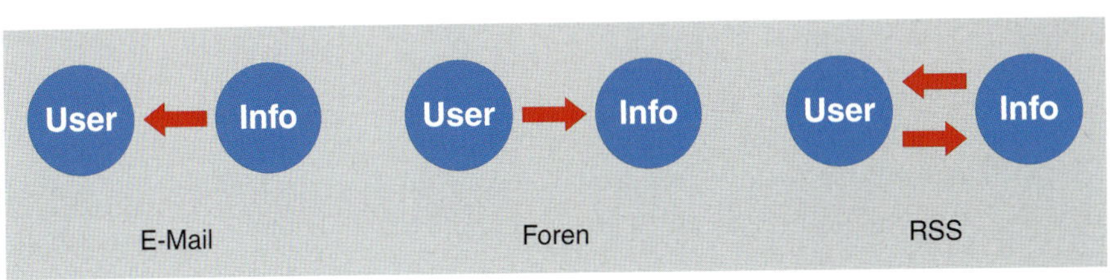

Vergleich der Kommunikationsprozesse zwischen E-Mail, Foren und RSS-Feeds.

Während bei E-Mails der Sender aktiv die Information zum Empfänger schickt und bei Foren der Empfänger aktiv die Information aussucht, so wird bei RSS-Feeds der Kommunikationsprozess durch das Abonnieren einmalig angestoßen und in Folge erhält der Empfänger dann automatisch die gewünschten Informationen, sobald sie beim Sender vorliegen. Als Alternative zu RSS gibt es das konkurrierende Format Atom, welches ebenfalls auf XML basiert, aber nicht kompatibel zu RSS ist.

13.6.4 Webcast

❶ Der Begriff **Webcast** ist die Kurzform von „Web Broadcast" und bezeichnet ein System, um Informationen von einer Person an viele Teilnehmer über das Internet zu verteilen.

Der **Webcast** ❶, auch **„Webinar"** oder „Onlineseminar" genannt, ist in der IT-Branche intern schon länger in Gebrauch, um aktuelle Informationen schnell, unkompliziert und möglichst kostengünstig einem beliebigen Kreis von Teilnehmern (Kunden, Interessenten, Partner) zugänglich zu machen.

Die typische Präsentationsform eines Webcast ist, dass ein Moderator bzw. Referent in einer Live-Veranstaltung mehreren eingeladenen Teilnehmern über das Medium Internet Informationen vorträgt. Dies können zum Beispiel Produkt-Neuigkeiten oder der Umgang mit Produkten sein.

Bei Webcasts unterscheidet man zwischen rein linearen Webcasts, die eine Live-Veranstaltung über einen Videostream präsentieren und interaktiven Webcasts, die einen speziellen Webcast-Client voraussetzen, dann aber die volle Funktionalität einer Webkonferenz bieten. Dazu gehört eine Chatfunktion, über der die Teilnehmer während der Veranstaltung dem Moderator Fragen stellen können und eine Teilnehmerliste, die zeigt, wer aktuell am Webcast teilnimmt.

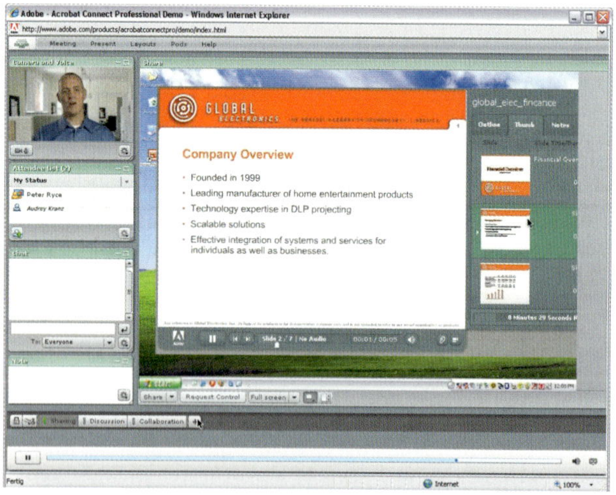

Interaktiver Webcast mit Acrobat Connect Professional (Quelle: Adobe).

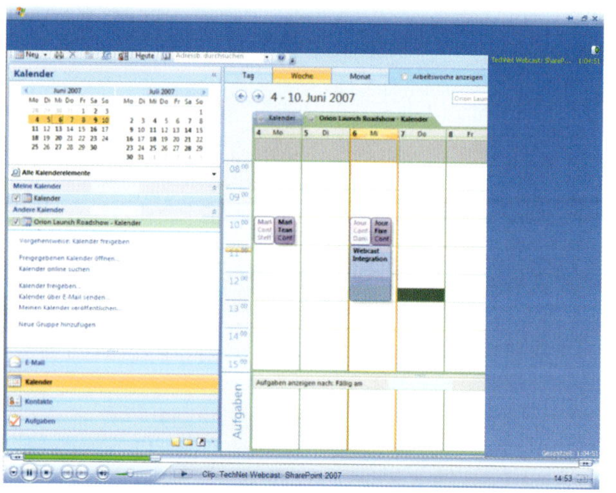

Linearer Webcast auf Basis eines Videostreams im Microsoft Medienplayer (Quelle: Microsoft TechNet Webcast).

Die primäre Informationsvermittlung geschieht dabei über Audio, dem Sprecherton des Referenten. Je nach verwendeter Webcast-Software geschieht dies über VoIP (Voice over IP) oder über eine hinzu geschaltete Telefonkonferenz.

Einige Veranstalter bieten ihre Webcasts auch nach der Veranstaltung als Aufzeichnungen in Form eines Webcast-Archivs an. Dies kann zum Beispiel als Windows Media File und als Powerpoint-Folien abrufbar sein.

13.6.5 Podcasting

Unter **Podcasting** ❶ versteht man das Anbieten von Audio- und Videodateien über das Internet. Dabei entspricht die inhaltliche Aufmachung von Podcasts denen einer Radiosendung bzw. bei Video-Podcasts denen einer Fernsehsendung. Themen werden redaktionell aufgearbeitet und in einer Serie von regelmäßigen Medienbeiträgen (Episoden) über RSS-Feeds zum Download angeboten.
Wer Podcasts nutzen will, braucht einen RSS-Reader, um die gewünschten RSS-Feeds mit den Podcasts zu abonnieren und abrufen zu können.

❶ Das Wort **Podcasting** ist ein Kunstwort und setzt sich aus den Begriffen „iPod" und „Broadcasting" zusammen.

Große Podcast-Verzeichnisse lassen sich mit iTunes durchsuchen (Quelle: iTunes von Apple).

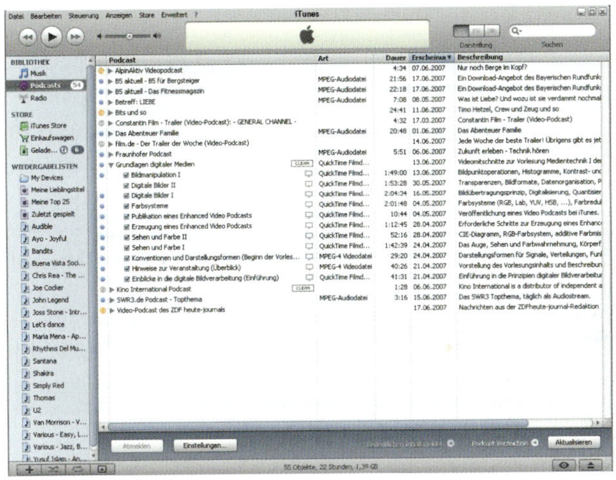

Die abonnierten Podcasts werden über die RSS-Reader-Funktion selbstständig geladen und direkt auf das Abspielgerät iPod übertragen (Quelle: iTunes von Apple).

Der interessante Aspekt von Podcasts ist, dass sie, auf mobile Endgeräte übertragen, ein individuell zusammengestelltes Informationsprogramm für unterwegs bieten können. Und das nicht nur mit Informationen von großen Anbietern, wie Fernsehanstalten oder Radiosendern, sondern ähnlich wie bei Weblogs, auch von jedem Podcaster, der über dieses Medium etwas mitteilen möchte.

Das Podcast-Logo.

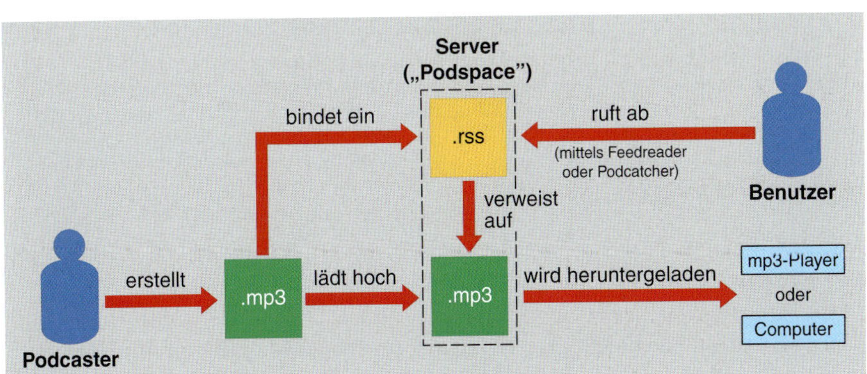

Die schematische Darstellung eines Podcasts-Produktionsprozesses, mit dem Podcast-Episoden im MP3-Format erstellt und mit Hilfe von RSS-Feeds bereitgestellt werden.

13.6.6 Social Networking

Durch die neuen Kommunikationsformen, die unter anderem durch Wikis, Foren und Weblogs geprägt werden, entstehen auch neue Internet-Gemeinschaften. Diese Virtuellen Gemeinschaften, oder auch Online-Communitys genannt, sind eingerichtete Plattformen für Menschen, die sich über das Internet begegnen und austauschen. In der Regel verfolgen die Teilnehmer dabei ähnlich gelagerte Interessen. Beziehen sich die gemeinsamen Interessen auch auf das Entwickeln und Pflegen von Bekanntschafts-Netzwerken, so spricht man von **Social Networking**. Hierzu haben sich mittlerweile viele Social Networking Plattformen etabliert.

Geschäfts-Netzwerke

In diesen Netzwerken steht das Beziehungsmanagement im Vordergrund. Es ermöglicht, Kontakte abzubilden, zu pflegen und neue zu knüpfen. Über Interessenangaben in den Mitglieder-Profilen und der Beziehungsstruktur lassen sich komplexe Vernetzungsstrukturen aufzeichnen und über Suchfunktionen abrufen. Das Netzwerk mit den meisten Mitgliedern mit mehr als 5 Millionen Benutzern ist im deutschsprachigem Raum „XING".

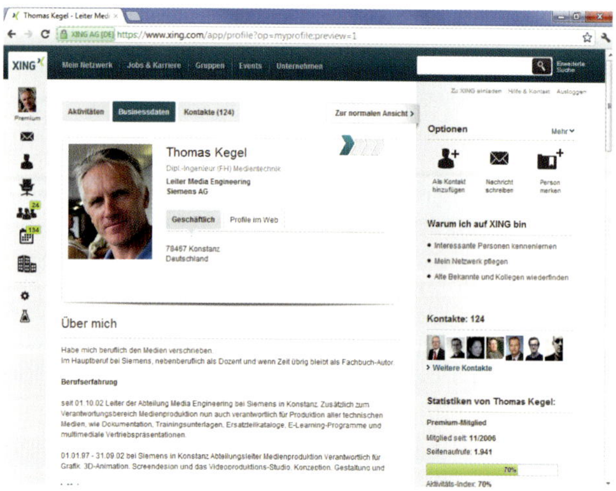

Jedes Mitglied erstellt ein aussagekräftiges Profil, um über das Geschäfts-Netzwerk Kontakte zu pflegen und neue zu knüpfen. (Quelle: XING.de).

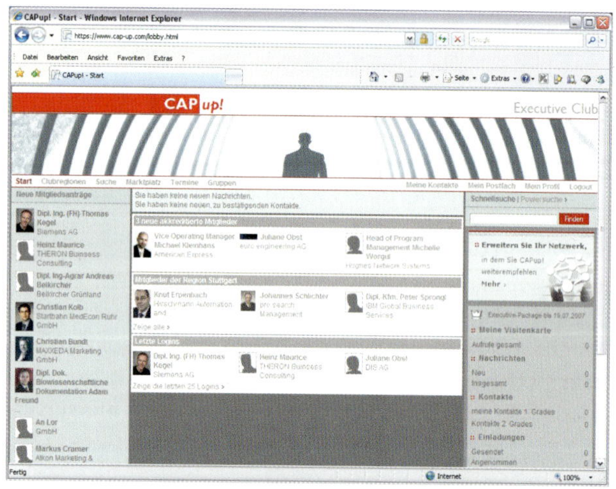

Untereinander können die Mitglieder über Geschäftsinteressen, Branchen, Regionen etc. vernetzt werden (Quelle: CAPup.de).

Freunde-Netzwerke

Auch hier steht das Beziehungsmanagement zu anderen Mitgliedern im Vordergrund. Nur geht es dabei um Kontakte und Freundschaften im privaten Bereich.

Typische Bestandteile dieser Netzwerk-Plattformen sind Mitgliederprofile, Kontaktlisten der Freunde, Suchfunktionen, Gruppen-Diskussionsforen, **Foto-Tagging** ❶, **Gruscheln** ❷ etc. Beispiele dieser Netzwerk-Plattformen sind „StudiVZ.net", „facebook.com", „piczo.com", „jappy.de" und „stayfriends.de".

❶ **Foto-Tagging** = Personen auf Fotos können mit deren Kontaktdaten verlinkt werden.

❷ **Gruscheln** = Kunstwort aus „grüßen" und „kuscheln". Dient zur Kontaktaufnahme mit anderen Mitgliedern.

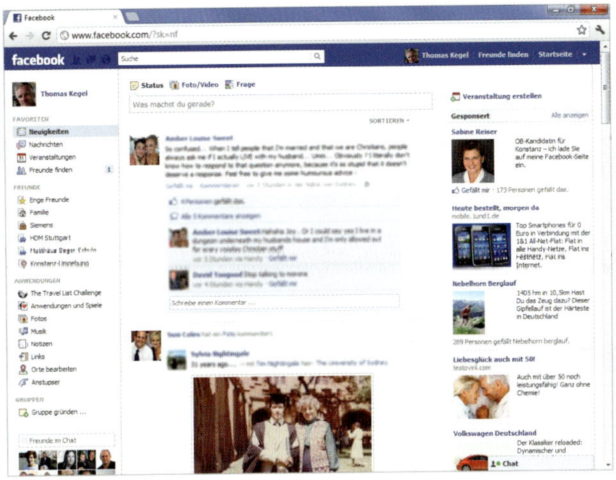

Die Netzwerke-Plattform „Facebook" hat 2012 mit weltweit über 900 Millionen Nutzern die größter Verbreitung (Quelle: facebook.com).

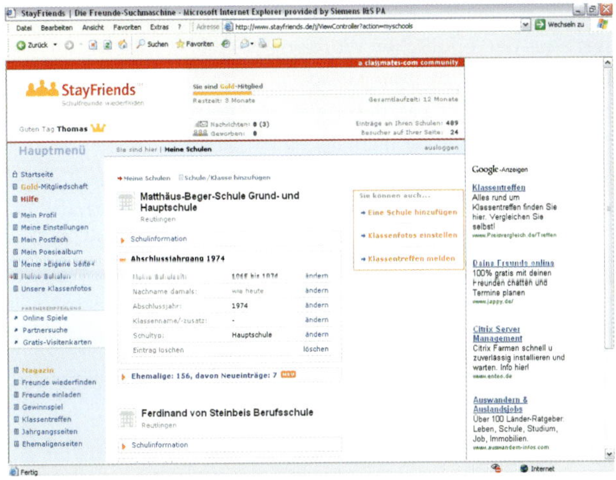

Auf frühere Schulfreunde spezialisierte Netzwerke dienen dem Auffinden alter Klassenkameraden/innen (Quelle: stayfriends.de).

Netzwerk zum Folgen von Kurznachrichten

Mit dem Erfolg von **„Twitter"** ❶ hat sich ein Kurznachrichtendienst etabliert, bei dem jeder Kurznachrichten **„Tweets"** bis maximal 140 Zeichen veröffentlichen kann.
Twitter ist ein öffentliches und kostenloses System, welches man auch als Blog ansehen kann. Hier spricht man von Microblogging, also dem bloggen mit kurzen Texten. Wer diese Nachrichten lesen will, muss sie abbonieren. Dadurch wird man zum sogenannten „Follower". Jeder Nutzer kann sich bei jedem anderen eintragen. Mit einer simplen Kurznachricht ist es somit möglich, auf einen Schlag zehn, 100 oder 10.000 Menschen zu erreichen. Jeder Follower kann seinerseits auf Tweets antworten, entweder öffentlich oder mit einer privaten Nachricht, die nur der Absender lesen kann. Die Stärken von Twitter liegen in der Aktualität der Beiträge und im mobilen Bereich, da „Twittern" mit den unterschiedlichsten Endgeräten möglich ist.

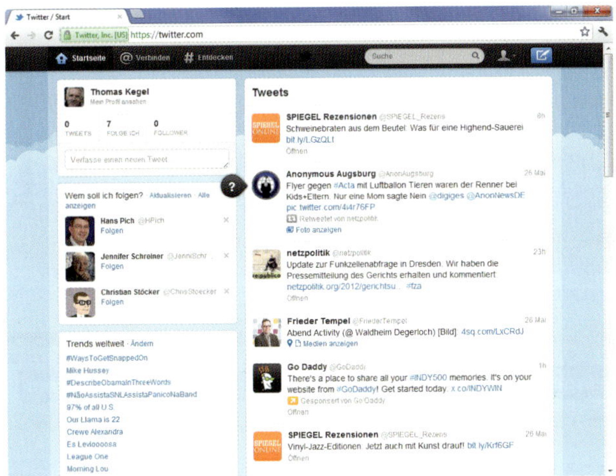

❶ Mit der Netzwerke-Plattform „Twitter" können Kurzmitteilungen schnell und kostenlos verbreitet werden (Quelle: twitter.com).

Netzwerke für gemeinschaftliches Bewerten und Indexieren

Plattformen, die Informationen, Themen, Bilder oder Bookmarks zum Bewerten durch die Gemeinschaft der Mitglieder anbieten, verfolgen das Ziel des gemeinschaftlichen Bewertens und Indexierens. Der daraus resultierende Mehrwert, der durch die Gemeinschaft geschaffen wird, kommt der Gemeinschaft auch wieder zu gute.

Beim gemeinschaftlichen Indexieren geht man davon aus, dass sich eine große Anzahl von Nutzern auf sinnvolle und schlüssige Zuordnungen einigen, aus denen dann automatisiert ein Schlagwortverzeichnis für spätere Suchanfragen generiert werden kann.

❶ **Folksonomy**, zusammengesetzt aus den englischen Wörtern folk (Volk) und taxonomy (Klassifizierung), drückt aus, dass beim Tagging jeder Nutzer im gleichen Maße an der Kategorisierung von Inhalten teilnehmen kann.

Dadurch entstehen ganze Sammlungen von Tags, auch **Folksonomien** ❶ genannt. Beispiel für diese Netzwerke sind „delicious.com“ und „mister-wong.de“.

Beim gemeinschaftlichen Bewerten werden Orte, Produkte, Medien oder andere Themen von Mitgliedern bewertet bzw. mit einer persönlichen Anmerkung versehen. Dadurch erhalten informationssuchende Mitglieder Hilfestellungen durch die Gemeinschaft. Beispiel für diese Netzwerke sind „Qype.com“ ❷, „Flickr.com“, „YouTube.com“ ❸, „fotocommunity.de“, „mister-wong.de“ ❹, „myspace.com“ ❺ und andere.

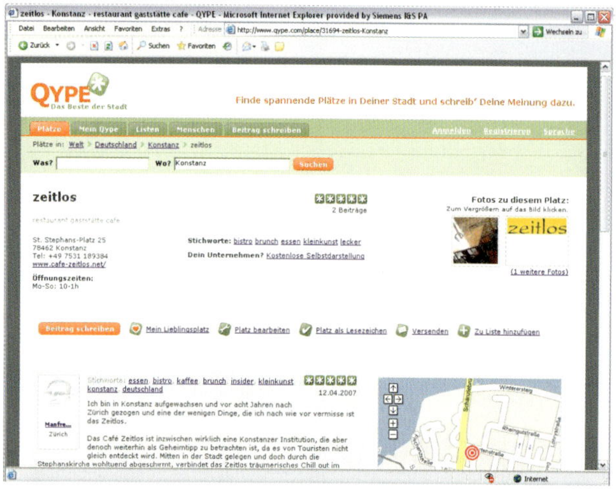

❷ Qype bietet als Social-Networking-Branchenbuch örtliche Tipps mit Bewertungen und Erfahrungen aus der Gemeinschaft (Quelle: qype.com).

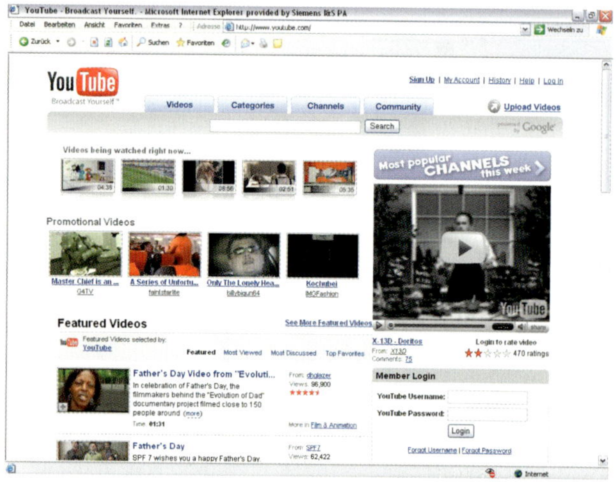

❸ YouTube erlaubt das Veröffentlichen von Videos. Die Gemeinschaft kann die Videos kommentieren und bewerten (Quelle: YouTube.com).

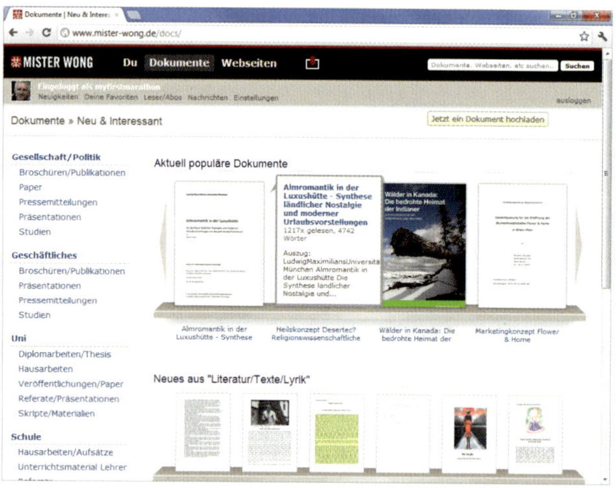

❹ Mr. Wong ist eine Art Online-Dokumenten-Sammlung, die von der Gemeinschaft bewertet und indexiert werden kann (Quelle: mister-wong.de).

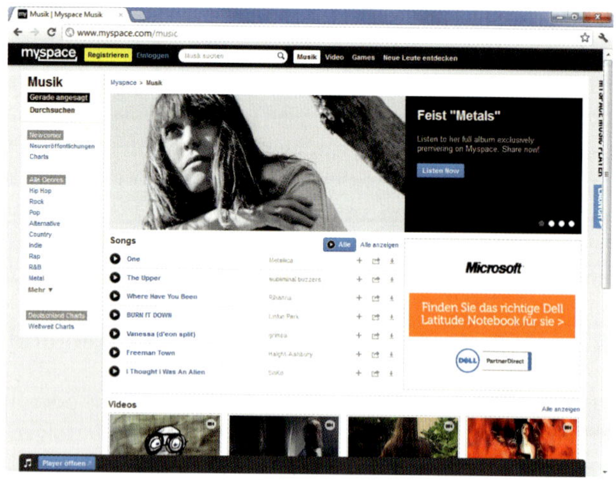

❺ MySpace hat seinen Schwerpunkt im Musikbereich mit Selbstdarstellen, musikalisch Gleichgesinnte finden und eigene Musik veröffentlichen (Quelle: myspace.com).

Aufgaben und Übungen, Literaturhinweise

Aufgaben und Übungen

1. Untersuchen Sie an einem frei gewählten Thema, wie der Informationsfluss bei Newslettern, Mailinglisten und Newsgroups zwischen den Internet-Nutzern abläuft.
2. Besuchen Sie Chats und Newsgroups und achten Sie auf die Verwendung von Akronymen und Emoticons. Übersetzen Sie die Kürzel in Fließtext.
3. Skizzieren Sie alle Hardware-Komponenten auf, die Sie für einen möglichst schnellen Internetzugang benötigen.
4. Vergleichen Sie an Hand von realen Beispielen das Leistungsangebot von einem reinen ISP gegenüber einem bekannten Onlinedienst.
5. Zeigen Sie die Darstellungsunterschiede der Browser Microsoft Internet Explorer, dem Google Chrome oder Firefox am Beispiel von zehn Internetauftritten.
6. Beschreiben Sie alle Maßnahmen, die notwendig sind, um möglichst viren- und datensicher E-Mails untereinander auszutauschen.

Literaturhinweise

Alby, Tom: Web 2.0: Konzepte, Anwendungen, Technologien. 3. Aufl., München 2008 (Carl Hanser Verlag)

Baumgart, Michael: Web Design, Berlin, Heidelberg, New York u. a. 2000 (Springer)

Beier, Markus; *Gizycki*, Vittoria von (Hrsg.): Usability – Nutzerfreundliches Webdesign, Berlin, Heidelberg, New York u. a. 2002 (Springer)

Gralla, Breston: So funktioniert das Internet, Ein visueller Streifzug durch das Internet, München 2001 (markt + Technik Verlag)

Grotenhoff, Maria; *Stylianakis*, Anna: Website-Konzeption. Von der Idee zum Storyboard. Bonn 2001 (Galileo)

Hofer, Klaus C.; *Zimmermann*, Hansjörg: Good Webrations, Eine Web Wirkungsanalyse, München 2000 (PROTEUS)

Langkau, Ralf: Webdesign und -publishing. Grundlagen und Designtechniken. 3. Aufl., München, Wien 2001 (Hanser)

Langkau, Ralf: Webdesign und -publishing. Projektmanagement für Websites. München, Wien 2000 (Hanser)

Möller, Erik: Die heimliche Medienrevolution. Wie Weblogs, Wikis und freie Software die Welt verändern, Hannover 2006 (Heise Zeitschriften-Verlag)

McKelvey, Roy: Hypergraphics, Reinbek bei Hamburg 2000 (Rowohlt)

Randerath, Detlef; *Neumann*, Christian: Streaming Media, Bonn 2001 (Galileo)

Renz, Florian: Praktiken des Social Networking, 2007 (Verlag Werner Hülsbusch)

Schenker, Amanda; *Meier*, Alexander: Internet-Konzept, Kilchberg 2000 (Smart Books Publishing)

Schieb, Jörg: Internet, Nichts leichter als das, Berlin 2001 (Stiftung Warentest)

Schnieders, Christian: Schnellkurs Internet, Köln 2001 (DuMont)

Schweibenz, Werner; *Thissen*, Frank: Qualität im Web, Berlin, Heidelberg, New York u. a. 2002 (Springer

Stocksmeier, Thorsten: Business Webdesign, Berlin, Heidelberg, New York u. a. 2002 (Springer)

14 Medieninformatik

Webcode: B1400

Für weitere Infos zu diesem Kapitel mit dem Smartphone einfach QR-Code scannen oder auf www.medien-verstehen.de den Webcode eingeben.

Als Teilgebiet der klassischen Informatik konzentriert sich die Medieninformatik auf den Schwerpunkt Multimedia und die digitale Informationsverarbeitung in den Medien. Dabei setzt sich die Medieninformatik in vielfältigen medialen Formen mit den Mensch-Computer-Schnittstellen auseinander.
In diesem Kapitel werden Grundlagen, Techniken und Werkzeuge behandelt, die im Rahmen der Medieninformatik benötigt werden, um Medien-Anwendungen zu erstellen.

14.1 Programmieren

Das Umsetzen und Realisieren einer Medien-Anwendungen erfolgt mit Werkzeugen, die in der Regel eine **Programmierung** mithilfe einer formalen Sprache erlaubt. Diese Programmiersprache dient der Erstellung von Informationsverarbeitungsanweisungen für das verwendete Computersystem.

14.1.1 Klassifizierung der Sprachen

Programmiersprachen lassen sich unterschiedlich klassifizieren, je nach Anwendungsgebiet, entsprechend der **Programmierparadigmen** ❶ oder hinsichtlich der Sprachgenerationen ❷.

❶ **Programmierparadigmen** beschreiben das zugrundeliegende Prinzip der Programmiertechnik. Beispiele sind die imperative und die objektorientierte Programmierung. Siehe Abschnitt 14.1.2.

❷ Über die **Generationen** der Programmiersprachen entwickelte sich die Benutzerfreundlichkeit der Computer-Mensch-Schnittstelle. Beginnend bei der 1. Generation, den direkten Prozessorbefehlen, gefolgt von den symbolischen Sprachen (2. Generation) entwickelten sich die problemorientierten Sprachen (3.-5. Generation), die der menschlichen Denkweise näher kommt.

Maschinensprachen sind Sprachen der **1. Generation**. Sie bestehen aus einer Folge von Befehlen und Anweisungen, die der Prozessor eines Computers direkt verarbeiten kann. Maschinensprache liegt immer in binärer Form vor, als Folge von Nullen und Einsen. Jede Maschinensprache muss genau auf den Prozessor abgestimmt sein.

Assemblersprachen sind Sprachen der **2. Generation**. Im Gegensatz zur Maschinensprache werden anstelle eines nur schwer zu merkenden Binärcodes die Befehle und Operanden durch leichter verständliche mnemonische Symbole (Mnemonik) dargestellt. Für jeden Computertyp gibt es spezielle, auf den Befehlsvorrat (Befehlssatz) des Computers zugeschnittene Assembler-Sprachen. Anstelle der Kodierung der Maschinenoperation „Addieren", die in einem 8-bit-Code z. B. durch das Bitmuster 00010111 festgelegt sein kann, lautet die entsprechende Assembler-Anweisung „add".

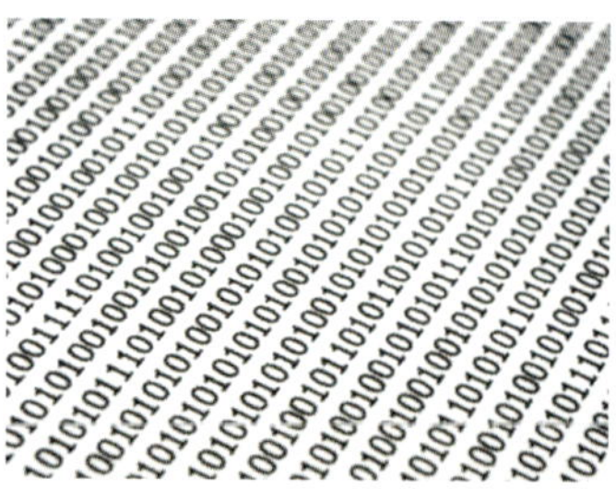
Der Prozessor des Computers versteht nur Maschinencode in Form von Nullen und Einsen.

Höhere Programmiersprachen bezeichnet man als Sprachen der **3. Generation**. Diese Sprachen werden unabhängig von Prozessoreigenschaften formuliert und vom Menschen wesentlich leichter „durchschaut". Eine in einer Hochsprache formulierte (abgeschlossene) Befehlsfolge nennt man Quellcode (Source Code). Programme in höheren Sprachen werden vor der Ausführung in einen Maschinencode gleicher Bedeutung übersetzt. Beispiel für höhere Programmiersprachen sind: C++ und Pascal.

Abfragesprachen sind typische Sprachen der **4. Generation**. Diese Sprachen bieten einfache Sprachmittel zur Auslösung von komplexen Operationen. Abfragesprachen dienen dem Suchen und Sortieren von Daten innerhalb einer Datenbank oder Internetsuchmaschinen. Einige Abfragesprachen ermöglichen es auch, Daten in einer Datenbank zu löschen, zu ändern oder neu aufzunehmen.

Beispiel für eine Abfragesprache: SQL (Structured Query Language)

Makrosprachen sind einfache Programmiersprachen, meist Interpreter-Sprachen, die es ermöglichen, häufig benutzte Folgen von Aktionen innerhalb eines Anwendungsprogramms in einem Makro zusammenzufassen, und teilweise sogar ganze Programme zu erstellen.
Eine der bekanntesten Makrosprachen ist VBA (Visual Basic for Applications), die Makrosprache für Microsoft Office Programme, Word und Excel.

Skriptsprachen sind einfach strukturierte und leicht zu erlernende Programmiersprachen, die es erlauben, innerhalb einer Anwendung Prozeduren (i. d. R. für die Verbindung zu einem Netz und zur Steuerung darin) zu schreiben. Beispiele für Skriptsprachen: JavaScript, Perl, PHP, VBScript.

Unter dem Begriff **Autorensysteme** versteht man spezialisierte Programme, die für das Erstellen von Multimedia-Software wie z. B. Schulungsunterlagen, Lern-Software, Edutainment-Programmen konzipiert sind. Mithilfe dieser Autorensysteme werden unterschiedliche Komponenten wie Text, Grafik, Sound und andere Elemente in Beziehung zueinander gesetzt und zu einem Ganzen verknüpft. Während bei den ersten Autorensystemen Programmierkenntnisse unabdingbar waren, können mit den neueren Versionen einfache Anwendungen durch Auswahl vorgegebener Elemente aus Menüleisten zusammengestellt werden. Aus diesem Grund eignen sich Autorensysteme nicht nur für Programmierer, sondern auch für Gestalter, Pädagogen und alle, die nach kurzer Einarbeitungszeit Inhalte in multimediale Anwendungen umsetzen wollen. Über eine integrierte Skriptsprache kann der Funktionsumfang des Autorensystems durch Autoren, die über Programmierkenntnisse verfügen, erweitert werden. Beispiele von Autorensystemen: Authorware, ToolBook, Director, Flash.

Seitenbeschreibungssprachen sind keine Programmiersprachen im klassischen Sinne, sondern dienen dazu, Dokumente mit Hilfe von mathematischen Objekten so exakt zu beschreiben, wie diese in einem speziellen Ausgabegerät, zum Beispiel einem Drucker oder auf einem Monitor, aussehen sollen. Es handelt sich dabei um Ausgabeformate, die in der Regel nicht zur weiteren Bearbeitung vorgesehen sind. Beispiele von Seitenbeschreibungssprachen sind: PostScript, PDF, PCL, XSL-FO.

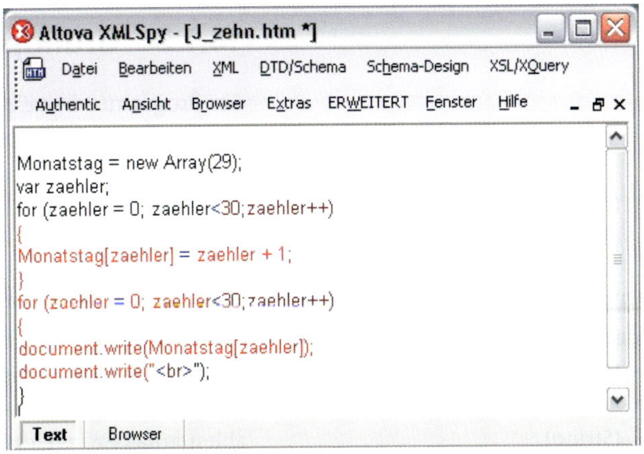

Skriptsprachen haben sich im Bereich der Web-Anwendungen durchgesetzt. Beispiel: JavaScript.

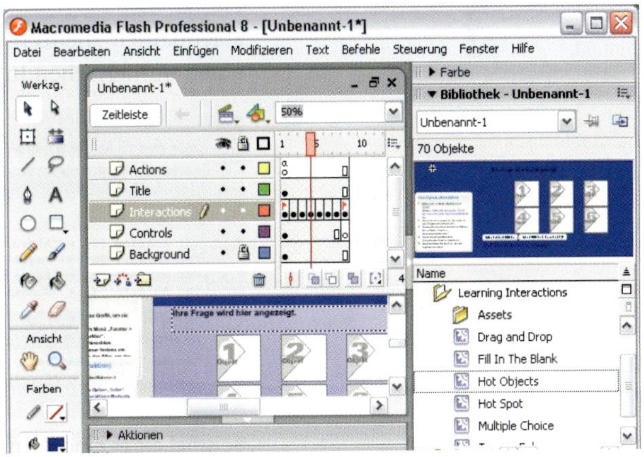

Autorensysteme bieten spezialisierte Komponenten für die Erstellung von Medien-Anwendungen. Beispiel: Adobe Flash.

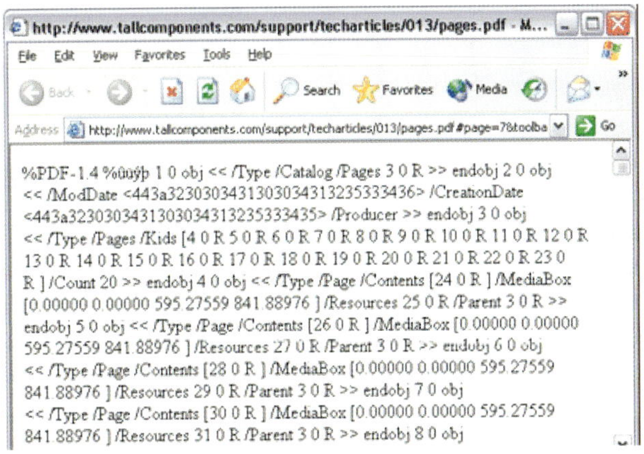

Seitenbeschreibungssprachen definieren die Medienausgabe, insbesondere für den Print-Bereich. Beispiel: PDF.

Typisch dafür sind Folgende:

- **If...else-Bedingungen** sorgen für eine Programmverzweigung, wenn bestimmte Bedingungen erfüllt sind. Diese Fallentscheidung kann auch ohne „else"-Pfad verwendet werden, durchläuft dann die Schleife bei Nichterfüllen der Bedingung ohne Abarbeiten einer Anweisung. Mehrere if...else-Bedingungen können auch ineinander verschachtelt werden.

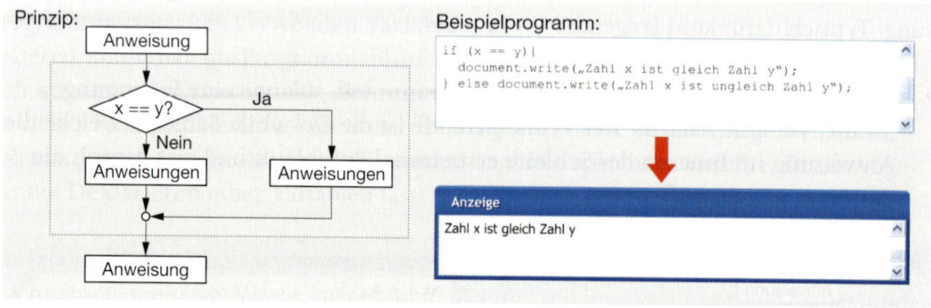

Beispiel einer if...else-Bedingung in JavaScript.

- **Switch-Bedingungen** verzweigen zu einem von mehreren Programmzweigen, je nach Zutreffen einer Bedingung. Falls keine vorgesehene Bedingung zutrifft, so greift der „Default"-Fall und führt die dafür vorgesehene Anweisung aus.

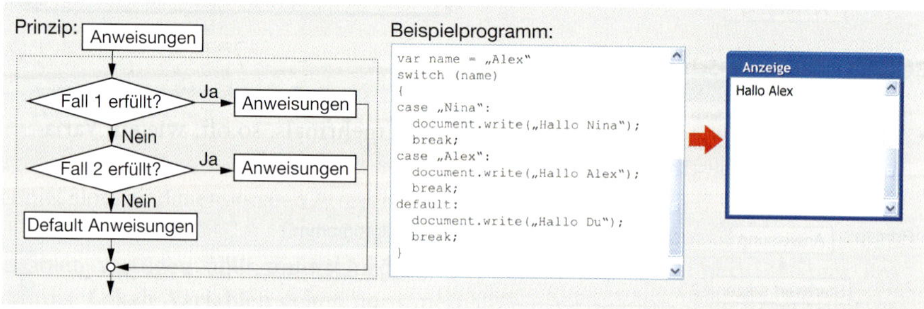

Beispiel einer Switch-Abfrage in JavaScript.

Bei einem Programm in C übernimmt die **Funktion** „main()" die Aufgabe des Hauptprogramms. Beliebig viele weitere Funktionen stellen dann das gesamte Programm dar, die von jeder Stelle aus aufgerufen werden können. Nach dem Durcharbeiten der Anweisungen in einer Funktion liefert diese einen Rückgabewert an das aufrufende Programm. Zum Beispiel den Ergebniswert einer mathematischen Berechnung.

Unterprogramm

Um eine Reihe von Anweisungen, die öfter verwendet werden sollen, nicht doppelt im Quellcode zu führen, werden diese zusammengefasst und mit einem Namen versehen. Diese als **Funktionen** benannten **Unterprogramme** (Subroutinen) können dann bei Bedarf von einer beliebigen Programmstelle aus aufgerufen werden und sind, da sie nur einmal gespeichert sind, leichter zu pflegen.

In einigen Programmiersprachen werden Funktionen, die keinen Rückgabewert an die aufrufende Stelle senden, **Prozeduren** genannt. Zum Beispiel kann dies die Anderung eines Schriftfonts sein. In der Programmiersprache C sind das Funktionen mit dem Datentyp „void". JavaScript kennt nur Funktionen und keine Prozeduren, da bei JavaScript der Rückgabewert nicht zwingend ist.

Imperative Programmierung

Die Programmiermethode, die eine Berechnung als Folge von Zustandsänderungen von Variablen betrachtet, wird **Imperative Programmierung** genannt. Ein Programm besteht dabei aus einer Folge von Befehlen an den Computer, wie z. B. „Schreibe in die Variable x den Wert 10" oder „Springe an die Stelle z im Programm". Dabei werden Eingabewerte in Variablen gespeichert und weiterverarbeitet. Dieses Verarbeiten wird in Funktionen oder Prozeduren zusammengefasst. Funktionen, bedingte Anweisung und Schleifen sind dabei ausreichend, um alle Algorithmen bei dieser Programmierung zu formulieren. Programmiersprachen-Beispiele sind: C, Pascal, Ada.

Objektorientierte Programmierung

Bei der **Objektorientierten Programmierung** (OOP) steht die Manipulation von sogenannten Objekten durch Funktionen und Prozeduren sowie die Verbindung von Objekten und deren Interaktion im Vordergrund. Unter einem **Objekt** kann man sich ein Software-Modell vorstellen, welches ein Gegenstand aus der realen Welt mit all seinen Eigenschaften und Verhaltensweisen beschreiben soll. Zum Beispiel ein Bildschirm, ein Drucker, ein Teil der Software selbst oder auch nur die Überschrift in einem Dokument kann dabei ein Objekt sein.
In der objektorientierten Programmierung werden Prozeduren und Funktionen mit dem Begriff **Methode** zusammengefasst. Methoden sind spezielle Funktionen, die einem Objekt zugeordnet sind und nur in Verbindung mit diesem vorkommen.

Ebenso verfügen die Objekte über verschiedene Eigenschaften. Diese Eigenschaften eines Objektes werden **Attribut** genannt.
In der Praxis muss sich der Programmierer bei den objektorientierten Programmiersprachen nicht mehr hauptsächlich um die technische Realisierung der Eigenschaften und Funktionen der Objekte kümmern, denn in Bibliotheken sind **Klassen** ❶ von Objekten gesammelt, aus denen der Programmierer für seine Aufgabe geeignete auswählt oder von diesen neue problemspezifische Objekte (**Instanzen** ❷) ableitet. Bei Bedarf kann der Programmierer auch vollkommen neue Objekte erstellen.
Programmiersprachen nach dieser Methode sind: C++, Turbo Pascal, Java, JavaScript

❶ In der OOP werden ähnliche Objekte zu Gruppierungen, sogenannten **Klassen**, zusammengefasst. Die Klassen können auch als Schablonen verstanden werden, die wie Baupläne für neue Objekte dienen.

❷ Die neuen Objekte, die aus vorhandenen Klassen entstehen, werden als **Instanzen** dieser Klasse bezeichnet. Durch eine **Vererbung** erhalten sie die Methoden und Attribute des Ursprungsobjektes mit auf den Weg.

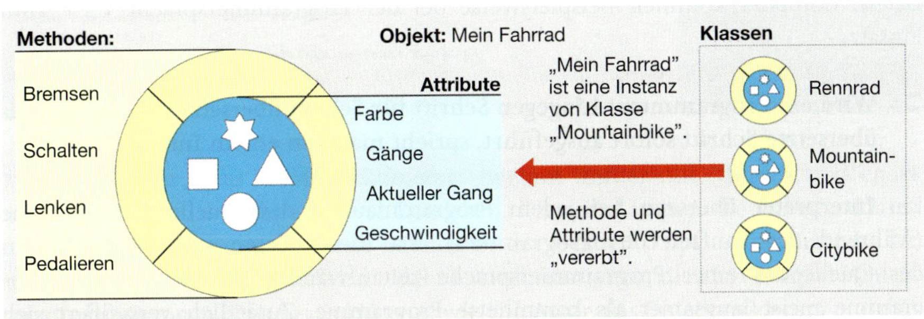

Veranschaulichung der Denkweise bei der objektorientierten Programmierung am Beispiel des Objektes „Fahrrad".

Dies können Texte, Formatierungen, Hyperlinks und Befehle zum Einbinden anderer Objekte sein.

➲ **Dabei muss beachtet werden, dass es grundlegende Layoutfaktoren gibt, die von den Einstellungen des verwendeten Browsers abhängen, und die der Gestalter nicht beeinflussen kann.**

Dies gilt besonders bei unformatiertem Text, der im Browser mit den browserspezifischen Einstellungen für Hintergrundfarbe, Textfarbe und Textgröße dargestellt wird. Auch eine Größenänderung des Browsers wirkt sich auf die Textlänge pro Zeile aus – verändert man die Größe des Browserfensters, so wird der Text anders umgebrochen. Um trotzdem auf die Gestaltung Einfluss zu nehmen, muss formatiert werden. Dies kann zum Einen mit Textstrukturierungen und zum Anderen mit dem Einsatz von Textattributen erfolgen.

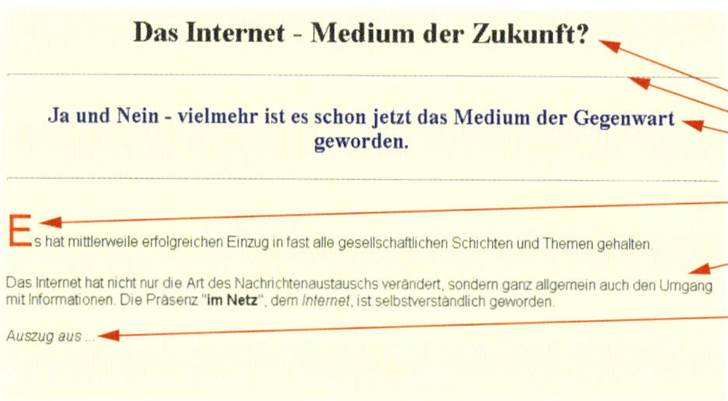

HTML-Code im Browser dargestellt.

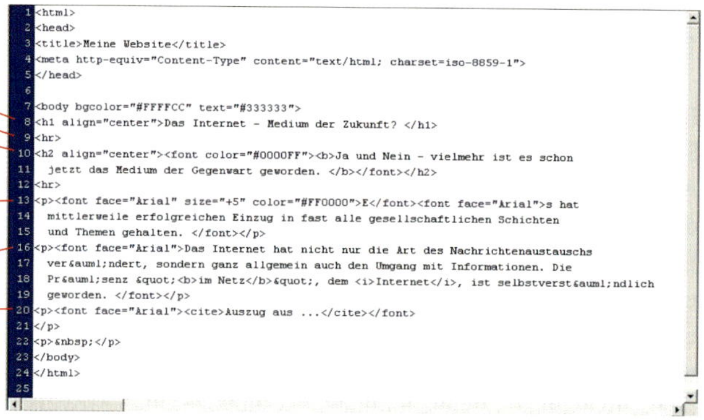

HTML-Code

❶ **HTML-Überschriften**:
<H1>...</H1> 1. Ordnung
<H2>...</H2> 2. Ordnung
<H3>...</H3> 3. Ordnung
<H4>...</H4> 4. Ordnung
<H5>...</H5> 5. Ordnung
<H6>...</H6> 6. Ordnung

❷ Die Größenangaben der Überschriften sind immer als relative Angaben zu verstehen, die von der Größe der Standardschrift des Browsers abhängen.

Eine einfache Art, den Text zu strukturieren, erreicht man mit der Zeilenschaltung, dem Tag
 (engl. „break"), und der Absatzschaltung, dem Tag <p> (engl. „paragraph"). Mit dem Tag <DIV> und einem dazugehörigen Parameter können Objekte im Broswer ausgerichtet werden. Die Grundeinstellung ist immer „linksbündig". Zum Beispiel zentriert der Tag <DIV align="center"> das folgende Objekt. Dem Objekt muss anschließend wieder ein </DIV> folgen. Auch einfache Trennlinien mit dem Tag <HR> können zum Strukturieren herangezogen werden.

Mit Überschriften kann zusätzlich logisch strukturiert werden. HTML kennt sechs **Überschriften** ❶, die sich üblicherweise nur durch ihre **Schriftgröße** ❷ unterscheiden. Innerhalb der Überschrift kann mit dem Parameter „align" zusätzlich eine Textausrichtung vorgenommen werden.

Zum Strukturieren verfügt HTML auch über weitere Funktionen, wie Listen, Aufzählungen und Tabellen.
Zum individuellen Gestalten von Textblöcken oder auch einzelnen Wörtern und Buchstaben setzt man Textattribute ein. Dabei wird zwischen logischen und physischen Anweisungen unterschieden. Logische Anweisungen beziehen sich auf die Bedeutung des Textinhaltes, werden jedoch über die Grundeinstellungen des verwendeten Browsers definiert. Beispiel: <cite> für ein Zitat.

Die physischen Anweisungen legen fest, wie ein Text aussehen soll. Dies kann zum Beispiel die **Schriftfarbe** ❶, die **Schriftgröße** ❷, die **Schriftart** ❸ oder die **Schriftauszeichnung** ❹ beeinflussen.

Für Schriftgestaltung wird der Tag <FONT> mit entsprechenden Parametern verwendet.

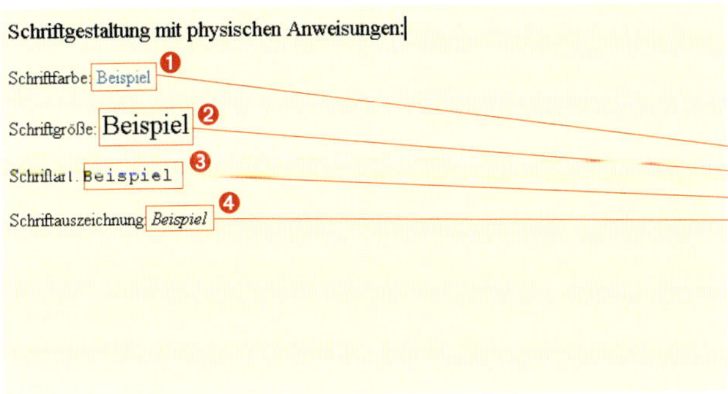

HTML-Code im Browser dargestellt.

```
<html>
<head>
<title>Schriftgestaltung</title>
<meta http-equiv="Content-Type" content="text/html; charset=iso-8859-1">
</head>

<body bgcolor="#FFFFCC" text="#000000">
<p><font size="4">Schriftgestaltung mit physischen Anweisungen:</font></p>
<p>Schriftfarbe: <font color="#0066FF">Beispiel </font></p>
<p>Schriftgr&ouml;&szlig;e: <font size="5">Beispiel</font></p>
<p>Schriftfont: <font face="Courier New, Courier, mono">Beispiel</font></p>
<p>Schriftauszeichnung: <i>Beispiel</i></p>
</body>
</html>
```

HTML-Code

HTML mit seinem international orientierten Zeichensatz kennt keine Sonderzeichen. Der bis zur Version HTML 3.2 gültige Zeichensatz stellt insgesamt 256 Zeichen zur Verfügung, wovon die ersten 128 identisch mit dem klassischen ASCII-Zeichensatz sind. Die zweite Hälfte beinhaltet Sonderzeichen, die jedoch nicht direkt über die Tastatur angesprochen werden können. Das heißt, landesspezifische Sonderzeichen, wie z. B. die deutschen Umlaute „ä, ö und ü", müssen verschlüsselt über das sogenannte **Maskieren** ❺ eingegeben werden. Zum Maskieren wird das spezielle Steuerzeichen „&" verwendet. Es teilt dem Browser mit, dass jetzt eine Maskierung folgt. Ein Semikolon (;) schließt die Maskierung ab. Ein Satz mit Umlauten kann dabei folgendermaßen aussehen:

„Die Fähre setzt über." wird in HTML „Die Fähre setzt über." geschrieben.

Aber nicht nur Text kann mit HTML geschrieben werden. In HTML-Dokumenten sind auch Grafiken und andere Objekte verwendbar. Grafiken müssen dabei in den Bildformaten **GIF**, **PNG** oder **JPEG** vorliegen. Sie werden nicht im Dokument gespeichert, da in HTML nur auf eine Grafikdatei referenziert wird. Der Browser lädt die Datei beim Darstellen automatisch hinzu. Dazu muss der Browser wissen, wo sich diese Grafikdatei befindet. Die Einbindung erfolgt mit Hilfe des Tag <IMG>. Als Parameter muss der Dateiname der Grafik mit dazugehörigem Pfad angegeben werden.

Beispiel: <IMG src="img src="Grafik/10_307-04.GIF" width="280" height="60">

Mögliche Parameter sind für
❶ die Schriftfarbe
z. B. <FONT color=„#0066FF">;
❷ die Schriftgröße
z. B. <FONT size=5> ;
❸ die Schriftart
z. B. <FONT face="Courier">.

❹ Schriftauszeichnungen sind Schrift-Eigenschaften wie „fett", „kursiv", „unterstrichen", sowie „hochgestellt" oder „tiefergestellt". Beispiel: <b> Fette Schrift </b>

❺ Beispiele für Maskierungen:
ä ä
Ä Ä
ü ü
Ü Ü
ß ß

Im Browser dargestellte Grafiken

```
<html>
<head>
<title>Grafikeinbindung</title>
<meta http-equiv="Content-Type" content="text/html; charset=iso-8859-1">
</head>

<body bgcolor="#FFFFFF" text="#000000">
<p align="center">Beispiel f&uuml;r Grafikeinbindung mit relativen Pfaden:</p>
<p align="center"><img src="Grafik/10_307-04.GIF" width="280" height="60"></p>
<p align="center"><img src="Grafik/10_307-03.GIF" width="340" height="25"></p>
</body>
</html>
```

Dazugehöriger HTML-Code

➲ **DHTML ist ein Konzept, um Inhalte einer Web-Seite in ihrer Position und ihrem Erscheinungsbild in Abhängigkeit von Benutzereingaben oder Skriptereignissen zu verändern.**

❶ Das **Document Object Model** beschreibt die Elemente einer Web-Seite nach einer Baumstruktur und erlaubt die skriptgesteuerte Veränderung von HTML Dokumenten.

DHTML verwendet zur dynamischen Darstellung von HTML

- Cascading Style Sheets (CSS)
- Document Object Model (DOM) ❶
- JavaScript oder VBScript

und setzt deshalb entsprechend kompatible Web-Browser voraus. Um trotzdem alle Web-Benutzer zu unterstützen, insbesondere für „barrierefreie" Angebote, kann ein paralleles, statisches HTML-Web eingesetzt werden.

Cascading-Style-Sheets

Eine effiziente Methode, Formatierungen über alle HTML-Seiten einer Website aus einer Quelle zu beeinflussen, sind die **Cascading-Style-Sheets (CSS)**, ein Standard zur Beschreibung der Layouteigenschaften von HTML-Dokumenten. Bei Cascading-Style-Sheets können Layoutinformationen auch für mehrere HTML-Seiten in separaten Dateien (Style Sheets) abgelegt werden. Sie sind vergleichbar mit Druckformatvorlagen von Textverarbeitungsprogrammen.

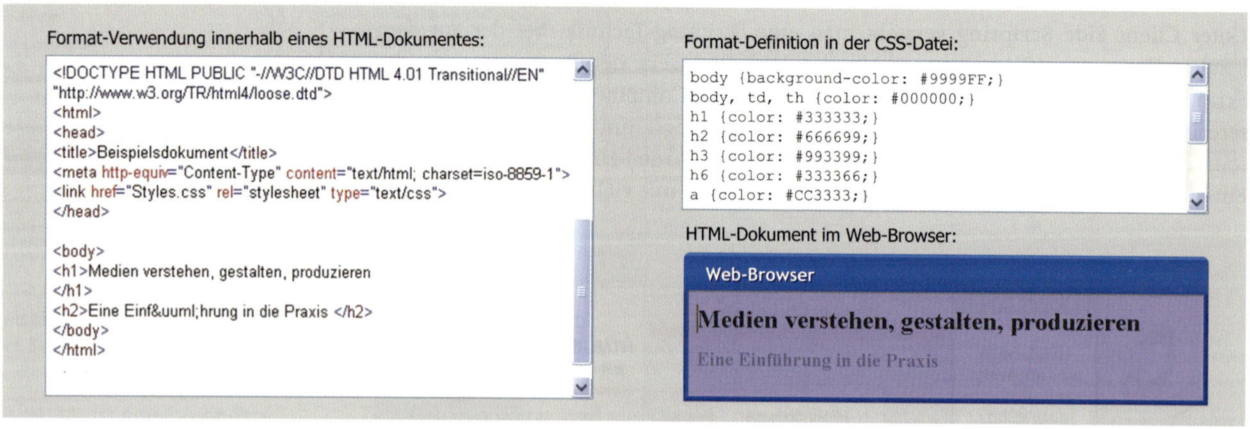

Im HTML-Dokument wird über <link href="Styles.css" rel="stylesheet"type="text/css"> auf eine externe CSS-Datei verlinkt, in der die Textattribute zentral definiert sind.

Mit der Einführung von CSS3 sind unter anderem auch eigenschaftsspezifische Stylesheets, sogenannte „Media Queries" möglich. Damit können Eigenschaften des darstellenden Endgerätes abgefragt werden. Zum Beispiel kann durch Auslesen der Breite und Höhe des Browserfensters sowie der Seitenorientierung die Web-Seite an das Endgerät angepasst werden. Über medienspezifische Stylesheets mit dem Attribut „media" kann die Gestaltung in Abhängigkeit des Ausgabemediums zum Beispiel zwischen Druckausgabe und Bildschirmausgabe unterschieden werden.

Java

Java ist eigentlich keine Skriptsprache, sondern eine von der Computer-Plattform unabhängige, objektorientierte Programmiersprache, die sich an die Syntax der weit verbreiteten Programmiersprache C/C++ anlehnt. Zur Unterstützung von HTML-Seiten wird Java ähnlich einer Skriptsprache eingesetzt, um HTML mit Programmfunktionalität zu erweitern. Dies erfolgt durch das Einbinden von kleinen Java-Anwendungen, die, wenn sie in einem Browser ablaufen, auch **Java-Applets** ❶ genannt werden.

Bei Java handelt es sich um eine Compiler-Sprache. Das bedeutet: Nachdem ein Programm geschrieben wurde, muss es kompiliert, das heißt, in einen speziellen, ausführbaren Binärcode übersetzt werden. Java-Applets sind auf fast allen Browsern, unter allen Betriebsystemen lauffähig.

```
{applet}
{applet license="development"}
|| My first java program
|| Version: 1.0
{title heading?=false, Hallo Welt-Applet}
{let hbox:HBox = {HBox
background="khaki",
color="blue",
font-size=24px,
"... mein Java-Applet Nr." & {value 0.5 | 0.5]
}
}
{paragraph
paragraph-justify="center",
paragraph-line-spacing=50px,
font-size=24pt,
font-family="Arial",
color="black",
{VBox
background="lightgray",
halign="center",
spacing=0.8cm,
font-size=10mm,
"Hurra, es funktioniert ... ",
hbox
}
{br} {italic Hallo Welt !!!}
}
```

❶ Beispiele eines Java-Applets

ActiveX

Im Gegensatz zu Java ist **ActiveX** eine Technologie, die von Microsoft entwickelt wurde und die primär nur unter dem Microsoft Internet Explorer lauffähig ist. Es handelt sich um eine Mischung aus Plug-in und Java-Applet, welche zu den Standardfunktionen des Browsers hinzugefügt wird.

ActiveX-Anwendungen, auch ActiveX-Steuerelemente genannt, können mit verschiedenen Programmierwerkzeugen, wie zum Beispiel Visual Basic oder C++, erstellt werden. Die Einbindung der ActiveX-Steuerelemente erfolgt mit dem HTML-Tag <object> und zusätzlichen Parametern.

Beispiele eines eingebundenen ActiveX-Steuerelementes:

```
<html>
<head>
<title>ActiveX Demo</title>
<meta http-equiv="Content-Type" content="text/html; charset=iso-8859-1">
</head>

<body bgcolor="#FFFFFF" text="#000000">
<object classid="clsid:D27CDB6E-AE6D-11cf-96B8-444553540000" width="220" height="191" >
  <param name=movie value="/swifs/BIKING.SWF">
  <param name=quality value=high>
  <embed src="/swifs/BIKING.SWF" quality=high width="220" height="191">
  </embed>
</object>
</body>
</html>
```

Dazugehöriger Quellcode:

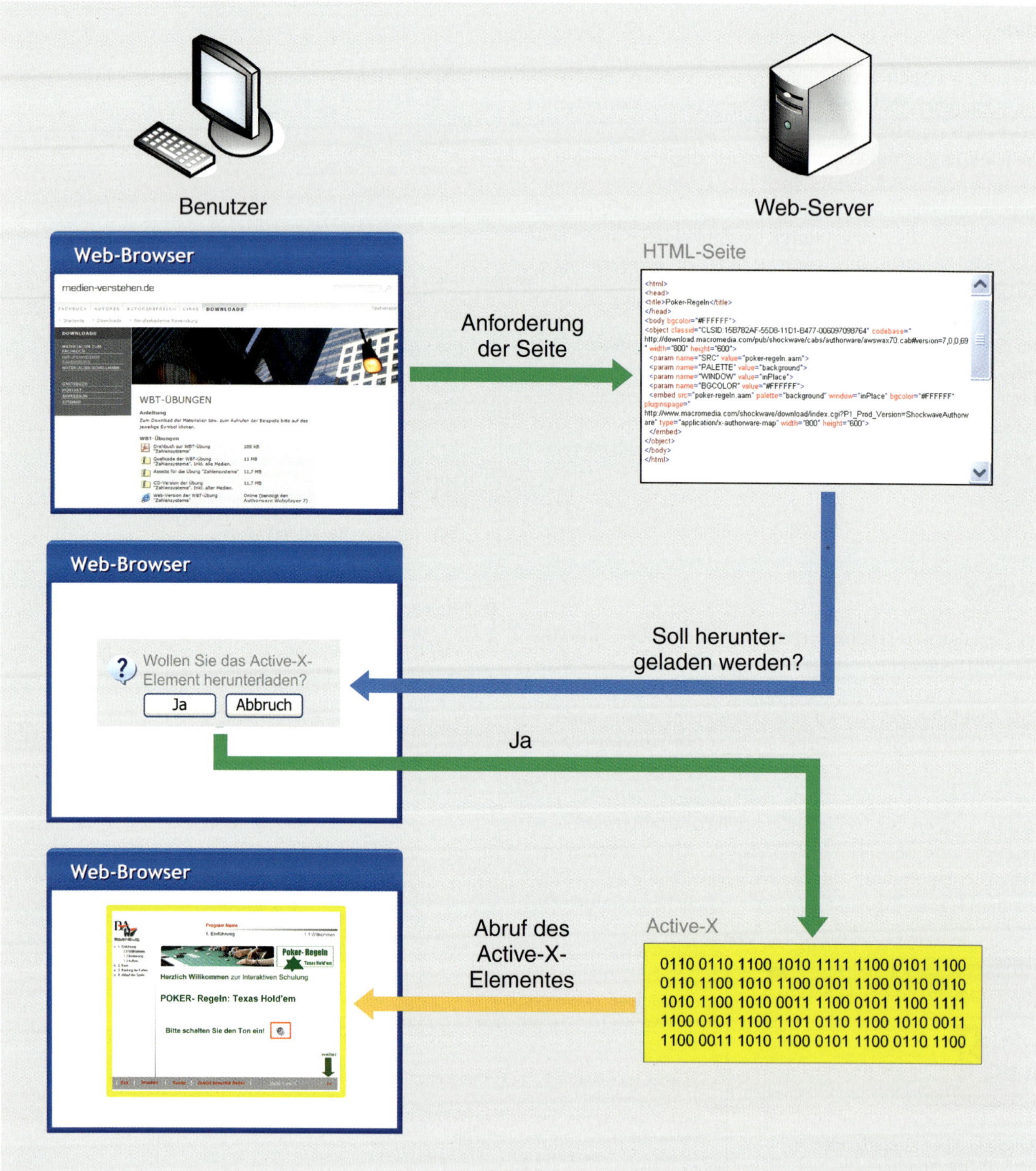

Wird die HTML-Seite mit dem Browser aufgerufen, so wird das eingebundene ActiveX- Steuerelement vom Web-Server abgerufen und auf dem lokalen Computer beim Benutzer gespeichert. Dabei erfolgt, je nach eingestellter Sicherheitsstufe im Browser, die Abfrage, ob das ActiveX-Steuerelement heruntergeladen werden soll oder nicht. Auf Grund seiner Funktionsvielfalt stellt jedes Programm eine mögliche Sicherheitslücke dar und sollte deshalb nur von vertrauenswürdigen Quellen akzeptiert werden. Ist das Element dann übertragen worden, so wird es auf dem lokalen Rechner ausgeführt.

JavaScript

Trotz seines Namens ist JavaScript keine Variante der Programmiersprache Java. JavaScript ist eine Scriptsprache, mit der die Funktionalität und Interaktivität von HTML-Seiten erweitert werden kann. **JavaScript** ❶ wird über spezielle Tags ❷ in Form von Klartext komplett in die HTML-Seite integriert. Dabei können die Befehle an mehreren Stellen in der Seite platziert sein. Befehle vor dem HTML-Tag <body> veranlassen deren Ausführung schon beim Laden der HTML-Seite.

Im Wesentlichen benutzt der Web-Designer JavaScript, um bestimmte Aktionen an Objekten der Website durchzuführen.

Die Grundsyntax nennt zuerst das Objekt, dann getrennt durch einen Punkt den Vorgang, der an dem Objekt (Empfänger) vorgenommen werden soll – die Methode.
Prinzip: Objekt.Methode(Argument)
Beispiel: document.write(„Hallo JavaScript !“);

❶ **JavaScript** wurde in Zusammenarbeit von Sun und Netscape entwickelt.

❷ JavaScript wird über Script-Container eingebunden, die mit <Script> beginnen und mit </Script> enden.
Beispiel:
<Script Language="Javascript">
<!-- >
</Script>

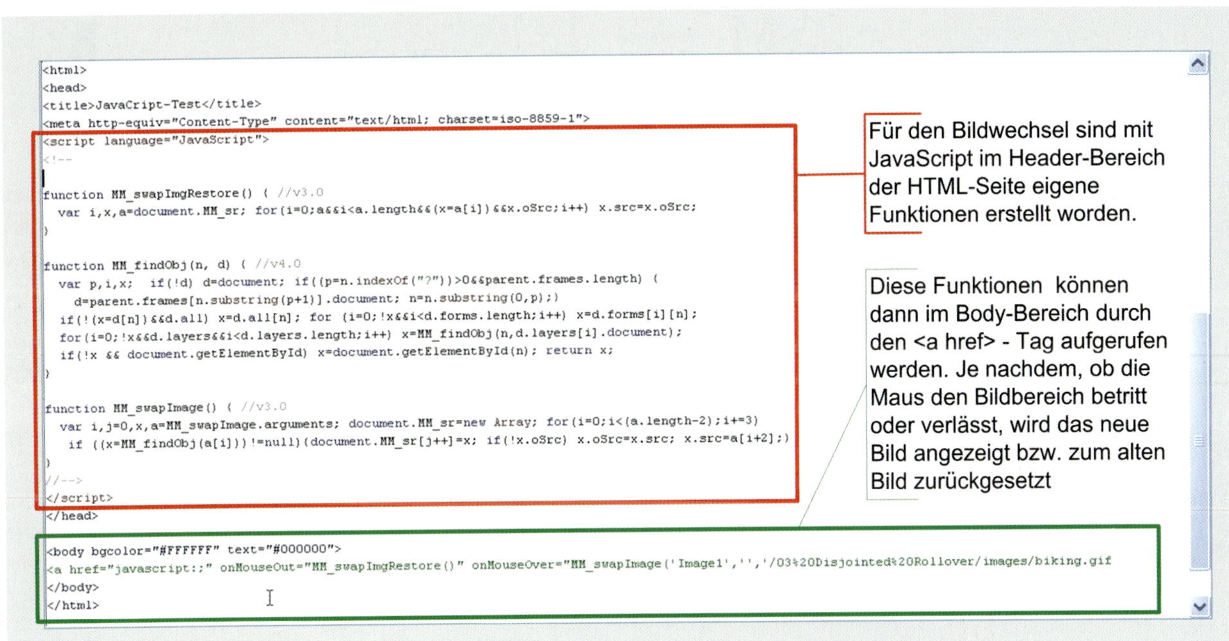

❸ Beispiel der JavaScript-Integration für den Bildwechsel als „Roll-over"-Effekt in einer HTML-Seite.

Will man beispielsweise bestimmten Navigationselementen (Buttons) auf der HTML-Seite zusätzliche Interaktivität, wie einen „Roll-over"-Effekt ❸, verleihen, so kann die JavaScript-Funktion in den <a href> - HTML-Tag eingebunden und das Skript damit aufgerufen werden.

AJAX

Traditionelle Interaktionen im Web erfolgen über eine Anforderung des Benutzers an den Server, der daraufhin eine neue HTML-Seite übermittelt. Dies hat zur Folge, dass jedes Mal eine komplett neue HTML-Seite übermittelt und im Web-Browser des Benutzers aufgebaut werden muss. Wartezeiten und jedes Mal ein komplett neuer Seitenaufbau sind die Folge.

❶ Die AJAX-Technologie setzt seitens des Web-Browsers lediglich die Unterstützung von JavaScript voraus.

Mit dem Konzept **AJAX** (**Asynchronous JavaScript and XML**) ❶ werden nur die Teile der HTML-Seite übertragen, die sich in Abhängigkeit der Benutzereingabe verändern. Dadurch wird die Datenübertragung reduziert und es ist kein komplett neuer Seitenaufbau im Web-Browser des Benutzers notwendig. Das Ergebnis ist eine dynamische Web-Seite, die sehr zügig auf Benutzereingaben reagiert.

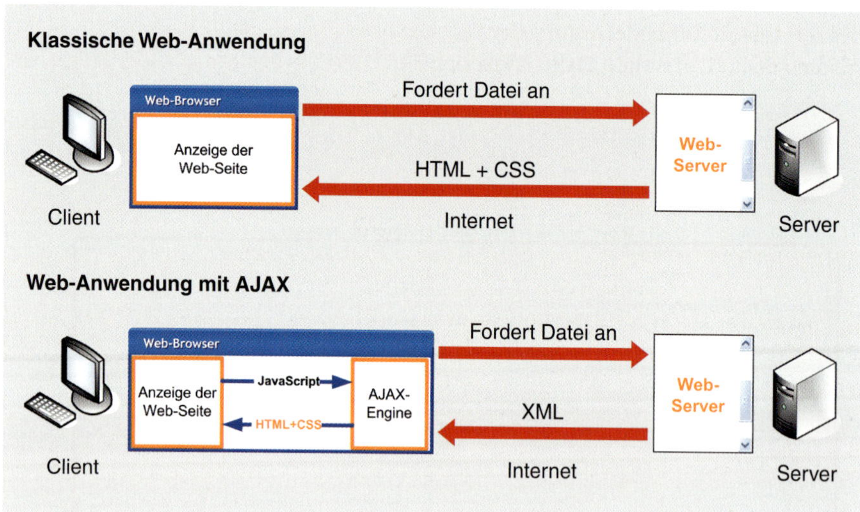

Vergleich einer klassischen Web-Anwendung mit einer auf AJAX basierenden Anwendung

Realisiert wird dies durch eine sogenannte **AJAX-Engine**, die auf der Client-Seite die Verarbeitung des Datentransports zwischen Client und Server übernimmt und die dynamische Anzeige der Web-Seite übernimmt. AJAX kombiniert bekannte Techniken wie JavaScript, DOM-Manipulation und XML zur dynamischen Darstellung der Inhalte einer Web-Seite.

Durch den Einsatz der AJAX-Technologie ist die Darstellung des Desktops im Web realisierbar.

Bekannte Beispiele sind „Google Maps", die Textverarbeitung „Ajax Write" und die Bildbearbeitung „nextImage".

14.3.3 Server Side Scripting

Unter **Server Side Scripting** versteht man eine Scripting-Technik, bei der auf dem **Server** der Programmcode des Skripts ausgeführt wird. Erst dessen Ausgabe wird an den Web-Browser geschickt. Da die HTML-Seite durch das Skript jeweils neu generiert wird, merkt der Benutzer gar nicht, dass die Seite dynamisch erzeugt wird.

Voraussetzung für das Ausführen von serverseitigen Skripten ist eine vorhandene Installation des Skript-Interpreters auf dem Web-Server des Providers.

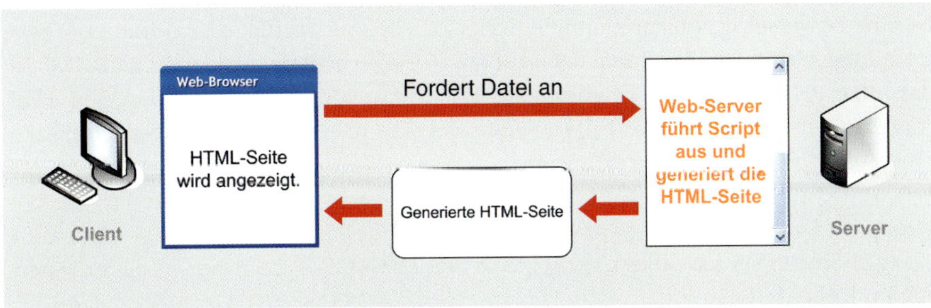

Prinzip-Darstellung des Server Side Scripting

In der Praxis sind verschiedene Skriptsprachen im Einsatz. Eine starke Verbreitung hat PHP und CGI erfahren, die in der Regel von den meisten Providern unterstützt werden.

CGI

Für Anwendungen, die mit Datenbanken kommunizieren sollen, werden meistens CGI-Programme verwendet. Das **Common Gateway Interface (CGI)** ist der Standard für interaktive Websites, bei denen ein Datenaustausch mit serverseitigen Ressourcen, z. B. Datenbanken, erfolgen soll. Ein CGI-Programm wird anders als Java, ActiveX oder JavaScript nicht auf dem lokalen Rechner, sondern auf dem Web-Server ausgeführt. CGI-Programme, bzw. CGI-Skripte, können in verschiedenen Programmiersprachen erstellt werden. Weit verbreitet ist dabei die Programmiersprache **Perl** ❶.

❶ **Perl (Practical Extraction and Report Language)** ist eine Skriptsprache, die hauptsächlich für den Datenaustausch von Servern mit anderen Anwendungsprogrammen eingesetzt wird.

```
#!/usr/bin/perl
# testform.cgi, Gaestebuchskript (Version 1.0)
require „cgi-lib.pl“; # „parsing“ der FORM-Daten und Ausgabe der Variablen
require „datum.pl“; # eine Routine fuer das Datum
$date = &ctime(time);
chop($date);
&parse_form;
print „Content-type: text/html\n\n“;
print „<HTML>\n“;
print „<head><title>Neueintrag in das Gästebuch</title></head>\n“;
print „<body>\n“;
print „<center>\n“;
print „<H2>Neueintrag in das Gästebuch</H2>\n“;
print „am $date<p>\n“;
print „<HR>\n“;
print „</center><p>\n“;
print „Wir haben von Ihnen folgende Angaben erhalten:<p> \n“;
print „<ul> \n“;
print „<li>Ihr Name lautet: <b>$in{‚username‘}</b> \n“;
print „<li>Ihre eMail Adresse ist: <b>$in{‚email‘}</b> \n“;
print „<li>Ihr Kommentar:<br> \n“;
print „<b>$in{‚comments‘}</b> \n“;
print „</ul><p> \n“;
print „<B>Vielen Dank für Ihre Eintragung in unser Gästebuch!</B><p> \n“;
print „</BODY>\n“;
print „</HTML>\n“;
$outfile = „>> /home/m/meinlogin/public_html/gaeste/gaestebuch.html“;
open(OUTFILE, $outfile);
print OUTFILE „
```

Beispiel einer Gästebuch-Formular-Maske als HTML-Seite (Abbildung unten), welches die Benutzerdaten an ein CGI-Programm (Abbildung links) übergibt, das die Eingabedaten auswertet und daraus den Gästebucheintrag als HTML-Seite generiert.

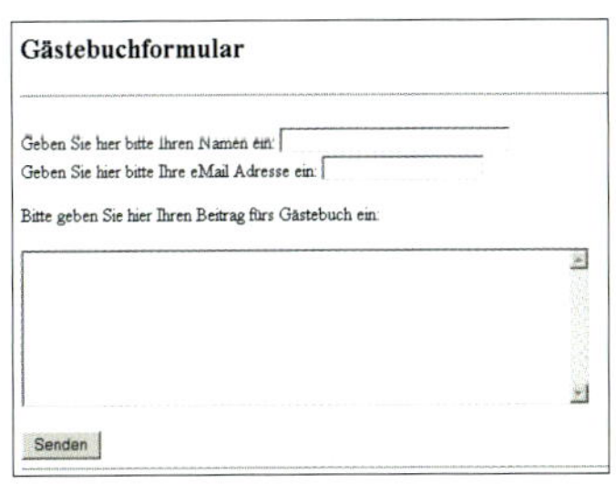

PHP

❶ Die Kennzeichnung des PHP-Codes erfolgt über:

```
<?php
// PHP-Anweisung
?>
```

PHP („Hypertext Preprocessor", ursprünglich „Personal Home Page Tools" genannt) ist eine serverseitig interpretierende Skriptsprache. Sie verfügt über eine an C bzw. C++ angelehnte Syntax. Einer der größten Vorteile gegenüber klassischem CGI ist, dass der PHP-Interpreter gewöhnliche HTML-Dateien akzeptiert, in denen PHP-Anweisungen ❶ stehen. Das folgende Beispiel gibt in Abhängigkeit einer Punktezahl einen entsprechenden Antworttext aus:

```
<?php if ($punkte > 100) { ?>
  <h2>Spitze. Du hast alles richtig gemacht!</h2>
<?php } else { ?>
  <h2>Nicht schlecht. Schaue es dir aber noch mal an!</h2>
<?php } ?>
```

PHP ist eine Open-Source-Software, die beliebt ist zur Erstellung von dynamischen Web-Inhalten. Bekannte Beispiele sind „MediaWiki", die Software von Wikipedia, und „WordPress" zum Erstellen von Weblogs.

ASP

❷ Die Kennzeichnung des ASP- bzw. JSP-Codes erfolgt über:

```
<%
// ASP- bzw. JSP-Anweisung
%>
```

ASP (Active Server Pages) ❷ ist eine serverseitige Technologie von Microsoft zur Erzeugung von dynamischen Web-Seiten. Als ASP wurde im Jahr 2002 ASP.NET von Microsoft abgelöst.

JSP

JSP (Java Server Pages) ❷ von Sun Microsystem erlaubt das serverseitige Einbauen von Java-Code in HTML- und XML-Seiten zur Erzeugung dynamischer Web-Seiten.

14.4 Auszeichnungssprachen

❸ Unter Tags (engl.) versteht man das Auszeichnen eines Datenbestandes mit zusätzlichen Informationen. Bei SGML, XML oder HTML geschieht dies durch Kürzel, die in Klein- und Größerzeichen eingeschlossen sind. Beispiel: <h2>

Zum Beschreiben von Daten werden Auszeichnungssprachen (**Markup Languages**) eingesetzt. Mit Hilfe von **Tags** ❸ markiert man Wörter, Sätze und Abschnitte eines Textes und weist ihnen Eigenschaften und Zugehörigkeiten zu. Es wird dabei zwischen **Descriptive Markup Languages** (Beschreibende Auszeichnungssprachen) und **Procedural Markup Languages** (Aufgabenorientierte Auszeichnungssprachen) unterschieden.

- Den Descriptive Markup Languages sind unter anderem **SGML**, **XML** und HTML zuzuordnen.
- **PostScript** und **PDF** sind typische Procedural Markup Languages.

14.4.1 SGML

Der ISO-Standard **SGML** (**Standard Generalized Markup Language**) ist eine Metasprache, mit deren Hilfe man verschiedene Anwendungen und Auszeichnungssprachen für Dokumente definieren kann. Die bekannteste Anwendung, die mit dieser Metasprache erstellt wurde, ist HTML. Die bekannteste und aktuellste Auszeichnungssprache ist XML, die hier näher vorgestellt werden soll.

14.4.2 XML

XML steht für **Extensible Markup Language** und ist eine Untermenge von SGML. XML ist ein von den Systemen und Anwendungen unabhängiges Datenformat, das dem Programmierer eine Möglichkeit bietet, strukturierte Dokumente in lesbarer Form zu erzeugen und zu verwalten, die auf vielfältige Weise dargestellt werden können. Dazu können eigene Tags und Attribute definiert werden. Diese Tags haben nichts mit der Darstellung am Bildschirm zu tun, sondern sind **semantische Tags** ❶.

❶ **Semantische Tags** sind inhaltliche Markierungen, welche die Möglichkeit unterstützen, sich so zu artikulieren, dass Computer diese Information inhaltlich interpretieren und austauschen können.

➲ **In XML wird Layout und Inhalt getrennt.**

Die vom World Wide Web Consortium (W3C) herausgegebene XML-Spezifikation definiert eine Metasprache, auf deren Basis durch strukturelle und inhaltliche Einschränkungen anwendungsspezifische Sprachen definiert werden. XML-Dokumente besitzen einen physischen und einen logischen Aufbau. Dazu müssen sie den XML-Syntax-Regeln entsprechen:

- Die Dokumente müssen **wohlgeformt** („well-formed") ❷ sein. Das heißt, alle Elemente mit Inhalt besitzen eine Beginn- und eine Ende-Kennung.
- Sie sollten gültig bzw. **validiert** („validated") sein. Das heißt, sie entsprechen einer **Document Type Definition** (**DTD**) ❸. Beim Datenaustausch mit XML ist es wichtig, dass die „Grammatik" des Element-Aufbaus über eine DTD überprüft wird, um festzustellen, ob alle Elemente und Attribute richtig verwendet werden. Diese DTD kann im Dokument oder besser in einer separaten Datei verwendet werden. Alternativ zur DTD kann die Definition auch über ein **XML-Schema** (**XSD**) erfolgen, welches selbst in XML geschrieben ist.
- Es muss genau ein Element, das sogenannte Wurzelelement, auf der obersten Ebene enthalten. Unterhalb von diesem Dokumentelement können weitere Elemente verschachtelt werden.

❷ Die Elemente besitzen einen Beginn-Tag (in < und > eingeschlossen) und einen Ende-Tag (mit vorangestelltem „/").
Beispiel:
<AUSGABE>Hallo</AUSGABE>

❸ Beispiel einer DTD:
<!DOCTYPE hallo [
<!ELEMENT AUSGABE (ANZEIGE)>
<!ELEMENT ANZEIGE (#PCDATA)>
]>

Kommen in den XML-Daten häufig wiederkehrende Texte vor, so können diese mit sogenannten **Entities** abgekürzt werden. Die Definition erfolgt in der DTD.

Zum Beispiel: <!ENTITY text „Konstanz">
Im XML-Dokument kann die Entity dann mehrfach verwendet werden.
Zum Beispiel: <Ort>&text</Ort>

Zur besseren Lesbarkeit der XML-Datei können Kommentare verwendet werden.
Beispiel: <!-- Jetzt kommt der Kommentar -->

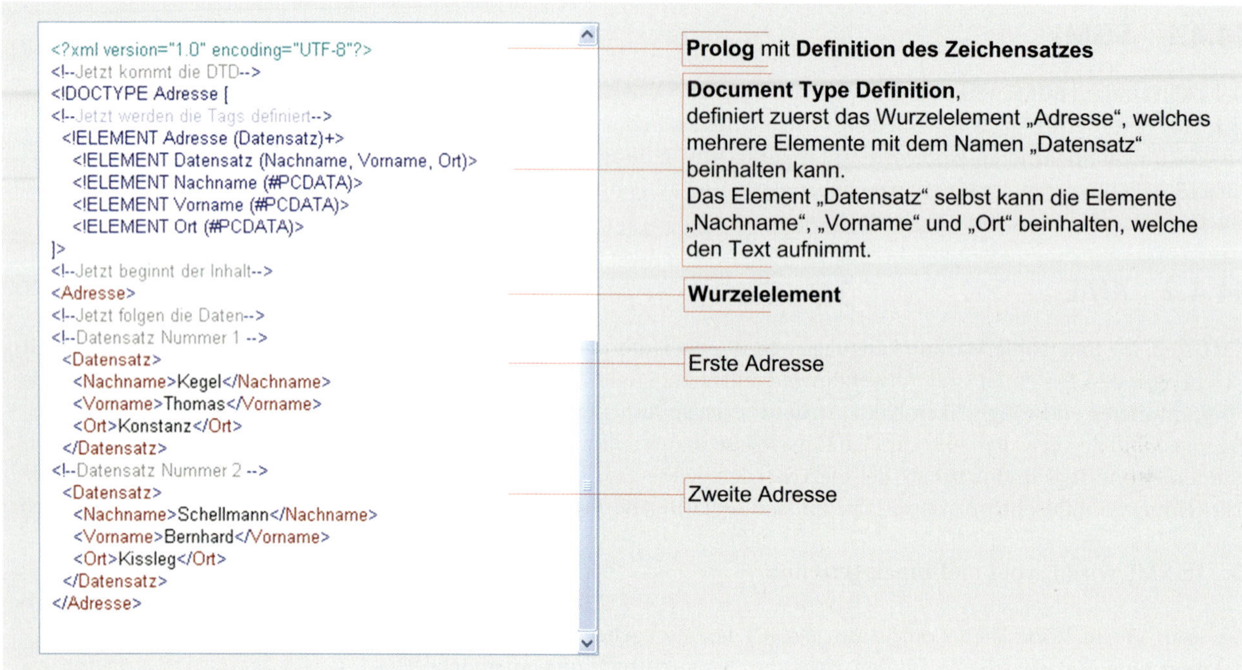

Beispiel eines XML-Dokumentenaufbaus an Hand einer Adressbuch-Datenbank mit den Feldern Nachname, Vorname und Ort

Datenausgabe und Formatierung über XSL

XML-Daten werden ohne Format-Informationen, unabhängig von der Datenausgabe, der Darstellung auf dem Bildschirm, oder einem Ausdruck gespeichert. Zur Formatierung kann wie bei HTML das CSS (Cascading Style Sheets) eingesetzt werden, oder besser das flexiblere XSL. **XSL** steht für **Extensible Stylesheet Language**.
Dazu erfolgt im Prolog des XML-Dokuments die Zuweisung auf eine XSL-Datei.
Beispiel: <?xml–stylesheet href=“style.xsl“ type=“text/xsl“?>

XSL besteht aus verschiedenen Komponenten:

- Die Beschreibung eines Dokuments als Baum mit Formatierungsanweisungen und Stilangaben übernimmt in XSL das XML-basierte **XSL-FO** (**XSL Formatting Objects**).
- Für die Umwandlung von XML-Dokumenten in andere XML-Dokumente kommt das XML-basierte **XSLT** (**XSL Transformation**) zum Einsatz.
- Zum Adressieren von bestimmten Bestandteilen im XML-Baum wird **XPath** (**XML Path Language**) eingesetzt.

An Hand des auf der nächsten Seite dargestellten Anwendungsbeispieles lässt sich das Zusammenspiel von Daten, Logik und Formatierung aufzeigen. Die Document Type Definition erfolgt über eine separate DTD-Datei (links im Bild), die Datensätze stehen in der XML-Datei (in der Mitte des Bildes) und die Darstellungsformatierung erfolgt über eine XSL-Datei (rechts im Bild). Soll nun die Darstellungsform verändert werden, so muss nur die XSL-Datei verändert werden. Die Textformatierung lässt sich einfach durch Textattribute in der Stilklasse „.design“ verändern.

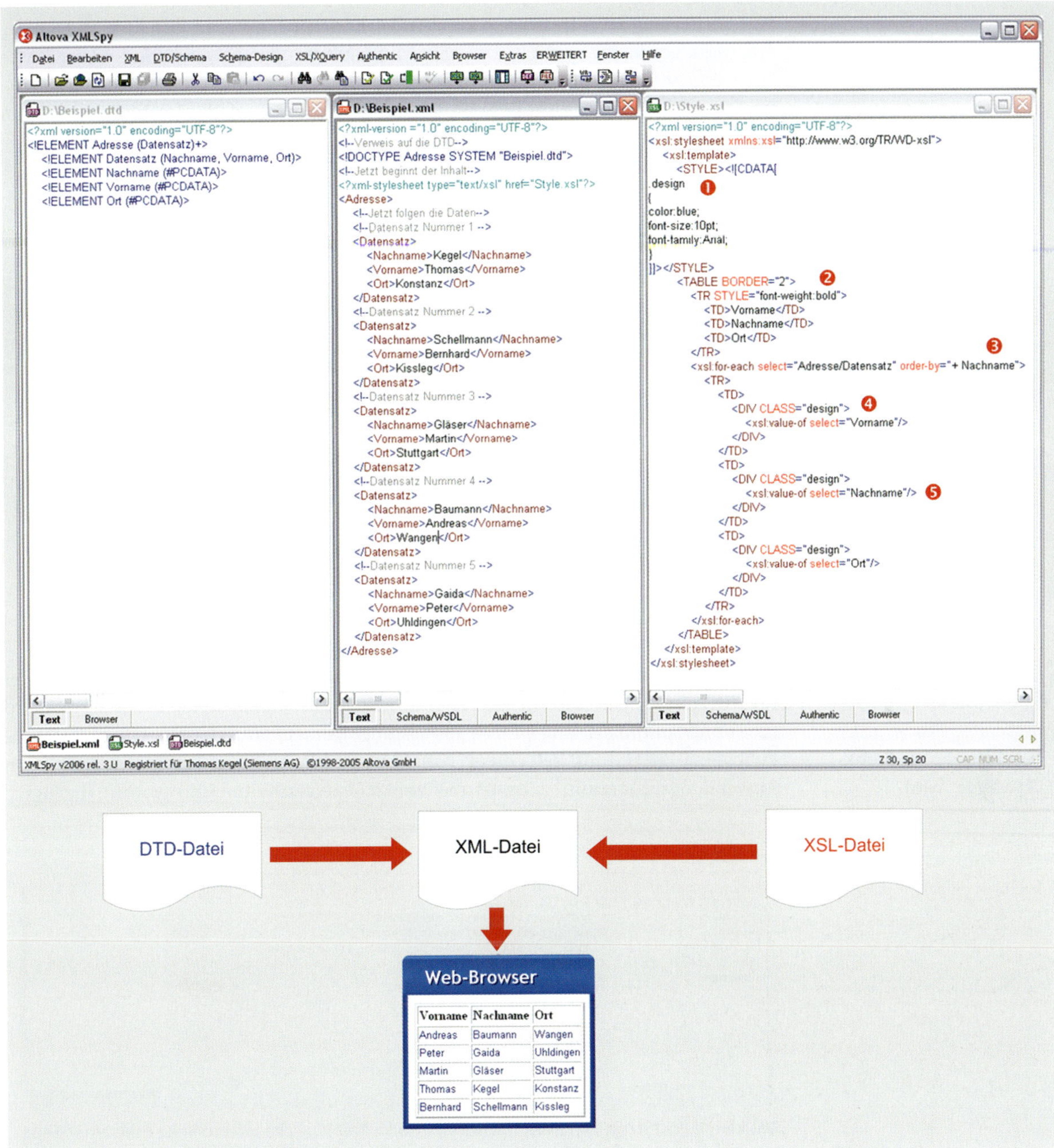

Beispiel einer Adressdatenbank in XML. Darstellungsformatierung über eine **XSL-Datei**:

❶ Definition der globalen Stilklasse „.design“

❷ Definition des Tabellenkopfs

❸ Durchsucht das Dokument nach allen Tags auf der Ebene „Datensatz“, liest alle Inhalte und sortiert durch das Attribut „order-by“ die Ausgabe nach den Nachnamen in aufsteigender Richtung.

❹ Ordnet dem Abschnitt den Style „design“ zu.

❺ Liest und gibt alle Inhalte des Tags „Nachname“ aus.

Im Web-Browser werden die Adressdaten formatiert und sortiert dargestellt.

Eine Sortierung der Adressliste nach dem Wohnort erreicht man durch Verändern des Attributes „order-by“ auf „+ Ort“. Eine Erweiterung der Daten erfolgt in der XML-Datei, indem weitere Datensätze hinzugefügt werde. Soll die Adressdatenbank-Struktur erweitert werden, zum Beispiel durch ein neues Datenfeld „Telefon“, so muss in der DTD-Datei das neue Element definiert werden kann dann in der XML-Datei verwendet werden.

Datenkonvertierung und Aufbereitung durch XSLT

Die **XSL-Transformation (XSLT)**, als Komponente von XSL, dient der Umwandlung (Transformation) von beliebigen XML-Dokumenten in andere Formate. Zielformate können zum Beispiel HTML oder PDF sein. Ein XSLT-Dokument beschreibt, wie die Elemente und Attribute des XML-Quelldokumentes in die Bestandteile des Zieldokumentes umgesetzt werden sollen. XSLT-Programme sind nach den Regeln des XML-Standards aufgebaut.

Um eine XSL-Transformation durchzuführen, werden spezielle XSLT-Prozessoren benötigt. Sie lesen XSLT-Stylesheets ein und transformieren ein oder mehrere XML-Dokumente nach den Stylesheet-Regeln in das gewünschte Ausgabeformat. XSLT-Prozessoren sind mittlerweile auch in Web-Browsern integriert.

14.4.3 Postscript

❶ Eine Variante des PostScript ist das Datenaustausch-Format EPS (Encapsulated PostScript), welches vorwiegend als Grafikformat verwendet wird.

PostScript ❶ ist eine von Adobe entwickelte Auszeichnungssprache, um Druckseiten für die Ausgabe auf Laserdruckern und Belichtern zu beschreiben. PostScript wird fast immer automatisch von Anwendungsprogrammen, zum Beispiel einem Desktop-Publishing-Programm, oder über PostScript-Druckertreibern aus jedem beliebigen Anwendungsprogramm, zum Beispiel einem Textverarbeitungsprogramm, erzeugt.

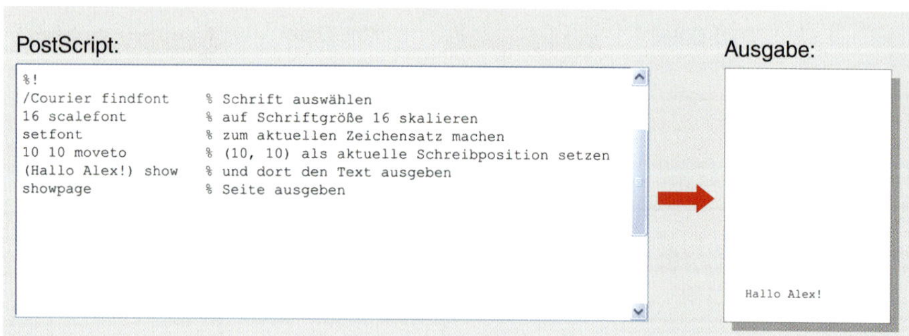

Das kleine PostScript-Programm schreibt „Hallo Alex!“ in die untere linke Ecke einer Seite.

Alle Schriften und grafischen Elemente werden in PostScript als skalierbare Vektorgrafik beschrieben und können daher in beliebiger Größe und Auflösung verlustfrei ausgegeben werden. PostScript Schriften sind qualitativ hochwertige Schriften, die Rundungen und Kurven sehr genau beschreiben können. Ein typischer PostScript-Schriftsatz besteht dabei immer aus einer PFM-Datei, welche technischen Informationen der einzelnen Buchstabenpaare enthält und der PFB-Datei, die die eigentliche Schriftinformation beinhaltet.

14.4.4 PDF

Das ebenfalls von Adobe entwickelte **PDF (Portable Document Format)** baut auf PostScript auf, verwendet jedoch nur einen eingeschränkten Befehlssatz. Es fehlen vor Allem die Strukturen einer Programmiersprache.

PDF ist ein plattformübergreifendes Dokumentenformat, welches sich mittlerweile zu einem Quasi-Standard für die Dokumentenweitergabe entwickelt hat. Obwohl PDF noch kein offizieller Standard ist, wurde die Verwendung von PDF hinsichtlich der Mindestanforderungen und Einschränkungen ❶ von der ISO (International Organization for Standardization) definiert.

❶ Spezifizierte Methoden beim Umgang mit PDF sind:

- PDF/X als Format für die Übermittlung von Druckvorlagen,
- PDF/A als Format für die Langzeitspeicherung und
- PDF/E als Format für technische Dokumente.

Zur Darstellung von PDF steht der kostenlose Reader von Adobe zur Verfügung, der auch als Integration in verschieden Web-Browsern weite Verbreitung gefunden hat.

Zusätzlich zur Schrift- und Grafikdarstellung ist PDF auch hyperlinkfähig. Das heißt, es können zum Einen innerhalb des Dokumentes Verknüpfungen aufgebaut werden und zum Anderen externe Links zu Websites oder anderen externen Dateien erstellt werden. Diese Funktionalität muss mit entsprechenden Editoren, zum Beispiel dem Adobe Acrobat, im PDF-Dokument aufgebaut werden, oder man übernimmt über Makros (z. B. dem PDFWriter) schon vorhandene Verlinkungen aus dem Quelldokument (z. B. Word oder Powerpoint).

Seit der Acrobat Version 7 lassen sich über PDF auch interaktive 3D-Objekte integrieren. Dieses **Acrobat 3D** eröffnet ganz neue Möglichkeiten für den Informationsaustausch im Bereich der CAD-Konstruktion, im Bauwesen, dem Marketing und der technischen Dokumentation.

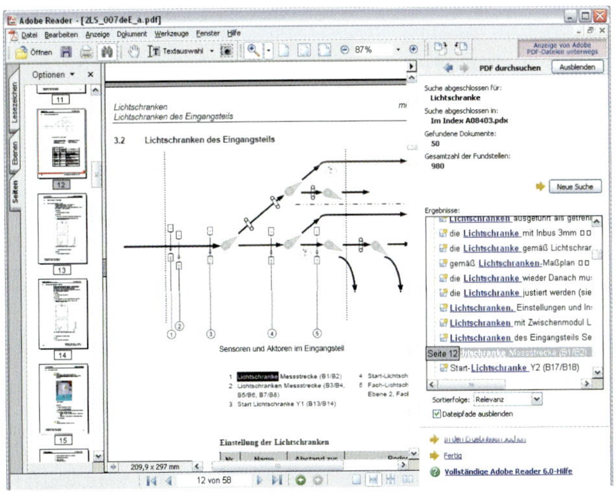

Die PDF-Darstellung im Adobe Reader erlaubt durch die Indexierung bei der „Catalog"-Funktion eine blitzschnelle Volltextsuche über viele PDF-Dokumente hinweg.
Quelle: Siemens AG.

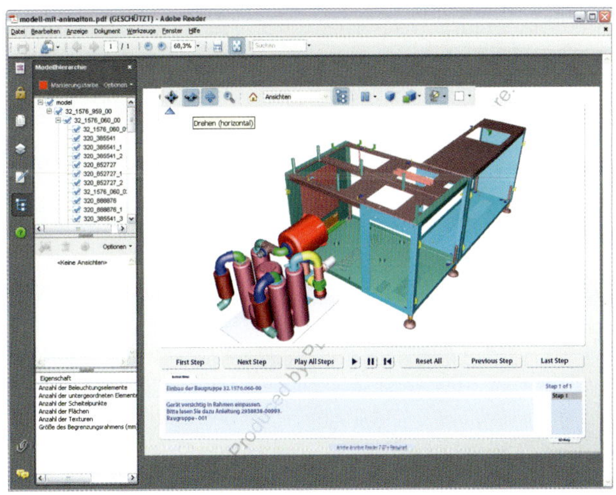

Über Acrobat 3D lassen sich interaktiv bewegbare Objekte mit Strukturbaum, vordefinierten Ansichten und Animationen in ein PDF-Dokument integrieren.
Quelle: Siemens AG.

14.5 Autorensysteme

Zum Erstellen von multimedialen Anwendungen bietet der Software-Markt ein breites Feld von Werkzeugen an. Hinsichtlich des Funktionsumfanges kann folgendermaßen klassifiziert werden:

Einfache Präsentationsprogramme mit dem Fokus auf Visualisierung ohne besondere Interaktions- und Erweiterungsmöglichkeiten.
Zum Beispiel Powerpoint von Microsoft, Impress von OpenOffice oder Keynote von Apple,

Spezialisierte Systeme, welche optimiert sind für einen speziellen Einsatz. Darunter fallen **Screenrecorder** (z. B. TechSmith Camtasia oder Adobe Captivate) zum Erstellen von SW-Erklärungen, **Rapid-Authoring-Tools** (z. B. Raptivity von Harbinger oder Rapid E-Learning Studio von Articulate) für die einfache Erstellung von E-Learning-Inhalten mit vordefinierten Funktionen und ein großes Spektrum von Webseiten-Erstellungs und -Pflege-Programme (z. B. Dreamweaver von Adobe oder WebtoDate von Data Becker).

Universelle Autorensysteme zum Erstellen von komplexen, interaktiven Anwendungen. Sie zeichnen sich aus durch eine Vielzahl vordefinierter Funktionen, die jedoch nahezu unbegrenzt erweiterbar sind.

In diesem Abschnitt soll primär auf „komplexe" **Autorensysteme** eingegangen werden. Mit einem solchen Autorensystem lassen sich einzelne multimediale Informationseinheiten zu multimedialen Anwendungen zusammensetzen. Dazu bieten sie dem Autor eine Arbeitsumgebung an, die in der Regel über grafische, interaktive Hilfsmittel verfügt und zusätzlich eine umfangreiche Programmierung ermöglicht. Autorenspezifische Anforderungen, wie zum Beispiel Interaktionen, Medieneinbindungen, etc. vereinfachen gegenüber reinen Programmiersprachen viele Aufgaben und sparen Zeit bei der Produktion.

14.5.1 Auswahl und Beschreibung

Drei unterschiedliche Ansätze

Autorensysteme sollten umfangreiche Importmöglichkeiten besitzen, Interaktionen und Benutzereingaben auswerten können und offene Schnittstellen besitzen, die externe Geräte ansteuern oder z. B. Datenbanken ankoppeln können. Durch eine interne Skriptsprache sollten Autorensysteme auch umfangreiche Programmieraufgaben abdecken können.

Eine Möglichkeit, Autorensysteme zu klassifizieren, ist die Betrachtung der grundsätzlichen Programm-Philosophie. Diese Betrachtungsweise kann in Metaphern ausgedrückt werden.

Metapher „Buch"

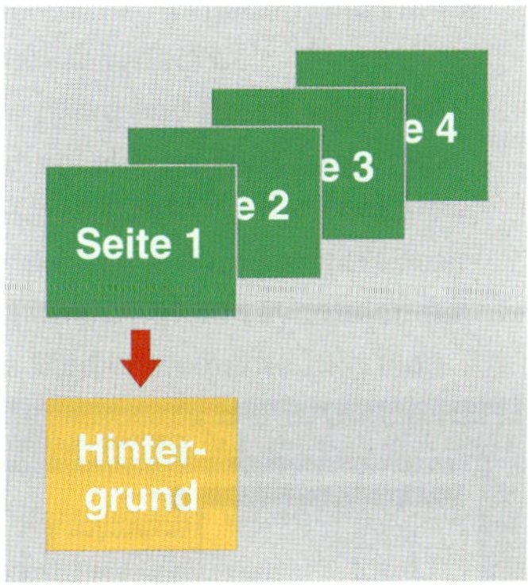

Nach dieser Metapher arbeitet „SuperCard" von Silicon Beach Software auf der Apple-Seite und „ToolBook" von SumTotal Systems auf der Windows-Seite.

Wie der Name schon verrät, liegt dieser Metapher das traditionelle Buch zu Grunde. In einem Programm (Buch) mit einem oder mehreren Hintergründen werden die Informationen mithilfe von unterschiedlichen Schichten bzw. Layern (Karten oder Seiten) aufgelegt.

➲ **Bei dieser Programm-Philosophie ist die Visualisierung der Struktur auf die Informationsschichten bezogen.**

Deshalb eignen sich Programme nach dieser Metapher besonders für statische Anwendungen, wie Informationssysteme, Hypermedia-Datenbanken, aber auch Lernprogramme.

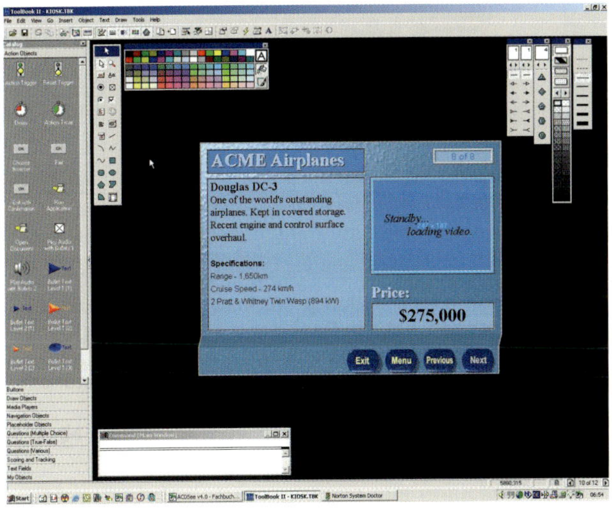

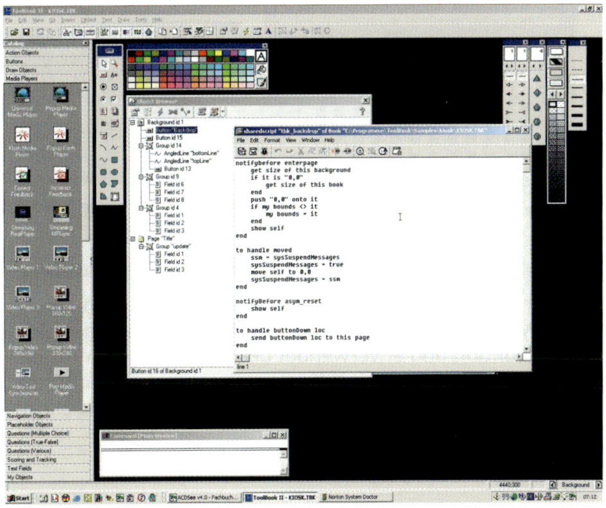

Das Autorensystem ToolBook von SumTotal Systems ist ein typisches Autorensystem, welches nach der „Buch"-Metapher arbeitet. Es verfügt über leistungsstarke Assistenten und Vorlagen. Als Skript-Sprache kommt OpenScript zum Einsatz. Man kann zwar bei kleineren Projekten auf OpenScript verzichten, aber schon bei etwas größeren Anwendungen kommt man um das Erlernen und Anwenden dieser Programmiersprache nicht herum. ToolBook-Anwendungen können als Offline-Anwendung auf CD-ROM oder als Online-Anwendung mit Hilfe eines Plug-Ins oder einer DHTML-Ausgabe für Web-Anwendungen verwendet werden.

Metapher „Zeit"

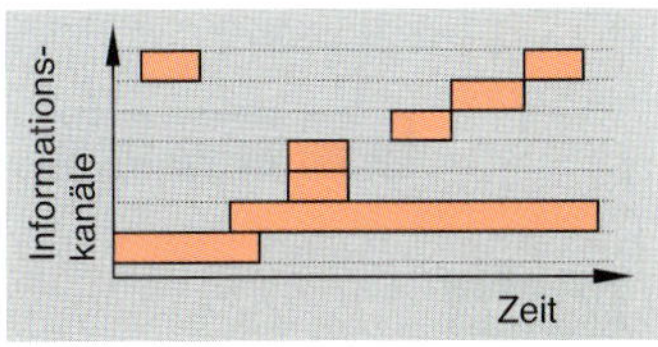

Bei Programmen, die nach dieser Metapher arbeiten, ist die Zeit der grundlegende Bezugspunkt. Die bekanntesten Autorensysteme, welche zeitorientiert arbeiten, sind das Programm „Director" und das Programm „Flash" von Adobe, die beide für die Apple- und die Windows-Welt verfügbar sind.

14.6 Multimedia im Internet

Das Internet ist anfänglich konzipiert worden, um textbasierte Informationen, wie Textdokumente und elektronische Post auszutauschen und an Diskussionsforen teilzunehmen. Mit steigender Leistungsfähigkeit der Personalcomputer und der Verbreitung schnellerer Internetzugänge ist die Verwendung von speicherintensiven Medienelementen, wie Videofilmen, Musik und Sprache, Animationen, sowie virtuelle Realitäten, möglich geworden.

14.6.1 Streaming-Audio und -Video

Musik, Sprache und Geräusche in hoher Qualität als digitale Dateien haben häufig einen hohen Speicherplatzbedarf. Kommt dazu noch die visuelle Komponente Video hinzu, so entstehen für ein paar Sekunden Videofilm schnell mehrere Megabyte an Daten – und das bedeutet auch bei schnellen Internetanbindungen teils enorme Download-Zeiten. Um dennoch Websites mit einem hohen Anteil von audio-visuellen Medien zu realisieren, bedarf es besonderer Komprimierungs-Algorithmen, um die Daten auf die notwendigste Größe zu reduzieren. Trotzdem beansprucht ein kompletter Download einer großen audio-visuellen Datei einige Zeit – Zeit, die der Benutzer mit Warten verbringen muss, bis die Medien am Bildschirm erscheinen. Deshalb setzt man sogenannte **Streaming-Verfahren** ein, die es erlauben, schon während des Downloads mit dem Abspielen der Medien zu beginnen.

Beispiel einer Internet-Seite mit Streaming-Video (Quelle: ZDF Mediathek)

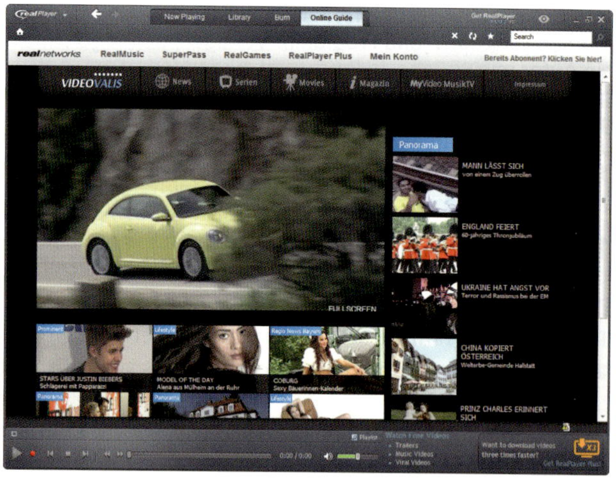

Beispiel eines Streaming-Player Programms (Quelle: Realplayer von RealNetworks).

Das Streaming-Verfahren erlaubt die Übertragung von Audio- und Videodaten quasi in Echtzeit. Dabei kommen spezielle Server und anstelle des TCP/IP-Protokolls das IP mit dem UDP (User Datagram Protocol) zum Einsatz. Das UDP erlaubt gegenüber dem TCP eine kontinuierliche Datenübertragung, die für Live-Audio und Live-Video notwendig ist.

Plug-Ins

Nicht nur Audio und Video gehören zu den multimedialen Medienelementen im Internet, sondern verschiedenste Grafik- und Bilddaten. Virtual Reality-Umgebungen und ganze interaktive Programme können zusätzlich in die HTML-Seiten eingebunden werden.
Um diese Medien anzeigen bzw. abspielen zu können, muss der Benutzer seinen Web-Browser mit den notwendigen Software-Erweiterungen ausrüsten. Diese Erweiterungen werden auch **Plug-Ins** ➊ genannt.

➊ Die meisten **Plug-Ins** funktionieren nur mit einem Browser. Das heißt, beim Download eines Plug-Ins muss der Anwender den Typ seines Browsers angeben, damit die richtige Plug-In-Version verwendet wird.

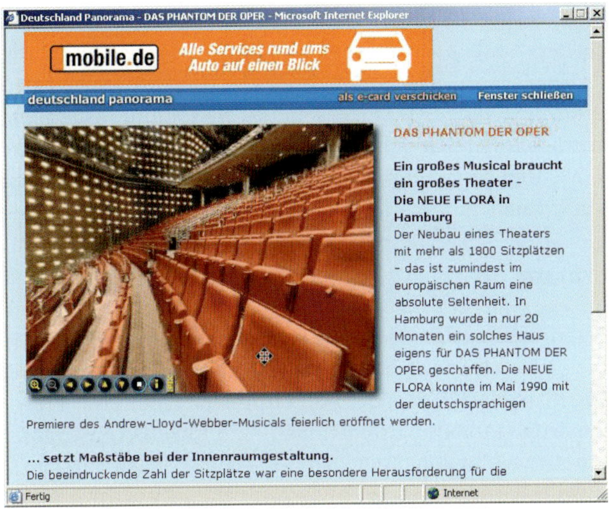

Virtueller Panorama-Rundgang mit dem IPIX-Viewer (Beispiel: Theater NEUE FLORA, Hamburg von Deutschland, Panorama.de)

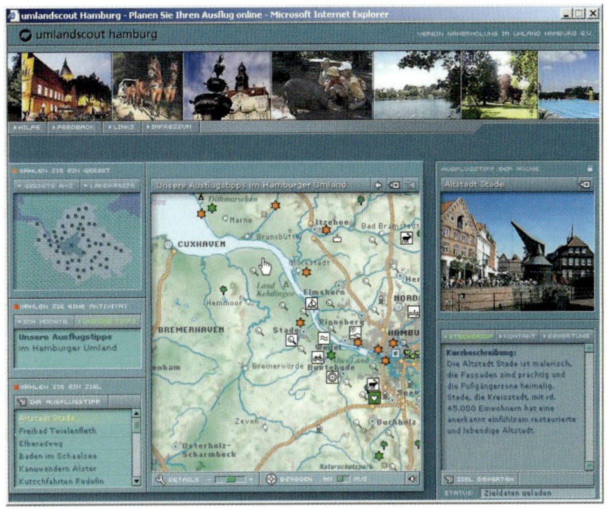

Komplette interaktive Anwendung in einem separaten Fenster mit Adobe Flash (Beispiel: Umlandscout – Reiseführer für Hamburg und Umland)

Üblicherweise werden die Plug-Ins bei Bedarf (engl. On demand) direkt vom Plug-In-Lieferant als Download geladen und teils automatisch als Software-Erweiterung im Browser installiert.

Weit verbreitete Plug-Ins sind zum Beispiel der Acrobat Reader von Adobe für das Anzeigen von Dokumenten, der Realplayer von RealNetworks für Streaming-Audio und -Video, die Plug-Ins für interaktive Anwendungen, wie Flash, Director und Authorware von Adobe, und QuickTimeVR von Apple oder IPIX Virtual Tour Viewer von IPIX zum Darstellen von Virtual Reality.

Mit Plug-Ins lässt sich das Internet nahezu unbegrenzt multimedial erweitern. Jede Erweiterung kann jedoch eine Sicherheitslücke darstellen. Deshalb sollte die Herkunft der Erweiterungen geprüft und der Download nur von vertrauenswürdigen Quellen akzeptiert werden.

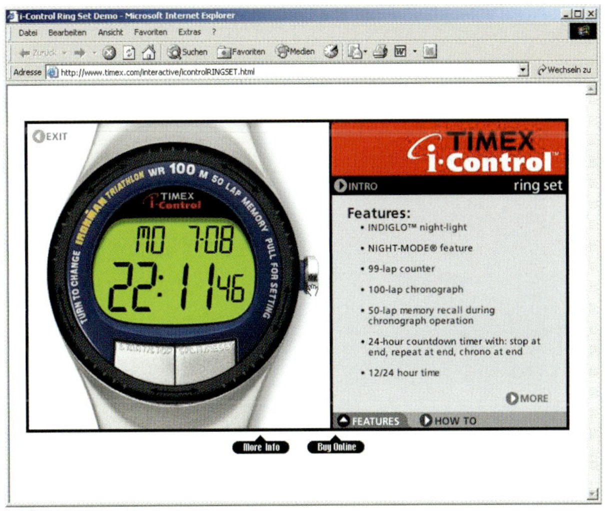

Interaktive Simulation mit dem Director. Das Pogramm-Element ist in eine HTML-Seite integriert (Beispiel: Timex)

14.6.2 3D-Visualisierung im Web

Standards zum Einbinden von Bildern, Sound und Video in Web-Seiten haben sich mittlerweile etabliert.

❶ **Web3D** ist keine Programmiersprache, sondern ein Oberbegriff für 3D-Sprachen.

Für dreidimensionale Anwendungen im Web, dem **Web3D** ❶, befinden wir uns noch in einer Sondierungsphase. Zum Einen gibt es die Bestrebungen des Web3D-Konsortiums ❷, offene Standards für 3D-Inhalte zu fördern und zu verbreiten. Zum Anderen versuchen Software-Hersteller in Kombination von 3D-Anwendungsprogrammen neue Formate zu verbreiten.

❷ Das **Web3D-Konsortium** ist ein nicht-kommerzieller Zusammenschluss aus Firmen und akademischen Einrichtungen, der sich der Entwicklung und Verbreitung von offenen Standards für dreidimensionale Inhalte im Internet widmet.

Standardisierte Formate

VRML97 ist ein einfaches und flexibles 3D-Format, welches aber wenig Akzeptanz und Verbreitung im kommerziellen Bereich gefunden hat. **X3D**, die Weiterentwicklung des **VRML**, basiert auf XML und könnte durch die Integration in das Videoformat MPEG4 stark an Bedeutung gewinnen.

Nichtstandardisierte Formate

Formate wie **Shockwave 3D** und **Acrobat 3D** von Adobe verfügen über mächtige Autorenwerkzeuge und nutzen die große Marktdurchdringung der Adobe Plug-Ins. **Java3D** von Sun Microsystems ist eine Klassenbibliothek der Programmiersprache Java. **Viewpoint**, spezialisiert auf hochwertige Produktpräsentationen, und **Cult3D** von Cycore, spezialisiert auf E-Commerce-Anwendungen, sind Technologien, die sich auf spezielle Anwendungsgebiete konzentrieren.

3D-Produktpräsentation im Web – realisiert mit Java3D (Quelle: Seiko, produziert von 3D-Scapes)

Anwendungsbereiche von 3D im Web

3D-Inhalte sind auf Web-Seiten noch nicht oft anzutreffen. Im Anwendungsbereich E-Commerce gibt es noch keine dreidimensionalen Einkaufszentren. Lediglich einzelne 3D-Produktpräsentatinen sind anzutreffen. Grund sind vorwiegend die hohen Erstellungskosten und das Fehlen von zielgruppenerprobten Benutzerschnittstellen.

Die größte Verbreitung von 3D-Inhalten findet derzeit im Unterhaltungsbereich statt. Dies ist auf die rasante Verbreitung von Online-Spielen im Web zurückzuführen. Auch im Bereich der Informationsvisualisierung, also der technischen Dokumentation, oder im Lehr- und Lernbereich, setzen sich 3D-Anwendungen immer stärker durch. Eine wichtige Plattform ist dabei Acrobat 3D, da dieses Format über das PDF-Plugin auf fast allen Web-Browsern verfügbar ist.

14.7 Daten-Management

Die Bedeutung des effizienten Umgangs mit Daten hat auch in der Medieninformatik einen besonderen Stellenwert. Informationen, Medienelemente und sonstige Daten sollen nicht nur einmal aufbereitet und in ein Zielmedium umgesetzt werden, sondern aus den Informationen und Medienelementen soll der bestmögliche Nutzen erzielt werden. Dazu gehören effiziente Datenspeicher-Verfahren, Mehrfachverwendungen und Prozesse, die wiederholbar und universell einsetzbar sind.

14.7.1 Cross Media und Single Source Publishing

Das Zusammentragen der Informationen und der Medien-Elemente, sowie das redaktionelle Aufbereiten nimmt bei einer Medienproduktion in der Regel den längsten Zeitabschnitt in Anspruch. Deshalb sollte diese Aufbereitung systematisch erfolgen, um Wiederholungen und ähnliche Arbeiten zu vermeiden.

Mit einem Erstellungsprozess nach dem **Single Source Publishing** – Prinzip erstellt man kleine Informationsmodule. Das „eigentliche Dokument" verweist auf diese Informationsmodule. Erst bei einer Produktion werden die verknüpften Informationsmodule zu einem Dokument zusammengefügt. Moderne Systeme setzen dabei auf die Datenhaltung in XML und die Verwaltung der Informationsmodule über Metadaten.

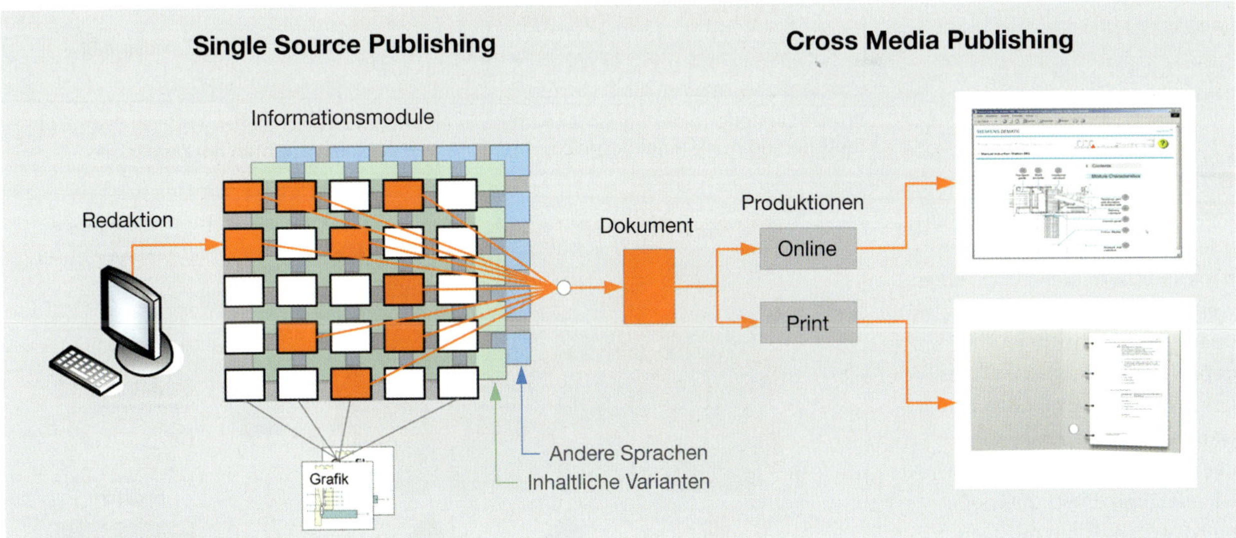

Beim Single Source Publishing werden die Inhalte als Informationsmodule gespeichert, auf die die Dokumenten-Produktion zugreift und dann beim Cross Media Publishing in das Zielmedium ausgibt.

Für die Ausgabe in verschiedene Zielmedien kann das sogenannte **Cross Media Publishing** zum Einsatz kommen. Hierunter versteht man die Produktionen verschiedener Zielmedien aus einer Informationsquelle, zum Beispiel die Produktion eines Handbuches und die Produktion einer Anleitung in Form von HTML-Seiten.

14.7.2 Content Management Systeme

❶ Beim Einsatz eines **CMS** ist darauf zu achten, dass
- die Inhalte stark modularisiert werden müssen,
- die „Atomisierung" der Information, also das Aufteilen in kleinste Informationsmodule, einen hohen Verwaltungsaufwand bedeutet,
- Anforderungen an die Benutzer höher sind als bei konventionellen Systemen.

Die Funktionalität von Single Source und Cross Media Publishing sind in der Regel in so genannten **Content Management Systemen (CMS)** ❶ gebündelt. Merkmale eines CMS sind die medienneutrale Datenhaltung von wiederverwendbaren Informationsbausteinen, „Content" genannt, sowie Ausgabewege für verschiedene Zielmedien.

Professionelle CMS verfügen über umfangreiche Funktionen, um Informationsbausteine zu konfigurieren und aus verschiedenen Perspektiven zu betrachten. Damit können zum Beispiel Versionen, inhaltliche Varianten und weitere Sprachen verwaltet werden. Durch die klare Strukturierung sind unter Anderem auch automatisierte Übersetzungs-Prozesse, z. B. in Verbindung mit einem **Translation Memory System** ❷ möglich.

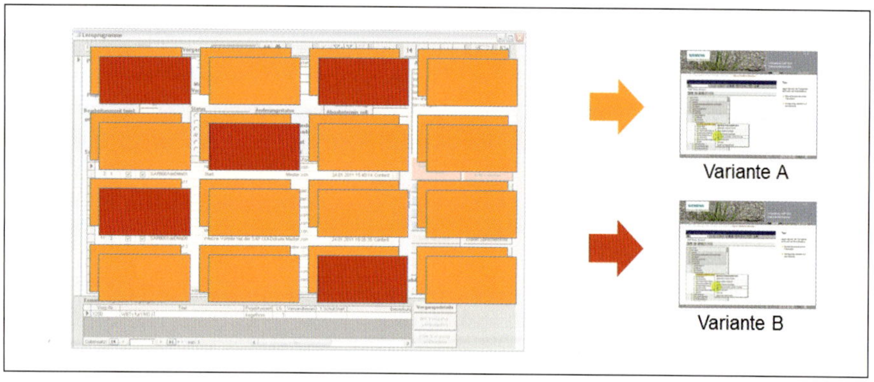

Prinzipdarstellung der Variantenbildung in einem CMS. Gleichbleibende Informationsmodule sind nur einmal gespeichert und werden für alle Varianten herangezogen.

❷ Translation Memory Systeme **TMS** sind Programme, die bereits übersetze Sätze in einer Datenbank speichern. Beim Übersetzen weiterer Texte wird jeder zu übersetzende Satz daraufhin geprüft, ob er bereits im Translation Memors vorhanden ist. Ist dies der Fall, so kann die in der Datenbank vorgefundene Übersetzung direkt übernommen werden. Somit muss ein Übersetzer keinen Satz zweimal übersetzen. Dies bietet ein hohes Einsparpotential bei Folge-Übersetzungen.

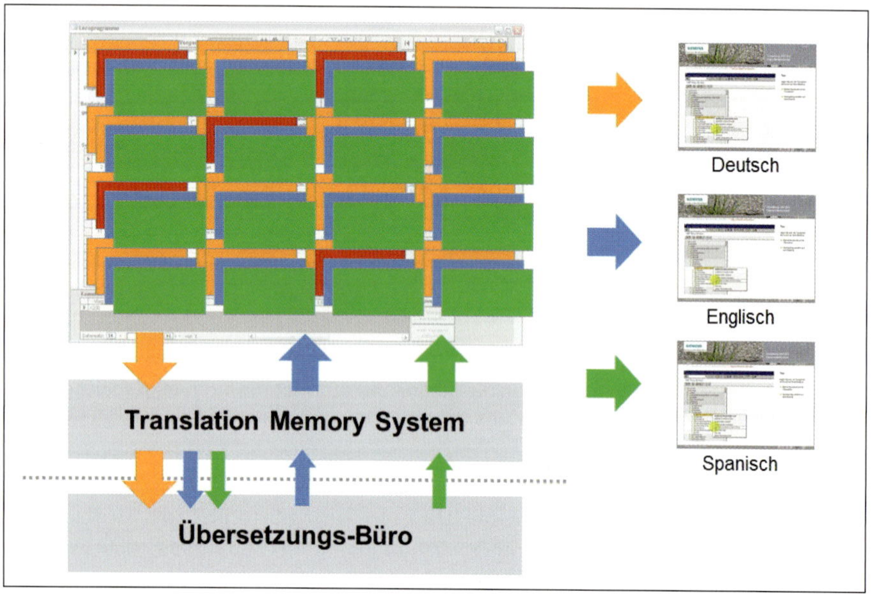

❷ Prinzipdarstellung des Übersetzungsprozesses mit einem Translation Memory System.

Dies ist beispielsweise für Redaktionssystem ❶ in der technischen Dokumentation wichtig.

Für die Verwaltung von Web-Auftritten kommen spezielle Web Content Management Systeme (WCMS) zum Einsatz, die serverseitig, wie auch clientseitig, dynamisch oder statisch arbeiten können.

- **Clientseitige CMS ❷ verwenden ein lokal installiertes Programm und laden die Daten per FTP auf den Web-Server.**
- **Serverseitige CMS ❸ hingegen laufen in Verbindung mit einer Datenbank auf einem Web-Server und werden über ein Web-Interface bedient.**

Dynamische CMS erstellen die HTML-Seiten bei jedem Aufruf der Web-Seite aus der CMS-Datenbank. Damit sind Änderungen an den Seiten sofort aktuell.

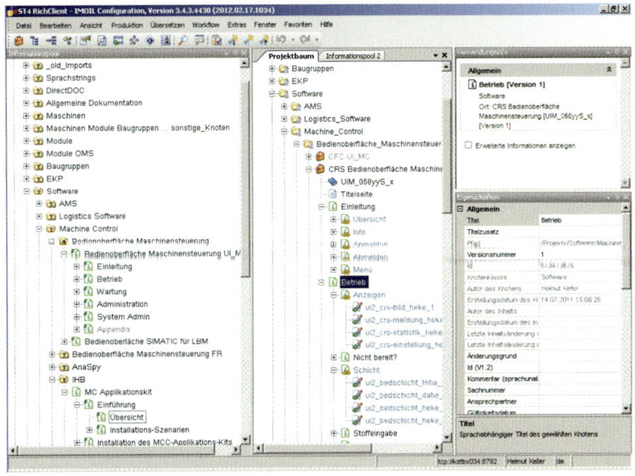

❶ Beispiel eines CMS für die Redaktion: Schema ST4 von Schema (Quelle: Siemens AG)

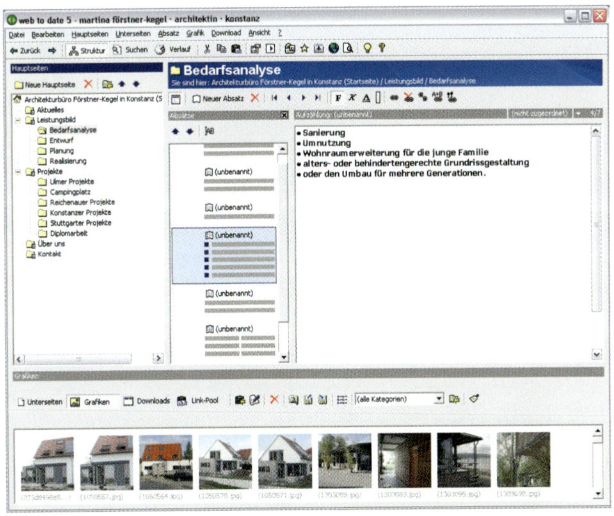

❷ Beispiel eines clientseitigen CMS für Websites: Web2Date von Data Becker. (Quelle: www.architektin-foerstner.de)

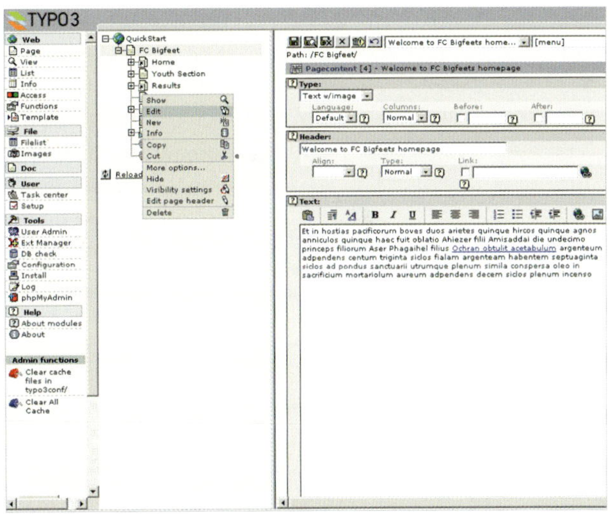

❸ Beispiel eines serverseitigen CMS für Websites: Open Source Software TYPO3 (Quelle: Typo3)

Statische Systeme erstellen die HTML-Seiten immer komplett neu und legen diese dann statisch auf dem Web-Server ab.

Neben der Darstellung einzelner Inhalte können CMS auch automatisch alternative Ausgabekanäle bedienen. Zum Beispiel als maschinenlesbare Ausgabe von Web-Inhalten für Feeds (z. B. RSS oder Atom), die über entsprechende Reader abonniert werden können.

Auch im Lernbereich müssen Inhalte verwaltet werden. Dies kann mit spezialisierten Content Management Systemen ❶ erfolgen, welche es erlauben lerngerechte Informationseinheiten für unterschiedlichen Lernszenarien und unterschiedliche Zielgruppen zu konfigurieren.

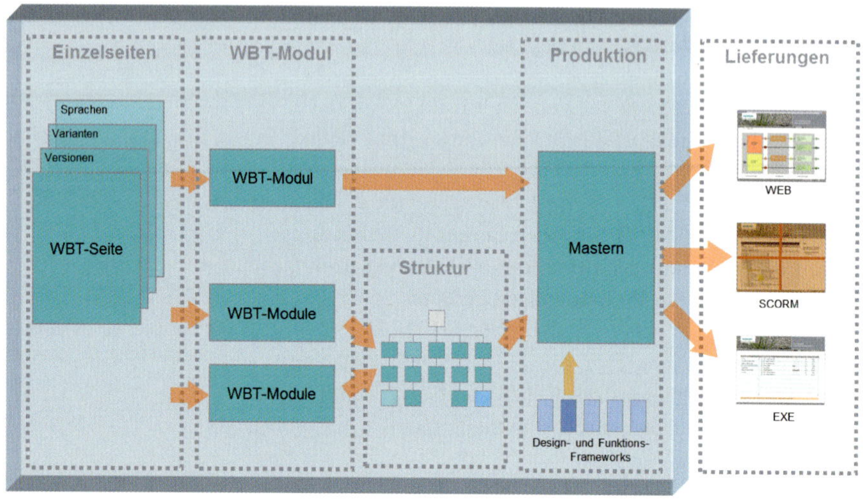

❶ Prinzipdarstellung eines CMS für Lernanwendungen mit unterschiedlichen Ausgabemöglichkeiten (Quelle: CMS PRODAT von Siemens AG).

Kommen zusätzlich zur Verwaltung der Inhaltsmodule umfangreiche Kommunikationsfunktionen und Benutzerverwaltungen für Lernende hinzu, so spricht man von **Learning Content Managementsystemen (LCMS)** ❷. Damit lassen sich komplette Lernprozesse online durchführen und verwalten.

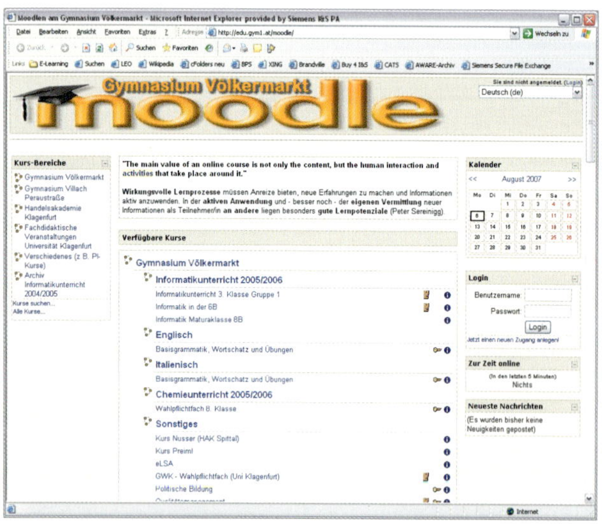

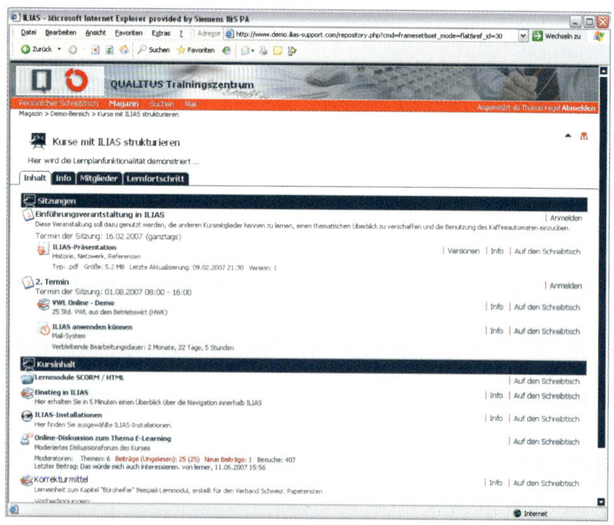

❷ Beispiele von LCMS aus dem Open Source Bereich. Links das LCMS Moodle (Quelle: Gymnasium Völkermarkt) und rechts das LCMS Ilias (Quelle: Qualitus).

Aufgaben und Übungen, Literaturhinweise

Aufgaben und Übungen

1. Programmiersprachen
   Beschreiben Sie den Unterschied zwischen einer höheren Programmiersprache und einem Autorensystem. Nennen Sie Softwarebeispiele und erläutern Sie mögliche Einsatzszenarien.
2. Grundprinzipien der Programmierung
   Wählen Sie für eine Skriptsprache (z. B. JavaScript) eine Kontrollstruktur aus, die geeignet ist, bei Erfüllung einer Bedingung eine Anweisung auszuführen und bei Nichterfüllung eine alternative Anweisung durchzuführen.
3. HTML
   Erstellen Sie das Grundgerüst eines HTML-Skriptes mit Texten in Überschriften unterschiedlicher Ordnung. Benutzen Sie Wörter mit Umlauten und bauen Sie Verknüpfungen über Hyperlinks innerhalb des Dokumentes auf.
4. Skriptsprachen
   Vergleichen Sie Client Side Scripting mit Server Side Scripting, zeigen Sie Vor- und Nachteile auf und nennen Sie typische Skriptsprachen dieser Prinzipien.
5. XML
   Nennen Sie Gründe für die Verwendung der Auszeichnungssprache XML.
6. Daten-Management
   Skizzieren und erläutern Sie das Prinzip des Single Source Publishing (SSP) bei einem Content Management System (CMS). Nennen Sie Kriterien, die bei einem CMS mit SSP beachtet werden sollten.

Literaturhinweise

Bruns, Kai; *Meyer-Wegener*, Klaus: Taschenbuch der Medieninformatik, München 2005 (Hanser Fachbuchverlag)

Dellwig, Elmar: JavaScript, München 2001 (Markt+Technik Verlag)

Steyer, Ralph: Jetzt lerne ich JavaScript und HTML, München 2005 (Markt+Technik Verlag)

Fuchs, Christian; *Gabriel*, Herbert; *Gailer*, Hannes; *Kleinbichler*, Arno: Medieninformatik 1, Wien 2004 (Manz Verlag Schulbuch)

Fuchs, Christian; *Gabriel*, Herbert; *Gailer*, Hannes; *Kleinbichler*, Arno: Medieninformatik 2, Wien 2004 (Manz Verlag Schulbuch)

Herold, Helmut; *Lurz*, Bruno; *Wohlrab*, Jürgen: Grundlagen der Informatik. Praktisch – Technisch – Theoretisch, München 2006 (Pearson Verlag)

Kersken, Sascha: Handbuch für Fachinformatiker, Bonn 2005 (Galileo Press GmbH)

Herczeg, Michael: Einführung in die Medieninformatik (Interaktive Medien), München 2006 (Verlag Oldenbourg)

Nation
29 August 2006 Tuesday
N3
orts in Penang
thousands to panic

C

Wirtschaft und Management

15 Projektmanagement 610
16 Akquisition und Präsentation . . 650
17 Medienrecht. 674
18 Kalkulation. 706
19 Medienproduktion 732
20 Marketing. 788

In Teil C geht es um die wirtschaftliche Seite der Medien und insbesondere um die Frage, was man alles berücksichtigen muss, wenn man Medienprojekte professionell und wirtschaftlich abwickeln möchte bzw. wie das „Management" von Medienprojekten funktioniert.

Die einzelnen Kapitel in diesem Teil C sind entsprechend dem sog. Wertschöpfungsprozess angeordnet. Danach muss ein Projekt zunächst konzipiert und geplant werden, bevor es gestartet wird. Kapitel 15 – überschrieben mit „Projektmanagement" – liefert das notwendige Know-how hierzu, indem es einen sehr kompakten, aber dennoch umfassenden Überblick über alle Schritte des Managements von Medienprojekten liefert.

Um einen Auftrag zu erlangen, ist es oft sehr wichtig, die Techniken der Akquisition und Präsentation zu kennen und anwenden zu können. Kapitel 16 liefert Grundkenntnisse hierzu. Unmittelbar nach der erfolgreichen Akquisition eines Auftrages stellen sich in der Regel vielschichtige Fragen des Rechteerwerbs und des Umgangs mit Rechten. Grundkenntnisse des Medienrechts sind daher erforderlich, wie sie in Kapitel 17 vermittelt werden.

Ferner muss jedes Projekt auf eine solide wirtschaftliche Basis gestellt werden, so dass sich die Frage stellt, wie man eine Kostenkalkulation erstellt. Die Techniken der Kalkulation werden mit zahlreichen Fallbeispielen in Kapitel 18 vorgestellt.

Die eigentliche Medienproduktion wird dann in Kapitel 19 beschrieben, gefolgt von der Darstellung der Vermarktungstechniken bzw. des Marketing in Kapitel 20. Eine besondere Beachtung wird dabei der Werbung geschenkt.

15 Projektmanagement

Webcode:
C1500

Für weitere Infos zu diesem Kapitel mit dem Smartphone einfach QR-Code scannen oder auf www.medien-verstehen.de den Webcode eingeben.

Einen Film, eine CD-ROM, einen Web-Auftritt oder ein anderes Medienprodukt herzustellen, ist eine komplexe Angelegenheit. Es ist nicht einfach, den Überblick zu behalten. Um auf Erfolgskurs zu bleiben, muss man den Ablauf straff organisieren, die richtigen Leute in einem Team vereinigen, den Kosten- und Zeitrahmen einhalten und ständig auf die Qualität achten. Das Rezept, um den Herausforderungen gerecht zu werden, heißt **Projektmanagement** ❶. Darunter wird ein Instrumentarium verstanden, mit dem es gelingt, außergewöhnliche und komplexe Vorhaben in den Griff zu bekommen.

❶ **Projektmanagement** ist ein Gesamtkonzept, mit dem man komplexe Vorhaben zum Erfolg führt.

Gutes Projektmanagement beginnt damit, dass man den Ablauf des Projekts übersichtlich strukturiert und den sog. **Projektlebenszyklus** sichtbar macht. Dabei können **sechs typische Phasen** unterschieden werden:

- Phase 1: Projekt-Entstehung
- Phase 2: Projekt-Definition
- Phase 3: Projekt-Start
- Phase 4: Projekt-Planung
- Phase 5: Projekt-Durchführung
- Phase 6: Projekt-Abschluss

Jede Phase wirft spezielle Fragen auf, auf die man sich gut vorbereiten muss, wenn man das Projekt im Griff behalten will. Im **Überblick** sind dies die folgenden Themen:

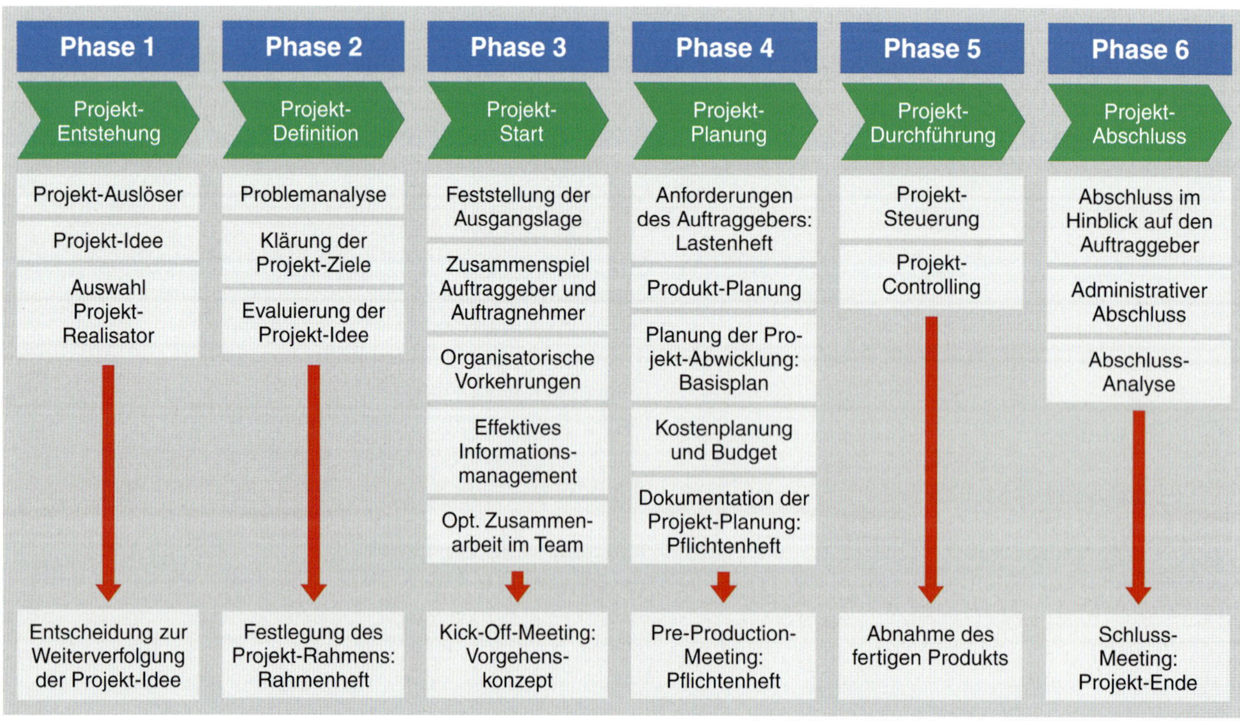

15.1 Projekt-Entstehung

15.1.1 Auslöser für Projekte

Projekte fallen nicht vom Himmel, sondern sie werden ins Leben gerufen. Auslöser für ein Projekt kann dabei ein externer oder ein interner Auftraggeber sein. Nachfolgende Abbildung zeigt die beiden voneinander zu unterscheidenden **Projekttypen**.

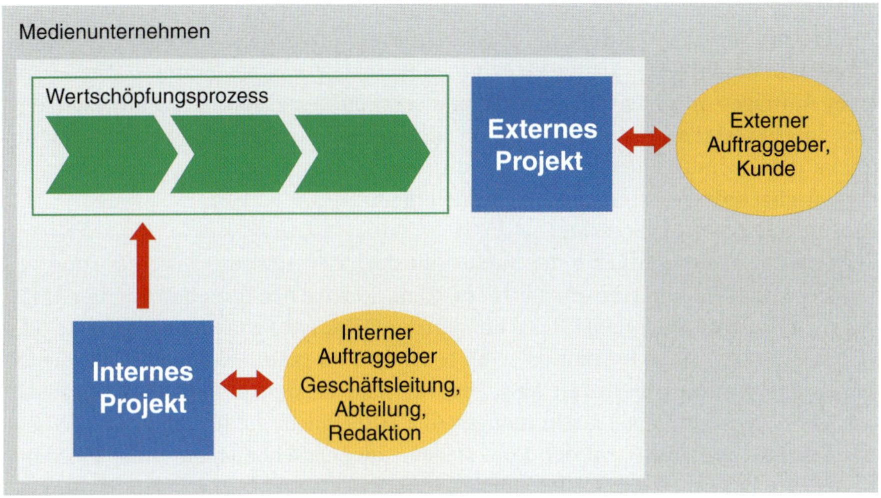

Externe Projekte

Auslöser für ein externes Projekt kann sein, dass ein **Auftraggeber von außen** an das Unternehmen herantritt und einen Auftrag erteilt. Das ist der Fall, wenn das betrachtete Medienunternehmen eine Filmproduktionsgesellschaft ist (z. B. Bavaria oder Studio Hamburg) und das ZDF oder RTL einen Auftrag zu einem Fernsehfilm vergibt ❶.

❶ In diesem Fall liegt eine klassische Auftragsproduktion vor. Projekte dieser Art werden als **Kundenauftragsprojekte** bezeichnet.

Beispiele: Das Radioprogramm SWR 3 veranstaltet ein „New Pop Festival“ und sucht nach einer Event-Agentur, die das Projektmanagement von A bis Z übernimmt. RTL hat unter Einsatz eines sehr großen Budgets die Sturmflut-Katastrophe in Hamburg im Jahr 1962 verfilmt und als großes TV-Event gezeigt; hierzu sucht RTL eine geeignete Produktionsfirma, die dieses Großprojekt stemmen könnte.

Weit verbreitet ist es auch, dass ein Auftraggeber einen Projektauftrag über eine **Ausschreibung** vergibt. In diesem Fall muss ein Angebot vorgelegt werden, über das der Auftraggeber befindet und es entweder ablehnt oder annimmt. Diese Art der Auftragsvergabe ist typisch für den Bereich von Werbe- und Kommunikationsmaßnahmen. Bei großen Werbekampagnen findet sogar ein sog. **Pitch** statt, bei dem Agenturen um die Gunst eines zumeist großen Auftraggebers (z. B. BMW, Telekom oder Unilever) werben ❷. Will eine Agentur in einem Pitch bestehen, muss sie in der Regel viel an Ressourcen und Know-how investieren, und läuft am Ende dennoch Gefahr, nicht zum Zuge zu kommen.

❷ Mit dem Begriff **Pitch** wird die Wettbewerbspräsentation einer (Werbe-)Agentur im Kampf um einen Auftrag („Etat“) bezeichnet.

❶ Unter **Akquisition** versteht man alle Maßnahmen und Anstrengungen zur Kundengewinnung. Die erstmalige Ansprache eines potenziellen Kunden wird als „Kalt-Akquise" bezeichnet. Gegenüber Privatkunden sind sog. Kaltanrufe in Deutschland nach dem Gesetz gegen den unlauteren Wettbewerb (UWG) verboten und dürfen nur mit ausdrücklicher Genehmigung des Kunden erfolgen. Gegenüber Gewerbetreibenden reicht deren mutmaßliche Einwilligung, die sich aus dem Geschäftsgegenstand ergeben kann.

Ein anderer Typus externer Projekte liegt vor, wenn die Entstehung des Projekts auf einem Anwerbevorgang beruht, den man als **Akquisition** bezeichnet ❶. Dies ist dann der Fall, wenn beispielsweise ein freier Autor sein Drehbuch verschiedenen Filmproduzenten vorlegt in der Hoffnung, dass einer davon „anbeißt" und ein Filmprojekt daraus entsteht. Ein anderes Beispiel ist der Filmhändler, der einer TV-Sendergruppe ein großes Filmpaket zum Kauf und zur Verwertung anbietet.

Interne Projekte

Bei internen Projekten kommt der **Auslöser** für ein Projekt aus den **eigenen Reihen**. Dabei wird das Projekt – analog zu externen Projekten – entweder durch die Vergabe eines Auftrages an einen Projektleiter bzw. eine Projektgruppe ausgelöst oder eine Einzelperson oder eine Abteilung bemüht sich um den Auftrag, ein Projekt durchführen zu dürfen. Auftraggeber ist häufig die Geschäftsführung oder entscheidungsbefugte nachgeordnete Bereiche des Unternehmens.

Beispiele für interne Projekte bei Medienunternehmen sind die Durchführung von Sonderprogrammen in Hörfunk und Fernsehen. So wird häufig zu bestimmten Anlässen (z. B. 10 Jahre deutsche Einheit, hundertster Geburtstag von Hermann Hesse oder 200 Jahre Französische Revolution) eine besondere Programmaktion geplant, die das Standardprogramm außer Kraft setzt. Manche Radiosender (z. B. SWR 3) veranstalten große, nach Umfragen zusammengestellte Hitparaden, die für eine ganze Woche das gesamte Programm „auf den Kopf stellen". Im Fernsehen ist an große TV-Events zu denken, bei denen ein großer eigener Film (z. B. bei ARD und ZDF: „Napoleon", „Die Vertreibung" oder „Stauffenberg") thematisch in Form eines großen Abends mit Dokumentationen, Interviews und Talk Shows aufbereitet wird. Solche großen TV-Events werden veranstaltet, um sich in der großen Vielfalt der Fernsehprogramme hervorzuheben und der Konkurrenz Zuschauer abzujagen, oft aber auch deshalb, um sein Image als „wichtiger Sender" aufzupolieren. Zu denken ist auch an große Sport-Ereignisse wie die Übertragung der Fußball-Weltmeisterschaft durch ARD und ZDF.

Für alle diese Projekte ist es wegen der hohen Komplexität der internen Abwicklung erforderlich, **interdisziplinäre Projektteams** einzusetzen, die alle Anforderungen (Programm, Marketing, Produktion und Technik, Finanzen) unter einen Hut bringen.

Andere Beispiele sind sog. „Change-Projekte", bei denen tiefgreifende Veränderungen in den Strukturen und Arbeitsabläufen vorgenommen werden sollen. Häufig geschieht dies im Zusammenhang mit der Einführung neuer Software, im Zuge von Rationalisierungsmaßnahmen oder bei Unternehmenszusammenschlüssen. Solche Projekte können eine **extreme Komplexität** annehmen, die dann oft nur noch durch eine externe Moderation von Consulting-Unternehmen gestemmt werden kann. Ein Beispiel ist die Einführung eines Intranet, das die gesamte Mitarbeiterschaft besser mit Informationen für die Arbeitsabläufe versorgt und zur besseren Kommunikation untereinander beiträgt. Als sehr großes internes Projekt kann eine Fusion von Unternehmen angesehen werden, z. B. die Fusion der beiden öffentlich-rechtlichen Sender Süddeutscher Rundfunk und Südwestfunk zum Südwestrundfunk im Jahr 1998. Um dieses Großprojekt zu beherrschen, war eine ganze „Projekt-Infrastruktur" notwendig.

15.1.2 Von der Projekt-Idee zur Basis-Entscheidung

Projekt-Idee

Zentraler Ausgangspunkt eines Projekts ist die **Idee**, die mit diesem Projekt verfolgt werden soll. Jedes Projekt lebt von der Projekt-Idee, die eine Antwort auf die Frage gibt, welches Problem damit gelöst werden kann oder welchen Vorteil das Unternehmen damit für sich erzeugen kann. Manchmal ist es die mehr zufällige Anregung eines Einzelnen, die den Vorgang ins Rollen bringt, oft entsteht die Projekt-Idee als Folge eines systematischen Innovationsprozesses (z. B. in der Abteilung „Forschung und Entwicklung") ❶.

Schon im ganz frühen Stadium der Entstehung eines Projekts ist es notwendig, die Idee zu präzisieren, die dem Projekt zugrunde liegen soll. Eine Idee ist nichts Nebulöses oder Abstraktes, sondern ist eine **präzise Vorstellung** dessen, was mit dem Projekt „bewegt" werden soll. Am besten ist es, man formuliert die Projekt-Idee in Form eines **Projekt-Antrages** ❷.

Mit einem Projektantrag schafft man eine Basis, auf der die Entscheidung zur Projekt-Durchführung leichter gefällt werden kann, und man hat eine gute Vorarbeit für die konkrete Auftragserteilung.

❶ Von innovativen Unternehmen ist bekannt, dass sie ihren Mitarbeitern Arbeitzeit zur Verfügung stellen (z. B. 10 %), in der diese nach Ideen suchen können, unabhängig davon, ob dies für das Unternehmen wertvoll erscheint. Durch diese Technik kommen deutlich mehr Initiativen für innovative Projekte zustande.

❷ Ein solcher Antrag sollte mindestens die folgenden Informationen beinhalten:
- Name des Projekts
- Kurzbeschreibung des Vorhabens
- Vorschlag zur Person, die die Projektleitung übernehmen soll
- Mögliche Partner: Unter-Auftragnehmer, Consultants, Experten
- Grobe Aussage zu Personalaufwand und Kostenrahmen
- Vorzusehender Fertigstellungstermin und Meilensteine
- Risikobetrachtung

Auswahl des Projekt-Realisators

Die Entscheidung, wer das Projekt durchführen soll, ist oft bereits in der Entstehungsphase des Projekts ein Thema. So stellt sich bei einem komplizierten, innovativen Filmprojekt beispielsweise die Frage, welcher Produzent überhaupt fähig ist, das Projekt umzusetzen, eine Frage, die insbesondere bei Projekten mit hohem technischen Einsatz in der Produktion und in der Nachbearbeitung (Special Effects) bedeutsam ist. Bei vielen solcher Projekte spielen bewährte und erfolgreiche Geschäftsbeziehungen der Vergangenheit bei der Auswahl des Projekt-Realisators eine große Rolle. Andererseits kommt es oft auch zu Ausschreibungen bis hin zu Pitches, um den richtigen Partner zu finden.

Bei internen Projekten ist es häufig so, dass schon sehr früh der Projektleiter bestimmt wird, der für die Realisation des Projekts verantwortlich sein soll. Das hat den Vorteil, dass diese Person schon früh in alle Erwägungen und Analysen, die im Vorfeld notwendig sind, einbezogen ist und es keiner unnötigen Einarbeitung zu einem späteren Zeitpunkt mehr bedarf.

Basis-Entscheidung zur Weiterverfolgung der Projekt-Idee

Alle Aktivitäten, die im Vorfeld eines Projekts ablaufen, haben zum Ziel, eine **verbindliche Entscheidung** über die Durchführung des Projekts zu erreichen. Diese Entscheidung kann aber üblicherweise erst getroffen werden, wenn das Projekt vollständig und im Detail definiert ist, was erst in der nächsten Projektphase – der Phase der Projekt-Definition – geschehen kann. Im Stadium der Entstehung des Projekts ist aber immerhin eine Basis-Entscheidung darüber möglich, ob die Idee zu einem Projekt weiterverfolgt werden soll oder ob man die Idee schon im Vorfeld „ad acta legen" will.

❶ Große Kino-Spielfilme, die sich zum Zeitpunkt ihrer Entstehung in den **technisch noch machbaren Grenzbereich** bewegten, sind z. B. „Jurassic Park" oder „Titanic", die dementsprechend hohe Produktionsbudgets zur Folge hatten. Berühmt geworden ist auch „Fitzcarraldo" mit dem Regisseur Werner Herzog und dem Hauptdarsteller Klaus Kinski, bei dem es um ein Opernhaus im Regenwald ging und um das abstruse Vorhaben, ein Dampfschiff über einen Berg zu schaffen. Der Film konnte nur mit größter Mühe realisiert werden.

❷ Bei Kino-Spielfilmen ist die **Prüfung der Wirtschaftlichkeit** besonders bedeutsam. Grund ist das sehr hohe Risiko, dass der Film am Markt scheitert. Beim deutschen Film kommt hinzu, dass man sich üblicherweise um Filmfördermittel bemüht, die eine äußerst penible Durchleuchtung der Kalkulation notwendig macht.

Operationalisierung von Zielen

Ziele muss man ganz konkret definieren, sonst sind sie keine Ziele, sondern nur Wünsche oder nette Vorstellungen, die keine Orientierung bringen. Den Vorgang der **Konkretisierung** von Zielen nennt man **Operationalisierung**. Hierzu gibt es verschiedene „Formeln", z. B. die „DARMAZ-Regel". Sie besagt: Ziele müssen deutlich, anspruchsvoll, realistisch, messbar, akzeptiert und zeitbezogen sein. Ähnlich die „IAT-Formel": Inhalt: Was soll genau erreicht werden? Ausmaß: Wie genau und mit wie viel Kraft soll das Ziel erreicht werden? Termin: Bis wann muss das Ziel erreicht werden?

Ein Beispiel für eine falsche Zieldefinition: „Die Anwender sind mit dem neuen Programm zufrieden." Richtig muss es heißen: „Die Anwendergruppe hat in einer Zufriedenheitsumfrage das Programm mit mindestens der Note „gut" bewertet."

15.2.3 Evaluierung der Projekt-Idee

Eine Projekt-Idee muss sorgfältig darauf hin geprüft („evaluiert") werden, ob sie tatsächlich in ein Projekt münden soll oder ob es nicht eher geboten ist, die Idee zu „begraben". Als **Kriterien** der Evaluierung einer Projekt-Idee sind anzulegen:

- Machbarkeit: Lässt sich die Idee überhaupt umsetzen? Ist sie machbar?
- Wirtschaftlichkeit: Kann die Idee wirtschaftlich vernünftig umgesetzt werden?
- Eigenschaften des Vorhabens: Ist das Vorhaben tatsächlich so komplex und anspruchsvoll, dass man ein Projekt einrichten muss oder reicht es vielleicht aus, das Vorhaben im „Normalbetrieb" des Unternehmens abzuwickeln?

Prüfung der Machbarkeit

Je komplexer ein Projekt ist, desto wichtiger wird es, bereits im Vorfeld zu überprüfen, ob das Projekt überhaupt durchführbar bzw. machbar ist. Bei der Prüfung der **Machbarkeit** spielen **drei Aspekte** eine besondere Rolle:

- Technische Machbarkeit: So kann es z. B. sein, dass ein innovatives Filmprojekt so hohe Anforderungen an Technik und Gestaltung stellt, dass es (noch) nicht realisierbar ist ❶. Zu denken ist auch an die Entwicklung neuer IT-Anwendungen, bei denen man zur Prüfung der technischen Umsetzbarkeit oft mit Prototypen arbeitet, um die Funktionalität eines Systems und die realisierbaren technischen Lösungen auszuloten.
- Wirtschaftliche Machbarkeit: Kern der Prüfung ist die Frage, ob das vom Auftraggeber ins Auge gefasste Budget ausreicht oder ob der Kostenrahmen völlig „aus dem Ruder läuft" ❷.
- Rechtliche Machbarkeit: Einem Projekt können sich hohe rechtliche Hürden entgegenstellen und es dadurch zum Scheitern bringen. Daher ist besonders sorgfältig zu prüfen, ob Gesetze oder zivilrechtliche Einschränkungen eine Gefährdung darstellen oder ob das Projekt durch rechtliche Hindernisse unverhältnismäßig teuer würde. Insbesondere bei Events spielt der rechtliche Aspekt eine große Rolle. Zu denken ist auch an Drehgenehmigungen, die in manchen Staaten manchmal nur schwer oder nur mit hohen bürokratischen Hürden erlangt werden können.

Bei sehr innovativen, sehr großen und hoch riskanten Projekten kann es erforderlich sein, eine sog. **Machbarkeitsstudie** (engl. **„Feasibility Study"**) durchzuführen, um die nötige Klarheit zu gewinnen. Eine solche Studie kann unter Umständen einen beachtlichen Geldbetrag verschlingen.

Stellt sich heraus, dass die Realisierbarkeit nicht gegeben oder stark eingeschränkt ist, müssen mögliche Alternativen („Optionen") geprüft werden. Wenn sich auch hierbei keine sinnvollen Alternativen der Problemlösung ergeben, müssen entweder die Ziele des Projekts revidiert werden oder die Beteiligten müssen erkennen, dass das Projekt nicht realisierbar ist. Problematisch ist es, wenn ein Projekt trotz erheblicher Zweifel an der Machbarkeit im Sinne eines „Augen zu und durch" und „schön Redens" dennoch gestartet wird.

Prüfung der Wirtschaftlichkeit

Eng mit der Frage der Machbarkeit ist die Prüfung der **Wirtschaftlichkeit** verbunden. Es geht darum, den vom Projekt erwarteten Nutzen den erwarteten Kosten gegenüberstellen und vergleichend zu bewerten. Dabei kann es vorkommen, dass ein Projekt aus wirtschaftlichen Gründen verändert oder gestrichen wird, obwohl die Machbarkeit prinzipiell gegeben ist.

Als Analyse-Instrument bietet sich ein „Nutzen-Kosten-Check" an, bei dem die vom Projekt zu **erwartenden Nutzen** den zu **erwartenden Kosten** gegenübergestellt werden. Besondere Schwierigkeiten bereiten die nicht unmittelbar fassbaren und in monetären Größen ausdrückbaren Nutzen und Kosten, die als „Intangibles" bezeichnet werden. Dabei handelt es sich z. B. bei einem neuen E-Commerce-Auftritt im Internet um Nutzenfaktoren wie die Verbesserung der strategischen Ausgangsposition des Unternehmens, die Verbesserung des Firmenimages beim Kunden und bei den eigenen Mitarbeitern, die Vereinfachung von Abläufen oder die Verbesserung der Kommunikation. Auf der Kostenseite geht es um verdeckte Kosten wie z. B. ein zunehmender Stress für Teile der Mitarbeiterschaft während der Einführung des Systems, Beeinträchtigungen des Betriebsklimas oder um verdeckten Mehraufwand durch Erhöhung des Arbeitstempos.

Keine oder geringere methodische Probleme bereitet die Ermittlung der direkten Nutzen und Kosten. Hierbei handelt es sich um die unmittelbaren und dem Projekt direkt zurechenbaren Auswirkungen (Beispiel Software-Entwicklung):

- Direkter Nutzen: Einsparungen beim Arbeitsaufwand, bei Material und Personal, Zunahme des erwirtschafteten Gewinns;
- Indirekter Nutzen: z. B. Steigerung der Arbeitsproduktivität;
- Einmalige Kosten: Unmittelbare Projektkosten, notwendige Anschaffungen an Hardware, Software, Räumen, Schulung der Mitarbeiter;
- Laufende Kosten: Personalkosten für die Redaktion der Inhalte, Wartung des Systems, Lizenzen, Materialkosten.

Insgesamt gesehen sind **Nutzen-Kosten-Analysen** eine schwierige Angelegenheit, aber dennoch unverzichtbar. Sie sind immer von subjektiven Einflüssen gekennzeichnet und bringen oft große Messprobleme mit sich.

15.3 Projekt-Start

15.3.1 Ausgangslage

Zum Projektstart ist es wichtig, sich die Ausgangposition bewusst zu machen, in der man sich befindet. Betroffen sind drei **Fragestellungen**:

- Wer sind die „Hauptdarsteller" des Projekts, also die wichtigsten Akteure?
- Welche Personen sind noch relevant für das Gelingen des Projekts? Das ist die Frage nach den Stakeholdern.
- Welches sind die kritischen Erfolgsfaktoren, also diejenigen Faktoren, die für das Gelingen des Projekts eine kritische Bedeutung haben?

Hauptdarsteller

Im Hinblick auf das Zusammenspiel aller am Projekt beteiligten Akteure erkennt man schnell, dass es sich bei einem Medienprojekt normalerweise um ein recht **kompliziertes Geflecht** von Auftraggeber, Zielgruppe, Agentur, Produktionsfirma und externen Dienstleistern handelt. Diese so zusammenzuführen, dass sie konstruktive Arbeit leisten können, ist eine große Aufgabe, vor der das Projektmanagement steht.

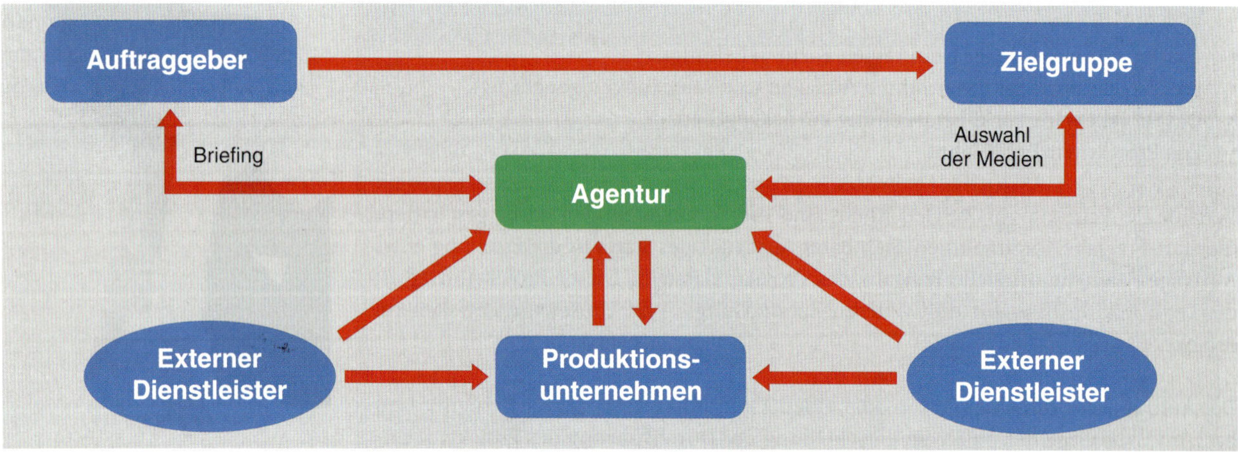

Stakeholder

Stakeholder sind Personen, auf die sich die Projektaktivitäten unmittelbar und mittelbar auswirken und die daher ein berechtigtes Interesse am Projektgeschehen haben. Sie haben einen Anspruch darauf, informiert und im gebotenen Umfang in das Geschehen einbezogen zu werden. Die Stakeholder nennt man daher auch „Anspruchsgruppen". Die Botschaft heißt: Betrachte nicht nur das Geschehen innerhalb des Projekts, sondern auch das direkte und das weitere Projektumfeld und sorge dafür, dass diese Außenstehenden ein positives Verhältnis zu deinem Projekt aufbauen. Entscheidend ist eine gute Kommunikation. Empfehlenswert ist es, eine genaue **Stakeholderanalyse** durchzuführen, die danach unterscheidet, welche Stakeholder dem Projekt gegenüber positiv oder eher negativ eingestellt sind und wie stark der Einfluss der jeweiligen Stakeholder ist.

Kritische Erfolgsfaktoren

Wenn das Projekt nun konkret gestartet wird, ist es gut, sich schon im Vorfeld die besonders kritischen Einflussfaktoren bewusst zu machen. Solche „Fallstricke" können im weiteren Projektablauf schwer zu schaffen machen. So haben zahlreiche Studien gezeigt, dass in Projekten immer wieder die gleichen typischen **Erfolgs-** und **Misserfolgsfaktoren** eine Rolle spielen ❶. Welche Faktoren besonders zum Erfolg eines Projektes beitragen, ist in zahlreichen Studien untersucht und verdeutlicht worden. Dabei hat sich die folgende „Hitliste" herauskristallisiert, wie man den Projekterfolg sicherstellen kann (vgl. Schelle/Ottmann/Pfeiffer 2005, S. 93):

1. Zieldefinition
2. Kommunikation
3. Planung
4. Topmanagement
5. Controlling
6. Projektleiterbefugnisse
7. Know-how Projektteam
8. Motivation Projektteam
9. Know-how Projektleiter
10. Planungs- und Steuerungsinstrumente
11. Partizipation

Hierbei wird deutlich, dass Projekte oft durch den **Faktor Mensch** zum Scheitern gebracht werden. Wichtig ist die Kompetenz und das Verhalten des Projektleiters. Ein besonderer Unruheherd ist erfahrungsgemäß aber auch die Kundenbeziehung. Blickt man beispielsweise auf den Agenturbereich, kann man als **typische Ursachen** für **mangelnde Kundenzufriedenheit** feststellen:

- Unbefriedigende Arbeitsergebnisse: Das Problem kann sein, dass die Agentur überfordert wurde (inhaltlich, kapazitätsmäßig, zeitlich). Meistens sind es aber unzulängliche und unpräzise Aufgabenstellungen, eine zu große Zurückhaltung der Agentur bei Rückfragen zu den Aufgabenstellungen und die fehlende Fähigkeit zum „Nein-Sagen" seitens der Agentur.
- Schlechtes Preis-Leistungsverhältnis: Oft ist ein mangelndes Verständnis des Kunden für die Kostenseite (v. a. bei Multimedia-Produktionen) festzustellen. Ebenso: fehlende Transparenz v. a. im Hinblick auf die Kosten; mangelndes Vertrauen (Gefühl, übervorteilt zu werden) und mangelnde Sachkenntnis
- Fehlerhafte bzw. zu hohe Abrechnungen: unklare Verträge, festgelegte Leistungen und Honorierungen waren nicht klar dokumentiert; fehlender KVA (Kostenvoranschlag); Änderungen seitens des Kunden wurden nicht dokumentiert
- Mangelnde Transparenz: fehlender „Klartext" über Erwartungen und Möglichkeiten; fehlende Partizipation und Einbindung des Kunden in die Abläufe; mangelhafte Kommunikation
- Unzuverlässigkeiten: sind sowohl auf Kunden- als auch auf Agenturseite zu beklagen
- Mangelnde „Chemie" zwischen Personen: kein Mut, Personen in verfahrenen Situationen auszutauschen.

❶ Die Liste der **Misserfolgsfaktoren**, die eine kritische Bedeutung haben, ist lang:
- Ziele sind unklar definiert.
- Teambildung wird nicht unterstützt.
- Konflikte im Team werden ignoriert.
- Im Team herrscht eine negative Stimmung.
- Gewachsene Kulturen werden nicht berücksichtigt.
- Experten sind „abgehoben", nehmen keine Kritik an und suchen nur anspruchsvolle statt pragmatische Lösungen.
- Fehler aus alten Projekten werden wiederholt.
- Die Kompetenzverteilung im Team ist unklar.
- Es gibt keinen Verlass auf mündliche Absprachen.
- Die Dokumentation ist mangelhaft.
- Risiken werden unterschätzt.

15.3.2 Zusammenspiel zwischen Auftraggeber und Auftragnehmer

Das Zusammenspiel aller Akteure muss im Projektmanagement reibungslos funktionieren. Dabei kommt dem **Auftraggeber** – aus Sicht z. B. einer Agentur ist das der Kunde – eine **Schlüsselrolle** zu. Dieser vergibt den Auftrag, verfolgt damit ein Ziel und hat mehr oder weniger klare Vorstellungen davon, in welchem Rahmen das Projekt ablaufen soll. Damit der Auftraggeber seine Ziele erreichen kann, steht ihm die Agentur als Helfer zur Seite. Sie arbeitet eine Konzeption aus, gibt Empfehlungen, macht Vorschläge und sorgt für die Effektivität der Aktion. Neben der Auswahl der Medien wird sie auch die Produktion z. B. des Films oder der CD-ROM veranlassen und überwachen. Es ist von größter Wichtigkeit für die erfolgreiche Projektabwicklung, dass das Zusammenspiel zwischen Auftraggeber und Auftragnehmer gut funktioniert. Eine besondere Rolle spielen dabei das **Briefing** und die **Vertragsgestaltung**.

Briefing

„Briefing" ist englisch und bedeutet „Anweisung" oder „Lagebesprechung". In diesem Wort steckt auch „brief", was so viel wie kurz und knapp heißt. Unter einem **Briefing** versteht man daher eine kurze und **genaue Aufgabenbeschreibung** für alle am Projekt beteiligten Partner. Es ist eine Kurzfassung dessen, worum es im Projekt geht. Ein Briefing wird vom Auftraggeber erstellt und soll immer in schriftlicher Form verfasst sein. Normalerweise wird das erste Briefing dem Auftragnehmer zur Stellungnahme vorgelegt, der im sog. „Re-Briefing" seine Änderungsvorschläge einbringen kann. Beim Briefing handelt es sich also um einen Prozess, der die Präzisierung der Rahmenbedingungen des Projekts zum Gegenstand hat ❶.

❶ Eine umfassende und pragmatische Definition für das **Briefing** lautet (vgl. Back/Beuttler 2003: S. 10): „Im Briefing beschreibt der Auftraggeber eine kommunikative Aufgabe, die der Dienstleister im Rahmen eines festgelegten kreativen Spielraums bis zu einem gesetzten Termin lösen soll. Um ihm dies zu ermöglichen, formuliert das Briefing so präzise wie möglich die Ziele, die erreicht werden sollen, definiert den kreativen Spielraum und liefert in hoch verdichteter, gut strukturierter Form alle zum Verständnis der Aufgabe nötigen Informationen über Produkt, Markt, übergeordnete wirtschaftliche und kommunikative Strategien und Ziele sowie über das Unternehmen. Soweit noch nicht im Vorfeld erfolgt, muss das Briefing Rollen, Kompetenzen und Befugnisse klären. Es sollte deshalb auch die Erwartungen und das Selbstverständnis des Auftraggebers enthalten. Das Briefing als Startpunkt einer Kooperation darf sich dabei nicht auf eine Einwegkommunikation beschränken, sondern muss kooperative Formen und Feedbackstrukturen umfassen."

Vertrag

Die gute Zusammenarbeit zwischen Auftraggeber und Auftragnehmer hängt neben dem Briefing auch von klaren Verträgen ab. Wie das Briefing kann man die **Vertragsgestaltung** auch als einen **Prozess** auffassen, da sich die Entwicklung der Vertragswerke üblicherweise über einen längeren Zeitraum hinzieht. Denkt man z. B. an ein großes Kinospielfilm-Projekt, wird schnell klar, dass hier viel juristische Kleinarbeit notwendig ist, damit alle Beteiligten zu ihrem Recht kommen und Zweifelsfragen geklärt werden können. Das beginnt mit der Frage, welchen gesellschaftsrechtlichen Rahmen der Filmproduzent wählt, in dem die Produktion verwirklicht wird. Bevorzugt wird hier zumeist die GmbH oder die GmbH & Co. KG, um die Haftung auf das eingesetzte Kapital zu beschränken. Sodann ist ein umfangreicher „Vertragssatz" notwendig, um die Kinofilmproduktion rechtlich abzusichern (vgl. Clevé 2004, S. 159 ff.):

- Autoren- und Drehbuchvertrag, Ko-Autorenvertrag
- Produktions- und Koproduktionsvertrag (Fernseh-Koproduktionsvertrag, Auftragsproduktionsvertrag, Produktionsservicevertrag)
- Filmförderungsvertrag
- Vertrag zum Completion Bond (Fertigstellungsgarantievertrag)
- Verträge betreffend Stab und Darsteller (Regievertrag, Darstellervertrag, Mitarbeitervertrag, Komponistenvertrag)
- Musiklizenzvertrag, Synchronisationsvertrag, Lizenz- und Verwertungsvertrag, Verleihvertrag, Filmversicherungsverträge, Geräteverleihverträge
- Postproduktions-Serviceverträge

Ein großes Problem bei der Vertragsgestaltung ist, dass man zwischen Auftraggeber und Auftragnehmer schon in der frühen Entstehungsphase des Projekts eine Vereinbarung benötigt, damit die Bereitschaft nicht erlahmt, weitere Zeit und Ressourcen in das Projekt zu investieren. Allerdings hat man zu diesem Zeitpunkt noch keine genauen Vorstellungen, was alles gemacht werden soll und welche Konsequenzen im Hinblick auf Kosten und Zeit auf einen zukommen. Um dieses Problem zu lösen, empfiehlt es sich, schon ganz früh in der Projekt-Entstehung einen sog. **Letter of Intent** abzuschließen ❶. Der ausgearbeitete Vertrag kann dann in aller Ruhe erarbeitet werden und spätestens in der Phase der konkreten Projekt-Planung – am besten unter Einschluss des Pflichtenhefts – von den Vertragsparteien unterzeichnet werden. Bei Bedarf kann zusätzlich auch noch ein Rahmen- bzw. Vorvertrag dazwischen geschaltet werden.

❶ Ein **Letter of Intent** ist eine rechtlich relevante Absichtserklärung, dass die Beteiligten weiter zusammenarbeiten wollen. Sollte die Zusammenarbeit jedoch dennoch vorzeitig enden, verpflichtet sich der Auftraggeber zur Abgeltung der entstandenen Kosten.

15.3.3 Organisatorische Vorkehrungen

Projektteam bilden

Ist der Auftrag erteilt, wird man beim Produzenten ein **Team** zusammenstellen, das die professionelle Umsetzung der Aufgabe garantiert. Von besonderem Interesse sind die Fragen: Zusammensetzung des Teams, Größe des Teams und Aufgabenverteilung innerhalb des Teams. Wie das Team zusammengesetzt werden soll, ist eine schwierige Frage. Die Regel lautet: Man muss sicherstellen, dass alle notwendigen Fachkompetenzen im Team vertreten sind. Bei einem Multimedia-Projekt sind zum Beispiel die folgenden **Fachkompetenzen** gefordert (sortiert nach den jeweiligen Fachgebieten):

- Inhalt: Autoren, Texter, Konzeptioner
- Gestaltung: Designer, Grafiker
- Produktion: Programmierer, Medienspezialisten (Video, Audio; wird oft an externe Dienstleister vergeben)
- Projektmanagement: Projektleiter

Häufig ist es so, dass die eine oder andere Kompetenz, die man für die Durchführung des Projekts benötigt, nur von außen erschlossen werden kann, indem man **externe Experten** engagiert. Für Filmprojekte ist es sogar typisch, dass das Produktionsteam und die Darsteller auf dem freien Markt rekrutiert werden. Wichtig ist es, eine übersichtliche Struktur zu schaffen, bei der klar ist, wer zum Team gehört und wer nicht.

Bei Bedarf kann man zusätzlich in ein **Kern**- und ein **Gesamt-Team** unterscheiden. Denkbar ist auch, dass für bestimmte Teilaufgaben spezielle Teams gegründet werden, die dem Projekt fallweise („ad hoc") zuarbeiten (**„Ad-Hoc-Teams"**). Alles in allem kann sich eine recht vielfältige Projektorganisation ergeben, was bei sehr großen Projekten ohnehin der Fall ist.

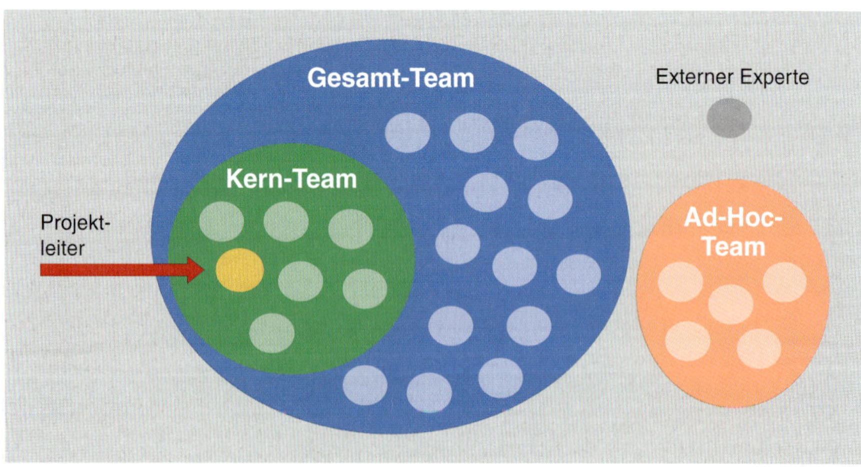

Wie **groß** das Team sein soll, hängt von der Komplexität und von der Schwierigkeit des Projekts ab:

- Für kleinere Projekte gilt eine **Teamgröße** von sieben Personen als günstig. Eine ungerade Zahl ist zu empfehlen ❶.
- Bei größeren und sehr großen Projekten lässt sich keine allgemeine Empfehlung aussprechen. Unter Umständen wird es notwendig sein, eine ganze „Infrastruktur" und das Gesamtteam in mehrere Teil-Teams zu untergliedern, z. B. in Steuerungsteam, Beratungsteam, Produktionsteam.

Wichtig ist schließlich, dass innerhalb des Teams eine klare **Aufgabenverteilung** und damit **Verantwortungsstruktur** hergestellt wird. Die folgenden Grundsätze sind dabei zu beachten:

- Jedes Teammitglied erfüllt die ihm zugeteilten Aufgaben in Eigenverantwortung.
- Alle Mitglieder sind gleichrangig.
- Der Projektleitung kommt eine Sonderrolle zu.

Damit das Team gut arbeiten kann, ist es wichtig, dass auf Seiten des Auftraggebers immer eine **konkrete Person** benannt ist, an die sich der Projektleiter jederzeit wenden kann.

Projektleitung bestimmen

Der Rolle des **Projektleiters** kommt eine **herausragende Bedeutung** für den Erfolg des Projekts zu. Daher muss die mit dieser Aufgabe betrauten Person über ausgeprägte **Fähigkeiten** verfügen. Neben Organisationstalent, Wirtschaftlichkeitsdenken und ergebnisorientiertem Denken und Handeln sind vor allem auch Fähigkeiten hinsichtlich der Menschenführung notwendig, das hat mit sogenannten „sozialen Kompetenzen" wie Kommunikationsfähigkeit und die Fähigkeit, mit Konflikten konstruktiv umzugehen und das Team zusammenzuhalten. Ob der Projektleiter erfolgreich arbeitet, hängt – theoretisch gesprochen – insbesondere von seiner **Rolle** ab, die er einnimmt ❷ sowie von seinem **Status** innerhalb des Teams ❸.

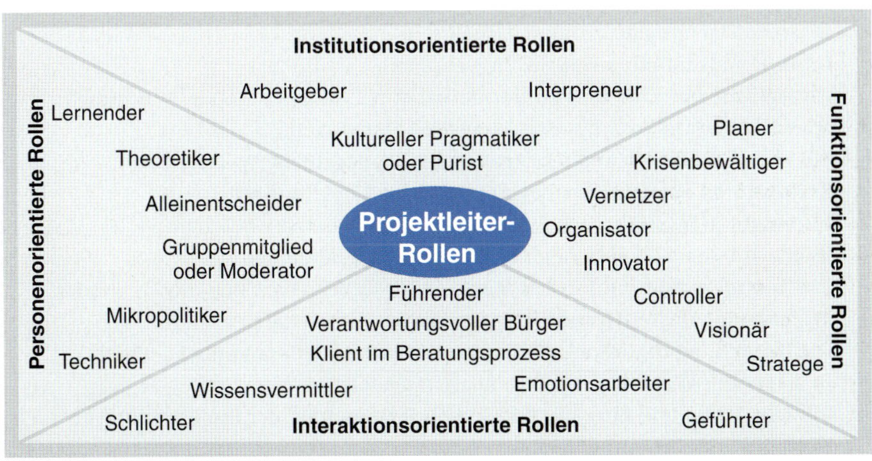

❶ Der Grund liegt darin, dass im Falle einer Abstimmung keine Patt-Situation entsteht. Allerdings sollten „Kampfabstimmungen" im Projektmanagement unbedingt vermieden werden. Besser ist es, Lösungen zu finden, bei denen alle Teammitglieder zustimmen können (Konsenslösungen).

❷ Unter einer **Rolle** wird ein Bündel von Erwartungen an das Verhalten einer Person verstanden. Daraus folgt die Interpretation von deren Aufgaben, Rechten und Pflichten sowie der Spielräume und Begrenzungen des Handelns. Die nebenstehende Darstellung stammt von Keßler/Winkelhofer.

❸ Der **Status** entscheidet über die hierarchische Positionierung des Projektleiters im Team. Unter „Status" wird verstanden, wie weit ein Mitglied von den Erwartungen der Gruppe abweichen kann, ohne Sanktionen von der Gruppe befürchten zu müssen. Dieses als „Idiosynkrasiekredit" bezeichnete Phänomen ist ein Indikator für das Ausmaß des Zusammenhalts in der Gruppe (Gruppenkohäsion). Je mehr Kredit der Projektleiter hat, desto höher ist sein Status.

❶ In der Kinofilmproduktion trägt die **Projektadministration** den Namen „Filmgeschäftsführung" oder „Production Accountant". Damit sind alle Personen bezeichnet, die für die finanzielle und buchhalterische Abwicklung der Filmproduktion verantwortlich sind.

❷ Ein **virtuelles Team** kann nicht regelmäßig an einem Ort zusammentreffen, sondern ist zur Verständigung untereinander auf technische Kommunikationsmittel angewiesen.

Projektadministration einrichten

Zu Beginn des Projektablaufs sollte man für eine schlagkräftige **administrative Infrastruktur** sorgen. Dieser Punkt wird nicht selten unterschätzt. Sinnvoll ist es – auch bei den kleineren Projekten – ein **Projektbüro** einzurichten, in dem alle Fäden zusammen laufen und insbesondere der ganze Verwaltungsapparat angesiedelt ist ❶. Hierzu gehört neben der Beauftragung qualifizierter Verwaltungskräfte auch die Schaffung geeigneter Räumlichkeiten, in denen sich das Projektteam regelmäßig treffen kann.

Im Projektbüro soll auch der sog. „Projekt-Ordner" geführt werden, der alle wichtigen Dokumente des Projekts beinhaltet. Auch wenn im Zeichen des Computers alle Dokumente digital gespeichert werden, empfiehlt es sich aus Sicherheitsgründen dennoch, sie in der Papierfassung verfügbar zu halten.

Arbeitet das Projektteam an verteilten Standorten, steht man vor dem Problem des **virtuellen Projektmanagements** ❷. Dies kann sehr große Dimensionen im Weltmaßstab annehmen. Zu denken ist beispielsweise an ein Unternehmen wie der Software-Hersteller SAP, der viele Projekte auf einer Achse Deutschland, Indien und USA abwickelt. Die Schwierigkeit dieser Art der Projektabwicklung besteht darin, dass die Mitglieder des Teams nicht so leicht eine gute „Team-Kultur" aufbauen können, da diese stark von der persönlichen Begegnung abhängt. Auch der Einsatz von Kommunikationstechnik wie Video- und Telefon-Konferenzen, die Einrichtung eines Projekt-Intranets oder der Einsatz von Projektmanagement-Software können dieses Defizit nicht vollständig ausgleichen. Daher gilt virtuelles Projektmanagement als besonders herausfordernd.

15.3.4 Effektive Information und Kommunikation

Eng mit der guten Organisation ist die Frage der Informationsversorgung der Mitglieder des Projekt-Teams verbunden. In jedem Projekt fallen eine Unmenge an Informationen mit Daten, Plänen, Listen, Grafiken, Schriftverkehr usw. an, die leicht zu einer unübersichtlichen Informationslage führen kann. Damit die Beteiligten des Projekts noch den Überblick behalten, ist es erforderlich, ein wirkungsvolles **Informations- und Kommunikationssystem** zu installieren. Dieses sollte den folgenden Anforderungen genügen:

- Informationen müssen immer aktuell sein.
- Informationsflut muss vermieden werden.
- Als Leitlinie gilt: „So wenig Informationen wie möglich, so viel wie nötig"
- Man arbeitet mit Zusammenfassungen und Auszügen.
- Man beschränkt sich auf den Sonderfall: „Management by Exception".
- Berichte sind auf den aktuellen Zeitbereich zu beschränken.
- Informationen sind je nach Empfänger stufenweise zu verdichten.
- Informationen sind entscheidungsorientiert aufzubereiten.
- Die Aussagekraft der Informationen soll durch Visualisierung erhöht werden.
- Wichtige (Schlüssel-)Informationen sind herauszustellen.
- Die Darstellung der Informationen erfolgt kurz, knapp und übersichtlich.
- In sinnvoller Weise werden Formulare eingesetzt.
- Informationen und Berichte sind sowohl Bringschuld der Projektleitung als auch Holschuld der Teammitglieder.

Projekt-Dokumentation

Effektives Informationsmanagement hängt stark von einer konsequenten **Projekt-Dokumentation** ab, die unbedingt sicher zu stellen ist. Eine Projekt-Dokumentation ist das entscheidende „Nachschlagewerk", das während des Projektablaufs und am Ende des Projekts die aktuellen Informationen liefert. Sie beruht auf einer Erfassung aller bedeutsamen Rahmen-, Planungs-, Beschluss- und Ergebnis-Daten in nachvollziehbarer Form. Sie ist notwendig, damit auch im Falle eines Wechsels in der Projektleitung oder in der Zusammensetzung des Teams die Umsetzung und der Transfer der Projekt-Erfahrungen in dokumentierter Form an die neuen Team-Mitglieder möglich ist. Auch der Transfer der Erfahrungen in Folgeprojekte wird durch eine gute Projekt-Dokumentation gewährleistet. Damit sind der aktuelle Projektstand und die getroffenen Entscheidungen permanent nachvollziehbar. Die Projekt-Dokumentation ist die umfassende Informationsgrundlage für alle Teammitglieder und Bearbeiter des Projekts. Für die lückenlose Projekt-Dokumentation sorgt die Projektleitung.

Adressatengerechte Aufbereitung

Besonders wichtig ist es, alle notwendigen Informationen **adressatengerecht** aufzubereiten. Der Auftraggeber hat einen anderen Informationsbedarf als die Projektleitung oder ein unternehmensinterner Steuerkreis, der über den Fortschritt des Projekts wacht. Ein Meilensteinbericht als Zwischenbericht ist für einen größeren Kreis interessant als ein Statusbericht, der ein einzelnes Arbeitspaket betrifft. Ein gutes Konzept der Informationsversorgung im Projekt könnte wie folgt aussehen (vgl. Schulz-Wimmer 2002, S. 261):

Art des Berichts	Verfasser	Empfänger	Wann?
Statusbericht Projekt	Projektleiter	Auftraggeber	monatlich
	Kernteam	Steuerkreis	(letzter Freitag)
		Projektteam	
Statusbericht Teilprojekt	Teilprojektleiter	Projektleiter	monatlich
			(3 Tage vor Statusbericht Projekt)
Statusbericht Arbeitspaket	AP-Verantwortlicher	Projektleiter	gemäß Vorgabe Projektleiter
Meilensteinbericht	Projektleiter	Auftraggeber	für festgelegte Meilensteine
	Kernteam	Steuerkreis	
		Projektteam	
Sofortbericht	Projektleiter	Auftraggeber	in Krisen
	Kernteam	Steuerkreis	
		Projektteam	
Ergebnisbericht	Projektleiter	Auftraggeber	zur Abnahme des Projekts
	Kernteam	Steuerkreis	
Abschlussbericht	Projektleiter	Auftraggeber	nach Abnahme des Projekts
	Projektteam	Steuerkreis	
Präsentation Phasenergebnis	Projektleiter	Auftraggeber	Ende einer Phase
	Kernteam	Steuerkreis	
Präsentation Projektergebnis	Projektleiter	Auftraggeber	Projektende
		Steuerkreis	

15.3.5 Optimale Zusammenarbeit im Team

Teamarbeit

❶ Anders ausgedrückt: Ein Team ist eine kleine Gruppe von Personen, deren Fähigkeiten sich einander ergänzen und die sich für eine gemeinsame Sache, für gemeinsame Leistungsziele und für einen gemeinsamen Arbeitsansatz engagieren und gegenseitig zur Verantwortung ziehen.

Projektarbeit ist **Teamarbeit**. Die anstehende Aufgabe kann nur gelöst werden, wenn mehrere Menschen zielorientiert und konstruktiv im Team zusammen arbeiten. Ein **Team** ist eine Gruppe von Personen, die gemeinsam eine Aufgabe bewältigt ❶. Die Betonung liegt auf „gemeinsam", da nur bei koordiniertem und auf ein Ziel ausgerichtetem Handeln der notwendige „Teamgeist" entstehen kann, der zum Projekterfolg führt. Haben die Beteiligten unterschiedliche Vorstellungen über Ziele, Wege und Methoden, kann die Gruppe nicht zu einem Team zusammen wachsen.

Nicht jede Arbeitsgruppe ist ein Team. Um dieses Prädikat zu erlangen, müssen einige Voraussetzungen gegeben sein. So ist ein Team eine Arbeitsgruppe, die formell ins Leben gerufen wurde und die ganz bestimmte **Merkmale** aufweist:

- Kleine, funktionsgegliederte Arbeitsgruppe
- Gemeinsame Zielsetzung
- Relativ intensive wechselseitige Beziehungen
- Spezifische Arbeitsform („team work")
- Ausgeprägter Gemeinschaftsgeist („team spirit")
- Relativ starker Gruppenzusammenhalt („Gruppenkohäsion")

Erfolgsfaktoren effektiver Teamarbeit

Es ist wichtig, sich vor Beginn der eigentlichen Projektarbeiten bewusst zu machen, welche Faktoren ein Team erfolgreich machen, um bei allen Team-Mitgliedern ein positives Bewusstsein zu schaffen. Als **Merkmale eines Erfolgsteams** können genannt werden (vgl. Francis/Young 1996, S. 18 ff):

- **Leistung:** Ein Team ist im Stande, Leistungen zu erzielen, die die Mitglieder jeweils für sich allein nicht erbringen könnten. Ein Team ist mehr als die Summe seiner Mitglieder.
- **Ziele:** Ein Team hat ein klares (Haupt-)Ziel, das alle Mitglieder kennen und mit dem sie einverstanden sind und das ihnen erstrebenswert erscheint. Die Mitglieder stellen ihre persönlichen Ziele in den Dienst des Hauptziels.
- **Dynamik:** Die Mitglieder des Teams spornen sich gegenseitig an. Ein Team produziert Synergie, die gezielt aufgebaut und nutzbar gemacht werden kann.
- **Struktur:** Ein Erfolgsteam hat eine genau auf die zu lösende Aufgabe abgestimmte Struktur. Alle notwendigen Faktoren sind geregelt: Teilaufgaben, Führungsansprüche, Arbeitsstil.
- **Klima:** Die Mitglieder identifizieren sich mit dem Team, es herrscht ein Klima des Vertrauens. Persönliche Schwierigkeiten werden offen besprochen. Das Team arbeitet einfühlsam, flexibel und im Geist der gegenseitigen Freude und Ermunterung.

Vor diesem Hintergrund kann ein Team auch bezeichnet werden als eine „aktive Gruppe von Menschen, die sich auf gemeinsame Ziele verpflichtet haben, harmonisch zusammenarbeiten, Freude an der Arbeit haben und hervorragende Leistungen bringen.".

Teamarbeit erfolgreich zu machen, fällt den beteiligten Personen nicht in den Schoß. Im Gegenteil: Nur wenn sie sich dafür einsetzen, stellt sich der Erfolg ein. Die Frage stellt sich, wie man das am besten macht und wo man am zweckmäßigsten ansetzen soll. Welche Faktoren sind für den Erfolg besonders wichtig? Eine Liste solcher **Erfolgsfaktoren** könnte z. B. wie folgt aussehen (vgl. Winkelhofer 1997, S. 433 f.):

- **Bekenntnis zum Team:** Die Team-Mitglieder verstehen sich nicht als Individuen, die unabhängig voneinander arbeiten, sondern als eine Einheit. Die persönlichen Ziele werden zugunsten der Team- bzw. Projektziele zurückgestellt.
- **Vertrauen**: Die Teammitglieder vertrauen einander. Jedes Mitglied vertraut darauf, dass die anderen ihre Verpflichtungen erfüllen, Freundschaften nicht missbrauchen, ihre Hilfe anbieten und akzeptieren sowie sich allgemein berechenbar und angemessen verhalten.
- **Zielbewusstsein:** Die Teammitglieder arbeiten zielgerichtet. Dem Team ist bekannt, wie es in die Gesamtstruktur des Unternehmens hineinpasst. Die Teammitglieder fühlen sich als Eigentümer ihrer Arbeiten und erfassen den Beitrag, den sie zum Projekt- und Unternehmenserfolg leisten.
- **Wirkungsvolle Kommunikation**: Die Teammitglieder kommunizieren durch Sprechen und Handeln wirkungsvoll. Die Kommunikation ist durch die Qualität und Menge der Interaktionen, die von den Teammitgliedern sowohl untereinander als auch mit Außenstehenden gepflegt werden, bestimmt. Die Interaktion kann auf der Gesprächsebene und auf der Handlungsebene stattfinden und umfasst im weiteren Sinn auch den Umgang mit Konflikten.
- **Kooperationsverhalten**: Die Teammitglieder entscheiden gemeinsam. Jeder im Team erfüllt seine Rolle. Es wird trotz aller Verschiedenheit partnerschaftlich miteinander umgegangen. Ebenso wird jeder Beitrag respektiert und im Team besprochen. Das Team entscheidet im Konsens.
- **Leistungsorientierte Methodik:** Die Teammitglieder verfolgen ihre Planung, Entscheidungsfindung und Qualitätsbewusstsein in systematischer Weise. Zur Methodik, die notwendig ist, um zum Zielbewusstsein, das eine Gruppe entwickelt hat, zu gelangen, zählen Instrumente der Problemlösung, Planungsverfahren sowie die regelmäßigen Besprechungen mit Tagesordnung und schriftlicher Zusammenfassung.

Professionelles Konfliktmanagement

Ein „starkes Team" ist darauf gefasst, dass es im Projektablauf immer wieder zu Konflikten kommt. Darauf bereitet es sich geistig vor und verhandelt im Vorfeld über Regelungen, wie die zu erwartenden Konflikte schonend und konstruktiv in den Griff zu bekommen sind. Dazu sind Grundkenntnisse der **Konflikttheorie** erforderlich. Konflikte lassen sich nicht immer leicht identifizieren, da ihre Ursachen vielfältiger Natur sein können. Zu unterscheiden sind **fünf Konfliktfelder**, die sich zum einen in Konflikte auf der Sachebene und zum anderen auf der psychosozialen Ebene klassifizieren lassen (vgl. Schelle 2004, S. 235).

Der Schwierigkeitsgrad der Konfliktlösung nimmt von links oben **(Zielkonflikt)** nach rechts unten **(Beziehungskonflikt)** beständig zu. Der Grund liegt auf der Hand: Je mehr „Unsachlichkeit" im Sinne von Antipathie, Misstrauen und Vorurteilen im Spiel ist, desto schwerer fällt es dem Team, den Konflikt rational zu behandeln.

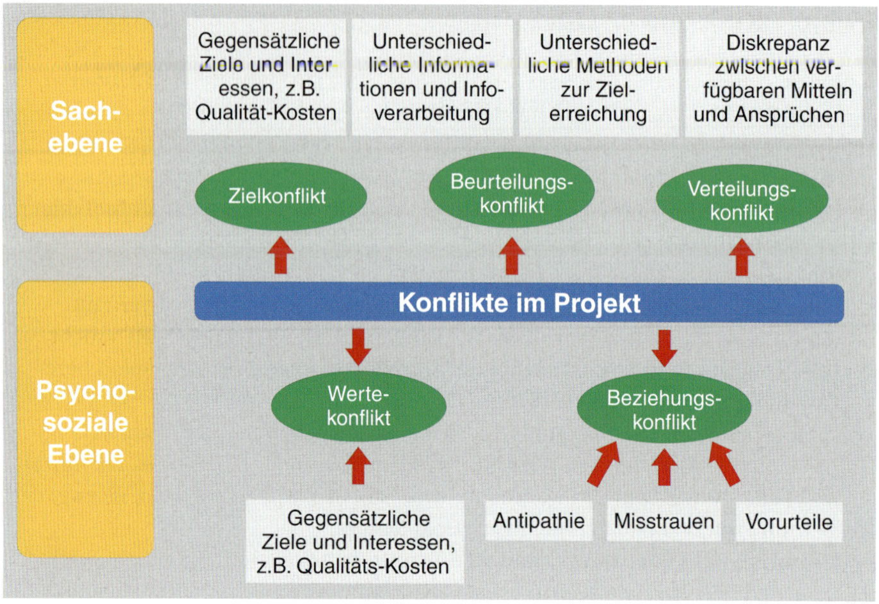

Phasenmodell der Teamentwicklung

Bei jedem Team ist festzustellen, dass sich seine „Kultur" im Zeitablauf verändert. Dabei hat man festgestellt, dass sich diese Veränderung im Zeitablauf nach einer gewissen Gesetzmäßigkeit vollzieht. Ein bekanntes **4-Phasen-Konzept** (nach Tuckman) besagt, dass ein Zustand hohen Zusammenhalts (Gruppenkohäsion) und hoher Leistungsfähigkeit (Performance) erst nach dem Durchlaufen von drei Stufen erreicht werden kann, ein nicht selten schmerzlicher Prozess für die Beteiligten. Gerade für Medienprojekte mit ihrer oftmals sehr divergierenden Teamstruktur spielt diese Gesetzmäßigkeit eine große Rolle. Ein Team durchläuft danach typischerweise die folgenden **vier Phasen** (vgl. Staehle 1999, S. 281):

- Phase 1 – **Forming**: Die Mitglieder definieren die Aufgaben, Regeln und geeigneten Methoden. Es herrscht allgemeine Unsicherheit, man probiert aus, welches Verhalten in der jeweiligen Situation akzeptabel ist. Die Führungsperson spielt eine große Rolle.
- Phase 2 – **Storming**: Konflikte entstehen. Es kommt zu emotionaler Ablehnung der Aufgabenanforderungen, zur Polarisierung der Meinungen und zum Aufstand gegen den Führer.
- Phase 3 – **Norming**: In einem Klima des offenen Austauschs von Meinungen und Gefühlen entsteht Kooperation. Es entwickelt sich Gruppenzusammenhalt, Gruppennormen und gegenseitige Unterstützung. Widerstände und Konflikte werden abgebaut bzw. bereinigt.
- Phase 4 – **Performing**: Die Energie der Beteiligten wird auf die konstruktive Bearbeitung der Aufgabe gelenkt. Man befindet sich nun (endlich) in der Hauptarbeitsphase, in der es zu Problemlösungen kommt. Die Probleme zwischen den Menschen sind gelöst, die Gruppenstruktur ist funktional zur Aufgabenerfüllung, das Rollenverhalten ist flexibel und konstruktiv.

15.3.6 Kick-Off-Meeting

Zum Ende der Phase des Projekt-Starts sind die entscheidenden Vorarbeiten geleistet, um die Projektaufgabe mit hoher Professionalität anzugehen. Man ist sensibilisiert, welche Anforderungen in sachlicher und menschlicher Hinsicht auf alle Beteiligten, auch auf den Auftraggeber, zukommen. Das Projekt kann nun konkret gestartet werden, was durch das sogenannte **Kick-Off-Meeting** geschieht. Das Kick-Off-Meeting ist von besonderer Wichtigkeit, da es das erste offizielle Zusammentreffen des Projektteams darstellt und bei dem eventuell auch Externe (z. B. eine Vertretung des Auftraggebers) beiwohnen.

Dieses Kick-Off-Meeting sollte sorgfältigst vorbereitet werden, nichts darf dem Zufall überlassen werden, gehen von ihm doch eine Reihe fundamentaler Signale aus, die das Zusammenwirken im Team und den weiteren Prozessablauf maßgeblich vorherbestimmen.

➲ **Ein bekannter Projektmanagement-Merkspruch lautet: „Sage mir, wie dein Projekt beginnt, und ich sage dir, wie es endet!"**

Das Kick-Off-Meeting hat für alle Beteiligten eine wichtige Orientierungs- und Formulierungsfunktion. Hier werden verschiedene „Pflöcke eingeschlagen", die das weitere Geschick des Projekts beeinflussen:

- Es wird klar, welche Arbeitsweise vorgesehen ist.
- Die Projektinhalte werden vorgestellt.
- Die Verbindlichkeit der Unternehmensführung kommt zum Ausdruck.
- Die Art der künftigen Zusammenarbeit der Beteiligten wird präzisiert.
- Es findet eine Verteilung der formalen und informellen Rollen der einzelnen Personen statt.

Empfehlungen

1. Wenn möglich, sollte die Auftaktsitzung vorrangig dem zwischenmenschlichen Kontakt vorzubehalten sein und der eigentlich sachliche Projektstart ist erst in der zweiten Sitzung vorzunehmen.
2. Man sollte überlegen, selbst bei kleineren Projekten, in einem vorgeschalteten Workshop („Projektstart-Workshop", vgl. Schelle/Ottmann/Pfeiffer 2005, S. 136) die Inhalte, die Dramaturgie und die Spielregeln des geplanten Auftakttreffens zu erarbeiten. Es gilt der Merksatz: „Ein guter Start des Projekts fällt dem Projektteam nicht in den Schoß, sondern muss hart erarbeitet werden". Hilfreich ist dabei z. B. die Verwendung von Checklisten für die Gestaltung von Sitzungen und Konferenzen.
3. Wer zum Kick-Off-Meeting einzuladen ist, ist nach dem Einzelfall zu entscheiden. Neben dem Projektteam und den unmittelbar beteiligten Entscheidungstragern (evtl. Entscheidungsgremium) sind dies die Vertretung des Auftraggebers, Ad-hoc-Gruppen, externe Experten oder Personalvertretungsorgane. In jedem Falle soll das Kick-Off-Meeting der Information aller wichtigen Stakeholder – also den wichtigsten Interessengruppen und -personen im und um das Projekt herum – dienen.
4. Die Sitzung ist professionell unter Anwendung moderner Kommunikationstechniken zu führen. Eine klare und durchdachte Tagesordnung muss der Sitzung zugrunde liegen.

15.4 Projekt-Planung

Die erste zentrale Aufgabe nach dem Projekt-Start ist die konkrete („operative") Planung, wie man das Projekt realisieren will. Dazu gilt es, ausgehend von den Anforderungen, die der Auftraggeber stellt, die Planung des Produkts, der Abwicklung des Projekts und der Kosten vorzunehmen. Alle diesbezüglichen Arbeiten münden in einer umfassenden Planungsdokumentation, für die sich in vielen Bereichen der Begriff des „Pflichtenhefts" eingebürgert hat.

15.4.1 Anforderungen des Auftraggebers: Lastenheft

Das **Lastenheft** wird vom Auftraggeber erstellt und umfasst die Zielsetzung, die Aufgabenstellung und alle **Eckdaten des Projekts**. Es zeigt den Ist-Zustand auf und erläutert den Soll-Zustand, wie er aus Sicht des Auftraggebers erreicht werden soll. Im Lastenheft sollen die Ziele klar definiert werden, es soll vollständig sein und eine gute Grundlage für den Auftragnehmer und das Projekt-Team sein, alle konkreten weiteren Vorgehensschritte auszuarbeiten.

❶ Hinzuweisen ist darauf, dass nicht in jedem Bereich der Medienprojekte der Begriff **Lastenheft** und auch der an anderer Stelle erklärte Begriff des **Pflichtenhefts** gebräuchlich ist. Stark verwendet werden sie bei technischen Projekten und in der Software-Entwicklung.

Die Erstellung des Lastenhefts steht im engen Zusammenhang mit dem in der Startphase besonders relevanten Briefing-Vorgangs. Vereinfachend kann man sagen, dass das Dokument, wie es im Prozess des **Briefing** und **Re-Briefing** zwischen Auftraggeber und Auftragnehmer entsteht, als Lastenheft bezeichnet werden kann ❶. Ein Lastenheft sollte die folgende **Gliederung** aufweisen:

- Aufgabenstellung
- Charakteristik des Unternehmens
- Beschreibung der Ausgangssituation (Ist-Zustand)
- Beschreibung der Aufgabenstellung (Soll-Zustand)
- Anforderungen an den Projektablauf
- Allgemeine Hinweise
- Anlagen

Aus dem Lastenheft entwickelt der Auftragnehmer das Pflichtenheft.

15.4.2 Produkt-Planung

Ziel von Medienprojekten ist es, ein Produkt zu erstellen, das eine Lösung für eine Kommunikationsaufgabe darstellt. Besonders deutlich wird dies bei einer Werbekampagne, bei einem Imagefilm oder bei einem Medien-Event, aber etwa auch bei Kinofilmproduktionen, mit denen Investoren eine Kapitalisierung am Markt erzielen wollen.

Der strategische Ausgangspunkt des Planungsprozesses ist daher die genaue Planung und Beschreibung des im Projekt herzustellenden **Produkts**. Dieses Produkt muss genau beschrieben und charakterisiert werden, um einen „Bauplan" bzw. eine „Konstruktionszeichnung" zu besitzen, nach der die Realisierung des Projekts ablaufen kann. Generell wird dieser Bauplan als „Produktbeschreibung" bzw. „Leistungsbeschreibung" bezeichnet, aber auch andere Begriffe sind gebräuchlich, so in der Filmproduktion der Begriff der „Stoffentwicklung".

Beispiel Stoffentwicklung in der Kinofilmproduktion

Bei einem Filmprojekt ist die Stoffentwicklung Ausgangspunkt für alle weiteren Realisationsschritte. Grundsätzlich kann der **Projektablauf** in **vier Phasen** gegliedert werden (vgl. Clevé 2004):

- Stoffentwicklung
- Packaging
- Vorproduktion, Produktion, Postproduktion
- Verwertung

Ziel der **Stoffentwicklung** ist es, ein Drehbuch „auf den Tisch zu bringen", das man ganz konkret filmisch umsetzen kann und auf dessen Basis man die konkrete, detaillierte Kalkulation erstellen kann. Bevor es dieses Drehbuch nicht gibt, können diese Schritte nicht unternommen werden.

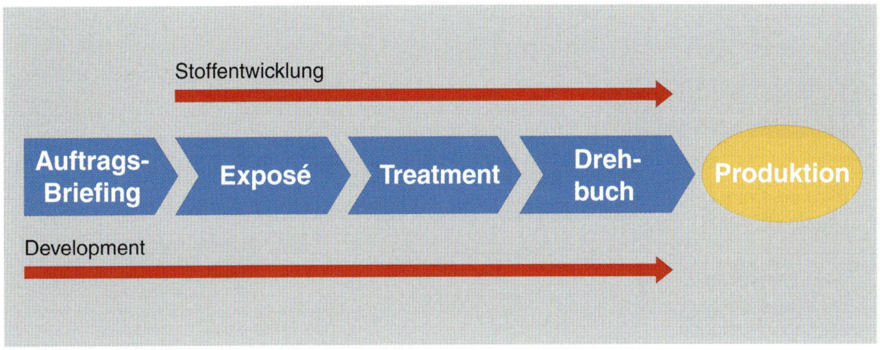

Die Stoffentwicklung, die im größeren Zusammenhang des „Development" steht, hat als Ausgangpunkt das (in welcher Form auch immer vorliegende) Briefing des Auftraggebers. Dort ist die Idee, die verfolgt werden soll, bereits so weit präzisiert, dass man sie weiterentwickeln kann. Dies geschieht in Form einer logischen Abfolge der permanenten Konkretisierung bzw. **Spezifikation** des Inhalts mit den **drei Schritten**:

- **Exposé:** Damit wird in der Filmproduktion eine umgangssprachliche Darstellung der Idee bezeichnet, die auf ein bis drei Seiten dargestellt ist. Beschrieben wird, um was es geht, welche Handlung mit welchen Akteuren gespielt wird, wann und wo diese ablaufen soll.
- **Treatment:** Im Exposé ist der fertige Film noch nicht vor dem inneren Auge erkennbar, da dieses noch nicht so detailliert und konkret den Inhalt beschreibt. Diese Aufgabe übernimmt das zumeist ca. 20- bis 40-seitige Treatment. Hierin werden die Akteure sehr detailliert und lebendig geschildert und der Handlungsablauf wird bereits ganz konkret beschrieben.
- **Drehbuch:** Aus dem Treatment wird nun das Drehbuch als konkrete Umsetzungsanleitung entwickelt. Als typische Faustregel gilt, dass eine Seite Drehbuch etwa eine Minute Spielfilm abbildet, was bedeutet, dass ein Drehbuch zumeist zwischen 90 und 120 Seiten umfasst ❶. Erfährt das Drehbuch eine bildhafte Darstellung (Visualisierung durch Zeichnungen), wie es vor allem beim Werbefilm üblich ist, spricht man vom „Storyboard".

❶ Der Begriff **Drehbuch** ist auch über den Bereich der Filmproduktion hinaus gebräuchlich, so auch z. B. in der Multimedia-Produktion.

Beispiel Leistungsbeschreibung bei Web-Projekten

Bei einem Web-Projekt entsteht die Beschreibung der Leistung ähnlich wie beim Film und durchläuft die Phasen der Spezifikation von der ersten Idee bis zur umsetzungsfähigen Produktionsvorlage, dem „Drehbuch". Was die Leistungsbeschreibung im engeren Sinne betrifft, kann man nach drei Aspekten unterscheiden, die als das „Magische Dreieck eines Web-Konzepts" bezeichnet werden kann (vgl. Lettau 2000, S. 47 ff.):

- Informationsarchitektur
- Navigationsarchitektur
- Screendesign

Die **Informationsarchitektur** repräsentiert dabei den Inhalt im eigentlichen Sinne. Als „goldene Regel" für Web-Auftritte kann dabei eine Trennung in einen Inhaltsblock, einen Kommunikationsblock und in Online-Mehrwerte („Add-Ons") gelten:

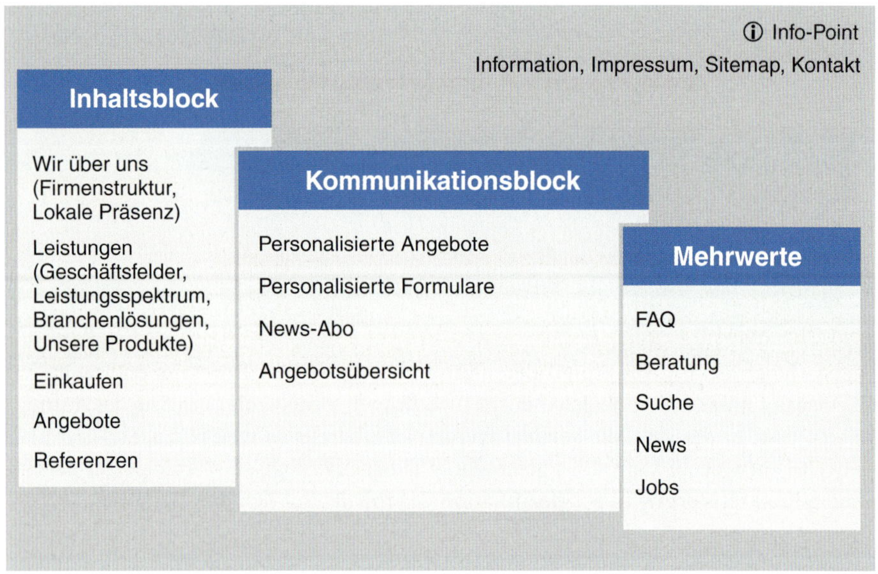

Bei der **Navigationsarchitektur** geht es darum, dem User eine schnelle und übersichtliche Informationsaufnahme zu ermöglichen und ihn konsequent mit möglichst wenigen Mausklicks durch die Anwendung zu führen. Dabei ist die „Usability", d. h. ein hohes Maß an Benutzerfreundlichkeit, von zentraler Bedeutung. Auf den Film übertragen geht es bei der Navigation um die Dramaturgie, im Hinblick auf das Feld von Lern-Software ist die Frage einer guten Didaktik angesprochen.

Das **Screendesign** schließlich betrifft die bestmögliche Gestaltung der Web-Site. Ziel ist es z. B., das Erscheinungsbild des Auftraggebers im Medium Internet gemäß dem offiziellen Corporate Design umzusetzen. Mit Blick auf die Nutzer geht es um deren Ansprüche an ein zeitgemäßes Design, die am besten mit einer „visuellen Provokation" beantwortet werden kann.

15.4.3 Planung der Projektabwicklung: Basisplan

Projektstrukturplan

Am Beginn der konkreten Ablaufplanung des Projekts steht der **Projektstrukturplan**, abgekürzt „PSP". Er ist als überaus wichtiges Planwerk anzusehen, weshalb er auch als „Plan der Pläne" bezeichnet wird. Er dient als Grundlage und Ausgangspunkt für alle weiteren Einzelplanungen. Aufgrund der Komplexität der Zusammenhänge ist es notwendig, dass das gesamte Projekt-Team in die Projektstrukturplanung eingebunden wird und einen übersichtlichen Projektstrukturplan sorgfältig erarbeitet. Es empfiehlt sich, dass das Team hierzu in Klausur geht.

Das Hauptergebnis der Projektplanung ist die Definition der sog. **Arbeitspakete**. Sie sind die kleinsten Einheiten im Projekt und entstehen auf der untersten Stufe des PSP. Auf der Grundlage der Arbeitspakete entwickelt man die Zeit- und Ressourcenplanung.

➲ **Um das Projekt überschaubar zu machen, erarbeitet man den Projektstrukturplan (PSP). Er ist der „Plan der Pläne" und zerlegt die Gesamtaufgabe in überschaubare Einzelaufgaben, die „Arbeitspakete" genannt werden.**

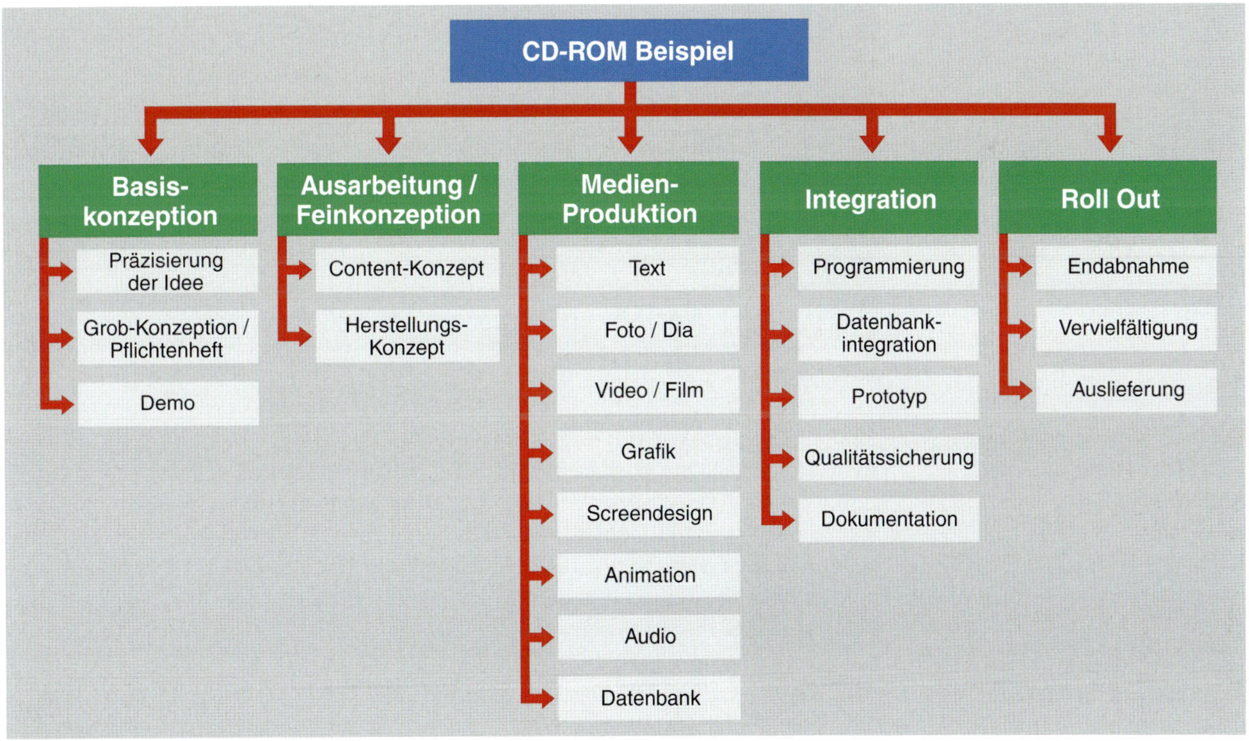

Normalerweise entstehen bei der Projektstrukturierung im Medienbereich zwischen 50 und 150 Arbeitspakete. Die Strukturierung sollte nicht zu tief gehen, damit das Projekt noch überschaubar bleibt. Aber auch ein zu grobes Raster ist andererseits nicht empfehlenswert.

Zeitplanung

Arbeitspakete sind der Ausgangspunkt für alle Planungen im Projekt. Sie sind die kleinsten Planungseinheiten. Jedes „AP" ist sorgfältig zu definieren und erhält eine genaue Beschreibung. Insbesondere ist festzulegen, wieviele Ressourcen notwendig sind und wie lange diese an Zeit benötigen, um es abzuarbeiten. Jedes Arbeitspaket bekommt eine „Visitenkarte":

Ausarbeitung Produktion	
12	2 Tage
Mi 15.03.00	Do 16.03.00

Das Beispiel drückt aus, dass das Arbeitspaket Nr. 12 die „Ausarbeitung der Produktion" ist, dass dafür 2 Tage erforderlich sind, die für den 15. und 16. März eingeplant sind.

Wenn der Projektstrukturplan mit den Arbeitspaketen vorliegt, kann die **Zeitplanung** erarbeitet werden. Bei der Zeitplanung fragt man zunächst danach, welchen Zeitbedarf jedes einzelne Arbeitspaket aufweist. Dazu listet man die Arbeitspakete in einer speziellen Liste auf, der sog. **Tätigkeitsliste**, und gibt an, wie lange sie voraussichtlich brauchen, bis sie abgearbeitet sind.

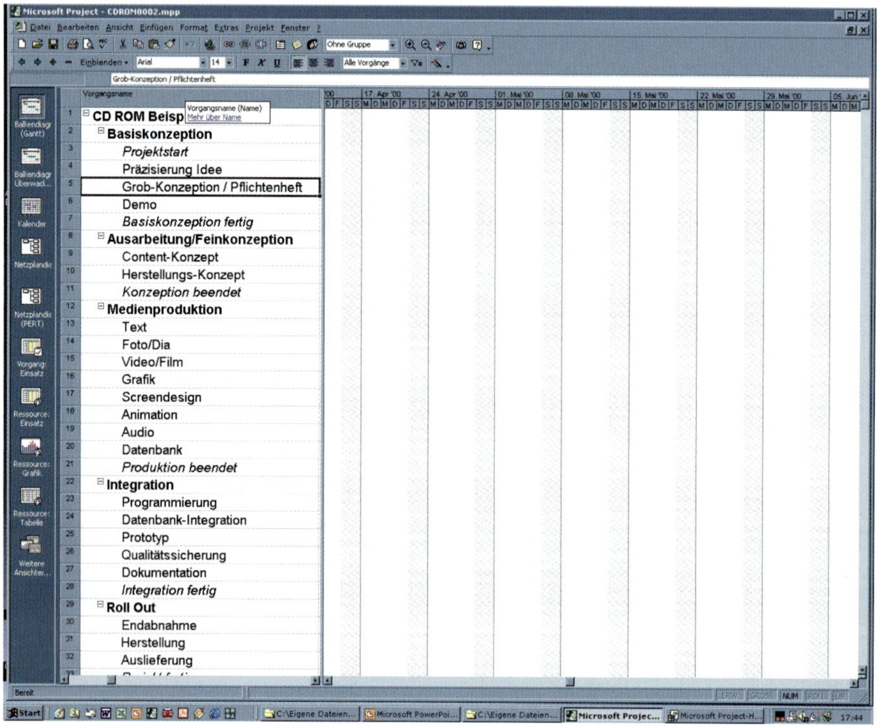

Screenshot MS Project: Tätigkeitsliste

❶ Die Gliederung der Arbeitspakete nach ihrer zeitlichen Abfolge nennt man auch **Projektablaufplan**.

Sind die Arbeitspakete mit ihrer Zeitdauer festgelegt, werden sie nun in eine zeitliche Reihenfolge gebracht ❶. Man überlegt sich, welche Arbeitspakete fertig sein müssen, bevor das nächste Arbeitspaket beginnen kann. Oder umgekehrt: Welche Arbeitspakete können gestartet werden, wenn ein bestimmtes Arbeitspaket erledigt ist? Dabei wird man feststellen, dass manche Arbeitspakete parallel nebeneinander abgearbeitet werden können, während andere es zwingend erfordern, dass ein vorhergehendes Arbeitspaket ❷ abgeschlossen ist.

❷ Ein vorhergehendes Arbeitspaket nennt man **Vorgänger**, ein nachfolgendes **Nachfolger**

Man kann nun die Arbeitspakete auflisten und sehr übersichtliche Darstellungen erzeugen, die für Ordnung im Projekt sorgen. Die entscheidenden Darstellungen sind das **Balkendiagramm** und der **Netzplan**.

Das **Balkendiagramm** ❶ ist ein sehr wirkungsvolles Instrument, um den zeitlichen Umfang der Arbeitspakete und deren logische Verknüpfung bildhaft und übersichtlich darzustellen. Es ist aus den verschiedensten Arbeitsgebieten bekannt, z. B. zur Darstellung von Dienstplänen, Einsatzplänen von Außendienstmitarbeitern oder Urlaubsplänen. Es folgt immer dem nachfolgenden Muster, bei dem die Arbeitspakete untereinander aufgelistet werden und deren zeitliche Länge horizontal sichtbar gemacht werden:

❶ Das Balkendiagramm wird nach seinem Erfinder auch **Gantt-Diagramm** genannt.

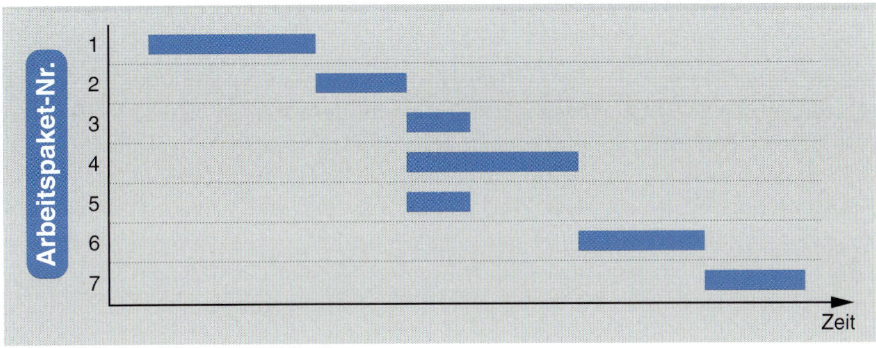

In MS-Project sieht das Balkendiagramm wie folgt aus, wobei die Arbeitspakete durch Pfeile miteinander verknüpft sind:

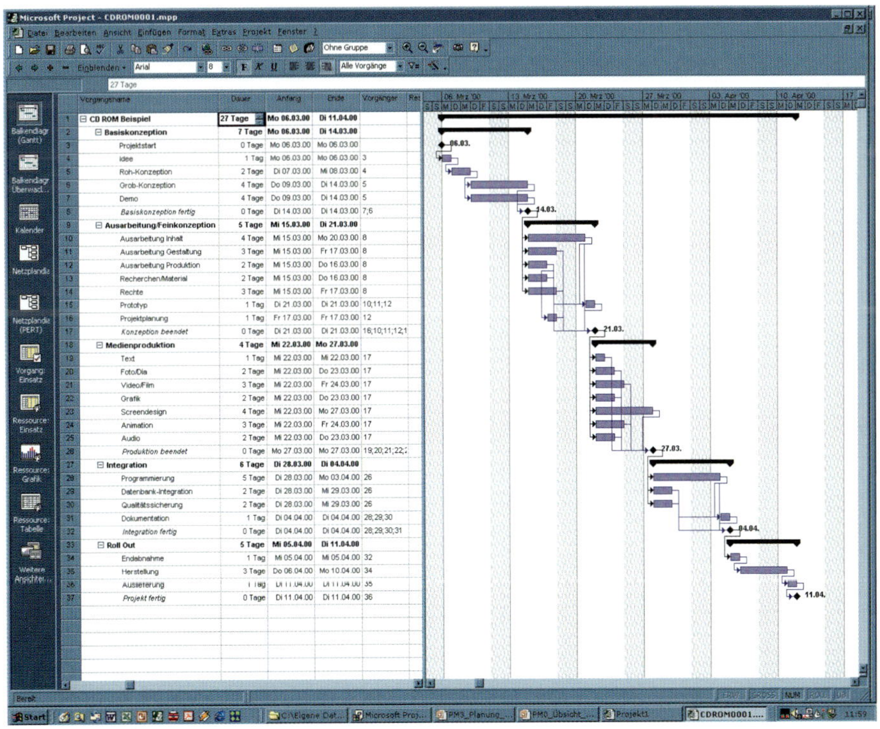

♦ Symbol für einen **Meilenstein**. Ein Meilenstein ist ein wichtiges Etappenziel im Projekt.

Grundsätzlich gibt es die folgenden Möglichkeiten der Verknüpfung:

- Die Arbeitspakete werden linear nacheinander abgearbeitet. Ein nachfolgende Arbeitspaket kann also nur starten, wenn das vorhergehende fertig gestellt ist. So muss z. B. die grafische Konzeption für einen Internet-Auftritt vorliegen, bevor man an die Ausarbeitung gehen kann.
- Arbeitspakete können auch parallel zueinander abgearbeitet werden, beispielsweise bei einer Multimediaproduktion, wenn das Foto-Shooting und die Erstellung des Screendesign zeitlich nebeneinander realisiert werden können.

❶ Dies ist allerdings nicht unbegrenzt, sondern nur innerhalb der gegebenen Voraussetzungen möglich.

Bei der parallelen Bearbeitung von Arbeitspaketen entstehen, sofern diese eine unterschiedlich lange Bearbeitungszeit erfordern, sog. **Pufferzeiten**. Besitzt ein Arbeitspaket eine gewisse Pufferzeit, kann der Startzeitpunkt desselben variabel gehalten werden, d. h. es muss nicht unbedingt zum frühest möglichen Zeitpunkt beginnen, sondern kann auch noch später starten ❶, ohne den ins Auge gefassten Endtermin des Projekts zu gefährden. Ausreichende Pufferzeiten senken das Risiko, von der Dynamik des Projekts in kritischen Phasen „überrollt" zu werden. Sie sind ein wichtiges Instrument, um innerhalb des Projekts ein wirkungsvolles Risikomanagement zu betreiben.

Das Balkendiagramm sorgt für eine übersichtliche Darstellung der geplanten Abfolge aller Arbeitspakete. Innerhalb dieses Beziehungsgeflechts gibt es eine Aneinanderreihung von Arbeitspaketen, die keinerlei Pufferzeit aufweisen. Diese spezielle Abfolge dieser Arbeitspakete – im nachfolgenden Screenshot von MS Project rot markiert – bezeichnet man auch als den **kritischen Pfad**.

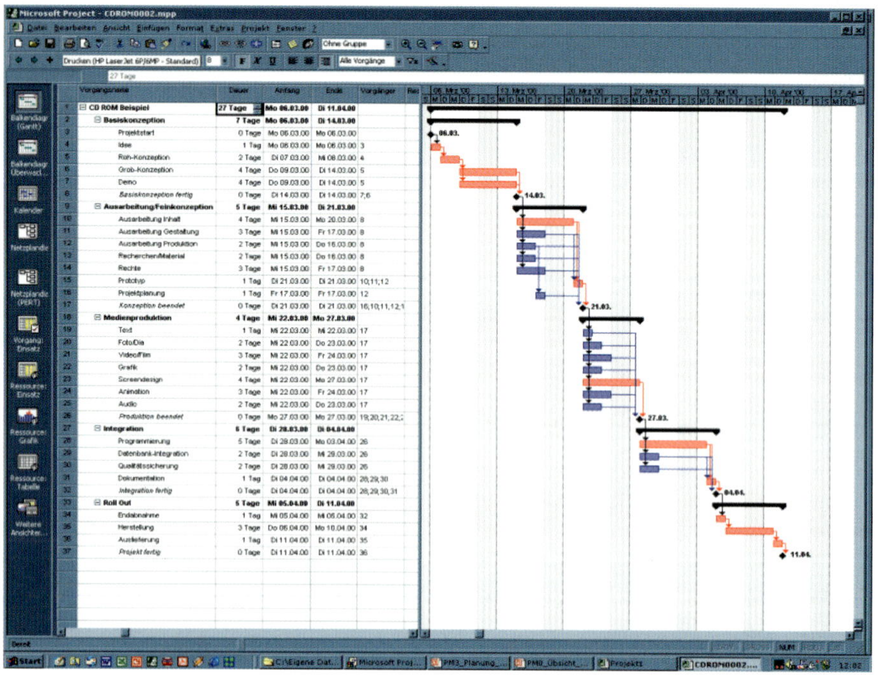

Screenshot MS Project: Kritischer Pfad

Der kritische Pfad wird deshalb als „kritisch“ bezeichnet, weil er alle diejenigen Arbeitspakete markiert, die zeitlich gesehen als kritisch einzustufen sind, denn eine Verzögerung bei diesen Arbeitspaketen führt unweigerlich zu einem Zeitverzug des ganzen Projekts. Ein solcher Zeitverzug ist aber in der Regel nicht hinnehmbar, steht doch bei einem Medienprojekt z. B. ein Messetermin, ein Ausstrahlungstermin oder der Start einer Kampagne zur Realisierung an ❶.

❶ Rein rechnerisch gilt: Die Summe der Pufferzeiten auf dem kritischen Pfad ist gleich Null.

Ein weiteres zentrales Hilfsmittel für die wirkungsvolle Projektplanung ist der sog. **Netzplan**. Er ist eine andere Art der Darstellung desselben Sachverhalts und insofern die „Kehrseite“ des Balkendiagramms. Im Netzplan werden die Arbeitspakete nicht als (liegende) Balken, sondern als Rechtecke dargestellt ❷.

❷ Der Begriff **Netzplan** leitet sich daraus ab, dass die Arbeitspakete durch Pfeile miteinander verknüpft („vernetzt“) werden und damit eine anschauliche Übersicht über den gesamten Projektablauf entsteht.

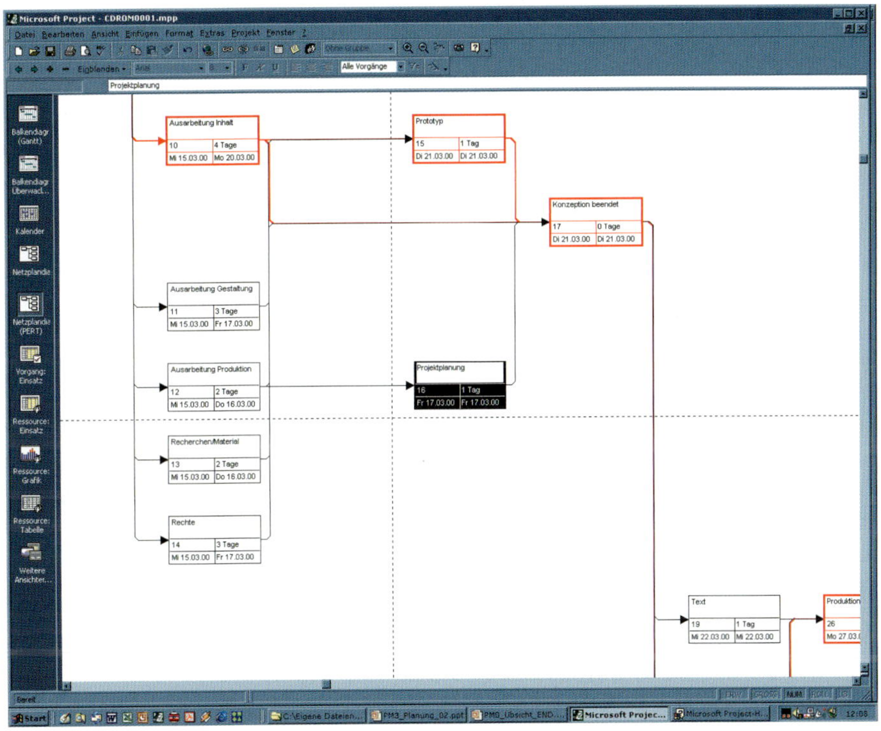

Screenshot MS Project: Netzplan

Der **Netzplan** ist eine optische Verknüpfung der Arbeitspakete. Er zeigt die logische Abfolge der Arbeitspakete (=Vernetzung) und den Typ der Arbeitspakete: Schwarz: „normale" Arbeitspakete rot: kritische Arbeitspakete. Bei letzteren darf kein Zeitverzug eintreten, ohne den Fertigstellungstermin des Projekts zu gefährden. Alle kritischen Arbeitspakete zusammengenommen bilden den sog. „Kritischen Pfad".

Bei der Erstellung eines Balkendiagramms bzw. Netzplans muss man sich fragen, nach welcher Methode man vorgehen will. Zur Auswahl steht die sogenannte Vorwärtsterminierung und die sog. Rückwärtsterminierung. Bei der **Vorwärtsterminierung** plant man die Arbeitspakete vom heutigen Zeitpunkt aus nach vorne, bei der **Rückwärtsterminierung** von einem definierten Endzeitpunkt aus rückwärts in die Gegenwart. In der Praxis kommt der Rückwärtsterminierung die größere Bedeutung zu, da in aller Regel feste Termine gegenüber dem Auftraggeber eingehalten werden müssen.

Ressourcenplanung

Im nächsten Schritt der Planungen überprüft man jedes einzelne Arbeitspaket darauf hin, welche Ressourcen notwendig sind, um es termingerecht fertig zu stellen. Unter Ressourcen versteht man alle Hilfsmittel, die zur Durchführung des Projekts erforderlich sind. Es gibt **zwei Typen von Ressourcen**:

- Personalressourcen, z. B. die geleisteten Arbeitsstunden des Programmierers oder des Projektleiters
- Sachressourcen, z. B. der Verbrauch an Material oder die Nutzungszeit eines Videostudios

Im Hinblick auf diese beiden Ressourcentypen werden die Arbeitspakete hinterfragt und der notwendige Ressourceneinsatz dokumentiert. Das Arbeitspaket „Prototyp erstellen" erfordert beispielsweise den Einsatz von vier Personen, die drei Tage tätig sind und in dieser Zeit entsprechende Computereinrichtungen nutzen.

Arbeitspakete spielen schließlich auch für die **Kostenplanung** eine wichtige Rolle. Wenn man den Bedarf an Ressourcen für das einzelne Arbeitspaket kennt, kann man diese mit Preisen versehen und den Ressourcenverbrauch bewerten. Man erhält dann die Kosten der Arbeitspakete, die eine wichtige Information für die Ermittlung der Gesamtkosten des Projekts sind.

15.4.4 Kostenplanung und Budget

Unter „Kosten" versteht man den Verbrauch an Ressourcen, bewertet in Geld. Die **Kostenplanung** schließt sich insofern direkt an die Planung der Ressourcen an, indem sie die im Projekt eingesetzten Ressourcen mit ihren Preisen bewertet. Aus Sicht des Projektmanagements bekommt man hierdurch einen Überblick, was die einzelnen Arbeitspakete kosten und wie sie sich diese sog. **Arbeitspaketkosten** auf Personal- und Sachressourcen verteilen.

Die Ermittlung der Arbeitspaketkosten ist hilfreich und liefert wertvolle Informationen über Kostenzusammenhänge im Ablauf des Projekts.

Dennoch findet die Kostenermittlung, auch „Kalkulation" genannt, weniger auf der Grundlage der Kategorien und Begriffe des Projektmanagements statt, sondern in einem eigenständigen Vorgang auf der Basis der üblichen Kategorien der **Kalkulation**. Dies ist im Rahmen der sog. **„Zuschlagskalkulation"** zum einen die Ermittlung der direkt dem Produkt zurechenbaren Kosten, die als **„Einzelkosten"** oder „direkte Kosten" bezeichnet werden, zum anderen die Ermittlung der **„Gemeinkosten"** oder „indirekten Kosten", die einem Produkt nur mittelbar zugerechnet werden können. Beide Kostenkategorien ergeben zusammen die sog. **„Selbstkosten"**, die als Grundlage für den Gewinnzuschlag dienen. Neben der Zuschlagskalkulation spielen im Medienbereich auch Teilkostenrechnungen eine große Rolle, bei denen der **Deckungsbeitrag** von Produkten ermittelt wird.

Wegen der großen Bedeutung der Kalkulation wird diese Thematik in einem gesonderten Kapitel dargestellt.

15.4.5 Dokumentation der Projekt-Planung: Pflichtenheft

Ein **Pflichtenheft** ist ein Dokument, in dem alle Punkte beschrieben sind, die für das Projekt wichtig sind. Es wird gelegentlich als „Gebetsbuch“ für das Projekt bezeichnet. Damit Auftraggeber und Auftragnehmer genau wissen, was bei dem ins Auge gefassten Projekt alles auf sie zukommt, „schreiben sie ihre Pflichten in ein Heft“ und haben so eine klare Vorstellung über die Aufgaben, die zu erledigen sind. Das Pflichtenheft ist der sichtbare Ausdruck für die Basiskonzeption des Projekts. Es ist ein absolutes Schlüsseldokument und sollte bei keinem Medienprojekt fehlen. Es verankert alle wichtigen Grund-Entscheidungen und ist sozusagen der „Grundriss“ für das Projekt. Ein Pflichtenheft sollte die folgenden **Bestandteile** haben:

- **Ziele:** Die Sach- und Formalziele sind sorgfältig auszuweisen.
- **Inhalte:** Festzulegen ist der Umfang der Anwendung (z. B. Länge des Films, Größe des Lernprogramms ❶), die Struktur der Inhalte (Welche Medienelemente – Text, Audio, Video, Animation, Grafik, Bild – sollen eingesetzt werden?), die Herkunft der Inhalte (Neuproduktion oder Archive), die **Interaktionsstrukturen** ❷, die **Interaktionselemente** ❸, und die Navigation (z. B. beim Film die Dramaturgie, bei Multimedia-Produktionen z. B. Schaltflächen, Platzierung auf dem Screen).
- **Gestaltung:** Festzulegen sind die Grundanforderungen an das Design, festgehalten im Style Guide ❹.
- **Produktion:** Zu dokumentieren ist das anzuwendende Produktionsverfahren, das wiederum von den einzusetzenden Medien abhängig ist. Bei multimedialen Produktionen ist die Wahl der Programmiertools ❺ von besonderer Wichtigkeit.
- **Technik:** Festzulegen ist die technische Plattform, was vor allem die Seite der Nutzung betrifft (z. B. Frage der PC-Ausstattung, bei Film Kinoproduktion oder nur Fernsehen).
- **Ökonomie:** Aufzuführen ist das Budget und seine grobe Aufteilung auf die einzelnen Zwecke (z. B. beim Film die Budgets ❻ für die Rechte, für Hauptdarsteller oder Effekte).
- **Management:** Zu zeigen ist eine grobe Vorstellung über den Projektverlauf (Entwurf Zeitplan, Meilensteine, wichtige Ecktermine).

Ein Pflichtenheft muss nicht in jedem Fall bis in alle Details ausgearbeitet sein. Bei kleineren Projekten bietet es sich an, nur eine einfache („schlanke“) Form des Pflichtenhefts anzufertigen. Für sehr große Projekte wie z. B. die Entwicklung einer Software für den betrieblichen Einsatz benötigt man eine detailliert ausgearbeitete Pflichtenheft-Grundlage. Drei Formen eines Pflichtenhefts kann man daher unterscheiden:

❶ Die Größe eines Lernprogramms kann z. B. in den erforderlichen Lernstunden ausgedrückt werden, die ein normaler Nutzer benötigt, um das ganze Programm durchzuarbeiten.

❷ **Interaktionsstrukturen** unterscheiden sich nach linearer und nicht-linearer Präsentation.

❸ Elemente der **Interaktion** sind vor allem: Klicken, Berührung (Touch) und Sprache (Spracheingabe).

❹ Unter **Style Guide** versteht man die das Dokument, das die gestalterischen Grundlinien der Anwendung festlegt (das „Look and Feel“).

❺ **Programmiertools** sind z. B. Autorenprogramme oder höhere Programmiersprachen.

❻ Ein **Budget** weist die für einen bestimmten Zweck bereitgestellten Mittel aus.

15.5.2 Projekt-Controlling

Was bedeutet Projekt-Controlling?

Unter **Projekt-Controlling** versteht man die Koordination des gesamten Führungssystems eines Projekts unter dem Blickwinkel, eine zielgerichtete Lenkung und Steuerung des Projekts sicherzustellen. Projekt-Controlling sorgt dafür, dass die Steuerung des Projekts „aus einem Guss“ erfolgt, also durchdacht ist, aufeinander abgestimmt und in der richtigen Dimensionierung erfolgt.

Im Fokus steht die Frage, wie man damit umgeht, wenn beim Soll-Ist-Vergleich Abweichungen der Ist-Werte von den Plan-Werten festzustellen sind. Haupt-Betätigungsfeld von Projekt-Controlling ist das **Änderungsmanagement**.

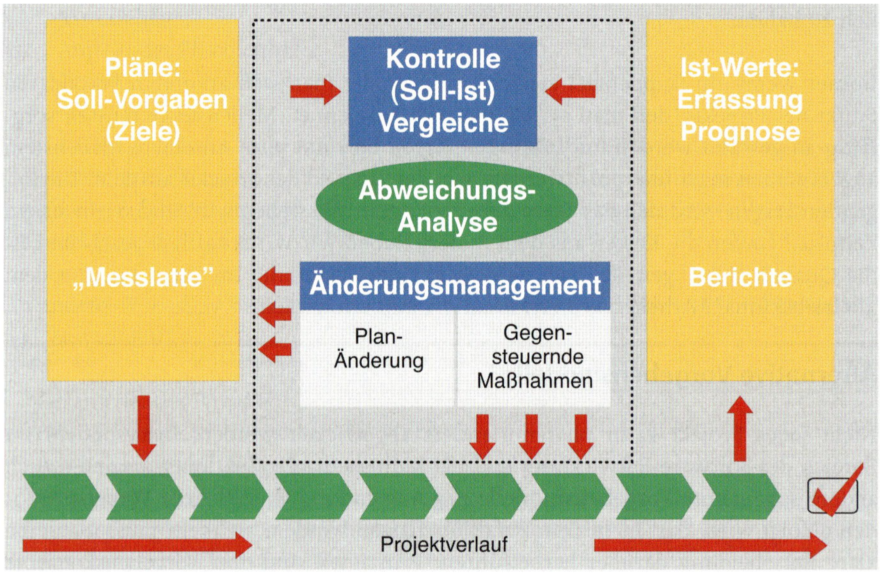

Abweichungen: Change Management

Trotz aller Bemühungen wird es nicht gelingen, den ausgestellten Plan minutiös einzuhalten. Abweichungen vom Plan wird es immer geben, so dass es im Projektverlauf immer wieder notwendig sein wird, Maßnahmen der **Gegensteuerung** zu ergreifen. Für diesen Fall bieten sich die folgenden Ansatzpunkte an:

- Leistung reduzieren: Der ursprünglich geplante Leistungsumfang wird auf das Machbare zurückgeführt, z. B. bei einem Film wird eine komplizierte Szene weggelassen oder nur vereinfachter Form gedreht.
- Aufwand reduzieren: Der Einsatz von Personal- oder Sachressourcen wird herabgesetzt, z. B. durch Ersatz einer ursprünglich vorgesehenen hochkarätigen Besetzung einer Nebenrolle durch einen preiswerteren Schauspieler.

- Kapazität erhöhen: Man setzt mehr Ressourcen ein oder verlängert die Zeit für die Herstellung des Produkts, z. B. durch Verlängerung der Drehzeit oder – wenn ein fixierter Endtermin ins Wanken gerät – durch Anordnung von Überstunden. Bei diesem Punkt kommt es eventuell zu der unliebsamen Erscheinung, dass der Auftraggeber das Projekt nachfinanzieren muss.
- Produktivität erhöhen: Man versucht, die Produktivität ❶ zu erhöhen, z. B. durch bessere Koordination, Umstellung der Pläne oder durch Rationalisierungsmaßnahmen, z. B. indem der Regisseur veranlasst wird, nicht unbedingt die letzte künstlerische Feinheit herauszuarbeiten und dadurch kostbare Zeit und knappes Geld zu „verbraten".

In einem Projekt das Ruder herumreißen zu müssen, kann für alle Beteiligten eine sehr schmerzhafte und konfliktträchtige Angelegenheit sein. An dieser Stelle ist in besonderem Maße das Verhandlungsgeschick und die Führungsstärke des Projektleiters gefordert.

Controlling-Instrumente

Als **Controlling-Instrumente** steht eine Vielzahl von Instrumenten zur Verfügung, angefangen von Instrumenten der Kostenrechnung bis zur „Balanced Scorecard" ❷.

Besonders bekannt geworden ist – als ein sehr einfaches Instrument – die Technik des „grünen Bereichs". Hierbei bilden die beiden besonders wichtigen Kategorien der Kosten und der Zeit die Dimensionen einer Positionierungsmatrix, bei der das innere Feld den grünen Bereich darstellt, in dem es keine Abweichungen vom Plan gibt. Bei geringen Abweichungen rutscht ein Projekt in den gelben Bereich, bei gravierenden Abweichungen in den roten Bereich.

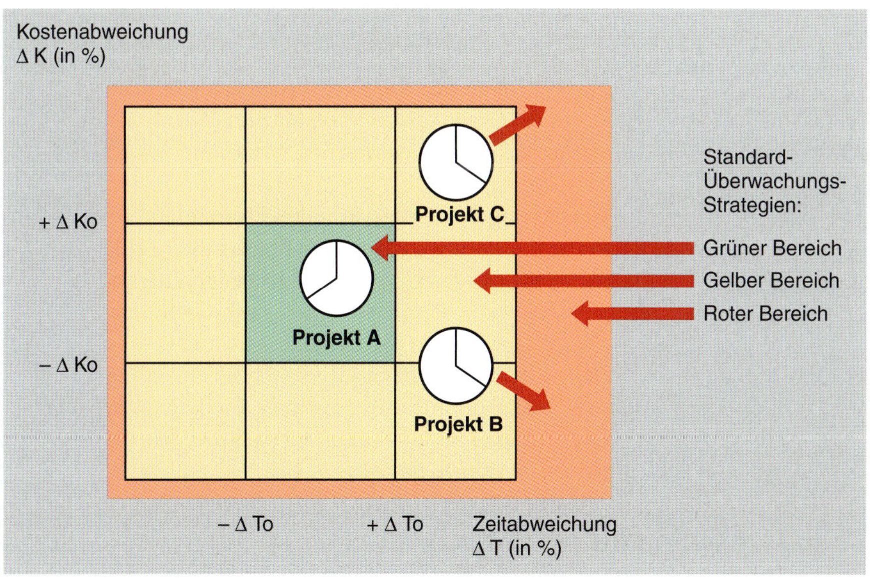

❶ **Produktivität** ist das Verhältnis zwischen dem Ergebnis (Output) und den eingesetzten Mitteln (Input).

❷ Die **Balanced Scorecard** ist ein modernes Führungs- und Controlling-Instrument, welches – im Projektmanagement – die Ausrichtung auf das strategisches Ziel sowohl über finanzielle als auch über nicht-finanzielle Leistungsindikatoren misst und steuert. Die Balanced Scorecard weist vier Dimensionen auf: die Kunden, das Personal, die Prozesse und die Finanzen.

15.6 Projekt-Abschluss

Der Abschluss eines Projekts ist entgegen einer simplen landläufigen Meinung kein einfacher Schlusspunkt, sondern ein vergleichsweise **komplizierter Prozess**. Bei professioneller Vorgehensweise muss das Projekt in mehreren Einzelschritten systematisch „heruntergefahren“ werden, um sämtliche offene administrative und rechtliche Punkte abzuarbeiten.

15.6.1 Abschluss im Hinblick auf den Auftraggeber

10-Stufen-Konzept

Gegenüber dem Auftraggeber bietet sich ein **10-Stufen-Konzept** für den **externen Abschluss** des Projekts an. Es sieht die folgenden Stufen vor:

- Stufe 1: Vor-Abnahme des fertigen Produkts durch den Auftraggeber
- Stufe 2: Nachbesserungen, Überarbeitungen
- Stufe 3: Lieferung aller fehlenden Unterlagen an den Auftraggeber
- Stufe 4: Abschluss-Präsentation mit Abnahme des Produkts vor dem Auftraggeber
- Stufe 5: Abnahme des überarbeiteten Produkts durch den Auftraggeber
- Stufe 6: Schriftliche Dokumentation der Abnahme und deren Übergabe
- Stufe 7: Rückgabe aller relevanten Unterlagen, Datenträger etc.
- Stufe 8: Übergabe der Projekt-Dokumentation (falls beauftragt)
- Stufe 9: Abschließendes Anschreiben mit Dank für Zusammenarbeit etc.
- Stufe 10: Übermittlung der Schlussrechnung

Abnahme des fertig gestellten Produkts

Bei Software- und Multimedia-Produkten ist ein **Abnahmetest** durchzuführen, bei dem Software einem Produkttest unterzogen wird (Funktionstest, Belastbarkeit, Ausfallsicherheit etc.), die Hardware einem Abschlusstest (Leistungsmerkmale, Geräteanschluss etc.) und die Systeme und Anlagen einem Akzeptanztest (Abnahme unter kundenspezifischen Bedingungen).

Empfehlenswert ist die Anfertigung eines **Abnahmetest-Protokolls**, bei dem Fehler erfasst und bewertet werden, eine ausführliche Erläuterung aller Fehler gegeben wird und angegeben wird, welche Maßnahmen zur Ursachenbeseitigung vorzusehen sind.

Nachforderungen an den Auftragnehmer können aufgrund von Fehlerbereinigungen, bei Preiskorrekturen oder Nachbesserungsfristen entstehen. Die wichtigste Anforderung an den Prozessschritt der Abnahme durch den Auftraggeber ist, dass die Produktübergabe in eindeutiger Weise erfolgen muss.

15.6.2 Administrativer Abschluss

Am Projektende sind eine Reihe von administrativen Arbeiten fällig, die sorgfältig erledigt werden müssen, um eventuellen Nachprüfungen und Nachfragen standhalten zu können. Gefordert ist eine saubere Archivierung aller projektrelevanten Unterlagen. **Zwei Phasen** sind dabei zu unterscheiden (vgl. Klose 1999, S. 168): Phase 1: Sichtung der kompletten Unterlagen (sofort nach der Präsentation); Phase 2: Abschließende Ablage (3-6 Monate nach offiziellem Projektende)

In **Phase 1** fallen die folgenden Abschlussarbeiten an:

- Abschlussrechnung, Information an Rechnungsabteilung
- Schließen des Projektkontos
- Abschlussmeldung
- Rückgabe von ausgeliehenen Unterlagen an Auftraggeber und an Dritte (z. B. Verbände, Institute, Verbände)
- Entsorgung nicht mehr benötigter Unterlagen (z. B. Zweitfassungen, Korrekturexemplaren)
- Vernichtung vertraulicher Unterlagen
- Zentrale Archivierung von Arbeitsunterlagen (z. B. Berichte, Software)
- Aufräumen (z. B. Löschen, Umkopieren, Zusammenfassen) von Dateien auf Projektspeicherplätzen
- Erarbeiten einer Projektdokumentation
- Personalrückführungsplan

Bei **Phase 2** muss beachtet werden:

- Kontrolle, inwieweit Phase 1 komplett durchgeführt wurde
- Aussortieren von Unterlagen, die nicht mehr benötigt werden

15.6.3 Abschlussanalyse

Projektabschlussbericht

Das Ergebnis der Abschlussanalyse ist der **Projektabschlussbericht**. In ihm werden alle wesentlichen Punkte des Projekts noch einmal zusammen gefasst und übersichtlich dargestellt. Die folgenden **Aspekte** sind zu berücksichtigen:

- Skizzierung des Auftrags
- Nachweis der Zielerreichung
- Beschreibung des fertigen Produkts
- Review der Projektplanung
- Statusbericht
- Ausblick
- Statistiken, Übersichten, Auswertungen

Um den Projektabschlussbericht erstellen zu können, sind eine Reihe von **Auswertungen** anzustellen, sowohl fachlich-inhaltlicher Natur als auch betriebswirtschaftlicher. Nachzuweisen ist insbesondere die Zielerreichung, also die Erreichung des Sachziels sowie der Formalziele Termin, Kosten und Qualität.

Erfahrungssicherung

Besondere Beachtung verdient die **Erfahrungssicherung**, die wegen der Aufwändigkeit und Zeitknappheit in der Regel sträflich vernachlässigt wird. Dabei verkennen die Beteiligten den hohen Nutzen, den ein Archiv der gemachten Erfahrungen für die weitere Projektarbeit stiftet. Die folgenden **Aspekte** sind bei der Erfahrungssicherung zu beachten:

- "Projektsteckbrief": Name, Nummer, Kurzbeschreibung, Status, Beginn-Ende, Projektleiter
- Welche Erfahrungsdaten sind besonders wichtig und müssen gesichert werden? Zu berücksichtigen auch „weiche" Faktoren
- Produkt- und Projektmessdaten, z. B. Plan- und Ist-Aufwand des Projekts, Dauer, Kosten, Prozentverteilung nach Phasen, Prozentualer Anteil für Qualitätssicherung, durchschnittliche Mitarbeiterzahl
- Zugrunde gelegte Aufwandsschätzverfahren
- Einflussgrößen: z. B. Enge des Etats, Enge der zur Verfügung stehenden Zeit, Grad der Arbeitsteiligkeit, Komplexität des Produkts, Anzahl externer Schnittstellen
- Kennzahlen, Kennzahlensysteme
- Erfahrungsdatenbanken: Nach technischen und betriebswirtschaftlichen Kriterien

15.6.4 Schluss-Meeting

Ein Schluss-Meeting ist genauso wichtig wie das **Kick-Off-Meeting**. Es beendet „mit Anstand" die meist lange Zeit gemeinsamer Arbeit, bei der dem zwischenmenschlichen Faktor eine hohe Bedeutung zukam. Dies sollte Grund genug sein, um am Ende eines Projekt nicht einfach „auseinander zu rennen", sondern nach einem würdigen Projektabschluss zu suchen. Notwendig ist das **Projektabschluss-Meeting** aber auch aus formalen Gründen, da hier die Entlastung der Verantwortlichen erfolgen muss. Die folgenden **Punkte** sollten im Schluss-Meeting thematisiert werden:

- Zielerreichung und Analyse
- Zufriedenheit des Kunden
- Einschätzung der „weichen Faktoren" (Klima im Team, Zusammenarbeit)
- Konsequenzen für künftige Projekte
- Entlastung von Projektteam und Projektleiter
- Erklärung der offiziellen Auflösung des Projekts

Zu erstellen ist ein **Projektabschlussbericht**, der an die an alle leitenden Projektbeteiligten und an den Auftraggeber verteilt wird. Weiterhin sind Abschlussfestlegungen, die Auflösung der Projektorganisation, eventuell die Überleitung von Personen in andere Funktionen und die Ressourcenauflösung zu vollziehen.

Ganz zum Schluss wird zu prüfen sein, ob die Beteiligten Raum und Kraft fur eine Projektfeier finden, um dem zwischenmenschlichen Faktor Rechnung zu tragen.

Aufgaben und Übungen, Literaturhinweise

Aufgaben und Übungen

1. Entwickeln Sie – überblicksartig – ein Konzept für das Management einer privaten Geburtstagsfeier.
2. Stellen Sie sich als Projekt die Erstellung und den Einsatz eines Imagefilms für Ihre Bildungseinrichtung vor. Nehmen Sie eine Wirtschaftlichkeitsuntersuchung für dieses Projekt in Form einer Nutzen-Kosten-Analyse vor.
3. Wählen Sie aus der aktuellen Fernsehwerbung einen beliebigen TV-Spot aus und stellen Sie Überlegungen an, welche Zielvorstellung die Agentur und der Auftraggeber wohl damit verfolgen.
4. Erstellen Sie eine Liste von Faktoren, die bei der Zusammenarbeit innerhalb eines Teams zu Schwierigkeiten führen können. Gehen Sie von Ihren eigenen Erfahrungen aus und bringen Sie Fallbeispiele zu Papier.
5. Erstellen Sie ein einfaches Pflichtenheft für eine „Media Night", die Ihre Bildungseinrichtung durchführen will.
6. Erstellen Sie eine Tagesordnung für das Kick-Off-Meeting für ein Projekt, bei dem Sie die Projektleitung innehaben.
7. Nehmen Sie Stellung zu der These, der menschliche, d. h. „weiche" Faktor sei für den Erfolg eines Projekts wichtiger als die „harten" Faktoren.

Literaturhinweise

Back, Louis/*Beuttler*, Stefan: Handbuch Briefing, Stuttgart 2003 (Schäffer-Poeschel)

Clevé, Bastian: Gib niemals auf. Filmökonomie in der Praxis. Konstanz 2004 (UVK)

Friedlein, Ashley: Web-Projektmanagement, Heidelberg 2002 (dpunkt.verlag)

Francis, Dave/*Young*, Don: Mehr Erfolg im Team, 5. Aufl., Hamburg 1996 (Windmühle)

Greunke, Uwe: Erfolgreiches Projektmanagement für Neue Medien. Ein Praxisleitfaden, Frankfurt am Main (Deutscher Fachverlag)

Kellner, Hedwig: Ganz nach oben durch Projektmanagement, München 2000 (Hanser)

Keßler, Heinrich/*Winkelhofer*, Georg A.: Projektmanagement, Berlin, Heidelberg, New York 2004 (Springer)

Klose, Burkhard: Projektabwicklung, 3. Aufl., Wien, Frankfurt (Ueberreuter)

Lettau, Claudia: Das Web-Pflichtenheft, Bonn 2000 (MITP-Verlag)

Litke, Hans-Dieter (Hrsg.): Projektmanagement, München, Wien 2005 (Hanser)

Schelle, Heinz: Projekte zum Erfolg führen. Projektmanagement systematisch und kompakt, 6. Aufl., München 2010 (dtv-Taschenbuch 5888)

Schelle, Heinz/*Ottmann*, Roland/*Pfeiffer*, Astrid: ProjektManager, 2. Aufl., Nürnberg 2005, Nachdruck 2007. Mit-Herausgeber: GPM Deutsche Gesellschaft für Projektmanagement e.V.

Schulz-Wimmer, Heinz: Projekte managen. Werkzeuge für effizientes Organisieren, Durchführen und Nachhalten von Projekten, Freiburg i. Br. 2005 (Haufe)

Staehle, Wolfgang H.: Management, 8. Aufl., München 1999 (Vahlen)

Stoyan, Robert (Hrsg.): Management von Webprojekten, 2. Aufl., Berlin, Heidelberg, New York 2007 (Springer)

Winkelhofer, Georg A.: Methoden für Management und Projekte, Berlin, Heidelberg, New York 1997 (Springer)

16 Akquisition und Präsentation

Webcode: C1600

Für weitere Infos zu diesem Kapitel mit dem Smartphone einfach QR-Code scannen oder auf www.medien-verstehen.de den Webcode eingeben.

Ein stets hart umkämpfter Wettbewerb um Marktanteile eines Produktes machen die Präsentation zu einem wichtigen Element, wenn es um die **USP**, die Unique selling proposition ❶, geht. Gerade bei der **Akquisition** ❷ neuer Kundenkreise kommt der spezifischen Präsentation eine wichtige Rolle zu. Wie man eine Präsentation plant, konzipiert und gestaltet sowie in der Praxis einsetzt, soll in diesem Kapitel betrachtet werden.

❶ **USP, Unique Selling Proposition**: Leistungsmerkmal, mit dem sich ein Angebot deutlich vom Wettbewerb abhebt.

❷ **Akquisition**: lat., alle Tätigkeiten von Verkaufsbereichen eines Unternehmens, um neue Kunden und Aufträge zu gewinnen oder weitere Geschäftsabschlüsse mit Altkunden zu tätigen.

16.1 Akquisition

16.1.1 Phasen-Modell der Projekt-Initiierung

Ausgangssituationen:
- Der Auftraggeber (Kunde) ergreift die Initiative und kontaktiert in Eigeninitiative den Auftragnehmer (Anbieter).
- Der Auftragnehmer wird vom Auftraggeber zum Kontakt aufgefordert.
- Der Auftragnehmer betreibt die Kontaktaufnahme von sich aus.

Akquisition

Gerade in den Vertriebs- und Angebotsabteilungen herrschen oft traditionelle Leistungsformen vor: Arbeitsteilung statt Arbeitsintegration, Informationszurückhaltung statt Informationsmarkt. Erfolgreiche Angebote sind stets das Ergebnis differenzierter **Managementprozesse**.

- Erkennen der Kundenanforderungen
- Effiziente Bearbeitung zahlreicher Kontakte
- Erarbeitung des strategisch und operativ richtigen Angebots
- Follow-Up bis zur Auftragsvergabe

Welche Schritte sind zu einer erfolgreichen Akquisition eines Projektauftrages zu gehen? Die folgenden Anhaltspunkte zeigen, dass es methodische Ansätze gibt, um die Erfolgswahrscheinlichkeit der Akquisitionsanstrengungen zu erhöhen

Methoden zur Unterstützung der erfolgreichen Akquisition

„100-10-1-Regel" = von 100 Ansprachen führen 10 zu einem Kontakt, wovon einer zum Erfolg führt.

Phase Vorlauf:
- Durchhaltevermögen aufbauen: „100-10-1-Regel".
- Selektion der eigenen Stärken und Fähigkeiten: Konzentration auf Kernkompetenzen, Unterstützung suchen.
- Branchenkenntnisse nutzen: Konzentration auf die geläufigen Branchen; Standortvorteile prüfen und ausnutzen.
- Adressen von potenziellen Kunden aufbauen: Zugängliche Handbücher nutzen, z. B. RedBox, Medienhandbücher, Nachschlagewerke, Adressverlage, Verbände.
- Persönliche Kontakte aktivieren: Messen, Veranstaltungen, Stammtische.
- Aufbau und Pflege einer Datenbank.

Phase Kontaktaufnahme:
- Erstellung eines individuellen Angebots: Ein individuelles Angebot löst fast immer Kundeninteresse aus!
- Akquisitionsbrief, Akquisitionstelefonat: Regeln der Ansprache beachten
- Persönliches Akquisitionsgespräch: Wichtig! Erster Eindruck („Primacy Effect“)
- Spontane Akquisition

Phase Commitment:
- Vertrauen aufbauen
- Schriftliche Bestätigung bzw. Letter of Intent
- Vertrag, Auftrag

Letter of Intent: Absichtserklärung, mit der eine Vertragspartei das Interesse am Abschluss eines Vertrages mitteilt.

Networking

Im Rahmen der Auftragsakquisition spielen konventionelle Vertriebsaktivitäten wie das Networking bzw. der Aufbau und die Pflege von Geschäftsbeziehungen eine große Rolle. Immer wichtiger werden internetbasierte Formen der Kontaktanbahnung und Auftragsakquisition.

Pitch

Mit dem Begriff „Pitch“ wird die Wettbewerbspräsentation einer (Werbe-) Agentur im Kampf um einen Etat bzw. einen Klienten bezeichnet. Mit „Pitching“ wird in der Medienbranche die Kontaktaufnahme zum Investor und die Präsentation der Idee bezeichnet. Hintergrund ist, dass z. B. eine gute Idee und ein gutes Drehbuch noch keinen guten Film ausmachen. Erforderlich sind Geld und ein Vertrieb.

Bevor die Zusammenarbeit mit einer Agentur beginnt, steht die Frage zur Entscheidung an, wem die Aufgabe anvertraut werden soll. Wettbewerbspräsentationen sind die aufwendigste Form der Agenturauswahl, aber nicht der einzige Weg. Auch große Etats werden durchaus vergeben, indem sich die ausgewählten Agenturen durch andere Formen des Kennenlernens qualifizieren konnten. Entscheidet sich der Auftraggeber aber zu einer Ausschreibung seines Etats durch eine Wettbewerbspräsentation, ist dies für alle Beteiligten mit einem hohen finanziellen und arbeitstechnischen Aufwand verbunden. In langjähriger Praxis haben sich Vorgehensweisen als besonders geeignet herausgestellt, um Wettbewerbspräsentationen für beide Seiten effizient zu gestalten – für den Auftraggeber, der das Risiko einer Fehlentscheidung minimieren will, für die beteiligten Agenturen, die unter fairen und transparenten Bedingungen antreten wollen.

Die GWA-Empfehlungen zur Agenturauswahl haben das Ziel, zu einer erfolgreichen Zusammenarbeit zwischen Kunden und Agenturen beizutragen. Die Agenturverbände in Großbritannien, Irland, Italien, der Niederlande, der Schweiz und Tschechien sowie der europäische Dachverband EACA haben gleichfalls Empfehlungen zur Agenturauswahl veröffentlicht.

Die nachfolgenden Regeln skizzieren den idealtypischen Ablauf einer **Wettbewerbspräsentation**. Die darin enthaltenen Empfehlungen haben sich in vielen Jahren der Praxis bewährt.

1. Es empfiehlt sich für den Werbungtreibenden, neben der Wettbewerbspräsentation die anderen Möglichkeiten der Agenturauswahl sorgfältig zu prüfen. Sie sind möglicherweise der spezifischen Situation angemessener.

2. Entscheidet er sich für eine Wettbewerbspräsentation, ist eine Vorauswahl von maximal zehn Werbeagenturen auf einer „Longlist" empfehlenswert.
3. Durch geeignete Verfahren (zum Beispiel Beratung oder Anhörung) empfiehlt sich die Herausbildung einer „Shortlist" mit höchstens drei bis fünf Agenturen.
4. Mit den Agenturen der Shortlist legt der Werbungtreibende fest, um welche Art der Wettbewerbspräsentation es sich handeln soll.
5. Das Honorar sollte sich für die Präsentation am Leistungsaufwand orientieren. Allen Agenturen sollte das gleiche Honorar gezahlt werden.
6. Die Agentur sollte für die Vorbereitung einer Präsentation mindestens vier Wochen, für eine strategisch/kreative Präsentation möglichst sechs bis acht Wochen Zeit erhalten.
7. Es hat sich bewährt, wenn für die eigentlichen Präsentationen ausreichend Zeit besteht (zwei Stunden pro Agentur) und wenn alle Entscheidungsträger persönlich anwesend sind.
8. Zwischen Werbungtreibenden und Agenturen sollte Vertraulichkeit mit den Daten des Auftraggebers und Nicht-Weitergabe der Nutzungsrechte bei Agenturen, deren Präsentationen nicht akzeptiert werden, vereinbart werden.
9. Es hat sich bewährt, wenn der Werbungtreibende alle beteiligten Agenturen möglichst am gleichen Tag informiert und mit der beauftragten Agentur abstimmt, wer in welcher Weise die Fachpresse informiert.

vgl: http://www.gwa.de/Pitch-Guide.750.0.html

16.1.2 Projekt-Start

Zusammenarbeit zwischen Auftraggeber und Auftragnehmer

Das gute Zusammenspiel von Auftraggeber und Auftragnehmer ist kein Zufallsprodukt, sondern hängt von der Schaffung von Erfolgsvoraussetzungen ab. Ein entscheidender Faktor ist die sog. Prozessevidenz.

Unter **Prozessevidenz** versteht man, welche Vorstellungen sowohl der Auftraggeber als auch der Auftragnehmer über den Verlauf eines Auftrages haben. Entscheidende Faktoren der Prozessevidenz sind das Prozessbewusstsein und die Prozesstransparenz. „Prozessbewusstsein beschreibt die grundsätzliche Erkenntnis einer beteiligten Partei, dass ein Auftrag Beiträge von allen Beteiligten erfordert und interaktiv abläuft. Prozesstransparenz beschreibt den Grad des exakten Wissens über Beiträge und Verläufe im einzelnen."

Defizite der Prozessevidenz können sowohl bei allen Beteiligten vorliegen. Systematisch gesehen ergeben sich die nebenstehenden „Transaktionssituationen" ❶, bei der lediglich Typ IV die reibungslose Zusammenarbeit zwischen Auftraggeber und Auftragnehmer garantiert: Typ I, II und III führen zu Unzufriedenheiten. Mit Engagement gelingt es, die Position von Typ IV zu erreichen.

❶ Ausmaß der Prozessevidenz auf Seiten des Auftraggebers (Nachfragers)

Ausmaß der Prozessevidenz auf Seiten des Auftragnehmers (Anbieters)	niedrig	hoch
niedrig	Typ I „Trial and Error"	Typ II Nachfrager-dominierter Prozess
hoch	Anbieter-dominierter Prozess Typ III	Reibungslose Zusammenarbeit zwischen Anbieter und Nachfrager Typ IV

Ursachen für Kundenunzufriedenheit

- Unbefriedigende Arbeitsergebnisse: Problem kann sein, dass die Agentur überfordert wurde (inhaltlich, kapazitätsmäßig, zeitlich); meistens aber: unzulängliche, unpräzise Aufgabenstellungen; zu große Zurückhaltung der Agentur bei Rückfragen zu den Aufgabenstellungen; fehlende Fähigkeit zum „Nein-Sagen" bei der Agentur.

Gründe für einen Agenturwechsel:
68 % zu wenig Aufmerksamkeit
14 % nicht die gewünschte Leistung erhalten
9 % besserer Preis bei Wettbewerber
5 % persönliche Gründe
4 % Zuliefererkündigung

- Schlechtes Preis-Leistungsverhältnis: zumeist unter dem Gesichtspunkt unbefriedigender Arbeitsergebnisse; oft mangelndes Verständnis des Kunden für die Kostenseite; fehlende Transparenz v. a. im Hinblick auf die Kosten; mangelndes Vertrauen (Gefühl, übervorteilt zu werden); mangelnde Sachkenntnis (Vergleich eines Fotoshootings im Wert von 8.000 Euro, all in all, mit einem 9 × 13 Color-Bild von Noname Fotoservice mit 20 Cent für das Umtauschrecht, wenn verwackelt!)
- Fehlerhafte/zu hohe Abrechnungen: unklare Verträge, festgelegte Leistungen und Honorierungen waren nicht klar dokumentiert; fehlender KVA (Kostenvoranschlag); Änderungen seitens des Kunden wurden nicht dokumentiert
- Mangelnde Transparenz: fehlender „Klartext" über Erwartungen und Möglichkeiten; fehlende Partizipation und Einbindung des Kunden in die Abläufe; mangelhafte Kommunikation
- Unzuverlässigkeiten: sind sowohl auf Kunden- als auch auf Agenturseite zu beklagen
- Mangelnde Chemie zwischen Personen: kein Mut, Personen in verfahrenen Situationen auszutauschen. Erwähnenswert ist ferner die Tatsache, dass nicht selten im vertragsfreien Raum agiert wird.

Erfolgsfaktor Transparenz

Auszug aus: Gläser, Martin (1996): Transparenz zahlt sich aus. Zum Qualitätsmanagement von Medien-Produkten, in: Wolfgang Wunden (Hrsg.): Wahrheit als Medienqualität (Beiträge zur Medienethik, Bd. 3), Frankfurt am Main 1996, S. 231-240:

Vom guten Kontakt zum Kunden lebt das ganze Projekt, – und vor allem der Auftragnehmer. Isoliertes Vorgehen ohne die ständige Rückkoppelung zum Auftraggeber verursacht riskante Sprachverwirrungen und möglicherweise teure Auseinandersetzungen über die Auftragserfüllung, besonders über die nachträgliche Beurteilung der Qualität. Der Kunde ist als entscheidender Ausgangspunkt der Projektarbeit anzusehen, und Qualität ist stets im Spiegel der Kundenwünsche zu definieren. Eine alte Hausregel sagt: „Wahr ist nie, was Sie sagen. Wahr ist immer, was der andere hört. Für ihn nämlich." Insofern steht der (subjektive) kundenzentrierte Qualitätsbegriff klar im Mittelpunkt.

Diesen Sachverhalt zu verinnerlichen, spielt schon deswegen eine große Rolle, weil die Kundenloyalität im allgemeinen drastisch abnimmt. Der moderne anspruchsvolle Kunde fühlt sich immer weniger an ein Produkt, einen Hersteller oder Anbieter gebunden – er verhält sich immer unverhohlener „multioptional". Umso entscheidender ist also dann der Aufbau einer guten und fruchtbaren Beziehung zum Kunden, die vom Geist der Partnerschaft und gegenseitigen Mitteilsamkeit getragen ist. Transparenz in den konstitutiven Bedingungen der Kundenbeziehung wird zum Erfolgsfaktor.

Für den Kunden ist der Kosten-Nutzen-Nachweis seines Auftrages das zentrale Anliegen. Eine durchschnittlich komplexe DVD-ROM kostet heute 50.000,– Euro, und es gibt wenig Chancen, den Preis wesentlich nach unten zu drücken. Schnell gerät man aber in die Zone von 250.000,– Euro, sobald das Vorhaben anspruchsvoller wird, z. B. durch den Einsatz neu produzierter Video-Sequenzen oder aufwendiger 3D-Animationen. Für sein gutes Geld will der Kunde berechtigterweise gute Qualität sehen. Er will sichergestellt wissen, dass er mit seiner DVD-ROM einen hohen Wirkungsgrad bei der Profilierung seiner Produkte oder seines Unternehmens erzielt.

Der gute Kontakt zum Kunden wird sich daher an der Nahtstelle des Leistungs- und Kostennachweises mitentscheiden. Transparenz und ungeschminkte Offenheit, even-

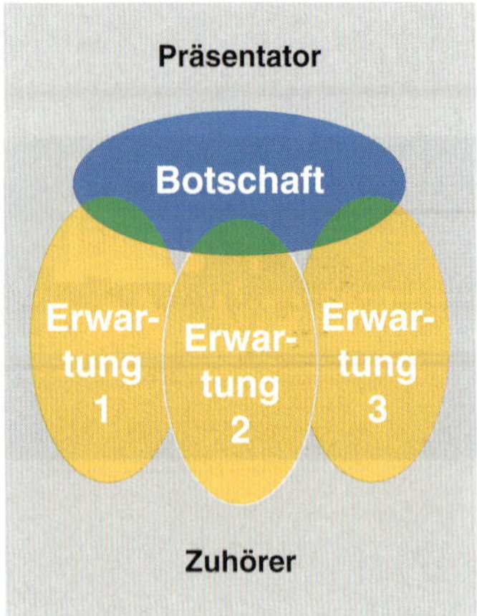

- Wie ist die Zusammensetzung der Gruppe? Ist sie homogen, z. B. nur Entscheider, oder heterogen, z. B. eine Abteilung mit allen Hierarchien?
- Mit welchen Vorkenntnissen und welcher persönlichen Vorbereitung gehen die Zuhörer in die Präsentationsveranstaltung?
- Welche Einstellung bringt der Zuhörer mit zur Veranstaltung? Muss er notgedrungen teilnehmen, weil es Vorgesetzte möchten oder sind es Eigeninteressen?
- Welche fachlichen Erwartungen setzen die Zuhörer in die Präsentation? Ist es die erste Informationsbeschaffung, soll eine Entscheidung getroffen werden, gibt es realen Bedarf an dem Präsentationsgegenstand, welchen Nutzen und welche Wünsche knüpfen die Zuhörer an die Präsentation?
- Welche persönlichen Erwartungen werden an die Präsentation und den Vortragenden gestellt? Bei dieser Frage geht es darum, die richtige Behandlungsweise des Zuhörers und dessen Wertschätzung zu finden sowie die Möglichkeit der aktiven Teilnahme (Interaktion). In diesem Zusammenhang nimmt auch die Seriosität, die Kompetenz und die Glaubwürdigkeit des Vortragenden zu.

16.2.2 Inhalte aufbereiten

In der Vorbereitungsphase zu einer Präsentation werden Ideen, Informationen und Bildmaterial zum Präsentationsthema gesammelt. Die Stoffsammlung kann beispielsweise in die Bereiche Wirtschaft, Technik, Mensch, Organisation und soziales Umfeld untergliedert werden. Je nach Zielgruppe werden die Inhalte auf der Basis der Argumentationsfolge aus den Bereichen zusammengestellt. Da während einer Präsentation davon ausgegangen werden kann, dass die Zuhörer aufgrund ihrer Vorkenntnisse, ihrer Stellung im Unternehmen und ihrer Interessen den Präsentationsgegenstand aus unterschiedlichen Blickwinkeln betrachten werden, muss der Vortragende seine Inhalte so wählen, dass er diesen unterschiedlichen Gesichtspunkten gerecht wird. Beispiele für inhaltliche Zuordnungen:

Wirtschaftliche Inhalte:	Umsatzzahlen, Kostenentwicklung, Gewinn- und Verlustrechnung, Absatzmarktbetrachtungen, Marketingstrategien.
Technische Inhalte:	Betrachtungen zur technischen Umsetzung, wissenschaftliche Untersuchungsergebnisse, Vergleichszahlen ähnlicher Projekte, verfahrenstechnische Gutachten.
Menschliche Inhalte:	Stellt den Menschen in den Mittelpunkt der Betrachtung des Produktes oder der Technologie.
Organisatorische Inhalte:	Stellt die Organisation eines Unternehmens in den Zusammenhang mit dem Präsentationsgegenstand. Dabei stehen beispielsweise Inhalte, die sich mit hierarchischen Strukturen oder der Planung des Produktionsablaufs beschäftigen, im Vordergrund.
Soziale Inhalte:	Aspekte der gesellschaftlichen und sozialen Auswirkung eines Produktes, einer Technologie, sowie die ökologische Wirkungsweise.

Zur besseren Veranschaulichung ist es hilfreich, mit praxisnahen Beispielen und Gegenbeispielen, mit realen Objekten, aber auch mit Zukunftsszenarien zu arbeiten.

Liegen alle Inhalte gesammelt vor, dann werden sie in drei Klassen eingeteilt. Um eine Auswahl für die Präsentation zu treffen, müssen die Inhalte gewichtet werden. Die wichtigsten Inhalte, die unbedingt vermittelt werden müssen, sind die Muss-Inhalte. Darunter sind die Kernkompetenzen des Unternehmens, wichtige Projekte, Produkt- und Leistungsangebote sowie Merkmale eines Produkts und die kundenspezifischen Nutzungsmöglichkeiten zu finden. Werden zusätzliche Beispiele, Gegendarstellungen aber auch Wiederholungen benötigt, dann fallen diese unter die Soll-Inhalte.

Karteikartensystem:
Kennzeichnung der Karten mit
M = Muss-Inhalte
S = Soll-Inhalte
K = Kann-Inhalte

Der Vortragende muss daran denken, dass der Zuhörer nicht mehr als 3 Aspekte gleichzeitig verarbeiten kann!

Lässt der zeitliche Rahmen es zu, dann lassen sich vertiefende Informationen, Beschreibungen technischer Detaillösungen oder auch schmückende Inhalte wie ergänzende Videos oder persönliche Erfahrungsberichte einfließen. Diese Inhalte bezeichnet man als Kann-Inhalte.

Bei der Abfolge der Inhalte ist nicht nur die Frage der Wichtigkeit von Inhalten zu klären, sondern sind auch didaktische Grundprinzipien einzuhalten. Diese didaktischen Abfolgen bieten dem Präsentationsanfänger schon eine gute Möglichkeit der Gliederung seiner Ziele und Inhalte. Jedes Teilziel wird mit einer Wiederholung zusammengefasst und so in sich abgeschlossen. Eine linear verlaufende Präsentation kann nachfolgende didaktische Struktur haben, jeweils von links nach rechts zu lesen.

- motivieren ——— aktivieren ——— informieren
- Überblick ——— Detail
- Bekannte Inhalte ——— Neue Inhalte
- Konkrete Sachverhalte ——— Abstrakte Sachverhalte
- Problematisierung ——— Lösungswege ——— Lösung

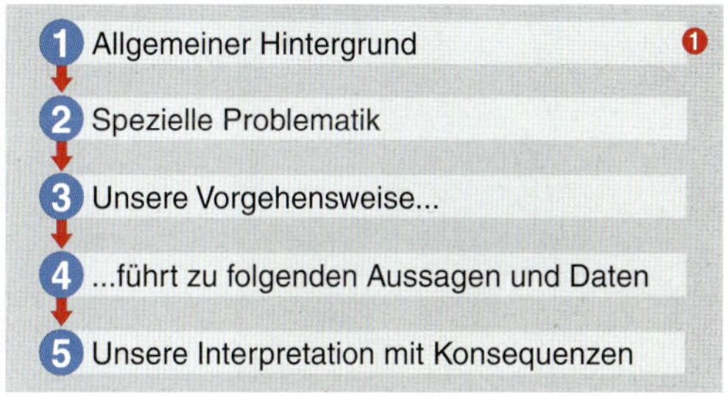

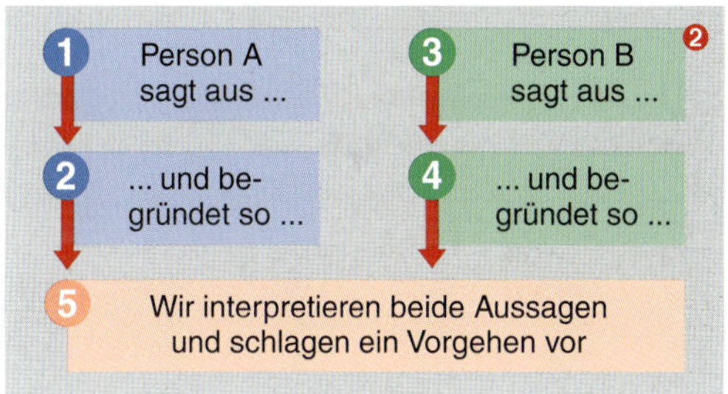

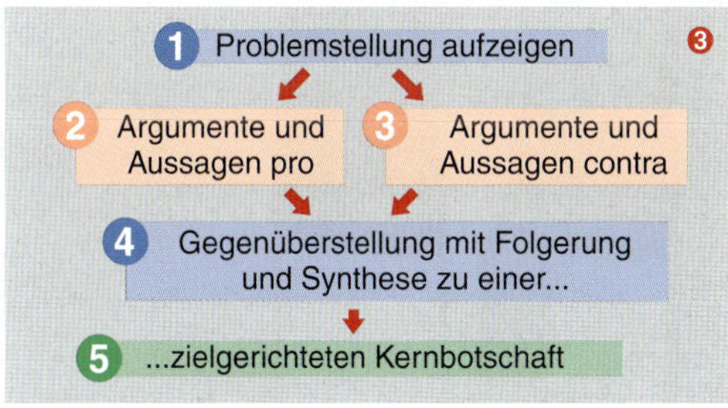

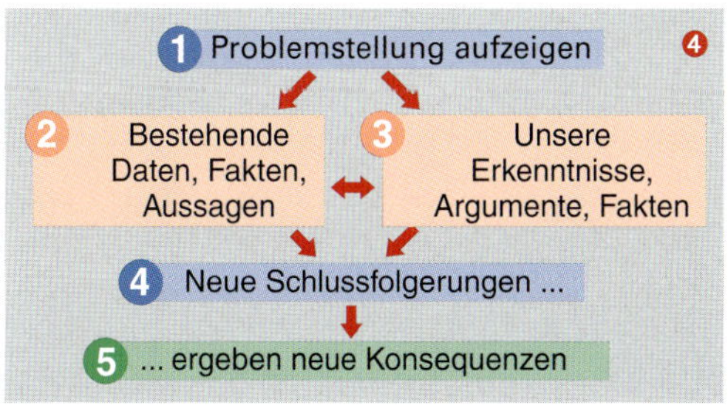

16.2.3 Präsentationen gliedern

Präsentationen bestehen im Grundsatz aus drei Abschnitten, einer Ausgangssituation mit einem Problem, die durch eine motivierende Einleitung aufgebaut wird, einem Hauptteil mit Problemlösungsstrategien und dem Schlussteil mit dem Fixieren der Lösung bzw. der gefundenen Ergebnisse. Der Schluss bleibt erfahrungsgemäß am längsten haften, so dass eine knappe Zusammenfassung, mit den wichtigsten Informationen und der Kernbotschaft, die Präsentation abrundet.

Der Ablauf einer Präsentation lässt sich nach den **Prinzipien des Fünfsatzes** gliedern. Neben dem schon oben angesprochenen Problemlösungsansatz, einem linearen Fünfsatz ❶, kennt man für den Aufbau von Vorträgen und Präsentationen den parallelen ❷, den dialektischen ❸ und den divergierenden ❹ Fünfsatz.

16.3 Durchführen von Präsentationen

16.3.1 Lampenfieber vor dem Auftritt

Präsentatoren werden durch Lampenfieber energiegeladen. Diese Energie wird beim Auftritt in der Bewegung und in der Stimme umgesetzt und abgebaut.

Die Angst vor dem Unbekannten, welche Menschen sitzen da im Saal, verliere ich den Faden, wie wird der Vortrag ankommen, werde ich als Vortragender das Gesicht verlieren, werde ich den Erwartungen nicht gerecht oder verfehle ich meine Präsentationsziele, all das schlägt sich in dem bekannten „Lampenfieber" nieder. Die Reaktion des Menschen auf Ängste und Gefahren ist die Flucht. Diese Fluchtbewegung wird mit einem Energieschub im Körper, durch Ausschütten von Adrenalin, eingeleitet. Nun bedeutet dies für den Vortragenden, dass er diese zusätzlich freiwerdende Energie nutzt, um sie im Vortrag positiv umzusetzen. Energieventile sind dann beispielsweise bildhafte Gesten mit Armen und Händen, die kontrollierte Ortsveränderung und eine kontrastreiche, laute Stimme.

Ungeübte Präsentatoren zeigen in solchen Stresssituationen hektische, unkontrollierte Bewegungen, Redehemmungen und sprachliche Unsicherheiten sowie Konzentrationsmängel. Damit ist ein sicherer und überzeugender Auftritt nicht möglich.

Welche Maßnahmen lassen sich gegen Lampenfieber ergreifen?

- Gewissenhafte Vorbereitung mit Testpräsentationen durchführen.
- Vor der Veranstaltung mit dem Publikum ein paar Worte wechseln.
- Mit einer interaktiven Phase, z. B. Erwartungsabfrage mit Kärtchen, oder Impulsfrage an die Zuhörer, wie „welchen Stellenwert hat die Printwerbung und die Onlinewerbung für die Produktpalette des Unternehmens?"
- Präsentationsgliederung auf der Folie oder am Flipchart entwickeln.
- Schaffen Sie für Ihre Tätigkeit als Vortragender eine positive Einstellung!
- Stehen Sie zu 100 % hinter dem Thema und Ihren Inhalten!
- Zeigen Sie dem Publikum gegenüber ungeteilte Aufmerksamkeit und Wertschätzung!

16.3.2 Körpersprache während des Vortrages

Die Glaubwürdigkeit und Überzeugung hängt stark davon ab, wie der Vortragende auftritt, d. h. wie seine Körpersprache ist, und wie sein äußeres Erscheinungsbild auf den Zuhörer wirkt. Wichtig erscheint, dass der Präsentator erkennt, dass die Zuhörer nicht wegen ihm allein kommen, sondern wegen den Inhalten, die er vermittelt und daneben noch wegen ihm. Das bedeutet, dass er unauffällig, seriös und gepflegt erscheinen sollte. Kleidung, Bewegung, sicherer Stand sowie positive Gestik und Mimik, sollen beim Zuhörer Vertrauen und Offenheit wecken und ihm signalisieren, dass hier ein Mensch vorträgt, der Stärke, Durchsetzungsvermögen und Engagement besitzt.

Der Zuhörer ist sehr sensibel für körperliche Signale, fühlt sich gegängelt, geringschätzig oder oberlehrerhaft behandelt oder kann Gefühle der Angst bekommen. Meist kommt es zu diesen negativen Auswirkungen, wenn der Vortragende die Gestik und Mimik schon im Vorfeld auf die Inhalte abstimmen und an entsprechenden Stellen im Vortrag einsetzen will und dadurch gekünstelt und unflexibel wirkt.

Grundsätzlich ist es besser, ein positives Verhalten und eine positive Körpersprache sich zu eigen zu machen, die man auch im alltäglichen Leben einsetzt. Dadurch wird der Vortragende während seiner Präsentation am Natürlichsten wirken, spontane Gesten und Verhaltensweisen zeigen und dann zum Sympathieträger beim Zuhörer avancieren.

Signale, die positiv wirken:

- Offene Körperhaltung, dem Zuhörer zugewandt.
- Fester, beidbeiniger Stand.
- Arme hängen locker seitlich oder Hände werden vor dem Körper ineinander gelegt.
- Bildhafte Gesten mit den Armen und Händen.
- Langsame, ruhige Bewegungen.
- Freundlicher, offener Blick allen Zuhörern entgegenbringen.
- Gezielte Ortsveränderung mit kontrollierten Bewegungen.
- Pausen während des Sprechens, laute Stimme, langsames Sprechtempo.

Signale, die man vermeiden sollte:

- Hände auf dem Rücken.
- Hände in der Hosentasche.
- Arme vor dem Körper verschränken.
- Schiefe Körperhaltung einnehmen.
- Breitbeinig stehen.
- Zeigefinger hochheben.
- Auf den Zuhörer zeigen.
- Auf den Boden blicken.
- Verstecken hinter einem Pult.

16.3.3 Wirkungsvoll sprechen

Inhalte müssen trotz aller Möglichkeiten der Visualisierung durch Sprache zum Zuhörer gelangen oder angekündigt werden. Aufgrund unterschiedlicher Voraussetzungen bei der Präsentation, große Räume mit viel Hall, Mikrofon und Verstärkeranlage, kleine oder große Zuhörerschaft u. a., muss die Stimme und die Art und Weise des Sprechens abgestimmt werden. Dazu ist es ratsam, vor der Präsentation die Räumlichkeiten zu besichtigen, eine Sprechprobe zu machen und sich über die Zahl der Zuhörer zu informieren.

Daneben sollte sich der Vortragende einige Grundsätze zu Eigen machen und dann seine Sprache in Testvorträgen überprüfen.

- Mit normaler, ruhiger Stimme die Präsentation beginnen.
- Zum ersten wichtigen Inhaltspunkt die Stimme und die Lautstärke verstärken.
- Wechsel der Lautstärke erzeugt Spannung und weckt die Aufmerksamkeit.
- Wichtige Worte im Vortrag betonen und stimmlich hervorheben.
- Wechsel des Sprechtempos erzeugt Dynamik und verhindert Monotonie.
- In wichtigen Passagen langsam und deutlich sprechen, damit die entscheidenden Inhalte nicht verloren gehen.
- Klare Artikulation und nicht „nuscheln".
- Keine Füllwörter wie „äh, mmh, also, dann" verwenden.
- Mit ausreichenden Sprechpausen sprechen, damit das Gesprochene auch verarbeitet werden kann.
- Pausen bieten die Möglichkeit, die Atmung zu kontrollieren und zu normalisieren
- Schnellsprechen und hektisches Formulieren vermeiden.
- Den Zuhörer zu Wort kommen lassen. Das sind aktive, erholende Pausen für den Vortragenden.
- Auf nichtsprachliche Signale der Unruhe, fehlender Blickkontakt, Schläfrigkeit achten und die Lautstärke sowie das Tempo variieren.
- Persönliche Erfahrungen, Zitate oder Wiederholungen lassen sich durch einen Rhythmuswechsel hervorheben.

16.3.4 Zuhörer begeistern

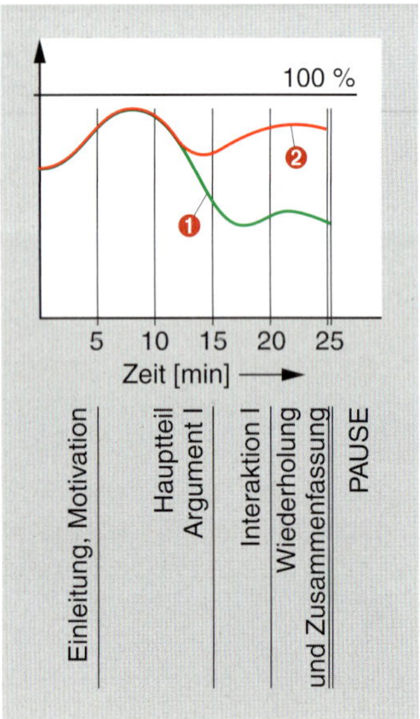

Die Aufmerksamkeit des Zuhörers ist starken Schwankungen unterworfen und muss zunächst geweckt und möglichst lange auf einem hohen Niveau gehalten werden. Wie die Kurve ❶ jedoch zeigt, fällt die Aufmerksamkeit schon nach relativ kurzer Zeit. Dieser Zeitpunkt ist jedoch nicht allgemeingültig und stellt zunächst einen Richtwert dar, der in der Planung der Präsentation berücksichtigt wird. Wie lassen sich diese 25 Minuten Präsentation so einteilen, dass der Abfall der Aufmerksamkeit bestmöglich kompensiert wird? Zunächst einmal erscheinen zwei Teilbereiche einer Präsentation entscheidend, um die Aufmerksamkeit zu steigern. Das ist zum einen die Zusammenfassung, die signalisiert, dass es dem Ende zugeht und die Inhalte abgeschlossen werden. Zum anderen ist es die Interaktion der Zuhörer, das aktive Einbeziehen in die inhaltliche Arbeit. Werden diese beiden Teile geschickt in den Zeitrahmen von 25 Minuten eingebaut, so lässt sich die Aufmerksamkeit wiedergewinnen ❷, gerade in einer Phase, da es stetig „bergab“ geht. Welche Ursachen hat nun die sinkende Aufmerksamkeit?

- Die inhaltliche Umsetzung ist unverständlich oder auch zu komplex.
- Der Vortragende lässt keine Gliederung erkennen.
- Der Nutzen und die Zielsetzung bleiben unklar.
- Der Zuhörer wird mit dem Einsatz der Medien überfordert.
- Die Präsentation ist langweilig und monoton.

Durch eine geeignete Aktivierung des Zuhörers lässt sich die Aufmerksamkeit über den Zeitraum von 25 Minuten weitgehend aufrecht erhalten. Danach benötigt der Rezipient eine Pause, um die gehörten und gesehenen Inhalte zu verarbeiten.

Möglichkeiten, den Zuhörer zu aktivieren:

- Attraktiver Einstieg mit dem Ziel, die Neugier zu wecken und ein erstes Spannungsfeld aufzubauen. Diese Neugier lässt sich mit aktuellen Meldungen aus der Presse, einer amüsanten Geschichte, einer rhetorischen Frage, durch Aufzeigen der Nutzeffekte oder auch durch eine grafische, fotografische oder animierte Darstellung mit entsprechendem Knalleffekt erzeugen.
- Der Vortragende stellt in jeder Phase der Präsentation den Nutzen dar, den der Zuhörer und sein Unternehmen hat, zeigen ihm neue Märkte auf, neue Betätigungsfelder für das Unternehmen u. v. a. Der Vortragende versetzt sich in die Firmensituation und in die Situation des Angestellten.
- Einbeziehen des Zuhörers durch offene Fragen mit den Fragewörtern „wer, wie, welche, was, wodurch, warum“.
- Aus Vorgesprächen Fakten, Wünsche und Fragen aufnehmen und diese im Verlauf der Präsentation einstreuen.
- Der Vortragende bewegt sich gezielt, um die Aufmerksamkeit zu lenken.
- Durch geschickten Medienwechsel von Flipchart auf Computerpräsentation und Video, lassen sich monotone Abläufe vermeiden.
- Der versierte Redner spielt mit Tempo, Lautstärke, Betonung in der Stimme mit Höhen und Tiefen und setzt durch diese Reize Spannungspunkte.
- Gezielt humoristische und geistreiche Geschichten, Anekdoten oder Zitate einbauen, lockert den Ablauf auf.

Anekdoten Beispiele:
Quelle: Puntsch, Eberhard: Das große Buch der Witze, Fabeln und Anekdoten, Esslingen 2000

- Das Fernsehen macht aus dem Kreis der Familie einen Halbkreis.
- Wenn ein Politiker sagt, wir säßen alle in einem Boot, dann heißt das: Er will den Kapitän spielen, und wir sollen rudern.
- Konsequenz = *Heute* so, *morgen* so
  Inkonsequenz = Heute *so*, morgen *so*

16.4 Präsentationen konzipieren und gestalten

16.4.1 Konzeptionelle Aspekte

Bei der Planung der Präsentation sind für die Folien, die Handouts, die Manuskripte und Bildschirmdarstellungen einheitliche Gestaltungsregeln aufzustellen. Das ist gerade dann ein wichtiger Punkt, wenn die Präsentation im Auftrag einer Firma produziert wird. In der Regel geben Firmen ihre Vorgaben in Form eines Style Guides heraus, in dem nähere Angaben zum Corporate Design gemacht werden. Für die eigene Präsentationsplanung ist es sinnvoll, die einzelnen Punkte der Checkliste durchzuarbeiten:

- Größe der Präsentation (Außenmaße)
- Position von Logo und Firmenname
- Position von Folientitel und Untertitel
- Aufteilung der Folie in Textblock, Bildteil
- Navigationssymbole oder -leiste anlegen; verwendete Symbole festlegen
- Position von Kernbotschaften, mit und ohne Hintergrundfarbe
- Farbendefinition
- Schriftdefinition
- Hinweise zur Abfolge einer Präsentation
- Standardfolien mit gleichbleibenden Inhalten für jede Präsentation
- Grafische Elemente zur Gliederung
- Vorgaben für Einsatz von Grafik und Bild im Inhaltsteil
- Angaben im Fußbereich zum Präsentator und Datum
- Position von Kernbotschaften,
- Style Guide mit Farbschemata ❶
- Schriftdefinition
- Hinweise zur Abfolge einer Präsentation
- Standardfolien mit gleichbleibenden Inhalten
- Grafische Elemente zur Gliederung
- Vorgaben für Einsatz von Grafik und Bild im Inhaltsteil
- Angaben im Fußbereich zum Präsentator und Datum

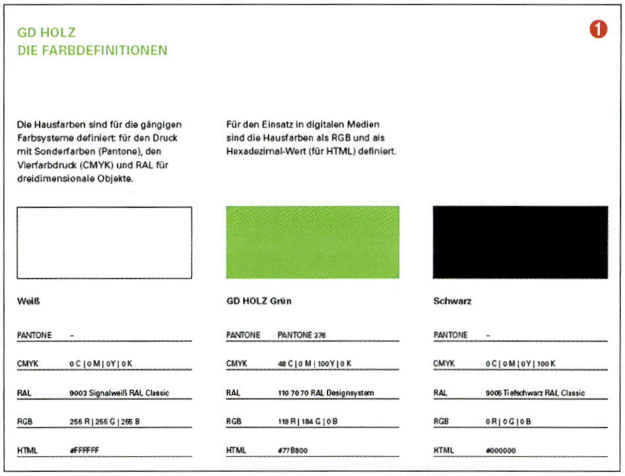

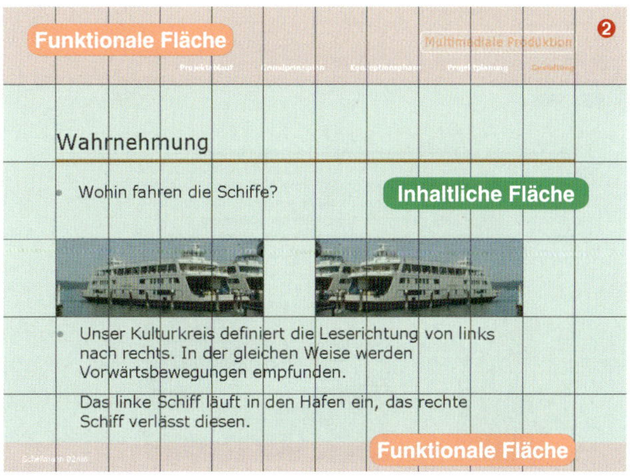

16.4.2 Funktionale und inhaltliche Flächen

Eine Folie teilt sich immer in funktionale und inhaltliche Flächen. Funktionale Flächen ❷ bilden den Rahmen um die Inhalte. Die **funktionale Fläche** nimmt beispielsweise die Schaltflächen (Buttons), Informationen über das „Wo bin ich?“, Titel und Untertitel, Name des Erstellers, Erstellungsdatum, Logo, Name der Firma u. a. auf. Das sind häufig sich wiederholende Informationen in gleicher Form oder wie bei der Seiten- und Kapitelnummerierung kontinuierlich aufbauend. Funktionale Flächen befinden sich immer im Randbereich Kopf-, Fuß- und Seitenränder der Folie. Es werden jedoch in der Praxis nicht alle Randbereiche benötigt.

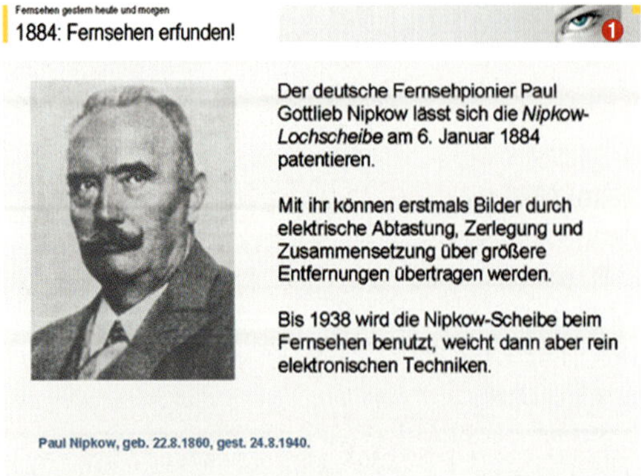

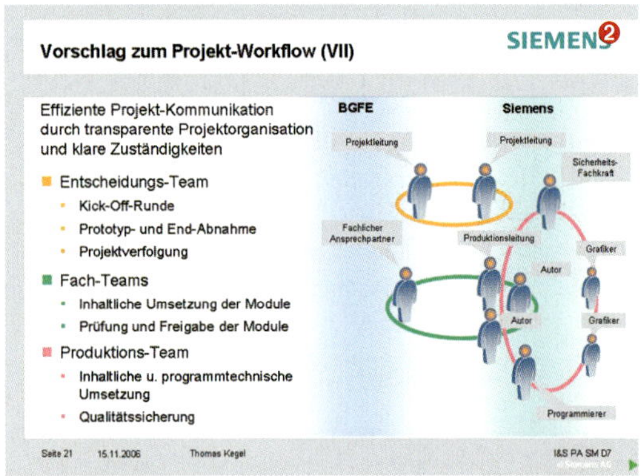

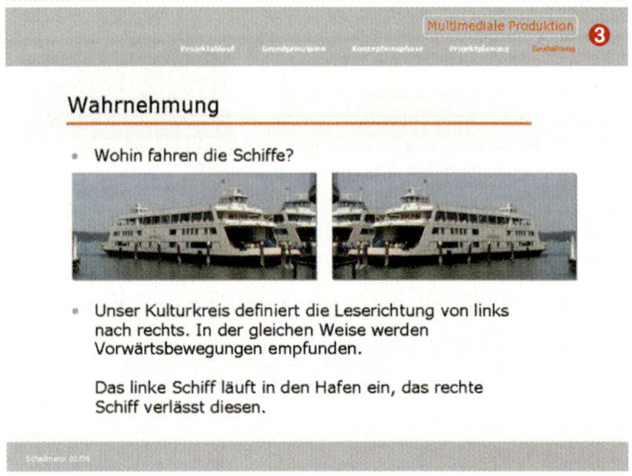

Inhaltliche Flächen stellen den Raum für Texte, Grafiken und Bilder dar, die Informationen zum Thema weitergeben.

Damit die Folien und Bildschirmseiten nach diesen Prinzipien aufgeteilt werden können, behilft man sich mit dem handschriftlichen Entwurf auf einem DIN-A4-Papier. Das Papier wird nach Bedarf mit einem Raster unterteilt, beispielsweise mit einem 6er- oder 12er-Raster mit einer beliebigen Zeilenzahl (Bild ❶, vorh. Seite). Folien sollten immer im Querformat angelegt werden.

Mit der Hilfslinienfunktion grafischer Programme sind solche Raster schnell und einfach umgesetzt. Die einzelnen Inhalte, ob Text, Grafik oder Bild lassen sich so in der Größe besser anpassen und schneller positionieren. Das hat vor allem den Vorteil, dass ein unschönes Merkmal schlampig produzierter Präsentationen nicht vorkommt, nämlich das Springen von Textkanten, Bildkanten und Navigationselementen, wenn von einer Seite zur nächsten Seite weitergeschaltet wird.

Positionierung von Text und Bild auf inhaltlichen Flächen

Wir lesen in unserem Kulturkreis von links nach rechts und nehmen daher auch die Inhalte von Folien und Bildschirmseite auf diese Weise wahr. Dadurch erhält die Anordnung von Text und Bild, von Bildfolgen und Flussdiagrammen eine entsprechende Bedeutung und eine logische Abfolge der Inhalte.

Die Texte werden sparsam eingesetzt, eher stichwortartig und sind bei einer Breite von maximal 60 Zeichen gut lesbar.

Bild links, Text rechts ❶: Das Bild führt auf den Text hin. Das Bild dient vielfach als Eyecatcher, muss auch nicht unbedingt Inhalte transportieren. Die Anordnung kommt häufig bei Auswahlmenüs und Inhaltsübersichten vor.

Text links, Bild rechts ❷: Text umfasst wichtige Inhalte. Das Bild vertieft oder visualisiert die geschriebenen Inhalte.

Bild oben, Text unten ❸: Die Anordnung wird dann benötigt, wenn die Inhalte im Bild einen größeren Platz benötigen. Das Bild hat dabei höhere Priorität.

Text oben, Bild unten ❹: Text dominiert die inhaltliche Umsetzung. Bilder ergänzen die Seite.

16.4.3 Gestalten mit Bild und Text

Die Aufnahme von Informationen gelingt dem Menschen besser, wenn er nicht nur das gesprochene Wort hört, sondern dieses Wort auch bildhaft dargestellt bekommt. Für die Planung der Präsentation bedeutet dies, dass drei Bereiche, Textdarstellung, Vortrag und Bild miteinander verknüpft werden müssen.

Nach einer amerikanischen Studie steigt die Entscheidungsfreudigkeit der Kunden mit dem Einsatz visueller Hilfsmittel. Dies ist nicht zuletzt dadurch begründet, dass ca. 80% der Entscheidungen emotional gefällt werden. Gerade Fotografien und Grafiken sind Übermittler von Emotionen und Stimmungen, die dramaturgisch gekonnt und zur rechten Zeit eingesetzt, die Aufmerksamkeit des Zuhörers wecken und Spannung erzeugen. Aufgrund der Verstärkung des Wortes durch das Bild wird die Behaltensleistung des Menschen gesteigert und Inhalte längerfristig verankert ❶. Im Übrigen wirken Präsentatoren nach Umfragen durch den wechselnden Einsatz der Medien und eine starke Visualisierung kompetenter und glaubwürdiger. Mit Hilfe der Vortragsstruktur lässt sich der Einsatz der Bilder optimal und ausgewogen planen.

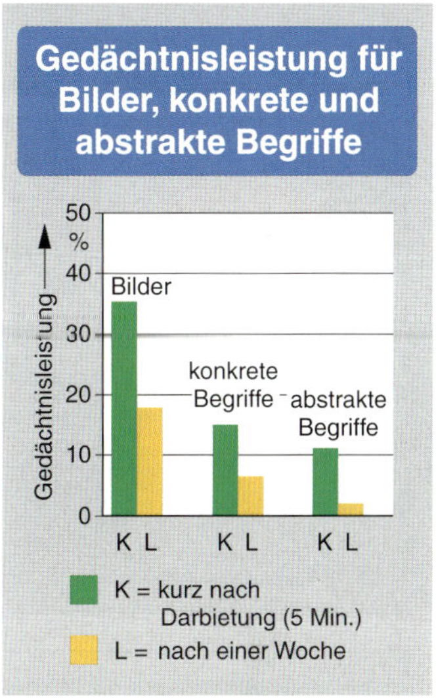

❶ Behaltensleistung (Kroeber-Riel)

Baustein Text

Das Schriftbild einer Präsentation muss vom Betrachter sofort erkannt und gelesen werden können. Auf den meisten Folien ist zum einen zu viel Text und dieser auch mit einer viel zu kleinen Schrift geschrieben. Die Schriftgröße muss der Zuhörer- und der Raumgröße angepasst sein. Es macht schon Unterschiede, ob man in einem Hörsaal oder in einem kleinen Konferenzraum präsentiert. Überladen Sie Ihre Folien nicht mit Texten, sondern reduzieren Sie Ihre Inhalte auf das Wesentliche.

Bedenken Sie beim „Texten", dass Text im Vergleich zum Bild vom Zuhörer sehr schlecht aufgenommen wird. Zunächst setzt man die Texte in einem Textfenster horizontal. Um der Folie mehr Dynamik zu verleihen, kann das Textfenster schräg gestellt werden ❷. Gleichzeitig fügt sich so der Text harmonisch oder auch verstärkend zum Inhalt des Bildes ein.

Werden Texte auf Bildern platziert, so kommt es häufig zu Problemen mit der Lesbarkeit. Das hängt zum einen daran, dass die Buchstaben meist zu dünn (Schriftschnitt regular oder normal) oder auch zu klein sind und sich nicht farblich abheben. Bilder verstärken diesen Effekt durch einen großen Kontrastumfang. Texte müssen dann entweder in flächendeckend dunkle oder helle Bereiche gesetzt oder mit einer farbigen, auch teiltransparenten Fläche ❸ hinterlegt werden.

Farbschemate mit Software erstellen und verteilen:

www.kuler.adobe.com
www.colourlovers.com
www. colourschemer.com

Speichern von Farben:
Plug-in Mondrianum,
www.lithoglyph.com/mondrianum

Baustein Farbe

Mit Farbe können Sie Aufmerksamkeit, Freude, Interesse, Abneigung, u.v.m beim Betrachter auslösen. Farben haben unterschiedliche emotionale Wirkung und sollten deshalb sehr gewissenhaft ausgewählt und eingesetzt werden. Durch Farbe lässt sich einerseits die funktionale von der inhaltlichen Fläche abgrenzen, anderseits wird durch die entsprechende Hintergrundfarbe der Kontrast zu Text und Bild verstärkt.

Hinweise und Regeln:

- Wählen Sie nach Möglichkeit helle oder dunkle Farben für den Hintergrund, keine Mitteltöne.
- Gesättigte Farben in grafischen Elementen, Diagrammen und Schaubildern wirken kräftiger und kontrastreicher.
- Farben können aus einem Farbtonbereich, komplementären Farben oder benachbarten Farben kombiniert werden.
- Bestimmt der Farbwert eines Objekts die Bilder, dann lässt sich diese Farbe in der Schrift und grafischen Elementen ebenfalls sehr anschaulich verwenden.
- Erstellen Sie sich ein Farbschema für Ihre Präsentation.

16.4.4 Gestaltungsprinzipien und Praxishinweise

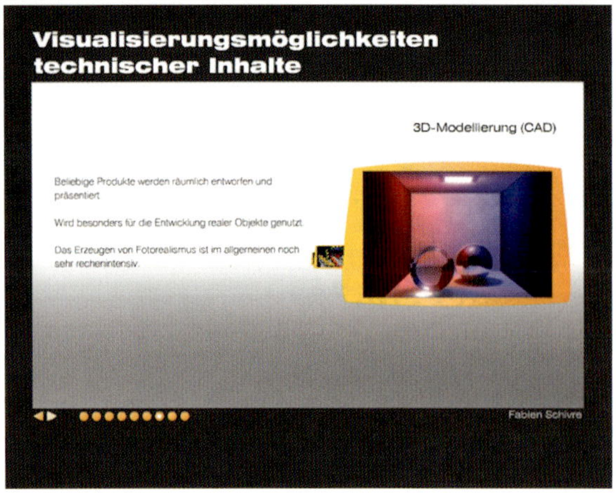

- Um selbst den Überblick zu behalten, geht die Interaktionsstruktur möglichst nicht tiefer als zwei Ebenen.
- Die Inhalte auf das Wesentliche beschränken, wie die Kerninformation, kurze Sätze und Schlagworte.
- Vermeiden Sie überladene Folien. Geben Sie Ihren Folien genügend Weißraum, damit sich Inhalte entfalten können, aber auch gleichzeitig das Auge des Betrachters erholen kann.
- Neben dem allgemeinen Gestaltungsgrundsatz der Symmetrie kommt der Asymmetrie in Präsentationen ein wichtige Rolle zu. Sie erzeugt Spannung, Größe, lässt Bilder über den Präsentationsrahmen hinaus wirken.
- Beachten Sie bei der Gestaltung die anderen Gestaltgesetze wie Gesetz der Prägnanz, Figur-Grund-Differenzierung, u. a. (s. Kapitel Elementares Gestalten)
- Stellen Sie die Schwerpunkte in Ihrer Präsentation deutlich und auffällig heraus.
- Achten Sie darauf, dass der Hintergrund, ob einfarbige Fläche oder Bild, den Inhalt nicht überstrahlt.
- Bauen Sie Schwarzfolien zur Unterbrechung der Computerpräsentation ein, wenn Sie während der Präsentation das Medium, zum Beispiel auf Flip-Chart, wechseln.
- Komplexe Aussagen und Sachverhalte auf mehrere Folien verteilen.
- Arbeiten Sie beim Aufbau der Folie mit einem Raster, im einfachsten Fall mit einem 3 × 3 - Raster.
- Gestalten Sie nach dem Motto: **Weniger ist mehr und übersichtlicher!**

16.5 Medieneinsatz

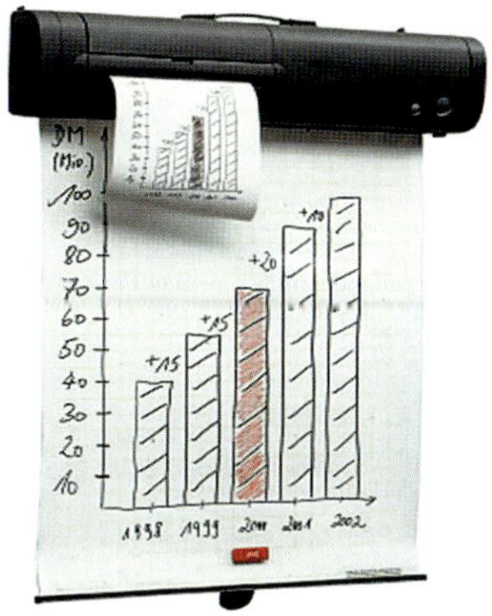

Der Einsatz von Medien soll helfen die Ziele zu erreichen, Aufmerksamkeit zu erzeugen und die wichtigen Informationen im Kopf des Rezipienten zu verankern.

Die unterschiedlichen Medien ermöglichen eine flexible Gestaltung, intensivere Interaktion mit dem Zuhörer, bessere Dokumentation von Aussagen, vielfältige Showeffekte. Die Wahl und der Einsatz entsprechender Medien richtet sich nach der Zielgruppe, nach den räumlichen Voraussetzungen und nach den zu vermittelnden Inhalten sowie nach dem geplanten Ablauf der Präsentation.

16.5.1 Folienpräsentation am Tageslichtprojektor

In allen Konferenzräumen dieser Welt sind Tageslichtprojektoren vorhanden, so dass jederzeit eine bildliche und textliche Darstellung mit Hilfe einer Folie umgesetzt werden kann. Bei kurzen Präsentationen mit geringem Folieneinsatz ist die Overheadprojektion günstiger und schneller als eine Computerpräsentation. Dabei muss man den technischen Aufwand durch den Einsatz von Computer und Beamer betrachten sowie die Vorbereitung der Dateien.

Wann kommt eine Folienpräsentation zum Einsatz?

- Bei Tageslicht sollen Bilder mit guter Qualität projiziert werden.
- Die Reihenfolge der Folien ist von Präsentation zu Präsentation beliebig.
- Bei Zeitproblemen lassen sich einzelne Folien problemlos überspringen.
- Bei Fragen können bestimmte Folien nochmals gezeigt werden.
- Folien lassen sich schriftlich ergänzen und markieren.
- Mit Blankofolien lassen sich Ergebnisse der Interaktion mit dem Zuhörer festhalten.

Vorbereitung von Folienpräsentationen

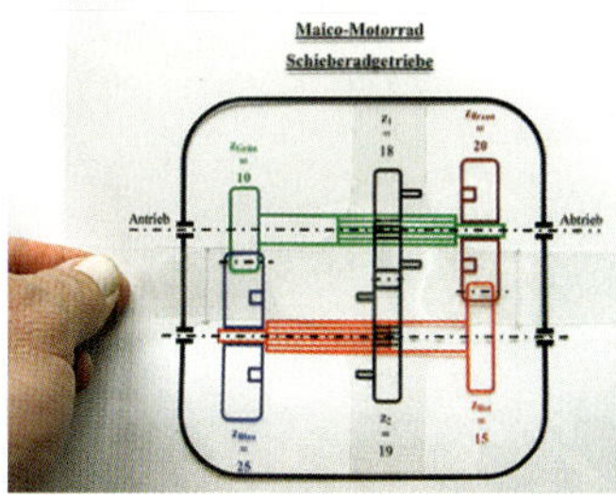

- Folien sollten immer im Querformat beschrieben werden, um die Höhe der Projektion nicht zu überschreiten.
- Glasfläche des Projektors mit einem Folienrahmen aus Pappe versehen. Zum Beschreiben der Folien den Rahmen verwenden. Folien wirken brillanter!
- Die Schrift so groß wählen, dass diese in der letzten Reihe des Präsentationsraumes gut lesbar ist. Schriftproben im Selbsttest prüfen.
- Notwendige Informationen ohne schmückendes Beiwerk liefern.
- Auf Verständlichkeit achten, Folien nicht überfrachten.
- Kernbotschaft deutlich herausstellen und visualisieren.
- Positionen der Leinwand und des Projektors sind meist vorgegeben, so dass die persönlichen Bewegungen sich nach den räumlichen Gegebenheiten richten muss. Vorher eine Raumbesichtigung durchführen!

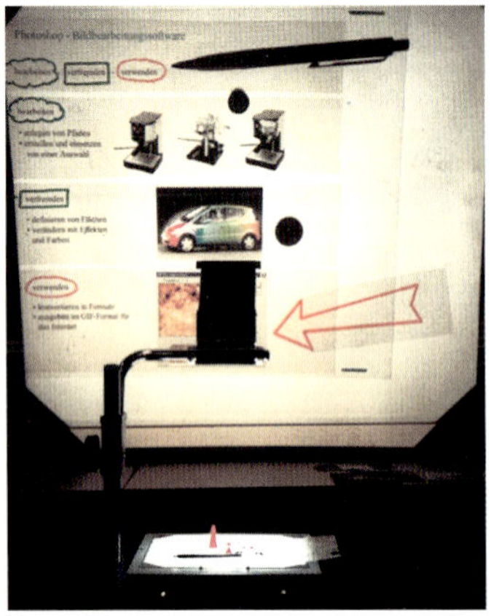

Tipps zur Durchführung

- Projektor zum Folienwechsel abdunkeln oder aus- und einschalten, damit wird die Aufmerksamkeit auf die Projektion gelenkt.
- Nicht im Projektionsstrahl stehen.
- Position neben dem Projektor einnehmen, mit Blickkontakt zum Publikum.
- Raschen Folienwechsel vermeiden, der Zuhörer muss Zeit zur Aufnahme der Informationen haben.
- Als Zeigehilfe einen Kugelschreiber oder eine am besten pfeilförmige, durchsichtige Zeigehilfe verwenden, jedoch nie den Finger.
- Niemals mit Fingern auf die Projektionsfläche zeigen und dort mit dem Rücken zum Publikum Sachverhalte erklären.
- Folienschlachten durch häufiges Folienwechseln unbedingt vermeiden!

Folien in vier Phasen präsentieren

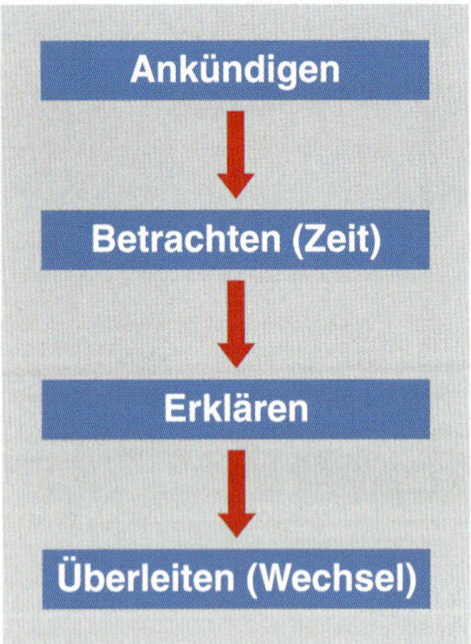

Phase 1: Folie dem Zuhörer ankündigen
Durch das Ankündigen des Folientitels oder durch eine kurze Einführung in die nachfolgende Darstellung, wird der Zuhörer auf die neuen Inhalte vorbereitet und seine Aufmerksamkeit auf die Folie ausgerichtet.

Phase 2: Zeit zum Betrachten geben
Nach dem Auflegen der Folie wird der Projektor eingeschaltet. Danach wird dem Betrachter kurze Zeit gegeben, die gesamte Folie zu betrachten. Neben dem Erfassen der Inhalte prägt sich die Folie wie ein Bild ein.

Phase 3: Erklären der Inhalte
Bei der Erläuterung der Folieninhalte geht es darum, zu erkennen, welche Vorkenntnisse beim Publikum bestehen und welche inhaltliche Elemente, Begriffe und Sätze der näheren Erklärung bedürfen. Der Präsentator sollte in Erfahrung bringen, wie ein Betrachter mit Flowchart, Diagrammen und Kennlinien umgehen kann.

Phase 4: Folie beenden und wechseln
Mit dem Abschluss der Folie durch eine Zusammenfassung wird eine Überleitung gefunden, um auf die Inhalte der nächsten Folie zu wechseln. Vor dem Folienwechsel muss unbedingt der Projektor abgedunkelt oder ausgeschaltet werden.

Präsentationstechniken

- **Aufdecktechnik**: Die Folie wird mit einem weißen Papier bedeckt und die Inhalte nach und nach freigegeben. Problem: Der Betrachter könnte sich gegängelt fühlen!
- **Überdecktechnik**: Mehrer Folien oder Teilstücke mit Inhalten werden so aufeinander gelegt, dass das vollständige Bild entsteht. Lichtstarker Projektor ist Voraussetzung!
- **Unterlegtechnik**: Die Folie mit einem unfertigen Bild wird unter einer Blankofolie platziert. Das Bild kann auf der Blankofolie mit Folienschreibern und Markern ergänzt werden.

16.5.2 Dia- und Videopräsentation

Die Präsentation von Stand- und Bewegtbildern hat ihren Stellenwert vor allem auf Messen sowie beispielsweise bei naturwissenschaftlichen und medizinischen Veranstaltungen und Kongressen. Die beiden Darstellungsformen kommen dann zum Einsatz, wenn in sich geschlossene Inhalte ohne Interaktion mit dem Publikum vorgestellt werden sollen. Dia- und Videopräsentationen werden aufgrund der Informationsfülle und -dichte in Form kleiner Blöcke bzw. Filmsequenzen vorgeführt.

Einsatzmöglichkeiten

- Einführen in das Präsentationsthema mit einer Bildfolge.
- Darstellen von komplexen Zusammenhängen, Prozessen und Entwicklungen.
- Visualisieren einer Unternehmenshierarchie.
- Abbilden verschiedener Objekte zum gleichen Thema.
- Zusammenfassen von Aussagen mehrerer Personen zum Thema (Interview).
- Hinzuschalten weiterer Vortragender mithilfe der Videokonferenz.

Hinweise zum Einsatz der Medien

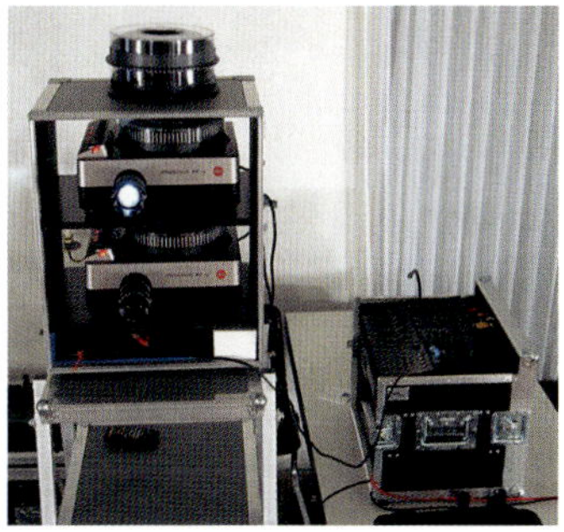

- In Verbindung mit Musik lassen sich eindrucksvolle Einleitungen mit einer Diaüberblendtechnik erzielen.
- Anmerkungen und Ergänzungen wie bei der Folienpräsentation sind hier nicht möglich. Der Vortragende wird in den Hintergrund gedrängt.
- Der Betrachter befindet sich in einer passiven Rolle und kann meist keine Informationen mitschreiben, da der Bildwechsel schnell erfolgt und der Präsentationsraum in der Regel abgedunkelt ist.
- Dias müssen übersichtlich und „leicht" sein. Das bedeutet für Textdarstellungen kurze Überschriften, höchstens drei bis fünf Zeilen Text.
- Dia- und Videoproduktionen eignen sich aufgrund ihrer brillanten und effektvollen Darstellungen als Stimulanzmittel in Situationen, in denen die Aufmerksamkeit abnimmt.
- Überwiegt der Einsatz von Dia und Video, kann der Vortrag schnell langweilig wirken.
- Diablöcke und Videofilm müssen genauso wie die einzelne Folie angekündigt, präsentiert und anschließend zusammengefasst werden.
- Diashow und Video können, sparsam und dramaturgisch an den richtigen Stellen eingesetzt, bereichernd für den Vortrag sein, da sie die Wirklichkeit besser darstellen als viele Grafiken geschmückt mit vielen Worten und sind damit für die Verständlichkeit förderlicher.
- Videos und Fotografien lassen sich in digitalisierter Form in Präsentationsprogrammen und Autorensoftware einbinden und präsentieren. Mit der geeigneten Schnittsoftware lassen sich Videos und Fotografien zusammenfassend bearbeiten und überblenden. In Verbindung mit der computerbasierenden Folienpräsentation, wäre für die Präsentationstechnik von Dia und Video nur Computer und Beamer notwendig.
- Wie beim Tageslichtprojektor, so gilt auch für den Dia- und Videoprojektor, dass die Gerätschaften in den meisten gut ausgestatteten Tagungsräumen zur Standardausstattung gehören. Wichtig für die Projektion ist es, den Raum abdunkeln zu können.

❶

16.5.3 Flip-Chart, Moderationskarten

Flip-Chart

Das Flip-Chart ❶ ist die richtige Ergänzung für die Computer- oder Folienpräsentation. Hier kann der Vortragende spontane Gedanken, Argumente aus dem Publikum, eine Gliederung des Vortrags oder eine Zusammenfassung festhalten. Mit Hilfe moderner Techniken lassen sich diese Aufschriebe direkt ausdrucken ❷. Komplexe Zusammenhänge, die aus der Hauptpräsentation nicht klar werden, können hier mittels Flow-Chart, Diagrammen, stichwortartigen Aufzählungen vertieft werden. Das gleiche betrifft Fragen im Anschluss an die Präsentation, die mithilfe der Visualisierung am Flip-Chart besser beantwortet werden, als durch Worte.

❷

Dazu sollte der Präsentator ein geübter Zeichner sein, der spontan Inhalte mittels Skizzen, ohne Vorbereitung, für das Publikum darstellt. Die festgehaltenen Informationen stehen dem Publikum über den Zeitraum der Präsentation zur Verfügung, so dass sich dieses Medium gut für den roten Faden, die Gliederung, für Kerninformationen eignet und die Teilziele mit der Computer- oder Folienpräsentation erarbeitet werden.

Damit erklären sich auch die Grenzen des Flipchart. Es begleitet den Vortrag und wird nicht als Hauptmedium eingesetzt. Aufgrund der geringen Abbildungsgröße sind sie nicht für große Gruppen geeignet.

❸
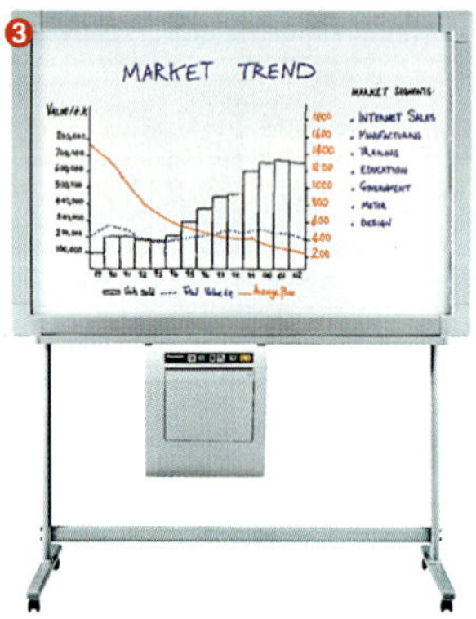

Neben der Zusatzeinrichtung zum Drucken des Flipchartaufschriebs kennt man in der Präsentationstechnik die sogenannten Copyboards ❸, die ein Mitschreiben während des Vortrags ebenso überflüssig macht. Die Schreibtafel besitzt zwei Schreibflächen, die auf Knopfdruck bewegt werden. Ein Lesekopf tastet, wie ein Scanner, das Bild ab und überträgt die Daten an den Drucker.

Moderationskarten

Interaktionen mit dem Publikum, zum Beispiel in einer Begrüßungs- und Einleitungsphase, werden mit Moderationskarten ❹ in Form von Rechtecken, Kreisen, Wolken u. a. durchgeführt. Die beschriebenen Karten werden von den Zuhörern an eine Pinwand geklebt oder können dort auch mit Magneten befestigt werden. Strukturen, Markierungen und Linien lassen sich im Anschluss auf dem Pinwandpapier herstellen ❺.

❹

❺

Arbeiten mit Flip-Chart und Moderationskarten

Um auf einem Flipchart oder mit Moderationskarten zu arbeiten bedarf es einiger Übung. Menschen, die es nicht gewohnt sind, vor einer Gruppe auf einer Tafel zu schreiben oder Skizzen zu entwerfen, werden diese Situation als unangenehm empfinden. Sie können sich den Kontrollblicken des Publikums ausgeliefert fühlen, die den Schreibstil beobachten, die Unsicherheit beim Skizzieren sehen oder auch den Fleck auf der Rückseite des Anzugs bemerken könnten, den man selber nicht sieht. Wenn der Vortragende mit dem Rücken zur Gruppe steht, werden ihm plötzlich solche Gedanken im Kopf herumgehen, die ablenken und unsicher machen. Wie arbeitet der Vortragende am Flip-Chart oder Pinnwand, damit die Pausen nicht zu groß werden, das Publikum unruhig und das Geschriebene dann nach Möglichkeit in guter Qualität erscheint?

Hinweise zum Einsatz ❶:

- Jeder Bogen erhält eine Überschrift.
- Kariertes Papier erleichtert die gerade Schreibweise.
- Kleinbuchstaben ein Karo hoch, Großbuchstaben zwei Karos.
- Einfache Sätze formulieren, keine Schachtelsätze.
- Kontrastreiche Farben wählen.
- Schlagworte mit Zeichen und Symbolen markieren.
- Fehler mit Tipp-Ex korrigieren, das wirkt nicht störend.
- In Druckbuchstaben schreiben, keine Schreib- oder Handschrift!
- Skizzen können schon in der Vorbereitung auf die Blätter gezeichnet und durch Umschlagen der Bögen aufgedeckt und dann beschriftet werden.
- Blatteinteilung vor der Präsentation vornehmen und Titel und Texte mit Bleistift leicht vorschreiben.
- Bei Moderationskarten den Platz für die Begriffe vorher grob einteilen ❷.

❶

❷

Präsentationsräume

In der Regel benötigen Pinwände und Flipcharts einen entsprechenden Platzbedarf vor allem, wenn sie frei stehen. Zur Grundausstattung sollte eine Projektionsfläche, ein Flipchart und eine Magnettafel, sowie eine Fernsehanlage mit Videorekorder gehören. In kleinen Räumen bietet es sich an, diese Gerätschaften an der Wand zu befestigen ❸. In großen Räumen können Pinwände auch als Raumteiler bei Kleingruppen-Veranstaltungen eingesetzt werden.

❸

16.5.4 Computerpräsentation

Die große Flexibilität, der Einsatz einer breiten Palette an medialen Bausteinen wie Text, Grafik, Fotografie, Animation, Video und Ton innerhalb der Computerpräsentation sind die Vorzüge, auf die heute keiner mehr verzichten möchte. Daneben lassen sich auch Realteile in die Präsentation mit einbauen. Zur Darstellung von Objekten vor einem größeren Publikum eignet sich eine kleine Tischkamera ❶, die in Verbindung mit Computer und Beamer eine vergrößerte Abbildung des Gegenstands ermöglicht.

Der Beamer ist mittlerweile zu einem leistungsstarken Projektionsgerät geworden mit durchaus passablen Auflösungen. Die Helligkeit des Bildes an der Projektionswand hängt von der Bildgröße und der Leistungsfähigkeit des Projektors ab. Der Lichtstrom sollte bei normalen Lichtverhältnissen größer als 400 Lumen/qm betragen. Der Raum sollte dann noch gegen direktes Sonnenlicht abgedunkelt werden. Damit die vollständige Bildschirmseite projiziert werden kann, muss die Auflösung des Bildschirms am Laptop auf die Beamerauflösung verringert werden (Eigenschaften | Anzeige - Einstellungen).

Beamer- / Bildschirmauflösungen:
SVGA 800 × 600
XGA 1024 × 768
SXGA 1280 × 1024
UXGA 1600 × 1200
MAC 720 × 480, 1440 × 900, 1680 × 1050 oder 1920 × 1200 Bildpunkte

Die zur Herstellung einer Bildschirmpräsentation verwendeten Programme zeichnen sich durch einfache Bedienbarkeit aus und sind in allen Officepaketen enthalten. Mit den klassischen Präsentationstools wie Powerpoint stellt man seitenbasierte Anwendungen zusammen. Diese Vorgehensweise kennen die meisten Benutzer aus der Arbeit mit Folien und sind es gewohnt eine Folie nach der anderen aufzulegen. In der gleichen Weise werden die Folien im Präsentationsprogramm dargestellt. Mit sogenannten Autorentools wie Director, Authorware und auch Flash werden umfangreiche multimediale Präsentationen, wie sie beispielsweise auf Messen gezeigt werden, Webauftritte oder Lernprogramme erstellt. Immer häufiger wird auch zum Herstellen einer kleinen Präsentation zu Flash gegriffen, da vielseitige Effekte möglich sind und die medialen Elemente zeitbasiert erscheinen.

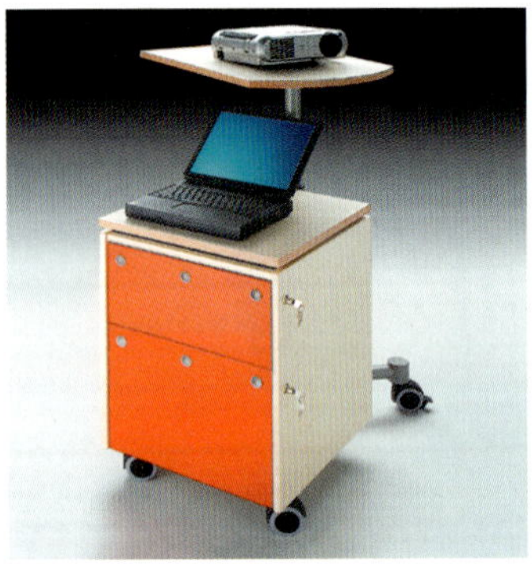

Eine kostengünstige Möglichkeit zwischen den teuren Autorenprogrammen und den Officeprogrammen bietet der Mediator von Matchware, der die Vorzüge der Folie mit einem zeitbasierten Erscheinen der Medienelemente verbindet. Daneben bietet sich für Präsentationen das PDF-Dokument an. Die Vorteile eines PDF´s liegen darin, dass es crossmedial einsetzbar ist. Das bedeutet, dass wir Medienelement einmal erstellen und über verschiedene Kanäle publizieren können. Die Darstellung eines Dokumentes ist auf jedem elektronischen Medium gleich, unabhängig von der Plattform und dem Betriebssystem und lässt sich als Druckprodukt ausgeben oder in einer Bildschirmdarstellung als Präsentation oder im Web wiedergeben (Single Source Publishing). Selbst Interaktivität und Verlinkung zwischen Seiten und Inhalten ist in PDF-Dokumenten möglich. Mit Hilfe von Lesezeichen lassen sich solche Verknüpfungen zu verschiedenen Inhalten der Präsentation herstellen.

Single Source Publishing:
Verfahren, um eine Vielzahl an Metadaten in verschiedenen Ausgabeformaten (cross medial) zur Verfügung zu stellen. Heute kommen dazu XML-Methoden zum Einsatz in Verbindung mit Content Management Systemen.

Aufgaben und Übungen, Literaturhinweise

Aufgaben und Übungen

1. Präsentationen werden nach ihrem Einsatzzweck unterschieden und spezifisch darauf aufgebaut. Unterscheiden Sie die drei Präsentationsanlässe Produkt-, Firmen-, Dienstleistungspräsentation hinsichtlich inhaltlicher Schwerpunkte. Stellen Sie die Schwerpunkte in einer Tabelle gegenüber und suchen Sie in der Praxis nach umgesetzten Beispielen (Internet, Firmenkontakt).
2. In einer Bildschirmpräsentation möchten Sie Ihre Lieblingssportart vorstellen. Schreiben Sie eine Gliederung nach dem Fünfsatz für die Inhalte der Präsentation.
3. Legen Sie Musterbildschirmseiten an, um das Zusammenwirken von Farbe und Typografie zu testen. Unterteilen Sie die Seite in inhaltliche und funktionale Bereiche mit Hilfe eines Gestaltungsrasters.
4. Erstellen Sie die Präsentation mit nicht mehr wie 10 Folien.
5. Vergleichen Sie die Präsentationsmedien Flipchart, Metaplan, Whiteboard/Tafel und Overhead-Projektor hinsichtlich der Visualisierungsmöglichkeiten.
6. Erstellen Sie eine Präsentation mit den Medien unter Aufgabe 5 zu einem im Alltag gebrauchten Produkt mit den hervorstechenden Merkmalen und technischen Daten des Produkts.

Literaturhinweise

Breger, Grob: Präsentieren und Visualisieren, München 2003 (dtv)

Hartmann, Funk, Nietmann: Präsentieren, 7. Aufl., Weinheim 2003 (Beltz)

Hertlein, Margit: Präsentieren – Vom Text zum Bild, Hamburg 2003 (Rowohlt)

Hierhold, Emil: Sicher präsentieren – wirksam vortragen, München, Wien 2005 (Redline)

Reynolds, Garr: Zen oder die Kunst des Präsentationsdesigns, 1. Aufl., München 2010 (Addison-Wesley-Verlag)

Schuhmann, Georg: Moderieren, Projektieren, Präsentieren, Haan 2006 (Europa-Lehrmittel)

Thiele, Albert: Überzeugend präsentieren, 2. Aufl., Berlin 2000 (Springer)

Thiele, Albert: Präsentieren Sie einfach, 1. Aufl., Frankfurt 2007 (Frankfurter Allgemeine Buch)

Thissen, Frank: Screen-Design, 3. Aufl., Berlin 2003 (Springer)

17 Medienrecht

Webcode: C1700

Für weitere Infos zu diesem Kapitel mit dem Smartphone einfach QR-Code scannen oder auf www.medien-verstehen.de den Webcode eingeben.

In einer Darstellung des Medienrechts heißt es (Fechner 2006, S. 241 f.): „Wer nicht selbst Jurist ist, sollte doch in der Lage sein, eine juristische Fragestellung in das richtige Rechtsgebiet einzuordnen und mit Hilfe von juristischer Literatur, insbesondere Kommentaren und Leitentscheidungen der Gerichte, eine Einschätzung vornehmen zu können. In den alltäglichen Entscheidungsfragen dürfte dies bereits ausreichend sein, bei Spezialproblemen wird der ausgebildete Jurist zu Rate zu ziehen sein. Jedoch auch in diesem Falle ist es sinnvoll, gezielt die Problematik des Einzelfalls ansprechen zu können. Zudem sind Fachsprache und Sachkenntnis in jeder Verhandlung mit Geschäftspartnern oder Anspruchstellern hilfreich. Noch wichtiger als der Gebrauch von Rechtskenntnissen in juristischen Auseinandersetzungen ist die Einbeziehung des Rechts im Vorfeld von Streitigkeiten."

Vor diesem Hintergrund und mit diesem Anspruch sollen in diesem Kapitel die **rechtlichen Rahmenbedingungen** für die Medien näher betrachtet werden. Die Darstellung ersetzt nicht tiefergehende Betrachtungen, sondern führt den Leser an die Materie heran, die es dann weiter zu vertiefen gilt.

Das **Medienrecht** gilt als eine sog. „Querschnittsmaterie", was ausdrücken soll, dass es sich nicht um ein in sich geschlossenes Rechtsgebiet handelt wie z. B. das Strafrecht oder das Familienrecht. Es ist vielmehr eine rechtliche Materie, die sich aus verschiedenen Rechtsgebieten zusammensetzt. Um die Vielfalt der Bezüge in den Griff zu bekommen, ist es zweckmäßig, zwischen **zwei großen Bereichen** zu unterscheiden,

- zum einen das allgemeine Grundlagenrecht, soweit es für die Medien relevant ist, hier insbesondere das Grundgesetz und das Urheberrecht,
- zum anderen das medienspezifische Recht, das die drei großen Teilbereiche des Presserechts, Rundfunkrechts und Multimediarechts umfasst, ergänzt um das internationale Medienrecht.

Im ersten Teil des Kapitels wird daher ein grober und sehr knapp gehaltener Überblick über die relevanten Regelungen beider Bereiche gegeben, also sowohl über das allgemeine Grundlagenrecht als auch über das medienspezifische Recht, während im zweiten Teil das Urheberrecht in den Fokus genommen und einer vertieften Darstellung unterzogen wird.

Letzteres folgt der Einsicht, dass im Hinblick auf die Schaffung von Medienprodukten die Frage der **Urheberrechte** von herausragender Bedeutung ist. Man denke zum Beispiel an die Abklärung aller Rechte bei einer Filmproduktion, beginnend mit dem Drehbuch über die Drehgenehmigung bis zum Regisseur und den Darstellern, oder an die Frage von illegalen Downloads und Weiterverbreitung von Musiktiteln im Rahmen von Peer-to-Peer-Netzwerken ❶.

❶ Mit **Peer-to-Peer (P2P)** bezeichnet man einen Verbund von Gleichberechtigten („Peers"), die sich gegenseitig Informationen zugänglich machen. Musterbeispiele sind legale und illegale Tauschbörsen für digitale Musik-Files im Internet, die man auch als „P2P-Tauschbörsen" bezeichnet.

17.1 Überblick über das Medienrecht

Die nachfolgende Übersicht gibt einen groben **Überblick** über besonders wichtige medienrelevante Rechtsbereiche im Zusammenhang:

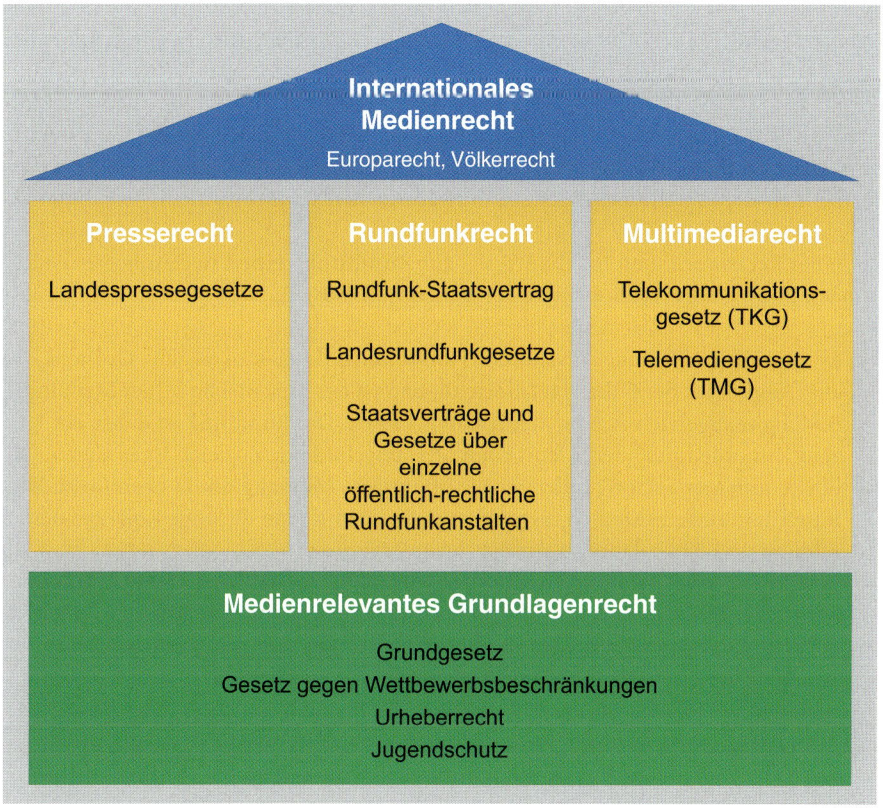

Dabei wird die angesprochene Feststellung deutlich, dass sich das Medienrecht aus höchst unterschiedlichen Bereichen zusammensetzt.

Erkennbar ist, dass die Basis des Medienrechts wesentlich vom Grundgesetz und dem Urheberrecht getragen wird und dann **drei große Säulen** das Medienrecht konstituieren:

- **Presserecht**
- **Rundfunkrecht**
- **Multimediarecht**

Von zunehmender Bedeutung fügt sich – gewissermaßen als Dach – das internationale Medienrecht hinzu.

„Medien spielten in der Geschichte der Menschheit seit jeher eine zentrale Rolle. Der Austausch von Informationen über Distanz gehört zu den Urbedürfnissen des Menschen. Bereits die großen Staaten der Frühzeit waren zur Abwehr äußerer und innerer Gefahren sowie für die Erfüllung verwaltungsmäßiger Aufgaben auf ein funktionierendes Nachrichtensystem angewiesen. Nicht zu übersehen ist von Anbeginn die Bedeutung der Medien als Mittel der Meinungsbeeinflussung zur Erlangung und Bewahrung von Macht. Charakteristisch für die rechtlichen Strukturen der Medien ist daher in geschichtlicher Hinsicht ihr Verhältnis zum Staat. Massenmedien sind bis heute ein verlockendes Instrument für Machthaber, um ihre Herrschaft zu festigen. Diktatorische Staaten sind durch eine Ausschaltung des freien Presse- und Rundfunkwesens gekennzeichnet. Eine funktionierende Demokratie beweist sich demgegenüber nicht nur durch einen freien Meinungsaustausch zwischen den Menschen, sondern vor allem auch durch einen freien Meinungsmarkt der Massenmedien" (Fechner 2012, Einleitung).

17.1.1 Medienrelevantes Grundlagenrecht

Grundgesetz

❶ **Artikel 5 GG**:
(1) Jeder hat das Recht, seine Meinung in Wort, Schrift und Bild frei zu äußern und zu verbreiten und sich aus allgemein zugänglichen Quellen ungehindert zu unterrichten. Die Pressefreiheit und die Freiheit der Berichterstattung durch Rundfunk und Film werden gewährleistet. Eine Zensur findet nicht statt.
(2) Diese Rechte finden ihre Schranken in den Vorschriften der allgemeinen Gesetze, den gesetzlichen Bestimmungen zum Schutze der Jugend und in dem Recht der persönlichen Ehre.
(3) Kunst und Wissenschaft, Forschung und Lehre sind frei. Die Freiheit der Lehre entbindet nicht von der Treue zur Verfassung.

Beim medienrelevanten Grundlagenrecht spielt die **Verfassung** und damit das **Grundgesetz** und dessen Auslegung durch das **Bundesverfassungsgericht** (BVerfG) eine herausragende Rolle. Es setzt die entscheidenden Normen für die Gestaltung der Medien und bindet alle staatliche Gewalt einschließlich den Gesetzgeber. Im Vordergrund steht Art. 5 Abs. 1 GG. Dort wird jedem Bürger dieses Landes die freie individuelle und öffentliche Meinungsbildung umfassend gewährleistet ❶. Kernbegriffe sind **Pressefreiheit** und **Rundfunkfreiheit**, die als schlechthin konstituierend für die freiheitlich-demokratische Grundordnung anzusehen sind.

In seiner Rechtsprechung hat das BVerfG zur **Rundfunkfreiheit** insbesondere die folgenden Punkte hervorgehoben (vgl. Hesse 2003, S. 60-76):

- Der Rundfunk übt eine wesentliche Funktion für die demokratische Ordnung aus: Angesichts der Fülle von Informationen ist der Einzelne zu seiner Meinungsbildung maßgeblich auf die Medien angewiesen. Der Rundfunk ist daher ein zentrales „Medium" der öffentlichen Meinungsbildung. Zugleich ist er aber auch ein „eminenter Faktor", indem er die öffentliche Meinung direkt beeinflusst. Der Rundfunk und die Medien insgesamt spielen damit eine wichtige Rolle bei der Bildung und Artikulation der öffentlichen Meinung.
- Eine besondere Bedeutung kommt dem Fernsehen zu, da es das einzige Medium ist, das zeitgleich in Bild und Ton zu berichten vermag und dadurch den Anschein der Authentizität erweckt, das Miterleben fördert und bequem verfügbar ist.
- Der Rundfunk besitzt eine Verantwortung für das kulturelle Leben in der Bundesrepublik.
- Rundfunkfreiheit setzt die Freiheit von staatlicher Beeinflussung voraus. Medien üben eine öffentliche Kontroll- und Kritikfunktion gegenüber der Staatsgewalt aus, deren Wirksamkeit nicht beeinträchtigt werden darf.
- Damit der Rundfunk seine Aufgabe als Medium und Faktor der öffentlichen Meinungsbildung ausüben kann, bedarf es einer Ordnung, die sicherstellt, dass eine Vielfalt der vorhandenen Meinungen im Rundfunk in möglichster Breite und Vollständigkeit Ausdruck findet (Gebot der Meinungsvielfalt). Rundfunkfreiheit hat damit eine dienende Funktion, sie ist „dienende Freiheit".

Das Grundgesetz schützt im Übrigen auch die interessengeleiteten kommunikativen Inhalte wie Werbung und Public Relations (PR). Meinungsfreiheit umfasst auch die Freiheit zur massenkommunikativen Vermittlung von Werbebotschaften. Werbung in den Medien jedweder Art ist damit direkt vom Grundgesetz geschützt.

Art. 30 GG besagt, dass die Ausübung staatlicher Befugnis und die Erfüllung der staatlichen Aufgaben Sache der **Länder** ist. Dem Bund steht die Aufgabenerfüllung nur dann zu, wenn sich dem Grundgesetz eine entsprechende Kompetenz entnehmen lässt. Vor diesem Hintergrund ist Presse und Rundfunk eine Angelegenheit der Länder, die die sog. ausschließliche Gesetzgebungskompetenz besitzen.

Eine wichtige Rolle im Kontext des Grundgesetzes spielt ferner das allgemeine **Persönlichkeitsrecht** nach Art. 2 Abs. 1 in Verbindung mit Art. 1 Abs. 1 GG ❶. Danach haben die Medien in ihren Veröffentlichungen die Persönlichkeitsrechte derjenigen zu wahren, über die sie berichten. Das Eindringen in die Privatsphäre stellt eine Rechtsverletzung dar und kann zivilrechtliche Gegenansprüche in Form von Gegendarstellung, Unterlassungsanspruch, Berichtigungsanspruch, Widerruf, Ergänzung und/oder Schadensersatz und Schmerzensgeld nach sich ziehen.

❶ **Artikel 2 GG**: (1) Jeder hat das Recht auf die freie Entfaltung seiner Persönlichkeit, soweit er nicht die Rechte anderer verletzt und nicht gegen die verfassungsmäßige Ordnung oder das Sittengesetz verstößt.

Artikel 1 GG: (1) Die Würde des Menschen ist unantastbar. Sie zu achten und zu schützen ist Verpflichtung aller staatlichen Gewalt.

Gesetz gegen den unlauteren Wettbewerb (UWG)

Von besonderer Relevanz für die Medien ist das Wettbewerbsrecht, insbesondere das Gesetz gegen den unlauteren Wettbewerb (UWG). Nach § 3 UWG sind alle unlauteren Wettbewerbshandlungen verboten.

Das UWG benennt als Beispiele unlauteren Wettbewerbs insbesondere die Vornahme von Wettbewerbshandlungen, die geeignet sind,

- die Entscheidungsfreiheit der Verbraucher oder sonstiger Marktteilnehmer durch Ausübung von Druck, in menschenverachtender Weise oder durch sonstigen unangemessenen unsachlichen Einfluss zu beeinträchtigen;
- die geschäftliche Unerfahrenheit insbesondere von Kindern oder Jugendlichen, die Leichtgläubigkeit, die Angst oder die Zwangslage von Verbrauchern auszunutzen.
- Unlauter ist es auch, den Werbecharakter von Wettbewerbshandlungen zu verschleiern.

Das UWG stellt also den **Wahrheitsgrundsatz** als besonders wichtig heraus. So muss z. B. ein Werbetreibender klar und verständlich kommunizieren, er darf nicht irreführen, er darf keine sog. „Mondpreise" setzen, „Lockvogelangebote" müssen mindestens zwei Tage lang vorrätig sein, E-Mail-Werbung ist ohne Einwilligung des Adressaten verboten u. v. m. Das Irreführungsverbot verlangt von den Medien größtmögliche Objektivität und Neutralität. Bereits durch das UWG wird damit z. B. die Grundlage für einen zentralen Grundsatz geschaffen, nach dem Werbebotschaften klar von redaktionell-programmlichen Inhalten getrennt werden müssen ❷.

❷ Dieser Grundsatz wird als **Trennungsgrundsatz von Werbung und Programm** bezeichnet.

Urheberrecht

Eine ebenfalls zentrale Rolle für die Medien spielt das **Urheberrecht**. Es verfolgt zwei **Ziele**: Zum einen soll es den Urheber gegen eine nicht zulässige Verwertung seines Werkes in den Medien schützen. Zum anderen bietet es Schutz des in den Medien veröffentlichten Werkes gegen die unzulässige Verwertung durch Dritte. Wichtige Punkte des Urheberrechts betreffen die folgenden **Aspekte**, die wegen ihrer hohen Bedeutung im zweiten Teil dieses Kapitels vertieft behandelt werden:

- Der entscheidende Ausgangspunkt und Schutzgegenstand ist eine individuelle schöpferische Leistung, die als „Werk" bezeichnet wird. Ein sog. „Allerweltserzeugnis" genießt keinen urheberrechtlichen Schutz. Zu unterscheiden sind Sprachwerke, Musikwerke, Werke der darstellenden, bildenden und angewandten Kunst, Fotografien, Filme, Darstellungen wissenschaftlicher oder technischer Art,

Computerprogramme, Sammelwerke, Datenbanken jeglicher Art. Als Sonderformen von Werken und damit als eigenständige Werke mit Urheberrechtsschutz sind Bearbeitungen, Umgestaltungen oder Übersetzungen anerkannt.

- Ein „Urheber“ ist der Schöpfer des Werkes und immer ein konkreter Mensch, d. h. eine natürliche Person. Je nach Werk spricht man von Autor, Schriftsteller, Verfasser, Komponist, Werbefilmer, Fotograf, Regisseur, Cutter, Kameramann, Verfasser, Software-Entwickler u. ä.
- **Urheberpersönlichkeitsrecht:** Rechtlicher Ausgangspunkt ist das Urheberpersönlichkeitsrecht, das dem Urheber als Werkschöpfer zufällt. Es ist unveräußerlich und umfasst das Veröffentlichungsrecht, das Recht auf Namensnennung und das Recht auf Verhinderung der Entstellung des Werkes.
- **Verwertungsrechte:** Der Urheber hat das alleinige Recht, über die Verwertung seines Werkes zu verfügen. Die wichtigsten Verwertungsrechte sind: Vervielfältigungsrecht, Verbreitungsrecht, Ausstellungsrecht, Vortrags-, Aufführungs- und Vorführungsrecht, Senderecht, Recht auf Wiedergabe durch Bild- und Tonträger.
- **Leistungsschutzrechte:** Diejenigen Personen, die ein Werk darstellen, vorführen, zur Aufführung bringen oder künstlerisch mitwirken, z. B. als Schauspieler, Sänger oder Musiker, sind sog. „ausübende Künstler“ die keine Urheber im eigentlichen Sinne sind, aber als „Inhaber verwandter Schutzrechte“ dennoch einen Schutz – allerdings eingeschränkt – genießen.
- Verwertungspraxis: Im Bereich von Texten, Bildern und Musik stehen die Autoren üblicherweise bei Verlagen unter Vertrag, wo dann auch die entsprechenden Rechte liegen. Bei bildenden Künstlern, Malern und Bildhauern liegen sie bei den Urhebern selbst. Für Komponisten kleinerer Werke, vor allem von Unterhaltungsmusik (sog. „Kleines Recht“) steht zur Durchsetzung der Rechte die **GEMA** („Gesellschaft für musikalische Aufführungsrechte und mechanische Vervielfältigungsrechte“) zur Verfügung, für Inhaber von Leistungsschutzrechten die GVL („Gesellschaft zur Verwertung von Leistungsschutzrechten“) und für den Bereich Literatur und Wissenschaft die VG Wort (Verwertungsgesellschaft Wort).

❶ Beim **Pay-TV** zum Beispiel wird das gesendete Signal vor seiner Ausstrahlung verschlüsselt (codiert) und beim Empfänger unter Einsatz der sog. **Set Top Box** wieder entschlüsselt (decodiert). Ziel ist es, den Zuschauer zu zwingen, für die Fernehsendungen einen Geldbetrag zu entrichten.

Alle Rechte (außer das Urheberpersönlichkeitsrecht) sind **eingeschränkt**: Die Werke der Urheber genießen eine Schutzfrist von 70 Jahren, gerechnet ab dem Tod des Urhebers, bei Leistungsschutzrechte sind es 50 Jahre nach der Veröffentlichung des Werkes (z. B. Aufführung).

❷ **Digital Rights Management (DRM)** bezeichnet alle technischen Maßnahmen zur digitalen Kontrolle von Urheber- und Verwertungsrechten an Inhalten (Content) aller Art. Der Schutz des Inhalts vor unerlaubter Nutzung erfolgt dabei durch Verschlüsselung.

Mediengüter lassen sich zumeist leicht **reproduzieren**, als Papierkopie und erst recht, wenn der Inhalt in digitaler Form vorliegt, weshalb es schwer fällt, einen wirksamen Schutz der Rechte der Urheber sicherzustellen. So ist es verständlich, dass das Urheberrecht im Hinblick auf die Medien als ein vergleichsweise „starkes Recht“ zu gelten hat, das bei Verletzung hohe Strafen androht. Verständlich ist es auch, dass mit dem Einsatz technologischer Mittel versucht wird, die Informationen zu verschlüsseln und die Urheberrechte durchzusetzen, ein Ansatz, der mit den Begriffen der Codierung ❶ und des Digital Rights Managements ❷ in Verbindung steht.

Kinder- und Jugendschutz

Ein letzter wichtiger Bereich von grundsätzlichem Charakter für die Medien umfasst die Vorschriften für den **Kinder- und Jugendschutz**. Hierbei sind aus medienrechtlicher Sicht **zwei Bereiche** besonders hervorzuheben:

- Bundesrecht: Jugendschutzgesetz (JuSchG), hier besonders Abschnitt 3 „Jugendschutz im Bereich der Medien"
- Landesrecht: Staatsvertrag über den Schutz der Menschenwürde und den Jugendschutz in den Telemedien – Jugendmedienschutz-Staatsvertrag (JMStV)

Das **Jugendschutzgesetz** dient dem Schutz von Kindern (Personen, die noch nicht 14 Jahre alt sind) und von Jugendlichen (Personen, die 14, aber noch nicht älter als 18 Jahre alt sind) in der Öffentlichkeit und enthält, was die Medien anbelangt, u. a. spezielle **Regelungen** für die Abgabe von Filmen und Computerspielen:

- Computerspiele und Bildschirmspielgeräte müssen wie Kino- und Videofilme mit einer Altersfreigabekennzeichnung versehen werden. Diese Bildträger dürfen nur an Kinder und Jugendliche abgegeben werden, die das gekennzeichnete Alter haben.
- Indizierte Trägermedien dürfen Kindern und Jugendlichen nicht zugänglich gemacht werden ❶.
- Für schwer jugendgefährdende Medien, insbesondere solche mit Gewaltdarstellungen, gelten besonders scharfe Verbote. So sind auch ohne Indizierung durch die Bundesprüfstelle Trägermedien (z. B. Bücher, Videos, CD, CD-ROM, DVD), die den Krieg verherrlichen, die Menschen in einer die Menschenwürde verletzenden Weise darstellen oder Jugendliche in unnatürlicher, geschlechtsbetonter Körperhaltung zeigen, mit weitreichenden Abgabe-, Vertriebs- und Werbeverboten belegt.

Zuwiderhandlungen gegen das Jugendschutzgesetz können als Straftaten oder Ordnungswidrigkeiten mit einem Bußgeld bis zu 50.000 Euro geahndet werden.

Ergänzend zum Jugendschutzgesetz des Bundes gibt es den **Jugendmedienschutz-Staatsvertrag der Länder** (JMStV), der eine einheitliche Rechtsgrundlage für den Jugendschutz in den elektronischen Medien (Fernsehen, Hörfunk, Internet) schafft. Durch Verzahnungsregelungen in beiden Gesetzen ist sichergestellt, dass Bundes- und Ländereinrichtungen nach einheitlichen Schutzstandards entscheiden.

§ 1 beleuchtet die Rolle dieses Staatsvertrags: „Zweck des Staatsvertrages ist der einheitliche Schutz der Kinder und Jugendlichen vor Angeboten in elektronischen Informations- und Kommunikationsmedien, die deren Entwicklung oder Erziehung beeinträchtigen oder gefährden, sowie der Schutz vor solchen Angeboten in elektronischen Informations- und Kommunikationsmedien, die die Menschenwürde oder sonstige durch das Strafgesetzbuch geschützte Rechtsgüter verletzen." ❷

Der JMStV gilt nur für elektronische Informations- und Kommunikationsmedien, das heißt für den Rundfunk (Hörfunk und Fernsehen) und für Telemedien. „Telemedien" sind alle Angebote im Internet (Webshops, Auktionshäuser, Suchmaschinen, E-Mail-Dienste, Informationsdienste, Podcasts, Communities, Portale, Blogs usw.).

❶ Die **Indizierung** eines Mediums bedeutet, dass das Medium weder beworben noch Kindern und Jugendlichen zugänglich gemacht werden darf. Es darf nicht an Kiosken oder im Versandhandel verkauft und nicht im Rundfunk und Fernsehen gesendet werden. Zuständig für die Indizierung ist die Bundesprüfstelle für jugendgefährdende Medien (BPjM). Jede Bürgerin, jeder Bürger kann bei einer Behörde oder anerkannten Jugendhilfeeinrichtung in ihrer/seiner Nähe auf ein Medium mit möglicherweise jugendgefährdendem Inhalt hinweisen und so auf die Einleitung eines Indizierungsverfahrens hinwirken. Die Indizierung hat nicht das generelle Verbot eines Mediums zur Folge. Sie verhindert aber, dass Kinder und Jugendliche mit jugendgefährdenden Medien konfrontiert werden.

❷ § 5 Abs. 1 stellt die Forderung: „Sofern Anbieter Angebote, die geeignet sind, die Entwicklung von Kindern oder Jugendlichen zu einer eigenverantwortlichen und gemeinschaftsfähigen Persönlichkeit zu beeinträchtigen, verbreiten oder zugänglich machen, haben sie dafür Sorge zu tragen, dass Kinder oder Jugendliche der betroffenen Altersstufen sie üblicherweise nicht wahrnehmen."

17.1.2 Presserecht

❶ Im absolutistischen Staat war das Presserecht ein Instrument zur Sicherung der Macht der Obrigkeit und zur Kontrolle der massenhaften Verbreitung von Gedankengut. Zentraler Grundwert des heutigen Presserechts ist die **Pressefreiheit**.

Das Presserecht hat eine doppelte Funktion, zum einen soll es den besonderen **Schutz** der redaktionellen Arbeit von **Journalisten** sicher stellen, zum anderen die **Pflichten** definieren, denen eben diese Journalisten unterworfen sind ❶.

Aufgrund der Gesetzgebungsbefugnis der Bundesländer (Art. 75 Abs. 1 Ziff. 2 GG i. V. m. Art. 72 GG) wird das Presserecht in Deutschland durch die Landespressegesetze bestimmt. Der Bund hat die Befugnis, ein Presserechtsrahmengesetz zu erlassen, wovon er bislang aber keinen Gebrauch gemacht hat, da die Landespressegesetze inhaltlich weitgehend übereinstimmen. Im Einzelnen sind die folgenden Regelungen zu den **Rechten** und **Pflichten der Journalisten** bedeutsam:

- Rechte: Die Presseangehörigen haben einen umfassenden Anspruch gegenüber den Behörden auf Auskunft, allerdings nicht, wenn die Behörden zur Geheimhaltung verpflichtet sind. Ein Auskunftsanspruch gegenüber privaten Unternehmen und Organisationen besteht nicht. Vor Gericht haben Journalisten ein Zeugnisverweigerungsrecht und besondere Rechte bei der Durchsuchung von Presseräumen und der Beschlagnahme von Materialien. Pressevertreter müssen Zugang zu allen öffentlichen staatlichen Veranstaltungen haben, ebenso zu Pressekonferenzen.
- Pflichten: Die Presseangehörigen haben eine besondere journalistische Sorgfaltspflicht bei der Recherche und Verbreitung von Nachrichten. Das Presseorgan ist von strafbaren Inhalten frei zu halten. Bei Zweifeln am Wahrheitsgehalt einer Meldung muss auf die Veröffentlichung verzichtet werden. Unter bestimmten Umständen besteht für den verantwortlichen Redakteur und für den Verleger die Verpflichtung zur Gegendarstellung. Ferner besteht eine Impressumpflicht, die dazu dient, die Verantwortung für die Inhalte klar zu fixieren. Verantwortliche Redakteure müssen ihren ständigen Aufenthalt innerhalb Deutschlands haben, die bürgerlichen Ehrenrechte besitzen und unbeschränkt geschäftsfähig sein. Der redaktionelle Teil und die Werbung müssen klar voneinander getrennt werden (Trennungsgebot).

❷ Der **Tendenzschutz** des Verlegers ist in § 118 Betriebsverfassungsgesetz (BetrVG) geregelt. Danach hat er das Recht, seinem Presseorgan eine bestimmte inhaltliche – auch politische – Meinung vorzuschreiben, womit die Mitwirkungsrechte des Betriebsrats zu Gunsten der publizistischen Unabhängigkeit beschnitten bzw. eingeschränkt werden. Dem steht diametral die Forderung (vor allem der Journalistenverbände und Gewerkschaften) entgegen, der Inhalt einer Zeitung müsse ganz und gar der Redaktion überlassen bleiben, eine Forderung, die als **innere Pressefreiheit** bezeichnet wird. In einer Entscheidung hat das Bundesverfassungsgericht festgelegt, dass es der öffentliche Auftrag der Presse erforderlich macht, die Grundsatzkompetenz dem Verleger zu überlassen.

Grundpfeiler aller Regelungen des Presserechts ist die **Pressefreiheit**, die über das Grundgesetz hinaus in allen Landespressegesetzen verankert ist. Hieraus ergeben sich die folgenden unmittelbaren **Konsequenzen**:

- **Recht auf Gründung:** Ein Presseunternehmen kann jederzeit frei und ohne staatliche Zulassung gegründet werden.
- **Redaktionsgeheimnis:** Die Redaktionsarbeit von Presseunternehmen ist in ihrer Vertraulichkeit geschützt. Die Presse darf daher ungehindert von staatlicher Einflussnahme Informationen sammeln und unterliegt nicht der Pflicht, Quellen offen zu legen. Allerdings dürfen keine Straftaten oder unzulässige Handlungen gerechtfertigt werden.
- **Tendenzschutz:** Wie jedermann, so steht auch einem Zeitungsverleger das Grundrecht der **Pressefreiheit** zu ❷.

Einschränkungen der Pressefreiheit können nur erfolgen, wenn sie vom Grundgesetz oder dem Landespressegesetz ausdrücklich zugelassen sind. Es herrscht ein **Zensurverbot** nach Art. 5 Abs. 1 Satz 3 GG.

17.1.3 Rundfunkrecht

Rundfunk wird – wie die Presse – in Deutschland als **Kulturgut** verstanden und fällt daher in die Kulturhoheit der Länder. Die folgenden **rechtlichen Grundlagen** – in nationaler Sicht – sind für den Rundfunk relevant:

❶ Genau heißt er: Staatsvertrag für Rundfunk und Telemedien (**Rundfunkstaatsvertrag** – RStV) vom 31.08.1991. Der Staatsvertrag wird laufend den Entwicklungen durch Änderungen angepasst.

- Rechtsprechung des Bundesverfassungsgerichts (BVerfG)
- Rundfunkstaatsvertrag (RStV) ❶
- Landesrundfunkgesetze
- Staatsverträge über ARD, ZDF und Deutschlandradio
- Gesetze bzw. Staatsverträge für die einzelnen Landesrundfunkanstalten der ARD (z. B. WDR-Gesetz, Staatsvertrag über den SWR)

Rechtsprechung des Bundesverfassungsgerichts

Der rechtliche Rahmen für den Rundfunk in Deutschland ist maßgeblich von der Rechtsprechung des Bundesverfassungsgerichts geprägt. In bisher insgesamt **zehn Urteilen** (seit 1961) sind die entscheidenden Vorgaben herausgearbeitet worden. Das Bundesverfassungsgericht hat insbesondere den Begriff der Grundversorgung als zentrales Kriterium für den Rundfunk herausgestellt ❷.

❷ „Der Begriff der Grundversorgung ist der Schlüssel für das Verständnis des geltenden Rundfunkrechts. Grundversorgung bedeutet, dass im Prinzip Sorge getragen sein muss, dass für die Gesamtheit der Bevölkerung Programme angeboten werden, die umfassend und in der vollen Breite des klassischen Rundfunkauftrags informieren und dass Meinungsvielfalt in der verfassungsrechtlich gebotenen Weise gesichert ist" (Fechner 2006, S. 250).

Mit **Grundversorgung** wird gleichzeitig auch der zentrale Funktionsbereich bzw. die Hauptaufgabe des öffentlich-rechtlichen Rundfunks beschrieben und festgeschrieben. Mit der Grundversorgung soll gewährleistet sein, dass der Rundfunk seine klassischen Aufgaben erfüllen kann, und zwar als Faktor und Forum der Meinungs- und politischen Willensbildung, als Unterhaltungsanbieter, als Einrichtung, die über die laufende Berichterstattung hinaus Informationsfunktionen erfüllt sowie als Kulturinstitution. Die Notwendigkeit des Grundversorgungsauftrags an den öffentlich-rechtlichen Rundfunk ergibt sich gemäß der Rechtsprechung des Bundesverfassungsgerichts unmittelbar aus Art. 5 Abs. 1 GG und kann vom Gesetzgeber nicht in Frage gestellt werden.

Rundfunkstaatsvertrag

Der **Rundfunkstaatsvertrag** (RStV) ist das zentrale Gesetzeswerk – sozusagen die „Bibel" – für den Rundfunk in Deutschland. Er schafft auf der Grundlage der Entscheidungen des Bundesverfassungsgerichts das konkret geltende Recht für den Rundfunk und enthält alle grundlegenden Regelungen sowohl für den öffentlich-rechtlichen als auch für den privaten Rundfunk.

Die **obersten Leitmaximen** des Rundfunkstaatvertrags heißen: freie Meinungsbildung, Meinungsvielfalt und Wettbewerb. In der Präambel des RStV heißt es daher: „Öffentlich-rechtlicher Rundfunk und privater Rundfunk sind der freien individuellen und öffentlichen Meinungsbildung sowie der Meinungsvielfalt verpflichtet. Beide Rundfunksysteme müssen in der Lage sein, den Anforderungen des nationalen und internationalen Wettbewerbs zu entsprechen. Im Zuge der Vermehrung der Rundfunkprogramme in Europa durch die neuen Techniken sollen Informationsvielfalt und kulturelles Angebot im deutschsprachigen Raum verstärkt werden."

Der Rundfunkstaatsvertrag heißt „Staatsvertrag“ und nicht „Gesetz“, weil **Rundfunk** eine **Angelegenheit der Bundesländer** ist und sich eine einheitlich für ganz Deutschland geltende Regelung nur in der Weise herstellen lässt, dass sich die Länder auf eine gemeinsame Grundlinie verständigen und für eine gemeinsame Regelung sorgen. Der rechtliche Zusammenschluss der Länder geschieht im Staatsvertrag. Geltendes Recht werden diese Regelungen allerdings erst, wenn die Parlamente der Länder diese staatsvertraglichen Regelungen in konkretes Landesrecht umsetzen. Werden Änderungen notwendig, muss dies in einem sog. „Rundfunkänderungsstaatsvertrag“ zwischen den Ländern geregelt werden. Derzeit befindet man sich auf dem „Parkett“ des 12. Rundfunkänderungsstaatsvertrags.

Der RStV enthält im Prinzip einen Katalog an allgemeinen Vorschriften, der für alle Rundfunkveranstalter im dualen System Deutschlands gleichermaßen Gültigkeit besitzt, sowie zwei spezielle Teile, die die grundlegenden Regelungen für den öffentlich-rechtlichen auf der einen Seite und für den privaten Rundfunk auf der anderen Seite beinhalten.

Die Allgemeinen Vorschriften legen den Rundfunkbegriff dar, sie formulieren allgemeingültige Programmgrundsätze und sorgen für einen Rahmen im Hinblick auf Berichterstattung, Produktionsanteile, Werbung und Sponsoring. Die Vorschriften für den öffentlich-rechtlichen Rundfunk regeln die „funktionsgerechte Finanzausstattung“, beschreiben das Verfahren zur Ermittlung des Finanzbedarfs und grenzt die Möglichkeiten für Werbung und Sponsoring ein. Die Vorschriften für den privaten Rundfunk schließlich umfassen Zulassungsvorschriften, die Messvorschriften, die den Maßnahmen zur Sicherung der Meinungsvielfalt zugrunde liegen (sog. Zuschaueranteilsmodell), beschreiben die Organisation der Medienaufsicht, formulieren Programmgrundsätze und die Regelwerke für die Durchführung von Werbung, Sponsoring und Teleshopping.

Die Rahmenregelungen des Rundfunkstaatsvertrages werden ergänzt und ausgefüllt durch die jeweiligen Landesrundfunkgesetze.

Weitere Regelwerke

Als weitere Regelwerke für den Rundfunk sind die **Landesrundfunkgesetze** bzw. **Landesmediengesetze** relevant, die spezielle Regelungen für die Zulassung von Veranstaltern, für die Sicherung der Meinungsvielfalt, für Programmgrundsätze und für die Organisation der Aufsicht durch eigens von den Ländern eingerichtete Landesanstalten enthalten.

Des weiteren sind die **Staatsverträge für ARD, ZDF** ❶ und Deutschlandradio zu nennen sowie die Gesetze bzw. Staatsverträge für die einzelnen Landesrundfunkanstalten der ARD. Gesetze gibt es für öffentlich-rechtliche Rundfunkanstalten, deren Sendegebiet mit dem Gebiet des Bundeslandes übereinstimmen, so für den Bayerischen Rundfunk, den Hessischen Rundfunk und den Westdeutschen Rundfunk. Ein Staatsvertrag zwischen einzelnen Bundesländern ist immer dann erforderlich, wenn – wie beim Südwestrundfunk, beim Norddeutschen Rundfunk oder beim Mitteldeutschen Rundfunk – die Zuständigkeit über zwei oder mehrere Bundesländer gegeben ist.

❶ Der rundfunkrechtliche Laie nimmt immer wieder fälschlicherweise an, das ZDF sei wegen seines bundesweiten Sendegebietes eine Bundeseinrichtung. Da Rundfunk eine Angelegenheit der Länder ist, ist das **ZDF** jedoch eine **Länderanstalt**, die von allen Bundesländern gemeinsam getragen wird.

17.1.4 Multimediarecht

Das Recht der „neuen Medien" – auch als „Multimediarecht" bezeichnet – wird durch zwei große **Rechtsvorschriften** geprägt:

- **Telekommunikationsgesetz** (TKG)
- **Telemediengesetz** (TMG)

Telekommunikationsgesetz

Der **Telekommunikationsgesetz** schafft den rechtlichen Rahmen für den technischen Vorgang der Telekommunikation. § 1 TKG lautet: „Zweck dieses Gesetzes ist es, durch technologieneutrale Regulierung den Wettbewerb im Bereich der Telekommunikation und leistungsfähige Telekommunikationsinfrastrukturen zu fördern und flächendeckend angemessene und ausreichende Dienstleistungen zu gewährleisten." Die Regulierung der Telekommunikation ist eine hoheitliche Aufgabe des Bundes. Um die Regulierungsziele zu erreichen, ist ein detailliertes und kompliziertes Regulierungsverfahren installiert worden, das vor allem die folgenden Maßnahmenbereiche umfasst:

- Regulierung des Zugangs zu den Netzen der Telekommunikation. Ziel ist es, für alle Anbieter einen gleichwertigen Zugang zu gewähren und Chancengleichheit sicherzustellen ❶.
- Regulierung des Entgelts. Ziel ist es nach § 27, „eine missbräuchliche Ausbeutung, Behinderung oder Diskriminierung von Endnutzern oder von Wettbewerbern durch preispolitische Maßnahmen von Unternehmen mit beträchtlicher Marktmacht zu verhindern."
- Missbrauchsaufsicht durchführen.
- Festlegen der Frequenzordnung.

❶ § 19 Abs. 1 TKG lautet: „Die Bundesnetzagentur kann einen Betreiber eines öffentlichen Telekommunikationsnetzes mit beträchtlicher Marktmacht dazu verpflichten, dass Vereinbarungen über Zugänge auf objektiven Maßstäben beruhen, nachvollziehbar sein, einen gleichwertigen Zugang gewähren und den Geboten der Chancengleichheit und Billigkeit genügen müssen." Im Kern geht es darum, die Monopolmacht der Deutschen Telekom zu regulieren und auch anderen Anbietern faire Bedingungen sicherzustellen. Als Aufsichtsbehörde ist die Bundesnetzagentur zuständig.

Telemediengesetz

Das am 01.03.2007 in Kraft getretene **Telemediengesetz des Bundes** – umgangssprachlich auch als **Internetgesetz** bezeichnet – dient der einheitlichen Regelung der rechtlichen Aspekte der „Dienste der Informationsgesellschaft, insbesondere des elektronischen Geschäftsverkehrs" ❷.

Unter **Telemedien** sind sämtliche Angebote im Internet zu verstehen. Dies sind Webshops (z. B. Amazon), Online-Auktionshäuser (z. B. eBay), Suchmaschinen (z. B. Google, Lycos), Webmail-Dienste, Informationsdienste (z. B. zu Wetter, Verkehrshinweisen), Podcasts, Chatrooms, Dating-Communities oder Web-Portale (z. B. Yahoo!, YouTube). Auch alle privaten Websites und Blogs fallen unter dieses Gesetz. Nicht als Telemedien gelten beispielsweise Live-Streams oder Webradios, da diese Rundfunk darstellen. Auch die bloße Internet-Telefonie („Voice over IP") ist kein Telemedium, sondern fällt unter die Telekommunikation. Telemedien sind im Gegensatz zu Rundfunkmedien zulassungs- und anmeldefrei. Allerdings haben die Diensteanbieter bestimmten Informationspflichten oder Impressumspflichten (wie z. B. Name und Anschrift, klare Erkennbarkeit von kommerzieller Kommunikation) zu genügen.

❷ In § 1 heißt es: „Dieses Gesetz gilt für alle elektronischen Informations- und Kommunikationsdienste, soweit sie nicht Telekommunikationsdienste nach § 3 Nr. 24 des Telekommunikationsgesetzes, die ganz in der Übertragung von Signalen über Telekommunikationsnetze bestehen, telekommunikationsgestützte Dienste nach § 3 Nr. 25 des Telekommunikationsgesetzes oder Rundfunk nach § 2 des Rundfunkstaatsvertrages sind (Telemedien)."

Stufe 1: Der Auftrag wird vergeben

Die Stadtmarketing GmbH Berlin als Auftraggeber hat zunächst ein Interesse daran, das fertige Werk möglichst uneingeschränkt zu nutzen. Dazu muss sie sich schon im Vertrag mit der Agentur alle notwendigen Verwertungsrechte sichern. Im Mittelpunkt steht das Recht zur Vervielfältigung und zum Verkauf.

Ferner soll der Titel „Berlin – Europäische Metropole der Zukunft" exklusiv für Berlin gesichert werden. Es wäre fatal, wenn z. B. die Städte Rom oder Paris mit dem selben Slogan aufwarten würden. Angesprochen ist damit die Frage eines möglichen Titelschutzes im europäischen Rahmen. Hier sieht es für Berlin gut aus: Seit der Reform des deutschen Markenrechts 1995 und der Einführung der EU-Gemeinschaftsmarkenverordnung 1996 ist der Markenschutz erheblich erweitert und kann einzelne Worte, kurze Musiksequenzen und sogar bestimmte Farben wie z. B. das Lila von Milka erfassen.

Berlin als Auftraggeber hat des Weiteren ein Interesse daran, dass im fertigen Werk das offizielle Logo, das Erscheinungsbild und alle Design-Elemente der äußeren Erscheinung von Berlin Verwendung finden. Den Herstellern wird man daher zwingend die richtige Verwendung der „Marke Berlin" vorschreiben.

❶ Das **Wettbewerbsrecht** sorgt für die Einhaltung der Grenzen des zulässigen Wettbewerbs. Die zentralen Vorschriften sind im „Gesetz gegen den unlauteren Wettbewerb" (UWG) enthalten.

Die Stadtmarketing Berlin GmbH muss schließlich darauf achten, dass sie keine anderen gesetzlichen Grundlagen verletzt. In Frage könnte z. B. das Wettbewerbsrecht ❶ kommen, das einen unlauteren (Städte-)Wettbewerb untersagt. Dort ist z. B. festgelegt, dass ein Ideenklau bzw. das „Abkupfern" von Ideen wettbewerbswidrig ist. Wenn es so wäre, dass Rom oder Paris bereits mit einem ähnlichen Slogan aufwartet, müsste man ganz genau prüfen, ob hier eine Rechtsverletzung vorliegt.

Stufe 2: Die beauftragte Agentur erstellt eine Konzeption

Um das Projekt zu realisieren, muss eine Agentur eingeschaltet werden, die die ganze Konzeption erarbeitet und den Produktionsprozess überwacht. Die Konzeption ist eine wesentliche Voraussetzung für das Gelingen des fertigen Produkts. Die Leistung der Agentur muss daher angemessen vergütet werden.

Die Kosten für die Erarbeitung der Konzeption können beachtlich sein, dies vor allem deshalb, weil sich die Agentur neben der reinen Arbeitsleistung auch die Nutzungsrechte bezahlen lässt.

❷ Unter **Briefing** versteht man den direkten Informationsaustausch zwischen Auftraggeber und Auftragnehmer mit dem Ziel der genauen Festlegung der Aufgabenstellung.

Die Agentur wird vom Auftraggeber mit dessen Vorstellungen und Anforderungen bekannt gemacht, die im sog. Briefing ❷ festgehalten werden. Rechtlich ist festzulegen, dass die Agentur nach Beendigung des Projekts nicht die Möglichkeit hat, die Konzeption oder Teile daraus für andere Zwecke zu verwenden.

Die Stadtmarketing Berlin GmbH muss sich also vor der ungerechtfertigten Weiterverwendung der erarbeiteten Konzeption schützen. Dies geschieht durch Übertragung sämtlicher Nutzungsrechte an der Konzeption von der Agentur an die Berliner Stadtmarketing GmbH.

Stufe 3: Ein Autor wird beauftragt, die Inhalte der Produktion zu verfassen

Die Inhalte, die auf der CD-ROM erscheinen sollen, werden vom Multimedia-Autor bzw. Drehbuch-Autor erstellt. Er arbeitet das Flowchart ❶ aus, entwickelt den Themenbaum, schafft Übersicht, kurz: er verfasst die umsetzungsfähige Produktionsvorlage für das Produkt. Eine Multimedia-Produktion stellt hohe Anforderungen, da prinzipiell alle Medienelemente betroffen sind.

❶ Mit dem **Flowchart** wird die Struktur einer interaktiven Anwendung visualisiert.

Der Autor tut gut daran, schon bei der Entwicklung der (komplexen) Inhalte die anfallenden Rechtekosten mit in Betracht zu ziehen. Von entscheidender Bedeutung ist die Frage, inwieweit die Medienelemente neu produziert werden müssen oder aber vorgefertigt vorliegen bzw. beschafft werden können. Der Autor entscheidet mit, wie hoch der Anteil an Neuproduktionen sein soll, und wie viele vorgefertigte Medienelemente benutzt werden können. Bereits fertiges Material kann aus verschiedenen Quellen wie z. B. Archive oder aus dem Netz bezogen werden.

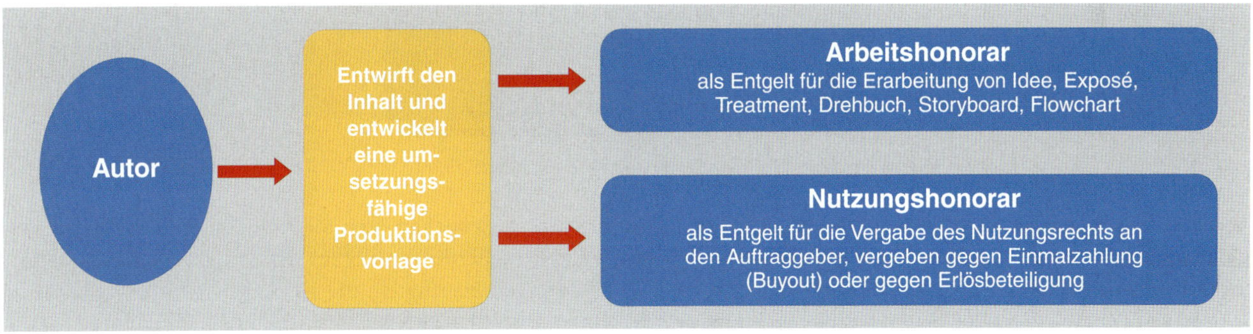

Dem Autor sollte klar sein, dass bei einer sehr umfangreichen Verwendung fremder vorgefertigter Elemente unter Umständen ein erheblicher Aufwand für die Rechteklärung entsteht, der bei multimedialen Produktionen geradezu „aus dem Ruder laufen" kann ❷.

❷ Allerdings gibt es die Hilfestellung von Agenturen. So wäre z. B. die Verwendung des Filmausschnitts aus der berühmten Kennedy-Rede 1963 „Ich bin ein Berliner" in einem vertretbaren finanziellen Rahmen zu realisieren.

Für den Autor selbst wird sich die Frage nach dem Honorar stellen. Dieses teilt sich nach zwei Bestandteilen auf:

- Arbeitshonorar: Entgelt für die Erarbeitung und Ausarbeitung von Idee, Exposé, Treatment, Drehbuch, Flowchart
- Nutzungshonorar: Honorar für die Vergabe des Nutzungsrechts der erstellten Inhalte an den Auftraggeber

Das Arbeitshonorar bemisst sich nach dem voraussichtlichen Aufwand, den der Autor einbringen muss, z. B. 10 Tage, die dann z. B. mit 500 Euro pro Tag vergütet werden. Davon zu trennen ist das Nutzungshonorar. Hier muss der Autor entscheiden, in welcher Form er das Nutzungsrecht erteilt: Zum einen kann er die Rechte gegen eine Einmalzahlung im Sinne eines „Buyout" ❸ abtreten, zum anderen wird er in Form einer regelmäßigen Lizenzzahlung am Erlös der Anwendung beteiligt. In der Praxis werden oft Arbeitshonorar und alle Nutzungsrechte incl. Buyout in einer gesamten Pauschale abgegolten.

❸ Unter **Buyout** versteht man die Entschädigung für die Überlassung des Veröffentlichungsrechts. In der Werbung wird es als prozentualer Aufschlag auf das Grundhonorar verrechnet.

❶ Üblicherweise wird der Videoteil bei Multimedia-Produktionen von externen Dienstleistern hergestellt.

Stufe 4: Das Werk wird von den dazu befähigten Spezialisten hergestellt
An der Herstellung der CD-ROM „Berlin – Europäische Metropole der Zukunft" ist eine Vielzahl von Spezialisten beteiligt. Auf der kreativen Seite sind dies vor allem die Mediendesigner, Screendesigner, Grafiker, Programmierer, auf der Produktionsseite der Vertreter des Multimedia-Produzenten, meist der Projektleiter, sowie Techniker und Operatoren. Wenn Video-Sequenzen eingeplant sind, wird ein Videoteam benötigt ❶. Eventuell kommen Darsteller hinzu. Erforderlich sind in jedem Fall Sprecher.

❷ Kreativleistungen genießen einen besonders starken urheberrechtlichen Schutz!

Man tut gut daran, zunächst davon auszugehen, dass die Arbeit aller Beteiligten einen urheberrechtlichen Schutz genießt – allerdings nicht im selben Umfang. Einen starken Schutz genießen vor allem diejenigen Beteiligten, die als Kreative mit der Schöpfung des neuen Werkes unmittelbar zu tun haben, und das können – wie oben gezeigt – eine ganze Reihe von Personen sein ❷. Geschützt ist das ganze Werk, aber auch jeder einzelne spezielle Beitrag einer Einzelperson zum Gesamtwerk.

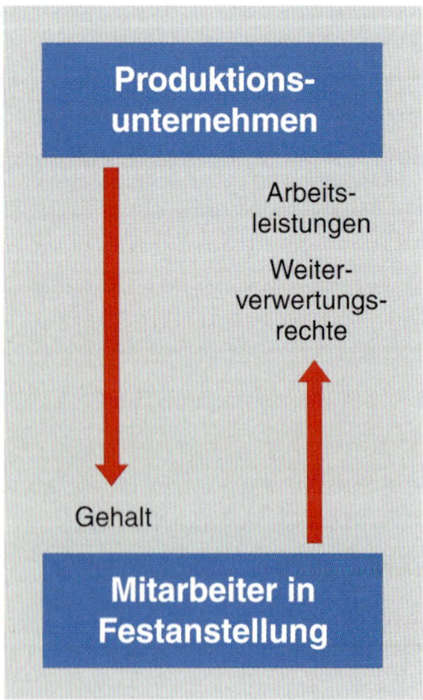

Will also jemand das fertige Werk nutzen, im vorliegenden Falle die Stadtmarketing Berlin GmbH, so ist das Einverständnis hierzu von jedem einzelnen Beteiligten einzuholen. Dieses Einverständnis einzuholen kann – muss aber nicht – zu einigen rechtlichen Schwierigkeiten führen. Zwei Situationen sind denkbar:

- Im ersten Fall wird das Produkt oder wesentliche Teile davon von der Stadtmarketing Berlin GmbH in Eigenregie produziert. Das führt dazu, dass sie mit allen Fragen der Rechteeinholung und Verhandlung über die Höhe der Vergütung der beteiligten Hersteller konfrontiert wird. Das könnte ein zeitraubendes und möglicherweise rechtlich spitzfindiges Unterfangen werden.
- Im vorliegenden Beispiel wird es jedoch wohl eher so sein, dass die Herstellung der Berlin-CD an ein professionelles Produktionsunternehmen (nennen wir es „Multimedia Production Berlin AG") als Auftrag fremd vergeben wird. In diesem (sehr wahrscheinlichen) Fall hat die Stadtmarketing GmbH Berlin normalerweise kein Problem. Sie kann davon ausgehen, dass das Produktionsstudio alle Rechte an den erbrachten Leistungen besitzt und auch berechtigt ist, die Rechte an ihre Auftraggeber weiter zu geben. Das wird sich die Stadtmarketing Berlin GmbH garantieren lassen.

Die Frage der Rechte ist im letzteren Fall ein internes Problem zwischen der „Multimedia Production Berlin AG“ und deren Angestellten und Mitarbeitern. Das Einverständnis der Weiterverwertung liegt normalerweise automatisch vor, wenn es sich um fest angestellte Mitarbeiter handelt, die dann im Rahmen ihres Arbeitsverhältnisses im Austausch gegen ihr Gehalt alle Rechte an ihren Auftraggeber abtreten. Bei freien Mitarbeitern und Subunternehmern sind die Rechte durch separate Vereinbarungen zu übertragen.

Nicht alle Teile der CD-ROM „Berlin – Europäische Metropole der Zukunft“ werden neu zu produzieren sein. Viele Medienbausteine liegen vermutlich schon in der einen oder anderen vorgefertigten Form vor. Die folgenden Quellen lassen sich unterscheiden:

- Material aus PR- und Marketing-Archiven von Berlin, z. B. Logos, offizielles Bild-, Grafik-, Film- und Tonmaterial. Es darf davon ausgegangen werden, dass dieses Material sogar schon in digitalisierter Form vorliegt und die Rechte für jede Form der Verwertung bei der Stadtmarketing Berlin liegen.
- Material, das in diversen anderen Archiven von Berlin betreffend vorliegt, aber erst noch recherchiert werden muss. Zu denken ist z. B. an historische Archive, Museen, Sammlungen, Dokumentationen. Hier ist möglicherweise ein aufwändiger Prozess der Sichtung notwendig, um geeignetes Material zu finden. Die Frage, wie es mit den Rechten für dieses Material aussieht, ist völlig offen. Sie muss genauestens geklärt werden.
- Material, das man von kommerziellen Bild-, Ton- und Film-Archiven beziehen kann, z. B. von Agenturen wie Mauritius, Bavaria, Selected Sound oder Central Order. Hier ist es so, dass eine geradezu gigantische Fülle von verwertbarem Material auf dem Markt zur Verfügung steht. Jeder Produzent wird genauestens prüfen, ob Archivmaterial einsetzbar ist, bevor man in die viel teurere Neuproduktion einsteigt. Allerdings verlangen die Archive selbstverständlich je nach Nutzungsart und Nutzungszeitraum mehr oder weniger hohe Honorare.
- Lizenzfreies Material. Dieses gibt es in der unterschiedlichsten Form, z. B. in Form von Sammlungen, die gegen ein Einmalentgelt genutzt werden dürfen, aber auch als völlig kostenfreie, da über Werbung finanzierte Angebote. Lizenzfrei sind vor allem aber alle Werke, deren urheberrechtliche Schutzfrist (spätestens 70 Jahre nach dem Tod des Urhebers) abgelaufen ist. Solche so genannten „gemeinfreien Werke“ können von jedem beliebig genutzt werden.

Abschließend eine Anmerkung zur Neuproduktion von Bildern und Filmsequenzen: Hier verdient die Frage, wie die im Werk abgebildeten Personen zu behandeln sind, eine besondere rechtliche Beachtung. Jede abgebildete Person besitzt nämlich ein unumstößliches und grundgesetzlich verankertes Persönlichkeitsrecht, das besagt, dass ein jeder das Recht auf eine Privatsphäre besitzt. Abgebildete Personen müssen daher der Veröffentlichung in einem Bild ausdrücklich zustimmen. Neben dem Grundgesetz sichert dieses Recht am eigenen Bild auch der Datenschutz und Spezialgesetze wie das Kunsturhebergesetz (KUG). Lediglich sehr bekannte Personen des öffentlichen Lebens müssen eine gewisse Einschränkung ihres Persönlichkeitsrechts hinnehmen.

Buch im Internet (1)
Ich besitze ein Originalbuch aus dem Jahre 1875, das eine Reisebeschreibung der Türkei zum Gegenstand hat. Der Verfasser ist Herbert P. Glott. Als freundlicher Zeitgenosse will ich das Werk kostenlos der Menschheit zugänglich machen und stelle das ganze Werk gescannt ins Internet. Darf ich das?
Antwort: Da sämtliche Schutzfristen für das Werk abgelaufen sind, sowohl was den Autor als auch den Verlag, der das Buch produziert hat, anbelangt, ist mein Handeln rechtmäßig.

Buch im Internet (2)
Ich als freundlicher Zeitgenosse bin der Meinung, dass man die Lesbarkeit erhöhen sollte und die Neuausgabe des Buches von Herbert P. Glott aus dem Jahr 1985 ins Netz stellen sollte. Immer noch rechtmäßig?
Antwort: Nein. Der herausgebende Verlag hat mit der Neuausgabe des Buches eine verlegerische Leistung erbracht und besitzt dadurch Rechte, gegen die ich nun bei der Veröffentlichung im Internet verstoßen würde.

Wagenfeld-Leuchte
Dem Bastler und Tüftler Sebastian Schlau fällt ein Konstruktionsplan einer Tischlampe im Bauhaus-Stil von Professor Wilhelm Wagenfeld (gest. 1990) aus dem Jahre 1924 in die Hände, von der er ganz begeistert ist. Würde er die Lampe kaufen wollen, müsste er eine Unsumme berappen. So entschließt er sich, diese Lampe selbst nachzubauen und sie der lieben Freundin zu Weihnachten zu schenken. Erlaubt?
Antwort: Ja. Es handelt sich um eine Vervielfältigung zu rein privatem Gebrauch. Die Weitergabe an die Freundin ist keine unerlaubte Verbreitung. Anders sähe es aus, wenn S. Schlau zehn Exemplare nachbauen und diese zum Verkauf anbieten würde, da die Erben des Schöpfers der Lampe Urheberschutz genießen.

Berliner Mauer
Die beiden Graffiti-Künstler Max und Moritz Mumm hatten in den 80er-Jahren in Berlin ein Mauerstück großflächig bemalt. Nach dem Abriss der Mauer kam ein großes Stück dieses Mauerabschitts in Monte Carlo zur Versteigerung. Erlös: eine Mio. Euro für die Firma XY. Die Graffiti-Künstler erfahren davon und verlangen Beteiligung am Versteigerungserlös. Ein berechtigtes Verlangen?
Antwort: Ja. Nach dem Urteil des Bundesgerichtshofs mussten die Künstler am Verkaufserlös angemessen beteiligt werden.

Anmerkung: Es handelt sich um einen wahren Fall (Namen geändert).

17.2.2 Bedeutung des Urheberrechts

Derjenige, der ein Werk schafft, z. B. ein Buch schreibt, ein Musikstück komponiert oder eine Multimedia-CD herstellt, geht zu Recht davon aus, dass er einen besonderen Schutz genießt. Es kann nicht sein, dass irgend jemand, ohne zu fragen und ohne sich die Erlaubnis zu holen, die Früchte harter Arbeit „abgreift" und für eigene Zwecke benutzt. Der Besitzer eines Autos würde ja auch heftig dagegen protestieren, wenn irgend jemand sich daran machen würde, sein Gefährt ungefragt für einen Personentransport zu benutzen!

Es geht also um die Frage der Nutzung von Eigentum, im Falle von Medienprodukten um die **Nutzung geistigen Eigentums**. Das fertige Medienprodukt ist ein eigenständiges **Werk**, das vor dem Zugriff unberechtigter Dritter geschützt ist. Nicht selten ist das Medienprodukt ja dazu da, einen finanziellen Erfolg zu erzielen, wie z. B. ein Fernsehwerbespot. Wenn die – u. U. sehr teure Produktion ❶ – einfach von einem Konkurrenten übernommen werden könnte, oder auch nur die Konzeption, wäre dies ein schwerer Schaden für das Werbung treibende Unternehmen, zumal sich der andere Wettbewerber einen ungerechtfertigten Zeit- und Kostenvorteil verschafft.

❶ Die Herstellungskosten eines Fernsehwerbespots können sich leicht auf 200 Tausend Euro und mehr belaufen.

Auch der Auftraggeber selbst, bzw. der Endkunde, kann das fertige Werk nicht nach Belieben nutzen. Auch er muss den Schutz des Werkes respektieren und kann sich nur das Recht zur Nutzung in einem genau festzulegendem Umfang sichern.

➲ **Das Urheberrecht ist das umfassende Recht des Schöpfers eines Werkes an seinem individuellen geistigen Werk.**

Dieses Recht hat den Charakter eines Eigentums ❷. Geschützt ist ein neu geschaffenes **Werk**, das eine persönliche **geistige Schöpfung** darstellt.

❷ Man sagt, das Urheberrecht ist ein „eigentumsähnliches Recht".

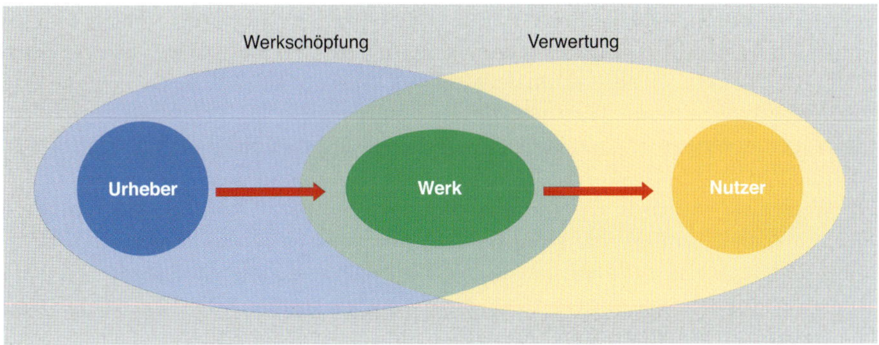

17.2.3 Werk als Schutzgegenstand

Definition Werk

❶ Der Schutzgegenstand im Urheberrecht ist das **Werk**.

Ein fremdes Werk oder auch nur Teile daraus ohne Genehmigung des Urhebers bzw. – wenn es mehrere sind – der Urheber zu verwenden, ist nicht erlaubt ❶. Dabei handelt es sich um ein schwerwiegendes Verbot, das dem Verbot gleichkommt, materielles Eigentum zu entwenden.

Allerdings ist nicht jedes erstellte Produkt und jede erbrachte Leistung gleich ein „Werk“, das wie Eigentum geschützt ist. Nach dem Urheberrecht werden, damit eine Leistung als ein „Werk“ eingestuft wird, bestimmte **Anforderungen** gestellt:

- Individuelle schöpferische Leistung
- Konkretisierung in einer eigenschöpferischen Form

Entscheidend ist vor allem die „individuelle schöpferische Leistung“. Ein Werk muss das Ergebnis einer geistigen Schöpfung sein und sich durch die individuelle Prägung seines Schöpfers auszeichnen.

Ist das Kriterium der „individuellen schöpferischen Leistung“ nicht erfüllt, spricht man von einem **Allerweltserzeugnis**, das keinen urheberrechtlichen Schutz genießt. Ein Allerweltserzeugnis wird als banal oder trivial angesehen, bei dem der Grad der Individualität und Originalität nicht ausreicht, um von einem „Werk“ sprechen zu können. Allerweltserzeugnisse dürfen von jedermann frei benutzt werden.

Forelle blau

Energiegehalt: 918 kJ (216 kcal) Fett: 12g Eiweiß´: 20g Kohlenhydrate: 1g

Zutaten	Zubereitung	Garzeit / Tipps
4 Forellen	waschen, gründlich säubern, in eine Schüssel legen	damit die Forellen eine schöne Blaufärbung bekommen, werden sie einige Zeit in Essig eingelegt.
1/4 l Essig	in einem Topf erwärmen, Fisch übergießen	
	Schüssel abdecken	Ruhezeit 30 Min.
1 1/2 l Wasser	in einem Topf zum kochen bringen	
1 El Salz	zufügen	
2 Zitronen	auspressen, Saft hinzufügen	statt Zitrone kann auch 1/8 l Essig verwendet werden.
1 Tl Zucker		
1 Lorbeerblatt	zufügen	
1 Zwiebel	schälen, halbieren, zufügen, Fisch in die kochende Flüssigkeit einlegen, unter dem Siedepunkt garziehen	15-30 Min. je nach Größe des Fisches
	Forellen herausschöpfen, auf einer Platte anrichten	
1 Zitrone	in Spalten schneiden, garnieren	
2 El Petersilie	waschen, fein wiegen, garnieren	Zur Forelle passen verschiedene Kartoffelbeilagen
50g Butter	in einem Topf erhitzen, in einem Saucengießer dazureichen	

Die Grenze vom Werk zum Allerweltserzeugnis ist weit gezogen, so dass auch noch scheinbar triviale Dinge wie Telefonbücher oder Sammlungen von Kochrezepten als Werk gelten und damit geschützt sind. Auch Datenbanken sind Werke, da sie auf Grund der Auswahl und Anordnung des Stoffes als eine eigene geistige Schöpfung ihres Urhebers anzusehen sind. Ebenso sind z. B. Werbegrafiken, die zu reinen Gebrauchszwecken dienen, normalerweise als Werke einzustufen, da eine geistige Schöpfung vorhanden ist. Gleiches gilt für Industriebauwerke, Bürohäuser oder Gartenanlagen, sofern es sich um künstlerische Schöpfungen handelt.

Ein Werk muss immer in einer „eigenschöpferischen Form“ konkretisiert sein. Eine Idee, die lediglich in Worten geäußert oder mit wenigen Sätzen hingeworfen wird, reicht üblicherweise nicht aus, um als Werk anerkannt zu werden. Erforderlich wäre z. B. eine ausgearbeitete Projektskizze, die dazu noch Dritten bekannt gemacht wird. Nur so gelänge es dem genialen Ideengeber, sich gegen Ideenklau zu schützen.

Die Idee zu einem Multimedia-Produkt ist praktisch nur in Form eines ausgearbeiteten Exposés, Treatments oder Drehbuches, der ausgearbeiteten Benutzer-Oberfläche oder des fertigen Produkts schutzfähig.

Arten von Werken

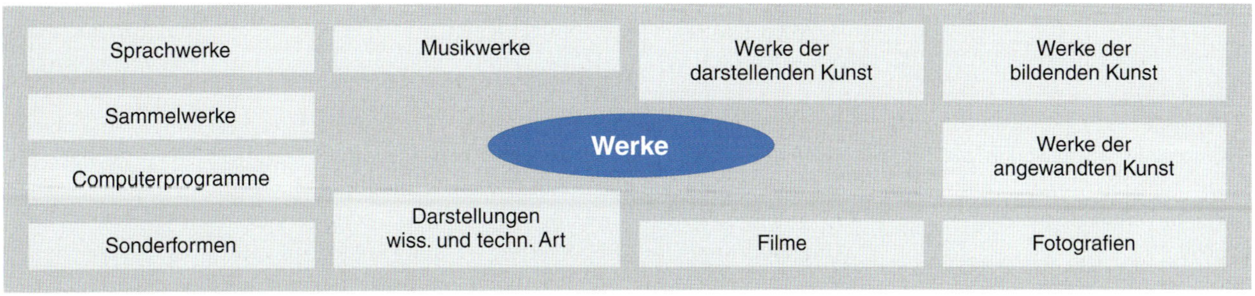

Das Urhebergesetz weist einen Katalog von Leistungen aus, in dem genau bezeichnet wird, was als Werk anzuerkennen ist. Dieser Katalog ist jedoch nicht abschließend zu verstehen. Im Einzelnen handelt es sich um die folgenden **Werke**:

- Sprachwerke: Texte jeder Art, mündliche Aufführungen (Reden). Übersetzungen, andere Bearbeitungen, Zusammenfassungen, Sammlungen von Werken sind selbständig neben den Originalwerken geschützt.
- Musikwerke: Alle Arten der „leichten" und „ernsten Musik" sowie bloße Improvisationen. Geschützt sind auch die Melodie und das Thema. Wenige einzelne Töne sind allerdings nicht mehr schutzfähig.
- Werke der darstellenden Kunst: Tanz, Pantomime, Theater, Choreographien.
- Werke der bildenden Kunst: Gemälde, Zeichnungen, Collagen, Skulpturen, Bauwerke usw.
- Werke der angewandten Kunst: Werbekonzeptionen, Werbetexte, Werbefotos, Werbefilme, Werbeplakate. Der Schutz von Werbeslogans und Warenetiketten wird überwiegend verneint.
- Fotografien: Geschützt sind nicht nur schöpferische Fotos („Lichtbildwerke"), sondern auch andere Fotos wie z. B. Schnappschüsse („Lichtbilder").
- Filme: Wie bei Fotografien wird zwischen schöpferischen Filmwerken und den sog. Laufbildern unterschieden. Bild- und Tonteile eines Filmes werden als eine Einheit betrachtet.
- Darstellungen wissenschaftlicher oder technischer Art: Pläne, Skizzen, Karten, Tabellen, Modelle, soweit sie geeignet sind, über technische oder wissenschaftliche Sachverhalte zu belehren. Darunter fallen z. B. auch Zeichnungen in Kindersachbüchern.
- Computerprogramme: Sie sind erst seit 1993 im Urheberrecht geschützt. Der Schutz umfasst nicht nur den Quellcode, sondern auch alles vorbereitende und begleitende Material.
- Sammelwerke: Sammlungen sind Werke, wenn sie durch Auslese oder Anordnung eine persönliche geistige Schöpfung sind.
- Datenbanken jeglicher Art: Hier handelt es sich um eine relativ neue Werkart. Es geht z. B. um den Katalog eines Shopping-Angebots, um eine Suchmaschine oder um ein Produktverzeichnis.

Neben den Werken sind deren Titel selbständig geschützt, ohne dass es einer Eintragung in das Markenregister beim Deutschen Patentamt bedarf.

Besondere Werke

Hinzuweisen ist auf einige **Sonderformen von Werken**. Die meisten, aber nicht alle aufgeführten Leistungen werden auch rechtlich als eigenständige Werke anerkannt:

- **Bearbeitungen** eines Werkes: Handelt es sich um eine eigenständige persönliche geistige Schöpfung, ist eine Bearbeitung wie ein selbständiges Werk geschützt ❶. Selbstverständlich bedarf die Veröffentlichung und Verwertung einer Bearbeitung der vorherigen Einwilligung des Urhebers des bearbeiteten Werkes.
- **Umgestaltung:** Eine Umgestaltung ist eine Veränderung eines bestehenden Werkes, das aber nicht die Qualität einer persönlichen geistigen Schöpfung erreicht und daher ungeschützt ist ❷.
- **Übersetzungen:** Die Übertragung eines Sprachwerkes in eine andere Sprache oder Mundart gilt stets als ein neues Werk und genießt daher einen eigenständigen Urheberschutz.
- **Parodie:** Hier handelt es sich um die Bearbeitung eines bestehenden Werkes mit dem Ziel, die übernommenen Werkteile komisch oder satirisch wirken zu lassen. Bis zur Grenze der Entstellung darf ein bestehendes Werk zum Zweck der Parodie frei benutzt werden. Einschränkungen sind aber im Musikbereich gegeben. Für musikalische Parodien sind die Grenzen sehr eng gezogen, weil es den sog. „starren Melodienschutz“ gibt, nach dem die Melodie eines Musikwerkes keinem anderen Musikwerk zugrunde gelegt werden darf. Auch eine Variation einer Melodie anderer Komponisten ist unzulässig. Eine freie Benutzung im Musikbereich ist daher praktisch ausgeschlossen.
- **Zitat:** Grundsätzlich hat jeder das Recht, einzelne Stellen aus einem Werk zu zitieren (Zitierfreiheit). Dies ist eine Einschränkung des Urheberrechts im Interesse der Allgemeinheit. Ein Zitat liegt vor, wenn einzelne Stellen eines bestehenden Werkes in einem neuen, selbständigen Werk verwendet werden. Dabei muss der Zweck vorliegen, eine Assoziation herbeizuführen, ohne zu einem tragenden Bestandteil des neuen Werkes zu werden.
- **Plagiat:** Hier handelt es sich um ein Produkt, dessen Erschaffer fremdes Geistesgut übernimmt und als sein eigenes ausgibt. Der Erschaffer ist ein Plagiator und macht sich einer Rechtsverletzung schuldig. Beispiel: Ein Sachbuch-Autor übernimmt ganze Passagen eines anderen Sachbuches wörtlich, ohne irgendeinen Hinweis, in sein Buch.
- **Gemeinfreie Werke:** Dies sind solche Werke, deren Schutzfrist (70 Jahre nach dem Tod des Urhebers) abgelaufen ist. Sie dürfen frei verwendet werden.

❶ Beispiele sind die Dramatisierung eines Schriftwerkes, die Schaffung eines Klavierauszugs oder eines musikalischen Potpourris.

❷ Eine **Umgestaltung** ist kein eigenständiges Werk – im Gegensatz zur „Bearbeitung“!

Benutzung von Werkpartikeln

Häufig wird bei Medienproduktionen nicht das vollständige Sprach-, Bild- oder Filmwerk benutzt, sondern nur kleine und kleinste **Partikel** aus diesen Werken. So werden z. B. im Musikbereich oft nur diverse Sounds kopiert oder nur Musikelemente wie Schlagzeugfiguren, Bassläufe oder Keyboard-Einstellungen. Nach allgemeiner Ansicht sind diese Partikel urheberrechtlich nicht geschützt, da sie nicht „melodietragend“ sind. Sie stellen lediglich „abstrakte Ideen ohne konkrete Form“ dar und sind nicht urheberrechtsfähig.

17.2.4 Urheber als Werkschöpfer

Begriff Urheber

Der **Urheber** ist der **Schöpfer eines Werkes**. Schöpfer wird man, wenn man ein Werk „mit eigenen Händen", auch unter Zuhilfenahme von Werkzeugen, geschaffen hat. Der Begriff „mit eigenen Händen" darf nicht wörtlich genommen werden, beim Werk eines Urheber handelt es sich vielmehr um eine **persönlich-geistige Schöpfung**, die selbständig geschaffen wurde. Ein rein maschinell und über eine Software erzeugte Informationsdarstellung ist daher nicht schutzfähig.

Ein **Urheber** ist immer ein **konkreter Mensch**, d. h. eine natürliche Person. Niemals kann eine juristische Person, also ein Unternehmen, eine staatliche oder private Institution, eine kommerzielle oder gemeinnützige Organisation, Träger eines Urheberrechts sein.

An der Erstellung einer Medienproduktion sind normalerweise eine ganze Reihe von Personen beteiligt, ohne deren Einsatz und Sachverstand das Werk nicht zustande kommen würde. Man steht also oft vor der Situation, dass mehrere Personen ein Werk gemeinsam geschaffen haben, ohne dass sich die Anteile der einzelnen gesondert verwerten lassen. Auch in diesem Fall erlangt nicht die Menschengruppe, z. B. ein Multimedia-Produktionsteam, den Urheberstatus, sondern **jeder einzelne** des Teams wird zum Urheber oder Miturheber.

Nur derjenige, der ein Werk geschaffen hat, ist Urheber ❶. Die Urheberschaft kann nicht an einen Vorgesetzten, an einen Auftraggeber oder einen sonstigen Dritten abgetreten werden. Die Urheberrechte sind also immer an die Person des Werkschöpfers gebunden. Das hat Bedeutung für Urheber, die in abhängigen Arbeitsverhältnissen stehen: So kann ein Arbeitgeber logischerweise von seinen Angestellten nicht verlangen, die Urheberschaft für geschaffene Werke abzutreten.

❶ Ohne Werk kein Urheber! Ohne Urheber kein Werk!

Der Schöpfer ist Urheber, so lange er lebt. Diese Rolle kann nicht übertragen werden, auch nicht durch Vererbung ❷. **Übertragbar** ist lediglich das **Nutzungsrecht** am geschaffenen Werk, das auch weiter vererbt werden kann.

❷ Die **Urheberschaft** ist also ein unveräußerliches Gut und eine Tatsache, über die man nicht streiten kann.

➲ **Der Urheber ist der Schöpfer eines Werkes. Er ist immer eine natürliche Person.**

Arten von Urhebern

Bei medialen Werken kommen eine Vielzahl von Personen in Betracht, die als **Urheber** anzusehen sind. Man kann dabei **nach Bereichen** unterscheiden:

- Text, Audio, Film: Textdichter, Drehbuchautor, Schriftsteller, Verfasser von Exposés, Treatments, Verfasser von wissenschaftlichen oder technischen Darstellungen, Komponist, Filmkomponist, Autor der Dialoge, Hauptregisseur
- Multimedia: Spezielle Urheber wie Drehbuchautoren, Programmierer, Screen-Designer, Konzeptionisten, Schöpfer von 3D-Animationen, Web-Designer

Umstritten und daher im Einzelfall zu beurteilen ist, inwieweit z. B. der Kameramann oder die Cutterin in die Rolle der Urheberschaft schlüpfen können. Das Urheberrecht sieht dies eher negativ und wirkt mit einem eigenen Abschnitt darauf hin, dass die Verwertungs- und Leistungsschutzrechte nicht auf die einzelnen Beteiligten verteilt werden, sondern sich letztlich in der Person des Filmproduzenten vereinigen. Dadurch soll verhindert werden, dass einzelne an der Gestaltung des Filmes Mitwirkende die Verwertung des Filmwerkes im Zweifel unnötig erschweren.

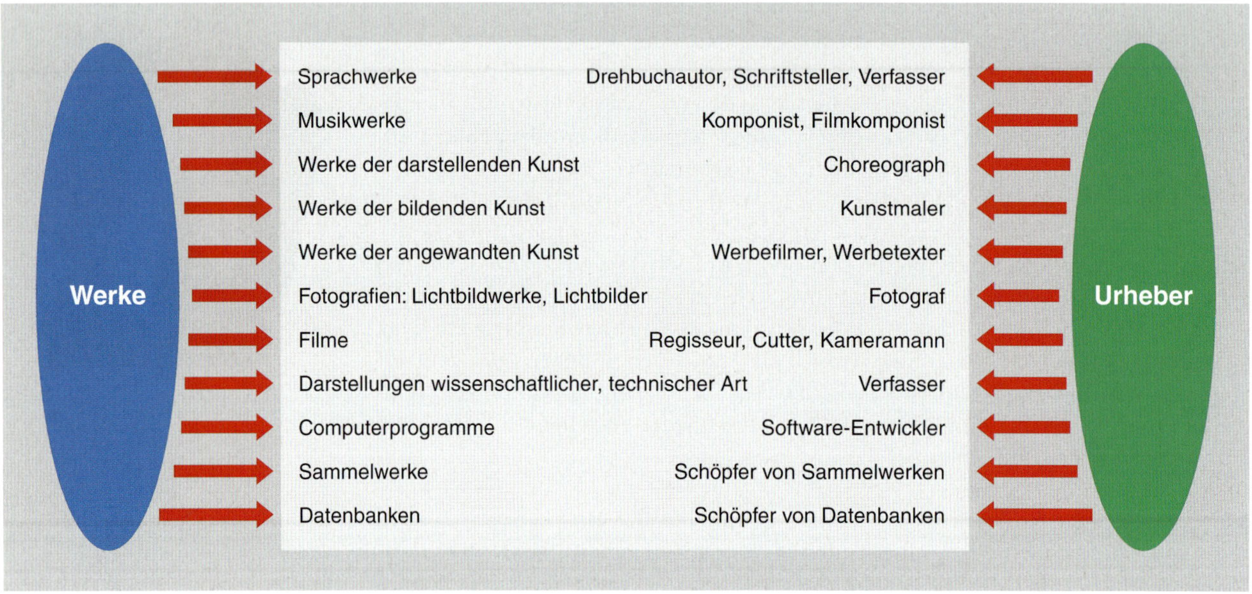

Leistungsschutzrechte der Mitwirkenden

❶ **Ausübende Künstler** sind:
- Schauspieler
- Sänger
- Musiker
- Tänzer
- Dirigenten
- Ensembles wie Orchester, Chöre, Musikgruppen, Ballett; vertreten durch den Vorstand
- Rezitatoren

Diejenigen Personen, die ein Werk darstellen, vorführen, zur Aufführung bringen, vortragen, präsentieren oder daran künstlerisch mitwirken, z. B. als Schauspieler, Sänger, Musiker oder als sonstige Mitwirkende, sind Ausübende Künstler, die sog. „Darbietungen" erbringen ❶. Sie sind keine Urheber im eigentlichen Sinne, sondern „Inhaber verwandter Schutzrechte" und genießen nur einen eingeschränkten Schutz.

Diese Schutzrechte werden auch **Leistungsschutzrechte** genannt ❷. Dass dieser Personenkreis überhaupt urheberrechtlich geschützt ist, darf nicht als selbstverständlich angenommen werden, denn nach dem Geist des Urhebergesetzes ist grundsätzlich nur die eigenständige schöpferische Leistung schutzwürdig. Der Schutz erklärt sich aus der Tatsache, dass die Leistungen der Mitwirkenden aber den Leistungen der Urheber in gewisser Weise ähnlich sind oder im Zusammenhang mit ihnen erbracht werden.

❷ **Leistungsschutzrechte** sind die Rechte der ausübenden Künstler, also derjenigen Personen, die ein Werk vortragen oder aufführen.

Kein ausübender Künstler (und schon gar nicht ein Werkschöpfer) ist z. B. ein Fernsehansager, da seine Äußerungen keine Wiedergabe eines schutzwürdigen Werkes sind. Mitwirkender ist im übrigen nur der, der auf die künstlerische Interpretation des Werkes einen bestimmenden Einfluss ausübt.

17.2.5 Geschützte Rechte

Das Urheberrecht schützt den Urheber zweifach: Zum einen ihn persönlich, zum anderen sein Werk. Die beiden Schutzbereiche sind daher zum einen das Persönlichkeitsrecht des Urhebers, zum anderen das Verwertungsrecht des Werkes.

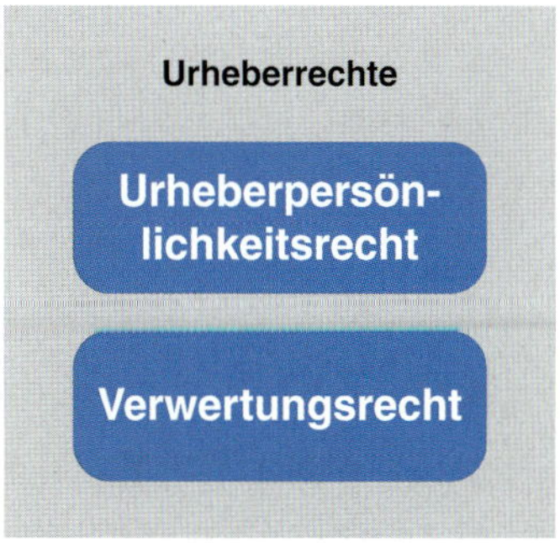

Urheberpersönlichkeitsrecht

Mit diesem Recht wird das Verhältnis des Urhebers zu seinem Werk bestimmt. Es ist ein Recht, das niemand dem Urheber nehmen kann. Zum Urheberpersönlichkeitsrecht gehören die folgenden **Teil-Rechte**:

- Veröffentlichungsrecht: Das ist das Recht des Urhebers, selbst darüber zu bestimmen, ob sein Werk überhaupt veröffentlicht wird, und wenn ja, wie.
- Recht auf Namensnennung: Ferner hat der Urheber das Recht, dass sein Name im Zusammenhang mit dem Werk genannt wird und mit welcher Urheberbezeichnung das Werk zu versehen ist.
- Recht auf Verhinderung der Entstellung des Werkes: Schließlich hat der Urheber das Recht, eine Entstellung oder Beeinträchtigung seines Werkes zu verbieten.

Verwertungsrechte

Die Verwertungsrechte schützen hauptsächlich die materiellen Interessen des Urhebers, im Gegensatz zu den angeführten persönlichen Interessen.

Danach hat der Urheber das alleinige Recht, über die Verwertung seines Werkes zu verfügen. Dieses Recht kann er anderen übertragen ❶. Die wichtigsten **Verwertungsrechte** sind:

❶ Nur das **Verwertungsrecht** ist übertragbar, nicht das **Persönlichkeitsrecht**!

- **Vervielfältigungsrecht:** Der Urheber hat das Recht, selbst darüber zu bestimmen, ob und in welcher Anzahl von seinem Werk Vervielfältigungsstücke hergestellt werden.
- **Verbreitungsrecht:** Dies ist das Recht, das Original-Werk oder Vervielfältigungsstücke des Werkes der Öffentlichkeit anzubieten, in Verkehr zu bringen, zu verkaufen, zu verschenken oder zu vermieten.
- **Ausstellungsrecht:** Es handelt sich um das Recht, das Original oder Vervielfältigungsstücke öffentlich zur Schau zu stellen (gilt besonders für Werke der bildenden Künste und der Fotografie).
- Vortrags-, Aufführungs- und **Vorführungsrecht:** Dies ist das Recht auf die unmittelbare öffentliche Wiedergabe des Werkes (ohne das Senderecht).
- **Senderecht:** Das Senderecht ist das Recht, das Werk durch Funk der Öffentlichkeit zugänglich zu machen. Der Begriff „Funk" ist als ein Oberbegriff zu verstehen, der alle technischen Verfahren erfasst, die Texte, Bilder und Töne von einer Sendestelle zu beliebig vielen Empfangsstellen übertragen. Darunter fallen auch das Internet und Online-Dienste.
- **Recht der Wiedergabe durch Bild- und Tonträger:** Hier handelt es sich um Zweitverwertungsrechte, da die Wiedergabe durch Bild- und Tonträger erst möglich ist, nachdem das Werk vervielfältigt worden ist.

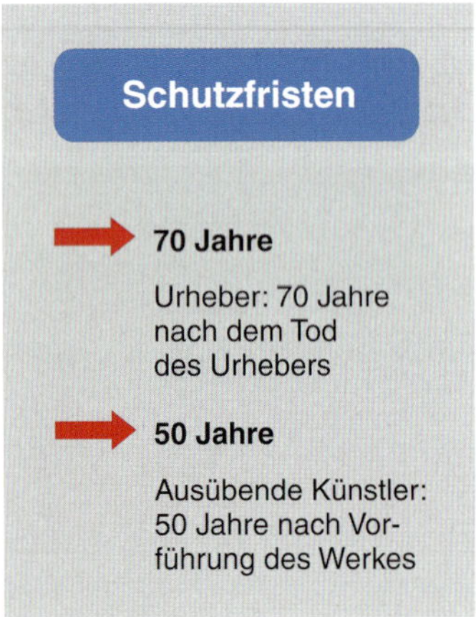

17.2.6 Einräumung von Nutzungsrechten

Dauer des Urheberrechts

Nutzungsrechte einzuräumen ist nur möglich innerhalb der **gesetzlichen Schutzfristen**. Sind die Schutzfristen abgelaufen, kann das Werk von jedermann frei genutzt werden. Man spricht dann von **gemeinfreien Werken**.

Die Schutzdauer für „Werke“ als die schöpferischen Leistungen beträgt 70 Jahre, gerechnet ab dem Tod des Urhebers. Für Inhaber von Leistungsschutzrechten (also z. B. Darsteller, Schauspieler, ausübende Künstler) werden nichtschöpferische Leistungen unterstellt und eine verkürzte Schutzfrist angesetzt. Sie beträgt grundsätzlich 50 Jahre nach Aufführung, Veröffentlichung oder Erscheinen des Werkes. Die Schutzfristen sind seit 1994 innerhalb der EU vereinheitlicht worden.

Beschränkung der Nutzungsrechte

exklusiv die reportage

Der Urheber kann die Nutzungsrechte an seinem Werk in freier Entscheidung vergeben. Dabei hat er eine Reihe von **Möglichkeiten**. Zunächst kann er die Rechte einfach oder exklusiv vergeben:

- Einfaches Nutzungsrecht: Vergibt der Urheber das einfache Nutzungsrecht, hat der Inhaber keinen Anspruch auf die alleinige, exklusive Nutzung des Werkes. Es kann also sein, dass mehrere Lizenznehmer das Nutzungsrecht gleichzeitig besitzen. Auch der Urheber selbst kann sein Werk weiterhin nutzen. In den meisten Fällen wird das einfache Nutzungsrecht wenig sinnvoll sein, da der Zweck des Rechteerwerbs untergraben würde. Man denke z. B. an eine TV-Werbekampagne oder eine Musikproduktion.
- Ausschließliches bzw. exklusives Nutzungsrecht: Der Erwerber dieses Rechts kann das Werk unter Ausschluss aller anderen Personen einschließlich des Urhebers nutzen. Er darf sogar – falls der Urheber zustimmt – weiteren Personen einfache Nutzungsrechte einräumen.

Die Nutzungsrechte können ferner auch noch räumlich, zeitlich und inhaltlich beschränkt sein. Zur Vermeidung von Irritationen müssen die Vertragspartner vor Auftragsbeginn genau festhalten, welche Rechte benötigt und eingeräumt werden.

- Räumliche Begrenzung: Hier erfolgt eine Beschränkung auf einzelne Länder, Sprachräume oder sogar Orte, z. B. für Berlin. Werden z. B. für eine Buchauflage nur die Rechte für den deutschsprachigen Raum erworben, ist bei einer weiteren Auflage in englischer Sprache eine zusätzliche Rechteeinräumung und Vergütung fällig.
- Zeitliche Begrenzung: Möglich ist die Beschränkung z. B. für die Dauer einer Werbekampagne, für eine bestimmte Anzahl von Monaten oder von Jahren.
- Inhaltliche Begrenzung: Die Beschränkung erfolgt hier im Hinblick auf die Nutzungsarten. So kann z. B. die Auflage eines Buches oder einer CD-ROM auf eine bestimmte Höhe begrenzt sein. Auch der Einsatz kann begrenzt sein, z. B. beschränkt auf die Kino- und Pay-TV-Ausstrahlung eines Filmes oder den Einsatz einer Archivszene nur für einen TV-Werbespot.

17.2.7 Verwertungspraxis

Verlage

Sollen z. B. in einer Multimedia-Produktion fremde Werkteile eingebaut werden, steht man vor der Frage, an wen man sich wenden soll, um sich das Nutzungsrecht zu sichern.

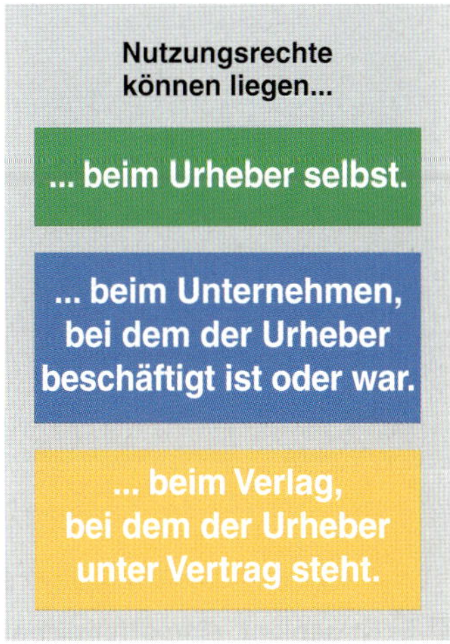

Bei bildenden Künstlern wie Malern und Bildhauern liegen die Rechte meist noch bei den **Urhebern selbst**. Geht es um Computer-Software, hat man es normalerweise mit **Arbeitnehmer-Urhebern** zu tun, und man muss sich an die betreffende Firma wenden.

Bei den Nutzungsrechten von Texten, Bildern und Musik liegen die Rechte demgegenüber normalerweise bei den **Verlagen**, bei denen die Autoren unter Vertrag stehen. Daher ist unbedingt der Verlag einzuschalten, wenn es um die Rechteklärung geht. Allerdings kann es hier zu unbefriedigenden Situationen kommen, da die Verlage die in Frage stehenden Rechte oft selbst nicht erworben haben, gerade wenn es um Multimedia-Produktionen geht. Daher muss die Rechtesituation bei Verlagen, Museen und Archiven besonders genau geprüft werden. Zu beachten ist, dass auch eine Haftungsklausel im Vertrag den Rechteverwerter vom Schadensersatz nicht freistellt, da es den „gutgläubigen Erwerb" ❶ im Urheberrecht nicht gibt.

❶ **Gutgläubiger Erwerb**: Jemand verleiht sein Auto an einen anderen und der verkauft es an einen Dritten. Der Dritte wird Eigentümer des Autos, da er dieses gutgläubig erworben hat.

Allerdings werden viele Autoren, die bei einem Verlag unter Vertrag stehen, häufig nicht bereit sein, ohne die Einschaltung des Verlags Rechte am Werk weiter zu geben. Daher empfiehlt es sich auf jeden Fall, mit dem Verlag Kontakt aufzunehmen, um auf der sicheren Seite zu stehen.

Verwertungsgesellschaften

Bedeutung der Verwertungsgesellschaften:
Die größte Rolle bei der Verwertung von Nutzungsrechten spielen die **Verwertungsgesellschaften**. Sie üben eine doppelte Funktion aus:

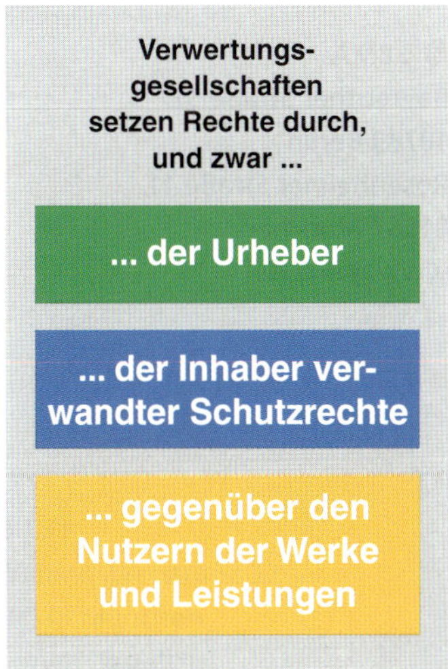

- Sie helfen denjenigen, die ein Nutzungsrecht suchen, die betreffenden Rechte ordnungsgemäß zu erwerben.
- Sie helfen vor allem aber den Urhebern, ihre Rechte durchzusetzen und nicht übervorteilt zu werden. Ohne ihre Hilfestellung würde es z. B. im musikalischen Bereich den Komponisten kaum gelingen, ihr Recht gegenüber den Konzertveranstaltern oder Restaurantbesitzern, die ihre Musikwerke zur Aufführung bringen oder abspielen, durchzusetzen. Nur weil sie sich der organisierten Form einer Verwertungsgesellschaft bedienen, können sie die systematische Abgeltung ihrer Ansprüche sicher stellen.

Unter den Begriff der Filmemacher fallen auch die Multimedia-Produzenten. Sollen die Rechte an einer fertigen Multimedia-Produktion von einer Verwertungsgesellschaft gesichert werden, bietet sich die VFF als Ansprechpartner an. Sollen fremde Multimedia-Produktionen oder Teile davon in die eigene Produktion eingebaut werden, ist die VFF ebenfalls relevant.

GVL:

Die Leistungsschutzrechte nimmt die GVL, die „Gesellschaft zur Verwertung von Leistungsschutzrechten mbH", wahr ❶. Sie vertritt die Rechte der folgenden Berufsgruppen:

❶ **GVL**
Heimhuder Straße 5
20148 Hamburg
www.gvl.de

- Ausübende Künstler
- Veranstalter
- Tonträgerhersteller
- Hersteller von Videoclips
- Schallplattenhersteller

Im Falle von Multimedia-Produktionen übertragen die ausübenden Künstler der GVL zur Wahrnehmung gegenüber Dritten das Senderecht sowie das Recht der Aufnahme, Vervielfältigung und öffentlichen Wiedergabe von Funksendungen. Tonträgerhersteller übertragen der GVL das Recht zur Aufnahme von Sendungen auf Bildtonträger (CD-ROM) und Übertragung von einem auf einen anderen Träger zum privaten Gebrauch und die unkörperliche, digitale Verbreitung, z. B. im Weg von Online.

VG Media:

Der offizielle Firmierung lautet: „VG Media zur Verwertung der Urheber- und Leistungsschutzrechte von Medienunternehmen mbH" ❷. Sie ist seit 1997 zugelassen und ist zuständig für die treuhänderische Wahrnehmung von Urheber- und Leistungsschutzrechten, die sich aus dem Urheberrechtsgesetz für private Medienunternehmen ergeben. Die VG Media nimmt die Interessen von derzeit 123 privaten Sendeunternehmen gegenüber unterschiedlichsten Nutzergruppen wahr. U. a. sind TV-Stationen beteiligt (v. a. Sat.1, ProSieben, N24, SPORT1, CNBC Europe, AL Jazeera, SBS 6, Eurosport, RTL und VIVA) sowie Radiosender (v. a. ANTENNE BAYERN, Klassik Radio, RTL RADIO, Hit Radio FFH und radio ffn).

❷ **VG Media**
Eichhornstraße 3
D-10785 Berlin
www.vgmedia.de

Die VG Media hat nach eigenen Angaben mit rund 34 000 Vertragspartnern, darunter Kabelnetz- und IPTV-Betreiber, Wohnungsunternehmen, Anbieter mobiler Dienstleistungen und elektronischer Programmführer (EPG), Beherbergungsbetriebe, Krankenhäuser und Fitnessstudios, umfangreiche Lizenzverträge geschlossen.

Aufgaben und Übungen, Literaturhinweise

Aufgaben und Übungen

1. Sammeln Sie Beispiele von Fernsehsendungen, von denen Sie der Auffassung sind, dass die „Würde des Menschen" nach Art. 1 Grundgesetz in Frage gestellt sein könnte.
2. Recherchieren Sie, wie die Indizierungspraxis der Bundesprüfstelle für jugendgefährdende Medien (BPjM) aussieht.
3. Recherchieren Sie den „Cicero-Fall" zum Thema Pressefreiheit.
4. Lesen Sie sorgfältig den Text des Rundfunkstaatsvertrages (RStV) durch.
5. Verfolgen Sie eine Woche lang eine Tageszeitung und sammeln Sie Fallbeispiele, die mit dem Urheberrecht zu tun haben.
6. Analysieren Sie die nächste private Fete darauf hin, was rechtlich passieren würde, wenn es sich um eine öffentliche Veranstaltung handelte.
7. Finden Sie heraus, welche GEMA-Gebühren anfallen würden, wenn Sie eine öffentliche Veranstaltung mit einer Kleinkunstgruppe durchführen. Treffen Sie entsprechende Annahmen.
8. Beobachten Sie den Abspann eines Kinofilms und erklären Sie, welche der Funktionen unter den Urheberschutz im eigentlichen Sinne und welche und die Leistungsschutzrechte fallen.
9. Schneiden Sie eine Anzeige aus der Zeitung aus und erklären Sie, was es im Zusammenhang mit dieser Anzeige an urheberrechtlichen Fragen geben könnte.

Literaturhinweise

Fechner, Frank: Medienrecht – Rechtsgrundlagen für Medienmanager, in: Scholz, Christian (Hrsg.): Handbuch Medienmanagement, Berlin, Heidelberg, New York 2006 (Springer), S. 239-260

Fechner, Frank: Medienrecht, 13. Aufl., Stuttgart 2012 (UTB)

Fechner, Frank; *Schipanski*, Tankred; *Rösler*, Albrecht: Fälle und Lösungen zum Medienrecht, 3. Aufl., Stuttgart 2012 (UTB)

Fricke, Ernst: Recht für Journalisten, 2. Aufl., Konstanz 2010 (UVK)

Hesse, Albrecht: Rundfunkrecht, 3. Aufl., München 2003 (Vahlen)

Homann, Hans-Jürgen: Praxishandbuch Filmrecht. Ein Leitfaden für Film-, Fernseh- und Medienschaffende. Berlin, Heidelberg, New York 2007 (Springer)

Jacobshagen, Patrick: Filmrecht – Die Verträge, Bergkirchen 2005 (Ppv Verlag)

Merx, Oliver; *Tandler*, Ernst; *Hahn*, Heinfried: Multimedia-Recht für die Praxis, Berlin, Heidelberg, New York 2002 (Springer)

Reisewitz, Perry (Hrsg.): Pressefreiheit unter Druck, Wiesbaden (VS Verlag)

Wilmer, Thomas: Ideen schützen lassen, 2. Aufl., München 2007 (dtv-Taschenbuch)

18 Kalkulation

Webcode: C1800

Für weitere Infos zu diesem Kapitel mit dem Smartphone einfach QR-Code scannen oder auf www.medien-verstehen.de den Webcode eingeben.

Ein Medienprodukt herzustellen erfordert nicht nur den geballten Sachverstand von Autoren, Gestaltern, Produzenten und Technikern, sondern auch den Sachverstand der Ökonomen und Projektmanager. Diese sorgen dafür, dass

- die Finanzierung des Projekts gesichert ist, was z. B. bei einem Kinofilm nicht selten eine besondere Herausforderung darstellt;
- das Gebot der Wirtschaftlichkeit beachtet wird, dass also z. B. der Film, das Buchprojekt oder der Internet-Auftritt kostengünstig und wirtschaftlich vertretbar hergestellt wird;
- dass der Produktionsvorgang, z. B. einer Multimedia-CD-ROM, einer Fernsehsendung oder einer Audio-CD gut organisiert ist und rationell und effektiv abläuft;
- dass die Vermarktung funktioniert, z. B. einer Spiele-CD, und daher die Chance auf Marktgewinne nicht vertan wird.

Eine besondere Herausforderung stellt die **Kalkulation** eines Medienproduktes dar, da es eine zentrale Voraussetzung für die Produktion ist: Erst wenn man weiß, was das Produkt kosten soll, kann man daran gehen, es herzustellen.

Methodisch gesehen ist die Kalkulation Teil der **Kosten- und Leistungsrechnung** und damit derjenige Teil des **Rechnungswesens** eines Unternehmens, der auf Informationen interner Art ausgerichtet ist. Zweck der Kosten- und Leistungsrechnung ist es, gesicherte Informationen für die Steuerung und das Management des betrieblichen („operativen") Bereiches zu gewinnen. Leitziel ist die Sicherstellung der **Wirtschaftlichkeit** des Wertschöpfungsprozesses.

Im Fokus der Betrachtung stehen die Endprodukte, also die zu erbringenden Leistungen, die in der Kosten- und Leistungsrechnung **Kostenträger** genannt werden ❶. Die Ermittlung der Kosten der Kostenträger bzw. Leistungen bzw. Produkte nennt man „Kalkulation". Vorrangige Aufgabe der Kosten- und Leistungsrechnung ist damit die Kalkulation der Kosten der Produkte, die hergestellt werden sollen. Im Überblick sind die folgenden **Zwecke der Kalkulation** zu unterscheiden:

❶ Ein **Kostenträger** ist also z. B. eine Buchauflage, eine Sendestrecke im Radio, eine einzelne TV-Sendung, ein Kino-Film oder ein Computerspiel.

- Schaffen einer Grundlage für die Abgabe eines Angebots und Ermittlung des Angebotspreises, Findung der Preisuntergrenze, Beherrschung der Kosten,
- Schaffen von Vergleichs- und Kontrollmöglichkeiten für das Kostencontrolling,
- Schaffen einer Grundlage für die Erfolgsermittlung und Erfolgskontrolle,
- Erarbeiten einer Unterlage für zukünftige Kalkulationen gleichartiger oder ähnlicher Leistungen, Aufbau eines Erfahrungsschatzes.

Endpunkt der Kalkulation ist die vollständige und transparente Aufbereitung der anfallenden oder angefallenen Kosten. Im vorliegenden Kapitel wird die Kalkulation von Medienprojekten näher beleuchtet. Das geschieht zum einen methodisch, indem ein 5-Schritte-Konzept der Kalkulation vorgestellt wird, das für jedes Medienprojekt angewandt werden kann. Zum anderen werden ausgewählte Medienbereiche im Sinne von Fallbeispielen vorgestellt.

18.1 Typische Kosten von Medienprodukten

Medienprodukte können sowohl in der Herstellung als auch in ihrer Verbreitung **beträchtliche Größenordnungen** annehmen. So stellte der Kinofilm „Titanic" im Jahr 1997 mit 200 Millionen Dollar Produktionskosten einen neuen „Weltrekord" auf, der zehn Jahre später durch Filme wie „Fluch der Karibik – Teil 3" (225 Millionen) und „Spider-Man 3" (258 Millionen) schon wieder übertroffen wurde ❶. Was die Kosten der Verbreitung von Medienprodukten anbelangt, bietet die Fernsehwerbung ein gutes Beispiel. Während die durchschnittlichen Herstellungskosten eines 30-Sekunden-TV-Spots, der für eine nationale Kampagne gedacht ist, immerhin stolze 150.000 Euro ausmachen, belaufen sich die Schaltkosten in den Medien auf ein Vielfaches. Die Schaltung eines einzigen 30-Sekunden-Spots z. B. in der Prime-Time von RTL kostet bis zu 70.000 Euro. Um eine ganze Fernsehkampagne zu fahren, kommt ein großer Markenartikler also schnell in eine Größenordnung eines zweistelligen Millionenbetrages.

❶ Wie rentabel solche Groß-Investitionen dennoch sein können, sieht man am weltweiten Einspiel-Erfolg der „Titanic", der sich bis heute auf mehr als zwei Milliarden Dollar beläuft!

18.1.1 Herstellungskosten

Die Welt der Kosten ❷ ist so bunt wie die Welt der Medienprodukte. Kein Fernsehwerbespot, kein Spielfilm, kein Computerspiel gleicht dem anderen. Jedes Medienprodukt hat seine ganz besondere Eigenart ❸, was zur Folge hat, dass es zwischen den einzelnen Formen vergleichsweise **große Kostenunterschiede** gibt. Zu unterscheiden sind dabei die Kosten für die Herstellung des Produkts sowie die Kosten, die für die Vervielfältigung, den Einsatz oder die Installation anfallen.

❷ Der **Begriff „Kosten"** ist durch drei Merkmale definiert:

- Verbrauch an Ressourcen
- bewertet in Geld und
- auf das Projekt bezogen.

Ein einfacher Videofilm kostet in der Herstellung z. B. deutlich weniger als eine komplexe CD-ROM, bei der viele Computeranimationen enthalten sind und ein hoher Programmieraufwand verursacht wird. Daher ist es nicht überraschend, dass es keine standardisierten Preise oder Listen gibt, aus denen sich die Kosten einer Medienproduktion ablesen lassen.

❸ Man spricht bei Medienprodukten von **Unikaten**, die in Einzelfertigung hergestellt werden müssen.

Präzise Vorstellungen über die Kosten bekommt man nur dann, wenn man das einzelne Medienprodukt genau definiert und in seine Bestandteile zerlegt. Immerhin gibt es gewisse Anhaltspunkte für typische Größenordnungen, die in der Branche bekannt sind.

Die nachfolgend genannten Zahlen verstehen sich als Herstellungskosten für durchschnittlich aufwändige („normale") Produktionen ohne die Kosten für Vervielfältigung, Montage, Vermarktung oder Einsatz. Einfache Produktionen (**„Low-Budget-Produktionen"**) mit wenigen Dreh- und Fototerminen und ohne Tricks und Grafiken können um einiges darunter liegen. Produktionen mit vielen Drehs, hohen Darstellergagen, Reise- und Übernachtungskosten und mit aufwändigen Tricks und Grafiken (**„High-Budget-Produktionen"**) liegen leicht um ein Vielfaches höher. Es ist wie beim Kauf eines Autos: Das Grundmodell ist erschwinglich, aber vergleichsweise langweilig. Das Salz in der Suppe sind die Extras, und die sind unter Umständen sehr teuer!

Typen von Produktionen

➡ **Low Budget**

Einfache Produktion ohne großen, insbesondere darstellerischen Aufwand

➡ **High Budget**

Aufwändige Produktion, meist szenischen Inhalts

Typische Größenordnungen für die Herstellungskosten von Medienprodukten (in Euro)

Hörfunk-Werbespot	8.000
1 Std. Aktuelles Magazin ARD Radio	3.000
Deutscher Kinofilm 90 Min.	2.000.000
Kauffilm 90 Min. Ausstrahlung ARD	200.000
Einfache Firmen-Dokumentation auf Video 20 Min.	25.000
Fernsehwerbespot 30 Sek.	150.000
Tagesschau ARD 15 Min./ Vollkosten	50.000
CD-ROM für PR, CBT / einfach (ohne Video, Animation)	5.000
CD-ROM für PR, CBT / mittlerer Aufwand	50.000
CD-ROM für PR, CBT / großer Aufwand	300.000
Spiele CD-ROM / komplex / internationale Vermarktung	3.000.000
Online-Erstauftritt / mittel / durch Agentur	25.000
Event-Dia AV: Multivision 10 Projektoren 15 Minuten	80.000
Einfache Computeranimation, pro Stück	50
mittel (z.B. Logo)	500
umfangreich (z.B. Mensch, Morphing-Szene)	3.000
extrem; pro Sekunde:	3.000

18.1.2 Einsatzkosten

❶ Kosten für den Einsatz werden auch **Roll-Out-Kosten** genannt

Je nach Medienprodukt kommen zu den dargestellten Herstellungskosten noch die Kosten für den Einsatz ❶ dazu. Man spricht in diesem Zusammenhang auch von den „Roll-Out-Kosten". Es handelt sich um:

❷ **POI** = „Point of Information", z. B. Bahnhöfe, öffentliche Plätze, Kulturzentren, Messen

❸ **POS** = „Point of Sale", z. B. Supermärkte, Verkaufsläden, Shopping Malls

- Kosten der Vervielfältigung, z. B. bei einem Buchprojekt, einer Audio-CD, einer Lern-CD-ROM für einen bestimmten Mitarbeiterkreis innerhalb eines Großunternehmens
- Kosten für den Verkauf, die Vermarktung und Verwertung, z. B. Werbung für das Buch, Kiosk-Provision beim Einzelverkauf von Zeitschriften
- Kosten für die Verbreitung, z. B. bei der Schaltung eines Fernsehwerbespots in einer Reihe von TV-Sendern („Media")
- Aufstellung eines interaktiven Kiosk-Terminals auf einer Messe oder an einem „POI" ❷ oder „POS" ❸

Typische Größenordnungen für ausgewählte Einsatzkosten von Medienprodukten (Schätzwerte in Euro)

Schaltung einer 4-Farben-Anzeige in "TV-Spielfilm"	11.000
Ganzseitige Farbanzeige im "Focus"	40.000
Schaltung eines einzigen TV-Werbespots, Prime Time RTL	7.000 bis 65.000
Schaltung eines TV-Werbespots im Nachrichtenumfeld von n-tv	700 bis 3.000
TKP für einen TV-Spot, Prime Time Pro7, je nach Zielgruppe	15 bis 50
(TKP, Tausend-Kontakt-Preis = Einschaltpreis im Verhältnis zur Zahl der Zuschauer = Relativer Preis)	
TKP bei der ARD für Zuschauer ab 14 Jahren	6 bis 9
Installation eines Kiosk-Terminals („Touch Screen") auf einer Messe	8.000
Vervielfältigung einer DVD, 5000 Exemplare	9.000
Technische Herstellung eines Taschenbuches 10.000 Exemplare, z.B.	15.000
Schaltung eines Banners auf der Homepage von Lycos, pro Tsd. Kontakte:	50
Buchung eines City Light Posters in Berlin, pro Tag:	12
Hallenmiete auf einer Messe, pro qm	50 bis 250

18.2 Ein 5-Schritte-Konzept der Kalkulation

18.2.1 Das Drehbuch – die Grundlage der Kalkulation

Wenn man herausfinden will, was ein Medienprodukt kostet, wird man schnell erkennen, dass es vom Typ und von der Beschaffenheit des Produkts abhängt, wie die Antwort auf diese Frage ausfällt.

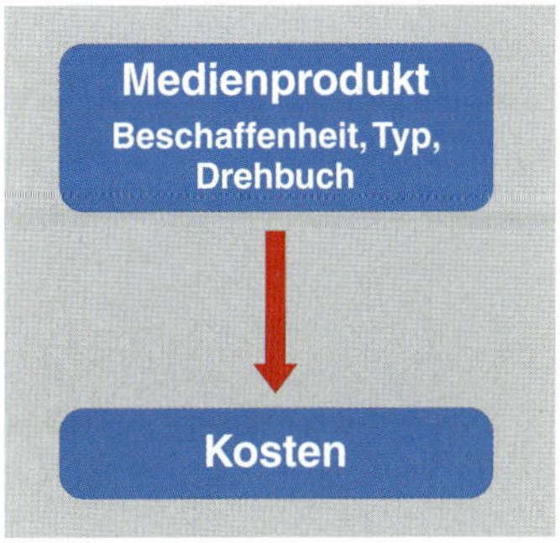

- Was kostet ein Haus?
- Was kostet ein Auto?
- Was kostet eine Urlaubsreise?

Solche Fragen sind viel zu pauschal und führen zu nichts. Erst der Bauplan des Architekten verrät, was das Haus kosten darf. Nur die Fahrzeugbeschreibung und der Leistungskatalog bringt Licht in das Dunkel, ob das Auto einen fairen Preis hat. Erst wenn man genau weiß, wohin die Reise gehen soll, kann man etwas Vernünftiges zu den Urlaubskosten sagen!

Genau so ist es bei einem Medienprodukt. Man denke z. B. an einen Kinospielfilm: Der Bauplan oder die **Leistungsbeschreibung** ist dort das sog. **Drehbuch** ❶. Das Drehbuch gibt Auskunft darüber, welche Handlung dem künftigen 90-Minuten-Streifen zugrunde liegt, wie viele Szenen die gesamte Handlung aufweist, wie die Szenen im einzelnen zu gestalten sind und wie sie dramaturgisch hintereinander ablaufen. Völlig zu Recht bezeichnet man das Drehbuch als die „Bibel" des Filmprojekts.

❶ Das **Drehbuch** ist die schriftliche Darlegung des Inhalts der Produktion.

Das Drehbuch liefert also die Informationen, die man haben muss, um überhaupt etwas zur Kostenseite sagen zu können. Je detaillierter das Drehbuch ausgearbeitet ist, um so genauer kann die Schätzung der Kosten ausfallen. Je weniger der Inhalt im Drehbuch festgelegt ist, um so eher muss man sich mit einer groben Kalkulation, eventuell sogar nur mit einer Schätzung „über den Daumen" begnügen.

❷ Das **Storyboard** stellt das Drehbuch in bebildeter Form dar.

➲ **Die Kalkulation eines Medienprodukts kann nur vorgenommen werden, wenn man eine klare Vorstellung vom herzustellenden Produkt hat. Ohne Drehbuch keine Kalkulation!**

In verschiedenen Medienbereichen ist es üblich, die Szenen des Drehbuchs durch Zeichnungen zu visualisieren, also bildhaft darzustellen. Das entsprechende Dokument heißt beim Spielfilm, beim Werbefilm sowie bei Multimedia-Produktionen **Storyboard** ❷. Allgemeiner gesagt wird eine Visualisierung auch als Layout bezeichnet.

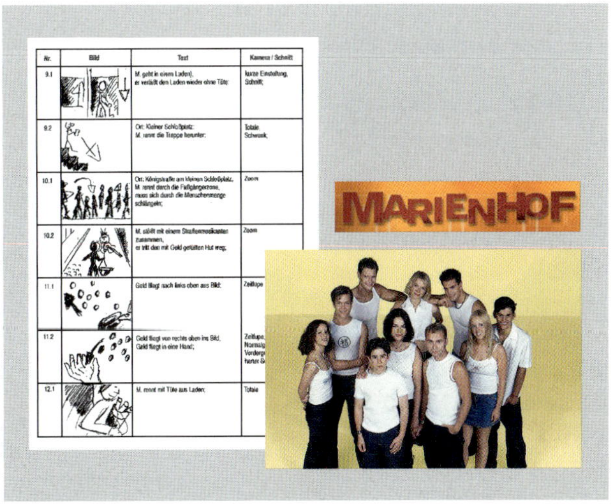

18.2.2 Ablauf der Kalkulation

In der Praxis der Film- und Medienproduktion ist die Vorgehensweise bei der **Kalkulation** grundsätzlich immer gleich. Sie lässt sich in **fünf Schritte** unterteilen:

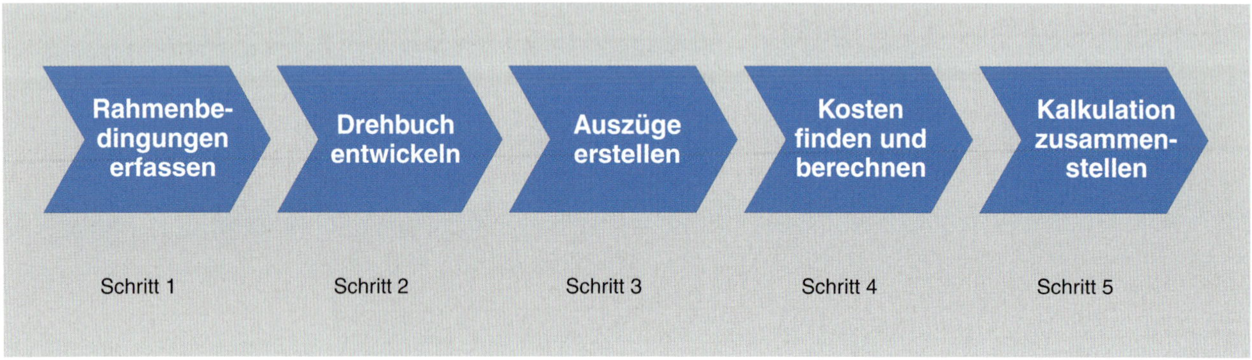

Schritt 1: Die Rahmenbedingungen erfassen

- Festlegung der Art der Produktion: z. B. Kino-Spielfilm, TV-Spiel, TV-Serie, Daily Soap etc.
- Festlegung des Bildträgerformats: z. B. bei Film 16 mm oder 35 mm ❶.
- Vorgaben des Auftraggebers: u. a. Termin, spezielle Normen im Hinblick auf Drehtage, Drehverhältnis, Höhe der Gagen, Person des Regisseurs.

❶ Relevant ist auch das 70 mm-Format, das dem IMAX-Kino zugrunde liegt.

Schritt 2: Das Drehbuch entwickeln

- Am Anfang steht die Idee zur Geschichte (**Stoffidee**).
- Aus ihr heraus wird das **Exposé** entwickelt. Anstatt von Exposé wird auch von Basisentwurf gesprochen.
- Es folgt das **Treatment**, das einen Grobentwurf des Inhalts darstellt.
- Schließlich wird das umsetzungsreife Drehbuch erarbeitet, das die Grundlage für die Produktion ist.
- Die Visualisierung erfolgt durch das **Storyboard**.

Schritt 3: Die Auszüge erstellen

- Hierunter versteht man die Analyse des Drehbuchs Bild für Bild. Bei einem Spielfilm entstehen oft mehr als 120 Auszüge. Ein Beispiel für einen Drehbuch-Auszug findet sich auf der nächsten Seite.
- Die Analyse erfolgt im Hinblick auf die notwendige Produktionstechnik: z. B. erforderliche Studiotechnik (Kamera, Licht, Aufbauten) oder Spezialausrüstung bei Außenaufnahmen,
- und im Hinblick auf die Faktoren, die für die Kosten verantwortlich sind: z. B. notwendiges Team, Spezialeffekte („SFX“ ❷), Musik, besondere Drehbedingungen (Wüste, Urwald).

❷ „SFX“ = lautmalerische Nachbildung von **Special Effects**. Musterbeispiel: Effekte in „Jurassic Park“

Drehbuch Auszug

Datum

Name der Filmproduktion | Titel | Nr. Auszug-Seite

Szenen-Nr. | Name der Szene | Innen / Außen

Beschreibung | Tag / Nacht

Drehbuchseite

Darsteller	Extras und Komparserie	Stunts
Ausstattung	Spezialeffekte	Requisiten
Autos / Tiere	Kostüm	Make-Up / Haare
Musik	Spezialausrüstung	Produktionsnotizen

Schritt 4: Die Kostenfindung

- Für jede Position, die Kosten verursacht, wird eine Schätzung vorgenommen. Hierzu ist viel Erfahrungswissen erforderlich, es müssen Recherchen vorgenommen werden, und Fachgespräche sind zu führen.
- Die Schätzung erfolgt in Form von Berechnungen (z. B. Filmmaterial),
- in Form von Näherungswerten (z. B. Drehort recherchieren),
- auf der Grundlage von Vergleichen (z. B. Drehverhältnis ❶)
- oder über Preislisten und Tarifverträge ❷.

Schritt 5: Die Kalkulation zusammenstellen

- Jede in der Kostenfindung ermittelte Kostenposition wird nach einem sinnvollen Schema zusammen gestellt und in eine übersichtliche Form gebracht.
- Dazu bietet sich z. B. für die Filmproduktion ein System von 10 Kostenblöcken an oder für Multimedia-Produktionen ein solches mit sechs (s. u.).

Die Ausarbeitung des Drehbuchs bis zur Kalkulation (Schritte 3 bis 5) obliegt dem Produktionsleiter ❸. Er ist der wirtschaftliche und organisatorische „Kopf" der Produktion. Wie sich jeder leicht vorstellen kann, handelt es sich bei der Produktionsleiterfunktion um eine höchst verantwortungsvolle Aufgabe.

❶ Das **Drehverhältnis** gibt das Verhältnis zwischen abgedrehtem Material und dem in der Produktion tatsächlich verwendeten Material an. Ein Verhältnis 1:10 besagt, dass von 10 Meter gedrehtem Film ein Meter in die Endversion eingeht.

❷ **Tarifverträge** werden zwischen Arbeitgebern und Arbeitnehmervertretungen (Gewerkschaften) für die einzelnen Branchen ausgehandelt.

❸ Die Arbeit des **Produktionsleiters** hat für die wirtschaftliche Steuerung von Medienprojekten Schlüsselbedeutung.

18.3 Kalkulationsbeispiele

18.3.1 Film-Kalkulation

Die Kalkulation dient der realistischen Einschätzung der finanziellen Seite des Filmprojekts. Von ihr hängt die effiziente Geschäftsführung, die Buchhaltung und der materielle Erfolg der Produktionsfirma ab. Sie einfach aus dem Bauch heraus zu entwickeln, birgt daher große Risiken.

Die Kalkulation muss mit größter Sorgfalt erstellt werden. Eine Hilfe ist ein klares und übersichtliches Kalkulationsschema, das sofort von allen verstanden wird und das wie eine Checkliste verwendet werden kann.

Ein solches Kalkulationsschema wird nachfolgend dargestellt. Es handelt sich um das **10-Kostenblöcke-Konzept**, das alle wichtigen Kosten einer Filmproduktion zusammenfasst und übersichtlich darstellt.

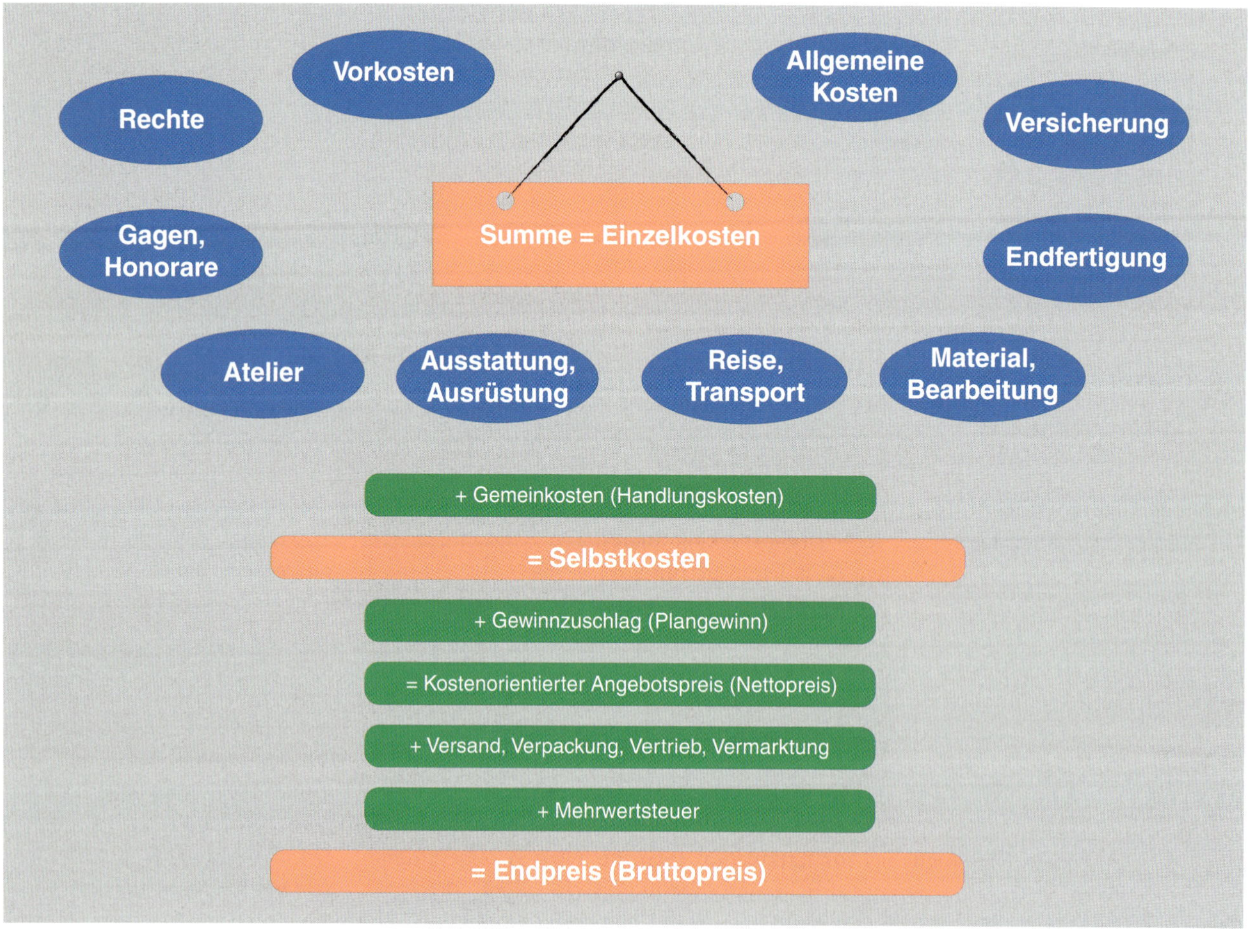

Kostenblock 1: Vorkosten

Zu Beginn eines Filmprojekts fallen aufwändige Vorarbeiten an. Bei einem Dokumentarfilm müssen z. B. Auslandsreisen zur Abklärung von Drehmöglichkeiten unternommen werden, es sind umfangreiche Recherchen notwendig ❶ oder es muss der Rat von Experten eingeholt werden. Das alles führt zu Reisekosten, Telefonkosten und Honorarkosten.

❶ Oft wird ein **Location Scout** eingesetzt, der dazu da ist, einen geeigneten Drehort ausfindig zu machen.

Kostenblock 2: Rechte und Manuskript

Vor Beginn der Spielfilmproduktion ist es wichtig, alle notwendigen Rechte lückenlos einzuholen. Keinesfalls darf in irgend einer Form fremdes geistiges Eigentum verwendet werden, wenn nicht die ausdrückliche Zustimmung des Rechteinhabers vorliegt. Rechte an fremden Werken, deren Nutzung man sich genehmigen lassen muss, können sein:

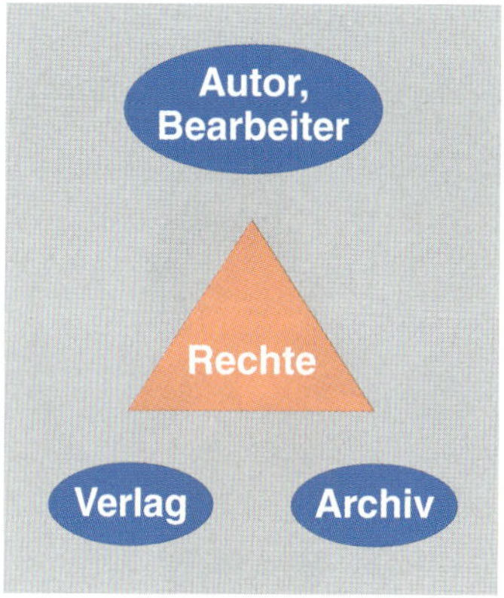

- Autorenrechte: z. B. für den **Drehbuchautor**, der das Original-Drehbuch schreibt, oder für den Komponisten der Filmmusik.
- Bearbeitungsrechte: z. B. für den Bearbeiter eines bereits vorliegenden Drehbuchs (das ist nicht selten der Regisseur oder ein anderer Autor). Das betrifft z. B. auch Übersetzungen oder das Synchrondrehbuch für Auslandsfassungen des Films.
- Verlagsrechte: wenn man eine literarische Vorlage verwendet, z. B. den Roman eines Erfolgsautors, aber auch bei Verwendung von Musik (Musikverlage). Viele (Wort- und Musik-)Autoren stehen bei Verlagen unter Vertrag, die dann die Verwertungsrechte besitzen.
- Nutzungsrechte von Film-, Ton-, Bildmaterial aus speziellen Archiven, z. B. bei Verwendung von historischem Material (z. B. Rede von Kennedy „Ich bin ein Berliner“ oder Alexanderplatz in Berlin um 1900) oder einzelner Szenen (z. B. Sonnenuntergang, Flug über den Grand Canyon).
- Nutzungsrechte von Mitschnitten aus Konzerten, Theater-, Opern- oder Kabarett-Aufführungen.

In den Rechteerwerb müssen häufig Verwertungsgesellschaften eingeschaltet werden, wenn die Rechteinhaber ihre Ansprüche entsprechend übertragen haben. Die bekannteste Verwertungsgesellschaft ist die **„GEMA“**, die die Rechte von Komponisten vertritt. Daneben gibt es zahlreiche weitere Verwertungsgesellschaften, z. B. die **„GVL“** (für die sog. Mitwirkenden wie Schauspieler oder Sprecher).

Die Nutzungsrechte können einen erheblichen Anteil an den Gesamtkosten ausmachen. So können sich die Kosten für ein Original-Drehbuch für einen deutschen Kino-Spielfilm leicht in die Größenordnung von 50 bis 100 Tausend Euro bewegen. Dieser Betrag ist nachzuvollziehen, muss doch ein Drehbuchautor einige Monate Zeit investieren, um ein gutes Drehbuch auszuarbeiten.

Eine besondere Rolle im Bereich der Rechte spielt das sog. **„Buyout“**. Darunter versteht man zusätzliche Zahlungen an Darsteller und Stabmitarbeiter, mit denen später eventuell fällige Wiederholungshonorare und Verkaufserlöse für immer abgegolten werden. Buyout-Zahlungen können das Drei- bis Vierfache des Grundhonorars oder sogar noch darüber ausmachen ❷.

❷ Beispiel: Ein Model erhält in der TV-Werbung ein Arbeits-Tageshonorar von 4.000 Euro. Bei zwei Tagen Einsatz sind das 8.000 Euro. Der **Buyout-Zuschlag** beträgt 400 Prozent, was einem Betrag von 32.000 Euro entspricht. Hinzu kommen noch andere Kosten (Agenturvergütung, Ausländerlohnsteuer), so dass der Einsatz des Models am Ende deutlich über 50.000 Euro kostet.

Personal-Ressourcen im Film

Cast

Alle Darsteller vor Kamera und Mikrofon

Staff

Der Stab hinter Kamera und Mikrofon

Kostenblock 3: Gagen und Honorare

Dieser Kostenblock bezieht sich auf den Aufwand aller am Filmprojekt beteiligten Personen sowohl vor als auch hinter der Kamera und des Mikrofons. Das sind zum einen die Darsteller, zum anderen ist es der Stab:

- Darsteller (vor Kamera und Mikrofon, auch **„Cast"** genannt): Hauptdarsteller, Kleine Rollen, Komparsen, Stuntmen, Doubles, Sprecher, Musiker.
- Stab (hinter Kamera und Mikrofon, auch **„staff"** genannt): Produktionsstab (v. a. Produzent, Herstellungsleiter, Produktionsleiter, Aufnahmeleiter), Regiestab (Regisseur, Kameramann, Tonmeister, Cutter), Ausstattungsstab (Architekt, Requisiteur, Kostümbildner, Maskenbildner), Sonstiger Stab (Beleuchter, Bühnenmeister).

Die Gagen und Honorare pro geleistetem Arbeitstag bzw. pro Arbeitswoche richten sich in weiten Teilen nach den Tarifverträgen, die zwischen den Produktionsfirmen und den Gewerkschaften (vor allem ver.di) abgeschlossen werden. Bei besonders wichtigen Mitwirkenden (Hauptrollen, Regisseur, Chef-Kameramann u. a.) werden jedoch spezielle Vereinbarungen getroffen. Die Höhe der zu kalkulierenden Gagen hängt ferner von der Beschäftigungszeit ab, die sich aus Vorbereitungszeit, Drehzeit, Reise- und Ruhetagen, Urlaubstagen sowie der Zeit für die Endfertigung zusammensetzt. Die typischen Beschäftigungszeiten für ein größeres Filmprojekt sind in einer gesonderten Übersicht dargestellt (s. u.).

Der Produzent und sein Produktionsleiter werden danach streben, mit allen beteiligten „Filmschaffenden" so weit wie möglich Pauschalverträge (meist auf Wochenbasis) abzuschließen. Dadurch erreichen sie, dass sämtliche Ansprüche abgegolten sind und später keine Zusatzforderungen erhoben werden. Die Gage für den Regisseur kann sich bei einem größeren Projekt leicht in die Größenordnung von 75.000 Euro bewegen. Dafür ist er freilich acht Monate mehr oder weniger intensiv für dieses Projekt im Einsatz.

Woody Allen	What's up, tiger lily?; Bananas; Der Stadtneurotiker; Radio Days; ...
Francis Ford Coppola	The Godfather I+II+III, Apocalypse Now; Cotton Club; Dracula; ...
Federico Fellini	La strada; La dolce vita; 8 $^{1}/_{2}$; F. Satyricon; Ginger und Fred; ...
Alfred Hitchcock	Rebecca; Verdacht; Das Fenster zum Hof; Psycho, Die Vögel; ...
Stanley Kubrick	Spartacus; 2001: A Space Odyssey; Clockwork Orange; Shining; ...
Martin Scorsese	Taxi Driver; New York, N.Y.; Goodfellas; Zeit der Unschuld; ...
Steven Spielberg	Jaws; 1941; E.T.; Die Farbe lila; Jurassic Park; Schindlers Liste; ...
Francois Truffaut	Antoine-Doinel-Zyklus; Fahrenheit 451; Die amerikanische Nacht; ...

❶ Unter Catering versteht man die Verpflegung des Teams während der Drehzeit.

Bei den Gagen und Honoraren spielen oft Zusatzkosten eine nicht unbeträchtliche Rolle. Zu denken ist z. B. an Überstunden- und Wochenendzuschläge (bis zu 100 Prozent Aufschlag), an Kosten für das Catering ❶ sowie an Beiträge zur Sozialversicherung, die vom Produzenten abzuführen sind.

Typische Beschäftigungszeiten in einem größeren Filmprojekt (in Wochen)

(in Anlehnung an Dress, Peter: Vor Drehbeginn, Berlin 1991, S. 179 f.)

Personal / Stab	Vorproduktion	Dreharbeiten	Nachbearbeitung
Regiestab	**Regiestab**	**Regiestab**	**Regiestab**
Regisseur	-------------------	----pauschal----	-------------------
Regie-Assistent	4	7	
Kameramann	-------------------	----pauschal----	-------------------
Kamera-Assistent	0,5	7	
Material-Assistent	0,5	7	
2. Kamera		0,5	
2. Kamera-Assistent		0,5	
Ton	0,5	7	0,5
Cutter		3	10
Cutter-Assistent		4	10
Cutter-Assistent		7	10
Standfotograf	-------------------	----pauschal----	-------------------
Script		7	
Trick		1	1
Ausstattungsstab	**Ausstattungsstab**	**Ausstattungsstab**	**Ausstattungsstab**
Architekt	-------------------	----pauschal----	-------------------
Ausstatter		3	
Kunstmaler	1		
Requisiteur Inland	2	4	
Requisiteur Inland	1	4	
Requisiteur Ausland	2	3	
Requisitenhilfe		3	
Kostümbildner	1,5	7	
Kostümbildner-Assistent	1,5	3	
Garderobier		7	
Maske	1	7	
Maske-Assistent			
Sonstiger Stab	**Sonstiger Stab**	**Sonstiger Stab**	**Sonstiger Stab**
Oberbeleuchter	1	7	1
Beleuchter 1		7	
Beleuchter 2		7	
Drehbühne Inland	1	4	
Drehbühne Ausland	1	4	
Baubühne	3	7	
Baubühnenhilfe	2	7	
Fahrer	3	7	1
Geräuschemacher			1
Geräuschemacher-Assistent			1
Pyrotechniker		1	
Hilfskräfte	2	7	1
Produktionsstab	**Produktionsstab**	**Produktionsstab**	**Produktionsstab**
Produktionsleiter	6	7	1
Produktionsleiter-Assistent	6	7	0,5
Aufnahmeleiter Inland	4	4	
Aufnahmeleiter Ausland	3	3	
Aufnahmeleiter Ausland	1	3	
Produktionssekretariat	6	7	2
Filmgeschäftsführung	-------------------	----pauschal----	-------------------

Gemeinkostenzuschlag

Die Kostenblöcke 1 bis 10 nennt man zusammen genommen die Einzelkosten. Manche Kosten können dem herzustellenden Produkt aber nicht direkt zugerechnet werden. Beispiele sind z. B. Kosten für Heizung, Strom, Gebäudemiete, allgemeine Versicherungen, Geschäftsfahrzeuge, Gehälter der Geschäftsleitung oder Beiträge zu Fachverbänden. Diese so genannten Gemeinkosten müssen pauschal auf die Kostenblöcke 1 bis 10 zugerechnet werden. Als Pauschale verwendet man normalerweise einen prozentualen Aufschlag. Solche Zuschläge bewegen sich in der Größenordnung von 10 bis 25 Prozent.

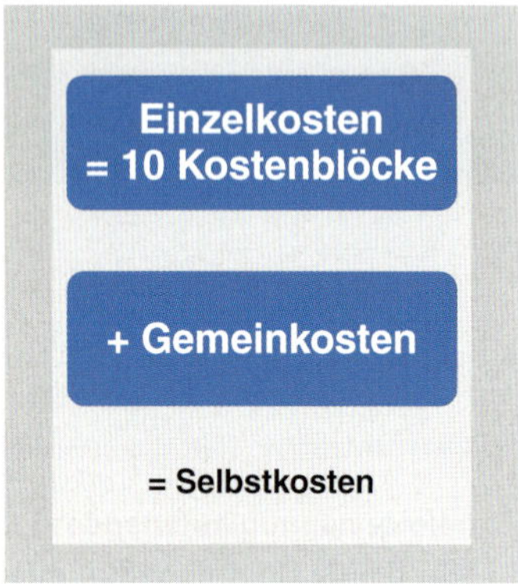

Filmkalkulationen arbeiten immer mit dieser Methodik. Es werden pauschal alle Kosten zugeschlagen, die dem Projekt nicht direkt zurechenbar sind. Solche Kalkulationen nennt man **Zuschlagskalkulationen**. Eine Zuschlagskalkulation verwendet man immer dann, wenn es sich um eine Einzelanfertigung oder „Maßanfertigung" handelt, also wie im vorliegenden Fall einer Filmkalkulation. Die Zuschlagskalkulation beruht auf dem folgenden **Grundraster**:

  Einzelkosten (direkt zurechenbare Kosten = Kostenblöcke 1 bis 10):
\+ Gemeinkosten (nicht direkt zurechenbare Kosten)

= Selbstkosten

Gewinn

Ein angemessener Gewinnzuschlag ist erforderlich, damit die herstellende Produktionsfirma ihren Geschäftszweck erreicht, nämlich Gewinn zu erzielen. Als angemessen wird – je nach Projekt – ein Zuschlag von 7,5 bis 15 Prozent angesehen. Das Thema des Gewinnzuschlags verweist bereits auf die Frage, welcher Angebotspreis gesetzt werden soll. Eine Filmproduktion soll Gewinn abwerfen, was nur möglich ist, wenn in den Endpreis (= Bruttopreis) ein angemessener Gewinn einkalkuliert wird (Ausnahme: über die Filmförderungsanstalt FFA finanzierte Filme).

Zusammenstellung der Kosten im Kalkulationsschema

Auf den folgenden Seiten wird auf der Grundlage des 10-Kostenblöcke-Konzepts das Fallbeispiel einer Kalkulation für einen deutschen Kino-Spielfilm mit durchschnittlichem Budget vorgestellt (in Anlehnung an Dress 1991, S. 39 ff. DM-Werte wurden auf Euro 2:1 umgerechnet. Beim verwendeten Formular handelt es sich um die Richtlinien der FFA). Die folgenden Annahmen sind dabei unterstellt:

- Länge des Films: 90 Minuten.
- Es handelt sich um eine reine Außenproduktion (also keine Studioproduktion).
- Es wird ein großer Darsteller- und Ausstattungsaufwand betrieben.

Dieses Beispiel unterscheidet sich wesentlich z. B. von einer Werbefilmproduktion, bei der die Produktionsbedingungen völlig anders sind. Ein Fernsehwerbespot hat ja nur eine durchschnittliche Länge von ca. 20 Sekunden (bei 25 Bildern pro Sekunde macht das nur 500 Einzelbilder aus!). Werbefilme werden in der Regel innerhalb einer Woche gedreht, in einer weiteren Woche geschnitten und fertiggestellt, basierend auf einer ausgedehnten Konzeptions- und Vorlaufphase.

1.	**Vorkosten**	
001	Vorkosten	50.000
	Summe Vorkosten	50.000
2.	**Rechte und Manuskript**	
002	Verfilmungsrechte	0
003	Treatment	0
004	Drehbuch	20.000
005	Synchronbuch	3.000
006	Archivrechte	3.500
007	Musikrechte	5.000
008	Textrechte	0
009	Komponist	12.500
010	Gema-Gebühren	0
011	(Dolby-Stereo incl.Tonmeister)	5.000
	Summe Rechte und Manuskript	*49.000*
3.	**Gagen**	
	a) Produktionsstab	
012	Produzent	27.500
013	Herstellungsleiter	0
014	Produktionsleiter	14.000
015	Produktionsleiter-Assistent	8.400
016	Aufnahmeleiter	9.600
017	Aufnahmeleiter	6.000
018	Aufnahmeleiter	3.000
019	Aufnahmeleiter (Synchron)	0
020	Produktionssekretärin	6.300
021	Produktionssekretärin	4.500
022	Kassierer	750
023	Filmgeschäftsführer	22.500
024	Buchhaltung	0
025	(offen)	0
	Summe Produktionsstab	*102.550*
	b) Regiestab	
026	Regisseur	30.000
027	Regie-Assistent	8.000
028	Regie-Assistent (Coach)	7.800
029	Regisseur (Synchron)	0
030	1. Kameramann	20.000
031	Kamera-Assistent	6.750
032	Kamera-Assistent	0
033	Material-Assistent	2.000
034	2. Kameramann	4.000
035	2. Kamera-Assistent	1.500
036	Tonmeister	8.000
037	Tonassistent	4.800
038	Cutter	17.600
039	Cutter-Assistent	10.800
040	2. Cutter-Assistent	4.000
041	Synchron-Cutter	0
042	Synchron-Cutter-Assistent	0
043	Standfotograf	3.500
044	Script	4.000
045	Fachmännischer Beirat	0
	Summe Regiestab	*132.750*

	c) Ausstattungsstab	
046	Szenenbildner	0
047	Szenenbildner-Assistent	0
048	Ausstatter	13.200
049	Kunstmaler	0
050	Bildhauer	400
051	Außenrequisiteur	8.000
052	Außenrequisiteur	0
053	Innenrequisiteur	5.600
054	Innenrequisiteur	0
055	Requisitienhilfe	2.500
056	Kostümbildner	10.000
057	Kostümbildner-Assistent	0
058	Garderobier	4.000
059	Garderobier	0
060	Garderobiere	0
061	Garderobiere	0
062	Garderoben-Aushilfe	2.000
063	Herrenmaskenbildner	6.400
064	Herrenmaskenbildner	0
065	Damenmaskenbildner	3.200
066	Damenmaskenbildner	0
067	Maskenbildner-Aushilfe	1.250
068	(offen)	0
069	(offen)	0
070	(offen)	0
	Summe Ausstattungsstab	*56.550*
	d) Sonstiger Stab	
071	Oberbeleuchter	6.400
072	Beleuchter	6.800
073	Beleuchter	5.950
074	Beleuchter	5.950
075	Aggregatfahrer	0
076	Drehbühnenmeister	6.400
077	Drehbühnenmann	0
078	Drehbühnenmann	0
079	Drehbühnenmann	0
080	Baubühnenmeister	6.750
081	Baubühnenmann	1.000
082	Baubühnenmann	1.000
083	Baubühnenmann	0
084	Baubühnenmann	0
085	Produktionsfahrer	4.800
086	Produktionsfahrer	4.000
087	Produktionsfahrer	0
088	Wachmann/Sanitäter	3.000
089	Geräuschemacher	6.000
090	Pyrotechniker, SFX	1.750
091	Pyrotechniker, SFX	0
092	Sonstiger Hilfskräfte	1.500
093	(Kinderbetreuung)	900
094	(Dolmetscher, Übersetzer)	500
095	(offen)	0
	Summe Sonstiger Stab	*62.700*

	e) Darsteller	
096	Hauptdarsteller	200.000
097	Kleine Rollen	212.500
098	Komparsen	25.050
099	Artisten/Stuntmen/Double	32.500
100	Choreograph	0
101	Ballett	0
102	Synchronsprecher	0
103	Kommentarsprecher	0
104	(offen)	0
	Summe Darsteller	*470.050*
	f) Musiker	
105	Musiker im Bild	0
106	Musiker im Aufnahmestudio	0
107	Dirigent	0
108	Sänger und Chor	0
109	Instrumentenmiete und Transport	0
110	Notenschreibarbeiten	0
111	(pauschal)	20.000
	Summe Musiker	*20.000*
	g) Zusatzkosten Gagen	
112	Samstags- und Sonntagsarbeit	6.500
113	Überstunden	20.000
114	Urlaubsabgeltung	17.180
115	Zusatzverpflegung	24.000
116	Berufsgenossenschaft	8.250
117	Sozialversicherung (Arbeitgeber)	35.870
118	Künstlersozialversicherung (AN)	3.000
119	(offen)	0
	Summe Zusatzkosten Gagen	*114.800*
4.	**Atelier**	
	a) Atelier-Bau	
120	Hallenmiete	0
121	Hallenmiete	0
122	Miete Vorbauhalle	0
123	Miete Nebenräume	0
124	Heizung	0
125	Reinigung	0
126	Feuerwehr	0
127	Telefonkosten	0
128	Löhne Baubühne	0
129	Material für Bau (Kauf)	0
130	Baufundus (Miete)	0
131	Geräte und Maschinen	0
132	Stromkosten	0
133	An- und Abtransporte	0
134	(offen)	0
135	(offen)	0
	Summe Atelier-Bau	*0*

Kalkulation Kinofilm (Seite 1) – Angaben in Euro

	b) Außenbau durch Atelier	
136	Löhne Baubühne	0
137	Material für Bau (Kauf)	0
138	Baufundus (Miete)	0
139	Geräte und Maschinen	0
140	Lastentransporte	0
141	Personentransporte	0
142	Tage- und Übernachtungsgelder	0
143	(offen)	0
144	(offen)	0
	Summe Außenbau Atelier	*0*
	c) Atelier Dreh	
145	Hallenmiete	0
146	Hallenmiete	0
147	Miete Nebenräume	0
148	Heizung	0
149	Reinigung	0
150	Feuerwehr	0
151	Telefon	0
152	Löhne Beleuchter	0
153	Löhne Drehbühne	0
154	Beleuchtungsgeräte	0
155	Bel.geräte Verbrauch, Schaden	0
156	Kran, Elemack, Dolly usw.	0
157	Stromkosten	0
158	Transportfahrzeuge	0
159	Aufpro-, Rückpro-Anlage	0
160	Blue-Screen-Anlage	0
161	(offen)	0
162	(offen)	0
163	*Summe Atelier Dreh*	*0*
	d) Abbau Atelier und Außenbau	
164	Hallenmiete	0
165	Löhne Abbau	0
166	Geräte und Maschinen	0
167	Reinigung, Müllabfuhr	0
168	Lastentransporte	0
169	Personentransporte	0
170	(offen)	0
	Summe Abbau At., Außenbau	*0*
5.	**Ausstattung und Technik**	
	a) Genehmigungen und Mieten	
171	Drehgenehmigungen	42.500
172	Drehgenehmigungen	0
173	Motivnebenkosten	16.500
174	Polizei- und Feuerwehreinsätze	7.500
175	Mieten für Büroräume	5.000
176	Mieten für sonstige Räume	3.400
177	Telefon, Telex	5.500
178	(Telefax)	1.250
179	(offen)	0
	Summe Genehmigungen, Mieten	*81.650*

	b) Bau und Ausstattung	
180	Material für Bau (Kauf)	30.000
181	Baufundus (Miete)	2.500
182	Geräte und Maschinen	2.000
183	An- und Abtransporte	6.000
184	Sonstige Baukosten	0
185	Reinigung, Müllabfuhr	4.000
186	Kostüm (Kauf)	15.000
187	Kostüm (Miete)	5.000
188	Kostümtransporte	1.250
189	Schminkmaterial, Haarteile (Kauf)	3.500
190	Schminkmaterial, Haarteile (Miete)	3.000
191	Requisiten (Kauf)	16.500
192	Requisiten (Miete)	7.500
193	Requisitentransporte	4.000
194	Fahrzeuge im Bild	21.000
195	Großrequisiten im Bild	0
196	Tiere und Nebenkosten	0
197	Gärtnerarbeiten	0
198	Pyrotechnik-Material	15.000
199	Spezialeffekt-Material	5.000
200	Modellbau	5.000
201	(LKW versenken)	4.250
202	(Bergung LKW)	3.400
203	(Schiff 5 Tage je 500)	2.500
204	(offen)	0
	Summe Bau, Ausstattung	*156.400*
	c) Technische Ausrüstung	
205	Kamera	35.145
206	Kamerazubehör und Verbrauch	0
207	Zusätzliche Kameraausrüstung	6.750
208	Hubschrauber, Aufnahmewagen	0
209	Tonapparatur	5.550
210	Tonzubehör und Verbrauch	0
211	Playbackanlage	0
212	Sprechfunkgeräte usw.	2.925
213	Beleuchtungsgeräte	46.342
214	Beleuchtungsgeräte Verbrauch	5.500
215	Bühnengeräte	6.750
216	Bühnengeräte Verbrauch	3.825
217	Kran, Elemack, Dolly usw.	5.800
218	Aggregat	3.500
219	Stromkosten incl. Anschluss	3.500
220	Lastwagen Beleuchtungsgeräte	2.573
221	Lastwagen für Bühnengeräte	0
222	Kameratransportwagen	2.062
223	Tongerätewagen	0
224	Produktionsfahrzeug	1.305
225	Produktionsfahrzeug	2.475
226	Produktionsfahrzeug	2.232
227	Wohnwagen, Herrenmaske	1.800
228	(Wohnwagen, Damenmaske)	1.800
229	(Regiewagen)	3.000
	Summe Techn. Ausrüstung	*142.834*

6.	**Reise- und Transportkosten**	
	a) Personen	
230	Reisekosten zum Drehort Inl.	24.215
231	Fahrtkosten am Drehort Inland	1.050
232	Reisekosten zum Drehort Ausl.	0
233	Fahrtkosten am Drehort Ausl.	0
234	Tage- und Übern.-Gelder Inl.	15.000
235	Tage- und Übern.-Gelder Ausl.	0
236	Reisekosten (Synchron)	1.750
237	Tage- und Übern.-Gelder Syn.	2.250
238	Sonstige Personentransporte	1.750
239	km-Geld und Benzin	4.744
240	(offen)	0
241	(offen)	0
	Summe Reise-/Transport Pers.	*50.759*
	b) Lasten	
242	Transport zum Drehort, Inland	4.900
243	Transport am Drehort, Ausland	0
244	Transport zum Drehort, Ausl.	0
245	Transport am Drehort, Ausl.	0
246	Sonstige Lastentransporte	0
247	Bahn- und Luftfracht	5.000
248	Zoll- und Grenzkosten	2.500
249	(offen)	0
	Summe Reise-/Transport Last.	*12.400*
7.	**Filmmaterial und Bearbeitung**	
250	Rohfilmmaterial	27.500
251	Tonbandmaterial	6.315
252	Kopierwerksleistungen	73.206
253	Tonüberspielung	5.700
254	Video- und MAZ-Bearbeitung	4.000
255	Fotomaterial	2.250
256	Fotobearbeitung	2.250
257	Trailer	5.000
258	(offen)	0
259	(offen)	0
	Summe Filmmaterial, Bearb.	*126.221*
8.	**Endfertigung**	
260	Vorführung	2.295
261	Schneideraum	5.000
262	Schneideraum	4.000
263	Schneideraummaterial	1.500
264	Numeriermaschine usw.	300
265	Sprachaufnahmen	30.000
266	Geräuschaufnahmen	3.559
267	Musikaufnahmen	1.947
268	Mischung	13.366
269	IT-Mischung	4.373
270	(offen)	
	Summe Endfertigung	*66.340*

Kalkulation Kinofilm (Seite 2) – Angaben in Euro

9.	**Versicherungen**	
271	Ausfallversicherung	27.500
272	Negativversicherung	15.000
273	Haftpflichtversicherung	2.500
274	Unfallversicherung	3.000
275	Feuerregressversicherung	0
276	Apparateversicherung	0
277	Kassenversicherung	0
278	Requisitenversicherung	0
279	Lampenversicherung	0
280	Reisegepäckversicherung	0
281	(offen)	0
282	(offen)	0
	Summe Versicherungen	*48.000*
10.	**Allgemeine Kosten**	
283	Vervielfältigungen	3.250
284	Büromaterial	3.000
285	Bürogeräte (Miete)	2.500
286	Telefon, Telex, Porto	3.500
287	Übersetzungen	2.000
288	Kleine Ausgaben	1.000
289	Bewirtungen	7.500
290	FSK-, FBW-Gebühren	4.200
291	Produzentenverband	0
292	Produktionspresse	7.500
293	PR-Kosten	20.000
294	Rechts- und Steuerberatung	8.000
295	Projektberatung	0
296	Projektüberwachung	0
	Summe Allgemeine Kosten	*62.450*
11.	**Kostenmindernde Erträge (abzüglich)**	
297	Löhne Abbau	0
298	Geräte und Maschinen	0
299	Reinigung, Müllabfuhr	0
300	Lastentransporte	0
	Summe Kostenmind. Erträge	*0*

Kostenzusammenstellung

1.	**Vorkosten**		50.000
2.	**Rechte und Manuskript**		49.000
3.	**Gagen**		
	a) Produktionsstab	102.550	
	b) Regiestab	132.750	
	c) Ausstattungsstab	56.550	
	d) Sonstiger Stab	62.700	
	e) Darsteller	470.050	
	f) Musiker	20.000	
	g) Zusatzkosten Gagen	114.800	
	Summe		959.400
4.	**Atelier**		
	a) Atelier-Bau	0	
	b) Außenbau durch Atelier	0	
	c) Atelier-Dreh	0	
	d) Abbau Atelier und Außenbau	0	
	Summe		0
5.	**Ausstattung und Technik**		
	a) Genehmigungen und Mieten	81.650	
	b) Bau und Ausstattung	156.400	
	c) Technische Ausrüstung	142.834	
	Summe		380.884
6.	**Reise- und Transportkosten**		
	a) Personen	50.759	
	b) Lasten	12.400	
	Summe		63.159
7.	**Filmmaterial und Bearbeitung**		126.221
8.	**Endfertigung**		66.340
9.	**Versicherungen**		48.000
10.	**Allgemeine Kosten**		62.450
11.	**Kostenmindernde Erträge**		0
A.	**Summe = (Netto-) Fertigungskosten**		**1.805.454**

A.	**Netto-Fertigungskosten**	**1.805.454**
B.	**Handlungskosten (12 % von A.)**	**108.327**
C.	**Zwischensumme**	**1.913.781**
D.	**Überschreitungsreserve**	**100.000**
E.	**Zwischensumme**	**2.013.781**
F.	**Finanzierungskosten**	**60.000**
G.	**Zwischensumme**	**2.073.781**
H.	**Treuhandgebühren**	**45.000**
I.	**Netto-Herstellungskosten**	**2.118.781**

Kalkulation Kinofilm (Seite 3) – Angaben in Euro

18.3.2 Multimedia-Kalkulation

Eine multimediale CD-ROM-Produktion unterscheidet sich von einer reinen Filmproduktion durch die grundsätzlich **höhere Komplexität** und sowie vor allem dadurch, dass es sich um eine interaktive Anwendung handelt. Die Stufen, die zur Kalkulation führen, sind im Prinzip die gleichen: Auch hier geht es darum, **fünf Stufen** zu durchlaufen, bis eine aussagefähige Kalkulation entstehen kann:

- Stufe 1: Rahmenbedingungen
- Stufe 2: Drehbuch
- Stufe 3: Auszüge
- Stufe 4: Kostenfindung
- Stufe 5: Kalkulation

Wie beim Film ist auch bei einer multimedialen Produktion das Drehbuch inkl. Storyboard das Basis-Dokument (Stufe 2: Drehbuch). Als erstes wird – analog den Auszügen beim Film – aus dem Drehbuch jeder einzelne Baustein, der auf dem Bildschirm (Screen) erscheinen soll, abgeleitet (Stufe 3). Baustein für Baustein werden nun die Inhalte beschrieben, differenziert nach den verschiedenen Medienelementen, den sog. Assets ❶, also Text, Bild, Grafik, Videosequenz, Audio oder Animation. Das Dokument, das die Assets auflistet, ist die sog. Medienliste. In der Medienliste kommt insbesondere zum Ausdruck, welche Teile der Produktion neu zu produzieren sind und welche Teile bereits als Archivmaterial vorliegen.

❶ Unter **Asset** versteht man das einzelne Datenobjekt einer Multimedia-Produktion, also Objekte der folgenden Art:
- Text
- Bild
- Grafik
- Videosequenz
- Audio
- Animation

Auf der Grundlage der Medienliste können nun die Kosten im einzelnen ermittelt werden (Stufe 4: Kostenfindung). Man schätzt für jeden Screen und dort für jedes Asset, welcher Aufwand erforderlich ist, um das Teil neu zu produzieren oder das vorliegende Archivmaterial zu bearbeiten. Daraus ergeben sich die erforderlichen „Manntage" für die Texterstellung, die Bildproduktion oder die Programmierung. Hinzu kommen die weiteren Kosten wie Urheberrechte, Konzeptionskosten und der Gemeinkostenzuschlag.

Alle Einzelpositionen werden anschließend in eine übersichtliche Form, also in ein Kalkulationsschema, gebracht und ergeben die Kalkulation (Stufe 5). Bei Multimedia ist es zweckmäßig, mit einem **6-Kostenblöcke-Konzept** zu arbeiten:

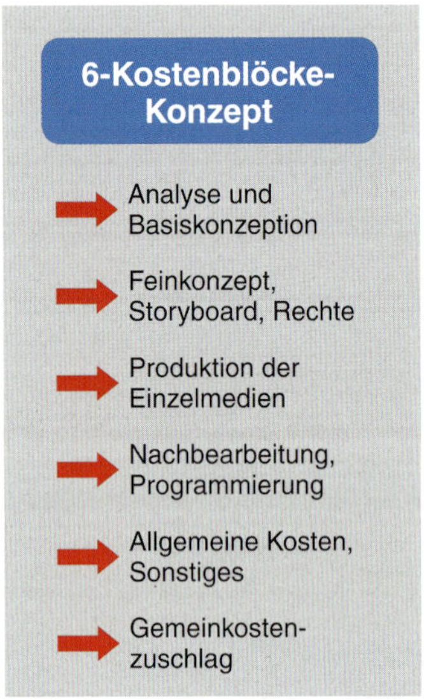

- Kostenblock 1: Analyse und Basis-Konzeption
- Kostenblock 2: Feinkonzept, Storyboard, Rechte
- Kostenblock 3: Produktion der Einzelmedien - Text, Ton, Bild, Grafik, Video und Animation
- Kostenblock 4: Integration: Nachbearbeitung, Programmierung
- Kostenblock 5: Sonstiges - Allgemeine Kosten
- Kostenblock 6: Zuschläge

Nachfolgend wird die Kalkulation für eine CD-ROM-Produktion wiedergegeben, bei der es sich um die interaktive Darstellung einer Kulturstätte handelt. Man kann die grundsätzlichen Unterschiede zur Filmkalkulation erkennen, sieht aber auch, dass sie vom Prinzip her ebenfalls der Methode der **Zuschlagskalkulation** folgt.

1	**Konzeption**	**Menge**	**Einzelpreis**	**Aufwand**	**Einzelpreis**	**Gesamtpreis**
1.1	Briefing/Workshop			1 Tage	1.100 €	1.100 €
1.2	Materialsichtung, Recherche			1 Tage	1.100 €	1.100 €
1.3	Exposé			1 Tage	1.100 €	1.100 €
1.4	Schnittstellendefinitionen			1 Tage	1.000 €	1.000 €
1.5	Grobdesign (Nutzerführung, Themenbaum)			1 Tage	1.000 €	1.000 €
	Zwischensumme Konzeption			*5 Tage*		*5.300 €*
2	**Ausarbeitung**	**Menge**	**Einzelpreis**	**Aufwand**	**Einzelpreis**	**Gesamtpreis**
2.1	Feinkonzept			1 Tage	1.000 €	1.000 €
2.2	Storyboard, Drehbuch, Screenbook, Flowchart	Seiten		5 Tage	700 €	3.500 €
2.3	Textredaktion für Specher und Screen (Autor)	Zeilen		2 Tage	700 €	1.400 €
2.4	Erwerb von Rechten (gesonderte Aufstellung)	GEMA etc.				
2.5	Projektplanung, Projektleitung, Freigabe			1 Tage	1.000 €	1.000 €
	Zwischensumme Ausarbeitung			*9 Tage*		*6.900 €*
3	**Produktion incl. Post-Produktion**					
3.1	**Produktion Video**	**Menge**	**Einzelpreis**	**Aufwand**	**Einzelpreis**	**Gesamtpreis**
3.1.1	Aufnahme einfachst, z.B. Moderation	10 min	500 €	1 Tage		5.000 €
3.1.2	Aufnahme einfach, z.B. Industrie, Sachvideo	10 min	800 €	1 Tage		8.000 €
3.1.3	Aufnahme szenisch, mittlerer Aufwand	min	3.000 €	Tage		
3.1.4	Aufnahme szenisch, großer Aufwand	min	5.000 €	Tage		
3.1.5	Videostudio			1 Tage	1.100 €	1.100 €
3.1.6	Digitalisierung (Einrichtung je Sequenz)	30 Sequ.	80 €	2 Tage		2.400 €
3.1.7	Digitalisierung MPEG offline Band (min. 5 Min.)	min	130 €	Tage		
3.1.8	Digitalisierung MPEG offline E-Bild (min. 5 Min.)	min	650 €	Tage		
3.1.9	Digitalisierung MPEG online Band (min. 5 Min.)	min	35 €	Tage		
3.1.10	Digitalisierung AVI vom Band (min. 5 Min.)	20 min	30 €	Tage		600 €
3.1.11	Konvertierung, Bearbeitung			1 Tage	1.100 €	1.100 €
3.1.12	Videoabnahme, ggf. Korrektur Kundenwünsche			0,5 Tage	1.000 €	500 €
	Zwischensumme Produktion Video			*6,5 Tage*		*18.700 €*
3.2	**Produktion Bild**	**Menge**	**Einzelpreis**	**Aufwand**	**Einzelpreis**	**Gesamtpreis**
3.2.1	Aufnahme (Fotograf)	Stück		Tage	500 €	
3.2.2	Aufnahme (Fotograf mit Studio)			1 Tage	800 €	800 €
3.2.3	Assistent			Tage	200 €	
3.2.4	Maske, Make Up, Haare, etc.			Tage	250 €	
3.2.5	Nebenkosten (Kleines Licht, Material, Requisiten)			Tage	250 €	
3.2.6	Modelle Laien			Tage	150 €	
3.2.7	Modelle Profis			Tage	500 €	
3.2.8	Scannen, Nachbearbeiten	Stück		0,5 Tage	1.000 €	500 €
3.2.9	Abnahme, ggf. Korrektur Kundenwünsche			0,5 Tage	1.100 €	550 €
	Zwischensumme Produktion Bild			*2 Tage*		*1.850 €*
3.3	**Produktion Grafik**	**Menge**	**Einzelpreis**	**Aufwand**	**Einzelpreis**	**Gesamtpreis**
3.3.1	Screendesign	75 Objekte		7 Tage	700 €	4.900 €
3.3.2	Texteingabe Screen			0,5 Tage	500 €	250 €
3.3.3	2D-Grafik	Objekte		Tage	950 €	
3.3.4	3D-Grafik	Objekte		Tage	700 €	
3.3.5	2D-Animation	min		Tage	800 €	
3.3.6	3D-Animation	min		Tage	850 €	
3.3.7	Abnahme, ggf. Korrektur Kundenwünsche			0,5 Tage	1.000 €	500 €
	Zwischensumme Produktion Grafik			*8 Tage*		*5.650 €*

		Menge	Einzelpreis	Aufwand	Einzelpreis	Gesamtpreis
3.4	**Produktion Ton**	**Menge**	**Einzelpreis**	**Aufwand**	**Einzelpreis**	**Gesamtpreis**
3.4.1	Sprecher	min		1 Tage	800 €	800 €
3.4.2	Sprachaufnahme Tonstudio	min		1 Tage	900 €	900 €
3.4.3	El. Musik u. Klang (Komposition und Aufnahme)	min/St.		0,5 Tage	700 €	350 €
3.4.4	Ton-Nachbearbeitung, Konvertierung, Schnitt	min		Tage	800 €	
3.4.5	Abnahme, ggf. Korrektur Kundenwünsche			0,5 Tage	1.000 €	500 €
	Zwischensumme Produktion Ton			*3 Tage*		*2.550 €*
3.5	**Programmierung**	**Menge**	**Einzelpreis**	**Aufwand**	**Einzelpreis**	**Gesamtpreis**
3.5.1	Programmierer A (C, Visual Basic etc.)			5 Tage	800 €	4.000 €
3.5.2	Programmierer B (Autorensysteme)			5 Tage	650 €	3.250 €
3.5.3	Programmierer C (HTML, PC-Grafik, Bilder)			Tage	500 €	
3.5.4	Komplettverschaltung			4 Tage	750 €	3.000 €
3.5.5	Funktionaler Test			1 Tage	500 €	500 €
3.5.6	Qualitätstest, Freigabe (Abnahme)			5 Tage	500 €	2.500 €
	Zwischensumme Programmierung			*20 Tage*		*13.250 €*
4	**Anteil Produktionsleitung**	10 %		4 Tage	1.200 €	8.690 €
5	**Herstellung**	**Menge**	**Einzelpreis**	**Aufwand**	**Einzelpreis**	**Gesamtpreis**
5.1	CD Einzelfertigung	1 Stück	100 €	0,2 Tage		100 €
5.2	CD Kleinauflage	20 Stück	3 €	Tage		60 €
5.3	CD-Mastering und Pressung	500 Stück	1 €	Tage		500 €
5.4	Begleitmaterial (Booklet, Inlaycard)	20 Stück		Tage		
5.5	Projektdokumentation	1 psch		1 Tage		
5.6	Abnahme, Versand	1 psch		0,2 Tage		
	Zwischensumme Herstellung			*1,4 Tage*		*660€*
6	**Nebenkosten des Auftragnehmers**	**Menge**	**Einzelpreis**	**Aufwand**	**Einzelpreis**	**Gesamtpreis**
6.1	Reisekosten	500 km	0,80 €	Tage		400 €
6.2	Kommunikation (Telefon, Fax, Porto)	psch		Tage		
6.3	Übernahme bestehender Projekte	psch		Tage		
6.4	Laborkosten	psch		Tage		
6.5	Gerätekosten	psch		Tage		
6.6	Verbrauchsmaterial	psch		Tage		
	Zwischensumme Nebenkosten Auftragnehmer			*0 Tage*		*400€*
7	**Zusatzkosten des Auftraggebers (z.B.POI)**	**Menge**	**Einzelpreis**	**Aufwand**	**Einzelpreis**	**Gesamtpreis**
7.1	Geräte (Miete)	1 psch		Tage		
7.2	Transport, Installation, Abbau	psch		Tage		
7.3	Standmiete (z.B. Zelt 5x5 m, 5 Tage)	1 psch	250 €	Tage		250 €
7.4	Betreuung	psch		5 Tage	500 €	2.500 €
	Zwischensumme Zusatzkosten Auftraggeber			*5 Tage*		*2.750 €*
	Summe					***66.700 €***
	Mehrwertsteuer				16 %	10.672 €
	Summe brutto					**77.372 €**

18.3.3 Buch-Kalkulation

Die Kalkulation eines Buchprojekts verläuft etwas anders als die beim Film und im Multimediabereich vorrangig angewandte Zuschlagskalkulation. Im Buchverlag, der sich dadurch auszeichnet, dass er viele (kleine, mittlere und größere) Projekte gleichzeitig abwickelt, ist das vorherrschende Kalkulationsverfahren die sog. **Deckungsbeitragsrechnung**. Während man bei der Zuschlagskalkulation sämtliche Kosten ermittelt und diejenigen Kosten, die dem Produkt nicht unmittelbar zurechenbar sind, über Gemeinkostenzuschläge den direkten Kosten hinzufügt, verzichtet man bei der Deckungsbeitragsrechnung auf diesen Zuschlag. Man begnügt sich damit, die direkt von einem Produkt verursachten Kosten ❶ zu ermitteln und stellt diese Kosten – die also nur einen Teil der gesamten Kosten des Produkts darstellen – dem von diesem Produkt erwarteten Umsatzerlös gegenüber. Die Differenz, die sich dann ergibt, nennt man **Deckungsbeitrag** ❷.

Der Begriff „Deckungsbeitrag“ bringt zum Ausdruck, dass dieser Betrag dazu dient, einen Beitrag zur Abdeckung der gesamten fixen Kosten des Verlags zu leisten. Alle Deckungsbeiträge aller Projekte zusammengenommen decken dann (hoffentlich) den gesamten Fixkosten-Block des Verlages ab und führen darüber hinaus zu einem Gewinn. Die nachfolgende Abbildung bringt den Zusammenhang bildhaft zum Ausdruck.

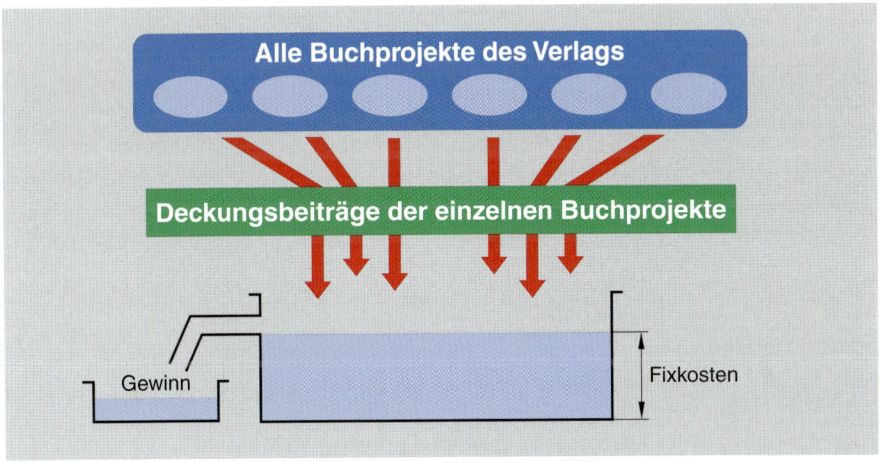

Nochmals zum Sinn der Deckungsbeitragsrechnung: Ein Buchprojekt eines Verlages steht neben vielen anderen gleichartigen Projekten, die zumeist hoch riskante Vorhaben darstellen. Es muss sorgfältig geprüft werden, ob das Projekt durchgeführt werden soll oder nicht. Die Deckungsbeitragsrechnung liefert den Ansatz zur Abschätzung der voraussichtlichen Wirtschaftlichkeit des Projekts. Gleichzeitig liefert sie den Hinweis, welcher Verkaufspreis verlangt werden muss, um aus dem Buchprojekt ein rentables Buchprojekt zu machen.

Das **nachfolgende Beispiel** zeigt die Deckungsbeitragskalkulation eines Taschenbuch-Projekts und stellt dieses der Zuschlagskalkulation gegenüber (Quelle: Schönstedt 1999, Teil D).

❶ Die von einem Projekt direkt verursachten Kosten nennt man **variable Kosten**. Typische variable Kosten im Medienbereich sind Kosten für Rechte, Honorare für freie Mitarbeiter, Materialverbrauch (Papier, Filmmaterial, CD-Rohlinge etc.), Reisekosten für Recherchen, Kommunikationskosten etc. Der Gegensatz zu den variablen Kosten sind die **Fixkosten**, die auch dann anfallen, wenn das Projekt nicht durchgeführt wird. Typische Fixkosten sind z. B. Gehälter für festangestellte Redakteure, Mieten, Versicherungen, „Flat Rates“ oder Steuern.

❷ Der **Deckungsbeitrag** ist definiert als Differenz zwischen dem Umsatzerlös und den variablen Kosten. Er gibt an, wie viel das Produkt zur Deckung der Fixkosten und zum Gewinn (Totalerfolg) beiträgt.

Es geht um das folgende Projekt: Herstellung eines Taschenbuchs in der Auflage von 10.000 Stück. Als Brutto-Ladenpreis sind 10 Euro vorgesehen.

Angaben zu den Kosten:

- Mehrwertsteuer: 7 % vom Netto-Ladenpreis
- Herstellkosten („Technische Herstellkosten“, „th“): 2,00 Euro
- Honorar/Lizenz („Pauschal-Honorar“): 5 % vom Netto-Ladenpreis
- Rabatt an Buchhandel („Durchschnittsrabatt“, „Sortimenter-Rabatt“): 45 % vom Netto-Ladenpreis
- Spezielle Angaben für die Zuschlagskalkulation: Gemeinkosten: 46 % vom Netto-Preis; Geplanter Gewinn („Plangewinn“) 0,31 Euro
- Spezielle Angaben für die Deckungsbeitragsrechnung: Vertreterprovision 8 % vom Netto-Preis; Auslieferung 12 % vom Netto-Preis; Werbung 10 % vom Netto-Preis

Begriffe:

- Brutto-Ladenpreis (Lp)
- Netto-Ladenpreis („Warenwert“) = Brutto-Ladenpreis abzgl. Mehrwertsteuer
- Netto-Preis („Netto-Abgabepreis“) = Netto-Ladenpreis abzgl. Rabatt

Kalkulation nach der Deckungsbeitragsrechnung

1.		Brutto-Ladenpreis (Lp)	10,00	Euro	
2.	./.	Mehrwertsteuer	0,65	Euro	
3.	=	Netto-Ladenpreis (Warenwert)	9,35	Euro	
4.	./.	Rabatt an Buchhandel	4,20	Euro	
5.	=	Netto-Preis („Netto-Abgabepreis“)	5,15	Euro	
6.	./.	Vertreterprovision 8 % von 5.	0,41	Euro	9,35 × 45 %
7.	./.	Auslieferung 12 % von 5.	0,62	Euro	
8.		Deckungsbeitrag I	**4,12**	**Euro**	
9.	./.	Pauschalhonorar 5 % von 3.	0,47	Euro	
10.	./.	Technische Herstellkosten (th)	2,00	Euro	
11.		Deckungsbeitrag II	**1,65**	**Euro**	9,35 × 5 %
12.	./.	Werbung 10 % von 5.	0,52	Euro	
13.		Deckungsbeitrag III (= eigentlicher Deckungsbeitrag pro Stück)	**1,13**	**Euro**	

Kalkulation nach der Zuschlagskalkulation (progressive Methode):

1.		Technische Herstellkosten (th)	2,00	Euro	
2.		Pauschalhonorar	0,47	Euro	
3.	=	Einzelkosten („Einstandskosten“)	2,47	Euro	
4.	+	Gemeinkosten	2,37	Euro	9,35 × 5 %
5.	=	Selbstkosten	4,84	Euro	
6.	+	Plangewinn	0,31	Euro	
7.	=	Netto-Preis („Netto-Abgabepreis“)	5,15	Euro	
8.	+	Rabatt an Buchhandel	4,20	Euro	
9.	=	Netto-Ladenpreis	9,35	Euro	
10.	+	Mehrwertsteuer	0,65	Euro	9,35 × 45 %
11.	=	Brutto-Ladenpreis (Lp)	**10,00**	**Euro**	

18.3.4 Kalkulation einer Drucksache

Faltblatt und Werbebroschüre

Drucksachen spielen sowohl im geschäftlichen als auch im privaten Bereich trotz der elektronischen Konkurrenz nach wie vor eine große Rolle. So sind beispielsweise im Direct Marketing gedruckte Medien als Werbeinstrument immer noch stark im Einsatz ❶. Dort unterscheidet man zwischen adressierten und unadressierten Werbesendungen:

- Adressierte Werbesendungen sind Mail Order Packages (Sendung mit Werbebrief, Prospekt, Rückantwortkarte und Versandkuvert), Kataloge, Kundenzeitschriften, Probezeitschriften, Prospekte, Geschenk-Mailings.
- Unadressierte Werbesendungen umfassen vor allem Handzettel, Prospekte, Warenproben, Hauswurfsendungen.

❶ Das Direct Marketing umfasst alle Kommunikationsinstrumente eines Unternehmen, die darauf ausgerichtet sind, einen direkten Kontakt zu den Kunden herzustellen. Dies reicht von einfachen Prospekten als Hauswurfsendung über Telefon-Marketing, E-Mail-Werbung, Beihefter in Zeitschriften mit Antwortkarten bis hin zu Fernsehwerbespots mit der Aufforderung zum Anruf (sog. „Response-Aufforderung"). Vgl. im Einzelnen Bruhn 2005, S. 651 ff.

Nachfolgend soll der Bereich kleinerer Werbe-Drucksachen näher betrachtet werden. Die einfachste Form ist ein **Image-Faltblatt**, das heute zum Standard selbst in kleinen Firmen, Verbänden und Vereinen gehört. Wer zum ersten Mal auf diesem Wege an die Öffentlichkeit geht, ist vermutlich mit einem Image-Faltblatt zum Start am besten beraten. Ein Faltblatt ist in der Regel nicht mehr als ein dreimal unterteiltes, entsprechend gefalztes Blatt Papier im DIN-A4-Format, das beidseitig bedruckt ist. Es hat mindestens fünf wichtige Vorteile:

- Das Faltblatt ist leicht zu verteilen und passt in jede Jacketttasche.
- Falls das Faltblatt ausgelegt werden soll, passt es in die meisten Auslageständе, da sie auf dieses Format genormt sind.
- Alle Informationen auf dem Faltblatt sind „kurz und knackig" nachzulesen.
- Für Bild und Text lässt sich auf einem Faltblatt ein optimales Layout finden.
- Das DIN-A4-Format wirkt sich optimal auf die Druck- und Papierkosten aus, weil es keinen „Verschnitt" gibt. Auch das Falzen ist einfach.

Zur Eigenherstellung von Faltblättern gibt es kostenlose einfache Tools, beispielsweise in „Word" von Microsoft oder im „Publisher". Im Internet finden sich für den Druck zudem preiswerte Online-Anbieter. Bei der Produktion des Faltblatts in der Hand eines Profis sollte man von folgendem **Kalkulationsbeispiel** ausgehen: Eine Agentur verlangt für ein 6-seitiges Standard-Faltblatt in DIN-A4, 4-farbig, mit einer Druckauflage von 10.000 Stück als „Komplettpaket" (Beratung, Gestaltung, Satz, Druck und Anlieferung) rund 1.200 € (zzgl. MwSt.). Dieser Preis ist freilich nur ein Orientierungswert, der differieren kann.

Bei einer Werbebroschüre handelt es sich um eine textbetonte Drucksache von geringem Umfang ohne Einband, die im Digitaldruck auch bei kleinen Auflagen sehr kostengünstig herzustellen ist. Broschüren sind in der Herstellung komplizierter und gewöhnlich teurer als Faltblatt. Sie haben ebenso wie Faltblatt in der Regel das DIN-A4-Format oder die Hälfte davon – DIN-A5. Zwischenformate sind auch gebräuchlich.

Kostenbereiche

Die Kalkulation einer Drucksache umfasst drei Kostenbereiche:
1. Entwicklung des Inhalts bis zur druckreifen Vorlage
2. Druck
3. Verbreitung

Bei der Entwicklung des Inhalts ist zwischen neuen und bereits bestehenden Inhalten zu unterscheiden. Um neue Inhalte zu generieren, bedarf es eines Ideengebers, ein Konzept muss entwickelt werden, der Fotograf entwickelt Bildmaterial, und Grafik und Design müssen konzipiert und umgesetzt werden. Bei der Verwendung bestehender Inhalte steht die Frage der Rechte an Bildern und Texten im Vordergrund.

Der Druck umfasst die folgenden drei Arbeitsschritte: (1) Druckvorstufe (mit Satz, Reproduktion und Montage und Druckformenherstellung, (2) Druck (Prozess der Übertragung von Farbe auf Papier oder einen anderen Bedruckstoff), (3) Druckweiterverarbeitung (Prozesse wie Schneiden, Falzen, Zusammentragen, Binden).

Bei der Verbreitung können höchst unterschiedliche Wege beschritten werden, die von der persönlichen Zustellung (Hauswurfsendungen) bis zu postalischen Zustellung bei Direct Mail-Aktion reichen.

Größere Drucksachen

Nachfolgend wird die **(Grob-)Kalkulation eines kleinen Reiseführers** für einen Landkreis wiedergegeben, der 64 Seiten Innenteil plus 4 Seiten Umschlag mit zahlreichen Farbfotos umfasst und bei dem Anzeigen vorgesehen sind (Quelle: Hermanni 2007, S. 193 ff.).

Interne Kosten (Verlag)		
1. Redaktion/Autor (Arbeitszeit 2 Wochen)	€	2.000,00
2. Lektorat (Arbeitszeit 3 Tage/24 Std. à € 25,–)	€	600,00
3. Fotograf (pauschal)	€	6.500,00
4. Grafik/Druckvorstufe (40 Std. à € 60,–)	€	2.400,00
5. Buchhaltung (pauschal)	€	500,00
Gesamtkosten intern (ohne MwSt)	€	12.000,00
Externe Kosten (Druckerei, Rechte, Distribution)		
1. Druckkosten (Auflage 5.000 Stück)	€	4.500,00
2. Anzeigenverkauf (Basishonorar + Provision 20 %)		
Basishonorar für 3 Monate (freie Zeiteinteilung)	€	3.000,00
3. Allgemeine Kosten	€	300,00
4. Titelschutz-Anzeige (www.titelschutzanzeiger,de)	€	150,00
5. Einkauf Fremdkommentare (2 ×)	€	1.000,00
6. Einkauf Karten/Ortspläne (5 × € 400,–)	€	2.000,00
7. ISBN-Nummer	€	67,79
8. Distribution (als Beilage eines Anzeigenblattes)		
(pro 1.000 Stück = € 67,–; bei 5.000 Stück Auflage)	€	335,00
Gesamtkosten extern (ohne MwSt)	€	11.952,779
Herstellungskosten gesamt (ohne MwSt)	**€**	**23.952,79**

18.3.5 Kalkulation eines Video-/ Computerspiels

Video- und Computerspiele gehören zu den **aufwändigsten Medienprodukten**. Spiele werden im internationalen Maßstab je nach technischem Aufwand und technischer Qualität in einer Raster von AAA (bestes Ergebnis) bis CCC (schlechtestes Ergebnis) eingestuft.

Das nachfolgende **Fallbeispiel** ❶ beruht auf der realen Kalkulation eines in Deutschland entwickelten, vergleichsweise einfachen Spielprojekts. Es ist als C/B-Projekt eingestuft, das sich also unterhalb des Durchschnitts befindet. Ein solches Produkt bewegt sich im mittleren Preissegment von ca. 30 Euro.

❶ Quelle: Müller-Lietzkow; Bouncken; Seufert 2006, S. 200 ff. Alle Angaben sind dieser sehr aufschlussreichen Studie entnommen.

Rahmendaten

Der Entwicklungszeitraum für dieses Projekt mittlerer Größe betrug 18 Monate. Bei größeren Projekten dauert die Entwicklung deutlich länger und erfordert mehr Personal. So liegt bei B/A-Projekten die Entwicklungszeit im Schnitt bei zwei Jahren und bei einem Personaleinsatz von 50 bis 60 Personen. AAA-Projekte („Triple-A-Produktionen“) agieren am oberen Limit und werden laut US-Experten mit einer Entwicklungszeit von drei Jahren und 100 bis 150 Personen kalkuliert. Großkonsolen-Spiele dieser Art bewegen sich in einem Budgetbereich, der jenseits der 10-Mio.-Dollar-Grenze liegt.

In der Kalkulation auf der folgenden Seite sind in der ersten Spalte von links die unterschiedlichen Kosten-Kategorien angegeben, die in der zweiten Spalte mit den entsprechenden Funktionen präzisiert werden. Die dritte Spalte gibt die Spannen von Monatsgehältern wieder, in denen sich die Leistungen bewegen. Die letzte Spalte schließlich zeigt die Berechnung der Kostenpositionen für das konkrete Projekt mit 18 Monaten und für die bestimmte Anzahl von Personen, die vor dem Doppelpunkt angegeben sind.

Die Kosten des Beispiel-Projekts summieren sich auf insgesamt 2.516.500 Euro und decken jedoch nur die Entwicklungskosten ab. Zu diesen Kosten sind für eine Gesamtkalkulation noch die Produktionskosten der Vervielfältigung der Träger, die Veröffentlichungskosten („Publishing“) und die After-Sales-Kosten zu ergänzen. Diese können bei Spielen dieser Art leicht noch einmal denselben Betrag wie die Entwicklungskosten erreichen, wenn nicht sogar überschreiten.

Das vorliegende Beispiel stellt – wie dargelegt – ein Beispiel der mittleren technischen Qualität dar. Das Spektrum der Spiele reicht jedoch auch in den Bereich von „Casual-Spielen“, die mit sehr kleinem Budget entwickelt wurden, aber dennoch sehr erfolgreich sein können, wie das Beispiel „Moorhuhn“ zeigt. Auch im Bereich von Kinderspielen sind die Budgets zumeist sehr viel geringer als das vorliegende Projektbeispiel. Übliche Produktionsbudgets liegen hier in einer Dimension von 100.000 bis 250.000 Euro.

Kostenkalkulation der Entwicklungskosten eines Spielprojekts

		Einzelkosten	Reales Projektbeispiel
Personal (Gehalt)		**Pro Kopf/Monat in Euro**	
	Management/ Executive Producer (2-3)	3.000 - 5.000 (Sek. 2.000 - 2.500)	2 : 144.000
	Grafiker (6-12)	2.500 - 4.000	6 : 342.000
	Programmierer (6-10)	3.000 - 6.000	6 : 432.000
	Gamedesign	3.000 - 5.000	1 : 72.000
	Leveldesigner (4-8)	2.500 - 3.000	4 : 180.000
	Musiker (1)	2.000 - 2.500	1 : 45.000
	Techniker (1)	2.000 - 3.000	1 : 36.000
	Personalnebenkosten	k.A.	350.000
Personal gesamt	**20-35 Personen**		**1.601.000**
Engines		**Preisspannen**	
	Grafik	100.000 - 500.000	250.000
	Physik	50.000 - 100.000	50.000
	Künstliche Intellegenz	25.000 - 50.000	25.000
	Sound & Musik	5.000 - 20.000	10.000
Engines gesamt		**180.000 - 670.000**	**335.000**
Ausstattungskosten pro Arbeitsplatz		**Einmalige Projektausstattung pro Arbeitsplatz**	
	Administration	2.500 - 3.000	5.000
	Grafiker/Designer	5.000 - 7.500	42.000
	Programmierer	3.000 - 5.000	24.000
	Leveldesigner	2.500 - 3.000	10.000
	Musiker	2.500 - 5.000	2.500
	Techniker	2.000 - 2.500	2.000
Ausstattungskosten gesamt		**85.500**	
Sonstige Kosten		**Monatsbasis**	
	Büroräume	2.000 - 3.000	45.000
	Laufende Kosten	10.000 - 20.000	270.000
	Reisekosten	4.000 - 6.000	90.000
	Kommunikationskosten	5.000	90.000
Sonstige Kosten gesamt		**21.000 - 34.000**	**495.000**
Kalkulationsbasis Beispielprojekt			**2.516.500**

Aufgaben und Übungen, Literaturhinweise

Aufgaben und Übungen

1. Nehmen Sie im Fernsehen eine Reihe von Fernsehwerbespots auf. Sortieren Sie diese danach, ob sie eher niedrige oder eher höhere Herstellungskosten verursacht haben (Low Budget vs. High Budget). Geben Sie Begründungen für Ihre Einschätzung.
2. Analysieren Sie fünf Ihnen bekannte Kinospielfilme darauf hin, ob sie eher Low-Budget- oder eher High-Budget-Produktionen darstellen.
3. Sie sollen eine kleine Szene mit einer Amateur-Videokamera drehen. Entwerfen Sie ein „Drehbuch" zu dieser Szene im Sinne einer groben Skizze. Entwickeln Sie nun aus diesem „Drehbuch" eine Kalkulation in grober Form.
4. Entwerfen Sie einen Image-Flyer für Ihre Bildungseinrichtung. Gehen Sie davon aus, dass von diesem Flyer 1.000 Exemplare gedruckt werden sollen, die aus Anlass einer großen Feierlichkeit verteilt werden sollen. Stellen Sie die Kalkulation für dieses Projekt dar.

Literaturhinweise

Beste, Johannes; *Hahn*, Hans; *Wolf*, Thomas: Rechnungswesen für Medienberufe, Troisdorf (Bildungsverlag EINS)

Bruhn, Manfred: Unternehmens- und Marketingkommunikation. Handbuch für ein integriertes Kommunikationsmanagement, München 2005 (Vahlen)

Bundesverband Druck und Medien e. V. (BVDM): Zahlreiche Publikationen zum Thema Kalkulation und Kosten- und Leistungsrechnung in den Bereichen Druck, Medien, Multimedia, Print- und Non-Print.

Clevé, Bastian: Gib niemals auf. Filmökonomie in der Praxis. Konstanz 2004 (UVK)

dmmv-Kalkulationssystematik. Leitfaden zur Kalkulation von Multimedia-Projekten. Autoren: *Dellingshausen*, Christoph von; *Gläser*, Martin; *Pracht*, Beate; *Walter*, Klaus; *Winkelhage*, Christoph, hrsg. v. dmmv und High Text-Verlag, München 2003.

Dress, Peter: Vor Drehbeginn. Effektive Planung von Film- und Fernsehproduktionen, Neuausgabe, Bergisch Gladbach 2002 (Bastei Lübbe)

Etat-Kalkulator, erscheint 2 mal im Jahr, creativ collection Freiburg i. Br.

Haberbecks Taschen-Kalkulator (www.haberbeck.de)

Hackenberg, Heidi: Kommunikationsdesign. Akquisition und Kalkulation, Mainz 2002 (Verlag Hermann Schmidt)

Hermanni, Alfred-Joachim: Medienmanagement. Grundlagen und Praxis für Film, Hörfunk, Internet, Multimedia und Print, München 2007 (Beck dtv-Taschenbuch)

Müller-Lietzkow, Jörg; *Bouncken*, Ricarda B.; *Seufert*, Wolfgang: Gegenwart und Zukunft der Computer- und Videospielindustrie in Deutschland, Dornach 2006 (Entertainment Media Verlag)

Schönstedt, Eduard: Der Buchverlag, 2. Aufl., Stuttgart, Weimar 1999 (J. B. Metzler)

Webcode: C1900

Für weitere Infos zu diesem Kapitel mit dem Smartphone einfach QR-Code scannen oder auf www.medien-verstehen.de den Webcode eingeben.

19 Medienproduktion

Dieses Kapitel befasst sich mit dem Herstellungsvorgang von Medienprodukten. Es präzisiert damit die in Kapitel 15.5 angesprochene Phase der Durchführung eines Projekts und folgt daher den Phasen der Projekt-Entstehung, der Projekt-Definition, dem Projekt-Start und der Projekt-Planung. Es geht darum, nun das im Projekt geplante Produkt konkret herzustellen. Welche Herstellungsvorgänge hierzu notwendig sind, wird nachfolgend in verallgemeinerter Form und anhand von Beispielen beleuchtet.

19.1 Medialer Produktionsprozess im Überblick

Die jeweiligen medialen Produktionsprozesse unterscheiden sich in vielerlei Hinsicht erheblich. So erfordert die Herstellung einer Zeitung, einer Zeitschrift oder eines Buches z. B. eine völlig andere Technik als die Herstellung eines Kinofilms. Im einen Fall sind komplizierte Druckmaschinen notwendig, während im anderen Fall Kameras, Effektgeräte und Schnittsysteme erforderlich sind. Wieder anders verlaufen Multimedia- und Internet-Produktionen, wo ein hoher Programmieraufwand mit spezifischem Software-Einsatz im Vordergrund steht. Ebenso unterschiedlich sind die eingesetzten Personengruppen, die völlig unterschiedliche Fähigkeiten mitbringen müssen, um in der jeweiligen Medienproduktion tätig werden zu können.

Ein weiteres wesentliches Merkmal produktionstechnischer Unterschiede ist, dass Medienprodukte typischerweise im unterschiedlichen Umfang intern bzw. extern produziert werden. So wird z. B. fiktionale Unterhaltung im Fernsehen (also Spielfilme, Serien, Reihen) durchweg extern von unabhängigen Produzenten erstellt, während Informationssendungen (Nachrichten, Magazine, Reportagen, Dokumentationen) in der Regel intern produziert werden. Bei Letzterem finden oft Zulieferungen von Nachrichtenagenturen, freien Mitarbeitern oder thematisch spezialisierten Anbietern (z. B. Reporter von Katastrophen oder der „High Society") statt. Im Gegensatz dazu wird nichtfiktionale TV-Unterhaltung (das sind vor allem Spielsendungen, Shows, Musik- und Sportübertragungen) sowohl intern als auch extern produziert, allerdings mit einem Trend zu verstärktem **Outsourcing**.

Trotz dieser höchst unterschiedlichen Ausgangslage lassen sich über alle Medienprodukte hinweg **Gemeinsamkeiten** in den Produktionsvorgängen ausmachen. Typisch ist ein **gemeinsames Grundmuster** des medialen Produktionsprozesses, das sich mit den folgenden **vier Produktionsschritten** beschreiben lässt (vgl. Krömker/Klimsa 2005, S. 19):

Content = Inhalt

- Pre-Production: Recherche, Planung, Erzeugung von Content
- Production: Anpassung von Content an das jeweilige technische Vermittlungssystem
- Post-Production Verfeinern, Bearbeiten und Testen von Content
- Distribution Transfer von Content an die Zielgruppen

Nachfolgende **Übersicht** (Quelle: Krömker/Klimsa 2005, S. 20) verdeutlicht die Gemeinsamkeiten im Hinblick auf diese vier Produktionsschritte, die als vier Säulen dargestellt sind. In horizontaler Richtung wird für jeden Medienbereich nach Content und Technik unterschieden. Diese Aufteilung macht klar, dass jeder einzelne mediale Produktionsprozess, in welchem Segment er auch stattfindet, immer aus einem Zusammenwirken der beiden Faktoren Content und Technik besteht und ein Produkt nur dann entstehen kann, wenn sich der kreative Prozess der Erstellung von Inhalten bzw. Content und der Einsatz technischer Systeme miteinander „verbünden". Einzelheiten dieser Darstellung werden in den einzelnen Unterkapiteln erläutert.

<table>
<tr><th colspan="2"></th><th>Pre-Production</th><th colspan="2">Production</th><th colspan="2">Post-Production</th><th>Distribution</th></tr>
<tr><td rowspan="2">Film</td><td>Content</td><td>Planung</td><td colspan="2">Dreharbeiten</td><td colspan="2">Material-Bearbeitung</td><td>Auslieferung/ Digitale Bereitstellung</td></tr>
<tr><td>Technik</td><td>Management-System</td><td colspan="2">Filmaufzeichnungs-System</td><td colspan="2">Postproduktions-System</td><td>Testumgebung/ Testsystem</td></tr>
<tr><td rowspan="2">Fernsehen Hörfunk</td><td>Content</td><td>Themen-Recherche</td><td>Material-Recherche</td><td>Material-Erstellung</td><td colspan="2">Material-Bearbeitung</td><td>Ausstrahlung</td></tr>
<tr><td>Technik</td><td>Redaktionssystem</td><td>Browsing-System</td><td>Aufzeichnungs-Wiedergabe-System</td><td colspan="2">Postproduktions-System</td><td>Sendeabwicklung</td></tr>
<tr><td rowspan="2">Musik</td><td>Content</td><td>Songwriting/ Komposition</td><td colspan="2">Musikaufnahme</td><td>Musik-Nachbearbeitung</td><td>CD-Erstellung/Vervielfältigung</td><td>Auslieferung/ Digitale Bereitstellung</td></tr>
<tr><td>Technik</td><td>Kompositions-System</td><td colspan="2">Aufzeichnungs-/ Wiedergabe-System</td><td>Postproduktions-System</td><td>Vervielfältigungs-System</td><td>Vertriebssystem</td></tr>
<tr><td rowspan="2">Internet</td><td>Content</td><td>Anforderungsanalyse</td><td>Storyboard/ Flowchart</td><td>Anwendungserstellung</td><td colspan="2">Anwendungs-Test</td><td>Digitale Bereitstellung</td></tr>
<tr><td>Technik</td><td>Management-System</td><td>Prototyping/ Design-System</td><td>Entwicklungsumgebung</td><td colspan="2">Testumgebung/ Testsystem</td><td>Provider-System</td></tr>
<tr><td rowspan="2">Print</td><td>Content</td><td>Themen-Recherche</td><td>Material-Recherche</td><td>Material-Erstellung</td><td colspan="2">Vervielfältigung (analog/digital)</td><td>Auslieferung/ Digitale Bereitstellung</td></tr>
<tr><td>Technik</td><td>Redaktions-System</td><td>Browsing-System</td><td>Schreib-/ Layout-System</td><td colspan="2">Drucksystem/ Content Management System</td><td>Provider-System</td></tr>
<tr><td rowspan="2">Mobilfunk</td><td>Content</td><td>Anforderungsanalyse</td><td colspan="2">Anwendungserstellung</td><td colspan="2">Anwendungs-Test</td><td>Digitale Bereitstellung</td></tr>
<tr><td>Technik</td><td>Management-System</td><td colspan="2">Programmier-System</td><td colspan="2">Testumgebung/ Testsystem</td><td>Provider-System</td></tr>
</table>

19.2 Produktion einer Tageszeitung

Zeitungen stellen an den Druckprozess hohe Anforderungen, da sie in großen Auflagen täglich erscheinen. Im Gegensatz zur gehefteten Zeitschrift wird die Tageszeitung in Lagen gefaltet. Die tägliche Informationsvermittlung läuft mittlerweile auf vielen Kanälen ab, und die Möglichkeiten, die das Internet bietet, sorgen dafür, dass die Tageszeitung nicht nur in Papier, sondern auch in elektronischer Form ins Haus kommt. Nach wie vor kommt der Tageszeitung eine wichtige Aufgabe zu, die der Wächterinstanz, und bildet damit eine entscheidende Säule demokratischer Gesellschaften.

Die Tageszeitung stellt für jeden Leser tagesaktuelle Informationen aus allen Bereichen des Lebens bereit. Die Fülle an Informationen, die Zeitpunkte der Geschehnisse auf der ganzen Welt zwingen die Verlage dazu, die Wege des Druckprodukts zum Leser kürzer und damit schneller zu machen. Rotationsmaschinen für den Sechsfarbendruck, moderne Sortier- und Verpackungsanlagen und Lokalredaktionen mit ausgelagerten Produktionsstätten können den Arbeitsfluss beschleunigen. Dazu sind die elektronischen Hilfsmittel wie Datenbanken, Redaktionsprogramme zur Text- und Bildverarbeitung sowie die Datenfernübertragung eine wertvolle Unterstützung. Tageszeitungen haben eine regional bezogene Zusammenstellung aus einem Mantelteil, der vor allem die internationalen und überregionalen Ereignisse abbildet, und dem Lokalteil.

19.2.1 Daten und Fakten

Stuttgarter Nachrichten / Stuttgarter Zeitung:

- 390.000 Exemplare (2005)
- In einem Haushalt lesen im Durchschnitt zwei Personen die Tageszeitung.
- Der Marktanteil der Stuttgarter Nachrichten und Stuttgarter Zeitung liegt im Stadtzentrum Stuttgart bei ca. 62%, Ballungsgebiet Stuttgart bei ca. 69%.

Die Stuttgarter Nachrichten haben eigene Lokalausgaben mit insgesamt ca. 78.000 Zeitungen mit der Kernauflage der Stadt und erstellen außerdem die überregionalen Mantelseiten für zahlreiche Lokalzeitungen in der Region Stuttgart.

Schwäbische Zeitung

- Erscheint in einer Gesamtauflage von nahezu 190.000 Exemplaren für die Regionen Schwarzwald-Bodensee-Oberschwaben-Ostalb.
- 22 Lokalausgaben

Frankfurter Allgemeine Zeitung

- Deutsche Abonnement-Tageszeitung, Ausrichtung liberal-konservativ
- ca. 364.000 Exemplare (2006)
- höchste Auslandsverbreitung aller deutschen Qualitäts-Zeitungen.
- Die FAZ ist seit 2001 mit einem eigenen redaktionellen Teil (FAZ.NET) im Internet. Dieser Service wird von 1,32 Mio. Lesern pro Monat genutzt.

Süddeutsche Zeitung
- Größte deutsche überregionale Abonnement-Tageszeitung, Ausrichtung liberal-kritisch
- 450.000 Exemplare pro Tag, ca. 1,2 Mio Leser pro Tag

Bildzeitung
- 3,8 Mio Jahresdurchschnitt (2005), 11,5 Millionen Leser
- Die Lesedauer beträgt ca. 10 Minuten (Quelle: Käuferanalyse BILD 2000)
- Der Anspruch von BILD lautet: Näher dran und schneller dran!
- 31 unterschiedliche Regional- und Lokalausgaben

Tageszeitung taz
- ca. 62.000 Exemplare, davon ca. 49.000 Abonnements
- seit 1979 am Markt, „gegründet ohne Verlag, ohne Kapital und ohne Erfahrung" (Zitat taz)
- Ausrichtung linksorientiert, kritisch

Ergänzt wird die Tageszeitung durch wöchentliche Magazine im Fernsehprogramm oder eine siebte Sonntagsausgabe bzw. zusätzliche monatliche Beilagen zum Thema Wirtschaft, Computertechnik, Schönheit, Medizin, Konzert, Kultur u. a. Bei der Samstagsausgabe einer Tageszeitung mit Magazinen und Beilagen können dann Spitzenauflagen bis zu 950.000 Exemplaren erreicht werden.

19.2.2 Herstellungsvorgang

Die einzelnen Fertigungsschritte bis zum Zeitungsprodukt, das der Leser in den Händen hält, sehen im Überblick sehr einfach aus und doch müssen sie exakt abgestimmt und geplant sein, damit ein Rad in das andere greift.

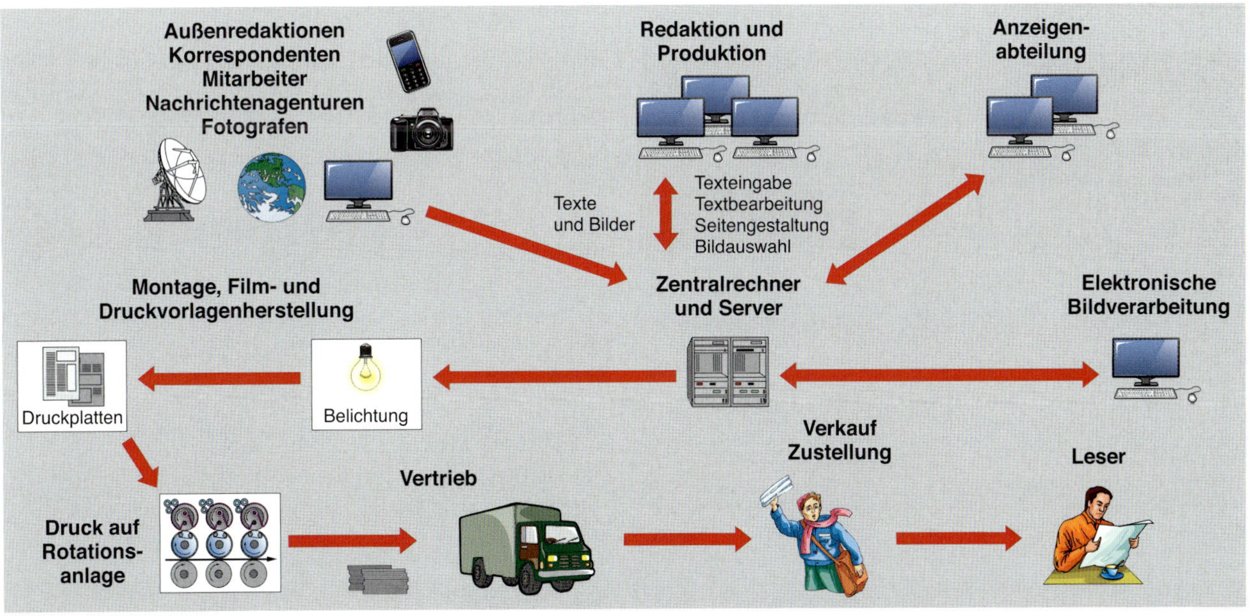

19.2.3 Von der Meldung zum Artikel

Am 13. Mai 1983 enthüllten die Stuttgarter Nachrichten den spektakulärsten Medienskandal der Nachkriegszeit. Konrad Kujau wurde als Fälscher der vom „Stern" veröffentlichten „Hitler-Tagebücher" entlarvt. Der Journalist Klaus-Ulrich Moeller erhielt für seine Enthüllungen den Theodor-Wolff-Preis.

Die Arbeitsweise hat sich für den Redakteur in vielen Bereichen verändert. Heute dominieren Datenbanken mit Korrespondentenberichten und Datenbanken der Agenturen wie SID, AP, KNA u. a. den Alltag der schreibenden Zunft. Aus der Fülle der bereit stehenden Informationen Wichtiges herauszufiltern und zu Artikeln, Glossen und Leitartikeln zu verarbeiten, ist die am häufigsten auftretende journalistische Arbeit, die Recherche vor Ort, mit dem Telefon oder über das Internet die andere und oft beschwerlichere Tätigkeit der Informationsbeschaffung.

So werden spektakuläre Nachforschungen, die beispielsweise zum Aufdecken der gefälschten Hitlertagebücher des Herrn Kujau führten, zu journalistischen Highlights, die nicht unbedingt den Alltag des Journalisten bestimmen.

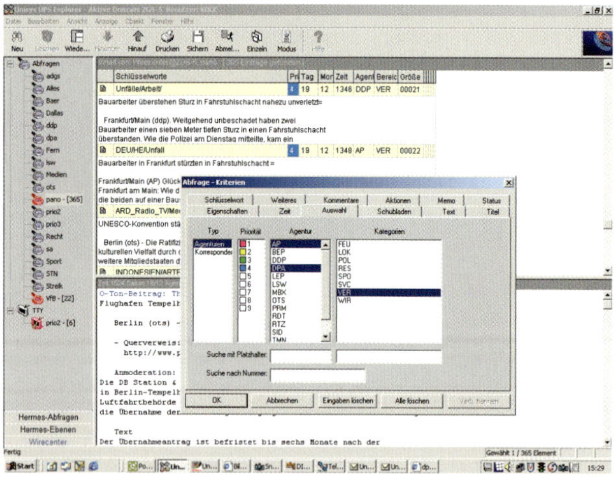

❶

Trotz unspektakulärer Routinearbeiten ist das journalistische Leben immer spannend, da man nie weiß, was an wichtigen Geschehnissen noch zur redaktionellen Weiterverarbeitung am Nachmittag eines jeden Tages eintrifft. Dann rückt die Zeit des Andrucks näher und die Seiten im Redaktionssystem füllen sich nach und nach mit den Inhalten.

Wie ein solches **Redaktionssystem** funktioniert, wollen wir uns im Folgenden näher anschauen. Agenturen auf der ganzen Welt und Korrespondenten stellen über Datenbanken Meldungen bereit, die der Redakteur mit Hilfe von Suchkriterien eingrenzen kann. Dabei hat er die Möglichkeit, verschiedene Einstellungen vorzunehmen, um die Informationen nach seinen Bedürfnissen zu filtern.

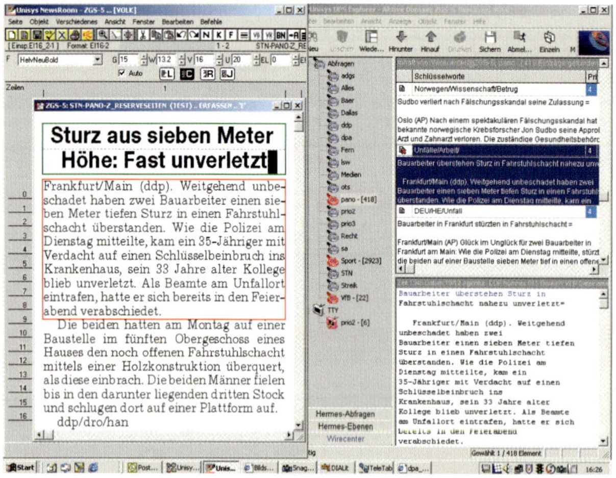

❸ ❷

Der Redakteur orientiert sich beispielsweise daran, wann die Meldung geschrieben wurde, mit welchen inhaltlichen Stichworten sie versehen ist, von welcher **Agentur** die Meldung kommt bzw. welchem Ressort sie zuzuordnen ist ❶.

Die ausgewählten Meldungen werden ihm dann in Blöcken mit den wichtigsten Schlagzeilen auf dem Bildschirm dargestellt ❷. Ein Textfenster gibt den ausführlichen Text der Meldung wieder. Hat sich der Redakteur für eine bestimmte Meldung entschieden, die zu einem Artikel ausgebaut werden soll, dann übernimmt er diese in das Layoutfenster ❸.

Der Text der Meldung fließt in das geöffnete Editierfenster und der Redakteur kann nun Überschrift und Texte hinzufügen, verändern bzw. löschen und damit nach seinen Vorstellungen einen vollständigen Artikel formulieren.

Der **Text** ist nun fertig und wird abgespeichert. Jetzt kann er im Ansichtsmodus gelesen und korrigiert werden ❶. Mit Hilfe der Zoomfunktion lassen sich einzelne Artikel einer Seite vergrößern, um sie Korrektur zu lesen. Sollte der Text zu einem späteren Zeitpunkt nochmals überarbeitet werden, so kann der Artikel mit einem Doppelklick im Editierfenster wieder geöffnet werden.

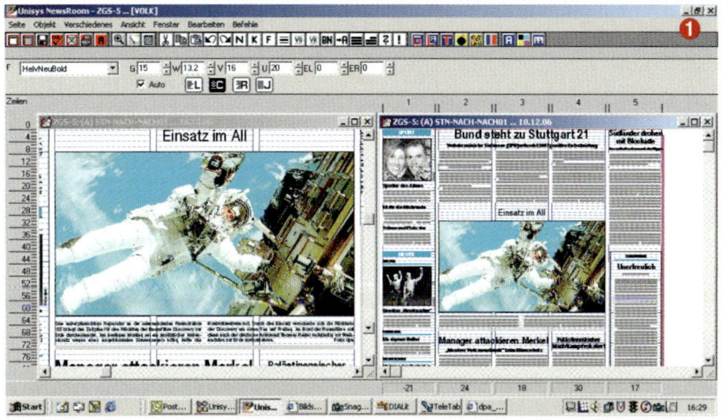

Die Inhalte der Zeitungsseiten werden zu unterschiedlichen Zeiten fertiggestellt, wobei mit der Schlusssitzung der Redaktion der Schlusspunkt der Editierarbeit gesetzt wird. Um zwischenzeitlich einen Überblick darüber zu erhalten, ob ein Artikel fertiggestellt, gerade geschrieben oder ein Layoutfeld für eine Meldung noch frei ist, kann jeder Redakteur über den Status-Modus des Redaktionssystems erfahren ❷. In der **Seitenübersicht** erhält man sofort den momentanen Zustand der Zeitungsseite. Die farbigen Felder haben folgende Bedeutung:

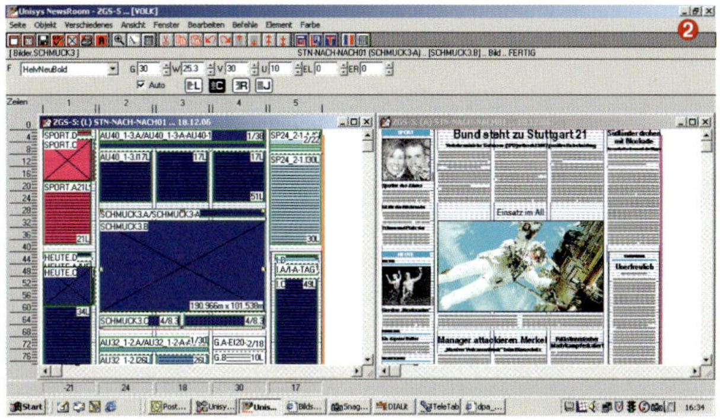

- weißes Feld: Meldung wurde noch nicht geschrieben.
- türkisfarbenes Feld: Meldung wird gerade geschrieben.
- hellblaues Feld: Artikel ist verfasst, wird aber noch redigiert.
- dunkelblaues Feld: Artikel ist fertiggestellt.

Bilder sind das Salz in der Suppe eines Berichts, sofern zur Meldung auch welche zur Verfügung stehen. Über eine **Bilddatenbank** kann der Redakteur nach Bildern suchen, die zur Meldung passen oder es werden mit der Meldung bereits Bilder angeboten. Aus dieser Bilddatenbank ❸ wählt der Redakteur das passende Bildmaterial aus und setzt es zur Kontrolle innerhalb des Layoutfensters in den Artikel ein. Im Ansichtsfenster bekommt man dann einen ersten Eindruck, wie die Seite im Endprodukt wirken wird.

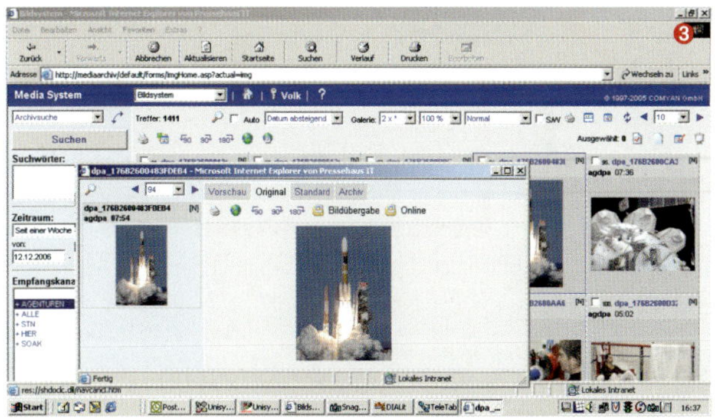

Die fertiggestellte Zeitungsseite wird nach der Freigabe durch die Redaktion auf einen Film (Computer-to-Film) oder direkt auf die Druckplatte (Computer-to-Plate) belichtet.

19.2.4 Druckprozess

Die Produktion einer Zeitung ist das Beispiel für ein sehr großes Druckprojekt. Betrachtet man den **Produktionsprozeess** von Druckprodukten ganz allgemein, so lassen sich die folgenden **drei klassischen Produktionsstufen** unterscheiden:

- die Druckvorstufe mit Reproduktion und Druckformherstellung (Prepress),
- der eigentliche Druckprozess (Press), und
- die Druckweiterverarbeitung (Postpress), sowie die Veredelung (Finishing).

Eine Übersicht über den hierbei entstehenden Material- und Datenfluss gibt die nachfolgende Abbildung (Quelle: Kipphan 2000, S. 14).

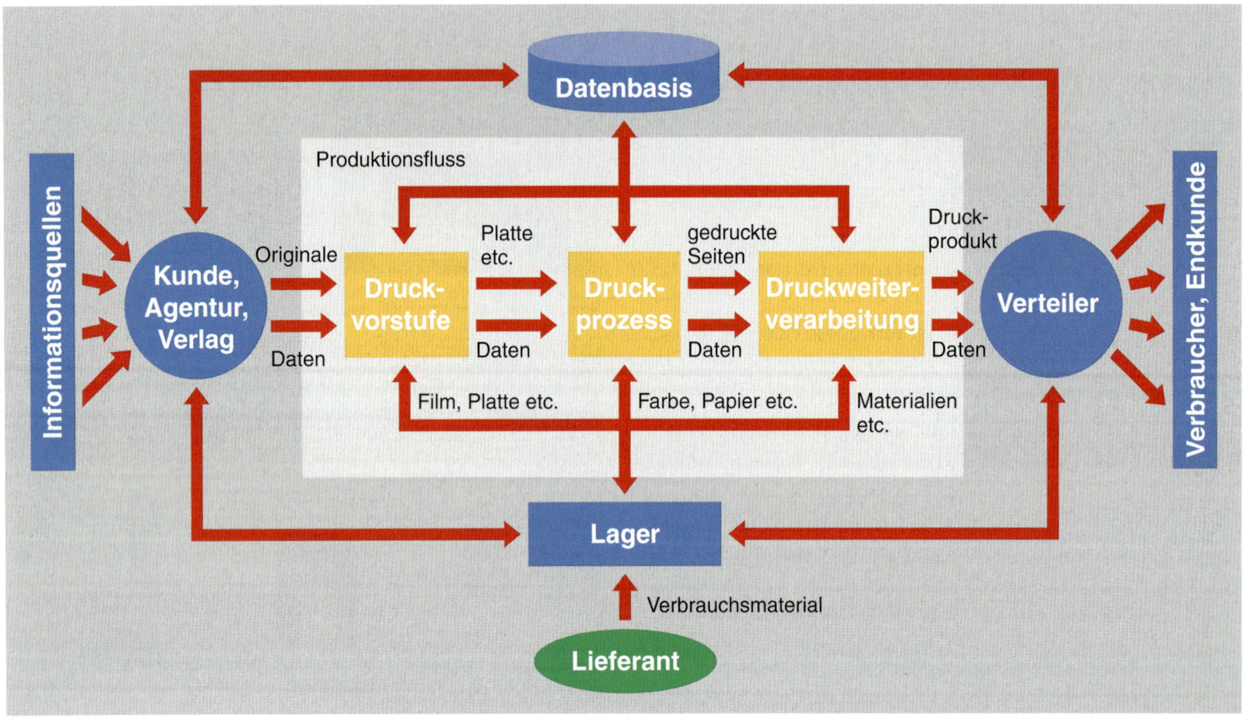

In dieser Darstellung wird deutlich, dass die ehemals strikte Trennung zwischen Print- und Non-Print-Techniken inzwischen aufgehoben ist. Die Entwicklung hierzu verlief geradezu dramatisch: Erst in den 70er-Jahren des vergangenen Jahrhunderts verdrängte der Fotosatz den Bleisatz und schaffte die Voraussetzung für den Offsetdruck. In den 80er-Jahren setzte sich Desktop-Publishing sowohl bei den Druckereien als auch bei deren Kunden durch, womit eine neue Technik der Bild- und Textverarbeitung zum Standard wurde. Die neuere Entwicklung wird nachhaltig durch die Digitalisierung angetrieben und macht die sog. „Computer-to-X"-Techniken möglich. Speziell spielt Computer-to-Plate eine wichtige Rolle, das ist die Bebilderung von Druckplatten direkt aus dem digitalen Datenbestand heraus.

19.2.5 Newsroom

Im Zeichen des Internet wird die **integrierte Nachrichten-Erzeugung** zu einer zunehmenden Herausforderung. Ein Schlüsselbegriff lautet: „One Source – multi media", was zum Ausdruck bringt, dass die Nachrichten an einer Stelle erzeugt werden müssen und diese dann für alle möglichen Medien aufbereitet werden, vor allem für die Zeitung und das Internet.

Vor diesem Hintergrund spielt bei den Tageszeitungen der sog. **Newsroom** eine immer wichtigere Rolle. Ein Musterbeispiel ist der Newsroom, wie er im Jahr 2006 bei der Tageszeitung „Die Welt" installiert wurde ❶:

❶ Nachfolgender Auszug stammt aus dem Beitrag „Zeitung, Internet, Fernsehen: Wie Deutschlands modernster Nachrichtenraum funktioniert" in der „Welt am Sonntag" vom 19.11.2006, S. 78 f.

„Was zunächst wie ein normales Großraumbüro aussieht, symbolisiert auf über 400 Quadratmetern Fläche zwei wichtige Innovationen auf einmal. Die erste Neuerung hat etwas mit dem Internet zu tun: Erstmals in der Geschichte der „Welt am Sonntag" arbeiten hier Zeitungsjournalisten Schulter an Schulter mit den Online-Kollegen. Die alten Grenzen zwischen Zeitung und Internet verschwimmen, ein neues Bewusstsein entsteht. Früher gab es Experten für das Zeitungsmachen und Experten für das Internet. Und diese Journalisten hatten wenig miteinander zu tun.
Aus Sicht der Profis war das damals eine sinnvolle Arbeitsteilung, aber die Ansprüche der Leser haben sich geändert. Sie wechseln zwischen den Zeitungen und Internet mühelos hin und her. Was sie in der Woche als Nachricht im Internet bei Welt.de finden, wollen sie am Sonntag vertieft in der Zeitung lesen. Umgekehrt möchten sie Themen, die sie in der Zeitung interessierten, online mit Hintergründen, Videos, Bildergalerien und Diskussionsforen vertiefen. Wenn Leser zwischen den Medien wechseln, können Journalisten nicht bei ihrem angestammten Berufsbild bleiben.
Viele Menschen verbringen heute mehr Zeit im Netz als mit der Zeitung. Das bedroht Zeitungen nicht in ihrer Existenz; sie besitzen viele einzigartige Stärken, die ihnen eine erfolgreiche Zukunft sichern. Aber Zeitungen müssen besser als bisher mit dem Internet verzahnt werden.
Genau das ermöglicht der neue Newsroom: Wirtschaftsredakteure, Sportreporter oder Parlamentskorrespondenten schreiben sowohl für die Zeitung als auch für Online. Ganz gleich, wer eine interessante Geschichte zu erzählen hat, kommt in die Nachrichtenzentrale und schildert sie Kollegen. Dort sitzen Chefredakteur, Ressortleiter, Fotoredakteure, Layouter, Infografiker – sie beraten gemeinsam, ob die Geschichte eher für die Zeitung oder für Online taugt, ob sie in beiden Medien erscheinen soll und wie sie dort jeweils aufbereitet wird.
... Die zweite wichtige Neuerung, für die der Newsroom steht, hat mit den Schwesterzeitungen der „Welt am Sonntag" zu tun: „Die Welt", „Berliner Morgenpost" und „Welt Kompakt". Über Jahrzehnte arbeitete die „Welt am Sonntag" völlig getrennt von ihren Schwestern. Die Redaktionen standen im Wettbewerb untereinander. Obwohl man eine gemeinsame Kantine besuchte und sich im Aufzug traf, wurden Informationen eifersüchtig gehütet. ... Wie sieht die Arbeit in der Zentrale aus? Sie beginnt morgens um 6 Uhr mit der ersten Schicht für das Webangebot Welt.de. Korrespondentenberichte von anderen Kontinenten laufen ein, Aufträge werden verteilt, Beiträge geschrieben, Videos produziert. Früh am Morgen werden die Seiten auf den neuesten Stand gebracht. Wenn die Redakteure von „Welt" und „Morgenpost" zur Arbeit kommen, sind die Geschehnisse bereits ein erstes Mal bewertet und aufbereitet worden.
Gegen halb zehn treffen sich die Ressorts, um 10 Uhr tagt die „Welt", um 11 Uhr die „Welt am Sonntag" um 12 Uhr die „Morgenpost". Im Laufe des Tages gibt es Sonderkonferenzen zur Gestaltung und zu den Kommentaren. Am Abend schließen die Tageszeitungen ihre Seiten ab. Parallel arbeitet die „Welt am Sonntag" an der Aufbereitung von Themen ... Gegen 20 Uhr beginnt dann die heiße Phase von „Welt Kompakt". Mit dem Redaktionsschluss um 0.30 Uhr ist dies Deutschlands aktuellste überregionale Zeitung. ...

An manchen Stellen blitzt ein Handlauf au

Zeitungsmachen ist ein Geschäft, das keinen Feiera
(aus einem Artikel von Michael Isenberg zum

An der Spitze in ein orange-farbenes, diffuses Licht getaucht, ragt der Gebäudekomplex nachts aus der Dunkelheit. Drinnen herrscht Hochbetrieb: Im Pressehaus in Stuttgart-Möhringen gehen die Lichter niemals aus. Die Bilder einer Nacht zeigen Menschen bei den unterschiedlichsten Tätigkeiten. Sie alle verbindet eines: Sie tragen ihren Teil dazu bei, daß von Montag bis Samstag die STUTTGARTER NACHRICHTEN erscheinen.

19.30 Uhr:
Die Druckerei gleicht dem Maschinensaal eines Ozeandampfers. Unter dem Metallgittersteg, der die Halle der Turmhausdruckerei in Längsrrichtung auf halber Höhe durchzieht, reihen sich die sieben Wifag OF5- und OF7-Rotationsdruckwerke wie mächtige Motorenblöcke in zwei Reihen hintereinander. An manchen Stellen blitzt ein von schwieligen Händen blankpolierter Handlauf auf und verstärkt den Eindruck von christlicher Seefahrt. Noch gilt „alle Maschinen stopp". Das Pfeifen der Druckluft-Kompressoren und Ölpumpen schneidet monoton durch den Raum. Eine Sirene gellt. Es riecht nach Öl und Farbe. Die Hast, mit der die Drucker in ihren blauen Overalls über die Maschinen hinweg – und manchmal durch schmale Luken hindurch – turnen, die Hast, in der sie die Farbwerke justieren und Druckplatten auf die Zylinder spannen, zeigt, daß in wenigen Minuten abgelegt wird. Die wenigen Anweisungen klingen barsch. Keine Zeit für Artigkeiten.

20.10 Uhr:
Vom Steuerpult aus bringt Maschinenführer Gerd Pamperl die vier aneinander gekoppelten Druckwerke auf Touren. Keine halbe Minute später jagen die Papierbahnen mit einer Geschwindigkeit, die Bilder und Texte zu einem bunten Streifen verwischen lässt, durch die Druckwerke. Mit einem ohrenbetäubenden, metallischen Hämmern werden die vier Bahnen im Falzapparat geschnitten und (in der heutigen Nacht) zu einer 48 Seiten starken Zeitung zusammengeführt. Nach rund 1000 Exemplaren Makulatur, die im Altpapiercontainer landen, gibt Pamperl seinem Drucker Uwe Nast ein Zeichen: Ab jetzt sind die Zeitungen in Ordung. Der erste Andruck, die Fernausgabe, hat die gewohnte Qualität.

20.46 Uhr:
Ein blinkendes Licht und eine unangenehm quäkende Sirene haben Gerhard Buisson in den Leitstand de Haustechnik gerufen. Kessel 2 der Heizungsanlage ha sich selbstständig abgeschaltet. Draußen hat es keir zehn Grad. Mit einer Taschenlampe in der Hand mach sich Buisson zur Fehlersuche auf den Weg in den Keller

22.02 Uhr:
Zwiebelbraten, Karottengemüse, Bandnudeln, Sala Saft. Adelheid Weihrer reicht das überladene Table über die Tresen. Rosa Judica poliert das Besteck. einer dreiviertel Stunde haben die beiden Frauen von d Cafeteria Feierabend. So lange gibt es auch noc warmes Essen. Wer seine Schicht um 19.30 U begonnen hat, der isst jetzt sozusagen zu Mittag. E Drucker kauft zwei Tafeln Schokolade. Nachtisch ur Nachtration.

22.15 Uhr:
Konstantin Wecker hat vor wenigen Minuten am Ranc seines Konzerts in Stuttgart bekanntgegeben, daß gegen seiner Verurteilung wegen Kokainmissbrauch Berufung einlegen wird. Der Nachtdienst in d Redaktion will diese Meldung noch im Feuilleto unterbringen, da macht ihnen das Computersystem eine Strich durch die Arbeit. Zunächst sind sie lahmgeleg Zur Untätigkeit verdammt sitzen die drei Redakteure v ihren Bildschirmen.

22.18 Uhr:
Im Untergeschoß der Versandabteilung rollt Günt Steffel die Paletten mit der bereits am Vortag gedruckte Buchbeilage in Position. Die rund zwei Meter hohe Türme mit den versetzt übereinander geschichtete Zeitungsseiten sehen aus wie die Bürsten einer Autowa chanlage. Ein Stockwerk höher wird die Beila maschinell in die fertige Zeitung eingeschoben.

23.22 Uhr:
Das Computersystem ist wieder da. Die Nachtredakteu stürzen an die Tastatur. Herr Wecker kommt doch no ins Blatt.

23.45 Uhr:
Nach dem Mittagessen ist Andreas Mücke in Leipzig b der Firma Sachsen-Papier vom Hof gefahren. Jetzt ste der Fahrer neben seinem 40-Tonner und überwacht d Abladen der kanalrohrdicken Papierrollen. Ein eisig Wind bläst den Männern ins Gesicht. Mücke fährt ger nachts nach Stuttgart – da ist die Bahn frei.

0.20 Uhr:
Jetzt noch schnell die Konstantin-Wecker-Nachric einbauen. Dazu wird der Artikel am Bildschirm in d Layout platziert und die gesamte Seite zum Plattenbe chter geschickt. Die alte Druckplatte raus, die neue de Plattenbelichter entnommen und ab geht es zur Rotatio

und lässt an christliche Seefahrt denken

d kennt: Momentaufnahmen aus einer langen Nacht
ährigen Jubiläum der Stuttgarter Nachrichten)

etzt sind schnelle Beine gefragt, dann können die Druckmaschinen mit der Stadtausgabe anlaufen

.19 Uhr:
Vie umgefallene Dominosteine ins Transportband efächert, verlassen die ersten Stadtexemplare die Druckerei in Richtung Versand.

.24 Uhr:
Eine Lautsprecherstimme schallt über das Flechtwerk er Transportbänder hinweg durch die Versandhalle. Alles ist in Bewegung. Zeitungen wandern von links ach rechts, von oben nach unten, von hinten nach vorn. ur manchmal sind Menschen zu sehen. Erinnert die otation an den Maschinensaal eines Dampfers, gäbe die zenerie im Versand die passable Kulisse für einen ames-Bond-Film ab – soviel High-Tech ballt sich hier der blitzsauberen Halle. In dieser Nacht werden sieben eilagen in die Zeitung gesteckt, entsprechend dick sind e Päckchen am Ausgabenband. Gerade wird die Tour ummer 464 zusammengestellt: die STUTTGARTER ACHRICHTEN für den Stuttgarter Osten.

.10 Uhr:
Ansichtssache: Der Autoparkplatz vor dem Haus ist jetzt, itten in der Nacht, halb leer – oder immer noch halb oll. Der Schriftzug „Pressehaus", von Scheinwerfern ngestrahlt und in einem orangefarbenen, diffusen Licht n Nachtnebel schwimmend, grüßt von oben herab.

.05 Uhr:
ei Günter Winkler klingelt das Telefon. Eine ältere ame ist am Apparat und fragt nach einem nördlichen onau-Zufluß in Ungarn mit drei Buchstaben. Winkler t Pförtner. Für nächtliche Anrufer ist er nur der „Mann on der Zeitung". Winkler und sein Kollege Wolfgang ink bemühen sich, alle nur erdenklichen Auskünfte zu eben, die die Leser wünschen. Der Name des andwirtschaftsministers von 1973 gehört noch zu den einfachen Fragen. Winkler und Fink sind die Höflichkeit in Person. Ihre eigentliche Aufgabe ist aber, für die Sicherheit des Gebäudes und der Menschen darin zu sorgen. Während Winkler beim Kreuzworträtsel-Problem behilflich ist, macht sich Fink auf zum Kontrollgang.

4.41 Uhr:
Maschinenführer Gerd Pamperl zieht den Reissverschluss seiner Jacke hoch. Er steht an der Haltestelle Landhaus. Gleich kommt die Stadtbahn U 3, mit der Pamperl nach Hause fährt. Unterm Arm trägt er eine druckfrische Zeitung. Machmal liest er sie auf der Heimfahrt. Während der Arbeit interessiert ihn nur die Druckqualität.

6.10 Uhr:
In der Küche türmen sich 500 Brötchen, Brezeln und Laugenstangen. Die beiden Köche Engelbert Knopf und Joachim Habiger beginnen jeden Tag mit Brötchen schmieren: Frühstücksservice in der Cafeteria. Im Hintergrund dampft der Kessel mit Rotkraut, brutzeln 45 Kilo Geschnetzeltes. Heute gibt es Chili con Carne mit Rösti, paniertes Kotelett mit Rotkraut und Schnittlauch-Kartoffeln oder Gemüsefrikadellen. Ein vegetarisches Gericht gehört zum Küchenstandard. Der absulote

Renner in der Kantine sind allerdings, wie könnte es anders sein, Linsen, Spätzle und Saiten.

8.01 Uhr:
Die Cafeteria öffnet ihre Pforten. Rasch bildet sich eine kleine Schlange von Frühaufstehern. In kleinen Grüppchen zumeist setzen sie sich an die lackierten Holztischchen und frühstücken. Wer alleine ist, liest Zeitung. Ein neuer Tag beginnt.

Hoch über den Köpfen laufen die soeben gedruckten Zeitungen in verschlungenen Transportbändern von der Druckerei direkt in den Versand. Bei der Montage und an der Reprokamera kommt es auf Schnelligkeit genauso an wie auf Präzision.

19.3 Buch-Produktion

19.3.1 Buch-Wertschöpfungsprozess im Überblick

Der **Wertschöpfungsprozess beim Buch** beginnt mit der Ideen- und Inhalte-Produktion des Autors und endet beim konsumierenden Leser. Dazwischen liegen zahlreiche Einzelschritte, die durchlaufen werden müssen, um das Buch herstellen zu können. Im Überblick lassen sich die Schritte in **vier Phasen** unterscheiden:

- Phase der Inhalte-Erstellung beim Autor und Überstellung an den Verlag, eventuell unter Einschaltung einer Agentur;
- Phase der eigentlichen Herstellung des Produkts, die von den Verlagen – dem sog. „Herstellenden Buchhandel" – vollzogen wird;
- Phase der Distribution, die der „Verbreitende Buchhandel" abwickelt;
- Phase des Konsums durch den Käufer des Buches und Leser des Inhalts.

Nachfolgende Darstellung gibt ein Bild über die **Teilprozesse**, wie sie sich in der Kette zwischen Autor und Leser abspielen (vgl. Kerlen 2003, S. 22):

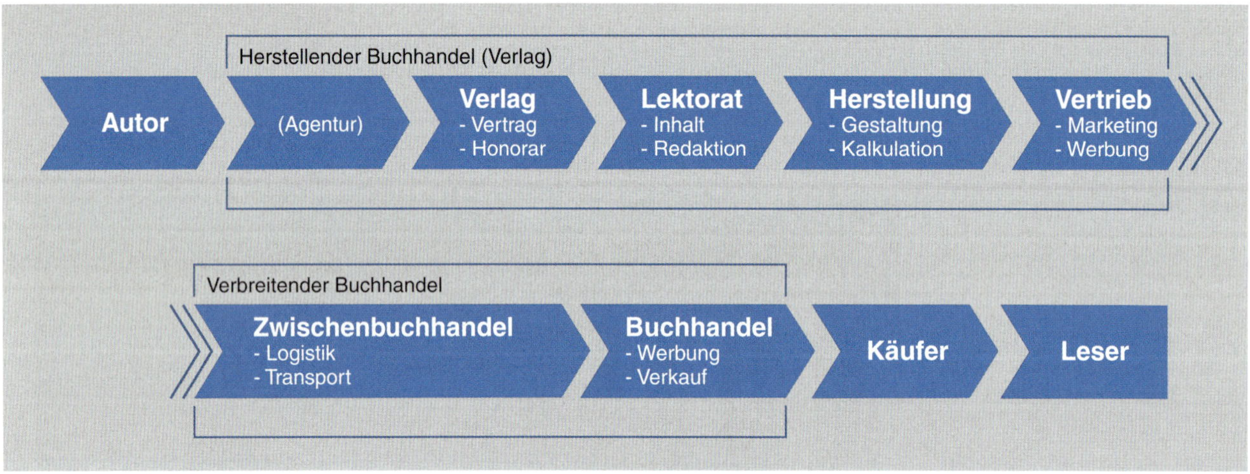

19.3.2 Produkterstellung durch den Verlag

Die Herstellung eines Buches durch einen Verlag erfordert einen umfangreichen und vielschichtigen **Managementprozess**, der typischerweise wie folgt abläuft (vgl. Kerlen 2003, S. 75):

- Auftragsbeurteilung
  1. Externe Informations-Beschaffung (Situations-Analyse, Konkurrenz-Analyse, Ressourcen-Analyse)
  2. Idee / Konzept mit Alternativen / Akquisition von Vor-Verantwortung (Herausgeber)
  3. Vor-Kalkulation: Kosten / zu erwartende Erlöse
  4. Interne Ressourcen-Analyse: Manpower, Finanzen, Zeit

- Beschluss über Durchführung (ja/nein) mit schriftlicher Begründung
- Auftragseröffnung
  1. Vertragswerk
  2. Akquisition der Haupt-Verantwortung (Autoren)
  3. Kostengerüst
  4. Zeitgerüst
  5. Vorschüsse auf Absatz- und Pauschalhonorare
- Auftragsdurchführung (Wer? Was? Wie? Wann? Wozu? Wie teuer?)
  1. Manuskriptphase: Herausgeber / Autoren-Konferenzen, sowie ständige Lektorats-Kommunikation mit Autoren und Herausgebern
  2. Redaktionsphase im Lektorat (oder Außendienstmitarbeiter)
  3. Satzvorbereitungsphase (im Hause)
  4. Herstellungsphase (außer Hause)
  5. Vertriebsphase / Marketing
- Auftragserfüllung
  Erlös, Controlling, Nachkalkulation, Soll-/Ist-Vergleich, Ergebnis

Blickt man speziell auf die eigentliche Herstellungsphase, so ergibt sich das folgende Bild eines **klassischen Herstellungsablaufes** (Quelle: Lucius 2005, S. 125):

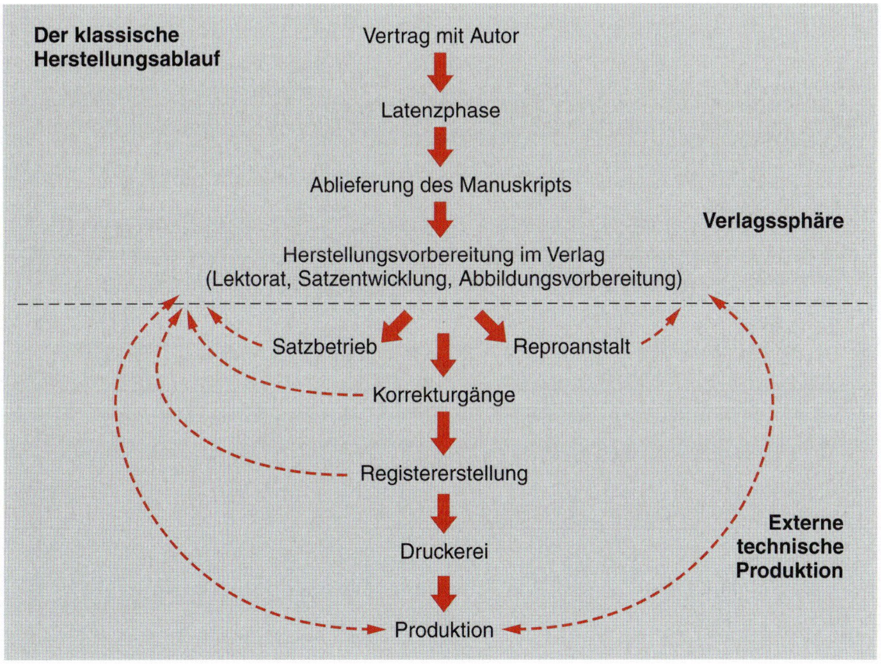

In der digitalen Welt erfolgt der Datenaustausch zwischen Autor, Verlag und Druckerei zunehmend über geeignete Datenformate, sofern die Kompatibilität der technischen Umgebung aller Beteiligten vorausgesetzt werden kann. Wenn dies funktioniert, werden herstellungstechnische Aspekte bereits in die Phase der Manuskripterstellung einbezogen, was zu erheblichen Kostenreduktionen beim Verlag führen kann.

19.4 Produktion von Radiosendungen

19.4.1 Radio-Workflow im Überblick

Radio machen ist eine komplexe Angelegenheit. Der **Wertschöpfungsprozess** („Workflow"), wie er bei einer **Radiosendung** abläuft, kann zum einen in die vier Teilprozesse der Preproduktion, Produktion, Postproduktion und Distribution differenziert werden, zum anderen in die Aspekte des Content-Prozesses, des produktionstechnischen Prozesses und des organisatorischen Prozesses. Die nachfolgende Abbildung verdeutlicht die einzelnen **Prozesselemente** (Quelle: Krömker / Klimsa 2005, S. 235 ff):

	Pre-Pro-duktion	Pro-duktion	Post-Pro-duktion	Distri-bution
Content Kreativer Prozess	Themen-Recherche Redaktion	Material-Recherche Material-erstellung	Material-bearbeitung	Ausstrahlung
Technik Produktions-technischer Prozess	Redaktions-system	Browsing-system Aufzeichnungs-Wiedergabe-system	Post-produktions-system	Sende-abwicklungs-system
Organisation Funktions-bereiche, Komplexe	Wort-redaktion Nachrichten-redaktion Musik-redaktion	Produktions-regie Sprecherraum Zentraler Geräteraum		Hauptsende-studio Sendeersatz-studio Nachrichten-studio

Um eine Hörfunksendung „fahren" zu können, müssen alle diese Prozesselemente in logischer Reihenfolge bearbeitet und aufeinander abgestimmt werden. Die Gesamtheit des kreativen Prozesses wird als „Content-System" bezeichnet, die Gesamtheit des produktionstechnischen Prozesses als „Technisches System", die organisatorischen Prozesse als „Organisationssystem". Alle Teilsysteme müssen optimal zusammenwirken.

In der **Gesamtschau** sind bei der Entwicklung und Ausstrahlung von Radiosendungen die folgenden Aspekte besonders relevant, die nachfolgend im Einzelnen näher beleuchtet werden sollen:

- Radio-Team
- Programmplanung
- Integration vorproduzierter Sendungselemente
- Sendeabwicklung

19.4.2 Radio-Team

Radio ist Teamarbeit. Viele verschiedene Menschen müssen zusammenwirken, damit am Ende die fertige Radiosendung „on air" gehen kann. Und eine Sendung reiht sich an die andere und bildet das Gesamtprogramm. 24 Stunden Radio am Tag wollen gemacht sein, was – dies sei nochmals betont – nur in besonders gut eingeübter Teamarbeit möglich ist.

Redaktion

Dreh- und Angelpunkt im Herstellungsprozess von Radiosendungen ist die **Redaktion**, die für den Inhalt dessen, was gesendet werden soll, verantwortlich zeichnet ❶. Die Redaktion verkörpert den Kernprozess des Sendebetriebs, so dass allen Beteiligten klar ist, dass innerhalb des Radio-Teams den redaktionellen Mitarbeitern die Schlüsselrolle zufällt. Im Hinblick auf die Art der zu sendenden Inhalte sind Wort-, Musik- und Nachrichtenredaktionen zu unterscheiden. Zentrales Steuerungs- und Koordinationsinstrument des redaktionellen Prozesses innerhalb eines Senders ist die tägliche Redaktionskonferenz, auf der das neue Programm besprochen und das gerade ausgestrahlte kritisch reflektiert wird.

❶ Der Begriff **Redaktion** drückt sowohl eine organisatorische Einheit als auch als den Prozess des Redigierens aus.
redigieren = stilistisches und inhaltliches Überarbeiten eines Textes.

Auf der **Ebene des Gesamtprogramms** eines Hörfunksenders trägt der Hörfunkdirektor die Gesamtverantwortung. Im konkreten **Sendebetrieb** ist es der „CvD", der **Chef vom Dienst**. Seine Funktion ist es, die Übersicht über alle Aktivitäten zu behalten, da in einer Redaktion viele unterschiedliche Leute unter großem Zeitdruck an einem gemeinsamen Produkt zusammenarbeiten. Der CvD plant die Sendung und sorgt dafür, dass die Reporter sich an verabredete Termine halten und dass alle einzelnen Elemente rechtzeitig zur Sendung fertig sind.

Eine wichtige Rolle spielen **Reporter**. Diese sind für das weite Feld der aktuellen Berichterstattung „draußen" unterwegs und bei wichtigen Ereignissen dabei. Sie recherchieren Ereignisse, Fakten und Hintergründe, führen Interviews durch, sammeln Original-Töne („O-Töne") und Geräusche, schreiben und sprechen Texte und fertigen schließlich aus dem Mix aller Elemente Beiträge, die auf Sendung gehen. Neben solchen „gestalteten Beiträgen" können sich Reporter auch live vom Ort des Geschehens in die Sendung einklinken. Im Hörfunk kann neben der aktuellen Berichterstattung als wichtigstes Programmelement die Musik gelten. Dauerhafter Erfolg eines Senders bestimmt sich maßgeblich über die gewählte „Musikfarbe". Notwendiges Glied im Radio-Team ist daher der **Musikredakteur**. Er wählt die Musikstücke einer Sendung aus, bringt sie in eine abwechslungsreiche Reihenfolge und spielt diejenigen, bei denen er davon ausgeht, dass sie bei der Zielgruppe ankommen. Eine Hauptaufgabe ist es dabei, die **Musikgestaltung** entsprechend der vorgegebenen musikalischen Formatierung des Senders vorzunehmen.

Die Aufgabe der redaktionellen Mitarbeiter ist es, den zu transportierenden Wort- und Musik-Inhalt bestmöglich zu gestalten. Dabei stehen sie vor zwei Kernfragen: 1. Welche Themen bzw. Inhalte sollen gebracht werden? 2. Wie soll das Thema bzw. der Inhalt umgesetzt bzw. präsentiert werden? Zum einen ist also über den Inhalt zu entscheiden, zum anderen über die Form, wobei beide Aspekte in enger Verbindung zueinander stehen und sich gegenseitig bedingen.

Ein Beispiel, welchen Spielraum man hat, ein Thema im Radio unterschiedlich „rüberzubringen", bietet der „Radioworkshop online" von BR-online.de:

„Ein gutes Thema kann man auf ganz unterschiedliche Art im Radio präsentieren. Zum Beispiel das Thema „Weihnachtsgeschenktipps in letzter Minute":

- Ihr könntet in die Fußgängerzone gehen und eine Umfrage machen. Dabei bekommt ihr ein buntes Ideenspektrum.
- Ihr könntet aber auch ein Interview mit dem Sprecher des Einzelhandelverbands machen, was denn so am Heiligabend noch über den Ladentisch geht – so bekommt ihr eine qualifizierte Experten-Aussage.
- Oder ihr geht in den Volkshochschulkurs „Weihnachtsgeschenke – selbst gemacht" und macht eine Reportage, das heißt, ihr beschreibt möglichst anschaulich, was die Leute so basteln.
- Oder ihr baut aus verschiedenen Elementen – Umfragen, Interviews, Musik und Geräuschen – eine Collage zusammen. Mit einem eigenen Text von euch als Verbindungsglied zwischen den Elementen – heißt so etwas „Gebauter Beitrag".
- Oder ihr denkt euch eine Szene aus, ein kleines Hörspiel rund um die Geschenke-Panik zu Weihnachten, entwickelt verschiedene Figuren und eine interessante Geschichte.
- Oder ihr recherchiert etwas zur Geschichte der Weihnachtsgeschenke und zu Weihnachts-Geschenk-Sitten in anderen Ländern. Solche Informationen könnt ihr prima als Nachrichtenmeldungen zusammenfassen.
- Oder ihr findet den ganzen Kommerz ganz furchtbar und schreibt euch euren Groll von der Seele – so etwas nennt man dann Kommentar. Der Kommentar muss aber immer als solcher gekennzeichnet werden. Denn er gibt die persönliche Meinung des Autors wieder – nicht die des Senders.

Wichtig ist auf jeden Fall, dass ihr euch überlegt, was bei eurem Beitrag rüberkommen soll – versucht also, die Aussage eures Beitrags als einen Satz zu formulieren. Diesen sogenannten Kernsatz behaltet ihr immer im Auge, dann wird euer Beitrag rund und schlüssig. Außerdem solltet ihr euch überlegen, welche Meinung ihr zu diesem Thema habt. Wenn ihr das für euch geklärt habt, fällt es euch leichter, im Kopf einen Schritt zur Seite zu machen und als Journalist einen möglichst unbeteiligten Standpunkt einzunehmen. Denn eure Hörer sollen sich schließlich selbst eine Meinung bilden können und nicht eure übergestülpt kriegen."

(http://www.br-online.de/wissen-bildung/thema/radioworkshop-radio-machen/...; 08.07.2007)

Technik

Um den Sendebetrieb zu ermöglichen, muss neben die Redaktion die Funktion der Produktion und Technik hinzutreten. Die entscheidende „Figur" ist dabei der **Tontechniker** (auch **Producer** genannt), der die ganze Breite des technischen Equipments wie Mikrofone, Mischpult, CD-Player, Audioschnittprogramme usw. steuert. Der Tontechniker ist dafür verantwortlich, dass alle Beiträge sauber produziert sind und gut klingen.

Präsentation

Für die Präsentation der Sendung ist der **Moderator** verantwortlich, der nicht selten – vor allem bei Informationssendungen – ein Redakteur ist („Redakteur im Studio"). Der Moderator präsentiert die Sendung und ist sozusagen ihre Stimme. Die Themen müssen so präsentiert werden, dass die Hörer gerne zuhören und möglichst „dran bleiben". Der Moderator „nimmt die Hörer an der Hand" und begleitet sie zielsicher durch die Sendung. Eine wichtige Aufgabe des Moderators ist es ferner, zwischen den einzelnen Beiträgen sinnvolle Verbindungen herzustellen und für den roten Faden der Sendung zu sorgen.

19.4.3 Programmplanung

Ziel und Ergebnis der redaktionellen Arbeit ist ein konkret umsetzbarer Programmplan. Für jeden Tag und für jede Stunde muss genau festgelegt werden, welche Art von Programm ausgestrahlt werden soll.

Rahmensetzungen für die Programmgestaltung

Bei der Gestaltung sind die Redaktionen nicht frei, sondern sie müssen sich in verschiedene Vorgaben einfügen. Eine wichtige Vorgabe ist die auf längere Sicht festgeschriebene Programmstruktur, die als **Programmschema** bezeichnet wird. Sie stellt die zeitliche Fixierung der Abfolge der vorgesehenen Sendungen und Sendestrecken dar.

alster radio 106!8 rock 'n pop
www.106acht.de

Programmschema

Das NEUE alster radio - 106!8 rock'n'pop

	Montag - Freitag	Samstag	Sonntag
05:00-10:00	**Maren und AC am Morgen - die explosivste Morningshow**	**rock'n'pop nonstop**	**rock'n'pop nonstop**
	Alle 30 Minuten Nachrichten und Wetter - Exklusiv: der Sofort-Verkehr inkl. Blitzer	**Die "damit Sie gut reinkommen" - Show**	
	6:05 / 8:05 Marens und AC's Schlacht der Geschlechter		**Kirche heute**
	7:05 / 9:05 ACs verrücktes Telefon	mit Maren und AC ins Wochenende ACs verrücktes Telefon, Wochenausblick	Eine Sendung in Zusammenarbeit mit den Hamburger Kirchen
10:00-18:00	**Mit rock'n'pop und Lars Lorenz durch den Tag**	Veranstaltungen und Gewinne	**106!8 rock'n'pop'n'sport**
	Immer um 10 vor: 106!8 Nachrichten - auch um: 16:20 / 17:20 Uhr	**106!8 rock'n'pop'n'sport**	Der Sonntag steht ganz im Zeichen des
	10:10 / 13:10 Jukebox - Nur Sie und der Zufall bestimmen, was läuft	Der Samstag steht ganz im Zeichen des	Sports: Bundesliga-Vorschau
	11:10 Job Top 3 / 12:10 ...mach lauter Lars - Die ganz besondere Platte 14:10 Der verlorene Song des Tages	Sports: Bundesliga-Vorschau Bundesliga-Ergebnisse	Bundesliga-Ergebnisse und andere Sporthighlights
	15:10 3 um 3: Das Mini-Konzert mit 3 Songs eines Künstlers 16:40 Hamburg Heute - Die Nachrichten aus Hamburg für Hamburg	Der Mini-Kaiser und andere Sporthighlights	
	17:40 Sport kompakt aus Hamburg, Deutschland und der Welt		
18:00-19:00	**Mit rock'n'pop in den Feierabend** 106!8 Nachrichten um 10 vor und 20 nach, Sport-News: 18:40 Uhr		**Bedo - live** rocKn'pop mit Musik-Highlights aus der Türkei
19:00-22:00	**Der lange Musikabend mit Mike Schneider**	**106!8 Samstag Party-Nacht**	
	19:10 Das Mini-Live-Konzert - Drei Liveaufnahmen eines Künstlers 20:00 Die 80er um 8 - Eine Stunde nur die besten 80er	Die Party-Klassiker der letzten Jahrzehnte mit Rudi Druve und Michael Wittig	**106!8 Sonntag Rock-Nacht** Die größten Rock-Hits der letzten 40 Jahre
	21:00 Die 90er um 9 - Eine Stunde nur die besten 90er 22:00 Die CD um 10 - Ein Album komplett ausgespielt		
23:00-00:00	**Schnack-Line mit Alex Schmidt**		
	Das Thema des Tages - Talken rund um die Uhr: 01805 / 88 106 8	**JACK FM**	**rock'n'pop nonstop**
00:00-05:00	**rock'n'pop nonstop die ganze Nacht**	Die etwas andere Show mit Roboter	

24 Stunden am Tag: 106!8 Nachrichten 10 Minuten früher auf den Punkt voll informiert (morgens und nachmittags auch um 20 nach)

In Ergänzung zur zeitlichen Strukturierung des Programms erfolgt eine Definition der inhaltlichen Struktur, die als **Formatierung** bezeichnet wird. Die meisten Sender definieren sich heute als Formatradio, was bedeutet, dass das Programm nach einem feststehenden Konzept über den ganzen Tag hinweg gestaltet ist. Dieses besteht z. B. aus Nachrichten zur vollen Stunde, aus regionalen Nachrichten zur halben Stunde, feststehenden Werbeblöcken und aus definiertem Raum für Musik, Jingles, Moderation, Interviews, Beiträge usw.

Definiert sich ein Radioprogramm z. B. als eine Musik- und Servicewelle mit einer Mischung aus Musik und Dienstleistungen (Information, Veranstaltungstipps, Verkehrshinweise), so kann die Formatierung in Richtung des Hauptformates „Contemporary Hit Radio (CHR)" gehen ❶.

❶ **Contemporay Hit Radio**:
- Alter der Zielgruppe: 15 bis 25 Jahre
- Musik: Top-40-Hits
- Präsentation: laut, fröhlich, hohes Tempo
- Wortanteil: gering, Nachrichten auf Schlagzeilen beschränkt

Als konkretes Ergebnis des Programmschemas und der Formatierung ist im Radio-Management die sog. **Sendeuhr** (auch als „Stundenuhr“, „Programmuhr“ oder „hot clock“ bezeichnet) gebräuchlich, die in standardisierter Form die Abfolge der verschiedenen Programmbestandteile innerhalb einer Sendestunde in übersichtlicher Form darstellt. Nachfolgend ein Beispiel für Radio NRW 1998 (Quelle: Wirtz 2006, S. 443):

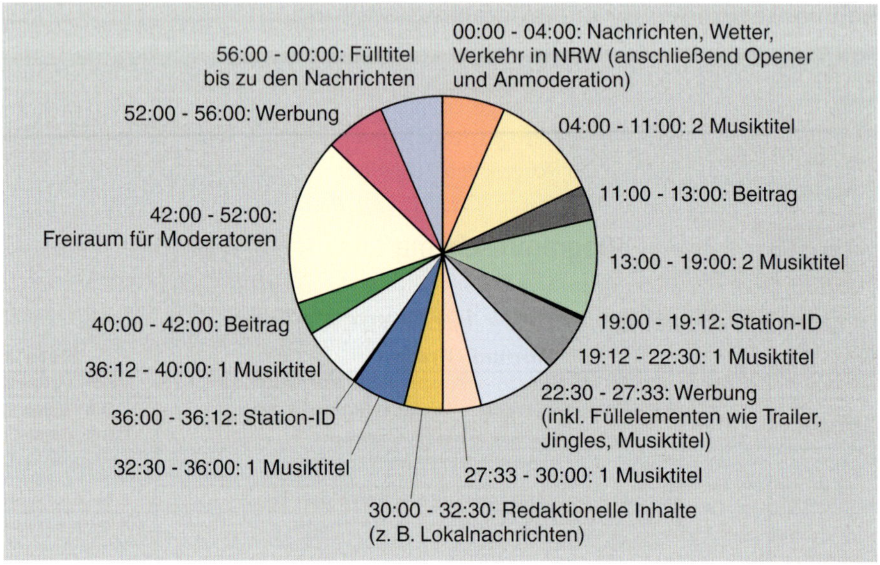

Die Sendeuhr wird am Computer erstellt und ist die Vorlage (das „Template“) für die konkrete Ausfüllung mit Musiktiteln, Beiträgen, Moderation, Werbung, Jingles ❶ und allen anderen Elementen. Eine Sendeuhr gilt immer nur für eine Stunde, kann sich aber wiederholen. Für unterschiedliche Sendungen sind unterschiedliche Sendeuhren definiert. Auch kann für ein und dieselbe Sendung die Sendeuhr nach Saison oder Anlass wechseln.

❶ Ein **Jingle** ist ein kurzer, flotter Werbespot, zusammengesetzt aus Musik, Geräuschen und einer kurzen Botschaft. Im Jingle geht es meistens darum, den Sendernamen und die Frequenz zu nennen (sog. „Station-ID“). Manchmal weisen Jingles aber auch auf spezielle Sendungen oder Aktionen hin.

Konkrete Programmgestaltung

Auf der Grundlage des Programmschemas, der Formatierung und deren Repräsentation in der Sendeuhr erfolgt die konkrete Programmgestaltung. Sichtbarer Ausdruck ist das **Wochenprogramm**, die auch als **Langablauf-Planung** bezeichnet wird. Mit dem Langablauf wird der Planungszeitraum von sechs bis zehn Wochen vor der Ausstrahlung erfasst und dient neben der internen Planung insbesondere auch der Mitteilung an die Programmzeitschriften. Hier erfolgt die genaue Festlegung aller auszustrahlenden Sendungen und die tagesgenaue Programmierung. Dieses Dokument ist besonders wichtig bei Kulturprogrammen, die sich mit anspruchsvollen Wort- und Musikprogrammen an ein Minderheitenpublikum richten. Dort werden in zahlreicher Form eigens für die jeweilige Sendung hergestellte Produkte erstellt, z. B. ein Hörspiel, aufwändig produzierte Features, Dokumentation usw.

Das Wochenprogramm ist Auslöser für die sog. **Programmbereitstellung**, die als die konkrete logistische Vorbereitung des Sendebetriebs fungiert.

Der Prozess der Programmbereitstellung endet mit der **Sendeablaufplanung**, die alle Planungen zu einem in sich geschlossenen, lückenlosen Sendetag zusammenfügt. Zu unterscheiden ist dabei zwischen festen Größen des Sendeablaufs, die nicht verändert werden dürfen, bedingt veränderlichen Größen und flexibel einsetzbaren Elementen.

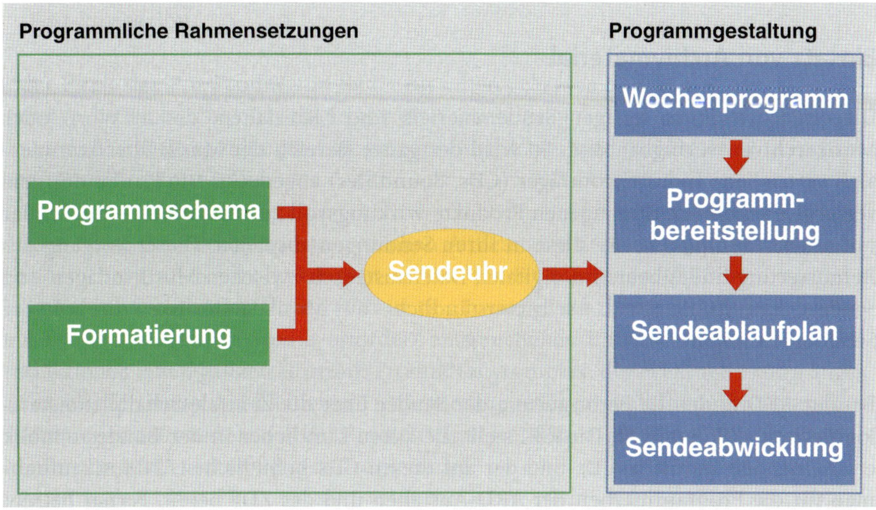

Digitalisierung der Redaktionsprozesse

Mit der Digitalisierung haben sich die Redaktionsprozesse im Hörfunk stark gewandelt. Insbesondere müssen die Redakteure heute ein hohes Verständnis und eine hohe Bereitschaft zur Anwendung der Digitaltechnik mitbringen. Ein Anschauungsbeispiel für diese Entwicklung liefert der folgende Textauszug (Quelle: (Blohmer/Erdmann 2005, S. 249): „Bereits nach einer kurzen Einweisung konnten Redakteure ihre Beiträge am Computer selbst schneiden und den Beitrag direkt in der Softwareapplikation, an den dafür vorgesehenen Platz im Sendeplan einfügen; ein vollkommen neuer Arbeitsablauf in der Hörfunkproduktion, der sich schnell in den Redaktionen durchsetzte und den klassischen Tontechniker überflüssig machte. Die Moderatoren im Sendestudio brauchen beispielsweise ihren Sendeablaufplan nicht mehr vor der Sendung auf Papier. Auch das Zusammenrechnen der Zeiten oder das Zusammenstellen der einzelnen Tonträger ist nicht mehr nötig. Der in der Musikredaktion erstellte Sendeablaufplan wird im Studio auf dem Bildschirm angezeigt und von der Sendeabwicklung ausgespielt. Für die „Radiomacher“ bedeutet die Arbeit mit digitalen Systemen mehr Zeit um kreativ zu sein und ihre Ideen dann einfach und schnell umsetzen zu können. Tontechniker hingegen werden mehr und mehr zu Systemadministratoren und übernehmen hochwertige Produktionen von Content-Elementen.“

Als **Vision** für die Zukunft kann man sich einen durchgängigen elektronischen Workflow ohne Medienbruch vorstellen, der von der Idee des Redakteurs über seine Recherchen zum Thema, die Suche und das Anhören von Archivmaterial über die Sendeplanung und Produktion bis hin zur Sendung, zur anschließenden Archivierung, Abrechnung und Sendeminutenstatistik sowie GEMA/GVL-Meldung reicht.

19.4.5 Sendeabwicklung

Am Ende der Kette steht die fertige Radiosendung. Eigentümlich für das Radio ist es, dass erst bei der Ausstrahlung der Sendung die eigentliche Herstellung des Endprodukts stattfindet. Im Vorfeld werden alle Elemente vorbereitet und gedanklich zu einem Paket zusammengestellt („Packaging"), die konkrete Umsetzung in das Produkt „Sendung" erfolgt aber erst zu dem Zeitpunkt, wo sie „on air" geht. Als besonders wichtige Aspekte im **Workflow des Sendebetriebs** sind anzusehen:

- Moderation
- Musik
- Sendeleitung
- Sendetechnik und Verbreitungswege

Moderation

Durch die Sendung führt der Moderator und sorgt für eine optimale **Präsentation**. Er hat eine hohe Bedeutung für das Sender- und Programm-Marketing, da er sozusagen der Verkäufer des Produkts ist, der unmittelbar mit dem Kunden – dem Hörer – in Kontakt tritt.

Vor allem aus technischen und kostenmäßigen Gründen, aber durchaus auch aus journalistischen Gründen, findet Radio-Moderation heute in sog. **Selbstfahrerstudios** statt. Moderatoren kümmern sich entsprechend der Vorgabe durch die Sendeuhr um die Texte, den Einsatz der Musik, von Jingles, Nachrichten und Werbung. Der Moderator im Selbstfahrerstudio ist in der Lage, völlig unabhängig von seinem gesprochenen Text die Technik zu bedienen und sämtliche Komponenten der Sendung zusammenzuführen. Er ist allein dafür verantwortlich, dass die Blenden zwischen zwei Musikstücken technisch sauber klingen, dass die vorgesehenen Jingles nach Sendeplan laufen und die Werbung und die Nachrichten pünktlich kommen. Nicht selten zeichnet der Moderator auch seine Hörer-Talks selbst auf.

Insofern ist der Moderator im Selbstfahrerstudio Senderegisseur, Präsentator und tontechnischer Producer in einer Person. Es ist verständlich, dass es einer erheblichen Übung und Kompetenz bedarf, ein Selbstfahrerstudio auf hohem Niveau zu bedienen. Bei den meisten Radiosendern in Deutschland ist das Selbstfahrerstudio inzwischen der reguläre Arbeitsplatz des Moderators. Damit gehört die bis vor nicht allzu langer Zeit als Standard praktizierte Variante der Sendung aus dem Studiokomplex, bestehend aus Regieraum und Sprecherstudio, in der ein Techniker die Sendung fährt und der Moderator „nur" spricht, weitgehend der Vergangenheit an.

Musik

Im Radiosendebetrieb wird der **Musikgestaltung** eine **herausragende Rolle** beigemessen, da man erkannt hat, dass die musikalische Formatierung maßgeblich den Erfolg einer Welle bestimmt. Musik ist für massenwirksame Hörfunkprogramme das wichtigste Programmelement, da die Zielgruppe sehr genau reagiert. Musik entscheidet über die Positionierung des gesamten Programms, so dass die Musik das am intensivsten formatierte Programmelement im Radio ist.

Der Einsatz von Musik als Programmelement erfolgt in hohem Maße computergestützt. Typischerweise sind bei der **Musikgestaltung** die folgenden **Aspekte** besonders interessant:

- Definition eines Musik-Pools: Zunächst muss die für das jeweilige Musikformat geeignete Musik ausgewählt werden. Eine Liste ist zu erstellen, die einen Musiktitel als „zulässig" definiert oder nicht. Die Ablage der formattauglichen Titel erfolgt im Musikspeicher. Wichtig ist es, dass die Studiotechnik über eine ausreichende Kapazität und Suchfunktionen verfügt und die Titel ohne lange Ladezeiten abrufbar sind.
- **Musikarchivierung**: Wichtig ist es, eine leistungsfähige Musikarchivierung zu betreiben, bei der die archivierten Musiktitel nach formatgerechten Meta-Daten wie Länge des Titels, Geschlecht des Interpreten, Musik-Epoche (z. B. Hit, Aktuell, 70er, 80er, 90er-Jahre), Tempo, Anmutung, Sprache, Art des Schlusses usw. geordnet sind. Nur so lassen sich zielgruppengerechte Informationen über geeignete Musiktitel gewinnen.
- **Musikuhr**: Die Strukturierung innerhalb der Sendung erfolgt über die sog. Musikuhr, die die Anzahl und Abfolge der Titel festlegt ❶.
- **Rotation**: Die zur Sendung freigegebenen formatgerechten Titel werden typischerweise in einem Rotationsverfahren zur Ausstrahlung gebracht. Hierzu wird eine Musikrotations-Software eingesetzt, über die Musiktitel nach vorgegebenen formatrelevanten Kategorien ausgewählt werden. Diese werden in die Musikuhren der Sendungen hinterlegt und generieren die konkrete Play List, die wiederum Teil des allumfassenden Sendeplans ist.

❶ Beispielsweise wird die Musikredaktion für eine Frühsendung in die – computergestützte – Musikuhr die Kriterien „schnell" und „kurz" eingeben, um für die Sendung einen frischen, munteren Eindruck zu erzeugen. Die Musikuhr sorgt dann dafür, dass nur Titel zum Zuge kommen, die diese Kriterien erfüllen.

Sendeleitung

Zur Gesamtsteuerung einer Sendung ist es notwendig, ein wirkungsvolles Management zu installieren. Dies geschieht durch die **Sendeleitung**, bei der alle Fäden zusammenlaufen. Überwacht wird, dass das Sendematerial vollständig vorliegt und der Sendungsworkflow gut funktioniert. Eventuell werden Korrekturen des Sendeablaufplans vorgenommen, wenn etwa der Sendebetrieb mit einem nicht planbaren Ereignis konfrontiert wird (z. B. große Ereignisse, Naturkatastrophen, technische Pannen). Dies kann zu Programmänderungen bis hin zur Abwicklung eines Notprogramms führen. Besonders kritisch ist bei solchen Notprogrammen, bei denen die standardmäßige Programmstruktur außer Kraft gesetzt ist, die gebuchte Werbung sicherzustellen.

Sendetechnik und Verbreitungswege

Um die Sendungen zum Hörer bringen zu können, ist nicht zuletzt viel Technik notwendig. Zum einen betrifft dies die **Technik im Studio**, aus dem das Signal auf Sendung geht (Sendestudio), zum anderen die weitere Verbreitung in die diversen Systeme. Hier ist der analoge Verbreitungsweg über **UKW** nach wie vor voll im Gebrauch, während **digitale terrestrische Verbreitungsformen** in der massenhaften Nutzung noch auf sich warten lassen. Inwieweit die Verbreitung von Radio über das Internet zu einer nachhaltigen Veränderung der Nutzung führt, ist eine weitere wichtige Frage künftiger Medienentwicklungen. Eine erhebliche Bedeutung haben bereits Produktionen erlangt, die als Podcasts im Internet verfügbar gemacht werden.

19.5 Film- und Fernsehproduktion

19.5.1 Phasen einer Filmproduktion im Überblick

Den Herstellungsprozess beim Film hat in sehr anschaulicher Weise Klaus Keil dargestellt und visualisiert (vgl. Iljine/Keil 1997, S. 208 f.):

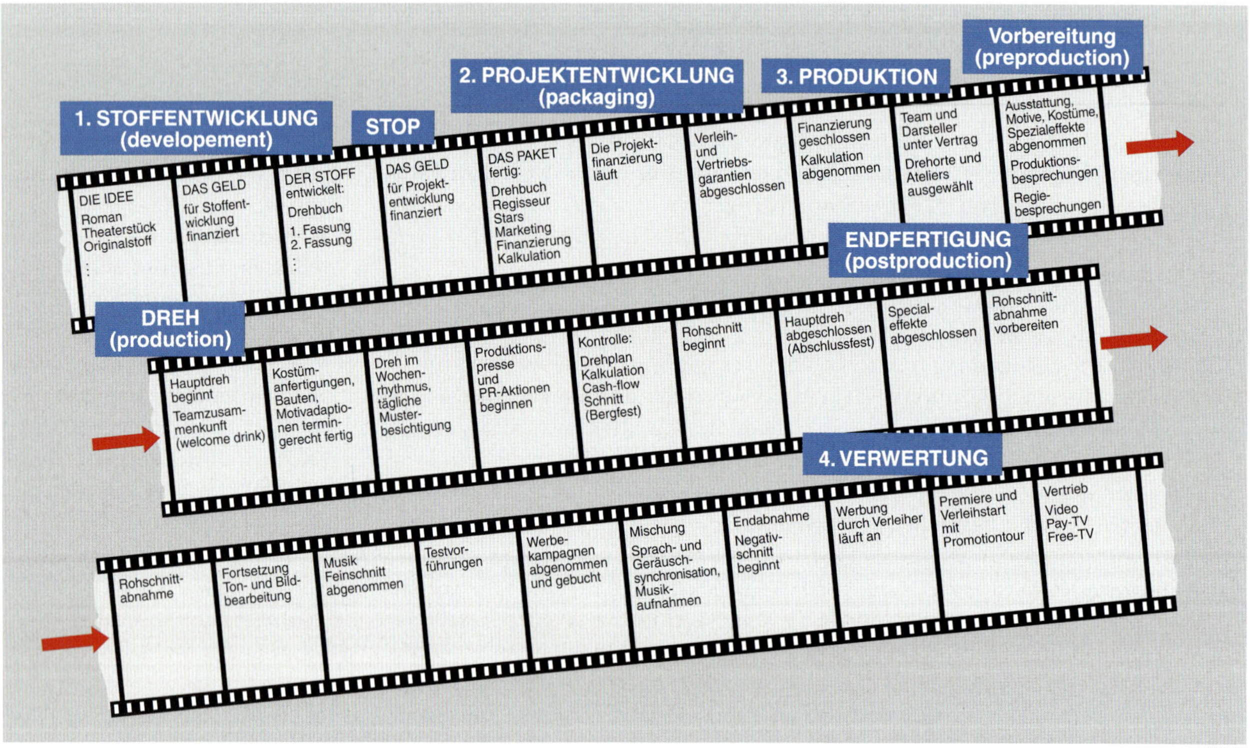

Danach wird der Produktionsprozess einer **großen Filmproduktion**, die für das Kino und/oder für das Fernsehen geplant ist, in die folgenden **vier Phasen** eingeteilt:

- Phase 1: **Stoffentwicklung (Development):** Aus der Idee entsteht ein fertiges Drehbuch, das finanziert ist.
- Phase 2: **Projektentwicklung (Packaging):** Das gesamte Filmpaket mit Drehbuch, Regisseur, Stars, Marketing, Finanzierung und Kalkulation steht und kann zur Umsetzung freigegeben werden.
- Phase 3: **Produktion** (Pre-Production, Production, Post-Production): Das fertige Filmprodukt liegt vorführungsreif und vermarktungsfähig vor.
- Phase 4: **Verwertung**: Das Produkt kann in den Kino-Verleih und in den Fernseh-Vertrieb gehen.

Nachfolgend wird der vorliegenden Thematik entsprechend die **Phase der Produktion** (Phase 3) näher betrachtet.

19.5.2 Pre-Production

Die Phasen der Stoffentwicklung und Projektentwicklung sind abgeschlossen, alle Hindernisse – insbesondere die finanziellen – sind aus dem Weg geräumt, so dass die konkrete Umsetzung des Filmprojekts beginnen kann.

Mit der Phase der Produktionsvorbereitung (Pre-Production) beginnt nun die entscheidende Phase des Filmprojekts. Sie ist definiert als der Zeitraum ab der gesicherten Finanzierung bis zum ersten Drehtag. Für die projektorientierte Vorbereitung sind mindestens 5 bis 6 Wochen zu kalkulieren.

Der Zeitraum der Pre-Production ist vorwiegend für die konkrete Organisation notwendig und dient weniger der künstlerischen Vorbereitung. Ziel der wochenlangen Bemühungen ist die Entwicklung des **Drehplans** ❶.

❶ Der **Drehplan** gibt an, an welchem Drehort mit welchen Darstellern welche Szenen gefilmt werden sollen.

Finanzierung und Kalkulation

Die Finanzierung ist geschlossen, die Kalkulation ist abgenommen. Das bedeutet, dass das nach dem **Finanzierungsplan** („**Cashflow-Plan**") vorgesehene Geld aus Förderungen, von Fernsehsendern, von Investoren, Filmfonds oder Verleihern auf Abruf zur Verfügung steht, und zwar konkret auf einem Bankkonto, das dem Produzenten zugänglich ist.

Team und Darsteller

Ein wesentlicher Vorgang der Pre-Production-Phase ist die vollständige und abschließende Auswahl des künstlerischen und technischen Stabes („staff") sowie der Darsteller („Cast"). Eine Schlüsselrolle spielt hierbei der **Regisseur** als Hauptfigur für die inhaltliche Umsetzung des Stoffes. Der Regisseur wird als erstes damit beginnen, den Zeitrahmen für die Realisierung des Films, in dem er sich bewegen will, möglichst präzise abzustecken. Da Regisseure pauschal bezahlt werden ❷, können sie sich aus persönlicher Sicht prinzipiell relativ frei fühlen, in welchem Zeitraum sie das Filmprojekt realisieren wollen und welchen Zeitbedarf die künstlerische Umsetzung beansprucht. Regisseure neigen aus dieser künstlerischen Sicht verständlicherweise dazu, eher Zeitpläne mit Luft „durchzudrücken" als in einem engen zeitlichen Korsett drehen zu müssen. Den Gegenpart zu dieser künstlerischen Funktion spielt der **Produzent** und sein unmittelbarer Vertrauter, der **Produktionsleiter**, die aus ökonomischer Sicht ein großes Interesse daran haben, dem Projekt möglichst enge zeitliche Vorgaben aufzuerlegen.

❷ Die **Höchstgagen** für die **Regie** belaufen sich auf fünf Prozent der Herstellungskosten bei Projekten bis zu 2.557.000 Euro, maximal jedoch 76.700 Euro, oberhalb dieses Betrages auf drei Prozent, maximal jedoch 128.000 Euro (vgl. Dress 2002, S. 99).

Als Ergebnis dieser Teilphase stehen das Team und die Darsteller unter Vertrag, die Verpflichtung der Mitwirkenden und des Produktionsstabes ist erfolgt.

Drehorte, Ateliers, Ausstattung, Technik

Eine weitere wichtige Aufgabe besteht in der Auswahl der **Drehorte** (bei Außenaufnahmen) und des Ateliers (bei Innenaufnahmen) einschließlich der notwendigen Technik. Als Ergebnis dieses Moduls liegen Verträge zur Atelier- und Motivanmietung vor, Drehgenehmigungen sind eingeholt, festgelegt sind die Motive und Kostüme, die geplanten Spezialeffekte sind abgenommen und werden zur Umsetzung vorbereitet.

Vielfalt der Arbeiten

Alle Vorarbeiten werden von zahlreichen Produktions- und Regiebesprechungen begleitet und erfordern einen hohen Einsatz aller Beteiligten. Um die Vielfalt der Arbeiten in der Pre-Production zu verdeutlichen, sei hier eine kleine Liste von anfallenden **Tätigkeiten** wiedergegeben (vgl. Clevé 2004, S. 165):

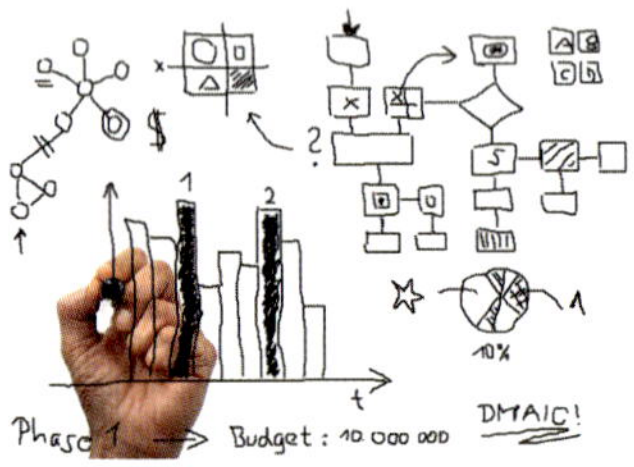

- Zahlung der ersten Rate des Verfilmungshonorars
- Verpflichtung von Mitarbeitern in den Bereichen Architektur, Bühnenbau, Artdesign, Ausstattung, Kostüm, Produktion, Regie, Kamera, Darsteller, Postproduction
- Finden von Drehorten und Sicherung derselben
- Entwurf und Erstellung von Bauten
- Design und Herstellung von Kostümen oder Suche in Fundi oder auf Flohmärkten
- Besetzung aller Rollen durch Regisseure und Casting-Agenturen
- Zusammenstellung des Kamera- und Lichtteams durch den Kameramann
- Buchung von Equipment
- Bestellung von Filmmaterial
- Organisation von Drehabwicklungen bei digitalen Bildeffekten

Oberstes Ziel der Pre-Production-Phase ist es, den allen Beteiligten vor Augen stehenden – strapaziösen und wochenlangen – Dreh so effizient, kräftesparend und nervenschonend, aber auch so kostengünstig wie möglich zu organisieren. Es versteht sich, dass eine entscheidende Rolle das umzusetzende **Drehbuch** spielt. Ist es besonders komplex, steigen die Anforderungen dramatisch an.

19.5.3 Produktion

Die Produktions- oder Drehphase (der „Dreh“) ist definiert als der Zeitraum vom ersten bis zum letzten Drehtag. Die Länge und der Ablauf der Drehphase richtet sich ebenfalls nach den Erfordernissen des Stoffs, wie er mit dem Drehbuch vorliegt. Im Durchschnitt liegt der Zeitbedarf für den Dreh bei ca. fünf Drehwochen ❶. Bereits eine Woche nach Drehende kann der Rohschnitt vorführfähig sein.

❶ Das macht deutlich, dass sich bei einem 90-minütigen Spielfilm die Tages-„Ausbeute“ – gemessen am Endprodukt – auf nur eine bis drei Minuten beläuft, ein Tatbestand, der vom Laien immer wieder bestaunt wird.

Start des Hauptdrehs

Die in der Vorproduktion in Auftrag gegebenen Kostümanfertigungen, Bauten und Motivadaptionen sind termingerecht fertig geworden. Der sog. „Hauptdreh“ kann beginnen. Der auch zwischenmenschlich bedeutsame Kick-Off findet mit der Teamzusammenkunft (dem „Welcome Drink“) statt. Aus Erfahrung weiß man, dass die Dreharbeiten niemals so verlaufen, wie es der Drehplan und die Planung des Produktionsleiters vorsieht, so dass die Kontrolle des Filmes höchste Anforderungen stellt. Die Schlüsselrolle in dieser Phase nimmt der **Regisseur** ein. Der Produzent kann in dieser für das Entstehen des Films höchst brisanten Phase gegen den Willen des Regisseurs kaum mehr einen verändernden Einfluss ausüben. An dieser Stelle des Films wird deutlich, eine welch wichtige Entscheidung die Auswahl des Regisseurs darstellt.

Der Dreh

Der konkrete Dreh steckt üblicherweise voller Tücken, Fallen, Unwägbarkeiten, Störungen und Problemen. Die Liste der **Schwierigkeiten** ist lang und kann unbegrenzt verlängert werden (vgl. Clevé 2004, S. 167 ❶):

❶ „Die Palette an Fehlerquellen ist von kosmischer Vielfalt …"

- Unvorhergesehene Straßenbauarbeiten, die zu Umleitungen und Verzögerungen führen
- technische Defekte an Geräten
- leere Batterien
- fehlende Requisiten
- schlechtes Wetter ❷
- Unpässlichkeiten von Darstellern
- Vergesslichkeiten
- menschliche Fehler
- persönliches Wohl- oder Unwohlbefinden
- Unfälle
- Kommunikationsprobleme

❷ Paradoxerweise kann im Film Sonnenschein schlechtes Wetter darstellen, und zwar dann, wenn das Drehbuch einen bewölkten Himmel oder Regen verlangt, ein Tatbestand, der den Einsatz teurer Effektgeräte (z. B. Nebelmaschinen) beim Dreh verständlich macht.

Um einen Eindruck in die Praxis zu bekommen, sei hier der Experte noch etwas ausführlicher zitiert (Clevé 2004, S. 167): „Alles findet unter enormem Zeit- und Gelddruck statt, jeder Drehtag kostet außerordentlich viel Geld, Überstunden oder Sonntagsarbeiten oder Nachtzuschläge können im Handumdrehen eine Kalkulation vollkommen aus dem Lot bringen und den Produzenten in den Ruin treiben. Viele der Beteiligten above-the-line wie auch below-the-line sind mit großem Selbstbewusstsein ausgestattet und der damit einhergehenden Unfehlbarkeit. Der Zusammenprall von Egos zeigt erst im täglichen Drehstress seine wahre Seite – während in der beginnenden Vorproduktion noch Differenzen übertüncht werden können, kommen Konflikte bei den Dreharbeiten garantiert zum Ausbruch. Dreharbeiten bedeuten zu einem großen Teil Krisenmanagement – nahezu der Normalzustand. Was andererseits natürlich für viele der Beteiligten auch den Reiz dieser Branche ausmacht, nach dem Motto: Genie beherrscht das Chaos. Nicht umsonst feiert man die Mitte von Dreharbeiten mit dem so genannten Bergfest."

Vor diesem Hintergrund ist es verständlich, dass so weit wie möglich **Sicherungen** in den Drehablauf eingebaut werden. So kann trotz hoher Kosten unter Umständen der Dreh im Atelier günstiger sein als die Außenaufnahme, da Risiken besser beherrscht werden können. Gebräuchlich ist es z. B. auch, dass der Grobschnitt schon bereits während der Drehphase beginnt, um Szenen eventuell nachdrehen zu können, solange die Darsteller noch vor Ort sind, die Kulissen noch nicht abgebaut sind und das Team beisammen ist. Über eine entsprechende Technik (z. B. mobile Schnitttechniken) kann eine Montage des Films direkt am Drehort erfolgen. Besonders wichtig ist ein gutes Briefing der Darsteller durch den Regisseur vor der zu drehenden Szene.

Kontrolle

Die Dreharbeiten verlaufen im Wochenrhythmus und beinhalten eine tägliche Musterbesichtigung. Bei den Dreharbeiten ist besonders zu beachten, dass die Chronologie eingehalten wird und bei szenischen Darstellungen die Anschlüsse stimmen. Stets sind der Zeitplan (Drehplan, Disposition), Kalkulation und der Cashflow-Plan entscheidende Kontrollinstrumente.

Für jeden Drehtag wird vom **Aufnahmeleiter** vorher eine **Tagesdisposition** (Dispo) erstellt und nach dem Dreh ein Tagesbericht. So haben alle Beteiligten stets einen genauen Überblick über den Stand und den Fortgang des Projekts.

Eine Dispo enthält alle wichtigen Details für den Dreh (vgl. Heid 2002, S. 159):

- Telefonnummern der für den Produktionsablauf verantwortlichen Personen und des Produktionsbüros,
- Nummern und Anschriften der zu drehenden Motive und Drehorte,
- Arbeitszeiten für jeden Bereich, Maske und Garderobe beginnen häufig früher, Beleuchter müssen möglicherweise ihre Geräte später abbauen,
- der Zeitpunkt des Drehbeginns (das ist nicht notwendigerweise der Zeitpunkt, zu dem die erste Klappe gedreht wird),
- alle an diesem Tag zu drehenden Bilder mit einer kurzen Beschreibung des Inhaltes und der Vorstoppzeit,
- Namen der Rollen und ihre Darsteller, der Zeitpunkt, wann sie abgeholt werden und wann sie drehfertig sein sollen,
- Anzahl der Komparsen,
- besondere technische Mittel, die benötigt werden,
- Aufgaben außerhalb des unmittelbaren Drehorts, z. B. eine Mustervorführung oder eine nachträgliche Motivbesichtigung,
- eine auf jede Fahrt und jeden Wagen bezogene Fahrdispo.

19.5.4 Post-Production

Die Phase der Post-Production („Nachbearbeitung") des Films nimmt einen vergleichsweise **langen Zeitraum** ein. Für einen durchschnittlichen Film benötigt man hierzu bereits meist bis zu drei Monaten. Bei Filmen, in denen komplizierte Special-Effects eingebaut werden, verlängern sich die Zeiten unter Umständen dramatisch. Empfehlenswert ist es daher, den entsprechenden „Effects Supervisor" bereits von Beginn an in die Phase der Umsetzung („Auflösung") des Drehbuchs, wenn nicht gar schon in die Drehbucherstellung einzubeziehen. Die visuelle Umsetzung des Stoffes ist in diesem Falle eine besondere Herausforderung für das Dreigestirn aus Regisseur, Kameramann und Special-Effects-Experte.

Auch die Produktionsabwicklung (Abrechnung, Rückbau, Abgabe von Leihmaterial etc.) kann einen erheblichen Zeitbedarf mit sich bringen und unter Umständen bis zu drei Wochen dauern. Geht die Filmproduktion an einen Fernsehsender, benötigt die Erstellung des kompletten Sendebandes ebenfalls bis zu drei Monaten, woran sich für den Pressevorlauf noch ein Zeitraum von mindestens noch sechs Wochen anschließt.

Rohschnitt

Die Post-Production kann in die beiden Phasen des Rohschnitts und des Feinschnitts eingeteilt werden. Der Rohschnitt beginnt wie gezeigt bereits in der Drehphase und wird in der ersten Stufe der Nachbearbeitung abgeschlossen. Im Einzelnen werden dabei die folgenden **Schritte** vollzogen:

- Sichten des Materials
- Kopierwerksarbeiten (Entwickeln, Lichtbestimmung, Arbeitskopie)
- Vorbereitung der Rohschnittabnahme
- Durchführung des Rohschnitts und Rohschnittabnahme

Feinschnitt

Während der Rohschnitt durch den Cutter nach einem Schnittplan vollzogen wird, findet der Feinschnitt nach dem Abschluss der Dreharbeiten statt. Da hier nun das endgültige „Gesicht" des Films entsteht, ist die Anwesenheit des Regisseurs und eventuell des Redakteurs des Fernsehsenders notwendig. Im Einzelnen werden die folgenden **Schritte** vollzogen:

- Ton- und Bild-Bearbeitung
- Abnahme der Musik-Komposition und Produktion, Musik-Feinschnitt
- Testvorführungen
- Mischung Sprach- und Geräuschsynchronisation, Musikaufnahmen
- Endabnahme (Negativschnitt beginnt).

Übersicht über die beteiligten Personen

Die Darstellung der Produktionsvorgänge beim Film hat deutlich gemacht, dass es sich um einen sehr komplizierten und von vielen Unwägbarkeiten begleiteten Herstellungsvorgang handelt. Es wurde deutlich, dass der Erfolg der Filmproduktion entscheidend von den beteiligten Personen abhängt. Abschließend sei daher noch eine **Übersicht** über den Personenkreis gegeben, der beim Film typischerweise am Werk ist. Zu trennen sind dabei der künstlerische und der organisatorisch-finanzielle Bereich.

19.6 Multimedia-Produktion

❶ **Multimedia-Agenturen** bieten unterschiedlichsten Kunden ihre Fähigkeiten und ihr Know-how als Dienstleistung an.

❷ Medien-Fachabteilungen von größeren Firmen unterstützen die Marketing-, Public Relations- und Schulungsaktivitäten der eigenen Firma.

❸ Beispiele von Tätigkeitsbezeichnungen aus Stellenangeboten in Fachzeitschriften:
Projektleiter, Interface Artist, New Media Kontakter, CBT-Autor, Multimedia Assistent, Mediengestalter, WebProfessional, Key-Account-Manager, Producer, Online-Redakteur, Medienberater, Senior Art Director, Konzepter, Screendesigner, Web-Developer, Content-Redakteur, Media Developer, New Media Designer, Coder, Programmierer Softcore, Texter, Content Integration Specialist, Technical Project Manager, Technical Consultant, Film- und Videodesigner, Web Based Application Developer, Shopdesigner, Junior Application Developer, Producer Foto & Multimedia, E-Commerce Manager, Flash-Entwickler, Director Marketing & Communications Projekt-Ingenieur, Unit-Director, Release Engineer, Lingo-Programmierer, Design new media, Softwarearchitekt, Systemintegrator Senior, Multimedia Developer. E-Consultant, Grafik-Designer, Portal-Manager, Senior Technologists, Information Architects, HTML-Spezialist, Creativ-Director ...

Bevor in diesem Kapitel der Ablauf einer Multimedia-Produktion behandelt wird, sollen die Mitarbeiter vorgestellt werden, die eine Medienproduktion durchführen. Die Tätigkeitsbereiche dieses Teams sind eine Weiterentwicklung aus dem Umfeld von audiovisuellen Medien; im Unterschied zu den klassischen Medien wie zum Beispiel Fernsehen und Film. Sie sind heute in den Multimedia-Agenturen ❶ und in speziellen Medien-Fachabteilungen ❷, die sich mit der Erstellung von digitalen Medien beschäftigen, tätig.

19.6.1 Projektbeteiligte

Die Aufgabenbereiche des Produktionsteams werden immer noch mit keinem klaren **Berufsbild** definiert. Ein eindeutiger Berufsstand hat bis vor kurzem in Deutschland gar nicht existiert. Seit einigen Jahren werden von Fachhochschulen spezifische Studiengänge im Bereich „Neue Medien" angeboten und Ausbildungsberufe speziell auf die Medienbranche ausgerichtet.

Im Bereich der Umschulung und der beruflichen Weiterbildung haben sich mehrere berufliche Akademien mit zertifizierten Ausbildungsgängen für die Medienbranche etabliert. Auch für berufliche Quereinsteiger bieten sogenannte Multimedia-Akademien interessante Möglichkeiten, die jedoch auf Grund der Qualitätsunterschiede und des teilweise vorhandenen Angebotswildwuchses von den Interessierten gründlich geprüft werden sollten.

Die gesamte Branche unterliegt so vielfältigen Funktionsabläufen und Aufgaben, dass eine klare Abgrenzung einzelner spezifischer **Berufsgruppen** und **Tätigkeitsbereiche** nur sehr schwer möglich ist. Auch die sehr unterschiedlichen Berufsbezeichnungen, die in ihrer „Kreativität" erstaunlich sind ❸, führen nicht gerade zu einer Transparenz der Berufsbilder in der Medienbranche.

Im Allgemeinen hängt es von der Größe der Agentur ab, wie breit das Aufgabenspektrum eines Mitarbeiters ist. In kleinen Agenturen sind **Generalisten** gefragt, die nahezu alle Aufgabenbereiche übernehmen. In größeren Unternehmen werden die anfallenden Tätigkeiten von Spezialisten ausgeführt. Je größer das Unternehmen, umso mehr bilden sich innerhalb der einzelnen Arbeitsgebiete Hierarchien heraus. Dort delegieren Chef-Designer, Teamleiter oder Redaktionsleiter die Aufgaben an entsprechende Spezialisten.

Generell ist jedoch festzustellen, dass viele der Aufgabenfelder der Multimediaproduktion mit denen einer audiovisuellen Medienproduktion oder der klassischen Film- und Fernsehproduktion zu vergleichen sind. Sie wurden lediglich ergänzt durch die mittlerweile sich rasant enwickelnden neuen technischen Möglichkeiten, die für die Branche spezifisch sind.

Produzent

In der Medienproduktion steht der Produzent an erster Stelle. Der Produzent sichert die finanzielle Basis für die Produktion und ermöglicht somit erst deren Realisierung. Erfolgt eine Medienproduktion als Dienstleistung, so ist üblicherweise der Auftraggeber der Produzent. Werden Medienprodukte hergestellt, die frei vermarktet werden, so tritt der Produzent als Verleger des Produktes auf. Das heißt, der **Produzent** kann sein:

- eine einzelne Person,
- eine Gruppe von Personen,
- ein Unternehmen oder ein Institut,
- eine Medienagentur oder ein Videostudio,
- eine Rundfunkanstalt,
- ein Verlag.

Produktionsteam

Der Produzent gilt allgemein als der „Hersteller" der Medien. Die eigentliche Umsetzung der Inhalte, das heißt das Konzipieren und Realisieren der Produktion, wird jedoch von einem ganzen Produktionsteam erarbeitet. Das Produktionsteam besteht aus Mitarbeitern verschiedenster Medienberufe. Je nach Größe der Produktion und je nach Produktionsart sind die Mitarbeiter unterschiedlich stark auf ein Tätigkeitsfeld spezialisiert.

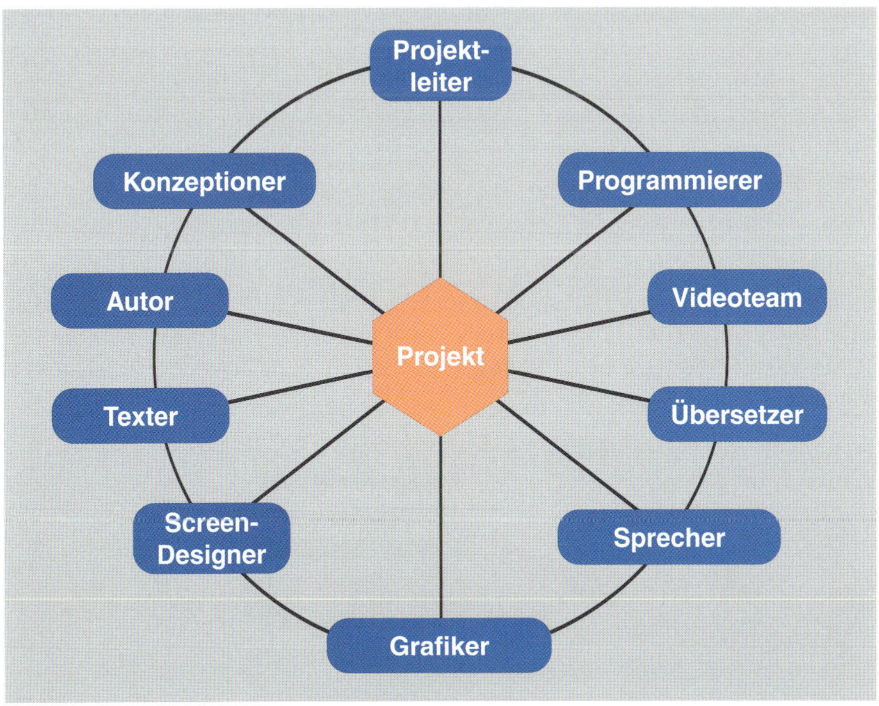

Wer macht was?

Interdisziplinär = mehrere Fachgebiete umfassend; die Zusammenarbeit mehrerer Fachgebiete betreffend.

Die Mitarbeiter bei einer Multimedia-Produktion verstehen sich als ein interdisziplinäres Team von Spezialisten.

➲ **Die Zusammensetzung des Produktionsteams hängt von der Art des Medien-Produktes und dessen Arbeitsanforderungen ab.**

Schon im Vorfeld der Produktion stellt der Produktionsleiter das für die Produktion notwendige Team zusammen. Jedes Teammitglied erfüllt als Spezialist die ihm zugeteilte Aufgabe mehr oder weniger in Eigenverantwortung.

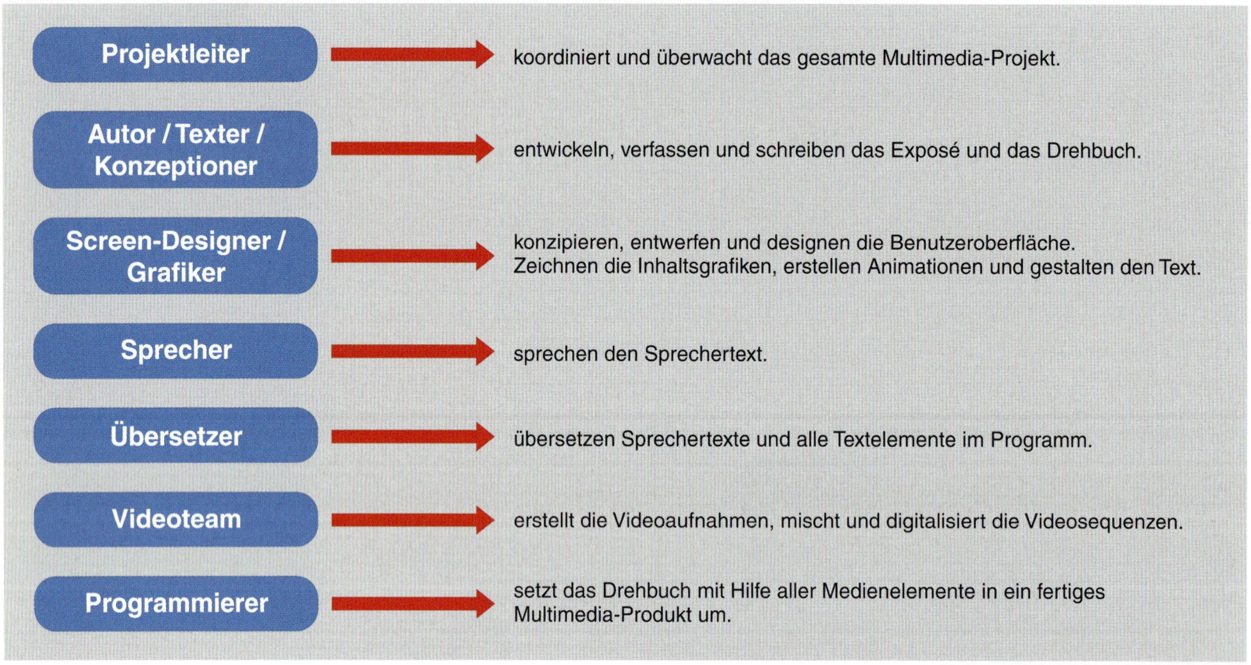

Medienproduktionen, die zum Beispiel Videosequenzen, 3D-Animationen, Sprecheraufnahmen etc. benötigen, können oft nicht komplett von einer Agentur in Eigenregie hergestellt werden. Dazu werden externe Dienstleister herangezogen, die sich auf diese Anforderungen spezialisiert haben. Die Verteilung der Aufgaben kann z. B. wie folgt aussehen:

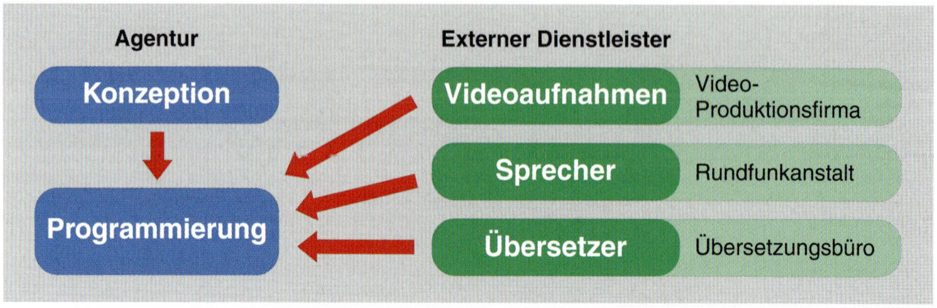

Projektleiter

Die Umsetzung des gesamten Projektes muss von einer Person gesteuert und überwacht werden. Das **Tätigkeitsgebiet** umfasst

- das Planen, Steuern und Überwachen der Produktion,
- das Bereitstellen qualifizierter Mitarbeiter und der erforderlichen Hardware- und Software-Ausrüstung,
- das Überwachen und Einhalten des finanziellen Rahmens und des Zeitplanes der gesamten Produktion.

Die Bezeichnung dieser Aufgabe variiert von „Projektleiter" über „Projektmanager" bis hin zu „Produktionsleiter", wobei letzterer sich mehr um die Realisierung und weniger um die Kosten der Produktion kümmert.

Gleichzeitig übernimmt der Projektleiter die Betreuung und Beratung des Auftraggebers während der gesamten Produktionsphase. Aber auch schon während der Akquisitionsphase, das heißt bevor der Auftrag zustande gekommen ist, bringt der Projektleiter sein Fachwissen im Rahmen von Vertriebsgesprächen mit ein.

Eine zusätzliche wichtige Aufgabe des Projektleiters ist die Betreuung des Produktionsteams, denn er ist gleichzeitig der Motivator des Teams. **Motivation** ist sehr wichtig, denn Projektarbeit unter Zeitdruck, lange Arbeitszeiten und ständige Wochenendarbeit belastet ein Projektteam außergewöhnlich. Nur ein hochmotiviertes Team kann solchen Belastungen über längere Zeit standhalten.

Der **Projektleiter** benötigt sehr gute Kenntnisse und Fähigkeiten
- im Produktionsmanagement,
- in der Medienproduktion,
- im kosten- und qualitätsbewusstem Denken,
- in der Personalführung und im Konfliktmanagement.

Konzeptionist / Autor

Den Entwurf einer Medienproduktion übernimmt der Konzeptionist. Dabei kann es sich um einen kreativen Mitarbeiter handeln, der Kundenanforderungen zielgruppen- und mediengerecht in ein Konzept umsetzen kann.

Diese Tätigkeiten werden in der Praxis von Mitarbeitern ausgeführt, die Berufsbezeichnungen wie „Konzeptionist", „Multimedia-Autor" oder „Storyboarder" führen. Das Spektrum des **Tätigkeitsbereichs** kann stark variieren und folgende Aufgaben umfassen:

- Erster Kundenkontakt und konzeptionelle Beratung des Kunden,
- Betreuung und Durchführung des Briefing-Workshops mit dem Kunden,
- Zielgruppenspezifisches Aufbereiten der Inhalte,
- Erarbeiten aller Ergebnisse und Produktionsunterlagen innerhalb der Konzeptionsphase, wie Exposé, Treatment, Flowchart und Drehbuch.

Dabei muss der Mitarbeiter über fundierte medientechnische, gestalterische und analytische Fähigkeiten verfügen. Da das Konzept maßgeblich über Erfolg und Misserfolg der Produktion entscheidet, kommt dem Konzeptionisten eine sehr zentrale Rolle innerhalb der gesamten Medienproduktion zu. Seine Ideen zur Umsetzung der Inhalte und der visuellen Gestaltung muss er dem Auftraggeber näher bringen; er muss ihn vom Konzept überzeugen und ihm ein Bild des möglichen Medienproduktes vermitteln.

Der **Konzeptionist** benötigt sehr gute Kenntnisse und Fähigkeiten
- im visuellen Gestalten,
- in der Medienproduktion,
- im Analysieren von Zusammenhängen,
- im kreativen Umsetzen von Ideen,
- in der Präsentationstechnik.

Mediendesigner

Der **Mediendesigner** benötigt sehr gute Kenntnisse und Fähigkeiten

- im grafischen Gestalten,
- der eingesetzten Grafiktools,
- der Softwareergonomie.

Mediendesigner setzen die Ideen des Konzeptionisten in ein visuelles und auditives Erscheinungsbild um. Sie sind für die **äußere Gestaltung des Mediums** verantwortlich. Dazu gehören

- die visuelle Gestaltung der Bildschirmoberfläche und der Navigationselemente,
- die visuelle Gestaltung der Inhalte in Form von Grafiken, Bildern, Animationen und Videosequenzen,
- die auditive Gestaltung der Geräusche, der Sprechertexte und der Musik.

Die Tätigkeiten des Mediendesigners werden in der Praxis von Mitarbeitern ausgeführt, die Berufsbezeichnungen wie „Mediengestalter“, „Screendesigner“, „3D-Grafiker“ oder „Soundeditor“ führen. Dabei muss der Mitarbeiter über fundierte Kenntnisse im professionellen Umgang mit Form, Farbe, Typografie und Layout verfügen und ausreichend Erfahrung im Umgang mit funktionalen Screendesign und der Software-Ergonomie gesammelt haben. Selbstverständlich müssen die aktuellen Bildbearbeitungswerkzeuge beherrscht werden. Mediendesigner, wie 3D-Grafiker, müssen zusätzlich umfangreiche 3D-Grafikerstellungs- und Animationswerkzeuge beherrschen.

Video- und Tonteam

Der **Video- und Ton-Spezialist** benötigt sehr gute Kenntnisse und Fähigkeiten

- in der Bildgestaltung,
- in der Medienproduktion,
- in der Kamera- und Schnitttechnik,
- in der Tonaufnahme und der Nachbearbeitung.

Zum Erstellen der Filmsequenzen und der Tonelemente für eine multimediale Produktion werden ebenfalls **Spezialisten** hinzugezogen. Regisseur, Kameramann, Kameraassistent, Beleuchter und Cutter sind typische Berufe von Mitarbeitern einer Videoproduktionsfirma. Diese stellt, meist als externe Produktionsfirma, die für die Multimedia-Produktion notwendigen Filmteile her. Auch die Erzeugung von Tonelementen wie Geräusche, Musik und Sprechertexte übernehmen Spezialisten aus dem Videoteam bzw. Tonfachleute eines Tonstudios.

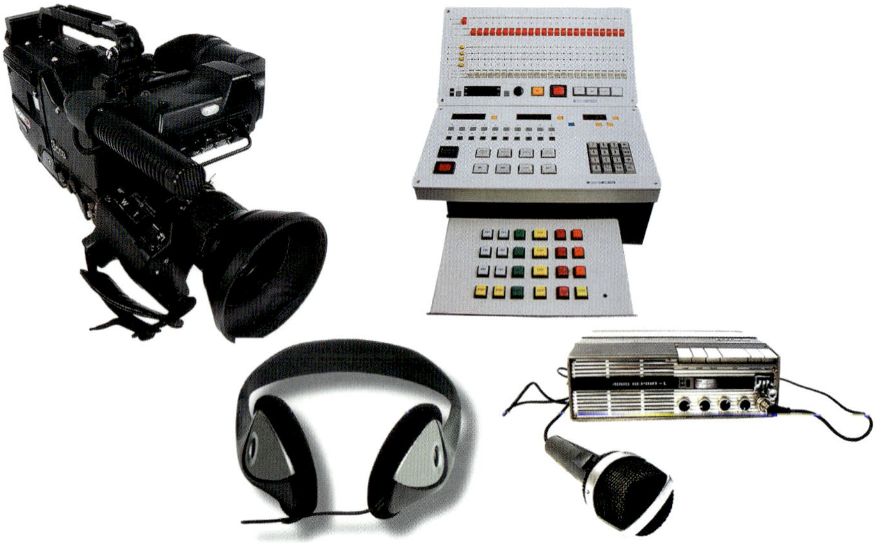

Programmierer

Der Programmierer ist zuständig für die **technische Realisierung des Gesamtproduktes** auf der Grundlage der Produktionsunterlagen Drehbuch und Flowchart. Er erstellt mit Hilfe eines Autorenwerkzeuges oder einer Programmiersprache die Struktur und Funktionalität des Programms. Dabei integriert er die Grafikelemente des Mediendesigners bzw. Screendesigners zu einem funktionierenden Screendesign und bindet die produzierten Inhaltselemente, wie Texte, Grafiken, Bilder, Videosequenzen, Animationen und Sound-Elemente, in das Programm ein.

Der Programmierer muss entsprechend den Produktionsanforderungen die notwendigen Autorenwerkzeuge und Software-Produkte einsetzen, um

- gemäß dem Drehbuch die Funktionalität und Inhalte des Programms umzusetzen,
- etwaige Kundenvorgaben bezüglich Erstellungswerkzeugen zu entsprechen,
- um effizient und schnell zum gewünschten Ergebnis zu kommen.

Unterschiedliche Produktions-Anforderungen bedingen auch unterschiedliche Arbeitsweisen und die Verwendung von unterschiedlichen Autorensystemen und Programmiersprachen. Klassische Multimedia-Anwendungen auf CD-ROM wird der Programmierer üblicherweise mit Autorensystemen, wie Macromedia Director und Authorware oder Toolbook u. a. herstellen. Bei Anwendungen für das Internet muss er teils noch sehr unterschiedliche Werkzeuge benutzen. Dies können Web-Editoren und Programmiersprachen, wie JavaScript oder Java von Sun Microsystem sein.

Der **Programmierer** benötigt sehr gute Kenntnisse

- der Autorenwerkzeuge,
- von regulären Programmiersprachen, wie z. B. C++,
- der Produktionstechnik,
- der Betriebssystemplattformen,
- der Web-Technologie.

Das Realisieren von Datenbankanbindungen, komplexen Simulationen und Animationen gehören genauso zu den programmiertechnischen Herausforderungen des Programmierers, wie das Entwickeln ganzer Redaktionssysteme für Autoren.

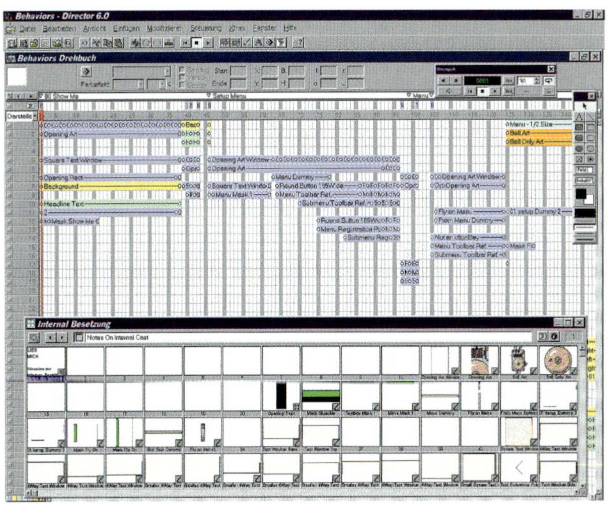

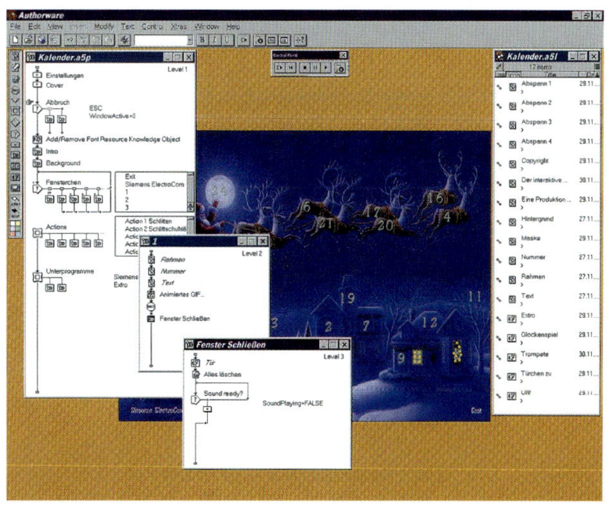

Der Programmierer von Multimedia-Anwendungen entwickelt sein Produkt mit Hilfe spezieller Autorensysteme

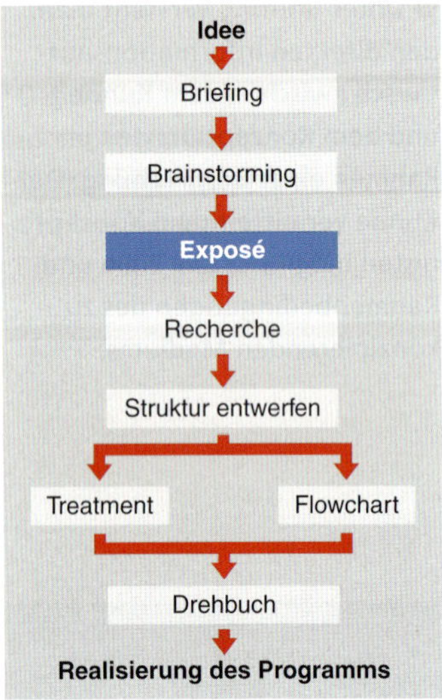

Exposé

Das Exposé sollte ausreichend Informationen über das eingesetzte System, über Form und Inhalt der Multimedia-Produktion und den Nutzen für Anwender und Auftraggeber beinhalten.

➲ **Unter dem Exposé versteht man eine detaillierte Ausarbeitung der inhaltlichen und formalen Ideen des Konzeptes.**

Produktdefinition:
Sie stellt eine Aussage über den Produkttyp, z. B. Computer Based Training, POI/POS, dar.

Programmaufbau mit Grundstruktur (Flowcharts):
Er soll dem Kunden einen Überblick über die Informationsvernetzung im Programm geben. Hierbei werden visuell die Navigationsmöglichkeiten zwischen den einzelnen Informationsblöcken aufgezeigt.

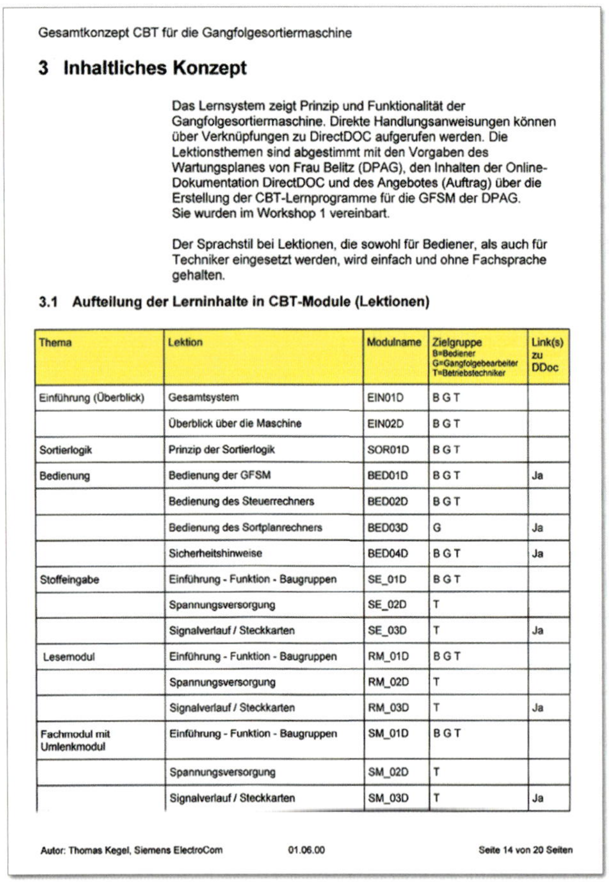

Gesamtkonzept CBT für die Gangfolgesortiermaschine

3 Inhaltliches Konzept

Das Lernsystem zeigt Prinzip und Funktionalität der Gangfolgesortiermaschine. Direkte Handlungsanweisungen können über Verknüpfungen zu DirectDOC aufgerufen werden. Die Lektionsthemen sind abgestimmt mit den Vorgaben des Wartungsplanes von Frau Belitz (DPAG), den Inhalten der Online-Dokumentation DirectDOC und des Angebotes (Auftrag) über die Erstellung der CBT-Lernprogramme für die GFSM der DPAG. Sie wurden im Workshop 1 vereinbart.

Der Sprachstil bei Lektionen, die sowohl für Bediener, als auch für Techniker eingesetzt werden, wird einfach und ohne Fachsprache gehalten.

3.1 Aufteilung der Lerninhalte in CBT-Module (Lektionen)

Thema	Lektion	Modulname	Zielgruppe B=Bediener G=Gangfolgebearbeiter T=Betriebstechniker	Link(s) zu DDoc
Einführung (Überblick)	Gesamtsystem	EIN01D	B G T	
	Überblick über die Maschine	EIN02D	B G T	
Sortierlogik	Prinzip der Sortierlogik	SOR01D	B G T	
Bedienung	Bedienung der GFSM	BED01D	B G T	Ja
	Bedienung des Steuerrechners	BED02D	B G T	
	Bedienung des Sortplanrechners	BED03D	G	Ja
	Sicherheitshinweise	BED04D	B G T	Ja
Stoffeingabe	Einführung - Funktion - Baugruppen	SE_01D	B G T	
	Spannungsversorgung	SE_02D	T	
	Signalverlauf / Steckkarten	SE_03D	T	Ja
Lesemodul	Einführung - Funktion - Baugruppen	RM_01D	B G T	
	Spannungsversorgung	RM_02D	T	
	Signalverlauf / Steckkarten	RM_03D	T	Ja
Fachmodul mit Umlenkmodul	Einführung - Funktion - Baugruppen	SM_01D	B G T	
	Spannungsversorgung	SM_02D	T	
	Signalverlauf / Steckkarten	SM_03D	T	Ja

Autor: Thomas Kegel, Siemens ElectroCom 01.06.00 Seite 14 von 20 Seiten

Beispiel einer Exposé-Seite für ein Computer Based Training (Lernprogramm)

Methodisches und didaktisches Konzept:
Das Konzept beschreibt, welche Inhalte mit welchen Mitteln und Medien umgesetzt werden. In welcher Weise die Informationsvermittlung abläuft, hängt von der Zielsetzung und der Zielgruppe ab.

Benutzerführung:
Sie gibt Aufschluss über das „User Interface".

- Wie kann die Benutzeroberfläche aussehen?
- Wie wird der Benutzer auf die Interaktionsmöglichkeiten aufmerksam gemacht?
- Kann dem Benutzer Unterstützung angeboten werden, z. B. in Form einer „lebendigen Informationszeile"?
- Welche Orientierungshilfen sind vorgesehen? Wie erkennt der Benutzer die Informationsebene, auf der er sich befindet?

Je nach Kunde und Produktion können auch mehrere Exposés vorbereitet werden, um so den Entscheidungsprozess des Kunden auf den Exposé-Präsentationstermin zu konzentrieren. Ein mehrmaliger sequenzieller Änderungsdurchlauf bis zur endgültigen Entscheidung kostet viel Zeit und Geld. Die nächsten Schritte der Konzeptionsphase behandeln die inhaltliche Recherche, das Erstellen der Programm-Struktur und, wenn notwendig, die Erstellung eines Treatments. Den Abschluss der Konzeptionsphase bildet das Drehbuch. Die Prozesse „Treatment", „Flowchart" und „Drehbuch" gehören zu der Phase, bei der das Konzept im Detail Gestalt annimmt.

Recherche

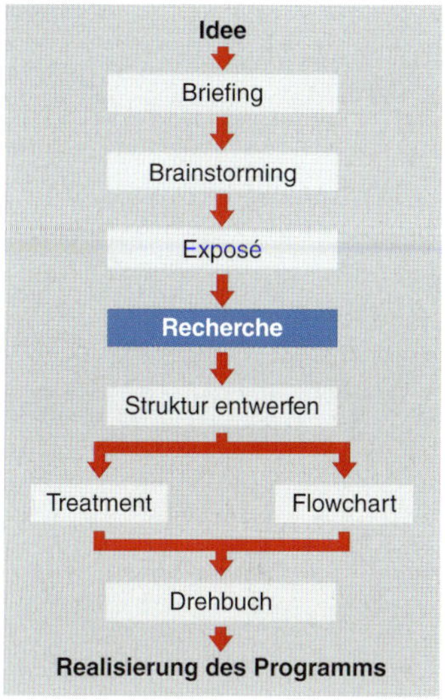

Um die Ideen zu konkretisieren, bedarf es der intensiven Aufarbeitung des Themas. Je nach herzustellendem Produkt variiert die Informationstiefe. Im Bereich von Public Relations (PR) wird man andere Maßstäbe an die Informationstiefe der Produkte ansetzen als bei einem Informationssystem oder Lernprogramm für ein Servicepersonal.

Wichtig ist auch, dass sich das Kreativteam über die betreffende Thematik hinweg mit der Branche im Allgemeinen beschäftigt. Nur so ist ein sogenanntes „Aufnorden" möglich, d. h. das Verwenden eines Präsentations- und Sprachstiles, der üblicherweise von der Zielgruppe (meist auch Branche) praktiziert und verstanden wird. Konkurrenzprodukte geben häufig Denkanstöße und machen deutlich, was sich am besten verkauft. Der Produzent (Agentur) sollte dann in der Lage sein, eine an die Zielgruppe orientierte, fachlich überzeugende Aussage in ein multimediales Produkt umzusetzen.

➲ **Für das Konzept muss sich der Autor intensiv mit der betreffenden Materie und deren Branche befassen.**

Im Bereich von Computer Based Training kann der **Wissenstransfer** zwischen Fachberatern des Kunden und dem CBT-Autor auf Grund der Informationstiefe auch größere Ausmaße annehmen. Steht dem Autor kein Fachberater zur Verfügung, so muss der Autor die erforderliche Informationsrecherche selbst in die Hand nehmen. Das kann z. B. bei komplexen technischen Zusammenhängen bedeuten, dass die Konzeptionsphase einen überproportionalen Anteil an der Gesamtproduktion einnimmt, was die Produktionskosten natürlich in die Höhe treibt.

Entwurf der Struktur

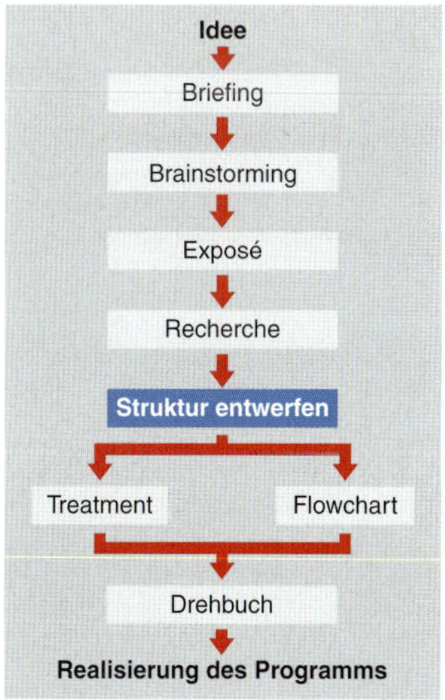

Bevor mit der eigentlichen Produktion begonnen werden kann, muss sich das Team über den eigentlichen Aufbau, der Struktur des Multimedia-Programms, klar werden.

Die Art des Multimedia-Programms gibt meist schon die **prinzipielle Grundstruktur** vor. So ergibt sich bei einem Informationssystem mit Hypertext-Funktionalität ein extrem verflochtenes Netzwerk der Verknüpfungen. Ein tutorielles Lernprogramm hingegen beinhaltet primär lineare Strukturen, da der Lernende „step by step" durch die Thematik geführt werden soll und hier das zu lernende Wissen oft aufeinander aufbaut.

In die Vorüberlegungen beim Entwerfen der Struktur muss unbedingt die betreffende **Zielgruppe** einbezogen werden.

- Ist die Zielgruppe mit derartigen Medien vertraut?
- In wie vielen verschachtelten Ebenen findet sich die Zielgruppe noch zurecht?
- Welche Einführungsphase ist für die Zielgruppe vorgesehen?
- Die Struktur sollte immer zielgruppenspezifisch konzipiert werden.

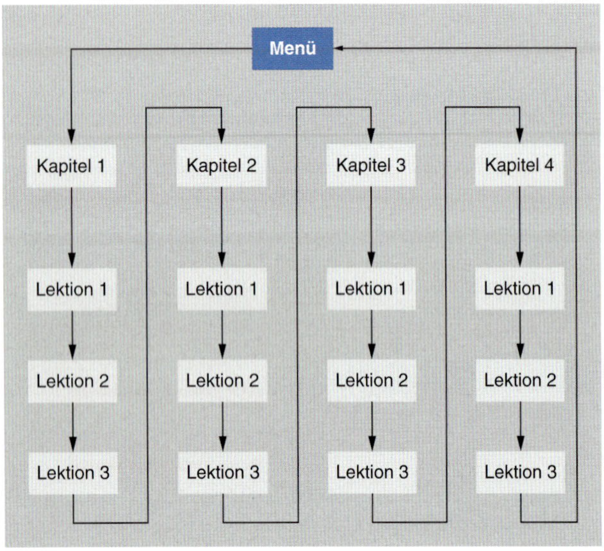

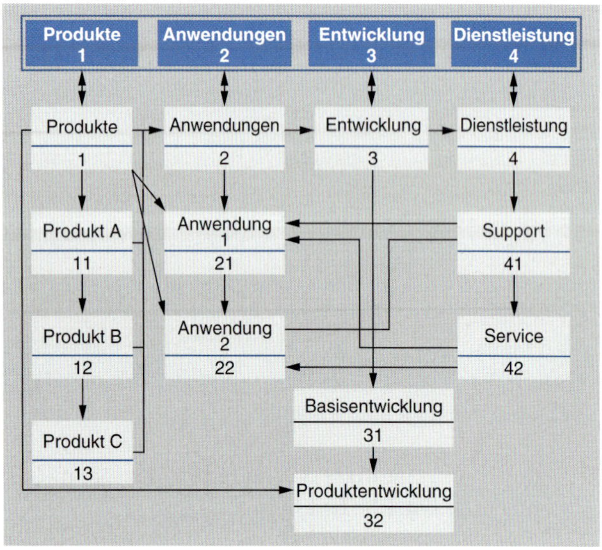

Unterschiedliche Anwendungen erfordern auch unterschiedlichste Programm-Strukturen.

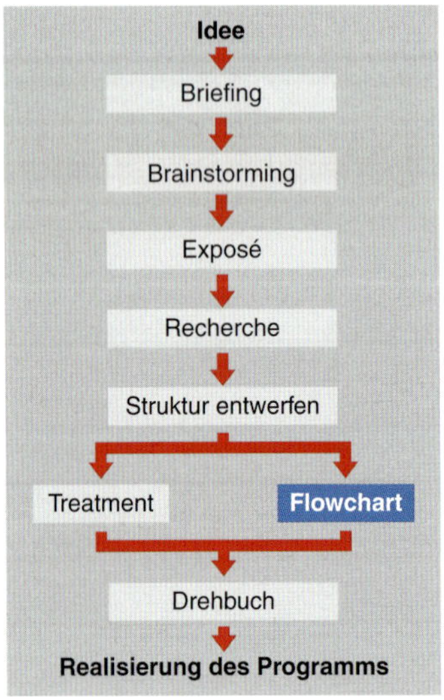

Flowchart

Der nichtlineare Ablauf von interaktiven Anwendungen erfordert vom Entwickler viel Vorstellungsvermögen. Die Gefahr einer unbeabsichtigten Sackgasse im Programm, d. h. eine Verzweigung ins Nichts, wird um so größer, je unübersichtlicher die Struktur des Programms ist. Um diese Gefahr zu vermeiden, wird das gesamte Netz der Informationseinheiten in visueller Form dargestellt. Das Produktionsteam erhält damit einen **Übersichtsplan**, auch „Flowchart“ genannt. In diesem Plan werden die Informationseinheiten bzw. Bildschirmeinheiten in Kästchen mit eindeutigen Bezeichnungen dargestellt. Zur Verknüpfung untereinander können Pfeile gezogen werden.

➲ **Mit einem „Flowchart“ kann die Struktur der interaktiven Anwendung visualisiert werden. Neben dem Flussdiagramm werden in der Praxis auch die Begriffe „Interaktionsdiagramm” oder „Struktogramm” verwendet.**

Ist die Struktur einmal festgelegt, so dient sie für das ganze Team zur allgemeinen Transparenz der Produktion und kann als Grundlage zur Informationsrecherche, zur Materialbeschaffung und zur Medienproduktion dienen. Der Programmierer hat mit dem „Flowchart“ einen visuellen Ablaufplan des Programms. Die Grafiker und das Videoteam sehen, wie viel, wann und wo Grafiken, Bilder und Videos verwendet werden sollen. Sie können damit die Bildschirmelemente besser aufeinander abstimmen. Natürlich ist ein Strukturplan ein veränderbares Medium, da auf Grund von späteren Kundenwünschen oder wegen eingeplantem Material, das nicht beschafft werden konnte, immer wieder Änderungen an der Tagesordnung sind.

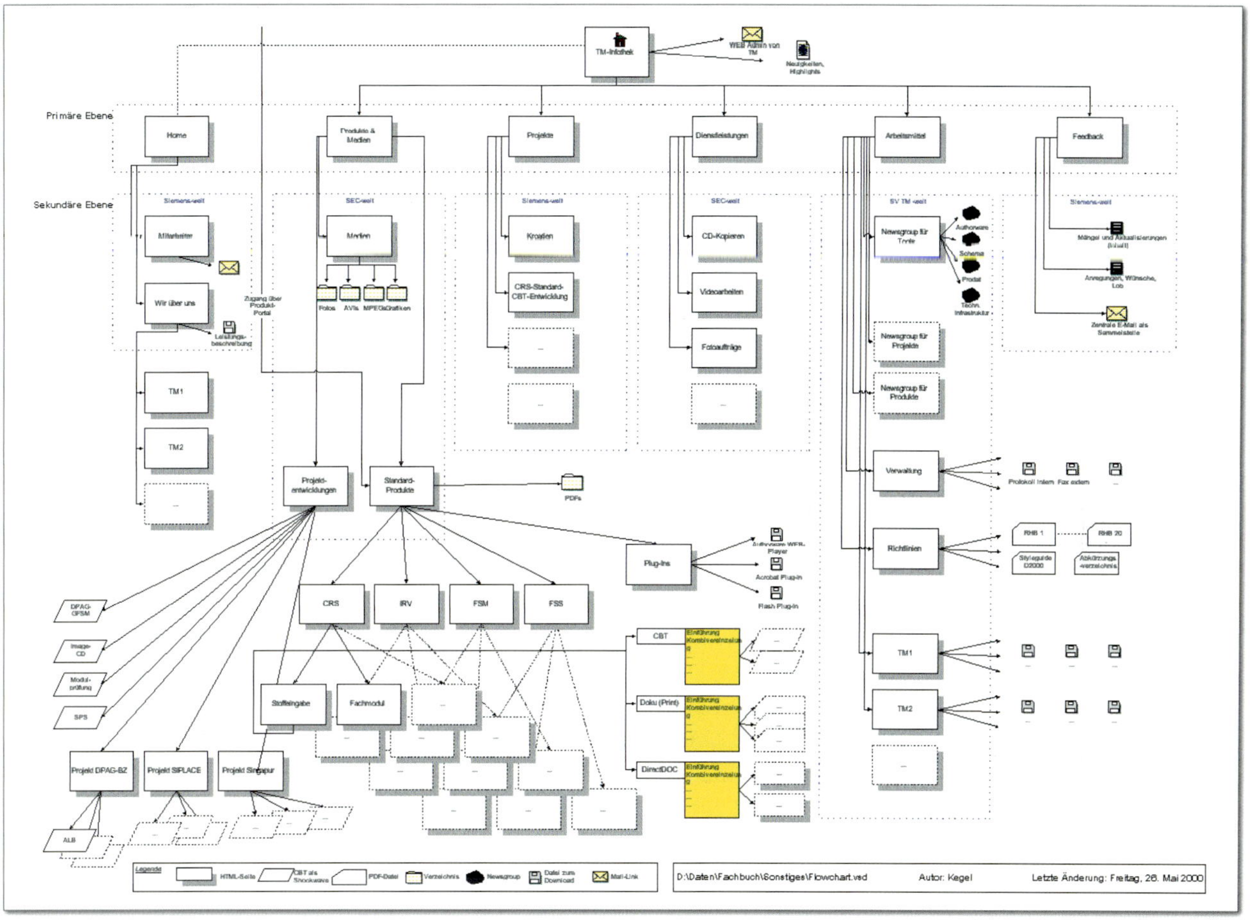

Beispiel eines Flowcharts für einen Intranet-Web-Auftritt

Treatment

Das **Treatment** ❶ legt den visuellen Stil fest und entwickelt bereits die Geschichte, bzw. den „roten Faden" der Produktion. Ein Treatment erläutert die **Hauptsequenzen einer Produktion** und gibt an, was bei der Entwicklung des Themas zu sehen und zu hören ist. Es gibt also schon wesentliche Einblicke in die Gestaltung des Mediums und lässt seine zukünftige Form bereits erahnen. Es ist gewissermaßen ein **Rohdrehbuch**.

❶ Das Treatment (engl. „Abhandlung") gibt genaue Auskunft über den inhaltlichen Zuschnitt des Themas.

Bei einem ausführlichen Exposé ist meist kein Treatment gefordert. Da der Detaillierungsgrad eines Treatments so hoch ist, sollte die Auftragsvergabe vorher erfolgen (auf Basis des Exposés), oder das Treatment wird gesondert in Rechnung gestellt. Es bleibt mit all seinen Ideen zur gestalterischen Umsetzung geistiges Eigentum des Autors.

Aus folgenden pragmatischen Gründen macht die Illustration eines Treatments Sinn:

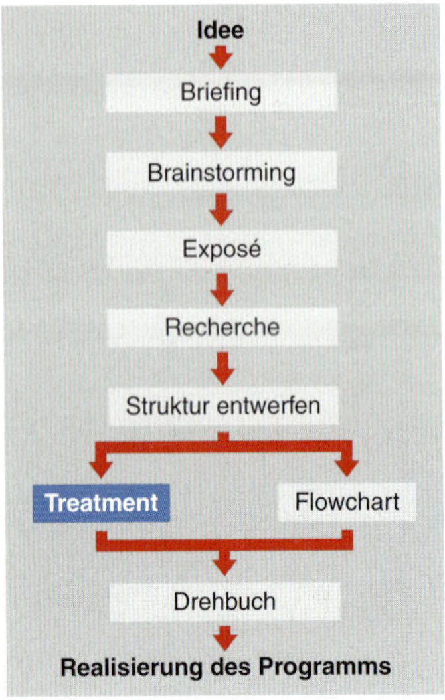

- Nicht jeder Auftraggeber verfügt über genügend Erfahrung mit dem Multimedia-Produktionsprozess und über ausreichend Vorstellungskraft, um sich auf Basis des Exposés den Ablauf und die Wirkung des gestalterischen Konzeptes in Form einer möglichen Produktion vorzustellen.
- Viele Entscheidungsträger verfügen nicht über die Zeit, sich in ein Konzept einzuarbeiten. Oftmals wird aber in wenigen Minuten über das Projekt entschieden, an dessen Vorbereitung und Konzeption das Team vielleicht Wochen oder Monate gearbeitet hat.

Ein möglichst guter Abgleich der Ergebnisvorstellungen zwischen Auftraggeber und Produktionsteam ist unbedingt notwendig. Grundlegende Änderungen im Drehbuch, oder noch extremer, im Prototyp bzw. in der ersten in Programmcode umgesetzten Fassung, sind verhältnismäßig zeitintensiv und dadurch teuer.

Mit Hilfe eines Treatments können sich alle an der Produktion Beteiligten bis zum Produzenten die Multimedia-Produktion besser vergegenwärtigen.

Konzept für Lernprogramm — Lernprogramm: SIPLACE Einführung

Kapitel 1: Der SMT-Prozeß

Lektion 3: Ihre Verantwortung und Präzision

Inhalte:
Sauberkeit und Konzentration beim Arbeiten

- Demonstration typischer Fehlerquellen
  - Förderer steht auf Bauteilen, folglich kommt es zu Abholfehlern. Maschinenstillstände drohen.
  - **Evtl. noch andere Fehlerquellen: z.B. : Unkonzentriertes Anspleißen führt zu sehr kostspieligen Serienfehlern, wenn zwar die richtige Bauform, aber das falsche Bauelement angespleißt wird. Werkzeug wird immer irgendwo abgelegt – die Folge ist unnötiges Suchen das Hektik in den Ablauf bringt. Schlechte Spleißstellen können die Förderer blockieren – Maschinenstillstand.**
- Maßnahmen
  - Säubern in und um die Maschine herum v.a. beim Rüstwechsel und während der Wartungsarbeiten
  - Saubere Werkzeuge, Ordnung mit den Klebestreifen, keine fettigen Finger,
  - **Bei der Arbeit konzentrieren**
  - **Arbeit gut durchorganisieren / auf Details achten**
- Appell an die Verantwortung
  - Schmutz wirkt sich in allen Bereichen negativ aus
  - **Exaktes** und **konzentriertes** Arbeiten ist extrem wichtig.

Lernziele:

- Das Bedienpersonal dafür sensibilisieren, daß es sich bei der SMT um einen sehr exakten Prozeß handelt.
- Eine hohe Bestückleistung und Qualität ist daher nur erreichbar, wenn das Peresonal exakt, sauber und konzentriert arbeitet.

Vorsicht! Nicht mit dem „erhobenen Zeigefinger", das blockiert die Bereitschaft

ALL2AD.DOC — 26.10.98 — - 4 -

Treatment als Feinkonzept

Drehbuch

Aufbauend auf dem Exposé wird das Drehbuch entwickelt. Das Drehbuch orientiert sich an den durch das Grobkonzept definierten Richtlinien.

Es beinhaltet, je nach Art der Produktion:

- die Gestaltung der einzelnen Bildschirmseiten,
- die Gestaltung der Aufgaben, Quiz, Hilfen, Feedbacks,
- die Gestaltung der Medien,
- den konkreten Programmablaufplan,
- das Video-Drehbuch,
- das Ton-Drehbuch.

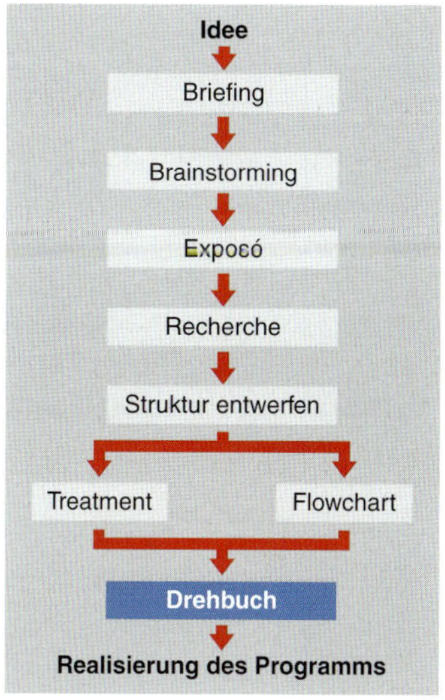

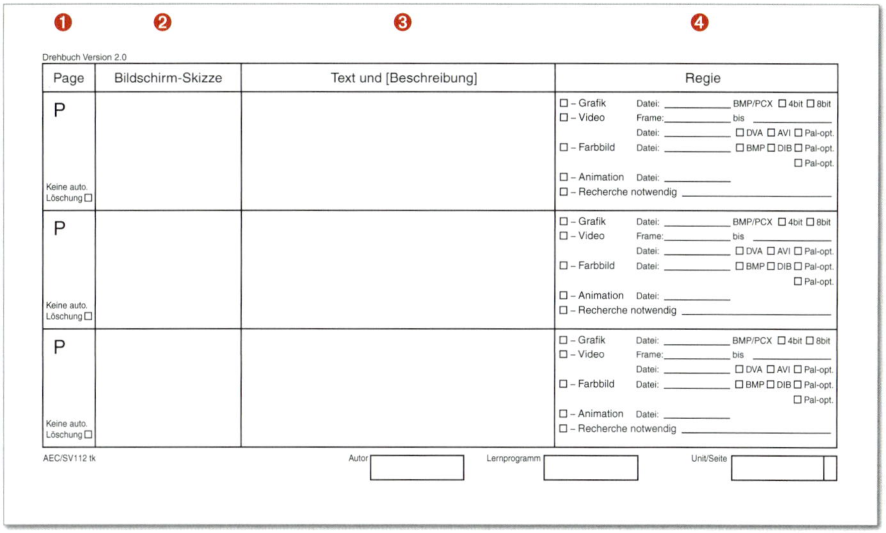

Page	Bildschirm-Skizze	Text und [Beschreibung]	Regie
P Keine auto. Löschung ☐			☐ – Grafik Datei: ____ BMP/PCX ☐ 4bit ☐ 8bit ☐ – Video Frame: ____ bis ____ Datei: ____ ☐ DVA ☐ AVI ☐ Pal-opt. ☐ – Farbbild Datei: ____ ☐ BMP ☐ DIB ☐ Pal-opt. ☐ Pal-opt. ☐ – Animation Datei: ____ ☐ – Recherche notwendig ____
P Keine auto. Löschung ☐			☐ – Grafik Datei: ____ BMP/PCX ☐ 4bit ☐ 8bit ☐ – Video Frame: ____ bis ____ Datei: ____ ☐ DVA ☐ AVI ☐ Pal-opt. ☐ – Farbbild Datei: ____ ☐ BMP ☐ DIB ☐ Pal-opt. ☐ Pal-opt. ☐ – Animation Datei: ____ ☐ – Recherche notwendig ____
P Keine auto. Löschung ☐			☐ – Grafik Datei: ____ BMP/PCX ☐ 4bit ☐ 8bit ☐ – Video Frame: ____ bis ____ Datei: ____ ☐ DVA ☐ AVI ☐ Pal-opt. ☐ – Farbbild Datei: ____ ☐ BMP ☐ DIB ☐ Pal-opt. ☐ Pal-opt. ☐ – Animation Datei: ____ ☐ – Recherche notwendig ____

AEC/SV112 tk Autor ____ Lernprogramm ____ Unit/Seite ____

Beispiel eines Drehbuchseiten-Formblattes.
Tabellarisches Layout mit:
❶ Seitenzähler der Bildschirmseite,
❷ Bildschirmskizze mit prinzipieller Darstellung und räumlicher Aufteilung der Bildelemente,
❸ Text, Sprechertext und Beschreibung eventueller Animationen und Interaktionen,
❹ Regieanweisungen.

Das Drehbuch ist nach Abnahme durch den Kunden die direkte Programmiergrundlage für das Programm. Die Gestaltung des Drehbuchs kann, je nach Produktion und Arbeitsweise des Teams, unterschiedlich vorgenommen werden.

Drehbuch: Outlook lernen

Screen-Bezeichnung	Text	Medienelemente	Interaktion
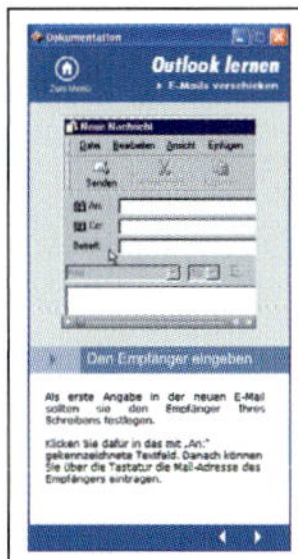 A020 lektion2.dir	[OD1TE020.rtf] **Den Empfänger eingeben** Als erste Angabe in der neuen E-Mail sollten sie den Empfänger Ihres Schreibens festlegen. Klicken Sie dafür in das mit „An:" gekennzeichnete Textfeld. Danach können Sie über die Tastatur die Mail-Adresse des Empfängers eintragen.	gonext.bmp goback.bmp home.bmp OD1VD006.mov	MouseUp → A021 MouseUp → A019 MouseUp → menu.dir

Datum 05.07.2002 Seite 25 von 60

Vereinfachte Gestaltung einer Drehbuchseite am Beispiel der multimedialen Dokumentation „Outlook lernen".

Beispiele aus Drehbüchern

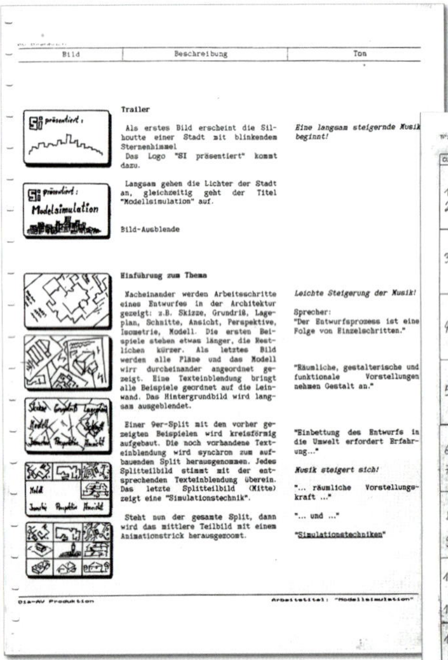

Drehbuchseite einer Multimedia-Präsentation

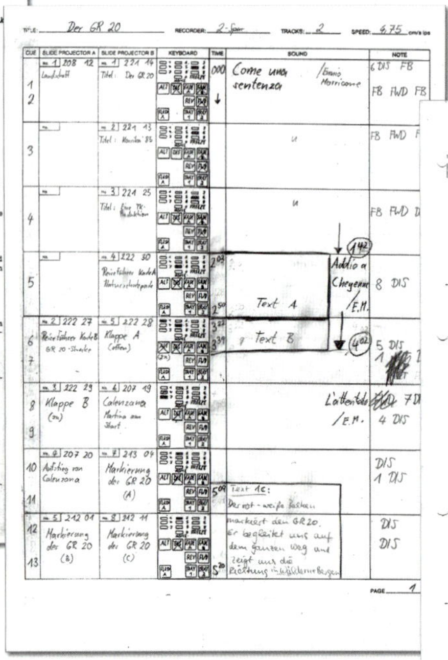

Drehbuchseite einer Tonbildschau

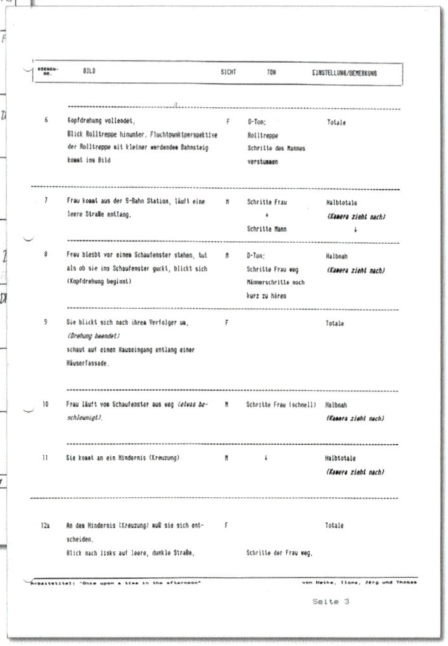

Drehbuchseite eines Filmwerbespots

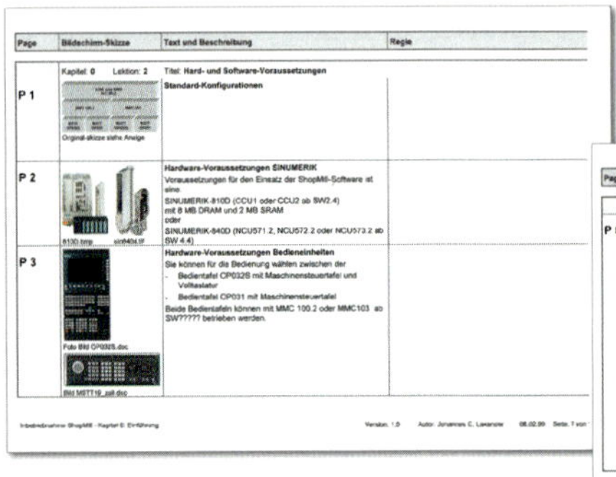

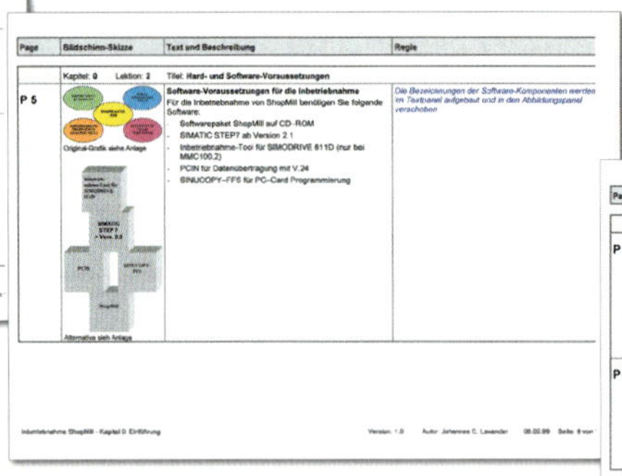

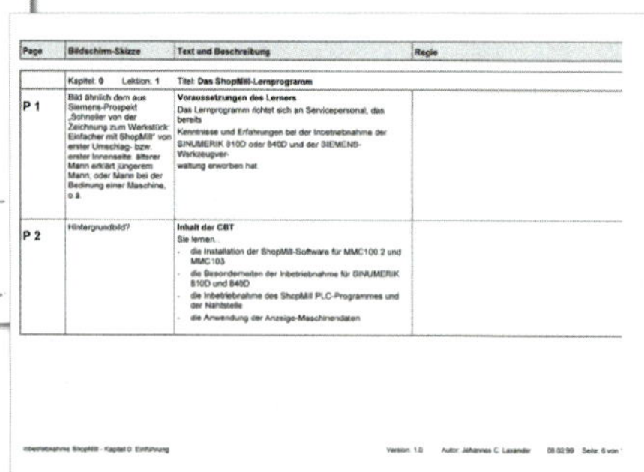

Drehbuchseiten eines technischen Lernprogramms

19.6.3 Realisierung

Ist das Drehbuch fertiggestellt, so kann mit der Umsetzung der Konzeption in die Multimedia-Produktion begonnen werden.

Medienproduktion

Zuerst müssen die erforderlichen Medien, die im Programm verwendet werden sollen, hergestellt werden. Dazu werden aus dem Drehbuch das Video-Drehbuch und das Ton-Drehbuch, bzw. der aufzunehmende Sprechertext extrahiert. Auf Basis des **Video-Drehbuches** werden die Videoaufnahmen hergestellt. Wenn die erforderlichen Ressourcen, wie Personal und Video-Equipment, nicht direkt von der Agentur aufgebracht werden können, muss ein externes Videoteam beauftragt werden.

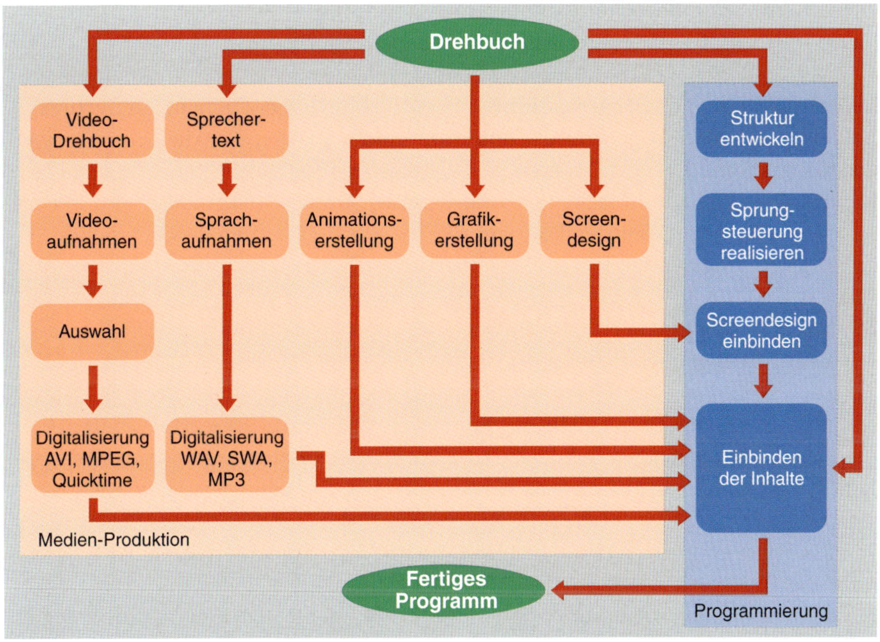

Prinzipieller Workflow vom Drehbuch bis zur Programmierung. Ausgehend vom Drehbuch werden die einzelnen Medien (Assets) hergestellt. Parallel dazu wird das Programmgerüst vom Programmierer aufgebaut. Mit den Screendesign-Elementen der Grafiker baut er die funktionierende Bedienungsoberfläche auf. Sobald die Assets produziert sind, können sie entsprechend der Drehbuch-Vorgaben in das Programm eingebaut werden.

Tonaufnahmen spalten sich üblicherweise in reine Sprecheraufnahmen, die auf Basis des aus dem Drehbuch extrahierten Sprechertextes entstehen, dem **O-Ton** ❶ und einer eventuellen Musikuntermalung. Der Sprechertext wird in einem speziellen Sprachaufnahme-Studio hergestellt. Ein professioneller Sprecher, z. B. vom Rundfunk, spricht die vorbereiteten Texte auf Band. O-Ton kann entweder während der Videoaufnahmen mitgeschnitten werden oder separat im Nachhinein aufgenommen werden. Hintergrund-Musik oder auch Trailer-Sounds werden entweder aus der Konserve, d. h. aus bestehenden Audio-CDs, oder individuell für diesen Anwendungszweck komponiert und produziert. Hierbei müssen selbstverständlich die üblichen GEMA-Bedingungen beachtet werden.

❶ Unter **Originalton (O-Ton)** versteht man Bild-Tonsynchrone, ursprüngliche Tonaufzeichnungen, die während den Dreharbeiten entstehen.

Die Arbeit der Screendesigner und Grafiker wird aufgeteilt in die Erstellung der Grafikelemente für das Screendesign und die Inhalts-Grafiken bzw. der Animationen.

Ist der Screendesigner bzw. Grafiker während der Konzeptionsphase nicht in die Produktion involviert worden, so ist das beschlossene Grafikkonzept zur Grafik- und Animationsherstellung mit dem Konzeptionisten durchzusprechen.

Dies ist deshalb von Bedeutung, da die Grafiken und Animationen nicht für sich allein betrachtet werden sollten, sondern immer in das visuelle Gesamtbild der Multimedia-Produktion einbezogen werden müssen.

Programmieren

Der Programmierprozess kann entweder nach Fertigstellung der einzelnen Medien (Grafiken, Videos, Ton etc.) erfolgen, oder, wie es in der Praxis üblich ist, **zeitgleich** mit der Medienproduktion.

Zuerst wird die entwickelte Struktur mit dem **Autorensystem** umgesetzt. Dabei wird die Sprungsteuerung mit allen Verknüpfungen vorangelegt.

Stehen die Buttons und Grafiken für die Benutzerführung noch nicht zur Verfügung, so können sie durch sogenannte „Dummies" ersetzt werden. Für die Dummies werden als grafische Elemente vorwiegend System-Standards des Autorensystems verwendet. Dies können einfache Standard-Buttons, simple Blockgrafiken und System-Schriften sein. Während der Programmierphase ist es immer wieder wichtig, die eigentlichen Programmteile ausführlich zu testen.

➲ **Wichtig ist, dass zuerst das gesamte Programmgerüst funktionsfähig ist und ausführlich getestet wurde.**

Nach dieser sehr wichtigen Phase der **Evaluation** ❶ wird das Screen-Layout in das fertige Gerüst implementiert. Jetzt sollte das Programm in einem größerem Kreis hinsichtlich der Benutzerführung und der Akzeptanz des Kunden getestet werden.

❶ Unter **Evaluation** versteht man die sachgerechte Bewertung des Medienprodukts hinsichtlich der Akzeptanz und der Wirkung beim Benutzer.

❷ **Digitale Assets** sind im allgemeinen Texte, Grafiken und andere Medienelemente, die den Inhalt (Content) der Medienproduktion darstellen.

Ist diese Phase erfolgreich bestanden, so kann mit dem **Implementieren** der Programminhalte begonnen werden. Hierzu werden sequentiell, auf Basis des Drehbuches, mit dem verwendeten Autorensystem die **Assets** ❷ (Medienelemente) in die vorgefertigte Struktur einprogrammiert und mit Animation und Interaktion so verknüpft, dass daraus ein multimediales, interaktives Programm entsteht.

Dem Testen der Benutzerführung (Usability-Test) kommt eine besondere Bedeutung zu. Ist nämlich die Benutzerführung des Programms zielgruppengerecht aufgebaut und einfach nachvollziehbar, hat man bereits die erste Stufe der Akzeptanz des Benutzers für das Programm gesichert.

Prototyp-Erstellung

Während des Programmierens ist es immer wieder wichtig, die einzelnen Phasen ausführlich zu testen. Zuerst wird intern für die Programmierung ein **Prototyp** für das Programmgerüst und die Sprungsteuerung erstellt. An ihm wird das Sprungverhalten, die Verknüpfungssicherheit und das Zeitverhalten der Navigation gestestet.

Als Testperson sollte nie der Programmierer fungieren, denn er ist von seinem Produkt zu befangen, um es neutral zu testen. Geeignet sind Personen, die zwar mit Multimedia-Produktionen vertraut sind, aber das spezielle Programm nicht kennen.

Als nächster Schritt sollte das **Design** überprüft werden. Hierzu werden die ersten Versionen der Buttons und aller sonstigen Navigationselemente in den ersten Prototyp implementiert und möglichst einer programmierneutralen Zielgruppe – im Idealfall einzelne Repräsentanten der späteren Programm-Nutzer – zum Testen vorgeführt. Dieser Prozess wird „Usability-Test" ❶ genannt. Dabei unterscheidet man die subjektive von objektiver Usability. Unter **subjektiver Usability** versteht man den persönlichen Eindruck der Testperson vom Programm. **Objektive Usability** hingegen ist der Eindruck, wie die Testperson das Programm gemäß den Erwartungen des Herstellers bedient. Je nach Projekt kann das in speziellen „Usability Labs" ❷ erfolgen, in denen Testpersonen unter realen Bedingungen den Prototyp bedienen:

- Es werden Aufgabenszenarien vorgegeben.
- Während der Nutzungsphase werden die Testpersonen beobachtet und die verschiedenen Parameter der Nutzung (Fehlversuche, spontane Äußerungen) protokolliert.
- Im Anschluss werden die Testpersonen schriftlich befragt.

❶ Nach der Norm ISO 9241 versteht man unter **Usability** die einfache Erlernbarkeit (intuitive Verständlichkeit) eines Systems, die Berücksichtigung von Vorwissen (Erwartungskonformität, und die Fehlerrobustheit (Fehlertoleranz).

❷ **Usability Labs** bieten simulierte Nutzungsumgebungen zum Testen von Programmen in möglichst realitätsnahen Bedingungen.

Danach wird der Prototyp entsprechend den Ergebnissen modifiziert und wenn möglich, in einem weiteren Testlauf evaluiert. Damit sollen Nutzungsbarrieren identifiziert und Optimierungspotenziale aufgedeckt werden, denn:

➲ **Die Technik soll sich am Menschen orientieren und nicht umgekehrt!**

Jetzt sollte das Programm mit aussagekräftigem Inhalt gefüllt werden. Das sollten Medienelemente wie Texte, Videos, Grafiken etc. sein, die für eine überschaubare Menge sachlich und fachlich dem Endprodukt entsprechen sollten. Die Prototyp-Prozedur, bei der der Kunde mit einbezogen sein soll, hängt individuell vom Kunden und dessen Anforderungen ab.

Bei größeren Medienproduktionen kann auch ein komplettes Thema als Prototyp zur Evaluation hergestellt werden. Dabei verfolgt der Auftraggeber das Ziel, die Akzeptanz des Medienprodukts bei der Zielgruppe sicherzustellen.

Vor der entgültigen Fertigstellung des Programms kann auch noch über eine **Beta-Version**, die an ausgewählte Kunden geliefert wird, eine letzte Qualitätssicherung erfolgen. Hierbei ist die Logistik und Gewichtung der Feedbacks unbedingt vorher zu planen und der Test-Zielgruppe entsprechend mitzuteilen.

Je früher mögliche Änderungen in den Produktionsprozess einfließen, desto kosteneffizienter können sie umgesetzt werden.

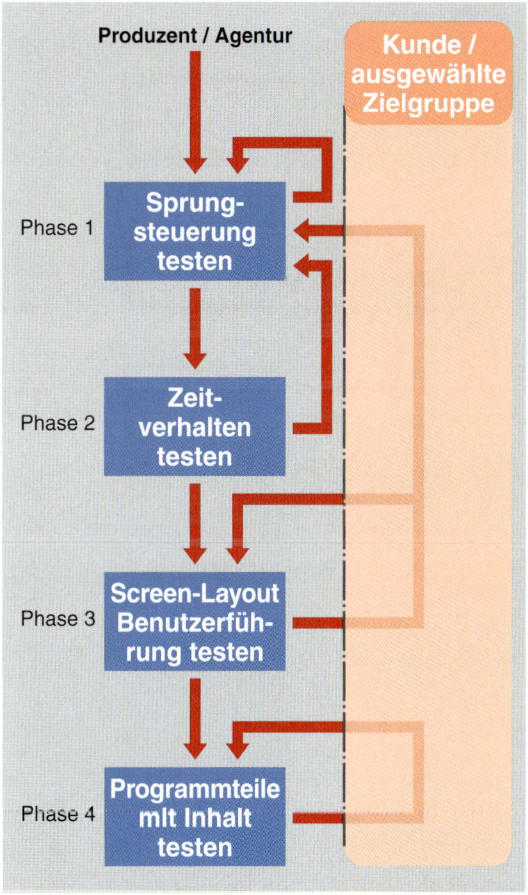

Unterschiedliche Prototypen begleiten den gesamten Produktionsprozess einer Multimedia-Anwendung. Beispiel einer mehrstufigen Überprüfung der Produktion, teils mit Einbeziehen des Kunden und auserwählten Zielgruppen.

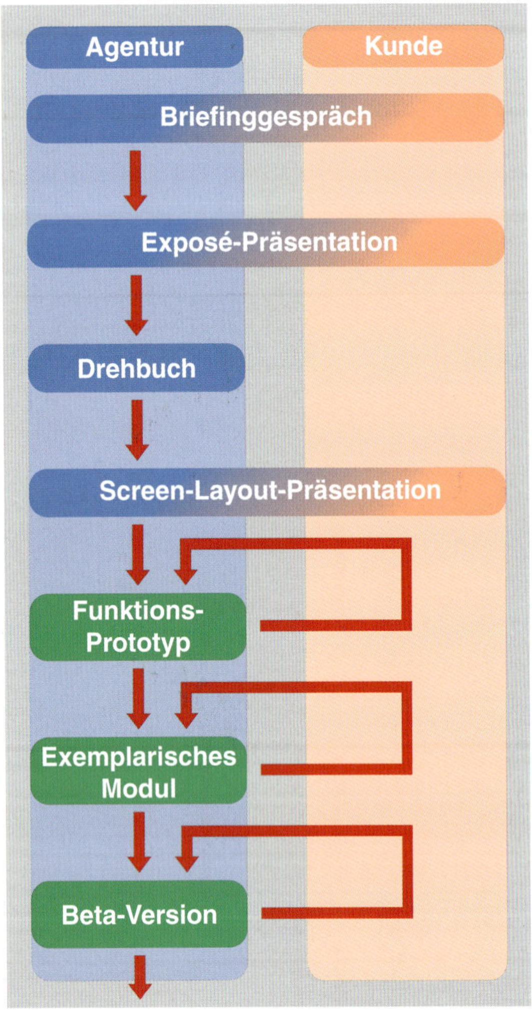

Beispiel einer Abnahme-Prozedur

Präsentationen und Abnahmen

Wenn die Multimedia-Produktion fertig gestellt und ausreichend getestet worden ist, muss die endgültige Version dem **Kunden** vorgeführt werden.

Es gilt, nicht nur die endgültige Version zu präsentieren, sondern auch alle aussagefähigen Zwischenschritte. Damit wird dem Kunden das Gefühl gegeben, jederzeit über den Stand der Produktion Bescheid zu wissen. Gleichzeitig kann der Dienstleister schon frühzeitig die Akzeptanz des Kunden abfragen, um auf Richtungsänderungen dynamisch reagieren zu können. Meist wird der Kunde nicht nur von einer einzigen Person verkörpert, sondern es sprechen mehrere Mitarbeiter mit, teils sogar aus unterschiedlichen Tätigkeitsfeldern, sei es der PR-Beauftragte, die eigene Werbeabteilung oder die Fachberater, die für die Inhalte zuständig sind. Präsentationen von Arbeitsergebnissen können je nach Projekt und Kunde sehr unterschiedlich sein.

➲ **Wichtig ist, dass die Präsentations- und Abnahmeprozedur im Vorfeld genau festgelegt wird.**

Grundlegende Änderungen in einem späteren Stadium der Produktion können den Aufwand überproportional in die Höhe treiben. Die Änderungsdurchläufe bei den Abnahmeprozeduren sollten durch Projektvereinbarungen definiert werden, da sonst der Änderungsaufwand nicht kalkulierbar ist. Diese Projektvereinbarungen sollten genau definierte Abnahmen der Teilergebnisse vorsehen. Diese Abnahmen erfordern aber auch vom Kunden ein besonderes Maß an Vorstellungsvermögen für die entstehende Produktion. Durch anschauliche Präsentationen der Teilergebnisse kann das Produktionsteam diesen Informationstransfer sicherstellen.

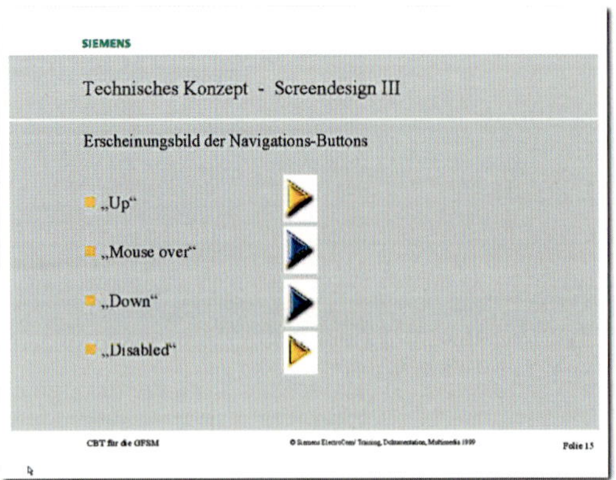

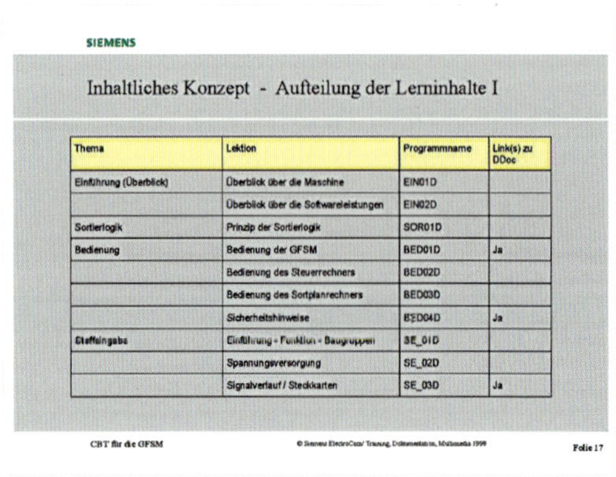

Thema	Lektion	Programmname	Link(s) zu DDoc
Einführung (Überblick)	Überblick über die Maschine	EIN01D	
	Überblick über die Softwareleistungen	EIN02D	
Sortierlogik	Prinzip der Sortierlogik	SOR01D	
Bedienung	Bedienung der GFSM	BED01D	Ja
	Bedienung des Steuerrechners	BED02D	
	Bedienung des Sortplanrechners	BED03D	
	Sicherheitshinweise	BED04D	Ja
Staffeingabe	Einführung - Funktion - Baugruppen	SE_01D	
	Spannungsversorgung	SE_02D	
	Signalverlauf / Steckkarten	SE_03D	Ja

Auszüge aus einer umfangreichen Exposé-Präsentation zur Abnahme beim Kunden

19.6.4 Einführung

Das Finishing

Ist das Programm fertiggestellt, abgenommen und getestet worden, so erfolgt der letzte Schritt der Produktion: Die Herstellung der Form und Prozedur, wie das Produkt den Kunden erreichen soll. Hierzu gehört z. B.:

- die Wahl des Datenträgers,
- die Installation des Programms,
- die Verpackung des Produktes.

Der Datenträger:
Welcher Datenträger gewählt werden soll, hängt von mehreren Kriterien ab:

- Wie umfangreich ist das Programm?
- Wie hoch ist die Auflage (Stückzahl)?
- Welche Datenträgerarten kann die Zielgruppe lesen?

Zur Auswahl stehen für den Offline-Bereich heutzutage primär **CD-ROMs** ❶, **DVDs** ❷ und **Blu-ray Disc** ❸. Im Online-Bereich kann das Programm entweder über das Internet angeschaut werden (z. B. als „Web Based Training" ❹), oder es wird über das Internet kopiert (Download-Vorgang) und dann lokal gestartet.

❶ Datenträger „CD-ROM / DVD"

❷ **DVDs** (Digital Versatile Disc) können zwischen 4,7 GB und 17 GB Daten aufnehmen.

❸ **BDs** (Blue-ray Disc) können als Single Layer bis zu 25 GB Daten aufnehmen.

❹ **Web Based Training** (WBT) ist die Online-Form von Computer Based Training (CBT).

Die Installation:
Um das Multimedia-Programm beim Kunden lauffähig zu machen, bedarf es üblicherweise einer Installations-Routine ❺, die je nach Installations-Konzept

- das Programm in die Benutzeroberfläche einbindet,
- zum Ablauf notwendige Runtime-Programme auf die lokale Festplatte installiert,
- das gesamte Programm auf die lokale Festplatte installiert.

Dem Endanwender (Zielgruppe) werden innerhalb dieser Prozedur gewisse Einflussmöglichkeiten angeboten. Dies erhöht die Transparenz der Installationsprozedur und sorgt für eine bessere Akzeptanz beim Benutzer.

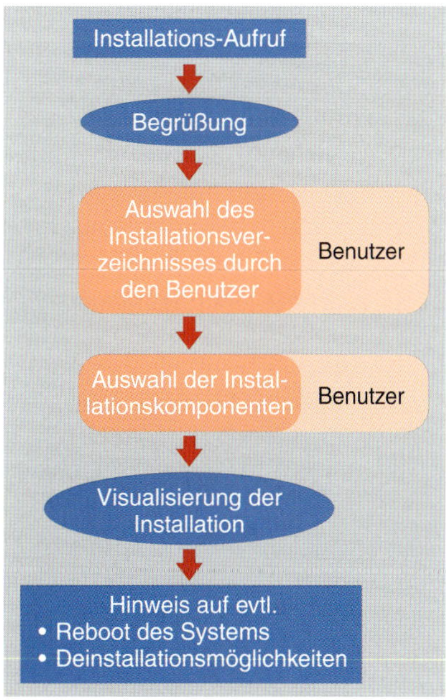

❺ Prinzip einer Installations-Routine

Jewelcase mit Booklet

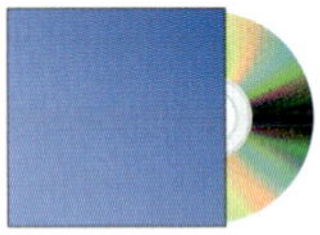

Hardcover

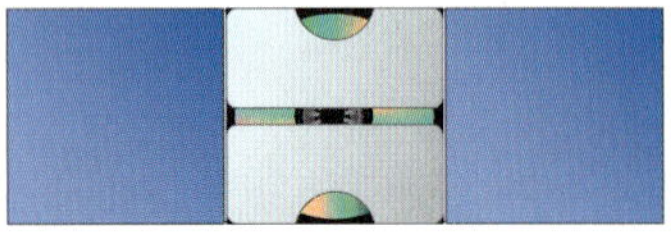

Sonderformat

Verpackungsbeispiel „Digipak“ (Beispiel: Deutsche Post AG)

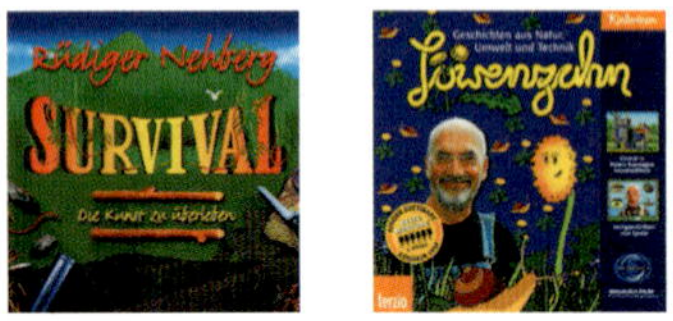

Booklet-Titelseiten (Beispiel: SURVIVAL - Rüdiger Nehberg und Löwenzahn – Terzio Verlag)

Beispiel: CD-ROM-Label eines Lernprogramms (Beispiel: Siemens AG)

Originelle Verpackungsart: CD-ROM, integriert in ein Mouse-Pad (Beispiel: Siemens ElectroCom)

Die Verpackung:
Nun gilt es, den Datenträger, auf dem das Multimedia-Programm gespeichert ist, zu verpacken. Der Datenträger kann auf die unterschiedlichsten Arten verpackt werden:

- Integriert im Begleitmaterial (Buch)
- Jewelcase mit Booklet
- Hardcover
- Buchähnliche Sonderformate z. B. „discArt“ oder „Digipak“

Die Evaluation:
Zusätzlich zu den Evaluationsstufen, die während einer Multimedia-Produktion durchgeführt werden können, wie Testing, Prototyping etc., kann eine nach Fertigstellung der Produktion folgende Evaluierung der Akzeptanz und des Produkterfolges stattfinden. Maßgeblich entscheidend an der Art und Weise dieser Evaluation sind zum einen die Produktart, z. B. CBT oder Informationssystem, und zum anderen die Rahmenbedingungen des Produkteinsatzes.

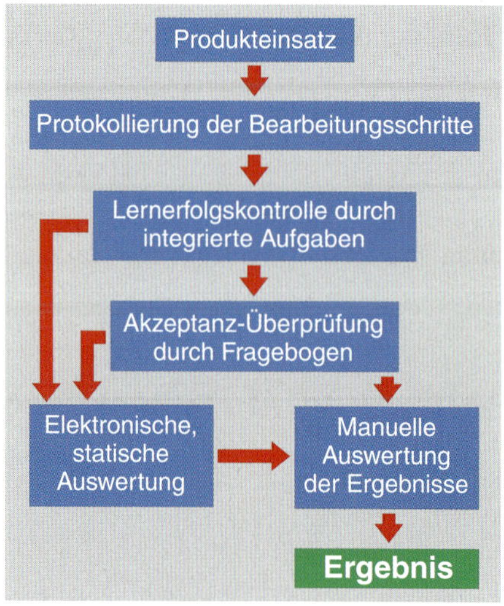

Beispiel von Evaluationsstufen bei CBT.

Die Evaluationsstufen können auf unterschiedliche Weise durchgeführt werden:

- Elektronische Navigations- und Bearbeitungsprotokollierung
- Elektronische Erfolgskontrolle durch Testaufgaben
- Elektronisches Quiz
- Elektronischer Fragebogen
- Schriftliche Auswertung über Fragebogenaktion

Wie diese Ergebnisse vom Benutzer des Systems zum Hersteller zurückgeleitet werden, hängt vom Einsatzumfeld des Produktes ab.
Beispiele für Rücklauf-Kanäle:

- Schriftliches Feedback über den Postweg
- Elektronisches Feedback über E-Mail
- Elektronisches Feedback über ein Web-Interface
- Lokales Feedback-Speichern und Selbstabholung durch den Hersteller

Akzeptanzüberprüfungen erfordern ein gewisses Maß an Aktivität und Bereitschaft vom Benutzer. Um dies zu fördern und zu unterstützen, gibt es die unterschiedlichsten Methoden der Anreizsteigerung, zum Beispiel:

- Preisausschreiben, bzw. Quiz
- Verlosungen
- Frei-Briefumschläge
- Werbegeschenke

19.7 Gestaltungsaspekte in der Produktentwicklung

Mit dem Begriff **Designprozess** beschreibt man die Entwicklungsphasen eines Produkts im Bereich der **Gestaltung**. Dieser Prozess sollte im Idealfall parallel zur Konstruktion, Entwicklung und Planung der Fertigung laufen.

Der Designer entwickelt jedoch nicht nur die äußere Gestalt nach Gesichtspunkten der Ästhetik, sondern trägt durch seine Entwürfe maßgeblich dazu bei, die Funktionalität positiv zu beeinflussen und verfahrenstechnische Abläufe zu optimieren.

Schlagworte zum Thema **Design**, **Produkt** und **Firma**:

- Innovationen brauchen Design
- Design erzeugt Höherwertigkeit
- Design formt Identität
- Design gibt Profil
- Design gestaltet Unternehmenskultur
- Design macht Marken

Quelle: Peter Zec: Mit Design auf Erfolgskurs, Köln 1998

Bei der Vielzahl der auf dem Markt befindlichen gleichartigen Produkte mit ähnlichen Funktionen wird es immer schwieriger, das eigene Produkt von den Konkurrenzprodukten abzuheben. In diesem Zusammenhang werden von den Produzenten **zwei Aspekte** verfolgt. Entweder wird der Gebrauchswert des Produkts konstant gehalten und die Herstellungskosten können gesenkt werden, oder der Gebrauchswert steigt bei möglichst gleichbleibenden Herstellungskosten. Unter diesen Gesichtspunkten kommt dem Gestalter nicht nur die Aufgabe zu, ein gutes Design zu entwickeln, er muss sich darüber hinaus verstärkt mit kalkulatorischen und konstruktiven Fragen bei Neuproduktionen und Überarbeitungen beschäftigen. Der für den Gestalter zentrale Designprozess gliedert sich in die **Phasen** Aufgabenstellung, Konzeptentwurf und Designentwurf. Mit der Umsetzung der Entwürfe und der Präsentation ist die gestalterische Arbeit abgeschlossen.

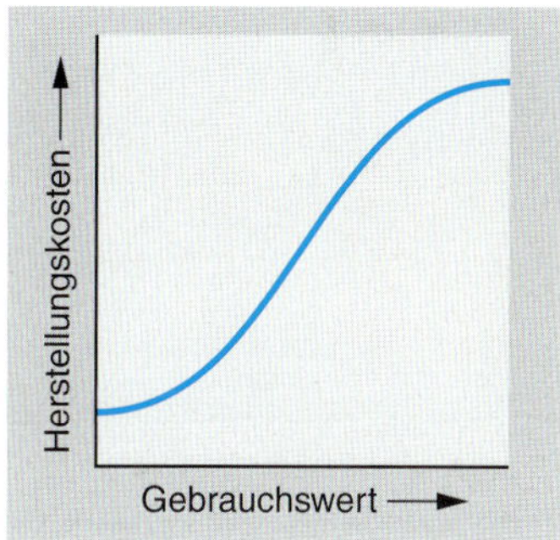

Steigen die Herstellungskosten, dann muss auch der Gebrauchswert steigen!

19.7.1 Phasen der Produktgestaltung

Aufgabe

Die Aufgabenstellung wird vom Auftraggeber in einem **Pflichtenheft** formuliert. Damit liegt die Zielvorstellung fest und der Designer kann erste Untersuchungen und Recherchen durchführen sowie Gestaltungsansätze entwickeln:

- Ist-Zustand erfassen und mit der neuen Zielvorstellung abgleichen.
- Erfassen der Einflüsse auf die Gestaltung durch firmenspezifische Vorgaben.
- Kulturelle und marktspezifische Einflüsse feststellen.
- Konkurrenzprodukte recherchieren und gegen das eigene Produkt abgrenzen.
- Zukünftige Entwicklungen und Anforderungen untersuchen.
- Richtlinien und Normen zum Produkt zusammenstellen.

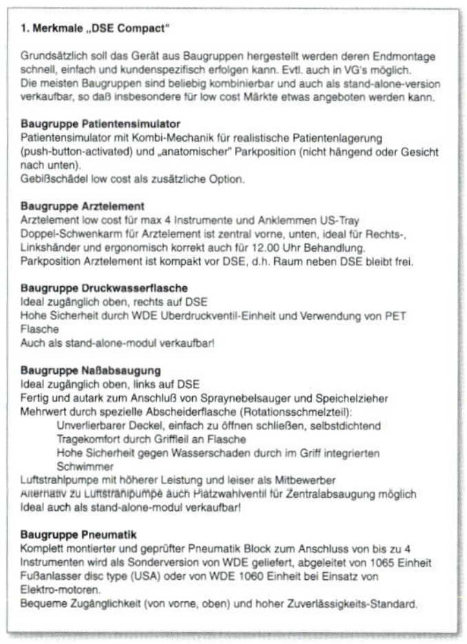

1. Merkmale „DSE Compact"

Grundsätzlich soll das Gerät aus Baugruppen hergestellt werden deren Endmontage schnell, einfach und kundenspezifisch erfolgen kann. Evtl. auch in VG's möglich. Die meisten Baugruppen sind beliebig kombinierbar und auch als stand-alone-version verkaufbar, so daß insbesondere für low cost Märkte etwas angeboten werden kann.

Baugruppe Patientensimulator
Patientensimulator mit Kombi-Mechanik für realistische Patientenlagerung (push-button-activated) und „anatomischer" Parkposition (nicht hängend oder Gesicht nach unten).
Gebißschädel low cost als zusätzliche Option.

Baugruppe Arztelement
Arztelement low cost für max 4 Instrumente und Anklemmen US-Tray
Doppel-Schwenkarm für Arztelement ist zentral vorne, unten, ideal für Rechts-, Linkshänder und ergonomisch korrekt auch für 12.00 Uhr Behandlung.
Parkposition Arztelement ist kompakt vor DSE, d.h. Raum neben DSE bleibt frei.

Baugruppe Druckwasserflasche
Ideal zugänglich oben, rechts auf DSE
Hohe Sicherheit durch WDE Uberdruckventil-Einheit und Verwendung von PET Flasche
Auch als stand-alone-modul verkaufbar!

Baugruppe Naßabsaugung
Ideal zugänglich oben, links auf DSE
Fertig und autark zum Anschluß von Spraynebelsauger und Speichelzieher
Mehrwert durch spezielle Abscheiderflasche (Rotationsschmelzteil):
Unverlierbarer Deckel, einfach zu öffnen schließen, selbstdichtend
Tragekomfort durch Griffleil an Flasche
Hohe Sicherheit gegen Wasserschaden durch im Griff integrierten Schwimmer
Luftstrahlpumpe mit höherer Leistung und leiser als Mitbewerber
Alternativ zu Luftstrahlpumpe auch Platzwahlventil für Zentralabsaugung möglich
Ideal auch als stand-alone-modul verkaufbar!

Baugruppe Pneumatik
Komplett montierter und geprüfter Pneumatik Block zum Anschluss von bis zu 4 Instrumenten wird als Sonderversion von WDE geliefert, abgeleitet von 1065 Einheit Fußanlasser disc type (USA) oder von WDE 1060 Einheit bei Einsatz von Elektro-motoren.
Bequeme Zugänglichkeit (von vorne, oben) und hoher Zuverlässigkeits-Standard.

Konzeption

In der Phase der Ideenfindung werden Skizzen angefertigt und verschiedene Lösungsansätze ❶ erarbeitet, die auf Funktionalität, Ästhetik und Einhaltung konstruktiver Merkmale geprüft werden. In dieser Phase beschäftigen sich die Gestalter mit folgenden Projektgrundlagen:

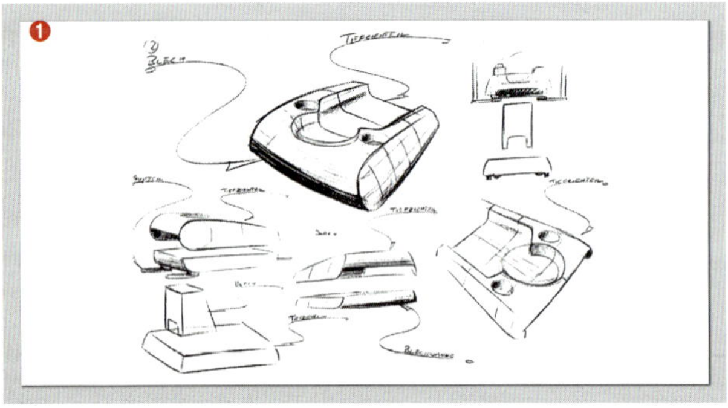

- Arbeitsablaufstudien
- Fragen der Bedienung
- Handhabungs- und Funktionssimulation
- Maßzeichnungen
- Fragen der Ergonomie und den zu erwarteten Kosten
- Material- und Farbauswahl, Gestaltung von Oberflächen
- Erste Modelle

Designentwurf

Im Konzeptentwurf werden häufig mehrere Ideen parallel aufgegriffen und weiterentwickelt. Mit der tiefergehenden Ausarbeitung des Projekts in den Bereichen Form, Farbe, Maße, Material, Oberfläche und Merkmale der Gestalt, wird ein Entwurf übrig bleiben, der auf das firmenspezifische Erscheinungsbild zugeschnitten wird ❷.

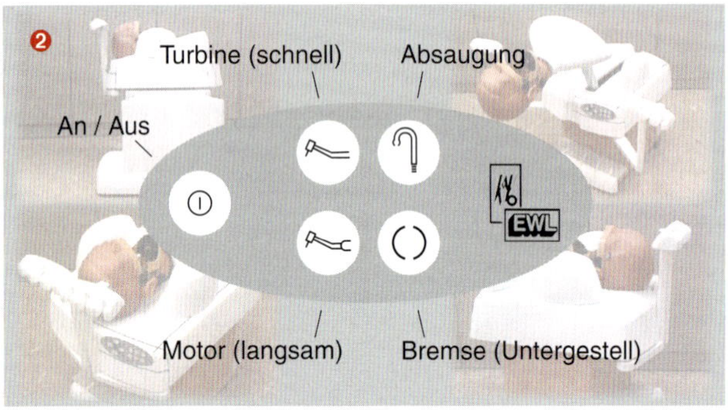

Dabei vermitteln die Maßzeichnungen der Einzelteile und die Gesamtzeichnung einen Eindruck von der späteren Gestalt und Größe des Produkts.
Folgende **Arbeiten** fallen in dieser dritten Phase an:

- Detailausarbeitungen von Griffen, Druckknöpfen u. a.
- Oberflächengestaltung
- Kostenrechnung und -prüfung
- Materialauswahl
- Abstimmung von Entwurf und Konstruktion
- Modellbau
- Einzelteilzeichnung zu den endgültigen Entwürfen

Den Abschluss der Arbeiten bildet eine **Dokumentation** ❸, in welcher der Kunde alle Designschritte nachvollziehen kann. In der abschließenden Präsentation wird der Entwicklungsprozess im Vortrag vorgestellt.

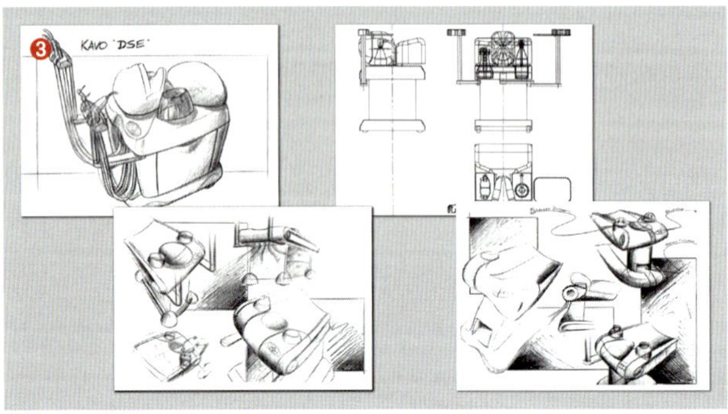

Für nachfolgende Werbemaßnahmen bedient man sich gerne der Entwürfe für das Produkt, wie das Beispiel des Prospekts zum dentalen Patienten-Simulator zeigt ❹. Dadurch können die verschiedenen Darstellungen mehrfach genutzt werden.

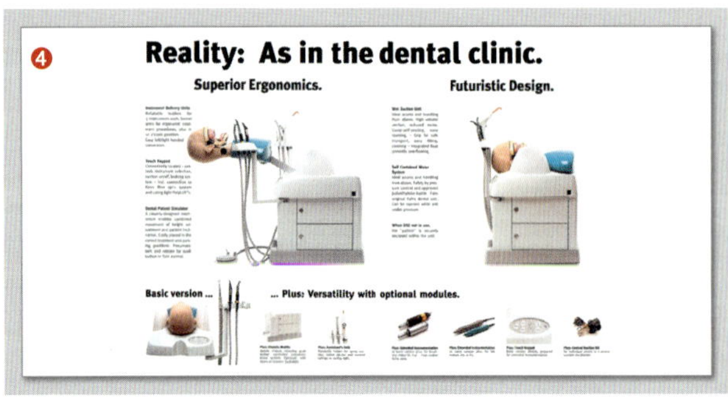

19.7.2 Produktbeispiele

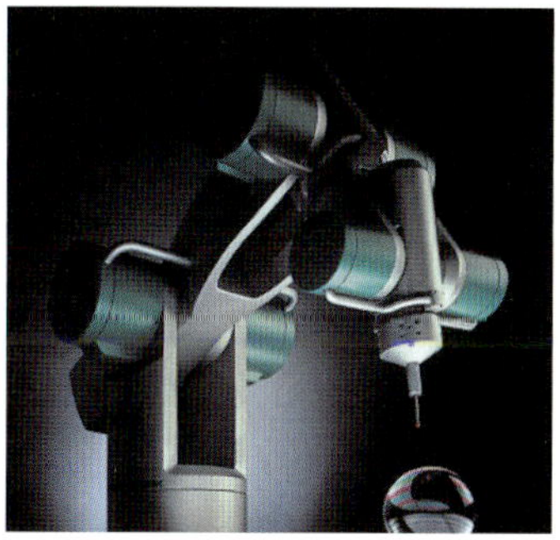

Auf der Basis der **Gliederung des Designprozesses** in die Phasen Aufgabe, Konzeption und Designentwurf entwickelten die Agenturen weitere Modelle, nach denen der Designprozess ablaufen kann. Um eine genauere Differenzierung der Projektschritte zu erhalten, lässt sich der Prozess grundsätzlich in insgesamt **sechs Phasen** unterteilen, die in sich abgeschlossen werden können:

- Phase 1: Untersuchung des Ist-Zustands
- Phase 2: Erarbeiten möglicher Lösungsansätze
- Phase 3: Festlegen des Lösungsweges
- Phase 4: Umsetzung in Entwürfen (Grafiken, Zeichnungen, Modelle)
- Phase 5: Vorproduktion: Erstellen von Teilzeichnungen, Dateien für Brands, Datenbanken für CD-Produktionen u. a.
- Phase 6: Produktion: Fertigung des Produkts, CD-Programmierung, Printproduktion

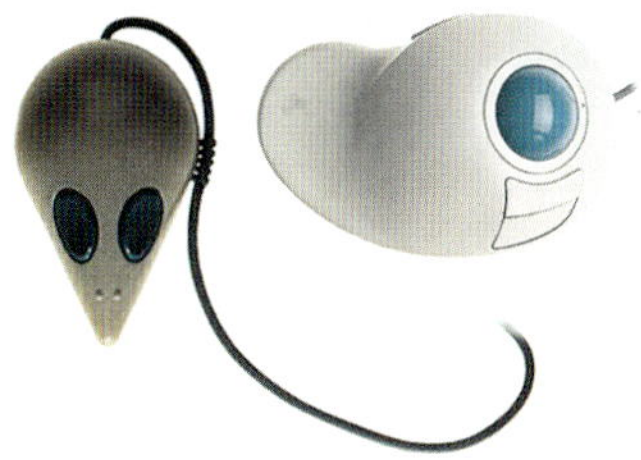

Je nach Mitarbeitergröße der Agentur und Vorhandensein fachlich geeigneter Mitarbeiter gestaltet sich das Dienstleistungsangebot und die daraus entstehenden Aufgabenstellungen, wie in der Bildleiste zu erkennen, unterschiedlich umfangreich. So kann es heute durchaus sein, dass große Designagenturen nicht allein den gestalterischen Teil des Produkts abdecken, sondern auch die gesamte Entwicklung mit den entsprechenden Ingenieurleistungen anbieten können. Damit lassen sich für eine große Agentur folgende Tätigkeitsfelder beschreiben:

- Klassisches Grafikdesign im Bereich Konzeption, Entwurf und Corporate Design
- Industriedesign mit Entwicklung und Gestaltung von Produkten
- Ingenieurdienstleistung in Entwicklung und Konstruktion, CAD
- CD-Präsentationen, Internetauftritte, Virtual Reality

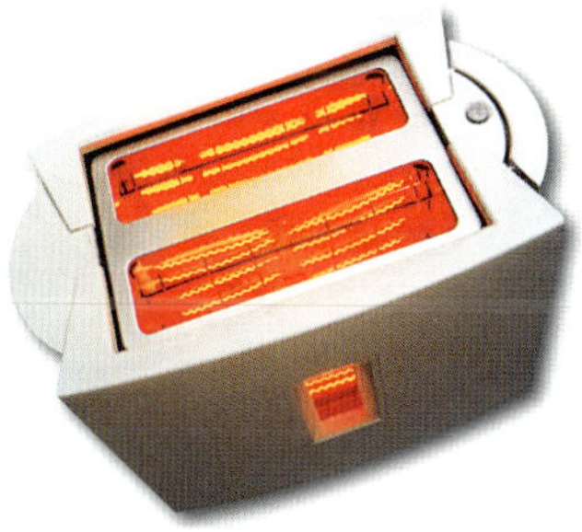

Anhand von drei Beispielen werden die möglichen Tätigkeitsfelder im Bild dargestellt und sind jeweils farbig markiert. Die Arbeiten sind in sechs Phasen gegliedert, wobei durch die Auftragsvergabe nicht immer alle Phasen durchlaufen werden müssen.

Produkt 1 Toaster: Die Aufgabe bestand darin, einen dem Markenzeichen verpflichteten Entwurf zu entwickeln, der zeitlos ist und der alle technologischen Vorteile eines modernen Toasters beinhaltet. Darüber hinaus entstand eine neuartige Idee, ein Sichtfenster einzubauen, um den Bräunungsgrad auch visuell wahrnehmen zu können.

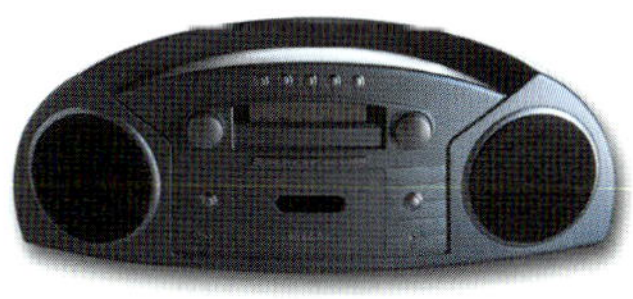

Produkt 2 Dual: Ziel dieser Aufgabenstellung war es, das Markenzeichen „Dual“ eines Konzerns wieder einzuführen. Die Aufgabe gliederte sich in die Überarbeitung des Schriftzugs und die Entwicklung einer Produktpalette von Radio- und Fernsehgeräten für den Endverbraucher.

Produkt 3 CD-ROM: Mit dem Einsatz von Video, 3-D-Animation und Virtual Reality werden auf einer CD-ROM die Produkte einer Computerfirma interaktiv vorgestellt.

Produktentwicklung

Die drei Beispiele werden in ihrer Entstehung durch eine Bildfolge dargestellt. Durch farbige Verlaufslinien sind die jeweiligen Tätigkeitsbereiche der Agentur frogdesign, das Grafikdesign, die Neuen Medien, das Industriedesign und die Ingenieurleistungen dargestellt. In den Spalten sind die sechs Entstehungsphasen, mit den entsprechenden Abbildungen, für den gesamten Designprozess dargestellt.

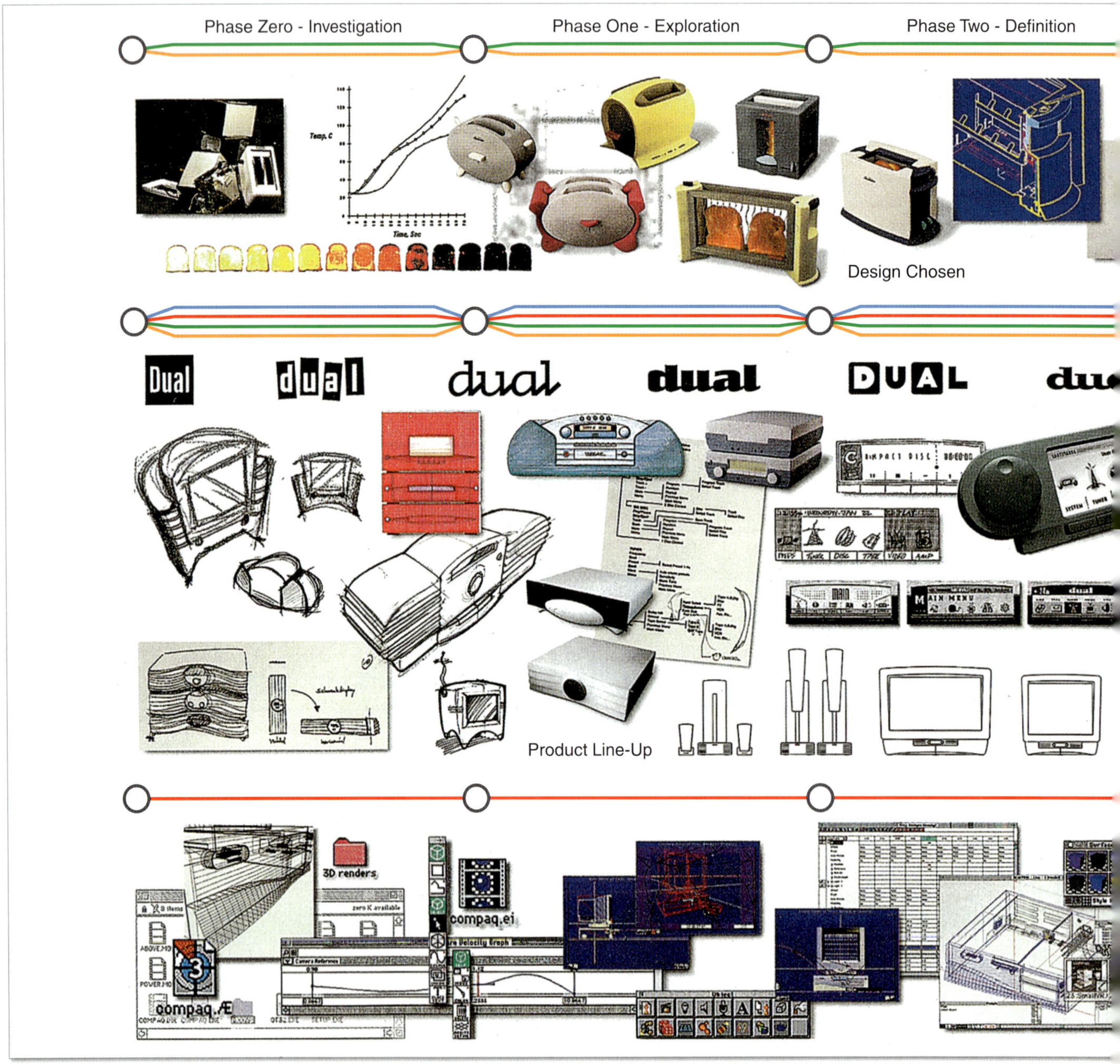

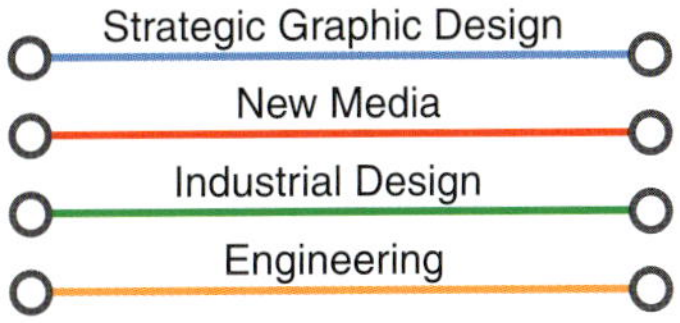

Strategic Graphic Design, Entwurf , Planung und Zeichnung
New Media, Neue Medien wie CD-ROM und Internet
Industrial Design, Industrie Design
Engineering, Ingenieurleistung und Konstruktion
Agentur frogdesign, Altensteig

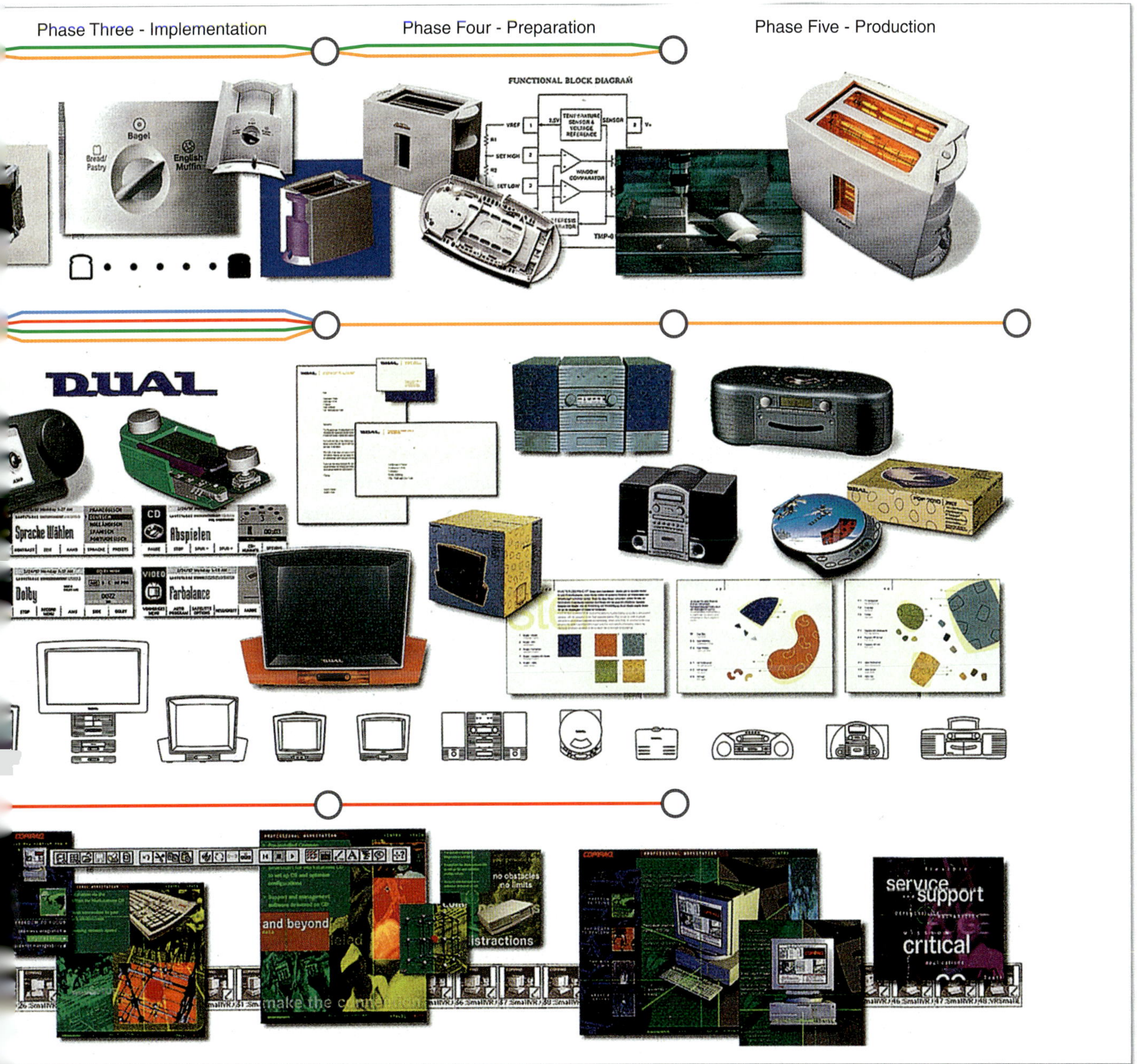

Aufgaben und Übungen, Literaturhinweise

Aufgaben und Übungen

1. Verfassen Sie zu einem Thema Ihrer Wahl einen Zeitungsartikel und stellen Sie dar, welche Schritte geschehen müssen, bis dieser Artikel in der Tageszeitung abgedruckt ist.
2. Beurteilen Sie das vorliegende Buch danach, welche Prozessschritte abgelaufen sind, bis es in fertiger Form in Ihrer Hand liegt.
3. Erstellen Sie einen Radio-Beitrag zu einem frei gewählten Thema unter Einsatz von Amateur-Equipment. Analysieren Sie Ihre Vorgehensweise.
4. Wählen Sie einen Kino-Spielfilm aus, den Sie gut kennen. Stellen Sie dar, welche Produktionsschritte vollzogen werden mussten, um diesen Film zu erstellen. Nehmen Sie Stellung zu den besonderen Schwierigkeiten, die mutmaßlich bei der Produktion aufgetreten sind.
5. Gehen Sie auf die Suche nach einem aus Ihrer Sicht „einfachen Fernsehfilm". Begründen Sie, warum Sie dieser Auffassung sind.
6. Sie planen eine Multimedia-Produktion für eine Selbstdarstellung. Verfassen Sie ein kleines Exposé.
7. Entwerfen Sie beispielhaft für einige Bildschirmseiten ein Drehbuch Ihrer Produktion.
8. Skizzieren Sie den notwendigen Produktionsprozess Ihrer Multimedia-Anwendung.
9. Bilden Sie für Ihre Produktion das notwendige Produktionsteam. Beschreiben Sie, welche Funktion und Aufgaben jedes Teammitglied hat.
10. Ordnen Sie die Verantwortlichkeit Ihrer Teammitglieder den einzelnen Produktionsprozess-Schritten zu. Verwenden Sie dazu die Skizze aus Aufgabe 8.
11. Ihr Programm ist fertig. Beschreiben Sie jetzt, wie das Programm zum Benutzer gelangt und wie es verpackt und „designt" werden soll.
12. Gestalten Sie Sitzmöbel für Schreibtische, von der Skizze bis zum fertigen Entwurf mit Einzelteilzeichnungen. Erstellen Sie dazu eine Dokumentation und eine Computer-Präsentation.

Literaturhinweise

Allgemein zur Medienproduktion:

Gläser, Martin: Medienmanagement, 2. Aufl., München 2010 (Vahlen)
Hermanni, Alfred-Joachim: Medienmanagement, München 2007 (dtv-Taschenbuch)
Klimsa, Paul: Produktionssteuerung – Grundlagen der Medienproduktion, in: Scholz, Christian (Hrsg.): Handbuch Medienmanagement, Berlin, Heidelberg, New York 2006 (Springer), S. 601-617
Krömker, Heidi; *Klimsa*, Paul (Hrsg.): Handbuch Medienproduktion, Wiesbaden 2005 (VS Verlag)
Wirtz, Bernd W.: Medien- und Internetmanagement, 7. Aufl., Wiesbaden 2011 (Gabler)

Produktionsprozesse Print:

Kerlen, Dietrich: Lehrbuch der Buchverlagswirtschaft, Stuttgart 2003 (Hauswedell)
Kipphan, Helmut (Hrsg.): Handbuch der Printmedien, Berlin et al. 2000 (Springer)
Lucius, Wolf D. von: Verlagswirtschaft, 2. Aufl., Stuttgart 2007 (UVK)
Röhring, Hans-Helmut: Wie ein Buch entsteht, Darmstadt 2003 (Wissenschaftliche Buchgesellschaft)

Produktionsprozesse Radio:

Blohmer, Helge; Erdmann, Matthias: Hörfunktechnik – Die digitale Radioproduktion, in: Krömker, Heidi; Klimsa, Paul (Hrsg.): Handbuch Medienproduktion, Wiesbaden 2005 (VS Verlag), S. 243-262
Müller, Dieter K.; Raff, Esther (Hrsg.): Praxiswissen Radio, Wiesbaden 2007 (VS Verlag)
Sturm, Robert; Zirbik, Jürgen: Die Radio-Station, Konstanz 1996 (UVK)

Produktionsprozesse Film:

Clevé, Bastian (Hrsg.): Von der Idee zum Film, 5. Aufl., Konstanz 2009 (UVK)
Clevé, Bastian: Gib niemals auf. Filmökonomie in der Praxis, Konstanz 2004 (UVK)
Dress, Peter: Vor Drehbeginn. Effektive Planung von Film- und Fernsehproduktionen, Bergisch Gladbach 2002 (Bastei Lübbe)
Kandorfer, Pierre: Lehrbuch der Filmgestaltung, 7. Aufl., Gau-Heppenheim 2010 (Schiele und Schoen)
Webers, Johannes: Handbuch der Film- und Videotechnik, 8. Aufl., München 2007 (Franzis Verlag).
Wendling, Eckhard: Filmproduktion, Konstanz 2008 (UVK)

Produktionsprozesse Fernsehen:

Geißendörfer, Hans W.; Leschinsky, Alexander (Hrsg.): Handbuch Fernsehproduktion, Neuwied, Kriftel 2002 (Luchterhand)
Hülsmann, Michael; Grapp, Jörn (Hrsg.): Strategisches Management für Film- und Fernsehproduktionen, München2009 (Oldenbourg)
Karstens, Eric; Schütte, Jörg: Praxishandbuch Fernsehen. Wie TV-Sender arbeiten, Wiesbaden 2005 (VS Verlag)
Schmidt-Matthiesen, Cornelia; Clevé, Bastian: Produktionsmanagement für Film und Fernsehen, Konstanz 2010 (UVK)

Produktionsprozesse Neue Medien:

Riser, Urs; Keuneke, Jürgen; Hoffmann, Bruni; Freibichler, Hans; hrsg. von Macromedia München: Konzeption und Entwicklung interaktiver Lernprogramme, Berlin, Heidelberg, New York 2002 (Springer)
Sydow, Jörg; Windeler, Arnold (Hrsg.): Organisation der Content-Produktion, Wiesbaden 2004 (VS Verlag)

20 Marketing

20.1 Marketing-Instrumentarium

20.1.1 Definition Marketing

Webcode:
C2000

Für weitere Infos zu diesem Kapitel mit dem Smartphone einfach QR-Code scannen oder auf www.medien-verstehen.de den Webcode eingeben.

Marketing ist die Summe aller Anstrengungen, das Unternehmen und seine Produkte konsequent auf die Wünsche der Kunden auszurichten. Das Ziel von Marketing ist es, einen Markterfolg zu erreichen. Dieser soll sich – direkt oder indirekt – in befriedigenden Verkaufs- und Gewinnzahlen niederschlagen.

Um das Ziel des Markterfolges zu erreichen, müssen geeignete Instrumente eingesetzt werden, die sog. **Marketing-Instrumente**. Sie lassen sich grundsätzlich in drei **Kategorien** einteilen:

Was ist Marketing?

- Das Unternehmen und seine Produkte...
- ...auf die Wünsche der Kunden ausrichten!
- Und zwar mit aller Konsequenz!

- **Produktpolitik:** Darunter werden alle Maßnahmen verstanden, die zu einem hervorragenden Produkt oder einer ganzen Produktpalette ❶ zu einem angemessenen Preis führen.
- **Präsenzpolitik:** Alle Maßnahmen, die das Produkt zum Kunden bringen, werden unter dem Titel Präsenzpolitik zusammen gefasst. Jedes Produkt braucht geeignete Absatzwege, um beim Kunden präsent zu sein ❷.
- **Profilpolitik:** Schließlich muss das Produkt in den Köpfen der Kunden als eine wertvolle Marke präsent sein. Ein Produkt braucht ein Profil. Alle Maßnahmen, die das Produkt „profilieren" sollen, nennt man Profilpolitik oder auch **Kommunikationspolitik**. Die wichtigsten Instrumente sind Werbung, Verkaufsförderung, Öffentlichkeitsarbeit ❸ und persönliche Kommunikation.

❶ Die Produktpalette wird auch **Sortiment** genannt.

❷ Um das sicher zu stellen, kann der Aufbau ganz neuer Vertriebskanäle wie das Internet notwendig sein.

❸ Mit der **Öffentlichkeitsarbeit** wirbt das Unternehmen um Vertrauen in der Öffentlichkeit. Anderer Name: **Public Relations**

Um erfolgreich zu sein, muss ein Unternehmen die „Klaviatur" aller drei Marketing-Instrumente beherrschen. Alle Instrumente stehen in einem engen Zusammenhang zueinander und müssen aufeinander abgestimmt sein. Die Kombination, für die sich ein Unternehmen entscheidet, nennt man **Marketing-Mix**.

Grundlage aller Marketingaktivitäten ist die Erkundung des Marktes und der eigenen Position im Markt. Zum Marketing-Instrumentarium gehört demnach auch die **Marktforschung**.

20.1.2 Produktpolitik

Die **Produktpolitik** umfasst alle Entscheidungen, die sich auf die marktgerechte Gestaltung der abzusetzenden Produkte ❶ beziehen. Der Begriff Produkt bezeichnet ein ganzes Bündel von Aspekten und darf nicht zu eng gesehen werden. **Drei Ebenen** sind zu unterscheiden, die ein erfolgreich vermarktetes Produkt aufweist:

- Ebene des Kernprodukts: Jedes Produkt weist in seinem Kern eine Einzigartigkeit auf, die dem Käufer oder Nutzer einen Kernvorteil, einen „USP" ❷, bringt. Dieser Kern des Produkts spricht beim Käufer ein ganz bestimmtes Bedürfnis, eine Hoffnung oder ein Problem an, das er gelöst haben will. So vermittelt z. B. der Besitz einer aktuellen Audio-CD dem jugendlichen Käufer das Gefühl, in seiner Clique „in" zu sein. Das Marketing im Sinne der Produktpolitik ist dazu da, diesen Kernvorteil klar herauszuarbeiten und der Zielgruppe mitzuteilen.
- Ebene des formalen Produkts: Jedes Produkt hat eine formale Seite, die gestaltet werden muss. Dazu gehören vor allem der Markenname, die Verpackung und das Styling. So muss die Audio CD zwar das Produktversprechen erfüllen und Qualität bieten, sie muss aber auch in einer attraktiven äußeren Aufmachung daherkommen und einen prägnanten Namen haben.
- Ebene des erweiterten Produkts: Jedes Produkt hat noch ein „Drumherum", das für den Käufer interessant ist. Zu denken ist vor allem an Serviceleistungen, Garantie und Installation. Bei der Audio-CD könnte z. B. ein Booklet mit Hintergrundmaterial über den Interpreten oder Hinweise auf Online-Links angefügt sein.

❶ **Produkte** sind Waren (= materielle Produkte), Dienstleistungen und Informationen.

❷ **USP = Unique Selling Proposition.** Man spricht in diesem Zusammenhang auch von „Produktversprechen".

➲ **Produkte sind niemals nur ein einfacher Gegenstand, sondern sind ein Mittel, mit dem der Nutzer ein ganzes Bündel von Vorteilen, Problemlösungen und Bedürfnisbefriedigungen verbindet!**

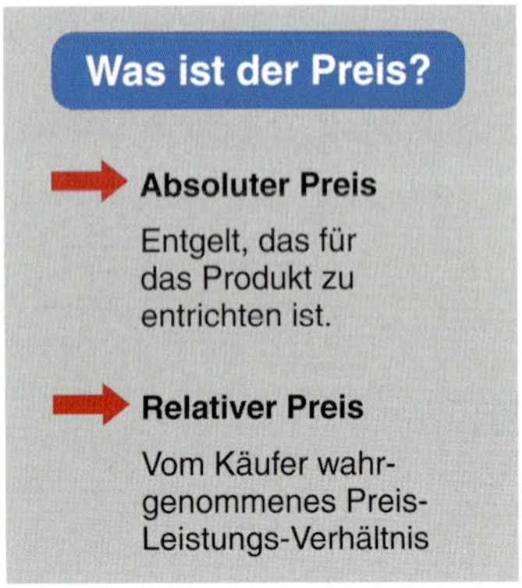

Ein wichtiger Bestandteil des Produkts ist auch sein **Preis**, also das Entgelt, das für das Produkt zu entrichten ist. Ein Produkt ist nur dann attraktiv, wenn es einen angemessenen Preis hat. Dabei ist weniger der absolute Preis wichtig, sondern der **relative Preis**.

Relativ heißt, dass der Produktpreis vom Käufer immer im Verhältnis zum gestifteten Nutzen bewertet wird. Er beurteilt das Produkt daraufhin, ob es ihm einen Leistungsvorteil, einen Preisvorteil oder beides bringt. In den vom Käufer wahrgenommenen Preis fließen oft auch noch andere Elemente ein wie z. B. gewährte Rabatte, die Lieferungs- und Zahlungsbedingungen oder Kreditmöglichkeiten.

❶ Ein **Relaunch** ist also ein Neustart eines bestehenden Produkts, der normalerweise von einem hohen Werbeeinsatz begleitet wird.

Ein letzter Aspekt der Produktpolitik ist die Tatsache, dass Produkte einem **Lebenszyklus** unterliegen und daher im Zeitablauf verändert werden müssen. Entweder werden sie eliminiert, weil sie nicht mehr Ertrag bringend sind, und durch völlig neue Produkte ersetzt. Man spricht von **Produktinnovation**. Oder die bestehenden Produkte werden verändert, was man als Produktvariation oder Relaunch ❶ bezeichnet. Eine Internetseite muss z. B. laufend verändert und weiter entwickelt werden, will der Anbieter im schnelllebigen Netz stand halten.

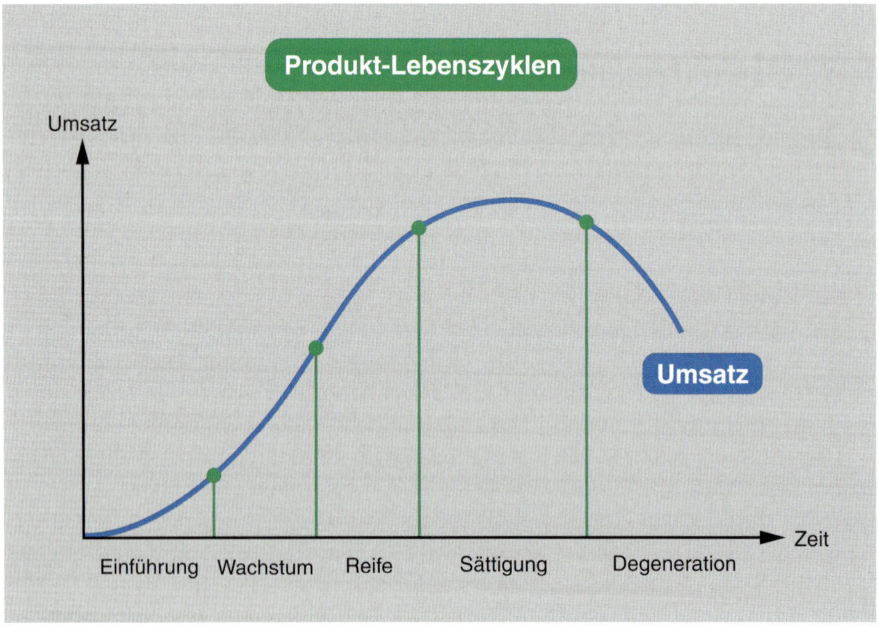

Produkt-Lebenszyklen

20.1.3 Präsenzpolitik

Die **Präsenzpolitik** – auch **Distributionspolitik** genannt – sorgt dafür, dass das Produkt vom produzierenden Unternehmen in die Verfügungsmacht des Verbrauchers bzw. Verwenders übergeht. Dabei muss sicher gestellt werden, dass das Produkt zur richtigen Zeit, im richtigen Zustand und in der erforderlichen Menge zur Verfügung steht. Zu unterscheiden sind **zwei Absatzwege**:

- **Direktabsatz:** Die Produkte werden über eigene Verkaufsfilialen und Läden („stores"), über Reisende, über Handelsvertreter oder über Franchising ❶ direkt an die Zielgruppen herangeführt. Eine zunehmende Bedeutung erlangen die elektronischen Medien als Instrument für den direkten Absatz von Produkten (z. B. der TV-Verkaufskanal H.O.T. oder Web-Shops im Internet).
- **Indirekter Absatz:** Hier erfolgt die Weitergabe der Produkte ❷ vom Hersteller über verschiedene Stufen des Handels, üblicherweise vom Großhandel über den Einzelhandel zum Nutzer.

❶ Beim **Franchising** verkauft der Händler (Franchise-Nehmer) im Namen des Herstellers (Franchise-Geber). Der Händler ist an den Namen, das Warenzeichen und die Ausstattung des Herstellers gebunden.

❷ Den körperlichen Transport des Produkts bezeichnet man als **Logistik**.

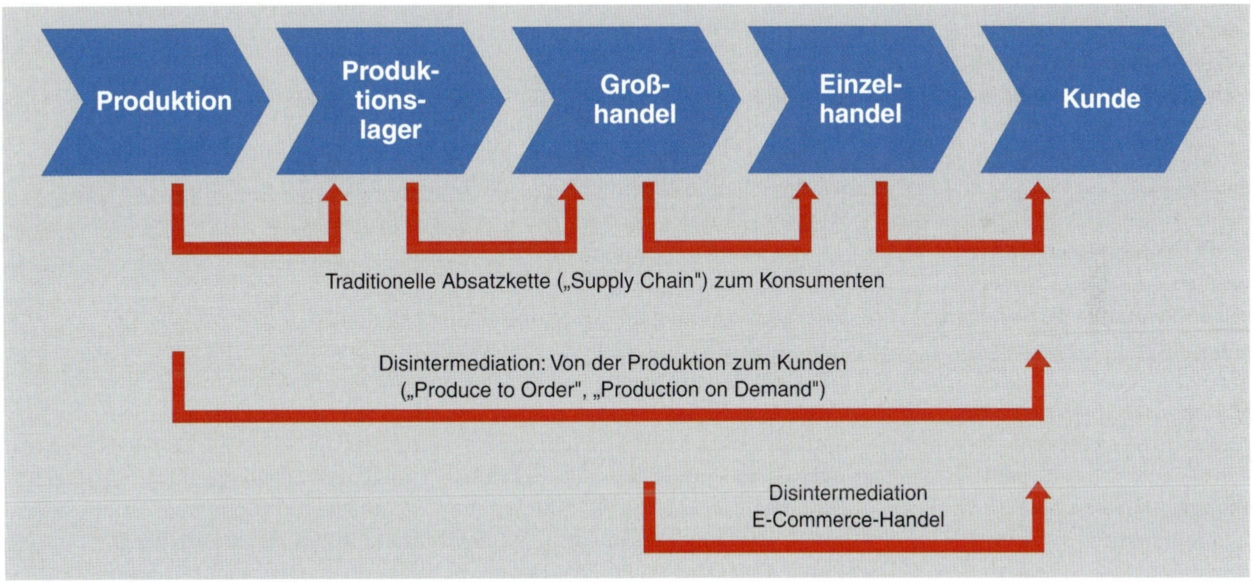

Absatzkette im Buchbereich unter Berücksichtigung des Internet

Im Hinblick auf die Medien ist als neues Vertriebssystem das Internet hoch bedeutend und vor allem auch brisant. Immer mehr Hersteller gehen dazu über, ihre Waren und Dienstleistungen durch die Eröffnung von Web-Shops direkt zu vermarkten und dadurch Handelsstufen zu überspringen oder auszuschalten ❸. Das führt dazu, dass der herkömmliche Groß- und Einzelhandel durch den Ausbau des Internet zu einem neuem Absatzkanal seine dominierende Stellung einbüßen könnte.

❸ Unter **Disintermediation** versteht man das Überspringen von Stufen in der Wertschöpfungskette, im Extrem aller Handelsstufen.

➲ **Produkte müssen beim Kunden präsent sein!**

20.1.4 Profilpolitik

Die **Profilpolitik** verfolgt das Ziel, den Produkten ein Profil zu verleihen und sie in den Köpfen der Käufer und Verwender als wichtige „Produkt-Persönlichkeiten" erscheinen zu lassen. Es geht darum, Einfluss zu nehmen auf die

- Meinungen
- Einstellungen
- Erwartungen
- Verhaltensweisen

der Abnehmer und diese positiv zu beeinflussen.

➲ **Produkte müssen Produkt-Persönlichkeiten sein. Sie brauchen ein Profil. Dies wird durch Kommunikationspolitik geschaffen.**

Die Einflussnahme auf die Käufer kann nur über Kommunikation erfolgen. Daher nennt man die Profilpolitik auch **Kommunikationspolitik**. **Vier Ansatzpunkte** sind zu unterscheiden:

- **Werbung:** Sie ist das bedeutendste aller kommunikationspolitischen Instrumente. Man versteht darunter die bezahlte Form der unpersönlichen Präsentation von Produkten. Zu unterscheiden ist klassische und alternative Werbung. Klassische Werbung ist Anzeigenwerbung, Werbung in Radio, TV und Kino oder Plakatwerbung. Online-Werbung kann mittlerweile bereits zur klassischen Werbung gezählt werden. Alternative Werbeformen sind Sponsoring ❶ oder Product Placement ❷. Eine immer größere Rolle spielt das Direktmarketing wie z. B. Mailings, Prospektverteilung oder Responsemedien ❸.
- **Verkaufsförderung:** Hierunter werden alle Maßnahmen verstanden, die zur punktuellen Aktivierung von Zielpersonen führen. Man spricht auch von Sales Promotion. Ansatzpunkt von Verkaufsförderung kann der Endkunde sein, der sich am Verkaufsort (POS = „Point of Sale") einfindet und z. B. eine kostenlose Probe oder einen Gutschein erhält. Es kann aber auch der Verkäufer sein, den man einer Schulung unterzieht, z. B. mittels einer CBT-Maßnahme (Computer Basiertes Training). Eine Sonderform von Verkaufsförderung ist das Merchandising ❹.
- **Public Relations** (kurz: PR): Der deutsche Begriff ist Öffentlichkeitsarbeit. Ziel ist es, durch gezielte Information ein gutes Verhältnis zwischen dem Unternehmen (z. B. dem Bertelsmann-Konzern) und der Öffentlichkeit aufzubauen mit dem Hintergedanken, das Image des Unternehmens zu verbessern. PR-Instrumente sind z. B. Pressekonferenzen, Interviews, Durchführung von Veranstaltungen, Betriebsbesichtigungen oder die Herstellung und Verteilung von Filmen, Broschüren, Schriften (z. B. Firmenjubiläum).
- **Persönliche Kommunikation:** Sie gilt als besonders interessant (aber auch als besonders kostenträchtig). Zu nennen ist die persönliche Beratung und Überzeugung, das Verkaufsgespräch beim Konsumenten (Außendienstverkauf) und der Telefonverkauf. Der persönliche Kontakt zum Kunden ist überaus wichtig bei Produkten, die erklärungsbedürftig sind (z. B. Software).

❶ Unter **Sponsoring** versteht man die Förderung von Personen oder Organisationen mit dem Ziel, das eigene Unternehmen zu kommunizieren. Im Vordergrund steht das Sponsoring in den Bereichen Sport, Kultur, Soziales und Umwelt.

❷ Mit **Product Placement** wird die Platzierung eines Markenartikels als Requisit in der Handlung eines Spielfilms bezeichnet.

❸ **Responsemedien** zielen auf die unmittelbare Reaktion der Konsumenten ab, z. B. bei TV-Shopping-Kanälen wie H.O.T. („Transaktionsfernsehen").

❹ **Merchandising** hat die Funktion, Waren am Point of Sale wirksam darzubieten und günstig zu platzieren.

20.1.5 Unterschiedliche Medienprodukte – anderes Marketing

Nach den vorstehenden begrifflichen Erläuterungen soll nun das **Medienmarketing** näher beleuchtet werden. Dabei handelt es sich um ein vielschichtiges Thema und es ist notwendig, Unterscheidungen zu treffen. Die wichtigste Unterscheidung bezieht sich auf die Medienprodukte, die sich in **zwei Typen** einteilen lassen:

- Medienprodukte als Endprodukte von Medienunternehmen
- Medienprodukte als Instrument zur Gestaltung der Geschäftsprozesse bei Wirtschaftsunternehmen

Im ersten Fall geht es um das Marketing von Medienprodukten, die als marktfähige Güter von Verlagen, Rundfunkanstalten oder Online-Anbietern auf den Markt gebracht werden. Diese Medienprodukte werden also publiziert. Sie sind **Publikationsprodukte**, die von Publikationsorganen auf den Markt gebracht werden.

Im zweiten Fall geht es um das Marketing mit Hilfe von Medienprodukten, um die Geschäftszwecke von Wirtschaftsunternehmen jedweder Art zu unterstützen. Dies ist im Gegensatz zum ersten Fall eine völlig andere Ausrichtung. Medien sind in diesem Fall ein Faktor im „Business“ ❶. Dieses Feld lässt sich in verschiedene Teilbereiche unterscheiden, insbesondere in die Felder „Business to Consumer“ („B-to-C-Medienprodukte“) und „Business to Business“ („B-to-B-Medienprodukte“).

❶ Wenn es sich um elektronische Medien handelt, spricht man von **E-Business**.

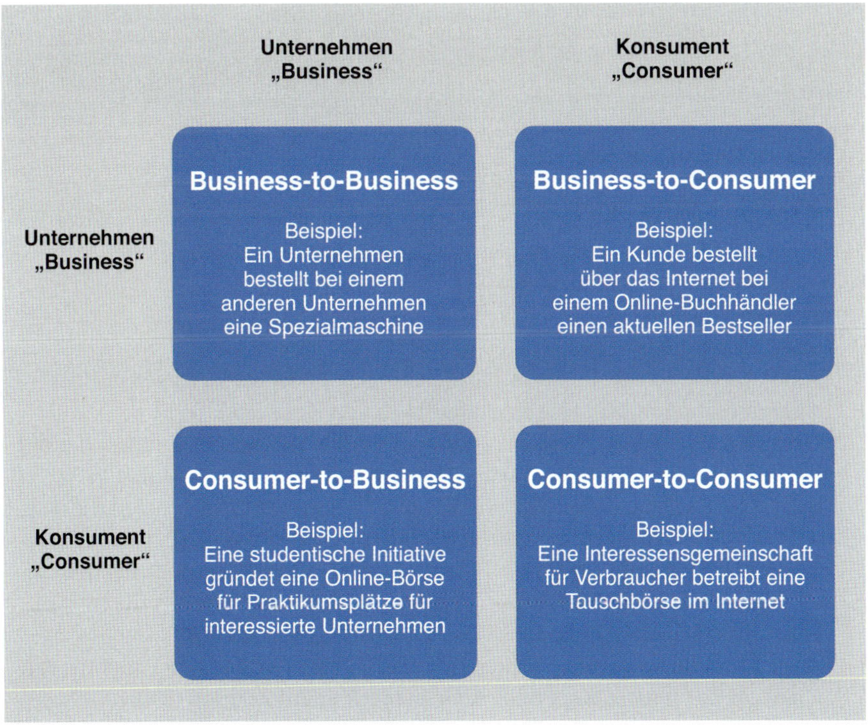

20.2 Medienprodukte als Publikation

20.2.1 Marketing-Mix bei Medienunternehmen

Medienprodukte, die für den Endverbraucher bestimmt sind, sind marktfähige Produkte, mit denen man möglichst hohe Verkaufszahlen und Gewinn erzielen will. Sie unterscheiden sich damit nicht von den herkömmlichen Gebrauchs- und Verbrauchsgütern wie Lebensmittel, Kraftfahrzeuge oder Dienstleistungen. Das Marketing der Medienprodukte folgt also den gleichen Grundsätzen und Instrumentarien.

Diejenigen Unternehmen, die Medienprodukte herstellen und vermarkten, sind die **Medienunternehmen**. Sie treten in den unterschiedlichsten Formen in Erscheinung. Das Spektrum reicht von kleinen Multimedia-Neugründungen bis zu den großen Unternehmen wie Bertelsmann, die im Weltmaßstab operieren.

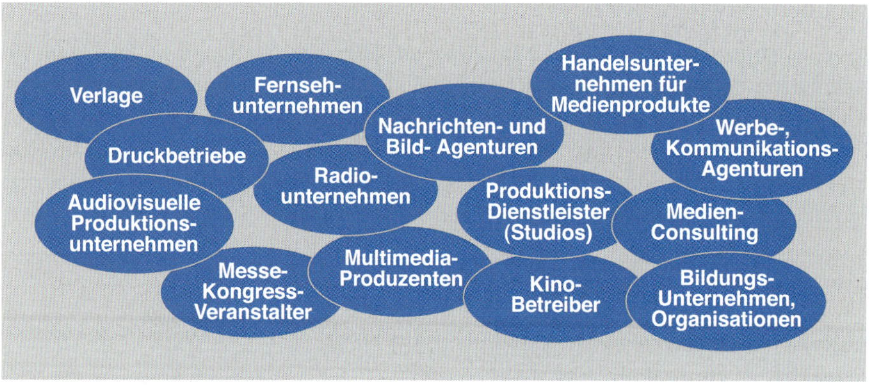

Die Welt der Medienunternehmen

Die **Produktpolitik** der Medienunternehmen ist darauf ausgerichtet, attraktive Produkte herzustellen, die sich auf den Medienmärkten behaupten können. Was sie anbieten, ist eine Frage der **Strategie**:

- Große Medienunternehmen zielen darauf ab, eine möglichst breit angelegte Produktpalette zu haben, um in möglichst vielen Bereichen vertreten zu sein. Dadurch verspricht man sich Krisenfestigkeit und Flexibilität. So ist es z. B. die Politik des Bertelsmann-Konzerns, auf allen Stufen der Wertschöpfungskette ❶ vertreten zu sein: Medienproduktion, Medienredaktion, Ausstrahlung, Verwertung. Oberstes Gebot ist es, in keine Engpass-Situationen hinein zu geraten und dann von anderen Lieferanten abhängig zu sein. Aus dem gleichen Grund versuchen große Medienunternehmen, über den engeren Bereich der Medien hinaus Allianzen mit starken Partnern einzugehen. Das wird befördert durch das Zusammenwachsen aller Bereiche der Informationswirtschaft ❷.
- Kleine Medienunternehmen ziehen sich eher in eine Nische zurück und spezialisieren sich auf ihre ganz spezielle Kompetenz. So wird z. B. ein CD-ROM-Produzent die notwendigen Video-Produktionsleistungen von einem Spezialdienstleister einkaufen und nicht selber herstellen wollen.

❶ In der **Wertschöpfungskette** werden die Produkte vom Ur-Zustand bis zum Endprodukt immer weiter entwickelt, bis sie zum Endkunden gelangen.

❷ Das Phänomen des Zusammenwachsens der einzelnen Bereiche der Informationswirtschaft (TIME: Telekommunikation, Informationstechnik, Medien, Consumer Electronics) nennt man auch **Konvergenz**.

Höchst unterschiedlich sieht auch die **Preispolitik** aus, die von den Medienunternehmen betrieben wird. Um die Finanzierung ihrer Produkte am Markt sicherzustellen, müssen sie für die einzelnen Medien unterschiedliche Ansätze verfolgen. Im Vordergrund stehen direkte Zahlungen der Nutzer und Erlöse aus der Werbung.

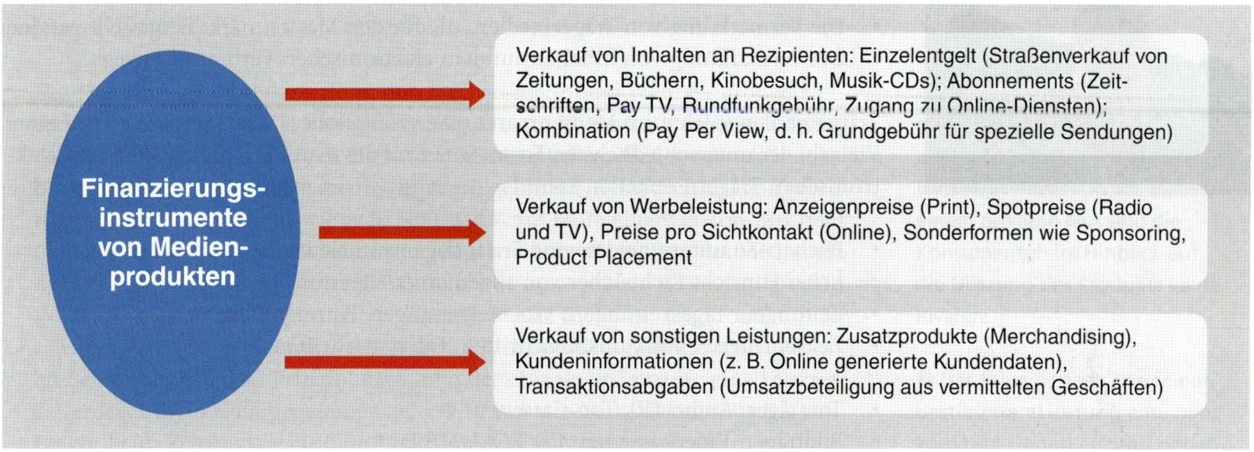

Was die **Präsenzpolitik** anbelangt, so haben die Medienunternehmen unterschiedliche Distributionskonzepte. Grundsätzlich ist zu sagen, dass mediale Produkte eine Ansammlung von Informationen darstellen und nicht materiell sind. Solche Produkte sind im Prinzip dazu geeignet, über Netze zu ihren Nutzern transportiert zu werden. So ist längst der Einstieg gemacht, Radio- und Fernsehsendungen über das Internet zu verbreiten. Große Texte wie Gutachten, Berichte, Verlautbarungen über das Netz zu verbreiten, ist eine gängige Angelegenheit. Alle großen Tages- und Wochenzeitungen sowie die Publikumszeitschriften und -magazine bieten umfassende Online-Informationen an. Prinzipiell gibt es keinen Hinderungsgrund, auch die Inhalte von Büchern über das Netz zu verschicken. Freilich wird es sich der Konsument nicht nehmen lassen, diejenige Form nachzufragen, die ihm am angenehmsten ist. So ist zu erwarten, dass es auch im Internet-Zeitalter weiterhin die gedruckte Form von Publikationen gibt.

Die elektronischen Massenmedien in Radio und Fernsehen verbreiten ihre Programme über drei Wege, zum einen terrestrisch über Sendernetze, was vor allem noch für den mobilen Radioempfang im Auto von großer Bedeutung ist, zum zweiten über Kabelnetze und schließlich über Satellit. Die Digitalisierung muss nicht unbedingt bedeuten, dass z. B. terrestrischer Transport überflüssig wird, auch über Sendernetze „durch die Luft" lassen sich digitale Botschaften transportieren.

Die **Profilpolitik** spielt für Medienunternehmen eine große Rolle. So rangiert der Mediensektor im Vergleich der Werbeaufwendungen nach Branchen ganz vorne. Hinzu kommen z. B. bei allen Fernseh- und Radiosendern große Anstrengungen hinzu, die eigenen Sendungen mit Trailern zu bewerben. Auch das Internet wird als Instrument verwendet, um die Programmangebote bekannt zu machen und z. B. vertiefende Informationen über die Sendungen anzubieten. Damit kommt dem Internet auch die Funktion zu, die Einschaltquote der Sendungen anzukurbeln.

20.3.2 Medienprodukte in Management, Beschaffung und Produktion

Medienprodukte im Management:

- Mitarbeiter-Zeitschrift: Die Führung eines Unternehmens hat ein Interesse daran, die Mitarbeiter gut zu informieren. Ein klassisches Instrument ist die Mitarbeiter-Zeitschrift, die meist sechsmal jährlich erscheint und sich an alle Mitarbeiter richtet.
- Schulungsmaterial: Nach wie vor interessant sind z. B. Management-Lehrgänge (Einsatz von Lern-Software auf CD-ROM, Intranet).
- **Business TV:** Bei diesem Medium übermitteln Unternehmen via TV-Satellit spezielle Informationen an ihre Mitarbeiter oder Außenstellen. Business TV bedeutet, das Medium Fernsehen für die geschäftliche Kommunikation zu nutzen. Die wesentlichen Einsatzbereiche von Business TV sind die Vermittlung von Wissen an die Mitarbeiter, sei es im Hinblick auf Produkteinführungen, Produktschulungen oder Verhaltenstraining. Mit dem Einsatz von Business TV gelingt es dem Management, die Schulung der Mitarbeiter und die interne Kommunikation zu verbessern. Zahlreiche, vor allem größere Firmen arbeiten intensiv mit diesem Medium. Zunehmend wird Business-TV durch Web-TV ersetzt.
- **Intranet:** Wie Business TV ist das Intranet ein unternehmensinternes Kommunikationssystem. Anders als Business TV arbeitet es aber auf der digitalen Plattform, was neue Möglichkeiten eröffnet, insbesondere Interaktion und Multimedialität. Intranets werden für alle Managementzwecke eingesetzt.

Medienprodukte in der Verwaltung:

- **Electronic Data Interchange (EDI):** Hierbei handelt es sich um den elektronischen Datenaustausch zwischen Geschäftspartnern. Es geht um die effiziente verwaltungstechnische Abwicklung von Geschäften. Das Medium ist bereits seit langem im Einsatz. Es wird zunehmend mit dem Internet verknüpft, um die Vorteile der digitalen Welt zu nutzen.
- Einsatz von Business-Software: In allen Unternehmen findet ein umfassender Software-Einsatz statt. Dabei ist zwischen vorgefertigter Standard-Software und maßgeschneiderten Lösungen zu unterscheiden.
- Dokumentenmanagement-Systeme: Der Einsatz von elektronischen Medien hilft mit, die papiergebundene Dokumentationen zu ersetzen, was zu einer Vereinfachung und Effizienzsteigerung führt.

Medienprodukte in der Beschaffung und Produktion:

- Internet als Einkaufsinstrument: Im Bereich des Einkaufs spielt das Internet eine zunehmend bedeutende Rolle. Der Grund liegt in der Fähigkeit des Internets, gewinnbringende Informationen schnell und umfangreich zu erzeugen. Mit dem Internet kann das Unternehmen sonst schwer zugängliche Informationen schnell auffinden, es kann elektronische Preisvergleiche anstellen oder elektronische Ausschreibungen veranstalten. Unter Einsatz von intelligenten Internet-Agenten lässt sich das Netz gezielt nach Informationen durchsuchen, weit über die Funktion von konventionellen Suchmaschinen hinausgehend.
- Software-Einsatz: Jedes Unternehmen ist interessiert daran, seine Geschäftsprozesse durch den Einsatz von Software zu unterstützen. Auch hier gibt es eine Vielzahl der unterschiedlichsten Programme.

20.3.3 Medienprodukte im Produkt- und Absatzbereich

Medienprodukte als Instrument der Produktgestaltung:

- Durch den Einsatz von Medien können die angebotenen Produkte aufgewertet werden. Ein Musterbeispiel ist die Einrichtung einer Online-Hotline für ein kompliziertes elektronisches Gerät oder eine multimediale Online-Gebrauchsanleitung. Medien in dieser Form eingesetzt, stellen Dienstleistungen dar, die das Kernprodukt um zusätzliche Leistungsbündel ergänzen und damit einen Zusatznutzen für den Nutzer erzeugen ❶.
- Mit digitalen Medien können Unternehmen ihr Produktangebot besser auf den einzelnen Kunden ausrichten. Sie eröffnen einen Weg, wie sie ihr Leistungsangebot auch im Falle von Massenproduktion maßgeschneidert gestalten können ❷. Ein Beispiel ist die Zusammenstellung des Produkts durch den Kunden via Online bei einem Computerkauf (Beispiel Dell-Computer).
- **Preispolitik:** Digitale Medien ermöglichen stärkere Differenzierungen in der Preisgestaltung und die Verbesserung der Zahlungsbedingungen für den Kunden (Rabattierung).

❶ Man spricht in diesem Zusammenhang von **Value Added Services**.

❷ Diese Personalisierung des Leistungsangebots wird als **Mass Customization** bezeichnet.

Medienprodukte in der Marktforschung:

- Internet als Instrument zum Data Mining und zur elektronische Marktforschung ❸: Das Internet ermöglicht völlig neue Formen der Informationserhebung wie z. B. virtuelle Testmärkte, Online-Befragungen, Diskussionsforen. Diese neuen Formen sind durchweg viel preiswerter als die herkömmlichen Marktforschungsinstrumente.
- Über Online-Protokollsysteme („elektronische Spuren") kann die sofortige und einfache Analyse von Daten erfolgen.

❸ Die **Marktforschung** ist eine wichtige Grundlage für das Marketing, bei der möglichst viele Informationen über die Märkte, die potenziellen Kunden oder über Konkurrenten in Erfahrung gebracht werden.

Medienprodukte im Verkauf, als verkaufsunterstützendes Mittel, als Vermarktungshilfe:

- Interaktive Kiosk-Terminals: Hier handelt es sich um Geräte, die den interaktiven Abruf von Informationen am POS, POI oder POF ❹ möglich machen, also z. B. auf Messen, Ausstellungen, in Diskotheken oder auf Bahnhöfen.
- Internet als Informationsinstrument: Das Internet dient hier z. B. dazu, die Produktpalette online zu präsentieren.
- Internet als Kommunikationsinstrument: Hier geht es um die Erhöhung der Kundenbindung und die Verbesserung des Kundenkontakts. Gute Möglichkeiten sind das laufende Zuspielen von Neuigkeiten aus dem Unternehmen über E-Mail-Newsletters oder die Einrichtung von Online-Kundenclubs („Communities").
- Internet als interaktiver Vertriebskanal: Das Internet dient auch zur Anbahnung und Abwicklung von geschäftlichen Transaktionen. Dies wird als „E-Commerce" bezeichnet. Ziel ist es, mit dem Absatzkanal Internet die Marktdurchdringung zu steigern.
- Lernprogramme im innerbetrieblichen Einsatz: Eine große Rolle spielen in der Verkaufsförderung das Training der Verkäufer und aller am Verkauf beteiligten Mitarbeiter. Medien helfen mit, Lerninhalte zu transportieren, z. B. durch CBT, WBT ❺ und Telelearning.

❹ **POS** = Point of Sales: der Ort des Verkaufs wie z. B. ein Einzelhandelsgeschäft oder Shopping-Zentrum
POI = Point of Information: der Ort, wo Informationen vermittelt werden wie z. B. Bahnhof oder Messe
POF = Point of Fun: der Ort, wo Spiel und Spaß dominieren wie z. B. Diskothek oder Freizeitpark

❺ **CBT = Computer Based Training**
WBT = Web Based Training

❶ Die Auswahl der Werbeträger nennt man **Mediaplanung** oder kurz **Media**.

❷ Wird auch als **Webvertising** bezeichnet, eine Wortschöpfung aus „Web“ und „Advertising“.

❸ In der Fachsprache als **One-to-one-Marketing** bezeichnet, also Marketing von einer Stelle (dem Unternehmen) zur anderen Stelle (dem einzelenen Kunden).

Medienprodukte als Kommunikationsmittel:

- Werbung: Medienprodukte spielen eine wesentliche Rolle in der Werbung. Dort wird das Produkt als „Werbemittel“ bezeichnet, z. B. eine gestaltete Anzeige oder ein TV-Spot, das in geeigneten Werbeträgern zu schalten ist ❶. Zu denken ist beispielsweise an die Herstellung eines Fernsehwerbespots, der von Agentur- und Produktionsseite entwickelt wird und den Umsatz eines Automobilherstellers ankurbeln soll.
- Internet-Werbung ❷: Durch das Internet gelingt es zunehmend, die Werbung auf die konkreten Bedürfnisse und Einstellungen der Zielgruppen hin maßzuschneidern. Das geht so weit, dass sogar völlig individualisierte Formen der Kommunikation zwischen Anbietern und Nachfragern möglich werden ❸.
- Öffentlichkeitsarbeit: In diesem Feld ist die Palette der Möglichkeiten besonders groß. Zu denken ist an Präsentations-CDs, Image-Broschüren oder Dia-AV. Letzteres ist die Verbindung von Bild und Ton in Form sog. Tonbildschauen oder Multivisionen, die auf Messen und bei Betriebsbesichtigungen nach wie vor Bedeutung haben.

Das Marketing mit Hilfe von Medienprodukten erweist sich damit als ein ausgesprochen vielschichtiges Gebiet. Es gibt kaum einen innerbetrieblichen Bereich und wohl kaum eine Verbindung zwischen Unternehmen, in dem nicht Medien eine Rolle spielen. Gerade der Business-Bereich ist es, der daher eine besondere Beachtung verdient, wenn man den Medieneinsatz untersuchen will.

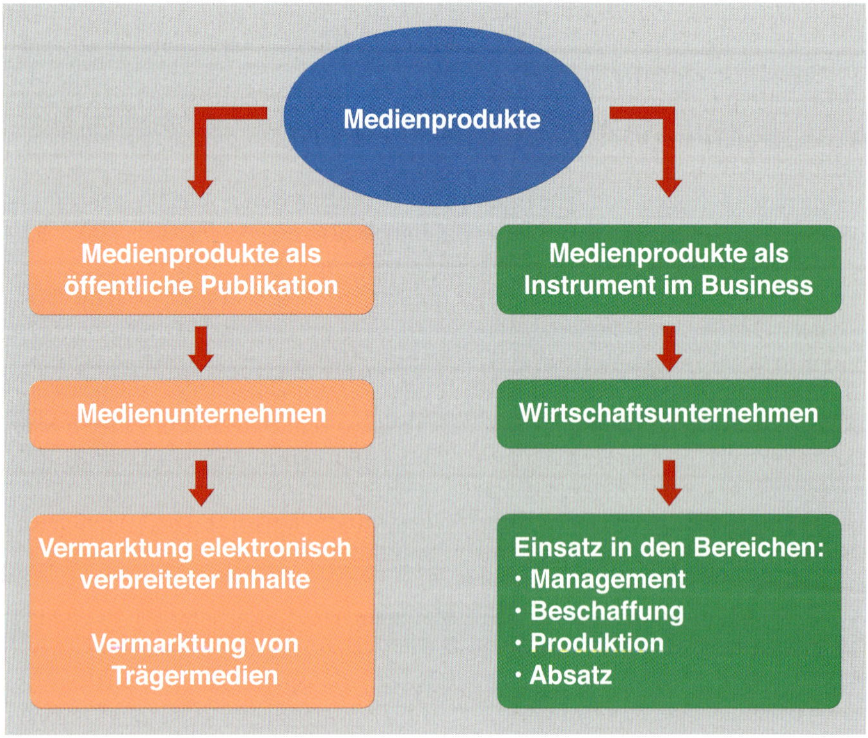

20.4 Im Fokus: Werbung

20.4.1 Rolle und Bedeutung der Werbung

Definition

Werbung begegnet uns auf Schritt und Tritt. Sie ist aus dem täglichen Leben nicht mehr wegzudenken. Manche Werbung wird als störend empfunden, nicht selten z. B. Fernsehwerbung, andere Werbeformen sind voll akzeptiert, z. B. Verkaufsprospekte für Lidl oder Aldi. Was oft nicht bedacht wird: **Werbung** ist eine **grundlegende Erscheinungsform des menschlichen Zusammenlebens** und nicht nur auf den Wirtschaftsbereich beschränkt. So gibt es Werbung z. B. auch bei der Begegnung zweier Menschen, die sich näher kommen wollen (der Mann „umwirbt" eine Frau), oder ein Abteilungsleiter in einem Unternehmen versucht seine Mitarbeiter von einer neuen Idee zu überzeugen (er „macht Werbung" für seine Vorstellungen) oder der junge Mensch sucht eine Stelle und stellt eine „Bewerbung" zusammen. Werbung ist also kein eng begrenztes wirtschaftliches Phänomen, das nur die Wirtschaftsunternehmen interessiert.

Ein kleines **Beispiel für Werbung**: Ein junger Mann will seinen Wagen verkaufen. Um die möglichen Käufer seine Absicht mitzuteilen, muss er Werbung für sein Anliegen machen. Zur Übermittlung inseriert er in einer Zeitung, von der er annimmt, dass seine Zielgruppe diese auch liest. Zusätzlich inseriert er in einem speziellen Online-Dienst.

➲ **Unter Werbung versteht man den bewussten Einsatz von Verfahren, mit denen Menschen in eine bestimmte Richtung ihres Denkens und Handelns beeinflusst werden sollen in der Absicht, die Ziele des Werbenden zu erfüllen.**

Die folgenden **Erscheinungsformen der Werbung** können unterschieden werden:

- Wirtschaftswerbung
- Politische Werbung (früher auch als „Propaganda" bezeichnet)
- Kulturelle Werbung
- Soziale Werbung

Werbung als **Wirtschaftswerbung** verstanden ist ein wichtiger Bestandteil des Marketing eines Unternehmens und dort ein zentraler Baustein dessen, was als „Kommunikationspolitik" bzw. „Profilpolitik" bezeichnet wurde. Werbung ist Teil des kommunikationspolitischen Instrumentenkastens, mit dem möglichst effizient Botschaften über die Produkte des Unternehmens an die Zielgruppen transportiert werden sollen. Als Transportwege stehen dabei eine Fülle von Werbeträgern zur Verfügung, die von den herkömmlichen („klassischen") Werbeträgern wie Zeitungen, Zeitschriften, Fernsehen, Radio, Kino und Plakate (Außenwerbung) bis zu den nicht-klassischen neueren Werbeträgern wie Direktwerbung, Sponsoring, Product Placement, Messen und Ausstellungen sowie die Belegung von Online-Werbeträgern (z. B. Suchmaschine „Google") reichen ❶.

❶ Klassische Wirtschaftswerbung wird auch als „Werbung **above the line**" bezeichnet, nicht-klassische als „Werbung **below the line**".

Von der Werbung muss man **Verkaufsförderung** und **Public Relations** unterscheiden. Beide zählen ebenfalls zu den kommunikationspolitischen Instrumenten, haben aber eine andere Ausrichtung: Verkaufsförderung ❷ bezeichnet kurzfristige Aktionen für den Handel und den Konsumenten, Aktionen am Verkaufsort („Point of Sale"), Preisausschreiben oder Proben etc., Public Relations umfasst alle Maßnahmen, mit denen ein Unternehmen in der Öffentlichkeit um Vertrauen wirbt.

❷ Die gebräuchliche Abkürzung für **Verkaufsförderung** lautet „VKF". Im Englischen spricht man von „Sales Promotion" oder nur von „Promotion".

Volkswirtschaftliche Bedeutung

❶ Alle hier genannten Zahlen entstammen dem offiziellen Jahresbericht des Zentralverbandes der deutschen Werbewirtschaft (ZAW) „Werbung in Deutschland 2011".

Die volkswirtschaftliche Bedeutung der Werbung ist groß. Allein die **Werbeaufwendungen** der Wirtschaft für die Schaltung in den Medien („Netto-Werbeumsätze Medien") betrugen im Jahr 2006 mehr als 20 Milliarden Euro ❶. Hinzu kommen noch einmal zehn Milliarden für die Entwicklung und **Herstellung der Werbebotschaften** (Konzeption, künstlerische Gestaltung und Produktion von Werbefilmen, Radiospots, Anzeigen, Plakaten). Das Volumen des Werbemarktes in Deutschland ist damit z. B. drei Mal so groß wie der Umsatz der gesamten deutschen Brauwirtschaft und macht einen Anteil von 1,36 Prozent des gesamten Bruttoinlandsprodukts aus.

Im Jahr 2010 sind in der Werbebranche rund 550.000 Menschen beschäftigt, das sind annähernd drei Viertel der Beschäftigten in der gesamten deutschen Automobilindustrie. Die **Berufsfelder** sind dabei sehr vielschichtig:

- Werbegestaltung (131.648 Beschäftigte): Werbefachleute in Werbeagenturen,
- Grafik-Ateliers, Schauwerber, Werbefotografen, Film- und Lichtwerbung
- Auftraggeber von Werbung (37.057 Beschäftigte): Werbefachleute in Werbeabteilungen der Anbieter (Hersteller, Dienstleister, Handel)
- Werbemittel-Verbreitung (13.652 Beschäftigte): Werbefachleute bei Verlagen, Funkmedien, Plakatanschlagunternehmen
- Zulieferbetriebe (169.680 Beschäftigte): Von Aufträgen der Werbewirtschaft abhängige Arbeitsplätze bspw. in der Papier- und Druckindustrie
- Telefonmarketing (199.233 Beschäftigte): nur Call-Center-Plätze

❷ Zu 100 Prozent aus Werbung finanzieren sich Anzeigenblätter und privates Free-TV (z. B. RTL oder ProSieben), zu Null Prozent das Buch, Pay-TV und der Kinofilm. Dazwischen liegen die Tageszeitungen und Wochenzeitungen (z. B. Die Zeit, Spiegel), die etwa ein Drittel aus dem direkten Verkauf an die Leser (Kiosk und Abonnement) und zwei Drittel aus dem Anzeigengeschäft erzielen. Bei Publikumszeitschriften (z. B. Bunte) ist das Verhältnis umgekehrt, also zwei Drittel aus Verkauf und ein Drittel aus Werbeanzeigen.

Verlage und **Rundfunksender** sind die Hauptnutznießer der Werbung. Für sie ist die Werbung ein wichtiger Finanzierungsfaktor, bei privaten TV-Sendern sogar praktisch das Hauptstandbein. Die Anteile der Finanzierung der Medienmärkte aus Werbung sind dabei sehr unterschiedlich ❷. Auch gemessen am gesamten Werbeaufkommen haben die einzelnen Medien einen unterschiedlich hohen Anteil, wobei die bis 2008 bestehende Vormachtstellung der Tageszeitungen mittlerweile zugunsten von Fernsehen abgebaut ist. Die Zahlen für die monetären Medienanteile am Werbemarkt im Einzelnen (2010) sehen wie folgt aus: Fernsehen 21 Prozent, Tageszeitungen 20, Werbung per Post 16, Anzeigenblätter 11, Publikumszeitschriften 8, Verzeichnis-Medien 6, Online-Angebote 5, Fachzeitschriften 5, Außenwerbung 4, Hörfunk 4, Wochen-/Sonntagszeitungen 1, Zeitungssupplements und Filmtheater <1.

Bei einem Blick auf die **Branchen**, die am meisten in Werbung investieren, fällt auf, dass die Liste von den Massen-Medien selbst angeführt wird. Sie profitieren also nicht nur von den Werbegeldern der Unternehmen, sie sind auch selbst sehr aktiv, Werbeausgaben zu tätigen. Ein Hauptgrund für diese auffällige Erscheinung ist die Tatsache, dass jede Form der Eigenwerbung (z. B. in Form von Trailern, Programmhinweisen oder Teasern bzw. „Anmachern" im Fernsehen oder von Eigenanzeigen in Zeitungen) als Geschäftsvorfall erfasst wird. Danach folgen vor allem die Handelsorganisationen, der Versandhandel, der Automarkt sowie Werbung für Arzneimittel, Schokolade und Süßwaren.

Gesellschaftliche Bedeutung

Die Rolle der Werbung allein anhand der rein wirtschaftlichen Zahlen beleuchten zu wollen, würde ihrer Bedeutung nicht gerecht. Werbung ist Kommunikation und leistet einen Beitrag zur **gesellschaftlichen Kommunikation**. Sie trägt damit zum Informationsaustausch und zum besseren Verständnis innerhalb der Gesellschaft bei, sie ist für das Funktionieren der Märkte unerlässlich. Ohne Werbung kann ein **Unternehmen** sich nicht artikulieren und seine Botschaften den Zielgruppen übermitteln. Ohne Werbung wären die Anbieter auf den Märkten „sprachlos", sie wären nicht fähig, ihre Produkte zu Marken zu entwickeln, die von den Konsumenten beachtet werden und eine so hohe Wertschätzung erfahren, dass sie gekauft werden. Mit Werbung ringt ein Unternehmen um die Sympathie und die Aufmerksamkeit ihrer potenziellen Kunden. Aus Sicht des **Verbrauchers** sorgt Werbung dafür, dass sie auf interessante Produkte aufmerksam werden, dass sie Preis- und Qualitätsvergleiche anstellen können und dass sie eine Garantie bekommen, die Produkte im ganzen Land auch in der beworbenen Form zu erhalten. Werbung ist damit ein wichtiger Teil eines freiheitlich organisierten marktwirtschaftlichen Wirtschaftssystems, das für ein hohes Wohlstandsniveau sorgt.

Werbung hat freilich auch ihre **Schattenseiten**. Es gibt Werbespots, die so sehr „nerven", dass man gerne die Fernbedienung benutzt, um ein anderes TV-Programm zu suchen. Es gibt Anzeigen, die so nichts sagend sind, dass man achtlos darüber hinwegblättert, es gibt Radiowerbung, die so marktschreierisch ist, dass man schleunigst einen anderen Sender einstellt. Hier muss die Branche dringend darauf achten, die Werbebotschaften in einer gefälligen Form aufzubereiten und zu präsentieren. Als großes Problem wird insbesondere die Unterbrecherwerbung in Fernsehfilmen angesehen.

Der Werbung wird auch nicht selten unterstellt, sie manipuliere den Konsumenten und verführe ihn zu Käufen, die er gar nicht will ❶. Noch weitergehend wird der Werbung das Vermögen unterstellt, dem Menschen ein Bewusstsein zu vermitteln, dass der Konsum sein eigentlicher zentraler Lebenszweck sei. Werbung sei insofern unmoralisch und gesellschaftlich wertlos, wenn nicht gar gefährlich.

Diesem Bild von der Werbung ist entgegenzuhalten, dass Werbung innerhalb der marktwirtschaftlichen Ordnung von einem **mündigen Konsumenten** ausgeht, der nach eigenen Vorstellungen die freie Konsumwahl ausübt. Danach ist der Verbraucher kein hilfloses, passives, ohnmächtiges und desorientiertes Wesen, das vor den Anbietern von Produkten und Dienstleistungen geschützt werden muss. Ein mündiger Konsument versteht sich als gleichwertiger Marktpartner, der mit seinen Entscheidungen die Anbieterseite zwingt, sich an seinen Bedürfnissen zu orientieren.

Hinzu kommt ein ganzes **System kontrollierender Regelungen**, die den Verbraucher gegen jede Form von Missbrauch schützt. Zu nennen sind eine Vielzahl von Spezialgesetzen und Verordnungen (insbesondere UWG, das Gesetz gegen unlautereren Wettbewerb), freiwillige Selbstbeschränkungsabkommen der Wirtschaft (z. B. Verzicht auf Tabakwerbung), Einrichtung des Deutschen Werberats, der Verhaltensregeln aufstellt und beaufsichtigt oder die Klagebefugnis von Verbraucherorganisationen.

❶ Vance Packard entwarf in seinem viel beachteten Werk „Die geheimen Verführer" 1957 ein Schreckensbild willenloser Konsumenten, die durch ins Unterbewusstsein eindringende Werbebotschaften gelenkt werden könnten. So schrieb er: „Mit oft eindrucksvollem Erfolg werden... Anstrengungen aufgewendet, um unsere gedankenlosen Gewohnheiten, unsere Kaufentschlüsse und unsere Denkvorgänge zu steuern, indem man sich der aus der Psychologie... aufgelesenen Einsichten bedient. Bezeichnenderweise gelten diese Anstrengungen einer Schicht unterhalb unserer Bewusstseinsebene, so dass die Antriebe, die uns bewegen... ‚verborgen' sind." Inzwischen ist die Möglichkeit der Effizienz unterschwellig wirkender Werbung weitgehend widerlegt worden (zitiert nach Focus Medienlexikon, Internet).

Ablauf einer Werbekampagne

Eine Werbekampagne zu entwickeln und durchzuführen, geschieht im engen Zusammenwirken eines **Auftraggebers** (z. B. das Unternehmen Mercedes-Benz) und einer **Werbeagentur** (z. B. Springer&Jacoby), wobei der Ausgangspunkt aller Arbeiten das Briefing darstellt. Unter einem **Briefing** wird der Prozess der Abstimmung sowie das zugrunde liegende Dokument verstanden, auf dessen Grundlage alle weiteren Arbeiten erfolgen. Die entscheidende Herausforderung besteht darin, eine Werbebotschaft zu gestalten und diese dann so effizient über geeignete Kanäle zu transportieren, dass die ins Auge gefasste Zielgruppe tatsächlich erreicht und zu einem gewünschten Verhalten (Einstellung, Kauf) veranlasst wird. Die zentralen **Bausteine eines Werbekonzepts** sind daher:

- Die Werbebotschaft, auch „Werbemittel" genannt. Sie gibt Antwort auf die folgenden Fragen: Welcher Inhalt soll mitgeteilt werden? Was will man sagen? Und: Wie soll es mitgeteilt werden?
- Die Werbeträger. Über welche Kanäle soll die Werbebotschaft transportiert werden? Wie soll die Werbung zu den Zielpersonen herangetragen werden? Werbeträger sind das Vehikel für den Transport der Werbebotschaft.

❶ vgl. GWA-Broschüre: Für Schülerinnen und Schüler: Einstieg in Kommunikation und Werbung, 2003

Prinzipiell erfolgt der **Ablauf einer Werbekampagne** nach einem immer ähnlichen Raster in den folgenden **sieben Stufen** ❶:

- Auftrag, Briefing des Kunden (des Auftraggebers) an die Agentur
- Beratung des Kunden
- Kreative Strategie und Umsetzung des Werbemittels
- Werbeträger-Auswahl, auch „Media-Strategie", „Media-Planung" oder nur „Media" genannt
- Produktion des Werbemittels
- Durchführung und Abrechnung der Werbekampagne
- Erfolgsmessung und Erfolgskontrolle

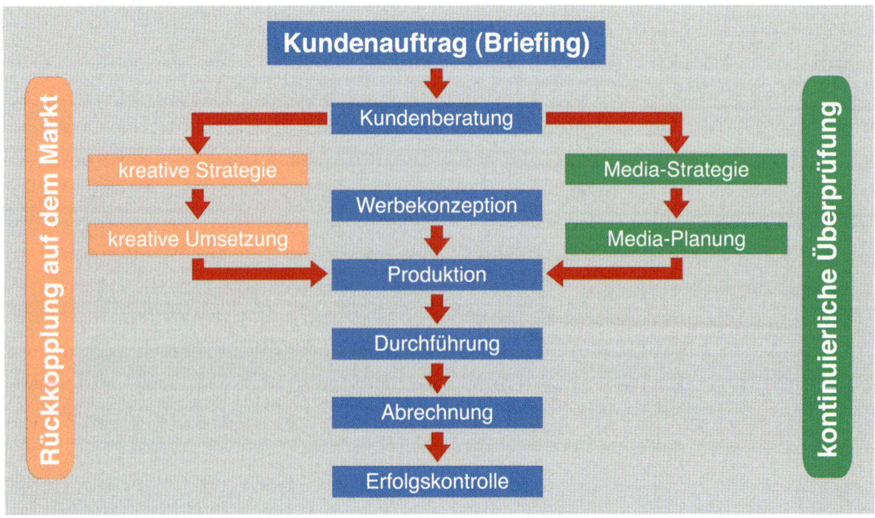

Werbeziele

Die zentrale Rolle im Briefing, das am Beginn jeder Werbekampagne steht, spielen die **Ziele**, die das Werbung treibende Unternehmen verfolgt. Grundsätzlich muss das Unternehmen dabei in einem zweistufigen Verfahren darüber entscheiden, welche **Kommunikationsziele** verfolgt werden sollen, und welche **wirtschaftlichen Ziele** angestrebt werden:

- Kommunikationsziele:
  1. Bekanntmachung: Erlangung, Erhaltung, Erhöhung einer einzigartigen Position in der Wahrnehmung durch die Zielgruppe („Unique Advertising Position"),
  2. Information über Funktion, Einsatz, Kosten-Nutzen-Differenzierung des beworbenen Produkts,
  3. Vertrauen: Imageverbesserung, Bindung an das Unternehmen, Vermeidung von ungewollten Wahrnehmungen (**„Kognitive Dissonanz"** ❶).
- Wirtschaftliche Ziele: Unterstützung des Absatzes durch Schaffung einer „Unique Selling Proposition" ❷, Vermittlung von Argumenten für den Kaufentschluss, Senkung der Vertriebskosten, gezieltes Kampagnen-Timing.

❶ Unter **kognitiver Dissonanz** versteht man eine als unbequem empfundene psychische Spannung, die entsteht, wenn zwischen dem Handeln und dem Wissen eines Menschen Widersprüche bestehen. Beispiel: Jemand raucht, obwohl er genau weiß, dass dies gesundheitsschädlich ist.

Je nachdem, in welcher Phase sich ein Produkt im sog. **Produktlebenszyklus** befindet, wird eine unterschiedliche Werbung notwendig sein:

- Ein Produkt wird neu im Markt eingeführt **(Einführungswerbung)**: erstmalige Werbung zur Bekanntmachung
- Ein Produkt soll in seiner Marktposition nach vorne geschoben werden **(Expansionswerbung)**: Erhöhung des Umsatzes/Marktanteils
- Ein Produkt soll in seiner Rolle im Markt gehalten werden **(Erhaltungswerbung)**: Erhaltung des Bekanntheitsgrades, Erinnerung, Aktualisierung
- Ein Produkt soll aufgefrischt werden **(Relaunch)** oder durch ein anderes ersetzt werden **(Reduktionswerbung)**: Verlagerung des Absatzes im Zeitablauf

❷ Der **USP** bringt präzise den Nutzen (Benefit) zum Ausdruck, den der Käufer hat, wenn er das Produkt erwirbt. Es handelt sich um den Verkaufsanspruch, der verkaufsstimulierend (selling) wirkt. Der USP beantwortet die Frage: „Warum soll ich das Produkt kaufen?"

Häufig wird der Werbung vorgeworfen, sie informiere den Konsumenten nicht oder nicht ausreichend. Diese Beobachtung ist zwar richtig, sollte aber nicht dazu verleiten, falsche Schlüsse zu ziehen. Grundsätzlich gibt es **zwei** mögliche **inhaltliche Ansätze**, Werbebotschaften zu gestalten und diese vom werbenden Unternehmen zum umworbenen Konsumenten zu transportieren:

- Werbung als Information: Vermittlung von Fakten (z. B. Preise, Qualitäten), Eigenschaften, rationale Gesichtspunkte – Beispiel: Computer, Lebensmittel in der Supermarkt-Werbung
- Werbung als Emotion: Ansprechen von Gefühlen (Sicherheit, Angst, Natur, soziale Bedürfnisse, Freude, Liebe, Hoffnung) – Beispiel: Automobilwerbung, Bier, Werbung mit Natur, Kindern, Tieren

Zur sicheren Erreichung des Werbeziels (z. B. der Einprägung des neuen Produktnamens) kann es zweckmäßig sein, voll auf **Emotion** zu setzen.

20.4.2 Werbemittel

Werbemittel für Film, Funk und Fernsehen bezeichnet man seit alters her auch als die **FFF-Werbemittel**.

Das Werbemittel ist eine durchdachte **Kombination aus werbewirksamen Elementen** wie Text, Bild, Ton, Video, Bewegung oder Grafik. Durch deren professionelle Gestaltung und Komposition zu einem überzeugenden Zusammenspiel soll die gewünschte **Werbewirkung** hervorgerufen werden.

Übersicht über die Werbemittel

Zu unterscheiden sind die folgenden **Werbemittel**:

- Presse: Anzeigen in Tageszeitungen, Anzeigen in Publikumszeitschriften
- Außenwerbung: Plakat
- Fernsehen: TV-Spot („harte Werbung"), Werbefilm, Sponsorsendung
- Radio: Radio-Spot, Sponsorsendung
- Kino: Kinofilm
- Internet: Online-Werbung als Banner, Online-Anzeige, Newsletter, EMail-Werbung
- Direktwerbung: Werbebrief („Direct Mail"), Prospekt, Katalog, Kundenzeitschrift, Preislisten, Geschenkgutschein, Aufkleber
- **3D-Werbemittel:** Werbegeschenke, Tragetasche, Packungen, Schaufensterdekoration, Displaymaterial am POS, Bedruckter Luftballon, Messestand, Mitarbeiter-Outfit, Firmenfahrzeug, Firmenfahne, Firmensymbol

Je nach Aufgabenstellung besitzt ein Werbemittel bestimmte **Vorzüge** und **Nachteile**. Kriterien für die Auswahl der Werbemittel sind z. B. die Möglichkeit einer gezielten Streuung, seine Kosten, die Wirkungsdauer oder die Möglichkeit des Konsumenten, der Werbung auszuweichen. Eine gezielte Streuung ist besonders gut bei Anzeigen in regionalen Tageszeitungen möglich, beim Plakat oder durch den Werbebrief. Hörfunkwerbung und Werbung in Zeitschriften ist relativ kostengünstiger als TV- und Kinowerbung. Im Hinblick auf die Wirkungsdauer sind im Vergleich zum flüchtigen TV- und Radiospot Anzeigen in Publikumszeitschriften als besonders günstig zu beurteilen. Ausweichmöglichkeiten bestehen am wenigsten beim Kinospot, am stärksten durch das „Zapping" im Fernsehen und die Möglichkeit des Überblätterns bei Anzeigen im einem separaten Anzeigenteil.

❶ Der Widerstand gegen die Werbung wird im Fachjargon auch als **Reaktanz** bezeichnet.

Je eindrucksvoller ein Werbemittel, desto weniger besteht die Gefahr, dass sich der Rezipient (Leser, Zuschauer, Zuhörer, User) von der Werbung abwendet. Für die Werbewirtschaft ist die Vermeidung von Werbung ❶ durch die Mediennutzer ein äußerst unangenehmer Vorgang. Sehr bekannt geworden ist das „Zapping".

➲ **Unter „Zapping" versteht man die Kontaktvermeidung durch den Zuschauer, indem er das Programm bei Werbeeinblendungen mit Hilfe der Fernbedienung auf einen anderen Kanal umschaltet.**

In der digitalen Fernsehlandschaft der Zukunft kommt der Werbevermeidung eine noch höhere Bedeutung zu, da es künftig möglich sein wird, über sog. Digitale Videorecorder (DVR) Werbung automatisch auszublenden.

Kreative Strategie und Umsetzung des Werbemittels

Um eine Konzeption für die Gestaltung eines Werbemittels zu entwickeln, empfiehlt es sich, vier **Fragen** zu stellen:

- Frage 1: Wer soll mit der Werbebotschaft erreicht werden?
- Frage 2: Was soll kommuniziert werden?
- Frage 3: Wie soll kommuniziert werden?
- Frage 4: Wo soll kommuniziert werden?

Frage 1, das „Wer", ist der Ausgangspunkt und betrifft die Frage nach der **Zielgruppe**. Nur wenn klar festgelegt ist, wer mit der Werbekampagne konkret angesprochen werden soll, kann man ein überzeugendes Gestaltungskonzept erarbeiten. Zielgruppen können nach den unterschiedlichsten Kriterien abgegrenzt werden, so z. B. nach soziodemografischen Kriterien wie Geschlecht, Alter, Einkommen, Schulbildung, Beruf, Familienstand oder Wohnortgröße ❶. Andere Kriterien setzen z. B. am Konsumverhalten der Menschen an oder am Lebensstil. Bei letzterem kommen in Frage: Freizeitaktivitäten, bevorzugte Urlaubsart, Musikinteressen, Wohnstil, Kleidungsstil, Einstellungen zu Essen und Trinken, Einstellungen zur Kleidung („Outfit") und zum eigenen Körper („Body-Image"), Werthaltungen, Lebensphilosophie und Moral, Zugehörigkeit zu sozialen Milieus, Arbeitszufriedenheit, Berufserwartungen, Einstellung zu Familie, Partnerschaft und Emanzipation, Wohnsituation, politisches Interesse.

❶ Ein Beispiel für eine **Zielgruppendefinition** nach soziodemografischen Kriterien: Alle verheirateten Frauen zwischen 20 und 49 Jahren mit Kindern zwischen 3 und 14 Jahren, bei einem Haushaltseinkommen von 3.000 Euro und mehr (netto).

Die eigentliche Gestaltung des Werbemittels ist mit den Frage 2 und 3 angesprochen. Um sie zu beantworten, bedient man sich der sog. **Copy-Strategie**. Sie ist das schriftliche Dokument, mit der man die inhaltliche Grundkonzeption einer Werbekampagne konkret fixiert. Eine Copy-Strategie besteht aus den folgenden **drei Elementen**:

- **Consumer Benefit:** Darunter versteht man den Nutzen, den besonderen Vorteil bzw. den einzigartigen Vorzug, den das beworbene Produkt für den Käufer besitzt. Diesen „Benefit" gilt es der Zielgruppe klar und verständlich mitzuteilen. Das zentrale Argument, warum die Zielpersonen das Produkt kaufen sollen, nennt man in diesem Zusammenhang auch das „Produktversprechen" bzw. die „Unique Selling Proposition" (USP). Häufig wird bei der USP zwischen Grundnutzen und Zusatznutzen unterschieden ❷. Die Umsetzung der USP erfolgt im sog. „Claim", mit dem der Kern der Werbeaussage auf ein Argument verkürzt wird und sich in allen Kommunikationsmaßnahmen wiederholt.
- **Reason Why:** Er bezeichnet die Begründung, die Glaubhaftmachung, den Beweis für die in der USP gemachten Behauptungen. Es ist also die Anspruchsbegründung für das Leistungsangebot. Je höher der Produktanspruch ist, eine desto größere Bedeutung erhält der Reason Why.
- **Tonality**, auch „Flair" genannt: Sie legt den Grundton der Werbung fest und bestimmt, wie das Produkt präsentiert werden soll. Beschrieben wird darin z. B., dass die Verpackung „atmosphärisch" sein soll z. B. im Sinne von jung und sportlich im Gegensatz zu traditionsgebunden und rustikal.

❷ **Grundnutzen** und **Zusatznutzen**: Produkte werden häufig nicht nur wegen ihrer Grundfunktion gekauft, sondern wegen eines interessanten Zusatznutzens wie Prestige, Ästhetik, Design, Wirtschaftlichkeit. Der Aspekt des Zusatznutzens gewinnt im Marketing eine immer größere Bedeutung, insbesondere im Hinblick auf die Möglichkeiten, die das Internet bietet.

Beispiel: Plakat, Anzeige, Broschüre

❶ **Kampagne „Schichtwechsel" EHG**

Auftraggeber: Energiehandelsgesellschaft märkische Stadtwerke mbH (EHG), eine Gemeinschaftsunternehmung von acht Stadtwerken
Produkt: Erdgas
Zielgruppe: Hauseigentümer, Nutzer des Energieträgers Erdöl
Positionierung: Die EHG-Stadtwerke versorgen die Region mit Erdgas
Consumer Benefit: Saubere und umweltschonende Energieversorgung
Werbeidee: Die Umstellung von Erdöl auf Erdgas durch die unterschiedlichen Erdschichten veranschaulichen
Kampagnen-Claim: „Schichtwechsel"
Tonality: bewusst irritierend und doppeldeutig (Slogan), seriös

❶ Quelle: T-Online- Business: BusinessPro: Marketingpraxis. Die besten Marketing- und Vertriebslösungen für den Mittelstand. E-Book 2004, S. 120 f. Die verantwortliche Agentur war die Fa. elementmedia GmbH, Schwerte.

Mit der Kampagne „Schichtwechsel2003" wollte die EHG eine hohe Aufmerksamkeit erzielen, informieren und dabei das Interesse für den modernen Energieträger Erdgas wecken. Die Zielsetzung der EHG lautete: „Die Zielkunden sollen für das Thema Umstellung auf Erdgas sensibilisiert oder – falls sie schon erdgasversorgt sind – in ihrer Entscheidung bestätigt werden".

Die Kampagne fand im Juni und Juli 2003 statt und umfasste die klassischen Werbeträger Großflächenplakate, Tageszeitungsanzeigen und Kampagnenbroschüren. Die Anzeigen und Plakate hatten die Aufgabe, die Vorteile von Erdgas in einer einzigen Botschaft auf den Punkt zu bringen. Begleitend dazu konnten in den Informationsbroschüren die Argumente, die für einen Wechsel zum Erdgas sprechen, ausführlich dargestellt werden. Die Broschüren wurden in einer Direktmailing-Aktion an die Zielgruppen verschickt. Flankierend zu den Printmedien gab es eine umfangreiche Hörfunk-Kampagne. Als Anlaufstelle wurde im Internet eine Kampagnen-Website eingerichtet (www.schichtwechsel2003.de).

Beispiel: TV-Werbespot

Persil-Kampagne

Produkt: Persil Supra

Zielgruppe: alle Konsumenten, die gepflegte Wäsche bei geringer Umweltbelastung wünschen

Positionierung: umweltschonendes Vollwaschmittel mit Wasserenthärter für die ganze Wäsche

Consumer Benefit: unübertroffene Reinheit und Pflege

Reason Why: Wasserenthärtung, neue Wirkstoffe

Tonality: vertrauenswürdig, informativ

Werbeidee: Präsenter-Spot für das Fernsehen

Ein **Präsenter-Spot** ist eine spezielle Gestaltungsform für die filmische Umsetzung der Copy-Strategie. Dabei stellt eine Person mit glaubwürdiger Autorität, der Präsenter, das zu bewerbende Produkt dem Publikum vor, sei es indem er die Qualitäten des Produkts demonstriert, sei es indem er geeignete Kommentare zu einer szenischen Handlung abgibt.

Die **Umsetzung der Werbeidee** könnte auch in völlig anderer Form erfolgen, so z. B. im Wege der sog. „Technik der Produktpersönlichkeit". Bei dieser Umsetzungstechnik (im Fachjargon: **„Copy-Technik"**) wird ohne irgendeine Präsentation durch einen Menschen das Produkt in Aktion gezeigt mit dem Ziel, die ganze Aufmerksamkeit auf den „Hauptdarsteller Produkt" zu lenken. Möglich wäre auch der Einsatz der sog. „Testimonial-Technik", die einen zufriedenen Käufer oder Benutzer des Produkts zeigt, der gewissermaßen ein Zeugnis über die Güte des Produkts ablegt. Gerne werden im Testimonial Film- und Fernsehstars eingesetzt, um deren Beliebtheit und Bekanntheit für Werbezwecke auszunutzen. Ein völlig anderer Copy-Technik-Ansatz ist schließlich der **„Slice of Life"**, bei dem nach einer klaren inhaltlichen Abfolge eine typische Szene, wie sie aus dem Leben gegriffen ist, vorgestellt wird ❶.

Soll ein Fernsehwerbespot seine maximale Wirkung erzeugen, müssen die **Gestaltungselemente**, aus denen er besteht, zu einer **organischen Einheit** verbunden werden. Dieses sind die Elemente Bild (Realbild, Grafik, Animation), Ton (Musik, Sprache, Geräusche) und Text. Von entscheidender Bedeutung ist die Dramaturgie, die dafür sorgen soll, dass die TV-Werbung „unter die Haut geht" und starke Gefühle auslöst. Als **Erfolgsfaktoren** für erfolgreiche Werbung im Fernsehen können gelten:

- Anregende und unterhaltsame Gestaltung
- Einfach, klar, verständlich
- Vermittlung produktrelevanter Eindrücke
- Verstärkung der vorhandenen Präferenzen der Zielgruppe
- Auslösung von persönlicher Betroffenheit
- Ausstrahlung von Glaubwürdigkeit

Eine weitere wichtige Gestaltungsfrage betrifft die **Länge des Spots**. Hier ist festzustellen, dass in den letzten Jahren eine deutliche Verkürzung der Spotlänge eingesetzt hat.

❶ Die **Dramaturgie** eines Slice-of-Life-Spots (nach Huth-Pflaum: Einführung in die Werbelehre):

1. Eine alltägliche Szene aus dem Leben der Zielgruppe
2. Eine Person hat ein Problem.
3. Ein freundlicher und glaubwürdiger Bekannter weiß Rat.
4. Ein bestimmtes Produkt wird als Problemlöser empfohlen.
5. Zweifel an der Produktleistung treten auf.
6. Es folgt eine Nutzendemonstration, die den endgültigen Beweis liefert.
7. Höhepunkt der Story: Das Produkt und dessen Leistung werden gelobt.
8. Schluss: Slogan oder Jingle (ein gesungener Werbespruch) und Packungsabbildung.

Beispiel: Crossmediale Kampagne

❶ Quelle: T-Online- Business: BusinessPro: Marketingpraxis. Die besten Marketing- und Vertriebslösungen für den Mittelstand. E-Book 2004, S. 116 f.

❶

Kampagne „Flaschenpost" von Coca-Cola 2003

Produkt: Marken der Coca-Cola Company

Zielgruppe: Mobiltelefonbesitzer („Generation SMS")

Positionierung: Fanta und die anderen Marken der Coca-Cola GmbH machen Spaß und bieten eine Markenwelt, mit der sich die Zielgruppe identifizieren kann.

Consumer Benefit: Wer Fanta oder andere Marken aus dem Coca-Cola-Sortiment trinkt, hat Spaß und liegt im Trend.

Reason Why: Die Freunde trinken ebenfalls die gleichen Coca-Cola-Marken und nutzen die originellen Fanta-Medien.

Tonality: bunt, schnell, laut

Werbeidee: Durch originelle Klingeltöne und Bildmotive sollen möglichst viele Handybesitzer zum Austausch von SMS-Grüßen und damit Markenbotschaften animiert werden.

Diese ungewöhnliche Werbekampagne wird inzwischen als eine der am besten vorbereiteten Kampagnen der Welt bezeichnet. Entwickelt wurden 150 Klingeltöne, Logos und Grußkarten in 500 Variationen. Im Zentrum standen die Getränkeflaschen. In der Coca-Cola-Pressemitteilung vom 06.03.2003 heißt es: „Handy-Spaß kommt jetzt beim Durstlöschen! Unter dem Motto Fanta Flaschenpost initiiert Coca-Cola eine der größten je in Deutschland gestarteten On-Pack-Kampagnen: Unter Führung der Marke Fanta geht am 1. April 2003 die markenübergreifende Fanta Flaschenpost an den Start. Bis zum 18. Mai 2003 finden sich auf den Innenseiten von rund 160 Millionen Flaschenetiketten der Marken Coca-Cola, Fanta, Coca-Cola light, Sprite, Mezzo Mix, Lift und Bonaqa individuelle Zahlencodes.

Wer diesen Code von seinem Handy an die angegebene Rufnummer schickt, erhält einen Service als Zugabe zum Herunterladen oder zum Verschicken an Freunde. Ob Logo, Klingelton oder mobile Grußkarte: Überraschung ist garantiert. Als Werbepartner für diese außergewöhnliche Kampagne konnten T-Mobile und Nokia gewonnen werden."

Zur nachhaltigen Unterstützung der Werbewirkung steht die Kampagne in einem **umfassenden integrierten Kommunikationskonzept**. So heißt es an anderer Stelle der Pressemitteilung: „Ein zentraler Bestandteil der Kampagne ist die Verbindung des jungen Kommunikationsmediums Handy mit den klassischen Kanälen im Kommunikations-Mix. Zum schnellen Bekanntheitsaufbau der Kampagne laufen parallel zur On-Pack-Kampagne von Anfang bis Ende April Werbespots im TV. Im Print-Bereich werden vor allem in Jugendtiteln und Programmzeitschriften Anzeigen geschaltet. Alle klassischen Werbeaktivitäten haben das Ziel, die Fanta Flaschenpost vorzustellen und auf die besondere Attraktivität der Zahlencodes hinzuweisen. Natürlich gehört auch das Medium Internet zum Kommunikations-Mix: Auf den jeweiligen sieben Marken-Websites (z. B. www.coca-cola.de oder www.fanta.de) finden sich Informationen zur Kampagne sowie allen technischen Aspekten. Beim Internetgewinnspiel können die User außerdem insgesamt 1.000 topaktuelle Nokia, 3.650 Handys oder 1.000 XtraCashs von T-Mobile gewinnen. Auch auf den Websites der Kooperationspartner Nokia (www.nokia.de) und T-Mobile (www.t-mobile.de) führen Teaser zu der multimedialen Welt der Fanta Flaschenpost."

Aus der Coca-Cola- Pressemitteilung: „Die Fanta Bundle Promotion ist weltweit die erste On-Pack-Kampagne, die sieben Erfolgsmarken unter einem gemeinsamen Titel markenindividuell bündelt und dabei intelligent die Möglichkeiten des Mobile Marketing nutzt. Mit der Fanta Flaschenpost erweitern wir den klassischen Kommunikations-Mix in bislang einmaliger Weise um das Kommunikationsmedium der jungen Erwachsenen, das Handy, so Jordi Queralt, Group Brand Manager Fanta zur zentralen Idee der Fanta Bundle Promotion."

Zum **Erfolg der Kampagne** ist in der FAZ vom 29.09.2003 zu lesen: „In der Kampagne „Fanta Flaschenpost", die von 12 Snap konzipiert wurde, hat der Konzern Zahlencodes auf den Innenseiten von mehr als 160 Millionen Getränkeflaschen angebracht. Die Kunden sollten den Code per SMS an die angegebene Rufnummer senden und erhielten dafür ein Logo, einen Klingelton oder eine mobile Grußkarte zum Herunterladen. „Wir sind mit den Ergebnissen unserer mobilen Marketing-Aktion sehr zufrieden. In den sieben Wochen der Kampagne sendeten unsere Kunden 5,9 Millionen Zahlencodes zurück", sagte Burggraeve. Das entspricht einer Antwort-Rate von 3,7 Prozent. Vor allem die kleinen Marken im Coca-Cola-Konzern hätten in dieser Zeit Marktanteile gewonnen. Zu den Kosten wollte Burggraeve keine genauen Angaben machen. „Es war nicht billig, hat sich aber gelohnt", sagte er. Zudem gaben 100.000 Menschen ihr Einverständnis, auch künftig an Werbeaktionen von Coca-Cola teilnehmen zu wollen. Daneben profitierten auch die Betreiber der Mobilfunk-Netze von der Werbeaktion: 1,3 Millionen Euro Zusatzumsatz flossen nach Angaben von Coca-Cola in die Taschen von T-Mobile, Vodafone, E-Plus und O2. Der direkt messbare Kundenkontakt per SMS oder Multimedia-Nachricht (MMS) wird nach Einschätzung der Marktforscher in den kommenden Jahren an Bedeutung gewinnen. „Das mobile Marketing wächst kräftig und wird seinen Höhepunkt in zwei Jahren erreichen", erwartet Michelle de Lussanet vom Marktforschungsunternehmen Forrester Research. ... Coca-Cola wird die Werbung in den interaktiven Medien bereits im Weihnachtsgeschäft erneut einsetzen. Im November soll die neue Kampagne starten, die Internet und Mobilfunk kombiniert. Werbepartner ist der Handy-Netzbetreiber Vodafone."

20.4.4 Werbeerfolgskontrolle

❶ Die **Werbeerfolgskontrolle** steht im Gegensatz zur Prüfung des Erfolgs im Vorfeld einer Kampagne. Bei dieser Art der Erfolgsmessung spricht man von „Werbeerfolgsprognose" oder von **Pre-Tests**.

Am Schluss einer Werbekampagne stellt sich die Frage nach deren Erfolg. Man schaut zurück und will wissen, ob die gesetzten Ziele erreicht wurden. Zu diesem Zweck stellt man Kontrollen des Werbeerfolgs an (sog. „Werbeerfolgskontrolle" bzw. „Post-Tests") ❶. Unter **Erfolg** versteht man das positive Resultat der Werbebemühungen im Hinblick auf die gesetzten Ziele. Gemäß der Unterscheidung der Werbeziele zum einen nach **außerökonomischen Zielen** bzw. Kommunikationszielen, zum anderen nach **ökonomischen Zielen**, trifft man bei der Werbeerfolgskontrolle die folgende Unterscheidung:

- Außerökonomischer Erfolg: Dabei geht es um die Messung des Kommunikationserfolgs. Es gilt die Frage zu beantworten, ob die Kampagne z. B. die Aufmerksamkeit, die Erinnerung, das Image oder die Einstellung der Zielgruppe gegenüber dem Produkt positiv verändert hat. Diese Art der Erfolgsmessung nennt man auch „Werbewirkungsforschung".
- Ökonomischer Werbeerfolg: Hier will man feststellen, ob die Werbekampagne die Kaufhandlungen der Zielgruppe positiv beeinflusst hat, ob also die Kampagne ein Mehr an Absatz und Umsatz gebracht hat.

„Wie wirkt Werbung?" Die berühmte anekdotische Antwort von Henry Ford lautet: „Die Hälfte des Geldes, das für Werbung ausgegeben wird, ist zum Fenster hinausgeworfen – unklar ist nur, welche Hälfte es ist!"

Es ist offenkundig, dass es sich bei der **Ermittlung des Werbeerfolgs** um eine hochgradig **komplexe Aufgabe** handelt. So steht man z. B. bei der Ermittlung des außerökonomischen Erfolgs vor der methodischen Frage, nach welcher Wirkungstheorie man bei der Messung vorgehen will. In Kapitel 1 des vorliegenden Lehrwerkes ist zwischen behavioristischen und konstruktivistischen Modellen unterschieden worden. Folgt man dem behavioristischen Ansatz (Stimulus-Response-Ansatz), so könnten die Abfolge der Werbewirkung in sechs Stufen beschrieben werden:

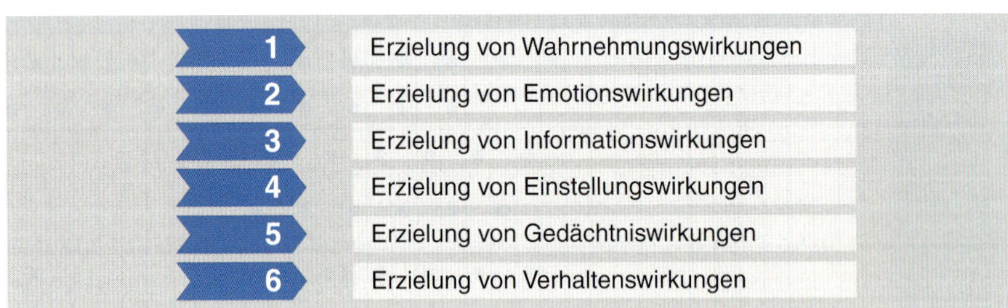

Zur Messung der Wirkungen sind die verschiedensten Ansätze im Einsatz. So überprüft man z. B., ob ein beworbenes Produkt und die Kommunikationsinhalte tatsächlich wahrgenommen wurden (erste Stufe), durch sog. **„Recall-Tests"**. Mit sog. **„Recognition-Tests"** prüft man die Wiedererkennung von Werbemitteln.

In der Praxis bereitet die Werbeerfolgskontrolle zudem erhebliche **methodische Schwierigkeiten**. So besagt z. B. das sog. Zurechnungsproblem, dass ein feststellbarer Werbeerfolg nicht unbedingt von der betreffenden Werbekampagne herrühren muss, sofern auch andere Faktoren wie das Verhalten der Konkurrenz, die Produkt-, Distributions- und Preispolitik als Einflussfaktor in Frage kommen könnten.

Aufgaben und Übungen, Literaturhinweise

Aufgaben und Übungen

1. Analysieren Sie, wie sich die Produktpolitik der Fernsehkanäle ZDF und MTV unterscheidet. Unterscheiden Sie dabei zwischen der Ebene des Kernprodukts, der Ebene des formalen Produkts und der Ebene des erweiterten Produkts.
2. Stellen Sie dar, über welche Wege die Tageszeitung „Frankfurter Allgemeine Zeitung" zum Leser gelangt.
3. Erstellen Sie ein Konzept, wie man aus einem neu gegründeten Hochschulradio, das auf UKW sendet, eine „Produktpersönlichkeit" machen kann.
4. Nehmen Sie Stellung zu der Frage, warum das ZDF in seinen Werbeblöcken die TV-Werbespots durch die „Mainzelmännchen" unterbricht.
5. Die Zahl der Kinobesuche nimmt seit einiger Zeit relativ gesehen stark ab. Stellen Sie dar, welche Möglichkeiten es gibt, diesen Trend umzukehren und dabei die Erträge der Kinobetreiber zu steigern.
6. Erklären Sie, warum eine crossmediale Werbekampagne für ein Unternehmen besonders attraktiv erscheint.
7. Nehmen Sie Stellung zum Thema „Marketing im Internet von Handwerksbetrieben".
8. Wählen Sie aus der aktuellen Fernsehwerbung einen beliebigen TV-Spot aus und stellen Sie Überlegungen an, welche Zielvorstellung die Agentur und der Auftraggeber wohl damit verfolgen.

Literaturhinweise

Beck, Joachim; Mödinger, Wilfried; Schmid, Sybille: Marketing. Grundlagen und Instrumente, 2. Aufl., Haan-Gruiten 2006 (Europa Lehrmittel)

Becker, Jochen: Marketing-Konzeption. Grundlagen des ziel-strategischen und operativen Marketing-Managements, 9. Aufl., München 2009 (Vahlen)

Breyer-Mayländer, Thomas; Seeger, Christof: Medienmarketing, München 2006 (Vahlen)

Bruhn, Manfred: Marketing, 11. Aufl., Wiesbaden 2012 (Gabler)

Bruhn, Manfred: Unternehmens- und Marketingkommunikation. Handbuch für ein integriertes Kommunikationsmanagement, München 2005 (Vahlen)

Hillebrecht, Steffen W.: Marketing für Presseverlage, 2. Aufl., Berlin 2009 (LIT)

Kloss, Ingomar: Werbung. Handbuch für Studium und Praxis, 5. Aufl., München 2011 (Vahlen)

Pezold, Kerstin; Sattler, Britta: Medienmarketing, Stuttgart 2009 (Lucius & Lucius)

Rota, Franco P.: Public Relations und Medienarbeit, 3. Aufl., München 2002 (dtv Taschenbuch)

Rota, Franco P.; Fuchs, Wolfgang: Lexikon Public Relations, München 2007 (Beck)

Schneider, Karl unter Mitarbeit von Dieter Pflaum (Hrsg.): Werbung in Theorie und Praxis, 6. Aufl., Waiblingen 2003 (M + S Verlag)

Unger, Fritz; Fuchs, Wolfgang: Management der Marketing-Kommunikation, 4. Aufl., Berlin, Heidelberg, New York 2007 (Springer)

Sachwortverzeichnis

3D-Animation 389 ff.
3D-Chat 528
3D-Darstellung 329
3D-Scanner 312
3D-Werbemittel 808
3GP 382
4-Phasen-Konzept nach Tuckmann 630

A

Abblenden 352
Abfragesprache 572
Abnahmetest 646
Abnahmetest-Protokoll 646
Above-the-Line-Werbung 803
Absatz, Direkt- 791
Absatz, indirekter 791
Absatzweg 86, 791
Abschlussanalyse 647
Absorption 213
Abspann 378
Abstrich 248
Abtastauflösung 458
Abtastfrequenz 434, 458
Access-Point 549
Achsensprung 365
Active Server Pages (ASP) 590
ActiveX 585
Ad-Hoc-Team 624
Adobe 242
ADSL 547
Advertainment 76
Agenda-Setting-Hypothese 112
Agentur 69, 736
Agenturnetzwerk 69
AGOF 81
Ähnlichkeit 199
Aicher, Otl 237, 340
Aicher-Scholl, Inge 237
AIFF-Dateiformat 424
AJAX 588
Akquisition 612, 650 ff., 799
Akronym 543
Aktivierung 308
Aktualisierung, instrumentelle 113
Aktualität 39, 144, 182
Akustische Bilder 306
Akzidenzdrucksache 456
Akzidenz-Grotesk 236
Allerweltserzeugnis 694
Allokation der Ressourcen 114
Alphabet 231, 340
Alphabet, griechisches 232
Alphabet, phönizisches 231
AM-Rasterung 458
Amtsblatt 72
Analog-digital-Wandlung 358, 433, 439
Analoge Fotografie 287 ff.
anamorph 379
Änderungsmanagement 644
Angeln von Ton 433
Animation 384 ff, 395
Animation, Cel- 387
Animation, Pfad- 387
Animation, Phasen- 385
Anstrich 248
Antiqua 235
Antiqua-Schrift 236, 240 ff.
Antiqua-Variante 241
Antivirenprogramm 553
Anzeige 45, 810
App 542
Apple 242
Äquivalenzprinzip 797
Arbeitspaket 635 ff.
Arbeitspaketkosten 640
Archiv 750
ARD 65 f., 90, 115, 158 f., 168, 682, 798
Aristoteles 200
ARPA 516
Array 574
ASCII-Standard 520
ASP 590
Assemblersprache 572
Assemble-Schnitt 376
Asset 722, 776
Assoziation 221, 246
Assoziations-Montage 496
Asymmetrie 205
Asynchrones DSL (ADSL) 547
Asynchronous JavaScript and XML (AJAX) 588
Atelier 755
Atelierkosten 716
Atmo 418
Atmosphäre 303
Attribut 577
Audio 404 ff.
Audio-Dateiformat 451 f.
Audio-Grabbing 424
Audiotechnik 426 ff.
Audio-Workstation 439
Aufblenden 352
Aufgabenverteilung 625
Aufhellung 314
Auflockerung 205
Auflösung 320, 456 ff.
Aufnahmeleiter 758
Aufnahmetechnik 367 ff.
Auftraggeber 615, 619 f., 622 ff., 632, 646
Auftragnehmer 622 ff.
Augmented Reality 402
Ausblenden 445
Aussage 54, 75
Aussagenforschung 76
Ausschießen 466
Ausschießschema 466
Ausschlussprinzip 115
Ausschnittvergrößerung 314, 316
Ausschreibung 611
Ausschwingphase 406 f.
Ausstattung 716, 755
Ausstellungsrecht 699
Aussteuerung 435
Auszeichnung 265
Auszug 710, 722
Autor 763
Autorensystem 573, 596 ff.
Autotypische Rasterung 458
Avatar 528
AVCHD 360
AVI 360
Axonometrie 333
axonometrische Darstellung 330, 333 f.

B

Badura-Modell 56
Balanced Scorecard 645
Balkendiagramm 344, 636 f.
Barock 235
Barock-Antiqua 235, 240
Barrierefreiheit 579
Barsortiment 86
Basismedium 144, 164
Basisplan 635
Bauhaus 236 f.
Baum-Metapher 501
Bearbeitung 696
Bedruckstoff 476 f.
Beeinflussungswirkung 102
Begleit-Medium 144
Behaviorismus 101
Bekanntheit 48, 99
Beleuchtung 366
Belichtung 277
Belichtungszeit 277
Belletristik 154
Below-the-Line-Werbung 46, 803
Bemusterung 750
Benutzerführung 504 ff.
Berichterstattung 125
Berthold AG 236
Berthold, Herrmann 250
Berufsbild 760
Beschaffung 62 f.
Beschäftigung 140
Beschichten 478
Betacam SP 356
Beurteilungskonflikt 630
Bewegtbild 350 ff.
Bewegung 363 ff., 384
Bewegungs-Tweening 388
Beziehungskonflikt 629 f.
Bild 74, 276 ff., 306 ff., 662 ff., 737
Bild, akustisches 306
Bildanalogie 309
Bildassoziation 309
Bildbearbeitung 310 ff.
Bilddatenbank 737
Bild, Digitalisierung 310 ff.
Bildebene 330
Bilderschrift 230
Bildformat 77, 322
Bild, Geruchs- 306
Bildgestaltung 297 ff.
Bild, haptisches 306
Bildkommunikation 33, 304
Bildkomposition 302 f.
Bildmetapher 309
Bildpositionierung 271
Bildrate 385
Bildsemiotik 304
Bildtransfer 294
Bildüberlegenheitswirkung 304
Bildumsetzung, direkte 309
Bildumsetzung, indirekte 309
Bildung 84, 152, 162
Bildungssendung 78
Bildverfremdung 318
Bildvorlage 455 ff.
Bildwechsel, dynamischer 351 ff.
Bildwechselfrequenz 77
Bildweite 281
Bildwiederholungsrate 385
Bildwirkung 308
Bill, Max 237
Binden 481
Bitmap 242
Bitmap-Schriftformat 243
BITNET 516
Blaupause 465
Bleikegel 251
Bleisatz 249
Blende 278, 351
Blended Learning 559 ff.
Blendenöffnung 277
Blendenwert 278
Blickkontakt 25
Blickverlauf 308
Blitzgerät 286
Blockheftung 481
Blocksatz 262
Blog, Blogger 73, 564
Blue Box 368
Blueprint 465
Blue-Screen-Technik 368
Blu-ray Disc 379, 779
BMP 321
Bodoni, Giambattista 236
Bogendruckmaschine 472
Bogenmontage 466
Book-on-Demand 89, 155
Botschaft 56, 74 ff., 256
Botschaft, wirkungsvolle Gestaltung 74 ff.
Brainstorming 767
Brennweite 278, 281
Bridge 517
Briefing 622, 632, 686, 767, 806
Broadcast-Qualität 361
Broschüre 810
Browser 449, 519, 551
Buch 89, 152 ff., 742 ff., 796
Buchdruck 132
Buchgattung 154
Buchhandel 155, 742
Buch-Kalkulation 725 f.
Buch-Produktion 742 ff.
Buchstabenabstand 258
Buch, Trends 155
Buch-Wertschöpfungsprozess 742
Budget 640 f
Bulletin Board 524
Bump-Mapping 394
Bundesverfassungsgericht 676, 681
Bundzuwachs 481
Buntfarben 216
Business-to-Busines 799
Business-to-Consumer 799
Business TV 800
Buyout 687, 713

C

Call-In 158
Camera Obscura 276
Capitalis Monumentalis 232
Capitalis Quadrata 233
Capitalis Rustica 233
Capturing 373
Cascading-Style-Sheet (CSS) 584
Cashflow-Plan 755, 757

Caslon, William 235, 250
Cast 714, 755
Catering 714
CBT 486, 491, 500, 559, 779, 801
CCD 310
CCD-Chip 291
CCD-Sensor 291
CD-ROM 779
CE 131, 141, 185
Cel-Animation 387
CGI 589
Change Management 644
Chat 525
Chatraum, Chatroom 525
Chef vom Dienst 745
Cicero 250
CIELAB-Farbmodell 460
CIF 359
Cinch-Stecker 429
Circuit Switched Data (CSD) 548
Clarendon 236
Client Side Scripting 583
CMM 460
CMS 556, 604 ff.
CMYK-System 219
Cocooning 106, 110
Codec 452
Cognitive Overload 504
Colormanagement 460 f.
Color-Management-Modul 460
Color-Proof 465
Common Gateway Interface (CGI) 589
Community 73, 528
CompactFlash 293
Compiler 578
Computer Based Training 486, 491, 500, 559, 779, 801
Computer Printing Control 474
Computer to Film 465
Computer to Plate 465
Computer to Press 465, 471
Computer to Print 471
Computer, Entwicklungsphasen 124
Computer, Geschichte 167
Computerpräsentation 672
Computerspiel s. Spiel
Connected TV 90
Constructive Solid Geometry (CSG) 391
Consumer Benefit 809
Consumer Electronics (CE) 131, 141, 184
Contemporay Hit Radio 747
Content 62, 160
Content Management System (CMS) 556, 604 ff.
Controlling 644 ff.
Cookie 553
Copy-Strategie 809
Copy-Technik 811
Corporate Behavior 47
Corporate Communication 47
Corporate Culture 47
Corporate Design 47, 266, 272
Corporate Identity 47, 273
Corporate Publishing 70
Courier 243
CPC 474
Cross Media Publishing 603
Crossmediale Werbekampagne 812 f.
CSD 548
CSS 584
Customer Relations 44
Customer Relationship Management 98
Customization 182, 801

D

DAB+ 91
Daguerre, Louis 123
Daily Soap 83
Darstellung, axonometrische 330, 333 f.
Darstellung, Dimensions- 328
Darstellung, ergonomische 327
Darstellung, Explosions- 329
Darstellung, gerenderte 329
Darstellung in Ansichten 330, 335
Darstellung, Informations- 342 ff.
Darstellung, perspektivische 330
Darstellung, Prinzip- 327
Darstellung, räumliche 330
Darstellung, schematische 328
Darstellungsform, journalistische 78
Darstellungsmethode 326
Datenhandschuh 401
Datenreduktion 445
Datenschutz 553
Datentyp 574
Datenübertragung, leistungsorientierte 516
Datenübertragung, paketorientierte 516
Datenübertragungsrate 445
DC-Offset-Tonsignal 442
Deckungsbeitrag 640, 725
Deckungsbeitragsrechnung 725
Decodierung 55
De-Esser-Zischlaut 442
Dehnrichtung 479
Deinkingprozess 477
Deklarieren 574
Demokratie 40, 87, 111
De-Noiser 444
Design 47, 69, 781
Designprozess 783
Desktop Publishing (DTP) 250
Development 754
DHTML 583
Dia-Audiovision 487
Diagramm 344, 665
Dialogführung 504
Diaprojektor 289
Diascanner 311
Dickte 248, 252
Didaktik 490 ff.
Didot, François Ambroise 249
Digital 8 359
Digital-Betacam 359
digitale Assets 776
digitale Fotografie 291 ff.
digitale Plattform 17
digitale Revolution 121
Digitalfotoprinter 296
Digitalisierung 160, 168, 186, 310, 749, 751
Digitalisierung, Kino 167
Digital Rights Management (DRM) 678
Digital Subscriber Line (DSL) 547
Digitaltechnik 454
Dimensionsdarstellung 328

Dimetrie 333 f.
DIN-Reihe 259
Direct Imaging 471
Direct Mailing 156
Direct Marketing 46, 727
Direktabsatz 791
Direktschall 413
Direktwerbung 46, 808
Disintermediation 791
Dispo, Disposition 757 f.
Dissonanz, kognitive 102, 807
Distanz 24
Distribution 63, 733, 744
Distributionspolitik 86
DivX 360
DNS 516, 518
Document Object Model 584
Document Type Definition (DTD) 591
Doku-Inszenierung 85
Dokumentation 78, 105, 782
Doku-Soap 85
Domain-Name 518
Domain Name System (DNS) 516, 518
Doppelmonopol 67
Dot 455
Download 449
Downloaddienst 174
Drahtringbindung 481
Dramaturgie 490, 493 ff., 811
Dreh 756 f
Drehbuch 85, 370 ff., 633, 709 ff., 722, 756, 773 f.
Drehbuch-Auszug 710 f.
Drehbuchautor 713
Drehbuchsoftware 372
Drehgenehmigung 716
Drehort 755
Drehplan 755, 757
Drehverhältnis 711
Dreifluchtpunktperspektive 333
DRM 678
Druck 454 ff.
Druckbogen 475
drucken 295 ff.
Drucker 295 f.
Druckindustrie 156 f.
Druckmaschine 472 ff.
Druckprozess 738
Druckpunkt 455
Druckqualität 455
Druckschrift 238
Druckschriften, Klassifikation 239
Druckschriften, Ordnungsprinzip 239
Druck- und Papierindustrie 156 f.
Druckverfahren 467 ff.
Druck-Workflow 454, 471
DSL 88, 547
DTD 591
DTP 250
DTP-Punkt 250
Durchschuss 254
Dürer, Albrecht 235, 330
DV 359
DVB 89, 160
DVCAM 359
DVCPro 359
DVD 779
DVD-Authoring 379
Dyade 21
Dynamic HTML (DHTML) 583
Dynamik 207 ff.

E

E-Book 89
E-Business 557
Echtfarbe 219
Echtzeitfähigkeit 440
E-Collaboration 561
E-Commerce 557, 791
EDGE 548
EDI 800
Edutainment 76, 489
Effekt, Bild 318 f.
E-Government 559
Eigenbewegung 363
Einblenden 445
Einblendung 353
Einfluchtpunktperspektive 331
Einführungswerbung 807
Eingabefrequenz 458
Einsatzkosten 708
Einschwingphase 406
Einstellgröße 298 f.
Einstellung 34, 77, 102, 297 ff.
Einstellung, amerikanische 298
Einstellung, Detail 298
Einstellung, groß 298
Einstellung, halbnah 299
Einstellung, Halbtotale 299
Einstellung, Kamera- 370
Einstellung, nah 298
Einstellungsgröße 77
Einstellung, Totale 299
Einstellung, Weite 299
Einzelkosten 640, 712, 718
Einzelphasenanimation 385
E-Learning 559
Electronic Data Interchange (EDI) 800
Electronic Program Guide (EPG) 163
Elektrofotografie 470
elektronische Bogenmontage 466
elektronisches Medium 142 f.
E-Mail 519 ff.
Emoticon 341, 543
Emotion 807
emotionaler Reiz 308
emotionale Wirkung 305
Emotionalisierung 85
Empfänger 26 ff., 56
Encapsulated PostScript (EPS) 594
Encodierung 55
Endfertigung 717
Endstrich 248
Enhanced Data Rates for GSM Evolution (EDGE) 548
Entgrenzung 93
Entrastern 459
Entwicklungslinie 370
Entwurf 326
Entwurfsprozess 192, 223, 258
Entwurfszeichnung 326
E-Paper 182
EPG 163
EPS 464, 471, 594
Equipment 716
Ereignis 113
Ereignis, genuines 113
Ereignis, mediatisiertes 113
Ereignis, Pseudo- 113
Erfahrungssicherung 648

Erfolgsfaktor, effektives Team 628 f.
Erfolgsfaktor, kritischer 621
Erfolgskontrolle 806
Erfolgsteam 628 f.
Ergonomie 327
ergonomische Darstellung 327
Erhaltungswerbung 807
Erkenntnistheorie 50
Erlebniswelt 488
Ersatzmontage 496
Erscheinungsbild, typografisches 266
Erscheinungsbild, visuelles 266, 272
Ethik, deskriptive 116
Ethik, journalistische 116
Ethik, normative 116
EUnet 516
Euroskala 219
Evaluation 616, 776, 780
Event 22
Event-Marketing 45
evolutionäres Modell 643
Exif 321
Expansionswerbung 807
Explosionsdarstellung 329
Exposé 633, 710, 767 f.
Exposition 370
Extensible HyperText Markup Language (XHTML) 582
Extensible Markup Language (XML) 591
Extensible Stylesheet Language (XSL) 592
Extranet 556
Extreme Digital 293

F

Facebook 73
Face-to-Face-Kommunikation 16, 21, 95
Fachbuch 154
Fachkompetenz 624
Fachzeitschrift 148 ff.
Factual Entertainment 85
Fade in 445
Fade out 445
Fadenheftung 481
Falzen 480 f.
Farbbalance 315
Farbe 212, 666
Farbe-an-sich-Kontrast 222
Farbeinsatz 258
Farben, indizierte 218
Farbensehen 212 f.
Farbgebung 258
Farbgestaltung 297
Farbharmonie 224 f.
Farbkombination 258
Farbkomponente 301
Farbkontrast 222
Farbkorrektur 314
Farbkreis 217
Farblaserdrucker 295 f.
Farb-Mapping 394
Farbmischung, additive 214
Farbmischung, subtraktive 215
Farbnegativfilm 289
Farbordnung 214 ff.
Farbordnungssystem 214
Farbproof 462
Farbsättigung 212
Farbsechseck 215
Farbseparation 462
Farbsystem 214
Farbtabelle 218
Farbtemperatur 284
Farbtiefe 321
Farbton 212, 219
Farbumkehrfilm 289
Farbwahrnehmung 213
Farbwert 218
Feasibility Study 617
Feinschnitt 759
Feldschema, Maletzke 57
Fernsehen 36, 78, 80 f, 83, 89 ff., 100, 130, 158 ff., 733, 808
Fernsehen, Bedeutung 104
Fernsehen, Geschichte 136
Fernsehen, Kritik am 105 ff.
Fernsehen, Trends 163
Fernsehfilm 83
Fernsehproduktion 754 ff.
Fernsehserie 83
Fernsehspiel 83
Fernseh-Standard 357
FFF-Werbemittel 808
Fiction 85
Figur-Grund-Beziehung 196, 198
Fiktion 105
File Transfer Protocol (FTP) 518, 532
Film 89, 164 ff., 354 ff., 733
Filmarchivierung 289
Filmemulsion 289
Filmentwicklung 290
Film, Geschichte 123, 133
Filmgestaltung 363
Filmindustrie 115
Film-Kalkulation 712 ff., 719 ff.
Filmmaterial 289, 717
Filmmusik 417
Filmnegativ 290
Filmproduktion 166, 754 ff.
Filmscanner 311
Filmtasche 289
Film, Trends 167
Filter 283 ff., 318
Filtereffekt 318
Finanzierung 755, 797
Firewire 360
First-Copy-Costs 796
Fixation 308
Fixiermedium 15
Fixkosten 725
Flachbettscanner 311
Flachdruck 468
Fläche 200, 203
Fläche, funktionale 661
Fläche, inhaltliche 662
Flash-Kartenformat 293
Flash Video (FLV) 381
Flattersatz 262
Fleisch 248
Flexodruck 468
Flip-Chart 670
Flowchart 501, 507, 687, 770 f.
Flowdesign 501
Flussdiagramm 598 f.
FLV 360
FM-Rasterung 458
FM-Synthese 438
Foerster, Wilhelm 250
Folienpräsentation 667
Folksonomy 570
Form 74, 192, 204, 302

Formalziel 615
Formanordnung 205 f., 211
Format, Radio 170
Formatierung 747
Formbeziehung 207 ff., 211
Form, dynamisch – richtungsweisend 210
Formelement 200, 211
Form, emporstrebend – ruhend 210
Form, geschlossen – umschlossen 210
Forming 630
Formmerkmal 241
Formsatz 263
Form, schützend – empfangend 210
Form, statisch – instabil 210
Form, steigend – fallend 210
Formwirkung 204, 210 f., 258
Forum, Foren 524
Fotografie 276
Fotografie, analoge 287 ff.
Fotografie, digitale 291 ff.
Fotografie, Geschichte 123, 133
Fotopapier 290
Foto-Tagging 568
Fournier, Pierre Simon 249
Fox, Benjamin 236
Fragmentierung 163, 183
Frame-by-Frame-Technik 385
Frame-Folge, Umkehrung 377
Franchising 791
Französische Renaissance-Antiqua 235, 240
Free-TV 67, 797 f.
Freeze-Frame-Technik 377
Freiwillige Selbstkontrolle Fernsehen 116
Fremdbeobachtung 38
Fremde Schriften 241
Fremdkontrolle 116
Frequenzgang 431 f.
frequenzmodulierte Rasterung 458
Froschperspektive 300, 332
Frutiger, Adrian 238, 247
FTP 518, 532
Führungslicht 366
Füll-Licht 366
Fundraising 71
Fundus 716
Fünfsatz, Prinzip 657
Funktion 576
Futura 237

G

Gage 714
Game Based Learning 489
Games, Gaming *s. Spiele*
Gammawert 461
Gantt-Diagramm 637
Garamond, Claude 235
Gatekeeper 40, 112
Gateway 517
GBL 489
GCR 461
Gebrochene Schriften 241 f.
Gedächtnis 305 f.
Gedächtnisbild 305 f.
Gedächtnisleistung 304
Gefühl 103
Gegenlicht 302, 366
Gegenschuss 365
Gegenstandsweite 281
Gehirn 305
geistige Schöpfung 693
GEMA 423, 678, 702 f., 713, 749
Gemeinkosten 640, 712, 718
Gemeinkostenzuschlag 718
Gemeinnützigkeit 65 f.
Gemeinschaft, virtuelle 489
General Packet Radio Service (GPRS) 548
Gensfleisch zu Gutenberg, Johannes 234, 454
Geräusch 56, 418 ff.
Geräuscharchiv 419, 423
gerenderte Darstellung 329
Geruchsbild 306
Gerücht 24
Geschäftsmodell 63
Geschichte der Medien 120 ff
Gesellschaft 13, 40, 61, 65, 93, 104 ff., 128 f., 805
Gesetz der Ähnlichkeit 197, 199
Gesetz der Erfahrung 198 f
Gesetz der Geschlossenheit 196, 198
Gesetz der Kontinuität 197, 199
Gesetz der Nähe 196, 198
Gesetz der Prägnanz 197, 199
Gesetz gegen den unlauteren Wettbewerb (UWG) 677
Gespräch 24, 29, 32
Gestalt 192, 302
Gestalten, elementares 192 ff.
Gestaltgesetz 195, 258
Gestaltpsychologie 195, 200
Gestaltung 192, 641, 781 ff.
Gestaltung, Film- 363
Gestaltung, Grundsätze 192 f.
Gestaltungselement 76
Gestaltungsmittel 208, 212
Gestaltungsprozess 192
Gestik 23, 25
Gewaltdarstellung 77, 100, 105, 109
Gewinn 718
GIF 321
Gill, Eric 247
Glätten 478
Gliederung, typografische 264 f.
Global System for Mobile Communication (GMS) 548
Globalisierung 93, 187
Goethe, Johann Wolfgang von 219
goldener Schnitt 259
Gotik 234
GPRS 548
Gradationskurve 314 f.
Grafik 324 ff.
Graustufen 457
Grauwert 254
griechisches Alphabet 232
Grobkonzept 767
Gropius, Walter 236
Großformatkamera 288
Grotesk-Schrift 236, 242
Groupware 16
Grundelement 200
Grundgesetz 675 ff.
Grundlinienraster 270
Grundnutzen 809
Grundsatz Trennung Werbung und Programm 81, 677
Grundschriftgröße 252
Gruppe 21 f., 61, 92 f., 97

Gruppierung 205
Gruscheln 568
GSM 548
Gut, meritorisches 115
Gut, öffentliches 115, 797
Gutenberg, Johannes Gensfleisch zu 128, 234, 454
GVL 678, 704, 713, 749

H

H.261 359
H.264-Codec 382
Habitualisierungsthese 109
Halbtonproof 465
Halbtotale 299
Halbunziale 233
Handschriftliche Antiqua 241
haptische Bilder 306
Harddisk-Recording 439 f.
Hardproof 464
Hauptlicht 366
Hausfarbe 221
Hausschrift 255, 272
HbbTV 90
HBCI-Standard 557
HDAV 487
HDTV 357
Hedonismus 175
Hell-Dunkel-Kontrast 222
Helligkeit 212, 219
Herstellungskosten 707
Hervorhebung 265
Hi-8 356
Hieroglyphen, ägyptische 230
High-Budget-Produktion 707
High Speed CSD (HSCSD) 548
High Speed Download Packet Access (HSDPA) 549
Hintergrundlicht 366
Hochdruck 467
Hochgeschwindigkeitskamera 288
Hochschule für Gestaltung Ulm 237
Holzstoff 477
Honorar 714
Hörereignis 405, 413
Hörfunk s. *Radio*
Horizontlinie 330
Hotspot 398, 549
HSB-Farbsystem 219
HSCSD 548
HSDPA 549
HTML 579
HTTP 451, 516, 518, 544
Hub 517
Human Relations 44 f.
Hybridformat 85
Hyperlink 502, 544
Hypermedium, Hypermedia 180, 544 f.
Hypermediasystem 502
Hypernet 183
Hypertext 502, 544 f.
Hypertext Markup Language (HTML) 579
Hypertext Preprocessor (PHP) 590
Hypertext Transfer Protocol (HTTP) 518, 544

I

ICC-Profil 460
ICE-Technologie 311
Idee 613, 691
Ideenskizze 326
Ideogramm 231
IEEE 1394-Schnittstelle 360
Ikon 338
IKT-Sektor 141
Illusion 108
Illustrationsprogramm 325
Image 48, 99
Image-Gestaltung, Beispiel 266 f.
Imagery 265, 304
IMAP4 520
Implementierung 776
Imposition-Proof 465
Independant 166
Index 338
Individualisierung 93
Individualkommunikation 21, 36
Indizierung 679
Industrialisierung 130, 236
Information 78 ff., 162
information richness 182
Informationsarchitektur 634
Informationsdarstellung 342 ff.
Informationsflut 105
Informationsgesellschaft 121
Informationsgrafik 342
Informationsorganisation 342 f.
Informationssystem 485, 500
Informationstechnik 184 f.
Informationstechnologie 17
Informationswirkung 102
Infotainment 76, 85, 489
Inhalt 74 ff.
inhaltliche Navigation 507
Inhaltsanalyse 76
Inhibitionsthese 109
Inkjetverfahren 470
inneres Bild 305
innere Pressefreiheit 680
Innovation 790
Insert-Schnitt 376
Installation 779
Instant Messaging 527
Instanz 577
Instruktionsdesign 492
Instruktionsmethode 492
Inszenierung, instrumentelle 113
Integrated Services Digital Network (ISDN) 546
Integration 105
Interaktion 20, 35, 95, 420, 503, 641
Interaktion, parasoziale 95
Interaktionsbeziehung 35
Interaktionselement 641
Interaktionsstruktur 641
interaktive Anwendung 420
Interaktivität 17, 36, 182, 484, 503
Interface-Agent 493
intermediäre Konkurrenz 122
internationales Medienrecht 684
Internationalisierung 187
Internet 45, 73, 81, 88, 90, 139, 160 f., 180 ff, 514 ff., 733
Internetagentur 69
Internetauftritt, Beispiel 198, 225
Internetgesetz 683
Internet, Leistungsmerkmale 182
Internet, mobiles 539 ff.
Internet, Nutzung 139
Internet, Nutzungsformen 182

Internet-Radio 451
Internet Relay Chat 525
Internet Service Provider (ISP) 550 f.
Internet, Trend 183
Internet-Werbung 80 f., 802, 814
InterNIC 515
Interpreter 578
Intranet 556, 800
Inverse Kinematik 393
Investor Relations 44
IP-Adresse 518
IPTC-Standard 321
IPTV 36, 160 f.
IRC 525
IRC-Client-Software 525
Irrelevanzreduktion 361, 446
ISDN 546
ISDN-Karte 546
Isometrie 333 f.
ISP 550 f.
iSRD-Technologie 311
IT-Branche 131, 141
ITK-Markt 141, 184
Itten, Johannes 216, 236
ITU 601 359

J

Java 585
Java-Applet 585
JavaScript 587
Java Server Pages (JSP) 590
Jingle 748
Joanna 247
Journalismus 38 ff., 127
Journalismus, investigativer 127
Journalismus, professioneller 39
journalistische Darstellungsformen 42, 78
journalistische Formen, Radio 170
JPEG 321
JSP 590
Jugendgefährdung 176
Jugendschutz 679
Junk-Mail 521

K

Kabel 88
Kabel Internet 545, 548
Kabel-TV 90
Kalkulation 640, 706 ff., 755, 757
Kalkulation, Buch- 725 f.
Kalkulation Computerspiel 729 f.
Kalkulation Drucksache 727 f.
Kalkulation, Film- 712 ff., 719 ff.
Kalkulation, Multimedia- 722 ff.
Kalkulationsschema 718 ff.
Kalt-Warm-Kontrast 222
Kamera 287 ff., 291 ff.
Kamera-Einstellung 370
Kameraführung 365
Kamera-Licht 366
Kamera, objektive 365
Kameraperspektive 77
Kamera, subjektive 365
Kampagne, crossmediale 812 f.
Kanal 525
Kandinsky, Wassily 236
Karolingische Minuskel 233
Kartenlesegerät 294
Kaschieren 478
Katalogisierung 534
Katharsisthese 109
Kaufzeitung 146
Kausalität 51
Kegelgröße 251
Kehlung 248
Keilschrift 230
Kepplinger, Hans Mathias 113
Kepplinger-Modell 113
Kerning 252
Kernprodukt 789
Kern-Team 624
Key-Color 461
Key Frame 388
Kick-Off 756
Kick-Off-Meeting 631, 648
Kinder 100, 105, 108
Kinderprogramm 83, 85
Kinder- und Jugendschutz 679
Kinematik, inverse 393
Kino 164 ff., 798, 808
Kinospielfilm 83
Kino, Trends 167
Kiosksystem 505
Klangfarbe 409
Klasse 577
Klassizismus 236
Klassizistische Antiqua 240
Klebebindung 481
Kleinbildkamera 287 f.
Kleingruppenkommunikation 16, 22
Kleinschrift, radikale 237
kognitive Dissonanz 102, 807
kognitive Wirkung 305
Kombinatorik 205
Kommunikation 13 ff., 228, 626, 629
Kommunikation, audiovisuelle 33
Kommunikation, auditive 33
Kommunikation, Bedeutung 18
Kommunikation, Begriff 18
Kommunikation, direkte 20 ff.
Kommunikation, dyadische 21
Kommunikation, Erfolgsbedingungen 26 ff.
Kommunikation, filmische 34
Kommunikation, Grundformen 16, 55 ff
Kommunikation, integierte 48
Kommunikation, interpersonale 16, 21
Kommunikation, mediale 21, 33 ff.
Kommunikation, multimodale 33
Kommunikation, natürliche 21
Kommunikation, nicht-personale 120
Kommunikation, non-verbale 23 ff., 120
Kommunikation, persönliche/personale 21 ff., 45, 120, 792
Kommunikation, Regeln für gute 29
Kommunikationsform 21
Kommunikationsinstrument 48
Kommunikationskanal 13
Kommunikationspolitik 45, 788, 792
Kommunikationsprozess 15, 18
Kommunikationsziel 807
Kommunikation, unvermittelte 21
Kommunikation, verbale 23 ff., 120
Kommunikation, visuelle 204, 256, 258, 338

MPEG 359, 446
MPEG-1 359
MPEG-2 359, 362
MPEG-4 359
Multimedia 17, 484 ff.
Multimedia-Agentur 760
MultimediaCard 293
Multimedia-Drehbuch 773 f.
Multimedia-Kalkulation 722 ff.
Multimedialität 182
Multimedia-Produktion 642, 760 ff.
Multimediarecht 675, 683
Multimedia-System 500
Multipurpose Internet Mail Extension 450
Multirow-Technik 399
Multitasking 97
Multivision 487
Musik 89, 172 ff., 417, 733, 752
Musikalien 64
Musikarchiv 423, 753
Musikgestaltung 745, 753
Musikredakteur 745
Musik, Trends 175
Musikuhr 753
Musikverlag 64
Muster 303

N

Nachbreite 248
Nachforderung 646
Nachricht 26 ff., 39, 55
Nachricht, Bauplan 26
Nachricht, die vier Seiten einer 26 ff.
Nachrichtenagentur 69
Nachrichtenfaktor 79
Nachrichtensendung 78
Nähe 24, 79, 196
Navigation 504 ff.
Navigation, inhaltliche 507
Navigationsarchitektur 634
Navigationselement 510 ff.
Navigation, strukturelle 506
NBTA 546
Nebenbei-Medium 144
Netiquette 543
Network Termination Basic Access (NBTA) 546
Networking 651
Netzebene 88
Netzeitung 43
Netzhaut 212
Netzplan 636, 639
Netzwerk 187
Netzwerk-Metapher 502
Neutralität 40
Newsgroup 522 ff.
Newsletter 521
Newsroom 739
NGO 71
Nicht-Rivalität im Konsum 115
Nickname 525
Nipkow, Paul Julius Gottlieb 124
NIP-Verfahren 471
NLE-Programm 373
Nodalpunkt 399
Noelle-Neumann, Elisabeth 112
Non-Fiction 85
Non-Governmental Organisation 71
Non-Impact-Printing 470
Non-Profit-Organisation 71
Normalize 443
Normalobjektiv 282
Normalperspektive 300, 332
Norming 630
NTBA 546
NTSC 357
NURBS-Verfahren 392
Nutzen 466
Nutzen-Kosten-Analyse 617
Nutzkanal 546
Nutzung 62, 162
Nutzungsrecht 690, 700

O

Oberlänge 248
Obertöne 406
Object-Movie 397, 399
Objekt 577
Objektiv 280 ff.
objektive Kamera 365
Objektivität 39 ff., 110, 125
objektorientierte Programmierung (OOP) 577
öffentliche Meinung 112
öffentliches Gut 115, 797
Öffentlichkeit 16, 40, 44, 72, 111
Öffentlichkeitsarbeit 47, 788, *s. auch Public Relations*
öffentlich-rechtlicher Rundfunk 115
Offsetdruck 454, 468
On-Demand-Nutzung 97
One-to-one-Marketing 802
Online 43, 798
Online-Banking 557
Online-Redaktion 43
OOP 577
Open Culture 127
OpenType 242
Opentype-Schriftformat 243
Operationalisierung 616
Operator 574
OPI-Bildaustausch 462
Opinion Leader 111
optische Mitte 207
optische Täuschung 195
optische Telegraphie 15
Ordnungspolitik 115
Ordnungsprinzip 239
Organisation 61, 70 f.
Organisationskommunikation 16
Orientierung 104
O-Ton 775
Outsourcing 732
Overwrite-Schnitt 376

P

P2P-Filesharing 174
Packaging 62 f., 633, 754, 799
PageRank 536
PAL 357
Panorama 397
Panoramakamera 288
Pantomimik 25
Papier 476
Papiereigenschaft 478 f.
Papierformat 259
Papierindustrie 156 f.
Papierpositiv 290

Papiersorte 479
Pappband 481
Paradigma 370
Parodie 696
Passergenauigkeit 474
Pay per Channel 67
Pay Per View 67, 797
Pay-TV 67, 158, 160, 166, 678, 797 f.
PC2PC 531
PC2Phone 531
PDA 539
PDF 471, 590, 595
Peer-to-Peer 167, 174, 674
Perceptual Coding 446
Performing 630
periodische Rasterung 458
Periodizität 39, 144
Perl 589
Permalink 564
Permission Marketing 814
Persönlichkeitsrecht 677, 699
Perspektive 77, 297, 300, 330 ff.
perspektivische Darstellung 330
Pfadanimation 387
Pfad, kritischer 638 f.
Pflichtenheft 623, 632, 641 f., 781
PGP 554
Phasenanimation 385
Phasenmodell 643
Phasenorientierung 643
Phönizisches Alphabet 231
Phonogramm 231
PHP 590
physischer Reiz 308
Pica-Point 250
Piktogramm 231, 340
Pitch 611, 651
Pixel 455
Pixelgrafik 324 f.
Plagiat 696
Plakat 45, 810
Plakatgröße 252
Plantreue 643
Plattenzylinder 469
Plattform 88
Playback Rate 385
PLC 545
Plot Point 370
Plug-In 441, 449, 582, 601
PNG 321
Podcast 160, 171, 567
POF 801
POI 708, 801
Point of Fun (POF) 801
Point of Information (POI) 708, 801
Point of Sale (POS) 44, 87, 708, 801, 808
Politik 40, 106, 111 ff., 125 ff.
Polygon-Verfahren 391
POP3 520
Pop-up-Menü 512
Portable Document Format (PDF) 590, 595
Portal 533
POS 44, 87, 708, 801, 808
Posting 524
Postman, Neil 76, 82, 105, 107
Postpress 738
Post-Production/Postproduktion 633, 732 f., 744, 751, 754, 758 ff.
PostScript 242, 250, 464, 590, 594
PostScript-Schriftformat 243
Powerline Communication (PLC) 545
PR 41, 44 f., 47, 70, 788, 792, 803
Practical Extraction and Report Language (Perl) 589
Prägen 478
Pragmatik 304, 340
Prägnanz 199
Präsentation 42, 650 ff., 778
Präsentationsraum 671
Präsentationssystem 487, 500
Präsentationsziel 655
Präsenter-Spot 811
Präsenzpolitik 788, 791, 795
Preispolitik 795, 801
Prepress 738
Pre-Production 732 f., 744, 751, 754 ff.
Pre-Production Meeting 642
Press 738
Presse 87, 808
Presse-Einzelhandel 87
Pressefreiheit 676, 680
Pressefreiheit, innere 680
Presse, Geschichte 132 f.
Presse-Grosso 87
Pressekodex 116
Pressekonferenz 41
Presserecht 675, 680
Pre-Test 816
Pretty Good Privacy (PGP) 554
Primärfarbe 216
Primitive 391
Print 733
printing on demand 470
Printmedien 142 ff.
Prinzipdarstellung 327
Privatpersonen als Kommunikatoren 61, 73
Problemanalyse 614
Production/Produktion 633, 641, 732 ff., 744, 751, 754
Product Placement 45, 67, 81, 104, 792
Produktentwicklung 781 ff.
Produktgestaltung 200
Produktinnovation 790
Produktion Buch 742 ff.
Produktion Fernsehen 754 ff.
Produktion Film 754 ff.
Produktion Multimedia 760 ff.
Produktion Radio 744 ff.
Produktion Tageszeitung 734 ff.
Produktionsleiter 711, 714, 755
Produktionsteam 761 ff.
Produktivität 645
Produktlebenszyklus 790, 807
Produkt-Planung 632
Produktpolitik 788 ff., 794
Produzent 755, 759, 761
Profilpolitik 788, 792, 795
Programmierer 765
Programmierparadigma 572
Programmiersprache, höhere 572
Programmiertool 641
Programmierung 572, 574 ff., 776
Programmierung, objektorientierte (OOP) 577
Programming 81, 163
Programmplanung 744, 747 ff.
Programmschema 747
Progressive Scan 355
Projekt 618

Projektablaufplan 636
Projekt-Abschluss 646 ff.
Projektabschlussbericht 647 f.
Projektabwicklung 635
Projektadministration 626
Projekt-Antrag 613
Projekt-Controlling 644
Projekt-Definition 614 ff.
Projekt-Dokumentation 627
Projekt-Durchführung 643 ff.
Projekt, externes 611
Projekt-Idee 613, 616
Projekt, internes 612
Projektion, kubische 398
Projektion, sphärische 398
Projektion, zylindrische 398
Projektlebenszyklus 610
Projektleiter 625, 762 f.
Projektmanagement 610 ff.
Projektmerkmal 618
Projekt-Planung 632 ff., 641 ff.
Projektrahmen 619
Projekt-Start 620 ff.
Projekt-Steuerung 643
Projektstrukturplan 635
Projektteam 612, 624 ff.
Projektziel 615
Proof 464
Proportion 207
Prototyp 776
Prototyping 643
Provider 515, 521, 550 f.
Proxy-Server 553
Prozedur 576
Prozessevidenz 652
Prozessfarbe 219
Prozesspolitik 115
Pseudo-Ereignis 113
Public-Key-Verfahren 554
Public Relations 41, 44 f., 47, 70, 788, 792, 803
Publikum 12, 38, 92, 95, 117
Publikum, disperses 95
Publikumsforschung 92
Publikumszeitschrift 148 ff.
Publizistik 38 ff.
Publizität 144
Pufferzeit 638
Pull-down-Menü 512
Punkt 200 f.
Punktdiagramm 345
Punkt, typografischer 249
Punktzuwachs 463
Punzen 248

Q

QCIF 359
Qualität 83, 615
Qualität, Fernsehen 83
Qualitätsfaktor 459
Qualitäts-Kontrast 222
Qualitätsverlust 325
Quantitäts-Kontrast 222
Quasistationäre Phase 406
QuickTime (MOV) 381

R

Radio 67, 80 f., 84, 91, 100, 160, 168 ff., 733, 744 ff., 798, 808
Radio, Format 170
Radio, Geschichte 135
Radio-Produktion 744 ff.
Radiosity 394
Radio, Trends 171
Radio-Workflow 744 ff.
Radius 317
Rahmenheft 619
Ranking-Verfahren 536
Rapid-Authoring-Tool 596
Rapid Prototyping 643
Raster 205
Rasterfrequenz 456
Rastergrafik 243
Raster Image Processor 463, 465, 471
Rasterproof 465
Rasterung, AM- 458
Rasterung, autotypische 458
Rasterung, FM- 458
Rasterung, frequenzmodulierte 458
Rasterung, periodische 458
Rasterweite 456
Rasterzelle 455
Raubkopie 172
Raumakustik 411 ff., 426, 430
Raumakustik, geometrische 414 f.
Raumakustik, statistische 415
räumliche Darstellung 330
Raumtiefe 297, 301, 303
Rausatz 263
RAW-Datei 313
RAW-Format 321
RAW-Konverter 313
Ray Tracing 394
Reaktanz 808
Realität s. *Wirklichkeit*
Realitätseindruck 419
Reality TV 82
RealServer 450
RealVideo (RV oder RM) 381
Reason Why 809
Re-Briefing 632
Recall-Test 816
Recherche 41, 769
Rechnungswesen 706
Recht 674 ff.
Rechte und Manuskript 713
Recognition-Test 816
Redaktion 42, 745
Redaktionsgeheimnis 680
Redaktionssystem 556, 736
Red Book 436
Red Button 90
Rede 31
Redekunst 24
Redigieren 42
Reduktionswerbung 807
Redundanzreduktion 361, 446
Reflexion 213, 413, 430
Regie 755
regionaler Raum 84
Regisseur 755 f.
Registerhaltigkeit 474
Reichweite 99, 162, 815
Reihung 205
Reinlayout 258, 326
Reisekosten 716
Reiz 308
Reiz, emotionaler 308
Reiz, physischer 308
Reiz-Reaktions-Schema 50 ff.
Reiz, überraschender 308
Rekreation 104

Relationship Marketing 98
Relaunch 790, 807
Remission 213
Remissionsrecht 87
Renaissance 235
Render-Farm 396
Rendering 329, 396
Renner, Paul 237
Repeater 517
Reporter 745
Resonanz 407
Response 51
Responsemedium 792
Ressourcenplanung 640
Rezension 558
Rezeptor 194, 212, 220
Rezipient 54, 57, 61, 92 ff.
RGB-Modus /-System 217, 460
Rhythmus 207 ff.
Richtcharakteristik 432
Richtung 365
Richtungswahrnehmung 411
Riepl'sches Gesetz 122
Rigging 393
RIP 463, 465, 471
Robot 534
Rohschnitt 758
Rolle 625
Rollendruckmaschine 473
Roll-Out-Kosten 708
Roll-over-Funktion 507
Rotation 753
Rotis 237
Router 517
RSS-Feed 565
RTP 451
RTSP 451
Rückkanalfähigkeit 182
Rückstichheftung 481
Rückwärtsterminierung 639
Rundfunk 681 f.
Rundfunkfreiheit 676
Rundfunk, öffentlich-rechtlicher 65 f., 130, 162
Rundfunk, privater 67 f., 162
Rundfunkrecht 675, 681 f.
Rundfunksender 804
Rundfunkstaatsvertrag 675, 681 f.

S

Saccade 308
Sachziel 615
Sales Promotion 46
Sammellinse 281
Sampling 433
Sampling Rate 385, 459
Satellit 88, 90, 545
Sättigung 219, 315
Satzart 262
Satzspiegel 258, 260 f.
Säulendiagramm 344
Scanner 311
Schaffensprozess 192
Schalldruckpegel 408
Schallereignis 405, 411, 413
Schärfe 297, 303
Schärfentiefe 283
Scharfzeichnen 317
Schatten 303, 336
Schaubild 665
Schaugröße 252
Scheinwelt 105, 108
Schema 308
schematische Darstellung 328
Schichtenmodell 517
Schlitzverschluss 277
Schlüsselbildtechnik 388
Schluss-Meeting 648
Schmuckfarbe 219
Schnitt 373 ff.
Schnittfolge 376
Schnitt, goldener 259
Schnitt, non-linearer 373
Schnitttechnik, besondere 377
Schön- und Widerdruck 466
Schöpfung, geistige 693
schräger Standpunkt 300
Schreiben 42
Schreibschrift 241 f.
Schrift 228
Schriftbreite 238
Schriftcharakter 245, 268
Schriftfamilie 238, 252
Schriftformat 243
Schrift, gebrochene 234
Schrift, Geschichte 123, 132
Schriftgrad 251
Schriftgröße 251 f., 258
Schriftlage 238
Schriftlinie 248
Schriftmischung 258
Schriftschnitt 238, 258
Schrift, serifenlose 236
Schriftstärke 238
Schriftstil 252
Schriftwahl 258
Schriftwirkung 244, 258
Schulbuch 154
Schulz von Thun, Friedemann 26 ff.
Schuss 365
Schützen 478
Schweizer Typografie 237
Schwellenwert 317
Schwenk 364
Schwerpunktbildung 207
SCORM 561
Screendesign 634
Screenrecorder 596
Scribble 326
Scrollbalken 512
SECAM 357
Second-Hand-Erfahrung 108
Secure Digital 293
Second Life 73
Secure Multipurpose Internet Mail Extension (S/MIME) 554
Secure Socket Layer (SSL) 557
Segmentierung 96
Segregation 93
Seitenbeschreibungssprache 573
Seitengestaltung 259
Seitenübersicht 737
Sekundärerfahrung 108
Sekundärfarbe 217
Selbstfahrerstudio 752
Selbstklebepapier 476
Selbstkosten 640, 712, 718
Selbstregulierung 115
Selbstverpflichtung 116
Semantik 304, 339
Semiotik 304, 338
Sendeablaufplanung 749
Sendeabwicklung 744, 752 ff.
Sendeleitung 753

Sender 26 ff., 56, 60
Senderecht 690, 699
Sendetechnik 753
Sendeuhr 748
sensorisches Zentrum 194
Sequenz 77, 498
Serife 232, 248
serifenbetonte Linear-Antiqua 240
serifenlose Linear-Antiqua 240
serifenlose Schrift 236
Serious Games 489
Server 450
Serverfarm 529
Server Side Scripting 588
Set Top Box 90, 678
SGML 591
Shading 394
Shannon-Weaver-Modell 55
Shopping-Mall 798
Shutter-Brille 401
Siebdruck 454, 469 f.
Simulationssystem 500
Simultan-Kontrast 222
Singlerow-Technik 399
Single Source Publishing 603
Sinnbild 338
Sinnesnerven 194
Sinnesorgan 193 f.
Sinneszellen 212
Sinus-Milieu 93 f.
Skalierung 314, 316, 325
Skizze 258, 326
Skriptsprache 573, 583 ff.
Skype 532
Slice of Life 811
Small Talk 24
SmartMedia-Karte 294
Smartphone 539
Smart-TV 90
S/MIME 554
SMPT 520
SMPTE-Timecode 374
Social Commerce 73
Social Media 73
Social Networking 568
Sofortbildkamera 288
Softproof 464
Software-Agent 534, 538
Software-Ergonomie 420
Sonderfarbe 219
S-O-R-Modell 51
Soundchip 438
Sounddesign 420
Soundkarte 426, 437
soziales Netzwerk 73
Sozialisation 104, 111
Spaltenbreite 253
Spam 521
Spannung 494
Special Effect 710
Speicherkarte 293
Speichermedium 15, 293 f.
Speicherung, anamorphe 379
Spezialkamera 288
sphärische Projektion 398
Spider 534
Spiegelreflexkamera 292
Spiegelreflex-System 279
Spiel 33, 89, 130, 176 ff., 488
Spielfilm 798
Spiel, Trends 179
Spiralbindung 481
Spline-Verfahren 392
Splitter 547
Sponsoring 45, 67, 81, 792
Sprache 23, 25, 306
sprechen 659
Sprechtext 416, 424, 444
S-R-Modell 51
SSL 554, 557
Staat 61, 72
Staatsunabhängigkeit 65
Stäbchen 212
staff 714, 755
Stakeholder 44, 620
Stakeholderanalyse 620
Standard Generalized Markup Language (SGML) 591
Standbild 297
Standproof 465
Standpunkt, schräger 300
Stankowski, Anton 204, 208
Stanzen 478
Stärke 317
Statistik 324
Stativ 285
Status 79, 625
Stereokamera 288
Stimulationsthese 105, 109
Stimulus 51
Stitching 397, 400
Stoffentwicklung 633, 754
Stoffidee 710
Storming 630
Störquelle 55
Storyboard 375, 633, 709 f.
Strategie 794
Strategie, crossmediale 43
Streaming 449, 600
Streichen 478
Streuplan 814 f.
Streuung 205
Struktur 205, 500
strukturelle Navigation 506
Strukturpolitik 115
Strukturwahl 500 f.
Style Guide 641
subjektive Kamera 365
Subvention 115
Sucherkamera 291
Suchersystem 279
Suchmaschine 534
Sujet 77
Supply Chain 791
S-VHS 356
Symbol 19 f., 338
Symmetrie 205
Syntagma 34
Syntaktik 304
Syntax 339
Systemprodukt 178
Szene 77, 364, 369

T

Tablet-PC 539
Tagesdisposition 758
Tageslichtfilm 289
Tageszeitung 43
Tageszeitung, regionale 146
Tageszeitung, überregionale 146
Tags 563, 579
Talkshow 83
Tarifvertrag 711

Tätigkeitsliste 636
Tauschbörse, illegale 167
TCP/IP 451, 516 ff.
Team 612, 624 ff., 755, 761 ff.
Teamarbeit 628
Teamentwicklung 630
Teamgröße 625
Team, virtuelles 626
Technik 121 ff., 755
Technikgeschichte der Medien 121 ff.
technischer Fortschritt 121
Telefon 186
Telefon, Geschichte 134
Telefongespräch 36
Telefon-Marketing 45
Telegrafie, Geschichte 134
Telekommunikation 17, 131, 141, 184 f.
Telekommunikationsgesetz (TKG) 675, 683
Telemediengesetz (TMG) 683
Telenovela 83, 163
Teleobjektiv 282
Teleshopping 45
Tendenzbetrieb 64
Tendenzschutz 680
Terrestrik 88, 90
Tertiärfarbe 217
Text 74, 306 f., 662 ff., 737
Text-Bild-Kommunikation 33
Textkommunikation 33
Textur 394
Theorie der Schweigespirale 112
Thermosublimationsdrucker 296
Thermosublimationsverfahren 464
Thermotransferdrucker 296
Thread 524
Tiefdruck 469
Tiefenanpassung, -korrektur 316
TIFF 321
Tilt 364
TIME Branche 17, 131, 141, 160, 180, 184 ff.
TIME-Branche, Trends 187
Timing 815
Tintenstrahldrucker 295, 470
Titel 378
TMS 604
Ton 74, 405 ff.
Tonality 809
Tonaufnahme 422 ff., 775
Tonbearbeitung 441
Tonhöhe 407, 409
Tonmischung 447 f.
Tonsignal 442
Tonstudio 428
Tonteam 764
Tonträger 174
Ton-Überspielung 436
Tonwertkorrektur 314
Tonwertstufe 455
Totale 299
Track 375
Trackback 564
Trägermedium 87, 796
Transformation, lineare 389
Transformationsreihe 206
Translation Memory System (TMS) 604
Transparent-Mapping 394
Transparenz 653
Transportkosten 716
Transportmedien 15
Transport, netzbasierter 88 ff.
Transport, physischer 87
Transportweg 61, 86 ff.
Trapping 462
Treatment 633, 710, 771 f.
Trennungsgrundsatz von Werbung und Programm 677
Trimmen 376
Triple Play 160, 547
Trommelscanner 311
True-Proof 465
TrueType 242
TrueType-Schriftformat 243
Trustcenter 554
Tschichold, Jan 237
TV-Nutzung, mobile 161
TV-Show 82
TV-Werbespot, Beispiel 811
Tweet 569
Twitter 569
Typografie 228 ff.
typografische Gliederung 264 f.
typografischer Punkt 249
typografisches Erscheinungsbild 266
Typologie 248
Typometer 251

U

Übereckperspektive 331
Überfüllen 462 f.
Übersetzung 696
Übertragungsmedium 15, 124
Überzeugungswirkung 102
Ubiquität 182
UCR 461
UDP 451
UKW 91, 753
Umgestaltung 696
Umschlagen 466
Umstülpen 466
UMTS 88, 549
Unbuntaufbau 461
Unbuntfarben 216
Uniform Resource Locator (URL) 518, 582
Unikat 707
Unique Selling Proposition (USP) 650, 789, 807, 809
Universal Mobile Telecommunication System (UMTS) 549
Universalität 39
Unschärfe 297, 303
Unterfarbenreduzierung 461
Unterfüllen 462 f.
Unterhaltung 82 ff., 152, 162
Unterhaltung, fiktionale 82
Unterhaltung, journalistische 85
Unterhaltung, nonfiktionale 82
Unterhaltungselektronik 17, 184
Unterhaltungsshow 83
Unterhaltungssystem 488
Unterlänge 248
Unternehmensethik 116 f.
Unternehmenskommunikation 44 ff.
Unterschneiden 252
Unziale 233
Urheber 697 ff.
Urheberpersönlichkeitsrecht 678, 699
Urheberrecht 674, 677 ff., 685 ff.

URL 518, 582
Usability 777
Usability Lab 777
USENET 516, 523
User-Generated Content 73, 171, 183
USP 642, 650, 789, 807, 809

V

Value Added Service 801
Variable 574
variable Kosten 725
VDSL2 547
Vektorgrafik 324 f.
Vektorgrafikprogramm 325
Venezianische Renaissance-Antiqua 235, 240
Verantwortung 116, 625
Verbreitungsrecht 690, 699
Veredeln 478
Verfremdung 318
Verkaufsförderung 46, 792, 803
Verkehrszeichen 340 f.
Verlag 64, 86, 742 f., 804
Verleih 754
Versalhöhe 248
Verschlusszeit 278
Versicherung 717
Verständigung 19, 22, 56
Verständlichkeit 497 f.
Verteilungskonflikt 630
Vertrag 623
Vertrauen 629
Vertrieb 86 f.
Vertrieb, direkter 86 f.
Vertrieb, indirekter 86 f.
Vervielfältigungsrecht 690, 699
Verwertung 633, 754
Verwertungsgesellschaft 701 ff.
Verwertungsrecht 678, 699
Very High Speed DSL (VDSL) 547
VG Bild-Kunst 703
VG Media 704
VG Wort 703
VHS 356
Video 354 ff.
Video-8 356
Video, analoges 354 ff.
Video-Ausgabe 379 ff.
Video, digitales 354
Video-DVD 379
Video-Format, analoges 356
Video-Format, digitales 359
Video on Demand 160, 163
Video-Produktion 369 ff.
Video-Spiel *s. Spiel*
Video-Streaming 381
Videoteam 764
Videotechnik, analoge 355 ff.
Videotechnik, digitale 358 ff.
da Vinci, Leonardo 235
Virtual Community 489
Virtual Reality 397 ff.
Virtual Reality Modeling Language 400
virtuelle Gemeinschaft 489
virtueller Marktplatz 798
virtueller Rundgang 398
virtuelles Team 626
virtuelle Welt 73, 489
Virus 552
Visualisierung 309
visuelles Erscheinungsbild 266, 272 f.
Vogelperspektive 300, 332
Voice over IP (VoIP) 530
Voice-Chat 526 f.
Volkswirtschaft 804
Volltonfarbe 219
Vorbreite 248
Vorführungsrecht 690, 699
Vorgehensmodell 643
Vorkosten 713
Vorproduktion 633, 750
Vorschaubild 512
Vortrag 24, 658
Vorwärtsterminierung 639
VRML 400, 602

W

Wahrnehmung 33, 77, 193, 229, 308
Wahrnehmungsart 195
Wahrnehmungseinheit 77
Wahrnehmungskette 193 f.
Wahrnehmung, visuelle 195
Walbaum 236
Wandler 433, 438
Wandlungsprinzip 430 f.
WAP 540
Warping 389
Wasserfall-Modell 166
Watzlawick, Paul 24
WAVE-Dateiformat 424
WBT 486, 491, 500, 559, 779, 801
Web 2.0 183, 562
Web Based Training (WBT) 486, 491, 500, 559, 779, 801
Web3D 602
WebCam 530
Webcast 566
Webchat 525 f.
Webinar 566
Webkatalog 534
Weblog 564
Web-Projekt 634
Web-Radio 91
Webserver 450
Web-TV 91, 161
Webvertising 802
Wegwerf-Prototyping 643
Weichzeichnen 317
Weitwinkelkamera 288
Weitwinkelobjektiv 282
Werbeagentur 69
Werbeanzeige 229
Werbebotschaft 80
Werbebudget 143, 814
Werbeerfolgskontrolle 816
Werbeholding 69
Werbekampagne, Ablauf 806
Werbemarkt 142 f.
Werbemittel 806, 808 ff.
Werbespot 45, 67, 170
Werbeträger 46, 142, 144, 166, 806, 814 ff.
Werbeziel 807
Werbung 46, 67, 69, 80 f., 115, 142 f., 162, 170, 306, 792, 803 ff.
Werk 677 f., 693 ff.
Werkpartikel 696
Wertekonflikt 630
Wertschöpfungskette 62 f., 164, 166, 794
Wertschöpfungskette Film 164, 166

Wertschöpfungskette Musik 174
Wertschöpfungsprozess 742
Wertschöpfungsverbund 184
Wettbewerb 67, 114
Wettbewerb, publizistischer 67
Wettbewerbspräsentation 651
Wettbewerbsrecht 686
Wickelfalz 480
Widerdruck 466
Wiki 563
Willberg, Hans-Peter 257
WiMAX 549
Windowing 166
Windows Media Video (WMV) 381
Wireless Application Protocol (WAP) 540
Wireless Local Network (WLAN) 549
Wireless Markup Language (WML) 540
Wirkfaktoren beim Rezipienten 103
Wirklichkeit 38 ff., 52, 79, 82, 105, 108, 112, 125, 305
Wirkung, affektive 103
Wirkung, kognitive 103
Wirkung, konative 103
Wirkungsmodell 103
Wirtschaft 114 ff., 130 f.
Wirtschaftlichkeit 616 f., 706
Wissen 103, 152
Wissenschaft 84
Wissenschaftssendung 78
Wissenskluft, wachsende 105, 110
WLAN 549
WML 540
WMV 359
Wochenprogramm 748
Wochenzeitung 146
Worldwide Interoperability for MicroWave (WiMAX) 549
World Wide Web (WWW) 515 ff., 544 ff., 554 ff.
Wortmarke 255, 272
Wortschrift, chinesische 231
WWW 515 ff., 544 ff., 554 ff.

X

XHTML 582
XLR-Stecker 429
XML 591
XML Path Language (XPath) 592
XML-Schema (XSD) 591
XPath 592
XSD 591
XSL 592
XSL-FO 592
XSL Formatting Objects (XSL-FO) 592
XSLT 592, 594
XSL Transformation (XSLT) 592, 594
Xvid 360

Y

YouTube 73

Z

Zahlungsbereitschaft 163
Zapfen 212
Zapping 162, 808
ZDF 65 f., 90, 115, 158 f. 682, 798
Zeichen 19, 230, 338
Zeichencode 340
Zeichensystem 338, 340 f.
Zeilenabstand 253, 258
Zeilenbreite 253
Zeilenfall 262
Zeilensprungverfahren 355
Zeitbudget 97
Zeitlupe 367
Zeitlupen-Effekt 377
Zeitplanung 636
Zeitraffer 367
Zeitraffer-Effekt 377
Zeitschrift 45, 80, 84, 87, 148 ff., 796
Zeitschrift, Geschichte 132 f.
Zeitschrift, Trends 151
Zeitung 45, 80, 84, 87, 130, 144 ff., 734, 796
Zeitung, Geschichte 132 f.
Zeitung, Produktion 734 ff.
Zeitung, Trends 147
Zellulose 477
Zentralperspektive 331
Zentralverschluss 277
Zerstreuungslinse 281
Zertifikat 554
Zielgruppe 92, 97 ff., 615, 620, 655, 690, 809
Zielkonflikt 629
Ziel, Werbung 807
Zischlaut 442
Zitat 696
Zoom 364
ZSK 750
Zusatznutzen 809
Zuschlagskalkulation 640, 718, 722
Zweifluchtpunktperspektive 331
zylindrische Projektion 398

Firmenverzeichnis

Die Autoren bedanken sich bei den nachfolgenden Firmen und Institutionen für ihre Unterstützung.

Agfa-Gevaert AG, Mortsel, Belgien
Anders & Kern Präsentationssysteme GmbH, © 667/1, 671/1–3, 672/1
Architekturbüro Förstner-Kegel, Konstanz

Barsortiment Lingenbrink, Norderstedt
Beyerdynamic, Heilbronn
Büttenpapierfabrik Gmund, Gmund am Tegernsee

Camgaroo AG, München
Claus Peter Dudek Photodesign, Hamburg
Coca-Cola GmbH, Berlin

Deutsche Bank AG, Frankfurt
Deutsche Post AG, Darmstadt
DVZ Druckmarkt Verlag Zürich GmbH, Zürich

Eberspächer GmbH & Co. KG, Esslingen
Engel Verbindungselemente, Weingarten
ERCO Leuchten GmbH, Lüdenscheid

Filmtheaterbetriebe Heinz Lochmann (Traumpalast), Rudersberg
Fotolia.com, Berlin, 12/1 © maxoido, 17/1 © Nmedia, 18/1 © Darren Baker, 22/1 © Rido, 29/1 © WavebreakMediaMicro, 30/1 © Kurhan, 31/1 © pojoslaw, 32/1 © Adam Gregor, 33/1 © Gennadiy Poznyakov, 34/1 © Benny Weber, 38/1 © Robert Kneschke, 39/1 © ashumskiy, 40/1 FotolEdhar, 41/2 © ashumskiy, 42/1 © Kzenon, 46/1 © Alexander Raths, 49/1 © olly, 49/2 © Gina Sanders, 50/1 © mentalrai, 52/1 © Robert Kneschke, 60/1 © Yuri Arcurs, 64/1 © asiln, 75/1 © Robert Kneschke, 78/2 © nightfly84, 79/1 © Marco2811, 80/1 © JiSIGN, 81/1 © vgstudio, 82/1 © Gennadiy Poznyakov, 84/1 © goce risteski, 87/1 © spinetta, 89/1 © Adam Borkowski, 89/2 © Thomas Jansa, 91/1 © kreativloft GmbH, 91/2 © Sergey Khakimullin, 92/1 © Photo_Ma, 95/1 © Fotol-Edhar, 101/1 © somenski, 104/1 © Andreas Wolf, 105/1 © BeTa-Artworks, 106/1 © contrastwerkstatt, 107/1 © Klaus-Peter Adler, 108/1 © Monkey Business, 110/1 © Monkey Business, 110/2 © somenski, 111/1 © Corgarashu, 112/1 © rico287, 114/1 © VRD, 114/2 © Gina Sanders, 115/1 © andreas130, 115/2 © Janina Dierks, 116/1 © Yuri Arcurs, 117/1 © Joachim Wendler, 117/2 © Tyler Olson, 139/1 © Mat Hayward, 143/1 © Picture-Factory, 144/1 © bellemedia, 152/1 © pressmaster, 158/1 © Gina Sanders, 163/1 © ispstock, 164/1 © Deklofenak, 168/2 © TheFinalMiracle, 170/1 © Benicce, 187/1 © by-studio, 220/2 © Lucky Dragon, 242/1 © Brett Mulcahy, 344/1 © BerlinStock, 414/2 © Gerd Reiber, 420/2 © Monkey Business, 615/1 © Yuri Arcurs, 624/1 © Andres Rodriguez, 628/1 © WavebreakMediaMicro, 650/1 © Swifter, 656/2 © vladgrin, 689/2 © Amir Kaljikovic, 691/1 © Guido Vrola, 697/1 © Amir Kaljikovic, 727/1 © Robert Kneschke, 729/1 © SanjMur, 744/2 © frank peters, 746/1 © spaxiax, 755/1 © fulgido, 756/1 © fotografiedk, 757/1 © Andrey Zyk, 758/1 © Conny Hagen, 794/1 © Gulien Diavel, 796/1 © diego cervo, 796/2 © luna, 800/1 © Viktor Pravdica, 800/2 © pressmaster, 808/1 © gravityimaging, 814/1 © rangizzz, 815/1 © Kzenon
Frogdesign, Altensteig

Georg Neumann GmbH, Berlin

Hans Kolb Wellpappe, Memmingen
Harald Küppers (www.kuepperscolor.de), Langen
Heidelberger Druckmaschinen AG, Heidelberg

Image-Affairs, Reutlingen
Informedia GmbH, Stuttgart

Jochen Wilfert Architekt, Fellbach

Kettenbach GmbH, © 667/2

Mobile Management GmbH, Kauferring

Neuland GmbH, Eichenzell, © 658/1–2
Norddeutscher Rundfunk, Hamburg

Piaggio & C. S.p.A., Italien

Radio-Technische Werkstätten GmbH, Köln
Realtech AG, Walldorf

Schnitt, Das Filmmagazin, Köln
Schuhwerk Grafikdesign, Bad Grönenbach
Seminarhotel Sonnenstrahl, Kißlegg
Sennheiser electronic GmbH, Wedemark
Shure Europe GmbH, Heilbronn
Siemens AG, Konstanz
Siemens AG, München
Siemens AG, Nürnberg
Sonoton Music GmbH, München
Staatliches Seminar für Didaktik und Lehrerbildung, Weingarten
Stankowski-Stiftung, Stuttgart
Studio Hamburg GmbH, Hamburg
Stuttgarter Nachrichten, Stuttgart
Südwestrundfunk SWR, Mainz

TerraTec Electronic GmbH, Nettetal

ullstein bild, Berlin, 100/1 © imagebroker.net / uwe umstätter, 330/1 © The Granger Collection

Verband Deutscher Papierfabriken, Bonn

Werbeagentur Topic, Christazhofen
Westdeutscher Rundfunk WDR, Köln

Zentrum für Familie, Umwelt und Kultur (Kloster Roggenburg), Roggenburg

Trotz großer Sorgfalt konnten die Urheber der Abbildungen nicht in allen Fällen ermittelt werden. Wir bitten gegebenenfalls um Mitteilung.